Call
Sky G

eCommerse

SEVENTH EDITION

Organizational Behavior

Science, the Real World, and You

Debra L. Nelson
Oklahoma State University

James Campbell Quick
University of Texas at Arlington

SOUTH-WESTERN
CENGAGE Learning™

Australia • Brazil • Japan • Korea • Mexico • Singapore • Spain • United Kingdom • United States

Organizational Behavior: Science, the Real World and You, Seventh Edition

Debra L. Nelson and James Campbell Quick

VP/Editorial Director: Jack W. Calhoun

Editor-in-Chief: Melissa Acuna

Executive Editor: Scott Person

Developmental Editor: Erin Guendelsberger

Senior Editorial Assistant: Ruth Belanger

Marketing Manager: Clinton Kernen

Marketing Coordinator: Julia Tucker

Senior Marketing Communications Manager: Jim Overly

Senior Content Project Manager: Diane Bowdler

Media Editor: Rob Ellington

Senior Manufacturing Buyer: Kevin Kluck

Production Service: Integra Software Services Pvt. Ltd

Copyeditor: Integra Software Services Pvt. Ltd

Compositor: Integra Software Services Pvt. Ltd

Senior Art Director: Tippy McIntosh

Cover and Internal Design: Joe Devine, Red Hangar Design

Cover Image: ©Santiago Cornejo, Shutterstock

Permissions Account Manager–Text: Roberta Broyer

Senior Permissions Account Manager–Image: Deanna Ettinger

Photo Researcher: Sarah Bonner

For product information and technology assistance, contact us at
Cengage Learning Customer & Sales Support, 1-800-354-9706

For permission to use material from this text or product,
submit all requests online at **www.cengage.com/permissions**
Further permissions questions can be emailed to
permissionrequest@cengage.com

Library of Congress Control Number: 2009943203

ISBN-13: 978-1-4390-4229-8

ISBN-10: 1-4390-4229-2

South-Western Cengage Learning
5191 Natorp Boulevard
Mason, OH 45040
USA

Cengage Learning products are represented in Canada by Nelson Education, Ltd.

For your course and learning solutions, visit **www.cengage.com**

Purchase any of our products at your local college store or at our preferred online store **www.CengageBrain.com**

Printed in the United States of America
1 2 3 4 5 6 7 13 12 11 10

Brief Contents

Contents

Preface

About the time the sixth edition of *Organizational Behavior: Science, the Real World, and You* appeared, the world experienced one of the most challenging financial downturns since the Great Depression of the 1930s. For many, these were scary times and for all they were challenging times. Universities saw major declines in endowments, but the core research and teaching continued, extending the 100-plus years of our profession. The ethics scandals that hit Wall Street in the midst of the crisis left the United States and the world looking for honest, authentic leaders and a more positive approach to understanding and leading people in organizations. However, while this was going on, the seventh edition emerged from the opportunities and optimism that form the heart of organizational behavior. Opportunity is "a favorable time" or "a chance for progress and advancement." In every crisis, there are both danger and opportunity: we choose to seek the opportunity, without ignoring possible dangers. More than responding to change, we encourage students of organizational behavior and leaders in organizations to be the instigators of positive change. Using the knowledge and insights offered in the study of organizational behavior, we can take responsible actions to create the kinds of organizations in which we thrive, grow strong, and experience fulfillment in the spirit of the happy/productive worker. No one can predict the future but everyone can help create the future. These are favorable times in which to advance the science and practice the art of organizational behavior in a manner that it is beneficial to all concerned. This includes workers and leaders, men and women, those of all ethnic groups and occupations, and all those of diverse faith traditions.

The distinctiveness of *Organizational Behavior* is reflected in its subtitle, *Science, the Real World, and You*. "Science" refers to the broad and deep research roots of our discipline. Our book is anchored in research tradition and contains not only classic research but also leading-edge scholarship in the field. This research and theory form the foundations of our knowledge base. "The Real World" reflects what is going on in organizations of all types: public and private, large and small, product and service oriented. In our text, these realities take shape as examples from all types of organizations. Some of the examples show success, whereas others show failure, in cases where managers apply organizational behavior knowledge in the real world. "You" features are the opportunities we have to grow and develop both as individuals and as organizations. In the book, they take the form of individual and group activities for proactive learning.

Organizational behavior is the study of individual behavior and group dynamics in organizational settings. It focuses on timeless topics like motivation, leadership, teamwork, and communication. Such issues have captured our attention for decades. Organizational behavior also encompasses contemporary issues in organizations. How do we encourage employees to act ethically, to engage in organizational citizenship behaviors, to go above and beyond the call of duty to exhibit exceptional performance? How do we restructure organizations in the face of increasing competition? What is the new psychological contract between employees and organizations? How have careers changed, and what can we expect in the future? How do you manage employee behavior in virtual organizations or teams? What happens when organizations with strong cultures and a need for constancy face the pressure to become current, competitive, and agile? *Organizational Behavior* thus engages both classic and emerging issues.

Our overarching theme of change continues to drive the book. We have streamlined the subthemes to focus on the human side of the organization. The three subthemes are globalization, diversity, and ethics. These subthemes continue to reflect the challenges that managers face. The sequence in which we address these subthemes and the ways in which we elaborate upon them *have* changed, however, as they should. The global marketplace continues to bring with it a world with no boundaries, with no constraints on time and distance. Diversity can be a tremendous asset, with its wealth of skills and knowledge, if managers can build organizational cultures that view differences as assets. Managing ethical behavior means doing the right thing in an age of increased white-collar crime and public scrutiny of organizations.

Organizations expect all employees to learn continually. Our book rests on the assumption that learning involves not only acquiring knowledge but also developing skills. The rich theory and research in organizational behavior must be translated into application. Thus, the text presents the opportunity to know concepts, ideas, and theories, and to practice skills, abilities, and behaviors to enhance the management of human behavior at work. Both knowledge and skills are essential for our future managers. We hope the knowledge and skills presented here empower them to succeed in the changing world of work.

SPECIAL FEATURES

Several special features of the book extend the subtitle *Science, the Real World, and You* to specific applications. These features are designed to enhance the application of theory and research in practice, to stimulate student interest and discussion, and to facilitate cognitive as well as skill-based learning. You learn in Chapter 1, Figure 1.4, that basic knowledge is concerned with Science, that skill application is concerned with the Real World, and that knowledge and skill development concern You directly. The pedagogical features included in each chapter are titled Science (Foundations), The Real World (Realities), and You (Challenges).

Science

Each chapter includes a Science feature that summarizes a leading-edge research study related to the chapter's topic. This feature exposes students to the way knowledge is advanced in organizational behavior and the scientific nature of the discipline. For example, the Science feature in Chapter 10 focuses on the way certain personalities tend to morally disengage from decisions that lead to unethical behavior.

Extensive Text References

The book is based on extensive classic and contemporary research literature. At the end of the book is a lengthy chapter-by-chapter reference list that students can refer to for in-depth treatments of the chapter topics. In this edition, over 200 new research studies, theory articles, and scholarly books have been reviewed and cited. In addition to this freshening of the content base for the text, chapters have new content and key terms that reflect positive changes. For example, Chapter 4 now has extensive coverage of emotions at work. Other research on emotions is integrated throughout the seventh edition. Chapter 7 brings attention to the continuing work/life balance issue of workaholism while the importance of heartfelt communication as an antidote to social isolation is emphasized in Chapter 8. Chapter 12 reflects enhanced coverage of the inspirational leadership theories (transformational, charismatic, authentic) along with emotional intelligence.

Thinking Ahead and Looking Back

The opening and closing features for the seventh edition, as in previous editions, frame the chapter with a vignette from one of six focus organizations. The organizations in the seventh edition are all new: CarMax, IKEA, Facebook, Nordstrom, Research in Motion, and Deloitte. As in the past, these companies represent manufacturing and service, profit and nonprofit, and large and small organizations. By featuring these six key organizations throughout the book, students can familiarize themselves with the companies in greater depth than a single appearance would allow. The Looking Back feature is a continuation of the Thinking Ahead feature on that particular organization and brings closure to the example.

The Real World

The purpose of including two new The Real World features in each chapter is to spotlight contemporary organizational life. The realities reflect the themes of globalization, diversity, and ethics. They include not only examples of successes, but also examples of failures, which are opportunities for learning. In Chapter 4, a Real World feature highlights Zappos, a company in which employees love their jobs, and shows how Zappos creates both job satisfaction and customer satisfaction. The Real World 12.2 presents Andrea Jung, CEO of Avon, and her unusual philosophy of leadership.

You

These self-assessment exercises provide the student with feedback on an important aspect of the topic. Examples are You 10.2, in which students can determine whether they are better at creative problem solving or logical problem solving, and You 13.2, in which students can discover their conflict-handling styles. Each You is designed to enhance self-knowledge or to promote skill development in the subject matter. The student is able to use the results of the You feature for self-discovery and behavioral change.

Diversity Dialogues

Faye Cocchiara has crafted a full set of Diversity Dialogues for the seventh edition. These are real-life stories drawn from news headlines that are presented in a way designed to stimulate frank dialogue and discussion. The aim is to present content that can be used to create a psychologically safe environment in which to discuss these often emotionally loaded and sensitive issues. There are Diversity Dialogues designed into the body of each chapter now, expanded from the nine that appeared in the sixth edition. Two examples are "When Domestic Violence 'Goes to Work' " in Chapter 7 and "Women Triumph in Times of Recession—Really?" in Chapter 1.

Discussion and Communication Questions

All students need help in developing their oral and written communication skills. Discussion and communication questions are included at the end of each chapter to give students practice in applying chapter material using some form of communication. The questions challenge students to write memos and brief reports, prepare oral presentations for class, interview experts in the field, and conduct research to gather information on important management topics for discussion in class.

Ethical Dilemmas

Joanne Gavin has conceived an entire new set of Ethical Dilemmas for the seventh edition. Learning to develop moral reasoning and the capacity to resolve ethical dilemmas is hard work. Simple answers to complex questions just do not exist. Therefore, an Ethical Dilemma has been crafted for each chapter that offers students an opportunity to engage in ethical debate and moral reasoning concerning tough decisions and situations. Each chapter's feature poses a scenario and then a series of questions for use in probing the ethical dilemma.

Experiential Exercises

Two group-oriented experiential exercises are included at the end of each chapter. They are designed for students to work in teams to learn more about an important aspect of the chapter's topic. The exercises give students opportunities to develop interpersonal skills and to process their thinking within a teamwork setting. In Experiential Exercise 4.2, for example, students are presented with twelve ethical issues faced in organizations, and they meet in groups to discuss all sides of the issue and a proposed resolution. Experiential Exercise 10.1 places students in the role of a manager who must make a layoff decision. Students are given summaries of their "employees'" résumés and asked to propose a decision in terms of who should be laid off.

Cases (New and Revised)

A case is included at the end of each chapter. Half of these chapter cases are completely new, and the other half have been updated. Each case is based on a real-world situation that has been modified slightly for learning purposes. Students have an opportunity to discuss and reflect on the content of the case, drawing on and then applying the content material of the chapter within the framework of the case. All of the Cohesion Cases that appear at the end of the four parts of the book are new and feature an ongoing scenario of the online retailer Zappos.com. The Workplace and BizFlix video cases are all new as well.

SOME DISTINCTIVE FEATURES STUDENTS LIKE

Organizational Behavior offers a number of distinctive, time-tested, and interesting features for students, as well as new and innovative features. Each chapter begins with a clear statement of learning objectives to provide students with expectations about what is to come. The chapter summaries are designed to bring closure to these learning objectives. Graphics and tables enhance students' ease in grasping the topical material and involve them actively in the learning process. Photos throughout each chapter reinforce and, in many cases, supplement the text.

Engaging and relevant end-of-chapter features such as the list of key terms, review questions, discussion questions, and cases reflect practical and applied aspects of organizational behavior.

Examples from diverse organizations (multinational, regional, nonprofit, public) and industries (manufacturing, service, defense) are included. These examples are integrated throughout the text. A unique feature of the book is its focus on the six organizations mentioned earlier. These represent many different types of organizations—large and small, profit and nonprofit, and product and service oriented. The purpose of this approach is to provide a sense of continuity and depth not achieved in single examples.

Study Aids

To help you learn, understand, and apply the material in *Organizational Behavior*, the seventh edition provides many unique and comprehensive study tools.

Web Site A rich Web site at www.cengage.com/management/nelson-quick complements the text, providing extras for students. Resources include chapter glossaries and interactive quizzes.

Student Premium Web Site (www.cengage.com/login) New to this edition, this optional premium Web site features text-specific resources that enhance student learning by bringing concepts to life. Dynamic interactive learning tools include online quizzes, flashcards, PowerPoint slides, concept tutorials, learning games, and more. Access to the Nelson/Quick Premium Student Web site is pincode protected. Learn more by adding this text to your bookshelf at www.cengage.com/login. Ask your local South-Western/Cengage Learning sales representative about this optional package item.

SOME DISTINCTIVE FEATURES INSTRUCTORS LIKE

Professors have demanding jobs. They should expect textbook authors and publishers to provide them with the support they need to do an excellent job for students. Among their expectations should be a well-integrated, complete ancillary package. *Organizational Behavior* has this package.

Ancillary Package

A comprehensive set of ancillaries supports the basic text: an Instructor's Manual with Video Guide, a Test Bank, ExamView (computerized testing software), PowerPoint® presentation files, a product support Web site, and a video program. The videos include clips about real companies with which your students may already be familiar as well as a variety of short vignettes from real Hollywood films. Using video in the classroom will enhance the text presentation and reinforce its themes, adding continuity and integration to the overall understanding of organizational behavior.

Instructor's Manual with Video Guide The Instructor's Manual with Video Guide for *Organizational Behavior* was prepared by David A. Foote (Middle Tennessee State University), Joseph E. Champoux (University of New Mexico), and B. J. Parker. For this edition, the Instructor's Manual is available only on the Instructor's

Resource CD-ROM and on the product support Web site, www.cengage.com/management/nelson-quick. Each chapter contains the following information:

- Chapter scan—a brief overview of the chapter.

- Learning objectives that are presented in the textbook.

- Key terms—a list of key terms from the chapter.

- The chapter summarized—an extended outline with narratives under each major point to flesh out the discussion and offer alternative examples and issues to bring forward. The extended outlines are several pages long and incorporate many teaching suggestions.

- Answer guidelines for end-of-chapter materials—detailed responses to the review questions, discussion and communication questions, and ethical dilemmas, with suggestions for keeping discussion on track in the classroom.

- Suggested answers for the You features, expanded for the seventh edition.

- Experiential exercises—a brief description of each exercise as well as a detailed summary of anticipated results. Also included are alternative experiential exercises not found in the text. Discussion questions are provided with selected experiential exercises. Finally, a list of sources for still more exercises may be found under "Extra Experiential Exercises."

- Cases—suggested answers for case discussion questions are provided in a detailed form.

- Integration of Myers–Briggs Type Indicator® material (optional)—including full descriptions and exercises in communication, leadership, motivation, decision making, conflict resolution, power, stress and time management, and managing change. For instructors unfamiliar with Myers–Briggs, a general introduction to this instrument is provided at the end of Chapter 3 of the Instructor's Manual. The introduction includes several good references for additional information about testing.

- Video cases—suggested answers to the Biz Flix and Workplace video cases are included for all chapters.

Test Bank The Test Bank, prepared by Jon G. Kalinowski (Minnesota State University, Mankato), has been thoroughly revised for this edition. The Test Bank contains more than 1,200 multiple-choice, true/false, matching, and essay questions. For this edition, a number of application-based questions have been added to the bank. Each question has been coded according to Bloom's taxonomy, a widely known testing and measurement device used to classify questions according to level (easy, medium, or hard) and type (application, recall, or comprehension). Each question has also been associated to AACSB learning standards. For this edition, the Test Bank is available only on the Instructor's Resource CD-ROM and on the product support Web site, www.cengage.com/management/nelson-quick.

ExamView This supplement contains all of the questions in the Test Bank. The program is easy-to-use test creation software compatible with Microsoft Windows and Macintosh. Instructors can add or edit questions, instructions, and answers and select questions (randomly or numerically) by previewing them on the screen. Instructors can also create and administer quizzes online, whether over the Internet, a local area network (LAN), or a wide area network (WAN). ExamView is available on the Instructor's Resource CD-ROM.

PowerPoint Presentation Files Donna Raleigh (University of Wisconsin, Eau Claire) has developed more than 300 PowerPoint slides for this text. These slides feature figures from the text, lecture outlines, and innovative adaptations to enhance classroom presentation. PowerPoint presentation files are available on the Instructor's Resource CD-ROM and on the product support Web site, www.cengage.com/management/nelson-quick.

Instructor's Resource CD-ROM (ISBN: 0-538-46711-8) Key instructor ancillaries (Instructor's Manual with Video Guide, Test Bank, ExamView, and PowerPoint slides) are provided on CD-ROM, giving instructors the ultimate tool for customizing lectures and presentations.

Web Site *Organizational Behavior* has its own product support Web site at www.cengage.com/management/nelson-quick. The full PowerPoint presentation is available for you to download as lecture support. The Instructor's Manual and Test Bank are also available for download.

WebTutor™ on WebCT® and on Blackboard® WebTutor is an interactive, Web-based learner supplement on WebCT and/or BlackBoard that harnesses the power of the Internet to deliver innovative learning aids that actively engage learners. Instructors can incorporate WebTutor as an integral part of their course, or the learners can use it on their own as a study guide. Benefits to learners include automatic feedback from quizzes and exams; interactive, multimedia-rich explanation of concepts; online exercises that reinforce what they have learned; flashcards that include audio support; and greater interaction and involvement through online discussion forums.

"Take 2" Video Program (ISBN: 1-439-07887-4) Available in DVD format, an updated video program has been developed for use with *Organizational Behavior.* Video segments have been selected to support the themes of the book and to deepen students' understanding of the organizational behavior concepts presented throughout the text. Brand new Biz Flix video cases, developed by Joseph E. Champoux of the University of New Mexico, incorporate clips from popular films including *Lost in Translation, Friday Night Lights,* and *Failure to Launch* into the classroom. Companies profiled in the Workplace video series include Evo, Numi Organic Tea, and Flight 001, among others. Information on using the videos can be found in the Instructor's Manual.

OUR REVIEWERS ARE APPRECIATED

We would like to thank our professional peers and colleagues who reviewed the text to evaluate scholarly accuracy, writing style, and pedagogy. The many changes we made are based on their suggestions. We gratefully acknowledge the help of the following individuals:

Angela Boston, *University of Texas at Arlington*

Beth Chung-Herrera, *San Diego State University*

Suzanne Crampton, *Grand Valley State University*

Roger A. Dean, *Washington and Lee University*

Lindsey Godwin, *Morehead State University*

Carol K. Johansen, *University of Southern Maine* and *Southern Maine Community College*

Clifton Mayfield, *University of Houston-Clear Lake*

Brenda McAleer, *University of Maine at Augusta*

Melissa Najera-Gonzales, *University of Houston-Clear Lake*

Daniel R. Sierchio, *Rutgers, the State University of New Jersey*

Laura Wolfe, *Louisiana State University*

For their assistance with recent editions, we would like to thank the following individuals:

Robert F. Abbey, Jr., *Troy State University*

Stephen R. Ball, *Cleary University*

Deborah Bashaw, *Harding University*

Talya Bauer, *Portland State University*

Mark C. Butler, *San Diego State University*

Ceasar Douglas, *Florida State University*

Tracey Rockett Hanft, *University of Texas, Dallas*

Theodore T. Herbert, *Rollins College*

Jacqueline A. Gilbert, *Middle Tennessee State University*

Don Jung, *San Diego State University*

Bryan Kennedy, *Athens State University*

Jalane M. Meloun, *Barry University*

Floyd S. Ormsbee, *Clarkson University*

Linda Beats Putchinski, *University of Central Florida*

Elizabeth C. Ravlin, *University of South Carolina*

Harriet L. Rojas, *Indiana Wesleyan University*

Chris John Sablynski, *California State University, Sacramento*

Marian C. Schultz, *University of West Florida*

M. Shane Spiller, *Morehead State University*

William H. Turnley, *Kansas State University*

ACKNOWLEDGMENTS

The seventh edition of **Organizational Behavior**, like its predecessors, is the product of great teamwork, and we are indebted to all of our team members who made the revision process a pleasure. Our editors Michele Rhoades and Scott Person were great creative resources and sounding boards, contributing terrific energy to the project. Erin Guendelsberger, our developmental editor, was a constant source of positive energy and ideas, and kept us going strong throughout the process.

Faye Cocchiara of Arkansas State University, a veteran colleague and collaborator, has worked with us since the fifth edition. Her voice can easily be detected throughout the book. Her voice and her research are most evident in the emphasis on diversity. Faye conceptualized, designed, authored, and executed the full set of Diversity Dialogues featured in each of the chapters in the book, starting with Chapter 1.

Laura Little of the University of Georgia joined the team for the seventh edition and her influence can be seen throughout the book. Her interest in emotions at work has shored up the coverage of emotions in this edition. Her teaching excellence translated into Science features that are interesting and timely, and to real-world examples that students can instantly relate to. Laura brought a contemporary flavor to the book and we are delighted to have her on board.

Joanne H. Gavin of the School of Management at Marist College continues to make her presence felt in her passion for moral and ethical action, which is a positive presence in the Ethical Dilemmas that she conceptualized and executed first in the fifth edition. The seventh edition features her latest conceptualization with an entire new set of Ethical Dilemmas. Her character continues to be with us and her own students as she leads them in national competition in the Ethics Bowl.

Speaking of ethics, John L. and Judy Goolsby's $2 million challenge gift directed to the College of Business at UT Arlington to found the Goolsby Leadership Academy, as noted in the ethics section of Chapter 2, places an exclamation point on the importance of ethics and integrity in business education. John has led by example, with personal integrity and humility.

Joseph Champoux of the University of New Mexico was kind enough to create a brand-new series of Biz Flix video cases, and B. J. Parker wrote our all-new Workplace video cases.

Michael McCuddy of Valparaiso University did his customary outstanding job on the cases that appear at the end of each chapter and the cohesion cases that appear at the end of each part. He has a way of making organizational problems fascinating to students. Jeff McGee was most helpful with small business and entrepreneurship advice and contacts as well as his support as chairman of the Department of Management. Additionally, Carol Byrne and Ruthie Brock, business librarians at the University of Texas at Arlington, provided much support in the preparation of this textbook.

Preparation of the ancillary materials to enhance classroom efforts required a host of people. David A. Foote, Middle Tennessee State University, Joseph E. Champoux, the University of New Mexico, and B. J. Parker created a superb Instructor's Manual and Video Guide. Jon Kalinowski of Minnesota State University, Mankato, was great in preparing the Test Bank that accompanies the textbook. Many thanks go to Donna Raleigh of University of Wisconsin, Eau Claire, for developing the PowerPoint presentation files.

We are fortunate to have several colleagues who have made helpful contributions and supported our development through all seven editions of the textbook: Mike Hitt of Texas A&M University; Ken Eastman of Oklahoma State University; Lisa Kennedy of Baylor College of Medicine; Janaki Gooty of Binghamton University; Jo Anne Wilson of AT&T; Tammy Manning of Galligan & Manning; David Mack, David Gray, Myrtle Bell, Ken Price, Wendy Casper, Yongmei Lu, and Jim Lavelle, all of the University of Texas at Arlington; Juliana Lilly of Sam Houston State University; and J. Lee Whittington of University of Dallas. Marilyn Macik-Frey has added so much in our collaborations on healthy communications, occupational health, and a deeper appreciation of personality preferences.

Our families and friends have encouraged us throughout the development of the book. They have provided us with emotional support and examples for the book and have graciously allowed us the time to do the book justice. We are truly grateful for their support.

This book has been a labor of love for both of us. It has made us better teachers and also better learners. And that is our wish for you!

Debra L. Nelson
James Campbell Quick

About the Authors

DEBRA L. NELSON

Dr. Debra L. Nelson is The Spears School of Business Associates' Professor of Business Administration and Professor of Management at Oklahoma State University. She received her Ph.D. from the University of Texas at Arlington, where she was the recipient of the R. D. Irwin Dissertation Fellowship Award. Dr. Nelson is the author of over ninety journal articles focusing on organizational stress management, gender at work, and leadership. Her research has been published in the *Academy of Management Executive, Academy of Management Journal, Academy of Management Review, MIS Quarterly, Organizational Dynamics, Journal of Organizational Behavior*, and other journals. In addition, she is coauthor/coeditor of several books, including *Organizational Behavior: Science, the Real World, and You* (6th ed., South-Western, Cengage Learning, 2009); *Positive Organizational Behavior* (Sage, 2007); *Organizational Leadership* (South-Western, Cengage Learning, 2004); *Gender, Work Stress, and Health* (American Psychological Association, 2002); *Advancing Women in Management* (Blackwell, 2002); and *Preventive Stress Management in Organizations* (American Psychological Association, 1997). Dr. Nelson has also served as a consultant to several organizations including AT&T, American Fidelity Assurance, Sonic, State Farm Insurance Companies, and Southwestern Bell. She has presented leadership and preventive stress management seminars for a host of organizations, including Blue Cross/Blue Shield, Conoco/Phillips, Oklahoma Gas and Electric, Oklahoma Natural Gas, and the Federal Aviation Administration. She has been honored with the Greiner Graduate Teaching Award, the Chandler-Frates and Reitz Graduate Teaching Award, the Regents' Distinguished Teaching Award, the Regents' Distinguished Research Award, and the Burlington Northern Faculty Achievement Award at OSU. Dr. Nelson also serves on the editorial review boards of the *Journal of Organizational Behavior, Journal of Leadership and Organizational Studies*, and *Leadership*. She is a partner in NelsonQuick Group.

JAMES CAMPBELL QUICK

Dr. James Campbell (Jim) Quick is John and Judy Goolsby Distinguished Professor in the Goolsby Leadership Academy, Distinguished Professor in the Academy of Distinguished Teachers, and Professor of Organizational Behavior in the Department of Management, College of Business at the University of Texas at Arlington. He is Visiting Professor, Lancaster University Management School and School of Health & Medicine, UK. He earned an A.B. with Honors from Colgate University, where he was a George Cobb Fellow and Harvard Business School Association intern. He earned an M.B.A. and a Ph.D. at the University of Houston. He completed postgraduate courses in behavioral medicine (Harvard Medical School) and combat stress (University of Texas Health Science Center at San Antonio). Dr. Quick is a Fellow of the Society for Industrial and Organizational Psychology, the American Psychological Association, the American Psychological Society, and the American Institute of Stress. He was awarded the 2002 Harry and Miriam Levinson Award by the American Psychological Foundation. With his brother (Jonathan D. Quick, M.D., M.P.H.), Dr. Quick framed the area of preventive stress management, a term now listed in the *APA Dictionary of Psychology* (2007). They, with Debra Nelson as first author, received the 1990 Distinguished Professional Publication Award for *Corporate Warfare: Preventing Combat Stress and Battle Fatigue*, published in the American Management Association's *Organizational Dynamics* and used in the curriculum of the United States Air Force Academy and the U.S. Army War College. His book *Managing Executive Health* (Cambridge University Press, 2008) emphasizes ethical, authentic leadership with Spotlights on Rebecca Chopp, president of Swarthmore College, and John L. Goolsby, who with his wife Judy founded the Goolsby Leadership Academy.

Dr. Quick's awards and recognitions include a listing in *Who's Who in the World*, 7th Edition (1984–85); The Maroon Citation (Colgate University Alumni Corporation, 1993); and a Presidential Citation from the American Psychological Association (2001). Dr. Quick won the 2008 Honors College Outstanding Faculty Award and 2009 Award for Distinguished Record of Research, both at UT Arlington.

Colonel Quick, United States Air Force Reserve (Retired), was the Senior Individual Mobilization Augmentee at the San Antonio Air Logistics Center (AFMC), Kelly AFB, Texas, in his last assignment. He was Distinguished Visiting Professor of Psychology, 59th Medical Wing (1999), and Visiting Scholar, United States Military Academy at West Point (2007). He is a graduate of the Air War College. His awards and decorations include the Legion of Merit, Meritorious Service Medal, and National Defense Service Medal with Bronze Star. He currently serves by appointment from Secretary of Defense Robert Gates on the Defense Health Board's Psychological Health External Advisory Subcommittee.

Dr. Quick is married to the former Sheri Grimes Schember; both are members of the Presidents' Club of Colgate University, the Silver Society of the American Psychological Foundation, and the Chancellor's Council of the University of Texas System, and are major donors to the Rotary Foundation. Jim is past president of the Great Southwest Rotary Club. Jim is a partner in NelsonQuick Group, LLC.

To our students, who challenge us to be better than we are, who keep us in touch with reality, and who are the foundations of our careers.

PART 1

© Brand X Pictures

Introduction

Organizational Behavior and Opportunity

LEARNING OBJECTIVES

After reading this chapter, you should be able to do the following:

1 Define *organizational behavior*.

2 Identify four action steps for responding positively in times of change.

3 Identify the important system components of an organization.

4 Describe the formal and informal elements of an organization.

5 Understand the diversity of organizations in the economy, as exemplified by the six focus organizations.

6 Recognize the opportunities that change creates for organizational behavior.

7 Demonstrate the value of objective knowledge and skill development in the study of organizational behavior.

CarMax decided to enter and change the used-car businesses.

THINKING AHEAD: CARMAX

Changing the Used-Car Business. . .

There are a variety of preconceptions and stereotypes about the used-car business in modern American mythology. Jokes about used-car salesmen have been kicked around for decades. CarMax decided to enter and change the used-car business.

Many of the industry's analysts were skeptical about the ability of the new kid on the block in the early 1990s. By the late 2000s, CarMax had in fact made a positive impact, one that AutoNation attempted to replicate and failed, exiting the used-car business in 1999. CarMax has succeeded through its own unique formula rather than through intensely competitive, cutthroat tactics. They are winning the game in the used-car industry and they are winning it the CarMax way, their way.[1]

The CarMax way is to emphasize ethical business dealings, no-haggle pricing, and customer service. These are the three pillars of the company's success. While most used-car dealers tell you that they do not put frame or structurally damaged cars on their lots, and most reputable dealers in fact do not, CarMax goes the extra mile in showing that it does not do so. Integrity is at the core of the company's ethical business practices. In addition to good used cars, CarMax does not engage in high pressure pricing or haggling. They are upfront about the pricing and explain to customers what is going to happen at every step along the path to owning that used car. The low-keyed sales approach was viewed very skeptically in the early years yet the company has done very well, with over 100 used-car superstores in their system by 2010. The low-key approach does not mean low profitability. CarMax averages $1,878 in gross profit on each used car, compared with $1,700 in gross profit for new car dealerships that sell used cars.

Customers are not going to pay extra for no reason; they are not stupid. The third leg in CarMax's three-pronged approach is to emphasize customer service. Customers walk into one of the company's superstores and most of them walk away very satisfied with the experience. They do not feel that the sales people are attempting to extract money from them. Along with the integrity of ethical business practices is the focus on the customer and the customer's needs. A satisfied customer is often a repeat customer over the long term. After more than a decade of success, however, CarMax faced a real challenge to its business model during the sharp 2008–2009 economic downturn. Would the company's three-way approach be enough to meet the challenges brought about by a weakening economy and slowing auto sales?

HUMAN BEHAVIOR IN ORGANIZATIONS

1 Define *organizational behavior.*

Human behavior in organizations is complex and often difficult to understand. Organizations have been described as clockworks in which human behavior is logical and rational, but they often seem like snake pits to those who work in them.[2] The clockwork metaphor reflects an orderly, idealized view of organizational behavior devoid of conflict or dilemma because all the working parts (the people) mesh smoothly. The snake pit metaphor conveys the daily conflict, stress, and struggle in organizations. Each metaphor reflects reality from a different perspective—the organization's versus the individual's point of view. These metaphors reflect the complexity of human behavior, the dark side of which is seen in cases of air rage and workplace violence. On the positive side, the Gallup Organization's Marcus Buckingham suggests that people's psychological makeup is at the heart of the emotional economy.[3]

This chapter is an introduction to organizational behavior. The first section provides an overview of human behavior in organizations, its interdisciplinary origins, and behavior in times of change. The second section presents an organizational context within which behavior occurs and briefly introduces the six focus companies used selectively in the book. The third section highlights the *opportunities* that exist in times of *change* and *challenge* for people at work.[4] The fourth section addresses the ways people learn about organizational behavior and explains how the text's pedagogical features relate to the various ways of learning. The final section of the chapter presents the plan for the book.

Organizational behavior is individual behavior and group dynamics in organizations. The study of organizational behavior is primarily concerned with the psychosocial, interpersonal, and behavioral dynamics in organizations. However,

opportunities
Favorable times or chances for progress and advancement.

change
The transformation or modification of an organization and/or its stakeholders.

challenge
The call to competition, contest, or battle.

organizational behavior
The study of individual behavior and group dynamics in organizations.

organizational variables that affect human behavior at work are also relevant to the study of organizational behavior. These organizational variables include jobs, the design of work, communication, performance appraisal, organizational design, and organizational structure. Therefore, although individual behavior and group dynamics are the primary concerns in the study of organizational behavior, organizational variables are also important.

This section briefly contrasts two perspectives for understanding human behavior, the external and the internal perspectives. The section then discusses six scientific disciplines from which the study of organizational behavior has emerged and concludes with a discussion of behavior in times of change.

Understanding Human Behavior

The vast majority of theories and models of human behavior fall into one of two basic categories. One category has an internal perspective, and the other has an external perspective. The internal perspective considers factors inside the person to understand behavior. This view is psychodynamically oriented. People who subscribe to this view understand human behavior in terms of the thoughts, feelings, past experiences, and needs of the individual. The internal perspective explains people's actions and behavior in terms of their history and personal value systems. The internal processes of thinking, feeling, perceiving, and judging lead people to act in specific ways. The internal perspective has given rise to a wide range of motivational and leadership theories. This perspective implies that people are best understood from the inside and that their behavior is best interpreted after understanding their thoughts and feelings.

The other category of theories and models of human behavior takes an external perspective. This perspective focuses on factors outside the person to understand behavior. People who subscribe to this view understand human behavior in terms of external events, consequences of behavior, and the environmental forces to which a person is subject. From the external perspective, a person's history, feelings, thoughts, and personal value systems are not very important in interpreting actions and behavior. This perspective has given rise to an alternative set of motivational and leadership theories, which are covered in Chapters 5 and 12 of the text. The external perspective implies that a person's behavior is best understood by examining the surrounding external events and environmental forces.

The internal and external perspectives offer alternative explanations for human behavior. For example, the internal perspective might say Mary is an outstanding employee because she has a high need for achievement, whereas the external perspective might say Mary is an outstanding employee because she is paid extremely well for her work. Kurt Lewin captured both perspectives in saying that behavior is a function of both the person and the environment.[5]

Interdisciplinary Influences

Organizational behavior is a blended discipline that has grown out of contributions from numerous earlier fields of study, only one of which is the psychological discipline from which Kurt Lewin came. These interdisciplinary influences are the roots for what is increasingly recognized as the independent discipline of organizational behavior. The sciences of psychology, sociology, engineering, anthropology, management, and medicine have each contributed to our understanding of human behavior in organizations.

Psychology is the science of human behavior and dates back to the closing decades of the nineteenth century. Psychology traces its own origins to philosophy and the

psychology
The science of human behavior.

Handwritten margin notes: #1; Feelings Internal motivational; External Surrounding Events; Examples of the Two science of physiology. One of the most prominent early psychologists, William James, actually held a degree in medicine (M.D.). Since its origin, psychology has itself become differentiated into a number of specialized fields, such as clinical, experimental, military, organizational, and social psychology. Organizational psychology includes the study of many topics, such as work motivation, which are also covered by organizational behavior.[6] Early psychological research for the American military during World War I had later implications for sophisticated personnel selection methods used by corporations such as Johnson & Johnson, Valero Energy, and Texas Instruments.[7]

Sociology, the science of society, has made important contributions to knowledge about group and intergroup dynamics in the study of organizational behavior. Because sociology takes society rather than the individual as its point of departure, the sociologist is concerned with the variety of roles within a society or culture, the norms and standards of behavior in groups, and the consequences of compliant and deviant behavior. For example, the concept of *role set*, a key contribution to role theory in 1957 by Robert Merton, was used by a team of Harvard educators to study the school superintendent role in Massachusetts.[8] More recently, the role set concept has been used to study the effects of codes of ethics in organizations.[9]

Engineering is the applied science of energy and matter. Engineering has made important contributions to our understanding of the design of work. By taking basic engineering ideas and applying them to human behavior at work, Frederick Taylor had a profound influence on the early years of the study of organizational behavior.[10] Taylor's engineering background led him to place special emphasis on human productivity and efficiency in work behavior. His notions of performance standards and differential piece-rate systems have had lasting impact. Taylor's original ideas are embedded in organizational goal-setting programs, such as those at Black & Decker, IBM, and Weyerhaeuser.[11]

Anthropology, the science of human learned behavior, is especially important to understanding organizational culture. Cultural anthropology focuses on the origins of culture and the patterns of behavior as culture is communicated symbolically. Research in this tradition has examined the effects of efficient cultures on organization performance[12] and how pathological personalities may lead to dysfunctional organizational cultures.[13] Schwartz used a psychodynamic, anthropological mode of inquiry in exploring corporate decay at General Motors and NASA.[14]

Management, originally called administrative science, is a discipline concerned with the study of overseeing activities and supervising people in organizations. It emphasizes the design, implementation, and management of various administrative and organizational systems. March and Simon take the human organization as their point of departure and concern themselves with the administrative practices that will enhance the effectiveness of the system.[15] Management is the first discipline to take the modern corporation as the unit of analysis, and this viewpoint distinguishes the discipline's contribution to the study of organizational behavior.

Medicine is the applied science of healing or treatment of diseases to enhance an individual's health and well-being. Medicine has long-standing concern for both physical and psychological health, as well as for industrial mental health.[16] More recently, as the war against acute diseases is being won, medical attention has shifted to more chronic diseases, such as hypertension, and to occupational health and well-being.[17] Individual behavior and lifestyle patterns play important roles in treating chronic diseases.[18] These trends have contributed to the growth of corporate wellness programs, such as Johnson & Johnson's "Live for Life Program." The surge in health care costs over the past two decades has contributed to increased organizational concern with medicine and health care in the workplace.[19]

sociology
The science of society.

engineering
The applied science of energy and matter.

anthropology
The science of the learned behavior of human beings.

management
The study of overseeing activities and supervising people in organizations.

medicine
The applied science of healing or treatment of diseases to enhance an individual's health and well-being.

Behavior in Times of Change

Early research with individuals, groups, and organizations in the midst of environmental change found that change is often experienced as a threat that leads to a reliance on well-learned and dominant forms of behavior.[20] That is, in the midst of change, people often become rigid and reactive, rather than open and responsive. This may be useful if the change is neither dramatic nor rapid because we are often effective at coping with incremental change. However, if significant change occurs, then rigid and well-learned behavior may be counterproductive. Leaders may interpret these responses as resistance to change. Strong leaders recognize these behaviors as an opportunity to learn from their critics, to understand the rigidity and resistance, and to facilitate positive pathways through the change.[21] The practice of outsourcing is a significant change in American industry that has been facilitated by dramatic advances in the Internet and networking technology.[22] Big changes disrupt people's habitual behavior and require learning if they are to be managed successfully. Eric Brown, ProLine International's VP of Global Business Development, offers some sage words of advice to see the opportunity in change.[23] He recommends adapting to change by seeing it as positive and seeing challenge as good rather than bad. His action steps for doing this are to (1) have a positive attitude, (2) ask questions, (3) listen to the answers, and (4) be committed to success. We see in the accompanying Science feature how important a positive attitude toward change is.

However, success is never guaranteed, and change sometimes results in failure. If this happens, do not despair. Some of the world's greatest leaders, such as Winston

2 Identify four action steps for responding positively in times of change.

Science

A Strong, Positive Attitude Toward Change

This research studied the dynamic and changing nature of organizations. There are a number of variables found to be associated with organizational changes that serve as mediators of outcomes of the change process. Not all changes result in good outcomes and not all change results in bad outcomes. What makes the difference? This study examined three variables that might affect the attitudes of 258 police officers toward a change aimed at restructuring its organizational design. The three variables were locus of control, growth need strength, and internal work motivation. Locus of control concerns one's personal beliefs about how much self-control one has versus how much control is due to chance or events in the environment. Growth need strength assesses how much a person needs to experience work as stimulating and challenging. Internal work motivation assesses one's self-initiative and personal drive. These three variables influence one's attitude toward change, which may be positive, as in looking forward to change, or weak, as in not looking forward to change. These all influence organizational commitment following the change. The results found that strong, positive attitudes toward change led to higher levels of organizational commitment as well as more successful implementation of change initiatives. The practical implications of this study suggest that employees with strong, positive attitude toward change work to ensure that a change initiative is successful. On the other hand, employees with weak attitudes toward change are likely to resist and potentially sabotage a change initiative.

SOURCE: S. M. Elias, "Employee Commitment in Times of Change: Assessing the Importance of Attitudes Toward Organizational Change," *Journal of Management* 35 (2009): 37–55.

Analyze Your Perceptions of a Change

Everyone perceives change differently. Think of a change situation you are currently experiencing. It can be any business, school-related, or personal experience that requires a significant change in your attitude or behavior. Rate your feelings about this change using the following scales. For instance, if you feel the change is more of a threat than an opportunity, you would circle 0, 2, or 4 on the first scale.

1. Threat	0	2	4	6	8	10	Opportunity
2. Holding on to the past	0	2	4	6	8	10	Reaching for the future
3. Immobilized	0	2	4	6	8	10	Activated
4. Rigid	0	2	4	6	8	10	Versatile
5. A loss	0	2	4	6	8	10	A gain
6. Victim of change	0	2	4	6	8	10	Agent of change
7. Reactive	0	2	4	6	8	10	Proactive
8. Focused on the past	0	2	4	6	8	10	Focused on the future
9. Separate from change	0	2	4	6	8	10	Involved with change
10. Confused	0	2	4	6	8	10	Clear

How positive are your perceptions of this change?

SOURCE: H. Woodward and S. Buchholz, *Aftershock: Helping People Through Corporate Change*, 15. Copyright © 1987 John Wiley & Sons, Inc. Reprinted by permission of John Wiley & Sons, Inc.

Churchill, experienced dramatic failure before achieving lasting success. The key to their eventual success was their capacity to learn from the failure and to respond positively to the opportunities presented to them. One venture capitalist with whom the authors have worked likes to ask those seeking to build a business to tell him about their greatest failure. What the venture capitalist is looking for in the answer is how the executive responded to the failure and what he or she learned from the experience. While change carries with it the risk of failure as well as the opportunity for success, it is often how we behave in the midst of change that determines which outcome results. Success can come through the accumulation of small wins and through the use of microprocesses, as has been found with middle managers engaged in institutional change.[24] What are your perceptions of change? Complete You 1.1 and assess your own behavior in times of change.

THE ORGANIZATIONAL CONTEXT

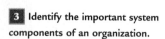

3 Identify the important system components of an organization.

A complete understanding of organizational behavior requires an understanding of both human behavior and the organizational context where behavior is enacted. This section discusses the organizational context. First, organizations are presented as systems. Second, the formal and informal organizations are discussed. Finally, six focus companies are presented as contemporary examples and drawn on throughout the text.

Organizations as Open Systems

As with human behavior, two different perspectives offer complementary explanations of organizations. Organizations are open systems of interacting components, which are people, tasks, technology, and structure. These internal components also interact with components in the organization's task environment. Organizations as open systems have people, technology, structure, and purpose, which interact with elements in the organization's environment.

What, exactly, is an organization? Today, the corporation is the dominant organizational form for much of the Western world, but other organizational forms have dominated other times and societies. Some societies have been dominated by religious organizations, such as the temple corporations of ancient Mesopotamia and the churches in colonial America.[25] Other societies have been dominated by military organizations, such as the clans of the Scottish Highlands and the regional armies of the People's Republic of China.[26,27] All of these societies are woven together by family organizations, which themselves may vary from nuclear and extended families to small, collective communities.[28,29] The purpose and structure of the religious, military, and family organizational forms may vary, but people's behavior in these organizations may be very similar. In fact, early discoveries about power and leadership in work organizations were remarkably similar to findings about power and leadership within families.[30]

Organizations may manufacture products, such as aircraft components or steel, or deliver services, such as managing money or providing insurance protection. To understand how organizations do these things requires an understanding of the open system components of the organization and the components of its task environment.

Katz, Kahn, and Leavitt set out open system frameworks for understanding organizations.[31] The four major internal components—task, people, technology, and structure—along with the organization's inputs, outputs, and key elements in the task environment, are depicted in Figure 1.1. The *task* of the organization is its mission, purpose, or goal for existing. The *people* are the human resources of the

task
An organization's mission, purpose, or goal for existing.

people
The human resources of the organization.

FIGURE

1.1   An Open Systems View of Organization

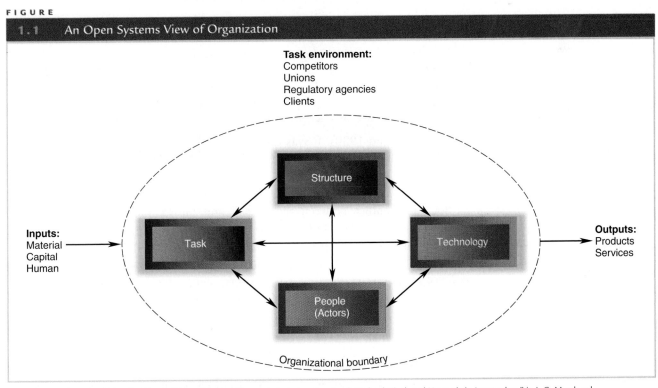

SOURCE: Based on Harold Leavitt, "Applied Organizational Change in Industry: Structural, Technological, and Humanistic Approaches," in J. G. March, ed., *Handbook of Organizations* (Chicago: Rand McNally, 1965), 1145. Reprinted by permission of James G. March.

organization. The *technology* is the wide range of tools, knowledge, and/or techniques used to transform the inputs into outputs. The *structure* is the systems of communication, the systems of authority, and the systems of workflow.

In addition to these major internal components, the organization as a system also has an external task environment. The task environment is composed of different constituents, such as suppliers, customers, and federal regulators. Thompson describes the task environment as that element of the environment related to the organization's degree of goal attainment; that is, it is composed of those elements of the environment related to the organization's basic task.[32] There are a number of organizations that are using or considering the use of Twitter as a way of networking elements of their task environments.[33] For example, NASA is using Twitter to update interested parties on the status of upcoming space shuttle flights. Originally a tool for personal networking and sharing daily life events, Twitter has become a powerful marketing and communication device for companies.

The organization system works by taking inputs, converting them into throughputs, and delivering outputs to its task environment. Inputs consist of the human, informational, material, and financial resources used by the organization. Throughputs are the materials and resources as they are transformed by the organization's technology component. Once the transformation is complete, they become outputs for customers, consumers, and clients. The actions of suppliers, customers, regulators, and other elements of the task environment affect the organization and the behavior of people at work. For example, Onsite Engineering and Management experienced a threat to its survival in the mid-1980s by being totally dependent on one large utility for its outputs. By broadening its client base and improving the quality of its services (i.e., its outputs) over the next several years, Onsite became a healthier, more successful small company. Transforming inputs into high-quality outputs is critical to an organization's success.

The Formal and Informal Organization

4 Describe the formal and informal elements of an organization.

technology
The tools, knowledge, and/or techniques used to transform inputs into outputs.

structure
The systems of communication, authority and roles, and workflow.

formal organization
The official, legitimate, and most visible part of the system.

informal organization
The unofficial and less visible part of the system.

Hawthorne studies
Studies conducted during the 1920s and 1930s that discovered the existence of the informal organization.

The open systems' view of organization may lead one to see the design of an organization as a clockwork with a neat, precise, interrelated functioning. The *formal organization* is the official, legitimate, and most visible part that enables people to think of organizations in logical and rational ways. The snake pit organizational metaphor mentioned earlier has its roots in the study and examination of the *informal organization,* which is unofficial and less visible. The informal elements were first fully appreciated as a result of the *Hawthorne studies,* conducted during the 1920s and 1930s. It was during the interview study, the third of the four Hawthorne studies, that the researchers began to develop a deeper understanding of the informal elements of the Hawthorne Works as an organization.[34] The formal and informal elements of the organization are depicted in Figure 1.2.

Potential conflict between the formal and informal organization makes an understanding of both important. Conflicts between these two elements erupted in many organizations during the early years of the twentieth century and were embodied in the union–management strife of that era. The conflicts escalated into violence in a number of cases. For example, during the 1920s, supervisors at the Homestead Works of U.S. Steel were issued pistols and boxes of ammunition "just in case" it became necessary to shoot unruly, dangerous steelworkers. Such potential formal–informal, management–labor conflict does not characterize all organizations. During the same era, Eastman Kodak was very progressive. The company helped with financial backing for employees' neighborhood communities, such as Meadowbrook in Rochester, New York. Kodak's concern for employees and attention to informal issues made unions unnecessary within the company.

1.2 Formal and Informal Organization

Formal organization (overt)
Goals and objectives
Policies and procedures
Job descriptions
Financial resources
Authority structure
Communication channels
Products and services

Social surface

Informal organization (covert)
Beliefs and assumptions
Perceptions and attitudes
Values
Feelings, such as fear,
    joy, anger, trust, and hope
Group norms
Informal leaders

The informal elements of the organization are frequent points of diagnostic and intervention activities in organization development, though the formal elements must always be considered as well because they provide the context for the informal.[35] These informal elements are important because people's feelings, thoughts, and attitudes about their work do make a difference in their behavior and performance. Individual behavior plays out in the context of the formal and informal elements of the system, becoming organizational behavior. The uncovering of the informal elements in an organization was one of the major discoveries of the Hawthorne studies. The importance of employees' moods, emotions, and dispositional affect is being re-recognized as a key influence on critical organizational outcomes, such as job performance, decision making, creativity, turnover, teamwork, negotiation, and leadership.[36]

Six Focus Organizations

Organizational behavior always occurs in the context of a specific organizational setting. Most attempts at explaining or predicting organizational behavior rely heavily on factors within the organization and give less weight to external environmental considerations.[37] Students can benefit from being sensitive to the industrial context of organizations and from developing an appreciation for each organization as a whole.[38] In this vein, six organizations each appear three times for a total of eighteen Thinking Ahead and Looking Back features. CarMax is illustrated in this chapter. We challenge you in each chapter to anticipate what is in the Looking Back feature once you read Thinking Ahead.

5 Understand the diversity of organizations in the economy, as exemplified by the six focus organizations.

The U.S. economy is the largest in the world, with a gross domestic product of more than $14.2 trillion in 2008. Figure 1.3 shows the major sectors of the economy. The largest sectors are service (43 percent) and product manufacture of nondurable goods (21 percent) and durable goods (7 percent). All together, the manufacture of products and the delivery of services account for 71 percent of the U.S. economy. Government and fixed investments account for the remaining 29 percent. Large and small organizations operate in each sector of the economy shown in Figure 1.3.

The private sectors are an important part of the economy. The manufacturing sector includes the production of basic materials, such as steel, and the production of finished products, such as automobiles and electronic equipment. The service sector includes transportation, financial services, insurance, and retail sales. The government sectors, which provide essential infrastructure, and nonprofit organizations are also important to our collective well-being because they meet needs not addressed in these economic sectors. We have chosen organizations that reflect a broad cross section of business: CarMax, Facebook, Nordstrom, IKEA, Research in Motion, and Deloitte.

Each of these six organizations makes an important and unique contribution to the manufacturing or service sectors of the national economy and/or to our national well-being. These organizations are not alone, however. Hundreds of other small, medium, and large organizations are making valuable and significant contributions to the economic health and human welfare of the United States. Brief examples from many organizations are used throughout the book. We hope that by better understanding these organizations, you may have a greater appreciation for your own organization and others within the diverse world of private business enterprises and nonprofit organizations.

FIGURE

1.3   U.S. Gross Domestic Product (Approximately $14.4 Trillion for 2008)

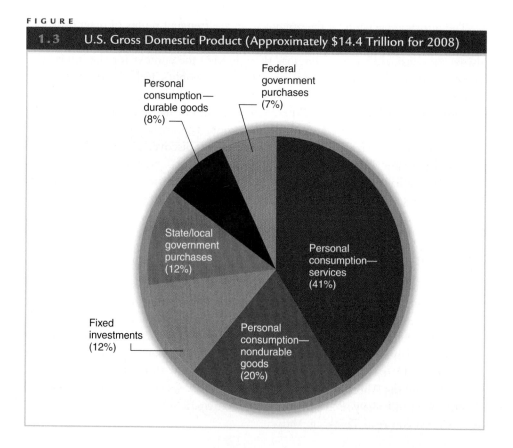

CarMax CarMax is a Fortune 500 company and is the largest retailer of used cars in the United States. Founded in 1992 as a concept for revolutionizing the way Americans buy cars, CarMax opened its first store in 1993 with a fleet of 500 used vehicles. The company recorded its first annual profit in the year 2000 and, five years later, was listed on *Fortune* magazine's "100 Best Companies to Work For" list. CarMax has earned that distinction each year since debuting on the list in 2005, advancing from number forty-six in 2008 to number thirty-one in 2009.

CarMax prides itself on changing the perception of the used car-buying experience, from the ordinary to the extraordinary. From the moment car shoppers step foot on the lot, they are met with a salesperson that remains with them throughout the entire process, from the greeting to the financing. Customers don't haggle for pricing. They don't have to haggle since the prices of vehicles are disclosed right away. CarMax goes out of its way to ensure customer confidence in the vehicles it sells by inspecting, reconditioning, and backing them with limited warranties. CarMax's goal is to make the car-buying experience painless and fun. According to its CEO, Tom Folliard, "CarMax was founded on the fundamental principle of integrity, reflected in the way we serve our customers, treat each other and deliver our products." This is evidenced by the company being only one of two North American companies to receive the Better Business Bureau's highest honor in recognition of ethical business practices, the International Torch Award for Marketplace Excellence.

CarMax is headquartered in Richmond, Virginia, and currently operates 100 used-car superstores in 46 markets. The company reported net sales and operating revenues of $6.97 billion and net earnings of $59.2 million in fiscal year 2009.[39]

Facebook Facebook is the second most-trafficked social networking Web site in the world. The company was founded in February 2004 by Mark Zuckerberg and his classmates from Harvard University, Chris Hughes, Dustin Moskovitz, and Eduardo Saverin. Facebook was first launched in their dorm room and was available for only Harvard students. Throughout 2004, Facebook expanded its network to other colleges and by the end of the year, the site had over 1 million active users. Now, anyone can join Facebook; the site has over 200 million active users and is available in 40 translations with 50 more in development.

Since inception, the company has developed numerous technologies to help the sharing of information through one's social graph, the digital mapping of user's real-world social connections, and has made an enormous impact on the way people communicate all over the world. Facebook has gone far beyond a communication tool for efficiently interacting with friends and families, and is now, for example, a marketing tool, a means to screen job candidates, and a way to rally support for political campaigns and policies. As a forum for over 200 million users and with so many uses, Facebook is navigating uncharted waters with issues such as user privacy and allowable content which they are addressing with innovative solutions such as customer participation in decision making.

Facebook has over 850 employees and is headquartered in Palo Alto, California, with its international headquarters in Dublin, Ireland. Additionally, the company has offices in Atlanta, Chicago, Dallas, Detroit, New York, Venice Beach, London, and Paris.[40]

Facebook.com worker Ginnie Chan, left, works at Facebook headquarters in Palo Alto, California.

Nordstrom Nordstrom is a fashion specialty chain with a focus on customer service, generous size ranges, and a selection of fine apparel, shoes, and accessories for the whole family. The first Nordstrom store was opened as a shoe store in Seattle, Washington, in 1901, under the name Wallin & Nordstrom. John W. Nordstrom and Carl Wallin founded this store on the principles of exceptional service, selection, quality, and value. In the late 1920s, both Wallin and Nordstrom sold their stake in the company to Nordstrom's sons, and members of the Nordstrom family have been involved in the company ever since.

Nordstrom also strives to be socially responsible. Every year, the company donates millions of dollars to nonprofits, it prints on Forest Stewardship Council (FSC)-certified paper with 30 percent recycled content, and in 2007, the company decided to pursue a more organized and comprehensive social responsibility strategy focusing on four primary areas: Supporting Communities, Sustaining the Environment, Protecting Human Rights, and Caring for our People.

Nordstrom has a long-standing philosophy for hiring personality and motivation and training the skills. When they find the right employee, they treat them well. They were one of the first companies to offer profit-sharing to employees. The company also has generous 401K, and in 2008, Nordstrom was listed on *Fortune* magazine's 2008 list of "100 Best Companies to Work For."

Today, Nordstrom is still headquartered in Seattle and is one of the nation's leading fashion specialty retailers with 177 U.S. stores in twenty-eight states.[41]

IKEA IKEA was founded in 1943 by Ingvar Kamprad in Sweden. The name IKEA came from the founders' initials (I.K.) and Elmtaryd (E) and Agunnaryd (A), the farm and village where he grew up. Kamprad started by buying small items such as pens, wallets, and picture frames in bulk and selling them by making individual sales calls. He sold the items for a profit but still at greatly reduced prices. He very quickly outgrew his ability to make sales calls and started a mail-order business using the local milk man to deliver products to the train station. In 1950s, Kamprad discovered the cost-saving and transportation advantages of not fully assembling its furniture. For the next fifty years, "flat-packs" have served IKEA well as the company has expanded throughout Europe, Asia, the Middle East, and North America as well as developed a Web presence.

IKEA takes corporate social responsibility seriously. Despite its low-cost model, IKEA does not cut costs at any price. They do not produce products with hazardous materials, they do not use wood from devastated forests, child labor is unacceptable, and suppliers must have a responsible attitude toward the environment. IKEA coworkers are on-site monitoring suppliers, monitoring forests, and discouraging child labor. Furthermore, IKEA supports initiatives of organizations such as UNICEF, Save the Children, and American Forests. Every new employee at IKEA goes through environmental training and each store has an environmental coordinator who actively works toward saving energy and educating employees and customers on reducing waste. For this focus on responsibility, in 2006, IKEA received the Foreign Policy Association Award for Global Corporate Social Responsibility.

IKEA has been recognized as a good place to work as well. For four consecutive years beginning in 2003, IKEA was on *Working Mother* magazine's annual list of the "100 Best Companies for Working Mothers." IKEA was also on *Training* magazine's annual list of top companies that excel at human capital development for five consecutive years beginning in 2002. Additionally, IKEA was listed on *Fortune*'s "100 Best Companies to Work For" in 2005, 2006, and 2007.

Currently, there are more than 250 IKEA stores in 34 countries, including 29 in the United States, where IKEA plans to open 3–5 stores a year. IKEA has about 128,000 employees in 39 countries and posted $21.2 billion in 2008 revenues.[42]

Research In Motion (RIM) RIM was founded in 1984 by its President and co-CEO Mike Lazaridis, who was joined by Jim Balsillie as co-CEO in 1992. What began as a wireless email solution for enterprise clients has evolved into a multifaceted and robust wireless platform that supports a wide range of communications, information, and entertainment applications for both businesses and consumers. RIM is the maker of the hugely popular BlackBerry (a favorite among many business executives) and a host of other wireless solutions for the worldwide mobile communications market.

The competition for the global converged device marketshare is heating up, and RIM is on pace to be a major contender. It opened its BlackBerry App World in April 2009 to compete directly for a piece of Apple's fast-growing iPhone business and broaden its appeal beyond its well-established base in the corporate world. The BlackBerry boasted approximately 3.9 million net new subscribers during the fourth quarter of 2009, bringing its total subscriber base to approximately 25 million. By 2009, RIM had shipped over 50 million BlackBerry smartphones and had grown its revenues by an impressive 170,000 percent. Strengthened by its core values of teamwork and egalitarianism, RIM is confident that it will continue to flourish and "stay in motion."

RIM is based in Waterloo, Ontario, Canada and has offices in North America, Europe, and Asia-Pacific. The firm posted revenues of $11.07 billion for fiscal year ended February 28, 2009.[43]

Deloitte Deloitte is one of the world's largest accounting and professional service delivery firms, providing audit, tax, consulting, and financial advisory services to some of the largest companies in more than twenty industries. It is currently number four of the top four auditing firms. But being number four of the "Big Four" doesn't intimidate Deloitte. Instead of selling off its consulting business as its major competitors have done, Deloitte expanded that side of its offerings and is by far the largest in terms of headcount, footprint of services, and global delivery.

Deloitte's origins can be traced from William Welch Deloitte's public accountancy apprenticeship in 1833 with London's Bankruptcy Court to the merger of his own accountancy office with George Touche's firm in 1990. This merger created Deloitte & Touche. Today, the "Deloitte" brand encompasses a global network of 70 firms in 142 countries operating under the name Deloitte Touche Tohmatsu. Sun Pharma, Reliance, and Tata Motors are among Deloitte's biggest clients.

As an employer, Deloitte has received praise for its culture of diversity and inclusion, professional development, and workplace flexibility. In 2008, it was named one of *Working Mother*'s "Best Companies for Multicultural Women" and marked its fifteenth consecutive year on *Working Mother*'s "100 Best Companies" list. Deloitte's emphasis on high-level recruiting, training programs, and attention to employee benefits has made it a top choice for Generation Y workers starting their professional careers.

Deloitte's leadership team includes its CEO James Quigley and U.S. CEO Barry Salzberg. Sharon Allen is the U.S. Chairman of the Board and sits on Deloitte Touche Tohmatsu's global board of directors. The firm is headquartered in New York and had a total headcount of 44, 375 employees in 2008, up nearly 3,400 in 2007. Deloitte reported $27.4 billion in total revenues in fiscal year 2008.[44]

The Real World 1.1

McDonald's Learns from Different Countries

American corporations typically do things the American way as they globalize and extend their reach into all parts of the world. The process of standardization is a uniquely American way of business since the advent of the Model T by Henry Ford. McDonald's has shown that it does not have to be that way. There was a time when McDonald's was vilified for pushing America onto the world, large sectors of which resented being Americanized. McDonald's has turned the tables and begun to learn about other countries and their unique tastes. McDonald's operations around the world are now able to invent their own buns, bags, and business practices. The approach has been a huge success for the company, most of whose business now comes from global markets. Rather than a Big Mac, the really successful Big Tasty was invented in Germany and

McDonald's has learned about countries and their unique tastes. Operations around the world are now able to invent their own unique products.

Manfred Bail/Photo Library

launched in Sweden. France, one of the company's best-performing and busiest countries, has the Croque McDo, which is ham and Swiss cheese on toast. The Netherlands has the McKroket, which is a deep-fried patty of beef. South Korea has the Bulgogi Burger, which is a pork patty marinated in soy-based sauce. Taiwan has the Rice Burger, which is shredded beef between two rice patties. Because many Indians do not eat beef, they have the Maharaja Mac, which is two chicken patties with smoke flavored mayo. McDonald's current global success is being achieved through accommodation, not through domination.

SOURCE: P. Gumbel, "Big Mac's Local Flavor," *Fortune* 157(9) (2008): 114–121.

CHANGE CREATES OPPORTUNITIES

6 Recognize the opportunities that change creates for organizational behavior.

Change creates opportunities and risks, as mentioned earlier in the chapter. Global competition is a leading force driving change at work and American companies can learn from the competition. McDonald's did just that as we see in The Real World 1.1. Competition in the United States and world economies has increased significantly during the past couple of decades, especially in industries such as banking, finance, and air transportation. Corporate competition creates performance and cost pressures, which have a ripple effect on people and their behavior at work. While one risk for employees is the marginalization of part-time professionals, good management practice can ensure the integration of these part-time professionals.[45] The competition may lead to downsizing and restructuring, yet it provides the opportunity for revitalization as well.[46] Further, small companies are not necessarily the losers in this competitive environment. Scientech, a small power and energy company, found it had to enhance its managerial talent and service quality to meet the challenges of growth and big-company competitors. Product and service quality is one tool that can help companies become winners in a competitive environment. Problem-solving skills are another tool used by IBM, Control Data Services, Inc., Northwest Airlines, and Southwest Airlines to help achieve high-quality products and services.

Too much change leads to chaos; too little change leads to stagnation. Some companies lead the way in creating change and transforming industries, as CarMax did in the used-car industry over the past two decades. Winning in a competitive industry can be a transient victory however; continuous change is required to stay ahead of the competition. One way that CarMax stayed ahead of the competition was through its ethical business practices as we saw in Thinking Ahead. CarMax has been a game changer in their industry.

Three Challenges for Managers Related to Change

Chapter 2 develops three challenges for managers related to change in contemporary organizations: globalization, workforce diversity, and ethics. These are three driving forces creating and shaping changes at work. Further, success in global competition requires organizations to be more responsive to ethnic, religious, and gender diversity as well as personal integrity in the workforce, in addition to responding positively to the competition in the international marketplace. Workforce demographic change and diversity are critical challenges in themselves for the study and management of organizational behavior.[47] The theories of motivation, leadership, and group behavior based on research in a workforce of one composition may not be applicable in a workforce of a very different composition.[48] This may be especially problematic if ethnic, gender, and/or religious differences lead to conflict between leaders and followers in organizations. For example, the Russian military establishment found ethnic and religious conflicts between the officers and enlisted corps a serious impediment to unit cohesion and performance.

Global Competition in Business

Managers and executives in the United States face radical change in response to increased global competition. According to noted economist Lester Thurow, this competition is characterized by intense rivalry between the United States, Japan, and Europe in core industries.[49] Economic competition places pressure on all categories of employees to be productive and to add value to the firm. The uncertainty of unemployment resulting from corporate warfare and competition is an ongoing feature of organizational life for people in companies or industries that pursue cost-cutting strategies to achieve economic success. The global competition in the automotive industry among the Japanese, U.S., and European car companies embodies the intensity that can be expected in other industries in the future.

Some people feel that the future must be the focus in coming to grips with this international competition; others believe we can deal with the future only by studying the past.[50] Global, economic, and organizational changes have dramatic effects on the study and management of organizational behavior. For example, American college students are found to have a much more positive attitude about globalization than the general public and older generations.[51] How positive were your perceptions of the change you analyzed in You 1.1? Are you an optimist who sees opportunity or a pessimist who sees threat?

Customer Focused for High Quality

Global competition has challenged organizations to become more customer focused, to meet changing product and service demands, and to exceed customers' expectations of high quality. Quality has the potential for giving organizations in viable industries a competitive edge in meeting international competition. In Thinking Ahead, we saw that CarMax has a strong customer focus.

Quality became a rubric for products and services of high status. Total quality is defined in many ways.[52] Total quality management (TQM) is the complete dedication to continuous improvement and to customers so that their needs are met and their expectations exceeded. Quality is a customer-oriented philosophy of management with important implications for virtually all aspects of organizational behavior. Quality cannot be optimized, because customer needs and expectations are always changing. It is a cultural value embedded in highly successful organizations. Ford Motor Company's dramatic metamorphosis as an automotive leader is attributable to the decision to "make quality Job One" in all aspects of the design and manufacture of cars. While TQM management consulting went through a boom-to-bust cycle, its solid technical foundation means that it is here to stay.[53]

Quality improvement enhances the probability of organizational success in increasingly competitive industries. One study of 193 general medical hospitals examined seven TQM practices and found them positively related to the financial performance of the hospitals.[54] Quality improvement is an enduring feature of an organization's culture and of the economic competition we face today. It leads to competitive advantage through customer responsiveness, results acceleration, and resource effectiveness.[55] The three key questions in evaluating quality improvement ideas for people at work are as follows: (1) Does the idea improve customer response? (2) Does the idea accelerate results? (3) Does the idea increase the effectiveness of resources? A "yes" answer means the idea should be implemented to improve quality.

Six Sigma is a philosophy for company-wide quality improvement developed by Motorola and popularized by General Electric. The Six Sigma program is characterized by its customer-driven approach, its emphasis on decision making based on quantitative data, and its priority on saving money.[56] It has evolved into a high-performance system to execute business strategy. Part of its quality program is a 12-step problem-solving method specifically designed to lead a Six Sigma "Black Belt" to significant improvement within a defined process. It tackles problems in four phases: (1) measure, (2) analyze, (3) improve, and (4) control. In addition, it demands that executives be aligned to the right objective and targets, quality improvement teams be mobilized for action, results be accelerated, and sustained improvement be monitored. Six Sigma is set up in a way that it can be applied to a range of problems and areas, from manufacturing settings to service work environments. Table 1.1 contrasts Six Sigma and TQM. One study compared Six Sigma with two other methods for quality improvement (specifically, Taguchi's methods and the Shainin system) and found it to be the most complete strategy of the three, with a strong emphasis on exploiting statistical modeling techniques.[57]

Six Sigma
A high-performance system to execute business strategy that is customer driven, emphasizes quantitative decision making, and places a priority on saving money.

TABLE 1.1 Contrasting Six Sigma and Total Quality Management

Six Sigma	Total Quality Management
Executive ownership	Self-directed work teams
Business strategy execution system	Quality initiative
Truly cross-functional	Largely within a single function
Focused training with verifiable	No mass training in statistics and quality
Return on investment	Return on investment
Business results oriented	Quality oriented

SOURCE: M. Barney, "Motorola's Second Generation," *Six Sigma Forum Magazine* (May 2002): 13.

Behavior and Quality at Work

Whereas total quality may draw on reliability engineering or just-in-time management, total quality improvement can be successful only when employees have the skills and authority to respond to customer needs.[58] Total quality has direct and important effects on the behavior of employees at all levels in the organization, not just on employees working directly with customers. Chief executives can advance total quality by engaging in participative management, being willing to change everything, focusing quality efforts on customer service (not cost cutting), including quality as a criterion in reward systems, improving the flow of information regarding quality improvement successes or failures, and being actively and personally involved in quality efforts. While serving as chairman of Motorola, George Fisher emphasized the behavioral attributes of leadership, cooperation, communication, and participation as important elements in the company's Six Sigma program.

Quality improvement continues to be important to our competitiveness. The U.S. Department of Commerce's sponsorship of an annual award in the name of Malcolm Baldrige, former secretary of commerce in the Reagan administration, recognizes companies excelling in quality improvement and management. The Malcolm Baldrige National Quality Award examination evaluates an organization in seven categories: leadership, information and analysis, strategic quality planning, human resource utilization, quality assurance of products and services, quality results, and customer satisfaction.

According to former President George H. W. Bush, quality management is not just a strategy. It must be a new style of working, even a new style of thinking. A dedication to quality and excellence is more than good business. It is a way of life, giving something back to society, offering your best to others.

Quality is one watchword for competitive success. Many factors can affect service quality, and one study in the airline industry found that multimarket contact led to delays in on-time arrivals, one key indicator of quality for airline passengers.[59] Organizations that do not respond to customer needs find their customers choosing alternative product and service suppliers who are willing to exceed their expectations. With this said, you should not conclude that total quality is a panacea for all organizations or that it guarantees unqualified success.

Managing Organizational Behavior in Changing Times

Over and above the challenge of quality improvement to meet international competition, managing organizational behavior during changing times is challenging for at least three reasons: (1) the increasing globalization of organizations' operating territory, (2) the increasing diversity of organizational workforces, and (3) the continuing demand for higher levels of moral and ethical behavior at work. These are the important issues to address in managing people. For example, a federal government study found diversity management strongly linked to both work group performance and job satisfaction.[60] In addition, people of color saw benefits from diversity management above and beyond those experienced by white employees.

Each of these three issues is explored in detail in Chapter 2 and highlighted throughout the text because they are intertwined in the contemporary practice of organizational behavior. For example, the issue of women in the workplace concerns workforce diversity and at the same time overlaps the globalization issue. Gender roles are often defined differently in various cultures, and sexual harassment is a frequent ethical problem for organizations in the United States, Europe, Israel, and South Africa. For another example, the public demand for ethical behavior in business is growing and the meaning of corporate codes of ethics can no longer be

The Real World 1.2

An Ethics Czar for President Obama . . . Will You Take the Job?

Early in his administration, President Obama appointed an impressive array of policy leaders to tackle the country's ever-mounting social and economic problems. Tough times call for creative solutions and so the president looked to the best and the brightest to help lead the nation. There was the Energy Czar, the Health Reform Czar, the Technology Czar, and the Green Czar; how about the Ethics Czar? Rather than federalizing the oversight of ethical behavior, the government could outsource the job. That is, make every American personally responsible for ethics and integrity. Will you be an Ethics Czar? That is right, you! CEOs, managers, leaders, entrepreneurs, and cabinetmakers can all set high standards in their companies and make a positive difference. Here is a Code of Conduct for Ethics Czars who accept the appointment. First, *lead by example*. The best way to promote ethics and integrity is

President Barack Obama announces a nomination.

© MICHAEL REYNOLDS/epa/Corbis

to demonstrate these qualities in all the things you think, say, and do. Second, *praise generously*. Providing corrective feedback at critical times can save lives and withholding praise when well deserved can kill initiative. Third, *criticize to build up, not tear down*. Legitimate criticism is linked to careful, accurate observation; it is not negative. Fourth, *be kind, unwind*. Learn to relax and let the small stuff go. Most of it is small stuff. Fifth, *punish fairly*. When punishment is needed, it must be administered justly. Sixth, *if it is to be, it is up to thee*. Some problems solve themselves. However, most problems are solved by problem solvers. Be a problem solver at work and take personal responsibility for what happens in your space and in your place of work.

SOURCE: B. Weinstein, "We Need an Ethics Czar to Battle Widespread Breakdown in Standards," *BusinessWeek* (March 16, 2009).

taken for granted, which means that integrating ethical reasoning into work is the only way to maximize business opportunities.[61] Should President Obama involve the federal government with an Ethics Czar? Read about it in The Real World 1.2. Therefore, students of organizational behavior must appreciate and understand these important issues.

LEARNING ABOUT ORGANIZATIONAL BEHAVIOR

7 Demonstrate the value of objective knowledge and skill development in the study of organizational behavior.

objective knowledge
Knowledge that results from research and scientific activities.

skill development
The mastery of abilities essential to successful functioning in organizations.

Organizational behavior is based on scientific knowledge and applied practice. It involves the study of abstract ideas, such as valence and expectancy in motivation, as well as the study of concrete matters, such as observable behaviors and medical symptoms of distress at work. Therefore, learning about organizational behavior includes at least three activities, as shown in Figure 1.4. First, the science of organizational behavior requires the mastery of a certain body of *objective knowledge*. Objective knowledge results from research and scientific activities, as reflected in the Science feature in each chapter. Second, the practice of organizational behavior requires *skill development* based on knowledge and an understanding of yourself in order to master the abilities essential to success. The You features in each chapter challenge you to know yourself and apply what you are learning. Third, both objective knowledge and skill development must be applied in real-world settings. The Real World features in each chapter open windows into organizational realities where science and skills are applied.

1.4 Learning about Organizational Behavior

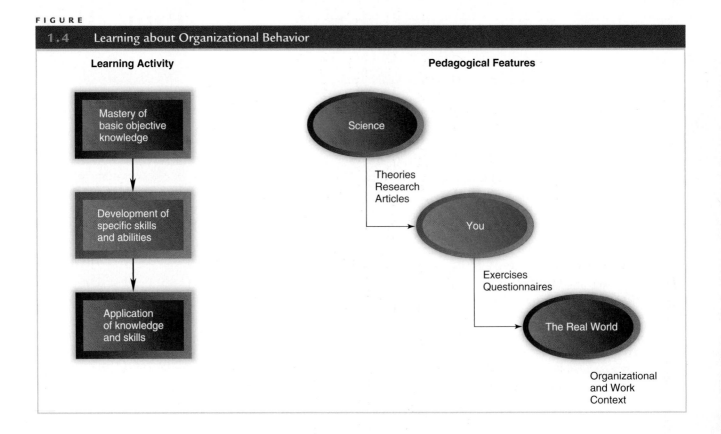

Learning is challenging and fun because we are all different. Some would deny our diversity, as the French have in not wanting to acknowledge differences in ethnic origin.[62] Within learning environments, student diversity is best addressed in the learning process through more options for students and greater responsibility on the part of students as coproducers in the effort and fun of learning.[63] For those who are blind or have vision impairments, learning can be a special challenge. The alignment of teaching styles with learning styles is important for the best fit, and teaching is no longer just verbal and visual but also virtual with a new generation of students.[64] To gain a better understanding of yourself as a learner, thereby maximizing your potential and developing strategies in specific learning environments, you need to evaluate the way you prefer to learn and process information. You 1.2 offers a quick way of assessing your learning style. If you are a visual learner, then use charts, maps, PowerPoint slides, videos, the Internet, notes, or flash cards, and write things out for visual review. If you are an auditory learner, then listen, take notes during lectures, and consider taping them so you can fill in gaps later; review your notes frequently; and recite key concepts out loud. If you are a tactile learner, trace words as you are saying them, write down facts several times, and make study sheets.

Objective Knowledge

Objective knowledge, in any field of study, is developed through basic and applied research. Research in organizational behavior has continued since early research on scientific management. Acquiring objective knowledge requires the cognitive mastery of theories, conceptual models, and research findings. In this book, the objective knowledge in each chapter is reflected in the notes that support the text and in the Science feature included in each chapter. Mastering the concepts and ideas that come from these notes enables you to intelligently discuss topics such as motivation, performance, leadership,[65] and executive stress.[66]

Learning Style Inventory

Directions: This 24-item survey is not timed. Answer each question as honestly as you can. Place a check on the appropriate line after each statement.

	OFTEN	SOMETIMES	SELDOM
1. Can remember more about a subject through the lecture method with information, explanations, and discussion.	____	____	____
2. Prefer information to be written on the chalkboard, with the use of visual aids and assigned readings.	____	____	____
3. Like to write things down or to take notes for visual review.			
4. Prefer to use posters, models, or actual practice and some activities in class.	____	____	____
5. Require explanations of diagrams, graphs, or visual directions.	____	____	____
6. Enjoy working with my hands or making things.			
7. Am skillful with and enjoy developing and making graphs and charts.	____	____	____
8. Can tell if sounds match when presented with pairs of sounds.			
9. Remember best by writing things down several times.			
10. Can understand and follow directions on maps.	____	____	____
11. Do better at academic subjects by listening to lectures and tapes.	____	____	____
12. Play with coins or keys in pockets.			
13. Learn to spell better by repeating the word out loud than by writing the word on paper.	____	____	____
14. Can better understand a news development by reading about it in the paper than by listening to the radio.	____	____	____
15. Chew gum, smoke, or snack during studies.			
16. Feel the best way to remember is to picture it in your head.	____	____	____
17. Learn spelling by "finger spelling" words.	____	____	____
18. Would rather listen to a good lecture or speech than read about the same material in a textbook.	____	____	____
19. Am good at working and solving jigsaw puzzles and mazes.			
20. Grip objects in hands during learning period.	____	____	____
21. Prefer listening to the news on the radio rather than reading about it in the newspaper.	____	____	____
22. Obtain information on an interesting subject by reading relevant materials.	____	____	____
23. Feel very comfortable touching others, hugging, hand-shaking, etc.	____	____	____
24. Follow oral directions better than written ones.	____	____	____

Scoring Procedures:

Score 5 points for each OFTEN, 3 points for each SOMETIMES, and 1 point for each SELDOM.

Visual Preference Score: 5 points for questions 2 + 3 + 7 + 10 + 14 + 16 + 19 + 22 = _____
Auditory Preference Score: 5 points for questions 1 + 5 + 8 + 11 + 13 + 18 + 21 + 24 = _____
Tactile Preference Score: 5 points for questions 4 + 6 + 9 + 12 + 15 + 17 + 20 + 23 = _____

SOURCE: Adapted from J. N. Gardner and A. J. Jewler, *Your College Experience: Strategies for Success, Third Concise Edition* (Belmont, CA: Wadsworth/ITP, 1998), 62–63; E. Jensen, *Student Success Secrets*, 4th ed. (Hauppauge, NY: Barron's, 1996), 33–36.

We encourage instructors and students of organizational behavior to think critically about the objective knowledge in organizational behavior. Only by engaging in critical thinking can one question or challenge the results of specific research and responsibly consider how to apply research results in a particular work setting. Rote memorization does not enable the student to appreciate the complexity of specific theories or the interrelationships among concepts, ideas, and topics. Good critical thinking, by contrast, enables the student to identify inconsistencies and limitations in the current body of objective knowledge.

Critical thinking, based on knowledge and understanding of basic ideas, leads to inquisitive exploration and is a key to accepting the responsibility of coproducer in the learning process. A questioning, probing attitude is at the core of critical thinking. The student of organizational behavior should evolve into a critical consumer of knowledge related to organizational behavior—one who is able to intelligently question the latest research results and distinguish plausible, sound new approaches from fads that lack substance or adequate foundation. Ideally, the student of organizational behavior develops into a scientific professional manager who is knowledgeable in the art and science of organizational behavior.

Skill Development

Learning about organizational behavior requires doing as well as knowing. The development of skills and abilities requires that students be challenged by the instructor and by themselves. Skill development is a very active component of the learning process. The You features in each chapter give you a chance to learn about yourself, challenge yourself, and developmentally apply what you are learning.

The U.S. Department of Labor wants people to achieve the necessary skills to be successful in the workplace.[67] The essential skills identified by the Department of Labor are (1) resource management skills such as time management; (2) information management skills such as data interpretation; (3) personal interaction skills such as teamwork; (4) systems behavior and performance skills such as cause–effect relationships; and (5) technology utilization skills such as troubleshooting. Many of these skills, such as decision making and information management, are directly related to the study of organizational behavior.[68]

Developing skills is different from acquiring objective knowledge in that it requires structured practice and feedback. A key function of experiential learning is to engage the student in individual or group activities that are systematically reviewed, leading to new skills and understandings. Objective knowledge acquisition and skill development are interrelated. The process for learning from structured or experiential activities is depicted in Figure 1.5. The student engages in an individual or group-structured activity and systematically reviews that activity, which leads to new or modified knowledge and skills.

If skill development and structured learning occur in this way, there should be an inherently self-correcting element to learning because of the modification of the student's knowledge and skills over time.[69] To ensure that skill development does occur and that the learning is self-correcting as it occurs, one must follow three basic assumptions that underlie the previous model..

First, each student must accept responsibility for his or her own behavior, actions, and learning. This is a key to the coproducer role in the learning process. A group cannot learn for its members. Each member must accept responsibility for what he or she does and learns. Denial of responsibility helps no one, least of all the learner.

Second, each student must actively participate in the individual or group-structured learning activity. Structured learning is an active process. In group activities,

1.5   Learning from Structured Activity

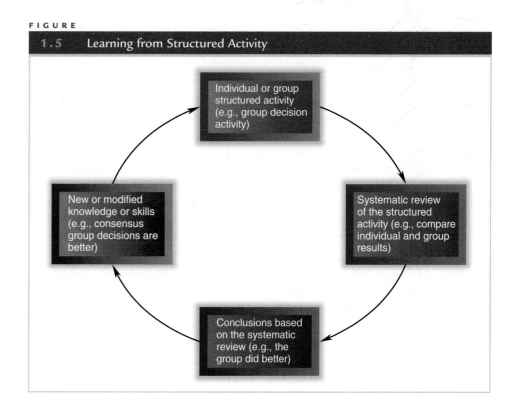

everyone suffers if just one person adopts a passive attitude. Hence, all must actively participate.

Third, each student must be open to new information, new skills, new ideas, and experimentation. This does not mean that students should be indiscriminate. It does mean that they should have a nondefensive, open attitude so that change is possible through the learning process.

Participating in group activities helps to ensure skill development and that learning is self-correcting as it occurs.

Application of Knowledge and Skills

The Real World features in each chapter give you a window into organizational realities and help you assess your own knowledge of the real world at work. Understanding the real world is one essential aspect of appreciating organizational behavior, the other two being understanding scientific knowledge and understanding yourself.

One of the advantages of structured, experiential learning is that a person can explore new behaviors and skills in a comparatively safe environment. Losing your temper in a classroom activity and learning about the potential adverse impact on other people will have dramatically different consequences from doing so with an important customer in a tense work situation. Learning spaces that encourage the interface of student learning styles with institutional learning environments create safe spaces to engage the brain to form abstract hypotheses, to actively test these hypotheses through concrete experience, and to reflectively observe the outcomes in behavior and experience.[70] The ultimate objective of skill application and experiential learning is that students be able to transfer the learning process they employed in structured classroom activities and learning spaces to unstructured opportunities in the workplace.

Although organizational behavior is an applied discipline, students are not "trained" in organizational behavior. Rather, they are "educated" in organizational

behavior and are a coproducer in learning. The distinction between these two modes of learning is found in the degree of direct and immediate applicability of either knowledge or skills. As an activity, training more nearly ties direct objective knowledge or skill development to specific applications. By contrast, education enhances a person's residual pool of objective knowledge and skills that may then be selectively applied later—sometimes significantly later—when the opportunity presents itself. Hence, education is highly consistent with the concept of lifelong learning. Especially in a growing area of knowledge such as organizational behavior, the student can think of the first course as the outset of lifelong learning about the topics and subject.

PLAN FOR THE BOOK

Challenge and opportunity are watchwords in organizations during these changing times. Managers and employees alike are challenged to meet change in positive and optimistic ways: change in how work gets done, change in psychological and legal contracts between individuals and organizations, change in who is working in the organization, and change in the basis for organization. Three challenges for managers are the global environment, workplace diversity, and ethical issues at work. These three challenges, which are discussed in detail in Chapter 2, are shaping the changes occurring in organizations throughout the world. For example, the increasing globalization of business has led to intense international competition in core industries, and the changing demographics of the workplace have led to gender, age, racial, and ethnic diversity among working populations.

The first two chapters compose Part 1 of the book, the introduction. Against the backdrop of the challenges discussed here, we develop and explore the specific subjects in organizational behavior. In addition to the introduction, the text has three major parts. Part 2 addresses individual processes and behavior. Part 3 addresses interpersonal processes and behavior. Part 4 addresses organizational processes and structure.

The five chapters in Part 2 are designed to help the reader understand specific aspects of human behavior. Chapter 3 discusses personality, perception, and attribution. Chapter 4 examines attitudes, values, and ethics. What was your attitude toward change in You 1.1? Chapters 5 and 6 address the broad range of motivational theories, learning, and performance management in organizations. Finally, Chapter 7 considers stress and well-being, including healthy aspects of life, at work.

Part 3 is composed of six chapters designed to help the reader better understand interpersonal and group dynamics in organizations. Chapter 8 addresses communication in organizations. Chapter 9 focuses on teamwork and groups as an increasingly prominent feature of the workplace. Chapter 10 examines how individuals and groups make decisions. Chapter 11 is about power and politics, one very dynamic aspect of organizational life. Chapter 12 addresses the companion topics of leadership and followership. Finally, Chapter 13 examines conflict at work, not all of which we consider bad.

The five chapters in Part 4 are designed to help the reader better understand organizational processes and the organizational context of behavior at work. Chapter 14 examines traditional and contemporary approaches to job design. Chapter 15 develops the topics of organizational design and structure, giving special attention to contemporary forces reshaping organizations and to emerging forms of organization. Chapter 16 addresses the culture of the organization. Chapter 17 focuses on the important issue of career management. Finally, Chapter 18 brings closure to the text and the main theme of change by addressing the topic of managing change.

MANAGERIAL IMPLICATIONS: FOUNDATIONS FOR THE FUTURE

Managers must consider personal and environmental factors to understand fully how people behave in organizations and to help them reach their maximum potential. Human behavior is complex and at times confusing. Characteristics of the organizational system and formal–informal dynamics at work are important environmental factors that influence people's behavior. Managers should look for similarities and differences in manufacturing, service-oriented, nonprofit, and governmental organizations.

Change may be seen as a threat or as an opportunity by contemporary managers. For example, hospital managers face not only clinical challenges but also organizational learning and the implementation of effective high involvement management practices with a professional workforce.[71] Changing customer demands for high-quality outputs in other industries challenges companies to beat the global competition. Globalization, workforce diversity, and ethics are three challenges for managers that are developed in Chapter 2. Another aspect of meeting the competition is learning. Managers must continually upgrade their knowledge about all

Diversity Dialogue

Women Triumph in Times of Recession—Really?

American women are finally in a position to surpass men in the workforce, but it took an economic recession for them to do it. The layoffs and plant closures experienced in the manufacturing and construction industries have hit working men terribly hard. Some estimate that 82 percent of the job losses during the recession have occurred for men. Why the difference? Women tend to hold jobs in "safer" recession-proof industries like healthcare and education.

Women's increased representation in the workforce should be cause for celebration. However, several issues loom beneath the surface that may damper the festivities. First, good benefits came with those good jobs in manufacturing and construction. This allowed men to support their families at much higher levels than women are able to do with their "safe" jobs. Women tend to work in part-time jobs with little or no health or unemployment insurance. And while the proportion of women in the workforce may be on pace to surpass that of men, their positions and salaries have not. The average salary of full-time women remains a fraction (between 77 and 80 percent) of men. Men continue to hold the majority of executive-level jobs. Finally, economists have found that even when both spouses work, working women devote much more time to child care and housework than men. Many agree that the job for laid off spouses—husbands especially—is not to settle into a new support role in which they help with cooking, cleaning, and running errands. His primary job is to find another job.

1. Do you believe an extended recession could completely change gender roles in the United States? Explain.
2. Do companies have a responsibility to raise women's salaries to accommodate their roles as primary breadwinners? Why or why not?

SOURCE: C. Rampell, "As Layoffs Surge, Women May Pass Men in Job Force," *New York Times* (February 6, 2009): A1; D. Cauchon, "Women Take Over Job Market," *ABCNews.com*.

aspects of their businesses, to include especially the human side of the enterprise. They must hone both their technical and interpersonal skills, engaging in a lifelong educational process. This is a fun and somewhat unpredictable process that can at times be frustrating, while always challenging and exciting.

Several business trends and ongoing changes are affecting managers across the globe. These include continuing industrial restructuring, a dramatic increase in the amount and availability of information, a need to attract and retain the best employees, a need to understand a wide range of human and cultural differences, and a rapid shortening of response times in all aspects of business activities. Further, the old company towns are largely relics of the past, and managers are being called on to re-integrate their businesses with communities, cultures, and societies at a much broader level than has ever been required before. Trust, predictability, and a sense of security become important issues in this context. Reweaving the fabric of human relationships within, across, and outside the organization is a challenge for managers today.

Knowledge becomes power in tracking these trends and addressing these issues. Facts and information are two elements of knowledge in this context. Theories are a third element of a manager's knowledge base. Good theories are tools that help managers understand human and organizational behavior, help them make good business decisions, and inform them about actions to take or to refrain from taking. Managers always use theories, if not those generated from systematic research, then those evolved from the manager's implicit observation. Theories tell us how organizations, business, and people work—or do not work. Therefore, the student is challenged to master the theories in each topic area and then apply and test the theory in the real world of organizational life. The challenge for the student and the manager is to see what works and what does not work in their specific work context.

LOOKING BACK: CARMAX

Real Success in Challenging Times

The sharp economic recession of 2008–2009 along with the accompanying financial crisis placed tremendous pressures on the global banking and auto industries, among others. The U.S. car manufacturing companies  experienced a full-blown crisis, General Motors required federal financial assistance to survive, and Chrysler went into bankruptcy court to dramatically restructure. Auto sales declined dramatically and many compared the crisis to that of the Great Depression of the 1930s. These were challenging times for managers and employees in a wide range of industries. Unemployment rates rose and people worried about making their home loan payments to avoid foreclosure. While some companies and industries were hurt much worse than others, no one was able to escape the pressures, changes, and challenges of this period.

In the midst of these challenging times, CarMax continued to display solid success. In early 2009, CarMax was named one of *Fortune*'s "100 Best Companies to Work For."[72] This distinction was for the fifth straight year, beginning in 2005. Ranked number 31 on the *Fortune* 2009 list, CarMax cited the dedication and innovativeness of its many associates who moved the company forward in the challenging times and difficult retail environment of the period. Rather than pulling in during this period, which is a common practice for companies in a crisis, CarMax associates reached out. Participation in the company's Volunteer Team-Builder Program, which is aimed at community service, rose significantly among associates. Giving to their communities is just one aspect of making CarMax a great place to work.

In addition to being a great place to work, CarMax invests in its associates and was named in *Training* magazine's "Training Top 125."[73] Each year, 125 organizations that excel at associate development are selected, and 2009 was the second consecutive year in which CarMax was named. The companies are chosen based on criteria such as best training practices, evaluation methods, and outstanding training initiatives. In the case of CarMax, the company was cited for three premier training programs: Extensive Sales Training, BASE Camp, and Culture of Integrity Training. During challenging and difficult times, some companies cut investment costs aimed at people development. That can make the company lean, and unfortunately weak. By investing in its associates during challenging times, CarMax aims to be fit and strong for the long run. Strong, competent people meet the challenges of difficult times more effectively and successfully.

Chapter Summary

1. Organizational behavior is individual behavior and group dynamics in organizations.

2. Change is an opportunity when one has a positive attitude, asks questions, listens, and is committed to succeed.

3. Organizations are open systems composed of people, structure, and technology committed to a task.

4. Organizations have formal and informal elements within them.

5. Manufacturing organizations, service organizations, privately owned companies, and nonprofit organizations all contribute to our national well-being.

6. The changes and challenges facing managers are driven by international competition and customer demands.

7. Learning about organizational behavior requires a mastery of objective knowledge, specific skill development, and thoughtful application.

Key Terms

anthropology (p. 6)
challenge (p. 4)
change (p. 4)
engineering (p. 6)

formal organization (p. 10)
Hawthorne studies (p. 10)
informal organization (p. 10)
management (p. 6)

medicine (p. 6)
objective knowledge (p. 20)
opportunities (p. 4)
organizational behavior (p. 4)

Review Questions

1. Define *organizational behavior*. What is its focus?

2. Identify the four action steps for responding positively to change.

3. What is an organization? What are its four system components? Give an example of each.

4. Briefly describe the elements of the formal and the informal organization. Give examples of each.

5. Discuss the six focus organizations used in the book.

6. Describe how competition and total quality are affecting organizational behavior. Why is managing organizational behavior in changing times challenging?

Discussion and Communication Questions

1. How do the formal aspects of your work environment affect you? What informal aspects of your work environment are important?

2. What is the biggest competitive challenge or change facing the businesses in your industry today? Will that be different in the next five years?

3. Describe the next chief executive of your company and what she or he must do to succeed.

4. Discuss two ways people learn about organizational behavior.

5. Which of the focus companies is your own company most like? Do you work for one of these focus companies? Which company would you most like to work for?

6. *(communication question)* Prepare a memo about an organizational change occurring where you work or in your college or university. Write a 100-word description of the change and, using Figure 1.1, identify how it is affecting the people, structure, task, and/or technology of the organization.

7. *(communication question)* Develop an oral presentation about the changes and challenges facing your college or university based on an interview with a faculty member or administrator. Be prepared to describe the changes and challenges. Are these good or bad changes? Why?

8. *(communication question)* Prepare a brief description of a service or manufacturing company, entrepreneurial venture, or nonprofit organization of your choice. Go to the library and read about the organization from several sources; then use these multiple sources to write your description.

Ethical Dilemma

Disco Global is an online and technology systems firm based out of Atlanta, Georgia; the company has been steadily acquiring a significant market share for the last five years. Founded by Melissa Young and Brian Whitman, Disco Global's current strategic goal is to penetrate international markets within the next three years. When Melissa and Brian first conceived of Disco Global, they envisioned growing a small niche company into one that served the widest market available, while they stay true to their professional values of corporate social responsibility.

Given Disco Global's positioning, the company has been advised to make inroads into the coveted Asian market at this time. Both co-CEO Melissa and Brian agree with this strategy and have secured a local

marketing team in Hong Kong to help facilitate their entrance into China's marketplace. Henry Chee Wan, their liaison in Hong Kong, has developed a very tight plan that everyone agrees will promote Disco Global in a positive and efficient manner.

During the course of their work with Henry, Melissa and Brian learn some facts about working within the Chinese governmental structure that have given them pause. In the company's vision statement, Melissa and Brian specifically included a mention of freedom to obtain knowledge. As they learn more about China's Internet censorship practices, they grow more concerned that in acquiescing to the government's conditions, they are moving too far away from their company's original goals and ethical compass. Henry explains to Melissa and Brian that the Internet is heavily regulated in China and that if their software or hardware was used with criminal, seditious intent, they would be liable for helping to reveal the user and culprit. Having their technology being used as filters for what Chinese people can read and hear seems contrary to the conception of Disco Global.

However, Melissa and Brian want to capitalize on the Asian market, and they agree that if Disco Global doesn't bring Internet and technology services to China, someone else will. Melissa and Brian now have to decide which the best decision for Disco Global is: stay true to their stated values or their strategic plan?

Questions:

1. Using consequential, rule-based and character theories, evaluate Melissa and Brian's options.

2. What should Melissa and Brian do? Why?

Experiential Exercises

1.1 What's Changing at Work?

This exercise provides an opportunity to discuss changes occurring in your workplace and university. These changes may be for the better or the worse. However, rather than evaluating whether they are good or bad changes, begin by simply identifying the changes that are occurring. Later, you can evaluate whether they are good or bad.

Step 1. The class forms into groups of approximately six members each. Each group elects a spokesperson and answers the following questions. The group should spend at least five minutes on each question. Make sure that each member of the group makes a contribution to each question. The spokesperson for each group should be ready to share the group's collective responses.

a. *What are the changes occurring in your workplace and university?* Members should focus both on internal changes, such as reorganizations, and on external changes, such as new customers or competitors. Develop a list of the changes discussed in your group.

b. *What are the forces that are driving the changes?* To answer this question, look for the causes of the changes members of the group are observing. For example, a reorganization may be caused by new business opportunities, by new technologies, or by a combination of factors.

c. *What signs of resistance to change do you see occurring?* Change is not always easy for people or organizations. Do you see signs of resistance, such as frustration, anger, increased absences, or other forms of discomfort with the changes you observe?

Step 2. Once you have answered the three questions in Step 1, your group needs to spend some time evaluating whether these changes are good or bad. Decide whether each change on the list developed in Step 1a is good or bad. In addition, answer the question "Why?" That is, why is this change good? Why is that change bad?

Step 3. Each group shares the results of its answers to the questions in Step 1 and its evaluation of the changes completed in Step 2. Cross-team questions and discussion follow.

Step 4. Your instructor may allow a few minutes at the end of the class period to comment on his or her perceptions of changes occurring within the university, or businesses with which he or she is familiar.

1.2 My Absolute Worst Job

Purpose: To become acquainted with fellow classmates.
Group size: Any number of groups of two.
Exercise schedule:

1. Write answers to the following questions:

   a. What was the worst job you ever had? Describe the following:

      (1) The type of work you did

      (2) Your boss

      (3) Your coworkers

      (4) The organization and its policies

      (5) What made the job so bad

   b. What is your dream job?

2. Find someone you do not know, and share your responses.

3. Get together with another dyad (pair), preferably new people. Partner "a" of one dyad introduces partner "b" to the other dyad; then "b" introduces "a." The same process is followed by the other dyad. The introduction should follow this format:

"This is Mary Cullen. Her very worst job was putting appliqués on bibs at a clothing factory, and she disliked it for the following reason. What she would rather do is be a financial analyst for a big corporation."

4. Each group of four meets with another quartet and is introduced, as before.

5. Your instructor asks for a show of hands on the number of people whose worst jobs fit into the following categories:

   a. Factory

   b. Restaurant

   c. Manual labor

   d. Driving or delivery

   e. Professional

   f. Health care

   g. Phone sales or communication

   h. Other

6. Your instructor gathers data on worst jobs from each group and asks the groups to answer these questions:

   a. What are the common characteristics of the worst jobs in your group?

   b. How did your coworkers feel about their jobs?

   c. What happens to morale and productivity when a worker hates the job?

   d. What was the difference between your own morale and productivity in your worst job and in a job you really enjoyed?

   e. Why do organizations continue to allow unpleasant working conditions to exist?

7. Your instructor leads a group discussion on Parts (a) through (e) of Question 6.

SOURCE: D. Marcic, "My Absolute Worst Job: An Icebreaker," *Organizational Behavior: Experiences and Cases* (St. Paul, MN: West, 1989), 5–6. Copyright 1988 Dorothy Marcic. All rights reserved. Reprinted by permission.

BizFlix | In Good Company

A corporate takeover brings star advertising executive Dan Foreman (Dennis Quaid) a new boss who is half his age. Carter Duryea (Topher Grace), Dan's new boss, wants to prove his worth as the new marketing chief at *Sports America*, Waterman Publishing's flagship magazine. Carter applies his unique approaches while dating Dan's daughter, Alex (Scarlett Johansson).

Organizational Behavior and Management: *Sports America* Magazine

This sequence starts with Carter Duryea entering Dan Foreman's office. It follows Foreman's reaction toward the end of a speech given by Globecom CEO Teddy K. (Malcolm McDowell). Carter Duryea enters while saying, "Oh, my God, Dan. Oh, my God." Mark Steckle (Clark Gregg) soon follows. The sequence ends with Carter asking, "Any ideas?" Dan Forman says, "One."

What to Watch for and Ask Yourself

- The film sequence shows three people interacting in a work environment. Which aspects of organizational behavior and management discussed earlier in this chapter appear in this sequence?

- The three people in this sequence represent different management levels in the company. Which levels do you attribute to Carter Duryea, Dan Foreman, and Mark Steckle?

- Critique the behavior shown in the sequence. What are the positive and negative aspects of the behavior shown?

Workplace Video | Evo: Managing in a Global Environment

Fast-growing online retailer Evo has an exciting new problem: It has more international customers than ever before. In 2001, the Seattle-based company began selling brand name ski-and-skate gear to U.S. consumers, and today Evo delivers products to places as far away as Bahrain, Turkey, Japan, and Bali.

Selling to global markets is loaded with difficulties, and Evo's customer service representatives tell stories about their challenging interactions with international shoppers. For starters, overseas callers are often disappointed to learn that they cannot order items due to international licensing and distribution agreements. In addition, language barriers between Evo's employees and international consumers make some orders impossible to transact.

Daily operations have unusual twists as well, especially in the area of supply chain management. "Manufacturers overseas can impact us," said Evo marketer Molly Hawkins. "There was a lock at all the ports in China and we couldn't import any of their products. Therefore, a lot of soft goods like jackets and pants couldn't be shipped."

And it's not just foreign ports that Evo must worry about: globalization affects products, too. In addition to selling skis, snowboards, and related gear, Evo now offers an international travel package for sport adventurers. Known as evoTRIP, the travel service provides guided ski, snowboarding, and surf expeditions to exotic destinations in South America, Japan, Indonesia, and Switzerland. "This concept is near and dear to what all of us value," said Bryce Phillips, Evo's founder. "It's getting out there, learning more about different cultures, doing the activities in different parts of the world, and seeing beautiful locations you've never seen before."

To offer the richest, most authentic cultural experience, evoTRIP hires local guides. Professional athletes from each country travel with groups so that evoTrippers can experience the cultural nuances from place to place.

Despite his early success marketing within the United States, Bryce Phillips is excited about expanding his company's global reach. As licensing practices change to reflect the boundary-free world of e-commerce, and as Evo becomes a global brand, ski-and-board enthusiasts all over the world may soon identify themselves as loyal Evo customers.

Questions

1. What political and economic challenges could evoTRIP encounter when conducting business in other countries?

2. How might globalization affect Evo's organizational context? Explain.

3. What cultural differences should Evo and evoTRIP participants pay attention to when traveling abroad?

Case

Facebook:
Just a Social Networking Site or an Opportunity for Entrepreneurs?

In May 2007, Facebook embarked on a venture to expand free services for members. The company invited software developers to write free software programs that Facebook members could utilize to inform and entertain one another. As of June 2008, a quarter-million developers requested Facebook's tools for building free software applications. Almost one-tenth (24,000) of those requests have resulted in actual software applications that enable Facebook users to play games, share movie preferences, and send each other virtual hugs, among many other things.[1]

Some of the 24,000 software applications have been successful while many others have failed to arouse user interest. According to Ben Ling, director of platform marketing at Facebook, the Facebook platform doesn't turn something that is not useful into something that is useful. Ling also says that "[e]ntrepreneurs need to ask themselves, 'What is the problem I'm trying to solve? What is the need I'm trying to address?'"[2]

One possible entrepreneurial venture that could use a platform such as Facebook to solve members' problems and satisfy their needs above and beyond social networking itself is group buying. This potential application focuses on group purchasing of products and services—something that started and failed elsewhere in the 1990s but which has arisen anew in a different form in China, where it is highly successful. The concept is called *tuangou*, and loosely translated it means "group buying."[3]

In the 1990s, when online businesses were springing up overnight, online group buying companies like LetsBuyIt.com and Mercata.com followed a simple business model that enabled online shoppers who were hunting for the same items to consolidate their orders in hopes of obtaining sizable discounts.[4] "It seemed like a great concept. The sites were free for consumers and made money by charging commissions and fees to the sellers of the products. Support was strong from investors, vendors and media. Within a few years, however, virtually all of the services failed. Traffic on the sites slowed after an initial boom. Most visitors didn't make purchases, and as the number of buyers went down, prices went up."[5]

Like the group buying Web sites of the 1990s, China's tuangou is based on the Web, but it has moved significantly beyond those earlier Web sites. China's experience with tuangou may help others to capitalize on Web-based social networking for group buying activities. "Lessons offered by tuangou suggest there are enormous opportunities for online services that are able to position themselves as intermediaries as people increasingly connect in online forums and social networks and demand more value via collective bargaining."[6]

Facebook offers to group buying the same potential that it has accorded to advertisers.

"Advertisers love the Internet because its mathematical and technological tools enable them to analyze anonymous data to detect patterns in peoples' interests and consumption habits and to match ads to them, adding precision, accountability and productivity [that] consumer marketers previously had lacked."[7]

Two major entrepreneurial opportunities may be on the horizon for merging information gleaned from Facebook with various group buying activities. One opportunity involves businesses using text-analytic software to probe the content of member profiles and posted messages with the intent of identifying their interests in specific products or services. The buying groups would then approach these Facebook members with tailor-made, already negotiated deals on services and products. Another opportunity exists in analyzing Facebook profiles and postings to identify people who are opinion leaders and therefore more likely to influence others. Group buying services could then provide these opinion leaders with incentives to recruit new members to the buying service.[8]

Are these two entrepreneurial opportunities an illusion or reality? The answer may hinge on how Facebook members react to their profiles and postings being used to glean the information needed by the group buying services.

Perhaps Facebook's previous experience with its *Beacon* feature in late 2007 provides an instructive perspective as Facebook, in conjunction with other entrepreneurs, seeks to mine, for commercial purposes, the wealth of information contained in member profiles and postings. Beacon, launched as an advertising scheme to provide the bang that marketers wanted from their advertising dollars, tracked Facebook members' activities and purchases on the Web,[9] as well as communicated them to their friends.[10] This provided a tremendous potential benefit to marketers by providing the means to pinpoint precisely the likes and dislikes of millions and millions of people.[11] However, members very quickly complained about invasion of their privacy[12] and that Facebook "was exploiting for commercial purposes personal information members hadn't intended to share."[13] Under increasing pressure, Facebook altered its implementation of the Beacon feature.[14]

Is the reaction to Beacon a harbinger of what may be in store for attempts to mine Facebook profiles and postings in order to serve the commercial interests of group buying services?

Discussion Questions

1. From your perspective, is the use of the Facebook platform to host more and different applications an appropriate and viable way for contemporary businesses to capitalize on social networking? Explain the reasoning behind your answer.

2. How has change created opportunities for entrepreneurs to develop businesses that utilize the Facebook platform?

3. Would you participate in a group buying experience on Facebook if one were available? Why or why not?

4. Do you think the two group buying business opportunities are genuine given Facebook's previous experience with Beacon? Explain your answer.

SOURCE: This case was written by Michael K. McCuddy, The Louis S. and Mary L. Morgal Chair of Christian Business Ethics and Professor of Management, College of Business Administration, Valparaiso University.

2

Challenges for Managers

LEARNING OBJECTIVES

After reading this chapter, you should be able to do the following:

1 Describe the dimensions of cultural differences in societies that affect work-related attitudes.

2 Explain the social and demographic changes that are producing diversity in organizations.

3 Describe actions managers can take to help their employees value diversity.

4 Discuss the assumptions of consequential, rule-based, and character theories of ethics.

5 Explain six issues that pose ethical dilemmas for managers.

RIM's BlackBerry has responded to the competition's challenge.

THINKING AHEAD: RESEARCH IN MOTION (RIM)

BlackBerry Battles Back

BlackBerrys have dominated the $12 billion annual U.S. market for smartphones with a 50 percent share since Mike Lazaridis began handing them out to chief information officers a decade ago. RIM, which created and sells the BlackBerry, doubled its global market share in 2008 from 7 percent to 14 percent. The BlackBerry still trails Nokia globally, the latter holding 42 percent of the global market in smartphones. The BlackBerry is still the favorite tool for e-mail among IT managers, and RIM clearly is holding a dominant position within the marketplace. However, given the lightening strike advances that occur in technological innovations, no company can establish a dominate position and then simply hold it. Success in advanced technologies requires active offensive strategies as well as turf protecting defensive ones.[1]

The assaults on RIM's dominate position are coming from several fronts. The company must compete with Apple, Nokia, and even Google in the consumer market with new, emerging, cutting-edge products. Apple's iPhone and other PDAs are replacing flip-phones in the hands of a whole lot of consumers. The competition has laid siege to RIM's turf and the company needs new products and new weapons to defend itself against the onslaught. BlackBerry has battled back with three new smartphones. First is the BlackBerry Pearl Flip that was launched by T-Mobile, looks a lot like Motorola's Razr, and takes on that angle of attack. Second is the Bold, a souped-up version of the Curve with a larger screen, which was brought out by AT&T at a premium price of $100 above the iPhone. Third is the Storm, a touch screen phone aimed to compete directly with Apple's iPhone, head-to-head.

BlackBerry has responded to the competition's challenge in the consumer market. How about the corporate market? The corporate market is a key strength for RIM and the company has engaged in a number of initiatives to strengthen its position in this arena. To make itself more indispensable to its corporate clients, RIM has produced software that lets the client seamlessly move between the office phone line and the BlackBerry. A call that begins in the car en route to work can end in the office with no one being the wiser. Good news for RIM is the number of CIOs and corporations that have passed up the iPhone because of security issues and because it is harder to customize its software for corporate use. Can RIM consolidate its lead in the corporate arena and buy some breathing room?

MANAGEMENT CHALLENGES IN A NEW TIME

1 Describe the dimensions of cultural differences in societies that affect work-related attitudes.

Most U.S. executives continue to believe that U.S. firms are encountering unprecedented global competition.[2] Globalization is being driven on the one hand by the spread of economic logics centered on freeing, opening, deregulating, and privatizing economies to make them more attractive for investment and, on the other hand, by the digitization of technologies that is revolutionizing communication.[3] The challenges for managers in this context are manifest in both opportunities and threats, as briefly touched upon in Chapter 1. The long, robust economic expansion in the United States during the 1990s led to a bubble that burst and several years of economic difficulty. Managers are challenged to lead people in the good times and the bad times, as Anne Mulcahy did in addressing Xerox's financial difficulties, because business cycles ultimately produce both. Over time, managers face both opportunities and threats.

What major challenges must managers overcome in order to remain competitive? Chief executive officers of U.S. corporations cite three issues that are paramount: (1) globalizing the firm's operations to compete in the global village; (2) leading a diverse workforce; and (3) encouraging positive ethics, character, and personal integrity.[4,5]

Successful organizations and managers respond to these three challenges as opportunities rather than as threats. Our six focus companies—CarMax, RIM, Nordstrom, Facebook, Deloitte, and IKEA—and their managers have wrestled with one or more of these three challenges as they pursue success and achievement. We see in the Looking Back feature that one of RIM's strengths is that it has embraced the uniqueness of being different, a key to success that cofounder Mike Lazaridis sees as one of the company's strengths. While CarMax, as we detailed in Chapter 1, was an industry changer, RIM has had a different challenge in being a technological pioneer. In this chapter, we focus on three challenges that, when well managed, lead to success and healthy organizational outcomes.

Globalization has led to the emergence of the global village in the world economy. The Internet, along with rapid political and social changes, has broken down old national barriers to competition. What has emerged is a world characterized by an ongoing process of integration and interconnection of states, markets, technologies, and firms. This world as a global macroeconomic village is a boundaryless market in which all firms, large and small, must compete.[6]

Managing a diverse workforce is something organizations like Alcon Laboratories and Coors Brewing Company do extremely well. Both companies reap success from their efforts. The workforce of today is more diverse than ever before. Managers are challenged to bring together employees of different backgrounds in work teams. This requires going beyond the surface to deep-level diversity.[7]

Good character, *ethical behavior*, and *personal integrity* are hallmarks of managers in organizations like Johnson & Johnson. The company's credo guides employee behavior and has helped employees do the right thing in tough situations. Ethical behavior in business has been at the forefront of public consciousness for some time now. Insider trading scandals, influence peddling, and contract frauds are in the news daily. It need not be that way. Many executives lead with a spirit of personal integrity.[8]

Organizations and managers who see opportunity in these three challenges will remain competitive, rather than just survive, in today's turbulent environment. Throughout the book, you'll see how organizational behavior can contribute to successfully managing these and other challenges.

THE GLOBAL VILLAGE

Only a few years ago, business conducted across national borders was referred to as "international" activity. The word *international* carries with it a connotation that the individual's or the organization's nationality is held strongly in consciousness.[9] *Globalization*, by contrast, implies that the world is free from national boundaries and that it is really a borderless world.[10] U.S. workers are now competing with workers in other countries. Foreign-based organizations are locating subsidiaries in the United States, such as the U.S. manufacturing locations of Honda, Toyota, Mazda, and Mercedes. The reverse is true as well. Volkswagen's German workers had to come to grips with globalization.[11]

Similarly, what were once referred to as multinational organizations (those doing business in several countries) are now called transnational companies. In *transnational organizations*, the global viewpoint supersedes national issues.[12] Transnational organizations operate over large global distances and are multicultural in terms of the people they employ. 3M, Dow Chemical, Coca-Cola, and other transnational organizations operate worldwide with diverse employee populations.

Changes in the Global Marketplace

Social and political upheavals have led organizations to change the way they conduct business and to encourage their members to think globally. Toyota is one Japanese company thinking big, thinking globally, and thinking differently by learning to speak to the 60-million-strong Generation Y, or millennials.[13] The collapse of Eastern Europe was followed quickly by the demise of the Berlin Wall. East and West Germany were united into a single country. In the Soviet Union, perestroika led to liberation and brought about many opportunities for U.S. businesses, as

transnational organization
An organization in which the global viewpoint supersedes national issues.

witnessed by the press releases showing extremely long waiting lines at Moscow's first McDonald's restaurant.

Business ventures in China have become increasingly attractive to U.S. companies. Coca-Cola has led the way. One challenge U.S. managers have faced is understanding the Chinese way of doing business. Chinese managers' business practices have been shaped by the Communist Party, socialism, feudalistic values, and *guanxi* (building networks for social exchange). Once *guanxi* is established, individuals can ask favors of each other with the expectation that the favor will be returned. For example, it is common in China to use *guanxi* to conduct business or to obtain jobs. *Guanxi* is sometimes a sensitive word, because Communist Party policies oppose the use of such practices to gain influence. In China, the family is regarded as being responsible for a worker's productivity, and in turn, the company is responsible for the worker's family. Because of socialism, Chinese managers have very little experience with rewards and punishments and are reluctant to use them in the workplace. The concept of *guanxi* is not unique to China. There are similar concepts in many other countries, including Russia and Haiti. It is a broad term that can mean anything from strongly loyal relationships to ceremonial gift-giving, sometimes seen as bribery. *Guanxi* is more common in societies with underdeveloped legal support for private businesses.[14]

To work with Chinese managers, Americans can learn to build their own *guanxi*; understand the Chinese chain of command; and negotiate slow, general agreements in order to interact effectively. Using the foreign government as the local franchisee may be effective in China. For example, KFC Corporation's operation in China is a joint venture between KFC (60 percent) and two Chinese government bodies (40 percent).[15]

In 1993, the European Union integrated fifteen nations into a single market by removing trade barriers. At that time, the member nations of the European Union were Belgium, Denmark, France, Germany, Greece, Ireland, Italy, Luxembourg, the Netherlands, Portugal, Spain, Austria, Finland, Sweden, and the United Kingdom. As of 2004, Estonia, Hungary, Latvia, Lithuania, Malta, Poland, Slovakia, and Slovenia were also members. The integration of Europe provides many opportunities for U.S. organizations, including 350 million potential customers. Companies like Ford Motor Company and IBM, which entered the market early with wholly owned subsidiaries, will have a head start on these opportunities.[16] Competition within the European Union will increase, however, as will competition from Japan and the former Soviet nations.

The United States, Canada, and Mexico have dramatically reduced trade barriers in accordance with the North American Free Trade Agreement (NAFTA), which took effect in 1994. Organizations have found promising new markets for their products, and many companies have located plants in Mexico to take advantage of low labor costs. DaimlerChrysler, for example, has a massive assembly plant in Saltillo. Prior to NAFTA, Mexico placed heavy tariffs on U.S. exports. The agreement immediately eliminated many of these tariffs and provided that the remaining tariffs be phased out over time.

All of these changes have brought about the need to think globally. Managers can benefit from global thinking by taking a long-term view. Entry into global markets requires long-term strategies.

Understanding Cultural Differences

One of the keys for any company competing in the global marketplace is to understand diverse cultures. Whether managing culturally diverse individuals within a single location or managing individuals at remote locations around the globe, an

guanxi

The Chinese practice of building networks for social exchange.

appreciation of the differences among cultures is crucial. Edgar Schein suggests that to understand an organization's culture, or more broadly any culture, it is important to dig below the surface of visible artifacts and uncover the basic underlying assumptions at the core of the culture.[17] His definition of organizational culture is the pattern of basic assumptions that a given group has invented, discovered, or developed in learning to cope with its problems of external adaptation and internal integration, and that have worked well enough to be considered valid. These basic assumptions are then taught to new members as the correct way to perceive, think, and feel in relation to those problems. We develop Schein's culture model of basic assumptions, values, visible artifacts, and creations more fully in Chapter 16.

Microcultural differences (i.e., differences within cultures) can play an important role in understanding the global work environment.[18] IBM sends management trainee teams around the globe to deepen their global awareness, as we see in The Real World 2.1. Knowing cultural differences in symbols is extremely important. Computer icons may not translate well in other cultures. The thumbs-up sign, for example, means approval in the United States. In Australia, however, it is an obscene gesture. And manila file folders, like the icons used in Windows applications, aren't used in many European countries and therefore aren't recognized.[19]

Do cultural differences translate into differences in work-related attitudes? The pioneering Dutch researcher Geert Hofstede focused on this question.[20] He and his colleagues surveyed 160,000 managers and employees of IBM who were working in 60 different countries.[21] In this way, the researchers were able to study

The Real World 2.1

IBM Uses the World as a Classroom

Traditional management development is done in a classroom and IBM still trains managers that way. In addition for top management prospects, IBM added the Corporate Service Corps. Modeled on the U.S. Peace Corps, this select IBM program aims to turn top management trainees into global citizens. IBM's human resources chief says this program helps future leaders understand how the world works, shows them how to network, and shows them how to work collaboratively with people who are far away. The Corporate Service Corps is selective, taking roughly the top 10 percent, maybe 500 of over 5,000 applications within the company. These 500 top management prospects are sent around the world in teams of 8–10. The teams spend three months before going overseas reading about their host countries, studying the problems they assigned to them, and getting to know

IBM building in Tel Aviv.

© Israel images/Alamy

their teammates via teleconferences and social networking Web sites. In the field, the teams work with local governments, universities, and business groups to do anything from upgrading technology for a government agency to improving public water quality. While the teams are only on location for about one month, good things happen. For example, one ten-member team working in the Philippines and traveling by minibus came upon a stalled water well project in the village of Carmen. They learned that the effort had run into engineering mistakes and a lack of money. The IBM team organized a meeting of the key project people and volunteered to pay $250 out of their own pockets for additional building materials. Two weeks later the well was completed.

SOURCE: S. Hamm, "The Globe is IBM's Classroom," *BusinessWeek* (March 23, 2009): 56.

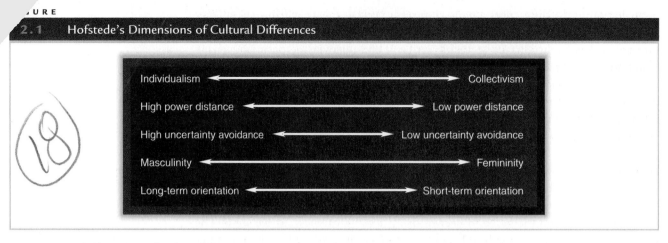

Individualism ⟵⟶ Collectivism

High power distance ⟵⟶ Low power distance

High uncertainty avoidance ⟵⟶ Low uncertainty avoidance

Masculinity ⟵⟶ Femininity

Long-term orientation ⟵⟶ Short-term orientation

SOURCE: Reprinted with permission of Academy of Management, PO Box 3020, Briar Cliff, NY 10510-8020. *Cultural Constraints in Management Theories* (Figure). G. Hofstede, *Academy of Management Executive 7* (1993). Reproduced by permission of the publisher via Copyright Clearance Center, Inc.

individuals from the same company in the same jobs, but working in different countries. Hofstede's work is important because his studies showed that national culture explains more differences in work-related attitudes than do age, gender, profession, or position within the organization. Thus, cultural differences do affect individuals' work-related attitudes. Hofstede found five dimensions of cultural differences that formed the basis for work-related attitudes. These dimensions are shown in Figure 2.1 and are described next.

Individualism versus Collectivism In cultures in which *individualism* predominates, people belong to loose social frameworks, but their primary concern is for themselves and their families. People are responsible for taking care of their own interests. They believe that individuals should make decisions. Cultures characterized by *collectivism* are tightly knit social frameworks in which individual members depend strongly on extended families or clans. Group decisions are valued and accepted.

The North American culture is individualistic in orientation. It is a "can-do" culture that values individual freedom and responsibility. By contrast, collectivist cultures emphasize group welfare and harmony. Israeli kibbutzim and Japanese culture are examples of societies in which group loyalty and unity are paramount. Organization charts show these orientations. In Canada and the United States, which are individualistic cultures, organization charts show individual positions. In Malaysia, which is a collectivist culture, organization charts show only sections or departments.

This dimension of cultural differences has other workplace implications. Individualistic managers, as found in the United Kingdom and the Netherlands, emphasize and encourage individual achievement. By contrast, collectivistic managers, such as in Japan and Colombia, seek to fit harmoniously within the group. They also encourage these behaviors among their employees. Further, there are cultural differences within regions of the world. Arabs are more collectivist than Americans. Within the Arab culture, however, Egyptians are more individualistic than Arabs from the Gulf States (Saudi Arabia, Oman, Bahrain, Kuwait, Qatar, and United Arab Emirates). This may be due to the fact that Egyptian businesspeople tend to have longer and more intensive exposures to Western culture.[22]

Power Distance The second dimension of cultural differences examines the acceptance of unequal distribution of power. In countries with a high *power distance*, bosses are afforded more power simply because they are the bosses. Titles are used,

individualism

A cultural orientation in which people belong to loose social frameworks, and their primary concern is for themselves and their families.

collectivism

A cultural orientation in which individuals belong to tightly knit social frameworks, and they depend strongly on large extended families or clans.

power distance

The degree to which a culture accepts unequal distribution of power.

formality is the rule, and authority is seldom bypassed. Power holders are entitled to their privileges, and managers and employees see one another as fundamentally different kinds of people. India is a country with a high power distance, as are Venezuela and Mexico.

In countries with a low power distance, people believe that inequality in society should be minimized. People at various power levels are less threatened by, and more willing to trust, one another. Managers and employees see one another as similar. Managers are given power only if they have expertise. Employees frequently bypass the boss in order to get work done in countries with a low power distance, such as Denmark and Australia.

Uncertainty Avoidance Some cultures are quite comfortable with ambiguity and uncertainty, whereas others do not tolerate these conditions well. Cultures with high *uncertainty avoidance* are concerned with security and tend to avoid conflict. People have a need for consensus. The inherent uncertainty in life is a threat against which people in such cultures constantly struggle.

Cultures with low uncertainty avoidance are more tolerant of ambiguity. People are more willing to take risks and are more tolerant of individual differences. Conflict is seen as constructive, and people accept dissenting viewpoints. Norway and Australia are characterized by low uncertainty avoidance, and this trait is seen in the value placed on job mobility. Japan and Italy are characterized by high uncertainty avoidance, so career stability is emphasized.

Masculinity versus Femininity In cultures that are characterized by *masculinity*, assertiveness and materialism are valued. Men are expected to be assertive, tough, and decisive and women to be nurturing, modest, and tender.[23] Money and possessions are important, and performance is what counts. Achievement is admired. Cultures that are characterized by *femininity* emphasize relationships and concern for others. Men and women are expected to assume both assertive and nurturing roles. Quality of life is important, and people and the environment are emphasized.

Masculine societies, such as in Austria and Venezuela, define gender roles strictly. Feminine societies, by contrast, tend to blur gender roles. Women may be the providers, and men may stay home with the children. The Scandinavian countries of Norway, Sweden, and Denmark exemplify the feminine orientation.

Time Orientation Cultures also differ in *time orientation,* that is, whether the culture's values are oriented toward the future (long-term orientation) or toward the past and present (short-term orientation).[24] In China, a culture with a long-term orientation, values such as thrift and persistence, which focus on the future, are emphasized. In Russia, the orientation is short-term. Values such as respect for tradition (past) and meeting social obligations (present) are emphasized.

U.S. Culture The position of the United States on these five dimensions is interesting. Hofstede found the United States to be the most individualistic country of any studied. On the power distance dimension, it ranked among the countries with weak power distance. Its rank on uncertainty avoidance indicated a tolerance of uncertainty. The United States also ranked as a masculine culture with a short-term orientation. These values have shaped U.S. management theory, so Hofstede's work casts doubt on the universal applicability of U.S. management theories. Because cultures differ so widely on these dimensions, management practices should be adjusted to account for cultural differences. Managers in transnational organizations must learn as much as they can about other cultures in order to lead their culturally diverse organizations effectively.

uncertainty avoidance
The degree to which a culture tolerates ambiguity and uncertainty.

masculinity
The cultural orientation in which assertiveness and materialism are valued.

femininity
The cultural orientation in which relationships and concern for others are valued.

time orientation
Whether a culture's values are oriented toward the future (long-term orientation) or toward the past and present (short-term orientation).

Planning for a Global Career

Think of a country you would like to work in, do business in, or visit. Find out about its culture, using Hofstede's dimensions as guidelines. You can use a variety of sources to accomplish this, particularly your school library, government offices, faculty members, or others who have global experience. You will want to answer the following questions:

1. Is the culture individualistic or collectivist?
2. Is the power distance high or low?
3. Is uncertainty avoidance high or low?
4. Is the country masculine or feminine in its orientation?
5. Is the time orientation short term or long term?
6. How did you arrive at your answers to the first five questions?
7. How will these characteristics affect business practices in the country you chose to investigate?

Careers in management have taken on a global dimension. Working in transnational organizations may well give managers the opportunity to work in other countries. *Expatriate managers,* those who work outside their home country, benefit from having as much knowledge as possible about cultural differences. Because managers are increasingly exposed to global work experiences, it is never too early to begin planning for this aspect of your career. You 2.1 asks you to begin gathering information about a country in which you would like to work, including information on its culture.

International executives are executives whose jobs have international scope, whether in an expatriate assignment or in a job dealing with international issues. What kind of competencies should an individual develop in order to prepare for an international career? There seem to be several attributes, all of them centering on core competencies and the ability to learn from experience. Some of the key competencies are integrity, insightfulness, risk taking, courage to take a stand, and ability to bring out the best in people. Learning-oriented attributes of international executives include cultural adventurousness, flexibility, openness to criticism, desire to seek learning opportunities, and sensitivity to cultural differences.[25] Further, strong human capital has a generally positive effect on internationalization.[26]

Understanding cultural differences becomes especially important for companies that are considering opening foreign offices, because workplace customs can vary widely from one country to another. A different language is part of it but managers and business owners really have to learn a different culture too.[27] Carefully searching out this information in advance can help companies successfully manage foreign operations. Consulate offices and companies operating within the foreign country are excellent sources of information about national customs and legal requirements. Table 2.1 presents a business guide to cultural differences in three countries: Japan, Mexico, and Saudi Arabia.

Another reality that can affect global business practices is the cost of layoffs in other countries. The practice of downsizing is not unique to the United States. Dismissing a forty-five-year-old middle manager with twenty years of service and a $50,000 annual salary can vary in cost from a low of $13,000 in Ireland to a high of $130,000 in Italy.[28] The cost of laying off this manager in the United States would be approximately $19,000. The wide variability in costs stems from the various legal protections that certain countries give workers. In Italy, laid-off employees

expatriate manager
A manager who works in a country other than his or her home country.

2.1 Business Guide to Cultural Differences

Country	Appointments	Dress	Gifts	Negotiations
Japan	Punctuality is necessary when doing business here. It is considered rude to be late.	Conservative for men and women in large to medium companies, though pastel shirts are common. May be expected to remove shoes in temples and homes, as well as in some *ryokan*-(inn) style restaurants. In that case, slip-on shoes should be worn.	Important part of Japanese business protocol. Gifts are typically exchanged among colleagues on July 15 and January 1 to commemorate midyear and the year's end, respectively.	Business cards (*meishi*) are an important part of doing business in Japan and key for establishing credentials. One side of your card should be in English and the reverse in Japanese. It is an asset to include information such as membership in professional associations.
Mexico	Punctuality is not always as much of a priority in Mexican business culture. Nonetheless, Mexicans are accustomed to North Americans arriving on time, and most Mexicans in business, if not government, will try to return the favor.	Dark, conservative suits and ties are the norm for most men. Standard office attire for women includes dresses, skirted suits, or skirts and blouses. Femininity is strongly encouraged in women's dress. Women business travelers will want to bring hosiery and high heels.	Not usually a requirement in business dealings though presenting a small gift will generally be appreciated as a gesture of goodwill. If giving a gift, be aware that inquiring about what the receiver would like to receive can be offensive.	Mexicans avoid directly saying "no." A "no" is often disguised in responses such as "maybe" or "We'll see." You should also use this indirect approach in your dealings. Otherwise, your Mexican counterparts may perceive you as being rude and pushy.
Saudi Arabia	Customary to make appointments for times of day rather than precise hours. The importance Saudis attach to courtesy and hospitality can cause delays that prevent keeping to a strict schedule.	The only absolute requirement of dress code in Saudi Arabia is modesty. For men, this means covering everything from navel to knee. Females are required to cover everything except the face, hands, and feet in public; they can wear literally anything they want providing they cover it with an *abaya* (standard black cloak) and headscarf when they go out.	Should only be given to the most intimate of friends. For a Saudi to receive a present from a lesser acquaintance is so embarrassing that it is considered offensive.	Business cards are common but not essential. If used, the common practice is to have both English and Arabic printed, one on each side, so that neither language is perceived as less important by being on the reverse of the same card.

SOURCE: Adapted from information obtained from business culture guides accessed online at http://www.executiveplanet.com.

must receive a "notice period" payment (one year's pay if they have nine years or more of service) plus a severance payment (based on pay and years of service). U.S. companies operating overseas often adopt the European tradition of training and retraining workers to avoid overstaffing and potential layoffs. An appreciation of the customs and rules for doing business in another country is essential if a company wants to go global.

Developing Cross-Cultural Sensitivity

As organizations compete in the global marketplace, employees must learn to deal with individuals from diverse cultural backgrounds. Stereotypes may pervade employees' perceptions of other cultures. In addition, employees may be unaware of others' perceptions of the employees' national culture. A potentially valuable exercise is to ask members of various cultures to describe one another's cultures. This provides a lesson on the misinterpretation of culture.

Intel wants interns and employees to understand the company's culture, but more importantly, it wants to understand the employees' cultures. In an effort to increase diversity, Intel's proportion of ethnic minorities in managerial positions increased from 13 percent in 1993 to 20 percent in 2003, and is still climbing.[29] Many individuals feel their cultural heritage is important and may walk into uncomfortable situations at work. To prevent this, Intel's new workers are paired carefully with mentors, and mentors and protégés learn about each others' cultures.

Cultural sensitivity training is a popular method for helping employees recognize and appreciate cultural differences. Another way of developing sensitivity is to use cross-cultural task forces or teams. The Milwaukee-based GE Medical Systems Group (GEMS) has 19,000 employees working worldwide. GEMS has developed a vehicle for bringing managers from each of its three regions (the Americas, Europe, and Asia) together to work on a variety of business projects. Under the Global Leadership Program, several work groups made up of managers from various regions of the world are formed. The teams work on important projects, such as worldwide employee integration to increase the employees' sense of belonging throughout the GEMS international organization.[30]

The globalization of business affects all parts of the organization, and human resource management is affected in particular. Companies have employees around the world, and human resource managers face the daunting task of effectively supporting a culturally diverse workforce. Human resource managers must adopt a global view of all functions, including human resource planning, recruitment and selection, compensation, and training and development. They must have a working knowledge of the legal systems in various countries, as well as of global economics, culture, and customs. Human resource managers must not only prepare U.S. workers to live outside their native country but also help foreign employees interact with U.S. culture. Global human resource management is a complex endeavor, but it is critical to the success of organizations in the global marketplace.

Globalization is one challenge managers must meet in order to remain competitive in the changing world. Related to globalization is the challenge of managing an increasingly diverse workforce. Cultural differences contribute a great deal to the diversity of the workforce, but there are other forms of diversity as well.

THE DIVERSE WORKFORCE

Workforce diversity is an important issue for organizations as Bell has so richly and clearly shown us.[31] The United States, as a melting pot nation, has always had a mix of individuals in its workforce. We once sought to be all alike, as in the melting pot, but we now recognize and appreciate individual differences. *Diversity* encompasses all forms of differences among individuals, including culture, gender, age, ability, religion, personality, social status, and sexual orientation. Catalyst's Sheila Wellington believed 2003 was the year in which business made the case for diversity and inclusion, and then matched it with action.

Attention to diversity has increased in recent years. This is largely because of the changing demographics of the working population. Managers feel that dealing

diversity
All forms of individual differences, including culture, gender, age, ability, religion, personality, social status, and sexual orientation.

with diversity successfully is a paramount concern for two reasons. First, managers need to know how to motivate diverse work groups. Second, managers need to know how to communicate effectively with employees who have different values and language skills.

Several demographic trends are affecting organizations. By the year 2020, the workforce will be more culturally diverse, more female, and older than ever. In addition, legislation and new technologies have brought more workers with disabilities into the workforce. Hence, learning to work together is an increasingly important skill, just as it is important to work with an open mind.[32] We learn more about team diversity in Chapter 9. Alcon Laboratories, the Swiss-owned and Fort Worth–based international company whose mission is to improve and preserve eyesight and hearing, creates an opportunity for learning to work together through diversity training.[33] Valuing diversity in organizations is an important issue.[34]

Workplace diversity is an important issue for organizations. Diversity encompasses all forms of differences among individuals, including culture, gender, age, and other factors.

Cultural Diversity

Cultural diversity in the workplace is growing because of the globalization of business, as we discussed earlier. People of diverse national origins—Koreans, Bolivians, Pakistanis, Vietnamese, Swedes, Australians, and others—find themselves cooperating in teams to perform the work of the organization. In addition, changing demographics within the United States significantly affect the cultural diversity in organizations. By 2020, minorities will constitute more than one-half of the new entrants to the U.S. workforce. The participation rates of African Americans and Hispanic Americans in the labor force increased dramatically in recent years. By 2020, white non-Hispanics will constitute 68 percent of the labor force (down from 83 percent in 2002); 14 percent of the workforce will be Hispanic (up from 12 percent); African Americans' share will remain at 11 percent; and 5 percent will be Asian.[35]

2 Explain the social and demographic changes that are producing diversity in organizations.

These trends have important implications for organizations. African Americans and Hispanic Americans are overrepresented in declining occupations, thus limiting their opportunities. Further, both groups tend to live in a small number of large cities that are facing severe economic difficulties and high crime rates. Because of these factors, minority workers are likely to be at a disadvantage within organizations. It does not have to be this way. For example, by monitoring its human resource systems, Coco-Cola has made substantial progress on diversity.[36]

The jobs available in the future will require more skill than has been the case in the past. Often, minority workers have not had opportunities to develop leading-edge skills. Minority skill deficits are large, and the proportions of African Americans and Hispanic Americans who are qualified for higher-level jobs are often much lower than the proportions of qualified whites and Asian Americans.[37]

Minority workers are less likely to be prepared because they are less likely to have had satisfactory schooling and on-the-job training. Educational systems within the workplace are needed to supply minority workers the skills necessary for success. Companies such as Motorola are already recognizing and meeting this need by focusing on basic skills training.

The globalization of business and changing demographic trends present organizations with a tremendously culturally diverse workforce. This represents both a challenge and a risk. The challenge is to harness the wealth of differences that cultural diversity provides. The risk is that prejudices and stereotypes may prevent managers and employees from developing synergies that can benefit the organization. As RIM grows its BlackBerry business into global markets as we saw in Thinking Ahead, the company must learn to meet the challenges that inevitably come with such growth.

Gender Diversity

The feminization of the workforce has increased substantially. The number of women in the labor force increased from 31.5 million in 1970 to 64 million in 2003. This increase accounts for almost 60 percent of the overall expansion of the entire labor force in the United States for this time period. In 2004, women made up over 60 percent of the labor force, and it is predicted that by the year 2010, 70 percent of new entrants into the workforce will be women and/or people of color. Women are better prepared to contribute in organizations than ever before. Women now earn 32 percent of all doctorates, 52 percent of master's degrees, and 50 percent of all undergraduate degrees. Thus, women are better educated, and more are electing to work. In 2004, almost 58 percent of U.S. women were employed.[38] However, women comprised only 14.7 percent of corporate board members in 2005.[39]

Women's participation in the workforce is increasing, but their share of the rewards of participation is not increasing commensurately. Women hold only 16.4 percent of corporate officer positions in the Fortune 500 companies.[40] In 2005, only eight Fortune 500 companies had women CEOs.[41] Xerox CEO Anne Mulcahy is a very positive example yet still the exception, not the rule. However, she paved the way at Xerox for Ursula Burns to become the first African American women to lead a Fortune 500 company.[42] Median weekly earnings for women persist at a level of 81 percent of their male counterparts' earnings.[43] Furthermore, because benefits are tied to compensation, women receive lower levels of benefits and are more likely to get hit the hardest in terms of promotions when companies restructure and layoffs during economic down times.[44]

In addition to lower earnings, women face other obstacles at work. The *glass ceiling* is an intangible barrier that keeps women (and minorities) from rising above a certain level in organizations. In the United States, it is rare to find women in positions above middle management in corporations.[45] The ultimate glass ceiling may well be the corporate board room and the professional partnership. One study found no substantive increase in female corporate board members between 1996 and 2002.[46] While women account for 40 percent of the legal professionals, they are not 40 percent of the law partners. The inclusion of women on corporate boards makes a positive difference in breaking gender stereotypes, enhancing communication, and changing group dynamics for the better.[47]

There is reason to believe that, on a global basis, the leadership picture for women is improving and will continue to improve. For example, the number of female political leaders around the world increased dramatically in recent decades. In the 1970s, there were only five such leaders. In the 1990s, twenty-one female leaders came into power. Countries such as Ireland, Sri Lanka, Iceland, and Norway all had female political leaders in the 1990s. Women around the world are leading major global companies, albeit not in the United States. These global female business leaders do not come predominantly from the West. In addition, a large number of women have founded entrepreneurial businesses. Women now own nearly 10.4 million of all American businesses, and these women-owned businesses employ more than 12.8 million people and generate $1.9 trillion in sales.[48]

Removing the glass ceiling and other obstacles to women's success represents a major challenge to organizations. Policies that promote equity in pay and benefits,

glass ceiling
An intangible barrier that keeps women and minorities from rising above a certain level in organizations.

encourage benefit programs of special interest to women, and provide equal starting salaries for jobs of equal value are needed in organizations. Corporations that shatter the glass ceiling have several practices in common. Upper managers clearly demonstrate support for the advancement of women, often with a statement of commitment issued by the CEO. Leaders incorporate practices into their diversity management programs to ensure that women perceive the organization as attractive.[49] Women are represented on standing committees that address strategic business issues of importance to the company. Women are targeted for participation in executive education programs, and systems are in place for identifying women with high potential for advancement.[50] Three of the best companies in terms of their advancement and development of women are Motorola, Deloitte & Touche, and the Bank of Montreal.[51]

Although women in our society have adopted the provider role, men have not been as quick to share domestic responsibilities. Managing the home and arranging for childcare are still seen as the woman's domain. In addition, working women often find themselves having to care for their elderly parents. Because of their multiple roles, women are more likely than men to experience conflicts between work and home. Organizations can offer incentives such as flexible work schedules, childcare, elder care, and work site health promotion programs to assist working women in managing the stress of their lives.[52]

More women in the workforce means that organizations must help them achieve their potential. To do less would be to underutilize the talents of half of the U.S. workforce.

The glass ceiling is not the only gender barrier in organizations. Males may suffer from discrimination when they are employed in traditionally female jobs such as nursing, elementary school teaching, and social work. Males may be overlooked as candidates for managerial positions in traditionally female occupations.[53]

Age Diversity

The graying of the U.S. workforce is another source of diversity in organizations. Aging baby boomers (those individuals born from 1946 through 1964) contributed to the rise of the median age in the United States to thirty-six in the year 2000—six years older than at any earlier time in history. This also means that the number of middle-aged Americans is rising dramatically. In the workforce, the number of younger workers is declining, as is the number of older workers (over age sixty-five). The net result will be a gain in workers aged thirty-five to fifty-four. By 2030, there will be 70 million older persons, more than twice their number in 1996. People over age sixty-five will comprise 13 percent of the population in 2010 and 20 percent of the population by 2030.[54]

This change in worker profile has profound implications for organizations. The job crunch among middle-aged workers will become more intense as companies seek flatter organizations and the elimination of middle-management jobs. Older workers are often higher paid, and companies that employ large numbers of aging baby boomers may find these pay scales a handicap to competitiveness.[55] However, a more experienced, stable, reliable, and healthy workforce can pay dividends to companies. The baby boomers are well trained and educated, and their knowledge can be a definite asset to organizations.

Another effect of the aging workforce is greater intergenerational contact in the workplace.[56] As organizations grow flatter, workers who were traditionally segregated by old corporate hierarchies (with older workers at the top and younger workers at the bottom) are working together. Four generations are cooperating: the silent generation (people born from 1930 through 1945), a small group that includes most organizations' top managers; the baby boomers, whose substantial numbers give them a strong influence; the baby bust generation, popularly known as Generation X (those born from 1965 through 1976); and the subsequent generation, tentatively called Generation Y, millennials, or the baby boomlet.[57] The millennials bring new challenges to the workplace because of their access to technology since a young age and a perpetual connection to parents.[58] While there is diversity among these various generations, there is diversity within each as well.

The differences in attitudes and values among these four generations can be substantial, and managers face the challenge of integrating these individuals into a cohesive group. Currently, as already noted, most positions of leadership are held by members of the silent generation. Baby boomers regard the silent generation as complacent and as having done little to reduce social inequities. Baby boomers strive for moral rights in the workplace and take a more activist position regarding employee rights. The baby busters, newer to the workplace, are impatient, want short-term gratification, and believe that family should come before work. They scorn the achievement orientation and materialism of the baby boomers. The millennials generate much controversy in both the definition of who they are and what constitute their distinguishing characteristics. Managing such diverse, conflicting perspectives is a challenge that must be addressed.

One company that is succeeding in accommodating the baby busters is Patagonia, a manufacturer of products for outdoor enthusiasts. Although the company does not actively recruit twenty-year-olds, approximately 20 percent of Patagonia's workers are in this age group because they are attracted to its products. To retain baby busters, the company offers several options, one of which is flextime. Employees can arrive at work as early as 6 A.M. and work as late as 6 P.M., as long as they work the core hours between 9 A.M. and 3 P.M. Workers also have the option of working at the office for five hours a day and at home for three hours.

Personal leaves of absence are also offered, generally unpaid, for as much as four months per year. This allows employees to take an extended summer break and prevents job burnout. Patagonia has taken into consideration the baby busters' desire for more time for personal concerns and has incorporated that desire into the company.[59]

Younger workers may have false impressions of older workers, viewing them as resistant to change, unable to learn new work methods, less physically capable, and less creative than younger employees. Research indicates, however, that older employees are more satisfied with their jobs, are more committed to the organization, and possess more internal work motivation than their younger cohorts.[60] Research also shows that direct experience with older workers reduces younger workers' negative beliefs.[61] Motivating aging workers and helping them maintain high levels of contribution to the organization is a key task for managers.

Ability Diversity

The workforce is full of individuals with different abilities, presenting another form of diversity. Individuals with disabilities are an underutilized human resource. An estimated 50 million individuals with disabilities live in the United States, and their unemployment rate is estimated to exceed 50 percent.[62] Nevertheless, the representation of individuals with disabilities in the workforce has increased because of the Americans with Disabilities Act, which went into effect in the summer of 1992. Under this law, employers are required to make reasonable accommodations to permit workers with disabilities to perform jobs. The act defines a person with a disability as "anyone possessing a physical or mental impairment that substantially limits one or more major life activities."[63] The law protects individuals with temporary, as well as permanent, disabilities. Its protection encompasses a broad range of illnesses that produce disabilities. Among these are acquired immune deficiency syndrome (AIDS), cancer, hypertension, anxiety disorders, dyslexia, blindness, and cerebral palsy, to name only a few.

Some companies recognized the value of employing workers with disabilities long before the legislation. Pizza Hut employs 3,000 workers with disabilities and plans to hire more. The turnover rate for Pizza Hut workers with disabilities is only one-fifth of the normal turnover rate.[64]

McDonald's created McJOBS, a program that has trained and hired more than 9,000 mentally and physically challenged individuals since 1981.[65] McJOBS is a corporate plan to recruit, train, and retain individuals with disabilities. Its participants include workers with visual, hearing, or orthopedic impairments; learning disabilities; and mental retardation. Through classroom and on-site training, the McJOBS program prepares individuals with disabilities for the work environment. Before McJOBS workers go on-site, sensitivity training sessions are held with store managers and crew members. These sessions help workers without disabilities understand what it means to be a worker with a disabling condition. Most McJOBS workers start part-time and advance according to their abilities and the opportunities available. Some McJOBS workers with visual impairments prefer to work on the back line, whereas others who use wheelchairs can work the drive-thru window.

Companies like Pizza Hut and McDonald's have led the way in hiring individuals with disabilities. One key to their success is helping able-bodied employees understand how workers with disabilities can contribute to the organization. In this way, ability diversity becomes an asset and helps organizations meet the challenge of unleashing the talents of workers with disabilities.

Differences Are Assets

Diversity involves much more than culture, gender, age, ability, or personality. It encompasses religion, social status, and sexual orientation. The scope of diversity is broad and inclusive. All these types of diversity lend heterogeneity to the workforce. Some programs aimed at enhancing appreciation and understanding diversity are required while some are voluntary. However, not everyone participates equally in voluntary diversity training. The degree to which individuals are open and receptive to diversity training depends on their level of diversity competence.[66] As we see in the Looking Back feature, Mike Lazaridis of RIM sees being different and pursuing your own path can be a real strength.

The issue of sexual orientation as a form of diversity has received increasing attention from organizations. Approximately 1.5 million households in the United States are identified as homosexual domestic partnerships.[67] Sexual orientation is an emotionally charged issue. Often, heterosexual resistance to accepting gay, lesbian, or bisexual workers is caused by moral beliefs. Although organizations must respect these beliefs, they must also send a message that all people are valued. The threat of job discrimination leads many gay men and lesbians to keep their sexual orientation secret at work. This secrecy has a cost, however. Closeted gay workers report lower job satisfaction and organizational commitment and more role conflict and conflict between work and home life issues than do openly gay workers or heterosexual workers.[68] To counteract these problems, companies like NCR are actively seeking gay job applicants. Other companies like IBM, Ford Motor Company, JPMorgan Chase, and American Airlines are offering benefits, training, support groups, and marketing strategies in support of gay rights. These initiatives help gay employees become more integrated and productive organizational members. Education and training can be supplemented by everyday practices like using inclusive language—for example, using the term *partner* instead of *spouse* in verbal and written communication.

Combating prejudice and discrimination is a challenge in managing diversity. Whereas prejudice is an attitude, discrimination is behavior. Both are detrimental to organizations that depend on productivity from every single worker. Often, in studies of ratings of promotion potential, minorities are rated lower than whites, and females are rated lower than males.[69] The disparity between the pay of women and minority-group members relative to white men increases with age.[70] It is to organizations' benefit to make sure that good workers are promoted and compensated fairly, but as the workforce becomes increasingly diverse, the potential for unfair treatment also increases.

Diversity is advantageous to the organization in a multitude of ways. Some organizations have recognized the potential benefits of aggressively working to increase the diversity of their workforces. Yum! Brands' Kentucky Fried Chicken (KFC) has a goal of attracting and retaining female and minority-group executives. A president of KFC's U.S. operations said, "We want to bring in the best people. If there are two equally qualified people, we'd clearly like to have diversity."[71]

In an effort to understand and encourage diversity, Alcon Laboratories developed a diversity training class called Working Together. The course takes advantage of two key ideas. First, people work best when they are valued and when diversity is taken into account. Second, when people feel valued, they build relationships and work together as a team.[72] Even majority group managers may be more supportive of diversity training if they appreciate their own ethnic identity. One evaluation of diversity training found that participants were more favorable if the training was framed with a traditional title and had a broad focus.[73] Further, women react more positively to diversity training than men. Companies can get positive pay-offs from diversity training and should, therefore, measure the effect of training.

Managing diversity is one way a company can become more competitive. It is more than simply being a good corporate citizen or complying with affirmative action.[74] It is also more than assimilating women and minorities into a dominant male culture. Managing diversity includes a painful examination of hidden assumptions that employees hold. Biases and prejudices about people's differences must be uncovered and dealt with so that differences can be celebrated and exploited to their full advantage.

Diversity's Benefits and Problems

Diversity can enhance organizational performance. Table 2.2 summarizes the main benefits, as well as problems, with diversity at work. Organizations can reap five main benefits from diversity. First, diversity management can help firms attract and retain the best available talent. The companies that appear at the top of "Best Places to Work" lists are usually excellent at managing diversity. Second, diversity can enhance marketing efforts. Just as workforces are becoming more diverse, so are markets. Having a diverse workforce can help the company improve its marketing plans by drawing on insights of employees from various cultural backgrounds. Third, diversity promotes creativity and innovation. The most innovative companies, such as HP (Hewlett Packard), deliberately put together diverse teams to foster creativity. Fourth, diversity results in better problem solving. Diverse groups bring more expertise and experience to bear on problems and decisions. They also encourage higher levels of critical thinking. Fifth, diversity enhances organizational flexibility. Inflexible organizations are characterized by narrow thinking, rigidity, and standard definitions of "good" work styles. By contrast, diversity makes an organization challenge old assumptions and become more adaptable. These five benefits can add up to competitive advantage for a company that manages diversity well.

2.2	Diversity's Benefits and Problems

Benefits	Problems
• Attracts and retains the best human talent	• Resistance to change
• Improves marketing efforts	• Lack of cohesiveness
• Promotes creativity and innovation	• Communication problems
• Results in better problem solving	• Interpersonal conflicts
• Enhances organizational flexibility	• Slowed decision making

Lest we paint an overly rosy picture of diversity, we must recognize its potential problems. Five problems are particularly important: resistance to change, lack of cohesiveness, communication problems, conflicts, and decision making. People are more highly attracted to, and feel more comfortable with, others like themselves. It stands to reason that diversity efforts may be met with considerable resistance when individuals are forced to interact with others unlike themselves. Managers should be prepared for this resistance rather than naively assuming that everybody supports diversity. (Managing resistance to change is presented at length in Chapter 18.) Another potential problem with diversity is the issue of cohesiveness, that invisible "glue" that holds a group together. Cohesive, or tightly knit, groups are preferred by most people. It takes longer for a diverse group of individuals to become cohesive. In addition, cohesive groups have higher morale and better communication. We can reason that it may take longer for diverse groups to develop high morale.

Another obstacle to performance in diverse groups is communication. Culturally diverse groups may encounter special challenges in terms of communication barriers. Misunderstandings can occur that can lower work group effectiveness. Conflicts can also arise, and decision making may take more time.[75]

In summary, diversity has several advantages that can lead to improved productivity and competitive advantage. In diverse groups, however, certain aspects of group functioning can become problematic. The key is to maximize the benefits of diversity and prevent or resolve the potential problems.

Pillsbury is one company that lays out the performance case for managing and valuing differences. Pillsbury's managers argue that the same business rationale for cross-functional teams is relevant to all kinds of diversity. Managing differences includes bringing race and gender, as well as marketing expertise, into a team. The company lacked the language expertise and cultural access to the Hispanic community. To open up a very profitable baked-goods market in a tough-to-crack niche, Pillsbury hired a group of Spanish-speaking Americans of Hispanic descent. Pillsbury's vice president of human resources conducted his own study of the food industry, asking an independent group to rate the diversity performance of ten companies and correlating it with financial performance over a ten-year period. Along with many other studies, the Pillsbury research suggests that diversity is a strong contributor to financial performance.[76]

Whereas the struggle for equal employment opportunity is a battle against racism and prejudice, managing diversity is a battle to value the differences that individuals bring to the workplace. Organizations that manage diversity effectively can reap the rewards of increased productivity and improved organizational health. Another aspect of a healthy organization is employees of good character, ethical behavior, and personal integrity.

ETHICS, CHARACTER, AND PERSONAL INTEGRITY

4 Discuss the assumptions of consequential, rule-based, and character theories of ethics.

In addition to the challenges of globalization and workforce diversity, managers frequently face ethical dilemmas and trade-offs. Some organizations display good character and their executives are known for personal integrity. Johnson & Johnson employees operate with an organizational credo, presented later in this section. Merck & Company is another organization that manages ethical issues well; its emphasis on ethical behavior has earned it recognition as one of America's most admired companies in *Fortune*'s polls of CEOs. However, in addition to formal codes of conduct, the exemplary words and actions of senior managers and supervisors go a long way in promoting a moral organization.[77] The tobacco industry and companies like Phillip Morris International have a unique ethics challenge in the sale of tobacco products given the known health risks, as we see in The Real World 2.2.

Despite the positive way some organizations handle ethical issues, however, unethical conduct can still occur. A few of the ethical problems that managers report as toughest to resolve include employee theft, environmental issues, comparable worth of employees, conflicts of interest, and sexual harassment.[78]

How can people in organizations rationally think through ethical decisions so that they make the "right" choices? Ethical theories help us understand, evaluate, and classify moral arguments; make decisions; and then defend conclusions about

The Real World 2.2

The Ethics of Selling Tobacco Products

Louis Camilleri got his dream job as CEO of Phillip Morris International (PMI), based in Switzerland overlooking Lake Geneva and the Alps of Savoie. What he left behind were 129 lawsuits involving the tobacco business in the United States. In his new position, he is able to sell cigarettes to the world and develop new products, such as Marlboro Black Menthol in Japan and a super-slim variant in Russia. Because PMI has less than 16 percent of the global market, there is room to grow. However, even in the international arena, there are forces aligning against smoking. Michael Bloomberg and Bill Gates have pledged $500 million to fund antismoking campaigns in emerging markets around the world. Smoking carries health risks and the scientific evidence is well established. However, that does not always stop people

In the international arena, forces are aligning against smoking.

Image copyright Stephen Coburn, 2009. Used under license from Shutterstock.com

from smoking. Camilleri argues that even if PMI shut down all of its production facilities, the tobacco industry would go underground because there would be continuing demand for tobacco products. The World Health Organization reports that over 5 million people annually die from the harmful effects of tobacco use. PMI aims to be more socially responsible and less blatant in its production promotion. The company engages in reducing the harmful effects of tobacco use for those who want to continue to use these products, as in the deal Camilleri signed with Stockholm-based Swedish Match to market smokeless tobacco worldwide.

SOURCE: N. Byrnes and F. Balfour, "Phillip Morris Unbound," *BusinessWeek* (May 4, 2009): 38.

what is right and wrong. Ethical theories can be classified as consequential, rule based, or character based.

Consequential theories of ethics emphasize the consequences or results of behavior. John Stuart Mill's utilitarianism, a well-known consequential theory, suggests that right and wrong are determined by the consequences of the action.[79] "Good" is the ultimate moral value, and we should maximize the most good for the greatest number of people. But do good ethics make for good business?[80] Right actions do not always produce good consequences, and good consequences do not always follow from right actions. And how do we determine the greatest good—in short-term or long-term consequences? Using the "greatest number" criterion can imply that minorities (less than 50 percent) might be excluded in evaluating the morality of actions. An issue that may be important for a minority but unimportant for the majority might be ignored. These are but a few of the dilemmas raised by utilitarianism.

By contrast, *rule-based theories* of ethics emphasize the character of the act itself, not its effects, in arriving at universal moral rights and wrongs.[81] Moral rights, the basis for legal rights, are associated with such theories. In a theological context, the Bible, the Talmud, and the Koran are rule-based guides to ethical behavior. Immanuel Kant worked toward the ultimate moral principle in formulating his categorical imperative, a universal standard of behavior.[82] Kant argued that individuals should be treated with respect and dignity and that they should not be used as a means to an end. He argued that we should put ourselves in the other person's position and ask if we would make the same decision if we were in his or her situation.

Corporations and business enterprises are more prone to subscribe to consequential ethics than rule-based ethics, in part due to the persuasive arguments of the Scottish political economist and moral philosopher Adam Smith.[83] He believed that the self-interest of human beings is God's providence, not the government's. Smith set forth a doctrine of natural liberty, presenting the classical argument for open market competition and free trade. Within this framework, people should be allowed to pursue what is in their economic self-interest, and the natural efficiency of the marketplace would serve the well-being of society. However, self-interest may cause business leaders to form inappropriate and even harmful attachments that lead to poor decision making.[84] Therefore, an alternative to those theories is offered through virtue-ethics.

Character theories of ethics emphasize the character of the individual and the intent of the actor, in contrast to either the character of the act itself or its consequences. These theories emphasize virtue-ethics and are based on an Aristotelian approach to character. Robert Solomon is the best-known advocate of this approach.[85] He supports a business ethics theory that centers on the individual within the corporation, thus emphasizing both corporate roles and personal virtues. The center of Aristotle's vision was on the inner character and virtuousness of the individual, not on her or his behavior or actions. Thus, the "good" person who acted out of virtuous and "right" intentions was one with integrity and ultimately good ethical standards. For Solomon, the six dimensions of virtue-ethics are community, excellence, role identity, integrity, judgment (*phronesis*), and holism. Further, "the virtues" are a shorthand way of summarizing the ideals that define good character. These include honesty, loyalty, sincerity, courage, reliability, trustworthiness, benevolence, sensitivity, helpfulness, cooperativeness, civility, decency, modesty, openness, and gracefulness, to name a few. Adam Smith might call these "the moral sentiments," and rewarding self-interest with economic incentives can backfire when appealing to the virtues can pay off.[86]

Cultural relativism contends that there are no universal ethical principles and that people should not impose their own ethical standards on others. Local

consequential theory
An ethical theory that emphasizes the consequences or results of behavior.

rule-based theory
An ethical theory that emphasizes the character of the act itself rather than its effects.

character theory
An ethical theory that emphasizes the character, personal virtues, and integrity of the individual.

standards should be the guides for ethical behavior. Cultural relativism encourages individuals to operate under the old adage "When in Rome, do as the Romans do." Unfortunately, strict adherence to cultural relativism can lead individuals to deny accountability for their decisions and to avoid difficult ethical dilemmas.

People need ethical theories to help them think through confusing, complex, difficult moral choices and ethical decisions. In contemporary organizations, people face ethical and moral dilemmas in many diverse areas. The key areas we address are employee rights, sexual harassment, romantic involvements, organizational justice, whistle-blowing, and social responsibility. We conclude with a discussion of professionalism and codes of ethics.

5 Explain six issues that pose ethical dilemmas for managers.

Employee Rights

Managing the rights of employees at work creates many ethical dilemmas in organizations. Some of these dilemmas are privacy issues related to technology. Computerized monitoring, discussed later in the chapter, constitutes an invasion of privacy in the minds of some individuals. The use of employee data from computerized information systems presents many ethical concerns. Safeguarding the employee's right to privacy and at the same time preserving access to the data for those who need it requires that the manager balance competing interests.

Drug testing, free speech, downsizing and layoffs, and due process are but a few of the issues involving employee rights that managers face. Perhaps no issue generates as much need for managers to balance the interests of employees and the interests of the organization as AIDS in the workplace. New drugs have shown the promise of extended lives for people with human immunodeficiency virus (HIV), and this means that HIV-infected individuals can remain in the workforce and stay productive. Managers may be caught in the middle of a conflict between the rights of HIV-infected workers and the rights of their coworkers who feel threatened.

Employers are not required to make concessions to coworkers but do have obligations to educate, reassure, and provide emotional support to them. Confidentiality may also be a difficult issue. Some employees with HIV or AIDS do not wish to waive confidentiality and do not want to reveal their condition to their coworkers because of fears of stigmatization or even reprisals. In any case, management should discuss with the affected employee the ramifications of trying to maintain confidentiality and should assure the employee that every effort will be made to prevent negative consequences for him or her in the workplace.[87]

Laws exist that protect HIV-infected workers. As mentioned earlier, the Americans with Disabilities Act requires employees to treat HIV-infected workers as disabled individuals and to make reasonable accommodations for them. The ethical dilemmas involved with this situation, however, go far beyond the legal issues. How does a manager protect the dignity of the person with AIDS and preserve the morale and productivity of the work group when so much prejudice and ignorance surround this disease? Many organizations, such as Wells Fargo, believe the answer is education.[88] Wells Fargo has a written AIDS policy because of the special issues associated with the disease—such as confidentiality, employee socialization, coworker education, and counseling—that must be addressed. The Body Shop's employee education program consists of factual seminars combined with interactive theater workshops. The workshops depict a scenario in which an HIV-positive worker must make decisions, and the audience decides what the worker should do. This helps participants explore the emotional and social issues surrounding HIV.[89] Many fears arise because of a lack of knowledge about AIDS.

You 2.2

How Much Do You Know About Sexual Harassment?

Indicate whether you believe each statement below is true (T) or false (F).

_____ 1. Sexual harassment is unprofessional behavior.

_____ 2. Sexual harassment is against the law in all fifty states.

_____ 3. Sexual advances are a form of sexual harassment.

_____ 4. A request for sexual activity is a form of sexual harassment.

_____ 5. Verbal or physical conduct of a sexual nature may be sexual harassment.

_____ 6. Sexual harassment occurs when submission to sex acts is a condition of employment.

_____ 7. Sexual harassment occurs when submission to or rejection of sexual acts is a basis for performance evaluation.

_____ 8. Sexual harassment occurs when such behavior interferes with an employee's performance or creates an intimidating, hostile, and offensive environment.

_____ 9. Sexual harassment includes physical contact of a sexual nature, such as touching.

_____ 10. Sexual harassment requires that a person have the intent to harass, harm, or intimidate.

All of the items are true except item 10, which is false. While somewhat ambiguous, sexual harassment is defined in the eyes of the beholder. Give yourself 1 point for each correct answer. This score reflects how much you know about sexual harassment. Scores can range from 0 (poorly informed) to 10 (well informed). If your score was less than 5, you need to learn more about sexual harassment.

SOURCE: See W. O'Donohue, ed., *Sexual Harassment* (Boston: Allyn and Bacon, 1997) for theory, research, and treatment. See http://www.eeoc.gov/stats/harass.html for the latest statistics.

Sexual Harassment

According to the Equal Employment Opportunity Commission, sexual harassment is unwelcome sexual attention, whether verbal or physical, that affects an employee's job conditions or creates a hostile working environment.[90] Court rulings, too, have broadened the definition of sexual harassment beyond job-related abuse to include acts that create a hostile work environment. In addition, Supreme Court rulings presume companies are to blame when managers create a sexually hostile working environment. Some organizations are more tolerant of sexual harassment. Complaints are not taken seriously, it is risky to complain, and perpetrators are unlikely to be punished. In such organizations, sexual harassment is more likely to occur. It is also more likely to occur in male-dominated workplaces.[91] Managers can defend themselves by demonstrating that they took action to eliminate workplace harassment and that the complaining employee did not take advantage of company procedures to deal with it. Even the best sexual harassment policy, however, will not absolve a company when harassment leads to firing, demotions, or undesirable working assignments.[92] How much do you know about sexual harassment? Complete You 2.2 to get an idea.

There are three types of sexual harassment. *Gender harassment* includes crude comments or sexual jokes and behaviors that disparage someone's gender or convey hostility toward a particular gender. *Unwanted sexual attention* involves unwanted touching or repeated unwanted pressures for dates. As we see in the Science feature, males high in likelihood to sexually harass may focus their attention more on female attractiveness than job performance data in completing performance ratings. *Sexual*

The Effect of Likelihood to Sexually Harass

Not all sexual harassment is male against female, but that is the dominant pattern. Further, not all males are equally likely to sexually harass a female. This research study investigated the effect of male differences in likelihood to sexually harass in terms of how they evaluated the job performance and attractiveness of high-performing and low-performing females. The researchers used an experimental design in which 92 twenty-year-old males were asked questions that assessed their tendency to sexually harass a female. Based on their answers, they were classified as high or low in the likelihood to sexually harass. Independently, the researchers had separate groups of ten and eleven males judge good and poor job performance descriptions and high and low attractiveness in a series of female photographs. The 92 males were then asked to rate the job performance and the attractiveness of females based upon the job performance descriptions and the photographs. The results showed that males high in likelihood to sexually harass reported much less performance rating distinction between high and low performing females than low in likelihood to sexually harass males. This suggests that those more likely to sexually harass may focus on female attractiveness rather than job performance data in completing performance ratings of females. Further, males less likely to sexually harass appear to focus on job performance data and are not distracted by attractiveness.

SOURCE: J. A. Lee, J. L. Welbourne, W. A. Hoke, and J. Beggs, "Examining the Interaction Among Likelihood to Sexually Harass, Ratee Attractiveness, and Job Performance," *Journal of Management* 35 (2009): 445–461.

coercion consists of implicit or explicit demands for sexual favors by threatening negative job-related consequences or promising job-related rewards.[93] A major review of over a decade of research on sexual harassment uses workplace aggression as a framework for making suggestions for the future.[94]

Sexual harassment costs the typical Fortune 500 company $6.7 million per year in absenteeism, turnover, and loss of productivity. Valeant Pharmaceuticals International has paid out millions to settle four sexual harassment complaints against former CEO Milan Panic. One U.S. airline reached a $2.6 million settlement with the EEOC in 2001 after the agency found widespread sexual harassment of female employees at the airline's New York JFK International Airport facility. Plaintiffs may now sue not only for back pay but also for compensatory and punitive damages. And these costs do not take into account the negative publicity that firms may encounter from sexual harassment cases, which can cost untold millions. Sexual harassment can have strong negative effects on victims. Victims are less satisfied with their work, supervisors, and coworkers and may psychologically withdraw at work. They may suffer poorer mental health and even exhibit symptoms of post-traumatic stress disorder in conjunction with the harassment experience. Some victims report alcohol abuse, depression, headaches, and nausea.[95]

Several companies have created comprehensive sexual harassment programs that seem to work. Atlantic Richfield (ARCO), owned by British Petroleum and a player in the male-dominated energy industry, has a handbook on preventing sexual harassment that includes phone numbers of state agencies where employees can file complaints. In essence, it gives employees a road map to the courthouse, and the openness seems to work. Lawsuits rarely happen at ARCO. When sexual harassment complaints come in, the company assumes the allegations are true and investigates thoroughly. The process has resulted in the firing of highly placed managers, including the captain of an oil tanker. Other companies believe in the power of training programs. Some of the best training programs use role-playing, videotapes, and group discussions of real cases to help supervisors recognize unlawful sexual harassment and investigate complaints properly.

Romantic Involvements

Hugging, sexual innuendos, and repeated requests for dates may constitute sexual harassment for some but a prelude to romance for others. This situation carries with it a different set of ethical dilemmas for organizations.

A recent fax poll indicated that three-fourths of the respondents felt it was okay to date a coworker, while three-fourths disapproved of dating a superior or subordinate. In *Meritor vs. Vinson*, the Supreme Court ruled that the agency principle applies to supervisor–subordinate relationships. Employers are liable for acts of their agents (supervisors) and can thus be held liable for sexual harassment. Other employees might claim that the subordinate who is romantically involved with the supervisor gets preferential treatment. Dating between coworkers poses less liability for the company because the agency principle does not apply. Policing coworker dating can also backfire: Wal-Mart lost a lawsuit when it tried to forbid coworkers from dating.

Workplace romances may result, for the participants, in experiences that can be positive or negative, temporary or permanent, exploitative to nonexploitative. The effects of office romances can similarly be positive or negative, or they can simply be mild diversions. Romances can be damaging to organizational effectiveness, or they can occasionally enhance effectiveness through their positive effects on participants. Two particular kinds of romances are hazardous in the workplace. Hierarchical romances, in which one person directly reports to another, can create tremendous conflicts of interest. Utilitarian romances, in which one person satisfies the needs of another in exchange for task-related or career-related favors, are potentially damaging in the workplace. Although most managers realize that workplace romance cannot be eliminated through rules and policies, they believe that intervention is a must when romance constitutes a serious threat to productivity or workplace morale.[96]

Organizational Justice

Another area in which moral and ethical dilemmas may arise for people at work concerns organizational justice, both distributive and procedural. *Distributive justice* concerns the fairness of outcomes individuals receive. For example, the salaries and bonuses of U.S. corporate executives became a central issue with Japanese executives when President George H. W. Bush and American CEOs in key industries visited Japan in 1992. The Japanese CEOs questioned the distributive justice in keeping the American CEOs' salaries at high levels at a time when so many companies were having financial difficulty and laying off workers.

Procedural justice concerns the fairness of the process by which outcomes are allocated. The ethical questions here do not concern the just or unjust distribution of organizational resources but rather, the process. Has the organization used the correct procedures in allocating resources? Have the right considerations, such as competence and skill, been brought to bear in the decision process? And have the wrong considerations, such as race and gender, been excluded from the decision process? One study in a work-scheduling context found voluntary turnover negatively related to advance notice and consistency, two dimensions of procedural justice.[97] Some research found cultural differences in the effects of distributive and procedural justice, such as between Hong Kong and the United States.[98]

distributive justice
The fairness of the outcomes that individuals receive in an organization.

procedural justice
The fairness of the process by which outcomes are allocated in an organization.

Whistle-Blowing

Whistle-blowers are employees who inform authorities of wrongdoings by their company or coworkers. Whistle-blowers can be perceived as either heroes or villains depending on the circumstances. For a whistle-blower to be considered a public hero, the situation the whistle-blower reports to authorities must be so serious as to be perceived as abhorrent by others.[99] By contrast, the whistle-blower is considered a villain if others see the act of whistle-blowing as more offensive than the situation being reported.

Whistle-blowing is important in the United States because workers sometimes engage in unethical behavior in an intense desire to succeed. Many examples of whistle-blowing can be found in corporate America. For example, one former Coca-Cola employee made a number of allegations against the company and issued an ultimatum: Coca-Cola must pay him nearly $45 million or he would go to the media.[100] While a Georgia state court dismissed most of the allegations, Coca-Cola still had to defend itself against claims related to wrongful termination. One of the former employee's allegations relating to a falsified marketing test did force Coca-Cola to make a public apology and offer to pay Burger King $21 million.

Organizations can manage whistle-blowing by communicating the conditions that are appropriate for the disclosure of wrongdoing. Clearly delineating wrongful behavior and the appropriate ways to respond are important organizational actions.

Social Responsibility

Corporate *social responsibility* is the obligation of an organization to behave in ethical ways in the social environment in which it operates. Ethical conduct at the individual level can translate into social responsibility at the organizational level. When Malden Mills, the maker of Polartec (fleece fabrics), burned down in 1995, the company's president, Aaron Feuerstein, paid workers during the months it took to rebuild the company. Although doing so cost the company a lot of money and was not required by law, Feuerstein said his own values caused him to do the socially responsible thing. Malden Mills recovered financially and continues its success with Polartec.

Socially responsible actions are expected of organizations. Current concerns include protecting the environment, promoting worker safety, supporting social issues, and investing in the community, among others. Some organizations, like IBM, loan executives to inner-city schools to teach science and math. Other organizations, like Patagonia, demonstrate social responsibility through environmentalism. Firms that are seen as socially responsible have a competitive advantage in attracting applicants.[101] For example, there can be a win-win for companies that go green by displaying a sense of community while improving economic performance.[102]

Codes of Ethics

One of the characteristics of mature professions is the existence of a code of ethics to which the practitioners adhere in their actions and behavior. An example is the Hippocratic Oath in medicine. Although some of the individual differences we address in Chapter 4 produce ethical or unethical orientations in specific people, a profession's code of ethics becomes a standard against which members can measure themselves in the absence of internalized standards.

The Four-Way Test No universal code of ethics or oath exists for business as it does for medicine. However, Paul Harris and four business colleagues, who founded Rotary International in 1905, addressed ethical and moral behaviors right from the beginning. Then Herbert J. Taylor developed the Four-Way Test in the 1930s,

whistle-blower
An employee who informs authorities of the wrongdoings of his or her company or coworkers.

social responsibility
The obligation of an organization to behave in ethical ways.

2.2 The Four-Way Test

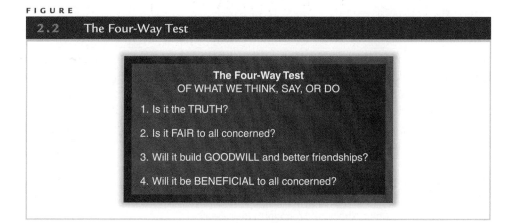

The Four-Way Test
OF WHAT WE THINK, SAY, OR DO

1. Is it the TRUTH?

2. Is it FAIR to all concerned?

3. Will it build GOODWILL and better friendships?

4. Will it be BENEFICIAL to all concerned?

shown in Figure 2.2, which is used in over 166 nations throughout the world by the 1.2 million Rotarians in more than 30,000 Rotary clubs. Figure 2.2 concerns all the things we think, say, and do.

DOD and the Johnson & Johnson Credo Beyond the individual and professional level, corporate culture is another excellent starting point for addressing ethics and morality. In Chapter 16 we examine how corporate culture and leader behavior trickle down the company, setting a standard for all below. In some cases, the corporate ethics may be captured in a regulation. For example, the Joint Ethics Regulation (DOD 5500.7-R, August 1993) specifies the ethical standards to which all U.S. military personnel are to adhere. In other cases, the corporate ethics may be in the form of a credo. Johnson & Johnson Credo, shown in Figure 2.3, helped hundreds of employees ethically address the criminal tampering with Tylenol products. In its 1986 centennial annual report, Johnson & Johnson attributed its success in this crisis, as well as its long-term business growth (a compound sales rate of 11.6 percent for 100 years), to "our unique form of decentralized management, our adherence to the ethical principles embodied in our credo, and our emphasis on managing the business for the long term."

Goolsby Leadership Academy As CEO of the key organization that emerged from the Howard Hughes estate, John Goolsby moved with support of his board of directors to implement an ethics policy for all employees. A strong ethics policy with clear guidelines and an enforcement mechanism were instrumental in insuring the financial integrity of the firm while combating self-serving behavior on the part of individuals.[103] He and his wife Judy subsequently established the Goolsby Leadership Academy as a place in which talented young men and women learn about ethical business practices. The Goolsby motto is: Integrity–Courage–Impact. Learning character strengths and virtues early in live can pay off later.

Individual codes of ethics, professional oaths, and organizational credos all must be anchored in a moral, ethical framework. They are always open to question and continuous improvement using ethical theories as a tool for reexamining the soundness of the current standard. Although a universal right and wrong may exist, it would be hard to argue that there is only one code of ethics to which all individuals, professions, and organizations can subscribe.

John L. Goolsby with Distinguished Goolsby Scholar Beatrice Wangari Njuguna

FIGURE

2.3   The Johnson & Johnson Credo

We believe our first responsibility is to the doctors, nurses, and patients,
to mothers and all others who use our products and services.
In meeting their needs everything we do must be of high quality.
We must constantly strive to reduce our costs
in order to maintain reasonable prices.
Customers' orders must be serviced promptly and accurately.
Our suppliers and distributors must have an opportunity
to make a fair profit.

We are responsible to our employees,
the men and women who work with us throughout the world.
Everyone must be considered as an individual.
We must respect their dignity and recognize their merit.
They must have a sense of security in their jobs.
Compensation must be fair and adequate,
and working conditions clean, orderly, and safe.
Employees must feel free to make suggestions and complaints.
There must be equal opportunity for employment, development
and advancement for those qualified.
We must provide competent management,
and their actions must be just and ethical.

We are responsible to the communities in which we live and work
and to the world community as well.
We must be good citizens—support good works and charities
and bear our fair share of taxes.
We must encourage civic improvements and better health and education.
We must maintain in good order
the property we are privileged to use,
protecting the environment and natural resources.

Our final responsibility is to our stockholders.
Business must make a sound profit.
We must experiment with new ideas.
Research must be carried on, innovative programs developed
and mistakes paid for.
New equipment must be purchased, new facilities provided,
and new products launched.
Reserves must be created to provide for adverse times.
When we operate according to these principles,
the stockholders should realize a fair return.

MANAGERIAL IMPLICATIONS: BEATING THE CHALLENGES

Organizational success depends on managers' ability to address the three challenges of globalization, workforce diversity, and ethics. Failure to address the challenges can be costly. Think about Pepsi's losses to Coke in the global cola wars. Coke is winning the battle and capitalizing on the huge opportunities and profits from global markets. A racial discrimination lawsuit against Texaco cost the company millions in a settlement and damaged its reputation. Managers' behavioral integrity (i.e., word-deed alignment) is judged by all employees, most especially African American employees.[104] Mitsubishi suffered a similar fate in a sexual harassment scandal. Failure to address these challenges can mean costly losses, damage to reputations, and ultimately an organization's demise.

These three challenges are important because the way managers handle them shapes employee behavior. Developing global mindsets among employees expands their worldview and puts competition on a larger scale. Knowing that diversity is

Diversity Dialogue

"You're Hired!" . . . Not . . . if You're Over 40

Donald Trump's hugely popular reality series, *The Apprentice*, was mired in controversy at the beginning of its sixth and final season. R. Joseph Hewett, a fifty-one-year-old technology manager, alleged in an age discrimination lawsuit that he never got a chance to hear the words, "You're fired!" because the show's organizers and producers felt he was too old to compete.

Hewett maintained that he was unjustifiably turned down for the reality show given his "many years of experience managing large commercial properties." Among his qualifications, Hewett graduated magna cum laude from college and worked as a technology manager at a commercial real estate company. He was also forty-nine years old at the time he applied for the show in 2005. In his lawsuit, Hewett asserted that only two of the finalists in the first six seasons of show had been over forty years of age, a claim that a Trump spokesman did not deny. According to the Trump organization, while they actively sought participants from "all age groups," few applicants were over the age of forty.

Hewett reached a settlement with the Trump organization that in his words was "satisfactory to all." He stated that the lawsuit was never about a disgruntled applicant trying to get back at Trump's organization but rather an opportunity to advocate on behalf of an entire class of people he believed had been victimized.

1. Was Hewett justified in bringing age discrimination litigation against *The Apprentice*? Why or why not?
2. What could the Trump organization have done to encourage more people over forty to apply for the show?

SOURCE: M. Pratt, "Apprentice Reject Who Claimed Age Discrimination Settles Suit," *Associated Press* (May 22, 2007).

---

valued and differences are assets causes employees to think twice about engaging in discriminatory behaviors. Sending a message that unethical behavior is not tolerated lets employees know that doing the right thing pays off.

These three challenges are recurring themes that you will see throughout our book. You will learn how companies are tackling these challenges and how organizational behavior can be used to create opportunity in organizations, which is a must if they are to remain competitive.

LOOKING BACK: RESEARCH IN MOTION (RIM)

Do One Thing Really Well—BlackBerry as Boss

There are companies that pursue success through a process of diversification. There are other companies that pursue success through a laser-like single-mindedness. RIM has pursued the latter strategy under the guidance of cofounder and co-CEO Mike Lazaridis. Mike and RIM have aimed to do one thing and do that one thing really well. The company has a

Courtesy of Research In Motion

singular vision. The focus is BlackBerry, just BlackBerry. RIM is not distracted by any notions of diversification. While some people would say that this is a weakness, Lazaridis' view is that RIM has nailed a trend judging by the growth of smartphones in today's world. The company is clear, focused, and on track with its singular vision.[105]

Singular vision is only one of the ingredients for success according to Lazaridis. Another success factor is the encouragement not to be afraid of taking an unconventional path. Being different may be a very good characteristic, enabling a person or a company to standout based on a distinctive competence or set of characteristics. Those who make their own paths are often called leaders and may well be pioneers. Another success factor for Lazaridis is thinking decades into the future. This is a companion to having a singular vision. Thinking into the future does require dreaming and in addition it requires rigorous research and analysis. Research, analysis, and careful planning lay the foundation for smart risks. Lazaridis encourages taking only smart risks, he does not encourage gambling, and there is an important difference.

Smart risks can pay off nicely in the marketplace. Lazaridis believes that RIM's singular vision is the firm's key strength and a key contributor to the growth of the BlackBerry smartphone, making it boss in the U.S. market. In all of North America, BlackBerry has 54 percent of the market. In Europe, Latin America, and Asia, BlackBerry is gaining ground. From great vision and big dreams followed by the hard, concrete thinking through research, analysis, and planning came RIM's success in the marketplace. RIM is not complacent however. The company contributed $150 million in venture capital to the Toronto-based BlackBerry Partners Fund to spur new software development. RIM is still on the move.

Chapter Summary

1. To ensure that their organizations meet the competition, managers must tackle three important challenges: globalization, workforce diversity, and ethical behavior.

2. The five cultural differences that affect work-related attitudes are individualism versus collectivism, power distance, uncertainty avoidance, masculinity versus femininity, and time orientation.

3. Diversity encompasses gender, culture, personality, sexual orientation, religion, ability, social status, and a host of other differences.

4. Managers must take a proactive approach to managing diversity so that differences are valued and capitalized upon.

5. Three types of ethical theories include consequential theories, rule-based theories, and character theories.

6. Ethical dilemmas emerge for people at work in the areas of employee rights, sexual harassment, romantic involvements, organizational justice, whistle-blowing, and social responsibility.

Key Terms

character theory (p. 55)

collectivism (p. 42)

consequential theory (p. 55)

distributive justice (p. 59)

diversity (p. 46)

expatriate manager (p. 44)

femininity (p. 43)

glass ceiling (p. 48)

guanxi (p. 40)

individualism (p. 42)

masculinity (p. 43)

power distance (p. 42)

procedural justice (p. 59)

rule-based theory (p. 55)

social responsibility (p. 60)

time orientation (p. 43)

transnational
    organization (p. 39)

uncertainty avoidance (p. 43)

whistle-blower (p. 60)

Review Questions

1. What are Hofstede's five dimensions of cultural differences that affect work attitudes? Using these dimensions, describe the United States.

2. What are the primary sources of diversity in the U.S. workforce?

3. What are the potential benefits and problems of diversity?

4. What is the reality of the glass ceiling? What would it take to change this reality?

5. What are some of the ethical challenges encountered in organizations?

6. Describe the difference between distributive and procedural justice.

Discussion and Communication Questions

1. How can managers be encouraged to develop global thinking? How can managers dispel stereotypes about other cultures?

2. Some people have argued that offshoring jobs is un-American and unethical. What do you think?

3. How do some companies accommodate the differing needs of a diverse workforce?

4. What effects will the globalization of business have on a company's culture? How can an organization with a strong "made in America" identity compete in the global marketplace?

5. Why is diversity such an important issue? Is the workforce more diverse today than in the past?

6. How does a manager strike a balance between encouraging employees to celebrate their own cultures and forming a single unified culture within the organization?

7. Do you agree with Hofstede's findings about U.S. culture? Other cultures? On what do you base your agreement or disagreement?

8. (*communication question*) Select one of the three challenges (globalization, diversity, ethics) and write a brief position paper arguing for its importance to managers.

9. (*communication question*) Find someone whose culture is different from your own. This could be a classmate or an international student at your university. Interview the person about his or her culture, using Hofstede's dimensions. Also ask what you might need to know about doing business in that person's culture (e.g., customs, etiquette). Be prepared to share this information in class.

Ethical Dilemma

Ryan McNamara is called into his manager's office at noon on a Tuesday and told that he is to report to Pryor Sterling Inc.'s Japan office immediately to oversee a crucial project with ties to three of the firm's major international accounts. Ryan has headed up similar projects in the firm's New York office, and he's had some contact with two of the managers in the Japan

office. Natalie Berman, Ryan's manager, gives him a file of information on the specifics of the project and a timetable for completion. She also impresses upon him how important it is that the project be completed seamlessly so the clients involved will be pleased.

He quickly packs a bag, boards a plane, and covers the material on his flight to Tokyo. Once there, Ryan has great difficulty getting a taxi driver to understand where he needs to go, because Ryan doesn't speak any Japanese. When he arrives at the firm's office, he is met by Kaito Ami, a mid-level supervisor also working on the project. Flustered, Ami tells Ryan that Kase Hisa, the executive with whom Ryan is to conference first, hasn't arrived yet. Ryan is immediately grateful, but does not notice Ami's discomfort.

Manager Anan Cho joins the men in the conference room to discuss the project. Ryan walks around the table so that the other men can sit nearer the head, but doesn't realize that he's left the most senior member, Hisa, sitting closest to the door, a clear insult in Japanese culture.

Ryan launches into his project timeline and his immediate goals, never noticing how his actions have translated to the people upon whom he is going to be dependant. Over the course of the next three days, Ryan is frustrated at each turn when people do not react to

him with positive energy. He is unable to get the project accomplished, and Pryor Sterling loses one of the international accounts as a result.

When Darcy Jenkins, COO of Pryor Sterling, demands to know what happened, Kase Hisa explains that McNamara insulted him and his staff at every turn and asks that he be fired. Ryan holds his boss, Natalie, accountable for not giving him any information or time to prepare to understand Japanese business customs. Natalie blames Ryan for not being honest about his limited knowledge of Japanese traditions and ultimately failing to get the job done. Darcy is unsure who to hold accountable but knows something needs to be done to prevent this from every happening again.

Questions:

1. Using consequential, rule-based, and character theories, evaluate Darcy's options.
2. What should Darcy do? Why?

Experiential Exercises

2.1 International Orientations

1. Preparation (preclass)

Read the background on the International Orientation Scale and the case study "Office Supplies International—Marketing Associate," complete the ratings and questions, and fill out the self-assessment inventory.

2. Group Discussions

Groups of four to six people discuss their answers to the case study questions and their own responses to the self-assessment.

3. Class Discussion

Instructor leads a discussion on the International Orientation Scale and the difficulties and challenges of adjusting to a new culture. Why do some people adjust more easily than others? What can you do to adjust to a new culture? What can you regularly do that will help you adjust in the future to almost any new culture?

Office Supplies International—Marketing Associate*

Jonathan Fraser is a marketing associate for a large multinational corporation, Office Supplies International (OSI), in Buffalo, New York. He is being considered for a transfer to the international division of OSI. This position will require that he spend between one and three

years working abroad in one of OSI's three foreign subsidiaries: OSI-France, OSI-Japan, or OSI-Australia. This transfer is considered a fast-track career move at OSI, and Jonathan feels honored to be in the running for the position.

Jonathan has been working at OSI since he graduated with his bachelor's degree in marketing ten years ago. He is married and has lived and worked in Buffalo all his life. Jonathan's parents are first-generation German Americans. His grandparents, although deceased, spoke only German at home and upheld many of their ethnic traditions. His parents, although quite "Americanized," have retained some of their German traditions. To communicate better with his grandparents, Jonathan took German in high school but never used it because his grandparents had passed away.

In college, Jonathan joined the German Club and was a club officer for two years. His other collegiate extracurricular activity was playing for the varsity baseball team. Jonathan still enjoys playing in a summer softball league with his college friends. Given his athletic interests, he volunteered to be the athletic programming coordinator at OSI, where he organizes the company's softball and volleyball teams. Jonathan has been making steady progress at OSI. Last year, he was named marketing associate of the year.

*"Office Supplies International—Marketing Associate" by Paula Caligiuri. Copyright © 1994 by Paula Caligiuri, Ph.D. Information for the International Orientation Scale can be obtained by contacting Paula Caligiuri, Ph.D. at 732-445-5228 or e-mail: paula@caligiuri.com. Reprinted by permission of the author. Dorothy Marcic and Sheila M. Puffer, *Management International: Cases, Exercises, and Readings* (Eagan, MN: West Publishing, 1994). *All rights reserved. May not be reproduced without written permission of the publisher.*

His wife, Sue, is also a Buffalo native. She teaches English literature at the high school in one of the middle-class suburbs of Buffalo. Sue took five years off after she had a baby but returned to teaching this year when Janine, their five-year-old daughter, started kindergarten. She is happy to be resuming her career. One or two nights a week, Sue volunteers at the city mission where she works as a career counselor and a basic skills trainer. For fun, she takes pottery and ethnic cooking classes.

Both Sue and Jonathan are excited about the potential transfer and accompanying pay raise. They are, however, also feeling apprehensive and cautious. Neither Sue nor Jonathan has ever lived away from their families in Buffalo, and Sue is concerned about giving up her newly reestablished career. Their daughter Janine has just started school, and Jonathan and Sue are uncertain whether living abroad is the best thing for her at her age.

Using the following three-point scale, try to rate Jonathan and Sue as potential expatriates. Write a sentence or two on why you gave the ratings you did.

Rating Scale

1. Based on this dimension, this person would adjust well to living abroad.

2. Based on this dimension, this person may or may not adjust well to living abroad.

3. Based on this dimension, this person would not adjust well to living abroad.

Jonathan's International Orientation

Rating dimension	Rating and reason for rating
International attitudes Foreign experiences Comfort with differences Participation in cultural events	

Sue's International Orientation

Rating dimension	Rating and reason for rating
International attitudes Foreign experiences Comfort with differences Participation in cultural events	

Discussion Questions: Office Supplies International

1. Imagine that you are the international human resource manager for OSI. Your job is to interview both Jonathan and Sue to determine whether they should be sent abroad. What are some of the questions you would ask? What critical information do you feel is missing? It might be helpful to role-play the three parts and evaluate your classmates' responses as Jonathan and Sue.

2. Suppose France is the country where they would be sent. To what extent would your ratings change? What else would you change about the way you are assessing the couple?

3. Now answer the same questions, except this time they are being sent to Japan. Repeat the exercise for Australia.

4. For those dimensions that you rated Sue and Jonathan either 2 or 3 (indicating that they might have a potential adjustment problem), what would you suggest for training and development? What might be included in a training program?

5. Reflect on your own life for a moment and give yourself a rating on each of the following dimensions. Try to justify why you rated yourself as you did. Do you feel that you would adjust well to living abroad? What might be difficult for you?

Rating dimension	Rating and reason for rating France, Japan, Australia (or other)
International attitudes Foreign experiences Comfort with differences Participation in cultural events	

6. Generally, what are some of the potential problems a dual-career couple might face? What are some of the solutions to those problems?

7. How would the ages of children affect the expatriate's assignment? At what age should the children's international orientations be assessed along with their parents?

International Orientation Scale

The following sample items are taken from the International Orientation Scale. Answer each question and give yourself a score for each dimension. The highest possible score for any dimension is 20 points.

Dimension 1: International Attitudes

Use the following scale to answer questions Q1 through Q4.

1 *Strongly agree*

2 *Agree somewhat*

3 *Maybe or unsure*

4 *Disagree somewhat*

5 *Strongly disagree*

Q1. Foreign language skills should be taught as early as elementary school. _____

Q2. Traveling the world is a priority in my life. _____

Q3. A yearlong overseas assignment (from my company) would be a fantastic opportunity for my family and me. _____

Q4. Other countries fascinate me. _____

Total Dimension 1 _____

Dimension 2: Foreign Experiences

Q1. I have studied a foreign language.

1 Never

2 For less than a year

3 For a year

4 For a few years

5 For several years

Q2. I am fluent in another language.

1 I don't know another language.

2 I am limited to very short and simple phrases.

3 I know basic grammatical structure and speak with a limited vocabulary.

4 I understand conversation on most topics.

5 I am very fluent in another language.

Q3. I have spent time overseas (traveling, studying abroad, etc.).

1 Never

2 About a week

3 A few weeks

4 A few months

5 Several months or years

Q4. I was overseas before the age of 18.

1 Never

2 About a week

3 A few weeks

4 A few months

5 Several months or years

Total Dimension 2 _____

Dimension 3: Comfort with Differences

Use the following scale for questions Q1 through Q4.

1 Quite similar

2 Mostly similar

3 Somewhat different

4 Quite different

5 Extremely different

Q1. My friends' career goals, interests, and education are ... _____

Q2. My friends' ethnic backgrounds are ... _____

Q3. My friends' religious affiliations are ... _____

Q4. My friends' first languages are ... _____

Total Dimension 3 _____

Dimension 4: Participation in Cultural Events

Use the following scale to answer questions Q1 through Q4.

1 Never

2 Seldom

3 Sometimes

4 Frequently

5 As often as possible

Q1. I eat at a variety of ethnic restaurants (e.g., Greek, Polynesian, Thai, German). _____

Q2. I watch the major networks' world news programs. _____

Q3. I attend ethnic festivals. _____

Q4. I visit art galleries and museums. _____

Total Dimension 4 _____

Self-Assessment Discussion Questions:

Do any of these scores suprise you?

Would you like to improve your international orientation?

If so, what could you do to change various aspects of your life?

2.2 Ethical Dilemmas

Divide the class into five groups. Each group should choose one of the following scenarios and agree on a course of action.

1. Sam works for you. He is technically capable and a good worker, but he does not get along well with others in the work group. When Sam has an opportunity to transfer, you encourage him to take it. What would you say to Sam's potential supervisor when he asks about Sam?

2. Your boss has told you that you must reduce your work group by 30 percent. Which of the following criteria would you use to lay off workers?

   a. Lay off older, higher-paid employees.

   b. Lay off younger, lower-paid employees.

    c. Lay off workers based on seniority only.

    d. Lay off workers based on performance only.

3. You are an engineer, but you are not working on your company's Department of Transportation (DOT) project. One day you overhear a conversation in the cafeteria between the program manager and the project engineer that makes you reasonably sure a large contract will soon be given to the ABC Company to develop and manufacture a key DOT subsystem. ABC is a small firm, and its stock is traded over the counter. You feel sure that the stock will rise from its present $2.25 per share as soon as news of the DOT contract gets out. Would you go out and buy ABC's stock?

4. You are the project engineer working on the development of a small liquid rocket engine. You know that if you could achieve a throttling ratio greater than 8 to 1, your system would be considered a success and continue to receive funding support. To date, the best you have achieved is a 4-to-1 ratio. You have an unproven idea that you feel has a 50 percent chance of being successful. Your project is currently being reviewed to determine if it should be continued. You would like to continue it. How optimistically should you present the test results?

5. Imagine that you are the president of a company in a highly competitive industry. You learn that a competitor has made an important scientific discovery that is not patentable and will give that company an advantage that will substantially reduce the profits of your company for about a year. There is some hope of hiring one of the competitor's employees who knows the details of the discovery. Would you try to hire this person?

Each group should present its scenario and chosen course of action to the class. The class should then evaluate the ethics of the course of action, using the following questions to guide discussion:

1. Are you following rules that are understood and accepted?

2. Are you comfortable discussing and defending your action?

3. Would you want someone to do this to you?

4. What if everyone acted this way?

5. Are there alternatives that rest on firmer ethical ground?

Scenarios adapted from R. A. DiBattista, "Providing a Rationale for Ethical Conduct from Alternatives Taken in Ethical Dilemmas," *Journal of General Psychology* 116 (1989): 207–214; discussion questions adapted with the permission of The Free Press, a Division of Simon & Schuster, Inc. from *The Manager as Negotiator: Bargaining for Cooperation and Competitive Gain* by David A. Lax and James K. Sebenius 0-02-918770-2. Copyright © 1986 by David A. Lax and James K. Sebenius.

BizFlix | Lost in Translation

Jet lag conspires with culture shock to force the meeting of Charlotte (Scarlett Johansson) and Bob Harris (Bill Murray). Neither can sleep after their Tokyo arrival. They meet in their luxury hotel's bar, forging an enduring relationship as they experience Tokyo's wonders, strangeness, and complexity. Based on director Sophia Coppola's Academy Award winning screenplay, this film was shot entirely on location in Japan. It offers extraordinary views of various parts of Japanese culture that are not available to you without a visit.

Cross-Cultural Observations: Visiting Japan

This sequence is an edited composite taken from different parts of the film. It shows selected aspects of Tokyo and Kyoto, Japan. Charlotte has her first experience with the complex and busy Tokyo train system. She later takes the train to Kyoto, Japan's original capital city for more than ten centuries.

What to Watch for and Ask Yourself

- While watching this sequence, pretend you have arrived in Tokyo, and you are experiencing what you are seeing. Do you understand everything you see?

- Is Charlotte bewildered by her experiences? Is she experiencing some culture shock?

- What aspects of Japanese culture appear in this sequence? What do you see as important values of Japanese culture? Review the earlier section, "Understanding Cultural Differences," to gain some insights about these questions.

Workplace Video | City of Greensburg, Kansas: Ethics and Social Responsibility

May 4, 2007, started out like any day for the 1,500 residents of Greensburg, Kansas. Weather forecasters predicted afternoon storms, but few residents paid much attention. By 6 P.M., the National Weather Service issued a tornado warning for Kiowa County. Around 9:20 P.M., storm sirens sounded, and residents took cover in bathrooms and basements. When they emerged from their shelters, their town was gone.

With 700 homes to rebuild, the residents were prepared to start with a clean slate. City Administrator Steve Hewitt and Mayor Lonnie McCollum rallied the people and vowed to rebuild a green town. Although both Hewitt and McCollum believed Greensburg should be rebuilt in a socially responsible way, using sustainable practices, designs, and materials, they faced some ethical dilemmas. Hewitt frequently explained his broad view of the stakeholders affected by their choices, "We're making 100-year decisions that will affect our children and our children's children."

Greensburg upped the cost of rebuilding when city council approved an ordinance declaring all municipal buildings would be built to the highest green building rating for sustainability: "LEED-Platinum." Leadership in Energy and Environmental Design (LEED) promotes a whole-building approach to sustainability by recognizing performance in five key areas of human and environmental health: materials selection, sustainable site development, energy efficiency, water savings, and indoor environmental quality. In Hewitt's mind, Greensburg had an economic responsibility to construct buildings that achieved maximum energy efficiency. So even if it cost more initially to build LEED-Platinum facilities, the town's energy costs as well as its operating costs would be significantly lower in the future.

Today, the initiative to rebuild Greensburg is a group effort. John Deere, BTI Greensburg, and Honda are but a few of the businesses aiding the cause. Greensburg GreenTown, a 501(c)(3) not-for-profit organization, is the town's central organizer, providing Greensburg with the information, support, and resources necessary to rebuild as a green community. Although many challenges lie ahead, leaders of the town will not be deterred. As they say in Greensburg: "Rebuilding green is the right thing to do."

Questions

Discussion Questions

1. In what ways do the activities of Greensburg exemplify good ethics and social responsibility? Explain.

2. What are the potential consequences of rebuilding Greensburg without concern for green practices?

3. Besides lowering energy costs, how else might Greensburg benefit from becoming a green town?

Case

The Timberland Company: Challenges and Opportunities

The Timberland Company, headquartered in Stratham, New Hampshire, characterizes itself as "a big company made up of a lot of small parts and incredibly talented people. We make boots, shoes, clothes and gear that are comfortable enough to wear all day and rugged enough for all year. We don't rest on our accomplishments. If we did, we'd only have ever made one waterproof leather boot."[1] Timberland sells its products around the world through department stores and athletic stores, as well in company-owned and franchised outlets in the United States, Canada, Latin America, Europe, the Middle East, and Asia.[2] In 2008, Timberland had $1.36 billion in revenue with a profit of $42.91 billion.[3]

According to the Timberland Web site, "Our place in this world is bigger than the things we put in it. So we volunteer in our communities. Making new products goes hand in hand with making things better. That means reducing our carbon footprint and being as environmentally responsible as we can."[4] Timberland's commitment to going beyond market success and corporate profitability is evident in the four pillars of its corporate social responsibility (CSR) strategy. These pillars are as follows: become carbon neutral by 2010; design recyclable products; have fair, safe, and nondiscriminatory workplaces; and focus employee service on community greening.[5] Timberland is committed to using "the resources, energy, and profits of a publicly traded footwear-and-apparel company to combat social ills, help the environment, and improve conditions for laborers around the globe."[6] Jeffrey Swartz, Timberland's CEO, believes that the best way to pursue social objectives is through a publicly traded company rather than through a privately owned company or a nonprofit organization because it forces commerce and justice—business interests and social/environmental interests—to be enacted in a public and transparent manner.[7]

One example of how this CSR strategy is implemented is provided by the company's manufacturing of biodegradable boots and shoes. Timberland even "lists the carbon footprint—or how much fossil fuel it took to create each pair of footwear—on every shoebox as a 'Green Index' label."[8]

Another example of Timberland's commitment to CSR is evident in how its deals with suppliers around the world with regard to fair labor practices and human rights. In addressing its commitment to global human rights, Timberland offers the following explanation: "Our Code of Conduct helps us ensure fair, safe and non-discriminatory workplaces around the world, and to create positive change in communities where Timberland® products are made. By reinforcing our Code of Conduct, engaging stakeholders, building local capacity, coming up with solutions as needed, and utilizing accurate and transparent reporting, we're doing what we can to improve the quality of life for approximately 175,000 workers in 290+ factories in 35 countries."[9]

Timberland tries to constructively engage suppliers who commit labor infractions; rather than immediately discharging such suppliers, Timberland works with suppliers to change their policies so as to keep the workers employed.[10]

Jeff Swartz recalls his introduction to volunteering during the regular workday in the late 1980s when he helped out at a center for young adults who were recovering from drug and alcohol addiction. Acknowledging that it changed his perspective regarding what can be accomplished during the workday, Swartz says, "I learned that serving strengthened our business from within and allowed us to accomplish not only the regular business agenda but more."[11] This helped set the course for the future of the Timberland Company.

An integral part of the corporate culture of Timberland is the *Path of Service*. This program provides employees with paid time off to do volunteer work in their community—and to do it during the busy workweek. Every Timberland employee around the globe receives forty hours of paid volunteer time a year. Employees also can apply for longer-term service sabbaticals.[12] And "[c]ompany meetings, which for many businesses include at least one afternoon of golf, are comprised of a day of service instead. ... Timberland also operates community stores in inner cities and donates a percentage of profits to needy groups."[13]

Another way in which Timberland comingles corporate success and social responsibility—along with a commitment to diversity—is through *Endless Possibilities*, a community outreach program that also involves retail partners Macy's and Dillard's. Endless Possibilities, among many other social initiatives, helps out at "New York-based Inwood House, which provides supportive environments for young women in distress."[14] Endless Possibilities was created to help support the revamping of Timberland's product line to make it more appealing to women. The reasoning behind the connection between the product and social responsibility is that women, as a consumer group, like to know that the products they purchase contribute in some way to the greater good.[15] The team's reasoning paid off not only in terms of Timberland's social activism but also in increased sales and a strengthened Timberland brand in the eyes of women.[16]

Still another way in which the Timberland Company pursues social justice initiatives is through its collaboration with nonprofit organizations. For instance, Timberland's long history of partnering with the nonprofit organization City Year has benefitted both organizations and has helped make employee involvement an integral part of Timberland's corporate culture. City Year engages people who are seventeen to twenty-four years old in community service and leadership development projects in the United States and South Africa—with the latter contributing to Timberland's global interests. Participants in the projects commit for one year, and Timberland provides clothing and equipment for over 1,000 City Year Corps members each year. Of its partnership with City Year, Timberland notes, "[w]e recognize that doing well while doing good helps the community and provides tangible benefits for the Timberland brand as more consumers look for brands that share their values."[17]

Does being socially responsible lead businesses to be more successful? Or does success provide the necessary resources for being socially responsible? Darrel Rigby and Suzanne Tager, in writing about the advantages of sustainable growth, point out that "[d]irect links between sustainability and profitability are somewhat tenuous; there's not much conclusive data proving the connection. ... The cause and effect may simply be that well-run companies also take pains to be good corporate citizens that opt for sustainable practices."[18]

In reflecting on the simultaneous pursuit of commercial success and CSR, Swartz opines, "[t]he social challenges that plague our world won't be solved by government or church alone. For-profit business can be part of the solution, as part of the everyday business agenda. We can earn our quarterly profits and take our share of responsibility for repairing the breaches in society at the same time."[19] Swartz also says, "[w]e believe in our guts that commerce and justice are not separate ideas; that doing well and doing good are not antithetical notions; that being cognizant of this quarter's earnings is part of what we are responsible for—just as being our brother's and sister's keeper is part of what we are responsible for, every business day."[20]

Discussion Questions

1. Jeffrey Swartz's approach to running Timberland is based on the belief that business success is compatible with corporate social and environmental responsibility. Do you share this belief? Why or why not?

2. How has the Timberland Company incorporated the four pillars of its corporate social responsibility (CSR) strategy into its day-to-day operations?

3. How does Timberland's CSR strategy and day-to-day operations respond to the globalization, diversity, and ethics challenges that it faces?

4. Consider the ethical, diversity, and globalization challenges that have confronted Timberland. How has Timberland converted these challenges into opportunities for the company?

SOURCE: This case was written by Michael K. McCuddy, The Louis S. and Mary L. Morgal Chair of Christian Business Ethics and Professor of Management, College of Business Administration, Valparaiso University.

Cohesion Case

Zappos.com: The Multiple Challenges of Growing an Unusual Company (A)

"Imagine a retailer with service so good its customers wish it would take over the Internal Revenue Service or start up an airline. It might sound like a marketing fantasy, but this scenario is reality for ... Zappos.com."[1] Headquartered in Henderson, Nevada, just a twenty-minute drive from the Las Vegas Strip, Zappos (a word play on zapatos, the Spanish word for shoes)[2] is an "e-commerce 'service provider' of shoes, apparel, handbags, accessories and more, representing about a thousand brands."[3] Zappos also has a distribution center (DC) in Louisville, Kentucky where it maintains an inventory of approximately 4 million items[4] and from which it provides rapid shipment to its customers.

In 1999, Tony Hsieh (pronounced Shay), the CEO of Zappos, invested $500,000 in a start-up online shoe store known as Shoesite.com that was founded in San Francisco by Nicholas Swinmurn, who was having trouble finding shoes that would fit him in his local mall.[5] In 2000, Hsieh became cochief executive with Swinmurn.[6] When Swinmurn left the company in 2006, Hsieh became the sole chief executive.[7]

Zappos wasn't Tony Hsieh's first entrepreneurial venture. Prior to Zappos, he cofounded LinkExchange, which Microsoft bought in 1998 for $265 million.[8] Then he cofounded a venture capital investment firm called Venture Frogs.[9] The $500,000 that Hsieh invested in Shoesite.com in 1999 was a combination of venture capital from Venture Frogs and his own personal funds.[10] Zappos still is a privately held company, with less than 50 percent being owned by CEO Hsieh and the remainder owned by Sequoia Capital.[11]

In its early days, Zappos could not afford to spend money on marketing; consequently, the company's "sales strategy involved making customers so happy that they bought again or told their friends or both. ... The defining aspect of the Zappos customer experience—free shipping and free returns—was concocted out of necessity. Hsieh figured that there was no other way to get people to try the [online] site."[12]

In 2004, Zappos, relocated from San Francisco to Las Vegas because "attracting and keeping high-quality customer service representatives was too difficult and expensive in the Bay Area."[13] Las Vegas seemed to be an ideal location, with cheaper real estate and abundant call-center workers.[14]

Zappos doesn't do anything quite the way other companies do.[15] For instance, the three buildings of the company's headquarters, which is located in a nondescript office park, are quite modest on the outside.[16] But inside is a different story! "There are the outlandish decorations adorning walls and cubicles, including jungle creepers that hang from the ceiling and a menagerie of toy monkeys and other creatures. There are the boisterous employees, some of whom rattle cowbells, shake pompoms and bellow greetings as visitors pass their desks. ... But this is no exercise in nostalgia. Instead, Zappos is the site of an ambitious business experiment ... [with] a corporate culture that allows Zappos to prosper by providing world-beating customer service, no matter what business it is involved in."[17] Emulating Amazon.com, Zappos has expanded beyond selling shoes, venturing as well into clothes, bedding, toys, cookware, electronics, and more—but the product offerings are slim in some of these categories.[18]

Zappos gets rave reviews for "its fast, free shipping—90% of orders arrive the next business day—and a 365-day return policy that allows footwear fans to order a bunch of shoes, try them on and return those that don't suit or fit. Three-quarters of sales are from repeat customers."[19] Hsieh views "customers as human beings, not just 'consumers,' and so makes customer service the defining feature of the brand."[20]

To gain another perspective on how Zappos differs from other companies, consider the experience of one shopper—unusual but a clear reflection of how Zappos employees deal with customer challenges: "A shopper visited the site to order a pair of shoes as a gift for her husband. Tragically, he was in a fatal car accident later that evening. [Subsequently,] [t]he Zappos call-center representative working on the order return was so touched by the story that she sent the customer a sympathy bouquet of flowers." Hsieh says the Zappos "philosophy is to do what's right for the customer even if it doesn't relate to a sale or if it costs a little bit more. We just want to go above and beyond for our customer."[21]

Hsieh believes that the success of Zappos is a direct reflection of the culture he has built and nourished. "A fun-loving, change-embracing culture drives the Zappos engine. Carefully nurtured by Hsieh, it provides a new workplace template for the future."[22] Hsieh's advice to other businesspeople: "Chase the vision. ... The money and profits will come."[23]

In 2000, Zappos had sales of $1.6 million; in 2008, the company's sales surpassed $1 billion.[24] Zappos was profitable in 2007 and 2008 after several years of just breaking even.[25] Tony Hsieh explains Zappos' growth this way: "We're aligned around one mission—to provide the best customer service possible. Rather than focus on maximizing short-term profits, we focus on how we can maximize the service to our customers. We are a service company that happens to sell shoes."[26] Hsieh sees the emphasis on customer service "as creating a platform for future growth."[27]

As Advertising Age writer Natalie Zmuda observes, "It seems that Zappos is really the poster child for this new age of consumer companies that truly are customer focused. A lot of companies like to say they are, but none of them is as serious as Zappos."[28]

Discussion Questions

1. What lessons about leading people and managing organizations does Zappos and its CEO, Tony Hsieh, provide?

2. What do you like about Zappos? What do you dislike about Zappos? Explain your answer.

3. Which of the management challenges—globalization; leading a diverse workforce; and ethics, character, and personal integrity—have had an important impact on the evolution of Zappos? Explain your answer.

4. How has Zappos CEO Tony Hsieh addressed the management challenges of globalization; leading a diverse workforce; and ethics, character, and personal integrity? Explain your answer.

5. Natalie Zmuda, a reporter for Advertising Age, concludes, "It seems that Zappos is really the poster child for this new age of consumer companies that truly are customer focused. A lot of companies like to say they are, but none of them is as serious as Zappos." Do you agree or disagree with Zmuda's assertion that Zappos is much different than other consumer companies? Explain the reasoning behind your answer.

6. What particular aspects of Zappos would other organizations do well to emulate? Explain your answer.

SOURCE: This case was written by Michael K. McCuddy, The Louis S. and Mary L. Morgal Chair of Christian Business Ethics and Professor of Management, College of Business Administration, Valparaiso University.

© Digital Vision

PART 2

Individual Processes and Behavior

3

Personality, Perception, and Attribution

LEARNING OBJECTIVES

After reading this chapter, you should be able to do the following:

1 Describe individual differences and their importance in understanding behavior.

2 Define *personality*.

3 Identify several personality characteristics and their influences on behavior in organizations.

4 Give examples of each personality characteristic from your own work experience and how you would apply your knowledge in managing personality differences.

5 Discuss Carl Jung's contribution to our understanding of individual differences, and explain how his theory is used in the Myers–Briggs Type Indicator (MBTI®) instrument.

6 Evaluate the importance of the MBTI® to managers.

7 Define *social perception* and explain how characteristics of the perceiver, the target, and the situation affect it.

8 Identify five common barriers to social perception.

9 Explain the attribution process and how attributions affect managerial behavior.

10 Evaluate the accuracy of managerial attributions from the standpoint of attribution biases and errors.

Nordstrom prides itself on customer service.

THINKING AHEAD: **NORDSTROM**

Salespeople Are the Top Priority

The key to Nordstrom's success over the last 100 years or so has been attributed to the employees and in particular the salespeople. Nordstrom prides itself on customer service and has a culture in which pleasing the customer is paramount.

The Nordstrom family, who still runs Nordstrom, understands this and treats their employees well so that they will treat the customers well. They have been consistently selected as one of the 100 Best Companies to Work For in America, and more than 3,000 of Nordstrom's employees have been with the company for more than ten years. Nordstrom uses an inverted pyramid to illustrate its structure. On this pyramid, the customers are on top but the salespeople are next—and the board of directors is at the bottom! This illustrates the value Nordstrom places in salespeople, and also their powerful positions in the organization. Salespeople are encouraged to make their own decisions and do whatever they think is appropriate to best serve their customers. For example, at a Seattle store a customer shopping right before a flight left her plane ticket behind. The salesperson who found it called the airline to ask them to print a new ticket. When they refused, the salesperson used some money from petty cash to hail a cab and deliver the ticket to the customer in person at the airport. In addition to empowering these employees, Nordstrom treats them well, offering profit-sharing and generous 401K plans, and has monthly recognition meetings to reward their salespeople.

Nordstrom has done an exceptional job focusing on programs aimed at retaining employees. What does it take to get a job at Nordstrom? In the Looking Back feature, you can see how they select people to join their award-winning sales team.

INDIVIDUAL DIFFERENCES AND ORGANIZATIONAL BEHAVIOR

1 Describe individual differences and their importance in understanding behavior.

In this chapter and continuing in Chapter 4, we explore the concept of *individual differences*. Individuals are unique in terms of their skills, abilities, personalities, perceptions, attitudes, emotions, and ethics. These are just a few of the ways people may be similar to or different from one another. Individual differences represent the essence of the challenge of management, because no two people are completely alike. Managers face the challenge of working with people who possess a multitude of individual characteristics, so the more managers understand those differences, the better they can work with others. Figure 3.1 illustrates how individual differences affect human behavior.

The basis for understanding individual differences stems from Lewin's early contention that behavior is a function of the person and the environment.[1] Lewin expressed this idea in an equation: $B = f(P, E)$, where B = behavior, P = person, and

individual differences
The way in which factors such as skills, abilities, personalities, perceptions, attitudes, values, and ethics differ from one individual to another.

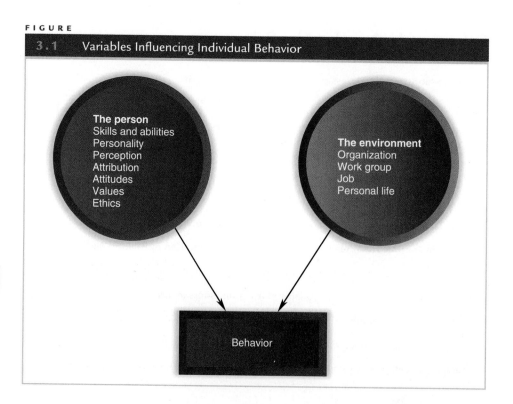

FIGURE

3.1 Variables Influencing Individual Behavior

The person
Skills and abilities
Personality
Perception
Attribution
Attitudes
Values
Ethics

The environment
Organization
Work group
Job
Personal life

Behavior

E = environment. This idea has been developed by the *interactional psychology* approach.[2] Basically, it says that in order to understand human behavior, we must know something about the person and the situation. There are four basic propositions of interactional psychology:

1. Behavior is a function of a continuous, multidirectional interaction between the person and the situation.

2. The person is active in this process and both changes, and is changed by, situations.

3. People vary in many characteristics, including cognitive, affective, motivational, and ability factors.

4. Two interpretations of situations are important: the objective situation and the person's subjective view of the situation.[3]

The interactional psychology approach points out the need to study both persons and situations. We will focus on personal and situational factors throughout the text. The person consists of individual differences such as those we emphasize in this chapter and Chapter 4: personality, perception, attribution, attitudes, emotions, and ethics. The situation consists of the environment the person operates in, and it can include things like the organization, work group, personal life situation, job characteristics, and many other environmental influences. We will briefly discuss skills and abilities which are individual differences that clearly impact behavior at work, and then move to a fascinating individual difference—personality.

SKILLS AND ABILITIES

There are many skills and abilities that relate to work outcomes. *General mental ability (GMA)* was introduced by Spearman (1904)[4] more than 100 years ago. It is defined as an individual's innate cognitive intelligence. It was the single best predictor of work performance across many occupations studied both here in the United States[5] and across different cultures,[6] and some would argue that intelligence testing should be the primary gauge for selecting employees.[7] But what about aspects of one's personality? Next, we will discuss personality characteristics that influence organizational outcomes.

PERSONALITY

What makes an individual behave in consistent ways in a variety of situations? Personality is an individual difference that lends consistency to a person's behavior. *Personality* is defined as a relatively stable set of characteristics that influence an individual's behavior. Although there is debate about the determinants of personality, there appear to be several origins. One determinant is heredity, and some interesting studies have supported this position. Identical twins who are separated at birth and raised apart in very different situations have been found to share personality traits and job preferences. For example, about half of the variation in traits like extraversion, impulsiveness, and flexibility was found to be genetically determined; that is, identical twins who grew up in different environments shared these traits.[8] In addition, the twins held similar jobs.[9] Thus, there does appear to be a genetic influence on personality.

Another determinant of personality is the environment a person is exposed to. Family, culture, education, and other environmental forces shape personality. Personality is therefore shaped by both heredity and environment.

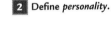 **2** Define *personality*.

interactional psychology
The psychological approach that says in order to understand human behavior, we must know something about the person and the situation.

personality
A relatively stable set of characteristics that influence an individual's behavior.

Personality Theories

Two major theories of personality are the trait theory and the integrative approach. Each theory has influenced the study of personality in organizations.

Trait Theory Some early personality researchers believed that to understand individuals, we must break down behavior patterns into a series of observable traits. According to *trait theory*, combining these traits into a group forms an individual's personality. Gordon Allport, a leading trait theorist, saw traits as broad, general guides that lend consistency to behavior.[10] Thousands of traits have been identified over the years. Raymond Cattell, another prominent trait theorist, identified sixteen traits that formed the basis for differences in individual behavior. He described traits in bipolar adjective combinations such as self-assured/apprehensive, reserved/outgoing, and submissive/dominant.[11]

Big Five Personality Model

Personality theorists have long argued that in order to understand individual behavior, people's behavioral patterns can be broken down into a series of observable traits. One popular personality classification is the "Big Five." The Big Five traits include extraversion, agreeableness, conscientiousness, emotional stability, and openness to experience.[12] These are broad, global traits that are associated with behaviors at work. Descriptions of the Big Five appear in Table 3.1.

From preliminary research, we know that students who are open to experience are more likely to be intrinsically motivated to learn or motivated to learn for the sake of learning whereas, extraverted students are more likely to be extrinsically motivated to learn or motivated to learn as a means to an end. Conscientious students are motivated both intrinsically and extrinsically.[13] We also know that introverted and conscientious employees are less likely to be absent from work.[14] In making peer evaluations, individuals with high agreeableness tend to rate others more leniently, while individuals with high conscientiousness tend to be tougher as raters.[15] Extraverts tend to have higher salaries, receive more promotions, and are more satisfied with their careers.[16] Across many occupations, people who are conscientious are more motivated and are high performers.[17] Viewing more specific

trait theory
The personality theory that states that in order to understand individuals, we must break down behavior patterns into a series of observable traits.

TABLE

3.1	The Big Five Personality Traits
Extraversion	The person is gregarious, assertive, and sociable (as opposed to reserved, timid, and quiet).
Agreeableness	The person is cooperative, warm, and agreeable (rather than cold, disagreeable, and antagonistic).
Conscientiousness	The person is hardworking, organized, and dependable (as opposed to lazy, disorganized, and unreliable).
Emotional stability	The person is calm, self-confident, and cool (as opposed to insecure, anxious, and depressed).
Openness to experience	The person is creative, curious, and cultured (rather than practical with narrow interests).

SOURCES: P. T. Costa and R. R. McCrae, *The NEO-PI Personality Inventory* (Odessa, FL: Psychological Assessment Resources, 1992); J. F. Salgado, "The Five Factor Model of Personality and Job Performance in the European Community," *Journal of Applied Psychology* 82 (1997): 30–43.

occupations, however, shows that different patterns of the Big Five factors are related to high performance. For customer service jobs, individuals high in emotional stability, agreeableness, and openness to experience perform best. For managers, emotional stability and extraversion are traits of top performers.[18] Recent research indicates that in work teams, the minimum level of agreeableness in a team as well as the mean levels of conscientiousness and openness to experience had a strong effect on overall team performance.[19] The Big Five framework has also been applied across cultures. It has held up well among Spanish and Mexican populations[20] and some cross-cultural research suggests that personality prevalence differs in different countries and that there may be good reason for these differences. For example, a recent study found that countries that have historically suffered from high levels of infectious diseases report lower mean levels of extraversion and openness to experience.[21]

The trait approach has been the subject of considerable criticism. Some theorists argue that simply identifying traits is not enough; instead, personality is dynamic and not completely stable. Further, early trait theorists tended to ignore the influence of situations.[22] Also, the trait theory tends to ignore process—that is, how we get from a trait to a particular outcome.

Integrative Approach Recently, researchers have taken a broader, more *integrative approach* to the study of personality.[23] To capture its influence on behavior, personality is described as a composite of the individual's psychological processes. Personality dispositions include emotions, cognitions, attitudes, expectancies, and fantasies.[24] *Dispositions*, in this approach, simply mean the tendencies of individuals to respond to situations in consistent ways. Influenced by both genetics and experiences, dispositions can be modified. The integrative approach focuses on both person (dispositions) and situational variables as combined predictors of behavior.

Personality Characteristics in Organizations

Managers should learn as much as possible about personality in order to understand their employees and how best to manage them. Hundreds of personality characteristics have been identified. We have selected three characteristics because of their particular influences on individual behavior in organizations: core self-evaluations (CSE), self-monitoring, and positive/negative affect. Because these characteristics affect performance at work, managers need to have a working knowledge of them.

Core Self-Evaluation (CSE) CSE is a broad set of personality traits that refers to self-concept.[25] It is comprised of locus of control, self-esteem, generalized self-efficacy, and emotional stability. CSE has been found to predict both goal-directed behavior and performance,[26] even in non-U.S. cultures (e.g., Japan).[27] Each characteristic comprising CSE with the exception of emotional stability (as we discussed in the Big Five approach) is addressed next.

Locus of Control An individual's generalized belief about internal (self) versus external (situation or others) control is called *locus of control*. People who believe they control what happens to them are said to have an internal locus of control, whereas people who believe that circumstances or other people control their fate have an external locus of control.[28] Research on locus of control has strong implications for organizations. Internals (those with an internal locus of control) have been found to have higher job satisfaction and performance, to be more likely to assume managerial positions, and to prefer participative management styles.[29] You can assess your locus of control in You 3.1.

3 Identify several personality characteristics and their influences on behavior in organizations.

4 Give examples of each personality characteristic from your own work experience and how you would apply your knowledge in managing personality differences.

integrative approach
The broad theory that describes personality as a composite of an individual's psychological processes.

locus of control
An individual's generalized belief about internal control (self-control) versus external control (control by the situation or by others).

What's Your Locus of Control?

Below is a short scale that can give you an idea of your locus of control. For each of the four items, circle either choice a or choice b.

1. a. Becoming a success is a matter of hard work; luck has little or nothing to do with it.
    b. Getting a good job depends mainly on being in the right place at the right time.
2. a. The average citizen can have an influence in government decisions.
    b. This world is run by the few people in power, and there is not much the little guy can do about it.
3. a. As far as world affairs are concerned, most of us are the victims of forces we can neither understand nor control.
    b. By taking an active part in political and social affairs, people can control world events.
4. a. With enough effort, we can wipe out political corruption.
    b. It is difficult for people to have much control over the things politicians do in office.

Scoring Key:

The internal locus of control answers are: 1a, 2a, 3b, 4a. The external locus of control answers are: 1b, 2b, 3a, 4b.

Determine which category you circled most frequently using the key to the left. This gives you an approximation of your locus of control.

SOURCES: T. Adeyemi-Bello, "Validating Rotter's Locus of Control Scale with a Sample of Not-for-Profit Leaders," *Management Research News* 24 (2001): 25–35; J. B. Rotter, "Generalized Expectancies for Internal vs. External Locus of Control of Reinforcement," *Psychological Monographs* 80, whole No. 609 (1966).

Internals and externals have similar positive reactions to being promoted, which include high job satisfaction, job involvement, and organizational commitment. The difference between the two is that internals continue to be happy long after the promotion, whereas externals' joy over the promotion is short-lived. This might occur because externals do not believe their own performance led to the promotion.[30]

Knowing about locus of control can prove valuable to managers. Because internals believe they control what happens to them, they will want to exercise control in their work environment. Allowing internals considerable voice in how work is performed is important. Internals will not react well to being closely supervised. Externals, in contrast, may prefer a more structured work setting, and they may be more reluctant to participate in decision making.

Self-Efficacy *General self-efficacy* is a person's overall view of himself/herself as being able to perform effectively in a wide variety of situations.[31] Employees with high general self-efficacy have more confidence in their job-related abilities and other personal resources (i.e., energy, influence over others, etc.) that help them function effectively on the job. People with low general self-efficacy often feel ineffective at work and may express doubts about performing a new task well. Previous success or performance is one of the most important determinants of self-efficacy. People who have positive beliefs about their efficacy for performance are more likely to attempt difficult tasks, to persist in overcoming obstacles, and to experience less

general self-efficacy
An individual's general belief that he or she is capable of meeting job demands in a wide variety of situations.

anxiety when faced with adversity.[32] People with high self-efficacy also value the ability to provide input, or "voice," at work. Because they are confident in this capability, they value the opportunity to participate.[33] High self-efficacy has also been recently related to higher job satisfaction and performance.

There is another form of self-efficacy, called task-specific self-efficacy, which we will cover in Chapter 6. *Task-specific self-efficacy* is a person's belief that he or she can perform a specific task ("I believe I can do this sales presentation today"). In contrast, general self-efficacy is broader ("I believe I can perform well in just about any part of the job"). Employees with high general self-efficacy have more confidence in their job-related abilities and personal resources. This "I think I can" attitude helps them function effectively on the job.

Self-Esteem *Self-esteem* is an individual's general feeling of self-worth. Individuals with high self-esteem have positive feelings about themselves, perceive themselves to have strengths as well as weaknesses, and believe their strengths are more important than their weaknesses.[34] Individuals with low self-esteem view themselves negatively. They are more strongly affected by what other people think of them, and they compliment individuals who give them positive feedback while cutting down people who give them negative feedback.[35]

Evaluations from other people affect our self-esteem. For example, you might be liked for who you are or for your achievements. Being liked for who you are is more stable, and people who have this type of self-esteem are less defensive and more honest with themselves. Being liked for your achievement is more unstable; it waxes and wanes depending on how high your achievements are.[36]

A person's self-esteem affects a host of other attitudes and has important implications for behavior in organizations. People with high self-esteem perform better and are more satisfied with their jobs.[37] For example, a recent study of 288 R&D engineers from four organizations found that self-esteem predicted supervisor ratings of job performance. This research indicates that self-esteem might be important to performance in knowledge-based occupations.[38] When they are involved in a job search, those with high self-esteem seek out higher-status jobs.[39] A work team made up of such individuals is more likely to be successful than a team with low or average self-esteem.[40]

Very high self-esteem may be too much of a good thing. When people with high self-esteem find themselves in stressful situations, they may brag inappropriately.[41] This may be viewed negatively by others, who see spontaneous boasting as egotistical. Very high self-esteem may also lead to overconfidence and to relationship conflicts with others who may not evaluate this behavior favorably.[42] Individuals with high self-esteem may shift their social identities to protect themselves when they do not live up to some standard. Take two students, Denise and Teresa, for example. If Denise outperforms Teresa on a statistics exam, Teresa may convince herself that Denise is not really a good person to compare against because Denise is an engineering major and Teresa is a physical education major. Teresa's high self-esteem is protecting her from this unfavorable comparison.[43]

Self-esteem may be strongly affected by situations. Success tends to raise self-esteem, whereas failure tends to lower it. Given that high self-esteem is generally a positive characteristic, managers should encourage employees to raise their self-esteem by giving them appropriate challenges and opportunities for success. These three characteristics, along with the effects of emotional stability as discussed in the section on the Big Five, then, constitute an important personality trait known as CSEs. CSE is a strong predictor of both job satisfaction and job performance next only to GMA.[44] In fact, individuals with high levels of CSE perform better on their jobs, are more successful in their careers, are more satisfied with their jobs and lives, report lower levels of stress and conflict, cope more effectively with setbacks, and

self-esteem
An individual's general feeling of self-worth.

Core Self-Evaluations and Life Success

Beginning in early childhood with books like *The Little Engine that Could*, which said, "I think I can, I think I can, I think I can," we grow up hearing how believing in yourself can make the difference between success and failure. But what about in real life, do positive self-evaluations lead to success?

Research supports this idea. Individuals with high CSEs have better job performance, are more satisfied in their work, are better able to recover from job loss, and are happier with life. And in a recent study conducted in all fifty states over the course of twenty-five years from 1979 to 2004, participants high in CSE started their careers on better footing and experienced steeper career paths over time. In fact, the advantages for people with high CSE doubled over the twenty-five-year period.

The researchers concluded that the effects of CSE were largely due to educational attainment and health. Individuals with low CSE acquired their education more slowly, which impacted pay, occupational status, and job satisfaction. These individuals also experienced more health problems, which negatively impacted their success at work and compromised pay and job satisfaction.

SOURCE: T.A. Judge and C. Hurst, "How the Rich (and Happy) Get Richer (and Happier): Relationship of Core Self-Evaluations to Trajectories in Attaining Work Success," *Journal of Applied Psychology* 93 (2008): 849–863.

better capitalize on advantages and opportunities.[45] In the Science feature, you can read about just how powerful CSE can be in leading to success.

Self-Monitoring A characteristic with great potential for affecting behavior in organizations is *self-monitoring*—the extent to which people base their behavior on cues from other people and situations.[46] High self-monitors pay attention to what is appropriate in particular situations and to the behavior of other people, and they behave accordingly. Low self-monitors, by contrast, are not as vigilant to situational cues and act from internal states rather than paying attention to the situation. As a result, the behavior of low self-monitors is consistent across situations. High self-monitors, because their behavior varies with the situation, appear to be more unpredictable and less consistent. One study amongst managers of a recruitment firm found that high self-monitors were more likely to offer emotional help to others in dealing with work-related anxiety. Low self-monitors, on the other hand, even when tasked with managerial responsibilities were less likely to offer such emotional support and help.[47] You can use You 3.2 to assess your own self-monitoring tendencies.

Research is currently focusing on the effects of self-monitoring in organizations. In one study, the authors tracked the careers of 139 MBAs for five years to see whether high self-monitors were more likely to be promoted, change employers, or make a job-related geographic move. The results were "yes" to each question. High self-monitors get promoted because they accomplish tasks through meeting the expectations of others and because they seek out central positions in social networks.[48] They are also more likely to use self-promotion to make others aware of their skills and accomplishments.[49] However, the high self-monitor's flexibility may not be suited for every job, and the tendency to move may not fit every organization.[50] Because high self-monitors base their behavior on cues from others and from the situation, they demonstrate higher levels of managerial self-awareness. This means that, as managers, they assess their own workplace behavior accurately.[51] Managers who are high self-monitors are also good at reading their employees' needs and changing the way they interact with employees depending on those needs.[52]

self-monitoring

The extent to which people base their behavior on cues from other people and situations.

You 3.2

Are You a High or Low Self-Monitor?

For the following items, circle T (true) if the statement is characteristic of your behavior. Circle F (false) if the statement does not reflect your behavior.

1. I find it hard to imitate the behavior of other people.   T   F
2. At parties and social gatherings, I do not attempt to do or say things that others will like.   T   F
3. I can only argue for ideas that I already believe.   T   F
4. I can make impromptu speeches even on topics about which I have almost no information.   T   F
5. I guess I put on a show to impress or entertain others.   T   F
6. I would probably make a good actor.   T   F
7. In a group of people, I am rarely the center of attention.   T   F
8. In different situations and with different people, I often act like very different persons.   T   F
9. I am not particularly good at making other people like me.   T   F
10. I am not always the person I appear to be.   T   F
11. I would not change my opinions (or the way I do things) in order to please others or win their favor.   T   F
12. I have considered being an entertainer.   T   F
13. I have never been good at games like charades or at improvisational acting.   T   F
14. I have trouble changing my behavior to suit different people and different situations.   T   F
15. At a party, I let others keep the jokes and stories going.   T   F
16. I feel a bit awkward in company and do not show up quite as well as I should.   T   F
17. I can look anyone in the eye and tell a lie with a straight face (if it is for a good cause).   T   F
18. I may deceive people by being friendly when I really dislike them.   T   F

Scoring:

To score this questionnaire, give yourself 1 point for each of the following items that you answered T (true): 4, 5, 6, 8, 10, 12, 17, and 18. Now give yourself 1 point for each of the following items that you answered F (false): 1, 2, 3, 7, 9, 11, 13, 14, 15, and 16.

Add both subtotals to find your overall score. If you scored 11 or above, you are probably a *high self-monitor*. If you scored 10 or under, you are probably a *low self-monitor*.

SOURCE: From M. Snyder, *Public Appearances, Private Realities: The Psychology of Self-Monitoring*. Copyright © 1987 by W. H. Freeman and Company. Used with permission.

Although research on self-monitoring in organizations has shown the positives associated with self-monitoring, recent research has also shown that high self-monitors are more likely to feel role conflict in that they are likely to span roles in organizations because of their socially adaptable nature.[53] So, although high self-monitors may respond more readily to work group norms, organizational culture, and supervisory feedback than do low self-monitors, who adhere more to internal guidelines for behavior ("I am who I am"), high self-monitors also have to be aware of possible stress and health consequences that role conflict can create. In addition, high self-monitors may be enthusiastic participants in the trend toward work teams because of their ability to assume flexible roles.

Positive/Negative Affect Recently, researchers have explored the effects of persistent mood dispositions at work. Individuals who focus on the positive aspects of themselves, other people, and the world in general are said to have *positive affect*.[54] By contrast, those who accentuate the negative in themselves, others, and the world are said to possess *negative affect* (also referred to as negative affectivity).[55] Positive affect is linked with job satisfaction, which we discuss at length in Chapter 4. Individuals with positive affect are more satisfied with their jobs.[56] In addition, those with positive affect are more likely to help others at work and also engage in more organizational citizenship behaviors (OCBs).[57] Employees with positive affect are also absent from work less often.[58] Positive affect has also been linked to more life satisfaction and better performance across a variety of life and work domains.[59] Individuals with negative affect report more work stress.[60] Individual affect also influences the work group. When top management team members have high levels of positive affectivity, the firm's financial performance is better, but when there are team members with both positive and negative affectivity, group conflict is frequent and less cooperation is seen.[61] Leader affectivity can have an impact on subordinate outcomes. For example, a recent study of leaders and subordinates found that leader negative affectivity had a negative effect on subordinate attitudinal outcomes such as organizational commitment, job satisfaction, and anxiety.[62] Positive affect and negative affect should be of interest to managers because of their impact on workplace behavior. Employees with positive affect perform better and they are more likely to engage in helping behaviors, but employees with negative affect are not only less likely to help others—they are more likely to be absent, to leave the organization, to incur an injury on the job, and to commit behaviors that are counterproductive.[63]

The characteristics previously described are but a few of the personality characteristics that affect behavior and performance in organizations. Negative affect, for example, affects work stress, as you'll see in Chapter 7. Another personality characteristic related to stress is Type A behavior, also presented in Chapter 7. Other personality characteristics are woven in throughout the book. Can managers predict the behavior of their employees by knowing their personalities? Not completely. You may recall that the interactional psychology model (Figure 3.1) requires both person and situation variables to predict behavior. Another idea to remember in predicting behavior is the strength of situational influences. Some situations are *strong situations* in that they overwhelm the effects of individual personalities. These situations are interpreted in the same way by different individuals, evoke agreement on the appropriate behavior in the situation, and provide cues to appropriate behavior. A performance appraisal session is an example of a strong situation. Employees know to listen to their boss and to contribute when asked to do so.

A weak situation, by contrast, is one that is open to many interpretations. It provides few cues to appropriate behavior and no obvious rewards for one behavior over another. Thus, individual personalities have a stronger influence in weak situations than in strong situations. An informal meeting without an agenda can be seen as a weak situation.

Organizations present combinations of strong and weak situations; therefore, personality has a stronger effect on behavior in some situations than in others.[64]

Measuring Personality

Several methods can be used to assess personality. These include projective tests, behavioral measures, and self-report questionnaires.

The *projective test* is one method used to measure personality. In these tests, individuals are shown a picture, abstract image, or photo and are asked to describe

---

positive affect
An individual's tendency to accentuate the positive aspects of himself or herself, other people, and the world in general.

negative affect
An individual's tendency to accentuate the negative aspects of himself or herself, other people, and the world in general.

strong situation
A situation that overwhelms the effects of individual personalities by providing strong cues for appropriate behavior.

projective test
A personality test that elicits an individual's response to abstract stimuli.

what they see or tell a story about it. The rationale behind projective tests is that each individual responds to the stimulus in a way that reflects his or her unique personality. The Rorschach inkblot test is a projective test commonly used to assess personality.[65] Like other projective tests, however, it has low reliability. The individual being assessed may look at the same picture and see different things at different times. Also, the assessor may apply his or her own biases in interpreting the information about the individual's personality.

There are *behavioral measures* of personality as well. Measuring an individual's behavior involves observing it in a controlled situation. We might assess a person's sociability, for example, by counting the number of times he or she approaches strangers at a party. The behavior is scored in some manner to produce an index of personality. Some potential problems with behavioral measures include the observer's ability to stay focused and the way the observer interprets the behavior. In addition, some people behave differently when they know they are being observed.

The most common method of assessing personality is the *self-report questionnaire*. Individuals respond to a series of questions, usually in an agree/disagree or true/false format. One of the more widely recognized questionnaires is the Minnesota Multiphasic Personality Inventory (MMPI). The MMPI is comprehensive and assesses a variety of traits, as well as various neurotic or psychotic disorders. Used extensively in psychological counseling to identify disorders, the MMPI is a long questionnaire. The Big Five traits we discussed earlier are measured by another self-report questionnaire, the NEO Personality Inventory. Self-report questionnaires also suffer from potential biases. It is difficult to be objective about your own personality. People often answer the questionnaires in terms of how they want to be seen, rather than as they really are.

Another approach to applying personality theory in organizations is the Jungian approach and its measurement tool, the MBTI® instrument. The MBTI® instrument has been developed to measure Jung's ideas about individual differences. Many organizations use the MBTI® instrument, and we will focus on it as an example of how some organizations use personality concepts to help employees appreciate diversity.

APPLICATION OF PERSONALITY THEORY IN ORGANIZATIONS: THE MBTI® INSTRUMENT

One approach to applying personality theory in organizations is the Jungian approach and its measurement tool, the MBTI® instrument.

Swiss psychiatrist Carl Jung built his work on the notion that people are fundamentally different, but also fundamentally alike. His classic treatise *Psychological Types* proposed that the population was made up of two basic types—Extraverted types and Introverted types.[66] He went on to identify two types of Perceiving (Sensing and Intuition) and two types of Judgment (Thinking and Feeling). Perceiving (how we gather information) and Judging (how we make decisions) represent the basic mental functions that everyone uses.

Jung suggested that human similarities and differences could be understood by combining preferences. We prefer and choose one way of doing things over another. We are not exclusively one way or another; rather, we have a preference for Extraversion or Introversion, just as we have a preference for right-handedness or left-handedness. We may use each hand equally well, but when a ball is thrown at us by surprise, we will reach to catch it with our preferred hand. Jung's type

5 Discuss Carl Jung's contribution to our understanding of individual differences, and explain how his theory is used in the Myers–Briggs Type Indicator® instrument.

6 Evaluate the importance of the MBTI® to managers.

behavioral measures
Personality assessments that involve observing an individual's behavior in a controlled situation.

self-report questionnaire
A common personality assessment that involves an individual's responses to a series of questions.

Participants in an MBTI® seminar.

theory argues that no preferences are better than others. Differences are to be understood, celebrated, and appreciated.

During the 1940s, a mother–daughter team became fascinated with individual differences among people and with the work of Carl Jung. Katharine Briggs and her daughter, Isabel Briggs Myers, developed the MBTI® instrument to put Jung's type theory into practical use. The MBTI® instrument is used extensively in organizations as a basis for understanding individual differences. More than 3 million people complete the instrument per year in the United States.[67] The MBTI® instrument has been used in career counseling, team building, conflict management, and understanding management styles.[68]

The Preferences

There are four scale dichotomies in type theory with two possible choices for each scale. Table 3.2 shows these preferences. The combination of these preferences makes up an individual's psychological type.

Extraversion/Introversion The *Extraversion/Introversion* preference represents where you get your energy. The Extraverted type (E) is energized by interaction with other people. The Introverted type (I) is energized by time alone. Extraverted types typically have a wide social network, whereas Introverted types have a more narrow range of relationships. As articulated by Jung, this preference has nothing to do with social skills. Many Introverted types have excellent social skills but prefer the internal world of ideas, thoughts, and concepts. Extraverted types represent approximately 49 percent of the U.S. population, and introverts 51 percent, indicating a fairly even split.[69] Does this mean all CEOs are extraverts? The answer can be found in Real World 3.1.

In work settings, Extraverted types prefer variety, and they do not mind the interruptions of the phone or visits from coworkers. Introverted types prefer quiet

Extraversion

A preference indicating that an individual is energized by interaction with other people.

Introversion

A preference indicating that an individual is energized by time alone.

T A B L E

3.2 Type Theory Preferences and Descriptions

Extraversion	Introversion	Thinking	Feeling
Outgoing	Quiet	Analytical	Subjective
Publicly expressive	Reserved	Clarity	Harmony
Interacting	Concentrating	Head	Heart
Speaks, then thinks	Thinks, then speaks	Justice	Mercy
Gregarious	Reflective	Rules	Circumstances
Sensing	**Intuition**	**Judging**	**Perceiving**
Practical	General	Structured	Flexible
Specific	Abstract	Time oriented	Open ended
Feet on the ground	Head in the clouds	Decisive	Exploring
Details	Possibilities	Makes lists/uses them	Makes lists/loses them
Concrete	Theoretical	Organized	Spontaneous

SOURCE: Modified and reproduced by special permission of the publisher, CPP, Inc., Mountain View, CA 94043 from the Introduction to Type® booklet by Isabel Briggs Myers. Copyright 1998 by Peter B. Myers and Katharine D. Myers. All rights reserved. Further reproduction is prohibited without the Publisher's written consent.

The Real World 3.1

Can an Introvert Be CEO? The Answer Is Yes!

One myth surrounding CEOs is that they are all extraverts. Bill Gates? Warren Buffett? Steven Spielberg? All introverts! In fact, four of ten CEOs in the United States are introverts. Among the many introverted CEOs is Brenda Barnes of Sara Lee. Formerly heading up Starwood Hotels and PepsiCo's North American operations, she took a four-year sabbatical to spend time with her two sons and a daughter, returning to the workforce as Sara Lee's COO and becoming CEO in 2005. Based on her own experience, she feels she has a role to play in making Corporate American aware of the talents of women who once stayed at home but want to reenter the workforce. "There's a large pool of women who chose to leave the workforce," she says. "But it doesn't mean they lost their brains."

Sara Lee Corp. has developed Returnships, a program for professionals returning to the workforce after having been away for a number of years. Not specifically for women but used by both sexes, Returnships are paid flexible internships of four to six months. Barnes is leading a transformation at Sara Lee that also includes focusing the product portfolio and moving the corporate culture to one based on integrity and teamwork. One of her key leadership lessons: listen to your employees, a skill that introverts are particularly good at.

Brenda Barnes, CEO of Sara Lee.

© John Zich /zr Images/Corbis

Other skills that introverts bring to the CEO job include thinking carefully before they speak and the capacity for reflective, creative thought. And the introversion/extraversion trait does not relate to social skills, only to energy. Introverts are refreshed and energized by time alone. For Brenda Barnes, who is bringing change to Sara Lee, listening, reflecting, and creative thinking will serve her well.

SOURCES: A. Fisher, "Job Hunting for Introverts," *Fortune* (February 13, 2009), accessed at http://money.cnn.com/2009/02/11/news/economy/introverts.fortune/index.htm; D. Winston, "A Woman CEO's View," *Forbes* (March 17, 2009), accessed at http://www.forbes.com/2009/03/17/work-life-ceo-leadership-careers-imbalance.html?partner-whiteglove_google.

for concentration, and they like to think things through in private. They do not mind working on a project for a long time and are careful with details. Introverted types dislike telephone interruptions, and they may have trouble recalling names and faces.

Sensing/Intuition The *Sensing/Intuition* preference represents perception, or how we prefer to gather information. In essence, it reflects what we pay attention to. The Sensing type (S) pays attention to information gathered through the five senses and to what actually exists. The Intuitive type (N) pays attention to a "sixth sense" and to what could be (possibilities) rather than what is.[70] Approximately, 73 percent of people in the United States are Sensing types.[71]

At work, Sensing types prefer specific answers to questions and can become frustrated with vague instructions. They like jobs that yield tangible results, and they enjoy using established skills more than learning new ones. Intuitive types like

Sensing
Gathering information through the five senses.

Intuition
Gathering information through "sixth sense" and focusing on what could be rather than what actually exists.

3.3   Characteristics Frequently Associated with Each Type

Sensing Types		Intuitive Types	
ISTJ	**ISFJ**	**INFJ**	**INTJ**
Quiet, serious, earn success by thoroughness and dependability. Practical, matter-of-fact, realistic, and responsible. Decide logically what should be done and work toward it steadily, regardless of distractions. Take pleasure in making everything orderly and organized—their work, their home, their life. Value traditions and loyalty.	Quiet, friendly, responsible, and conscientious. Committed and steady in meeting their obligations. Thorough, painstaking, and accurate. Loyal, considerate, notice and remember specifics about people who are important to them, concerned with how others feel. Strive to create an orderly and harmonious environment at work and at home.	Seek meaning and connection in ideas, relationships, and material possessions. Want to understand what motivates people and are insightful about others. Conscientious and committed to their firm values. Develop a clear vision about how best to serve the common good. Organized and decisive in implementing their vision.	Have original minds and great drive for implementing their ideas and achieving their goals. Quickly see patterns in external events and develop long-range explanatory perspectives. When committed, organize a job and carry it through. Skeptical and independent, have high standards of competence and performance for themselves and others.
ISTP	**ISFP**	**INFP**	**INTP**
Tolerant and flexible, quiet observers until a problem appears, then act quickly to find workable solutions. Analyze what makes things work and readily get through large amounts of data to isolate the core of practical problems. Interested in cause and effect, organize facts using logical principles, value efficiency.	Quiet, friendly, sensitive, and kind. Enjoy the present moment, what's going on around them. Like to have their own space and to work within their own time frame. Loyal and committed to their values and to people who are important to them. Dislike disagreements and conflicts, do not force their opinions or values on others.	Idealistic, loyal to their values and to people who are important to them. Want an external life that is congruent with their values. Curious, quick to see possibilities, can be catalysts for implementing ideas. Seek to understand people and to help them fulfill their potential. Adaptable, flexible, and accepting unless a value is threatened.	Seek to develop logical explanations for everything that interests them. Theoretical and abstract, interested more in ideas than in social interaction. Quiet, contained, flexible, and adaptable. Have unusual ability to focus in depth to solve problems in their area of interest. Skeptical, sometimes critical, always analytical.

solving new problems and are impatient with routine details. They enjoy learning new skills more than actually using them. Intuitive types tend to think about several things at once, and they may be seen by others as absentminded. They like figuring out how things work just for the fun of it.

Thinking/Feeling The *Thinking/Feeling* preference represents the way we prefer to make decisions. The Thinking type (T) makes decisions in a logical, objective fashion, whereas the Feeling type (F) makes decisions in a personal, value-oriented way. The general U.S. population is divided 40/60 on the Thinking/Feeling type preference, but it is interesting that the majority of all males are Thinking types, whereas two-thirds of all females are Feeling types. It is the one preference in type theory that has a strong gender difference. Thinking types tend to analyze decisions, whereas Feeling types sympathize. Thinking types try to be impersonal, while Feeling types base their decisions on how the outcome will affect the people involved.

Thinking
Making decisions in a logical, objective fashion.

Feeling
Making decisions in a personal, value-oriented way..

TABLE
3.3 (Continued)

Sensing Types		Intuitive Types	
ESTP Flexible and tolerant, they take a pragmatic approach focused on immediate results. Theories and conceptual explanations bore them—they want to act energetically to solve the problem. Focus on the here-and-now, spontaneous, enjoy each moment that they can be active with others. Enjoy material comforts and style. Learn best through doing.	**ESFP** Outgoing, friendly, and accepting. Exuberant lovers of life, people, and material comforts. Enjoy working with others to make things happen. Bring common sense and a realistic approach to their work and make work fun. Flexible and spontaneous, adapt readily to new people and environments. Learn best by trying a new skill with other people.	**ENFP** Warmly enthusiastic and imaginative. See life as full of possibilities. Make connections between events and information very quickly, and confidently proceed based on the patterns they see. Want a lot of affirmation from others, and readily give appreciation and support. Spontaneous and flexible, often rely on their ability to improvise and their verbal fluency.	**ENTP** Quick, ingenious, stimulating, alert, and outspoken. Resourceful in solving new and challenging problems. Adept at generating conceptual possibilities and then analyzing them strategically. Good at reading other people. Bored by routine, will seldom do the same thing the same way, apt to turn to one new interest after another.
ESTJ Practical, realistic, matter-of-fact. Decisive, quickly move to implement decisions. Organize projects and people to get things done, focus on getting results in the most efficient way possible. Take care of routine details. Have a clear set of logical standards, systematically follow them and want others to also. Forceful in implementing their plans.	**ESFJ** Warmhearted, conscientious, and cooperative. Want harmony in their environment, work with determination to establish it. Like to work with others to complete tasks accurately and on time. Loyal, follow through even in small matters. Notice what others need in their day-by-day lives and try to provide it. Want to be appreciated for who they are and for what they contribute.	**ENFJ** Warm, empathetic, responsive, and responsible. Highly attuned to the emotions, needs, and motivations of others. Find potential in everyone, want to help others fulfill their potential. May act as catalysts for individual and group growth. Loyal, responsive to praise and criticism. Sociable, facilitate others in a group, and provide inspiring leadership.	**ENTJ** Frank, decisive, assume leadership readily. Quickly see logical and inefficient procedures and policies, develop and implement comprehensive systems to solve organizational problems. Enjoy long-term planning and goal setting. Usually well informed, well read, enjoy expanding their knowledge and passing it on to others. Forceful in presenting their ideas.

NOTE: I = Introversion; E = Extraversion; S = Sensing; N = Intuition; T = Thinking; F = Feeling; J = Judging; and P = Perceiving.

SOURCE: Modified and reproduced by special permission of the publisher, CPP, Inc., Mountain View, CA 94043 from the Introduction to Type® booklet by Isabel Briggs Myers. Copyright 1998 by Peter B. Myers and Katharine D. Myers. All rights reserved. Further reproduction is prohibited without the Publisher's written consent.

In work settings, Thinking types tend to show less emotion, and they may become uncomfortable with more emotional people. They are likely to respond more readily to other people's thoughts. They tend to be firm minded and like putting things into a logical framework. Feeling types, by contrast, tend to be more comfortable with emotion in the workplace. They enjoy pleasing people as well as frequent praise and encouragement.

Judging/Perceiving The *Judging–Perceiving* dichotomy reflects one's orientation to the outer world. The Judging type (J) loves closure. Judging types prefer to lead a planned, organized life and like making decisions. A Perceiving type (P), by contrast, prefers a more flexible and spontaneous life and wants to keep options open. Imagine two people, one with a preference for Judging and the other for Perceiving,

Judging Preference
Preferring closure and completion in making decisions.

Perceiving Preference
Preferring to explore many alternatives and flexibility.

going out for dinner. The J asks the P to choose a restaurant, and the P suggests ten alternatives. The J just wants to decide and get on with it, whereas the P wants to explore all the options. In the United States, Js comprise 54 percent of the population, with Ps making up 46 percent.

In all arenas of life, and especially at work, Judging types love getting things accomplished and delight in marking off the completed items on their calendars. Perceiving types tend to adopt a wait-and-see attitude and to collect new information rather than draw conclusions. Perceiving types are curious and welcome new information. They may start too many projects and not finish them.

The Sixteen Types

The preferences combine to form sixteen distinct types, as shown in Table 3.3. For example, let's examine ESTJ. This type has Extraversion, Sensing, Thinking, and Judging preferences. ESTJs see the world as it is (S); make decisions objectively (T); and like structure, schedules, and order (J). Combining these qualities with their preference for interacting with others makes them naturally attracted to managing others. ESTJs are seen by others as dependable, practical, and able to get any job done. They are conscious of the chain of command and see work as a series of goals to be reached by following rules and regulations. They may have little tolerance for disorganization and have a high need for control. Research results from the *MBTI® Atlas* show that most frequent type among the 7,463 managers studied were ESTJs.[72]

There are no good and bad types, and each type has its own strengths and weaknesses. There is a growing volume of research on type theory. The MBTI® instrument has been found to have good reliability and validity as a measurement instrument for identifying type.[73,74] Type has been found to be related to learning style, teaching style, and choice of occupation. For example, the MBTI® types of engineering students at Georgia Tech were studied in order to see who was attracted to engineering and who was likely to leave the major. STs and NTs were more attracted to engineering. Es and Fs were more likely to withdraw from engineering courses.[75] Type has also been used to determine an individual's decision-making style and management style.

Recent studies have begun to focus on the relationship between type and specific managerial behaviors. The Introverted type (I) and the Feeling type (F), for example, have been shown to be more effective at participative management than their counterparts, the Extraverted type and the Thinking type.[76] Companies like AT&T, ExxonMobil, and Williams Companies use the MBTI® instrument in their management development programs to help employees understand the different viewpoints of others in the organization. The MBTI® instrument can also be used for team building. Hewlett-Packard and Armstrong World Industries use the MBTI® instrument to help teams realize that diversity and differences lead to successful performance.

Type theory is valued by managers for its simplicity and accuracy in depicting personalities. It is a useful tool for helping managers develop interpersonal skills. Managers also use type theory to build teams that capitalize on individuals' strengths and to help individual team members appreciate differences.

It should be recognized that there is the potential for individuals to misuse the information from the MBTI® instrument in organizational settings.[77] Some inappropriate uses include labeling one another, providing a convenient excuse that they simply can't work with someone else, and avoiding responsibility for their own personal development with respect to working with others and becoming more flexible. One's type is not an excuse for inappropriate behavior.

We turn now to another psychological process that forms the basis for individual differences. Perception shapes the way we view the world, and it varies greatly among individuals.

SOCIAL PERCEPTION

Perception involves the way we view the world around us. It adds meaning to information gathered via the five senses of touch, smell, hearing, vision, and taste. Perception is the primary vehicle through which we come to understand ourselves and our surroundings. *Social perception* is the process of interpreting information about another person. Virtually all management activities rely on perception. In appraising performance, managers use their perceptions of an employee's behavior as a basis for the evaluation.

One work situation that highlights the importance of perception is the selection interview. The consequences of a bad match between an individual and the organization can be devastating for both parties, so it is essential that the data gathered be accurate. Typical first interviews are brief, and the candidate is usually one of many seen by an interviewer during a day. How long does it take for the interviewer to reach a decision about a candidate? In the first four to five minutes, the interviewer often makes an accept or reject decision based on his or her perception of the candidate.[78]

In one study among CEOs and top management teams, it was found that perceptions of dissimilarity in values among CEOs and top management teams can lead to increased conflict. More interestingly, even if in reality there were no differences in values, just the perception that there were value differences led to increased conflict. This study highlights the importance of perception in organizations by recommending that managers pay attention to how their employees perceive organizational decisions because this (more than reality) might have an impact on behavior.[79]

Perception is also culturally determined. Based on our cultural backgrounds, we tend to perceive things in certain ways. Read the following sentence:

Finished files are the result of years of scientific study combined with the experience of years.

Now quickly count the number of *f*s in the sentence. Individuals for whom English is their second language see all six *f*s. Most native English speakers report that there are three *f*s. Because of cultural conditioning, *of* is not an important word and is ignored.[80] Culture affects our interpretation of the data we gather, as well as the way we add meaning to it.

Valuing diversity, including cultural diversity, has been recognized as a key to international competitiveness.[81] This challenge and others make social perception skills essential to managerial success.

Three major categories of factors influence our perception of another person: characteristics of ourselves, as perceivers; characteristics of the target person we are perceiving; and characteristics of the situation in which the interaction takes place. Figure 3.2 shows a model of social perception.

Characteristics of the Perceiver

Several characteristics of the perceiver can affect social perception. One such characteristic is *familiarity* with the target (the person being perceived). When we are familiar with a person, we have multiple observations on which to base our impression of him or her. If the information we have gathered during these observations is

7 Define *social perception* and explain how characteristics of the perceiver, the target, and the situation affect it.

social perception
The process of interpreting information about another person.

FIGURE

3.2   A Model for Social Perception

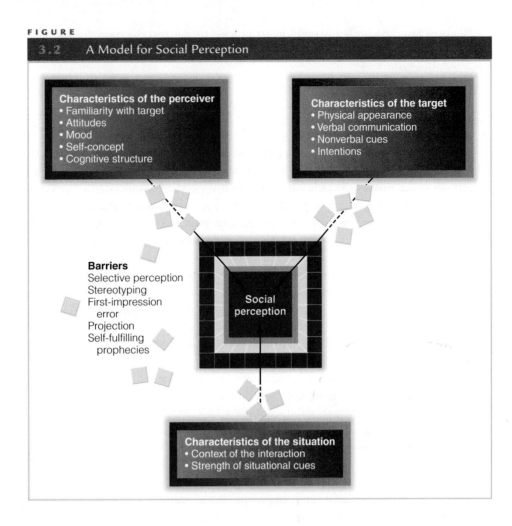

accurate, we may have an accurate perception of the other person. Familiarity does not always mean accuracy, however. Sometimes, when we know a person well, we tend to screen out information that is inconsistent with what we believe the person is like. This is a particular danger in performance appraisals where the rater is familiar with the person being rated.

The perceiver's *attitudes* also affect social perception. Suppose you are interviewing candidates for a very important position in your organization—a position that requires negotiating contracts with suppliers, most of whom are male. You may feel that women are not capable of holding their own in tough negotiations. This attitude will doubtless affect your perceptions of the female candidates you interview.

Mood can have a strong influence on the way we perceive someone.[82] We think differently when we are happy than we do when we are depressed. In addition, we remember information that is consistent with our mood state better than information that is inconsistent with our mood state. When in a positive mood, we form more favorable impressions of others. When in a negative mood, we tend to evaluate others unfavorably.

Another factor that can affect social perception is the perceiver's *self-concept*. An individual with a positive self-concept tends to notice positive attributes in another person. By contrast, a negative self-concept can lead a perceiver to pick out negative traits in another person. Greater understanding of self provides more accurate perceptions of others.

Cognitive structure, an individual's pattern of thinking, also affects social perception. Some people have a tendency to perceive physical traits, such as height, weight, and appearance, more readily. Others tend to focus more on central traits,

or personality dispositions. Cognitive complexity allows a person to perceive multiple characteristics of another person rather than attending to just a few traits.

Characteristics of the Target

Characteristics of the target—the person being perceived—influence social perception. *Physical appearance* plays a big role in our perception of others. The perceiver will notice the target's physical features like height, weight, estimated age, race, and gender. Clothing says a great deal about a person. Blue pin-striped suits, for example, are decoded to mean banking or Wall Street. Perceivers tend to notice physical appearance characteristics that contrast with the norm, that are intense, or that are new or unusual.[83] A loud person, one who dresses outlandishly, a very tall person, or a hyperactive child will be noticed because he or she provides a contrast to what is commonly encountered. In addition, people who are novel can attract attention. Newcomers or minorities in the organization are examples of novel individuals.

Physical attractiveness often colors our entire impression of another person. Interviewers rate attractive candidates more favorably, and attractive candidates are awarded higher starting salaries.[84,85] People who are perceived as physically attractive face stereotypes as well. We will discuss these and other stereotypes later in this chapter.

Verbal communication from targets also affects our perception of them. We listen to the topics they speak about, their tone of voice, and their accent and make judgments based on this input.

Nonverbal communication conveys a great deal of information about the target. Eye contact, facial expressions, body movements, and posture all are deciphered by the perceiver in an attempt to form an impression of the target. It is interesting that some nonverbal signals mean very different things in different cultures. The "okay" sign in the United States (forming a circle with the thumb and forefinger) is an insult in South America. Facial expressions, however, seem to have universal meanings. Individuals from different cultures are able to recognize and decipher such expressions the same way.[86]

The *intentions* of the target are inferred by the perceiver based on observation. We may see our boss appear in our office doorway and think, "Oh no! She's going to give me more work to do." Or we may perceive that her intention is to congratulate us on a recent success. In any case, the perceiver's interpretation of the target's intentions affects the way the perceiver views the target.

Characteristics of the Situation

The situation in which the interaction between the perceiver and the target takes place also influences the perceiver's impression of the target. The *social context* of the interaction is a major influence. Meeting a professor in his or her office affects your impression in a certain way that may contrast with the impression you would form had you met the professor in a local restaurant. In Japan, social context is very important. Business conversations after working hours or at lunch are taboo. If you try to talk business during these times, you may be perceived as rude.[87]

The *strength of situational cues* also affects social perception. As we discussed earlier in the chapter, some situations provide strong cues as to appropriate behavior. In these situations, we assume that the individual's behavior can be accounted for by the situation, and that it may not reflect her or his disposition. This is the *discounting principle* in social perception.[88] For example, you may encounter an automobile salesperson who has a warm and personable manner, asks about your work and hobbies, and seems genuinely interested in your taste in cars. Can you assume that this behavior reflects the salesperson's personality? You probably cannot, because

discounting principle
The assumption that an individual's behavior is accounted for by the situation.

of the influence of the situation. This person is trying to sell you a car, and in this particular situation, he or she probably treats all customers in this manner.

You can see that characteristics of the perceiver, the target, and the situation all affect social perception. It would be wonderful if all of us had accurate social perception skills. Unfortunately, barriers often prevent us from perceiving another person accurately.

Barriers to Social Perception

8 Identify five common barriers to social perception.

Several factors lead us to form inaccurate impressions of others. Five of these barriers to social perception are selective perception, stereotyping, first-impression error, projection, and self-fulfilling prophecies.

We receive a vast amount of information. *Selective perception* is our tendency to choose information that supports our viewpoints. Individuals often ignore information that makes them feel uncomfortable or threatens their viewpoints. Suppose, for example, that a sales manager is evaluating the performance of his employees. One employee does not get along well with colleagues and rarely completes sales reports on time. This employee, however, generates the most new sales contracts in the office. The sales manager may ignore the negative information, choosing to evaluate the salesperson only on contracts generated. The manager is exercising selective perception.

A *stereotype* is a generalization about a group of people. Stereotypes reduce information about other people to a workable level, and they are efficient for compiling and using information. Stereotypes become even stronger when they are shared with and validated by others.[89] Stereotypes can be accurate; when they are accurate, they can be useful perceptual guidelines. Sometimes, however, stereotypes are inaccurate. They harm individuals when inaccurate impressions of them are inferred and are never tested or changed.[90] What is your stereotype of the typical CEO? Meet PepsiCo's CEO, who dispels these stereotypes, in the Real World feature.

In multicultural work teams, members often stereotype foreign coworkers rather than getting to know them before forming an impression. Team members from less developed countries are often assumed to have less knowledge simply because their homeland is economically or technologically less developed.[91] Stereotypes like these can negatively impact performance[92] as well as deflate the productivity of the work team and create low morale.

Attractiveness is a powerful stereotype. We assume that attractive individuals are also warm, kind, sensitive, poised, sociable, outgoing, independent, and strong. Are attractive people really like this? Certainly, all of them are not. A study of romantic relationships showed that most attractive individuals do not fit the stereotype, except for possessing good social skills and being popular.[93]

Some individuals may seem to us to fit the stereotype of attractiveness because our behavior elicits from them behavior that confirms the stereotype. Consider, for example, a situation in which you meet an attractive fellow student. Chances are that you respond positively to this person, because you assume he or she is warm, sociable, and so on. Even though the person may not possess these traits, your positive response may bring out these behaviors in the person. The interaction between the two of you may be channeled such that the stereotype confirms itself.[94]

Stereotyping pervades work life. When there is a contrast against a stereotype, the member of the stereotyped group is treated more positively (given more favorable comments or pats on the back). For example, a female softball player may be given more applause for a home run hit than a male teammate. This occurs because some people may stereotype women as less athletic than men, or because they hold female players to a lower standard. Either way, the contrast is still part of stereotyping.[95]

selective perception
The process of selecting information that supports our individual viewpoints while discounting information that threatens our viewpoints.

stereotype
A generalization about a group of people.

The Real World 3.2

Not Your Stereotypical CEO

She loves music, plays electric guitar, and sings karaoke. Known for her spontaneity and humor, she ascribes positive intent to everything people do or say. She is a product of her native India and is passionate about globalization. Indra Nooyi, PepsiCo's CEO, is a different kind of CEO, and she is taking the role of change agent at the company, pushing for healthier snacks (she was a key player in the national efforts to eliminate trans fats from products). Along with that goal, she is striving for a net-zero impact on the environment and taking good care of Pepsi's massive workforce.

Indra Nooyi, CEO of PepsiCo.

The battle against obesity is one she thinks Pepsi should take on, and encouraged the entire food industry to do so. In a speech, Nooyi exhorted food company executives, "Do you remember campaigns like 'Keep America Beautiful?' What about 'Buckle Up?' I believe we need an approach like this to attack obesity. Let's be a good industry that does 100% of what it possibly can—not grudgingly, but willingly." Her mantram "Performance with a Purpose" represents how she wants PepsiCo to conduct business both at home and abroad.

Under Nooyi's leadership, Pepsi has boosted its lineup of products that fit the wellness lifestyle, enhanced its drinks with vitamins and antioxidants, and offered products in calorie-specific serving sizes to discourage overconsumption. It has introduced low-calorie Gatorade, and reformulated Propel, Aquafina, and SoBe drinks. A life-long vegetarian, she spent $1.3 billion on acquisitions like Naked Juice, a maker of soy drinks and organic juices.

Can a CEO who advocates healthy reforms be successful as CEO of a company that is famous for soft drinks and salty snacks? The answer could be yes, in the case of this CEO who goes against the stereotype.

SOURCES: A. Moore, "Indra Nooyi Puts Her Brand on Pepsi's Pressing Global Challenges," *MarketWatch* (May 14, 2009), accessed at http://www.marketwatch.com; B. Morris, "The Pepsi Challenge," *Fortune* (February 19, 2008), accessed at http://money.cnn.com/2008/02/18/news/companies/morris_nooyi.fortune/.

First impressions are lasting impressions, so the saying goes. Individuals place a good deal of importance on first impressions, and for good reason. We tend to remember what we perceive first about a person, and sometimes we are quite reluctant to change our initial impressions.[96] *First-impression error* occurs when we observe a very brief bit of a person's behavior in our first encounter and infer that this behavior reflects what the person is really like. Primacy effects can be particularly dangerous in interviews, given that we form first impressions quickly and that they may be the basis for long-term employment relationships.

What factors do interviewers rely on when forming first impressions? Perceptions of the candidate, such as whether they like the person, whether they trust the person, and whether or not the person seems credible, all influence the interviewer's decision. Something seemingly as unimportant as the pitch of your voice can leave a lasting impression. Speakers with higher vocal pitch are believed to be more competent, more dominant, and more assertive than those with lower voices. This belief can be carried too far; men whose voices are high enough that they sound feminine are judged the

first-impression error
The tendency to form lasting opinions about an individual based on initial perceptions.

least favorably of all by interviewers. This finding is ironic, given that research has found that students with higher vocal pitch tend to earn better grades.[97]

Projection, also known as the false-consensus effect, is a cause of inaccurate perceptions of others. It is the misperception of the commonness of our own beliefs, values, and behaviors such that we overestimate the number of others who share these things. We assume that others are similar to us, and that our own values and beliefs are appropriate. People who are different are viewed as unusual and even deviant. Projection occurs most often when you surround yourself with others similar to you. You may overlook important information about others when you assume everyone is alike and in agreement.[98]

Self-fulfilling prophecies are also barriers to social perception. Sometimes our expectations affect the way we interact with others such that we get what we wish for. Self-fulfilling prophecy is also known as the Pygmalion effect, named for the sculptor in Greek mythology who prayed that a statue of a woman he had carved would come to life, a wish that was granted by the gods.

Early studies of self-fulfilling prophecy were conducted in elementary school classrooms. Teachers were given bogus information that some of their pupils had high intellectual potential. These pupils were chosen randomly; there were really no differences among the students. Eight months later, the "gifted" pupils scored significantly higher on an IQ test. The teachers' expectations had elicited growth from these students, and the teachers had given them tougher assignments and more feedback on their performance.[99] Self-fulfilling prophecy has been studied in many settings, including at sea. The Israeli Defense Forces told one group of naval cadets that they probably wouldn't experience seasickness, and even if they did, it wouldn't affect their performance. The self-fulfilling prophecy worked! These cadets were rated better performers than other groups, and they also had less seasickness. The information improved the cadets' self-efficacy—they believed they could perform well even if they became seasick.[100]

The Pygmalion effect has been observed in work organizations as well.[101]

A manager's expectations of an individual affect both the manager's behavior toward the individual and the individual's response. For example, suppose your initial impression is that an employee has the potential to move up within the organization. Chances are you will spend a great deal of time coaching and counseling the employee, providing challenging assignments, and grooming him or her for success.

Managers can harness the power of the Pygmalion effect to improve productivity in the organization. It appears that high expectations of individuals come true. Can a manager extend these high expectations to an entire group and have similar positive results? The answer is yes. When a manager expects positive things from a group, the group delivers.[102]

Impression Management

Most people want to make a favorable impression on others. This is particularly true in organizations, where individuals compete for jobs, favorable performance evaluations, and salary increases. The process by which people try to control the impressions others have of them is called *impression management*. Individuals use several techniques to control others' impressions of them.[103]

Some impression management techniques are self-enhancing. These techniques focus on enhancing others' impressions of the person using the technique. Name-dropping, which involves mentioning an association with important people in the hopes of improving one's image, is often used. Managing one's appearance is another technique for impression management. Individuals dress carefully for interviews

projection
Overestimating the number of people who share our own beliefs, values, and behaviors.

self-fulfilling prophecy
The situation in which our expectations about people affect our interaction with them in such a way that our expectations are confirmed.

impression management
The process by which individuals try to control the impressions others have of them.

because they want to "look the part" in order to get the job. Self-descriptions, or statements about one's characteristics, are used to manage impressions as well.

Another group of impression management techniques are *other-enhancing*. These techniques focus on the individual one is trying to impress rather than on one's self. Flattery is a common other-enhancing technique whereby compliments are given to an individual in order to win his or her approval. Favors are also used to gain the approval of others. Agreement with someone's opinion is a technique often used to gain a positive impression. People with disabilities, for example, often use other-enhancing techniques. They may feel that they must take it upon themselves to make others comfortable interacting with them. Impression management techniques are used by individuals with disabilities as a way of dealing with potential avoidance by others.[104]

A final type of impression management technique called *social identity–based impression management*. This type of impression management is based on managing others' impressions of some basic aspect of an individuals' identity. Minorities may use this type of impression management by acting more like the majority. Women, for example, may hide their more feminine qualities and discuss topics that are typically considered more masculine.[105]

Are impression management techniques effective? Most research on this topic has focused on employment interviews; the results indicate that candidates who engage in impression management by self-promoting performed better in interviews, were more likely to obtain site visits with potential employers, and were more likely to get hired.[106,107] In addition, employees who engage in impression management are rated more favorably in performance appraisals than those who do not.[108]

Impression management seems to have an impact on others' impressions. As long as the impressions conveyed are accurate, this process can be beneficial to organizations. If the impressions are found to be false, however, a strongly negative overall impression may result. Furthermore, excessive impression management can lead to the perception that the user is manipulative or insincere.[109] We have discussed the influences on social perception, the potential barriers to perceiving another person, and impression management. Another psychological process that managers should understand is attribution.

ATTRIBUTION IN ORGANIZATIONS

As human beings, we are innately curious. We are not content merely to observe the behavior of others; rather, we want to know why they behave the way they do. We also seek to understand and explain our own behavior. *Attribution theory* explains how we pinpoint the causes of our own behavior and that of other people.[110]

The attributions, or inferred causes, we provide for behavior have important implications in organizations. In explaining the causes of our performance, good or bad, we are asked to explain the behavior that was the basis for the performance.

Internal and External Attributions

Attributions can be made to an internal source of responsibility (something within the individual's control) or an external source (something outside the individual's control). Suppose you perform well on an exam in this course. You might say you aced the test because you are smart or because you studied hard. If you attribute your success to ability or effort, you are making an *internal attribution*.

Alternatively, you might make an *external attribution* for your performance. You might say it was an easy test (you would attribute your success to degree of task difficulty) or that you had good luck. In this case, you are attributing your

9 Explain the attribution process and how attributions affect managerial behavior.

attribution theory
A theory that explains how individuals pinpoint the causes of their own behavior and that of others.

performance to sources beyond your control, or external sources. You can see that internal attributions include such causes as ability and effort, whereas external attributions include causes like task difficulty or luck.

Attribution patterns differ among individuals.[111] Achievement-oriented individuals attribute their success to ability and their failures to lack of effort, both internal causes. Failure-oriented individuals attribute their failures to lack of ability, and they may develop feelings of incompetence as a result of their attributional pattern. Evidence indicates that this attributional pattern also leads to depression.[112] Women managers, in contrast to men managers, are less likely to attribute their success to their own ability. This may be because they are adhering to social norms that compel women to be more modest about their accomplishments or because they believe that success has less to do with ability than with hard work.[113]

Attribution theory has many applications in the workplace. The way you explain your own behavior affects your motivation. For example, suppose you must give an important presentation to your executive management group. You believe you have performed well, and your boss tells you that you've done a good job. To what do you attribute your success? If you believe careful preparation and rehearsal were the cause, you're likely to take credit for the performance and to have a sense of self-efficacy about future presentations. If, however, you think you were just lucky, you may not be motivated to repeat the performance because you believe you had little influence on the outcome.

One situation in which a lot of attributions are made is the employment interview. Candidates are often asked to explain the causes of previous performance ("Why did you perform poorly in math classes?") to interviewers. In addition, candidates often feel they should justify why they should be hired ("I work well with people, so I'm looking for a managerial job"). Research shows that successful and unsuccessful candidates differ in the way they make attributions for negative outcomes. Successful candidates are less defensive and make internal attributions for negative events. Unsuccessful candidates attribute negative outcomes to things beyond their control (external attributions), which gives interviewers the impression that the candidate failed to learn from the event. In addition, interviewers fear that the individuals would be likely to blame others when something goes wrong in the workplace.[114]

Attributional Biases

10 Evaluate the accuracy of managerial attributions from the standpoint of atttribution biases and errors.

The attribution process may be affected by two very common errors: the fundamental attribution error and the self-serving bias. The tendency to make attributions to internal causes when focusing on someone else's behavior is known as the *fundamental attribution error*.[115] The other error, *self-serving bias*, occurs when focusing on one's own behavior. Individuals tend to make internal attributions for their own successes and external attributions for their own failures.[116] In other words, when we succeed, we take credit for it; when we fail, we blame it on other people.

Both of these biases were illustrated in a study of health care managers who were asked to cite the causes of their employees' poor performance.[117] The managers claimed that internal causes (their employees' lack of effort or lack of ability) were the problem. This is an example of the fundamental attribution error. When the employees were asked to pinpoint the cause of their own performance problems, they blamed a lack of support from the managers (an external cause), which illustrates self-serving bias.

There are cultural differences in these two attribution errors. As described previously, these biases apply to people from the United States. In more fatalistic cultures, such as India's, people tend to believe that fate is responsible for much that happens. People in such cultures tend to emphasize external causes of behavior.[118]

fundamental attribution error
The tendency to make attributions to internal causes when focusing on someone else's behavior.

self-serving bias
The tendency to attribute one's own successes to internal causes and one's failures to external causes.

In China, people are taught that hard work is the route to accomplishment. When faced with either a success or a failure, Chinese individuals first introspect about whether they tried hard enough or whether their attitude was correct. In a study of attributions for performance in sports, Chinese athletes attributed both their successes and failures to internal causes. Even when the cause of poor athletic performance was clearly external, such as bad weather, the Chinese participants made internal attributions. In terms of the Chinese culture, this attributional pattern is a reflection of moral values that are used to evaluate behavior. The socialistic value of selfless morality dictates that individual striving must serve collective interests. Mao Zedong stressed that external causes function only through internal causes; therefore, the main cause of results lies within oneself. Chinese are taught this from childhood and form a corresponding attributional tendency. In analyzing a cause, they first look to their own effort.[119]

The way individuals interpret the events around them has a strong influence on their behavior. People try to understand the causes of behavior in order to gain predictability and control over future behavior. Managers use attributions in all aspects of their jobs. In evaluating performance and rewarding employees, managers must determine the causes of behavior and a perceived source of responsibility. One tough call managers often make is whether allegations of sexual harassment actually resulted from sexual conduct, and if harassment did occur, what should be done about it. To make such tough calls, managers use attributions.

Attribution theory can explain how performance evaluation judgments can lead to differential rewards. A supervisor attributing an employee's good performance to internal causes, such as effort or ability, may give a larger raise than a supervisor attributing the good performance to external causes, such as help from others or good training. Managers are often called on to explain their own actions as well, and in doing so they make attributions about the causes of their own behavior. We continue our discussion of attributions in Chapter 6 in terms of how they are used in managing employee performance by presenting Kelley's attribution theory.

MANAGERIAL IMPLICATIONS: USING PERSONALITY, PERCEPTION, AND ATTRIBUTION AT WORK

Managers need to know as much as possible about individual differences in order to understand themselves and those with whom they work. An understanding of personality characteristics can help a manager appreciate differences in employees. With the increased diversity of the workforce, tools like the MBTI® can be used to help employees see someone else's point of view. These tools can also help make communication among diverse employees more effective.

Managers use social perception constantly on the job. Knowledge of the forces that affect perception and the barriers to accuracy can help the manager form more accurate impressions of others.

Determining the causes of job performance is a major task for the manager, and attribution theory can be used to explain how managers go about determining causality. In addition, knowledge of the fundamental attribution error and self-serving bias can help a manager guard against these biases in the processes of looking for causes of behavior on the job.

In this chapter, we have explored the psychological processes of personality, perception, and attribution as individual differences. In the next chapter, we will continue our discussion of individual differences in terms of attitudes, values, and ethics.

Diversity Dialogue

Say it Loud—I'm Fat and I'm Proud!

"Pure awesome." That's how thirty-one-year-old Marianne Kirby describes herself. Weighing in at a hefty 319 pounds, Kirby likes what she sees when she looks in the mirror. Twenty-one-year-old Marianne Gregg feels the same way. While Gregg is considerably lighter than Kirby, she uses the "F word" freely when describing herself. According to Gregg, "I'm not necessarily curvy and not chubby. I'm fat. I'm 220 pounds."

Gregg and Kirby are part of a small but growing "fat acceptance" movement in the United States where being fat is a physical characteristic to be celebrated. Members of this new movement not only accept their bodies, they embrace them. It's okay for them to be fat as long as their mental and spiritual health remains intact. They are not embarrassed by their size. Neither are they necessarily concerned about how others might perceive them. In fact, both women are actively trying to change the diet-crazed culture "one fat girl at a time." Kirby founded the Web site, TheRound.com and recently authored a book entitled *Lessons from the Fatosphere*, while Gregg writes a blog called "Young, Fat and Fabulous" that is dedicated to plus-sized women pursuing careers in fashion.

Gregg and Kirby are not without their critics. The National Action Against Obesity says that promoting this type of lifestyle is "reckless" and can lead to dire health consequences. Rebecca Puhl, a weight expert at Yale University's Rudd Center for Food Policy and Obesity, agrees but acknowledges that fad dieting can also lead to physical and psychological complications.

Although Gregg and Kirby have accepted their fatness, they are not against being physically healthy. Quite the contrary, Gregg admits that she tries to eat a balanced diet and watch her calorie intake, and Kirby remains active—jogging, roller skating, and doing Pilates and yoga. The message that Gregg and Kirby is trying to get across is that there is nothing wrong with being fat. It doesn't mean that they're lazy or smelly. They're just fat.

1. What role does weight play in your impression of others?
2. Does your attribution of *how* a person became fat affect your perceptions? Explain.

SOURCE: M. Pflum, "Fat Acceptance: 'Young, Fat and Fabulous' Say No to Yo-Yo Diets," *ABCNews.com* (June 15, 2009), http://abcnews.go.com.

LOOKING BACK: NORDSTROM

Hiring the Personality and the Attitude

At Nordstrom, the focus is on hiring the personality and the attitude and training the skill. They focus on hiring nice people with a positive, motivated, and committed attitude. Neither previous retail experience nor a college degree has ever been a prerequisite for succeeding at Nordstrom. Nordstrom makes a great effort in the hiring process to understand the potential employee's personality, how that employee feels about themselves, and their attitudes toward serving customers. When Nordstrom

Courtesy of Nordstrom

NORDSTROM

expanded into Southern California in the 1970s and needed new employees, they ran a newspaper ad that simply read, "Wanted: People Power" and then described the attributes that Nordstrom wanted. The ad did not mention what job was available or even the company, but the ad was successful in that it attracted the personality and attitude the company was looking for. In fact, that ad attracted Len Kuntz, who became one of those original employees. Kuntz was hired based on these attributes and used them to work his way up to executive vice president/regional manager of the Washington–Alaska region. Managers are also encouraged to notice people outside of Nordstrom with a great personality; they will give them a business card. Personality and attitude are keys to success at Nordstrom.[120]

Chapter Summary

1. Individual differences are factors that make individuals unique. They include personalities, perceptions, skills and abilities, attitudes, values, and ethics.

2. The trait theory and integrative approach are two personality theories.

3. Managers should understand personality because of its effect on behavior. Several characteristics affect behavior in organizations, including locus of control, self-esteem, self-monitoring, and positive/negative affect.

4. Personality has a stronger influence in weak situations, where there are few cues to guide behavior.

5. One useful framework for understanding individual differences is type theory, developed by Carl Jung and measured by the Myers–Briggs Type Indicator (MBTI®).

6. Social perception is the process of interpreting information about another person. It is influenced by characteristics of the perceiver, the target, and the situation.

7. Barriers to social perception include selective perception, stereotyping, first-impression error, projection, and self-fulfilling prophecies.

8. Impression management techniques such as name-dropping, managing one's appearance, self-descriptions, flattery, favors, and agreement are used by individuals to control others' impressions of them.

9. Attribution is the process of determining the cause of behavior. It is used extensively by managers, especially in evaluating performance.

Key Terms

attribution theory (p. 101)
behavioral measures (p. 89)
discounting principle (p. 97)
extraversion (p. 90)
Feeling (p. 92)
first-impression error (p. 99)
fundamental attribution error (p. 102)
general self-efficacy (p. 84)
impression management (p. 100)

individual differences (p. 80)
integrative approach (p. 83)
interactional psychology (p. 81)
introversion (p. 90)
intuition (p. 91)
Judging Preference (p. 92)
locus of control (p. 83)
Myers–Briggs Type Indicator
   (MBTI®) (p. 78)

negative affect (p. 88)
Perceiving Preference (p. 92)
personality (p. 81)
positive affect (p. 88)
projection (p. 100)
projective test (p. 88)
selective perception (p. 98)
self-esteem (p. 85)
self-fulfilling prophecy (p. 100)

Review Questions

1. What are individual differences, and why should managers understand them?

2. Define *personality* and describe its origins.

3. Describe two theories of personality and explain what each contributes to our knowledge of personality.

4. Describe the eight preferences of the Myers–Briggs Type Indicator instrument. How does this measure Carl Jung's ideas?

5. What factors influence social perception? What are the barriers to social perception?

6. Describe the errors that affect the attribution process.

Discussion and Communication Questions

1. What contributions can high self-monitors make in organizations? Low self-monitors?

2. How can managers improve their perceptual skills?

3. Which has the stronger impact on personality: heredity or environment?

4. How can managers make more accurate attributions?

5. How can managers encourage self-efficacy in employees?

6. How can self-serving bias and the fundamental attribution error be avoided?

7. *(communication question)* You have been asked to develop a training program for interviewers. An integral part of this program focuses on helping interviewers develop better social perception skills. Write an outline for this section of the training program. Be sure to address barriers to social perception and ways to avoid them.

8. *(communication question)* Form groups of four to six; then split each group in half. Debate the origins of personality, with one half taking the position that personality is inherited and the other half that personality is formed by the environment. Each half should also discuss the implications of its position for managers.

Ethical Dilemma

Juanita Maxwell devotes a great deal of time and energy to getting to know her employees. She pays attention to what they say when she asks them how they're doing, and she remembers incidental facts like pet's names and favorite days of the week. Juanita has found that these kinds of details help her match her employees to projects that bring out their best skill sets and internal motivations. She knows, for example, that her office manager, Marcy, is a true morning person, so Juanita schedules their meetings as early as possible to maximize their effectiveness.

Juanita has a new employee on the sales team, Sandra, who is not as easy for her to read. When Sandra first started at Trumbell and Son, she was very quiet, bordering on introverted. Juanita chalked some of it, certainly, to Sandra being new, and many of the other office workers having been colleagues for over five years. At the company picnic a month later, however,

Sandra matched the level of laughter and outgoingness of employees like Willy, the most senior salesperson. She engaged in games and exhibited spirited competitiveness.

Back in the office on Monday, though, Sandra kept her eyes down and avoided small talk in the office break room. She wasn't impolite to Juanita, but gone was the vivacious person who appeared at the picnic.

Juanita assumed Sandra was a naturally shy person until the first 8 A.M. staff meeting to discuss Trumbell's new product line. As voices rose with suggestions and questions, Sandra didn't hesitate to add hers to the fray. Juanita was surprised at Sandra's sudden assertive nature, given that only two days ago she had barely mumbled out "Good evening" as Juanita had waved good bye.

This ebb and flow of energy and assertiveness continued for three months, during which Juanita tries to discern which "Sandra" is the "real" one. Is she a dynamic go-getter who just didn't like mornings or a complete introvert? So far Sandra has done an excellent job, but Juanita is uncomfortable having an employee whose personality seems so inconsistent. She begins to question if Sandra is really a good fit for Trumbell and Son.

Experiential Exercises

3.1 Management Styles*

Part I. This questionnaire will help you determine your preferences. For each item, circle either a or b. If you feel both a and b are true, decide which one is more like you, even if it is only slightly more true.

1. I would rather
   a. solve a new and complicated problem.
   b. work on something I have done before.
2. I like to
   a. work alone in a quiet place.
   b. be where the action is.
3. I want a boss who
   a. establishes and applies criteria in decisions.
   b. considers individual needs and makes exceptions.
4. When I work on a project, I
   a. like to finish it and get some closure.
   b. often leave it open for possible changes.
5. When making a decision, the most important considerations are
   a. rational thoughts, ideas, and data.
   b. people's feelings and values.
6. On a project, I tend to
   a. think it over and over before deciding how to proceed.
   b. start working on it right away, thinking about it as I go along.
7. When working on a project, I prefer to
   a. maintain as much control as possible.
   b. explore various options.
8. In my work, I prefer to
   a. work on several projects at a time and learn as much as possible about each one.
   b. have one project that is challenging and keeps me busy.
9. I often
   a. make lists and plans whenever I start something and may hate to seriously alter my plans.
   b. avoid plans and just let things progress as I work on them.

Questions:

1. Using consequential, rule-based, and character theories, evaluate Juanita's options.
2. What should Juanita do? Why?

10. When discussing a problem with colleagues, it is easy for me to
    a. see "the big picture."
    b. grasp the specifics of the situation.
11. When the phone rings in my office or at home, I usually
    a. consider it an interruption.
    b. do not mind answering it.
12. Which word describes you better?
    a. Analytical
    b. Empathetic
13. When I am working on an assignment, I tend to
    a. work steadily and consistently.
    b. work in bursts of energy with "downtime" in between.
14. When I listen to someone talk on a subject, I usually try to
    a. relate it to my own experience and see if it fits.
    b. assess and analyze the message.
15. When I come up with new ideas, I generally
    a. "go for it."
    b. like to contemplate the ideas some more.
16. When working on a project, I prefer to
    a. narrow the scope so it is clearly defined.
    b. broaden the scope to include related aspects.
17. When I read something, I usually
    a. confine my thoughts to what is written there.
    b. read between the lines and relate the words to other ideas.
18. When I have to make a decision in a hurry, I often
    a. feel uncomfortable and wish I had more information.
    b. am able to do so with available data.
19. In a meeting, I tend to
    a. continue formulating my ideas as I talk about them.
    b. only speak out after I have carefully thought the issue through.

20. In work, I prefer spending a great deal of time on issues of

    a. ideas.

    b. people.

21. In meetings, I am most often annoyed with people who

    a. come up with many sketchy ideas.

    b. lengthen meetings with many practical details.

22. I am a

    a. morning person.

    b. night owl.

23. What is your style in preparing for a meeting?

    a. I am willing to go in and be responsive.

    b. I like to be fully prepared and usually sketch an outline of the meeting.

24. In a meeting, I would prefer for people to

    a. display a fuller range of emotions.

    b. be more task oriented.

25. I would rather work for an organization where

    a. my job is intellectually stimulating.

    b. I am committed to its goals and mission.

26. On weekends, I tend to

    a. plan what I will do.

    b. just see what happens and decide as I go along.

27. I am more

    a. outgoing.

    b. contemplative.

28. I would rather work for a boss who is

    a. full of new ideas.

    b. practical.

In the following, choose the word in each pair that appeals to you more:

29. a. Social

    b. Theoretical

30. a. Ingenuity

    b. Practicality

31. a. Organized

    b. Adaptable

32. a. Active

    b. Concentration

Scoring Key

Count one point for each item listed below that you have circled in the inventory.

Score for I	Score for E	Score for S	Score for N
2a	2b	1b	1a
6a	6b	10b	10a
11a	11b	13a	13b
15b	15a	16a	16b
19b	19a	17a	17b
22a	22b	21a	21b
27b	27a	28b	28a
32b	32a	30b	30a

Total

Circle the one with with more points—I or E.

Circle the one more points—S or N.

Score for T	Score for F	Score for J	Score for P
3a	3b	4a	4b
5a	5b	7a	7b
12a	12b	8b	8a
14b	14a	9a	9b
20a	20b	18b	18a
24b	24a	23b	23a
25a	25b	26a	26b
29b	29a	31a	31b

Total

Circle the one with more points—T or F.

Circle the one with more points—J or P.

Your score is

I or E _____   T or F _____

S or N _____   J or P _____

Part II. The purpose of this part of the exercise is to give you experience in understanding some of the individual differences that were proposed by Carl Jung.

Step 1. Your instructor will assign you to a group.

Step 2. Your group is a team of individuals who want to start a business. You are to develop a mission statement and a name for your business.

Step 3. After you have completed Step 2, analyze the decision process that occurred within the group. How did you decide on your company's name and mission?

Step 4. Your instructor will have each group report to the class the name and mission of the company, and then the decision process used. Your instructor will also give you some additional information about the exercise and provide some interesting insights about your management style.

*Note: The "Personality Inventory" instrument is not in any way associated with CPP, Inc., Isabel Myers Briggs, or the MBTI® or Myers–Briggs Type Indicator® trademarks.

SOURCE: From D. Marcic and P. Nutt, "Personality Inventory," in D. Marcic, ed., *Organizational Behavior: Experiences and Cases* (St. Paul, MN: West, 1989), 9–16. Reprinted by permission.

3.2 Stereotypes in Employment Interviews

Step 1. Your instructor will give you a transcript that records an applicant's interview for a job as a laborer. Your task is to memorize as much of the interview as possible.

Step 2. Write down everything you can remember about the job candidate.

Step 3. Your instructor will lead you in a discussion.

SOURCE: Adapted from D. A. Sachau and M. Hussang, "How Interviewers' Stereotypes Influence Memory: An Exercise," *Journal of Management Education* 16 (1992): 391–396. Copyright © 1992 by Sage Publications. Reprinted with permission of Sage Publications, Inc.

BizFlix | Because I Said So

Meet Daphne Wilder (Diane Keaton)—your typical meddling, overprotective, and divorced mother of three daughters. Two of her three beautiful daughters have married. That leaves Millie (Mandy Moore) as the focus of Daphne's undivided attention and compulsive need to find Millie a mate. Daphne places some online advertising, screens the applicants, and submits those she approves to Millie. Along the way, Daphne meets Joe (Stephen Collins), the father of one applicant. Romance emerges and the film comes to a delightful, though expected, conclusion.

Personality Assessment: Daphne and Millie

This scene starts after Daphne answers her cellular telephone and says the person has the wrong number. It follows the frantic rearrangement of the sofa, which ends up in the same place it started. The film cuts to Millie and Jason (Tom Everett Scott) dining at his place.

What to Watch for and Ask Yourself

- Which Big Five personality traits best describe Daphne? Give examples of behavior from the film scene to support your observations.

- Which Big Five personality traits best describe Millie? Give examples of behavior from the film scene to support your observations.

- Review the discussion of the "Myers–Briggs Type Indicator® instrument" earlier in this chapter. Assess both Daphne and Millie with the content of Table 3.3, "Characteristics Frequently Associated with Each Type."

Recycline Preserve: | Strategy and the Partnership Advantage

When Recycline set out to differentiate itself from conventional consumer goods manufacturers, the company had no idea how the public would perceive its green marketing efforts. The company began in 1996 when founder Eric Hudson designed an innovative toothbrush out of all-recycled material. Today, Recycline's eco-friendly product line, Preserve, includes a range of personal care items, tableware, and kitchen goods.

Recycline's materials may be recycled, but its strategy is completely new. By offering products that makes consumers feel good about their purchases, Recycline not only delivers products of higher value, but it also introduces fresh ideas in the industry. The company's partnership with Stonyfield Farm is a good example: During one Earth Day in Boston, an employee from Stonyfield approached Recycline to ask if the company had a use for scrap plastic from its yogurt containers. Recycline saw the benefit of working with Stonyfield Farm, and now the scrap plastic is used to create Preserve brand products, including toothbrushes and razors.

Although the partnership with Stonyfield Farm has yielded amazing results, Recycline wouldn't be where it is today without Whole Foods. "Our company was born in the natural channel," noted C.A. Webb, Recycline's director of marketing. "Whole Foods has been our number one customer. Not only have they done an amazing job of telling our story in their stores, they are the ultimate retail partner for us because they are so trusted. Customers have a sense that when they enter a Whole Foods Market, every product has been carefully hand selected in accordance with Whole Food's mission."

In 2007, Whole Foods Market and Recycline launched a line of kitchenware products that included colanders, cutting boards, mixing bowls, and storage containers. "Together we did the competitive research, we speced out the products, and we developed the pricing strategy and designs," Webb said. "It created less risk on both sides."

Through its partnerships, Recycline was able to take an untested product and sell it at the nation's largest and most respected natural foods store. Whole Foods Market in turn used its experience and resources to ensure the product sold well. "We gave Whole Foods a 12-month exclusive on the line," Webb said, "which in turn gave them a great story to tell."

Discussion Questions

1 What is your perception of CEO Eric Hudson? On what do you base your perception?

2 What is the public's perception of green products according to Marketing Director C.A. Webb? Why do some people have that perception, and what can Recycline do to change it?

3 To what do you attribute Recycline's success?

Case

Finding and Developing Employee Talent at Deloitte

Recruiting and retaining talented employees is a challenge faced by all businesses, and many of them go to extraordinary lengths to recruit the "best and brightest" as well as to retain talented employees. How do companies go about doing this? Are these extraordinary efforts worth it? Do these efforts have a demonstrable pay-off for the businesses that use them?

Consider Deloitte, a "Big Four" accounting firm. "'Deloitte' is the brand under which 165,000 dedicated professionals in independent firms throughout the world collaborate to provide audit, consulting, financial advisory, risk management, and tax services to selected clients. These firms are members of Deloitte Touche Tohmatsu."[1] Deloitte uses a variety of approaches and techniques to recruit talented people and ensure that their talents are effectively utilized within the company.

In England, for instance, Deloitte is one of many firms that benefit from an educational initiative that is achieving extraordinary results in developing talented young people. The program, known as *Teach First*, was launched in 2002 and is loosely modeled on the *Teach for America* program in the United States. "Teach First recruits top [university] graduates by offering them a challenge: intensive training, full teacher certification, and the chance to help turn around a failing school—all within two years."[2] Each year approximately 1,300 applicants compete for the 200 Teach First positions; characteristically, program participants are in the top 3 percent of their graduating classes, and they have degrees in finance, math, engineering, and philosophy.[3]

Teach First recruits highly talented young people by promising them the opportunity to make a substantial impact within two years, which Brett Wigdortz, CEO of Teach First, says is "a very powerful message for young people." Wigdortz also observes that today's graduates want to make a difference and have real leadership opportunities to prove themselves, and that they value social responsibility.[4] "Teach First graduates demonstrate skills that often take years to learn on the job," says Jo Owen, a former partner with Accenture, the business consulting firm, and now the director of strategy for Teach First. Owen notes most graduates are learning technical skills early in their business careers, but these are not the skills that people must have in order to succeed in the long term. "Future leaders learn early on the tough lessons of managing people, leadership, initiative and entrepreneurialism. The Teach First program helps graduates gain these lifetime skills," observes Owen.[5] All of these skills are ones that many businesses, including Deloitte, want in their employees. And the Teach First experience is often a stepping-stone to another career, which enables companies like Deloitte to benefit without making a substantial additional investment in training and development.

Deloitte seeks out talented people in other ways as well. As an aid to identifying prospective employees who have the potential to be successful, the accounting firm requires applicants to take a verbal reasoning aptitude test. Sarah De Carteret, national graduate recruitment manager for the U.S. offices of Deloitte, says, for example, that "[v]erbal reasoning is hugely important because we are not looking for bean counters."[6] She adds that Deloitte employees perform a lot of advisory work that requires writing reports and analyzing information.[7] Screening prospective employees with testing devices such as the verbal reasoning aptitude test helps to ensure that new hires have the requisite skills for success.

Deloitte's concern about employee talent is not just limited to the recruiting process. In its U.S. locations, the firm has developed internal mechanisms for assessing the skills, interests, knowledge, and career objectives of existing employees who are dissatisfied with their present situation. The Deloitte Career Connections (DCC) program helps "dissatisfied staff to figure out interests and skills that might be a better fit somewhere else in the organization."[8] The DCC program employs a variety of assessment tools, including "an online Myers Briggs personality test, [a] Strong Interest-type tool, and a values-based exercise to help staff consider strengths and interests that may fit with their personalities."[9] Subsequent to this thorough assessment, Deloitte helps these employees to discover the most feasible way to address the sources of their dissatisfaction and to accomplish their career objectives within the organization.

Has the DCC program benefitted the company? The most obvious impact has been on developing and retaining talented employees, rather than having to recruit new employees. In financial terms, "DCC estimates that the firm has saved about $83.4 million, calculated with a turnover cost of twice the average annual salary of $76,000."[10]

On balance then, do these various programs really help Deloitte in recruiting and retaining people who are really the "best and brightest"?

Discussion Questions

1. Using the descriptions of different behaviors, attitudes, and abilities that Deloitte seems to deem desirable in its applicants, describe the key personality characteristics that you think the company is seeking in its employees? Explain the reasoning behind your answer.

2. How might the characteristics of the perceiver, the target, and the situation affect the social perceptions that employers like Deloitte likely have regarding participants in the Teach First program?

3. What attributions are prospective employers like Deloitte likely making regarding participants in the Teach First program? Why are employers making these attributions?

4. How can the use of personality and vocational interest testing benefit Deloitte? What risks might be associated with Deloitte's use of these testing devices?

5. How might social perception and attribution processes factor into the operation of the Deloitte Career Connections (DCC) program?

SOURCE: This case was written by Michael K. McCuddy, The Louis S. and Mary L. Morgal Chair of Christian Business Ethics and Professor of Management, College of Business Administration, Valparaiso University.

4

Attitudes, Emotions, and Ethics

LEARNING OBJECTIVES

After reading this chapter, you should be able to do the following:

1 Explain the ABC model of an attitude.

2 Describe how attitudes are formed.

3 Identify sources of job satisfaction and commitment and suggest tips for managers to help build these two attitudes among their employees.

4 Distinguish between organizational citizenship and workplace deviance behaviors.

5 Identify the characteristics of the source, target, and message that affect persuasion.

6 Discuss the definition and importance of emotions at work.

7 Justify the importance of emotional contagion at work.

8 Contrast the effects of individual and organizational influences on ethical behavior.

9 Discuss how value systems, locus of control, Machiavellianism, and cognitive moral development affect ethical behavior.

Facebook has to make judgment calls based on its ethics and value system.

THINKING AHEAD: FACEBOOK

Offensive Content versus Free Speech

The social networking site Facebook has over 200 million active members and is translated into 40 languages, with 50 languages more in development. Seventy percent of Facebook users live outside the United States, less than a

Courtesy of Facebook

third are college students, and the fastest growing demographic is individuals thirty-five years and older.[1] With this kind of diversity in membership, there are often opposing viewpoints as to what content is acceptable to post. Facebook has rules prohibiting hateful, threatening, or pornographic content or content that contains nudity or graphic or gratuitous violence.[2] Some content, however, resides in the gray area between natural and obscene or profane and between inflammatory and hateful. When an issue does reside in this gray area, Facebook has to make a judgment call based on its ethics and value system, which may be at odds with its users' values.

In January 2009, Facebook removed pictures of nursing women from these individuals' personal pages, citing that these pictures violated their policy against nudity.[3] In 2008, Facebook received criticism for *not* removing content. Socialist deputies in the European Parliament condemned Facebook for allowing anti-gypsy groups on its site. Members of the UK parliament condemned Facebook for hosting pages that include images of the Ku Klux Klan.[4] And in 2009, Facebook was pressured to remove groups that denied the Holocaust.[5] Facebook is not the only company dealing with hate speech on the Web. The Simon Wisenthal Center, a human rights organization, found that online documents promotion racism or other forms of hatred surged to 10,000, a 25 percent increase from the previous year.[6]

No doubt Facebook is in a tough position. They would like to maintain freedom of speech on the Web, but critics argue that Facebook has the ability to decide what is appropriate for users within its terms of service and that hate groups should not be tolerated.[7] Issues like these are likely to continue as Facebook adds users with diverse backgrounds and viewpoints. What steps has Facebook taken to deal with these ethical dilemmas? Our Looking Back feature continues the story at the end of the chapter.

In this chapter, we continue the discussion of individual differences we began in Chapter 3 with personality, perception, and attribution. Persons and situations jointly influence behavior, and individual differences help us to better understand the influence of the person. Our focus now is on three other individual difference factors: attitudes, emotions, and ethics.

ATTITUDES

An *attitude* is a psychological tendency that is expressed by evaluating a particular entity with some degree of favor or disfavor.[8] We respond favorably or unfavorably toward many things: coworkers, our own appearance, and politics are some examples.

Attitudes are important because of their links to behavior. Attitudes are also an integral part of the world of work. Managers speak of workers who have a "bad attitude" and conduct "attitude adjustment" talks with employees. Often, poor performance attributed to bad attitude really stems from lack of motivation, minimal feedback, lack of trust in management, or other problems. These are areas that managers must explore.

It is important for managers to understand the antecedents to attitudes as well as their consequences. Managers also need to understand the different components of attitudes, how attitudes are formed, the major attitudes that affect work behavior, and how to use persuasion to change attitudes.

The ABC Model

Attitudes develop on the basis of evaluative responding. An individual does not have an attitude until he or she responds to an entity (person, object, situation, or issue) on an affective, cognitive, or behavioral basis. To understand the complexity of an attitude, we can break it down into three components, as depicted in Table 4.1.

1 Explain the ABC model of an attitude.

attitude
A psychological tendency expressed by evaluating an entity with some degree of favor or disfavor.

	Component	Measured by	Example
A	Affect	Physiological indicators Verbal statements about feelings	I don't like my boss.
B	Behavioral intentions	Observed behavior Verbal statements about intentions	I want to transfer to another department.
C	Cognition	Attitude scales Verbal statements about beliefs	I believe my boss plays favorites at work.

4.1 The ABC Model of an Attitude

SOURCE: Adapted from M. J. Rosenberg and C. I. Hovland, "Cognitive, Affective, and Behavioral Components of Attitude," in M. J. Rosenberg, C. I. Hovland, W. J. McGuire, R. P. Abelson, and J. H. Brehm, eds., *Attitude Organization and Change* (New Haven, CT: Yale University Press, 1960). Copyright 1960 Yale University Press. Used with permission.

These components—affect, behavioral intentions, and cognition—compose what we call the ABC model of an attitude.[9] *Affect* is the emotional component of an attitude. It refers to an individual's feeling about something or someone. Statements such as "I like this" or "I prefer that" reflect the affective component of an attitude. Affect is measured by physiological indicators such as galvanic skin response (changes in electrical resistance of skin that indicate emotional arousal) and blood pressure. These indicators show changes in emotions by measuring physiological arousal. An individual's attempt to hide his or her feelings might be shown by a change in arousal.

The second component is the intention to behave in a certain way toward an object or person. Our attitudes toward women in management, for example, may be inferred from observing the way we behave toward a female supervisor. We may be supportive, passive, or hostile, depending on our attitude. The behavioral component of an attitude is measured by observing behavior or by asking a person about behavior or intentions. The statement "If I were asked to speak at commencement, I'd be willing to try to do so, even though I'd be nervous" reflects a behavioral intention.

The third component of an attitude, cognition (thought), reflects a person's perceptions or beliefs. Cognitive elements are evaluative beliefs and are measured by attitude scales or by asking about thoughts. The statement "I believe Japanese workers are industrious" reflects the cognitive component of an attitude.

The ABC model shows that to thoroughly understand an attitude, we must assess all three components. Suppose, for example, you want to evaluate your employees' attitudes toward flextime (flexible work scheduling). You would want to determine how they feel about flextime (affect), whether they would use flextime (behavioral intention), and what they think about the policy (cognition). The most common method of attitude measurement, the attitude scale, measures only the cognitive component.

Attitude Formation

Attitudes are learned. Our responses to people and issues evolve over time. Two major influences on attitudes are direct experience and social learning.

2 Describe how attitudes are formed.

Direct experience with an object or person is a powerful influence on attitudes. How do you know that you like biology or dislike math? You have probably formed these attitudes from experience in studying the subjects. Research has shown that attitudes that are derived from direct experience are stronger, held more confidently, and more resistant to change than attitudes formed through indirect experience.[10] One reason attitudes derived from direct experience are so powerful is their availability. This means that the attitudes are easily accessed and are active in our cognitive processes.[11] When attitudes are available, we can call them quickly into consciousness. Attitudes that are not learned from direct experience are not as available, so we do not recall them as easily.

In *social learning,* the family, peer groups, religious organizations, and culture shape an individual's attitudes in an indirect manner.[12] Children learn to adopt certain attitudes by the reinforcement they are given by their parents when they display behaviors that reflect an appropriate attitude. This is evident when very young children express political preferences similar to their parents'. Peer pressure molds attitudes through group acceptance of individuals who express popular attitudes and through sanctions, such as exclusion from the group, placed on individuals who espouse unpopular attitudes.

Substantial social learning occurs through *modeling,* in which individuals acquire attitudes by merely observing others. After overhearing other individuals expressing an opinion or watching them engaging in a behavior that reflects an attitude, the observer adopts the attitude.

For an individual to learn from observing a model, four processes must take place:

1. The learner must focus attention on the model.
2. The learner must retain what was observed from the model. Retention is accomplished in two basic ways. In one way, the learner "stamps in" what was observed by forming a verbal code for it. The other way is through symbolic rehearsal, by which the learner forms a mental image of himself or herself behaving like the model.
3. Behavioral reproduction must occur; that is, the learner must practice the behavior.
4. The learner must be motivated to learn from the model.

Culture also plays a definitive role in attitude development. Consider, for example, the contrast in the North American and European attitudes toward vacation and leisure. The typical vacation in the United States is two weeks, and some workers do not use all of their vacation time. In Europe, the norm is longer vacations; and in some countries, *holiday* means everyone taking a month off. The European attitude is that an investment in longer vacations is important to health and performance.

Attitudes and Behavior

If you have a favorable attitude toward participative management, will your management style be participative? As managers, if we know an employee's attitude, to what extent can we predict his or her behavior? These questions illustrate the fundamental issue of attitude–behavior correspondence, that is, the degree to which an attitude predicts behavior.

This correspondence has concerned organizational behaviorists and social psychologists for quite some time. Can attitudes predict behaviors like being absent from work or quitting your job? Some studies suggested that attitudes and behavior are closely linked, while others found no relationship at all or a weak relationship

affect
The emotional component of an attitude.

social learning
The process of deriving attitudes from family, peer groups, religious organizations, and culture.

at best. Attention then became focused on when attitudes predict behavior and when they do not. Attitude–behavior correspondence depends on five things: attitude specificity, attitude relevance, timing of measurement, personality factors, and social constraints.

Individuals possess both general and specific attitudes. You may favor women's right to reproductive freedom (a general attitude) and prefer pro-choice political candidates (a specific attitude) but not attend pro-choice rallies or send money to Planned Parenthood. That you don't perform these behaviors may make the link between your attitude and behaviors on this issue seem weak. However, given a choice between a pro-choice and an anti-abortion political candidate, you will probably vote for the pro-choice candidate. In this case, your attitude seems quite predictive of your behavior. The point is that the greater the attitude specificity, the stronger its link to behavior.[13]

Another factor that affects the attitude–behavior link is relevance.[14] Attitudes that address an issue in which we have some self-interest are more relevant for us, and our subsequent behavior is consistent with our expressed attitude. Suppose there is a proposal to raise income taxes for those who earn $150,000 or more. If you are a student, you may not find the issue of great personal relevance. Individuals in that income bracket, however, might find it highly relevant; their attitude toward the issue would be strongly predictive of whether they would vote for the tax increase.

The timing of the measurement also affects attitude–behavior correspondence. The shorter the time between the attitude measurement and the observed behavior, the stronger the relationship between the attitude and the behavior. For example, voter preference polls taken close to an election are more accurate than earlier polls.

Personality factors also influence the attitude–behavior link. One personality disposition that affects the consistency between attitudes and behavior is self-monitoring. Recall from Chapter 3 that low self-monitors rely on their internal states when making decisions about behavior, while high self-monitors are more responsive to situational cues. Low self-monitors therefore display greater correspondence between their attitudes and behaviors.[15] High self-monitors may display little correspondence between their attitudes and behavior because they behave according to signals from others and from the environment.

Finally, social constraints affect the relationship between attitudes and behavior.[16] The social context provides information about acceptable attitudes and behaviors.[17,18] New employees in an organization, for example, are exposed to the attitudes of their work group. Suppose a newcomer from Afghanistan holds a negative attitude toward women in management because in his country the prevailing attitude is that women should not be in positions of power. He sees, however, that his work group members respond positively to their female supervisor. His own behavior may therefore be compliant because of social constraints. This behavior is inconsistent with his attitude and cultural belief system.

As rational beings, individuals try to be consistent in everything they believe in and do. They prefer consistency (consonance) between their attitudes and behavior. Anything that disrupts this consistency causes tension (dissonance), which motivates individuals to change either their attitudes or their behavior to return to a state of consistency. The tension produced when there is a conflict between attitudes and behavior is *cognitive dissonance*.[19]

Suppose, for example, a salesperson is required to sell damaged televisions for the full retail price, without revealing the damage to customers. She believes, however, that doing so constitutes unethical behavior. This creates a conflict between her attitude (concealing information from customers is unethical) and her behavior (selling defective TVs without informing customers about the damage).

cognitive dissonance
A state of tension that is produced when an individual experiences conflict between attitudes and behavior.

The salesperson, experiencing the discomfort from dissonance, will try to resolve the conflict. She might change her behavior by refusing to sell the defective TV sets. Alternatively, she might rationalize that the defects are minor and that the customers will not be harmed by not knowing about them. These are attempts by the salesperson to restore equilibrium between her attitudes and behavior, thereby eliminating the tension from cognitive dissonance.

Managers need to understand cognitive dissonance because employees often find themselves in situations in which their attitudes conflict with their behavior. They manage the tension by changing their attitudes or behavior. Employees who display sudden shifts in behavior may be attempting to reduce dissonance. Some employees find the conflicts between strongly held attitudes and required work behavior so uncomfortable that they leave the organization to escape the dissonance.

Work Attitudes

Attitudes at work are important because, directly or indirectly, they affect work behavior. Chief among the things that negatively affect employees' work attitudes are jobs that are very demanding, combined with a lack of control on the part of the employee.[20] A positive psychological climate at work, on the other hand, can lead to positive attitudes and good performance.[21] A study found that when hotel employees offered helpful, concerned service, hotel customers developed a warmer, more positive attitude toward the hotel itself. This attitude resulted in greater customer loyalty, greater likelihood that the customers would stay at the hotel, and even a willingness to pay more for the same service. Customer attitudes were strongly influenced by employee gestures, facial expressions, and words. In this study, customer attitudes were crucial to the success of the firm, and employee behaviors were crucial in forming customer attitudes, meaning firms can "train" their employees to "train" customers to have better attitudes![22] At Zappos, the online retailer of shoes, happy employees translate into happy customers. Read how Zappos makes it happen in The Real World 4.1.

Although many work attitudes are important, two attitudes in particular have been emphasized. Job satisfaction and organizational commitment are key attitudes of interest to managers and researchers.

3 Identify sources of job satisfaction and commitment and suggest tips for managers to help build these two attitudes among their employees.

Job Satisfaction Most of us believe that work should be a positive experience. *Job satisfaction* is a pleasurable or positive emotional state resulting from the appraisal of one's job or job experiences.[23] It has been treated both as a general attitude and as satisfaction with five specific dimensions of the job: pay, the work itself, promotion opportunities, supervision, and coworkers.[24] You can assess your own job satisfaction by completing You 4.1.

An individual may hold different attitudes toward various aspects of the job. For example, an employee may like his or her job responsibilities but be dissatisfied with the opportunities for promotion. Personal characteristics also affect job satisfaction.[25] Those with high negative affectivity are more likely to be dissatisfied with their jobs. Challenging work, valued rewards, opportunities for advancement, competent supervision, and supportive coworkers are dimensions of the job that can lead to satisfaction.

There are several measures of job satisfaction. One of the most widely used measures comes from the Job Descriptive Index (JDI). This index measures the specific facets of satisfaction by asking employees to respond yes, no, or cannot decide to a series of statements describing their jobs. Another popular measure is the Minnesota Satisfaction Questionnaire (MSQ).[26] This survey also asks employees

job satisfaction
A pleasurable or positive emotional state resulting from the appraisal of one's job or job experiences.

The Real World 4.1

Delighted Employees, Delighted Customers at Zappos

Working at a call center may not be your idea of a dream job, but think again. Zappos staffers, from the call center representatives, to bloggers, to warehouse workers, absolutely LOVE their jobs. CEO Tony Hsieh believes it all starts with the culture and a focus on employees. Among the core values at Zappos is "create fun and a little weirdness," including parades, pajama parties, and happy hours. A typical interview question is "How weird are you?" After a four-week training session, new employees are offered a $2,000 to quit, which is rarely accepted. This helps Zappos ensure culture fit by offering a way out to employees who don't buy into the culture. There's a nap room, profit, fully paid medical and dental benefits, and flexible work hours. Free food and drinks are provided, but it's not exactly the gourmet health cuisine offered at Google—it's typically sandwiches. Zappos also provides a full-time life coach, and employees who consult the coach must sit on a red velvet throne. The rationale for the coach is that workers can't provide great customer service if they're upset. And, there is evidence that employees have great attitudes toward their jobs and Zappos. Each year, the company publishes unedited commentary from workers about life working at Zappos and everyone gets a copy. Last year's version totaled 480 pages.

Another Zappos value is "deliver wow." Wowing customers is the top priority. Although some companies outsource their call centers, Hsieh has refused, because customer service is too important. Call center employees don't use a script, and they're encouraged

Zappos provides a unique culture. Its core values include creating "fun and a little weirdness."

above all to be creative. Shipping is free in both directions, and if Zappos doesn't have the shoe you want, they'll direct you to a competitor who has it. There is a 365-day returns policy, and "surprise" upgrades to overnight delivery. A customer who reveals he/she is having a tough time might find flowers delivered from a Zappos employee. There's also evidence that customers are happy: 75 percent of Zappos purchases are from repeat business.

Do positive work attitudes lead to positive customer attitudes? Zappos thinks so, because both employees and customers are delighted.

SOURCES: M. Borden, "#20 Zappos," *Fast Company* (February 11, 2009), accessed at http://www.fastcompany.com/fast50_09/profile/list/zappos; J. O'Brien, "Zappos Knows How to Kick It," *Fortune* (February 2, 2009): 55–58.

to respond to statements about their jobs, using a five-point scale that ranges from very dissatisfied to very satisfied. Figure 4.1 presents some sample items from each questionnaire.

Managers and employees hold a common belief that happy or "satisfied" employees are more productive at work. Most of us feel more satisfied than usual when we believe that we are performing better than usual.[27] Interestingly, the relationship between job satisfaction and performance is quite a bit more complex than that. Are satisfied workers more productive? Or are more productive workers more satisfied? The link between satisfaction and performance has been widely explored. One view holds that satisfaction causes good performance. If this were true, the manager's job would simply be to keep workers happy. Although this may be the case for certain individuals, job satisfaction for most people is one of several causes of good performance. Another view holds that good performance causes

You 4.1

Assess Your Job Satisfaction

Think of the job you have now or a job you've had in the past. Indicate how satisfied you are with each aspect of your job below, using the following scale:

1 = Extremely dissatisfied
2 = Dissatisfied
3 = Slightly dissatisfied
4 = Neutral
5 = Slightly satisfied
6 = Satisfied
7 = Extremely satisfied

1. The amount of job security I have.
2. The amount of pay and fringe benefits I receive.
3. The amount of personal growth and development I get in doing my job.
4. The people I talk to and work with on my job.
5. The degree of respect and fair treatment I receive from my boss.
6. The feeling of worthwhile accomplishment I get from doing my job.
7. The chance to get to know other people while on the job.
8. The amount of support and guidance I receive from my supervisor.
9. The degree to which I am fairly paid for what I contribute to this organization.
10. The amount of independent thought and action I can exercise in my job.
11. How secure things look for me in the future in this organization.
12. The chance to help other people while at work.
13. The amount of challenge in my job.
14. The overall quality of the supervision I receive on my work.

SOURCE: *Work Redesign* by Hackman/Oldham, © 1980. Reprinted by permission of Pearson Education, Inc., Upper Saddle River, NJ.

Now compute your scores for the facets of job satisfaction.

Pay satisfaction:

Q2 + Q9 = Divided by 2

Security satisfaction:

Q1 + Q1 = Divided by 2

Social satisfaction:

Q4 + Q7 + Q12 = Divided by 3

Supervisory satisfaction:

Q5 + Q8 + Q14 = Divided by 3

Growth satisfaction:

Q3 + Q6 + Q10 + Q13 = Divided by 4

Scores on the facets range from 1 to 7. (Scores lower than 4 suggest there is room for change.)

This questionnaire is an abbreviated version of the Job Diagnostic Survey, a widely used tool for assessing individuals' attitudes about their jobs. Compare your scores on each facet with the following norms for a large sample of managers.

Pay satisfaction:	4.6
Security satisfaction:	5.2
Social satisfaction:	5.6
Supervisory satisfaction:	5.2
Growth satisfaction:	5.3

How do your scores compare? Are there actions you can take to improve your job satisfaction?

satisfaction. If this were true, managers would need to help employees perform well, and satisfaction would follow. However, some employees who are high performers are not satisfied with their jobs.

The research shows modest support for both views, but no simple, direct relationship between satisfaction and performance has been found.[28] One reason for these results may be the difficulty of demonstrating the attitude–behavior links we

4.1   Sample Items from Satisfaction Questionnaires

Job Descriptive Index

Think of the work you do at present. How well does each of the following words or phrases describe your work? In the blank beside each word given below, write

___Y___ for "Yes" if it describes your work
___N___ for "No" if it does NOT describe it
___?___ if you cannot decide

WORK ON YOUR PRESENT JOB:

_____ Routine
_____ Satisfying
_____ Good

Think of the majority of the people that you work with now or the people you meet in connection with your work. How well does each of the following words or phrases describe these people? In the blank beside each word, write

___Y___ for "Yes" if it describes the people you work with
___N___ for "No" if it does NOT describe them
___?___ if you cannot decide

COWORKERS (PEOPLE):

_____ Boring
_____ Responsible
_____ Intelligent

Minnesota Satisfaction Questionnaire

1 = Very dissatisfied
2 = Dissatisfied
3 = I can't decide whether I am satisfied or not
4 = Satisfied
5 = Very satisfied

On my present job, this is how I feel about:

_____ The chance to work alone on the job (independence)
_____ My chances for advancement on this job (advancement)
_____ The chance to tell people what to do (authority)
_____ The praise I get for a good job (recognition)
_____ My pay and the amount of work I do (compensation)

SOURCES: The Job Descriptive Index is copyrighted by Bowling Green State University. The complete forms, scoring key, instructions, and norms can be obtained from Dr. Patricia C. Smith, Department of Psychology, Bowling Green State University, Bowling Green, OH 43403. Minnesota Satisfaction Questionnaire from D. J. Weiss, R. V. Davis, G. W. England, and L. H. Lofquist, *Manual for the Minnesota Satisfaction Questionnaire* (University of Minnesota Vocational Psychology Research, 1967).

described earlier in this chapter. Future studies using specific, relevant attitudes and measuring personality variables and behavioral intentions may be able to demonstrate a link between job satisfaction and performance.

Another reason for the lack of a clear relationship between satisfaction and performance is the intervening role of rewards. Employees who receive valued rewards are more satisfied. In addition, employees who receive rewards that are contingent on performance (the higher the performance, the larger the reward) tend to perform better. Rewards thus influence both satisfaction and performance. The key to influencing both satisfaction and performance through rewards is that the rewards are valued by employees and are tied directly to performance.

Job satisfaction has been shown to be related to many other important personal and organizational outcomes. It is related to *organizational citizenship behavior* (OCB)—behavior that is above and beyond the call of duty. Satisfied employees are more likely to make positive comments about the company, refrain from

4 Distinguish between organizational citizenship and workplace deviance behaviors.

organizational citizenship behavior
Behavior that is above and beyond the call of duty.

complaining when things at work do not go well, and help their coworkers.[29] Going beyond the call of duty is especially important to organizations using teams to get work done. Employees depend on extra help from each other to get things accomplished. When massive wildfires swept through California in 2003, most businesses in the San Diego area closed for one or more days as choking black smoke filled the air and thousands of homes were threatened. Aplus.net, an Internet service provider, chose to remain open; however, due to the danger involved, the company did not require its employees to report to work. Yet, in spite of thick smoke, most of the firm's employees came to work anyway, even though some were unsure if their homes would be waiting for them when they left work that evening.[30] Because of their willingness to go the extra mile, Aplus.net and its customers remained up and running throughout the fires. The firm reported in November that the massive fires had no negative impact on its financial results for the quarter.

Satisfied workers are more likely to want to give something back to the organization because they want to reciprocate their positive experiences.[31] Often, employees may feel that citizenship behaviors are not recognized because they occur outside the confines of normal job responsibilities. OCBs do, however, influence performance evaluations. Employees who exhibit behaviors such as helping others, making suggestions for innovations, and developing their skills receive higher performance ratings.[32] And different parts of an attitude relate to different targets of OCBs. Affect tends to direct OCBs toward other people, while job cognitions direct OCBs toward the organization.[33]

Individuals who identify strongly with the organization are more likely to perform OCBs.[34] High self-monitors, who base their behavior on cues from the situation, are also more likely to perform OCBs.[35] Good deeds, in the form of OCBs, can be contagious. One study found that when a person's close coworkers chose to perform OCBs, that person was more likely to reciprocate. When the norm among other team members was to engage in OCBs, the individual worker was more likely to offer them. The impact of one worker's OCBs can spread throughout an entire department.[36]

Although researchers have had a tough time demonstrating the link between job satisfaction and individual performance, this has not been the case for the link between job satisfaction and organizational performance. Companies with satisfied workers have better performance than companies with dissatisfied workers.[37] This may be due to the more intangible elements of performance, like OCB, that contribute to organizational effectiveness but aren't necessarily captured by just measuring individual job performance.

Job satisfaction is related to some other important outcomes. People who are dissatisfied with their jobs are absent more frequently. The type of dissatisfaction that most often causes employee absenteeism is dissatisfaction with the work itself. In addition, unhappy workers are more likely to quit their jobs, and turnover at work can be very costly to organizations. Such workers also report more psychological and medical problems than do satisfied employees.[38]

Researchers have consistently demonstrated a link between job satisfaction and turnover intentions; that is, unhappy employees tend to leave the organization. One thing that leads to dissatisfaction at work is a misfit between an individual's values and the organization's values, which is called a lack of person–organization fit. People who feel that their values don't mesh with the organization's experience job dissatisfaction and eventually leave the company when other job opportunities arise.[39]

Like all attitudes, job satisfaction is influenced by culture. One study compared job satisfaction across forty-nine countries. Job characteristics and job satisfaction were more tightly linked in richer countries, more individualistic countries, and smaller power-distance countries. These findings suggest that cultural differences have strong influences on job satisfaction and the factors that produce it.[40]

Because organizations face the challenge of operating in the global environment, managers must understand that job satisfaction and other job attitudes are significantly affected by culture. Employees from different cultures may have differing expectations of their jobs; thus, there may be no single prescription for increasing the job satisfaction of a multicultural workforce. Researchers are currently studying job attitudes around the world. In China's hotel and restaurant industry, for example, researchers found that high-performance human resource practices led to service-oriented OCBs. Examples of such practices include promotions from within, flexibility in job assignments, long-term-results-oriented appraisals, and job security. Such OCBs were in turn linked to lower turnover and higher productivity at the organizational level.[41] So, it appears that high-performance human resource practices have very positive impacts in China.

Workplace deviance behavior (WDB)—counterproductive behavior that violates organizational norms and causes harm to others or the organization—is another outcome of attitudes at work.[42] Deviance is garnering attention due to negative events in the business world such as downsizing, technological insecurities, and other challenges being faced by many organizations. Layoffs, for example, may cause employees to develop negative attitudes and to feel anger and hostility toward the organization and to indulge in retaliatory behaviors. Even when an employee keeps his or her job but believes the procedure used to determine the layoff is unfair, workplace deviance such as bad-mouthing the employer or revenge against the manager may occur.[43,44] Unfairness at work is a major cause of deviance, sabotage, and retaliation. Positive attitudes about the work environment lead to reduced deviance. Preventing and managing WDB is important because it harms department and organizational performance. Supervisors can positively influence deviance behavior as well, particularly when employees intend to quit. Abusive supervision is related to increased deviance behavior, particularly deviance behavior directed at the supervisor.[45] You can assess your own WDBs with the questionnaire in You 4.2.

Organizational Commitment The strength of an individual's identification with an organization is known as *organizational commitment*. There are three kinds of organizational commitment: affective, continuance, and normative.

Affective commitment is an employee's intention to remain in an organization because of a strong desire to do so. It consists of three factors:

- A belief in the goals and values of the organization.
- A willingness to put forth effort on behalf of the organization.
- A desire to remain a member of the organization.[46]

Affective commitment encompasses loyalty, but it is also a deep concern for the organization's welfare.

Continuance commitment is an employee's tendency to remain in an organization because he or she cannot afford to leave.[47] Sometimes employees believe that if they leave, they will lose a great deal of their investments in time, effort, and benefits and that they cannot replace these investments.

Normative commitment is a perceived obligation to remain with the organization. Individuals who experience normative commitment stay with the organization because they feel that they should.[48]

Certain organizational conditions encourage commitment. Participation in decision making and job security are two such conditions. Certain job characteristics also positively affect commitment. These include autonomy, responsibility, role clarity, and interesting work.[49,50]

workplace deviance behavior
Any voluntary counterproductive behavior that violates organizational norms and causes some degree of harm to organizational functioning.

organizational commitment
The strength of an individual's identification with an organization.

affective commitment
A type of organizational commitment based on an individual's desire to remain in an organization.

continuance commitment
A type of organizational commitment based on the fact that an individual cannot afford to leave.

normative commitment
A type of organizational commitment based on an individual's perceived obligation to remain with an organization.

You 4.2

Do You Engage in Workplace Deviance Behavior?

Think of the job you have now or a job you've had in the past. Indicate to what extent you engaged in the behaviors below. Use the following scale:

1 Very slightly or not at all
2 A little
3 Moderately
4 Quite a bit
5 Definitely

1. Worked on a personal matter instead of work for your employer.
2. Taken property from work without permission.
3. Spent too much time fantasizing or daydreaming instead of working.
4. Made fun of someone at work.
5. Falsified a receipt to get reimbursed for more money than you spent on business expenses.
6. Said something hurtful to someone at work.
7. Taken an additional or a longer break than is acceptable at your workplace.
8. Repeated a rumor or gossip about your company.
9. Made an ethnic, religious, or racial remark or joke at work.
10. Come in late to work without permission.
11. Littered your work environment.
12. Cursed at someone at work.
13. Called in sick when you were not.
14. Told someone about the lousy place where you work.
15. Lost your temper while at work.
16. Neglected to follow your boss's instructions.
17. Intentionally worked slower than you could have worked.
18. Discussed confidential company information with an unauthorized person.
19. Left work early without permission.
20. Played a mean prank on someone at work.
21. Left your work for someone else to finish.
22. Acted rudely toward someone at work.
23. Repeated a rumor or gossip about your boss or coworkers.
24. Made an obscene comment at work.
25. Used an illegal drug or consumed alcohol on the job.
26. Put little effort into your work.
27. Publicly embarrassed someone at work.
28. Dragged out work in order to get overtime.

SOURCE: R. J. Bennett and S. L. Robinson, "Development of a Measure of Workplace Deviance," *Journal of Applied Psychology* 85 (2000): 349–360.

Affective and normative commitments are related to lower rates of absenteeism, higher quality of work, increased productivity, and several different types of performance.[51] Managers should encourage affective commitment because committed individuals expend more task-related effort and are less likely than others to leave the organization.[52]

Managers can increase affective commitment by communicating that they value employees' contributions and that they care about employees' well-being.[53] Affective commitment also increases when the organization and employees share the same values and when the organization emphasizes values like moral integrity, fairness, creativity, and openness.[54] Negative experiences at work can undoubtedly diminish affective commitment. One such experience is discrimination. Perceived age discrimination, whether for being too old or too young, can dampen affective commitment.[55] Managers' affective commitment can also directly impact firm performance. In a recent study investigating human resource practices, researchers found that

are differentiated by the amount of elaboration, or scrutiny; the target is motivated to give the message.

The *central route* to persuasion involves direct cognitive processing of the message's content. When an issue is personally relevant, the individual is motivated to think carefully about it. The listener may nod his/her head when the argument is strong and shake his or her head if the argument is weak.[68] In the central route, the content of the message is very important. If the arguments presented are logical and convincing, attitude change will follow.

In the *peripheral route* to persuasion, the individual is not motivated to pay much attention to the message's content. This is because the message may not be perceived as personally relevant, or the target may be distracted. Instead, the individual is persuaded by characteristics of the persuader—for example, expertise, trustworthiness, and attractiveness. In addition, he or she may be persuaded by statistics, the number of arguments presented, or the method of presentation—all of which are nonsubstantial aspects of the message. Interestingly, people are more likely to carefully consider a message's content (the central route) when their social networks are diverse and include people with a variety of different views. Individuals whose social networks include people who have similar viewpoints do not scrutinize this information as carefully, making the peripheral route more important.[69]

The elaboration likelihood model shows that the target's level of involvement with the issue is important. That involvement also determines which route to persuasion will be more effective. In some cases, attitude change comes about through both the central and the peripheral routes. To cover all of the bases, managers should structure the content of their messages carefully, develop their own attributes that will help them be more persuasive, and choose a method of presentation that will be attractive to the audience.[70]

We have seen that the process of persuading individuals to change their attitudes is affected by the source, the target, the message, and the route. When all is said and done, however, managers are important catalysts for encouraging attitude change. This is a difficult process. Recently, researchers have proposed that people hold attitudes at two different levels.

MOODS AND EMOTIONS AT WORK

Traditional management theories did not place a premium on studying the effects of employee emotions at work. This was largely because emotions were thought to be "bad" for rational decision making. Ideas about management centered around the stereotypic ideal employee who kept her or his emotions in check and behaved in a totally rational rather than emotional manner. Because of recent research, we know that emotions and cognitions are intertwined and that both are normal parts of human functioning and decision making.

What are moods and emotions? Moods are typically regarded as feeling states that are more enduring than emotions but have no clear cause and yet are made up of the variety of emotions one is experiencing.[71] *Emotions* (e.g., anger, joy, pride, hostility) are short-lived, intense reactions to an event that affect work behaviors. Individuals differ in their capacity to experience both positive emotions (e.g., happiness, pride) and negative emotions (e.g., anger, fear, guilt).[72] Employees have to cope with both positive and negative events at work almost daily, and these events lead to moods and emotions. When events at work are positive and goals are being met, employees experience positive emotions.[73]

Events that threaten or thwart the achievement of goals cause negative emotions, which then threaten job satisfaction and commitment. Positive moods lead to better

6 Discuss the definition and importance of emotions at work.

emotions
Mental states that typically include feelings, physiological changes, and the inclination to act.

work performance and OCBs and decreased deviance.[74–76] Positive mood may be particularly important in the workplace because moods last longer. A recent study showed positive mood was positively related to OCBs on the same day the positive mood was recorded as well as OCBs on the day after.[77]

As we discussed earlier, negative emotions lead to workplace deviance. The use of power and influence in organizations, even if it is routine, can spark several forms of deviance. Such deviance could be targeted at both the organization and other individuals in the work environment.[78] Positive emotions produce better cognitive functioning, physical and psychological health, and coping mechanisms.[79] People who experience positive emotions tend to do so repeatedly, and they are more creative.[80] Overall, people who experience positive emotions are more successful across a variety of life domains and report higher life satisfaction. Negative emotions, on the other hand, lead to unhealthy coping behaviors and lowered cardiovascular function and physical health.

7 Justify the importance of emotional contagion at work.

There is another reason that emotions need to be managed at work: emotions are very infectious. They spread through emotional contagion. What is *emotional contagion*? It is a dynamic process through which the emotions of one person are transferred to another either consciously or unconsciously through nonverbal channels. Emotional contagion occurs primarily through nonverbal cues and is affected through a basic human tendency of mimicry. We tend to mimic each other's facial expressions, body language, speech patterns, and vocal tones. Emotional contagion is an important work process because most jobs today require some degree of interpersonal interaction. Examples of such interactions could be dealing with a customer who is angry, a coworker who is fearful of a layoff decision, a leader who praises an employee's work, and so on. Emotional contagion could occur in many of these instances and travel throughout the work group. Positive emotions that spread through a work group through this process produce cooperation and task performance.[81] The opposite can occur as well. Negative emotions can permeate a work group and destroy morale and performance.

When organizations and their employees go through change and/or huge losses, the pain caused by such trauma is not always eased by reason. Good leaders learn how to use compassion to heal and rebuild employee morale.[82] You will recall the tragedy of 9/11 in New York City. Examples abound of organizational leaders who stood by their people with strength and empathy in times of tragedy. Yet other companies there refused, for example, to give their employees the next day off. These organizations failed to create a comfortable place for their employees to share their grief and trauma. Undoubtedly, these are not issues that could be resolved by a sound business strategy alone but by compassionate leaders who are not afraid to let their emotions and mood show appropriately and are not disdainful of employee feelings.

The impact of mood and emotion is far-reaching in workplace behavior. We know that employees experience both positive and negative emotions at work. In the Science feature, read how employees use different strategies to deal with negative emotions at work.

emotional contagion
A dynamic process through which the emotions of one person are transferred to another either consciously or unconsciously through nonverbal channels.

ethical behavior
Acting in ways consistent with one's personal values and the commonly held values of the organization and society.

ETHICAL BEHAVIOR

Ethics is the study of moral values and moral behavior. *Ethical behavior* is acting in ways consistent with one's personal values and the commonly held values of the organization and society.[83]

There is evidence that paying attention to ethical issues pays off for companies. In the early 1990s, James Burke, then the CEO of Johnson & Johnson (J&J), put together a list of companies that devoted a great deal of attention to ethics. The

Science

How Do You Manage Negative Emotions at Work?

Research suggests that positive emotions have very positive outcomes at work but oftentimes work events lead to employees feeling negatively. Understanding what work events lead to negative feelings and how individuals deal with these feelings might help organizations better reap the benefits of positive emotions. What triggers the need to manage emotions at work? A recent study showed that interpersonal work events most often triggered the need to regulate one's emotions and personal problems brought to work was the second most-reported trigger. When people experience negative emotions, they use five strategies to regulate them. The first four, situation selection, situation modification, attentional deployment, and cognitive change, are strategies aimed at affecting what is causing the negative emotion. The fifth, modulating the emotional response, is focused on altering the response to the negative emotion.

Situation selection involves approaching or avoiding whatever causes a negative emotion—for example, avoiding a coworker who is very insulting. Situation modification involves changing the situation so it doesn't cause negative emotions. For example, an employee may ask for help from a coworker to avoid being overloaded and feeling distressed. Attentional deployment involves distracting yourself from the problem by concentrating on something else or doing something more enjoyable.

For example, an employee may think about his or her fun plans for the evening to avoid thinking about negative things at work. Cognitive change involves thinking about the situation differently by putting yourself in another person's shoes, by thinking about how the situation could be worse, or by reframing the situation. For example, after making a major mistake at work, an employee may imagine ways the mistake could have been worse as well as chalk it up to a learning experience. Finally, modulating the emotional response involves faking unfelt emotions and hiding negative emotions. For example, an employee who is angry at his or her boss may pretend to be happy when interacting with the boss, hiding his or her anger.

The study mentioned above found that the situation selection strategy of seeking out people who make employees feel good is the most commonly used, followed by attentional deployment strategies. This study suggests that employees do make attempts to manage their emotions and do so using a variety of different strategies. Understanding these strategies help organizations provide resources and tools to reduce the occurrence of negative emotions as well as increase the likelihood of successfully regulating them.

SOURCE: J. M. Diefendorff, E. M. Richard, and J. Yang, "Linking Emotion Regulation Strategies to Affective and Negative Emotions at Work," *Journal of Vocational Behavior* 73 (2008): 498–508.

---

group included J&J, Coca-Cola, Gerber, Kodak, 3M, and Pitney Bowes. Over a forty-year period, the market value of these organizations grew at an annual rate of 11.3 percent, as compared with 6.2 percent for the Dow Jones industrials as a whole.[84] Doing the right thing can have a positive effect on an organization's performance.[85] J&J Credo (presented in Chapter 2) has stood the test of time. You can read about how the company integrates its credo into its activities in Real World 4.2.

Ethical behavior in firms can also lead to practical benefits, particularly in attracting new talent. Firms with better reputations are able to attract more applicants, creating a larger pool from which to hire, and evidence suggests that respected firms are able to choose higher quality applicants.[86]

Failure to handle situations in an ethical manner can cost companies. Employees who are laid off or terminated are very concerned about the quality of treatment they receive. Honestly explaining the reasons for the dismissal and preserving the dignity of the employee will reduce the likelihood that he or she will initiate a claim against the company. One study showed that less than 1 percent of employees who felt the company was being honest filed a claim; more than 17 percent of those who felt the company was being less than honest filed claims.[87]

The Real World 4.2

Johnson & Johnson: Credo in Action

You know its products—Tylenol, Band-Aids, Splenda, Listerine—but you may not realize that J&J is the sixth most profitable company in the Fortune 500 and the fifth most valuable. This ranks J&J ahead of some big players like IBM, Procter & Gamble, and General Electric. Besides having great products, what makes J&J a market leader? A big contributor to the company's success is its emphasis on the credo (featured in Chapter 2). Many companies have ethics codes or statements, but that doesn't necessarily mean that the guiding principles contained in these documents are translated into ethical behavior. What separates J&J from the rest of the pack is that it actually follows the principles in the credo. Those principles include responsibilities to doctors, nurses and patients, employees, communities, and stockholders, in that order.

CEO Bill Weldon travels worldwide to talk with employees moving into new leadership positions about the real-life application of the credo. (He does so on a high-tech artificial knee built by J&J's medical devices group.) J&J's spot-on response to the Tylenol crisis is legendary, but there are many other notable examples of the credo in action. An early leader in the sustainability movement, J&J began setting environmental goals in 1990, and since then it has reduced water and energy usage and raw materials use, and continues to tie environmental improvements to its credo.

J&J's community work in Africa goes back seventy-five years. Today its efforts in twenty African countries target life-changing, long-term solutions to major health problems. For example, J&J partners with the Elizabeth Glaser Pediatric Foundation to prevent mother-to-child transmission of HIV/AIDS in Cameroon, Malawi, Lesotho, Swaziland, and Zimbabwe. This partnership

Johnson and Johnson is guided by the real-life application of its credo. For example, J&J provides education and orphan support resources for Project Mercy., Inc., a program to promote education, health care, and other projects to communities in Yetebon, Ethiopia.

has provided prenatal counseling, HIV/AIDS testing, and antiretroviral medicines to several hundred thousand women. In Kenya, J&J partners with Operation Smile to provide free reconstructive surgeries for cleft lips and cleft palates. J&J donates financial support and medical supplies for the surgeries, and helps to mobilize doctors and hospitals to donate their time to operate on needy children.

The secret to J&J's is not its credo—it is the steadfast application of the credo's principles in everyday business life.

SOURCE: G. Colvin and J. Shambora, "J&J: Secrets of Success," *Fortune* (May 4, 2009): 117–119; Johnson & Johnson: Our Community Work in Africa, accessed at http://www.jnj.com/wps/wcm/connect/0d9 1c9804f5563329da8bd1bb31559c7/our-community-work-in-africa. pdf?MOD=AJPERES).

Unethical behavior by employees can affect individuals, work teams, and even the organization. Organizations thus depend on individuals to act ethically. For this reason, more and more firms are starting to monitor their employees' Internet usage. "Little Brother" and "SurfControl Web Filter" are just two of several software packages that allow system administrators to easily monitor employee Web usage, flagging visits to specific Web sites by using neural network technology to classify URL content and block Web traffic.

Although some employees have complained that this type of monitoring violates their privacy, the courts have generally disagreed, arguing that employees are using company hardware and software; hence the company is entitled to monitor what employees do with it. In one such case, Michael Smyth was fired from his job with

Pillsbury Co. after company employees read inflammatory comments he made in several e-mails to his supervisor. Smyth sued for wrongful termination, claiming that his right to privacy was violated because the firm had told employees their e-mail would remain confidential. Despite these promises, the court ruled that Smyth had no reasonable expectation of privacy while using the firm's equipment; further, it said, Smyth's right to privacy was outweighed by the firm's need to conduct business in a professional manner. Only future court cases will clarify where a firm's effort to monitor potentially unethical behavior actually crosses its own ethical line.[88]

Today's high-intensity business environment makes it more important than ever to have a strong ethics program in place. In a survey of more than 4,000 employees conducted by the Washington, D.C.–based Ethics Resource Center, one-third of the employees said that they had witnessed ethical misconduct in the past year. If that many employees actually saw unethical acts, imagine how many unethical behaviors occurred behind closed doors! The most common unethical deeds witnessed were lying to supervisors (56 percent), lying on reports or falsifying records (41 percent), stealing or theft (35 percent), sexual harassment (35 percent), drug or alcohol abuse (31 percent), and conflicts of interest (31 percent).[89]

One of the toughest challenges managers face is aligning the ideal of ethical behavior with the reality of everyday business practices. Violations of the public's trust are costly. When Mattel recalled 20.5 million toys that were manufactured in China for toxic lead paint and magnets that if swallowed can create serious intestinal problems likened to a gunshot, its image suffered.[90] To counter negative effects, Mattel launched a national advertising campaign to try to undo the damages. Firms experience lower accounting returns and slow sales growth for as long as five years after being convicted of a corporate illegality.[91,92]

The ethical issues that individuals face at work are complex. A review of articles appearing in the *Wall Street Journal* during just one week revealed more than sixty articles dealing with ethical issues in business.[93] As Table 4.2 shows, the themes appearing throughout the articles were distilled into twelve major ethical issues. You can see that few of these issues are clear-cut. All of them depend on the specifics of

TABLE

4.2   Ethical Issues from One Week in the *Wall Street Journal*

1. **Stealing:** Taking things that don't belong to you.
2. **Lying:** Saying things you know aren't true.
3. **Fraud and deceit:** Creating or perpetuating false impressions.
4. **Conflict of interest and influence buying:** Bribes, payoffs, and kickbacks.
5. **Hiding versus divulging information:** Concealing information that another party has a right to know or failing to protect personal or proprietary information.
6. **Cheating:** Taking unfair advantage of a situation.
7. **Personal decadence:** Aiming below excellence in terms of work performance (e.g., careless or sloppy work).
8. **Interpersonal abuse:** Behaviors that are abusive of others (e.g., sexism, racism, emotional abuse).
9. **Organizational abuse:** Organizational practices that abuse members (e.g., inequitable compensation, misuses of power).
10. **Rule violations:** Breaking organizational rules.
11. **Accessory to unethical acts:** Knowing about unethical behavior and failing to report it.
12. **Ethical dilemmas:** Choosing between two equally desirable or undesirable options.

SOURCE: Kluwer Academic Publishers, by J. O. Cherrington and D. J. Cherrington, "A Menu of Moral Issues: One Week in the Life of *The Wall Street Journal*," *Journal of Business Ethics* 11 (1992): 255–265. Reprinted with kind permission of Springer Science and Business Media.

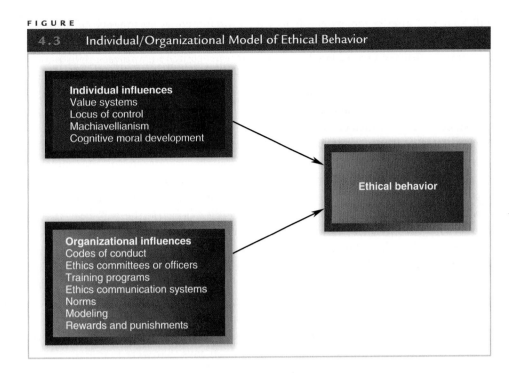

FIGURE

4.3   Individual/Organizational Model of Ethical Behavior

Individual influences
Value systems
Locus of control
Machiavellianism
Cognitive moral development

Ethical behavior

Organizational influences
Codes of conduct
Ethics committees or officers
Training programs
Ethics communication systems
Norms
Modeling
Rewards and punishments

the situation, and their interpretation depends on the characteristics of the individuals examining them. For example, look at issue 2: lying. We all know that "white lies" are told in business. Is this acceptable? The answer varies from person to person.

Ethical behavior is influenced by two major categories of factors: individual characteristics and organizational factors.[94] This section looks at the individual influences. We examine organizational influences throughout the remainder of the book—particularly in Chapter 15, in which we focus on creating an organizational culture that reinforces ethical behavior.

The model that guides our discussion of individual influences on ethical behavior is presented in Figure 4.3. It shows both individual and organizational influences.

Making ethical decisions is part of each manager's job. It has been suggested that ethical decision making requires three qualities of individuals:[95]

8 Contrast the effects of individual and organizational influences on ethical behavior.

1. The competence to identify ethical issues and evaluate the consequences of alternative courses of action.

2. The self-confidence to seek out different opinions about the issue and decide what is right in terms of a particular situation.

3. Tough-mindedness—the willingness to make decisions when all that needs to be known cannot be known and when the ethical issue has no established, unambiguous solution.

9 Discuss how value systems, locus of control, Machiavellianism, and cognitive moral development affect ethical behavior.

What are the individual characteristics that lead to these qualities? Our model presents four major individual differences that affect ethical behavior: value systems, locus of control, Machiavellianism, and cognitive moral development.

VALUES

values
Enduring beliefs that a specific mode of conduct or end state of existence is personally or socially preferable to an opposite or converse mode of conduct or end state of existence.

One important source of individual differences in ethical behavior is values. We use them to evaluate our own behavior and that of others. As such, they vary widely among individuals. *Values* are enduring beliefs that a specific mode of conduct or

end state of existence is personally or socially preferable to an opposite or converse mode of conduct or end state of existence.[96] This definition was proposed by Rokeach, an early scholar of human values. As individuals grow and mature, they learn values, which may change over the life span as an individual develops a sense of self. Cultures, societies, and organizations shape values. Parents and others who are respected by the individual play crucial roles in value development by providing guidance about what is right and wrong. Because values are general beliefs about right and wrong, they form the basis for ethical behavior. For example, Whole Foods Market is committed to environmentally friendly causes and has created a foundation for the compassionate treatment of animals. The CEO of Whole Foods Market, John Mackey, was recently named one of the top 30 corporate leaders in American businesses. Mackey has set an extraordinary example by ignoring conventional wisdom and refusing to compete with Wal-Mart. Instead he has led Whole Foods Market through five consecutive years of 21 percent sales gains by strongly adhering to what he believes in and being environmentally and socially responsible. Visit the wholefoods.com Web site to learn more about how being values driven can lead to success.

John Mackey, CEO of Whole Foods Market, was recently named one of the top 30 corporate leaders in American businesses.

Instrumental and Terminal Values

Rokeach distinguished between two types of values: instrumental and terminal. *Instrumental values* reflect the means to achieving goals; that is, they represent the acceptable behaviors to be used in achieving some end state. Instrumental values identified by Rokeach include ambition, honesty, self-sufficiency, and courage. *Terminal values*, by contrast, represent the goals to be achieved or the end states of existence. Rokeach identified happiness, love, pleasure, self-respect, and freedom among the terminal values. A complete list of instrumental and terminal values is presented in Table 4.3. Terminal and instrumental values work in concert to provide individuals with goals to strive for and acceptable ways to achieve the goals.

Americans' rankings of instrumental and terminal values have shown remarkable stability over time.[97] The highest ranked instrumental values were honesty, ambition, responsibility, forgiving nature, open-mindedness, and courage. The highest ranked terminal values were world peace, family security, freedom, happiness, self-respect, and wisdom.

Age also affects values. Baby boomers' values contrast with those of the baby busters, who are beginning to enter the workforce. The baby busters value family life and time off from work and prefer a balance between work and home life. This contrasts with the more driven, work-oriented value system of the boomers. The baby boomers placed a huge emphasis on achievement values. Their successors in Generation X and Generation Y, however, are markedly different in what they value at work. For example, Generation X values self-reliance, individualism, and balance between family and work life. Generation Y, on the other hand, values freedom in scheduling so much that most are employed only part-time. Furthermore, they have a work-to-live mindset rather than the live-to-work philosophy of the baby boomers.[98]

Work Values

Work values are important because they affect how individuals behave on their jobs in terms of what is right and wrong.[99] Four work values relevant

instrumental values
Values that represent the acceptable behaviors to be used in achieving some end state.

terminal values
Values that represent the goals to be achieved or the end states of existence.

TABLE		
4.3	Instrumental and Terminal Values	

Instrumental Values		
Honesty	Ambition	Responsibility
Forgiving nature	Open-mindedness	Courage
Helpfulness	Cleanliness	Competence
Self-control	Affection/love	Cheerfulness
Independence	Politeness	Intelligence
Obedience	Rationality	Imagination

Terminal Values		
World peace	Family security	Freedom
Happiness	Self-respect	Wisdom
Equality	Salvation	Prosperity
Achievement	Friendship	National security
Inner peace	Mature love	Social respect
Beauty in art and nature	Pleasure	Exciting, active life

SOURCE: Table adapted with the permission of The Free Press, a Division of Simon & Schuster, Inc., from *The Nature of Human Values* by Milton Rokeach. Copyright © 1973 by The Free Press.

to individuals are achievement, concern for others, honesty, and fairness.[100] Achievement is a concern for the advancement of one's career. This is shown in such behaviors as working hard and seeking opportunities to develop new skills. Concern for others is shown in caring, compassionate behaviors such as encouraging other employees, or helping others work on difficult tasks. These behaviors constitute organizational citizenship, as we discussed earlier. Honesty is providing accurate information and refusing to mislead others for personal gain. Fairness emphasizes impartiality and recognizes different points of view. Individuals can rank-order these values in terms of their importance in their work lives.[101] Although individuals' value systems differ, sharing similar values at work produces positive results. Employees who share their supervisor's values are more satisfied with their jobs and more committed to the organization.[102] Values also have profound effects on the choice of jobs. Traditionally, pay and advancement potential have been the strongest influences on job choice decisions. One study, however, found that three other work values—achievement, concern for others, and fairness—exerted more influence on job choice decisions than did pay and promotion opportunities.[103]

This means that organizations recruiting job candidates should pay careful attention to individuals' values and to the messages that organizations send about company values. A new "name and shame" report published in Australia by RepuTex is designed to embarrass companies that behave unethically. Nineteen groups graded each of Australia's top companies on corporate governance policies, environmental friendliness, and workplace practices. The 500-page report named Westpac, a major bank, as the most ethical firm in Australia. Westpac was the only company in the country's top 100 to receive the AAA rating.[104]

Cultural Differences in Values

As organizations face the challenges of an increasingly diverse workforce and a global marketplace, it becomes more important than ever for them to understand the influence of culture on values. Doing business in a global marketplace often means that managers encounter a clash of values among different cultures. Take the value of loyalty, for example. In Japan, loyalty means "compassionate overtime." Even though you have no work to do, you should stay late to give moral support to your peers who are working late.[105] By contrast, Koreans value loyalty to the person for whom one works.[106] In the United States, family and other personal loyalties are more highly valued than is loyalty to the company or one's supervisor.

Cultures differ in what they value in terms of an individual's contributions to work. Collectivist cultures such as China and Mexico value a person's contributions to relationships in the work team. By contrast, individualist cultures like the United States and the Netherlands value a person's contributions to task accomplishment. Both collectivist and individualist cultures value rewards based on individual performance.[107] Iran also represents a collectivist culture. Iranian managers' values, which include little tolerance for ambiguity, high need for structure, and willingness to sacrifice for the good of society, are greatly influenced by Islam. Belonging, harmony, humility, and simplicity are all values promoted by Islam.[108]

Values also affect individuals' views of what constitutes authority. French managers value authority as a right of office and rank. Their behavior reflects this value, as they tend to use power based on their position in the organization. By contrast, managers from the Netherlands and Scandinavia value group inputs to decisions and expect their decisions to be challenged and discussed by employees.[109]

Value differences between cultures must be acknowledged in today's global economy. We may be prone to judging the value systems of others, but we should resist the temptation to do so. Tolerating diversity in values can help us understand other cultures. Value systems of other nations are not necessarily right or wrong—merely different. The following suggestions can help managers understand and work with the diverse values that characterize the global environment:[110]

1. Learn more about and recognize the values of other peoples. They view their values and customs as moral, traditional, and practical.

2. Avoid prejudging the business customs of others as immoral or corrupt. Assume they are legitimate unless proved otherwise.

3. Find legitimate ways to operate within others' ethical points of view—do not demand that they operate within your value system.

4. Avoid rationalizing "borderline" actions with excuses such as the following:
   - "This isn't really illegal or immoral."
   - "This is in the organization's best interest."
   - "No one will find out about this."
   - "The organization will back me up on this."

5. Refuse to do business when stakeholder actions violate or compromise laws or fundamental organizational values.

6. Conduct relationships as openly and aboveboard as possible.

Locus of Control

Another individual influence on ethical behavior is locus of control. In Chapter 3, we introduced locus of control as a personality variable that affects individual behavior.

Recall that people with an internal locus of control believe that they control events in their lives and that they are responsible for what happens to them. By contrast, people with an external locus of control believe that outside forces such as fate, chance, or other people control what happens to them.[111]

Internals are more likely than externals to take personal responsibility for the consequences of their ethical or unethical behavior. Externals are more apt to believe that external forces caused their ethical or unethical behavior. Research has shown that internals make more ethical decisions than do externals.[112] Internals also are more resistant to social pressure and are less willing to hurt another person, even if ordered to do so by an authority figure.[113]

Machiavellianism

Another individual difference that affects ethical behavior is Machiavellianism. Niccolò Machiavelli was a sixteenth-century Italian statesman. He wrote *The Prince*, a guide for acquiring and using power.[114] The primary method for achieving power that he suggested was manipulation of others. *Machiavellianism*, then, is a personality characteristic indicating one's willingness to do whatever it takes to get one's own way.

A high-Mach individual behaves in accordance with Machiavelli's ideas, which include the notion that it is better to be feared than loved. High-Machs tend to use deceit in relationships, have a cynical view of human nature, and have little concern for conventional notions of right and wrong.[115] They are skilled manipulators of other people, relying on their persuasive abilities. Low-Machs, by contrast, value loyalty and relationships. They are less willing to manipulate others for personal gain and are concerned with others' opinions.

High-Machs believe that the desired ends justify any means. They believe that manipulation of others is fine if it helps achieve a goal. Thus, high-Machs are likely to justify their manipulative behavior as ethical.[116] They are emotionally detached from other people and are oriented toward objective aspects of situations. And high-Machs are likelier than low-Machs to engage in behavior that is ethically questionable.[117] Employees can counter Machiavellian individuals by focusing on teamwork instead of on one-on-one relationships where high-Machs have the upper hand. It is also beneficial to make interpersonal agreements public and thus less susceptible to manipulation by high-Machs.

Cognitive Moral Development

An individual's level of *cognitive moral development* also affects ethical behavior. Psychologist Lawrence Kohlberg proposed that as individuals mature, they move through a series of six stages of moral development.[118] With each successive stage, they become less dependent on other people's opinions of right and wrong and less self-centered (acting in one's own interest). At higher levels of moral development, individuals are concerned with broad principles of justice and with their self-chosen ethical principles. Kohlberg's model focuses on the decision-making process and on how individuals justify ethical decisions. His model is a cognitive developmental theory about how people think about what is right and wrong and how the decision-making process changes through interaction with peers and the environment.

Cognitive moral development occurs at three levels, and each level consists of two stages. In level I, called the premoral level, the person's ethical decisions are based on rewards, punishments, and self-interest. In stage 1, the individual obeys rules to avoid punishment. In stage 2, the individual follows the rules only if it is in his or her immediate interest to do so.

Machiavellianism
A personality characteristic indicating one's willingness to do whatever it takes to get one's own way.

cognitive moral development
The process of moving through stages of maturity in terms of making ethical decisions.

In level II, the conventional level, the focus is on the expectations of others (parents, peers) or society. In stage 3, individuals try to live up to the expectations of people close to them. In stage 4, they broaden their perspective to include the laws of the larger society. They fulfill duties and obligations and want to contribute to society.

In level III, the principled level, what is "right" is determined by universal values. The individual sees beyond laws, rules, and the expectations of other people. In stage 5, individuals are aware that people have diverse value systems. They uphold their own values despite what others think. For a person to be classified as being in stage 5, decisions must be based on principles of justice and rights. For example, a person who decides to picket an abortion clinic just because his religion says abortion is wrong is not a stage 5 individual. A person who arrives at the same decision through a complex decision process based on justice and rights may be a stage 5 individual. The key is the process rather than the decision itself. In stage 6, the individual follows self-selected ethical principles. If there is a conflict between a law and a self-selected ethical principle, the individual acts according to the principle.

As people mature, their moral development passes through these stages in an irreversible sequence. Research suggests that most adults are in stage 3 or 4. Most adults thus never reach the principled level of development (stages 5 and 6).

Since it was proposed more than thirty years ago, Kohlberg's model of cognitive moral development has received a great deal of research support. Individuals at higher stages of development are less likely to cheat,[119] more likely to engage in whistle-blowing,[120] and more likely to make ethical business decisions.[121,122]

Kohlberg's model has also been criticized. Gilligan, for example, has argued that the model does not take gender differences into account. Kohlberg's model was developed from a twenty-year study of eighty-four boys.[123] Gilligan contends that women's moral development follows a different pattern—one that is based not on individual rights and rules but on responsibility and relationships. Women and men face the same moral dilemmas but approach them from different perspectives—men from the perspective of equal respect and women from the perspective of compassion and care. Researchers who reviewed the research on these gender differences concluded that the differences may not be as strong as originally stated by Gilligan. Some men use care reasoning, and some women may use justice reasoning, when making moral judgments.[124]

There is evidence to support the idea that men and women view ethics differently. A large-scale review of sixty-six studies found that women were more likely than men to perceive certain business practices as unethical. Young women were more likely to see breaking the rules and acting on insider information as unethical. Both sexes agreed that collusion, conflicts of interest, and stealing are unethical. It takes about twenty-one years for the gender gap to disappear. Men seem to become more ethical with more work experience; the longer they are in the workforce, the more their attitudes become similar to those held by women. There is an age/experience effect for both sexes: experienced workers are more likely to think lying, bribing, stealing, and colluding are unethical.[125]

Individual differences in values, locus of control, Machiavellianism, and cognitive moral development are important influences on ethical behavior in organizations. Given that these influences vary widely from person to person, how can organizations use this knowledge to increase ethical behavior? One action would be to hire those who share the organization's values. Another would be to hire only internals, low-Machs, and individuals at higher stages of cognitive moral development. This strategy obviously presents practical and legal problems.

There is evidence that cognitive moral development can be increased through training.[126] Organizations could help individuals move to higher stages of moral development by providing educational seminars. However, values, locus of control, Machiavellianism, and cognitive moral development are fairly stable in adults.

The best way to use the knowledge of individual differences may be to recognize that they help explain why ethical behavior differs among individuals and to focus managerial efforts on creating a work situation that supports ethical behavior.

Most adults are susceptible to external influences; they do not act as independent ethical agents. Instead, they look to others and to the organization for guidance. Managers can offer such guidance by encouraging ethical behavior through codes of conduct, ethics committees, ethics communication systems, training, norms, modeling, and rewards and punishments, as shown in Figure 4.3. We discuss these areas further in Chapter 16.

MANAGERIAL IMPLICATIONS: ATTITUDES, VALUES, AND ETHICS AT WORK

Managers must understand attitudes because of their effects on work behavior. By understanding how attitudes are formed and how they can be changed, managers can shape employee attitudes. Attitudes are learned through observation of other employees and by the way they are reinforced. Job satisfaction and organizational commitment are important attitudes to encourage among employees, and participative management is an excellent tool for doing so.

Diversity Dialogue

Michael Phelps—When Age and Values Collide

The world had barely finished celebrating the start of 2009 when photographs of Michael Phelps flooded the media outlets. Seeing photos of Phelps was nothing new. After all, he was an Olympic gold medalist who had just won a record eight medals for swimming the previous summer in Beijing. But seeing Phelps smoking cannabis (an illegal drug) from a glass pipe WAS new. The image of Phelps with bong in hand was in stark contrast to his *Sports Illustrated* cover draped with a necklace of gold medals. The public could not believe its collective eyes. What possessed Phelps to do such a thing? What was he thinking? Didn't he realize that this could destroy his Olympic career or at the very least, ruin his "hero" image?

Twenty-three-year-old Phelps had gotten into trouble before. At age nineteen, he received eighteen months' probation for driving while under the influence. According to published reports, Phelps had developed quite a reputation for partying during lulls in the swimming calendar. The night after the bong incident, witnesses told reporters that Phelps showed up at yet another nightclub "throwing back shots two at a time." Fellow partygoers described his behavior as "loud," "obnoxious," and "wild." This was very different from his rather disciplined public persona of eating, sleeping, and swimming.

Acknowledging his mistake, Phelps apologized stating, "I'm 23 years old and despite the successes I've had in the pool, I acted in a youthful and inappropriate way, not in a manner people have come to expect from me." Despite engaging in an illegal act, Phelps was neither charged with a criminal offence nor did he face any action by the United States Olympic Committee (USOC).

1. In what ways might Generation Y's "work-to-live" philosophy have contributed to Phelps' behavior?

2. What effect will the USOC's (in) action have on Phelps' future behavior?

SOURCE: G. Dickinson, "What a Dope," *News of the World* (January 2, 2009).

Emotions are also important because of their influence on employee behaviors. Managers should be trained to perceive emotions in employees and manage them effectively. They should watch for burnout and emotional exhaustion, specifically in service occupations. Such emotion management can help foster OCBs and prevent workplace deviance in the organization.

Ethical behavior at work is affected by individual and organizational influences. A knowledge of individual differences in value systems, locus of control, Machiavellianism, and cognitive moral development helps managers understand why individuals have diverse views about what constitutes ethical behavior.

This chapter concludes our discussion of individual differences that affect behavior in organizations. Attitudes, emotions, and ethics combine with personality, perception, and attribution to make people unique. Individual uniqueness is a major managerial challenge, and it is one reason there is no single best way to manage people.

LOOKING BACK: FACEBOOK

Ethics and Subjective Judgment

Courtesy of Facebook

Facebook has come under fire recently for "content allowed" as well as "content disallowed" on its site. Currently, Facebook does not actively search its site for content that doesn't adhere to their policies. Instead, they rely on users to flag this content. Questionable items go before a team that is trained to delete or allow each item based on the team's interpretation of the company's guidelines. Facebook also seeks outside counsel, meeting regularly with human rights organizations, and the state department for advice on these issues.[127] In the end, the delete or allow decision is a judgment call based on the company's values which are clearly not always going to be in line with every user—and as a result, Facebook has received some criticism for their decisions. However, like ethics and ethical dilemmas in most organizations and jobs, it is exceedingly difficult to develop rules that can ethically deal with all issues that arise; subjective judgment will always be necessary.

Chapter Summary

1. The ABC model of an attitude contends that an attitude has three components: affect, behavioral intentions, and cognition. Cognitive dissonance is the tension produced by a conflict between attitudes and behavior.

2. Attitudes are formed through direct experience and social learning. Direct experience creates strong attitudes because the attitudes are easily accessed and active in cognitive processes.

3. Attitude–behavior correspondence depends on attitude specificity, attitude relevance, timing of measurement, personality factors, and social constraints.

4. Two important work attitudes are job satisfaction and organizational commitment. There are cultural differences in these attitudes, and both attitudes can be improved by providing employees with opportunities for participation in decision making.

5. A manager's ability to persuade employees to change their attitudes depends on characteristics of the manager (expertise, trustworthiness, and attractiveness); the employees (self-esteem, original attitude, and mood); the message (one-sided versus two-sided); and the route (central versus peripheral).

6. Emotions can strongly affect an individual's behavior at work.

7. Instrumental values reflect the means to achieving goals; terminal values represent the goals to be achieved.

8. Ethical behavior is influenced by the individual's value system, locus of control, Machiavellianism, and cognitive moral development.

Key Terms

affect (p. 118)

affective commitment (p. 125)

attitude (p. 116)

cognitive dissonance (p. 119)

cognitive moral development (p. 138)

continuance commitment (p. 125)

emotions (p. 129)

emotional contagion (p. 130)

ethical behavior (p. 130)

instrumental values (p. 135)

job satisfaction (p. 120)

Machiavellianism (p. 138)

normative commitment (p. 125)

organizational citizenship behavior (p. 123)

organizational commitment (p. 125)

social learning (p. 118)

terminal values (p. 135)

values (p. 134)

workplace deviance behavior (p. 125)

Review Questions

1. How are attitudes formed? Which source is stronger?

2. Discuss cultural differences in job satisfaction and organizational commitment.

3. What are the major influences on attitude–behavior correspondence? Why do some individuals seem to exhibit behavior that is inconsistent with their attitudes?

4. What should managers know about the emotions at work?

5. Define *values*. Distinguish between instrumental values and terminal values. Are these values generally stable, or do they change over time?

6. What is the relationship between values and ethics?

7. How does locus of control affect ethical behavior?

8. What is Machiavellianism, and how does it relate to ethical behavior?

9. Describe the stages of cognitive moral development. How does this concept affect ethical behavior in organizations?

Discussion and Communication Questions

1. What jobs do you consider to be most satisfying? Why?

2. How can managers increase their employees' job satisfaction?

3. Suppose you have an employee whose lack of commitment is affecting others in the work group. How would you go about persuading the person to change this attitude?

4. In Rokeach's studies on values, the most recent data are from 1981. Do you think values have changed since then? If so, how?

5. What are the most important influences on an individual's perceptions of ethical behavior? Can organizations change these perceptions? If so, how?

6. How can managers encourage organizational citizenship?

7. (*communication question*) Suppose you are a manager in a customer service organization. Your group includes seven supervisors who report directly to you. Each supervisor manages a team of seven customer service representatives. One of your supervisors, Linda, has complained that

Joe, one of her employees, has "an attitude problem." She has requested that Joe be transferred to another team. Write a memo to Linda explaining your position on this problem and what should be done.

8. *(communication question)* Select a company that you admire for its values. Use the resources of your university library to answer two questions. First, what are the company's values? Second, how do employees enact these values? Prepare an oral presentation to present in class.

9. *(communication question)* Think of a time when you have experienced cognitive dissonance. Analyze your experience in terms of the attitude and behavior involved. What did you do to resolve the cognitive dissonance? What other actions could you have taken? Write a brief description of your experience and your responses to the questions.

Ethical Dilemma

Sarah Kovacs supervises a team of ten employees in the human resources department of Paddington, Inc. She strives to match each member of her team's strengths with appropriate tasks, and for the last five years, Sarah has created a pleasant working environment for everyone.

The newest member of her team, Kim Evans, excels at meeting deadlines and works at a level above her peers. However, since she was hired a year ago, Kim has managed to find problems or downsides to everything, and never fails to share her moody nit-picking with others. Often, Kim points out legitimate issues that need to be dealt with, but she does it with an air of negativity and misery that stymies the team's enthusiasm and puts Sarah in a challenging position from which to motivate her team. Sarah's frustration has become difficult to contain, and meetings with Kim have not produced any change in her attitude.

Last week in her supervisor's meeting, Sarah became aware of a position opening up in the marketing department that requires the skills at which Kim excels. The position hasn't been advertised yet, but Sarah thinks that she could fast-track Kim into an interview.

However, Sarah knows that Kim's negative affect will possibly be an even greater problem for the marketing department, because of that team's interaction with Paddington's clientele. Not only could Kim sour her new team's relationships, she could pass that negativity onto current and potential clients. Of course, Sarah's never seen Kim dealing with clients—Kim may have the ability to set aside her negative outlook when necessary. But she's certainly seen Kim openly criticize Paddington's policies to her peers and in front of Sarah and other managers. She's heard Kim complain about workloads, vacation time, cafeteria food, the weather…

But if Kim gets the position on the marketing team, the HR team could begin to function again like a cohesive group with focus and vision. Sarah is not sure what would be best for Paddington and her department or what she should do.

Questions:

1. Using consequential, rule-based and character theories, evaluate Sarah's options.

2. What should Sara do? Why?

Experiential Exercises

4.1 Chinese, Indian, and American Values

Purpose

To learn some differences among Chinese, Indian, and American value systems.

Group size

Any number of groups of five to eight people.

Time required

50+ minutes

Exercise Schedule

1. **Complete rankings (preclass)**
   Students rank the fifteen values either for Chinese and American orientations or for Indian and American systems. If time permits, all three can be done.

	Unit time	Total time
2. Small groups (optional)	15 min	15 min

   Groups of five to eight members try to achieve consensus on the ranking values for both Chinese and American cultures.

| 3. Group presentations (optional) | 15 min | 30 min |

   Each group presents its rankings and discusses reasons for making those decisions.

4. Discussion 20 min 50 min

Instructor leads a discussion on the differences between Chinese and American value systems and presents the correct rankings.

Value Rankings

Rank each of the fifteen values below according to what you think they are in the Chinese, Indian (from India), and American cultures. Use "1" as the most important value for the culture and "15" as the least important value for that culture.

Value	American	Chinese	Indian
Achievement			
Deference			
Order			
Exhibition			
Autonomy			
Affiliation			
Intraception			
Succorance			
Dominance			
Abasement			
Nurturance			
Change			
Endurance			
Heterosexuality			
Aggression			

Some Definitions

Intraception: The tendency to be governed by subjective factors, such as feelings, fantasies, speculations, and aspirations; the other side of extraception, where one is governed by concrete, clearly observable physical conditions.

Succorance: Willingness to help another or to offer relief.

Abasement: To lower oneself in rank, prestige, or esteem.

Internal/External Locus of Control

Consider American and Chinese groups. Which would tend to have more internal locus of control (tend to feel in control of one's destiny, that rewards come as a result of hard work, perseverance, and responsibility)? Which would be more external (fate, luck, or other outside forces control destiny)?

Machiavellianism

This concept was defined by Christie and Geis as the belief that one can manipulate and deceive people for personal gain. Do you think Americans or Chinese would score higher on the Machiavellian scale?

Discussion Questions

1. What are some main differences among the cultures? Did any pattern emerge?

2. Were you surprised by the results?

3. What behaviors could you expect in business dealings with Chinese (or Indians) based on their value system?

4. How do American values dictate Americans' behaviors in business situations?

SOURCE: "Chinese, Indian, and American Values" by Dorothy Marcic, copyright 1993. Adapted from Michael Harris Bond, ed., *The Psychology of the Chinese People*, Hong Kong: Oxford University Press, 200 Madison Ave., NY 10016, 1986. The selection used here is a portion of "Chinese Personality and Its Change," by Kuo-Shu Yang, pp. 106–170. Reprinted by permission.

4.2 Is This Behavior Ethical?

The purpose of this exercise is to explore your opinions about ethical issues faced in organizations. The class should be divided into twelve groups. Each group will randomly be assigned one of the following issues, which reflect the twelve ethical themes found in the *Wall Street Journal* study shown in Table 4.3.

1. Is it ethical to take office supplies from work for home use? Make personal long-distance calls from the office? Use company time for personal business? Or do these behaviors constitute stealing?

2. If you exaggerate your credentials in an interview, is it lying? Is lying in order to protect a coworker acceptable?

3. If you pretend to be more successful than you are in order to impress your boss, are you being deceitful?

4. How do you differentiate between a bribe and a gift?

5. If there are slight defects in a product you are selling, are you obligated to tell the buyer? If an advertised "sale" price is really the everyday price, should you divulge the information to the customer?

6. Suppose you have a friend who works at the ticket office for the convention center where Shania Twain will be appearing. Is it cheating if you ask the friend to get you tickets so that you won't have to fight the crowd to get them? Is buying merchandise for your family at your company's cost cheating?

7. Is it immoral to do less than your best in terms of work performance? Is it immoral to accept workers' compensation when you are fully capable of working?

8. What behaviors constitute emotional abuse at work? What would you consider an abuse of one's position of power?

9. Are high-stress jobs a breach of ethics? What about transfers that break up families?

10. Are all rule violations equally important? Do employees have an ethical obligation to follow company rules?

11. To what extent are you responsible for the ethical behavior of your coworkers? If you witness unethical behavior and don't report it, are you an accessory?

12. Is it ethical to help one work group at the expense of another? For instance, suppose one group has excellent performance and you want to reward its members with an afternoon off. In that case, the other group will have to pick up the slack and work harder. Is this ethical?

Once your group has been assigned its issue, you have two tasks:

1. First, formulate your group's answer to the ethical dilemmas.

2. After you have formulated your group's position, discuss the individual differences that may have contributed to your position. You will want to discuss the individual differences presented in this chapter as well as any others that you feel affected your position on the ethical dilemma.

Your instructor will lead the class in a discussion of how individual differences may have influenced your positions on these ethical dilemmas.

SOURCE: Kluwer Academic Publishers, by J. O. Cherrington and D. J. Cherrington, "A Menu of Moral Issues: One Week in the Life of *The Wall Street Journal*," *Journal of Business Ethics* 11 (1992): 255–265. Reprinted with kind permission of Springer Science and Business Media.

BizFlix | The Emperor's Club

William Hundert (Kevin Kline), a professor at the exclusive Saint Benedict's Academy for Boys, believes in teaching his students about living a principled life. He also wants them to learn his beloved classical literature. A new student, Sedgewick Bell (Emile Hirsch), challenges Hundert's principled ways. Bell's behavior during the seventy-third annual Mr. Julius Caesar Contest causes Hundert to suspect that Bell leads a less-than-principled life, a suspicion confirmed years later during a reenactment of the competition.

Ethics and Ethical Behavior: An Assessment of Sedgewick Bell

Mr. Hundert is the honored guest of his former student Sedgewick Bell (Joel Gretsch) at Bell's estate. Depaak Mehta (Rahul Khanna), Bell, and Louis Masoudi (Patrick Dempsey) compete in a reenactment of the Julius Caesar competition. Bell wins the competition, but Hundert notices that Bell is wearing an earpiece. Earlier in the film, Hundert had suspected that young Bell wore an earpiece during the competition, but Headmaster Woodbridge (Edward Herrmann) urged him to ignore his suspicion.

This scene appears near the end of the film after the competition reenactment. Bell announced his candidacy for the U.S. Senate just before he talks to Hundert in the bathroom. In his announcement, he carefully described his commitment to specific values he would pursue if elected.

What to Watch for and Ask Yourself

- Does William Hundert describe a specific type of life that one should lead? If so, what are its elements?

- Does Sedgewick Bell lead that type of life? At what level of cognitive moral development do you perceive Sedgewick Bell? Support your response with specific moments in the film scene.

- What consequences or effects do you predict for Sedgewick Bell because of the way he chooses to live his life?

Workplace Video | Numi Organic Tea: Dynamics of Behavior in Organizations

Getting a job offer from Numi Organic Tea is similar to getting accepted into a big mafia family, minus the illegal activities and violence. Fierce loyalty is critical for survival. A willingness to work long and strange hours is non-negotiable.

When asked about Numi's hiring practices, co-founder Ahmed Rahim responded that "People are everything for a company. You can have a great product and great mission, but without the right people, you don't have the right formula."

Numi hasn't had much trouble finding and retaining talent. Approximately fifty people work for the progressive Oakland-based company, and Rahim has reduced the potential for turnover by making sure every candidate has the right skills and experience and fits well with the organization's culture.

Jen Mullin, vice president of marketing, recently hired a public relations assistant to help connect with customers through social networking sites like MySpace and Facebook.

In particular, Mullin was looking for someone who was passionate about Numi tea and shared the organizational commitment to organics, sustainability, and fair trade. Employees who share Numi's values can effectively represent the organization in any situation. According to Mullin, the company can tell within sixty days whether or not someone is going to work out. In the case of the new PR assistant, Numi scored. When asked to help with a marketing research project, the new assistant, Tish, went above and beyond the call of duty.

Regardless of how many people join the staff, Numi's growth makes it difficult for anyone to feel on top of his or her workload. To destress, many employees take breaks in the company's tea garden, where they sip tea and cultivate an inner calm. Mullin's team meets weekly to prioritize and, if necessary, change project due dates so people don't feel continuously behind and overwhelmed. Flextime helps a lot of Numi folks manage their daily stress, too.

Although many companies have employees who come across as ambitious and hard-working, Numi seems to be fully populated with high-achieving and high-performance types that will do whatever it takes to make Numi the most successful brand in the world.

Questions

1. Are Numi's expectations for organizational citizenship realistic? Explain.

2. How is Numi susceptible to hiring the wrong people in spite of its efforts?

3. What qualities are hardest to assess given the limited contact possible through interviews? What are some possible solutions to this challenge?

Case

Rahodeb (or John Mackey): Internet Postings about Whole Foods Market and Wild Oats

Started as one small store in Austin, Texas in 1980, Whole Foods Market has grown into the world's leading retailer of natural and organic foods, with hundreds of locations in North America and the United Kingdom.[1] Whole Foods Market was founded by Craig Weller, Mark Skiles, and John Mackey, who serves as the company's CEO. Whole Foods Market has expanded through the acquisition of numerous companies, including but not limited to Wellspring Grocery, Fresh Fields, Bread of Life, Merchant of Vino, Allegro Coffee, Nature's Heartland, and Harry's Farmers Market, among others. The most recent acquisition was Wild Oats Markets.[2]

However, the acquisition of Wild Oats was not without its problems. The Federal Trade Commission (FTC) filed suit in June 2007 to block Whole Foods Market's acquisition of Wild Oats; the acquisition was challenged on antitrust grounds.[3] Then in late August 2007, a federal appeals court turned down the FTC's request to overturn a federal district court ruling allowing Whole Foods Market to complete its purchase of rival grocer Wild Oats.[4]

Interestingly, while conducting its antitrust review, the FTC discovered that, over a period of several years, John Mackey had posted comments about Whole Foods Market and its competitors in the online stock forums of Yahoo!® Finance. Mackey used the screen name "Rahodeb"—an anagram of Deborah, the name of Mackey's wife—to conceal his true identity as CEO of Whole Foods Market.[5] At least 240 of Rahodeb's 1,300 or so posts mentioned Wild Oats, a company with which Mackey had an increasingly bitter rivalry.[6]

The acrimony between Mackey and Perry Odak, CEO of Wild Oats, can be traced to the first time the two men met at a retailing conference in Manhattan in 2001. "I'm going to destroy you," Mackey shouted at Odak. Whole Foods' officials tell a different version of the story—with milder language—but the confrontation has persisted as a food-industry legend.[7]

For nearly eight years, John Mackey posted numerous comments about Whole Foods Market using the pseudonym Rahodeb. In some of his postings, Mackey lauded Whole Foods' stock, cheered its financial results, and castigated Wild Oats Markets, the company on which

Whole Foods Market had acquisition designs.[8] In January 2005, Rahodeb posted this opinion: "No company would want to buy Wild Oats Markets Inc." Rahodeb continued, "Would Whole Foods Market buy OATS? Almost surely not at current prices. What would they gain? OATS locations are too small. . . . [Wild Oats management] clearly doesn't know what it is doing . . . OATS has no value and no future."[9] Other comments that Mackey posted under the Rahodeb alias included the following: "While I'm not a Mackey groupie . . . I do admire what the man has accomplished." "I love the company and I'm in it for the long haul. I shop at Whole Foods Market. I own a great deal of its stock. I'm aligned with the mission and the values of the company . . . is there something wrong with this?"[10]

Mackey asserts that his online comments were personal, not professional. However, Mackey's friends and colleagues say there is little distinction between his personal and professional sides,[11] and that he is straightforward and transparent.[12] Mackey's defenders also say, "his anonymous comments—though boastful, provocative and impulsive—were no different from his public ones, and were never intended to disclose insider information or move stock prices."[13]

In a statement published in mid-July 2007 on the Whole Foods' Web site, Mackey "said his anonymous statements didn't reflect his or the company's policies or beliefs. Some of the views Rahodeb expressed, Mr. Mackey said, didn't match his own beliefs." Mackey further stated that he made the anonymous comments on Yahoo Finance because he "had fun doing it."[14]

Rahodeb's (or Mackey's) online postings were investigated by the Securities and Exchange Commission (SEC) and the FTC. As the legal wrangling unfolded, charges and countercharges were slung—not just by the direct participants, but by interested observers as well—and utterly delicious twists and turns kept emerging. FTC lawyers were shocked that their "'gotcha' haul of off-color statements by . . . *Mackey* wasn't enough to block his merger with Wild Oats . . . in the absence of serious antitrust evidence."[15] However, Mackey asserted that the FTC was "running 'a rigged game' that handcuffs retailers and other companies under its jurisdiction."[16]

Some commentators castigated Mackey; others were less critical. For instance, John Hollon, editor of the *Business of Management* blog characterizes Mackey as "a delusional apologist for his own bad behavior."[17] Another blogger, Andres Acosta, disagrees with Hollon. Acosta says, "I look at it differently. I appreciate his transparency and willingness to admit to making a mistake. It's the sign of a great leader who can pick himself up after taking a hard fall and keep moving forward."[18] Chiming in with a nuanced argument that could be interpreted as supporting either a positive or negative view of Mackey is Adam Sarner, an analyst at Gartner Inc., who says, "[t]he need for executive online transparency depends on the context of the post."[19]

Has John Mackey been vindicated in Whole Foods Market's acquisition of Wild Oats? Hallie Mummert, writing in *Target Marketing*, says, "[w]at some chalked up to a bizarre display of self-aggrandizement, others pegged as unethical and possibly illegal behavior."[20] And business blogger Laurie Ruettimann writes, "Great companies operate on the right side of the ethical spectrum and have little tolerance for 'spin.' "[21] Mackey himself, quoted in the *Wall Street Journal*, says, "If I could get the money back, I'd take it. . . . We would be better off today if we hadn't done this deal—taking on all this debt right before the economy collapsed."[22] Even though Mackey has been described as "an opinionated iconoclast," he "succeeded in buying out his largest competitor, Wild Oats Markets, and has expanded overseas to London, the next stop on his quest for global dominance."[23]

Discussion Questions

1. Using the ABC model of an attitude, analyze what John Mackey's online comments about Wild Oats reveal about his attitudes.

2. Using the concepts of instrumental values and terminal values, explain John Mackey's blogging behavior relative to the Wild Oats acquisition. Using the same concepts explain the reaction of the SEC, FTC, and interested observers to Mackey's blogging behavior.

3. From your perspective, did John Mackey act in an ethical or unethical manner? Explain the reasoning behind your answer.

4. At what level of cognitive moral development is John Mackey apparently operating? Explain your answer.

5. What insights regarding John Mackey's attitudes, values, and ethics are provided by his use of the pseudonym "Rahodeb" to disguise his extensive online commentary about Wild Oats?

SOURCE: This case was written by Michael K. McCuddy, The Louis S. and Mary L. Morgal Chair of Christian Business Ethics and Professor of Management, College of Business Administration, Valparaiso University.

5

Motivation at Work

LEARNING OBJECTIVES

After reading this chapter, you should be able to do the following:

1 Define motivation.

2 Explain how Theory X and Theory Y relate to Maslow's hierarchy of needs.

3 Discuss the needs for achievement, power, and affiliation.

4 Describe the two-factor theory of motivation.

5 Explain two new ideas in human motivation.

6 Describe how inequity influences motivation and can be resolved.

7 Describe the expectancy theory of motivation.

8 Describe the cultural differences in motivation.

Deloitte Headquarters in Copenhagen.

THINKING AHEAD: DELOITTE

Focused on People, with Appreciation

When Ian Steele became the partner in charge of Deloitte's Glasgow office, he set out to discover what people liked and did not like about working there.[1] He realized that people remember how you make them feel. So, he focused on the people. People join Deloitte for the training and future prospects. The numbers are good. Eighty percent say their Deloitte job is good for personal growth and 82 percent say their experience is good for their future. Seventy-three percent find their work stimulating and 72 percent are excited about Deloitte's future. On a personal note, Deloitte was flexible in helping executive assistant Cath Mitchell move to the Glasgow office to be near her sister. The work results were very positive too with Mitchell winning four outstanding contribution awards as diversity coordinator for Scotland, each award worth nearly $5,000.

Ian Steele displayed excellent leadership when he took over Deloitte's Glasgow office. He is a reflection of leadership excellence for Deloitte in the UK. People are proud to work for the company as reflected in the 80 percent positive score earned in employee responses. There is high confidence in senior management as shown in the 80 percent rating and in the personal example we see displayed by Ian Steele in Glasgow. This is reflected too in a top-four score earned by Deloitte's senior partner and chief executive of the company's UK operations John Connolly. Sixty-nine percent of the people say that more than motivated, they are inspired by Connolly. When the 2008 credit crunch hit, Connolly actively provided regular voicemail updates on how the company was doing in the crisis, another sign of excellent leadership.

Managing in good times is a good deal less difficult than doing so in hard times. Every company and every industry has hard times that challenge leaders and employees alike. We see Connolly's active, engaged response at the outset of the credit crunch, which became one of the most severe financial crises in a generation or more. During these times, people's basic needs may become severely threatened and their insecurities can stir deep emotions. Having a partner in charge like Ian Steele and a chief executive like John Connolly who focus on the people and find ways to display appreciation can go a long way to providing reassurance and a sense of felt security. Is that enough? In the Looking Back feature on page 174, we take a closer look at leading in hard times and staying focused on what you want most.

This is the first of two chapters about motivation, behavior, and performance at work. A comprehensive approach to understanding these topics must consider three elements of the work situation—the individual, the job, and the work environment—and how these elements interact.[2] This chapter emphasizes internal and process theories of motivation. It begins with individual need theories of motivation, turns to the two-factor theory of motivation, and finishes by examining two individual–environment interaction or process theories of motivation. Chapter 6 emphasizes external theories of motivation and focuses on factors in the environment to help understand good or bad performance.

MOTIVATION AND WORK BEHAVIOR

1 Define *motivation*.

Motivation is the process of arousing and sustaining goal-directed behavior. It is one of the more complex topics in organizational behavior. Motivation comes from the Latin root word *movere*, which means "to move."

Motivation theories attempt to explain and predict observable behavior. The wide range and variety of motivation theories result from the great diversity of people and the complexity of their behavior in organizations. Motivation theories may be broadly classified into internal, process, and external theories of motivation. Internal theories of motivation give primary consideration to variables within the individual that give rise to motivation and behavior. The hierarchy of needs theory exemplifies the internal theories. Process theories of motivation emphasize the

motivation
The process of arousing and sustaining goal-directed behavior.

nature of the interaction between the individual and the environment. Expectancy theory exemplifies the process theories. External theories of motivation focus on the elements in the environment, including the consequences of behavior, as the basis for understanding and explaining people's behavior at work. Any single motivation theory explains only a small portion of the variance in human behavior. Therefore, alternative theories have developed over time in an effort to account for the unexplained portions of the variance in behavior.

Internal Needs

Philosophers and scholars have theorized for centuries about human needs and motives. During the past century, attention narrowed to understanding motivation in businesses and other organizations.[3] Max Weber, an early German organizational scholar, argued that the meaning of work lay not in the work itself but in its deeper potential for contributing to a person's ultimate salvation.[4] From this Calvinistic perspective, the Protestant ethic was the fuel for human industriousness. The Protestant ethic said people should work hard because those who prospered at work were more likely to find a place in heaven. You 5.1 lets you evaluate how strongly you have a pro-Protestant versus a non-Protestant ethic. Although Weber, and later Blood, both used the term *Protestant ethic*, many see the value elements of this work ethic in the broader Judeo-Christian tradition. We concur.

A more complex motivation theory was proposed by Sigmund Freud. For him, a person's organizational life was founded on the compulsion to work and the power of love.[5] He saw much of human motivation as unconscious by nature. *Psychoanalysis* was Freud's method for delving into the unconscious mind to better understand a person's motives and needs. Freud's psychodynamic theory offers explanations for irrational and self-destructive behavior, such as suicide or workplace violence. The motives underlying such traumatic work events may be understood by analyzing a person's unconscious needs and motives. The psychoanalytic approach also helps explain deviant workplace behavior, which can have a negative impact on business unit performance.[6] Freud's theorizing is important as the basis for subsequent need theories of motivation. Research suggests that people's deeper feelings may transcend culture, with most people caring deeply about the same few things.[7]

Internal needs and external incentives both play an important role in motivation. Although extrinsic motivation is important, so too is intrinsic motivation, which varies by the individual.[8] Four drives or needs, which are to acquire, to bond, to comprehend, and to defend, underlie employee motivation and organizations that meet these needs can improve performance.[9] Intrinsic work motivation is linked to spillover effects from work to home, with mothers transmitting the emotions of happiness, anger, and anxiety from work to home.[10] Interestingly, fathers who have high intrinsic work motivation tended to report greater overall anxiety at home after the workday. Therefore, it is important for managers to consider both internal needs and external incentives when attempting to motivate their employees. Further, managers who are more supportive and less controlling appear to elicit more intrinsic motivation from their employees.

External Incentives

Early organizational scholars made economic assumptions about human motivation and developed differential piece-rate systems of pay that emphasized external incentives. They assumed that people were motivated by self-interest and economic gain. The Hawthorne studies confirmed the positive effects of pay incentives on productivity and also found that social and interpersonal motives were important.[11]

psychoanalysis
Sigmund Freud's method for delving into the unconscious mind to better understand a person's motives and needs.

Protestant Ethic

Rate the following statements from 1 (for *disagree completely*) to 6 (for *agree completely*).

_____1. When the workday is finished, people should forget their jobs and enjoy themselves.

_____2. Hard work makes us better people.

_____3. The principal purpose of people's jobs is to provide them with the means for enjoying their free time.

_____4. Wasting time is as bad as wasting money.

_____5. Whenever possible, a person should relax and accept life as it is rather than always striving for unreachable goals.

_____6. A good indication of a person's worth is how well he or she does his or her job.

_____7. If all other things are equal, it is better to have a job with a lot of responsibility than one with little responsibility.

_____8. People who "do things the easy way" are the smart ones.

_____Total your score for the pro-Protestant ethic items (2, 4, 6, and 7).

_____Total your score for the non-Protestant ethic items (1, 3, 5, and 8).

A non-Protestant ethic score of 20 or over indicates you have a strong nonwork ethic; 15–19 indicates a moderately strong nonwork ethic; 9–14 indicates a moderately weak nonwork ethic; 8 or less indicates a weak nonwork ethic.

A pro-Protestant ethic score of 20 or over indicates you have a strong work ethic; 15–19 indicates a moderately strong work ethic; 9–14 indicates a moderately weak work ethic; 8 or less indicates a weak work ethic.

SOURCE: M. R. Blood, "Work Values and Job Satisfaction," *Journal of Applied Psychology* 53 (1969): 456–459. Copyright © 1969 by the American Psychological Association. Reprinted with permission.

However, there are those who raise the question about where self-interest ends and the public interest begins. For example, public service employees may respond more positively to perceptions of the benefit their agencies provide to the public than to self-interest economic incentives such as merit pay.[12]

Those who made economic assumptions about human motivation emphasized financial incentives for behavior. The Scottish political economist and moral philosopher Adam Smith argued that a person's *self-interest* was God's providence, not the government's.[13] More recently, executives have focused on "enlightened" self-interest. Self-interest is what is in the best interest and benefit to the individual; enlightened self-interest additionally recognizes the self-interest of other people. Adam Smith laid the cornerstone for the free enterprise system of economics when he formulated the "invisible hand" and the free market to explain the motivation for individual behavior. The "invisible hand" refers to the unseen forces of a free market system that shape the most efficient use of people, money, and resources for productive ends. Smith's basic assumption was that people are motivated by self-interest for economic gain to provide the necessities and conveniences of life. Thus, employees are most productive when motivated by self-interest.

Technology is an important concept in Smith's view because he believed that a nation's wealth is determined primarily by the productivity of its labor force. Therefore, a more efficient and effective labor force yields greater abundance for the

self-interest
What is in the best interest and benefit to an individual.

nation. Technology is important as a force multiplier for the productivity of labor.[14]

Frederick Taylor, the founder of scientific management, was also concerned with labor efficiency and effectiveness.[15] His central concern was to change the relationship between management and labor from one of conflict to one of cooperation.[16]

Taylor believed the basis of their conflict was the division of the profits. Instead of continuing this conflict over the division of profits, labor and management should form a cooperative relationship aimed at enlarging the total profits.

External incentives may take a material form, such as plaques or certificates.

Employee Recognition and Ownership

Modern management practices—such as employee recognition programs, flexible benefit packages, and stock ownership plans—build on Smith's and Taylor's original theories. These practices emphasize external incentives, which may take either strictly economic form or more material form, such as "outstanding employee" plaques, gold watches, and other organizational symbols of distinction. Whataburger has developed the WhataGames, in which the best employees compete for bragging rights as well as cash, prizes, and even medals.[17] This corporate Olympics is a training-and-loyalty exercise that helps significantly reduce turnover and build commitment. One bridge approach to employee motivation that considers both psychological needs and external incentives is psychological ownership. An increasing number of scholars and managers emphasize the importance of "feelings of ownership" for the organization. One study of 800 managers and employees in three different organizations found that psychological ownership increased organizational citizenship behavior, a key contextual performance beyond the call of duty as discussed in Chapter 3.[18]

MASLOW'S NEED HIERARCHY

Psychologist Abraham Maslow proposed a theory of motivation emphasizing psychological and interpersonal needs in addition to physical needs and economic necessity. Kenexa is the leading human resources services company that excels at understanding employees needs through a blend of psychology and technology, as we see in The Real World 5.1. Maslow's theory was based on a need hierarchy later applied through Theory X and Theory Y, two sets of assumptions about people at work. In addition, his need hierarchy was reformulated in an ERG (Existence, Relatedness, Growth) theory of motivation using a revised, three-tier classification scheme for basic human needs. The three are Existence needs, Relatedness needs, and Growth needs.

The Hierarchy of Needs

The core of Maslow's theory of human motivation is a hierarchy of five need categories.[19] Although he recognized that there were factors other than one's needs (e.g., culture) that were determinants of behavior, he focused his theoretical attention on specifying people's internal needs. Maslow labeled the five hierarchical categories as physiological needs, safety and security needs, love (social) needs, esteem needs, and the need for self-actualization. Maslow's *need hierarchy* is depicted in Figure 5.1, which also shows how the needs relate to Douglas McGregor's assumptions about people, which will be discussed next.

good final paper.

need hierarchy
The theory that behavior is determined by a progression of physical, social, and psychological needs, including lower-order needs and higher-order needs.

The Real World 5.1

Beyond Motivated to Inspired

Kenexa is the leading human resources services company in America with 60 percent of the Fortune 100 companies as its clients. Caterpillar, Time Warner, and Wachovia are among the leading companies that Kenexa serves. The company's success rests on a blend of psychology and technology that enables it to understand employee needs, often taking these employees beyond motivation to inspiration. Kenexa believes that employees do want to have fun and even laugh their way through problems inevitably encountered on the job. The company gets into the minds of client organization employees and helps build strong loyalty by listening deeply to the people. Kenexa does this through interviews and surveys aimed at enabling them to understand what truly inspires client employees. Employees love sessions in which they are simply listened to fully, accurately, and deeply. Based upon their interview and survey data, Kenexa

helps Fortune 100 companies and other clients devise strategies that are responsive to employee needs and their aspirations. Measuring employee motivation and inspiring employees to excel and be loyal has more than feel-good results. Turnover is 21 percent lower among managers who experience pride in their company, and unwanted turnover is expensive. In addition to this sort of cost avoidance, Kenexa has found that companies with higher employee satisfaction scores had 700 percent higher shareholder return. That is financial performance! Therefore, understanding employee needs and motivation leads to employee inspiration, manager loyalty, and great financial returns. This is Triple Crown, winning performance.

SOURCE: K. Rockwood, "Employee Whisperer," *Fast Company* (November 2008): 72–72.

Maslow conceptually derived the five need categories from the early thoughts of William James[20] and John Dewey,[21] coupled with the psychodynamic thinking of Sigmund Freud and Alfred Adler.[22] Maslow's need theory was later tested in research with working populations. For example, one study reported that middle managers and lower-level managers had different perceptions of their need deficiencies and the importance of their needs.[23] One distinguishing feature of Maslow's need hierarchy

FIGURE

5.1   Human Needs, Theory X, and Theory Y

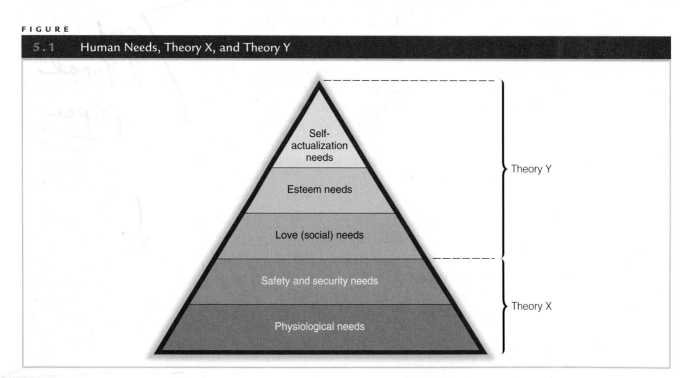

is the following progression hypothesis. Although some research has challenged the assumption, the theory says that only ungratified needs motivate behavior.[24] Further, it is the lowest level of ungratified needs in the hierarchy that motivates behavior. As one level of need is met, a person progresses to the next higher level of need as a source of motivation. Hence, people progress up the hierarchy as they successively gratify each level of need.

Theory X and Theory Y

One important organizational implication of the need hierarchy concerns how to manage people at work (see Figure 5.1). Douglas McGregor understood people's motivation using Maslow's need theory. He grouped the physiological and safety needs as "lower order" needs and the social, esteem, and self-actualization needs as "higher order" needs, as shown in Figure 5.1. McGregor proposed two alternative sets of assumptions about people at work based on which set of needs were the motivators.[25] His *Theory X* and *Theory Y* assumptions are included in Table 5.1. McGregor saw the responsibility of management as the same under both sets of assumptions. Specifically, "management is responsible for organizing the elements of productive enterprise—money, materials, equipment, people—in the interest of economic ends."[23]

McGregor believed that Theory X assumptions are appropriate for employees motivated by lower order needs. Theory Y assumptions, by contrast, are appropriate for employees motivated by higher order needs. Employee participation programs are one consequence of McGregor's Theory Y assumptions. Therefore, Fortune 1000 corporations use employee involvement as one motivation strategy for achieving high performance.[27] Whole Foods Market founder and CEO John Mackey relies on Maslow's hierarchy of needs in leading the company.[28]

Gordon Forward, founding CEO of world-class Chaparral Steel Company, considered the assumptions made about people central to motivation and management.[29]

2 Explain how Theory X and Theory Y relate to Maslow's hierarchy of needs.

Theory X
A set of assumptions of how to manage individuals who are motivated by lower-order needs.

Theory Y
A set of assumptions of how to manage individuals who are motivated by higher-order needs.

TABLE

| 5.1 | McGregor's Assumptions about People |

Theory X	Theory Y
• People are by nature indolent. That is, they work as little as possible.	• People are not by nature passive or resistant to organizational needs. They have become so as a result of experience in organizations.
• People lack ambition, dislike responsibility, and prefer to be led.	• The motivation, the potential for development, the capacity for assuming responsibility, and the readiness to direct behavior toward organizational goals are all present in people. Management does not put them there. It is a responsibility of management to make it possible for people to recognize and develop these human characteristics for themselves.
• People are inherently self-centered and indifferent to organizational needs.	
• People are by nature resistant to change.	
• People are gullible and not very bright, the ready dupes of the charlatan and the demagogue.	• The essential task of management is to arrange conditions and methods of operation so that people can achieve their own goals best by directing their own efforts toward organizational objectives.

SOURCE: From "The Human Side of Enterprise" by Douglas M. McGregor; reprinted from *Management Review*, November 1957. Copyright 1957 American Management Association International. Reprinted by permission of American Management Association International, New York, NY. All rights reserved. http:// www. amanet.org.

He viewed employees as resources to be developed. Using Maslow's need hierarchy and Theory Y assumptions about people, he cultivated and developed a productive, loyal workforce in Texas Industries Inc's Chaparral Steel unit. Similarly, we saw in Thinking Ahead that Ian Steele of Deloitte focused positive attention and appreciation on his people.

ERG Theory

Clayton Alderfer recognized Maslow's contribution to understanding motivation, but he believed that the original need hierarchy was not quite accurate in identifying and categorizing human needs.[30] As an evolutionary step, Alderfer proposed the ERG theory of motivation, which grouped human needs into only three basic categories: existence, relatedness, and growth.[31] Alderfer classified Maslow's physiological and physical safety needs in an existence need category; Maslow's interpersonal safety, love, and interpersonal esteem needs in a relatedness need category; and Maslow's self-actualization and self-esteem needs in a growth need category.

In addition to the differences in categorizing human needs, ERG theory added a regression hypothesis to go along with the progression hypothesis originally proposed by Maslow. Alderfer's regression hypothesis helped explain people's behavior when frustrated at meeting needs at the next higher level in the hierarchy. Specifically, the regression hypothesis states that people regress to the next lower category of needs and intensify their desire to gratify these needs. Hence, ERG theory explains both progressive need gratification and regression when people face frustration.

MCCLELLAND'S NEED THEORY

3 Discuss the needs for achievement, power, and affiliation.

A second major need theory of motivation focuses on personality and learned needs. Henry Murray developed a long list of motives and manifest needs in his early studies of personality.[32] David McClelland was inspired by Murray's early work.[33] McClelland identified three learned or acquired needs, called *manifest needs*. These were the needs for achievement, for power, and for affiliation. Some individuals have a high need for achievement, whereas others have a moderate or low need for achievement. The same is true for the other two needs. Hence, it is important to emphasize that different needs are dominant in different people.

For example, a manager may have a strong need for power, a moderate need for achievement, and a weak need for affiliation. Each need has quite different implications for people's behavior. The Murray Thematic Apperception Test (TAT) was used as an early measure of the achievement motive and was further developed by McClelland and his associates.[34] The TAT is a projective test, and projective tests were discussed in Chapter 3.

Need for Achievement

The *need for achievement* concerns issues of excellence, competition, challenging goals, persistence, and overcoming difficulties.[35] A person with a high need for achievement seeks excellence in performance, enjoys difficult and challenging goals, and is persevering and competitive in work activities. Example questions that address the need for achievement are as follows: Do you enjoy difficult, challenging work

Image copyright Galyna Andrusko, 2009. Used under license from Shutterstock.com

A person with a high need for achievement enjoys difficult and challenging goals.

activities? Do you strive to exceed your performance objectives? Do you seek out new ways to overcome difficulties?

McClelland found that people with a high need for achievement perform better than those with a moderate or low need for achievement, and he has noted national differences in achievement motivation. Individuals with a high need for achievement have three unique characteristics. First, they set goals that are moderately difficult yet achievable. Second, they like to receive feedback on their progress toward these goals. Third, they do not like having external events or other people interfere with their progress toward the goals. How individuals interpret goal performance may depend on whether the goal is personal or societal.[36] When evaluating goal progress, especially when failure occurs, feedback should minimize triggering a negative mood and frustration.[37]

High achievers often hope and plan for success. They may be quite content to work alone or with other people—whichever is more appropriate to their task. High achievers like being very good at what they do, and they develop expertise and competence in their chosen endeavors. Research shows that need for achievement generalizes well across countries with adults who are employed full-time.[38] In addition, international differences in the tendency for achievement have been found. Specifically, achievement tendencies are highest for the United States, an individualistic culture, and lowest for Japan and Hungary, collectivistic societies.[39]

Need for Power

The *need for power* is concerned with the desire to make an impact on others, influence others, change people or events, and make a difference in life. The need for power is interpersonal because it involves influence with other people. Individuals with a high need for power like to control people and events. McClelland makes an important distinction between socialized power, which is used for the benefit of many, and personalized power, which is used for individual gain. The former is a constructive force, whereas the latter may be a very disruptive, destructive force.

A high need for power was one distinguishing characteristic of managers rated the "best" in McClelland's research. Specifically, the best managers had a very high need for socialized power, as opposed to personalized power.[40] These managers are concerned about others; have an interest in organizational goals; and have a desire to be useful to the larger group, organization, and society. For example, on the McClelland need profile, Management Sciences for Health CEO Jonathan D. Quick, M.D., displayed a high need for interactive power, or socialized power, which is very positive. This contrasts with the need for imperial power, a need in which he was very low, which is again very positive.

While successful managers have the greatest upward velocity in an organization and rise to higher managerial levels more quickly than their contemporaries, they benefit their organizations most if they have a high socialized power need.[41] The need for power is discussed further in Chapter 11, on power and politics.

Need for Affiliation

The *need for affiliation* is concerned with establishing and maintaining warm, close, intimate relationships with other people.[42] Those with a high need for affiliation are motivated to express their emotions and feelings to others while expecting them to do the same in return. They find conflicts and complications in their relationships disturbing and are strongly motivated to work through any such barriers to

need for achievement
A manifest (easily perceived) need that concerns individuals' issues of excellence, competition, challenging goals, persistence, and overcoming difficulties.

need for power
A manifest (easily perceived) need that concerns an individual's need to make an impact on others, influence others, change people or events, and make a difference in life.

need for affiliation
A manifest (easily perceived) need that concerns an individual's need to establish and maintain warm, close, intimate relationships with other people.

FIGURE

5.2   Need Theories of Motivation

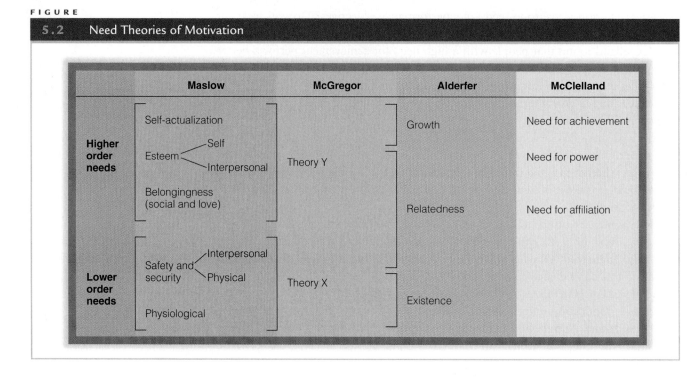

closeness. The relationships they have with others are therefore close and personal, emphasizing friendship and companionship.

Over and above these three needs, Murray's manifest needs theory included the need for autonomy. This is the desire for independence and freedom from any constraints. People with a high need for autonomy prefer to work alone and to control the pace of their work. They dislike bureaucratic rules, regulations, and procedures. The need for relationships is important in each theory. A study of 555 nurses in specialized units found that intrinsic motivation increased with supportive relationships on the job.[43] Figure 5.2 summarizes Maslow's hierarchy of needs with its two extensions in the work of McGregor and Alderfer. The figure also summarizes McClelland's need theory of motivation. The figure shows the parallel structures of these four motivational theories.

HERZBERG'S TWO-FACTOR THEORY

4 Describe the two-factor theory of motivation.

Frederick Herzberg departed from the need theories of motivation and examined the experiences that satisfied or dissatisfied people at work. This motivation theory became known as the two-factor theory.[44] Herzberg's original study included 200 engineers and accountants in western Pennsylvania during the 1950s. Herzberg asked these people to describe two important incidents at their jobs: one that was very satisfying and made them feel exceptionally good at work, and another that was very dissatisfying and made them feel exceptionally bad at work.

Herzberg and his colleagues believed that people had two sets of needs—one related to the avoidance of pain and one related to the desire for psychological growth. Conditions in the work environment would affect one or the other of these needs. Work conditions related to satisfaction of the need for psychological growth were labeled *motivation factors*. Work conditions related to dissatisfaction caused by discomfort or pain were labeled *hygiene factors*. Each set of factors related to one aspect of what Herzberg identified as the human being's dual nature regarding the

motivation factor
A work condition related to satisfaction of the need for psychological growth.

hygiene factor
A work condition related to dissatisfaction caused by discomfort or pain.

5.3   The Motivation–Hygiene Theory of Motivation

Hygiene: Job dissatisfaction	Motivators: Job satisfaction
	Achievement
	Recognition of achievement
	Work itself
	Responsibility
	Advancement
	Growth
Company policy and administration	
Supervision	
Interpersonal relations	
Working conditions	
Salary*	
Status	
Security	

*Because of its ubiquitous nature, salary commonly shows up as a motivator as well as hygiene. Although primarily a hygiene factor, it also often takes on some of the properties of a motivator, with dynamics similar to those of recognition for achievement.

SOURCE: Reprinted from Frederick Herzberg, *The Managerial Choice: To Be Efficient or to Be Human* (Salt Lake City: Olympus, 1982). Reprinted by permission.

work environment. Thus, motivation factors relate to job satisfaction, and hygiene factors relate to job dissatisfaction,[45] as shown in Figure 5.3.

Motivation Factors

Job satisfaction is produced by building motivation factors into a job, according to Herzberg. This process is known as job enrichment. In the original research, the motivation factors were identified as responsibility, achievement, recognition, advancement, and the work itself. When these factors are present, they lead to superior performance and effort on the part of job incumbents.

Figure 5.3 also shows that salary is a motivational factor in some studies. Many organizational reward systems now include other financial benefits, such as stock options, as part of an employee's compensation package. A long-term study of young men in the United States and the former West Germany found job satisfaction positively linked to earnings and changes in earnings, as well as voluntary turnover.[46]

Motivation factors lead to positive mental health and challenge people to grow, contribute to the work environment, and invest themselves in the organization. According to the theory and original research, the absence of these factors does not lead to dissatisfaction. Rather, it leads to the lack of satisfaction. The motivation factors are the more important of the two sets of factors because they directly affect a person's motivational drive to do a good job. When they are absent, the person is demotivated to perform well and achieve excellence. The hygiene factors are a completely distinct set of factors unrelated to the motivation to achieve and do excellent work.

Hygiene Factors

Job dissatisfaction occurs when the hygiene factors are either not present or not sufficient. In the original research, the hygiene factors were company policy and administration; technical supervision; salary; interpersonal relations with one's supervisor; working conditions; and status. These factors relate to the context of the job and may be considered support factors. They do not directly affect a person's motivation to work but influence the extent of the person's discontent. They cannot stimulate psychological growth or human development but may be thought of as maintenance factors. Excellent hygiene factors result in employees' being *not dissatisfied* and contribute to the absence of complaints about these contextual considerations. Organizational justice might be considered a hygiene factor and when present can yield exponential positive responses such as good organizational citizenship, though that is influenced by the quality of the employee–supervisor relationship.[47]

When these hygiene factors are poor or absent, the person complains about "poor supervision," "poor medical benefits," or whatever hygiene factor is poor. Employees experience a deficit and are dissatisfied when the hygiene factors are not present. Many companies have initiated formal flextime policies as a way to reduce dissatisfaction and persuade women leaders to come back to work.[48] Even in the absence of good hygiene factors, employees may still be very motivated to perform their jobs well if the motivation factors are present. Although this may appear to be a paradox, it is not because the motivation and hygiene factors are independent of each other.

The combination of motivation and hygiene factors can result in one of four possible job conditions. First, a job high in both motivation and hygiene factors leads to high motivation and few complaints among employees. Second, a job low in both factors leads to low motivation and many complaints among employees. Third, a job high in motivation factors and low in hygiene factors leads to high employee motivation to perform coupled with complaints about aspects of the work environment. Fourth, a job low in motivation factors and high in hygiene factors leads to low employee motivation to excel but few complaints about the work environment.

Two conclusions can be drawn at this point. First, hygiene factors are of some importance up to a threshold level, but beyond the threshold there is little value in improving them. Second, the presence of motivation factors is essential to enhancing

You 5.2

What's Important to Employees?

There are many possible job rewards that employees may receive. Listed below are ten possible job reward factors. Rank these factors three times. First, rank them as you think the average employee would rank them. Second, rank them as you think the average employee's supervisor would rank them for the employee. Finally, rank them according to what you consider important.

Your instructor has normative data for 1,000 employees and their supervisors that will help you interpret your results and put them in the context of Maslow's need hierarchy and Herzberg's two-factor theory of motivation.

Employee   **Supervisor**   **You**

1. Job security
2. Full appreciation of work done
3. Promotion and growth in the organization
4. Good wages
5. Interesting work
6. Good working conditions
7. Tactful discipline
8. Sympathetic help with personal problems
9. Personal loyalty to employees
10. A feeling of being in on things

employee motivation to excel at work. You 5.2 asks you to rank a set of ten job reward factors in terms of their importance to the average employee, supervisors, and you.

Critique of the Two-Factor Theory

Herzberg's two-factor theory has been critiqued. One criticism concerns the classification of the two factors. Data have not shown a clear dichotomization of incidents into hygiene and motivator factors. For example, employees almost equally classify pay as a hygiene factor and a motivation factor. A second criticism is the absence of individual differences in the theory. Specifically, individual differences such as age, sex, social status, education, or occupational level may influence the classification of factors. A third criticism is that intrinsic job factors, such as the work flow process, may be more important in determining satisfaction or dissatisfaction on the job. Psychological climate can impact job satisfaction as well, though it is important to consider both organizational and individual level referents.[49] Finally, almost all of the supporting data for the theory come from Herzberg and his students using his peculiar critical-incident technique. These criticisms challenge and qualify, yet do not invalidate, the theory. Independent research found his theory valid in a government research and development environment.[50]

Herzberg's two-factor theory has important implications for the design of work, as discussed in Chapter 14.

TWO NEW IDEAS IN MOTIVATION

5 Explain two new ideas in human motivation.

While executives like Whole Foods Market's CEO John Mackey value traditional motivation theories such as Maslow's, others like PepsiCo's CEO Steve Reinemund use new motivational ideas with their employees. Two new ideas in motivation have emerged in the past decade. One centers on eustress, strength, and hope. This idea comes from the new discipline of positive organizational behavior.[51] A second new idea centers on positive energy and full engagement. This idea translates what was learned from high-performance athletes for Fortune 500 executives and managers, such as those at PepsiCo. Both new ideas concern motivation, behavior, and performance at work.

Eustress, Strength, and Hope

Our detailed discussion of stress and health at work will come in Chapter 7. The positive side of stress discussed in Chapter 7 concerns its value as a motivational force, as in eustress. *Eustress* is healthy, normal stress.[52] Aligned with eustress in the new discipline of positive organizational scholarship are investing in strengths, finding positive meaning in work, displaying courage and principled action, and drawing on positive emotions at work.[53] This new, positive perspective on organizational life encourages optimism, hope, and health for people at work. Rather than focusing on the individual's needs, or alternatively on the rewards or punishment meted out in the work environment, this new idea in motivation focuses on the individual's interpretation of events.

Eustress is one manifestation of this broad, positive perspective. People are motivated by eustress when they see opportunities rather than obstacles, experience challenges rather than barriers, and feel energized rather than frustrated by the daily experiences of organizational life. Thus, eustress is a healthy and positive motivational force for individuals who harness its energy for productive work and organizational contributions.

Positive Energy and Full Engagement

The second new idea in motivation takes lessons learned from professional athletes and applies them in order to develop corporate athletes.[54] Jim Loehr's central tenets are the management of energy rather than time and the strategic use of disengagement to balance the power of full activity engagement.[55] This approach to motivation suggests that individuals do not need to be activated by unmet needs but are already activated by their own physical, emotional, mental, and spiritual energy. A manager's task is to help individuals learn to manage their energy so that they can experience periodic renewal and recovery and thus build positive energy and capacity for work.

A key to positive energy and full engagement is the concept that energy recovery is equally important to, if not more important than, energy expenditure. One way to recover energy may be through a twenty-minute nap, as we see in The Real World 5.2. Individuals may be designed more as sprinters than long-distance runners, putting forth productive energy for short periods and then requiring time for recovery to reenergize. This approach to motivation and work is based on a balanced approach to the human body's potential to build or enhance its capacity, thus enabling the individual to sustain a high level of performance in the face of increasing work demands.

eustress
Healthy, normal stress.

The Real World 5.2

Need Energy, Take a Nap

Some people may wonder if toy manufacturer Worlds Apart is practicing bizarre HR. The company has an approved human resource practice for employees who get fatigued and low on energy during the workday. Worlds Apart says that it is fine to take out your inflatable bed at the office and take a twenty-minute nap. The practice does not replace a good night's sleep nor is it designed for a two-hour siesta. This is an energy recovery practice that has been practiced over the ages by accomplished and talented people, such as, interestingly, Lieutenant General George C. Patton. While some companies may have a separate sleep room into which employees may retreat for several hours of sleep so as to work late into the night, this is a practice to discourage because it can create lethargy, just the opposite of the desired effect, and interfere with work-home balance. The Worlds Apart practice is a targeted, focused strategy consistent with the practice of high-performance athletes who engage in short energy recovery activities so that they can then achieve peak performance when fully engaged in an event. Worlds Apart has found that this practice is especially appropriate for new parents and those employees engaged in long-hour work stretches. Falling asleep at the desk is a bad practice because poor posture prevents appropriate relaxation and recovery. So, when low on energy, the company says pull out your inflatable mattress, take a twenty-minute nap, wake up refreshed and energized, and go back to work.

Short naps refresh and energize employees who are low on energy.

SOURCE: Staff, "Bizarre HR: A 20-Minute Nap Leaves Staff Perky and Motivated," *Human Resources* (May 2009): 11.

SOCIAL EXCHANGE AND EQUITY THEORY

Equity theory is a social exchange process theory of motivation that focuses on the individual–environment interaction. In contrast to internal needs theories of motivation, equity theory is concerned with the social processes that influence motivation and behavior. Power and exchange are important considerations in understanding human behavior.[56] In the same vein, Amitai Etzioni developed three categories of exchange relationships that people have with organizations: committed, calculated, and alienated involvements.[57] The implications of these relationships for power are discussed in detail in Chapter 11. Etzioni characterized committed relations as moral ones of high positive intensity, calculated relationships as ones of low positive or low negative intensity, and alienated relationships as ones of high negative intensity. Committed relationships may characterize a person's involvement with a religious group, and alienated relationships may characterize a person's incarceration in a prison. Social exchange theory may be the best way to understand effort–reward relationships and the sense of fairness at work as seen in a Dutch study.[58] Moral principles in workplace fairness are important because failures in fairness, or unfairness, lead to such things as theft, sabotage, and even violence.[59]

Demands and Contributions

Calculated involvements are based on the notion of social exchange in which each party in the relationship demands certain things of the other and contributes accordingly to the exchange. Business partnerships and commercial deals are excellent examples of calculated involvements. When they work well and both parties to the exchange benefit, the relationship has a positive orientation. When losses occur or conflicts arise, the relationship has a negative orientation. A model for examining these calculated exchange relationships is set out in Figure 5.4. We use this model to examine the nature of the relationship between a person and his or her employing organization.[60] The same basic model can be used to examine the relationship between two individuals or two organizations.

Demands Each party to the exchange makes demands upon the other. These demands express the expectations that each party has of the other in the relationship. The organization expresses its demands on the individual in the form of goal or mission statements, job expectations, performance objectives, and performance feedback. These are among the primary and formal mechanisms through which people learn about the organization's demands and expectations of them.

The organization is not alone in making demands of the relationship. The individual has needs to be satisfied as well, as we have previously discussed. These needs form the basis for the expectations or demands placed on the organization by the individual. Employee need fulfillment and the feeling of belonging are both important to a healthy exchange and to organizational membership.[61] These needs may be conceptualized from the perspective of Maslow, Alderfer, Herzberg, or McClelland. In the Looking Back feature at the end of the chapter we see Deloitte's response when employee needs are threatened.

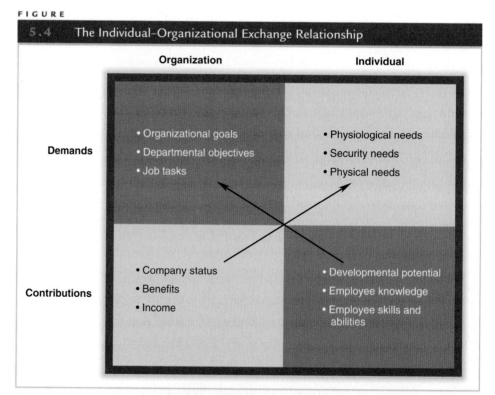

FIGURE

5.4 The Individual–Organizational Exchange Relationship

SOURCE: J. P. Campbell, M. D. Dunnette, E. E. Lawler III, and K. E. Weick, Jr., *Managerial Behavior, Performance, and Effectiveness* (New York: McGraw-Hill, 1970). Reproduced with permission from McGraw-Hill, Inc.

Science

Social and Economic Exchange in Transition

The People's Republic of China is a market economy aspiring to enter the World Trade Organization. These processes have prompted the use of various kinds of organizational forms and management mechanisms by companies. This research was designed to examine the relative importance of these multiple mechanisms for inducing employee commitment and performance in an emerging economic context and rising world economic power. Two studies were conducted, one with graduate business students in Chinese universities and the other with middle and top managers in thirty-one companies located in a variety of large Chinese cities such as Beijing. The two studies together examined the effects of executive leadership style, organizational culture, and employment approaches on both social and economic exchange relationship perceptions. These exchange relationship perceptions were expected to influence employee commitment, task

performance, and organizational citizenship behavior. The results of the tests suggest that social exchange relationship perceptions are influenced by executive leadership style, organizational culture, and employment approach, which in turn has an effect on commitment and performance, but not organizational citizenship behavior. The results further suggest that economic exchange relationship perceptions have partial mediating influences too yet are not as important at social exchange perceptions. The research does make an important contribution to employee-organization linkages and social exchange theory. In addition, the research suggests the universality of social exchange theory.

SOURCE: L. J. Song, A. S. Tsui, and K. S. Long, "Unpacking Employee Responses to Organizational Exchange Mechanisms: The Role of Social and Economic Exchange Perceptions," *Journal of Management* 35 (2009): 56–93.

Contributions Just as each party to the exchange makes demands upon the other, each also has contributions to make to the relationship. These contributions are the basis for satisfying the demands expressed by the other party in the relationship. Employees are able to satisfy organizational demands through a range of contributions, including their skills, abilities, knowledge, energy, professional contacts, and native talents. As people grow and develop over time, they are able to increasingly satisfy the range of demands and expectations placed upon them by the organization.

In a similar fashion, organizations have a range of contributions available to the exchange relationship to meet individual needs. These contributions include salary, benefits, advancement opportunities, security, status, and social affiliation. Some organizations are richer in resources and better able to meet employee needs than others. Thus, one of the concerns that individuals and organizations alike have is whether the relationship is a fair deal or an equitable arrangement for both members. What we see in the Science feature is a study of social and economic exchange in the People's Republic of China.

6 Describe how inequity influences motivation and can be resolved.

Adams's Theory of Inequity

Blau's and Etzioni's ideas about social process and exchange provide a context for understanding fairness, equity, and inequity in work relationships. Stacy Adams explicitly developed the idea that *inequity* in the social exchange process is an important motivator. Adams's theory of inequity suggests that people are motivated when they find themselves in situations of inequity or unfairness.[62] Inequity occurs when a person receives more, or less, than the person believes is deserved based on

inequity
The situation in which a person perceives he or she is receiving less than he or she is giving, or is giving less than he or she is receiving.

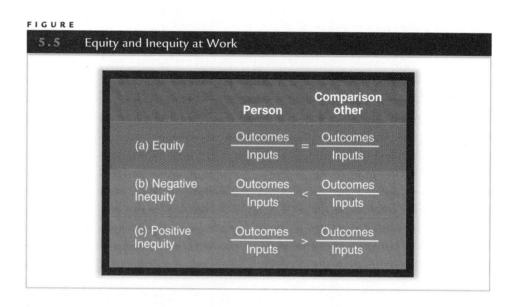

5.5   Equity and Inequity at Work

	Person	Comparison other
(a) Equity	$\dfrac{\text{Outcomes}}{\text{Inputs}}$ =	$\dfrac{\text{Outcomes}}{\text{Inputs}}$
(b) Negative Inequity	$\dfrac{\text{Outcomes}}{\text{Inputs}}$ <	$\dfrac{\text{Outcomes}}{\text{Inputs}}$
(c) Positive Inequity	$\dfrac{\text{Outcomes}}{\text{Inputs}}$ >	$\dfrac{\text{Outcomes}}{\text{Inputs}}$

effort and/or contribution. Inequity leads to the experience of tension, and tension motivates a person to act in a manner to resolve the inequity.

When does a person know that the situation is inequitable or unfair? Adams suggests that people examine the contribution portion of the exchange relationship just discussed. Specifically, individuals consider their inputs (their own contributions to the relationship) and their outcomes (the organization's contributions to the relationship). They then calculate an input/outcome ratio, which they compare with that of a generalized or comparison other. Figure 5.5 shows one equity situation and two inequity situations, one negative and one positive. For example, inequity in (b) could occur if the comparison other earned a higher salary, and inequity in (c) could occur if the person had more vacation time, in both cases all else being equal. Although not illustrated in the example, nontangible inputs, like emotional investment, and nontangible outcomes, like job satisfaction, may well enter into a person's equity equation.

Pay inequity has been a particularly thorny issue for women in some professions and companies. Eastman Kodak and other companies have made real progress in addressing the problem through pay equity.[63] As organizations become increasingly international, it may be difficult to determine pay and benefit equity/inequity across national borders.

Adams would consider the inequity in Figure 5.5(b) to be a first level of inequity. A more severe, second level of inequity would occur if the comparison other's inputs were lower than the person's. Inequalities in one (inputs or outcomes) coupled with equality in the other (inputs or outcomes) are experienced as a less severe inequity than inequalities in both inputs and outcomes. Adams's theory, however, does not provide a way of determining if some inputs (such as effort or experience) or some outcomes are more important or weighted more than others, such as a degree or certification.

The Resolution of Inequity

Once a person establishes the existence of an inequity, a number of strategies can be used to restore equity to the situation. Adams's theory provides seven basic strategies: (1) alter the person's outcomes, (2) alter the person's inputs, (3) alter the comparison other's outcomes, (4) alter the comparison other's inputs, (5) change who is used as a comparison other, (6) rationalize the inequity, and (7) leave the organizational situation.

Within each of the first four strategies, a wide variety of tactics can be employed. For example, if an employee has a strategy to increase his or her income by $11,000 per year to restore equity, the tactic might be a meeting between the employee and his or her manager concerning the issue of salary equity. The person would present relevant data on the issue. Another tactic would be to work with the company's compensation specialists. A third tactic would be to bring the matter before an equity committee in the company. A fourth tactic would be to seek advice from the legal department.

The selection of a strategy and a set of tactics is a sensitive issue with possible long-term consequences. In this example, a strategy aimed at reducing the comparison other's outcomes may have the desired short-term effect of restoring equity while having adverse long-term consequences in terms of morale and productivity. Similarly, the choice of legal tactics may result in equity but have the long-term consequence of damaged relationships in the workplace. Therefore, as a person formulates the strategy and tactics to restore equity, the range of consequences of alternative actions must be taken into account. Hence, not all strategies or tactics are equally preferred. The equity theory does not include a hierarchy predicting which inequity reduction strategy a person will or should choose.

Field studies on equity theory suggest that it may help explain important organizational behaviors. For example, one study found that workers who perceived compensation decisions as equitable displayed greater job satisfaction and organizational commitment.[64] In addition, equity theory may play an important role in labor–management relationships with regard to union-negotiated benefits.

New Perspectives on Equity Theory

Since the original formulation of the theory of inequity, now usually referred to as equity theory, a number of revisions have been made in light of new theories and research. One important theoretical revision proposes three types of individuals based on preferences for equity.[65] *Equity sensitives* are those people who prefer equity based on the originally formed theory. Equity sensitivity contributes significantly to variation in free time spent working.[66] *Benevolents* are people who are comfortable with an equity ratio less than that of their comparison other, as exhibited in the Calvinistic heritage of the Dutch.[67] These people may be thought of as givers. *Entitleds* are people who are comfortable with an equity ratio greater than that of their comparison other, as exhibited by some offspring of the affluent who want and expect more.[68] These people may be thought of as takers. Females and minorities have not always been equitably treated in business and commerce.

Research on organizational justice has a long history.[69] One study suggests that a person's organizational position influences self-imposed performance expectations.[70] Specifically, a two-level move up in an organization with no additional pay creates a higher self-imposed performance expectation than a one-level move up with modest additional pay. Similarly, a two-level move down in an organization with no reduction in pay creates a lower self-imposed performance expectation than a one-level move down with a modest decrease in pay. In addition, procedural justice can predict task performance, though the effect can be influenced by intrinsic motivation.[71]

One of the unintended consequences of inequity and organizational injustice is dysfunctional behavior. Organizational injustice caused by payment inequity can even lead to insomnia, though the effects are reduced by training in interactional justice.[72] More seriously, workplace injustice can trigger aggressive reactions or other forms of violent and deviant behavior that do harm to both individuals and the organization. Fortunately, only a small number of individuals respond to such unfairness through dysfunctional behavior.[73]

equity sensitive
An individual who prefers an equity ratio equal to that of his or her comparison other.

benevolent
An individual who is comfortable with an equity ratio less than that of his or her comparison other.

entitled
An individual who is comfortable with an equity ratio greater than that of his or her comparison other.

Although most studies of equity theory take a short-term perspective, equity comparisons over the long term should be considered as well. Increasing, decreasing, or constant experiences of inequity over time may have very different consequences for people.[74] For example, do increasing experiences of inequity have a debilitating effect on people? In addition, equity theory may help companies implement two-tiered wage structures, such as the one used by American Airlines in the early 1990s. In a two-tiered system, one group of employees receives different pay and benefits than another group. A study of 1,935 rank-and-file members in one retail chain using a two-tiered wage structure confirmed the predictions of equity theory.[75] The researchers suggest that unions and management may want to consider work location and employment status (part-time versus full-time) prior to the implementation of a two-tiered system.

EXPECTANCY THEORY OF MOTIVATION

7 Describe the expectancy theory of motivation.

Whereas equity theory focuses on a social exchange process, Vroom's expectancy theory of motivation focuses on personal perceptions of the performance process. His theory is founded on the basic notions that people desire certain outcomes of behavior and performance, which may be thought of as rewards or consequences of behavior, and that they believe there are relationships between the effort they put forth, the performance they achieve, and the outcomes they receive. Expectancy theory is a cognitive process theory of motivation.

The key constructs in the expectancy theory of motivation are the *valence* of an outcome, *expectancy*, and *instrumentality*.[76] Valence is the value or importance one places on a particular reward. Expectancy is the belief that effort leads to performance (e.g., "If I try harder, I can do better"). Instrumentality is the belief that performance is related to rewards (e.g., "If I perform better, I will get more pay"). A model for the expectancy theory notions of effort, performance, and rewards is depicted in Figure 5.6.

Valence, expectancy, and instrumentality are all important to a person's motivation. Expectancy and instrumentality concern a person's beliefs about how effort, performance, and rewards are related. For example, a person may firmly believe that an increase in effort has a direct, positive effect on performance and that a reduced

valence
The value or importance one places on a particular reward.

expectancy
The belief that effort leads to performance.

instrumentality
The belief that performance is related to rewards.

FIGURE

5.6   An Expectancy Model for Motivation

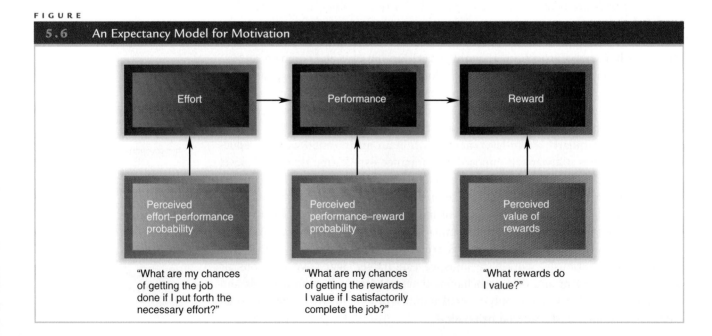

amount of effort results in a commensurate reduction in performance. Another person may have a very different set of beliefs about the effort–performance link. The person might believe that regardless of the amount of additional effort put forth, no improvement in performance is possible. Therefore, the perceived relationship between effort and performance varies from person to person and from activity to activity.

In a similar fashion, people's beliefs about the performance–reward link vary. One person may believe that an improvement in performance has a direct, positive effect on the rewards received, whereas another person may believe that an improvement in performance has no effect on the rewards received. Again, the perceived relationship between performance and rewards varies from person to person and from situation to situation. Where people attach symbolic meaning to monetary rewards, there is a positive effect over and above the economic value of the reward.[77] From a motivation perspective, it is the person's belief about the relationships between these constructs that is important, not the actual nature of the relationship. During volatile times in business, the performance–reward linkage may be confusing.

Expectancy theory has been used by managers and companies to design motivation programs.[78] Sometimes called *performance planning and evaluation systems*, these motivation programs are designed to enhance a person's belief that effort would lead to better performance and that better performance would lead to merit pay increases and other rewards. Valence and expectancy are particularly important in establishing priorities for people pursuing multiple goals.[79]

A person's motivation increases along with his or her belief that effort leads to performance and that performance leads to rewards, assuming the person wants the rewards. This is the third key idea within the expectancy theory of motivation. It is the idea that the valence, or value, that people place on various rewards varies. One person prefers salary to benefits, whereas another person prefers the reverse. All people do not place the same value on each reward. Expectancy theory has been used in a wide variety of contexts, including test-taking motivation among students.[80]

Motivational Problems

Within the expectancy theory framework, motivational problems stem from three basic causes: disbelief in a relationship between effort and performance, disbelief in a relationship between performance and rewards, and lack of desire for the rewards offered. Interestingly, defensive pessimism may motivate if the act of worrying that it triggers leads to an active planning process that reduces anxiety and prevents performance problems.[81]

If the motivational problem is related to the person's belief that effort will not result in performance, the solution lies in altering this belief. The person can be shown how an increase in effort, or an alteration in the kind of effort put forth, can be converted into improved performance. For example, the textbook salesperson who does not believe more calls (effort) will result in greater sales (performance) might be shown how to distinguish departments with high-probability sales opportunities from those with low-probability sales opportunities. Hence, more calls (effort) can be converted into greater sales (performance).

If the motivational problem is related to the person's belief that performance will not result in rewards, the solution lies in altering this belief. The person can be shown how an increase in performance or a somewhat altered form of performance will be converted into rewards. For example, the textbook salesperson who does not believe greater sales (performance) will result in overall higher commissions

(rewards) might be shown computationally or graphically that a direct relationship does exist. Hence, greater sales (performance) are directly converted into higher commissions (rewards).

If the motivational problem is related to the value the person places on, or the preference the person has for, certain rewards, the solution lies in influencing the value placed on the rewards or altering the rewards themselves. For example, the textbook salesperson may not particularly want higher commissions, given the small incremental gain he would receive at his tax level. In this case, the company might establish a mechanism for sheltering commissions from being taxed or alternative mechanisms for deferred compensation.

Research results on expectancy theory have been mixed.[82] The theory has been shown to predict job satisfaction accurately.[83] However, the theory's complexity makes it difficult to test the full model, and the measures of instrumentality, valence, and expectancy have only weak validity.[84] In addition, measuring the expectancy constructs is time consuming, and the values for each construct change over time for an individual. Finally, a theory assumes the individual is totally rational and acts as a minicomputer, calculating probabilities and values. In reality, the theory may be more complex than people as they typically function.

Motivation and Moral Maturity

Expectancy theory would predict that people work to maximize their personal outcomes. This is consistent with Adam Smith's ideas of working for one's own self-interest. Ultimately, Smith and expectancy theories believe that people work to benefit themselves alone. Expectancy theory would not explain altruistic behavior for the benefit of others. Therefore, it may be necessary to consider an individual's *moral maturity* in order to better understand altruistic, fair, and equitable behavior. Moral maturity is the measure of a person's cognitive moral development, which was discussed in Chapter 4. Morally mature people act and behave based on universal ethical principles, whereas morally immature people act and behave based on egocentric motivations.[85]

Cultural Differences in Motivation

8 Describe the cultural differences in motivation.

Most motivation theories in use today have been developed by, and are about, Americans.[86] When researchers have examined the universality of these theories, they have found cultural differences, at least with regard to Maslow's, McClelland's, and Herzberg's theories. For example, while self-actualization may be the pinnacle need for Americans in Maslow's need hierarchy, security may be the most important need for people in cultures such as Greece and Japan who have a high need to avoid uncertainty.[87] Although achievement is an important need for Americans, research noted earlier in the chapter suggested that other cultures do not value achievement as much as Americans do.

The two-factor theory has been tested in other countries as well. Results in New Zealand did not replicate the results found in the United States; supervision and interpersonal relationships were important motivators in New Zealand rather than hygienic factors as in America.[88] Equity theory is being examined in cross-cultural contexts, leading to a reexamination of equity preferences, selection of referent others, and reactions to inequity.[89] Finally, expectancy theory may hold up very nicely in cultures that value individualism but break down in more collectivist cultures that value cooperative efforts. In collectivist cultures, rewards are more closely tied to group and team efforts, thus rendering unnecessary the utility of expectancy theory.

moral maturity
The measure of a person's cognitive moral development.

Diversity Dialogue

Balance: Not Just for Working Moms Anymore

"Once upon a time—several decades ago—there was a clear divide between the roles of mothers and fathers. Mothers stayed home and took care of the kids and fathers went to work." That was the lead-in to an ABC television news story in June 2007. According to the story, the number of mothers working outside the home doubled to 80 percent in the past forty years. This increase of women in the workforce has led many men to break from their traditional roles as the sole breadwinners of the family and embrace their new roles as "co-parents."

Bryan and Lisa Levey of Lexington, Massachusetts, are prime examples of how gender roles have converged. They both have careers yet they both share equally in the household duties—cooking, doing the laundry, helping with homework, and chauffeuring their two young children. Sharing the responsibilities takes the pressure off Lisa to be the primary caregiver and Bryan to be the primary breadwinner. Says Bryan,

"Having the work/life balance is very critical to both of our [his and Lisa's] happiness."

Bryan's happiness has not come without a price, however. He has had to forgo at least one promotion in order to spend less time at the office and more time at home with his family. Bryan is fine with the choices that he's made. "Maybe I could have been at the top of a business at a young age, but I probably wouldn't have been very happy, so what's the point?"

1. What effect will gender convergence have on the ways in which companies motivate and reward its employees?
2. Do you think men who have chosen to spend more time at home will be stigmatized at work for the choice they've made? Why or why not? If so, how can they address such stigmatization?

SOURCE: B. Stark, "Dad: 'I Can't Stay for That Meeting,'" *ABC News* (June 16, 2007), http://abcnews.go.com.

MANAGERIAL IMPLICATIONS: MANY WAYS TO MOTIVATE PEOPLE

Managers must realize that all motivation theories are not equally good or equally useful. The later motivation theories, such as the equity and expectancy theories, may be more scientifically sound than earlier theories, such as the two-factor theory. Nevertheless, the older theories of motivation have conceptual value, show us the importance of human needs, and provide a basis for the later theories. The individual, internal theories of motivation and the individual–environment interaction process theories uniquely contribute to our overall understanding of human behavior and motivation at work.

Managers cannot assume they understand employees' needs. They should recognize the variety of needs that motivate employee behavior and ask employees for input to better understand their needs. Individual employees differ in their needs, and managers should be sensitive to ethnic, national, gender, and age differences in this regard. Employees with high needs for power must be given opportunities to exercise influence, and employees with high needs for achievement must be allowed to excel at work.

Managers can increase employee motivation by training (increased perceptions of success because of increased ability), coaching (increased confidence), and task assignments (increased perceptions of success because of more experience). Managers should ensure that rewards are contingent on good performance and that valued rewards, such as time off or flexible work schedules, are available. Managers must understand what their employees want.

Finally, managers should be aware that morally mature employees are more likely to be sensitive to inequities at work. At the same time, these employees are less likely to be selfish or self-centered and more likely to be concerned about equity issues for all employees. Morally mature employees will act ethically for the common good of all employees and the organization.

LOOKING BACK: DELOITTE

A Lattice, not a Ladder

© Clive Sawyer/Alamy

When Deloitte's UK operations hit nearly $4 billion in revenues, everyone received about a $2,000 bonus, a bottle of champagne at Christmas, and an extra day off. Those were the good times. How about the hard times?[90] Both for the hard times and for the changing generational differences and needs of people, Deloitte needs to look at meeting different kinds of employee needs. A recession is an opportune time for a company to explore creative ways to manage and lead people. Deloitte engaged in experimentation with reduced hours, unpaid furloughs, and lateral career moves. Crises are times in which to seek out new opportunities while being attentive to the dangers and pitfalls that are most often the focus. Going up the career ladder in hard times may be difficult, even impossible, but is it a dead-end at work?

People's needs change because of circumstances and because of life demands. Therefore, after some experimentation, Deloitte implemented a Mass Career Customization (MCC) Program as a way to motivate talented women and men to remain in the workforce. Rather than being stuck with the pressure of a career ladder, Deloitte employees may move up, down, or across what is a career lattice, depending on their life goals. Lattice is a career-path metaphor much preferred by Deloitte vice chair Cathy Benko. The MCC concept worked wonders for Deloitte tax accountant Chris Keehn in the Chicago office who was frustrated by the very long hours that cut into time with his four-year-old daughter. With support of his senior manager and two of Deloitte's partners, Keehn shifted gears and began telecommuting four days each week.

Deloitte is displaying flexibility in Chicago just as we saw it doing in the UK. The key to the success of MCC arrangements is a win-win outcome of positive social exchanges. At the center of the concept is the employee's life goal(s). What do you want most? Answering that question is a key to the Deloitte program. Career customization is not for everyone. About 10 percent of Deloitte employees "dial-up" or "dial-down" their career at any given point, but 80 percent of employees want the flexibility. Each employee's lattice is nailed together by twice-a-year evaluations that consider career targets and larger life goals. Career customization is especially good in meeting the needs of millennials who want more work-life balance, young parents like Keehn who want more time with children, and boomers who are easing into retirement. Deloitte focuses on and appreciates its people.

Chapter Summary

1. Early economic theories of motivation emphasized extrinsic incentives as the basis for motivation and technology as a force multiplier.

2. Maslow's hierarchy of needs theory of motivation was the basis for McGregor's Theory X and Theory Y assumptions about people at work.

3. According to McClelland, the needs for achievement, power, and affiliation are learned needs that differ among diverse cultures.

4. The two-factor theory found that the presence of motivation factors led to job satisfaction, and the presence of hygiene factors prevented job dissatisfaction.

5. New ideas in motivation emphasize eustress, hope, positive energy, and full engagement.

6. Social exchange theory holds that people form calculated working relationships and expect fair, equitable, ethical treatment.

7. Expectancy theory says that effort is the basis for motivation and that people want their effort to lead to performance and rewards.

8. Theories of motivation are culturally bound, and differences occur among nations.

Key Terms

benevolent (p. 169)
entitled (p. 169)
equity sensitive (p. 169)
eustress (p. 164)
expectancy (p. 170)
hygiene factor (p. 160)
inequity (p. 167)

instrumentality (p. 170)
moral maturity (p. 172)
motivation (p. 152)
motivation factor (p. 160)
need for achievement (p. 159)
need for affiliation (p. 159)
need for power (p. 159)

need hierarchy (p. 155)
psychoanalysis (p. 153)
self-interest (p. 154)
Theory X (p. 157)
Theory Y (p. 157)
valence (p. 170)

Review Questions

1. How can knowledge of motivation theories help managers?

2. What are the five categories of motivational needs described by Maslow? Give an example of how each can be satisfied.

3. What are the Theory X and Theory Y assumptions about people at work? How do they relate to the hierarchy of needs?

4. What three manifest needs does McClelland identify?

5. How do hygiene and motivational factors differ? What are the implications of the two-factor theory for managers?

6. What are two new ideas in motivation that managers are using?

7. How is inequity determined by a person in an organization? How can inequity be resolved if it exists?

8. What are the key concepts in the expectancy theory of motivation?

Discussion and Communication Questions

1. What do you think are the most important motivational needs for the majority of people? Do you think your needs differ from those of most people?

2. At what level in Maslow's hierarchy of needs are you living? Are you basically satisfied at this level?

3. Assume you are leaving your current job to look for employment elsewhere. What will you look for that you do not have now? If you do not have a job, assume you will be looking for one soon. What are the most important factors you will seek?

4. If you were being inequitably paid in your job, which strategy do you think would be the most helpful to you in resolving the inequity? What tactics would you consider using?

5. Do you believe you can do a better job of working or studying than you are currently doing? Do you think you would get more pay and benefits or better grades if you did a better job? Do you care about the rewards (or grades) in your organization (or university)?

6. What important experiences have contributed to your moral and ethical development? Are you working to further your own moral maturity at this time?

7. (communication question) Prepare a memo describing the two employees you work with who most closely operate according to Theory X and Theory Y assumptions about human nature. Be as specific and detailed in your description as you can, using quotes and/or observational examples.

8. (communication question) Develop an oral presentation about the most current management practices in employee motivation. Find out what at least four different companies are doing in this area. Be prepared to compare these practices with the theory and research in the chapter.

9. (communication question) Interview a manager and prepare a memo summarizing the relative importance she or he places on the needs for achievement, power, and affiliation. Include (a) whether these needs have changed over time and (b) what job aspects satisfy these needs.

Ethical Dilemma

Bill Lawrence has been an employee at Huntington Manufacturing for nearly fifteen years; he's steadily worked his way up a frontline worker to management. Plaques and awards hang on the walls of his office, and he's received excellent remarks on past annual reviews.

In short, Bill was an exemplary employee. Until six months ago, the normally prompt Bill began arriving at least fifteen minutes late and now he is always the first to leave, whether the day's work was done or not. He stopped arriving to meetings with ideas fully formulated, and slowly he stopped offering ideas or comments. Bill had always been committed to working weekends during the times when labor was particularly busy, to make sure the products got out one way or another—now, Bill is content to sign a piece of paper and rest the project completion on hope and the efforts of the foremen beneath him.

Jim Donavan is Bill's direct supervisor, and is completely befuddled by the drastic changes in Bill. Jim's never had to worry about motivating Bill, because Bill was the first to energize everyone else on the team. But now Bill is not only not meeting his previous standard of achievement, he's falling below the minimum

standard of performance. Jim has always valued Bill as an employee, and beyond that, he personally likes Bill.

First, Jim tried simply talking with Bill about current goals and objectives, but Bill's performance has not changed. Jim reminded Bill frequently about how many people were depending on his leadership, but Bill did not change his work pattern. Jim wondered if, after fifteen years, Bill was finding himself bored in his current position, so Jim proposed a lateral move within Huntington or the opportunity for professional development. Neither have seemed to change Bill's behavior.

Jim knew that Bill's youngest child just left for college about six months ago, but Bill hadn't expressed any concern about that prior to the event. Jim wonders if there was something else going on at home that was deeply affecting his once model employee's motivation to achieve. Jim begins to wonder how much longer he could afford to retain Bill in his current situation?

Questions:

1. Using consequential, rule-based and character theories, evaluate Jim's options.

2. What should Jim do? Why?

Experiential Exercises

5.1 What Do You Need from Work?

This exercise provides an opportunity to discuss your basic needs and those of other students in your class. Refer back to You 5.2, and look over your ranking of the ten possible job reward factors. Think about basic needs you may have that are possibly work related and yet would not be satisfied by one or another of these ten job reward factors.

Step 1. The class will form into groups of approximately six members each. Each group elects a spokesperson and answers the following questions. The group should spend at least five minutes on the first question and make sure each member of the group makes a contribution. The second question will probably take longer for your group to answer, up to fifteen minutes. The spokesperson should be ready to share the group's answers.

a. *What important basic needs do you have that are not addressed by one or another of these ten job reward factors?* Members should focus on the whole range of needs discussed in the different need theories of motivation covered in Chapter 5. Develop a list of the basic needs overlooked by these ten factors.

b. *What is important to members of your group?* Rank-order all job reward factors (the original ten and any new ones your group came up with in Step 1) in terms of their importance for your group. If group members disagree about the rankings, take time to discuss the differences among group members. Work for consensus and also note points of disagreement.

Step 2. Each group will share the results of its answers to the questions in Step 1. Cross-team questions and discussion follow.

Step 3. If your instructor has not already shared the normative data for 1,000 employees and their supervisors mentioned in You 5.2, the instructor may do that at this time.

Step 4 (Optional). Your instructor may ask you to discuss the similarities and differences in your group's rankings with the employee and supervisory normative rankings. If so, spend some time addressing two questions.

a. *What underlying reasons do you think may account for the differences that exist?*

b. *How have the needs of employees and supervisors changed over the past twenty years? Are they likely to change in the future?*

5.2 What to Do?

According to Stacy Adams, the experience of inequity or social injustice is a motivating force for human behavior. This exercise provides you and your group with a brief scenario of an inequity at work. Your task is to consider feasible actions for redress of this inequity.

John and Mary are full professors in the same medical school department of a large private university. As a private institution, neither the school nor the university makes the salaries and benefits of its faculty a matter of public record. Mary has pursued a long-term (fourteen years) career in the medical school, rising through the academic ranks while married to a successful businessman with whom she has raised three children. Her research and teaching contributions have been broad ranging and award winning. John joined the medical school within the last three years and was recruited for his leading-edge contribution to a novel line of research on a new procedure. Mary thought he was probably attracted with a comprehensive compensation package, yet she had no details until an administrative assistant gave her some information about salary and benefits a month ago. Mary learned that John's base contract salary is 16 percent higher than hers ($250,000 versus $215,000), that he was awarded an incentive pay component for the commercialization of his new procedure, and that he was given an annual discretionary travel budget of $35,000 and a membership in an exclusive private club. Mary is in a quandary about what to do. Given pressures from the board of trustees to hold down costs associated with public and private pressure to keep tuition increases low, Mary wonders how to begin to close this $70,000 inequity gap.

Step 1. Working in groups of six, discuss the equity issues in this medical school department situation using the text material on social exchange and equity theory. Do the outcome differences here appear to be based on gender, age, performance, or marital status? Do you need more information? If so, what would it be?

Step 2. Consider each of the seven strategies for the resolution of inequity as portrayed in this situation. Which ones are feasible to pursue based on what you know? Which ones are not feasible? Why? What are the likely consequences of each strategy or course of action? What would you advise Mary to do?

Step 3. Once your group has identified feasible resolution strategies, choose the best strategy. Next, develop a specific plan of action for Mary to follow in attempting to resolve the inequity so that she can achieve the experience and reality of fair treatment at work.

Step 4 (Optional). Your group may be asked to share its preferred strategy for this situation and your rationale for it.

BizFlix | Friday Night Lights (I)

The Odessa, Texas passion for Friday night high school football (Permian High Panthers) comes through clearly in this cinematic treatment of H. G. (Buzz) Bissinger's well-regarded book of the same title.[1] Coach Gary Gaines (Billy Bob Thornton) leads them to the 1988 semifinals where they must compete against a team of much larger players. Fast-moving pace in the football sequences and a slower pace in the serious, introspective sequences give this film many fine moments.

Motivation: "Can you get the job done, Mike?"

This scene starts with a panning shot of the Winchell's house. Coach Gaines says to Mike Winchell (Lucas Black), "Can you get the job done, Mike?" The scene follows a harsh practice and Mike talking to someone from a telephone booth. The film continues with the Odessa-Permian vs. Cooper football game.

What to Watch for and Ask Yourself

- This chapter defined motivation as "the process of arousing and sustaining goal-directed behavior." Does Mike Winchell show the characteristics of this definition early in the scene? Do you expect him to show any of the characteristics after the scene ends and he returns to the team?

- Which needs discussed earlier in this chapter does Mike appear focused on early in the scene? Which needs can become his focus later in the scene? See the "The Hierarchy of Needs" and "ERG Theory" sections earlier in this chapter for some suggestions.

- Apply "McClelland's Need Theory" to this scene. Which parts of that theory appear in this scene? Give specific examples.

- "Cultural Differences," to gain some insights about these questions.

Workplace Video | Flight 001: Motivating Employees

All retail jobs are not created equal. Just ask Amanda Shank. At a previous job, a store-owner bluntly told her, "You're just a number. You can be replaced at any time." Shank said, "When you're told something like that, why would you want to put any effort in?" That sort of callous treatment is hardly an incentive. Luckily, after landing a job at Flight 001, Shank started to feel motivated again.

Flight 001 cofounder Brad John frequently visits his New York stores to talk with staff about what's happening. While visiting Shank's Brooklyn store, where she had recently been promoted to assistant store manager, John asked if customers were shopping differently after the airlines had added new fees for checked luggage. Shank confirmed John's suspicions and gave him a full report along with recommendations for how they might make adjustments in inventory and merchandising.

Shank is thrilled to have found a place where she can make a contribution and be challenged. "At this company they make an effort to show you you're appreciated; you have a say in what goes on. You're given compliments and feedback about what you could be better at," she explained.

---

[1]J. Craddock, ed., *VideoHound's Golden Movie Retriever* (Detroit: Gale Cengage Learning, 2008), 368.

Although growth opportunities might seem limited in retail, store leader Claire Rainwater involves crew members in projects that use their strengths. If someone excels at organization and operations, she asks that person to identify and implement an improvement that excites him or her. She gives visually talented associates free reign to create new merchandising displays. Rainwater could easily provide direction on how to approach these tasks, but she allows her crew members the autonomy to determine how they want to approach and execute tasks, which ultimately creates a greater sense of empowerment and engagement.

Although retail offers careers, crew development chief Emily Griffin says that the industry is temporary for many people. Most associates just want to make some money while pursuing other interests as students, photographers, musicians, etc. Usually Griffin can tell which associates are passing through and who might stick around. What is interesting is that when she started at Flight 001, Griffin thought she was passing through.

Discussion Questions

1. According to Maslow's hierarchy, which basic needs did Shank's old boss fail to meet?

2. How might feeling underpaid affect the work of a Flight 001 associate?

3. Speculate the possible reasons Griffin stayed at Flight 001 to pursue a career.

Case

Controversial Retention Bonuses at AIG

American International Group (AIG), a behemoth insurance and financial services company, became notoriously famous in early 2009 for the payment of $165 million in retention bonuses to employees in its Financial Products unit—the business unit that was instrumental in bringing AIG to its knees and necessitating the infusion of many billions of dollars in U.S. government bailout money, beginning in September 2008. Although the near collapse of AIG was significantly influenced by "soured trades entered into by the company's Financial Products division," the operations of other AIG units, such as the financial gambles of its 2,000-employee Investments unit, helped cripple the company as well.[1]

Rapidly mounting financial losses had been occurring in the Financial Products unit for some time. Consequently, AIG decided to unwind the business and shut it down. In early 2008, employees in the Financial Products unit were asked to remain with the company through the unit's shutdown and, essentially, to work themselves out of a job.[2] To entice talented employees to stay and work through the shutdown, a contractual retention bonus plan was instituted.[3] According to a report in the *Washington Post*, the Financial Products employees were repeatedly assured, subsequent to the plan's implementation decision being made in March 2008, that AIG would honor these contractual obligations.[4]

The bonus plan was highly favorable to AIG's Financial Products employees—and the bonuses were not really linked to the employees' performance. The unit's employees were paid bonuses totaling $423 million in 2007, despite a paper loss of $11.5 billion on toxic real estate assets.[5] The 2008 bonus plan, which was approved in March of that year by the board of AIG's Financial Products unit just as the unit's losses were beginning to surface,[6] was "designed to kick in without regard to paper losses."[7] For 2008, paper losses on the toxic real estate assets ballooned to $28.6 billion, and total losses were more than $40 billion.[8]

According to New York Attorney General Andrew Cuomo, who was threatening legal action against AIG, seventy-three Financial Products employees received $1 million or more in bonus payments. The top recipient, identified by the *Wall Street Journal* as Douglas Poling, received more than $6.4 million, whereas the next half-dozen top bonus recipients got more than $4 million each. In addition, another fifteen employees received $2 million or more, and fifty-one other employees received $1 million or more.[9] "Of those people collecting more than $1 million, eleven have already left the company, Mr. Cuomo's office said."[10]

When the retention bonuses were paid in March 2009, the U.S. Congress, President Obama's administration, and the public were outraged. Under intense political pressure, AIG's CEO Edward Liddy, who was working for only $1 a year, asked the "bonus recipients to cough up half their pay, despite fearing that resignations would follow."[11] In defense of the bonuses, however, Gerry Pasciucco, head of the Financial Products unit, observed that the "top bonus recipient, Douglas Poling, had successfully sold off several holdings in his area of responsibility, infrastructure and energy investments. He's done an excellent job at the task of unwinding his book, of realizing value."[12]

In the ensuing emotionally charged days, employees of the Financial Products unit pondered what to do. According to one account, "employees have huddled in small groups in conference rooms off the division's main trading floor in Wilton, Conn., debating what to do. Some have expressed worries about retaliation. One employee said he had instructed his wife to call the police in the event his identity became known and a news truck appeared at his home. Others commiserated that their children have been verbally abused in school. Employees have passed around emails from colleagues who opposed returning the payments."[13]

Some Financial Products employees decided to return their bonuses. Mr. Poling indicated he intended to return his bonus.[14] "Fifteen of the top 20 recipients of the retention bonuses have agreed to give back a total of more than $30 million in payments."[15]

Others Financial Products employees opted to keep their bonuses, perhaps the most notable of whom is Jake DeSantis, a Financial Products unit executive who received an after-tax bonus of $742,006.40. On March 25, 2009, in an op-ed contribution to the *New York*

Times, DeSantis published an open letter to AIG's CEO, Edward Liddy, wherein he resigned his AIG position. DeSantis's letter read in part:

> After 12 months of hard work dismantling the company—during which A.I.G. reassured us many times we would be rewarded in March 2009—we in the financial products unit have been betrayed by A.I.G. and are being unfairly persecuted by elected officials. In response to this, I will now leave the company. . . . I take this action after 11 years of dedicated, honorable service to A.I.G. I can no longer effectively perform my duties in this dysfunctional environment, nor am I being paid to do so. Like you, I was asked to work for an annual salary of $1, and I agreed out of a sense of duty to the company and to the public officials who have come to its aid. Having now been let down by both, I can no longer justify spending 10, 12, 14 hours a day away from my family for the benefit of those who have let me down.[16]

With respect to his intention to not return the retention bonus, DeSantis wrote,

> I have decided to donate 100 percent of the effective after-tax proceeds of my retention payment directly to organizations that are helping people who are suffering from the global downturn. This is not a tax-deduction gimmick; I simply believe that I at least deserve to dictate how my earnings are spent, and do not want to see them disappear back into the obscurity of A.I.G.'s or the federal government's budget. Our earnings have caused such a distraction for so many from the more pressing issues our country faces, and I would like to see my share of it benefit those truly in need.[17]

DeSantis's op-ed piece stimulated much discussion regarding the proper response to the retention bonus fiasco. Did DeSantis do the right thing?

Discussion Questions

1. What types of work behaviors did AIG intend to encourage through its retention bonus plan?

2. Which needs seem to be important to the employees of AIG's Financial Products unit?

3. Using the model of the individual–organizational exchange relationship, explain the relationship that employees of AIG's Financial Products unit believed they had with the company. How was this exchange relationship violated?

4. Which motivation theory do you think has the most relevance for understanding the responses of the Financial Product employees to the implementation and unraveling of the retention bonus plan? Explain the reasoning behind your answer.

5. The amount of compensation earned by executives—as well as by professional athletes and famous actors/actresses and musicians—often sparks emotionally charged debate. Do you believe the $1 million plus retention bonuses received by seventy-three employees of AIG's Financial Products was excessive? Why or why not?

6. What would you have done if you were one of the seventy-three Financial Products employees who received a retention bonus of $1 million or more? Explain the reasoning behind your answer.

SOURCE: This case was written by Michael K. McCuddy, The Louis S. and Mary L. Morgal Chair of Christian Business Ethics and Professor of Management, College of Business Administration, Valparaiso University.

6

Learning and Performance Management

LEARNING OBJECTIVES

After reading this chapter, you should be able to do the following:

1 Define *learning, reinforcement, punishment, extinction*, and *goal setting.*

2 Distinguish between classical and operant conditioning.

3 Explain the use of positive and negative consequences of behavior in strategies of reinforcement and punishment.

4 Identify the purposes of goal setting and five characteristics of effective goals.

5 Describe 360-degree feedback.

6 Compare individual and team-oriented reward systems.

7 Describe strategies for correcting poor performance.

Nordstrom salespeople are motivated to give extraordinary service.

THINKING AHEAD: NORDSTROM

Motivation by Competition and Contest

Like competitive athletes, Nordstrom salespeople are motivated **NORDSTROM** in many ways to give extraordinary service because extraordinary service produces extraordinary sales volumes.[1] The image of competitive athletes may elicit an image of salespeople rushing around at a frantic, high-speed pace. This would be the wrong image. Think focused, eye-on-the-prize athletes who pay full and careful attention to the customer right in front of them. Nordstrom regularly distributes videotaped interviews with top salespeople who share tips and advice with others. Staff meetings become workshops in which associates compare, examine, and discuss sales techniques or perform skits in which one plays salesperson to a second associate's "customer." For example, the STEP (Sales Training Education Program) was developed by Washington State's regional personnel department for associates seeking information from salespeople and department managers.

Like competitive athletes, Nordstrom associates play in teams yet in a paradoxical way. The company insists that all associates be team players who compete on a level playing field while at the same time the company encourages everyone to become a star performer. The company must engage in well-managed competition so that associates are highly competitive yet do not destroy or damage each other in the competitive process. The company has done this from its very early days in business through a series of contexts. All of the Nordstroms were very keenly interested in sports, hence the athletic and competitive model. The aim is creative tension rather than destructive tension. Elmer Nordstrom recollected that early competitive process in which everyone worked hard to do their best so as not to be at the bottom of the list.

Star performers among team players? Yes, herein lays a creative paradox that energizes the Nordstrom culture. The company manages and motivates by contest. The company encourages creative tension among associates through publically available information about the performance of associates on their own floor and on sales floors around the country. Every associate can know where they stand and how their performance compares with others' performance. Twice a month, every associate's sales-per-hour numbers are posted for all to see; there is no place to hide in this wide open environment. Rewards follow performance. There are cash prizes, trips, and awards for outstanding sales-per-hour and sales-per-month performances. Associates can earn rewards the old-fashioned way; they earn them. Star performance means something very concrete and tangible within the Nordstrom environment. How about goal setting, recognition, and praise? We explore these and the rest of the Nordstrom story in the Looking Back feature.

This is the second of two chapters addressing motivation and behavior. Chapter 5 emphasized internal and process theories of motivation. This chapter focuses on external theories of motivation and factors in the work environment that influence good and bad performance, such as the competitiveness within Nordstrom's sales environment. The first section addresses learning theory and the use of reinforcement, punishment, and extinction at work. It also touches on Bandura's social learning theory and Jung's personality approach to learning. The second section presents theory, research, and practice related to goal setting in organizations. The third section addresses the definition and measurement of performance. The fourth section is concerned with rewarding performance. The fifth and concluding section addresses how to correct poor performance.

LEARNING IN ORGANIZATIONS

1 Define learning, reinforcement, punishment, extinction, and goal setting.

learning
A change in behavior acquired through experience.

Learning is a change in behavior acquired through experience. Learning may begin with the cognitive activity of developing knowledge about a subject, which then leads to a change in behavior. Alternatively, the behaviorist approach to learning assumes that observable behavior is a function of its consequences. According to the behaviorists, learning has its basis in classical and operant conditioning. Learning helps guide and direct motivated behavior.

Classical Conditioning

Classical conditioning is the process of modifying behavior so that a conditioned stimulus is paired with an unconditioned stimulus and elicits an unconditioned response. It is largely the result of the research on animals (primarily dogs) by the Russian physiologist Ivan Pavlov.[2] Pavlov's professional exchanges with Walter B. Cannon and other American researchers during the early 1900s led to the application of his ideas in the United States.[3] Classical conditioning builds on the natural consequence of an unconditioned response to an unconditioned stimulus. In dogs, this might be the natural production of saliva (unconditioned response) in response to the presentation of meat (unconditioned stimulus). By presenting a conditioned stimulus (e.g., a bell) simultaneously with the unconditioned stimulus (the meat), the researcher caused the dog to develop a conditioned response (salivation in response to the bell).

Classical conditioning may occur in a similar fashion in humans.[4] For example, a person working at a computer terminal may get lower back tension (unconditioned response) as a result of poor posture (unconditioned stimulus). If the person becomes aware of that tension only when the manager enters the work area (conditioned stimulus), then the person may develop a conditioned response (lower back tension) to the appearance of the manager.

Although this example is logical, classical conditioning has real limitations in its applicability to human behavior in organizations for at least three reasons. First, humans are more complex than dogs and less amenable to simple cause-and-effect conditioning. Second, the behavioral environments in organizations are complex and not very amenable to single stimulus–response manipulations. Third, complex human decision making makes it possible to override simple conditioning.

2 Distinguish between classical and operant conditioning.

Operant Conditioning

Operant conditioning is the process of modifying behavior through the use of positive or negative consequences following specific behaviors. It is based on the notion that behavior is a function of its consequences,[5] which may be either positive or negative. The consequences of behavior are used to influence, or shape, behavior through three strategies: reinforcement, punishment, and extinction.

Organizational behavior modification (O.B. Mod., commonly known as OBM) is a form of operant conditioning used successfully in a variety of organizations to shape behavior by Luthans and his colleagues.[6] The three types of consequences used in OBM to influence behavior are financial reinforcement, nonfinancial reinforcement, and social reinforcement. A major review of the research on the influence of OBM in organizations found that it had significant and positive influence on task performance in both manufacturing and service organizations, but that the effects were most powerful in manufacturing organizations.[7] In a study of pay for performance, more productive employees chose pay for performance over fixed compensation when given a choice.[8] However, regardless of which pay scheme employees chose, all produced more under a pay for performance scheme.

3 Explain the use of positive and negative consequences of behavior in strategies of reinforcement and punishment.

The Strategies of Reinforcement, Punishment, and Extinction

Reinforcement is used to enhance desirable behavior, and punishment and extinction are used to diminish undesirable behavior. The application of reinforcement theory is central to the design and administration of organizational reward systems. Well-designed reward systems help attract and retain the very best employees. Strategic rewards help motivate behavior, actions, and accomplishments, which advance the organization toward specific business goals.[9] Strategic rewards go beyond cash

classical conditioning
Modifying behavior so that a conditioned stimulus is paired with an unconditioned stimulus and elicits an unconditioned response.

operant conditioning
Modifying behavior through the use of positive or negative consequences following specific behaviors.

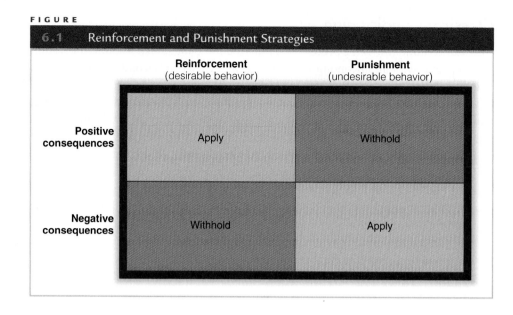

FIGURE

6.1   Reinforcement and Punishment Strategies

	Reinforcement (desirable behavior)	**Punishment** (undesirable behavior)
Positive consequences	Apply	Withhold
Negative consequences	Withhold	Apply

to include training and educational opportunities, stock options, and recognition awards such as travel. Strategic rewards are important positive consequences of people's work behavior.

Reinforcement and punishment are administered through the management of positive and negative consequences of behavior. *Positive consequences* are the results of a person's behavior that he or she finds attractive or pleasurable. They might include a pay increase, a bonus, a promotion, a transfer to a more desirable geographic location, or praise from a supervisor. *Negative consequences* are the results of a person's behavior that he or she finds unattractive or aversive. They might include disciplinary action, an undesirable transfer, a demotion, or harsh criticism from a supervisor. Positive and negative consequences must be defined for the person receiving them. Therefore, individual, gender, and cultural differences may be important in their classification.

The use of positive and negative consequences following a specific behavior either reinforces or punishes that behavior.[10] Thorndike's law of effect states that behaviors followed by positive consequences are more likely to recur, and behaviors followed by negative consequences are less likely to recur.[11] Figure 6.1 shows how positive and negative consequences may be applied or withheld in the strategies of reinforcement and punishment.

Reinforcement *Reinforcement* is the attempt to develop or strengthen desirable behavior by either bestowing positive consequences or withholding negative consequences. Positive reinforcement results from the application of a positive consequence following a desirable behavior. Bonuses paid at the end of successful business years are an example of positive reinforcement. Marriott International provides positive reinforcement by honoring ten to twenty employees each year with its J. Willard Marriott Award of Excellence. Each awardee receives a medallion engraved with the words that express the basic values of the company: dedication, achievement, character, ideals, effort, and perseverance. Nordstrom uses cash and other positive rewards to reinforce sales achievements, as we saw in the Thinking Ahead feature.

Negative reinforcement results from withholding a negative consequence when a desirable behavior occurs. For example, a manager who reduces an employee's pay (negative consequence) if the employee comes to work late (undesirable behavior) and refrains from doing so when the employee is on time (desirable behavior) has negatively reinforced the employee's on-time behavior. The employee avoids

positive consequences
Results of a behavior that a person finds attractive or pleasurable.

negative consequences
Results of a behavior that a person finds unattractive or aversive.

reinforcement
The attempt to develop or strengthen desirable behavior by either bestowing positive consequences or withholding negative consequences.

PART 2 INDIVIDUAL PROCESSES AND BEHAVIOR

6.1   Schedules of Reinforcement

Benefits	Description	Effects on Responding
Continuous	Reinforcer follows every response.	1. Steady high rate of performance as long as reinforcement follows every response 2. High frequency of reinforcement may lead to early satiation 3. Behavior weakens rapidly (undergoes extinction) when reinforcers are withheld 4. Appropriate for newly emitted, unstable, low-frequency responses
Intermittent	Reinforcer does not follow every response.	1. Capable of producing high frequencies of responding 2. Low frequency of reinforcement precludes early satiation 3. Appropriate for stable or high-frequency responses
Fixed Ratio	A fixed number of responses must be emitted before reinforcement occurs.	1. A fixed ratio of 1:1 (reinforcement occurs after every response) is the same as a continuous schedule 2. Tends to produce a high rate of response that is vigorous and steady
Variable Ratio	A varying or random number of responses must be emitted before reinforcement occurs.	Capable of producing a high rate of response that is vigorous, steady, and resistant to extinction
Fixed Interval	The first response after a specific period of time has elasped is reinforced.	Produces an uneven response pattern varying from a very slow, unenergetic response immediately following reinforcement to a very fast, vigorous response immediately preceding reinforcement
Variable Interval	The first response after varying or random periods of time have elapsed is reinforced.	Tends to produce a high rate of response that is vigorous, steady, and resistant to extinction

SOURCE: Table from *Organizational Behavior Modification* by Fred Luthans and Robert Kreitner. Copyright © 1985, p. 58, by Scott Foresman and Company and the authors. Reprinted by permission of the authors.

the negative consequence (a reduction in pay) by exhibiting the desirable behavior (being on time to work).

Either continuous or intermittent schedules of reinforcement may be used. These reinforcement schedules are described in Table 6.1. When managers design organizational reward systems, they consider not only the type of reinforcement but also how often the reinforcement should be provided.

Punishment *Punishment* is the attempt to eliminate or weaken undesirable behavior. It is used in two ways. One way to punish a person is to apply a negative consequence following an undesirable behavior. For example, a professional athlete who is excessively offensive to an official (undesirable behavior) may be ejected from a game (negative consequence). The other way to punish a person is to withhold a positive consequence following an undesirable behavior. For example, a salesperson who makes few visits to companies (undesirable behavior) and whose sales are well

punishment
The attempt to eliminate or weaken undesirable behavior by either bestowing negative consequences or withholding positive consequences.

below the quota (undesirable behavior) is likely to receive a very small commission check (positive consequence) at the end of the month.

One problem with punishment is that it may have unintended results. Because punishment is discomforting to the individual being punished, the experience of punishment may result in negative psychological, emotional, performance, or behavioral consequences. For example, the person being punished may become angry, hostile, depressed, or despondent. From an organizational standpoint, this result becomes important when the punished person translates negative emotional and psychological responses into negative actions. Threat of punishment can elicit fear, a management tool used by some leaders but not at Southwest Airlines, a company that emphasizes positive relationships.[12] Too much actual punishment may lead to a generalized negative response and decreased motivation to work better.[13]

Extinction An alternative to punishing undesirable behavior is *extinction*—the attempt to weaken a behavior by attaching no consequences (either positive or negative) to it. It is equivalent to ignoring the behavior. The rationale for using extinction is that a behavior not followed by any consequence is weakened. However, some patience and time may be needed for extinction to be effective.

Extinction may be practiced, for example, by not responding (no consequence) to the sarcasm (behavior) of a colleague. Extinction may be most effective when used in conjunction with the positive reinforcement of desirable behaviors. Therefore, in the example, the best approach might be to compliment the sarcastic colleague for constructive comments (reinforcing desirable behavior) while ignoring mocking comments (extinguishing undesirable behavior).

Extinction is not always the best strategy, however. In cases of dangerous behavior, punishment might be preferable to deliver a swift, clear lesson. It might also be preferable in cases of seriously undesirable behavior, such as employee embezzlement and other illegal or unethical behavior.

Bandura's Social Learning Theory

A social learning theory proposed by Albert Bandura is an alternative and complement to the behaviorist approaches of Pavlov and Skinner.[14] Bandura believes learning occurs through the observation of other people and the modeling of their behavior. Executives might teach their subordinates a wide range of behaviors, such as leader–follower interactions and stress management, by exhibiting these behaviors. Since employees look to their supervisors for acceptable norms of behavior, they are likely to pattern their own responses on the supervisor's.[15] For example, in the transfer of learning, a considerate or support style is more strongly related to employee motivation than is a structuring style.

Central to Bandura's social learning theory is the notion of *task-specific self-efficacy*, an individual's beliefs and expectancies about his or her ability to perform a specific task effectively. (Generalized self-efficacy was discussed in Chapter 3.) Individuals with high self-efficacy believe that they have the ability to get things done, that they are capable of putting forth the effort to accomplish the task, and that they can overcome any obstacles to their success. Self-efficacy is higher in a learning context than in a performance context, especially for individuals with a high learning orientation.[16] There are four sources of task-specific self-efficacy: prior experiences, behavior models (witnessing the success of others), persuasion from other people, and assessment of current physical and emotional capabilities.[17] Believing in one's own capability to get something done is an important facilitator of success. There is strong evidence that self-efficacy leads to high performance

extinction
The attempt to weaken a behavior by attaching no consequences to it.

task-specific self-efficacy
An individual's beliefs and expectancies about his or her ability to perform a specific task effectively.

on a wide variety of physical and mental tasks.[18] High self-efficacy has also led to success in breaking addictions, increasing pain tolerance, and recovering from illnesses. Conversely, success can enhance one's self-efficacy. For example, women who trained in physical self-defense increased their self-efficacy, both for specific defense skills and for coping in new situations.[19]

Alexander Stajkovic and Fred Luthans draw on Bandura's ideas of self-efficacy and social learning in expanding their original work in behavioral management and OBM into a more comprehensive framework for performance management.[20] Bandura saw the power of social reinforcement, recognizing that financial and material rewards often occur following, or in conjunction with, the approval of others, whereas undesirable experiences often follow social disapproval. Thus, self-efficacy and social reinforcement can be powerful influences over behavior and performance at work. A comprehensive review of 114 studies found that self-efficacy is positively and strongly related to work performance, especially for tasks that are not too complex.[21] Stajkovic and Luthans suggest that managers and supervisors can be confident that employees with high self-efficacy are going to perform well. The challenge managers face is how to select and develop employees so that they achieve high self-efficacy.

Managers can help employees in this process. The strongest way for an employee to develop self-efficacy is to succeed at a challenging task. Managers can help by providing job challenges, coaching and counseling for improved performance, and rewarding employees' achievements. Given the increasing diversity of the workforce, managers may want to target their efforts toward women and minorities in particular. Research has indicated that these groups tend to have lower than average self-efficacy.[22] Counterintuitively in a training context, self-efficacy was negatively related to motivation and exam performance for students taking a series of five class exams despite a significant positive relationship with exam performance at the between-person level for these students.[23]

Learning and Personality Differences

The cognitive approach to learning mentioned at the beginning of the chapter is based on the *Gestalt* school of thought and draws on Jung's theory of personality differences (discussed in Chapter 3). Two elements of Jung's theory have important implications for learning and subsequent behavior.

The first element is the distinction between introverted and extraverted people. Introverts need quiet time to study, concentrate, and reflect on what they are learning. They think best when they are alone. Extraverts need to interact with other people, learning through the process of expressing and exchanging ideas with others. They think best in groups and while they are talking.

The second element is the personality functions of intuition, sensing, thinking, and feeling. These functions are listed in Table 6.2, along with their implications for learning by individuals. The functions of intuition and sensing determine the individual's preference for information gathering. The functions of thinking and feeling determine how the individual evaluates and makes decisions about newly acquired information.[24] Each person has a preferred mode of gathering information and a preferred mode of evaluating and making decisions about that information. For example, an intuitive thinker may want to skim research reports about implementing total quality programs and then, based on hunches, decide how to apply the research findings to the organization. A sensing feeler may prefer viewing videotaped interviews with people in companies that implemented total quality programs and then identify people in the organization most likely to be receptive to the approaches presented.

6.2 Personality Functions and Learning

Personality Preference	Implications for Learning by Individuals
Information Gathering	
Intuitors	Prefer theoretical frameworks. Look for the meaning in material. Attempt to understand the grand scheme. Look for possibilities and interrelations.
Sensors	Prefer specific, empirical data. Look for practical applications. Attempt to master details of a subject. Look for what is realistic and doable.
Decision Making	
Thinkers	Prefer analysis of data and information. Work to be fair-minded and evenhanded. Seek logical, just conclusions. Do not like to be too personally involved.
Feelers	Prefer interpersonal involvement. Work to be tenderhearted and harmonious. Seek subjective, merciful results. Do not like objective, factual analysis.

SOURCE: O. Kroeger and J. M. Thuesen, *Type Talk: The 16 Personality Types That Determine How We Live, Love, and Work* (New York: Dell, 1989).

GOAL SETTING AT WORK

4 Identify the purposes of goal setting and five characteristics of effective goals.

Goal setting is the process of establishing desired results that guide and direct behavior. Goal-setting theory is based on laboratory studies, field research experiments, and comparative investigations by Edwin Locke, Gary Latham, John M. Ivancevich, and others.[25] Goals help crystallize the sense of purpose and mission that is essential to success at work. Priorities, purpose, and goals are important sources of motivation for people at work, often leading to collective achievement, even in difficult times. While goals have robust effects on performance, it is important to consider task demands that may influence the magnitude and direction of the effects.[26] We explore Nordstrom's unique approach to goal setting in the Looking Back feature at the end of the chapter. In The Real World 6.1, we see how Hyundai Motor Company (HMC) used goal setting to mount an impressive comeback.

Characteristics of Effective Goals

Various organizations define the characteristics of effective goals differently. For the former Sanger-Harris, a retail organization, the acronym SMART communicated the approach to effective goals. SMART stands for *Specific, Measurable, Attainable, Realistic,* and *Time-bound*. Five commonly accepted characteristics of effective goals are specific, challenging, measurable, time-bound, and prioritized.

Specific and challenging goals serve to cue or focus the person's attention on exactly what is to be accomplished and to arouse the person to peak performance. In a wide range of occupations, people who set specific, challenging goals consistently outperform those who have easy or unspecified goals, as shown in Figure 6.2. The unconscious may have a positive effect here too. Two studies of subconscious goal motivation found that subconscious goals significantly enhanced task performance for consciously difficult and do-best goals, though not for easy goals.[27] How difficult

goal setting
The process of establishing desired results that guide and direct behavior.

The Real World 6.1

Aggressive Goal Setting... and More

The history of the Korean automotive industry has been a "rags to riches" story beginning with the establishment of the Hyundai Motor Company in 1967 to assemble American-designed cars for local consumption. By 2005, it had become the sixth largest automobile producer in the world and a major competitor to GM, Ford, and Toyota. HMC's growth has been remarkable. No Korean companies had previous experience of automobile assembly and there were no supporting industries, yet within thirty years HMC has become one of the world's leading automobile manufacturer and the company used a practice of internally generated crises as a catalyst for organizational resilience. The company rebounded from failures and used aggressive goal setting. HMC set aggressive construction deadlines as goals for its five major overseas production facilities that composed its global production network. The company set demanding production targets as goals for its manufacturing workforce. The company set stringent quality benchmarks as goals for its vehicles. Ultimately, HMC had an overarching goal to become a Top Five global carmaker by 2007. That is aggressive goal setting. The company succeeded by learning from

Hyundai factory in Beijing, China.

© Gideon Mendel/Corbis

failures, localizing production, internally transferring experienced staff, and codifying previous experience. Learning from experience became a key enabling mechanism for the aggressive goal setting and ultimate company success.

SOURCE: B. Friel, "If at First You Don't Succeed: Globalized Production and Organizational Learning at the Hyundai Motor Company," *Asia Pacific Business Review* 15(2) (April 2009): 163–180.

FIGURE

6.2 Goal Level and Task Performance

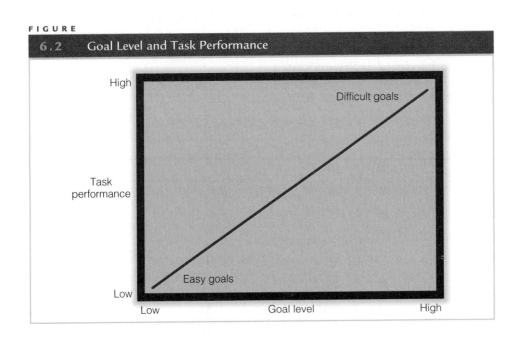

and challenging are your work or school goals? You 6.1 gives you an opportunity to evaluate your goals for five dimensions.

Measurable, quantitative goals are useful as a basis for feedback about goal progress. Qualitative goals are also valuable. The Western Company of North America (now part of BJ Services Company) allowed about 15 percent of a manager's goals to be of a qualitative nature.[28] A qualitative goal might be to improve relationships with customers. Further work might convert the qualitative goal into quantitative measures such as number of complaints or frequency of complimentary letters. In this case, however, the qualitative goal may well be sufficient and most meaningful.

Time-bound goals enhance measurability. The time limit may be implicit in the goal, or it may need to be made explicit. For example, without the six-month time limit, an insurance salesperson might think the sales goal is for the whole year rather than for six months. Many organizations work on standardized cycles, such as quarters or years, where very explicit time limits are assumed. If there is any uncertainty about the time period of the goal effort, the time limit should be explicitly stated.

The priority ordering of goals allows for effective decision making about resource allocation.[29] As time, energy, or other resources become available, a person can move down the list of goals in descending order. The key concern is with achieving the top-priority goals. Priority helps direct a person's efforts and behavior. Although these characteristics help increase motivation and performance, that is not the only function of goal setting in organizations. One new study of goal setting suggests that it may be a theory of ability as well as a theory of motivation, especially in a learning context versus a performance context.[30]

Goal setting serves one or more of three functions. First, it can increase work motivation and task performance.[31] Second, it can reduce the role stress that is associated with conflicting or confusing expectations.[32] Third, it can improve the accuracy and validity of performance evaluation.[33]

Increasing Work Motivation and Task Performance

Goals are often used to increase employee effort and motivation, which in turn improve task performance. The higher the goal, the better the performance; that is, people work harder to reach difficult goals. The positive relationship between goal difficulty and task performance is depicted in Figure 6.2.

Three important behavioral aspects of enhancing performance motivation through goal setting are employee participation, supervisory commitment, and useful performance feedback. Employee participation in goal setting leads to goal acceptance by employees. Goal acceptance is thought to lead to goal commitment and then to goal accomplishment. Special attention has been given to factors that influence commitment to difficult goals, such as participation in the process of setting the difficult goals.[34] Even in the case of assigned goals, goal acceptance and commitment are considered essential prerequisites to goal accomplishment.

Supervisory goal commitment is a reflection of the organization's commitment to goal setting. Organizational commitment is a prerequisite for successful goal-setting programs, such as management by objectives (MBO) programs.[35] The organization must be committed to the program, and the employee and supervisors must be committed to specific work goals as well as to the program. (MBO is discussed in more detail later in the chapter.)

You 6.1

Task–Goal Attribute Questionnaire

Listed below is a set of statements that may or may not describe the job or school objectives toward which you are presently working. Please read each statement carefully and rate each on a scale from 1 (agree completely) to 7 (disagree completely) to describe your level of agreement or disagreement with the statement. *Please answer all questions.*

_____ 1. I am allowed a high degree of influence in the determination of my work/school objectives.

_____ 2. I should not have too much difficulty in reaching my work/school objectives; they appear to be fairly easy.

_____ 3. I receive a considerable amount of feedback concerning my quantity of output on the job/in school.

_____ 4. Most of my coworkers and peers try to outperform one another on their assigned work/school goals.

_____ 5. My work/school objectives are very clear and specific; I know exactly what my job/assignment is.

_____ 6. My work/school objectives will require a great deal of effort from me to complete them.

_____ 7. I really have little voice in the formulation of my work/school objectives.

_____ 8. I am provided with a great deal of feedback and guidance on the quality of my work.

_____ 9. I think my work/school objectives are ambiguous and unclear.

_____ 10. It will take a high degree of skill and know-how on my part to attain fully my work/school objectives.

_____ 11. The setting of my work/school goals is pretty much under my own control.

_____ 12. My boss/instructors seldom let(s) me know how well I am doing on my work toward my work/school objectives.

_____ 13. A very competitive atmosphere exists among my peers and me with regard to attaining our respective work/school goals; we all want to do better than anyone else in attaining our goals.

_____ 14. I understand fully which of my work/school objectives are more important than others; I have a clear sense of priorities on these goals.

_____ 15. My work/school objectives are quite difficult to attain.

_____ 16. My supervisor/instructors usually ask(s) for my opinions and thoughts when determining my work/school objectives.

Scoring:

Place your response (1 through 7) in the space provided. For questions 7, 12, 9, and 2, subtract your response from 8 to determine your adjusted score. For each scale (e.g., participation in goal setting), add the responses and divide by the number of questions in the scale.

Participation in Goal Setting:
Question 1 _____
Question 7 (8 – _____) = _____
Question 11 _____
Question 16 _____
Total divided by 4 = _____

Feedback on Goal Effort:
Question 3 _____
Question 8 _____
Question 12 (8 – _____) = _____
Total divided by 3 = _____

Peer Competition:
Question 4 _____

Question 13 _____
Total divided by 2 = _____

Goal Specificity:
Question 5 _____
Question 9 (8 – _____) = _____
Question 14 _____
Total divided by 3 = _____

Goal Difficulty:
Question 2 (8 – _____) = _____
Question 6 _____
Question 10 _____
Question 15 _____
Total divided by 4 = _____

Interpreting your average scale scores: 6 or 7 is very high on this task–goal attribute. 4 is a moderate level on this task–goal attribute. 1 or 2 is very low on this task–goal attribute.

SOURCE: Adapted from R. M. Steers, "Factors Affecting Job Attitudes in a Goal-Setting Environment," *Academy of Management Journal* 19 (1976): 9. Permission conveyed through Copyright Clearance Center, Inc.

The supervisor plays a second important role by providing employees with interim performance feedback on progress toward goals. Performance feedback is most useful when the goals are specific, and specific goals improve performance most when interim feedback is given.[36] When done correctly, negative performance feedback can lead to performance improvement.[37] For example, assume an insurance salesperson has a goal of selling $500,000 worth of insurance in six months but has sold only $200,000 after three months. During an interim performance feedback session, the supervisor may help the salesperson identify his problem—that he is not focusing his calls on the likeliest prospects. This useful feedback coupled with the specific goal helps the salesperson better focus his efforts to achieve the goal. Feedback is most helpful when it is useful (helping the salesperson identify high-probability prospects) and timely (halfway through the performance period). Individuals with strong mastery motivation may focus particular attention on those areas with the most discrepancy from goal achievement as deadline near.[38]

Reducing Role Stress, Conflict, and Ambiguity

A second function of goal setting is to reduce the role stress associated with conflicting and confusing expectations. This is done by clarifying the task–role expectations communicated to employees. Supervisors, coworkers, and employees are all important sources of task-related information. A fourteen-month evaluation of goal setting in reducing role stress found that conflict, confusion, and absenteeism were all reduced through the use of goal setting.[39]

The improved role clarity resulting from goal setting may be attributable to improved communication between managers and employees. An early study of the MBO goal-setting program at Ford Motor Company found an initial 25 percent lack of agreement between managers and their bosses concerning the definition of the managers' jobs. Through effective goal-setting activities, this lack of agreement was reduced to about 5 percent.[40] At FedEx, managers are encouraged to include communication-related targets in their annual MBO goal-setting process.[41]

Improving Performance Evaluation

The third major function of goal setting is improving the accuracy and validity of performance evaluation. One of the best methods of doing so is to use *management by objectives (MBO)*—a goal-setting program based on interaction and negotiation between employees and managers. MBO programs have been pervasive in organizations for nearly thirty years.[42]

According to Peter Drucker, who originated the concept, the objectives-setting process begins with the employee writing an "employee's letter" to the manager. The letter explains the employee's general understanding of the scope of the manager's job, as well as the scope of the employee's own job, and lays out a set of specific objectives to be pursued over the next six months or year. After some discussion and negotiation, the manager and the employee finalize these items into a performance plan.

Drucker considers MBO a participative and interactive process. This does not mean that goal setting begins at the bottom of the organization. It means that goal setting is applicable to all employees, with lower level organizational members and professional staff having a clear influence over the goal-setting process.[43] (The performance aspect of goal setting is discussed in the next section of the chapter.)

management by objectives (MBO)
A goal-setting program based on interaction and negotiation between employees and managers.

Goal-setting programs have operated under a variety of names, including goals and controls at Purex (now part of Dial Corporation), work planning and review at Black & Decker and General Electric, and performance planning and evaluation at IBM. Most of these programs are designed to enhance performance,[44] especially when incentives are associated with goal achievement.

The two central ingredients in goal-setting programs are planning and evaluation. The planning component consists of organizational and individual goal setting. Organizational goal setting is an essential prerequisite to individual goal setting; the two must be closely linked for the success of both.[45] At FedEx, all individual objectives must be tied to the overall corporate objectives of people, service, and profit.

In planning, discretionary control is usually given to individuals and departments to develop operational and tactical plans to support the corporate objectives. The emphasis is on formulating a clear, consistent, measurable, and ordered set of goals to articulate *what* to do. It is also assumed that operational support planning helps determine *how* to do it. The concept of intention is used to encompass both the goal (*what*) and the set of pathways that lead to goal attainment (*how*), thus recognizing the importance of both what and how.[46]

The evaluation component consists of interim reviews of goal progress, conducted by managers and employees, and formal performance evaluation. The reviews are midterm assessments designed to help employees take self-corrective action. They are not designed as final or formal performance evaluations. The formal performance evaluation occurs at the close of a reporting period, usually once a year. To be effective, performance reviews need to be tailored to the business, capture what goes on in the business, and be easily changed when the business changes.[47]

Because goal-setting programs are somewhat mechanical by nature, they are most easily implemented in stable, predictable industrial settings. Although most programs allow for some flexibility and change, they are less useful in organizations where high levels of unpredictability exist, as in basic research and development, or where the organization requires substantial adaptation or adjustment. While overprescribing goal setting to solve every organizational problem is foolish, goal letting does remain an effective technique to motivate performance.[48] Finally, individual, gender, and cultural differences do not appear to threaten the success of goal-setting programs.[49] Thus, goal-setting programs may be widely applied and effective in a diverse workforce.

PERFORMANCE: A KEY CONSTRUCT

Goal setting is designed to improve work performance, an important organizational behavior directly related to the production of goods or the delivery of services. Performance is most often thought of as task accomplishment, the term *task* coming from Taylor's early notion of a worker's required activity.[50] Some early management research found performance standards and differential piece-rate pay to be key ingredients in achieving high levels of performance, while other early research found stress helpful in improving performance up to an optimum point.[51] Hence, outcomes and effort are both important for good performance. Predicting job performance has been a concern for over 100 years. Early theories around the time of World War I focused on the importance of intelligence and general mental ability (GMA). Research has found GMA highly predictive of job knowledge in both civilian and military jobs.[52] Equally important to predicting job performance is defining the term.

Performance Management

Performance management is a process of defining, measuring, appraising, providing feedback on, and improving performance.[53] The skill of defining performance in behavioral terms is an essential first step in the performance management process. Once defined, performance can be measured and assessed. This information about performance can then be fed back to the individual and used as a basis for setting goals and establishing plans for improving performance. Positive performance behaviors should be rewarded, and poor performance behaviors should be corrected. This section of the chapter focuses on defining, measuring, appraising, and providing feedback on performance. The last two sections of the chapter focus on rewarding, correcting, and improving performance.

Defining Performance

Performance must be clearly defined and understood by the employees who are expected to perform well at work. Performance in most lines of work is multidimensional. For example, a sales executive's performance may require administrative and financial skills along with the interpersonal skills needed to motivate a sales force. Or a medical doctor's performance may demand the positive interpersonal skills of a bedside manner to complement the necessary technical diagnostic and treatment skills for enhancing the healing process. Each specific job in an organization requires the definition of skills and behaviors essential to excellent performance. Defining performance is a prerequisite to measuring and evaluating performance on the job.

Although different jobs require different skills and behaviors, organizational citizenship behavior (OCB) is one dimension of individual performance that spans many jobs. OCB was defined in Chapter 4 as behavior that is above and beyond the call of duty. OCB involves individual discretionary behavior that promotes the organization and is not explicitly rewarded; it includes helping behavior, sportsmanship, and civic virtue. According to supervisors, OCB is enhanced most through employee involvement programs aimed at engaging employees in the work organization rather than through employee involvement in employment decisions in nonunion operations.[54] OCB emphasizes collective performance in contrast to individual performance or achievement. OCB is just one of a number of performance dimensions to consider when defining performance for a specific job within an organization.

Performance appraisal is the evaluation of a person's performance once it is well defined. Accurate appraisals help supervisors fulfill their dual roles as evaluators and coaches. As a coach, a supervisor is responsible for encouraging employee growth and development. As an evaluator, a supervisor is responsible for making judgments that influence employees' roles in the organization. Using social comparisons to rate employee performance has somewhat of an advantage over simple absolute rating standards in making such judgments.[55] Although procedural justice is often thought of as a unidimensional construct, recent research shows that in the performance appraisal content it can be conceptualized as two-dimensional.[56] A manager's assumptions about whether an employee can change or not influence the employees' perceptions of the procedural justice with which their last performance appraisal was conducted.[57]

Cross-cultural research has found that North American, Asian, and Latin American managers' perceptions of their employees' motivation are different and that their perceptions affect their appraisals of employee performance.[58]

The major purposes of performance appraisals are to give employees feedback on performance, identify the employees' developmental needs, make promotion and reward decisions, make demotion and termination decisions, and develop information about the organization's selection and placement decisions. For example, a review of 57,775 performance appraisals found higher ratings on appraisals done for administrative reasons and lower ratings on appraisals done for research or for employee development.[59]

Measuring Performance

Ideally, actual performance and measured performance are the same. Practically, this is seldom the case. Measuring operational performance is easier than measuring managerial performance because of the availability of quantifiable data. Measuring production performance is easier than measuring

Measuring operational performance is easier than measuring managerial performance because of the availability of quantifiable data.

research and development performance because of the reliability of the measures. Research focused on measuring motivation for task performance found that wording and context influence the validity of direct self-reports.[60] The accompanying Science feature shows the effects of accuracy in performance evaluations on subsequent task performance.

Performance appraisal systems are intended to improve the accuracy of measured performance and increase its agreement with actual performance. The extent

Science

The Effects of Accuracy in Performance Evaluations

This research was based on two studies, an experimental laboratory study and a field study. The performance evaluations include both self-evaluations and, in some cases, evaluations from an external authority. An interesting pattern of results emerged that showed the effects of accuracy in performance evaluation on subsequent task performance. The main finding was that when individuals more accurately evaluated their performance on a task, the better was their performance on a subsequent task. In addition, the first study found that for those individuals who overestimated their performance on a task, the lower their performance on the next task. Interestingly, underestimating performance on a task had no apparent effect on performance of the subsequent task. The second study found that these effects were dampened by the presence of an external authority. Specifically, when individuals received feedback from an external authority, the effects of the inaccuracy of their own self-performance evaluations had a reduced effect on subsequent performance. Therefore, accuracy in self-performance evaluation has a positive effect on the next task performance, and overestimation in self-performance evaluation has a negative effect on the task performance that follows. However, both of these effects are reduced, though not eliminated, when there is an external authority engaged in the role of performance evaluation.

SOURCE: S. Ellis, R. Mendel, and M. Aloni-Zohar, "The Effect of Accuracy of Performance Evaluation on Learning from Experience: The Moderating role of After-Event Reviews," *Journal of Applied Social Psychology* 39(3) (2009): 541–563.

6.3 Actual and Measured Performance

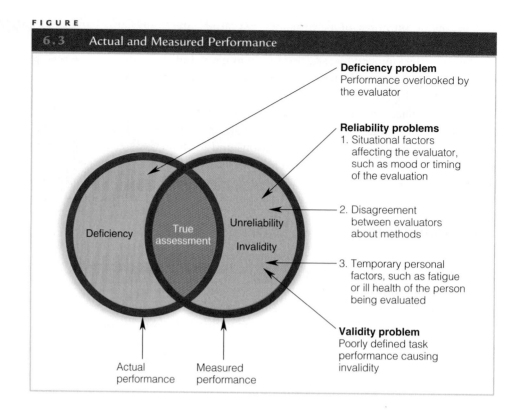

Deficiency problem
Performance overlooked by the evaluator

Reliability problems
1. Situational factors affecting the evaluator, such as mood or timing of the evaluation

2. Disagreement between evaluators about methods

3. Temporary personal factors, such as fatigue or ill health of the person being evaluated

Validity problem
Poorly defined task performance causing invalidity

Deficiency
True assessment
Unreliability
Invalidity

Actual performance
Measured performance

of agreement is called the true assessment, as shown in Figure 6.3. The figure also identifies the performance measurement problems that contribute to inaccuracy. These include deficiency, unreliability, and invalidity. Deficiency results from overlooking important aspects of a person's actual performance. Unreliability results from poor-quality performance measures. Invalidity results from inaccurate definition of the expected job performance.

Early performance appraisal systems were often quite biased. See, for example, Table 6.3, which is a sample of officer effectiveness reports from an infantry company

TABLE

6.3 Officer Effectiveness Reports, Circa 1813

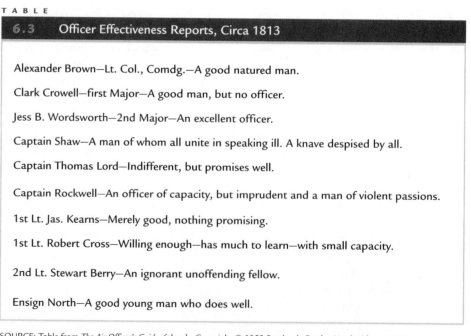

Alexander Brown—Lt. Col., Comdg.—A good natured man.

Clark Crowell—first Major—A good man, but no officer.

Jess B. Wordsworth—2nd Major—An excellent officer.

Captain Shaw—A man of whom all unite in speaking ill. A knave despised by all.

Captain Thomas Lord—Indifferent, but promises well.

Captain Rockwell—An officer of capacity, but imprudent and a man of violent passions.

1st Lt. Jas. Kearns—Merely good, nothing promising.

1st Lt. Robert Cross—Willing enough—has much to learn—with small capacity.

2nd Lt. Stewart Berry—An ignorant unoffending fellow.

Ensign North—A good young man who does well.

SOURCE: Table from *The Air Officer's Guide*, 6th ed., Copyright © 1952 Stackpole Books. Used with permission.

in the early 1800s. Even contemporary executive appraisals have a dark side, arousing managers' and executives' defenses. Addressing emotions and defenses is important to making appraisal sessions developmental.[61] Some performance review systems lead to forced rankings of employees, which may be controversial.

Performance-monitoring systems using modern electronic technology are sometimes used to measure the performance of vehicle operators, computer technicians, and customer service representatives. For example, such systems might record the rate of keystrokes or the total number of keystrokes for a computer technician. The people subject to this type of monitoring are in some cases unaware that their performance is being measured. What is appropriate performance monitoring? What constitutes inappropriate electronic spying on the employee? Are people entitled to know when their performance is being measured? The ethics of monitoring performance may differ by culture. The United States and Sweden, for example, respect individual freedom more than Japan and China do. The overriding issue, however, is how far organizations should go in using modern technology to measure human performance.

Goal setting and MBO are results-oriented methods of performance appraisal that do not necessarily rely on modern technology. Like performance-monitoring systems, they shift the emphasis from subjective, judgmental performance dimensions to observable, verifiable results. Goals established in the planning phase of goal setting become the standard against which to measure subsequent performance. However, rigid adherence to a results-oriented approach may risk overlooking performance opportunities.

FedEx has incorporated a novel and challenging approach to evaluation in its blueprint for service quality. All managers at FedEx are evaluated by their employees through a survey-feedback-action system. Employees evaluate their managers using a five-point scale on twenty-nine standard statements and ten local option ones. Low ratings suggest problem areas requiring management attention. For example, the following statement received low ratings from employees in 1990: "Upper management pays attention to ideas and suggestions from people at my level." CEO Fred Smith became directly involved in addressing this problem area. One of the actions he took to correct the problem was the development of a biweekly employee newsletter.

Performance Feedback: A Communication Challenge

Once clearly defined and accurate performance measures are developed, there is still the challenge of performance feedback. Feedback sessions are among the more stressful events for supervisors and employees. Early research at General Electric found employees responded constructively to positive feedback and were defensive over half the time in response to critical or negative feedback. Typical responses to negative feedback included shifting responsibility for the shortcoming or behavior, denying it outright, or providing a wide range of excuses for it.[62] In a study of 499 Chinese supervisor–subordinate dyads, supervisors responded positively to employees who sought performance feedback if their motive was performance enhancement or improvement.[63] However, if the employee's motive was impression management, supervisors responded less positively.

In a performance feedback session, both parties should try to make it a constructive learning experience, since positive and negative performance feedback has long-term implications for the employee's performance and for the working relationship. American Airlines follows three guidelines in providing evaluative feedback so that the experience is constructive for supervisor and employee alike.[64] First, refer to specific, verbatim statements and specific, observable behaviors displayed by the person receiving the feedback. This enhances the acceptance of the feedback while reducing the chances of denial. Second, focus on changeable behaviors, as opposed to intrinsic or personality-based attributes. People are often more defensive about who they are than about what they do. Third, plan and organize for the session ahead of time. Be sure to notify the person who will receive the feedback. Both the leader and the follower should be ready.

In addition to these ideas, many companies recommend beginning coaching and counseling sessions with something positive. The intent is to reduce defensiveness and enhance useful communication. There is almost always at least one positive element to emphasize. Once the session is underway and rapport is established, the evaluator can introduce more difficult and negative material. Because people are not perfect, there is always an opportunity for them to learn and grow through performance feedback sessions. Critical feedback is the basis for improvement and is essential to a performance feedback session. Specific feedback is beneficial for initial performance but discourages exploration and undermines the learning needed for later, more independent performance.[65]

360-Degree Feedback

5 Describe 360-degree feedback.

Many organizations use *360-degree feedback* as a tactic to improve the accuracy of performance appraisals because it is based on multiple sources of information. When self-evaluations are included in this process, there is evidence that the evaluation interviews can be more satisfying, more constructive, and less defensive.[66] One of the criticisms of self-evaluations is their low level of agreement with supervisory evaluations.[67] However, high levels of agreement may not necessarily be desirable if the intent of the evaluation is to provide a full picture of the person's performance. This is a strength of the 360-degree feedback method, which provides a well-rounded view of performance from superiors, peers, followers, and customers.[68]

An example of a 360-degree feedback evaluation occurred in a large military organization for a midlevel civilian executive. The midlevel executive behaved very differently in dealing with superiors, peers, and followers. With superiors, he was positive, compliant, and deferential. With peers, he was largely indifferent, often ignoring them. With followers, he was tough and demanding, bordering on cruel and abusive. Without each of these perspectives, the executive's performance would not have been accurately assessed. When the executive received feedback, he was able to see the inconsistency in his behavior.

Two recommendations have been made to improve the effectiveness of the 360-degree feedback method. The first is to add a systematic coaching component to the 360-degree feedback.[69] By focusing on enhanced self-awareness and behavioral management, this feedback-coaching model can enhance performance as well as satisfaction and commitment, and reduce intent to turnover. The second is to separate the performance feedback component of the 360-degree appraisal from the management development component.[70] The feedback component should emphasize quantitative feedback and performance measures, while the management development component should emphasize qualitative feedback and competencies for development.

While 360-degree feedback generates actionable knowledge, its effectiveness has been found to vary across cultures. One study examining the 360-degree feedback process found 360-degree feedback to be most effective in cultures with low-power distance and individualistic values.[71]

Developing People and Enhancing Careers

A key function of a good performance appraisal system is to develop people and enhance careers. Developmentally, performance appraisals should emphasize individual growth needs and future performance. If the supervisor is to coach and develop employees

360-degree feedback
A process of self-evaluation and evaluations by a manager, peers, direct reports, and possibly customers.

effectively, there must be mutual trust. The supervisor must be vulnerable and open to challenge from the subordinate while maintaining a position of responsibility for what is in the subordinate's best interests.[72] The supervisor must also be a skilled, empathetic listener who encourages the employee to talk about hopes and aspirations.[73]

The employee must be able to take active responsibility for future development and growth. This might mean challenging the supervisor's ideas about future development as well as expressing individual preferences and goals. Passive, compliant employees are unable to accept responsibility for themselves or to achieve full emotional development. Individual responsibility is a key characteristic of many organization work cultures that treat employees like adults and expect them to act and behave like adults. This contrasts with work cultures in which leaders treat employees more paternalistically.

Key Characteristics of an Effective Appraisal System

An effective performance appraisal system has five key characteristics: validity, reliability, responsiveness, flexibility, and equitability. Its validity comes from capturing multiple dimensions of a person's job performance. Its reliability comes from capturing evaluations from multiple sources and at different times over the course of the evaluation period. Its responsiveness allows the person being evaluated some input into the final outcome. Its flexibility leaves it open to modification based on new information, such as federal requirements. Its equitability results in fair evaluations against established performance criteria, regardless of individual differences.

REWARDING PERFORMANCE

One function of a performance appraisal system is to provide input for reward decisions. If an organization wants good performance, it must reward good performance. If it does not want bad performance, it must not reward bad performance. If companies talk "teamwork," "values," and "customer focus," they need to reward behaviors related to these ideas. Employees may be more satisfied with monetary rewards if they understand the functions of the pay system and if the pay system is used to provide performance feedback.[74] Although this idea is conceptually simple, it can become very complicated in practice. Reward decisions are among the most difficult and complicated decisions made in organizations, and among the most important decisions. When leaders confront decisions about pay every day, they should know that it is a myth that people work for money.[75] While pay and rewards for performance have value, so too do trust, fun, and meaningful work.

Employees may be more satisfied with monetary rewards if the pay system is used to provide performance feedback.

Image copyright Bob Ainsworth, 2009. Used under license from Shutterstock.com

A Key Organizational Decision Process

Reward and punishment decisions in organizations affect many people throughout the system, not just those being rewarded or punished. Reward allocation involves sequential decisions about which people to reward, how to reward them, and when to reward them. Taken together, these decisions shape the behavior of everyone in the organization because of the vicarious learning that occurs as people watch what happens to others, especially when new programs or initiatives are implemented. People carefully watch what happens to peers who make mistakes or have problems with the new system; then they gauge their own behavior accordingly. As we saw in the Thinking Ahead feature, Nordstrom's creative competition fosters an environment in which associates may even learn from watching others.

Individual versus Team Reward Systems

6 Compare individual and team-oriented reward systems.

One of the distinguishing characteristics of Americans is the value they place on individualism. Systems that reward individuals are common in organizations in the United States. One strength of these systems is that they foster autonomous and independent behavior that leads to creativity, to novel solutions to old problems, and to distinctive contributions to the organization. Individual reward systems directly affect individual behavior and encourage competitive striving within a work team. However, different types of employees may have different reward preferences. For example, award seekers may prefer travel awards, nesters may prefer days off, bottom-liners may prefer cash bonuses, freedom yearners may prefer flextime, praise cravers may prefer written praise, and upward movers may prefer status awards.[76] Motivation and reward systems outside the United States are often group focused.[77]

Too much competition within a work environment, however, may be dysfunctional. At the Western Company of North America, individual success in the MBO program was tied too tightly to rewards, and individual managers became divisively competitive. For example, some managers took last-minute interdepartmental financial actions in a quarter to meet their objectives, but by doing so, they caused other managers to miss their objectives. Actions such as these raise ethical questions about how far individual managers should go in serving their own self-interest at the expense of their peers.

Team reward systems solve the problems caused by individual competitive behavior. These systems emphasize cooperation, joint efforts, and the sharing of information, knowledge, and expertise. The Japanese and Chinese cultures, with their collectivist orientations, place greater emphasis than Americans on the individual as an element of the team, not a member apart from the team. Digital Equipment Corporation (now part of Hewlett-Packard) used a partnership approach to performance appraisals. Self-managed work group members participated in their own appraisal process. Such an approach emphasizes teamwork and responsibility.

Some organizations have experimented with individual and group alternative reward systems.[78] At the individual level, these include skill-based and pay-for-knowledge systems. Each emphasizes skills or knowledge possessed by an employee over and above the requirements for the basic job. At the group level, gain-sharing plans emphasize collective cost reduction and allow workers to share in the gains achieved by reducing production or other operating costs. In such plans, everyone shares equally in the collective gain. Avnet, Inc. found that collective profit sharing improved performance.

The Power of Earning

The purpose behind both individual and team reward systems is to shape productive behavior. Effective performance management can be the lever of change that boosts individual and team achievements in an organization. So, if one wants the rewards available in the organization, one should work to earn them. Performance management and reward systems assume a demonstrable connection between performance and rewards. Organizations get the performance they reward, not the performance they say they want.[79] Further, when there is no apparent link between performance and rewards, people may begin to believe they are entitled to rewards regardless of how they perform. The concept of entitlement is very different from the concept of earning, which assumes a performance–reward link. This connection between performance and rewards must be openly visible and tied to metrics with which employees can identify.[80]

You 6.2

Correcting Poor Performance

At one time or another, each of us has had a poor performance of some kind. It may have been a poor test result in school, a poor presentation at work, or a poor performance in an athletic event. Think of a poor performance event that you have experienced and work through the following three steps.

Step 1. Briefly describe the specific event in some detail. Include why you label it a poor performance (bad score? someone else's evaluation?).

Step 2. Analyze the Poor Performance

a. List all the possible contributing causes to the poor performance. Be specific, such as the room was too hot, you did not get enough sleep, you were not told how to perform the task, etc. You might ask other people for possible ideas, too.

1. _____
2. _____
3. _____
4. _____
5. _____
6. _____
7. _____

b. Is there a primary cause for the poor performance? What is it?

Step 3. Plan to Correct the Poor Performance

Develop a step-by-step plan of action that specifies what you can change or do differently to improve your performance the next time you have an opportunity. Include seeking help if it is needed. Once your plan is developed, look for an opportunity to execute it.

The notion of entitlement at work is counterproductive when taken to the extreme because it counteracts the power of earning.[81] People who believe they are entitled to rewards regardless of their behavior or performance are not motivated to behave constructively. Merit raises in some organizations, for example, have come to be viewed as entitlements, thus reducing their positive value in the organizational reward system. People believe they have a right to be taken care of by someone, whether that is the organization or a specific person. Entitlement engenders passive, irresponsible behavior, whereas earning engenders active, responsible, adult behavior. If rewards depend on performance, people must perform responsibly to receive them. The power of earning rests on a direct link between performance and rewards.

CORRECTING POOR PERFORMANCE

Often a complicated, difficult challenge for supervisors, correcting poor performance is a three-step process. First, the cause or primary responsibility for the poor performance must be identified. Second, if the primary responsibility is a person's, then the source of the personal problem must be determined. Third, a plan of action to correct the poor performance must be developed. You 6.2 gives you an opportunity to examine a poor performance you have experienced. Poor performance may result from a variety of causes, the more important being poorly designed work systems, poor selection processes, inadequate training and skills development, lack of personal motivation, and personal problems intruding on the work environment. Not all poor performance is self-motivated; some is induced by the work system. Therefore, a good diagnosis should precede corrective action. For example, it may be that an employee is subject to a work design or selection system that does not allow the person to exhibit good performance. Identifying the cause of the poor performance comes first and should be done in communication with the employee. If the problem is with the system and the supervisor can fix it, everyone wins as a result.

7 Describe strategies for correcting poor performance.

If the poor performance is not attributable to work design or organizational process problems, then attention should be focused on the employee. At least three possible causes of poor performance can be attributed to the employee. The problem may lie in (1) some aspect of the person's relationship to the organization or supervisor, (2) some area of the employee's personal life, or (3) a training or developmental deficiency. In the latter two cases, poor performance may be treated as a symptom as opposed to a motivated consequence. In such cases, identifying financial problems, family difficulties, or health disorders may enable the supervisor to help the employee solve problems before they become too extensive. Employee assistance programs (EAPs) can be helpful to employees managing personal problems. These are discussed in Chapter 7 in relation to managing stress.

Poor performance may also be motivated by an employee's displaced anger or conflict with the organization or supervisor. In such cases, the employee may or may not be aware of the internal reactions causing the problem. In either event, sabotage, work slowdowns, work stoppages, and similar forms of poor performance may result from such motivated behavior. The supervisor may attribute the cause of the problem to the employee, and the employee may attribute it to the supervisor or organization. To solve motivated performance problems requires treating the poor performance as a symptom with a deeper cause. Resolving the underlying anger or conflict results in the disappearance of the symptom (poor performance).

Performance and Kelley's Attribution Theory

According to attribution theory, managers make attributions (inferences) concerning employees' behavior and performance.[82] The attributions may not always be accurate. For example, an executive with Capital Cities Communications/ABC (now part of the Disney Company) who had a very positive relationship with his boss was not held responsible for profit problems in his district. The boss blamed the problem on the economy. Supervisors and employees who share perceptions and attitudes, as in the Capital Cities situation, tend to evaluate each other highly.[83] Supervisors and employees who do not share perceptions and attitudes are more likely to blame each other for performance problems.

Harold Kelley's attribution theory aims to help us explain the behavior of other people. He also extended attribution theory by trying to identify the antecedents of internal and external attributions. Kelley proposed that individuals make attributions based on information gathered in the form of three informational cues: consensus, distinctiveness, and consistency.[84,85] We observe an individual's behavior and then seek out information in the form of these three cues. *Consensus* is the extent to which peers in the same situation behave the same way. *Distinctiveness* is the degree to which the person behaves the same way in other situations. *Consistency* refers to the frequency of a particular behavior over time.

We form attributions based on whether these cues are low or high. Figure 6.4 shows how the combination of these cues helps us form internal or external attributions. Suppose you have received several complaints from customers regarding one of your customer service representatives, John. You have not received complaints about your other service representatives (low consensus). Upon reviewing John's records, you note that he also received customer complaints during his previous job as a sales clerk (low distinctiveness). The complaints have been coming in steadily for about three months (high consistency). In this case, you would most likely make an internal attribution and

consensus
An informational cue indicating the extent to which peers in the same situation behave in a similar fashion.

distinctiveness
An informational cue indicating the degree to which an individual behaves the same way in other situations.

consistency
An informational cue indicating the frequency of behavior over time.

6.4 Informational Cues and Attributions

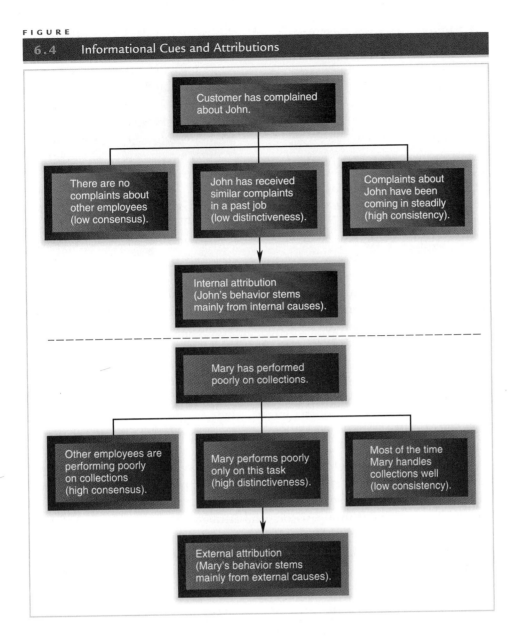

conclude that the complaints must stem from John's behavior. The combination of low consensus, low distinctiveness, and high consistency leads to internal attributions.

Other combinations of these cues, however, produce external attributions. High consensus, high distinctiveness, and low consistency, for example, produce external attributions. Suppose one of your employees, Mary, is performing poorly on collecting overdue accounts. You find that the behavior is widespread within your work team (high consensus) and that Mary is performing poorly only on this aspect of the job (high distinctiveness), and that most of the time she handles this aspect of the job well (low consistency). You will probably decide that something about the work situation caused the poor performance—perhaps work overload or an unfair deadline.

Consensus, distinctiveness, and consistency are the cues used to determine whether the cause of behavior is internal or external. The process of determining the cause of a behavior may not be simple and clear-cut, however, because of some biases that occur in forming attributions.

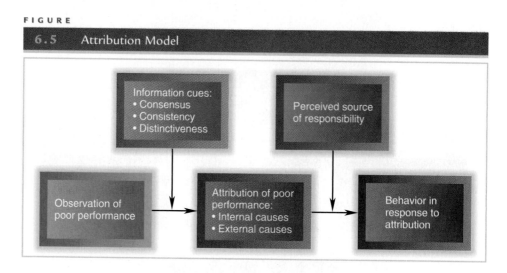

6.5 Attribution Model

Figure 6.5 presents an attribution model that specifically addresses how supervisors respond to poor performance. A supervisor who observes poor performance seeks cues about the employee's behavior in the three forms discussed above: consensus, consistency, and distinctiveness.

On the basis of this information, the supervisor makes either an internal (personal) attribution or an external (situational) attribution. Internal attributions might include low effort, lack of commitment, or lack of ability. External attributions are outside the employee's control and might include equipment failure or unrealistic goals. The supervisor then determines the source of responsibility for the performance problem and tries to correct the problem.

Supervisors may choose from a wide range of responses. They can, for example, express personal concern, reprimand the employee, or provide training. Supervisors who attribute the cause of poor performance to a person (an internal cause) will respond more harshly than supervisors who attribute the cause to the work situation (an external cause). Supervisors should try not to make either of the two common attribution errors discussed in Chapter 3: the fundamental attribution error and the self-serving bias.

Coaching, Counseling, and Mentoring

Supervisors have important coaching, counseling, and mentoring responsibilities to their subordinates. Supervisors and coworkers have been found to be more effective in mentoring functions than assigned, formal mentors from higher up in the organizational hierarchy.[86] Success in the mentoring relationship also hinges on the presence of openness and trust.[87] This relationship may be one where performance-based deficiencies are addressed or one where personal problems that diminish employee performance, such as depression, are addressed.[88] In either case, supervisors can play a helpful role in employee problem-solving activities without accepting responsibility for the employees' problems. One important form of help is to refer the employee to trained professionals.

Coaching and counseling are among the career and psychosocial functions of a mentoring relationship.[89] *Mentoring* is a work relationship that encourages development and career enhancement for people moving through the career cycle. Mentor relationships typically go through four phases: initiation, cultivation, separation, and redefinition. For protégés, mentoring offers a number of career benefits.[90] The relationship can significantly enhance the early development of a newcomer and the midcareer development of an experienced employee. IBM, for example, expanded its mentoring program to include employees at all levels.[91]

mentoring

A work relationship that encourages development and career enhancement for people moving through the career cycle.

The Real World 6.2

Try Mentoring: New Spin, Old Practice

Tri-mentoring is a formalized peer-mentoring system that recognizes implicit learning in organizations. Employees can and do learn from each other in the normal performance of daily tasks, regardless of their individual levels of competency. This is a process of leveraging tacit knowledge that can be formalized, as it is in tri-mentoring, and promoted. Organizations benefit as do individual employees. Williams' knowledge management company created and advances the concept. This is how it works. Three employees get together and share their tacit, implicit knowledge to build organizational capability. Pairings of two are less effective because one frequently dominates or is more influential. On the other hand, four or more can lead to coordination and lack of agreement problems. The trio offers flexibility, healthy discussion, and covers overlaps while the trio self-selects, managers provide direction, and experts assess outcomes. An example occurred in a paint shop where the painter, the finisher, and the quality control officer all had the same instructions. Each interpreted the instructions differently, resulting in rejects, stress, wasted time and materials, and organizational frustration. When a manager put the painter, finisher, and quality control officer into a tri-mentoring context, they talked through tacit knowledge that led to a uniform acceptable standard with agreed upon targets. Positive results were found in fewer rejects, less wasted time and materials, as well as less stress and frustration. As the example shows, tri-mentoring is a targeted approach to peer-mentoring and information sharing that has potential for positive pay-offs.

SOURCE: D. Williams, "Tri-Mentoring: A New Spin on an Old Practice," *New Zealand Management* 56(2) (March 2009): 28.

One study found that good newcomer performance resulted in their receiving more delegation from their leaders.[92] Career development can be enhanced through peer relationships as an alternative to traditional mentoring relationships.[93] Executive coaching is increasingly being used as a way of outsourcing the business mentoring functions.[94] The Real World 6.2 describes a tri-mentoring approached developed by a New Zealand knowledge-management company. Informational, collegial, and special peers aid the individual's development through information sharing, career strategizing, job-related feedback, emotional support, and friendship. Hence, mentors and peers may both play constructive roles in correcting an employee's poor performance and in enhancing overall career development.

MANAGERIAL IMPLICATIONS: PERFORMANCE MANAGEMENT IS A KEY TASK

People in organizations learn from the consequences of their actions. Therefore, managers must exercise care in applying positive and negative consequences to ensure that they are connected to the behaviors the managers intend to reward or punish. Managers should also be judicious in the use of punishment and should consider extinction coupled with positive reinforcement as an alternative to punishment for shaping employee behavior. The strategic use of training and educational opportunities, stock options, and recognition awards is instrumental to successful organizational reward systems. Managers can serve as positive role models for employees' vicarious learning about ethical behavior and high-quality performance.

Goal-setting activities may be valuable to managers in bringing out the best performance from employees. Managers can use challenging, specific goals for this purpose and must be prepared to provide employees with timely, useful feedback on goal progress so that employees will know how they are doing. Goal-setting activities that are misused may create dysfunctional competition in an organization and lead to lower performance.

Good performance management systems are a valuable tool for providing employees with clear feedback on their actions. Managers who rely on valid and reliable performance measures may use them in employee development and to correct poor performance. Managers who use high-technology performance monitoring systems must remember that employees are humans, not machines. Managers are responsible for creating a positive learning atmosphere in performance feedback sessions, and employees are responsible for learning from these sessions. 360-degree feedback is especially effective when combined with coaching.

Finally, managers can use rewards as one of the most powerful positive consequences for shaping employee behavior. If rewards are to improve performance, managers must make a clear connection between specific performance and the rewards. Employees should be expected to earn the rewards they receive; they should expect rewards to be related to performance quality and skill development.

Diversity Dialogue

Race and Rewards at the Harlem Patrol Borough

Omar J. Edwards of the New York City Police Department (NYPD) was accidentally shot and killed by a fellow officer on May 28, 2009. While off duty, Edwards was chasing a suspected car thief in East Harlem, New York, with his gun drawn when the incident occurred. While accidents such as this are unfortunate, they are not unusual, especially in the line of police work. This particular accident, however, would affect rank-and-file minority police officers in a very significant way. After the accident, New York City Police Commissioner Raymond Kelly vowed to increase the number of minority officers in top-level Harlem patrol borough positions. By all accounts, Commissioner Kelly is "a fair-minded leader of a hierarchical organization," so why the emphasis on promoting minority officers, and why now?

For one thing, the off-duty police officer was black; the shooter is white. This fact "resurrected the volatile cross section of race, politics, and the use of deadly force by police officers." Conventional wisdom suggests that public servants should represent the community in which they serve so that they might have a better understanding of the residents and vice versa. While the number of blacks and Hispanic captains and higher rose significantly since 2001, whites make up the majority of the Harlem patrol borough's executive corps.

Harlem patrol borough's reward system operates in much the same way as it does in all police departments. Promotion of rank-and-file officers to captain depends on their performance on civil service exams. Promotions above the captain rank are discretionary. And while Commissioner Kelly admits that minority officers have enjoyed a quicker promotion than white officers of the same rank; Roy Richter, the president of the Captain's Endowment Association, points out that "[T]his police commissioner rewards performance regardless of race or gender."

1. How will Commissioner Kelly's vow to increase minority representation in the top command affect the rank-and-file officers?
2. Should service organization managers consider their "market" when promoting employees to higher levels? Why or why not?

SOURCE: A. Baker, "Police Commissioner Plans to Put More Minority Officers in Top Posts," *New York Times* (June 26, 2009); A. Gendar, E. Pearson, B. Paddock, and L. Standora, "Black Cop Killed by White Officer: Horror in East Harlem as Off-Duty Rookie Is Shot Pursuing Suspect," *New York Daily News* (May 29, 2009).

LOOKING BACK: NORDSTROM

Hit Your Goals, Win Your Praise

In the Thinking Ahead feature, we saw the competitiveness, the athletic competitiveness, of Nordstrom's sales

NORDSTROM

environment. This competitive environment is a disciplined one in contrast to a free-for-all one. Goal setting is what undergirds this intensely competitive sales environment.[95] The company is organized as an inverted pyramid, with sales associates at the top of this inverted design. Below the sales associates are the buyers and below the buyers are the managers. This makes the managers the heavy lifters within the Nordstrom design and what binds every one of these three tiers together is goal setting. Each member of each tier strives to meet personal, departmental, store, and regional goals. There are goals for each day, goals for each month, and goals for each year. That is a disciplined, well ordered, and competitive structure within which performance expectations are clear, feedback clear, and results understandable.

The caution in this environment is that if you take the goal too seriously, it can ruin the fun of achieving the goal. Achieving is fun. At the same time, it is not the end of the world if you miss, or fail to make, a goal. This becomes an opportunity to talk to yourself about next time. When you work a little bit harder, you then hit that goal. Half the challenge is in making the goal. When you do make the goal, self-reinforcement is in order to compliment the cash and other rewards the company provides. Pat yourself on the back, you did a great job and hit your goals. The power of the goal is that it provides focus, direction, and provides perspective why you are part of the Nordstrom team.

Now that you are a successful competitive sales athlete who effectively uses goal setting to achieve great performance and receive the resulting rewards of cash and trips, now what? Yes, you can praise yourself and engage in self-reinforcement. Nordstrom understands the importance of recognition and praise. You have earned them and you should receive them. Within the company, the best salespeople achieve the status of Pacesetter. Pacesetters meet or beat the sales-volume goal for their own department for the one-year period from December 16 through December 15 of the following year. Pacesetters are presented with a certificate of merit, and more, in a public ceremony. Being a Pacesetter takes hard work, success, and time! For monthly periods, Customer Service All-Star recognition comes from your store manager. So, hit your goals, win your praise, and become an All-Star, then a Pacesetter.

Chapter Summary

1. Learning is a change in behavior acquired through experience.

2. The operant conditioning approach to learning states that behavior is a function of positive and negative consequences.

3. Reinforcement is used to develop desirable behavior; punishment and extinction are used to decrease undesirable behavior.

4. Bandura's social learning theory suggests that task-specific self-efficacy is important to effective learning.

5. Goal setting improves work motivation and task performance, reduces role stress, and improves the accuracy and validity of performance appraisal.

6. Performance management and 360-degree feedback can lead to improved performance.

7. Making accurate attributions about the behavior of others is an essential prerequisite to correcting poor performance.

8. High-quality performance should be rewarded, and poor performance should be corrected.

9. Mentoring is a relationship for encouraging development and career enhancement for people moving through the career cycle.

Key Terms

classical conditioning (p. 185)
consensus (p. 204)
consistency (p. 204)
distinctiveness (p. 204)
extinction (p. 188)
goal setting (p. 190)
learning (p. 184)

management by objectives (MBO) (p. 194)
mentoring (p. 206)
negative consequences (p. 186)
operant conditioning (p. 185)
performance appraisal (p. 196)
performance management (p. 196)

positive consequences (p. 186)
punishment (p. 187)
reinforcement (p. 186)
task-specific self-efficacy (p. 188)
360-degree feedback (p. 200)

Review Questions

1. Define the terms *learning, reinforcement, punishment,* and *extinction.*

2. What are positive and negative consequences in shaping behavior? How should they be managed? Explain the value of extinction as a strategy.

3. How can task-specific self-efficacy be enhanced? What are the differences in the way introverted and extraverted and intuitive and sensing people learn?

4. What are the five characteristics of well-developed goals? Why is feedback on goal progress important?

5. What are the purposes of conducting performance appraisals? What are the benefits of 360-degree feedback?

6. What are the two possible attributions of poor performance? What are the implications of each?

7. How can managers and supervisors best provide useful performance feedback?

8. How do mentors and peers help people develop and enhance their careers?

Discussion and Communication Questions

1. Which learning approach—the behavioral approach or Bandura's social learning theory—do you find more appropriate for people?

2. Given your personality type, how do you learn best? Do you miss learning some things because of how they are taught?

3. What goals do you set for yourself at work? In your personal life? Will you know if you achieve them?

4. If a conflict occurred between your self-evaluation and the evaluation given to you by your supervisor or instructor, how would you respond? What, specifically, would you do? What have you learned from your supervisor or instructor during the last reporting period?

5. What rewards are most important to you? How hard are you willing to work to receive them?

6. *(communication question)* Prepare a memo detailing the consequences of behavior in your work or university environment (e.g., grades, awards, suspensions, and scholarships). Include in your memo your classification of these consequences as positive or negative. Should your organization or university change the way it applies these consequences?

7. *(communication question)* Develop an oral presentation about the most current management practices in employee rewards and performance management.

Find out what at least four different companies are doing in this area. Be prepared to discuss their fit with the text materials.

8. *(communication question)* Interview a manager or supervisor who is responsible for completing performance appraisals on people at work. Ask the manager which aspects of performance appraisal and the performance appraisal interview process are most difficult and how he or she manages these difficulties.

Ethical Dilemma

Margaret Dawson supervises a team of six salespeople within Smith & Yardley, Inc., and she's been with the company for five years. As her team was assembled, Margaret worked assertively to make sure everyone was clear on how to complete the sometimes complicated expense report forms. Since her sales force was on the road for approximately 60 percent of the time, filling out expense reports completely was essential. The sales people were dependent on getting reimbursements quickly for living expenses and the extensive mileage accrued; the accounting team needed to process the forms quickly in order to avoid a critical backlog of debt. Margaret's team consistently submits their reports on time, a fact that pleases both Margaret and her boss. The team receives their reimbursements promptly, which meets their needs.

For her entire time with Smith & Yardley, Inc., Margaret has used a rounding system to make the numbers reconcile more easily when inputted into the excel spreadsheet expense report. She has consistently shared this procedure with her salespeople as a method of reconciliation that also quickens the process. Margaret is also aware that when her subordinates complete their reports this way, they often get a little extra money in their reimbursement check. Since that's the procedure Margaret was taught when she was new to the company, she feels comfortable passing that information on.

At the last managers' meeting, Margaret's supervisor, Henry, reviewed the correct procedures for completing expense reports. She learned that the rounding system that she was taught and has consequently taught to her sales force isn't exactly the way the company would like outstanding expenses reconciled. The way in which Margaret and her team complete their reports isn't specifically wrong, but it does err in favor of awarding the employees extra money. Margaret has to decide if she should gather her team and inform them that expense reports have to be completed in a new, more time-consuming manner, or if she should simply allow the team to keep submitting the forms in the way in which they've all become accustomed.

Questions:

1. Using consequential, rule-based and character theories, evaluate Margaret's options.

2. What should Margaret do? Why?

Experiential Exercises

6.1 Positive and Negative Reinforcement

Purpose: To examine the effects of positive and negative reinforcement on behavior change.

1. Two or three volunteers are selected to receive reinforcement from the class while performing a particular task. The volunteers leave the room.

2. The instructor identifies an object for the student volunteers to locate when they return to the room. (The object should be unobtrusive but clearly visible to the class. Some that have worked well are a small

triangular piece of paper that was left behind when a notice was torn off a classroom bulletin board, a smudge on the chalkboard, and a chip in the plaster of a classroom wall.)

3. The instructor specifies the reinforcement contingencies that will be in effect when the volunteers return to the room. For negative reinforcement, students should hiss, boo, and throw things (although you should not throw anything harmful) when the first volunteer is moving away from the object;

cheer and applaud when the second volunteer is getting closer to the object; and if a third volunteer is used, use both negative and positive reinforcement.

4. The instructor should assign a student to keep a record of the time it takes each of the volunteers to locate the object.

5. Volunteer number one is brought back into the room and is instructed: "Your task is to locate and touch a particular object in the room, and the class has agreed to help you. You may begin."

6. Volunteer number one continues to look for the object until it is found while the class assists by giving negative reinforcement.

7. Volunteer number two is brought back into the room and is instructed: "Your task is to locate and touch a particular object in the room, and the class has agreed to help you. You may begin."

8. Volunteer number two continues to look for the object until it is found while the class assists by giving positive reinforcement.

9. Volunteer number three is brought back into the room and is instructed: "Your task is to locate and touch a particular object in the room, and the class has agreed to help you. You may begin."

10. Volunteer number three continues to look for the object until it is found while the class assists by giving both positive and negative reinforcement.

11. In a class discussion, answer the following questions:

   a. How did the behavior of the volunteers differ when different kinds of reinforcement (positive, negative, or both) were used?

   b. What were the emotional reactions of the volunteers to the different kinds of reinforcement?

   c. Which type of reinforcement—positive or negative—is most common in organizations? What effect do you think this has on motivation and productivity?

6.2 Correcting Poor Performance

This exercise provides an opportunity for you to engage in a performance diagnosis role-play as either the assistant director of the Academic Computing Service Center or as a member of a university committee appointed by the president of the university at the request of the center director. The instructor will form the class into groups of five or six students and either ask the group to select who is to be the assistant director or assign one group member to be the assistant director.

Performance diagnosis, especially where some poor performance exists, requires making attributions and determining causal factors as well as formulating a plan of action to correct any poor performance.

Step 1. (five minutes) Once the class is formed into groups, the instructor provides the assistant director with a copy of the role description and each university committee member with a copy of the role context

information. Group members are to read through the materials provided.

Step 2. (fifteen minutes) The university committee is to call in the assistant director of the Academic Computing Service Center for a performance diagnostic interview. This is an information-gathering interview, not an appraisal session. The purpose is to gather information for the center director.

Step 3. (fifteen minutes) The university committee is to agree on a statement that reflects their understanding of the assistant director's poor performance and to include a specification of the causes. Based on this problem statement, the committee is to formulate a plan of action to correct the poor performance. The assistant director is to do the same, again ending with a plan of action.

Step 4. (ten to fifteen minutes, optional) The instructor may ask the groups to share the results of their work in Step 3 of the role-play exercise.

BizFlix | Take the Lead

Dance academy owner and instructor Pierre Dulaine (Antonio Banderas) offers to help troubled detention students in a South Bronx high school. His formal ballroom style sharply differs from their hip-hop moves. After watching a hot tango sequence between Pierre and instructor Morgan (Katya Virshilas), the students begin to warm up to Pierre's approach. His work with the students proves successful and they compete in the 25th Annual Grand Ballroom Competition.

Behavior Modification: Learning Ballroom Dancing

This film sequence has two parts with a title screen between them. The first part starts with Pierre saying, "So, as your principal has made me your executioner, you will report to me every morning here at 7:30 A.M." This part ends after Pierre sings, "You're dancing, you're dancing . . . "

The second part begins with Pierre saying "The waltz. It cannot be done without trust between partners." This sequence ends with Rock (Rob Brown) and LaRhette (Yaya DaCosta) continuing with their practice.

What to Watch for and Ask Yourself

- Rock and LaRhette are trying to learn the waltz. Which of the two approaches to learning described earlier in this chapter best apply to this film sequence? Do you see examples of classical conditioning or operant conditioning? Why?

- This chapter discussed strategies of reinforcement, punishment, and extinction. Which of those strategies appear in the film sequence? Give examples from the film sequence to support your answer.

- Apply the concepts described in the earlier section of this chapter, "Performance: A Key Construct," to the film sequence. Which performance concepts do you see? Give specific examples of the concepts from the film sequences.

Workplace Video | Flight 001: Planning and Goal Setting

Until the late 1990s, Brad John and John Sencion had been working in different areas of the fashion industry in New York. Both traveled often between the United States, Europe, and Japan for work. No matter how many times they began a trip, they spent the days and hours racing all over town picking up last-minute essentials. By the time they got to the airport, they were sweaty, stressed, and miserable—not exactly the glamorous existence they envisioned when they got into the fashion industry.

On a 1998 flight from New York to Paris, the weary travelers came up with an idea for a one-stop travel shop targeted at fashion-forward globetrotters like themselves. They called it Flight 001 and began selling guidebooks, cosmetics, laptop bags, luggage, electronic gadgets, passport covers, and other consumer products.

Today, after celebrating its 10-year anniversary, Flight 001 is being hailed as one of the most exciting new businesses in the industry. In addition to selling useful travel merchandise, the New York-based retailer offers a unique shopping experience: Flight 001 stores are shaped like airplane fuselages tricked out with retro airport décor and accessories. The company has multiple stores in the United States and a boutique in Harvey Nichols—an upscale department store in the United Arab Emirates. In the years ahead, the founders expect to be in every major city in the United States, Europe, and Asia.

But as the company embarks on a new five-year plan, the stretch goal of opening as many as 30 new stores in the U.S. and overseas is beginning to hit turbulence—especially in the area of financial management. Cofounder Brad John is determined to make Flight 001 the international authority on travel, but ambitious plans will require changes to the company's staffing, merchandising strategy, and methods for assessing organizational performance.

With all the talk about expansion and new product lines, it will be increasingly important that Flight 001 not become distracted from what makes it special in the first place: location, design, and an impeccable product line.

Discussion Questions

1. Identify Flight 001's mission and goals.

2. Do goals at Flight 001 possess the characteristics of effective goal setting? Explain your answer using the "SMART" acronym mentioned in the chapter.

3. What problem is hampering Flight 001's growth plans, and how does co-founder Brad John assess his company's performance?

Case

Learning Programs in the American Express Learning Network

American Express (AmEx), a company with operations around the world, was founded in 1850 to provide freight forwarding and delivery services. Since then AmEx has evolved into a global financial services company, perhaps best known for its American Express charge card.[1] With about 65,000 employees worldwide,[2] enhancing the performance capabilities of employees is an important concern at AmEx, and this concern is addressed through the activities of the American Express Learning Network (AELN). Jeanette Harrison, vice president of AELN, explains the importance of superior employee performance in the financial services industry. She says, "[a]nytime you're touching your own money—let alone anyone else's—you want control and compliance to be top of mind. That includes privacy of data, data integrity and ensuring appropriate adherence to all regulations and legislation. That has always been fundamental to the learning network's curriculum."[3]

How does AELN go about fostering learning and promoting superior performance among its employees? Examination of AELN's programs for customer service training and leadership development provides some answers.

CUSTOMER SERVICE TRAINING

The stated mission of AELN is to "ready all those who serve"—a mission that is very close to the "approximately 15,000 customer-care professionals within the company's Service Delivery Network, which is responsible for assisting card members and merchants with needs ranging from processing new accounts to card remittance."[4]

According to Harrison, AELN's VP, the initial learning for customer-care employees focuses on ensuring that "everyone has a solid understanding of how they introduce themselves, how they ensure the appropriate privacy and security levels for all of our customers and how they proceed into the interaction."[5] Harrison explains further that employees' interaction with customers is about solving problems, whether it's a customer's question, a request for a replacement credit card, a request for information, or some other issue. Consequently, customer service learning is oriented toward training scenarios that involve problem resolution.[6]

AELN provides both technical training and soft skills training. Technical training focuses on learning the specific job, how to use different software applications, and how to process forms, among other skills. Soft skills training addresses such topics as customer care principles, speaking and listening skills, dispute resolution, and others.[7]

In summarizing the desired outcomes of AELN's customer service training, Harrison emphasizes, "We're not looking for service—we're looking for extraordinary service."[8]

LEADERSHIP DEVELOPMENT

Leadership development is another important learning and performance management responsibility of AELN. In an effort to discover the most effective method of developing leaders for American Express, AELN implemented a new model of leadership development across the entire AmEx organization in 2006, but did so experimenting with three different training venues. One group of trainees (or learners) experienced only online delivery of learning materials, and these were studied through self-direction without any supporting events like peer discussion, formal meetings, or talks by senior organizational leaders. Another group of learners experienced traditional classroom training without any support of online materials or other formal events. The third group of learners experienced a *blended learning* approach that combined classroom or Web-based interaction with senior leaders, self-directed online learning, and encouragement of discussion among learners.[9]

In evaluating the three different approaches, AELN assessed employee training responses—called learner responses—at six different levels. Level 1 measured learner reaction, wherein the trainees indicated the level of satisfaction they had with the learning experience. Level 2 focused on learner knowledge, or an assessment of the acquisition of new knowledge and skills. Level 3 addressed the learners' behavior by evaluating their observed improvement in leadership skills three months after the training sessions. Level 4 targeted the business impact of the training on the learners in terms of improved productivity of the learners' direct reports (i.e., those people for whom the learner has immediate supervisory responsibility). Level 5 targeted return on investment (ROI) via a cost/benefit analysis of the sales productivity of a learner's direct reports relative to the cost of the learner's training. Level 6 focused on assessing the transfer climate, or the extent to which the leadership training actually would be applied and sustained on the job.[10]

Assessments at levels 1 and 2 were based upon the learner's self-report; at levels 3 and 4 the assessments were conducted via self-report from the learners and reports from the learners' supervisor and direct reports; at level 5 it was based upon objective data; and at level 6 the evaluation was carried out through on-the-job observations. For levels 1 and 2 all three modes of delivery were rated extremely high—an average of 4.5 on a 5.0 scale. For level 3, "high improvement" was achieved by 51 percent of the blended learning participants versus 42 percent for those experiencing instructor-led delivery and 32 percent for online delivery. At Level 4, the direct reports of "high improvement leaders" indicated an average 42 percent increase in productivity, with similar results across the three learning venues. For Level 5, the ROI was 923 percent for online learning, 972 percent for instructor-led learning, and 1,599 percent for blended learning. At Level 6, the blended learning approach was more effective due to its creation of higher leader involvement.[11] Clearly, blended learning has the upper hand in AELN's leadership development program.

THE JEANETTE HARRISON LEARNING PHILOSOPHY

Whether it is customer service training or leadership development, Jeanette Harrison's learning philosophy is infused into the learning and performance management programs of the AELN. And what is her learning philosophy? "Learning literally changes lives, and not just in the workplace. My hope is that what we do in the classroom is not only changing the lives of those we interact with at work on a day-to-day basis, but also their families, neighbors and communities. I really believe education is the road to a better life."[12]

Discussion Questions

1. What applications of learning theory and goal-setting theory do you see in AELN's customer service training program?

2. What applications of learning theory and goal-setting theory do you see in AELN's leadership development program?

3. Using relevant concepts from Chapter 6, explain why you think the blended learning approach to leadership development turned out to be the superior training venue.

4. Do you agree or disagree with Jeanette Harrison's learning philosophy that the effects of learning within a business organization should change lives both within and outside the workplace? Explain the reasoning behind your answer.

SOURCE: This case was written by Michael K. McCuddy, The Louis S. and Mary L. Morgal Chair of Christian Business Ethics and Professor of Management, College of Business Administration, Valparaiso University.

7

Stress and Well-Being at Work

LEARNING OBJECTIVES

After reading this chapter, you should be able to do the following:

1 Define *stress, distress,* and *strain*.

2 Compare four different approaches to stress.

3 Explain the psychophysiology of the stress response.

4 Identify work and nonwork causes of stress.

5 Describe the benefits of eustress and the costs of distress.

6 Discuss individual differences in the stress–strain relationship.

7 Distinguish the primary, secondary, and tertiary stages of preventive stress management.

8 Discuss organizational and individual methods of preventive stress management.

IKEA faced the stress of an economic downtown and pervasive corruption in the Russian government.

©Greg Balfour Evans/Alamy.

THINKING AHEAD: IKEA

An Economic Downturn and a Problem of Corruption

During the prolonged recession that began in 2008, IKEA ran into the duel stressors of decreasing product demand that came from the economic downturn and of unpredictability in

Norbert Michalke/ Photolibrary

the Russian market.[1] Every business encounters challenge and hard times. These are rarely the defining events of the business, as in IKEA's case. Rather, the defining nature of the business is how it responds to the stress and challenge of difficulties or hard time. From its founding in 1951, Sweden's IKEA has enjoyed steady growth and expansion to a workforce of roughly 120,000. The company was unable to sustain its growth in the face of the severe economic downturn, and, further, IKEA had to engage in its largest cutback ever by releasing about 5,000 personnel to maintain the company's overall health.

IKEA faced two stressors simultaneously, as mentioned. In addition to the economic downturn, the company ran into the problem of corruption in Russia. This lack of integrity in business transactions and exchanges creates unpredictability for any business, as IKEA quickly learned. The public stance on the Russian issue by IKEA's eighty-three-year-old founder Ingvar Kamprad was particularly notable because IKEA is clearly an international business that operates stores in dozens of countries. To his credit, Russian President Demitri A. Medvedev acknowledged that corruption is a national problem and that curbing official corruption is one of the goals of his tenure. While official corruption did not become a personal source of stress for IKEA's Mr. Kamprad, it did for some of his executives and employees when Russian officials engaged in shakedowns and bribe-taking.

If the Russian president can solve the official corruption problem in his country, that certainly removes an acute source of stress for IKEA in its Russian operations. Further, it opens the opportunity in Russia for growth and expansion. In the short term, the best strategy may be the one taken, which is to defend its own corporate integrity and the well-being of its executives and employees. How about the economic downturn? That larger source of stress for the company requires a much different kind of coping response for not as well-defined a problem. A long, successful history does not guarantee a bright future for any business, as we have seen in previous corporate icons who have failed in other industries. How will minimalist retailer IKEA cope with this economic challenge?

1 Define *stress*, *distress*, and *strain*.

Stress is an important topic in organizational behavior, in part due to the increase in competitive pressures that take a toll on workers and managers alike. Poor leadership, work–family conflicts, and sexual harassment are among the leading causes of work stress.[2] This chapter has five major sections, each addressing one aspect of stress. The first section examines the question "What is stress?" The discussion includes four approaches to the stress response. The second section reviews the demands and stressors that trigger the stress response at work. The third section examines the performance and health benefits of stress and the individual and organizational forms of distress. The fourth section considers individual difference factors, such as gender and personality hardiness, that help moderate the stress–distress relationship. The fifth section presents a framework for preventive stress management and reviews a wide range of individual and organizational stress management methods.

WHAT IS STRESS?

Stress is one of the most creatively ambiguous words in the English language, with as many interpretations as there are people who use the word. In some languages, the term *stress* has a variety of meanings, and Spanish does not even have a direct translation of it. Even the stress experts do not agree on its definition. Stress carries a negative connotation for some people, as though it were something to be avoided. This is unfortunate because stress is a great asset in managing legitimate emergencies and achieving peak performance. *Stress*, or the stress response, is the unconscious preparation to fight or flee that a person experiences when faced with any demand.[3] A *stressor*, or demand, is the person or event that triggers the stress response. *Distress*

stress

The unconscious preparation to fight or flee that a person experiences when faced with any demand

stressor

The person or event that triggers the stress response.

distress

The adverse psychological, physical, behavioral, and organizational consequences that may arise as a result of stressful events.

strain

Distress.

You 7.1

The Frazzle Factor

Read each of the following statements and rate yourself on a scale of 0–3, giving the answer that best describes how you generally feel (3 points for *always*, 2 points for *often*, 1 point for *sometimes*, and 0 points for *never*). Answer as honestly as you can, and do not spend too much time on any one statement.

Am I Overstressed?

_____ 1. I have to make important snap judgments and decisions.

_____ 2. I am not consulted about what happens on my job or in my classes.

_____ 3. I feel I am underpaid.

_____ 4. I feel that no matter how hard I work, the system will mess it up.

_____ 5. I do not get along with some of my coworkers or fellow students.

_____ 6. I do not trust my superiors at work or my professors at school.

_____ 7. The paperwork burden on my job or at school is getting to me.

_____ 8. I feel people outside the job or the university do not respect what I do.

Am I Angry?

_____ 1. I feel that people around me make too many irritating mistakes.

_____ 2. I feel annoyed because I do good work or perform well in school, but no one appreciates it.

_____ 3. When people make me angry, I tell them off.

_____ 4. When I am angry, I say things I know will hurt people.

_____ 5. I lose my temper easily.

_____ 6. I feel like striking out at someone who angers me.

_____ 7. When a coworker or fellow student makes a mistake, I tell him or her about it.

_____ 8. I cannot stand being criticized in public.

Scoring

To find your level of anger and potential for aggressive behavior, add your scores from both quiz parts.

40–48: The red flag is waving, and you had better pay attention. You are in the danger zone. You need guidance from a counselor or mental health professional, and you should be getting it now.

30–39: The yellow flag is up. Your stress and anger levels are too high, and you are feeling increasingly hostile. You are still in control, but it would not take much to trigger a violent flare of temper.

10–29: Relax, you are in the broad normal range. Like most people, you get angry occasionally, but usually with some justification. Sometimes you take overt action, but you are not likely to be unreasonably or excessively aggressive.

0–9: Congratulations! You are in great shape. Your stress and anger are well under control, giving you a laid-back personality not prone to violence.

SOURCE: Questionnaire developed by C. D. Spielberger. Appeared in W. Barnhill, "Early Warning," *Washington Post* (August 11, 1992): B5.

or *strain* refers to the adverse psychological, physical, behavioral, and organizational consequences that *may* occur as a result of stressful events. You 7.1 gives you an opportunity to examine how overstressed and angry you may be.

Four Approaches to Stress

The stress response was discovered by Walter B. Cannon, a medical physiologist, early in the twentieth century.[4] Later researchers defined stress differently than Cannon. We will review four different approaches to defining stress: the homeostatic/medical, cognitive appraisal, person–environment fit, and psychoanalytic approaches. These four approaches will give you a more complete understanding of what stress really is.

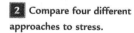
The Homeostatic/Medical Approach When Walter B. Cannon originally discovered stress, he called it "the emergency response" or "the militaristic response," arguing that it was rooted in "the fighting emotions." His early writings provide the basis for calling the stress response the *fight-or-flight* response. According to Cannon, stress results when an external, environmental demand upsets the person's natural steady-state balance.[5] He referred to this steady-state balance, or equilibrium, as *homeostasis*. Cannon believed the body is designed with natural defense mechanisms to keep it in homeostasis. He was especially interested in the role of the sympathetic nervous system in activating a person under stressful conditions.[6]

The Cognitive Appraisal Approach Richard Lazarus was more concerned with the psychology of stress. He de-emphasized the medical and physiological aspects, emphasizing instead the psychological and cognitive aspects of the response.[7] Like Cannon, Lazarus saw stress as a result of a person–environment interaction, and he emphasized the person's cognitive appraisal in classifying persons or events as stressful or not. Individuals differ in their appraisal of events and people. What is stressful for one person may not be stressful for another. Perception and cognitive appraisal are important processes in determining what is stressful. One study found culture-specific differences in perceptions of the causes of job stress between China and the United States.[8] For example, American employees reported lack of job control as a source of stress while Chinese employees reported job evaluations as a source. In addition to cognitive appraisal, Lazarus introduced problem-focused and emotion-focused coping. Problem-focused coping emphasizes managing the stressor, and emotion-focused coping emphasizes managing your response. People with positive core self-evaluations tend to use emotion-focused coping when faced with stressors. These people view themselves as capable, worthy, and in control of their lives.[9]

The Person–Environment Fit Approach Robert Kahn was concerned with the social psychology of stress. His approach emphasized how confusing and conflicting expectations of a person in a social role create stress for the person.[10] He extended the approach to examine a person's fit in the environment. A good person–environment fit occurs when a person's skills and abilities match a clearly defined, consistent set of role expectations. This results in a lack of stress for the person. Stress occurs when the role expectations are confusing and/or conflicting or when a person's skills and abilities are not able to meet the demands of the social role. After a period of this stress, the person can expect to experience strain, such as strain in the form of depression.

The Psychoanalytic Approach Harry Levinson defined stress based on Freudian psychoanalytic theory.[11] Levinson believes that two elements of the personality interact to cause stress. The first is the *ego-ideal*—the embodiment of a person's perfect self. The second is the *self-image*—how the person really sees himself or herself, both positively and negatively. Although not sharply defined, the ego-ideal encompasses admirable attributes of parental personalities, wished-for and/or imaginable qualities a person would like to possess, and the absence of any negative or distasteful qualities. Stress results from the discrepancy between the idealized self (ego-ideal) and the real self-image; the greater the discrepancy, the more stress a person experiences. More generally, psychoanalytic theory helps us understand the role of unconscious personality factors as causes of stress within a person.

homeostasis
A steady state of bodily functioning and equilibrium.

ego-ideal
The embodiment of a person's perfect self.

self-image
How a person sees himself or herself, both positively and negatively.

The Stress Response

Whether activated by an ego-ideal/self-image discrepancy, a poorly defined social role, cognitive appraisal suggesting threat, or a lack of balance, the resulting stress response is characterized by a predictable sequence of mind and body events. The stress response begins with the release of chemical messengers, primarily adrenaline, into the bloodstream. These messengers activate the sympathetic nervous system and the endocrine (hormone) system. These two systems work together and trigger four mind–body changes to prepare the person for fight or flight:

Psychoanalytic theory helps us understand the role of unconscious personality factors as causes of stress.

1. The redirection of the blood to the brain and large-muscle groups and away from the skin, internal organs, and extremities.

2. Increased alertness by way of improved vision, hearing, and other sensory processes through the activation of the brainstem (ancient brain).

3 Explain the psychophysiology of the stress response.

3. The release of glucose (blood sugar) and fatty acids into the bloodstream to sustain the body during the stressful event.

4. Depression of the immune system, as well as restorative and emergent processes (such as digestion).

This set of four changes shifts the person from a neutral, or naturally defensive, posture to an offensive posture. The stress response can be very functional in preparing a person to deal with legitimate emergencies and to achieve peak performance. It is neither inherently bad nor necessarily destructive.

SOURCES OF WORK STRESS

Work stress is caused by factors in the work environment. In addition, pressures from outside the workplace can have spillover effects into the workplace and cause additional stress. An example of this would be when a working mother or father is called at work to come and pick up a sick child from the day-care center so that the child does not expose other children to a health risk. Therefore, the two major categories of sources of work stress are the work demands and nonwork demands shown in Table 7.1. As the table suggests, one of the most complex causes of work stress is role conflict. An innovative study by Pam Perrewé and her colleagues examined the dysfunctional physical and psychological consequences of role conflict.[12] The researchers found political skill to be an antidote for role conflict, one of a range of preventive stress management strategies discussed later in the chapter.

4 Identify work and nonwork causes of stress.

Work Demands

Table 7.1 organizes work demands into four major categories, which are task demands, role demands, interpersonal demands, and physical demands as shown. The table does not present an exhaustive list of work demands but rather aims to show major causes of work stress in each of the four major domains of the work

| 7.1 | Work and Nonwork Demands |

Work Demands

Task Demands	Role Demands
Change	Role conflict:
Lack of control	Interrole
Career progress	Intrarole
New technologies	Person–role
Time pressure	Role ambiguity
Interpersonal Demands	**Physical Demands**
Emotional toxins	Extreme environments
Sexual harassment	Strenuous activities
Poor leadership	Hazardous substances
	Global travel

Nonwork Demands

Home Demands	Personal Demands
Family expectations	Workaholism
Child-rearing/day-care arrangements	Civic and volunteer work
Parental care	Traumatic events

environment. The Science feature includes a different way of categorizing stressors, either as challenge stressors and hindrance stressors. The research examines the effects of these stressors and the positive impact of organizational support.

Task Demands Globalization is creating dramatic changes at work, causing on-the-job pressure and stress.[13] Change leads to uncertainty, a lack of predictability in a person's daily tasks and activities, and may be caused by job insecurity related to difficult economic times. Even as the U.S. economy recovered strongly in 2004, creating hundreds of thousands of jobs, nearly 80,000 U.S. workers continue to lose their jobs monthly. For those who do not lose their jobs, underemployment, monotony, and boredom may be problems. Technology and technological innovation create further change and uncertainty for many employees, requiring adjustments in training, education, and skill development. Intended to make life and work easier and more convenient, information technology may have a paradoxical effect and be a source of stress rather than a stress reliever.

Lack of control is a second major source of stress, especially in work environments that are difficult and psychologically demanding. The lack of control may be caused by inability to influence the timing of tasks and activities, to select tools or methods for accomplishing the work, to make decisions that influence work outcomes, or to exercise direct action to affect the work outcomes. One study found that male workers in occupations with low job autonomy (lack of control) and high job demands (heavy workloads) experienced more heart attacks than other male workers.[14]

Science

The Benefits of Challenge Stress and Organizational Support

This study was conducted in the Louisiana Office of Motor Vehicles using responses from 215 employees and their direct supervisors in 61 offices throughout the state. The purpose was to examine the effects of challenge stressors and hindrance stressors. Challenge stressors included items like the amount of responsibility that an employee had, time pressure, and the number of projects and/or assignments that an employee had. Hindrance stressors included items like the degree to which politics rather than performance affects organizational decisions and the amount of red tape required to get through in order to get the job done. The researchers thought that challenge stressors would have a positive effect on role-based performances of task performance, citizenship performance, and customer service performance. They thought that hindrance stressors would have a negative effect of

these same three role-based performances. The results showed that hindrance stressors did have a negative effect on performance. In addition, the results showed that challenge stressors had a positive effect on performance that was moderated by organizational support. The researchers concluded that companies can benefit from increasing challenges in the workplace if they are supportive of employees working to meet the challenges and if they remove hindrances that interfere with employees' ability to perform their work. While most job stress research has focused on the negative consequences of work stressors, this study shows the positive aspects of some stressors.

SOURCE: J. C. Wallace, B. D. Edwards, T. Arnold, M. L. Frazier, and D. M. Finch, "Work Stressors, Role-Based Performance, and the Moderating Influence of Organizational Support," *Journal of Applied Psychology* 94 (2009): 254–262.

Concerns over career progress, new technologies, and time pressures (or work overload) are three additional task demands triggering stress for the person at work. Career stress is related to the career gridlock that has occurred in many organizations as the middle-manager ranks have been thinned due to mergers, acquisitions, and downsizing during the past two decades.[15] Leaner organizations, unfortunately, often leave work overload for those who are still employed. Time pressure is a leading cause of stress and is often associated with work overload, but may result from poor time management skills. Challenge stressors that promote personal growth and achievement, however, are positively related to job satisfaction and organizational commitment.[16] New technologies create both career stress and "technostress" for people at work who wonder if "smart" machines will replace them.[17] Although they enhance the organization's productive capacity, new technologies may be viewed as the enemy by workers who must ultimately learn to use them. This creates a real dilemma for management.

Role Demands The social–psychological demands of the work environment may be every bit as stressful as task demands at work. People encounter two major categories of role stress at work: role conflict and role ambiguity.[18] Role conflict results from inconsistent or incompatible expectations being communicated. The conflict may be an interrole, intrarole, or person–role conflict.

Interrole conflict is caused by conflicting expectations related to two separate roles, such as employee and parent. For example, the employee with a major sales presentation on Monday and a sick child at home Sunday night is likely to experience interrole conflict. Work–family conflicts like these can lead individuals to withdrawal behaviors.[19]

Intrarole conflict is caused by conflicting expectations related to a single role, such as employee. For example, the manager who presses employees for both very fast *and* high-quality work may be viewed at some point as creating a conflict for employees.

Ethics violations are likely to cause person–role conflicts. This is the problem created for IKEA employees by the Russian officials who shake them down, as we saw in the Thinking Ahead feature. Employees expected to behave in ways that violate personal values, beliefs, or principles experience conflict. The unethical acts of committed employees exemplify this problem. Organizations with high ethical standards, such as Johnson & Johnson, are less likely to create ethical conflicts for employees. Person–role conflicts and ethics violations create a sense of divided loyalty for an employee.

The second major cause of role stress is role ambiguity. Role ambiguity is the confusion a person experiences related to the expectations of others. Role ambiguity may be caused by not understanding what is expected, not knowing how to do it, or not knowing the result of failure to do it. For example, a new magazine employee asked to copyedit a manuscript for the next issue may experience confusion because of lack of familiarity with the magazine's copyediting procedures and conventions.

A twenty-one-nation study of middle managers examined their experiences of role conflict, role ambiguity, and role overload. The results indicated that role stress varies more by country than it does by demographic and organizational factors. For example, non-Western managers experience less role ambiguity and more role overload than do their Western counterparts.[20] In a study of work–family and family–work conflict, job demand and control, social support, and work-hour flexibility among Indian and Norwegian doctors and nurses, the predictors of job stress in India differed from those in Norway and the predictors for doctors differed from those of nurses.[21] A study of U.S. military personnel found that when role clarity was high in a supportive work group, psychological strain was low.[22] A study of 2,273 Norwegian employees found that role conflict, role ambiguity, and conflict with coworkers actually increased under laissez-faire leadership, suggesting that this leadership style and behavior is destructive, even toxic.[23]

Interpersonal Demands Emotional toxins, sexual harassment, and poor leadership in the organization are interpersonal demands for people at work. Emotional toxins are often generated at work by abrasive personalities.[24] They can spread through a work environment and cause a range of disturbances. Even emotional dissonance can be a cause of work stress.[25] Organizations are increasingly less tolerant of sexual harassment, a gender-related interpersonal demand that creates a stressful working environment both for the person being harassed and for others. The vast majority of sexual harassment is directed at women in the workplace and is a chronic yet preventable workplace problem.[26] Poor leadership in organizations and excessive, demanding management styles are a leading cause of work stress for employees. Employees who feel secure with strong, directive leadership may be anxious with an open management style. Those comfortable with participative leaders may feel restrained by a directive style. Trust is an important characteristic of the leader–follower interpersonal relationship, and a threat to a worker's reputation with her or his supervisor may be especially stressful.[27] Functional diversity in project groups also causes difficulty in the establishment of trusting relationships, thus increasing job stress, which leads to lower cohesiveness within the group.[28]

Physical Demands Extreme environments, strenuous activities, hazardous substances, and global travel create physical demands for people at work. Work environments that are very hot or very cold place differing physical demands on people and create unique risks. One cross-cultural study that examined the effects of national culture and ambient temperature on role stress concluded that ambient temperature does affect human well-being, leading to the term *sweatshop* for inhumane working conditions.[29] Dehydration is one problem of extremely hot climates, whereas frostbite is one problem of extremely cold climates. The strenuous job of a steelworker and the hazards associated with bomb disposal work are physically demanding in different ways. The unique physical demands of work are often occupation specific, such as the risk of gravitationally induced loss of consciousness for military pilots flying high-performance fighters[30] or jet lag and loss of sleep for globe-trotting CEOs like IBM's Samuel J. Palmisano and Carlos Ghosn, CEO of two auto companies, Renault and Nissan, that are a half a world apart. The demands of business travel are increasingly recognized as sources of stress.[31] However, the positive aspects of business trips are also increasingly recognized.[32]

Office work has its physical hazards as well. The World Health Organization suggests that even noisy, crowded offices, such as those of some stock brokerages, can prove stressful as well as harmful.[33] Working with a computer terminal can also be stressful, especially if the ergonomic fit between the person and machine is not correct. Eyestrain, neck stiffness, and arm and wrist problems can occur. Office designs that use partitions (cubicles) rather than full walls can create stress. These systems offer little privacy for the occupant (e.g., to conduct employee counseling or performance appraisal sessions) and little protection from interruptions. Stress audits by Roberson Cooper Ltd. aim to take the ambiguity out of the stress concept and provide detailed assessments for companies. As we see in The Real World 7.1, your office may actually make you sick. In The Real World 7.1, the focus is on the overlooked stress risks of the office setting, as just discussed.

Nonwork Demands

Nonwork demands also create stress, which may carry over into the work environment, or vice versa.[34] Nonwork demands may be broadly identified as home demands from an individual's personal life environment and personal demands that are self-imposed.

Home Demands Not all workers are subject to family demands related to marriage, child rearing, and parental care. The wide range of home and family arrangements in contemporary American society has created great diversity in this arena. For those in traditional families, these demands may create role conflicts or overloads that are difficult to manage. For example, the loss of good day care for children may be especially stressful for dual-career and single-parent families.[35] The tension between work and family may lead to a struggle to achieve balance in life. This struggle led Rocky Rhodes, cofounder of Silicon Graphics, to establish four priorities for his life: God, family, exercise, and work.[36] These priorities helped him reallocate his time to achieve better balance in his life. As a result of the maturing of the American population, an increasing number of people face the added demand of parental care. Even when a person works to achieve an integrative social identity, combining many social roles into a "whole" identity for a more stress-free balance in work and nonwork identities, the process of integration is not an easy one.[37]

Personal Demands Self-imposed, personal demands are the second major category of nonwork demands identified in Table 7.1. While self-imposed and personal, they

The Real World 7.1

Can Your Office Make You Sick?

Stress audits conducted by Roberson Cooper Ltd. throughout the world help companies understand stress risks at work. How about the individual office setting? While construction sites have visible risks to health and safety, many employees consider their office a safe haven. Actually, your office may cause stress and in other ways be risky. Open office designs expose you to germs and contagious diseases that can be combated by regular hand washing. Your boss could actually be killing you, a little bit at a time. An angry boss places people under psychological stress and an incompetent boss increases the risk of cardiovascular disorders. Burning the midnight oil through over fifty-five hours of work each week exposes you to the risk of decreased mental skills and memory problems while

Open office designs expose employees to germs and contagious diseases that can be combated by regular hand washing.

Image copyright Yuri Arcurs, 2009. Used under license from Shutterstock.com

working forty-one hours a week or less is much healthier. Vertebrae-skewing chairs and poor posture put stress on the lower back and create one of the most debilitating occupational health problems. Computer work places the entire muscular-skeletal system under stress, most especially the upper arms and hands. In addition, the increase in computer work has significantly decreased the amount of physical activity in the office for those tied to their terminals. The important message about your office is to increase the awareness of causes of stress and health risks. To do this does not require thinking of your office as a dangerous place.

SOURCE: R. Sharp, "How Your Office Makes You Sick," *The Independent* (March 3, 2009).

can and do contribute to work stress on the job. *Workaholism* may be the most notable of these personal demands that causes stress at work and has been identified as a form of addiction.[38] Some of the early warning signs of workaholism include overcommitment to work, inability to enjoy vacations and respites from work, preoccupation with work problems when away from the workplace, and constantly taking work home on the weekend. Another type of personal demand comes from civic activities, volunteer work, and nonwork organizational commitments, such as in churches, synagogues, and public service organizations. These demands become more or less stressful depending on their compatibility with the person's work and family life and their capacity to provide alternative satisfactions for the person. Finally, traumatic events, such as 9/11, and their aftermath are stressful for people who experience them.[39] Not all traumatic events are as catastrophic as 9/11, however. Job loss, examination failures, and termination of romantic attachments are all traumatic, though less catastrophic, and may lead to distress if not addressed and resolved.

THE CONSEQUENCES OF STRESS

workaholism
An imbalanced preoccupation with work at the expense of home and personal life satisfaction.

Stress can be good or bad. Some managers and executives thrive under pressure because they practice what world-class athletes already know.[40] That is, to bring mind, body, and spirit to peak condition requires recovering energy, which is just as important as expending energy. Hence, world-class athletes and managers who practice what they know get high marks on any "stress test" because they use stress-induced energy in positive, healthy, and productive ways. One study found motivation as a mediator of the emotional exhaustion and job performance relationship.[41] The consequences of healthy, normal stress (called *eustress*, for "euphoria + stress") include a number of performance and health benefits to be balanced against the more commonly known costs of individual and organizational distress.[42] The benefits of eustress and the costs of distress are listed in Table 7.2. An organization striving for high-quality products and services needs a healthy workforce to support the effort. Eustress is a characteristic of healthy people; distress is not.

5 Describe the benefits of eustress and the costs of distress.

Performance and Health Benefits

The Yerkes–Dodson law, shown in Figure 7.1, indicates that stress leads to improved performance up to an optimum point.[43] Beyond the optimum point, further stress and arousal have a detrimental effect on performance. Therefore, healthy amounts of eustress are desirable to improve performance by arousing a person to action. It is in the midrange of the curve that the greatest performance benefits from stress are achieved. Joseph McGrath has suggested that performance declines beyond the midpoint in the Yerkes–Dodson curve because of the increasing difficulty of the task to be performed.[44] The stress response does provide momentary strength and physical force for brief periods of exertion, thus providing a basis for peak performance in athletic competition or other events. In addition, psychological well-being contributes positively to job performance.[45]

Specific stressful activities, including aerobic exercise, weight training, and flexibility training, improve health and enhance a person's ability to manage stressful demands or situations. Cannon argued that the stress response better prepares soldiers for combat.[46]

The stress response is not inherently bad or destructive. The various individual and organizational forms of distress often associated with the word *stress* are the result of prolonged activation of the stress response, mismanagement of the energy induced by the response, or unique vulnerabilities in a person. We next examine the forms of individual distress and then the forms of organizational distress.

TABLE

7.2 Benefits of Eustress and Costs of Distress	
Benefits of Eustress	
Performance	**Health**
Increased arousal	Cardiovascular efficiency
Bursts of physical strength	Balance in the nervous system
Full engagement	Enhanced focus in an emergency
Costs of Distress	
Individual	**Organizational**
Psychological disorders	Participation problems
Medical illnesses	Performance decrements
Behavioral problems	Compensation awards

FIGURE

7.1   Yerkes–Dodson Law

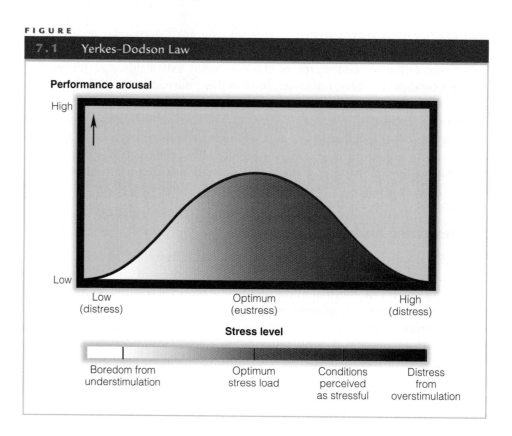

Individual Distress

An extreme preoccupation with work may result in acute individual distress, such as the unique Japanese phenomenon of *karoshi*, or death by overwork.[47] In general, individual distress usually takes one of the three basic forms shown in Table 7.2. Work-related psychological disorders are among the ten leading health disorders and diseases in the United States, according to the National Institute for Occupational Safety and Health.[48] The most common types of psychological distress are depression, burnout, and psychosomatic disorders. Depression and burnout can lead to emotional exhaustion with its associated negative consequences.[49] Emotional exhaustion may also be caused by the requirements for emotional expression on the job.[50] Burnout contrasts with rust-out, which is a form of psychological distress caused by the lack of challenge, inspiration, and opportunity on the job.[51] Psychosomatic disorders are physical disorders with a psychological origin. For example, the intense stress of public speaking may result in a speech disorder; that is, the person is under so much stress that the mind literally will not allow speech to occur.

A number of medical illnesses have a stress-related component.[52] The most significant such illnesses are heart disease and strokes, backaches, peptic ulcers, and headaches. Ford Motor Company found that cardiovascular diseases, the leading cause of death in the United States since 1910, constituted only 1.5 percent of the medical incidents among 800 salaried employees at its headquarters but accounted for 29 percent of the reported medical costs.[53] On the positive side, premature death and disability rates have dropped 24–36 percent since the mid-1970s. Backaches are a nonfatal medical problem to which stress contributes through the strong muscular contractions related to preparation for fight or flight. Headaches may be related to eyestrain or have a migraine component, but tension headaches are caused by the contraction of the head and neck muscles under stressful conditions. Finally, stress is a contributing factor to peptic ulcers. A popular comedian commented, "I don't get angry; I just grow a tumor!" There is no clear evidence that stress is a direct causal agent in the onset of cancer. However, stress may play an indirect role in the progression of the disease.[54]

Behavioral problems are the third form of individual distress. These problems include workplace aggression, substance abuse of various kinds, and accidents. Workplace aggression may be triggered by perceptions of injustice in the workplace.[55] Interpersonal conflicts can be a form of nonphysical aggression. One study found that conflicts with workmates, neighbors, and other "nonintimates" account for about 80 percent of our bad moods.[56] Ethnic and cultural differences are too often a basis for interpersonal conflicts and may escalate into physical violence in the workplace. For example, some U.S. employees of Arab descent experienced ethnic slurs and bullying at work during the War on Terror with Iraq, a largely Arab nation. Psychological detachment from work can be a successful strategy for coping with work stressors and reduce the psychological strain associated with workplace bullying.[57]

Substance abuse ranges from legal behaviors such as alcohol abuse, excessive smoking, and the overuse of prescription drugs to illegal behaviors such as heroin addiction. Former surgeon general C. Everett Koop's war on smoking was warranted based on health risk information reported by the American Heart Association. However, the war on smoking also raises an ethical debate about the restriction of individual behavior. How far can the government or society go in restricting individual behavior that has adverse health consequences for many? This is even more problematic in light of recent research results showing the adverse health effects nonsmokers experience as a result of secondhand smoke.

Accidents, both on and off the job, are another behavioral form of distress that can sometimes be traced to work-related stressors. For example, an unresolved problem at work may continue to preoccupy or distract an employee driving home and result in an automobile accident.

These three forms of individual distress—psychological disorders, medical illnesses, and behavioral problems—cause a burden of personal suffering. They also cause a collective burden of suffering reflected in organizational distress.

Organizational Distress

The University of Michigan studies on organizational stress identified a variety of indirect costs of mismanaged stress for the organization, such as low morale, dissatisfaction, breakdowns in communication, and disruption of working relationships. Subsequent research at the Survey Research Center at Michigan established behavioral costing guidelines, which specify the direct costs of organizational distress.[58] New research suggests that even positive performance stereotypes can have an adverse effect on organizational health.[59]

Participation problems are the costs associated with absenteeism, tardiness, strikes and work stoppages, and turnover. In the case of absenteeism, the organization may compensate by hiring temporary personnel who take the place of the absentee, thus elevating personnel costs. When considering turnover, a distinction should be made between dysfunctional and functional turnover. Dysfunctional turnover occurs when an organization loses a valuable employee. It is costly for the organization. Replacement costs, including recruiting and retraining, for the valued employee range from five to seven months of the person's monthly salary. Functional turnover, by contrast, benefits the organization by creating opportunities for new members, new ideas, and fresh approaches. Functional turnover occurs when an organization loses an employee who has little or no value or is a problem. Functional turnover is good for the organization. The "up or out" promotion policy for members of some organizations is designed to create functional turnover.

participation problem
A cost associated with absenteeism, tardiness, strikes and work stoppages, and turnover.

Performance decrements are the costs resulting from poor quality or low quantity of production, grievances, and unscheduled machine downtime and repair. As in the case of medical illnesses, stress is not the only causal agent in these performance decrements. Stress does play a role, however, whether the poor quality or low quantity of production is motivated by distressed employees or by an unconscious response to stress on the job. In California, some employees have the option of taking a "stress leave" rather than filing a grievance against the boss.

Compensation awards are the organizational costs resulting from court awards for job distress.[60] One former insurance employee in Louisiana filed a federal suit against the company, alleging it created a high-strain job for him that resulted in an incapacitating depression.[61] A jury awarded him a $1.5 million judgment that was later overturned by the judge. Job stress–related claims have skyrocketed and threaten to bankrupt the workers' compensation system in some states, although claims and costs are down in other states.[62] However, employers need not panic because fair procedures go a long way toward avoiding legal liability, and legal rulings are setting realistic limits on employers' obligations.[63]

INDIVIDUAL DIFFERENCES IN THE STRESS–STRAIN RELATIONSHIP

6 Discuss individual differences in the stress–strain relationship.

The same stressful events may lead to distress and strain for one person and to excitement and healthy results for another. Individual differences play a central role in the stress–strain relationship. The weak organ hypothesis in medicine, also known as the Achilles' heel phenomenon, suggests that a person breaks down at his or her weakest point. As the Looking Back feature on IKEA notes, we can look within for sources of strength as well. Some individual differences, such as gender and Type A behavior pattern, enhance vulnerability to strain under stressful conditions. Other individual differences, such as personality hardiness and self-reliance, reduce vulnerability to strain under stressful conditions. One study of personality and emotional performance found that individuals high on extraversion experienced elevated heart rates when asked to express personality incongruent emotions, such as anger, and that neuroticism was associated with increased heart rate and poor performance more generally.[64] This suggests that extraversion and neuroticism affect the stress–strain relationship.

Gender Effects

While prevailing stereotypes suggest that women are the weaker sex, the truth is that the life expectancy for American women is approximately seven years longer than for American men. This implies that women may be stronger. The stereotype is challenged by research in public accounting, which finds that female public accountants have no higher turnover rates than males even though they report more stress, thus suggesting that women respond differently to stress.[65] This is further supported by research that finds women's behavioral responses to stress are in fact different from men's responses to stress.[66]

Some literature indicates that there are differences in the stressors to which the two sexes are subject.[67] For example, sexual harassment is a gender-related source of stress for many working women. Interestingly, a study found that men, more than women, experienced increased problem drinking as a result of workplace harassment, probably because harassment is a nonnormal occurrence for men.[68] There is also substantive evidence that the important differences in the sexes are

performance decrement
A cost resulting from poor quality or low quantity of production, grievances, and unscheduled machine downtime and repair.

compensation award
An organizational cost resulting from court awards for job distress.

7.3	Type A Behavior Pattern Components

1. Sense of time urgency (a kind of "hurry sickness").

2. The quest for numbers (success is measured by the number of achievements).

3. Status insecurity (feeling unsure of oneself deep down inside).

4. Aggression and hostility expressed in response to frustration and conflict.

in vulnerabilities.[69] Males, for instance, are more vulnerable at an earlier age to fatal health problems, such as cardiovascular disorders, whereas women report more nonfatal, but long-term and disabling, health problems. Although we can conclude that gender indeed creates a differential vulnerability between the two sexes, it may actually be more important to examine the differences *among* women or *among* men.

Type A Behavior Pattern

Type A behavior pattern, also labeled *coronary-prone behavior*,[70] is a complex of personality and behavioral characteristics, including competitiveness, time urgency, social status insecurity, aggression, hostility, and a quest for achievements. Table 7.3 lists four primary components of the Type A behavior pattern.

There are two primary hypotheses concerning the lethal part of the Type A behavior pattern. One hypothesis says that the problem is time urgency, whereas the other suggests that it is hostility and aggression. The weight of evidence indicates the latter.[71] Look back at your result in You 7.1. Are you too angry and overstressed?

The alternative to the Type A behavior pattern is the Type B behavior pattern. People with Type B personalities are relatively free of the Type A behaviors and characteristics identified in Table 7.3. Type B people are less coronary prone, but if they do have a heart attack, they do not appear to recover as well as those with Type A personalities. Organizations can also be characterized as Type A or Type B.[72] Type A individuals in Type B organizations and Type B individuals in Type A organizations experience stress related to a misfit between their personality type and the predominant type of the organization. However, preliminary evidence suggests that Type A individuals in Type A organizations are most at risk of health disorders.

Type A behavior can be modified. The first step is recognizing that an individual is prone to this pattern. Another possible step is to spend time with Type B individuals. Type B people often recognize Type A behavior and can help them take hassles less seriously and see the humor in situations. Type A individuals can also pace themselves, manage their time well, and try not to do multiple things at once. Focusing only on the task at hand and its completion, rather than worrying about other tasks, can help them cope more effectively.

Personality Hardiness

People who have personality hardiness resist strain reactions when subjected to stressful events more effectively than do people who are not hardy.[73] The components of *personality hardiness* are commitment (versus alienation), control (versus powerlessness), and challenge (versus threat). Commitment is a curiosity and engagement with one's environment that leads to the experience of activities as interesting and enjoyable. Employees with high levels of commitment are less

Type A behavior pattern
A complex of personality and behavioral characteristics, including competitiveness, time urgency, social status insecurity, aggression, hostility, and a quest for achievements.

personality hardiness
A personality resistant to distress and characterized by commitment, control, and challenge.

Commitment, control, and challenge are components of personality hardiness.

likely to leave the organization and experience promotion stress.[74] Control is an ability to influence the process and outcomes of events that lead to the experience of activities as personal choices. Challenge is the viewing of change as a stimulus to personal development, which leads to the experience of activities with openness.

The hardy personality appears to use these three components actively to engage in transformational coping when faced with stressful events.[75] *Transformational coping* is the act of actively changing an event into something less subjectively stressful by viewing it in a broader life perspective, by altering the course and outcome of the event through action, and/or by achieving greater understanding of the process. The alternative to transformational coping is regressive coping, a much less healthy form of coping with stressful events characterized by a passive avoidance of events by decreasing interaction with the environment. Regressive coping may lead to short-term stress reduction at the cost of long-term healthy life adjustment. In addition, more resilient employees have the ability to bounce back from stressful events more readily than those not as resilient.[76]

Self-Reliance

There is increasing evidence that social relationships have an important impact on health and life expectancy.[77] *Self-reliance* is a personality attribute related to how people form and maintain supportive attachments with others. Self-reliance was originally based in attachment theory, a theory about normal human development.[78]

The theory identifies three distinct patterns of attachment, and research suggests that these patterns extend into behavioral strategies during adulthood, in professional as well as personal relationships.[79] Self-reliance results in a secure pattern of attachment and interdependent behavior. Interpersonal attachment is emotional and psychological connectedness to another person. The two insecure patterns of attachment are counterdependence and overdependence.

Self-reliance is a healthy, secure, *interdependent* pattern of behavior. It may appear paradoxical, because a person appears independent while maintaining a host of supportive attachments.[80] Self-reliant people respond to stressful, threatening situations by reaching out to others appropriately. Self-reliance is a flexible, responsive strategy of forming and maintaining multiple, diverse relationships. Self-reliant people are confident, enthusiastic, and persistent in facing challenges. Their flexibility allows them to form healthy partner relationships that can be a buffer against work-related stress.[81]

Counterdependence is an unhealthy, insecure pattern of behavior that leads to separation in relationships with other people. When faced with stressful and threatening situations, counterdependent people draw into themselves, attempting to exhibit strength and power. Counterdependence may be characterized as a rigid, dismissing denial of the need for other people in difficult and stressful times. Counterdependent people exhibit a fearless, aggressive, and actively powerful response to challenges.

Overdependence is also an unhealthy, insecure pattern of behavior. Overdependent people respond to stressful and threatening situations by clinging to other people in any way possible. Overdependence may be characterized as a desperate, preoccupied attempt to achieve a sense of security through relationships. Overdependent people exhibit an active but disorganized and anxious response to challenges. Overdependence prevents a person from being able to organize and maintain healthy relationships and thus creates much distress. It is interesting to note that both counterdependence and overdependence are exhibited by some military personnel who are experiencing adjustment difficulties during the first thirty days of

transformational coping
A way of managing stressful events by changing them into less subjectively stressful events.

self-reliance
A healthy, secure, *interdependent* pattern of behavior related to how people form and maintain supportive attachments with others.

counterdependence
An unhealthy, insecure pattern of behavior that leads to separation in relationships with other people.

overdependence
An unhealthy, insecure pattern of behavior that leads to preoccupied attempts to achieve security through relationships.

You 7.2

Are You Self-Reliant?

Each of the following questions relates to how you form relationships with people at work, at home, and in other areas of your life. Read each statement carefully and rate each on a scale from 0 (strongly disagree) to 5 (strongly agree) to describe your degree of disagreement or agreement with the statement. *Answer all 15 questions.*

_____ 1. It is difficult for me to delegate work to others.
_____ 2. Developing close relationships at work will backfire on you.
_____ 3. I avoid depending on other people because I feel crowded by close relationships.
_____ 4. I am frequently suspicious of other people's motives and intentions.
_____ 5. Asking for help makes me feel needy, and I do not like that.
_____ 6. It is difficult for me to leave home or work to go to the other.
_____ 7. People will always be there when I need them.
_____ 8. I regularly and easily spend time with other people during the workday.
_____ 9. I trust at least two other people to have my best interests at heart.
_____ 10. I have a healthy, happy home life.
_____ 11. I need to have colleagues or subordinates close in order to feel secure about my work.
_____ 12. I become very concerned when I have conflict with family members at home.
_____ 13. I get very upset and disturbed if I have conflicts in relationship(s) at work.
_____ 14. I prefer very frequent feedback from my boss to know I am performing well.
_____ 15. I always consult others when I make decisions.

Scoring:

Follow the instructions to determine your score for each subscale of the Self-Reliance Inventory. *Note: Question 6 is used twice in scoring.*

Self-Reliance/Counterdependence

Step 1: Total your responses to Questions 1–6 _____
Step 2: Total your responses to Questions 7–10 _____
Step 3: Subtract your Step 2 total from 20 (20 – _____) = _____
Step 4: Add your results in Steps 1 and 3 _____

Self-Reliance/Overdependence

Step 5: Total your responses to Questions 6 and 11–15 _____

A score lower than 16 in Step 4 or Step 5 indicates self-reliance on that particular subscale.

A score higher than 20 in Step 4 suggests possible counterdependence, and a score higher than 20 in Step 5 suggests possible overdependence.

SOURCE: Adapted from J. C. Quick, D. L. Nelson, and J. D. Quick, "The Self-Reliance Inventory," in J. W. Pfeiffer, ed., *The 1991 Annual: Developing Human Resources* (San Diego: Pfeiffer & Co., 1991), 149–161.

basic training.[82] In particular, basic military trainees who have the most difficulty have overdependence problems and find it difficult to function on their own during the rigors of training.

You 7.2 gives you an opportunity to examine how self-reliant (interdependent), counterdependent, and/or overdependent you are.

PREVENTIVE STRESS MANAGEMENT

7 Distinguish the primary, secondary, and tertiary stages of preventive stress management.

preventive stress management
An organizational philosophy that holds that people and organizations should take joint responsibility for promoting health and preventing distress and strain.

Stress is an inevitable feature of work and personal life. It is neither inherently bad nor destructive. Stress can be managed. The following is the central principle of *preventive stress management:* Individual distress and organizational distress are not inevitable. Preventive stress management is an organizational philosophy about people and organizations taking joint responsibility for promoting health and preventing distress and strain. Preventive stress management is rooted in the public health notions of prevention, which were first used in preventive medicine. The three stages of prevention are primary, secondary, and tertiary prevention. A framework for understanding preventive stress management is presented in Figure 7.2, which includes the three stages of prevention in a preventive medicine context, as well as an organizational context.

Primary prevention is intended to reduce, modify, or eliminate the demand or stressor causing stress. The idea behind primary prevention is to eliminate or ameliorate the source of a problem. True organizational stress prevention is largely primary in nature, because it changes and shapes the demands the organization places on people at work. *Secondary prevention* is intended to alter or modify the individual's or the organization's response to a demand or stressor. People must learn to manage the inevitable, inalterable work stressors and demands so as to avert distress and strain while promoting health and well-being. *Tertiary prevention* is intended to heal individual or organizational symptoms of distress and strain. The symptoms may range from early warning signs (such as headaches or absenteeism) to more severe forms of distress (such as hypertension, work stoppages, and strikes). One innovative approach used by the computer company DriveSavers blends treatment

FIGURE

7.2 A Framework for Preventive Stress Managemen

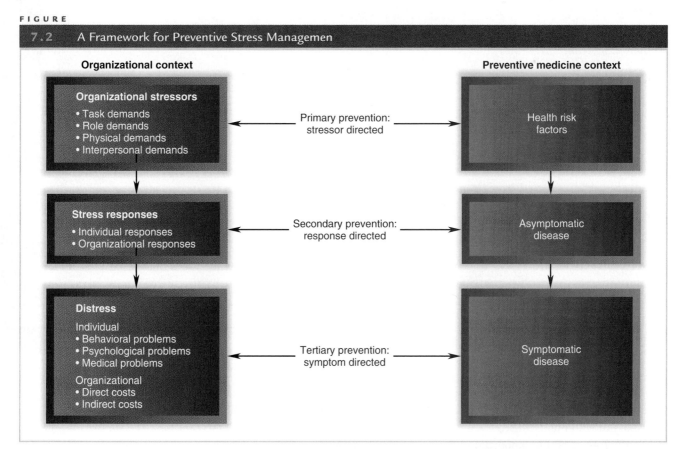

SOURCE: Figure 1 in J. D. Quick, R. S. Horn, and J. C. Quick, "Health Consequences of Stress," *Journal of Organizational Behavior Management* 8(2) (Fall 1986): 21. Reprinted with permission of Haworth Press, Inc., 10 Alice Street, Binghamton, NY 13904. Copyright 1986.

and prevention with a full-time former grief counselor.[83] We discuss the stages of prevention in the context of organizational prevention, individual prevention, and comprehensive health promotion.

Organizational Stress Prevention

Some organizations are low-stress, healthy environments, whereas others are high-stress environments that may place their employees' health at risk. The experience of organizational justice and fairness is emerging as one contextual factor at work that leads to a positive low-stress work environment.[84] One comprehensive approach to organizational health and preventive stress management was pioneered in the U.S. Air Force by Colonel Joyce Adkins, who developed an Organizational Health Center (OHC) within the Air Force Materiel Command.[85] The OHC's goal is to keep people happy, healthy, and on the job, while increasing efficiency and productivity to their highest levels by focusing on workplace stressors, organizational and individual forms of distress, and managerial and individual strategies for preventive stress management. This comprehensive, organizational health approach addresses primary, secondary, and tertiary prevention. Most organizational prevention, however, is primary prevention, including job redesign, goal setting, role negotiation, and career management. Two organizational stress prevention methods, team building and social support at work, are secondary prevention. While we discuss team building in Chapter 9, we should note here that team structure under stress may influence team effectiveness. Specifically, teams experiencing quantitative demands are more effective when more tightly structured, while teams experiencing qualitative demands are more effective when more loosely structured.[86] Finally, companies such as Kraft Foods (a subsidiary of Altria Group, Inc.) and Hardee's Food Systems (part of CKE Restaurants, Inc.) have developed specific violence prevention programs to combat the rise in workplace violence. Violence in organizations is a category of dysfunctional behaviors that are often motivated by stressful events and whose negative consequences organizations want to prevent.[87] Other employers are using return-to-work interviews and phased return to work programs to combat the negative effects of stress-related employee absences.[88]

Job Redesign The job strain model presented in Figure 7.3 suggests that the combination of high job demands and restricted job decision latitude or worker control leads to a high-strain job. A major concern in job redesign should be to enhance worker control. Increasing worker control reduces distress and strain without necessarily reducing productivity in many cases. The exception to this is for employees with more traditional values, because an increase in job control for them actually has detrimental effects on their health.[89]

Job redesign to increase worker control is one strategy of preventive stress management. It can be accomplished in a number of ways, the most common being to increase job decision latitude. Increased job decision latitude might include greater decision authority over the sequencing of work activities, the timing of work schedules, the selection and sequencing of work tools, or the selection of work teams. A second objective of job redesign should be to reduce uncertainty and increase predictability in the workplace. Uncertainty is a major stressor.

Goal Setting Organizational preventive stress management can also be achieved through goal-setting activities. These activities are designed to increase task motivation, as discussed in Chapter 6, while reducing the degree of role conflict and ambiguity to which people at work are subject. Goal setting focuses a person's attention

8 Discuss organizational and individual methods of preventive stress management.

primary prevention
The stage in preventive stress management designed to reduce, modify, or eliminate the demand or stressor causing stress.

secondary prevention
The stage in preventive stress management designed to alter or modify the individual's or the organization's response to a demand or stressor.

tertiary prevention
The stage in preventive stress management designed to heal individual or organizational symptoms of distress and strain.

FIGURE

7.3   Job Strain Model

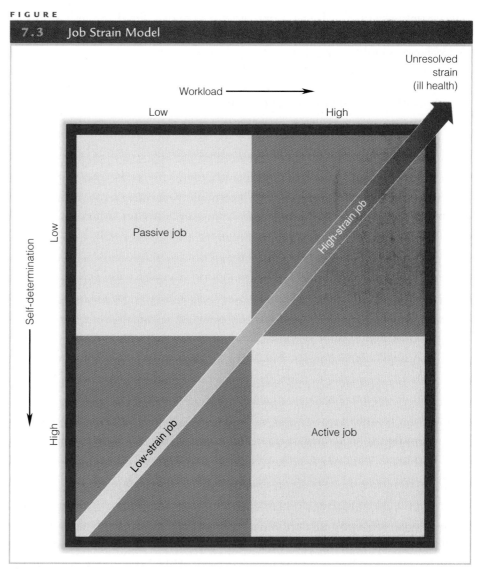

SOURCE: B. Gardell, "Efficiency and Health Hazards in Mechanized Work," in J. C. Quick, R. S. Bhagat, J. E. Dalton, and J. D. Quick, eds., *Work Stress: Health Care Systems in the Workplace*. Copyright © 1987. Reproduced with permission of Greenwood Publishing Group, Inc., Westport, CT.

while directing energy into a productive channel. Implicit in much of the goal-setting literature is the assumption that people participate in, and accept, their work goals. Chapter 6 addressed goal setting in depth.

Role Negotiation The organizational development technique of role negotiation has value as a stress management method because it allows people to modify their work roles.[90] Role negotiation begins with the definition of a specific role, called the focal role, within its organizational context. The person in the focal role then identifies the expectations understood for that role, and key organizational members specify their expectations of the person in the focal role. The actual negotiation follows from the comparison of the role incumbent's expectations and key members' expectations. The points of confusion and conflict are opportunities for clarification and resolution. The final result of the role negotiation process should be a clear, well-defined focal role with which the incumbent and organizational members are all comfortable.

Social Support Systems Team building, discussed in Chapter 9, is one way to develop supportive social relationships in the workplace. However, team building is primarily task oriented, not socioemotional, in nature. Although employees may receive much of their socioemotional support from personal relationships outside the workplace, such support within the workplace is also necessary for psychological well-being.

Social support systems can be enhanced through the work environment in a number of ways. Interpersonal communication is the key to unlocking social support for preventive stress management.[91] Figure 7.4 identifies key elements in a person's work and nonwork social support system. These relations provide emotional caring, information, evaluative feedback, modeling, and instrumental support.

Individual Prevention

Clinical research shows that individuals may use a number of self-directed interventions to help prevent distress and enhance positive well-being.[92] Individual prevention can be of a primary, secondary, or tertiary nature. The primary prevention activities we discuss are learned optimism, time management, and leisure-time activities. The secondary prevention activities we discuss are physical exercise, relaxation, and diet. The tertiary prevention activities we discuss are opening up and professional help. These eight methods and their benefits are summarized in Table 7.4.

Positive Thinking Positive thinking is an optimistic approach used by people to explain the good and bad events in their lives to themselves.[93] It is a habit of thinking learned over time, though some people are predisposed to positive thinking. Pessimism is an alternative explanatory style leading to depression, physical health problems, and low levels of achievement. By contrast, positive thinking

FIGURE

7.4   Social Support at Work and Home

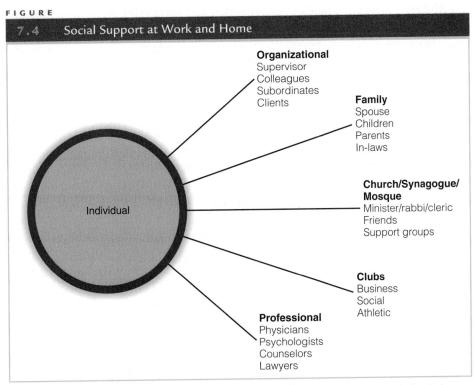

SOURCE: From J. C. Quick, J. D. Quick, D. L. Nelson, and J. J. Hurrell, Jr., in *Preventive Stress Management in Organizations*, 1997, p. 198. Copyright © 1997 by The American Psychological Association. Reprinted with permission.

7.4   Individual Preventive Stress Management

Primary Prevention

Positive thinking:	Optimistic, nonnegative self-talk that reduces depression.
Time management:	Improves planning and prioritizes activities.
Leisure-time activity:	Balances work and nonwork activities.

Secondary Prevention

Physical exercise:	Improves cardiovascular function and muscular flexibility.
Relaxation training:	Lowers all indicators of the stress response.
Diet:	Lowers the risk of cardiovascular disease and improves overall physical health.

Tertiary Prevention

Opening up:	Releases internalized traumas and emotional tensions.
Professional help:	Provides information, emotional support, and therapeutic guidance.

SOURCE: M. Barney, "Motorola's Second Generation," *Six Sigma Forum Magazine* (May 2002): 13

and optimism enhance physical health and achievement and avert susceptibility to depression. Positive thinking does not mean ignoring real stress and challenge. Optimistic people avoid distress by viewing the bad events and difficult times in their lives as temporary, limited, and caused by something other than themselves. They face difficult times and adversity with hope. Optimistic people take more credit for the good events in their lives; they see these good events as more pervasive and generalized. Learned optimism begins with identifying pessimistic thoughts and then distracting oneself from these thoughts or disputing them with evidence and alternative thoughts. Learned optimism is nonnegative thinking. This is one of the five dimensions of positive organizational behavior (POB), the other four being confidence/self-efficacy, hope, subjective well-being/happiness, and emotional intelligence.[94]

Time Management Time pressure is one of the major sources of stress listed in Table 7.1 for both workers and students. The leading symptoms of poor time management include constant rushing, missed deadlines, work overload and the sense of being overwhelmed, insufficient rest time, and indecision. Good time managers are "macro" time managers who use a GP³ method of time management.[95] This method includes (1) setting *goals* that are challenging yet attainable; (2) *prioritizing* these goals in terms of their relative importance; (3) *planning* for goal attainment through specific tasks, activities, scheduling, and even delegation; and (4) *praising* oneself for specific achievements along the way. Setting concrete goals and prioritizing them are the most important first steps in time management skills, ensuring that the most critical work and study activities receive enough time and attention. This system of time management enables a person to track his or her success over time and goes a long way toward reducing unnecessary stress and confusion.

Leisure-Time Activities Unremitted striving characterizes many people with a high need for achievement. Leisure-time activities provide employees an opportunity for rest and recovery from strenuous activities either at home or at work. Many

The Real World 7.2

Marathon Training Not Required

The Cooper Aerobics Center does not require marathon-intensity training for those who want to achieve the health and stress-resistant benefits of the physically fit individual. The biggest benefits of physical exercise actually come at the low-intensity level, and brisk walking does not require changing into athletic clothes. If there is only one thing to do for yourself during the course of the work week, it is to go outside and take a brisk walk. Fresh air, deep breaking, and physical activity for 15 or 20 minutes is all that is required. Lunchtime or after-work walking clubs can be a great way to combine the physical exercise benefits with social support exchanges. Some executives walk to meet colleagues at an agreed upon lunch place after which they walk back to their office settings. Building physical exercise into daily living in this way overcomes the hurdle for people who do not have the interest or motivation for more strenuous sports and physical activities, such as racquetball, squash, tennis...or marathon training. The brisk walk can be more stimulating than a cup of coffee while being healthier at the same time. An added benefit of getting outside in the fresh air for a brisk walk is the exposure to sunshine. The exposure can make you happier because exposure to sunlight is linked to the production of the feel-good chemical serotonin and is needed for the body to produce vitamin D.

SOURCE: Staff, "If You Only Do One Thing This Week, Go Outside," *Guardian Unlimited* (June 29, 2009).

individuals, when asked what they do with their leisure time, say that they clean the house or mow the lawn. These activities are fine, as long as they produce the stress-reducing benefit of pleasure. Some say our work ethic is a cultural barrier to pleasure. We work longer hours, and two-income families are the norm. Leisure is increasingly a luxury among working people. The key to the effective use of leisure time is enjoyment. Leisure time can be used for spontaneity, joy, and connection with others in our lives. While vacations can be a relief from job burnout, they may suffer fade-out effects.[96] Hence, leisure time and vacations must be periodic, recurring activities.

Physical Exercise Different types of physical exercise are important secondary stress prevention activities. Colleges and universities often implement physical exercise through physical education classes, while military organizations implement it through physical fitness standards. Aerobic exercise improves a person's responsiveness to stressful activities. Kenneth Cooper has long advocated aerobic exercise.[97] Research at the Aerobics Center in Dallas has found that aerobically fit people (1) have lower levels of adrenaline in their blood at rest; (2) have a slower, stronger heart functioning; and (3) recover from stressful events more quickly. As we see in The Real World 7.2, it does not require marathon training to achieve these benefits as a shield against the adverse effects of stress.

Flexibility training is an important type of exercise because of the muscular contractions associated with the stress response. One component of the stress response is the contraction of the flexor muscles, which prepares a person to fight or flee. Flexibility training enables a person to stretch and relax these muscles to prevent the accumulation of unnecessary muscular tension.[98] Flexibility exercises help maintain joint mobility, increase strength, and play an important role in the prevention of injury.

Relaxation Training Herbert Benson was one of the first people to identify the relaxation response as the natural counterresponse to the stress response.[99] In studying Western and Eastern peoples, Benson found that Judeo-Christian people have elicited this response through their time-honored tradition of prayer, whereas Eastern people have elicited it through meditation. The relaxation response does not require a theological or religious component. If you have a practice of regular prayer or meditation, you may already elicit the relaxation response regularly. Keep in mind that digestion may interfere with the elicitation of the response, so avoid practicing relaxation shortly after eating.

Diet Diet may play an indirect role in stress and stress management. High sugar content in the diet can stimulate the stress response, and foods high in cholesterol can adversely affect blood chemistry. Good dietary practices contribute to a person's overall health, making her or him less vulnerable to distress. In his nonsurgical, nonpharmacological approach to reversing heart disease, Dean Ornish proposes a very stringent "reversal diet" for people with identifiable blockage of the arteries.[100] Ornish recommends a somewhat less stringent "prevention diet" as one of four elements for opening up the arteries. Another element in his program is being open in relationships with other people.

Opening Up Everyone experiences a traumatic, stressful, or painful event in life at one time or another. One of the most therapeutic, curative responses to such an event is to confide in another person.[101] Discussing difficult experiences with another person is not always easy, yet health benefits, immune system improvement, and healing accrue through self-disclosure. In one study comparing those who wrote once a week about traumatic events with those who wrote about nontraumatic events, significant health benefits and reduced absenteeism were found in the first group.[102] Confession need not be through a personal relationship with friends. It may occur through a private diary. For example, a lawyer might write each evening about all of his or her most troubling thoughts, feelings, and emotions during the course of the day. The process of opening up and confessing appears to counter the detrimental effects of stress.

Professional Help Confession and opening up may occur through professional helping relationships. People who need healing have psychological counseling, career counseling, physical therapy, medical treatment, surgical intervention, and other therapeutic techniques available. Employee assistance programs (EAPs) may be very helpful in referring employees to the appropriate caregivers. Even combat soldiers who experience battle stress reactions severe enough to take them out of action can heal and be ready for subsequent combat duty.[103] The early detection of distress and strain reactions, coupled with prompt professional treatment, can be instrumental in averting permanent physical and psychological damage.

Comprehensive Health Promotion

Whereas organizational stress prevention is aimed at eliminating health risks at work, comprehensive health promotion programs are aimed at establishing a "strong and resistant host" by building on individual prevention and lifestyle change.[104] Physical fitness and exercise programs characterize corporate health promotion programs in the United States and Canada.[105] A health promotion and wellness survey of accredited medical schools in the United States, Canada, and Puerto Rico found that these programs place the most emphasis on physical well-being and the least emphasis on spiritual well-being.[106] A new approach to comprehensive health promotion places the focus on the organization and organizational wellness.[107] Still, social and cognitive processes are key considerations in the successful implementation of stress prevention programs.[108]

Johnson & Johnson developed a comprehensive health promotion program with a significant number of educational modules for individuals and groups. These modules addressed a specific topic, such as Type A behavior, exercise, diet (through cooperative activities with the American Heart Association), stress, and risk assessment (through regular risk assessments and health profiles for participants). Johnson & Johnson

Diversity Dialogue

When Domestic Violence "Goes to Work"

Rachel was assaulted by her partner when she was eight months pregnant. Not only did he assault her, he snatched the telephone out of the wall, leaving Rachel with no way to call for help. By the time she cleaned up her head wound and got to a pay phone to call in sick, her shift had already begun.

This wasn't the first time that Rachel had to miss work. She regularly called in sick due to the physical and emotional effects of the abuse she suffered at the hands of her partner. In fact, Rachel had become a pro at making excuses to explain away her cuts, strangle marks, and bruises to her colleagues. When the "I fell" and "I hurt myself in a sporting event" explanations wore thin, she began to cover up the telltale marks on her neck and arms with long sleeves and sweaters even during the summer. All of the other times, Rachel had gotten away with calling in sick so often, but this time was different. This time she lost her job.

Rachel is not alone. She is one of the 57 percent of women who have reported domestic abuse at some time in their lives. Although they struggle to keep their personal and professional lives separate, women who experience domestic trauma often find it very difficult if not impossible to concentrate at work. Because these women often suffer in silence, their employers may feel they have no other alternative but to fire them.

1. Is domestic violence a workplace issue?
2. What can employers do if they suspect an employee's poor performance is related to stress stemming from domestic abuse?

SOURCE: B. Pennings, "Domestic Violence: A Workplace Issue," *New Matilda* (June 6, 2007).

found that the health status of employees who are not participating in health promotion programs in the workplace improves if the worksite does have such a program.

MANAGERIAL IMPLICATIONS: STRESS WITHOUT DISTRESS

Stress is an inevitable result of work and personal life. Distress is not an inevitable consequence of stressful events, however; in fact, well-managed stress can improve health and performance. Managers must learn how to create healthy stress for employees to facilitate performance and well-being without distress. Managers can help employees by adjusting workloads, avoiding ethical dilemmas, being sensitive to diversity among individuals concerning what is stressful, and being sensitive to employees' personal life demands.

New technologies create demands and stress for employees. Managers can help employees adjust to new technologies by ensuring that their design and implementation are sensitive to employees and that employee involvement is strong.

Managers can be sensitive to early signs of distress at work, such as employee fatigue or changes in work habits, in order to avoid serious forms of distress. The serious forms of distress include violent behavior, psychological depression, and cardiovascular problems. Distress is important to the organization because of the costs associated with turnover and absenteeism, as well as poor-quality production.

Managers should be aware of gender, personality, and behavioral differences when analyzing stress in the workplace. Men and women have different vulnerabilities when it comes to distress. Men are at greater risk of fatal disorders, for example, and women are more vulnerable to nonfatal disorders, such as depression. Managers should be aware that even positive performance stereotypes may place undue stress on employees, leading to chronic disorders such as hypertension. Personality hardiness and self-reliance are helpful in managing stressful events.

Managers can use the principles and methods of preventive stress management to create healthier work environments. They can practice several forms of individual stress prevention to create healthier lifestyles for themselves, and they can encourage employees to do the same. Large organizations can create healthier workforces through the implementation of comprehensive health promotion programs. Setting an example is one of the best things a manager can do for employees when it comes to preventive stress management.

LOOKING BACK: IKEA

Look Within for Sources of Strength

Norbert Michalke/
Photolibrary

Yes, IKEA faced external challenges in the economic downturn and the Russian corruption problem. There is a saying that the strong survive. If that is so, what is the source of strength for survival? In IKEA's case, even the company's business model has been challenged. Specifically, the question has been posed: Is IKEA's business modeling coming apart?[109] This is both a legitimate and an important question, one for any business to be able to answer in the negative. Just because the company's sales may be sluggish does not mean that the core business model of minimalist flat-pack furniture is dead or outdated. The core business model must be a source of strength and survivability in a competitive, demanding marketplace. IKEA's competitors, such as Kingfisher's B & Q, seek to emulate the one-size-fits-all approach to global retailing.

Duke behavioral economist Dan Ariely has a theory that IKEA's build-it-yourself furniture creates long-term customer loyalty.[110] Why? Because you like the furniture even more after struggling to put it all together with a minimum of useful instructions. No one would suggest that the instructions are overly detailed. This mild ambiguity creates a customer opportunity. Specifically, the opportunity is for the customer to engage, or invest, in the whole process of creating the furniture. Engagement and involvement lead to commitment. That may be the underpinning for Ariely's theory about IKEA's model for creating loyalty and business. His theory is born too of personal experience as an IKEA customer. The company's do-it-yourself strategy has succeeded for over half a century, one indicator of strength, and across dozens of countries, another indicator of strength.

IKEA's new Tampa, Florida store is the size of two Wal-Mart Supercenters, suggesting that the company believes in its business model and its internal strength to compete. If every customer that visits the IKEA store in Tampa spends a few hours inside, this might become a weekend pastime for thousands of Florida's West Coast citizens. A store this size becomes a big target. Maybe the customer loyalty that IKEA generates through the do-it-yourself strategy results from appealing to these customers' sense of achievement. While the company's business model may be an internal

source of strength to survive and thrive in a very competitive retail environment, IKEA may draw

strength too from its loyal and lasting customer base who has displayed their own strength and

achievement in assembling IKEA furniture.

Chapter Summary

1. Stress is the unconscious preparation to fight or flee when faced with any demand. Distress is the adverse consequence of stress.

2. Four approaches to understanding stress are the homeostatic/medical approach, the cognitive appraisal approach, the person–environment fit approach, and the psychoanalytic approach.

3. The stress response is a natural mind–body response characterized by four basic mind–body changes.

4. Employees face task, role, interpersonal, and physical demands at work, along with nonwork demands. Globalization, international competition, and advanced technologies create new stresses at work.

5. Nonwork stressors, such as family problems and work–home conflicts, can affect an individual's work life and home life.

6. Stress has health benefits, including enhanced performance.

7. Distress is costly to both individuals and organizations.

8. Individual diversity requires attention to gender, Type A behavior, personality hardiness, and self-reliance in determining the links between stress and strain.

9. Preventive stress management aims to enhance health and reduce distress or strain. Primary prevention focuses on the stressor, secondary prevention focuses on the response to the stressor, and tertiary prevention focuses on symptoms of distress.

Key Terms

compensation award (p. 232)
counterdependence (p. 234)
distress (p. 220)
ego-ideal (p. 222)
homeostasis (p. 222)
overdependence (p. 234)
participation problem (p. 231)
performance decrement (p. 232)
personality hardiness (p. 233)
preventive stress management (p. 236)
primary prevention (p. 237)

secondary prevention (p. 237)
self-image (p. 222)
self-reliance (p. 234)
strain (p. 220)
stress (p. 220)
stressor (p. 220)
tertiary prevention (p. 237)
transformational coping (p. 234)
Type A behavior pattern (p. 233)
workaholism (p. 228)

Review Questions

1. Define *stress*, *distress*, and *strain*.

2. Describe four approaches to understanding stress. How does each add something new to our understanding of stress?

3. What are the four changes associated with the stress response?

4. List three demands of each type: task, role, interpersonal, and physical.

5. What is a nonwork demand? How does it affect an individual?

6. Describe the relationship between stress and performance.

7. What are the major medical consequences of distress? The behavioral consequences? The psychological consequences?

8. Why should organizations be concerned about stress at work? What are the costs of distress to organizations?

9. How do individual differences such as gender, Type A behavior, personality hardiness, and self-reliance moderate the relationship between stress and strain?

10. What are primary prevention, secondary prevention, and tertiary prevention? Describe major organizational stress prevention methods.

11. Describe eight individual preventive stress management methods.

12. What is involved in comprehensive health promotion programs?

Discussion and Communication Questions

1. Why should organizations help individuals manage stress? Isn't stress basically the individual's responsibility?

2. Is there more stress today than in past generations? What evidence is available concerning this question?

3. Discuss the following statement: Employers should be expected to provide stress-free work environments.

4. If an individual claims to have job-related anxiety or depression, should the company be liable?

5. Do you use any stress prevention methods that are not discussed in the chapter? If so, what are they?

6. (*communication question*) Write a memo describing the most challenging demands and/or stressors at your workplace (or university). Be specific

in describing the details of these demands and/ or stressors. How might you go about changing them?

7. (*communication question*) Interview a medical doctor, a psychologist, or another health care professional about the most common forms of health problems and distress seen in their work. Summarize your interview and compare the results to the categories of distress discussed in the chapter.

8. (*communication question*) Do research on social support and diaries as ways to manage stressful and/ or traumatic events. Develop an oral presentation for class that explains the benefits of each of these approaches for preventive stress management. Include guidelines on how to practice each.

Ethical Dilemma

Neil Murray has been working for a small accounting firm for the last eight months—he left a grueling position with one of the major firms in New York City in favor of a chance to work at Johnston & Marcus. Even though Neil makes a little less money, he truly values the other "perks" of the job. Neil appreciates how the founding partners have established a supportive environment. The firm maintains a warm, family atmosphere, where people feel legitimately cared for. Neil no longer works long nights or weekends, and he's been able to reconnect with his young family by eating dinner together every night and volunteering as a Little League coach. That extra time has also allowed Neil to pick up a workout regimen to get his health back in order. He also loves how the firm encourages their staff to volunteer their accounting talents to local nonprofits

by rewarding them with paid vacation time for their efforts. In short, Neil has found his new job extremely rewarding, both professionally and personally.

Once a month, however, Neil has to file a status report on the firm's standing and financials to a clearing house. It isn't a long or complicated report, but Neil dreads completing it, because his boss requires Neil to falsify information that needs to be included.

Neil hasn't challenged his boss—he has simply complied with the request.

During the last two months, as the report date looms, Neil finds himself getting depressed. He has begun to get sick to his stomach when he thinks about completing the forms using incorrect information. Neil doesn't even want to sign his name to the document, because he knows that he is committing a crime.

If this were occurring at Neil's former job, Neil would have quit the first time he was asked to lie. However, he feels so strongly about how well he loves everything else at Johnston & Marcus that it's hard for him to imagine leaving.

Questions:

1. Using consequential, rule-based and character theories, evaluate Neil's options.

2. What should Margaret do? Why?

Experiential Exercises

7.1 Gender Role Stressors

The major sources of stress are not necessarily the same for men and women. This exercise will help you identify the similarities and differences in the stressors and perceptions of men and women.

Step 1. Individually list the major sources of stress for you because of your gender. Be as specific as possible, and within your list, prioritize your stressors.

Step 2. Individually list what you think are the major sources of stress for those of the opposite gender. Again, be as specific as possible, and prioritize your list.

Step 3. In teams of five or six members of the same sex, share your two lists of stressors. Discuss these stressors, and identify the top five sources of stress for your group because of your gender and the top five sources of stress for those of the opposite gender. Again, be as specific as possible, and prioritize your list.

Step 4. The class will then engage in a cross-team exchange of lists. Look for similarities and differences among the teams in your class as follows. Select one gender to be addressed first. If the females are first, for example, the male groups will post their predictions. This will be followed by the actual stressor lists from the female groups. Then do the same for the other gender.

7.2 Workplace Stress Diagnosis

The following exercise gives you an opportunity to work within a group to compare the work demands and job stressors found in different work settings. Intervention for preventive stress management should always be based on a good diagnosis. This exercise gives you a start in this direction.

Step 1. Rate the degree to which each of the following work demands is a source of stress for you and your coworkers at work. Use a 7-point rating scale for assigning the stressfulness of the work demand, with 7 = very high source of stress, 4 = moderate source of stress, and 1 = very little source of stress.

_____ Uncertainty about various aspects of the work environment

_____ Lack of control over people, events, or other aspects of work

_____ Lack of career opportunities and progress

_____ The implementation of new technologies

_____ Work overload; that is, too much to do and not enough time

_____ Conflicting expectations from one or more people at work

_____ Confusing expectations from one or more people at work

_____ Dangerous working conditions and/or hazardous substances

_____ Sexual harassment by supervisors, coworkers, or others

_____ Abrasive personalities and/or political conflicts

_____ Rigid, insensitive, unresponsive supervisors or managers

Step 2. Write a brief description of the most stressful event that has occurred in your work environment during the past twelve-month period.

Step 3. The class will form into groups of approximately six members each. Each group elects a spokesperson and then compares the information developed by each person in Steps 1 and 2. In the process of this comparison, answer the following questions:

a. What are the similarities between work environments in terms of their most stressful work demands?

b. What are the differences among work environments in terms of their most stressful work demands?

c. Are there similarities in the descriptions of the most stressful events? If so, what are they?

Step 4. Each group will share the results of its answers to the questions in Step 3. Cross-team questions and discussion follow.

Step 5 (Optional). Your instructor may ask you to choose one or another of the work environments in which to develop some preventive stress management strategies. Complete parts a and b below in your group.

a. Identify one to three preventive stress management strategies that you think are the best to use in the work environment. Why have you chosen them?

b. How should the effectiveness of these strategies be evaluated?

BizFlix | The Upside of Anger

Terry Ann Wolfmeyer (Joan Allen) turns to ferocious anger and alcohol after her husband leaves for his secretary. Neighbor Denny Davies (Kevin Costner), a retired Detroit Tigers pitcher and host of a radio talk show, tries to befriend Terry and help her cope as a drinking buddy. Add four beautiful daughters and the interpersonal interactions become complex and sometimes comedic.

Stress and Stressors: Terry and Denny

This sequence has two parts with a title screen separating them. Part I follows the family dinner with Denny as a guest. Terry is standing on the porch holding her drink against her forehead as Denny arrives. Part I ends with Terry saying, "Then leave. Any other reason than that for you to be here, frankly, is just pitiful." She returns to the house while Denny stays on the porch.

Part II follows the bungee jumping scene and Denny driving Lavender "Popeye" Wolfmeyer (Evan Rachel Wood) home. It begins with Terry and Denny eating ice cream from the same container. Denny tells her that "Popeye" suggested he marry her mother. This scene ends after Denny kicks down the bathroom door. Terry screams, jumps into the bathtub, and Denny approaches silently.

What to Watch for and Ask Yourself

- Separately assess the stressors affecting Terry and Denny. View Part I for Terry and Part II for Denny.

- Are Terry and Denny having a distress or eustress response? Give examples of behavior in the film sequences to support your observations.

- Review the earlier section, "The Consequences of Stress." What consequences do you observe or predict for Terry and Denny?

Workplace Video | Mitchell Gold + Bob Williams: The Evolution of Management Thinking

When Mitchell Gold and Bob Williams started their furniture company in 1989, the rules governing the upholstery industry were so outdated that the business partners had to write their own. New management philosophies taking hold in the larger business world were far from the minds of most furniture executives, and service throughout the industry was undependable. When a customer placed an order for a custom upholstery couch, a representative would estimate delivery any time within ten weeks—and rarely did the piece arrive on time or according to plan.

But Gold and Williams had a clear sense of how they wanted to run their business. Their goal was to guarantee comfort, minimize costs, enact rigorous controls, and create styles they desired for their own homes. Most importantly, they would never skimp on quality. True to that vision, the Mitchell Gold + Bob Williams furniture company (MG+BW) uses only high-quality kiln-dried hardwoods for new products.

Early on in their venture, the entrepreneurial duo began producing private-label furniture for Pottery Barn. They soon added Crate & Barrel, Restoration Hardware, and Chambers. Gold and Williams supplemented that business with robust sales to business clients such as W Hotels.

But the partners also wanted to provide a workplace where employees could perform jobs unburdened by stress. To achieve that goal, they set out to devise creative benefits and worker-friendly facilities. Indeed, MG+BW has a reputation for offering generous benefits to employees, spouses, partners, and other family members. For employees who seek better integration between work and everyday living, the company offers a health-conscious café, indoor walking track, gym, and on-site daycare—the first in the furniture industry. MG+BW even offers college scholarships for children of employees.

Gold and Williams have become respected leaders in their industry, and competitors must now play by the rules they set. As the partners celebrate 20 years in business and $100 million in sales, it's clear that their people-focused business strategies have paid off.

Discussion Questions

1. Identify sources of stress that Mitchell Gold and Bob Williams aim to alleviate in their organization.

2. In what way does MG + BW use benefits to promote a healthy workforce?

3. Why is it necessary for MG + BW to monitor and manage the stress levels of workers?

Case

Dealing with Stress the Genentech Way

Genentech, founded in 1976 by Dr. Herbert W. Boyer, a biochemist, and Robert A. Swanson, a venture capitalist, has a mission "to be the leading biotechnology company, using human genetic information to discover, develop, manufacture and commercialize medicines to treat people with serious or life-threatening medical conditions."[1] Headquartered in South San Francisco, California, Genentech "launched the biotechnology industry, which engineers drugs from living cells instead of test tubes."[2] The company manufactures and markets biotherapeutic products in the areas of oncology, immunology, and disorders of tissue growth and repair.[3] Over the years Genentech has become a leading biotechnology company, noted as much for its human resources programs as for its development and commercialization of new biotherapeutic products.

In 2007, Genentech CEO Arthur Levinson said, "… we place a huge emphasis on making Genentech a great place to work. Eight or nine years ago, we didn't appear on many lists of the best places [to work].… [Then we started asking employees questions like:] 'What do you like; and more importantly, what do you not like about the company? What bothers you?'"[4]

This concern for making the company a great place to work has resulted in Genentech being recognized multiple times as one of the top places to work in the United States. In early 2009, for example, *Fortune* magazine included Genentech on its list of the "100 Best Companies to Work For" for the eleventh year in a row. In September 2008, *Working Mother* magazine identified the company as one of the "100 Best Companies for Working Mothers" for the sixteenth consecutive time. Also in late 2008, *Science* magazine tagged Genentech as "the top employer in the biopharmaceutical industry" for the seventh consecutive year.[5]

The management philosophy and corporate culture of Genentech play important roles in the company's human resource policies and practices. Insights into these philosophical and cultural underpinnings can be discovered on the company's Web site. Genentech's Web site states, "We don't wonder about the purpose of our jobs at Genentech. Helping people with difficult-to-treat diseases provides a common mission for all of us and drives us to work hard and with a sense of urgency. We focus our drug discovery efforts on unmet medical needs—serious or life-threatening illnesses where there is a need for safer and more effective therapies—because we believe these are the areas where we can make the biggest difference. We spend every day thinking about matters of life and death, and we feel a great responsibility to do our best work. However, we counterbalance this seriousness with an environment that is casual.… We refer to this combination of gravity and informality as 'casual intensity,' and we believe it is part of what has made us successful."[6] The company's Web site goes on to indicate that "We place great importance on our employees, and we strive to make each individual feel valued for his/her contributions to the company's mission.… We aim for every employee to feel that their unique ways of thinking are welcomed and that they can take the initiative to propose projects they believe are important to the company's success. We also encourage employees to bring their idiosyncratic and playful ways of expressing themselves and celebrating life to our demanding workplace."[7]

Genentech has numerous programs that provide employees with a unique workplace as well as diverse opportunities to enhance their personal learning, achieve personal and professional goals, and enable them to manage the sometimes difficult task of juggling their work lives and their personal lives.[8] What are some of the specific Genentech programs that make it such a good place to work?

Being a leading company in the biotechnology industry requires Genentech to maintain a corporate culture that fosters creativity and innovation. Genentech's "commitment to innovation has to be underscored at every turn. Since its founding in 1976, *Genentech* has allowed its researchers to publish their findings in academic journals, an important career status marker for scientists. That's different from most pharma companies, which tightly guard their research secrets. As a result, *Genentech* can compete with the Harvard and Stanford universities of the world when recruiting top scientists."[9]

Genentech also promotes emotional health among its employees by creating a connection culture. One example of this connection culture involves bringing cancer patients into the company's facilities to meet with employees; doing so reinforces for the employees the importance of the work they do, and they have a face-to-face understanding of how their work impacts the lives of people. A connection

PART 3

© Digital Vision

Interpersonal Processes and Behavior

8

Communication

LEARNING OBJECTIVES

After reading this chapter, you should be able to do the following:

1 Understand the roles of the communicator, the receiver, perceptual screens, and the message in interpersonal communication.

2 Practice good reflective listening skills.

3 Describe the five communication skills of effective supervisors.

4 Explain five communication barriers and gateways through them.

5 Distinguish between defensive and nondefensive communication.

6 Explain positive, healthy communication.

7 Describe Information Communication Technology (ICT) used by managers.

CarMax found a window of opportunity in the midst of a difficulty economy.

THINKING AHEAD: CARMAX

Challenge Meets Optimism

The automotive industry in the United States had two very difficult years during 2008 and 2009, possibly the worst in industry history. The federal government weighed in with financial support for General Motors Corporation and Chrysler LLC,

Courtesy of CarMax

yet both companies were forced into bankruptcy court. Ford was the only one of the three major American automotive makers that met the challenge without federal bailout money. The economic difficulties of this two-year period did not start in the automotive industry, even though the industry was dramatically affected. Financial institutions were among the worst impacted and Wall Street was dramatically transformed. This severe economic downturn was compared to the Great Depression of the 1930s. This challenging external environment threw CarMax some serious punches.

Crises create opportunities as well as pose danger for all those in the midst of them. The worst case danger in an environment like this is the complete loss of the business through liquidation. Companies not prepared for challenge and difficulty run that risk. Companies and leaders who understand that all businesses meet challenging times are often better prepared to find a silver lining in the rain clouds of adversity. Windows of opportunity may open during these times, windows may appear to open, and then again windows of opportunity may not be as they appear. In the midst of a very difficult economy, CarMax saw a window of opportunity for a new used-car location off of Scholls Ferry Road in Oregon.[1] While the land was part of a designated "regional center," the local Oregon city had failed to update its zoning. So, was this a real window of opportunity for the company? The message for CarMax: exercise caution.

In the midst of these challenging times, CarMax CEO Tom Folliard communicated with optimism and nondefensively with shareholders and employees alike.[2] His blend of realistic optimism communicated his vision of the path through the difficult challenges in the industry. He set out an active response to help position CarMax for the economic rebound to come. Several actions helped the company endure the tough economy while making it stronger for the future. For example, by cutting $100 per vehicle in reconditioning costs, CarMax would save $30 million annually on the 300,000 or more cars they sell. CarMax CEO's optimism helped employees and shareholders alike understand that the company is strong enough to take any punch the external environment throws and still come out on top. What other moves did CarMax make to overcome the challenges of the economic crisis?

Communication is the evoking of a shared or common meaning in another person. *Interpersonal communication* occurs between two or more people in an organization. Reading, listening, managing and interpreting information, and serving clients are among the interpersonal communication skills identified by the Department of Labor as being necessary for successful functioning in the workplace.[3] In Chapter 7, we noted that interpersonal communication is the key to social support for preventive stress management.[4] Interpersonal communication is central to health and well-being.

This chapter addresses the interpersonal and technological dimensions of communication in organizations. The first section presents an interpersonal communication model and a reflective listening technique intended to improve communication. The next section of the chapter addresses the five communication skills that characterize effective supervisors. The third section examines five barriers to effective communication and gives suggestions for overcoming them. The fourth section compares defensive and nondefensive communication. The fifth section discusses kinds of nonverbal communication. The final section gives an overview of the latest technologies for information management in organizations.

1 Understand the roles of the communicator, the receiver, perceptual screens, and the message in interpersonal communication.

communication
The evoking of a shared or common meaning in another person.

interpersonal communication
Communication between two or more people in an organization.

INTERPERSONAL COMMUNICATION

Interpersonal communication is important in building and sustaining human relationships at work. This kind of communication cannot be replaced by the advances in information technology and data management that have taken place during the past several decades. The model in this section of the chapter provides a basis for understanding the four key elements of interpersonal communication: the communicator, the receiver, perceptual screens, and the message. Reflective listening is a valuable tool for improving interpersonal communication.

An Interpersonal Communication Model

Figure 8.1 presents an interpersonal communication model as a basis for the discussion of communication. The model has four basic elements: the communicator, the receiver, perceptual screens, and the message. The *communicator* is the person originating the message. The *receiver* is the person receiving the message. The receiver must interpret and understand the message. *Perceptual screens* are the windows through which we interact with people in the world. The communicator's and the receiver's perceptual screens influence the quality, accuracy, and clarity of the message. The screens influence whether the message sent and the message received are the same or whether distortion occurs in the message. Perceptual screens are composed of the personal factors each person brings to interpersonal communication, such as age, gender, values, beliefs, past experiences, cultural influences, and individual needs. The extent to which these screens are open or closed significantly influences both the sent and received messages.

The *message* contains the thoughts and feelings that the communicator intends to evoke in the receiver. The message has two primary components. The thought or conceptual component of the message (its content) is contained in the words, ideas, symbols, and concepts chosen to relay the message. The feeling or emotional component of the message (its affect) is contained in the intensity, force, demeanor, and sometimes the gestures of the communicator. Language and emotion expressed in initial claims were both important to the likelihood of online dispute resolution.[5] This component of the message adds the emotional overtones, such as joy, anger, fear, or pain, to the conceptual component. This addition often enriches and clarifies the message. The feeling component gives the message its full meaning.

Feedback may or may not be activated in the model. Feedback occurs when the receiver provides the communicator with a response to the message. More broadly, it occurs when information is fed back that completes two-way communication.

The *language* of the message is increasingly important because of the multinational nature of many organizations. Language is the words, their pronunciation, and the methods of combining them used by a community of people. Language will be addressed as a possible barrier to communication. For example, special language barriers arise for non–Japanese-speaking Americans who work with Japanese

communicator
The person originating a message.

receiver
The person receiving a message.

perceptual screen
A window through which we interact with people that influences the quality, accuracy, and clarity of the communication.

message
The thoughts and feelings that the communicator is attempting to elicit in the receiver.

feedback
Information fed back that completes two-way communication.

language
The words, their pronunciation, and the methods of combining them used and understood by a group of people.

FIGURE

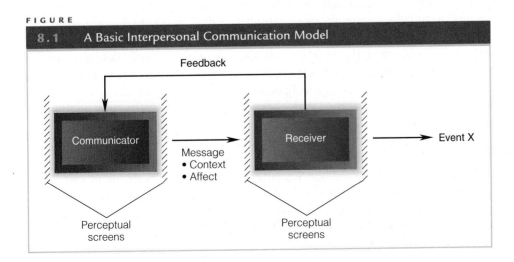

8.1 A Basic Interpersonal Communication Model

8.1 Communication Media: Information Richness and Data Capacity		
Medium	Information Richness	Data Capacity
Face-to-face discussion	Highest	Lowest
Telephone	High	Low
Electronic mail	Moderate	Moderate
Individualized letter	Moderate	Moderate
Personalized note or memo	Moderate	Moderate
Formal written report	Low	High
Flyer or bulletin	Low	High
Formal numeric report	Lowest	Highest

SOURCE: Created by E. A. Gerloff from "Information Richness: A New Approach to Managerial Behavior and Organizational Design" by Richard L. Daft and R. H. Lengel in *Research in Organizational Behavior* 6 (1984): 191–233. Reprinted by permission of JAI Press Inc.

employees and for non-Spanish-speaking Canadians who work with Spanish-speaking employees.

Data are the uninterpreted, unanalyzed elements of a message. *Information* is data with meaning to some person who has interpreted or analyzed them. Messages are conveyed through a medium, such as a telephone or face-to-face discussion. Messages differ in *richness*, the ability of the medium to convey the meaning.[6] Table 8.1 compares different media with regard to data capacity and information richness. Attributes of communication media affect how influence-seeking behavior is generated and perceived in organizations.[7] The Science feature focuses our attention on personality effects on communication media preferences in threatening and nonthreatening situations.

Reflective Listening

Reflective listening is the skill of carefully listening to another person and repeating back to the speaker the heard message to correct any inaccuracies or misunderstandings. This kind of listening emphasizes the role of the receiver or audience in interpersonal communication. Managers use it to understand other people and help them solve problems at work.[8] Reflective listening enables the listener to understand the communicator's meaning, reduce perceptual distortions, and overcome interpersonal barriers that lead to communication failures. Reflective listening ensures that the meanings of the sent and received messages are the same. Reflecting back the message helps the communicator clarify and sharpen the intended meaning. It is especially useful in problem solving. Reflective listening can be learned in a short time with positive effects on behaviors and emotions in corporate settings.[9]

Reflective listening can be characterized as personal, feeling oriented, and responsive.[10] First, reflective listening emphasizes the personal elements of the communication process, not the impersonal or abstract elements of the message. The reflective listener demonstrates empathy and concern for the communicator as a person, not an inanimate object. Second, reflective listening emphasizes the feelings communicated in the message. Thoughts and ideas are often the primary focus of a receiver's response, but that is not the case in reflective listening. The receiver should

2 Practice good reflective listening skills.

data
Uninterpreted and unanalyzed facts.

information
Data that have been interpreted, analyzed, and have meaning to some user.

richness
The ability of a medium or channel to elicit or evoke meaning in the receiver.

reflective listening
A skill intended to help the receiver and communicator clearly and fully understand the message sent.

Science

The Effects of Extraversion and Neuroticism

Current technological developments, in particular the Internet, have significantly increased the number of communication media and the way we communicate with other people. This research study focused on personality effects in the choice of communication media, especially extraversion and neuroticism. The research is based on data from two subsamples in Germany, one composed primarily of university students and the other recruited via the Internet. The subsamples were found to have virtually no differences on the main variable measures and so were combined into a single sample of 228. The investigators expected that the two personality variables would impact the choice of communication media. They further expected that social skills and social anxiety would moderate the effects of personality. The results did confirm that extraverts and those low in neuroticism preferred media with high-richness levels, such as face-to-face communication, while introverts and individuals high in neuroticism preferred media with low-richness levels, such as e-mail. These personality effects were moderated by the situation. Specifically, these effects were pronounced in threatening situations that required high social skills and entailed social anxiety or conflicts. By contrast, when challenges and potential threat of a communication situation were low, no significant personality effects occurred. The conclusion is that there are significant trait personality effects from extraversion and neuroticism in situations of social conflict.

SOURCE: G. Hertel, J. Schroer, B. Batinic, and S. Naumann, "Do Shy People Prefer to Send E-Mail?" *Social Psychology* 39(4): 231–243.

pay special attention to the feeling component of the message. Third, reflective listening emphasizes responding to, not leading, the communicator. Receivers should distinguish their own feelings and thoughts from those of the speaker so as not to confuse the two. The focus must be on the speaker's feelings and thoughts in order to respond to them. A good reflective listener does not lead the speaker according to the listener's own thoughts and feelings.

Four levels of verbal response by the receiver are part of active reflective listening: affirming contact, paraphrasing expressed thoughts and feelings, clarifying implicit thoughts and feelings, and reflecting "core" feelings not fully expressed. Nonverbal behaviors also are useful in reflective listening. Specifically, silence and eye contact are responses that enhance reflective listening.

Each reflective response is illustrated through the case of a software engineer and her supervisor. The engineer has just discovered a major problem, which is not yet fully defined, in a large information system she is building for a very difficult customer.

Affirming Contact The receiver affirms contact with the communicator by using simple statements such as "I see," "Uh-huh," and "Yes, I understand." The purpose of an affirmation response is to communicate attentiveness, not necessarily agreement. In the case of the software engineer, the supervisor might most appropriately use several affirming statements as the engineer begins to talk through the problem. Affirming contact is especially reassuring to a speaker in the early stages of expressing thoughts and feelings about a problem, particularly when there may be some associated anxiety or discomfort. As the problem is more fully explored and expressed, it is increasingly useful for the receiver to use additional reflective responses.

Paraphrasing the Expressed After an appropriate time, the receiver might paraphrase the expressed thoughts and feelings of the speaker. Paraphrasing is useful because it reflects back to the speaker the thoughts and feelings as the receiver heard them. This verbal response enables the receiver to build greater empathy, openness, and acceptance into the relationship while ensuring the accuracy of the communication process.

In the case of the software engineer, the supervisor may find paraphrasing the engineer's expressed thoughts and feelings particularly useful for both of them in developing a clearer understanding of the system problem. For example, the supervisor might say, "I hear you saying that you are very upset about this problem and that you are not yet clear about what is causing it." It is difficult to solve a problem until it is clearly understood.

Clarifying the Implicit People often communicate implicit thoughts and feelings about a problem in addition to their explicitly expressed thoughts and feelings. Implicit thoughts and feelings are not clearly or fully expressed. The receiver may or may not assume that the implicit thoughts and feelings are within the awareness of the speaker. For example, the software engineer may be anxious about how to talk with a difficult customer concerning the system problem. This may be implicit in her discussion with her supervisor because of the previous discussions about this customer. If her anxiety feelings are not expressed, the supervisor may want to clarify them. For example, the supervisor might say, "I hear that you are feeling very upset about the problem and may be worried about the customer's reaction when you inform him." This would help the engineer shift the focus of her attention from the main problem, which is in the software, to the important and related issue of discussing the matter with the customer.

Reflecting "Core" Feelings Next, the receiver should go beyond the explicit or implicit thoughts and feelings that the speaker is expressing. The receiver, in reflecting the core feelings that the speaker may be experiencing, is reaching beyond the immediate awareness level of the speaker. "Core" feelings are the deepest and most important ones from the speaker's perspective. For example, if the software engineer had not been aware of any anxiety in her relationship with the difficult customer, her supervisor's ability to sense the tension and bring it to the engineer's awareness would exemplify reflecting core feelings.

The receiver runs a risk of overreaching in reflecting core feelings if a secure, empathetic relationship with the speaker does not already exist or if strongly repressed feelings are reflected back. Even if the receiver is correct, the speaker may not want those feelings brought to awareness. Therefore, it is important to exercise caution and care in reflecting core feelings to a speaker.

Silence Long, extended periods of silence may cause discomfort and be a sign or source of embarrassment, but silence can help both speaker and listener in reflective listening. From the speaker's perspective, silence may be useful in moments of thought or confusion about how to express difficult ideas or feelings. The software engineer may need some patient, silent response as she thinks through what to say next. Listeners can use brief periods of silence to sort out their own thoughts and feelings from those of the speaker. Reflective listening focuses only on the latter. In the case of the software engineer's supervisor, any personal, angry feelings toward the difficult customer should not intrude on the engineer's immediate problem. Silence provides time to identify and isolate the listener's personal responses and exclude them from the dialogue.

Eye Contact Eye contact is a nonverbal behavior that may help open up a relationship and improve communication between two people. The absence of any direct eye contact during an exchange tends to close communication. Cultural and individual

two-way communication
A form of communication in which the communicator and receiver interact.

one-way communication
Communication in which a person sends a message to another person and no feedback, questions, or interaction follow.

differences influence what constitutes appropriate eye contact. For example, some cultures, such as in India, place restrictions on direct eye contact initiated by women or children. Too much direct eye contact, regardless of the individual or culture, has an intimidating effect. We see President Obama use eye contact very effectively in The Real World 8.2.

Moderate direct eye contact, therefore, communicates openness and affirmation without causing either speaker or listener to feel intimidated. Periodic aversion of the eyes allows for a sense of privacy and control, even in intense interpersonal communication.

One-Way versus Two-Way Communication Reflective listening encourages two-way communication. *Two-way communication* is an interactive form of communication in which there is an exchange of thoughts, feelings, or both and through which shared meaning often occurs. Problem solving and decision making are often examples of two-way communication. *One-way communication* occurs when a person sends a message to another person and no feedback, questions, or interaction follow. Giving instructions or giving directions are examples of one-way communication. One-way communication occurs whenever a person sends a one-directional message to a receiver with no reflective listening or feedback in the communication.

One-way communication is faster, although how much faster depends on the amount and complexity of information communicated and the medium chosen. Even though it is faster, one-way communication is often less accurate than two-way communication. This is especially true for complex tasks in which clarifications and iterations may be required for task completion. Where time and accuracy are both important to the successful completion of a task, such as in combat or emergency situations, extensive training prior to execution enhances accuracy and efficiency of execution without two-way communication.[11] Firefighters and military combat personnel engage extensively in such training to minimize the need for communication during emergencies. These highly trained professionals rely on fast, abbreviated, one-way communication as a shorthand for more complex information. However, this communication only works within the range of situations for which the professionals are specifically trained.

It is difficult to draw general conclusions about people's satisfaction with one-way versus two-way communication. For example, communicators with a stronger need for feedback or who are not uncomfortable with conflicting or confusing questions may find two-way communication more satisfying. By contrast, receivers who believe that a message is very straightforward may be satisfied with one-way communication and dissatisfied with two-way communication because of its lengthy, drawn-out nature.

FIVE KEYS TO EFFECTIVE SUPERVISORY COMMUNICATION

Interpersonal communication, especially between managers and employees, is a critical foundation for effective performance in organizations, as well as for health and well-being as seen later in the chapter. As we see in The Real World 8.1, AstraZeneca has developed a unique model of effective leadership communication. Language and power are intertwined in the communication that occurs between managers and their employees.[12] This is especially critical when leaders are articulating vision and achieving buy-in from employees.[13] One large study of managers in a variety of jobs and industries found that managers with the most effective work units engaged in

3 Describe the five communication skills of effective supervisors.

routine communication within their units, whereas the managers with the highest promotion rates engaged in networking activities with superiors.[14] Another study of male and female banking managers suggested that higher performing managers are better and less apprehensive communicators than lower performing managers.[15] Oral communication (voice) and cooperative behaviors are important contextual performance skills that have positive effects on the psychosocial quality of the work environment.[16]

A review of the research on manager–employee communication identified five communication skills that distinguish "good" from "bad" supervisors.[17] These skills include being expressive speakers, empathetic listeners, persuasive leaders, sensitive people, and informative managers. Some supervisors are effective without possessing each of these skills, and some organizations value one or another skill over the others. Thus, dyadic (two-person) relationships are at the core of much organization-based communication.[18]

Expressive Speakers

Better supervisors express their thoughts, ideas, and feelings and speak up in meetings. They are comfortable expressing themselves. They tend toward extraversion and are perceived as possessing charisma, a concept discussed in Chapter 12.[19] Supervisors who are not talkative or who tend toward introversion may at times leave their employees wondering what their supervisors are thinking or how they feel about certain issues. Supervisors who speak out let the people they work with know where they stand, what they believe, and how they feel.

Empathetic Listeners

In addition to being expressive speakers, the better supervisors are willing, empathetic listeners. They use reflective listening skills; they are patient with, and responsive to, problems that employees, peers, and others bring to them about their work. They respond to and engage the concerns of other people. For example, the president of a health care company estimated that he spent 70 percent of his interpersonal time at work listening to others.[20] He listens empathetically to personal and work dilemmas without taking responsibility for others' problems. Empathetic listeners are able to hear the feelings and emotional dimensions of the messages people send them, as well as the content of the ideas and issues. Better supervisors are approachable and willing to listen to suggestions and complaints. In the case of physicians, those with high perceived control were more open in their communication, and patients found them more empathetic.[21] You 8.1 gives you an opportunity to evaluate how active a listener you are. Active listening is one key communication skill that closes the feedback gap between managers and employees.[22]

Persuasive Leaders (and Some Exceptions)

Better supervisors are persuasive leaders rather than directive, autocratic ones. All supervisors and managers must exercise power and influence in organizations if they are to ensure performance and achieve results. These better supervisors are distinguished by their use of persuasive communication when influencing others. Specifically, they encourage others to achieve results instead of telling others what to do. They are not highly directive or manipulative in their influence attempts. Patience may be a virtue in this context because the sleeper effect, or delayed influence, may be active in some situations.[23]

The Real World 8.1

The FAME Model of Leadership Communication

When AstraZeneca R&D was faced with major and sustained change, the company decided to coach, equip, and support its leadership teams to engage employees through the challenging time. AstraZeneca R&D used a FAME model of leadership communication that is based on Focus, Articulate, Model, and Engage. First, effective leaders communicate a clear focus for what they want to help employees think, feel and do in the midst of change. Second, leaders turn their vision into articulate words that employees can remember and repeat. Third, leaders model and provide an example for employees, using their own communication style strengths. Fourth, effective leaders help employees see how they fit into the bigger picture and involve them effectively. AstraZeneca R&D found that using the FAME model enabled their leaders to understand their own communication styles and those of others, and then display flexibility in getting on other people's wavelengths quickly. The company found that leaders need to think about their message from the audience's point of view and then display consistency in communicating that message. Finally, large-scale meetings were found to be effective in sending a consistent message when they were followed by small-scale discussions for question clarification and reinforcement of the message. AstraZeneca R&D found that leadership communication is a learned skill that can be developed with the benefits that leaders are more self-aware and confident in their communication style, thus maximizing their strengths and minimizing their weaknesses.

SOURCE: D. Walters and D. Norton, "Leadership Communication—The AstraZeneca Way," *Strategic Communication Management* 12 (December 2007–January 2008): 16–19.

The exceptions to this pattern of communication occur in emergency or high-risk situations, such as life-threatening traumas in medical emergency rooms or in oil rig firefighting. In these cases, the supervisor must be directive and assertive.

Sensitivity to Feelings

Better supervisors are also sensitive to the feelings, self-image, and psychological defenses of their employees. Although the supervisor is capable of giving criticism and negative feedback to employees, he or she does it confidentially and constructively. Incorporating criticism with a dose of praise can minimize negative reactions to negative feedback.[24] In addition, avoid giving critical feedback or reprimanding employees in public. Those settings are reserved for the praise of employees' accomplishments, honors, and achievements. In this manner, the better supervisors are sensitive to the self-esteem of others. They work to enhance that self-esteem as appropriate to the person's real talents, abilities, and achievements.

Informative Managers

Finally, better supervisors keep those who work for them well informed and appropriately and selectively disseminate information. This role involves receiving large volumes of information through a wide range of written and verbal communication media and filtering it before distributing it. The failure to do so can lead to either information overload for the employees or a lack of sufficient information for performance and task accomplishment. Better supervisors favor giving advance notice of organizational changes and explaining the rationale for organizational policies.

A person may become a good supervisor even in the absence of one of these communication skills. For example, a person with special talents in planning and

You 8.1

Are You an Active Listener?

Reflective listening is a skill that you can practice and learn. Here are ten tips to help you become a better listener.

1. Stop talking. You cannot listen if your mouth is moving.
2. Put the speaker at ease. Break the ice to help the speaker relax. Smile!
3. Show the speaker you want to listen. Put away your work. Do not look at your watch. Maintain good eye contact.
4. Remove distractions. Close your door. Do not answer the telephone.
5. Empathize with the speaker. Put yourself in the speaker's shoes.
6. Be patient. Not everyone delivers messages at the same pace.
7. Hold your temper. Do not fly off the handle.
8. Go easy on criticism. Criticizing the speaker can stifle communication.
9. Ask questions. Paraphrase and clarify the speaker's message.
10. Stop talking. By this stage, you are probably very tempted to start talking, but do not. Be sure the speaker has finished.

Think of the last time you had a difficult communication with someone at work or school. Evaluate yourself in that situation against each of the ten items. Which one(s) do you need to improve on the most?

organizing or in decision making may compensate for a shortcoming in expressiveness or sensitivity. Further, when supervisors and employees engage in overt behaviors of communication and forward planning, they have a greater number of agreements about the employee's performance and behavior.[25] Overall, interpersonal communication is a key foundation for human relationships.

BARRIERS AND GATEWAYS TO COMMUNICATION

4 Explain five communication barriers and gateways through them.

Barriers to communication are factors that block or significantly distort successful communication. About 20 percent of communication problems that cause organizational problems and drain profitability can be prevented or solved by communication policy guidelines.[26] *Gateways to communication* are pathways through these barriers and serve as antidotes to the problems caused by communication barriers. These barriers may be temporary and can be overcome. Awareness and recognition are the first steps in formulating ways to overcome them. Five communication barriers are physical separation, status differences, gender differences, cultural diversity, and language. The discussion of each concludes with one or two ways to overcome it.

Physical Separation

barriers to communication
Aspects of the communication content and context that can impair effective communication in a workplace.

gateways to communication
Pathways through barriers to communication and antidotes to communication problems.

The physical separation of people in the work environment poses a barrier to communication. Telephones and technology, such as e-mail, often help bridge the physical gap. We address a variety of new technologies in the closing section of the chapter. Although telephones and technology can be helpful, they are not as information rich as face-to-face communication (see Table 8.1).

Periodic face-to-face interactions are one antidote to physical separation problems because the communication is much richer, largely due to nonverbal cues. The richer the communication, the lower the potential for confusion or misunderstandings. Another gateway through the barrier of physical separation is regularly scheduled meetings for people who are organizationally interrelated.

Status Differences

Status differences related to power and the organizational hierarchy pose another barrier to communication among people at work, especially within manager–employee pairs.[27] Because the employee is dependent on the manager as the primary link to the organization, the employee is more likely to distort upward communication than either horizontal or downward communication.

Effective supervisory skills, discussed at the beginning of the chapter, make the supervisor more approachable and remedy the problems related to status differences. In addition, when employees feel secure, they are more likely to be straightforward in upward communication. The absence of status, power, and hierarchical differences, however, is not a cure-all. New information technologies provide another way to overcome status-difference barriers because they encourage the formation of nonhierarchical working relationships.[28]

Gender Differences

Communication barriers can be explained in part by differences in conversational styles.[29] Thus, when people of different ethnic or class backgrounds talk to one another, what the receiver understands may not be the same as what the speaker meant. In a similar way, men and women have different conversational styles, which may pose a communication barrier between those of opposite sexes. For example, women prefer to converse face to face, whereas men are comfortable sitting side by side and concentrating on some focal point in front of them. Research finds that women prefer the direct face-to-face communication because it facilitates shared understanding.[30] These differences in conversation style between men and women may result in a failure to communicate. Again, what is said by one may be understood to have an entirely different meaning by the other. Male–female conversation is really cross-cultural communication. In a work context, one study found that female employees sent less information to their supervisors and experienced less information overload than did male employees.[31]

Women and men have different conversational styles. For example, women prefer to converse face to face.

An important gateway through the gender barrier to communication is developing an awareness of gender-specific differences in conversational style. These differences can enrich organizational communication and empower professional relationships.[32] A second gateway is to actively seek clarification of the person's meaning rather than freely interpreting meaning from one's own frame of reference.

Cultural Diversity

Cultural values and patterns of behavior can be very confusing barriers to communication. Important international differences in work-related values exist among people in the United States, Germany, the United Kingdom, Japan, and other nations.[33] These value differences have implications for motivation, leadership, and teamwork in work organizations.[34] Habitual patterns of interaction within a culture often substitute for communication. Outsiders working in a culture foreign to them often find these habitual patterns confusing and at times bizarre. For example, the German culture places greater value on authority and hierarchical differences. It is therefore more difficult for German workers to engage in direct, open communication with their supervisors than it is for U.S. workers.[35]

These types of cultural stereotypes can be confusing and misleading in cross-cultural communications. When people from one culture view those in another culture through the lens of stereotypes, they in effect are discounting the individual differences within the other culture. For example, an Asian stereotype of Americans may be that they are aggressive and arrogant and, thus, insensitive and unapproachable. Or an American may stereotype the Chinese and Japanese as meek and subservient, unable to be appropriately strong and assertive. Individuals who depend on the accuracy of these forms of cultural stereotypes may be badly misled in communicating with those in other cultures.

One gateway through cultural diversity as a communication barrier is increasing awareness and sensitivity. In addition, companies can provide seminars for expatriate managers as part of their training for overseas assignments. Bernard Isautier, chairman, president, and CEO of PetroKazakhstan, believes that understanding and communication are two keys to success with workplace diversity, which is an essential ingredient for success in international markets.[36] A second gateway is developing or acquiring a guide, map, or beacon for understanding and interacting with members of other cultures. One approach to doing this is to describe a nation in terms of a suitable and complex metaphor.[37] For example, Irish conversations, the Spanish bullfight, and American football are consensually derived metaphors that can enable those outside the culture to understand its members.

Language

Language is a central element in communication. It may pose a barrier if its use obscures meaning and distorts intent. Although English is the international language of aviation, it is not the international language of business. Where the native languages of supervisors and employees differ, the risk of barriers to communication exists. However, increasing numbers of businesspeople are bilingual or multilingual. For example, Honeywell former CEO Michael Bonsignore's ability to speak four languages helped him conduct business around the world more fluently. Less obvious are subtle distinctions in dialects within the same language, which may cause confusion and miscommunication. For example, the word *lift* means an elevator in Great Britain and a ride in the United States. In a different vein, language barriers are created across disciplines and professional boundaries by technical terminology. Acronyms may be very useful to those on the inside of a profession or discipline as means of shorthand communication. Technical terms can convey precise meaning between professionals. However, acronyms and technical terms may only confuse, obscure, or derail any attempt at clear understanding for people unfamiliar with their meaning and usage. For example, while *probable* is a meaningful word for the forecaster, *likely* is a better term for the layperson to avoid miscommunication.[38] Use simple, direct, declarative language. Speak in brief sentences and use terms or words you have heard from your audience. As much as possible, speak in the language of the listener. Do not use jargon or technical language except with those who clearly understand it.

DEFENSIVE AND NONDEFENSIVE COMMUNICATION

5 Distinguish between defensive and nondefensive communication.

Defensive communication in organizations also can create barriers between people, whereas nondefensive communication helps open up relationships.[39] *Defensive communication* includes both aggressive, attacking, angry communication and passive, withdrawing communication. *Nondefensive communication* is an assertive, direct, powerful form of communication. It is an alternative to defensive communication. Although aggressiveness and passiveness are both forms of defensive communication, assertiveness is nondefensive communication. Organizations are increasingly engaged in courtroom battles and media exchanges, which are especially fertile settings for defensive communication. Catherine Crier had extensive experience as a trial lawyer and judge in dealing with defensive people. She carried this knowledge over into her position as a news anchor for CNN, ABC, and Fox News and during her years on Court TV. Her four basic rules are (1) define the situation, (2) clarify the person's position, (3) acknowledge the person's feelings, and (4) bring the focus back to the facts. Defensive communication in organizations leads to a wide range of problems, including injured feelings, communication breakdowns, alienation in working relationships, destructive and retaliatory behaviors, nonproductive efforts, and problem-solving failures. When such problems arise in organizations, everyone is prone to blame everyone else for what is not working.[40] The defensive responses of counter attack or sheepish withdrawal derail communication. Such responses tend to lend heat, not light, to the communication. An examination of eight defensive tactics follows the discussion of the two basic patterns of defensiveness in the next section.

Nondefensive communication, by contrast, provides a basis for asserting and defending oneself when attacked, without being defensive. There are appropriate ways to defend oneself against aggression, attack, or abuse. An assertive, nondefensive style restores order, balance, and effectiveness in working relationships. A discussion of nondefensive communication follows the discussion of defensive communication. In the Thinking Ahead feature, we saw CarMax CEO Tom Folliard use optimism and nondefensive communication with shareholders and employees.

Defensive Communication at Work

Defensive communication often elicits defensive communication in response. The two basic patterns of defensiveness are dominant defensiveness and subordinate defensiveness. One must be able to recognize various forms of defensive communication before learning to engage in constructive, nondefensive communication. You 8.2 helps you examine your defensive communication. Complete it before reading the following text material.

Subordinate Defensiveness Subordinate defensiveness is characterized by passive, submissive, withdrawing behavior. The psychological attitude of the subordinately defensive person is "You are right, and I am wrong." People with low self-esteem may be prone to this form of defensive behavior, as well as people at lower organizational levels. When people at lower levels fear sending bad news up the organization, information that is sensitive and critical to organizational performance may be lost.[41] People who are subordinately defensive do not adequately assert their thoughts and feelings in the workplace. Passive-aggressive behavior is a form of defensiveness that begins as subordinate defensiveness and ends up as dominant defensiveness. It is behavior that appears very passive but, in fact, masks underlying aggression and hostility.

defensive communication
Communication that can be aggressive, attacking, and angry, or passive and withdrawing.

nondefensive communication
Communication that is assertive, direct, and powerful.

You 8.2

What Kind of a Defender Are You?

Not all of our communication is defensive, but each of us has a tendency to engage in either subordinate or dominant defensiveness. The following table presents twelve sets of choices that will help you see whether you tend to be more subordinate or dominant when you communicate defensively.

Complete the questionnaire by allocating 10 points between the two alternatives in each of the twelve rows.

For example, if you never ask permission when it is not needed, but you do give or deny permission frequently, you may give yourself 0 and 10 points, respectively, in the third row. However, if you do each of these behaviors about equally, though at different times, you may want to give yourself 5 points for each alternative.

Add your total points for each column. Whichever number is larger identifies your defensive style.

Subordinate Defensiveness

_____ Explain, prove, and justify your actions, ideas, or feelings more than is required for results wanted.

_____ Ask why things are done the way they are, when you really want to change them. *Why don't they . . .?*

_____ Ask permission when not needed. *Is it okay with you if . . .?*

_____ Give away decisions, ideas, or power when it would be appropriate to claim them as your own. *Don't you think that . . .?*

_____ Apologize, feel inadequate, say *I'm sorry* when you're not.

_____ Submit or withdraw when it's not in your best interest. *Whatever you say . . .*

_____ Lose your cool, lash out, cry where it's inappropriate (turning your anger toward yourself).

_____ Go blank, click off, be at a loss for words just when you want to have a ready response. *I should've said . . .* (afterwards)

_____ Use coping humor, hostile jocularity, or put yourself down when "buying time" or honest feedback would get better results. *Why don't you lay off?*

_____ Use self-deprecating adjectives and reactive verbs. *I'm just a . . . I'm just doing what I was told.*

_____ Use the general *you* and *they* when I and personal names would state the situation more clearly. *They really hassle you here.*

_____ Smile to cover up feelings or put yourself down since you don't know what else to do and it's nice.

_____ TOTAL Subordinate Points

Dominant Defensiveness

_____ Prove that you're right. *I told you so. Now see, that proves my point.*

_____ Give patient explanations but few answers. *It's always been done this way. We tried that before, but . . .*

_____ Give or deny permission. *Oh, I couldn't let you do that.*

_____ Make decisions or take power as your natural right. *The best way to do it is . . . Don't argue, just do as I say.*

_____ Prod people to get the job done. *Don't just stand there . . .*

_____ Take over a situation or decision even when it's delegated; get arbitrary. *My mind is made up.*

_____ Lose your cool, yell, pound the desk where it's inappropriate (turning your anger toward others).

_____ Shift responsibility for something you should have taken care of yourself. *You've always done it before. What're you all of a sudden upset for now?*

_____ Use coping humor, baiting, teasing, hostile jocularity, mimicry to keep other people off balance so you don't have to deal with them. *What's the matter, can't you take it?*

_____ Impress others with how many important people you know. *The other night at Bigname's party when I was talking to . . .*

_____ Don't listen: interpret. Catch the idea of what they're saying, then list rebuttals or redefine their point. *Now what you really mean is . . .*

_____ Use verbal dominance, if necessary, to make your point. Don't let anyone interrupt what you have to say.

_____ TOTAL Dominant Points

Dominant Defensiveness Dominant defensiveness is characterized by active, aggressive, attacking behavior. It is offensive in nature: "The best defense is a good offense." The psychological attitude of the dominantly defensive person is "I am right, and you are wrong." People who compensate for low self-esteem may exhibit this pattern of behavior, as well as people who are in higher level positions within the organizational hierarchy.

Junior officers in a regional banking organization described such behavior in the bank chairman, euphemistically called "The Finger." When giving orders or admonishing someone, he would point his index finger in a domineering, intimidating, emphatic manner that caused defensiveness on the part of the recipient.

Defensive Tactics

Unfortunately, defensive tactics are all too common in work organizations. Eight major defensive tactics are summarized in Table 8.2. They might be best understood in the context of a work situation: Joe is in the process of completing a critical report for his boss, and the deadline is drawing near. Mary, one of Joe's peers at work, is to provide him with some input for the report, and the department secretary is to prepare a final copy of it. Each work example in the table is related to this situation.

Until defensiveness and defensive tactics are recognized for what they are, it is difficult either to change them or to respond to them in nondefensive ways. Defensive tactics are how defensive communication is acted out. In many cases, such tactics raise ethical dilemmas and issues for those involved. For example, is it ethical to raise doubts about another person's values, beliefs, or sexuality? At what point does simple defensiveness become unethical behavior?

Power plays are used by people to control and manipulate others through the use of choice definition (defining the choice another person is allowed to make), either/ or conditions, and overt aggression. The underlying dynamic in power plays is that of domination and control.

A put-down is an effort by the speaker to gain the upper hand in the relationship. Intentionally ignoring another person or pointing out his or her mistakes in a meeting is a kind of put-down.

TABLE

8.2 Defensive Tactics		
Defensive Tactic	**Speaker**	**Work Example**
Power play	The boss	"Finish this report by month's end or lose your promotion."
Put-down	The boss	"A capable manager would already be done with this report."
Labeling	The boss	"You must be a slow learner. Your report is still not done?"
Raising doubts	The boss	"How can I trust you, Joe, if you can't finish an easy report?"
Misleading	Joe	"Mary has not gone over with me the information I need from her for the report." (She left him a copy.)
Scapegoating	Joe	"Mary did not give me her input until just today."
Hostile jokes	Joe	"You can't be serious! The report isn't that important."
Deception	Joe	"I gave it to the secretary. Did she lose it?"

Labeling is often used to portray another person as abnormal or deficient. Psychological labels are often used out of context for this purpose, such as calling a person "paranoid," a word that has a specific, clinical meaning.

Raising doubts about a person's abilities, values, preferential orientations, or other aspects of her or his life creates confusion and uncertainty. This tactic tends to lack the specificity and clarity present in labeling.

Giving misleading information is the selective presentation of information designed to leave a false and inaccurate impression in the listener's mind. It is not the same as lying or misinforming. Giving misleading information is one form of deception.

Scapegoating and its companion, buck-passing, are methods of shifting responsibility to the wrong person. Blaming other people is another form of scapegoating or buck-passing.

Hostile jokes should not be confused with good humor, which is both therapeutic and nondefensive. Jokes created at the expense of others are destructive and hostile.

Deception may occur through a variety of means, such as lying or creating an impression or image that is at variance with the truth. Deception can be very useful in military operations, but it can be a destructive force in work organizations.

Nondefensive Communication

Nondefensive communication is a constructive, healthy alternative to defensive communication in working relationships. The person who communicates nondefensively may be characterized as centered, assertive, controlled, informative, realistic, and honest. Nondefensive communication is powerful, because the speaker is exhibiting self-control and self-possession without rejecting the listener. Converting defensive patterns of communication to nondefensive ones enhances relationship building at work. Relationship building behaviors and communication help reduce adverse responses, such as blame and anger, following negative events at work.[42]

The subordinately defensive person needs to learn to be more assertive. This can be done in many ways, of which two examples follow. First, instead of asking for permission to do something, report what you intend to do and invite confirmation. Second, instead of using self-deprecating words, such as "I'm just following orders," drop the *just*, and convert the message into a self-assertive, declarative statement. Nondefensive communication should be self-affirming without being self-aggrandizing. Some people overcompensate for subordinate defensiveness and inadvertently become domineering.

The person prone to be domineering and dominantly defensive needs to learn to be less aggressive. This may be especially difficult because it requires overcoming the person's sense of "I am right." People who are working to overcome dominant defensiveness should be particularly sensitive to feedback from others about their behavior. There are many ways to change this pattern of behavior. Here are some examples. First, instead of giving and denying permission, give people free rein except in situations where permission is essential as a means of clearing approval or ensuring the security of the task. Second, instead of becoming inappropriately angry, provide information about the adverse consequences of a particular course of action.

NONVERBAL COMMUNICATION

nonverbal communication
All elements of communication that do not involve words.

Much defensive and nondefensive communication focuses on the language used. However, most of the meaning in a message (an estimated 65–90 percent) is conveyed through nonverbal communication.[43] *Nonverbal communication* includes all elements of communication, such as gestures and the use of space, that do not involve words or language.[44] The four basic kinds of nonverbal communication are proxemics, kinesics, facial and eye behavior, and paralanguage. They are important

The Real World 8.2

Eye Contact and Voice Tone Proved to be Wind under His Wings

Barack Obama usually chooses eloquent words for his messages, and he certainly did that for his inaugural address as President of the United States. Words are important, but up to 93 percent of the emotional meaning behind what is said comes through nonverbal communication. President Obama gave his inaugural against the backdrop of a severe recession marked by massive layoffs, foreclosures, bankruptcies, and other economic difficulties. He achieved success using eye contact and tone of voice rather than more frequently used hand gestures. Rather than limiting his eye contact to particular places or segments in the audience, he intelligently used eye contact by constantly spanning the entire crowd present, from extreme left to extreme right. This communicated his awareness of the enormity of the audience, beyond those present to the viewing audience.

President Barack Obama gives his inaugural address.

Photo by Alex Wong/Getty Images

In addition, President Obama chose tone of voice as his most evocative and powerful nonverbal behavior. He altered it frequently to match his message. While the taking of the oath had some awkward moments of confusion between him and Chief Justice Roberts, Obama's confident tone during his inaugural speech gave him an air of command and imparted strong meaning to his words. His forceful tone of voice conveyed appropriate gravity at the right moments. His tone of voice later conveyed a powerful sense of optimism and compelling vision of a brighter future. These key nonverbal behaviors were wind under his wings in what became an inspiring inaugural address.

SOURCE: W.A. Gentry, "Nonverbal Obama: Aside From His Words," *Business Week Online* 21 January 2009: 4.

---

topics for managers attempting to understand the types and meanings of nonverbal signals from employees. Nonverbal communication is influenced by both psychological and physiological processes. [45] The Office of the President of the United States has been called a bully pulpit and President Reagan was called the Great Communicator. The Real World 8.2 discusses President Obama's nonverbal communication to create his inspiring inaugural address.

Some of the scientific research in nonverbal communication is interesting. One study in particular found that one's body posture and position informs internal subjective experience and consequently influences behavior. [46] In any case, the interpretation of nonverbal communication is specific to the context of the interaction and the actors. That is, nonverbal cues only give meaning in the context of the situation and the interaction of the actors. For example, some federal and state judges attempt to curb nonverbal communication in the courtroom. The judges' primary concern is that nonverbal behavior may unfairly influence jurors' decisions. It is important to note that nonverbal behavior is culturally bound. Gestures, facial expressions, and body locations have different meanings in different cultures. Nonverbal behavior may contribute to culturally shared attitudes and beliefs, but can be biased to favor certain social groups while disparaging others.[47] The globalization of business means managers should be sensitive to the nonverbal customs of other cultures in which they do business.

Proxemics

The study of an individual's perception and use of space, including territorial space, is called *proxemics*.[48] *Territorial space* refers to bands of space extending outward from the body. These bands constitute comfort zones. In each comfort zone, different cultures prefer different types of interaction with others. Figure 8.2 presents four zones of territorial space based on U.S. culture.

The first zone, intimate space, extends outward from the body to about 1-1/2 feet. In this zone, we interact with spouses, significant others, family members, and others with whom we have an intimate relationship. The next zone, the personal distance zone, extends from 1-1/2 feet outward to 4 feet. Friends typically interact within this distance. The third zone, the social distance zone, spans the distance from 4 to 12 feet. We prefer that business associates and acquaintances interact with us in this zone. The final zone is the public distance zone, extending 12 feet from the body outward. Most of us prefer that strangers stay at least 12 feet from us, and we become uncomfortable when they move closer.

Territorial space varies greatly across cultures. People often become uncomfortable when operating in territorial spaces different from those with which they are familiar. Edward Hall, a leading proxemics researcher, says Americans working in the Middle East tend to back away to a comfortable conversation distance when interacting with Arabs. Because Arabs' comfortable conversation distance is closer than that of Americans, Arabs perceive Americans as cold and aloof. One Arab wondered, "What's the matter? Does he find me somehow offensive?"[49] Personal space tends to be larger in cultures with cool climates, such as the United States, Great Britain, and northern Europe, and smaller in cultures with warm climates, such as southern Europe, the Caribbean, India, or South America.[50]

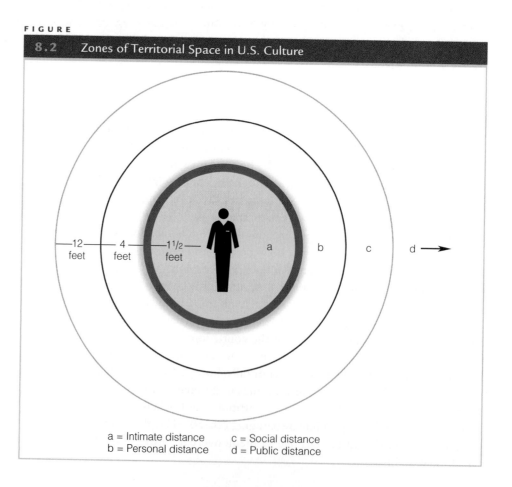

FIGURE

8.2   Zones of Territorial Space in U.S. Culture

a = Intimate distance   c = Social distance
b = Personal distance   d = Public distance

proxemics

The study of an individual's perception and use of space, including territorial space.

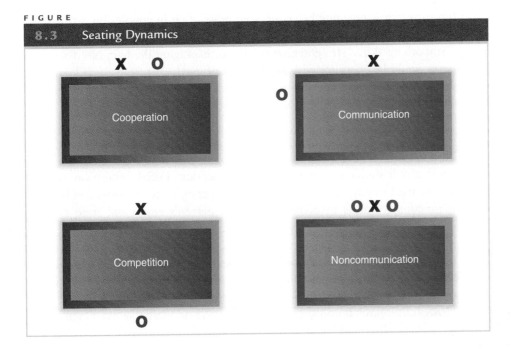

8.3 Seating Dynamics

Cooperation

Communication

Competition

Noncommunication

Our relationships shape our use of territorial space. For example, we hold hands with, or put an arm around, significant others to pull them into intimate space. Conversely, the use of territorial space can shape people's interactions. A 4-foot-wide business desk pushes business interactions into the social distance zone. An exception occurred for one SBC manager who met with her seven first-line supervisors around her desk. Being elbow to elbow placed the supervisors in one another's intimate and personal space. They appeared to act more like friends and frequently talked about their children, favorite television shows, and other personal concerns. When the manager moved the staff meeting to a larger room and the spaces around each supervisor were in the social distance zone, the personal exchanges ceased, and they acted more like business associates again.

Seating dynamics, another aspect of proxemics, is the art of seating people in certain positions according to their purpose in communication. Figure 8.3 depicts some common seating dynamics. To encourage cooperation, you should seat the other party beside you, facing the same direction. To facilitate direct and open communication, seat the other party across a corner of your desk from you or in another place where you will be at right angles. This allows for more honest disclosure. To take a competitive stand with someone, position the person directly across from you. Suppose you hold a meeting around a conference table, and two of the attendees are disrupting it. Where should you seat them? If you place one on each side of yourself, it should stifle the disruptions (unless one is so bold as to lean in front of you to keep chatting).

Kinesics

Kinesics is the study of body movements, including posture.[51] Like proxemics, kinesics is culturally bound; there is no single universal gesture. For example, the U.S. hand signal for "okay" is an insult in other countries. With this in mind, we can interpret some common U.S. gestures. Rubbing one's hands together or exhibiting a sharp intake of breath indicates anticipation. Stress is indicated by a closed hand position (i.e., tight fists), hand wringing, or rubbing the temples. Nervousness may be displayed through drumming fingers, pacing, or jingling coins in the pocket. Perhaps

kinesics
The study of body movements, including posture.

most fun to watch is preening behavior, seen most often in couples on a first date. Preening communicates, "I want to look good for you" to the other party and consists of smoothing skirts, straightening the tie, or arranging the hair. No discussion of gestures would be complete without mention of insult gestures—some learned at an early age, much to the anxiety of parents. Sticking out one's tongue while waving fingers with one's thumbs in the ears is a common childhood insult gesture.

Facial and Eye Behavior

The face is a rich source of nonverbal communication. Facial expression and eye behavior are used to add cues for the receiver. A person's facial expression has two distinct functions. One is to communicate the person's emotional state and the other is to act as a messenger, revealing the person's behavioral intentions.[52] The face may give unintended clues to emotions the sender is trying to hide. Dynamic facial actions and expressions in a person's appearance are key clues of truthfulness, especially in deception situations.[53] In legal proceedings, laypeople and professionals alike assume nonverbal behaviors, such as avoiding eye contact, are displayed while lying. However, research found support for only three nonverbal behaviors in regard to lying: nodding, foot and leg movements, and hand movements.[54]

Although smiles have universal meaning, frowns, raised eyebrows, and wrinkled foreheads must all be interpreted in conjunction with the actors, the situation, and the culture. One study of Japanese and U.S. students illustrates the point. The students were shown a stress-inducing film, and their facial expressions were videotaped. When alone, the students had almost identical expressions. However, the Japanese students masked their facial expressions of unpleasant feelings much better than did the American students when another person was present.[55]

As mentioned earlier, eye contact can enhance reflective listening and, along with smiling, is one good way of displaying positive emotion.[56] However, eye contact must be understood in a cultural context. A direct gaze indicates honesty, truthfulness, and forthrightness in the United States. This may not be true in other cultures. For example, Barbara Walters was uncomfortable interviewing Muammar al-Qaddafi in Libya because he did not look directly at her. However, in Libya, it is a serious offense to look directly at a woman.[57] In Asian cultures, it is considered good behavior to bow the head in deference to a superior rather than to look in the supervisor's eyes.

Paralanguage

Paralanguage consists of variations in speech, such as pitch, loudness, tempo, tone, duration, laughing, and crying.[58] People make attributions about the sender by deciphering paralanguage cues. A high-pitched, breathy voice in a female may contribute to the stereotype of the "dumb blonde." Rapid, loud speech may be taken as a sign of nervousness or anger. Interruptions such as "mmm" and "ah-hah" may be used to speed up the speaker so that the receiver can get in a few words. Clucking of the tongue or the "tsktsk" sound is used to shame someone. All these cues relate to how something is said.

How Accurately Do We Decode Nonverbal Cues?

People's confidence in their ability to decode nonverbal communication is greater than their accuracy in doing so. Judges with several years' experience in interviewing were asked in one study to watch videotapes of job applicants and to rate the applicants' social skills and motivation levels.[59] The judges were fairly accurate about the social skills, but not about motivation. They relied on smiling, gesturing, and speaking as cues to motivation, yet none of these cues are motivation indicators. Smiles are a very interesting nonverbal cue. Research suggests that smiles may be communicated vocally in the absence of visual cues but cannot always be taken as a sign of genuine affect. [60] Thus, incorrectly interpreting nonverbal codes leads to inaccuracy.

Studies of deception emphasize how to use nonverbal cues to interpret whether someone is lying. In one simulation study, customers were asked to detect whether or not automobile salespeople were lying. The customers' ability to detect lies in this study was no better than chance. Does this suggest that salespeople are skilled deceivers who control nonverbal behaviors to prevent detection? [61] A person's mood may affect the ability to detect deception on the part of others.[62]

Paul Ekman, a psychologist who has trained judges, Secret Service agents, and polygraphers to detect lies, says that the best way to detect lies is to look for inconsistencies in the nonverbal cues. Rapidly shifting facial expressions and discrepancies between the person's words and body, voice, or facial expressions are some clues.[63]

Nonverbal communication is important for managers because of its impact on the meaning of the message. However, a manager must consider the total message and all media of communication. A message can only be given meaning in context, and cues are easy to misinterpret. Table 8.3 presents common nonverbal behaviors exhibited by managers and how employees may interpret them. Nonverbal cues can give others the wrong signal.

TABLE 8.3   Common Nonverbal Cues from Manager to Employee

Nonverbal Communication	Signal Received	Reaction from Receiver
Manager looks away when talking to the employee.	Divided attention	My supervisor is too busy to listen to my problem or simply does not care.
Manager fails to acknowledge greeting from fellow employee.	Unfriendliness	This person is unapproachable.
Manager glares ominously (i.e., gives the evil eye).	Anger	Reciprocal anger, fear, or avoidance, depending on who is sending the signal in the organization.
Manager rolls the eyes.	Not taking person seriously	This person thinks he or she is smarter or better than I am.
Manager sighs deeply.	Disgust or displeasure	My opinions do not count. I must be stupid or boring to this person.
Manager uses heavy breathing (sometimes accompanied by hand waving).	Anger or heavy stress	Avoid this person at all costs.
Manager does not maintain eye contact when communicating.	Suspicion or uncertainty	What does this person have to hide?
Manager crosses arms and leans away.	Apathy or closed-mindedness	This person already has made up his or her mind; my opinions are not important.
Manager peers over glasses.	Skepticism or distrust	He or she does not believe what I am saying.
Manager continues to read a report when employee is speaking.	Lack of interest	My opinions are not important enough to get the supervisor's undivided attention.

SOURCE: From "Steps to Better Listening" by C. Hamilton and B. H. Kleiner. Copyright © February 1987. Reprinted with permission, *Personnel Journal*, all rights reserved.

POSITIVE, HEALTHY COMMUNICATION

6 Explain positive, healthy communication.

The absence of heartfelt communication in human relationships leads to loneliness and social isolation and has been labeled *communicative disease* by James Lynch.[64] Communicative disease has adverse effects on the heart and cardiovascular system and can ultimately lead to premature death. According to Lynch, heartfelt communication is a healing dialogue and central antidote for communicative disease. Positive, healthy communication is central to health and well-being. While communication may often be thought of as a cognitive activity of the head, Lynch suggests that the heart may be more important in the communications process.

Positive, healthy communication is one important aspect of working together when the term *working together* is taken for its intrapersonal meaning as well as its interpersonal meaning.[65] The balance between head and heart is achieved when a person displays positive emotional competence and is able to have a healthy internal conversation between his or her thoughts and feelings, ideas, and emotions. In addition, working together occurs when there are cooperative work behaviors between people based on positive, healthy, and open communication that is in turn based on trust and truthfulness. Honest competition within the workplace is not inconsistent with this notion of working together; forthright, well-managed, honest competition can bring out the best in all those involved.

Positive, healthy communication is at the core of personal integrity as displayed by healthy executives.[66] As president, the late Ronald Reagan was a great communicator who displayed strong ethical character, personal integrity, and simplicity in his communication. He exemplified communication from the heart in the sense that his messages came from his core values, beliefs, and aspirations for himself and others. His optimism shone through from the core of his person, displaying a continuing positive attitude that drew even his opponents to like him. Communication from core values and beliefs is communication anchored in personal integrity and ethical character.

Courtesy of Karol Wasylyshyn

Karol Wasylyshyn (pictured) has shown that one dimension of coaching star executives is to enhance their emotional competency and capacity to talk through challenging issues.

Personal integrity in positive, healthy communication is achieved through emotional competence and the head-to-heart dialogue mentioned earlier. In addition to the public self, as is familiar in the case of Ronald Reagan, all executives have a private self. Karol Wasylyshyn has shown that one dimension of coaching star executives is to enhance their emotional competence and capacity to talk through challenging issues, both personally and professionally.[67] Quick and Macik-Frey focus on the private-self aspect of positive, healthy communication in developing their model of executive coaching through deep interpersonal communication.[68] This model relies on what Lynch might call a healing dialogue between executive and coach. However, their model of deep interpersonal communication is one that can enhance positive, healthy communication in a wider range of human relationships.

COMMUNICATING THROUGH NEW TECHNOLOGIES

7 Describe Information Communication Technology (ICT) used by managers.

Nonverbal behaviors can be important in establishing trust in working relationships, but modern technologies may challenge our ability to maintain that trust. Many organizations around the world are now plugging into the Internet, which allows for the easy transfer of information and data across continents. Managers in today's business world have access to more communication tools than ever before.

All of these new technologies are, surprisingly, having relatively little impact on work culture. In addition, security concerns since 9/11 have complicated wireless access. An understanding of the use of these new technologies facilitates effective, successful communication. In addition, it is important to understand how these new technologies affect others' communication and behavior. Finally, information technology can encourage or discourage moral dialogue, and moral conversations are central to addressing ethical issues at work.[69]

Written Communication

Many organizations are working toward paperless offices and paperless interfaces with their customers. Some written communication is still required, however. Forms are one category of written communication. Manuals are another. Policy manuals are important in organizations because they set out guidelines for decision making and rules of actions for organizational members. Operations and procedures manuals explain how to perform various tasks and resolve problems that may occur at work. Reports are a third category of written communication; company annual reports are an example. Reports may summarize the results of a committee's or department's work or provide information on progress toward certain objectives.

Letters and memorandums are briefer, more frequently used categories of written communication in organizations. Letters are a formal means of communication—often with people outside the organization—and may vary substantially in length. Memorandums are another formal means of communication, often to constituencies within the organization. Memos are sometimes used to create a formal, historical record of a specific event or occurrence to which people in the organization may want to refer at some future date. Looking back at Table 8.1, we can conclude that written communication has the advantage of high to moderate data capacity and the possible disadvantage of moderate to low information richness.

Communication Technologies

Computer-mediated communication was once used only by technical specialists but now influences virtually all managers' behavior in the work environment. Informational databases are becoming more commonplace. These databases provide a tremendous amount of information with the push of a button. Another example of an informational database is the type of system used in many university libraries, in which books and journals are available through an electronic card catalog. In addition, the Internet seems to be everywhere. We see in the Looking Back feature that CarMax has designed a new Advanced Search option on their Web site to allow customers to more effectively meet their needs.

E-mail systems represent another technology; users can leave messages via the computer to be accessed at any time by the receiver. This eliminates the time delay of regular mail and allows for immediate reply. Research comparing e-mail to face-to-face communication on choices individuals make found that the effects vary with the nature of the decisions and may depend on the complexity and content of what needs to be communicated.[70] Thus, e-mail has strengths and advantages in communication as well as limitations with which to exercise caution. Relative to face-to-face interaction, people who communicate via e-mail are less cooperative and feel more justified in being noncooperative.[71] Unfortunately, some people feel much less inhibited when using e-mail and end up sending caustic messages they would never consider saying in person. The MoodWatch software system helps guard against "flaming" e-mails by notifying users if their message contains hostile, abusive, or bullying content (flames). The bottom line is that people cannot communicate as effectively over e-mail as they think.[72] In addition and on a positive note, there are

communicative disease
The absence of heartfelt communication in human relationships leading to loneliness and social isolation.

also devices that enable international e-mail users to have their messages translated to and from French, German, Spanish, Portuguese, and English.

Voice mail systems are another widely used communication mode, especially in sales jobs where people are away from the office. Voice behavior influences the quality of the work environment. This has implications for the quality of voice mail as well. Some voice mail systems allow the user to retrieve messages from remote locations. Timely retrieval of messages is important. One manager in the office furniture industry had a problem with her voice mail when first learning to use it. She would forget to check it until late in the day. Employees with problems early in the day felt frustrated with her slow response time. When using voice mail, it is important to remember that the receiver may not retrieve the messages in a timely manner. Urgent messages must be delivered directly.

Facsimile (fax) machine systems allow the immediate transmission of documents. This medium allows the sender to communicate facts, graphs, and illustrations very rapidly. Fax machines are used in cars as well as offices and remote locations.

Cell phones are also commonplace, permitting communication while away from the office and on the commute to and from work. They are used extensively in sales jobs involving travel. Not all reactions to car phones are positive. For example, one oil producer did not want his thinking time disturbed by a cell phone while driving. Using a cell phone while driving is also risky, with some estimates suggesting it is as risky as driving under the influence of alcohol. For this reason, some states have outlawed the use of cell phones while driving a motor vehicle. Social networking sites such as Twitter have emerged to track customer perceptions of products. For example, all of online shoe retailer Zappos' 429 employees, to include the CEO, have Twitter accounts.[73]

How Do Communication Technologies Affect Behavior?

Information Communication Technology (ICT) offers faster, more immediate access to information than was available in the past. It provides instant exchange of information in minutes or seconds across geographic boundaries and time zones. Schedules and office hours become irrelevant. The normal considerations of time and distance become less important in the exchange. Hence, these technologies have important influences on people's behavior.

One aspect of computer-mediated communication is its impersonal nature. The sender interacts with a machine, not a person. As mentioned earlier, studies show that using these technologies results in an increase in flaming, or making rude or obscene outbursts by computer.[74] Interpersonal skills like tact and graciousness diminish, and managers are more blunt when using electronic media. People who participate in discussions quietly and politely when face to face may become impolite, more intimate, and uninhibited when they communicate using computer conferencing or e-mail.[75]

Another effect of the new technologies is that the nonverbal cues we rely on to decipher a message are absent. Gesturing, touching, facial expressions, and eye contact are not available, so the emotional element of the message is difficult to access. In addition, clues to power, such as organizational position and departmental membership, may not be available, so the social context of the exchange is altered.

Communication via technologies also changes group interaction. It tends to equalize participation, because group members participate more equally, and charismatic or higher status members may have less power.[76] Studies of groups that make decisions via computer interaction (computer-mediated groups) have shown that the computer-mediated groups took longer to reach consensus than face-to-face groups. In addition, they were more uninhibited, and there was less influence from any one dominant person. It appears that groups that communicate by computer experience a breakdown of social and organizational barriers. However, one study found that ICTs, especially e-mail, teleconferencing combined with e-meetings, and team

Information Communication Technology (ICT)

The various new technologies, such as e-mail, voice mail, teleconferencing, and wireless access, which are used for interpersonal communication.

rooms, reduced the tension created by intercultural communication and increased effective decision making of virtual teams.[77]

The potential for overload is particularly great with the new communication technologies. Not only is information available more quickly, the sheer volume of information at the manager's fingertips also is staggering. An individual can easily become overwhelmed by information and must learn to be selective in accessing it.

A paradox created by the new, modern communication technology lies in the danger it may pose for managers. The danger is that managers cannot get away from the office as much as in the past, because they are more accessible to coworkers, subordinates, and the boss via telecommunications. Interactions are no longer confined to the 9 to 5 work hours.

In addition, the use of new technologies encourages polyphasic activity (i.e., doing more than one thing at a time). Managers can simultaneously make phone calls, send computer messages, and work on memos. Polyphasic activity has its advantages in terms of getting more done—but only up to a point. Paying attention to more than one task at a time splits a person's attention and may reduce effectiveness. Constantly focusing on multiple tasks can become a habit, making it psychologically difficult for a person to let go of work.

Finally, the new technologies may make people less patient with face-to-face communication. The speed advantage of the electronic media may translate into an expectation of greater speed in all forms of communication. However, individuals may miss the social interaction with others and may find their social needs unmet. Communicating via computer means an absence of small talk; people tend to get to the point right away.

With many of these technologies, the potential for immediate feedback is reduced, and the exchange can become one-way. Managers can use the new technologies more effectively by keeping the following hints in mind:

1. Strive for completeness in your message.
2. Build in opportunities for feedback.
3. Do not assume you will get an immediate response.
4. Ask yourself if the communication is really necessary.
5. "Disconnect" yourself from the technology at regular intervals.
6. Provide opportunities for social interaction at work.

MANAGERIAL IMPLICATIONS: COMMUNICATE WITH STRENGTH AND CLARITY

Interpersonal communication is important for the quality of working relationships in organizations. Managers who are sensitive and responsive in communicating with employees encourage the development of trusting, loyal relationships. Managers and employees alike benefit from secure working relations. Managers who are directive, dictatorial, or overbearing with employees, by contrast, are likely to find such behavior counterproductive, especially in periods of change.

Encouraging feedback and practicing reflective listening skills at work can open up communication channels in the work environment. Open communication benefits decision-making processes, because managers are better informed and more likely to base decisions on complete information. Open communication encourages nondefensive relationships, as opposed to defensive relationships, among people at work. Defensive relationships create problems because of the use of tactics that trigger conflict and division among people.

Managers benefit from sensitivity to employees' nonverbal behavior and territorial space, recognizing that understanding individual and cultural diversity is

Diversity Dialogue

Don Imus: Cross-Cultural Miscommunication or Insensitivity?

When Don Imus referred to members of the Rutgers University women's basketball team as "nappy-headed hos," he ignited a firestorm of criticism from a wide variety of sources including the NAACP and the National Organization for Women—culminating in his dismissal from the *Imus in the Morning* radio show.

As a result of Imus's remarks, six of ten of the nation's largest advertisers pulled their support from the show, putting MSNBC's $163 million-plus in total annual advertising revenue at risk. As the owners of the radio station that originated the Imus broadcast, NBC and CBS were responsible for taking any disciplinary action against the host. First NBC, then CBS fired Imus and yanked his program off the air. According to NBC CEO Jeff Zucker, this was done to preserve the organization's strong reputation for integrity, not due to pressure from advertisers.

By the time he was fired in 2007, the sixty-six-year-old Imus had been no stranger to pushing the envelope.

In fact, former *60 Minutes* host Mike Wallace termed *Imus in the Morning* as "dirty and sometimes racist" back in 1998. Similar to those of other radio shock jocks such as Howard Stern and Opie & Andy, the show regularly included talk that seemed to some like social satire but to others more like racism and sexism. Many wondered why it took his employers so long to discipline him.

1. Should organizations be held responsible for their employees' communications? Discuss any factors that might enhance or diminish their level of responsibility.
2. Were NBC and CBS justified in ending *Imus in the Morning*? Why or why not?

SOURCE: B. Steinberg, B. Barnes, and E. Steel, "Facing Ad Defection, NBC Takes Don Imus Show Off TV," *Wall Street Journal* (April 12, 2007): B1; A. Neuharth, "Does Imus' Trash Talk Hurt First Amendment?," *USA Today* (April 12, 2007), http://www.usatoday.com/news/opinion/columnist/neuharth/2007-04-12-imus_N.htm.

important in interpreting a person's nonverbal behavior. Seeking verbal clarification on nonverbal cues improves the accuracy of the communication and helps build trusting relationships. In addition, managers benefit from an awareness of their own nonverbal behaviors. Seeking employee feedback about their own nonverbal behavior helps managers provide a message consistent with their intentions.

Managers may complement good interpersonal contact with the appropriate use of new information technology. New information technologies' high data capacity is an advantage in a global workplace. The high information richness of interpersonal contacts is an advantage in a culturally diverse workforce. Therefore, managers benefit from both interpersonal and technological media by treating them as complementary modes of communication, not as substitutes for each other.

LOOKING BACK: CARMAX

An Advanced Search Tool for Customers

CarMax has a history of being a great place to work. Even during the economic difficulties of 2008 and 2009, CarMax made a positive move from the No. 46 spot to the No. 21 spot on the list of America's 100 Best Places to Work. This sends a clear, positive message both within the company and to the whole business community. An important aspect of this recognition is undoubtedly how the

company treats its employees, especially during times of economic difficulty. CarMax did have to cut jobs to endure the very tough economy. This reduction in staffing came through attrition and labor hour savings. The company cautioned the news of job loss with a generous severance package of 4 to 26 weeks' pay. That sends a message to those who stay as well as those who must leave.

Courtesy of CarMax

How CarMax treats employees in difficult times is one element of internal business integrity. The company shows integrity in the marketplace too and with customers. For example, the Better Business Bureau of Central Virginia awarded CarMax its Torch Award for Marketplace Integrity. These awards are presented regionally to companies that practice fair, honest, and ethical business practices. CarMax won Torch Awards for Marketplace Integrity in six other markets as well: Chicago and Northern Illinois; Louisville, southern Indiana, and Western Kentucky; greater Maryland; central Ohio; greater Houston and south Texas; and metro Atlanta, Athens, and northeast Georgia. [78] That is an impressive array of awards for fair, honest, and ethical business practices around the country.

Treating employees well in difficult times and ethical business practices are strength factors to broadcast during difficult times. In addition, CarMax launched a new advanced search tool for customers as a way for them to search CarMax's thousands of vehicles online. This new, optimal Advanced Search available at carmax.com is for used car shoppers who want to enter multiple criteria into one search right from the start. Any combination of makes, features, colors, and more can be entered into one search field with an update instantly available to the customer. This flexible, full-featured online vehicle search makes the process quick and easy for the company customers. [79] Successfully meeting the challenge of difficult times requires optimism, empathy for employees, ethics and integrity in the marketplace, and the creation of easy to use Web site technology for customers. That is the CarMax way.

Chapter Summary

1. The perceptual screens of communicators and listeners either help clarify or distort a message that is sent and received. Age, gender, and culture influence the sent and received messages.

2. Reflective listening involves affirming contact, paraphrasing what is expressed, clarifying the implicit, reflecting "core" feelings, and using appropriate nonverbal behavior to enhance communication.

3. The best supervisors talk easily with diverse groups of people, listen empathetically, are generally persuasive and not directive, are sensitive to a person's self-esteem, and are communication minded.

4. Physical separation, status differences, gender differences, cultural diversity, and language are potential communication barriers that can be overcome.

5. Active or passive defensive communication destroys interpersonal relationships, whereas assertive, nondefensive communication leads to clarity.

6. Nonverbal communication includes the use of territorial space, seating arrangements, facial gestures, eye contact, and paralanguage. Nonverbal communication varies by nation and culture around the world.

7. Communicative disease is the absence of heartfelt communication in human relationship and can lead to loneliness and social isolation.

8. Information Communication Technology (ICT) includes e-mail, voice mail, and cell phones. High-tech innovations require high-touch responses.

Key Terms

barriers to communication (p. 266)
communication (p. 258)
communicative disease (p. 277)
communicator (p. 259)
data (p. 260)
defensive communication (p. 269)
feedback (p. 259)
gateways to communication (p. 266)

information (p. 260)
Information Communication Technology (ICT) (p. 280)
interpersonal communication (p. 258)
Kinesics (p. 275)
language (p. 259)
message (p. 259)
nondefensive communication (p. 269)

nonverbal communication (p. 272)
one-way communication (p. 263)
perceptual screen (p. 259)
receiver (p. 259)
reflective listening (p. 260)
richness (p. 260)
two-way communication (p. 263)

Review Questions

1. What different components of a person's perceptual screens may distort communication?

2. What are the three defining features of reflective listening?

3. What are the four levels of verbal response in reflective listening?

4. Compare one-way and two-way communication.

5. What are the five communication skills of effective supervisors and managers?

6. Describe dominant and subordinate defensive communication. Describe nondefensive communication.

7. What four kinds of nonverbal communication are important in interpersonal relationships?

8. What are helpful nonverbal behaviors in the communication process? Unhelpful behaviors?

9. What is communicative disease?

10. Describe at least five new communication technologies in terms of data richness.

Discussion and Communication Questions

1. Who is the best communicator you know? Why do you consider that person to be so?

2. Who is the best listener you have ever known? Describe what that person does that makes him or her so good at listening.

3. What methods have you found most helpful in overcoming barriers to communication that are physical? Status-based? Cultural? Linguistic?

4. Who makes you the most defensive when you talk with that person? What does the person do that makes you so defensive or uncomfortable?

5. With whom are you the most comfortable and nondefensive in conversation? What does the person do that makes you so comfortable or nondefensive?

6. What nonverbal behaviors do you find most helpful in others when you are attempting to talk with them? When you try to listen to them?

7. (communication question) Identify a person at work or at school who is difficult to talk to and arrange an interview in which you practice good reflective listening skills. Ask the person questions about a topic you think may interest her or him. Pay particular attention to being patient, calm, and nonreactive. After the interview, summarize what you learned.

8. (communication question) Go to the library and read about communication problems and barriers. Write a memo categorizing the problems and barriers you find in current literature (last five years). What changes do organizations or people need to make to solve these problems?

9. (communication question) Develop a role-playing activity for class that demonstrates defensive (dominant or subordinate) and nondefensive communication. Write brief role descriptions that classmates can act out.

10. (communication question) Read everything you can find in the library about a new communication technology. Write a two-page memo summarizing what you have learned and the conclusions you draw about the new technology's advantages and disadvantages.

Ethical Dilemma

Dan Neville is the manager for a team of engineers at RFC, Inc. He is responsible for coordinating his team's efforts on a daily, weekly, and monthly basis, as well as assuring that they are keeping on schedule with teams in other offices around the country. Dan regularly communicates with his own team via e-mail, attaching memos and instructions prior to their regular face-to-face meetings. Clear, consistent, and timely communication is an essential element of Dan's job.

Dan usually has no trouble with any member of the team understanding his instructions, except for Kyle Trenton. Kyle always seems to misunderstand or misinterpret Dan's messages, even during face-to-face meetings. Kyle doesn't seem to be deliberately being obstinate; he honestly derives other meanings from Dan's communications, reading into the words Dan chooses and coming up with implied ideas that Dan never intended.

Inevitably, Dan has to meet with Kyle separately to be certain that Kyle understands the tasks at hand. If left to his own devices, Kyle wouldn't come to Dan to question his interpretation of the message, because he sincerely believes he "gets it." However, Kyle is rarely clear about Dan's meanings, and Dan must devote extra time and energy to reorient Kyle. Dan tries to be sympathetic, because Kyle is a nice person and a good worker, but Kyle requires twice as much time from Dan as everyone else and it is frustrating. Dan does worry that if Kyle would happen to misunderstand critical directions on a building project which are not corrected, someone could legitimately get hurt.

Dan has an opportunity to move Kyle onto a new position, where he would no longer have to work with Dan's current team and Dan would no longer have to communicate with Kyle. However, Dan knows that Ken Rothberg is the head of that team, and Ken is known for being a very poor communicator. Dan suspects that Ken wouldn't take any additional time to make certain that Kyle understood his instructions, and that could cause even more critical problems.

Questions:

1. Using consequential, rule-based and character theories, evaluate Dan's options.

2. What should Dan do? Why?

Experiential Exercises

8.1 Communicate, Listen, Understand

The following exercise gives you an opportunity to work within a three-person group to do a communication skill-building exercise. You can learn to apply some of the reflective listening and two-way communication materials from the early sections of the chapter, as well as some of the lessons managing difficult communication in a nondefensive manner.

Step 1. The class is formed into three-person groups and each group designates its members "A," "B," and "C." There will be three 5- to 7-minute conversations among the group members: first, between A and B; second, between B and C; third, between C and A. During each conversation, the nonparticipating group member is to observe and make notes about two communicating group members.

Step 2. Your instructor will give you a list of controversial topics and ask A to pick a topic. A is then asked to discuss his or her position on this topic, with the rationale for the position, with B. B is to practice reflective listening and engage in listening checks periodically by paraphrasing what he or she understands to be A's position. C should observe whether B is practicing good listening skills or becoming defensive. C should also observe whether A is becoming dominantly defensive in the communication. This should be a two-way communication.

Step 3. Repeat Step 2 with B as communicator, C as listener, and A as observer.

Step 4. Repeat Step 2 with C as communicator, A as listener, and B as observer.

Step 5. After your instructor has had all groups complete Steps 1 through 4, your three-person group should answer the following questions.

a. *Did either the listener or the communicator become visibly (or internally) angry or upset during the discussion?*

b. *What were the biggest challenges for the listeners and the communicator in the controversial communication?*

c. *What are the most important skill improvements (e.g., better eye contact or more patience) the listener and communicator could have made to improve the quality of understanding achieved through the communication process?*

8.2 Preparing for an Employment-Selection Interview

The purpose of this exercise is to help you develop guidelines for an employment selection interview. Such interviews are one of the more important settings in which supervisors and job candidates use applied communication skills. There is always the potential for defensiveness and confusion as well as lack of complete information exchange in this interview. This exercise allows you to think through ways to maximize the value of an employment selection interview, whether you are the supervisor or the candidate, so that it is a productive experience based on effective applied communication.

Your instructor will form your class into groups of students. Each group should work through Steps 1 and 2 of the exercise.

Step 1. *Guidelines for the Supervisor*
Develop a set of guidelines for the supervisor in preparing for and then conducting an employment selection interview. Consider the following questions in developing your guidelines.

a. What should the supervisor do before the interview?

b. How should the supervisor act and behave during the interview?

c. What should the supervisor do after the interview?

Step 2. *Guidelines for the Employee*
Develop another set of guidelines for the employee in preparing for and then being involved in an employment selection interview. Consider the following questions in developing your guidelines.

a. What should the employee do before the interview?

b. How should the employee act and behave during the interview?

c. What should the employee do after the interview?

Once each group has developed the two sets of guidelines, the instructor will lead the class in a general discussion in which groups share and compare their guidelines. Consider the following questions during this discussion.

1. What similarities are there among the groups for each set of guidelines?

2. What unique or different guidelines have some of the groups developed?

3. What are essential guidelines for conducting an employment selection interview?

BizFlix | Friday Night Lights (II)

The Odessa, Texas passion for Friday night high school football (Permian High Panthers) comes through clearly in this cinematic treatment of H. G. (Buzz) Bissinger's well-regarded book of the same title.[1] Coach Gary Gaines (Billy Bob Thornton) leads them to the 1988 semifinals where they must compete against a team of much larger players. Fast-moving pace in the football sequences and a slower pace in the serious, introspective sequences give this film many fine moments.

Communication: Half-Time

This sequence[2] begins with a shot of Coach Gaines and the team gathered around him during the half-time break. He starts his speech to the team by saying, "Well, it's real simple. You got two more quarters and that's it." It ends after Gaines says, "Boys, my heart is full. My heart's full." He calls to Ivory Christian (Lee Jackson) to begin the team prayer.

What to Watch for and Ask Yourself

- This chapter defines communication as creating "a shared or common meaning in another person." Do you perceive Coach Gaines as having reached that communication goal? Why or why not?

- The chapter described an Interpersonal Communication Model. What are examples from this film sequence of each part of the model?

- Assess the effectiveness of this communication event. How do you expect team members and the assistant coaches to react in the second half of the game?

Workplace Video | Greensburg Public Schools: Communication

Greensburg superintendent Darrin Headrick was driving home the night the tornado hit town. He stopped at Greensburg High School principal Randy Fulton's house to take cover. He soon discovered the entire school system was wiped out. Every building was gone. Textbooks were scattered all over town, and computers were destroyed.

Along with 95 percent of the town's 1,500 residents, Headrick was homeless. With only four months to restore Greensburg Unified School District #422, Headrick went to work. All he had to work with was his laptop and cell phone, so he got in his truck and started looking for a wireless signal.

For the first three months after the tornado, no one could live in Greensburg. Because the tornado had affected telephone service, no one had a home telephone; people were either in shelters or staying with friends and family out of town. Everyone was eager to reconnect and get information. The Federal Emergency Management Agency (FEMA) provided primary crisis communications by distributing flyers, but residents had to come to town to get them.

Unable to access the school's normal communication channels, Headrick took a lesson from his students who preferred to communicate via text messaging because of

---

[1]J. Craddock, ed., *VideoHound's Golden Movie Retriever* (Detroit, MI: Gale Cengage Learning, 2008), p. 368.
[2]This sequence draws from DVD Chapter 27, "Half-Time." However, we edited in scenes from other parts of the film to reduce the number of identifiable talent to whom we must pay a fee. If you have seen this film, you will know that this exact sequence does not exist at any point in the film.

its capacity for rapid exchange. Headrick realized text messaging was the perfect new channel for disseminating formal school communications. Few people had computers or landlines, but most folks had cell phones. Headrick set up a centralized network in which families were able to subscribe to a text service and receive important updates instantly wherever they were.

When things stabilized, Headrick set up forums at which students, parents, and teachers could participate in two-way, face-to-face communication. The text service was fabulous, but it didn't allow for real feedback or personal dialogue.

Rebuilding will take several years, but thanks to a temporary campus of trailers, the Greensburg schools started on time that fall. Communications within the school have continued to change. Every Greensburg High student now has a laptop and hands in assignments via e-mail. Teachers provide instant feedback on homework through instant messaging. The administration, teachers, students, and parents of Greensburg schools still talk to each other in person when it makes sense. The rest of the time, they happily communicate using the latest technologies.

Discussion Questions

1. Describe the advantages of text messaging as the preferred communication channel in Greensburg after the tornado.

2. Describe the disadvantages of text messaging as the preferred communication channel in Greensburg after the tornado.

3. What lessons can managers take from this story?

Case

RIM's BlackBerry: Problems and Prospects for Business Communications

Communication in the contemporary business world increasingly relies on technology—technology that is reliable, that works when it is supposed to work. When the technology does not work as it is supposed to, business communication is disrupted—potentially to someone's detriment.

One of the very popular communication devices is Research In Motion's BlackBerry smart phone. Based in Ontario, Canada, Research In Motion (RIM) provides wireless Internet and e-mail services to support the BlackBerry. "The company has long argued that its delivery system, which ties back to a central network-operations center, improves the security and reliability of its service. But the center is a choke point that can create massive problems, with wide ramifications for its partners."[1]

Indeed, twice in a recent ten-month period, the reliability of RIM's wireless services challenged BlackBerry users and RIM's partners. In April 2007 and then again in February 2008, BlackBerry users in North America experienced the frustration of having an e-mail blackout—at least a nine-hour outage in the April incident and about a three-hour outage in the 2008 event.[2] "Several IT administrators and email-monitoring companies said the problem appeared to be related to the failure of one of the main pathways that connect corporate email servers to RIM's network."[3]

With these two service outages in less than a year, a potentially troubling pattern could be emerging for RIM. "[T]he latest incident could undermine BlackBerry's reputation for dependable service which has won it strong loyalty. While its last widespread outage didn't have a discernible impact on its growth rate, rivals are growing more formidable and RIM can't afford to lose its edge."[4]

The blackout may have less of an impact on BlackBerry users than on RIM's business partners. As Jessica Vascellaro, writing in the *Wall Street Journal* about the February 2008 blackout, observed, "[m]any BlackBerry users may have already forgotten Monday's three-hour e-mail outage. But Research In Motion Ltd., maker of the popular e-mail device and service, may soon learn that its business partners aren't as forgiving."[5]

According to Julie Ask, a wireless analyst at Jupiter Research, "the outage could weaken RIM's negotiating position with carriers and other wireless partners, who are likely to demand assurances that the pattern won't continue to repeat itself."[6] The *Wall Street Journal's* Jessica Vascellaro writes that the e-mail blackout "could create friction between RIM and the growing network of businesses that support and promote its service.... Keeping those relationships intact is critical to the wireless company's ability to expand.... RIM can't afford to alienate these companies, which have a growing number of options for wireless email services to offer subscribers."[7]

Although an e-mail blackout can be problematic, the impact of interrupted wireless service can be more devastating when the array of BlackBerry applications is considered. For instance, Verizon Communications, in an effort to phase out field technicians' use of laptops and proprietary but awkward hand-held devices, has been testing BlackBerry smart phones for online applications directed at managing daily work flow and testing the condition of telephone lines.[8] Bob Mudge, executive vice president and chief operating officer of Verizon, indicates that the company plans to switch about 12,000 of Verizon's field technicians over to BlackBerries, a move that likely will replace 1,500 laptops that Verizon technicians are currently using and will eliminate the need to buy 5,000–7,000 laptops as the company continues phasing out its proprietary hand-held devices.[9] Of course, such a shift requires continuously reliable wireless service.

There are numerous other potential applications for smart phones like the BlackBerry. Nick Wingfield, writing in the *Wall Street Journal*, notes that "mobile workers have been ditching their desktop computers for laptops that they can take wherever they go. Now road warriors are starting to realize that they can get even more portability—and lots of computing punch—from smart phones," like the BlackBerry that have e-mail and other Internet functions.[10] Many business "travelers are now using smart phones the way they once used laptops—and laptops the way they once used desktop computers," and some traveling business people are even "ditching their

289

laptops entirely and doing all their mobile work from smart phones."[11] Again, the increasing reliance of mobile workers—or road warriors—on smart phone technology places a premium on reliable wireless.

As a premier provider of wireless services for the BlackBerry smart phones, is Research In Motion up to the challenges, given its two service outages?

Discussion Questions

1. Can the basic interpersonal communication model be used as an aid in understanding the impact of the two wireless e-mail outages on BlackBerry users? If so, how?

2. How are wireless technology and the Internet transforming the way business people communicate with regard to fulfilling their job responsibilities?

3. What are the advantages and disadvantages of relying to an increasing degree on technology to facilitate communications between people?

4. Why is the reliability of RIM's services crucial to its ongoing success as a leader in communications technology?

SOURCE: This case was written by Michael K. McCuddy, The Louis S. and Mary L. Morgal Chair of Christian Business Ethics and Professor of Management, College of Business Administration, Valparaiso University.

Work Teams and Groups

LEARNING OBJECTIVES

After reading this chapter, you should be able to do the following:

1 Define *group* and *work team*.

2 Explain four important aspects of group behavior.

3 Describe group formation, the four stages of a group's development, and the characteristics of a mature group.

4 Explain the task and maintenance functions in groups.

5 Identify the social benefits of group and team membership.

6 Discuss diversity and creativity in teams.

7 Discuss teamwork and self-managed teams.

8 Explain the importance of upper echelons and top management teams.

Mike Lazaridis and Jim
Balsillie, co-CEOs of RIM.

THINKING AHEAD: RESEARCH IN MOTION (RIM)

Partnership and Teamwork

Jim Balsille and Mike Lazaridis are co-CEOs of Research in
Motion (RIM). They have forged a great partnership.[1] Is this
the ultimate in teamwork? Each contributes equally to the
company's success that rests largely on the two men's long-

standing partnership. As co-CEOs, they share authority like two parents in a family, complementing

each other's strengths, power, and influence. When it comes to responsibility, the two men divide the

workload. Lazaridis is the unofficial chief technologist of the company, while Balsille, an accountant

by training, has taken the lead in business strategy since the early 1990s. From their differences, the

two have drawn strength, and from their common passion they have bonded in partnership. For many

Canadians, this is a story too good to be true.

What effect does Jim Balsille's pursuit of the Phoenix Coyotes hockey team have on the partner-

ship and their teamwork?[2] Hockey is a Canadian national pastime in a similar way that baseball is an

American pastime. Therefore, the legal battle to relocate the National Hockey League (NHL) team

from Phoenix, Arizona, in the Southwestern United States to Hamilton, Ontario, Canada, might be considered very "Canadian" with national pride on the line. As a late-forties billionaire, Balsille is in a reasonable position to consider courting an NHL team for Hamilton. On the other hand, legal battles take time, energy, money, and other resources. How much can he keep his eye on the hockey puck and allow his attention to be diverted from RIM and BlackBerry success? Pursuing a Canadian national pastime might be a positive for the partnership while being too distracted by hockey may negatively affect teamwork.

In a second legal action beyond the Phoenix Coyotes hockey team, Jim Balsille arrived at a settlement with Canadian regulators over a controversy involving stock options. One of the conditions of the settlement reached with the Ontario Securities Commission was that Balsille had to step down from the Board of RIM for a least one year. In addition, the two co-CEOs had to make penalty payments. In the case of Balsille, the payment was $5 million Canadian while in the case of Lazaridis, the payment was $1.5 million Canadian. Every partnership and team has its challenges that stretch the relationship and threaten the success of the collaboration. A key question here is what effect does Balsille's departure from the RIM Board have on his work performance and on the work performance of his co-CEO Mike Lazaridis?

In the aircraft industry, Northrop Grumman was able to achieve teamwork among employees, customers, and partners through knowledge sharing in integrated product teams.[3] Not all teams and groups work face to face. In today's information age, advanced computer and telecommunications technologies enable organizations to be more flexible through the use of virtual teams.[4] Virtual teams also address new workforce demographics, enabling companies to access expertise and the best employees who may be located anywhere in the world. Whether a traditional groups or a virtual teams, groups and teams continue to play a vital role in organizational behavior and performance at work.

1 Define *group* and *work team*.

A *group* is two or more people having common interests, objectives, and continuing interaction. Table 9.1 summarizes the characteristics of a well-functioning, effective group.[5] A *work team* is a group of people with complementary skills who are committed to a common mission, performance goals, and approach for which they hold themselves mutually accountable.[6] All work teams are groups, but not all groups are work teams. Groups emphasize individual leadership, individual accountability, and individual work products. Work teams emphasize shared leadership, mutual accountability, and collective work products.

The chapter begins with a traditional discussion of group behavior and group development in the first two sections. The third section discusses teams. The final two sections explore the contemporary team issues of empowerment, self-managed teams, and upper echelon teams.

GROUP BEHAVIOR

Group behavior has been a subject of interest in social psychology for a long time, and many different aspects of group behavior have been studied over the years. We now look at four topics relevant to groups functioning in organizations: norms of behavior, group cohesion, social loafing, and loss of individuality. Group

group
Two or more people with common interests, objectives, and continuing interaction.

work team
A group of people with complementary skills who are committed to a common mission, performance goals, and approach for which they hold themselves mutually accountable.

9.1 Characteristics of a Well-Functioning, Effective Group

- The atmosphere tends to be relaxed, comfortable, and informal.
- The group's task is well understood and accepted by the members.
- The members listen well to one another; most members participate in a good deal of task-relevant discussion.
- People express both their feelings and their ideas.
- Conflict and disagreement are present and centered around ideas or methods, not personalities or people.
- The group is aware and conscious of its own operation and function.
- Decisions are usually based on consensus, not majority vote.
- When actions are decided, clear assignments are made and accepted by members of the group

behavior topics related to decision making, such as polarization and groupthink, are addressed in Chapter 10.

Norms of Behavior

The standards that a work group uses to evaluate the behavior of its members are its *norms of behavior*. These norms may be written or unwritten, verbalized or not, implicit or explicit. As long as individual members of the group understand them, the norms can be effective in influencing behavior. Norms may specify what members of a group should do (such as a stated dress code for men and women), or they may specify what members of a group should not do (such as executives not behaving arrogantly with employees). Morality norms are more important than competence norms when it comes to making decisions to work at improving the status of one's in-group.[7]

Norms may exist in any aspect of work group life. They may evolve informally or unconsciously within a group, or they may arise in response to challenges, such as the norm of disciplined behavior by firefighters in responding to a three-alarm fire to protect the group.[8] Performance norms are among the most important group norms from the organization's perspective. Even when group members work in isolation on creative projects, they display conformity to group norms.[9] Group norms of cooperative behavior within a team can lead to members working for mutual benefit, which in turn facilitate team performance.[10] On the other hand, verbal expressions of negativity within the group can be detrimental to team performance and a violation of group norms.[11] We discuss performance standards further in a later section of this chapter. Organizational culture and corporate codes of ethics, such as Johnson & Johnson's Credo (see Chapter 2), reflect behavioral norms expected within work groups. Finally, norms that create awareness of, and help regulate, emotions are critical to groups' effectiveness.[12]

Group Cohesion

The "interpersonal glue" that makes the members of a group stick together is *group cohesion*. Group cohesion can enhance job satisfaction for members and improve

norms of behavior
The standards that a work group uses to evaluate the behavior of its members.

group cohesion
The "interpersonal glue" that makes members of a group stick together.

organizational productivity.[13] Highly cohesive groups are able to control and manage their membership better than work groups low in cohesion. In one study of 381 banking teams in Hong Kong and the United States, increased job complexity and task autonomy led to increased group cohesiveness, which translated into better performance.[14] In addition to performance, highly cohesive groups are strongly motivated to maintain good, close relationships among the members. We examine group cohesion in further detail, along with factors leading to high levels of it, when discussing the common characteristics of well-developed groups.

Social Loafing

Social loafing occurs when one or more group members rely on the efforts of other group members and fail to contribute their own time, effort, thoughts, or other resources to a group.[15] This may create a drag on the group's efforts and achievements. Some scholars argue that, from the individual's standpoint, social loafing, or free riding, is rational behavior in response to an experience of inequity or when individual efforts are hard to observe. However, it shortchanges the group, which loses potentially valuable resources possessed by individual members.[16]

A number of methods for countering social loafing exist, such as having identifiable individual contributions to the group product and member self-evaluation systems. For example, if each group member is responsible for a specific input to the group, a member's failure to contribute will be noticed by everyone. If members must formally evaluate their contributions to the group, they are less likely to loaf.

Loss of Individuality

Social loafing may be detrimental to group achievement, but it does not have the potentially explosive effects of *loss of individuality*. Loss of individuality, or deindividuation, is a social process in which individual group members lose self-awareness and its accompanying sense of accountability, inhibition, and responsibility for individual behavior.[17]

When individuality is lost, people may engage in morally reprehensible acts and even violent behavior as committed members of their group or organization. For example, loss of individuality was one of several contributing factors in the violent and aggressive acts that led to the riot that destroyed sections of Los Angeles following the Rodney King verdict in the early 1990s. Loss of individuality is not always negative or destructive, however. The loosening of normal ego control mechanisms in the individual may lead to prosocial behavior and heroic acts in dangerous situations.[18] A group that successfully matures may not encounter problems with loss of individuality.

GROUP FORMATION AND DEVELOPMENT

3 Describe group formation, the four stages of a group's development, and the characteristics of a mature group.

After its formation, a group goes through predictable stages of development. If successful, it emerges as a mature group. One logical group development model proposes four stages following the group's formation:[19] mutual acceptance, decision making, motivation and commitment, and control and sanctions. To become a mature group, each of the stages in development must be successfully negotiated.

According to this group development model, a group addresses three issues: interpersonal issues, task issues, and authority issues.[20] The interpersonal issues include matters of trust, personal comfort, and security. The task issues include the mission or purpose of the group, the methods the group employs, and the outcomes expected of the group. The authority issues include decisions about who is in charge, how power and influence are managed, and who has the right to tell whom to do what. This section addresses group formation, each stage of group development, and the characteristics of a mature group.

Group Formation

Formal and informal groups form in organizations for different reasons. Formal groups are sometimes called official or assigned groups, and informal groups may be called unofficial or emergent groups. Formal groups gather to perform various tasks and include an executive and staff, standing committees of the board of directors, project task forces, and temporary committees. An example of a formal group was the task force at The University of Texas at Arlington, whose mission was to design the Goolsby Leadership Academy, which bridges academics and practice. Chaired by the associate dean of business, the task force was composed of seven members with diverse academic expertise and business experience. The task force envisioned a five-year developmental plan to create a national center of excellence in preparing Goolsby Scholars for authentic leadership in the twenty-first century.

Diversity is an important consideration in the formation of groups. For example, Monsanto Agricultural Company, now simply Monsanto Company, created a task force titled "Valuing Diversity" to address subtle discrimination resulting from workforce diversity.[21] The original task force was titled "Eliminating Subtle Discrimination (ESD)" and was composed of fifteen women, minorities, and white males. Subtle discrimination might include the use of gender- or culture-specific language. Monsanto and the task force's intent was to build on individual differences—whether in terms of gender, race, or culture—in developing a dominant heterogeneous culture. Diversity can enhance group performance. One study of gender diversity among U.S. workers found that men and women in gender-balanced groups had higher job satisfaction than those in homogeneous groups.[22]

Jorge Callado, 2009 Goolsby Scholar, teams with Goolsby Scholars Patrick Espinosa and Kristen King. Scholars are selected for authentic leadership in the twenty-first century.

Used with permission by The University of Texas at Arlington College of Business.

Ethnic diversity has characterized many industrial work groups in the United States since the 1800s. This was especially true during the early years of the 1900s, when waves of immigrant workers arrived from Germany, Yugoslavia, Italy, Poland, Scotland, the Scandinavian countries, and many other nations. Organizations were challenged to blend these culturally and linguistically diverse peoples into effective work groups.

In addition to ethnic, gender, and cultural diversity, there is interpersonal diversity. Highly effective work groups achieve compatibility through interpersonal diversity. Successful interpersonal relationships are the basis of group effort, a key foundation for business success. Effective, productive work groups often differ in their needs for inclusion in activities, control of people and events, and interpersonal affection from others. This diversity within the work group allows the members to find strength through balance and complementary interpersonal needs.

Informal groups evolve in the work setting to gratify a variety of member needs not met by formal groups. For example, organizational members' inclusion and affection needs might be satisfied through informal athletic or interest groups. Athletic teams representing a department, unit, or company may achieve semiofficial status, such as the AT&T National Running Team, which uses the corporate logo on its race shirts.

social loafing
The failure of a group member to contribute personal time, effort, thoughts, or other resources to the group.

loss of individuality
A social process in which individual group members lose self-awareness and its accompanying sense of accountability, inhibition, and responsibility for individual behavior.

Stages of Group Development

All groups, formal and informal, go through stages of development, from forming interpersonal relationships among the members to becoming a mature and productive unit. Mature groups are able to work through the necessary interpersonal, task, and authority issues to achieve at high levels. Demographic diversity and group fault lines (i.e., potential breaking points in a group) are two possible predictors of the sense-making process, subgroup formation patterns, and nature of group conflict at various stages of group development.[23] Hence, group development through these stages may not always be smooth.

There are a number of group development models in the literature, and we look at two of these models in particular. These two well-known models are Tuckman's and Gersick's. Each of these models looks at the evolution of behavior in teams, and Tuckman's model also focuses on leadership.

The Five-Stage Model Bruce Tuckman's five-stage model of group development proposes that team behavior progresses through five stages: forming, storming, norming, performing, and adjourning.[24] These stages and the emphasis on relationships and leadership styles in each are shown in Figure 9.1.

Dependence on guidance and direction is the defining characteristic in the *forming* stage. Team members are unclear about individual roles and responsibilities and tend to rely heavily on the leader to answer questions about the team's purpose, objectives, and external relationships. Moving from this stage requires that team members feel they are part of the team.

Team members compete for position in the *storming* stage. As the name suggests, this is a stage of considerable conflict as power struggles, cliques, and factions within the group begin to form. Clarity of purpose increases, but uncertainties still exist. This is also the stage when members assess one another with regard to trustworthiness, emotional comfort, and evaluative acceptance. For the "Valuing Diversity" task force at Monsanto, trust was one of the early issues to be worked through. A coaching style by the leader is key during this stage of group development as team members may challenge him or her.

Agreement and consensus are characteristic of team members in the *norming* stage. It is in this stage that roles and responsibilities become clear and accepted with big decisions being made by group agreement. The focus turns from interpersonal relations to decision-making activities related to the group's task accomplishment. Small decisions may be delegated to individuals or small teams within the group. The group addresses authority questions like these: Who is responsible for what aspects of the group's work? Does the group need one primary leader and spokesperson? Wallace Supply Company, an industrial distributor of pipes, valves, and fittings, has found employee teams particularly valuable in this aspect of work

FIGURE

9.1 Tuckman's Five-Stage Model of Group Development

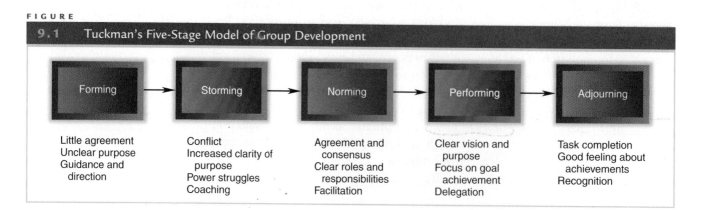

Forming	Storming	Norming	Performing	Adjourning
Little agreement	Conflict	Agreement and	Clear vision and	Task completion
Unclear purpose	Increased clarity of	consensus	purpose	Good feeling about
Guidance and	purpose	Clear roles and	Focus on goal	achievements
direction	Power struggles	responsibilities	achievement	Recognition
	Coaching	Facilitation	Delegation	

life.[25] Leadership is facilitative with some leadership responsibilities being shared by the team.

As a team moves into the *performing* stage, it becomes more strategically aware and clear about its mission and purpose. In this stage of development, the group has successfully worked through the necessary interpersonal, task, and authority issues and can stand on its own with little interference from the leader. Primarily, the team makes decisions, and disagreements are resolved positively with necessary changes to structure and processes attended to by the team. A mature group is able to control its members through the judicious application of specific positive and negative sanctions based on the evaluation of specific member behaviors. Recent research shows that evaluation biases stemming from liking someone operate in face-to-face groups but not in electronic groups, such as virtual teams.[26] Members at this stage do not need to be instructed but may ask for assistance from the leader with personal or interpersonal development. The team requires a leader who delegates and oversees.

The final stage of group development is the *adjourning* stage. When the task is completed, everyone on the team can move on to new and different things. Team members have a sense of accomplishment and feel good knowing that their purpose is fulfilled. The leader's role is primarily one of recognition of the group's achievements. Unless the group is a task force or other informal team, most groups in organizations remain at the performing stage and do not disband as the adjourning stage suggests.

Punctuated Equilibrium Model Although it is still highly cited in team and group research, Tuckman's "forming–norming–storming–performing–adjourning" model may be unrealistic from an organizational perspective. In fact, research has shown that many teams experience relational conflicts at different times and in different contexts. Connie Gersick proposes that groups do not necessarily progress linearly from one step to another in a predetermined sequence but alternate between periods of inertia with little visible progress toward goal achievement *punctuated* by bursts of energy as work groups develop. It is in these periods of energy that the majority of a group's work is accomplished.[27] For example, a task force given nine months to complete a task may use the first four months to choose its norms, explore contextual issues, and determine how it will communicate.

Characteristics of a Mature Group

The description of a well-functioning, effective group in Table 9.1 characterizes a mature group. Such a group has four distinguishing characteristics: a clear purpose and mission, well-understood norms and standards of conduct, a high level of group cohesion, and a flexible status structure. The Mayo Clinic exemplifies the characteristics of a mature group and the power of teamwork as featured in The Real World 9.1.

Purpose and Mission The purpose and mission may be assigned to a group (as in the previous example of the Goolsby Leadership Academy task force) or emerge from within the group (as in the case of the AT&T National Running Team). Even in the case of an assigned mission, the group may reexamine, modify, revise, or question the mission. It may also embrace the mission as stated. The importance of mission is exemplified in IBM's Process Quality Management, which requires that a process team of not more than twelve people develop a clear understanding of mission as the first step in the process.[28] The IBM approach demands that all members agree to go in the same direction. The mission statement is converted into a specific agenda, clear goals, and a set of critical success factors. Stating the purpose

The Real World 9.1

No Stars Here, Just World-Class Teamwork

The Mayo Clinic began as a family medical practice in Rochester, Minnesota, in the late 1800s and still acts like one. While the Mayo Clinic is now a large business with a world-class medical brand, the face of the clinic is the patient treatment team of doctors, nurses, and allied health professionals who always put the patient first. The clinic hires no stars. Mayo ardently searches for team players and hires for values as well as talent. As a result, the clinic has a highly cohesive, cooperative culture. This is reinforced by paying everyone on a salary system. Clinic patients get more than a doctor; they get the whole Mayo team, as needed. Everyone is clear that the mission of the clinic is to put the needs of the patient first. In addition, all of the staff practices medicine as a cooperative science, not a competitive science. This makes collaboration the norm and expected behavior. Collaboration and teamwork are further reinforced by the boundarylessness throughout the clinic. There is flexibility and seamlessness in the group and team structures that form to serve the patient. The team concept underlies Mayo's clinical excellence, its superb personal service, and its highly efficient care. That the Mayo family medical practice has survived for more than a century is impressive. That it continues to feel like a family medical practice while achieving a world-class reputation in medicine is truly remarkable. What maturity…what teamwork!

Source: L. L. Berry and K. D. Seltman, "The Power of Teamwork at Mayo Clinic," *Mworld* (Winter 2008–2009): 37–39.

and mission in the form of specific goals enhances productivity over and above any performance benefits achieved through individual goal setting.[29]

Behavioral Norms Behavioral norms, which evolve over a period of time, are well-understood standards of behavior within a group.[30] They are benchmarks against which team members are evaluated and judged by other team members. Some behavioral norms become written rules, such as an attendance policy or an ethical code for a team. Other norms remain informal, although they are no less understood by team members. Dress codes and norms about after-hours socializing may fall into this category. Behavioral norms also evolve around performance and productivity.[31] Productivity norms even influence the performance of sports teams.[32] The group's productivity norm may or may not be consistent with, and supportive of, the organization's productivity standards. A high-performance team sets productivity standards above organizational expectations with the intent to excel. Average teams set productivity standards based on, and consistent with, organizational expectations. Noncompliant or counterproductive teams may set productivity standards below organizational expectations with the intent of damaging the organization or creating change. On the positive side, behavioral norms can permeate an entire organizational culture for the benefit of all and positive affectivity of members can be contagious in workgroups.[33]

Group Cohesion Group cohesion was earlier described as the interpersonal attraction binding group members together. It enables a group to exercise effective control over its members in relation to its behavioral norms and standards. Goal conflict, unpleasant experiences, and domination of a subgroup are among the threats to a group's cohesion. Groups with low levels of cohesion have greater difficulty exercising control over their members and enforcing their standards of behavior. A classic study of cohesiveness in 238 industrial work groups found cohesion to be an important factor influencing anxiety, tension, and productivity within the

9.2 Cohesiveness and Work-Related Tension*

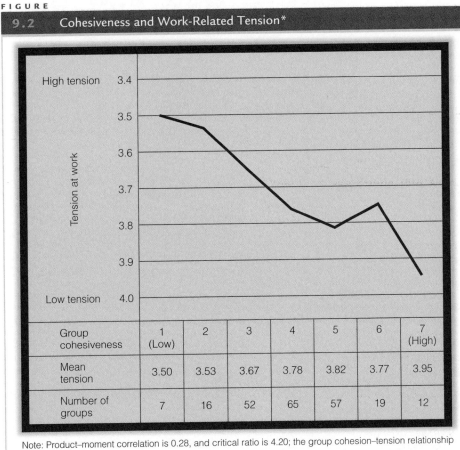

Group cohesiveness	1 (Low)	2	3	4	5	6	7 (High)
Mean tension	3.50	3.53	3.67	3.78	3.82	3.77	3.95
Number of groups	7	16	52	65	57	19	12

Note: Product–moment correlation is 0.28, and critical ratio is 4.20; the group cohesion–tension relationship is highly significant at the .001 level.

*The measure of tension at work is based on group mean response to the question "Does your work ever make you feel 'jumpy' or nervous?" A low numerical score represents relatively high tension.

SOURCE: From S. E. Seashore, *Group Cohesiveness in the Industrial Work Group*, 1954. Research conducted by Stanley E. Seashore at the Institute for Social Research, University of Michigan. Reprinted by permission.

groups.[34] Specifically, work-related tension and anxiety were lower in teams high in cohesion, and they were higher in teams low in cohesion, as depicted in Figure 9.2. This suggests that cohesion has a calming effect on team members, at least concerning work-related tension and anxiety. In addition, actual productivity was found to vary significantly less in highly cohesive teams, making these teams much more predictable with regard to their productivity. The actual productivity levels were primarily determined by the productivity norms within each work group. That is, highly cohesive groups with high production standards are very productive. Similarly, highly cohesive groups with low productivity standards are unproductive. Member satisfaction, commitment, and communication are better in highly cohesive groups. Groupthink may be a problem in highly cohesive groups and is discussed in Chapter 10. You 9.1 includes the three group cohesion questions from this research project. Complete You 9.1 to determine the level of cohesion in a group of which you are a member.

Group cohesion is influenced by a number of factors, most notably time, size, the prestige of the team, external pressure, and internal competition. Group cohesion evolves gradually over time through a group's normal development. Smaller groups—those of five or seven members, for example—are more cohesive than those of more than twenty-five, although cohesion does not decline much with size after forty or more members. Prestige or social status also influences a group's

How Cohesive Is Your Group?

Think about a group of which you are a member. Answer each of the following questions in relation to this group by circling the number next to the alternative that most reflects your feelings.

1. Do you feel that you are really a part of your group?
    5—Really a part of the group.
    4—Included in most ways.
    3—Included in some ways, but not in others.
    2—Do not feel I really belong.
    1—Do not work with any one group of people.

2. If you had a chance to do the same activities in another group, for the same pay if it is a work group, how would you feel about moving?
    1—Would want very much to move.
    2—Would rather move than stay where I am.
    3—Would make no difference to me.
    4—Would rather stay where I am than move.
    5—Would want very much to stay where I am.

3. How does your group compare with other groups that you are familiar with on each of the following points?

- The way people get along together.
  5—Better than most.
  3—About the same as most.
  1—Not as good as most.

- The way people stick together.
  5—Better than most.
  3—About the same as most.
  1—Not as good as most.

- The way people help one another on the job.
  5—Better than most.
  3—About the same as most.
  1—Not as good as most.

Add up your circled responses. If you have a number of twenty or above, you view your group as highly cohesive. If you have a number between ten and nineteen, you view your group's cohesion as average. If you have a number of seven or less, you view your group as very low in cohesion.

SOURCE: From S. E. Seashore, *Group Cohesiveness in the Industrial Work Group*, University of Michigan, 1954. Reprinted by permission.

cohesion, with more prestigious groups, such as the U.S. Air Force Thunderbirds or the U.S. Navy Blue Angels, being highly cohesive. However, even groups of very low prestige may be highly cohesive in how they stick together. Finally, external pressure and internal competition influence group cohesion. The external pressures of the Ontario Securities Commission discussed in the Thinking Ahead feature might be expected to increase the cohesiveness in the Balsille–Lazaridis team. Whereas external pressures tend to enhance cohesion, internal competition usually decreases cohesion within a team. One study found that company-imposed work pressure disrupted group cohesion by increasing internal competition and reducing cooperative interpersonal activity.[35]

Status Structure *Status structure* is the set of authority and task relations among a group's members. The status structure may be hierarchical or egalitarian (i.e., democratic), depending on the group. Successful resolution of the authority issue within a team results in a well-understood status structure of leader–follower relationships. Where leadership problems arise, it is important to find solutions and build team leader effectiveness.[36] Whereas groups tend to have one leader, teams tend to share leadership. For example, one person may be the team's task master who sets the agenda, initiates much of the work activity, and ensures that the team meets its deadlines. Another team member may take a leadership role in maintaining effective interpersonal relationships in the group. Hence, shared leadership is very feasible

status structure
The set of authority and task relations among a group's members

in teams. An effective status structure results in role interrelatedness among group members,[37] such as that displayed by Bill Perez and Bill Wrigley. Their tag-team style of cooperation in leading Wm. Wrigley Jr. Company has served the company well.

Diversity in a group is healthy, and members may contribute to the collective effort through one of four basic styles:[38] the contributor, the collaborator, the communicator, and the challenger. The contributor is data driven, supplies necessary information, and adheres to high performance standards. The collaborator sees the big picture and is able to keep a constant focus on the mission and urge other members to join efforts for mission accomplishment. The communicator listens well, facilitates the group's process, and humanizes the collective effort. The challenger is the devil's advocate who questions everything from the group's mission, purpose, and methods to its ethics. Members may exhibit one or more of these four basic styles over a period of time. In addition, an effective group must have an integrator.[39] This can be especially important in cross-functional teams, where different perspectives carry the seeds of conflict. However, cross-functional teams are not necessarily a problem. Effectively managing cross-functional teams of artists, designers, printers, and financial experts enabled Hallmark Cards to cut its new-product development time in half.[40]

Emergent leadership in groups was studied among sixty-two men and sixty women.[41] Groups performed tasks not classified as either masculine or feminine, that is, "sex-neutral" tasks. Men and women both emerged as leaders, and neither gender had significantly more emergent leaders. However, group members who described themselves in masculine terms were significantly more likely to emerge as leaders than group members who described themselves in feminine, androgynous (both masculine and feminine), or undifferentiated (neither masculine nor feminine) terms. Hence, gender stereotypes may play a role in emergent leadership.

Task and Maintenance Functions

An effective group or team carries out various task functions to perform its work successfully and various maintenance functions to ensure member satisfaction and a sense of team spirit.[42] Teams that successfully fulfill these functions afford their members the potential for psychological intimacy and integrated involvement. Table 9.2 presents nine task and nine maintenance functions in teams or groups.

4 Explain the task and maintenance functions in groups.

TABLE

9.2 Task and Maintenance Functions in Teams or Groups

Task Functions	Maintenance Functions
Initiating activities	Supporting others
Seeking information	Following others' leads
Giving information	Gatekeeping communication
Elaborating concepts	Setting standards
Coordinating activities	Expressing member feelings
Summarizing ideas	Testing group decisions
Testing ideas	Consensus testing
Evaluating effectiveness	Harmonizing conflict
Diagnosing problems	Reducing tension

Task functions are those activities directly related to the effective completion of the team's work. For example, the task of initiating activity involves suggesting ideas, defining problems, and proposing approaches and/or solutions to problems. The task of seeking information involves asking for ideas, suggestions, information, or facts. A study of security analysts found that the quality of colleagues' work helped to improve and maintain the quality of individual member performance.[43] Effective teams have members who fulfill various task functions as they are required.

Some task functions are more important at one time in the life of a group, and other functions are more important at other times. For example, during the engineering test periods for new technologies, the engineering team needs members who focus on testing the practical applications of suggestions and those who diagnose problems and suggest solutions.

The effective use of task functions leads to the success of the group, and the failure to use them may lead to disaster. For example, the successful initiation and coordination of an emergency room (ER) team's activities by the senior resident saved the life of a knife wound victim.[44] The victim was stabbed one-quarter inch below the heart, and the ER team acted quickly to stem the bleeding, begin intravenous fluids, and monitor the victim's vital signs.

Following another group member's lead may be as important as leading others.

Maintenance functions are those activities essential to the effective, satisfying interpersonal relationships within a group or team. For example, following another group member's lead may be as important as leading others. Communication gatekeepers within a group ensure balanced contributions from all members. Because task activities build tension into teams and groups working together, tension reduction activities are important to drain off negative or destructive feelings. For example, in a study of twenty-five work groups over a five-year period, humor and joking behavior were found to enhance the social relationships in the groups.[45] The researchers concluded that performance improvements in the twenty-five groups indirectly resulted from improved relationships attributable to the humor and joking behaviors. Maintenance functions enhance togetherness, cooperation, and teamwork, enabling members to achieve psychological intimacy while furthering the success of the team. Team optimism is an important predictor of team outcomes particularly for newly formed teams as we see in the Science feature. As a leader, Jody Grant's optimism and supportive attitude as chairman and CEO of Texas Capital Bancshares enabled him to build a vibrant bank in the aftermath of the great Texas banking crash of 1982–1992. Grant was respected for his expertise *and* his ability to build relationships. Both task and maintenance functions are important for successful groups and teams.

task function

An activity directly related to the effective completion of a team's work.

maintenance function

An activity essential to effective, satisfying interpersonal relationships within a team or group.

WORK TEAMS IN ORGANIZATIONS

Work teams are task-oriented groups, though in some organizations the term *team* has a negative connotation for unions and union members. Work teams make important and valuable contributions to the organization and are important to the member need satisfaction. For example, an idea to implement a simple change in packaging from a work team at Glenair, a UK-based aerospace and defense contractor, saved the company twenty-five minutes of packaging time per unit. Additionally,

Science

Positive Effects of Team Optimism

For a decade, positive psychology, positive organizational behavior, and positive organizational scholarship have uncovered the important role that positivity plays in both individual and organizational success. It is therefore surprising that few researchers have investigated positivity at the team level. The present study examines the emergence of team-level positive psychological capacities and their relationship with team functioning. The research included over 300 students working for two sessions of three-member or four-member teams. The final results were based upon data from 101 teams, each of which completed four projects during the course of the research. In addition to information on previous teammate knowledge and task interdependency, the researchers measured three positive psychological attributes from Luthans' PsyCap framework. These were team efficacy, team resilience, and team optimism. The key team outcomes considered in the research were cohesion, cooperation, coordination, and conflict and team satisfaction. The results showed that team optimism is an important predictor of many team outcomes when teams are newly formed. However, after the completion of several projects, team resilience and team efficacy show greater explanatory power concerning team outcomes. Team optimism seems to be the most functional positive organizational behavior (POB) capacity for newly formed teams. The research concluded that more is not necessarily better and that level of teammate interactions is important in team processes and team outcomes.

SOURCE: B. J. West, J. L. Patera and M. K. Carsten, "Team Level Positivity: Investigating Positive Psychological Capacities and Team Level Outcomes," *Journal of Organizational Behavior* 30 (2009): 249-267.

a job that used to take one worker half an hour to complete was reduced to only five minutes, freeing the worker to perform other work in the factory.[46]

Several kinds of work teams exist. One classification scheme uses a sports analogy. Some teams work like baseball teams with set responsibilities, other teams work like football teams through coordinated action, and still others work like doubles tennis teams with primary yet flexible responsibilities. In addition, crews are a distinct type of work team that can be studied using the concept of "crewness."[47] Although each type of team may have a useful role in the organization, the individual expert should not be overlooked.[48] That is, at the right time and in the right context, individual members must be allowed to shine.

Why Work Teams?

Teams are very useful in performing work that is complicated, complex, interrelated, and/or more voluminous than one person can handle. Harold Geneen, while chairman of ITT, said, "If I had enough arms and legs and time, I'd do it all myself." Obviously, people working in organizations cannot do everything because of the limitations of arms, legs, time, expertise, knowledge, and other resources. Individual limitations are overcome and problems are solved through teamwork and collaboration. World-class U.S. corporations, such as Motorola, Inc., are increasingly deploying work teams in their global affiliates to meet the competition and gain an advantage.[49] Motorola's "Be Cool" team in the Philippines has a family atmosphere and may even begin a meeting with a prayer, yet is committed to improving individual and team performance.

Teams make important contributions to organizations in work areas that lend themselves to teamwork. *Teamwork* is a core value at Hewlett-Packard. Complex, interdependent work tasks and activities that require collaboration particularly lend themselves to teamwork. Teams are appropriate where knowledge, talent, skills, and

teamwork
Joint action by a team of people in which individual interests are subordinated to team unity.

abilities are dispersed across organizational members and require integrated effort for task accomplishment. The recent emphasis on team-oriented work environments is based on empowerment with collaboration, not on power and competition. Teams with experience working together may produce valuable innovations, and individual contributions are valuable as well.[50] Larry Hirschhorn labels this "the new team environment" founded on a significantly more empowered workforce in the industrial sectors of the American economy. This new team environment is compared with the old work environment in Table 9.3. Beyond the new team environment is the emergence of virtual teams.

That teams are necessary is a driving principle of total quality efforts in organizations. Total quality efforts often require the formation of teams—especially cross-functional teams composed of people from different functions, such as manufacturing and design, who are responsible for specific organizational processes. Former Eastman Kodak CEO George Fisher believed in the importance of participation and cooperation as foundations for teamwork and a total quality program. In a study of forty machine crews in a northeastern U.S. paper mill, organizational citizenship behaviors (OCBs), specifically helping behavior and sportsmanship, contributed significantly to the quantity and quality of work group performance.[51]

Work Team Structure and Work Team Process

Work team effectiveness in the new team environment requires attention by management to both work team structure and work team process.[52] The primary structural issues for work teams are goals and objectives, operating guidelines, performance measures, and the specification of roles. A work team's goals and objectives specify what must be achieved, while the operating guidelines set the organizational boundaries and decision-making limits within which the team must function. A new theory suggests a "core" set of roles in teams and that the characteristics of the role holders in the core are more important for overall team performance.[53] The goal-setting process was discussed in Chapter 6 and has applicability for work teams, too. In addition to these two structural elements, the work team needs to know what performance measures are being used to assess its task accomplishment. For example, a medical emergency team's performance measures might include the success rate in saving critically injured patients and the average number of hours a patient is in the ER before being transferred to a hospital bed. Finally, work team structure requires a clearly specified set of roles for the executives and managers who oversee

TABLE

9.3 A Comparison of the New Team Environment versus the Old Work Environment

New Team Environment	Old Work Environment
Person comes up with initiatives.	Person follows orders.
Team has considerable authority to chart its own steps.	Team depends on the manager to chart its course.
Members form a team because people learn to collaborate in the face of their emerging right to think for themselves. People both rock the boat and work together.	Members were a team because people conformed to direction set by the manager. No one rocked the boat.
People cooperate by using their thoughts and feelings. They link up through direct talk.	People cooperated by suppressing their thoughts and feelings. They wanted to get along.

SOURCE: *Managing in the New Team Environment*, by L. Hirschhorn, © 1991. Reprinted by permission of Prentice Hall, Inc., Upper Saddle River, NJ.

the work of the team, for the work team leaders who exercise influence over team members, and for team members. These role specifications should include information about required role behaviors, such as decision making and task performance, as well as restrictions or limits on role behaviors, such as the limitations on managerial interventions in work team activities and decision making. Expectations as well as experience may be especially important for newcomer role performance in work teams.[54]

Work team process is the second important dimension of effectiveness. Two of the important process issues in work teams are the managing of cooperative behaviors and the managing of competitive behaviors. Both sets of behaviors are helpful in task accomplishment, and they should be viewed as complementary sets of behaviors. Cooperative teamwork skills include open communication, trust, personal integrity, positive interdependence, and mutual support. On the other hand, positive competitive teamwork skills include the ability to enjoy competition, to play fair, to be a good winner or loser, to have access to information for monitoring where the team and members are in the competition, and not to overgeneralize or exaggerate the results of any specific competition. In a study of reward structures in 75 four-member teams, competitive rewards enhanced speed of performance, while cooperative rewards enhanced accuracy of performance.[55]

Work team process issues have become more complex in the global workplace with teams composed of members from many cultures and backgrounds. This is enhanced by the presence of virtual work teams operating on the global landscape. Our discussions of diversity earlier in the text have particular relevance to multicultural work teams. In this new environment, teams must increasingly bring together members with different specialties and knowledge to work on complex problems. The ability to do so affects team performance and psychological safety.[56] In addition to the process issues of cooperation, competition, and diversity, three other process issues are related to topics we discuss elsewhere in the text. These are empowerment (discussed in the next major section of this chapter), team decision making (discussed in Chapter 10), and conflict management and resolution (discussed in Chapter 13).

Quality Teams and Circles

Quality teams and quality circles (QCs) are part of a total quality program. Decision making in *quality teams* is discussed in detail in Chapter 10. Quality teams are different from QCs in that they are more formal and are designed and assigned by upper level management. Quality teams are not voluntary and have formal power, whereas QCs have less formal power and decision authority. Although less commonly used than a decade ago, QC principles continue to have value.

Quality circles (QCs) are small groups of employees who work voluntarily on company time—typically one hour per week—to address work-related problems such as quality control, cost reduction, production planning and techniques, and even product design. Membership in a QC is typically voluntary and is fixed once a circle is formed, although some changes may occur as appropriate. QCs are trained in various problem-solving techniques and use them to address the work-related problems.

QCs were popularized as a Japanese management method when an American, W. Edwards Deming, exported his thinking about QCs to Japan following World War II.[57] QCs became popular in the United States in the 1980s, when companies such as Ford, Hewlett-Packard, and Eastman Kodak implemented them. The Camp Red Cloud Garrison in South Korea saved $2 million by implementing the Six Sigma quality program that involved all garrison supervisors and looked at

quality team
A team that is part of an organization's structure and is empowered to act on its decisions regarding product and service quality.

quality circle (QC)
A small group of employees who work voluntarily on company time, typically one hour per week, to address work-related problems such as quality control, cost reduction, production planning and techniques, and even product design.

efficiencies from the customer's perspective. Some of the money saved from technology improvements has gone back to employees in an effort to improve safety equipment, work facilities, and employee recreation.

Quality teams and QCs must deal with substantive issues if they are to be effective; otherwise, employees begin to believe the quality effort is simply a management ploy. QCs do not necessarily require final decision authority to be effective if their recommendations are always considered seriously and implemented when appropriate. One study found that QCs are effective for a period of time, and then their contributions begin to diminish.[58] This may suggest that quality teams and QCs must be reinforced and periodically reenergized to maintain their effectiveness over long periods of time.

Social Benefits

5 Identify the social benefits of group and team membership.

Two sets of social benefits are available to team or group members. One set accrues from achieving psychological intimacy. The other comes from achieving integrated involvement.[59]

Psychological intimacy is emotional and psychological closeness to other team or group members. It results in feelings of affection and warmth, unconditional positive regard, opportunity for emotional expression, openness, security and emotional support, and giving and receiving nurturance. Failure to achieve psychological intimacy results in feelings of emotional isolation and loneliness. This may be especially problematic for chief executives who experience loneliness at the top. Although psychological intimacy is valuable for emotional health and well-being, it need not necessarily be achieved in the work setting.

Integrated involvement is closeness achieved through tasks and activities. It results in enjoyable and involving activities, social identity and self-definition, being valued for one's skills and abilities, opportunity for power and influence, conditional positive regard, and support for one's beliefs and values. Failure to achieve integrated involvement results in social isolation. Whereas psychological intimacy is more emotion based, integrated involvement is more behavior and activity based. Integrated involvement contributes to social psychological health and well-being.

Psychological intimacy and integrated involvement each contribute to overall health. It is not necessary to achieve both in the same team or group. For example, while chief executive at Xerox Corporation, David Kearns, was also a marathon runner, he found integrated involvement with his executive team and psychological intimacy with his athletic companions on long-distance runs.

Teams and groups have two sets of functions that operate to enable members to achieve psychological intimacy and integrated involvement. These are task and maintenance functions.

DIVERSITY AND CREATIVITY IN TEAMS

6 Discuss diversity and creativity in teams.

psychological intimacy
Emotional and psychological closeness to other team or group members.

integrated involvement
Closeness achieved through tasks and activities.

Diversity and creativity are important, emerging issues in the study of teams and teamwork. Recent research in diversity has focused on the issue of dissimilarity and its effect within the team itself. This is often studied based on social identity theory and self-categorization theory. Later in the chapter, we specifically address the issue of multicultural diversity in upper echelons, or top management teams, in the global workplace. Creativity concerns new and/or dissimilar ideas or ways of doing things within teams. Novelty and innovation are creativity's companions. While creativity is developed in some detail in Chapter 10, we treat it briefly here in the context of teams.

Dissimilarity

We defined diversity in Chapter 1 in terms of individual differences. Recent relational demography research finds that demographic dissimilarity influences employees' absenteeism, commitment, turnover intentions, beliefs, work group relationships, self-esteem, and organizational citizenship behavior (OCB).[60] Thus, dissimilarity may have positive or negative effects in teams and on team members. Racial dissimilarity may also impact the extent to which team members communicate with each other and develop a sense of group identity.[61] Structural diversity can enhance team performance.[62] While value dissimilarity may be positively related to task and relationship conflict, it is negatively related to team involvement.[63] This highlights the importance of managing dissimilarity in teams, being open to diversity, and turning conflicts over ideas into positive outcomes. With the U.S. population becoming increasingly diverse, odds are high that employees will be working in multicultural teams right here in the United States, as we see in The Real World 9.2.

Functional background is one way to look at dissimilarity in teams. We saw in Thinking Ahead that Balsille and Lazaridis complement each other based on their functional background differences. One study of 262 professionals in 37

The Real World 9.2

Leading Differently at Parker Hannifin, Time Warner Cable...

Sharon Powell of Parker Hannifin Corporation, a provider of motion and control technologies, thinks about diversity in a different way from many leaders and managers. She understands that it is not just what country an employee comes from but what part of America one comes from that can make a difference. Team members from New York, the Midwest, and the Deep South can display differences in communication, language, idioms, business etiquette, and attire as diverse as team members from different countries, if somewhat more subtle. In contrast to Sharon Powell, some leaders assume that because their company's operations do not go outside the U.S., training employees to work in multicultural teams is not important. Multicultural teams are no longer limited to those rooted in an international

Assembly area for Boeing 737 and 747 airplanes at a Parker Hannifin complex in California.

© Tom Carroll/PHOTOTAKE/Alamy

context with members from different countries and with different languages. Teams may be 100 percent American and still multicultural. Time Warner Cable finds that the diversity among its customers has demanded that diversity be represented in every aspect of the company if it is going to serve these diverse customers well. Hence, leaders who are sensitive to such differences then have the potential to build bridges across the cultural divides in such a way as to forge a strong and productive unit. Training can be a key to learning how to achieve this. At Parker Hannifin, senior leaders are trained to operate in a global culture, work virtually, and develop a deeper self-awareness.

Source: S. Gupta, "Mine the Potential of Multicultural Teams," *HR Magazine* (October 2008): 279–284.

cross-functional teams found that promoting functional background social iden-tification helped individuals perform better as team members.[64] Another study of multifunctional management teams in a *Fortune* 100 company found that functional background predicted team involvement.[65] Finally, in a slightly different study of 129 members on twenty multidisciplinary project teams, informational dissimilarity had no adverse effects when there was member task and goal congruence.[66] Where there was incongruence, dissimilarity adversely affected team identification and OCBs.

Creativity

Creativity is often thought of in an individual context rather than a team context. However, there is such a thing as team creativity. In a study of fifty-four research and development teams, one study found that team creativity scores would be explained by aggregation processes across both people and time.[67] The investigators concluded that it is important to consider aggregation across time as well as across individuals when one is attempting to understand team creativity. In another study of creative behavior, a Korean electronics company found that individual dissimilarity in age and performance as well as functional diversity within the team positively affect individual employees' creative behavior.

Some think that the deck is stacked against teams as agents of creativity. Leigh Thompson disagrees and suggests that team creativity and divergent thinking can be enhanced through greater diversity in teams, brainwriting, training facilitators, membership change in teams, electronic brainstorming, and building a playground.[68] These practices can overcome social loafing, conformity, and downward norm set-ting in teams and organizations. Team members might exercise care in timing the insertion of their novel ideas into the team process so as to maximize the positive impact and benefits.[69]

TEAMWORK AND SELF-MANAGED TEAMS

7 Discuss teamwork and self-managed teams.

Quality teams and QCs, as we discussed earlier, are one way to implement team-work in organizations. Self-managed teams are broad-based work teams that deal with issues beyond quality. Decision making in self-managed teams is also discussed in Chapter 10. On a dysfunctional note, employee resistance behavior can emerge in self-managed work teams. It is influenced by cultural values and can affect employee attitudes.[70] However, self-managed teams have an overall positive history and are increasingly used by U.S. multinational corporations in global operations.

Teamwork is an essential feature of programs like total quality management.[71] As an attribute of organizational culture, teamwork relies on leadership skills and encourages participation to insure team success.[72] Quality action teams (QATs) at FedEx are the primary quality improvement process (QIP) technique used by the company to engage management and hourly employees in four- to ten-member problem-solving teams.[73] The teams are empowered to act and solve problems as specific as charting the best route from the Phoenix airport to the local distribution center or as global as making major software enhancements to the online package-tracking system.

Teamwork

Teamwork is a core value in many organizations, such as Hewlett Packard, as men-tioned earlier in the chapter. Successful teamwork rests on three foundations that are: working together, team diversity and empowerment skills. In this chapter we discuss working together and team diversity. In Chapter 11 we include a discussion of empowerment skills in the context of power and politics. Working together actually carries a double message, one for the team member and one for the team as a whole.[74] The working together message for the team member is that emotional competence is important and requires clear communication between one's head and heart, between one's thoughts and ones feelings. The working together message for the team as a whole is that cooperative behavior within the team is a key to success, in contrast to internally competitive behavior. Cooperative action within the team relies on open communication, trust and trustworthiness, and interpersonal support.[75] The benefits of working together are positive interdependence, the experience of interpersonal security, and win–win performance outcomes. As we will see in Looking Back, teamwork combined with imagination has no limits.

Working together was a foundation for the successful racial integration of the U.S. Army.[76] Charles Moskos and John Sibley Butler tell a real success story that has its caveats. They conclude that the U.S. Army has good race relations, but not perfect ones. They suggest that what they learned can be transferred to other organizations. Another example of working together comes from an educational context and is called Jigsaw learning, which teaches cooperative learning without denying the existence of competitive behaviors and a competitive society. Central to the Jigsaw cooperative learning are listening skills, especially reflective listening as discussed in Chapter 8, that build cooperation.[77] These examples of working together rest on team member emotional competence and cooperative behavior in a team.

Team diversity is the second foundation for successful teamwork. *Team diversity* is the differences in ability, skills, experience, personality, and demographic characteristics within a team. Chapter 2 explored diversity more broadly. Team diversity includes surface-level diversity and deep-level diversity.[78] Surface-level diversity is defined as heterogeneity based on relational demography characteristics such as sex, race/ethnicity, and age. Deep-level diversity is defined as heterogeneity based on personality preferences, interpersonal needs, attitudes, beliefs, and values. Both levels of team diversity are important considerations in developing a successful team with a rich, heterogeneous, broad base of resources, perspectives, and experiences to draw upon. Team members may relate well based on their similarities while finding great strength in their differences that complement each other. Complete You 9.2 to explore how much team diversity you experience.

Self-Managed Teams

Self-managed teams make decisions that were once reserved for managers. They are also called *self-directed teams* or *autonomous work groups*. Self-managed teams are one way to implement empowerment in organizations. Even so, managers have an important role in providing leadership and influence.[79] In doing so, there is strong support for the use of soft influence tactics in managers' communication with self-directed teams, which yields more positive results.[80] A one-year study of self-managed teams suggests that they have a positive impact on employee attitudes but not on absenteeism or turnover.[81] Evaluative research is helpful in achieving a better understanding of this relatively new way of approaching teamwork and the design of work. Research can help in establishing expectations for self-managed teams. For example, one study of autonomous work teams found that a key ingredient to enhancing organizational commitment and job satisfaction involves the perception that one has the required skills and abilities to perform well.[82] Further, there are risks, such as groupthink, in self-managing teams that must be prevented or managed if the team is to achieve full development and function.[83] Finally, one evaluation of empowerment, teams, and TQM programs found that companies associated with these popular management techniques did not have higher economic performance.[84]

team diversity
The differences in ability, skills, experience, personality, and demographic characteristics within a team.

self-managed team
A team that makes decisions that were once reserved for managers.

How Much Diversity Is on Your Team?

This exercise allows you to explore the level of diversity on your team. Listed below are words that describe a variety of individual differences in the workplace.

Categories and Types of Diversity

Surface-Level	Deep-Level
Social-category differences	*Differences in knowledge or skills*
Race	Education
Ethnicity	Functional knowledge
Gender	Information or expertise
Age	Training
Religion	Experience
Sexual orientation	Abilities
Physical abilities	
	Differences in values or beliefs
	Cultural background
	Ideological beliefs
	Personality differences
	Cognitive style
	Affective disposition
	Motivational factors
	Organizational- or community-status differences
	Tenure or length of service
	Position title
	Differences in social and network ties
	Work-related ties
	Friendship ties
	Community ties
	In-group memberships

Think about the level of diversity you have on your team.

1. Which of the above-listed attributes are in your team?
2. What attributes contribute to team effectiveness/performance?
3. What diversity characteristics need to be added to your team to make it more effective?

SOURCE: Adapted from E. Mannix and M. A. Neale, "What Differences Make a Difference?" *Psychological Science in the Public Interest* 6 (2005): 31–55.

Other evaluations of self-managed teams are more positive. Southwest Industries, a high-technology aerospace manufacturing firm, embarked on a major internal reorganization in the early 1990s that included the creation of self-managed teams to fit its high-technology production process. Southwest's team approach resulted in a 30 percent increase in shipments, a 30 percent decrease in lead time, a 40 percent decrease in total inventory, a decrease in machinery downtime, and almost a one-third decrease in production costs.[85] Self-managed teams were also the foundation for the miraculous resurrection of the former Chrysler (now DaimlerChrysler)

Corporation's oldest plant in New Castle, Indiana, as the United Auto Workers' union and company management forged a partnership for success.[86]

A game called Learning Teams is available to help people create self-directed teams, learn cooperatively, and master factual information.[87] With no outside help, an engineering team in the Defense Systems and Electronics Group (DSEG), now part of Raytheon, developed themselves into a highly effective, productive, self-managed team. They then helped DSEG in its successful effort to win a Malcolm Baldrige National Quality Award.

UPPER ECHELONS: TEAMS AT THE TOP

Self-managed teams at the top of the organization—top-level executive teams—are referred to as *upper echelons*. Organizations are often a reflection of these upper echelons.[88] Upper echelon theory argues that the background characteristics of the top management team can predict organizational characteristics. Furthermore, upper echelons are one key to the strategic success of the organization.[89] Within the team, performance is affected by the leader's displays of both anger and happiness.[90] Teams at the top are instrumental in defining the organization over time such that the values, competence, ethics, and unique characteristics of the top management team are eventually reflected throughout the organization. This ability to exert organization-wide power and influence makes the top management team a key to the company's success. This ability may be compromised if the top team sends mixed signals about teamwork and if executive pay systems foster competition, politics, and individualism.[91]

For example, when Lee Iacocca became CEO at the former Chrysler Corporation, his top management team was assembled to bring about strategic realignment within the corporation by building on Chrysler's historical engineering strength. The dramatic success of Chrysler during the early 1980s was followed by struggle and accommodation during the late 1980s. This raises the question of how long a CEO and the top management team can sustain organizational success.

Hambrick and Fukutomi address this question by examining the dynamic relationship between a CEO's tenure and the success of the organization.[92] They found five seasons in a CEO's tenure: (1) response to a mandate, (2) experimentation, (3) selection of an enduring theme, (4) convergence, and (5) dysfunction. A summary of each season is shown in Table 9.4. All else being equal, this seasons model has significant implications for organizational performance. Specifically, organizational performance increases during a CEO's tenure to a peak, after which performance declines. This relationship is depicted in Figure 9.3. The peak has been found to come at about seven years—somewhere in the middle of the executive's seasons. As indicated by the dotted lines in the figure, the peak may be extended, depending on several factors, such as diversity in the executive's support team.

Diversity at the Top

From an organizational health standpoint, diversity and depth in the top management team enhance the CEO's well-being.[93] From a performance standpoint, the CEO's top management team can influence the timing of the performance peak, the degree of dysfunction during the closing season of the CEO's tenure, and the rate of decline in organizational performance. Diversity and heterogeneity in the top management team help sustain high levels of organizational performance at the peak and help maintain the CEO's vitality. The presence of a "wild turkey" in the top management team can be a particularly positive force. The wild turkey is a devil's advocate who challenges the thinking of the CEO and other top executives and

8 Explain the importance of upper echelons and top management teams.

upper echelon
A top-level executive team in an organization.

9.4   The Five Seasons of a CEO's Tenure

Critical CEO Characteristics	1 Response to Mandate	2 Experimentation	3 Selection of an Enduring Theme	4 Convergence	5 Dysfunction
Commitment to a Paradigm	Moderately strong	Could be strong or weak	Moderately strong	Strong; increasing	Very strong
Task Knowledge	Low but rapidly increasing	Moderate; somewhat increasing	High; slightly increasing	High; slightly increasing	High; slightly increasing
Information Diversity	Many sources; unfiltered	Many sources but increasingly filtered	Fewer sources; moderately filtered	Few sources; highly filtered	Very few sources; highly filtered
Task Interest	High	High	Moderately high	Moderately high but diminishing	Moderately low and diminishing
Power	Low; increasing	Moderate; increasing	Moderate; increasing	Strong; increasing	Very strong; increasing

SOURCE: D. Hambrick and G. D. S. Fukutomi, "The Seasons of a CEO's Tenure," *Academy of Management Review* 16 (1991): 729. Permission conveyed through Copyright Clearance Center, Inc.

provides a counterpoint during debates. If not shouted down or inhibited, the wild turkey helps the CEO and the team sustain peak performance and retard the CEO's dysfunction and decline. For example, President George W. Bush had his administration enhanced by the independent voice of Secretary of State Colin Powell. Often taking a more moderate position on policy issues than either the secretary of defense or the vice president, Powell brought variance and value to the voice of President Bush's administration.

FIGURE

9.3   Executive Tenure and Organizational Performance

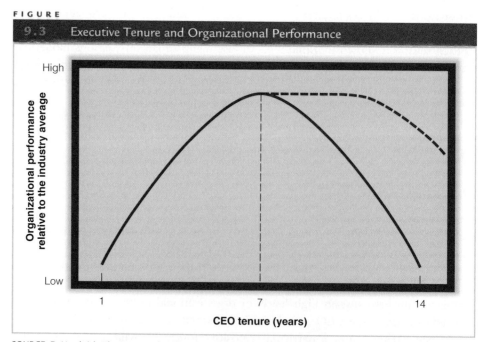

SOURCE: D. Hambrick, The Seasons of an Executive's Tenure, keynote address, the Sixth Annual Texas Conference on Organizations, Lago Vista, TX, April 1991.

No organization can succeed without a senior team that, collectively, captures a diversity of attributes: vision, task mastery, stewardship, and facilitation.[94] Leaders must evolve communication strategies to bring together a team that is functionally diverse, intellectually diverse, demographically diverse, temperamentally diverse, and so on, in order to complement each other. Dissimilarity develops strength, while similarity builds connections. A study of 207 U.S. firms in 11 industries found that functional diversity of top management teams had a positive effect on firm performance as the proportion of leaders in the same location increased.[95]

We can conclude that the leadership, composition, and dynamics of the top management team have an important influence on the organization's performance. In some cases, corporations have eliminated the single CEO. Current research has shown a dramatic increase in the number of co-CEO arrangements in both public and private corporations.[96] While more common in Europe than in the United States in the past, historical U.S. examples exist as well, such as when Walter Wriston created a three-member team when he was chairman at Citicorp (now part of Citigroup). At Southwest Airlines, the new top management team is emerging from the long shadow of legendary founder Herb Kelleher. This new top team led Southwest successfully through the terrorist crisis of September 2001.

Multicultural Top Teams

The backgrounds of group members may be quite different in the global workplace. Homogeneous groups in which all members share similar backgrounds are giving way to token groups in which all but one member come from the same background, bicultural groups in which two or more members represent each of two distinct cultures, and multicultural groups in which members represent three or more ethnic backgrounds.[97] Diversity within a group may increase the uncertainty, complexity, and inherent confusion in group processes, making it more difficult for the group to achieve its full, potential productivity.[98] On the positive side, Merck attributes its long-term success to its leadership model that promotes and develops the leadership skills of all Merck employees. Ray Gilmartin, former chairman, president, and CEO, valued diversity in Merck's top management team because he believed that diversity sparks innovation when employees with different perspectives work together to offer solutions. The design and function of top management teams in Great Britain, Denmark, and the Netherlands have been studied by international researchers.[99] The age and educational specialization of top management teams were found to have a positive effect on team performance especially when members have a need to participate in cognitive tasks.[100] The advantages of culturally diverse groups include the generation of more and better ideas while limiting the risk of groupthink, a subject to be discussed in Chapter 10.

MANAGERIAL IMPLICATIONS: TEAMWORK FOR PRODUCTIVITY AND QUALITY

Work groups and teams are important vehicles through which organizations achieve high-quality performance. The current emphasis on the new team environment, shown in Table 9.3, places unique demands on managers, teams, and individuals in leading, working, and managing. Managing these demands requires an understanding of individual diversity and the interrelationships of individuals, teams, and managers, as depicted in the triangle in Figure 9.4. Expectations associated with these three key organizational roles for people at work are different. The first role is as an individual, empowered employee. The second is as an active member of one

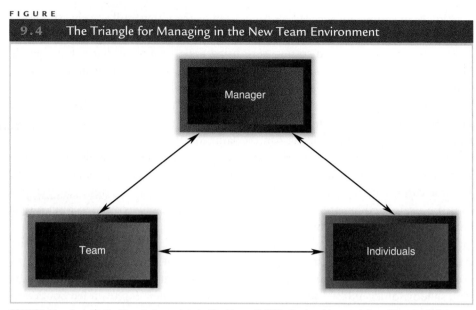

SOURCE: *Managing in the New Team Environment*, by L. Hirschhorn, © 1991. Reprinted by permission of Prentice Hall, Inc., Upper Saddle River, NJ.

or more teams. The third is the role of manager or formal supervisor. Earlier in the chapter, we discussed the foundations for teamwork, empowerment, and working in the new team environment. Individual empowerment must be balanced with collaborative teamwork.

The manager in the triangle is responsible for creating a receptive organizational environment for work groups and teams. This requires that she or he achieve a balance between setting limits (so that individuals and teams do not go too far afield) and removing barriers (so that empowered individuals and self-managed teams can accomplish their work). In addition, the manager should establish a flexible charter for each team. Once the charter is established, the manager continues to be available to the team as a coaching resource, as necessary. The manager establishes criteria for evaluating the performance effectiveness of the team, as well as the individuals, being supervised. In an optimum environment, this involves useful and timely performance feedback to teams that carries a sense of equity and fairness with it. The manager's responsibilities are different from those of the team leader.

Effective team leaders may guide a work group or share leadership responsibility with their teams, especially self-managed teams. Team leaders are active team members with responsibility for nurturing the development and performance of the team.[101] They require skills different from those of the manager. Whereas the manager establishes the environment in which teams flourish, the team leader teaches, listens, solves problems, manages conflict, and enhances the dynamics of team functioning to ensure its success. It is the team leader's task to bring the team to maturity; help it work through interpersonal, task, and authority issues; and be skilled in nurturing a cohesive, effective team. A team leader requires the hands-on skills of direct involvement and full membership in the team. Flexibility, delegation, and collaboration are characteristics of healthy teams and their leaders. Increasing globalization requires team leaders to be skilled at forging teamwork among diverse individuals, whereas managers must be skilled at forging collaboration among diverse groups.

Diversity Dialogue

Diverse Duo Seals the Deal

Kerry Cannella and Selma Bueno are from two different worlds—literally. Cannella is from Rhode Island, while Bueno is from Brazil. Although they have different geographic and cultural backgrounds, Kerry and Selma are both bankers at Merrill Lynch; Cannella is a managing director; Bueno, a junior associate.

Earlier in the year, Merrill Lynch was involved in a deal potentially worth several million dollars. The firm had been representing Brazilian investors who were selling their stake in a multibillion-dollar Latin American company to potential U.S. investors. The deal was in process, but each side was moving slowly and cautiously. Merrill Lynch needed to do something to step up the pace of negotiations and close the deal.

Enter the team of Cannella and Bueno. The two bankers made frequent trips between New York and Brazil. Bueno analyzed financial papers and put together an offering document for investors in her native Portuguese. In addition, she selected hotels and restaurants and translated during negotiations, making both sides feel at ease. The result was a successful deal for Merrill Lynch worth hundreds of millions of dollars and one that met everyone's satisfaction. Cannella considers his partnership with Bueno "a perfect match." According to Cannella, "She [Bueno] bridged the gap between the U.S. party, the Brazilian party, and me."

1. Could Merrill Lynch have achieved similar success without having someone on the team with Selma Bueno's cultural background? Explain.
2. What risks and rewards can employers expect by placing representatives with diverse backgrounds on work groups and teams?

SOURCE: E. Iwata, "Companies Find Gold inside Melting Pot," *USA Today* (July 9, 2007): B1.

LOOKING BACK: RESEARCH IN MOTION (RIM)

Partners Who Changed the World

Courtesy of Research In Motion

At the end of the day, the Balsille–Lazaridis partnership remains intact. All partnerships and teams experience challenges, two of which we considered in Thinking Ahead with regard to RIM co-CEOs. Strong bonds, secure relationships, and committed partners are able to transcend the challenges to insure that the integrity of the relationship continues and overcomes the problems that work and life present. The story that Canadians thought too good to be true did become a reality. More than that, the partnership and teamwork both underpinned the company and transformed the world. Change has come to how we work together, how we communicate, and how we get things done because of the BlackBerry and the success of the Balsille–Lazaridis partnership.

The BlackBerry has challenged a number of very basic concepts in work and life. The BlackBerry has challenged the concept of the work day in terms of its definition by time. The BlackBerry has challenged the boundary between work and home. The BlackBerry has challenged the concept of time itself, virtually eliminating dead time, and even space. The BlackBerry has enabled things that would have been ludicrous before its creation. For example, an executive admiring the terra cotta army of Xi'an received a flash message that negotiations on a key agreement in India had hit a roadblock. Within two hours, the executive had coordinated his team in India with key partners in Canada and obtained all required approvals. One has to marvel at how far technology moved in such a short time to facilitate such successful teamwork.

When the Balsille–Lazaridis team set forth in January 1999, the two had vision but could not fully conceive of how far they might go in a ten-year period.[102] The ensuing decade proved to be transformative for each of the partners, for RIM as a company, and for the broader world of work. Balsille says that the BlackBerry has changed the latency of collaboration. The world and work are much more fluid as a result of BlackBerry, making possible that which was impossible a decade ago. The combination of imagination and teamwork truly know no limits. Balsille and Lazaridis have changed the world with the BlackBerry, quite literally, along a wide range of dimensions. A 2007 survey estimated that an average corporate BlackBerry user converted sixty-three minutes of downtime into productive time while the BlackBerry returned $58,380 to the company for each employee making $100,000 per year.

Chapter Summary

1. Groups are often composed of diverse people at work. Teams in organizations are key to enhancing quality and achieving success.

2. Important aspects of group behavior include norms of behavior, group cohesion, social loafing, and loss of individuality.

3. Once a group forms, it generally goes through five stages of development. If successful, the group can function independently, with little interference from its leader.

4. Quality circles, originally popularized in Japan, and quality teams contribute to solving technological and quality problems in the organization.

5. Teams provide social benefits for team members, as well as enhancing organizational performance.

6. Functional and value dissimilarity may have positive or negative effects on teams. Managing dissimilarity in teams and being open to diversity are highly important for promoting creativity.

7. Teamwork requires specific organizational design elements and individual psychological characteristics and skills.

8. Upper echelons and top management teams are key to the strategy and performance of an organization. Diversity and a devil's advocate in the top team enhance performance.

9. Managing in the new team environment places new demands on managers, teams, and individuals. Managers must create a supportive and flexible environment and nurture the team's development.

Key Terms

group (p. 294)
group cohesion (p. 295)
integrated involvement (p. 308)
loss of individuality (p. 296)
maintenance function (p. 304)
norms of behavior (p. 295)

psychological intimacy (p. 308)
quality circle (QC) (p. 307)
quality team (p. 307)
self-managed team (p. 311)
social loafing (p. 296)
status structure (p. 302)

task function (p. 304)
team diversity (p. 311)
teamwork (p. 305)
upper echelon (p. 313)
work team (p. 294)

Review Questions

1. What is a group? A work team?
2. Explain four aspects of group behavior. How can each aspect help or hinder the group's functioning?
3. Describe what happens in each stage of a group's development according to Tuckman's Five-Stage Model. What are the leadership requirements in each stage?
4. Describe the four characteristics of mature groups.
5. Why are work teams important to organizations today? How and why are work teams formed?
6. Describe at least five task and five maintenance functions that effective work teams must perform.
7. Discuss diversity and creativity in teams.
8. Describe the necessary skills for empowerment and teamwork.
9. What are the benefits and potential drawbacks of self-managed teams?
10. What is the role of the manager in the new team environment? What is the role of the team leader?

Discussion and Communication Questions

1. Which was the most effective group (or team) of which you have been a member? What made that group (or team) so effective?
2. Have you ever felt peer pressure to act more in accordance with the behavioral norms of a group? Have you ever engaged in a little social loafing? Have you ever lost your head and been caught up in a group's destructive actions?
3. Name a company that successfully uses teamwork and empowerment. What has that company done that makes it so successful in this regard? Has its team approach made a difference in its performance? How?
4. Name a person you think is a particularly good team member. What makes him or her so? Name someone who is a problem as a team member. What makes this person a problem?
5. Think about your current work environment. Does it use quality circles or self-managed teams? What are the barriers to teamwork and empowerment in that environment? What elements of the environment enhance or encourage teamwork and empowerment? (If you do not work, discuss this question with a friend who does.)
6. (*communication question*) Prepare a memo describing your observations about work teams and groups in your workplace or university. Where have you observed teams or groups to be most effective? Why? What changes might be made at work or in the university to make teams more effective?
7. (*communication question*) Develop an oral presentation about what the most important norms of behavior should be in an academic community and workplace. Be specific. Discuss how these norms should be established and reinforced.
8. (*communication question*) Interview an employee or manager about what he or she believes contributes to cohesiveness in work groups and teams. Ask the person what the conclusions are based on. Be prepared to discuss what you have learned in class.
9. Do you admire the upper echelons in your organization or university? Why or why not? Do they communicate effectively with groups and individuals throughout the organization?

Ethical Dilemma

Hank Krendle, account manager for Craven Marketing, believes that Jason Krueger is a great candidate for promotion—Jason has consistently met the expectations set for his position, has initiated cost-saving procedures, and is a consummate team player. Jason has met with Hank regularly to make certain that he's on target for advancement, and Hank has encouraged Jason that his productivity and ability to lead make him an excellent candidate. The team with which Jason currently works collaborates very well, and Hank believes that Jason has the skills to become a competent manager and to go grow and develop within the company.

Just as Hank is set to make his recommendations to his boss to consider Jason for a newly opened account manager position, he becomes aware that Jason's team is next scheduled to work on the Maxim Factory account, which is one of Craven's largest clients. Hank worked hard to earn that account for his section, and Jason and his team are the best people at Craven to get the work done efficiently. Hank knows that the people in his department are all capable, but Jason is really the stand-out, and certainly the only person who can manage this complex and high-profile project to the satisfaction of the management team at Maxim Factory.

If Hank recommends Jason for the account manager's position, it would leave his team without his invaluable talents. However, Hank has been promising Jason that he would fully back him for the next opening. If Hank holds off recommending Jason for this current opening, there may not be another for quite some time. Is it fair to overlook Jason for something he has worked so hard to get? That could really hurt Jason's career

advancement. But, is it fair not to give Maxim the best possible attention? Maxim is one of Craven's largest and oldest clients.

Questions:

1. Using consequential, rule-based and character theories, evaluate Hank's options.

2. What should Hank do? Why?

Experiential Exercises

9.1 Tower Building: A Group Dynamics Activity

This exercise gives you an opportunity to study group dynamics in a task-oriented situation. Each group must bring materials to class for building a tower. All materials must fit in a box no greater than eight cubic feet (i.e., 2 ft. × 2 ft. × 2 ft. or 1 ft. × 2 ft. × 4 ft.).

Step 1. Each group is assigned a meeting place and a workplace. One or two observers should be assigned in each group. The instructor may assign a manager to each group.

Step 2. Each group plans for the building of the paper tower (no physical construction is allowed during this planning period). Towers will be judged on the basis of height, stability, beauty, and meaning. (Another option is to have the groups do the planning outside of class and come prepared to build the tower.)

Step 3. Each group constructs its tower.

Step 4. Groups inspect other towers, and all individuals rate towers other than their own. See the evaluation sheet at the right. Each group turns in its point totals (i.e., someone in the group adds up each person's total for all groups rated) to the instructor, and the instructor announces the winner.

Step 5. Group dynamics analysis. Observers report observations to their own groups, and each group

analyzes the group dynamics that occurred during the planning and building of the tower.

Step 6. Groups report on major issues in group dynamics that arose during the tower planning and building. Complete the tower building aftermath questionnaire as homework if requested by your instructor.

CRITERIA	GROUPS							
	1	2	3	4	5	6	7	8
Height								
Stability/Strength Beauty								
Meaning/ Significance								
TOTALS								

Rate each criterion on a scale of 1–10, with 1 being lowest or poorest, and 10 being highest or best.

SOURCE: From *Organizational Behavior and Performance*, 5e by Szilagyi and Wallace, © 1997. Reprinted by permission of Prentice Hall, Inc., Upper Saddle River, NJ.

9.2 Design a Team

The following exercise gives you an opportunity to design a team. Working in a six-person group, address the individual characteristics, team composition, and norms for an effective group whose task is to make recommendations on improving customer relations. The president of a small clothing manufacturer is concerned that his customers are not satisfied enough with the company's responsiveness, product quality, and returned-orders process. He has asked your group to put together a team to address these problems.

Step 1. The class will form into groups of approximately six members each. Each group elects a spokesperson and answers the following questions. The group should spend an equal amount of time on each question.

a. *What characteristics should the individual members of the task team possess?* Members may consider

professional competence, skills, department, and/ or personality and behavioral characteristics in the group's discussion.

b. *What should the composition of the task team be?* Once your group has addressed individual characteristics, consider the overall composition of the task team. Have special and/or unique competencies, knowledge, skills, and abilities been considered in your deliberations?

c. *What norms of behavior do you think the task team should adopt?* A team's norms of behavior may evolve, or they may be consciously discussed and agreed upon. Take the latter approach.

Step 2. Each group will share the results of its answers to the questions in Step 1. Cross-team questions and discussion follow.

Biz Flix | Friends with Money

This film focuses on four female friends at various stages of life development. Three are married; some with children. Some couples are extremely wealthy, others are not. Olivia (Jennifer Aniston), a former school teacher and now a maid, is single. The film focuses on interactions among them and the dynamics of their lives.

A Small Team: The Aaron Team in Action

These sequences come from two different places in the film. A titling screen separates the sequences.

The first sequence begins with The Other Aaron (Ty Burrell) saying to Aaron (Simon McBurney), "I've—Excuse me, I've …. I've seen you in here a lot." This sequence ends after they discuss Aaron's socks.

Sequence 2 is DVD Chapter 15, "Friendship Grows." The two Aarons come out of a movie theater. Aaron says, "On top of it, I don't get the part where the guy tells the other guy not to come to the house." The sequence ends as The Other Aaron says, "I love your shirt, by the way."

What to Watch for and Ask Yourself

- This chapter defined a group as "two or more people having common interests, objectives, and continuing interaction." Does this film sequence have examples of each part of that definition? Identify specific moments that fit the definition.

- Review the section "Stages of Group Development." Apply that discussion to both film sequences. You should see examples of each stage.

- Does the small group in these film sequences appear cohesive? Cite some specific moments from the film sequences to support your conclusion.

Workplace Video | Evo: Teamwork

For years Evo has supported athletic teams, but only recently did the Seattle-based e-commerce company launch a formal workplace team. Like many organizations, the online retailer of snowboard, ski, skate, and wake gear used team metaphors loosely to describe anything involving random groups of employees. But Evo got an education on real work teams when the company formed a team for its creative services employees.

The new group, which is comprised of a photographer, designer, and copywriter, is responsible for producing Evo's magazine ads, promotions, and Web site content. Although the individuals' roles are not generally interchangeable, photographer Tre Dauenhauer might dabble in design, graphic designer Pubs One may write a few lines of copy, and copywriter Sunny Fenton might snap photos on occasion. Most team projects require a combination of eye-grabbing photos, clever words, and a compelling design, and the teammates are committed to a common purpose.

When the creative services team launched, group members moved into their own space, away from Evo's chaotic, open-plan work areas. Being together every day enabled the team members to become better acquainted and move through the "forming" stage more quickly. But even with close quarters, Dauenhauer, One, and Fenton needed help navigating the conflict-ridden, storming stage of their team's development. Before joining the team, they functioned individually and weren't used to sharing power or making decisions as a group. To help the members learn to work together, Nathan Decker, director of e-commerce, became the team leader. As a skilled negotiator, Decker makes sure his talented trio steers clear of dysfunction and delivers the goods. Any time the team finishes a project, Decker brings members together for a postmortem discussion—a method of reviewing what was learned, and how things could be executed differently. It's here that the team members identify new routines and rituals to incorporate into their process for future improvement.

Due to Decker's leadership and skillful negotiation of conflicts, members of the creative services team are learning how to communicate in ways never before possible. Having a skilled leader to facilitate work processes has helped build team cohesiveness and deliver a collective output that is greater than the sum of its parts.

Discussion Questions

1. What organizational dilemma was hurting Evo's creative output, and how did management resolve the conflict?

2. How can Decker effectively lead when the team starts "norming"?

3. How might the team benefit from having a leader with a creative background?

Case

Teamwork Challenges at Stryker Corporation

The Stryker Corporation was built on innovation. "When Dr. Homer Stryker, an orthopedic surgeon from Kalamazoo, Michigan, found that certain medical products were not meeting his patients' needs, he invented new ones. As interest in these products grew, Dr. Stryker started a company in 1941 to produce them. The company's goal was to help patients lead healthier, more active lives through products and services that make surgery and recovery simpler, faster and more effective."[1]

Homer Stryker started Orthopedic Frame Company to sell devices for moving patients with spinal injuries.[2] A short time later he invented the first power tool—the oscillating cast saw—for removing plaster casts after patients' broken bones had healed. After that the company began providing hospital beds. These early initiatives, but especially the oscillating cast saw, formed the foundation of what is now the Stryker Corporation, one of the leading companies in the worldwide market for orthopedic devices.[3] Stryker, headquartered in Kalamazoo, Michigan, employs over 15,000 people with most of its operations being in the United States, Europe, and Japan. As a leading medical technology company and one of the largest in the multibillion dollar worldwide orthopedic market, Stryker manufactures replacement joints such as shoulders, knees, and hips; high-technology tools like imaging systems that help surgeons reconstruct body parts; and a variety of other medical devices and products, including surgical tools and hospital beds.[4]

One of Stryker's recent orthopedic innovations was a navigation system for hip replacement surgery that permitted surgeons to observe via a computer screen the precise positioning of a hip replacement prosthesis. Due to the nature of hip replacement, the navigation system had to have the capability of withstanding the various physical stresses put on the equipment, including pounding with a surgical hammer. In addition, the navigation system—especially its sophisticated electronics—had to survive repeated sterilization under 270-degree-Fahrenheit steam pressure. However, shortly after field testing of the hip replacement navigation system began, significant problems with the system were discovered. Numerous complaints were received from surgeons, and the systems were returned to Stryker. Examination of the returned units revealed that the precision electronics of the system frequently failed and metal parts were broken or damaged.[5]

Finding a solution to the navigation system problems was assigned to Klaus Welte, vice president and plant manager for Stryker's Freiburg, Germany facility, which was acquired in 1998. Under its previous owner, Leibinger, the Freiburg facility had developed a magnetic imaging navigation system for use in neurosurgery. After the acquisition by Stryker, the Freiburg facility applied its navigation system technology and expertise to developing other surgical tools, including ones for orthopedics. Thus, the Freiburg facility was given the responsibility for solving the problems with the hip replacement navigation system.[6]

Welte's first challenge was assembling a team to work on solving the navigation system problem. Welte believed that the team's success would require both a clear view of what had to be accomplished and a deep understanding of each team member's abilities."[7] Welte assembled a team of the best people at Freiburg in operations, computer-aided design, engineering, and research. One team member was talented in structural analysis, communication, and follow-through. Another member provided the "social glue" for the team and would never stop until all tasks were complete. Still another team member was an organizer who helped keep the team on task and from rushing ahead before it was ready. Yet another team member was especially knowledgeable regarding how a product design will successfully survive the manufacturing process. Another person was noted for highly innovative—indeed visionary—product design ideas.[8]

Although each team member's abilities were important, how those abilities fit together was equally important. According to Welte, "Creating an effective team requires more than just filling all the job descriptions with someone who has the right talent and experience.... By no means can you substitute one engineer for another. There are really very, very specific things that they are good at...and how well the team members' abilities combine is as important as the abilities themselves."[9] How well the Stryker team jelled became evident in their approach to problem solving.

Due to the number of problems with the hip replacement navigation system, the Freiburg team addressed each problem separately, beginning with the most crucial issue and working down to the relatively minor problems. The solution for each problem was thoroughly tested before moving on to the next issue. Consequently, the team did not have a fully assembled prototype until all the problems were addressed. This approach proved successful, both in terms of the ultimate success of the prototype design and the team working effectively together as problem solvers. In the first nine months after the redesigned hip replacement navigation system was released, the company did not receive a single complaint from surgeons—an incredible achievement for complex surgical equipment.[10] Additionally, the navigation system quickly contributed to double-digit growth in worldwide sales in Stryker's medical and surgical equipment segment.[11]

Although the redesigned hip replacement navigation system proved reliable and essentially problem-free, not the same can be said for the orthopedic hip implants themselves—the surgical insertion of which is guided by the navigation system. There were ongoing problems with the actual hip replacement joints manufactured by Stryker. The U.S. Food and Drug Administration (FDA) issued a total of three warning letters in less than a year regarding recurring quality problems. As Jon Kamp, a reporter for the *Wall Street Journal*, observes, "[s]uch letters require demanding and sometimes-costly changes and can be hard to shake. They also may crimp approval for certain new products, although Stryker doesn't have many new products likely to feel an impact."[12] As an incentive for managers to "resolve quality control deficiencies and achieve world-class systems, Stryker...[decided to] link 25% of each senior executive's and division president's annual bonus to this issue."[13]

In addition to the quality issue, Stryker, as well as four other companies—Zimmer Holdings Inc. and Biomet Inc. of Warsaw, Indiana; the DePuy Orthopedics unit of Johnson & Johnson, New Brunswick, New Jersey; and Smith & Nephew PLC of London, England—were charged by the U.S. government of financially rewarding "doctors who selected a company's hip and knee implants, even when they weren't necessarily the best for a particular patient."[14] All but Stryker agreed to pay $310 million to settle the government's claims of the companies violating antikickback laws, whereas Stryker only agreed to government supervision; none of the companies admitted any wrongdoing.[15] A subsequent subpoena from the U.S. Department of Health and Human Services (HHS) sought information on the antikickback settlement;[16] Stryker characterized the HHS request for information as "oppressive and overly broad."[17] The matter is still playing out in court as this case is being written.

Given the challenges that are plaguing Stryker's orthopedic hip implants, could the company perhaps benefit from a team effort similar to that used in redesigning the hip replacement navigation system?

Discussion Questions

1. Discuss the extent to which the characteristics of well-functioning, effective groups accurately describe the Freiburg hip replacement navigation system team.

2. Explain why teamwork is important to effectively solve the problems which field testing of the hip replacement navigation system revealed.

3. Describe how the task functions and maintenance functions are operating within the Freiburg team.

4. Explain why diversity and creativity are important to the effective functioning of the Freiburg team.

5. How could Stryker utilize insights gained from the experiences of the Freiberg team to address the ongoing quality problems with the actual orthopedic implants?

6. Obviously, close working relationships need to exist between companies that design, manufacture, and market surgical implants and the surgeons who use those implants. What impact might the antikickback issue have on the working relationship between Stryker and the surgeons who use its orthopedic hip implants?

SOURCE: This case was written by Michael K. McCuddy, The Louis S. and Mary L. Morgal Chair of Christian Business Ethics and Professor of Management, College of Business Administration, Valparaiso University.

10

Decision Making by Individuals and Groups

LEARNING OBJECTIVES

After reading this chapter, you should be able to do the following:

1 Explain the assumptions of bounded rationality.

2 Describe Jung's cognitive styles and how they affect managerial decision making.

3 Describe and evaluate the role of intuition and creativity in decision making.

4 Critique your own level of creativity and list ways of improving it.

5 Compare and contrast the advantages and disadvantages of group decision making.

6 Discuss the symptoms of groupthink and ways to prevent it.

7 Evaluate the strengths and weaknesses of several group decision-making techniques.

8 Explain the emerging role of virtual decision making in organizations.

9 Utilize an "ethics check" for examining managerial decisions.

Mark Zuckerman (left),
founder of Facebook.

THINKING AHEAD: FACEBOOK

Facebook's New Focus on Customer Participative Decision Making

Since creating Facebook in 2004 in a Harvard University dorm room, Facebook founders Mark Zuckerman and colleagues have, for the most part, followed a decision-making style not uncommon in business in the United States. Decisions are made internally by employees within the organization. However, after user backlashes over the last several years, Facebook seems to have realized this strategy may not be working. Facebook allows its users an unprecedented ability to express and publicize their satisfaction or lack thereof with the company—and Facebook users haven't been shy in expressing their opinions. Facebook users protested changes made to Facebook by creating a group called "We Hate the New Facebook, So Stop Changing It," which has well over a million members.[1] In 2007, Facebook introduced Beacon, which allowed users to see what Web sites were visited by their friends and showed their online purchases.[2] Members protested and Facebook apologized. And in 2009, Facebook altered its privacy policy to include Facebook's right to archive user content even after the user chooses to remove it. Members

protested and Facebook scrambled to put a positive spin on the issue.[3] Facebook is one of the companies leading the edge in how we communicate. Now that this tool is being used to express disfavor regarding the provider, how will Facebook respond? The Looking Back feature tells the rest of the story.

THE DECISION-MAKING PROCESS

Decision making is a critical activity in the lives of managers. The decisions a manager faces can range from very simple, routine matters for which he or she has an established decision rule (*programmed decisions*) to new and complex decisions that require creative solutions (*nonprogrammed decisions*).[4] Scheduling lunch hours for one's work group is a programmed decision. The manager performs the decision activity on a daily basis, using an established procedure with the same clear goal in mind. By contrast, decisions like buying out another company are nonprogrammed. For example, Facebook's decision to use Beacon was a nonprogrammed decision. The decision to acquire a company is another situation that is unique and unstructured and requires considerable judgment. Regardless of the type of decision made, it is helpful to understand as much as possible about how individuals and groups make decisions.

Decision making is a process involving a series of steps, as shown in Figure 10.1. The first step is recognition of the problem; that is, the manager realizes that a decision must be made. Identification of the real problem is important; otherwise, the manager may be reacting to symptoms and firefighting rather than dealing with the root cause of the problem. Next, a manager must identify the objective of the decision—in other words, determine what is to be accomplished by it.

The third step in the decision-making process is gathering information relevant to the problem. The manager must pull together sufficient information about why the problem occurred. This involves conducting a thorough diagnosis of the situation and going on a fact-finding mission.

The fourth step is listing and evaluating alternative courses of action. During this step, a thorough "what-if" analysis should also be conducted to determine the various factors that could influence the outcome. It is important to generate a wide range of options and creative solutions in order to be able to move on to the fifth step.

In the fifth step, the manager selects the alternative that best meets the decision objective. If the problem has been diagnosed correctly and sufficient alternatives have been identified, this step is much easier.

Finally, the solution is implemented. The situation must then be monitored to see whether the decision met its objective. Consistent monitoring and periodic feedback are essential parts of the follow-up process.

MODELS OF DECISION MAKING

The success of any organization depends on managers' abilities to make *effective decisions*. An effective decision is timely, is acceptable to the individuals affected by it, and meets the desired objective.[5] This section describes three models of decision making: the rational model, the bounded rationality model, and the garbage can model.

programmed decision
A simple, routine matter for which a manager has an established decision rule.

nonprogrammed decision
A new, complex decision that requires a creative solution.

effective decision
A timely decision that meets a desired objective and is acceptable to those individuals affected by it.

FIGURE

10.1   The Decision-Making Process

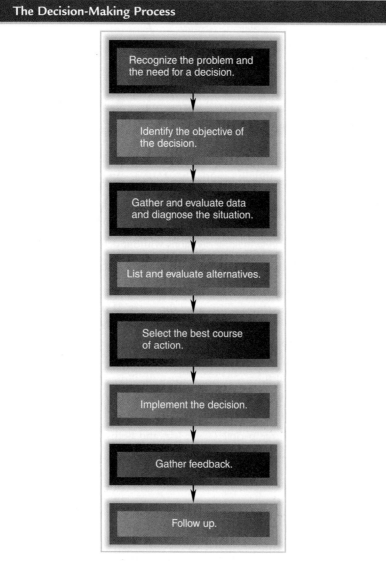

Rational Model

Rationality refers to a logical, step-by-step approach to decision making, with a thorough analysis of alternatives and their consequences. The rational model of decision making comes from classic economic theory and contends that the decision maker is completely rational in his or her approach. The rational model has the following important assumptions:

1. The outcome will be completely rational.

2. The decision maker has a consistent system of preferences, which is used to choose the best alternative.

3. The decision maker is aware of all the possible alternatives.

4. The decision maker can calculate the probability of success for each alternative.[6]

In the rational model, the decision maker strives to optimize, that is, to select the best possible alternative.

Given its assumptions, the rational model is unrealistic. There are time constraints and limits to human knowledge and information-processing capabilities. In addition, a manager's preferences and needs change often. The rational model is thus

rationality
A logical, step-by-step approach to decision making, with a thorough analysis of alternatives and their consequences.

an ideal that managers strive for in making decisions. It captures the way a decision should be made but does not reflect the reality of managerial decision making.[7]

Bounded Rationality Model

1 Explain the assumptions of bounded rationality.

Recognizing the deficiencies of the rational model, Herbert Simon suggested that there are limits on how rational a decision maker can actually be. His decision theory, the bounded rationality model, earned a Nobel Prize in 1978.

Simon's model, also referred to as the "administrative man" theory, rests on the idea that there are constraints that force a decision maker to be less than completely rational. The bounded rationality model has four assumptions:

1. Managers select the first alternative that is satisfactory.
2. Managers recognize that their conception of the world is simple.
3. Managers are comfortable making decisions without determining all the alternatives.
4. Managers make decisions by rules of thumb or heuristics.

Bounded rationality assumes that managers *satisfice*; that is, they select the first alternative that is "good enough," because the costs of optimizing in terms of time and effort are too great.[8] Further, the theory assumes that managers develop shortcuts, called *heuristics*, to make decisions in order to save mental activity. Heuristics are rules of thumb that allow managers to make decisions based on what has worked in past experiences.

Heuristics can help us make decisions, but they can also cause errors in judgment. To illustrate this, please consider the following:

1. Imagine a group of three people (Tom, Joe, and Beth) want to form a two-person team. They can create three different teams: Tom and Joe, Tom and Beth, or Joe and Beth. There are three different two-person teams. Now imagine you have ten people who want to form two-person teams and ten people who want to form eight-person teams. You need to determine if there are there more two-persons teams possible or more eight-person teams possible.[9]

2. On one day in a large metropolitan hospital, eight births were recorded by gender in the order of arrival. Which of the following orders of births (B = boy, G = girl) was most likely reported?
   a. BBBBBBBB   b. BBBBGGGG   c. BGBBGGGB.[10]

The majority of people's response for number one is two-person teams and for number two is c. However, closer investigation indicates that these answers are incorrect. There are as many two-person teams as eight-person teams in a group of ten, and any combination of birth order (boys or girls) at a given hospital is equally likely. These incorrect answers are subject to two of the many common heuristic biases.

The first question relates to the availability heuristic, in which individuals tend to make decisions based on the frequency, probability, or likelihood of an event based on how easily they can remember it.[11] In the preceding example, two-person teams are more available than eight-person teams because ten can easily be split into two groups of five and there is only one eight-person team at a time in a group of ten. The second question illustrates the representative heuristic or gambler's fallacy, in which decisions of probability are based on similarity of occurrence to others.[12] Despite the roughly 50 percent chance of any one woman having a boy or girl, many people relate the probability of one gender being born on what the preceding birth gender happened to be.

These heuristics can play an important role not only in answering correctly or incorrectly but also in other aspects of decision making such as ethics. A recent study found that the availability of information relating to severe consequences

bounded rationality
A theory that suggests there are limits to how rational a decision maker can actually be.

satisfice
To select the first alternative that is "good enough," because the costs in time and effort are too great to optimize.

heuristics
Shortcuts in decision making that save mental activity.

10.2 The Garbage Can Model

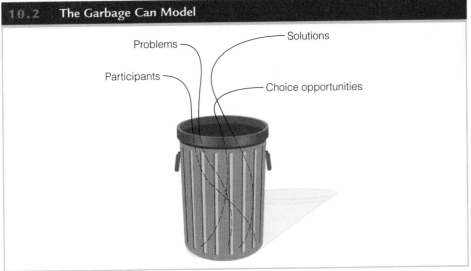

Problems

Solutions

Participants

Choice opportunities

SOURCE: From M. D. Cohen, J. G. March, and J. P. Olsen in *Administrative Science Quarterly* 17 (March 1972): 1–25. Reprinted by permission of the *Administrative Science Quarterly*.

for an unethical decision reduced the likelihood that one would make that decision; however, this study also found that the availability of others who believed that a particular act was morally acceptable increased the perceptions that this act was viewed as socially acceptable.[13] Thus, individuals and managers need to be aware of how heuristics are used and take care that these short cuts in decision making are not leading to poor decisions. Do using satisficing, and heuristics in the bounded rationality model more realistically portray the managerial decision process? Research indicates that they do.[14] One of the reasons managers face limits to their rationality is that they must make decisions under risk and time pressure. The situation they find themselves in is highly uncertain, and the probability of success is not known.

Garbage Can Model

Sometimes the decision-making process in organizations appears to be haphazard and unpredictable. In the *garbage can model*, decisions are random and unsystematic.[15] Figure 10.2 depicts the garbage can model. In this model, the organization is a garbage can in which problems, solutions, participants, and choice opportunities are floating around randomly. If the four factors happen to connect, a decision is made.[16] The quality of the decision depends on timing. The right participants must find the right solution to the right problem at the right time.

The garbage can model illustrates the idea that not all organizational decisions are made in a step-by-step, systematic fashion. Especially under conditions of high uncertainty, the decision process may be chaotic. Some decisions appear to happen out of sheer luck.

On the high-speed playing field of today's businesses, managers must make critical decisions quickly, with incomplete information, and must also involve employees in the process.

DECISION MAKING AND RISK

garbage can model
A theory that contends that decisions in organizations are random and unsystematic.

Many decisions involve some element of risk. For managers, hiring decisions, promotions, delegation, acquisitions and mergers, overseas expansions, new product development, and other decisions make risk a part of the job.

Risk and the Manager

Individuals differ in terms of their willingness to take risks. Some people experience *risk aversion*. They choose options that entail fewer risks, preferring familiarity and certainty. Other individuals are risk takers; that is, they accept greater potential for loss in decisions, tolerate greater uncertainty, and in general are more likely to make risky decisions. Risk takers are also more likely to take the lead in group discussions.[17]

Research indicates that women are more averse to risk taking than men and that older, more experienced managers are more risk averse than younger managers. There is also some evidence that successful managers take more risks than unsuccessful ones.[18] However, the tendency to take risks or avoid them is only part of behavior toward risk. Risk taking is influenced not only by an individual's tendency but also by organizational factors. In commercial banks, loan decisions that require the assessment of risk are made every day.

Upper level managers face a tough task in managing risk-taking behavior. By discouraging lower level managers from taking risks, they may stifle creativity and innovation. If upper level managers are going to encourage risk taking, however, they must allow employees to fail without fear of punishment. One way to accomplish this is to consider failure "enlightened trial and error."[19] The key is establishing a consistent attitude toward risk within the organization.

When individuals take risks, losses may occur. Suppose an oil producer thinks there is an opportunity to uncover oil by reentering an old drilling site. She gathers a group of investors and shows them the logs, and they chip in to finance the venture. The reentry is drilled to a certain depth, and nothing is found. Convinced they did not drill deep enough, the producer goes back to the investors and requests additional financial backing to continue drilling. The investors consent, and she drills deeper, only to find nothing. She approaches the investors, and after lengthy discussion, they agree to provide more money to drill deeper. Why do decision makers sometimes throw good money after bad? Why do they continue to provide resources to what looks like a losing venture?

risk aversion

The tendency to choose options that entail fewer risks and less uncertainty.

escalation of commitment

The tendency to continue to support a failing course of action.

Escalation of Commitment

Continuing to support a failing course of action is known as *escalation of commitment*.[20] In situations characterized by escalation of commitment, individuals who make decisions that turn out to be poor choices tend to hold fast to them, even when substantial costs are incurred.[21] An example of escalation is the price wars that often occur between airlines. The airlines reduce their prices in response to competitors until at a certain stage, both airlines are in a "no-win" situation. Yet they continue to compete despite the heavy losses they are incurring. The desire to win is a motivation to continue to escalate, and each airline continues to reduce prices (lose money) based on the belief that the other airline will pull out of the price war. Another example of escalation of commitment is NASA's enormous International Space Station. Originally estimated to cost $8 billion, the Space Station has been redesigned five times and remains unfinished. Its estimated cost topped $30 billion, and some pundits speculate that the total bill may reach $130 billion for what physicist Robert Park describes as "the biggest technological blunder in history." Despite the station's

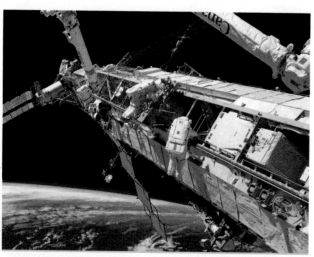

NASA's International Space Station is an example of escalation of commitment.

drain on virtually every other NASA program, it remains a focal point of NASA's work and continues to consume vast resources.[22]

Why does escalation of commitment occur? One explanation is offered by cognitive dissonance theory, as we discussed in Chapter 4. This theory assumes that humans dislike inconsistency, and that when there is inconsistency among their attitudes or between their attitudes and behavior, they strive to reduce the dissonance.[23]

Other reasons why people maintain a losing course of action are optimism and control. Some people are overly optimistic and overestimate the likelihood that positive things will happen to them. Other people operate under an illusion of control—that they have special skills to control the future that other people don't have.[24] In addition, sunk costs may encourage escalation. Individuals think, "Well, I've already invested this much . . . what's a few dollars more?" And the closer a project is to completion, the more likely escalation is to occur.[25]

Clinging to a poor decision can be costly to organizations. While many foreign automakers saw promise in the green movement and urgent trends to build cars back in 2002, Rick Wagoner and General Motors stuck with a cost cutting strategy that streamlined their operations and focused on SUVs and trucks. Over the last four years with Wagoner as its CEO, GM lost $82 billion and even these losses did not change GM's strategy.[26] When Wagoner finally showed signs of de-escalating and recognizing SUVs and trucks were not the answer, it was too late and despite a multibillion dollar government bailout, GM declared bankruptcy.

Recent research investigating what characteristics make an individual more likely to de-escalate found that individuals with a higher self-esteem and individuals that are given an opportunity to affirm an important value were more likely to de-escalate.[27] Organizations can use this information to deal with escalation of commitment. Another way to reduce escalation of commitment is to split the responsibility for decisions about projects. One individual can make the initial decision, and another can make subsequent decisions. Companies have also tried to eliminate escalation of commitment by closely monitoring decision makers.[28] Another suggestion is to provide individuals with a graceful exit from poor decisions so that their images are not threatened. One way of accomplishing this is to reward people who admit to poor decisions before escalating their commitment to them. A study also suggested that having groups, rather than individuals, make an initial investment decision would reduce escalation. Support has been found for this idea. Participants in group decision making may experience a diffusion of responsibility for the failed decision rather than feeling personally responsible; thus, they can pull out of a bad decision without threatening their image.[29]

We have seen that there are limits to how rational a manager can be in making decisions. Most managerial decisions involve considerable risk, and individuals react differently to risk situations.

JUNG'S COGNITIVE STYLES

In Chapter 3, we introduced Jungian theory as a way of understanding and appreciating differences among individuals. This theory is especially useful in pointing out that individuals have different styles of making decisions. Carl Jung's original theory identified two styles of information gathering (sensing and intuiting) and two styles of making judgments (thinking and feeling). You already know what each individual preference means. Jung contended that individuals prefer one style of perceiving and one style of judging.[30] The combination of a perceiving style and a judging style is called a *cognitive style*. There are four cognitive styles: sensing/thinking (ST), sensing/feeling (SF), intuiting/thinking (NT), and intuiting/feeling (NF). Each of the cognitive styles affects managerial decision making.[31]

2 Describe Jung's cognitive styles and how they affect managerial decision making.

cognitive style
An individual's preference for gathering information and evaluating alternatives.

STs rely on facts. They conduct an impersonal analysis of the situation and then make an analytical, objective decision. The ST cognitive style is valuable in organizations because it produces a clear, simple solution. STs remember details and seldom make factual errors. Their weakness is that they may alienate others because of their tendency to ignore interpersonal aspects of decisions. In addition, they tend to avoid risks.

SFs also gather factual information, but they make judgments in terms of how they affect people. They place great importance on interpersonal relationships but also take a practical approach to gathering information for problem solving. The SFs' strength in decision making lies in their ability to handle interpersonal problems well and to take calculated risks. SFs may have trouble accepting new ideas that break the organization's rules.

NTs focus on the alternative possibilities in a situation and then evaluate them objectively and impersonally. NTs love to initiate ideas, and they like to focus on the long term. They are innovative and will take risks. This makes NTs good at things like new business development.[32] Weaknesses of NTs include their tendencies to ignore arguments based on facts and to ignore the feelings of others.

NFs also search out alternative possibilities, but they evaluate the possibilities in terms of how they will affect the people involved. They enjoy participative decision making and are committed to developing their employees. However, NFs may be prone to making decisions based on personal preferences rather than on more objective data. They may also become too responsive to the needs of others.

Research supports the existence of these four cognitive styles and their influences on managerial decision making.[33] One study asked managers to describe their ideal organization, and the researchers found strong similarities in the descriptions of managers with the same cognitive style.[34] STs wanted an organization that relied on facts and details and that exercised impersonal methods of control. SFs focused on facts, too, but they did so in terms of the relationships within the organization. NTs emphasized broad issues and described impersonal, idealistic organizations. NFs described an organization that would serve humankind well and focused on general, humanistic values.

All four cognitive styles have much to contribute to organizational decision making.[35] Isabel Briggs Myers, creator of the MBTI®, also developed the Z problem-solving model, which capitalizes on the strengths of the four separate preferences (sensing, intuiting, thinking, and feeling). By using this model, managers can use both their preferences and nonpreferences to make decisions more effectively. The Z model is presented in Figure 10.3.

According to this model, good problem solving has four steps:

1. *Examine the facts and details.* Use sensing to gather information about the problem.

2. *Generate alternatives.* Use intuiting to develop possibilities.

3. *Analyze the alternatives objectively.* Use thinking to logically determine the effects of each alternative.

4. *Weigh the impact.* Use feeling to determine how the people involved will be affected.

Using the Z model can help an individual develop his or her nonpreferences. Another way to use the Z model is to rely on others to perform the nonpreferred activities. For example, an individual who is an NF might want to turn to a trusted NT for help in analyzing alternatives objectively.

10.3   The Z Problem-Solving Model

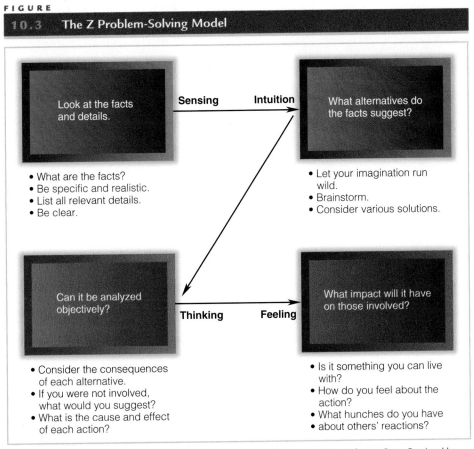

Look at the facts and details.

Sensing → **Intuition**

What alternatives do the facts suggest?

- What are the facts?
- Be specific and realistic.
- List all relevant details.
- Be clear.

- Let your imagination run wild.
- Brainstorm.
- Consider various solutions.

Can it be analyzed objectively?

Thinking → **Feeling**

What impact will it have on those involved?

- Consider the consequences of each alternative.
- If you were not involved, what would you suggest?
- What is the cause and effect of each action?

- Is it something you can live with?
- How do you feel about the action?
- What hunches do you have
- about others' reactions?

SOURCE: Excerpted from *Type Talk at Work* by Otto Kroeger and Janet M. Thuesen, 1992, Delacorte Press. Reprinted by permission of Otto Kroeger Associates.

OTHER INDIVIDUAL INFLUENCES ON DECISION MAKING

In addition to the cognitive styles just examined, many other individual differences affect a manager's decision making. Other personality characteristics, attitudes, and values, along with all of the individual differences variables that were discussed in Chapters 3 and 4, have implications for managerial decision making. Managers must use both their logic and their creativity to make effective decisions. Most of us are more comfortable using either logic or creativity, and we show that preference in everyday decision making. You 10.1 is an activity that will tell you which process, logic or creativity, is your preferred one. Take You 10.1 now, and then read on to interpret your score.

Brain hemispheric dominance is related to students' choices of college majors. Left-brained students gravitate toward business, engineering, and sciences, whereas right-brained students are attracted to education, nursing, communication, and literature.[36]

Our brains have two lateral halves (Figure 10.4). The right side is the center for creative functions, while the left side is the center for logic, detail, and planning. There are advantages to both kinds of thinking, so the ideal situation is to be "brain-lateralized" or to be able to use either logic or creativity or both, depending on the situation. There are ways to develop the side of the brain you are not accustomed to using. To develop your right side, or creative side, you can ask "what-if" questions, engage in play, and follow your intuition. To develop the left side, you can set goals for completing tasks and work to attain these goals. For managers, it is important to see the big picture, craft a vision, and plan strategically—all of which require right-brain skills. It is equally important to be able to understand day-to-day operations and flow chart work processes, which are left-hemisphere brain skills.

Which Side of Your Brain Do You Favor?

There are no "right" or "wrong" answers to this questionnaire. It is more of a self-assessment than a test. Do not read the questions more than once. Don't overanalyze. Merely circle "a" or "b" to indicate which answer is more typical of you.

1. Typically, when I have a problem to solve,
   a. I make a list of possible solutions, prioritize them, and then select the best answer.
   b. I "let it sit" for a while or talk it over with someone before I attempt to reach a solution.

2. When I sit with my hands clasped in my lap (FOLD YOUR HANDS THAT WAY RIGHT NOW BEFORE GOING ON, THEN LOOK AT YOUR HANDS), the thumb that is on top is
   a. my right thumb.
   b. my left thumb.

3. I have hunches
   a. sometimes, but do not place much faith in them.
   b. frequently and I usually follow them.

4. If I am at a meeting or lecture, I tend to take extensive notes.
   a. True
   b. False

5. I am well organized, have a system for doing things, have a place for everything and everything in its place, and can assimilate information quickly and logically.
   a. True
   b. False

6. I am good with numbers.
   a. True
   b. False

7. Finding words in a dictionary or looking up names in a telephone book is something I can do easily and quickly.
   a. True
   b. False

8. If I want to remember directions or other information,
   a. I make notes.
   b. I visualize the information.

9. I express myself well verbally.
   a. True
   b. False

10. To learn dance steps or athletic moves,
   a. I try to understand the sequence of the steps and repeat them mentally.
   b. I don't think about it; I just try to get the feel of the game or the music.

Interpretation:

- Four, five, or six "a" answers indicate lateralization—an ability to use either hemisphere easily and to solve problems according to their nature rather than according to a favored manner.

- One, two, or three "a" answers indicate right-hemisphere dominance; corresponding traits include inventiveness, creativity, innovation, risk taking, whimsy, and an ability to see the "big picture."

- Seven, eight, or nine "a" answers indicate a left-hemisphere dominance—a tendency toward attention to detail, the use of logic, and traits of thoroughness and accuracy.

SOURCE: "Which Side of the Brain Do You Favor?" from *Quality Driven Designs*. Copyright 1992 Pfeiffer/Jossey-Bass. Reprinted by permission of Jossey-Bass, Inc., a subsidiary of John Wiley & Sons, Inc.

Two particular individual influences that can enhance decision-making effectiveness will be highlighted next: intuition and creativity.

The Role of Intuition

3 Describe and evaluate the role of intuition and creativity in decision making.

There is evidence that managers use their *intuition* to make decisions.[37] Henry Mintzberg, in his work on managerial roles, found that in many cases managers do not appear to use a systematic, step-by-step approach to decision making.

FIGURE

10.4 Functions of the Left and Right Brain Hemispheres

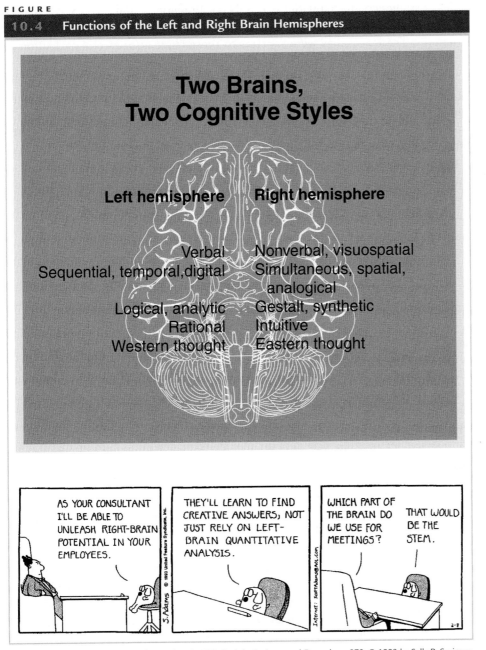

SOURCES: Created based on ideas from *Left Brain, Right Brain* by Springer and Deutsch, p. 272. © 1993 by Sally P. Springer and Georg Deutsch (New York: W. H. Freeman and Company, 1993). DILBERT reprinted by permission of United Feature Syndicate, Inc.

Rather, Mintzberg argued, managers make judgments based on "hunches."[38] Daniel Isenberg studied the way senior managers make decisions and found that intuition was used extensively, especially as a mechanism to evaluate decisions made more rationally.[39]

Robert Beck studied the way managers at BankAmerica (now Bank of America) made decisions about the future direction of the company following the deregulation of the banking industry. Beck described their use of intuition as an antidote to "analysis paralysis," or the tendency to analyze decisions rather than developing innovative solutions.[40]

Dr. Gary Klein, a renowned cognitive psychologist, has written a book on the power of intuition. Dr. Klein and his colleagues insist that skilled decision makers rely on patterns of learned information in making quick and efficient decisions. In a

intuition

A fast, positive force in decision making that is utilized at a level below consciousness and involves learned patterns of information.

series of studies conducted with the U.S. Navy, firefighters, and the U.S. Army, they found that decision makers normally relied on intuition in unfamiliar, challenging situations. These decisions were superior to those made after careful evaluation of information and potential alternatives.[41]

Just what is intuition? In Jungian theory, intuiting (N) is one preference used to gather data. This is only one way that the concept of intuition has been applied to managerial decision making, and it is perhaps the most widely researched form of the concept of intuition. There are, however, many definitions of *intuition* in the managerial literature. Chester Barnard, one of the early influential management researchers, argued that intuition's main attributes were speed and the inability of the decision maker to determine how the decision was made.[42] Other researchers have contended that intuition occurs at an unconscious level, and that this is why the decision maker cannot verbalize how the decision was made.[43]

Intuition has been variously described as follows:

- The ability to know or recognize quickly and readily the possibilities of a situation.[44]

- Smooth automatic performance of learned behavior sequences.[45]

- Simple analyses frozen into habit and into the capacity for rapid response through recognition.[46]

These definitions share some common assumptions. First, there seems to be a notion that intuition is fast. Second, intuition is utilized at a level below consciousness. Third, there seems to be agreement that intuition involves learned patterns of information. Fourth, intuition appears to be a positive force in decision making.

The use of intuition may lead to more ethical decisions. Intuition allows an individual to take on another's role with ease, and role taking is a fundamental part of developing moral reasoning. You may recall from Chapter 4 the role of cognitive moral development in ethical decision making. One study found a strong link between cognitive moral development and intuition. The development of new perspectives through intuition leads to higher moral growth, and thus to more ethical decisions.[47]

One question that arises is whether managers can be taught to use their intuition. Weston Agor, who has conducted workshops on developing intuitive skills in managers, has attained positive results in organizations such as the city of Phoenix and entertainment powerhouse Walt Disney Enterprises. After giving intuition tests to more than 10,000 executives, he has concluded that in most cases, higher management positions are held by individuals with higher levels of intuition. Just as the brain needs both hemispheres to work, Agor cautions that organizations need both analytical and intuitive minds to function at their peak. Consider Grant Tinker, former head of NBC. "Sometimes the boss has to go by his gut, hold his nose, and jump," Tinker writes in *Tinker in Television*. Lee Iacocca, in his autobiography, spends pages extolling intuition: "To a certain extent, I've always operated by gut feeling."[48] Agor suggests relaxation techniques, using images to guide the mind, and taking creative pauses before making a decision.[49] A review of the research on intuition suggests that although intuition itself cannot be taught, managers can be trained to rely more fully on the promptings of their intuition.[50]

Intuition is an elusive concept, and one with many definitions. There is an interesting paradox regarding intuition. Some researchers view "rational" methods as preferable to intuition, yet satisfaction with a rational decision is usually determined by how the decision feels intuitively.[51] Intuition appears to have a positive effect on managerial decision making, but it is not without controversy. Some writers argue that intuition has its place and that instincts should be trusted, but not

The Real World 10.1

What's that Cool Building?

Can you believe this is a parking garage? Moore Ruble Yudell won numerous awards, including an American Architecture Award and a Design Green honor award for the Santa Monica Civic Center parking structure pictured here. Recycled steel was used, and reflective glass panels not only look good—they allow the maximum use of natural lighting and greatly reduce the consumption of electricity. Photovoltaic panels on the ceiling of the garage use solar energy, and the panels generate a third of the electricity used in the garage. A water recycling system is used in the sprinklers.

The company has long been committed to green practices, integrating strict energy conservation guidelines and the use of healthy building materials into its designs all over the world. The firm's projects include

Santa Monica Civic Center parking structure.

© Arcaid/Alamy

the U.S. Embassy in Berlin and the Wanhao Century Center office and hotel complex in Beijing, among a host of others. The "reduce-reuse-recycle" mantra is woven into all the company's projects and is shared by its staff of sixty professionals. Many of these employees are long-term (fifteen years or more) Moore Ruble Yudell staffers, which is a testament to the firm's commitment to fostering creativity and professional growth among individuals.

Projects like this one illustrate that creative ideas can be used to address social and environmental challenges—in essence, green business is creative business.

SOURCES: D. Philadelphia, "Green Business," *Fortune Small Business* (October 2008): 23; www.moorerubleyudell.com.

---

as a substitute for reason. With new technologies, managers can analyze a lot more information in a lot less time, making the rational method less time-consuming than it once was.[52]

Creativity at Work

Creativity is a process influenced by individual and organizational factors that results in the production of novel and useful ideas, products, or both.[53] The social and technological changes that organizations face require creative decisions.[54] Architectural firm Moore Ruble Yudell has long been committed to sustainability and green practices. In Real World 10.1, you can see the creativity that went into their design of an award-winning building—a parking garage!

Creativity is a process that is at least in part unconscious. The four stages of the creative process are preparation, incubation, illumination, and verification.[55] Preparation means seeking out new experiences and opportunities to learn, because creativity grows from a base of knowledge. Travel and educational opportunities of all kinds open the individual's mind. Incubation is a process of reflective thought and is often conducted subconsciously. During incubation, the individual engages in other pursuits while the mind considers the problem and works on it. Illumination occurs when the individual senses an insight for solving the problem. Finally, verification is conducted to determine if the solution or idea is valid. This is accomplished by thinking through the implications of the decision, presenting it to another person, or trying it out. Sleep is an important contributor to creative problem solving. Momentary quieting of the brain through relaxation can also increase "coherence"

creativity
A process influenced by individual and organizational factors that results in the production of novel and useful ideas, products, or both.

or the ability of different parts of the brain to work together.[56,57] Both individual and organizational influences affect the creative process.

Individual Influences Several individual variables are related to creativity. One group of factors involves the cognitive processes that creative individuals tend to use. One cognitive process is divergent thinking, meaning the individual's ability to generate several potential solutions to a problem.[58] In addition, associational abilities and the use of imagery are associated with creativity.[59] Unconscious processes such as dreams are also essential cognitive processes related to creative thinking.[60]

Personality factors have also been related to creativity in studies of individuals from several different occupations. These characteristics include intellectual and artistic values, breadth of interests, high energy, concern with achievement, independence of judgment, intuition, self-confidence, and a creative self-image.[61] Tolerance of ambiguity, intrinsic motivation, risk taking, and a desire for recognition are also associated with creativity.[62]

There is also evidence that people who are in a good mood are more creative.[63] Positive affect is related to creativity in work teams because being in a positive mood allows team members to explore new ways of thinking.[64] Positive emotions enhance creativity by broadening one's cognitive patterns and resources. For example, repeated experiences of love, interest, courage, and gratitude cause one to discard old theories and automatic ways of doing things. Instead, these positive emotions initiate thoughts and actions that are novel and unscripted.[65,66] Moreover, it is a cyclical process, because creative thoughts and incidents lead to more positive affect. You might say that thinking positively makes us more creative, and being more creative makes us think positively.[67] In tasks involving considerable cognitive demands, however, it has been found that people in negative moods perform better. When an individual experiences negative moods or emotions, it is a signal that all is not well, which leads to more attention and vigilance in cognitive activity. Positive moods signal that all is well with the status quo, which can lead to decreased performance on some decision-making tasks involving complex mental activity.[68,69]

Organizational Influences The organizational environment people work in can either support or impede creativity. Creativity killers include focusing on how work is going to be evaluated, being closely monitored while you are working, and competing with other people in win–lose situations. By contrast, creativity facilitators include feelings of autonomy, being part of a team with diverse skills, and having creative supervisors and coworkers.[70] High-quality, supportive relationships with supervisors are related to creativity.[71] High-quality social networks that are cohesive can have a positive impact on creative decision making. Such social networks encourage creative decision making by facilitating shared sense-making of relevant information and consensus building.[72] Flexible organizational structures and participative decision making have also been associated with creativity. An organization can also present impediments to creativity. These barriers include internal political problems, harsh criticism of new ideas, destructive internal competition, and avoidance of risk.[73] The physical environment can also hamper creativity. Companies like Oticon, a Danish hearing-aid manufacturer, and Ethicon Endo-Surgery, a division of Johnson & Johnson, use open-plan offices that eliminate office walls and cubicles so that employees interact more frequently. When people mix, ideas mix as well.[74]

Studies of the role of organizational rewards in encouraging creativity have mixed results. Some studies have shown that monetary incentives improve creative performance, whereas others have found that is not the case.[75] Still other studies have indicated that explicitly contracting to obtain a reward led to lower levels of creativity when compared with contracting for no reward, being presented with just the task,

You 10.2

Creative or Logical Problem Solving: What Is Your Preference?

Try the following creative problem-solving challenge.

Each of the following problems is an equation that can be solved by substituting the appropriate words for the letters. Have fun with them!

Examples: 3F = 1Y (3 feet = 1 yard.)
4LC = GL (4 leaf clover = Good luck.)

1. M + M + NH + V + C + RI = NE.
2. "1B in the H = 2 in the B."
3. 8D − 24H = 1W.
4. 3P = 6.
5. HH & MH at 12 = N or M.
6. 4J + 4Q + 4K = All the FC.
7. S & M & T & W & T & F & S are D of W.
8. A + N + AF + MC + CG = AF.
9. T = LS State.
10. 23Y − 3Y = 2D.
11. E − 8 = Z.
12. Y + 2D = T.
13. C + 6D = NYE.
14. Y − S − S − A = W.
15. A & E were in the G of E.
16. My FL and South P are both MC.
17. "NN = GN."
18. N − P + SM = S of C.
19. 1 + 6Z = 1M.
20. "R = R = R."
21. AL & JG & WM & JK were all A.
22. N + V + P + A + A + C + P + I = P of S.
23. S + H of R = USC.

SOURCE: From *A Whack on the Side of the Head* by Roger Von Oech. Copyright © 1983, 1990, 1998 by Roger Von Oech. By permission of Warner Books.

Now try the following logical problem-solving exercise, entitled "Who Owns the Fish?", which is attributed to Albert Einstein.

There are five houses in a row and in five different colors. In each house lives a person from a different country. Each person drinks a certain drink, plays a certain game, and keeps a certain pet. No two people drink the same drink, play the same game, or keep the same pet.

- The Brit lives in a red house.
- The Swede keeps dogs.
- The Dane drinks tea.
- The green house is on the left of the white house.
- The green house owner drinks coffee.
- The person who plays tennis rears birds.
- The owner of the yellow house plays chess.
- The man living in the house right in the center drinks milk.
- The Norwegian lives in the first house.
- The man who plays poker lives next to the man who keeps cats.
- The man who keeps horses lives next to the one who plays chess.
- The man who plays billiards drinks beer.
- The German plays golf.
- The Norwegian lives next to the blue house.
- The man who plays poker has a neighbor who drinks water.

Question: Who owns the fish?
Answer: Your instructor can provide the solutions to this exercise.

SOURCE: By E. O. Welles, © 2004 Gruner + Jahr USA Publishing. "The Billionaire Next Door," first published in *Inc. Magazine* 23(6) (May 2001): 80–85. Reprinted with permission.

or being presented with the task and receiving the reward later.[76] Organizations can therefore enhance individuals' creative decision making by providing a supportive environment, participative decision making, and a flexible structure.

Individual/Organization Fit Research has indicated that creative performance is highest when there is a match, or fit, between the individual and organizational influences on creativity. For example, when individuals who desire to be creative are matched with an organization that values creative ideas, the result is more creative performance.[77]

A common mistaken assumption regarding creativity is that either you have it or you do not. Research refutes this myth and has shown that individuals can be trained to be more creative.[78] The Disney Institute features a wide range of programs offered to companies, and one of their bestsellers is creativity training. You 10.2 allows you to determine whether you prefer creative or logical problem solving.

Part of creativity training involves learning to open up mental locks that keep us from generating creative alternatives to a decision or problem. The following are some mental locks that diminish creativity:

- Searching for the "right" answer.
- Trying to be logical.
- Following the rules.
- Avoiding ambiguity.
- Striving for practicality.
- Being afraid to look foolish.
- Avoiding problems outside our own expertise.
- Fearing failure.
- Believing we are not really creative.
- Not making play a part of work.[79]

4 Critique your own level of creativity and list ways of improving it.

Note that many of these mental locks stem from values within organizations. Organizations can facilitate creative decision making in many ways. Rewarding creativity, allowing employees to fail, making work more fun, and providing creativity training are a few suggestions. Also, companies can encourage creativity by exposing employees to new ideas. This can be done in several ways, including job rotation, which moves employees through different jobs and gives them exposure to different information, projects, and teams. Employees can also be assigned to work with groups outside the company, such as suppliers or consultants. Finally, managers can encourage employees to surround themselves with stimuli that they have found to enhance their creative processes. These may be music, artwork, books, or anything else that encourages creative thinking.[80]

We have seen that both individual and organizational factors can produce creativity. Creativity can also mean finding problems as well as fixing them. Recently, four different types of creativity have been proposed, based on the source of the trigger (internal or external) and the source of the problem (presented versus discovered). Responsive creativity means responding to a problem that is presented to you by others because it is part of your job. Expected creativity is discovering problems because you are expected to by the organization. Contributory creativity is responding to problems presented to you because you want to be creative. Proactive creativity is discovering problems because you want to be creative.[81]

3M consistently ranks among the top ten in *Fortune*'s annual list of most admired corporations. It earned this reputation through innovation: More than one-quarter of 3M's sales are from products less than four years old. Post-It Notes, for example, were created by a worker who wanted little adhesive papers to mark hymns for church service. He thought of another worker who had perfected a light adhesive, and the two spent their free time developing Post-It Notes. 3M has continued its tradition of innovation with Post-It Flags, Pop-Up Tape Strips, and Nexcare Ease-Off Bandages.

Leaders can play key roles in modeling creative behavior. Sir Richard Branson, founder and chairman of UK-based Virgin Group, believes that if you do not use your employees' creative potential, you are doomed to failure. At Virgin Group, the culture encourages risk taking and rewards innovation. Rules and regulations are not overvalued, nor is analyzing ideas to death. Branson says an employee can have an idea in the morning and implement it in the afternoon.[82]

Creativity is a global concern. Poland, for example, is undergoing a major shift from a centrally planned economy and monoparty rule to a market economy and Western-style democracy. One of the major concerns for Polish managers is creativity. Finding ingenious solutions and having the ability to think creatively can be a question of life or death for Polish organizations, which are making the transition to a faster pace of learning and change.[83]

Both intuition and creativity are important influences on managerial decision making. Both concepts require additional research so that managers can better understand how to use them as well as how to encourage employees to use them to make more effective decisions.

Sir Richard Branson, founder and chairman of the Virgin Group, encourages risk taking and innovation. Pictured is WhiteKnightTwo, an aircraft with which he hopes to begin creating a commercial space travel business.

PARTICIPATION IN DECISION MAKING

Effective management of people can improve a company's economic performance. Firms that capitalize on this fact share several common practices. Chief among them is participation of employees in decision making.[84] Many companies do this through highly empowered self-managed teams like the ones we discussed in Chapter 9. Even in situations where formal teams are not feasible, decision authority can be handed down to front-line employees who have the knowledge and skills to make a difference. At Hampton Inn hotels, for example, guest services personnel have the power to do whatever is necessary to make guests happy—without consulting their superiors.

The Effects of Participation

Participative decision making occurs when individuals who are affected by decisions influence the making of those decisions. Participation buffers employees from the negative experiences of organizational politics.[85] Participation in decisions such as how technology is developed at one's organization has also been found to relate to people's attitudes toward the technology and how they use it.[86] In addition, participative management has been found to increase employee creativity, job satisfaction, and productivity.[87]

GE Capital believes in participation. Each year it holds dreaming sessions, and employees from all levels of the company attend strategy and budget meetings to discuss where the company is heading. As a result, young employees came up with e-commerce ideas through Web sites like http://www.financiallearning.com and http://www.gefn.com, which were highly successful.[88]

As our economy becomes increasingly based on knowledge work, and as new technologies make it easier for decentralized decision makers to connect, participative decision making will undoubtedly increase.[89] Consider the city and county of San Francisco, a combined city/county government organization. When the city and county of San Francisco needed to adopt a single messaging system to meet the needs of more than 20,000 users, it faced a huge challenge in getting all the users to provide input into the decision. Technology helped craft a system that balanced

participative decision making
Decision making in which individuals who are affected by decisions influence the making of those decisions.

the needs of all the groups involved, and IT planners developed a twenty-eight-page spreadsheet to pull together the needs and desires of all sixty departments into a focused decision matrix. Within two years, 90 percent of the users had agreed on and moved to a single system, reducing costs and complexity.[90]

Foundations for Participation in Decision Making

What conditions must be in place in order for participative decision making to work? The organizational foundations include a supportive organizational culture and a team-oriented work design. A supportive work environment is essential because of the uncertainty within the organization. Lower level organizational members must be able to make decisions and take action on them. As operational employees are encouraged to take part in making decisions, fear, anxiety, or even terror can be created among middle managers in the organization.[91] Senior leadership must create an organizational culture that is supportive and reassuring for these middle managers as the power dynamics of the system change. If not supported and reassured, the middle managers can become a restraining, disruptive force to participative decision-making efforts.

A second organizational foundation for participative decision making concerns the design of work. Team-oriented work designs are a key organizational foundation because they lead to broader tasks and a greater sense of responsibility. For example, Volvo builds cars using a team-oriented work design in which each person does many different tasks, and each person has direct responsibility for the finished product.[92] These work designs create a context for effective participation as long as the empowered individuals meet necessary individual prerequisites.

The three individual prerequisites for participative decision making are (1) the capability to become psychologically involved in participative activities, (2) the motivation to act autonomously, and (3) the capacity to see the relevance of participation for one's own well-being.[93] First, people must be psychologically equipped to become involved in participative activities if they are to be effective team members. Not all people are so predisposed. For example, Germany has an authoritarian tradition that runs counter to participative decision making at the individual and group level. General Motors encountered significant difficulties implementing quality circles in its German plants, because workers expected to be directed by supervisors, not to engage in participative problem solving. The German initiatives to establish supervisory/worker boards in corporations are intended to change this authoritarian tradition.

A second individual prerequisite is the motivation to act autonomously. People with dependent personalities are predisposed to be told what to do and to rely on external motivation rather than internal, intrinsic motivation.[94] These dependent people are not effective contributors to decision making.

Finally, if participative decision making is to work, people must be able to see how it provides a personal benefit to them. The personal pay-off for the individual need not be short term. It may be a long-term benefit that results in people receiving greater rewards through enhanced organizational profitability.

What Level of Participation?

Participative decision making is complex, and one of the things managers must understand is that employees can be involved in some, or all, of the stages of the decision-making process. For example, employees could be variously involved in identifying problems, generating alternatives, selecting solutions, planning implementations, or evaluating results. Research shows that greater involvement in all five of these stages has a cumulative effect. Employees who are involved in all five processes have higher satisfaction and performance levels. And all decision processes are not created equal. If employees can't be provided with full participation in all stages, the highest pay-offs seem to come with involvement in generating alternatives, planning implementations, and evaluating results.[95] Styles of participation in decision making may need to change as the company grows or as its culture changes.

THE GROUP DECISION-MAKING PROCESS

Managers use groups to make decisions for several reasons. One is *synergy*, which occurs when group members stimulate new solutions to problems through the process of mutual influence and encouragement within the group. Another reason for using a group is to gain commitment to a decision. Groups also bring more knowledge and experience to the problem-solving situation.

Group decisions can sometimes be predicted by comparing the views of the initial group members with the final group decision. These simple relationships are known as *social decision schemes*. One social decision scheme is the majority-wins rule, in which the group supports whatever position is taken by the majority of its members. Another scheme, the truth-wins rule, predicts that the correct decision will emerge as an increasing number of members realize its appropriateness. The two-thirds-majority rule means that the decision favored by two-thirds or more of the members is supported. Finally, the first-shift rule states that members support a decision represented by the first shift in opinion shown by a member.

Research indicates that these social decision schemes can predict a group decision as much as 80 percent of the time.[96] Current research is aimed at discovering which rules are used in particular types of tasks. For example, studies indicate that the majority-wins rule is used most often in judgment tasks (i.e., when the decision is a matter of preference or opinion), whereas the truth-wins rule predicts decisions best when the task is an intellective one (i.e., when the decision has a correct answer).[97]

Advantages and Disadvantages of Group Decision Making

Both advantages and disadvantages are associated with group decision making. The advantages include (1) more knowledge and information through the pooling of group member resources; (2) increased acceptance of, and commitment to, the decision, because the members had a voice in it; and (3) greater understanding of the decision, because members were involved in the various stages of the decision process. The disadvantages of group decision making include (1) pressure within the group to conform and fit in; (2) domination of the group by one forceful member or a dominant clique, who may ramrod the decision; and (3) the amount of time required, because a group makes decisions more slowly than an individual.[98]

Given these advantages and disadvantages, should an individual or a group make a decision? Substantial empirical research indicates that whether a group or an individual should be used depends on the type of task involved. For judgment tasks requiring an estimate or a prediction, groups are usually superior to individuals because of the breadth of experience that multiple individuals bring to the problem.[99] On tasks that have a correct solution, other studies have indicated that the most competent individual outperforms the group.[100] This finding has been called into question, however. Much of the previous research on groups was conducted in the laboratory, where group members interacted only for short periods of time. Researchers

5 Compare and contrast the advantages and disadvantages of group decision making.

synergy
A positive force that occurs in groups when group members stimulate new solutions to problems through the process of mutual influence and encouragement within the group.

social decision schemes
Simple rules used to determine final group decisions.

wanted to know how a longer experience in the group would affect decisions. Their study showed that groups who worked together for longer periods of time outperformed the most competent member 70 percent of the time. As groups gained experience, the best members became less important to the group's success.[101] This study demonstrated that experience in the group is an important variable to consider when evaluating the individual versus group decision-making question.

Research is just beginning on the role of trust and trustworthiness in team decision making. One study was conducted for six weeks on student teams that were involved in designing an information systems project. The teams' trust of each other and risk-taking actions were cyclical. When teams saw the other team as trustworthy, they took a risk; then the other team, based on their perception of the first team's trustworthiness, decided whether or not to take a risk, and so on. The study showed that the trust process works between teams much the same as it does between individuals.[102]

Given the emphasis on teams in the workplace, many managers believe that groups produce better decisions than do individuals, yet the evidence is mixed. It is clear that more research needs to be conducted in organizational settings to help answer this question.

Two potential liabilities are found in group decision making: groupthink and group polarization. These problems are discussed in the following sections.

Groupthink

6 Discuss the symptoms of groupthink and ways to prevent it.

One liability of a cohesive group is its tendency to develop *groupthink*, a dysfunctional process. Irving Janis, the originator of the groupthink concept, describes groupthink as "a deterioration of mental efficiency, reality testing, and moral judgment" resulting from pressures within the group.[103]

Certain conditions favor the development of groupthink. One of the conditions is high cohesiveness. Cohesive groups tend to favor solidarity because members identify strongly with the group.[104] High-ranking teams that make decisions without outside help are especially prone to groupthink because they are likely to have shared mental models; that is, they are more likely to think alike.[105] And homogeneous groups (ones with little to no diversity among members) are more likely to suffer from groupthink.[106] Two other conditions that encourage groupthink are having to make a highly consequential decision and time constraints.[107] A highly consequential decision is one that will have a great impact on the group members and on outside parties. When group members feel that they have a limited time in which to make a decision, they may rush through the process. These antecedents cause members to prefer concurrence in decisions and to fail to evaluate one another's suggestions critically. A group suffering from groupthink shows recognizable symptoms. Table 10.1 presents these symptoms and makes suggestions on how to avoid groupthink.

An incident cited as a prime example of groupthink is the 1986 *Challenger* disaster, in which the shuttle exploded and killed all seven crew members. A presidential commission concluded that flawed decision making was the primary cause of the accident. Sadly, organizations often struggle to learn from their mistakes. In 2003, the shuttle *Columbia* exploded over Texas upon reentering the Earth's atmosphere, killing all seven crew members. Within days of the *Columbia* disaster, questions began to surface about the decision-making process that led flight engineers to assume that damage caused to the shuttle upon take-off was minor and to continue the mission. Subsequent investigation led observers to note that NASA's decision-making process appears just as flawed today as it was in 1986, exhibiting all the classic symptoms of groupthink. The final accident report blamed the NASA culture that downplayed risk and suppressed dissent for the decision.[108, 109]

groupthink
A deterioration of mental efficiency, reality testing, and moral judgment resulting from pressures within the group.

10.1   Symptoms of Groupthink and How to Prevent It

Symptoms of Groupthink

- *Illusions of invulnerability.* Group members feel that they are above criticism. This symptom leads to excessive optimism and risk taking.

- *Illusions of group morality.* Group members feel they are moral in their actions and therefore above reproach. This symptom leads the group to ignore the ethical implications of their decisions.

- *Illusions of unanimity.* Group members believe there is unanimous agreement on the decisions. Silence is misconstrued as consent.

- *Rationalization.* Group members concoct explanations for their decisions to make them appear rational and correct. The results are that other alternatives are not considered, and there is an unwillingness to reconsider the group's assumptions.

- *Stereotyping the enemy.* Competitors are stereotyped as evil or stupid. This leads the group to underestimate its opposition.

- *Self-censorship.* Members do not express their doubts or concerns about the course of action. This prevents critical analysis of the decisions.

- *Peer pressure.* Any members who express doubts or concerns are pressured by other group members who question their loyalty.

- *Mindguards.* Some members take it upon themselves to protect the group from negative feedback. Group members are thus shielded from information that might lead them to question their actions.

Guidelines for Preventing Groupthink

- Ask each group member to assume the role of the critical evaluator who actively voices objections or doubts.

- Have the leader avoid stating his or her position on the issue prior to the group decision.

- Create several groups that work on the decision simultaneously.

- Bring in outside experts to evaluate the group process.

- Appoint a devil's advocate to question the group's course of action consistently.

- Evaluate the competition carefully, posing as many different motivations and intentions as possible.

- Once consensus is reached, encourage the group to rethink its position by reexamining the alternatives.

SOURCE: Irving L. Janis, *Groupthink: Psychological Studies of Policy Decisions and Fiascoes,* 2nd ed. Copyright © 1982 by Houghton Mifflin Company. Used with permission.

Consequences of groupthink include an incomplete survey of alternatives, failure to evaluate the risks of the preferred course of action, biased information processing, and a failure to work out contingency plans. The overall result of groupthink is defective decision making. Groupthink may be a contributor to corruption in organizations. Beech-Nut sold millions of dollars of phony apple juice, and investigations indicated that employees were aware that the company had been using cheap concentrate. Employees rationalized their actions by saying that other companies were selling fake juice, and that it was safe to consume. Ultimately, after incurring $25 million in fines and legal costs, the company was almost destroyed.[110]

Table 10.1 presents Janis's guidelines for avoiding groupthink. Many of these suggestions center around the notion of ensuring that decisions are evaluated completely, with opportunities for discussion from all group members. This strategy helps encourage members to evaluate one another's ideas critically. Groups that are educated about the value of diversity tend to perform better at decision-making tasks. On the other hand, groups that are homogenous and are not educated about the value of diversity do not accrue such benefits in decision making.[111]

Janis has used the groupthink framework to conduct historical analyses of several political and military fiascoes, including the Bay of Pigs invasion, the Vietnam War, and Watergate. One review of the decision situation in the *Challenger* incident proposed that two variables, time and leadership style, are important to include.[112] When a decision must be made quickly, there is more potential for groupthink. Leadership style can either promote groupthink (if the leader makes his or her opinion known up-front) or avoid groupthink (if the leader encourages open and frank discussion).

There are few empirical studies of groupthink, and most of these involved students in a laboratory setting. More applied research may be seen in the future, however, as a questionnaire has been developed to measure the constructs associated with groupthink.[113] Janis's work on groupthink has led to several interdisciplinary efforts at understanding policy decisions.[114] The work underscores the need to examine multiple explanations for failed decisions. Teams that experience cognitive (task-based) conflict are found to make better decisions than teams that experience affective (emotion-based) conflict. As such, one prescription for managers has been to encourage cognitive conflict while minimizing affective conflict. However, these two forms of conflict can also occur together, and more research is needed on how one can be encouraged while minimizing the other.[115]

Group Polarization

Another group phenomenon was discovered by a graduate student. His study showed that groups made riskier decisions; in fact, the group and each individual accepted greater levels of risk following a group discussion of the issue. Subsequent studies uncovered another shift—toward caution. Thus, group discussion produced shifts both toward more risky positions and toward more cautious positions.[116] Further research revealed that individual group member attitudes simply became more extreme following group discussion. Individuals who were initially against an issue became more radically opposed, and individuals who were in favor of the issue became more strongly supportive following discussion. These shifts came to be known as *group polarization*.[117]

The tendency toward polarization has important implications for group decision making. Groups whose initial views lean a certain way can be expected to adopt more extreme views following interaction.

Several ideas have been proposed to explain why group polarization occurs. One explanation is the social comparison approach. Prior to group discussion, individuals believe they hold better views than the other members. During group discussion, they see that their views are not so far from average, so they shift to more extreme positions.[118] A second explanation is the persuasive arguments view. It contends that group discussion reinforces the initial views of the members, so they take a more extreme position.[119] Both explanations are supported by research. It may be that both processes, along with others, cause the group to develop more polarized attitudes.

Group polarization leads groups to adopt extreme attitudes. In some cases, this can be disastrous. For instance, if individuals are leaning toward a dangerous decision, they are likely to support it more strongly following discussion. Group polarization impacts group discussions on hiring. A recent study investigated how group discussions affected raters during hiring decisions, and results indicated that after discussing as a group, employers were less accurate in their ratings and had greater contrast effects and increased halo effects.[120] Both groupthink and group

group polarization
The tendency for group discussion to produce shifts toward more extreme attitudes among members.

polarization are potential liabilities of group decision making, but several techniques can be used to help prevent or control these two liabilities.

TECHNIQUES FOR GROUP DECISION MAKING

Once a manager has determined that a group decision approach should be used, he or she can determine the technique that is best suited to the decision situation. Seven techniques will be briefly summarized: brainstorming, nominal group technique, Delphi technique, devil's advocacy, dialectical inquiry, quality circles and quality teams, and self-managed teams.

7 Evaluate the strengths and weaknesses of several group decision-making techniques.

Brainstorming

Brainstorming is a good technique for generating alternatives. The idea behind *brainstorming* is to generate as many ideas as possible, suspending evaluation until all of the ideas have been suggested. Participants are encouraged to build on the suggestions of others, and imagination is emphasized. One company that uses brainstorming intensively is IDEO, a world-class new product design firm. In Real World 10.2, you can see their brainstorming recommendations.

One recent trend is the use of electronic rather than verbal brainstorming in groups. Electronic brainstorming overcomes two common problems that can produce group brainstorming failure: production blocking and evaluation apprehension. In verbal brainstorming, individuals are exposed to the inputs of others.

> **brainstorming**
> A technique for generating as many ideas as possible on a given subject, while suspending evaluation until all the ideas have been suggested.

The Real World 10.2

Brainstorming at Ideo: Are Cookies the Secret?

Brainstorming is so much a part of the culture at Ideo that it has its own set of beliefs about what makes it work best. First, morning meetings are best for creativity. Second, group sizes of three to ten people are most productive for brainstorming. And third, cookies always help people be more productive. These three simple beliefs have helped Ideo Product Development become a leading product design firm. Some of its most famous creations include the Apple mouse, the Palm V, the Oral-B toothbrush for kids, and a lifelike mechanical whale used in the movie Free Willy.

At Ideo, the brainstorming sessions are designed around fluency and flexibility. Fluency is a rapid-fire succession of ideas, so silence is minimized. Flexibility is looking at the idea from as many viewpoints as possible. Ideo's business has shifted from designing products to designing experiences and designing for behavioral change. For example, Ideo designed a Smart Gauge for the Ford Fusion that teaches people to drive the car in ways that maximize fuel efficiency, making using the Smart Gauge, and therefore saving fuel, fun for the driver. Ideo also created an interactive music experience for (RED)™ that allows subscribers to connect with friends and design a video with new music. While the subscribers are creating the video, they can see how many lives they've saved through (RED)'s Global Fund.

Fast Company named Ideo tenth on the list of the world's most innovative companies. Evidently, cookie-fueled brainstorming sessions work!

SOURCES: L. Tishler, "Seven Secrets to Good Brainstorming," *Fast Company* (December 19, 2007), accessed at http://www.fastcompany.com/node/63818/print; R. Saflan, "Presenting the 50 Most Innovative Companies," *Fast Company* (February 3, 2009), accessed at http://www.fastcompany.com/fast50_09/profile/list/ideo.

While listening to others, individuals are distracted from their own ideas.[121] This is referred to as production blocking. When ideas are recorded electronically, participants are free from hearing the interruptions of others; thus, production blocking is reduced. Some individuals suffer from evaluation apprehension in brainstorming groups. They fear that others might respond negatively to their ideas. In electronic brainstorming, input is anonymous, so evaluation apprehension is reduced. Studies indicate that anonymous electronic brainstorming groups outperform face-to-face brainstorming groups in the number of ideas generated.[122]

Nominal Group Technique

A structured approach to decision making that focuses on generating alternatives and choosing one is called *nominal group technique (NGT)*. NGT involves the following discrete steps:

1. Individuals silently list their ideas.
2. Ideas are written on a chart one at a time until all ideas are listed.
3. Discussion is permitted but only to clarify the ideas. No criticism is allowed.
4. A written vote is taken.

NGT is a good technique to use in a situation where group members fear criticism from others.[123]

Delphi Technique

The *Delphi technique*, which originated at the Rand Corporation, involves gathering the judgments of experts for use in decision making. Experts at remote locations respond to a questionnaire. A coordinator summarizes those responses, and the summary is sent back to the experts. The experts then rate the various alternatives generated, and the coordinator tabulates the results. The Delphi technique is valuable in its ability to generate a number of independent judgments without the requirement of a face-to-face meeting.[124]

Devil's Advocacy

In the *devil's advocacy* decision method, a group or individual is given the role of critic. This devil's advocate has the task of coming up with the potential problems of a proposed decision. This helps organizations avoid costly mistakes in decision making by identifying potential pitfalls in advance.[125] As we discussed in Chapter 9, a devil's advocate who challenges the CEO and top management team can help sustain the vitality and performance of the upper echelon.

Dialectical Inquiry

Dialectical inquiry is a debate between two opposing sets of recommendations. Although it sets up a conflict, it is a constructive approach, because it brings out the benefits and limitations of both sets of ideas.[126] When using this technique, it is important to guard against a win–lose attitude and to concentrate on reaching the most effective solution for all concerned. Research has shown that the way a decision is framed (i.e., win–win versus win–lose) is very important. A decision's outcome could be viewed as a gain or a loss, depending on the way the decision is framed.[127]

Quality Circles and Quality Teams

As you recall from Chapter 9, quality circles are small groups that voluntarily meet to provide input for solving quality or production problems. Quality circles are

nominal group technique (NGT)
A structured approach to group decision making that focuses on generating alternatives and choosing one.

Delphi technique
Gathering the judgments of experts for use in decision making.

devil's advocacy
A technique for preventing groupthink in which a group or individual is given the role of critic during decision making.

dialectical inquiry
A debate between two opposing sets of recommendations.

also a way of extending participative decision making into teams. Managers often listen to recommendations from quality circles and implement the suggestions. The rewards for the suggestions are intrinsic—involvement in the decision-making process is the primary one.

Quality circles are often generated from the bottom up; that is, they provide advice to managers, who still retain decision-making authority. As such, quality circles are not empowered to implement their own recommendations. They operate in parallel fashion to the organization's structure, and they rely on voluntary participation.[128] In Japan, quality circles have been integrated into the organization instead of added on. This may be one reason for Japan's success with this technique. By contrast, the U.S. experience is not as positive. It has been estimated that 60–75 percent of the quality circles have failed. Reasons for the failures have included lack of top management support and lack of problem-solving skills among quality circle members.[129]

Quality teams, by contrast, are included in total quality management and other quality improvement efforts as part of a change in the organization's structure. Quality teams are generated from the top down and are empowered to act on their own recommendations. Whereas quality circles emphasize the generation of ideas, quality teams make data-based decisions about improving product and service quality. Various decision-making techniques are employed in quality teams. Brainstorming, flow charts, and cause-and-effect diagrams help pinpoint problems that affect quality.

Some organizations have moved toward quality teams, but Toyota has stuck with quality circles. The company has used them since 1963 and was the second company in the world to do so. Toyota's quality circles constitute a limited form of empowerment—and they like it that way. The members want to participate but not be self-directed. They would rather leave certain decisions to managers who are trusted to take good care of them. Toyota attributes its success with quality circles to the longevity of their use and to its view of them as true methods of participation.[130]

Quality circles and quality teams are methods for using groups in the decision-making process. Self-managed teams take the concept of participation one step further.

Self-Managed Teams

Another group decision-making method is the use of self-managed teams, which we also discussed in Chapter 9. The decision-making activities of self-managed teams are more broadly focused than those of quality circles and quality teams, which usually emphasize quality and production problems. Self-managed teams make many of the decisions that were once reserved for managers, such as work scheduling, job assignments, and staffing. Unlike quality circles, whose role is an advisory one, self-managed teams are delegated authority in the organization's decision-making process.

Many organizations have claimed success with self-managed teams. At Northern Telecom (now Nortel Networks), revenues rose 63 percent and sales increased 26 percent following the implementation of self-managed teams.[131] Research evidence shows that such teams can lead to higher productivity, lower turnover among employees, and flatter organization structure.[132]

Self-managed teams, like any cohesive group, can fall victim to groupthink. The key to stimulating innovation and better problem solving in these groups is welcoming dissent among members. Dissent breaks down complacency and sets in motion a process that results in better decisions. Team members must know that dissent is permissible so that they won't fear embarrassment or ridicule.[133] Before choosing a group decision-making technique, the manager should carefully evaluate the group members and the decision situation. Then the best method for accomplishing the objectives of the group decision-making process can be selected. If the goal is generating a large number of alternatives, for example, brainstorming would be a good choice. If group members are reluctant to contribute ideas, the nominal group technique would be appropriate. The need for expert input would be best facilitated by the Delphi technique. To guard against groupthink, devil's advocacy or dialectical inquiry would be effective. Decisions that concern quality or production would benefit from the advice of quality circles or the empowered decisions of quality teams. Moreover, recent research suggests that if individuals within a team are made accountable for the process of decision making (rather than for the end decision itself), then such teams are more likely to gather diverse information, share information, and eventually make better decisions.[134] Finally, a manager who wants to provide total empowerment to a group should consider self-managed teams.

DIVERSITY AND CULTURE IN DECISION MAKING

Styles of decision making vary greatly among cultures. Many of the dimensions proposed by Hofstede that were presented in Chapter 2 affect decision making. Uncertainty avoidance, for example, can affect the way people view decisions. In the United States, a culture with low uncertainty avoidance, decisions are seen as opportunities for change. By contrast, cultures such as those of Indonesia and Malaysia attempt to accept situations as they are rather than to change them.[135] Power distance also affects decision making. In more hierarchical cultures, such as India, top-level managers make decisions. In countries with low power distance, lower-level employees make many decisions. The Swedish culture exemplifies this type.

The individualist/collectivist dimension has implications for decision making. Japan, with its collectivist emphasis, favors group decisions. The United States has a more difficult time with group decisions because it is an individualistic culture. Time orientation affects the frame of reference of the decision. In China, with its long-term view, decisions are made with the future in mind. In the United States, many decisions are made considering only the short term.

The masculine/feminine dimension can be compared to the Jungian thinking/feeling preferences for decision making. Masculine cultures, as in many Latin American countries, value quick, assertive decisions. Feminine cultures, as in many Scandinavian countries, value decisions that reflect concern for others.

Managers should learn as much as possible about the decision processes in other cultures. NAFTA, for example, has eliminated many barriers to trade with Mexico. In Mexican organizations, decision-making authority is centralized, autocratic, and retained in small groups of top managers. As a consequence, Mexican employees are reluctant to participate in decision making and often wait to be told what to do rather than take a risk. Significant differences exist amongst Hispanic work-related ethics and non-Hispanic work-related ethics as well. These differences need be managed effectively by managers to help individuals make decisions that are aligned with organizational values and ethics.[136] In addition, joint ventures with family-owned *grupos* (large groups of businesses) can be challenging. It may be difficult to identify the critical decision maker in the family and to determine how much decision-making authority is held by the *grupo's* family board.[137] Mexican managers may be more likely to engage in escalation of commitment or continue to invest in a losing venture. However, because lower level managers in Mexico have control over smaller amounts of resources, they tend to invest in smaller increments than do U.S. managers.[138]

Recent research examining the effects of cultural diversity on decision making has found that when individuals in a group are racially dissimilar, they engage in more open information sharing, encourage dissenting perspectives, and arrive at better decisions than racially similar groups.[139] Other kinds of diversity such as functional background have been studied as well. Top management teams that have members who come from a variety of functional backgrounds (e.g., marketing, accounting, information systems) engage in greater debate in decision making that top management teams in which the members come from similar backgrounds. This diversity results in better financial performance for the firm.[140] Research also indicates than strategic decision making in firms can vary widely by culture. For example, one such source of variation stems from the differential emphasis placed on environmental scanning in different cultures. Furthermore, strategic decision making might appear rational but is also informed by firm level and national characteristics.[141]

DECISION MAKING IN THE VIRTUAL WORKPLACE

Managers today are working in flexible organizations—so flexible in fact that many workplaces are unconstrained by geography, time, and organizational boundaries. Virtual teams are emerging as a new form of working arrangement. Virtual teams are groups of geographically dispersed coworkers who work together using a combination of telecommunications and information technologies to accomplish a task. Virtual teams seldom meet face to face, and membership often shifts according to the project at hand.

8 Explain the emerging role of virtual decision making in organizations.

How are decisions made in virtual teams? These teams require advanced technologies for communication and decision making. Many technologies aid virtual teams in decision making: desktop videoconferencing systems (DVCS), group decision support systems (GDSS), Internet/intranet systems, expert systems, and agent-based modeling (ABM).[142]

DVCS are the major technologies that form the basis for other virtual team technologies. DVCS recreate the face-to-face interactions of teams and go one step beyond by supporting more complex levels of communication among virtual team members. Small cameras on top of computer monitors provide video feeds, and voice transmissions are made possible through earpieces and microphones. High-speed data connections are used for communication. All team members can be connected, and outside experts can even be added. A local group can connect with up to fifteen different individuals or groups. Users can simultaneously work on documents, analyze data, or map out ideas.

Managers use decision support systems (DSS) as tools to enhance their ability to make complex decisions. DSS are computer and communication systems that process incoming data and synthesize pertinent information for managers to use. Another tool for decision making focuses on helping groups make decisions. A GDSS uses computer support and communication facilities to support group decision-making processes in either face-to-face meetings or dispersed meetings. The GDSS has been shown to affect conflict management within a group by depersonalizing the issue and by forcing the group to discuss its conflict management process.[143] Team decisions often improve by using a GDSS because members share information more fully when they use a GDSS.[144]

GDSS make real-time decision making possible in the virtual team. They are ideal systems for brainstorming, focus groups, and group decisions. By using support tools within the GDSS, users can turn off their individual identities and interact with anonymity, and can poll participants and assemble statistical information relevant to the decision being made. GDSS are thus the sophisticated software that makes collaboration possible in virtual teams.

Internal internets, or intranets, are adaptations of Internet technologies for use within a company. For virtual teams, the Internet and intranets can be rich communication and decision-making resources. These tools allow virtual teams to archive text, video, audio, and data files for use in decision making. They permit virtual teams to inform other organization members about the team's progress and enable the team to monitor other projects within the organization.

By using DVCS, GDSS, and Internet/intranet technologies, virtual teams can capitalize on a rich communications environment for decision making. It is difficult, however, to duplicate the face-to-face environment. The effectiveness of a virtual team's decision making depends on its members' ability to use the tools that are available. Collaborative systems can enhance virtual teams' decision quality if they are used well.[145]

ABM is an agent-based simulation in which a computer creates thousands, even millions, of individual actors known as agents. Each of these virtual agents makes virtual decisions, thus providing an estimate of how each decision type might affect outcomes.[146]

Several organizations have adopted ABM to evaluate potential consequences of important decisions. For example, when Macy's was considering a major remodeling of their store space, they enlisted the services of PricewaterhouseCoopers to develop an ABM system that virtually modeled the changes in floor plans and consumer's responses to these changes. This simulation helped Macy's experiment with differing layout plans in cyberspace, thus predicting consumer behavior before it risked costly changes in the real world. You can see that for organizations like Macy's, ABM is a software simulation that can be very useful in making complex, nonroutine decisions involving some degree of uncertainty.

Decision making in the virtual workplace is characterized by the use of sophisticated technologies to assist in decision making. Some of these technologies, like videoconferencing, DSS, and GDSS, simply assist humans in making the decision. Others, like expert systems and some forms of ABM, play a greater role in making the decision. Regardless of the degree to which they play a role, all of these technologies make decision making in today's virtual workplace easier.

ETHICAL ISSUES IN DECISION MAKING

9 Utilize an "ethics check" for examining managerial decisions.

One criterion that should be applied to decision making is the ethical implications of the decision. Ethical decision making in organizations is influenced by many factors, including individual differences and organizational rewards and punishments.

Kenneth Blanchard and Norman Vincent Peale proposed an "ethics check" for decision makers in their book *The Power of Ethical Management*.[147] They contend that the decision maker should ponder three questions:

1. *Is it legal?* (Will I be violating the law or company policy?)

2. *Is it balanced?* (Is it fair to all concerned in the short term and long term? Does it promote win–win relationships?)

3. *How will it make me feel about myself?* (Will it make me proud of my actions? How will I feel when others become aware of the decision?)

General Dynamics, a major defense contractor that builds weapons ranging from submarines to fighter jets, faced charges of defrauding the government out of more than $2 billion on the Los Angeles class submarine project. While the company ultimately admitted no guilt, the scandal cost Admiral Hyman Rickover his career. And audiotapes of the firm's CEO and CFO discussing their plans to "screw the Navy," combined with revelations that a company vice president billed the Navy for the cost of kenneling his dog while he was out of town, started a long downhill slide that ultimately cost the two executives their jobs and cost General Dynamics its reputation.[148, 149] Research shows that some individuals morally disengage when

Science

Why Do People Make Unethical Decisions?

Recently, it seems, there have been stories of unethical behavior in all aspects of society from business to sports to religious institutions. These tales beg the question of why people are making unethical decisions. It seems that any many of these cases, what would normally stop an individual from making unethical decisions, is for some reason deactivated. This process has been called moral disengagement.

In a recent study investigating what influences people to morally disengage, researchers found that an individual's personality can influence whether they morally disengage and then make unethical decisions. Individuals who are empathetic for others and individuals who perceive themselves to be moral will engage in less moral disengagement; but individuals who are cynical and individuals who believe most things occur by chance rather than personal initiative will more likely become morally disengaged. These findings suggest that organizations may be able to identify people who are more likely to morally disengage and avoid putting these individuals in ethically sensitive positions. Organizations may also be able to put in place more specific decision-making processes like group decision making that could lessen the impact of any individual decision maker's personality.

SOURCE: J. R. Detert, L. K. Trevino, and V. L. Sweitzer, "Moral Disengagement in Ethical Decision Making: A Study of Antecedents and Outcomes," *Journal of Applied Psychology* 93 (2008): 374–391.

making decisions, and this leads them to make unethical decisions. Read about who is most likely to do this in the Science feature.

In summary, all decisions, whether made by individuals or by groups, must be evaluated for their ethics. Organizations should reinforce ethical decision making among employees by encouraging and rewarding it. Socialization processes should convey to newcomers the ethical standards of behavior in the organization. Groups should use devil's advocates and dialectical methods to reduce the potential for groupthink and the unethical decisions that may result.

MANAGERIAL IMPLICATIONS: DECISION MAKING IS A CRITICAL ACTIVITY

Decision making is important at all levels of every organization. At times managers may have the luxury of optimizing (selecting the best alternative), but more often they are forced to satisfice (select the alternative that is good enough). And, at times, the decision process can even seem unpredictable and random.

Individuals differ in their preferences for risk, as well as in their styles of gathering information and making judgments. Understanding individual differences can help managers maximize strengths in employee decision styles and build teams that capitalize on strengths. Creativity is one such strength. It can be encouraged by providing employees with a supportive environment that nourishes innovative ideas. Creativity training has been used in some organizations with positive results.

Some decisions are best made by individuals and some by teams or groups. The task of the manager is to diagnose the situation and implement the appropriate level of participation. To do this effectively, managers should know the advantages and disadvantages of various group decision-making techniques and should minimize the potential for groupthink. Finally, decisions made by individuals or groups should be analyzed to see whether they are ethical.

Diversity Dialogue

Functional Diversity Comes Through in a Pinch

Jim Amoss is the editor of the *Times-Picayune* in New Orleans. Ordinarily, the newspaper's staffers would look to him or the senior editors to make the decisions. As the publication's leader, Amoss would be the most likely person to know what to do in case of an emergency. But on the morning of August 30, 2005, he did not know what to do. That was no ordinary day. It was the day that Hurricane Katrina struck New Orleans.

Like most organizations in the area, the staff at the *Times* had prepared for natural disasters. Extra generators were in place, and the staff had practiced emergency drills many times. In fact, the *Times* had even written articles detailing what to expect during a major hurricane. Unfortunately, all that planning literally went out the window during Hurricane Katrina. Water had flooded the generators and phones weren't working so no one could communicate. But this was the biggest story of their lives, and it had to be covered.

The staffers responded quickly without waiting for Amoss to hand out assignments. A functionally diverse team of about a dozen journalists, which included an editorial page editor, an art critic, and a religion writer, made the decision to return to the city's downtown area to gather supplies. They then went door to door searching for phone lines. The members of the team had never worked together before, but each of them went outside their comfort zones to make a decision that Amoss referred to as "an extraordinary moment of spontaneous leadership."

1. Discuss the effect of the team's functional heterogeneity on their decision to cover the Hurricane Katrina story.
2. What was Amoss' role in the team's ultimate decision?

SOURCE: J. Alexander, "Out of Disaster, Power in Numbers," *U.S. News & World Report* 141(16) (October 30, 2006): 75–77.

LOOKING BACK: FACEBOOK

User Commitment and Satisfaction at Facebook

Courtesy of Facebook

Instead of ignoring Facebook protestors and other less vocal customers, Facebook has decided to formally include them in the decision-making process. Facebook founder and CEO Zuckerman wants users to meaningfully participate in Facebook's future. As a result, Facebook will hold virtual town hall meetings for thirty days following any change to their principles and statement of rights and responsibilities. Users will be able to comment on these changes, Facebook will review and consider these submissions and then republish the statements. Facebook will also consolidate the comments and post the most common ones. Once these principles and statements are republished, all users will be able to vote on their adoption.[150,151]

This sort of customer participative decision making is unprecedented and it's not going to be easy as more than 100 million users log onto Facebook *daily*.

What does Facebook hope to gain from this type of participative decision making? Facebook hopes to reap the same benefits from customer participative management that research has found for employee participative management: namely user commitment and satisfaction through engagement and trust in the company.

Chapter Summary

1. Bounded rationality assumes that there are limits to how rational managers can be.

2. The garbage can model shows that under high uncertainty, decision making in organizations can be an unsystematic process.

3. Jung's cognitive styles can be used to help explain individual differences in gathering information and evaluating alternatives.

4. Intuition and creativity are positive influences on decision making and should be encouraged in organizations.

5. Empowerment and teamwork require specific organizational design elements and individual characteristics and skills.

6. Techniques such as brainstorming, nominal group technique, Delphi technique, devil's advocacy, dialectical inquiry, quality circles and teams, and self-managed teams can help managers reap the benefits of group methods while limiting the possibilities of groupthink and group polarization.

7. Technology is providing assistance to managerial decision making, especially through expert systems and group decision support systems. More research is needed to determine the effects of these technologies.

8. Managers should carefully weigh the ethical issues surrounding decisions and encourage ethical decision making throughout the organization.

Key Terms

bounded rationality (p. 328)
brainstorming (p. 347)
cognitive style (p. 331)
creativity (p. 337)
Delphi technique (p. 348)
devil's advocacy (p. 348)
dialectical inquiry (p. 348)
effective decision (p. 326)

escalation of commitment (p. 332 ~~330~~)
garbage can model (p. 329)
group polarization (p. 346)
groupthink (p. 344)
heuristics (p. 328)
intuition (p. 334)
nominal group technique (NGT) (p. 348)

nonprogrammed decision (p. 326)
participative decision making (p. 341)
programmed decision (p. 326)
rationality (p. 327)
risk aversion (p. 330)
satisfice (p. 328)
social decision schemes (p. 343)
synergy (p. 343)

Review Questions

1. Compare the garbage can model with the bounded rationality model. Compare the usefulness of these models in today's organizations.

2. List and describe Jung's four cognitive styles. How does the Z problem-solving model capitalize on the strengths of the four preferences?

3. What are the individual and organizational influences on creativity?

4. What are the individual and organizational foundations of empowerment and teamwork?

5. Describe the advantages and disadvantages of group decision making.

6. Describe the symptoms of groupthink, and identify actions that can be taken to prevent it.

7. What techniques can be used to improve group decisions?

Discussion and Communication Questions

1. Why is identification of the real problem the first and most important step in the decision-making process? How does attribution theory explain

mistakes that can be made as managers and employees work together to explain why the problem occurred?

2. How can organizations effectively manage both risk taking and escalation of commitment in the decision-making behavior of employees?

3. How will you most likely make decisions based on your cognitive style? What might you overlook using your preferred approach?

4. How can organizations encourage creative decision making?

5. What are some organizations that use expert systems? Group decision support systems? How will these two technologies affect managerial decision making?

6. How do the potential risks associated with participating in quality circles differ from those associated with participating in quality teams? If you were a member of a quality circle, how would management's decisions to reject your recommendations affect your motivation to participate?

7. *(communication question)* Form a team of four persons. Find two examples of recent decisions made in organizations: one that you consider a good decision, and one that you consider a bad decision. Two members should work on the good decision, and two on the bad decision. Each pair should write a brief description of the decision. Then write a summary of what went right, what went wrong, and what could be done to improve the decision process. Compare and contrast your two examples in a presentation to the class.

8. *(communication question)* Reflect on your own experiences in groups with groupthink. Describe the situation in which you encountered groupthink, the symptoms that were present, and the outcome. What remedies for groupthink would you prescribe? Summarize your answers in a memo to your instructor.

Ethical Dilemma

Aaron Chomsky, Jr. has been CEO of Varnett Publishing for twenty-five years; his father, Aaron Sr., founded the company in 1921. In the last thirty years, Varnett has acquired many smaller publishing companies in an effort to dominate the whole of the Northeast publishing industry. The small family company has grown into a publishing house that produces daily, weekly, and monthly news publications, as well as magazines and other print media for communities in New York, Connecticut, New Hampshire, and Vermont. Aaron Jr. took over as CEO during the high point in the life cycle of the news paper industry; that industry has, however, been in decline since 1998.

Aaron has just received word from the CFO that most of Varnett's acquisitions are failing individually, and that because of the decline in the market, Varnett will not be able to easily unload them. Consequently, Varnett is facing bankruptcy.

Varnett has many employees who have been with the company for more than thirty years, and many employees have family members also employed by Varnett. Aaron's father always promoted a sense of family within the company, even as Varnett grew well beyond a small town-single newspaper organization.

Aaron values his employees greatly, but if he alerts them to the severity of the situation, he knows that they will be compelled to search for employment elsewhere. If too many employees leave, however, Aaron knows that Varnett will not be able to produce the newspapers that are still operating. If Varnett stops producing newspapers, the company will absolutely fail, devastating shareholders. If Varnett absolutely fails, his employees will absolutely be out of work, and he will be able to offer them nothing.

Aaron feels great loyalty to his employees, but he also feels great loyalty to run Varnett in the most profitable way for his shareholders for as long as possible. He feels that he cannot protect one without sacrificing the other.

Time is passing quickly—if he doesn't commit to an action one way or the other, both will suffer equally. He must make a decision soon.

Questions:

1. Using consequential, rule-based and character theories, evaluate Arron's options.

2. What should Arron do? Why?

Experiential Exercises

10.1 Making a Layoff Decision

Purpose

In this exercise, you will examine how to weigh a set of facts and make a difficult personnel decision about laying off valued employees during a time of financial hardship. You will also examine your own values and criteria used in the decision-making process.

The Problem

Walker Space Institute (WSI) is a medium-sized firm located in Connecticut. The firm essentially has been a subcontractor on many large space contracts that have been acquired by firms like Alliant Techsystems and others.

With the cutback in many NASA programs, Walker has an excess of employees. Stuart Tartaro, the head of one of the sections, has been told by his superior that he must reduce his section of engineers from nine to six. He is looking at the following summaries of their vitae and pondering how he will make this decision.

1. *Roger Allison*, age twenty-six, married, two children. Allison has been with WSI for a year and a half. He is a very good engineer, with a degree from Rensselaer Polytech. He has held two prior jobs and lost both of them because of cutbacks in the space program. He moved to Connecticut from California to take this job. Allison is well liked by his coworkers.

2. *Dave Jones*, age twenty-four, single. Jones is an African American, and the company looked hard to get him because of affirmative action pressure. He is not very popular with his coworkers. Because he has been employed less than a year, not much is known about his work. On his one evaluation (which was average), Jones accused his supervisor of bias against African Americans. He is a graduate of the Detroit Institute of Technology.

3. *William Foster*, age fifty-three, married, three children. Foster is a graduate of "the school of hard knocks." After serving in the Vietnam War, he started to go to school but dropped out because of high family expenses. Foster has worked at the company for twenty years. His ratings were excellent for fifteen years. The last five years they have been average. Foster feels his supervisor grades him down because he does not "have sheepskins covering his office walls."

4. *Donald Boyer*, age thirty-two, married, no children. Boyer is well liked by his coworkers. He has been at WSI five years, and he has a B.S. and M.S. in engineering from Purdue University. Boyer's ratings have been mixed. Some supervisors rated him high and some average. Boyer's wife is an M.D.

5. *Ann Shuster*, age twenty-nine, single. Shuster is a real worker, but a loner. She has a B.S. in engineering from the University of California. She is working on her M.S. at night, always trying to improve her technical skills. Her performance ratings have been above average for the three years she has been at WSI.

6. *Sherman Soltis*, age thirty-seven, divorced, two children. He has a B.S. in engineering from Ohio State University. Soltis is very active in community affairs: Scouts, Little League, and United Way. He is a friend of the vice president through church work. His ratings have been average, although some recent ones indicate that he is out of date. He is well liked and has been employed at WSI for fourteen years.

7. *Warren Fortuna*, age forty-four, married, five children. He has a B.S. in engineering from Georgia Tech. Fortuna headed this section at one time. He worked so hard that he had a heart attack. Under doctor's orders, he resigned from the supervisory position. Since then he has done good work, though because of his health, he is a bit slower than the others. Now and then he must spend extra time on a project because he did get out of date during the eight years he headed the section. His performance evaluations for the last two years have been above average. He has been employed at WSI for fourteen years.

8. *Robert Treharne*, age forty-seven, single. He began an engineering degree at MIT but had to drop out for financial reasons. He tries hard to stay current by regular reading of engineering journals and taking all the short courses the company and nearby colleges offer. His performance evaluations have varied, but they tend to be average to slightly above average. He is a loner, and Tartaro thinks this has negatively affected Treharne's performance evaluations. He has been employed at WSI for sixteen years.

9. *Sandra Rosen*, age twenty-two, single. She has a B.S. in engineering technology from the Rochester Institute of Technology. Rosen has been employed less than a year. She is enthusiastic, a very good worker, and well liked by her coworkers. She is well regarded by Tartaro.

Tartaro does not quite know what to do. He sees the good points of each of his section members. Most have been good employees. They all can pretty much do one another's work. No one has special training.

He is fearful that the section will hear about the downsizing and morale will drop. Work would fall off. He does not even want to talk to his wife about it, in case she would let something slip. Tartaro has come to you, Edmund Graves, personnel manager at WSI, for some guidelines on this decision—legal, moral, and best personnel practice.

Assignment

You are Edmund Graves. Write a report with your recommendations for termination and a careful analysis of the criteria for the decision. You should also carefully explain to Tartaro how you would go about the terminations and what you would consider reasonable termination pay. You should also advise him about the pension implications of this decision. Generally, fifteen years' service entitles you to at least partial pension.

SOURCE: W. F. Glueck, *Cases and Exercises in Personnel* (Dallas: Business Publications, 1978), 24–26.

10.2 Dilemma at 29,000 Feet

Purpose

Making ethical decisions often requires taking decisive actions in ambiguous situations. Making these decisions entails not just weighing options and making rational choices but making choices between competing yet equally important demands. Managers must not only take action but also provide compelling reasons that make their choices rationally accountable to others. This exercise requires you to think through an ethical situation, take an action, and create a convincing justification for your action. The exercise is designed to encourage critical thinking about complex problems and to encourage thinking about how you might resolve a dilemma outside your area of expertise.

The Problem

Imagine you are the sole leader of a mountain-climbing expedition and have successfully led a group of three climbers to the mountain summit. However, on your descent, trouble sets in as a fierce storm engulfs the mountain and makes progression down nearly impossible. One climber collapses from exhaustion at 24,000 feet and cannot continue down the mountain. The two stronger climbers insist on continuing down without you because they know if they stay too long at high altitude death is certain. No one has ever survived overnight on the mountain. A rescue attempt is impossible because helicopters cannot reach you above 18,000 feet.

As the leader, you are faced with a difficult choice: abandon your teammate and descend alone or stay with your dying teammate and face almost certain death. On one hand, you might stay with your dying teammate in hopes that the storm might clear and a rescue party will be sent. However, you know that if you stay both of you will most likely die. On the other hand, you are still strong and may be able to make it down to safety, abandoning your teammate to die alone on the mountain.

Assignment

Your assignment is to make an argument for one of the actions: staying with your teammate or descending alone. The technical aspects of mountain climbing are not important, nor is it good enough to state that you would not get in this situation in the first place! What is important is that you provide a well-reasoned argument for your action. A good argument might address the following points:

1. A discussion of the pros and cons of each action: staying with your teammate or descending alone.
2. A discussion of the underlying values and assumptions of each action. For example, staying with the teammate implies that you have a particular obligation as the leader of a team; descending alone suggests that you may place a higher value on your own life.
3. A discussion of your own values and viewpoints on the topic. In other words, take a stand and justify your position. How, for example, might you justify to the family of the abandoned climber your decision to descend alone? How might you justify to your own family your decision to stay with the ailing climber?
4. What prior experience, knowledge, or beliefs lead you to your conclusion?
5. How might this situation be similar to or different from the dilemmas faced in more typical organizations? For example, do leaders need to take actions that require them to make similar difficult decisions? Have you experienced any similar dilemmas that had no easy answer in the workplace, and how did you resolve them?

Final Thoughts

Remember, there is no right or wrong answer to this case. The point is to consider and make clear your own ethical choices by evaluating all relevant information, evaluating the underlying assumptions of each, and creating a clear and convincing argument for action. A quote by philosopher Martha Craven Nussbaum might act as a starting point for your study. She writes,

Both alternatives make a serious claim on your practical attention. You might sense that no matter how you choose, you will be left with some regret that you did not do the other thing. Sometimes you may be clear about which is the better choice and yet feel pain over the frustration of the other significant concerns. It is extremely important to realize that the problem is not just one difficult decision but that conflicts arise when the final decision itself is perfectly obvious.

Good luck in your decision!

SOURCE: D. C. Kayes, "Dilemma at 29,000 Feet: An Exercise in Ethical Decision Making Based on the 1996 Mt. Everest Climbing Disaster," *Journal of Management Education* 26 (2002): 307–321. Reprinted by permission of Sage Publications.

BizFlix | Failure to Launch

Meet Tripp (Matthew McConaughey), thirty-five years old, has a nice car, loves sailing, and lives in a nice house—his parents'. Tripp's attachment to his family usually annoys any woman with whom he becomes serious. Mother Sue (Kathy Bates) and father Al (Terry Bradshaw) hire Paula (Sarah Jessica Parker). She specializes in detaching people like Tripp from their families. The term *failure to launch* refers to the failure to move out of the family home at an earlier age.

The Bird Problem: Fast Decision Making!

This fast-moving sequence begins with the sound of a bird chirping as it perches on a tree limb. Kit (Zooey Deschanel) and Ace (Justin Bartha) have waited patiently for the bird's arrival. This bird has annoyed Kit for many days. Ace believes that Kit only pumped the shotgun twice. The sequence ends after the bird leaves the house.

What to Watch for and Ask Yourself

- Does "The Bird Problem" present Kit and Ace with a programmed or nonprogrammed decision? What features of their decision problem led to your choice?

- Review the earlier section describing the decision-making process. Which steps in that process appear in "The Bird Problem?" Note the examples of each step that you see.

- Assess the degree of certainty, uncertainty, and risk that Kit and Ace face in this decision problem. What factors set the degree of certainty, uncertainty, and risk?

Workplace Video | Greensburg, Kansas: Decision Making

It's almost impossible to assign credit or blame to any one person for Greensburg's decision to rebuild the small Kansas town as a model green community after a tornado decimated 95 percent of its buildings. Many folks in Greensburg would assert that whoever made the decision, made a good one. Other residents make a different case.

Former mayor Lonnie McCollum expressed interest in exploring the possibilities of running Greensburg's municipal buildings on solar and wind power well before the EF5 tornado hit in May 2004. After the storm, he saw the tragedy as an opportunity to reinvent the dying town and put it back on the map. But McCollum was not the sole decision maker; instead, he was the leader of a small community facing endless uncertainties. Ultimately, the Greensburg City Council would have to vote on this matter.

After multiple rounds of community meetings in which residents engaged in rigorous debate, Greensburg's City Council voted in favor of rebuilding the town using green methods and materials. And when the council members voted on the specifics of implementation, they decided to build all municipal buildings to the Leadership in Energy and Environmental Design (LEED) Platinum standard, which is the highest nationally accepted benchmark for the design, construction, and operation of high-performance green buildings.

But residents were divided over the decision, and the town meetings generated rancor and politicking. Mayor McCollum eventually resigned, city administrators dug in, and many residents checked out. But the rebuilding plan went forward, and today a collaborative effort among business and nonprofit groups is putting Greensburg back on the map.

There is no way to convince every Greensburg resident that going green was a good decision. Perhaps all the City Council can hope for is support from a majority of residents. In their minds, what were the alternatives? The town was dying. But Greensburg is rebuilding thanks to generous corporate sponsorships and government grants. The town also stars in a TV show on Planet Green. The TV show is aptly named *Greensburg*.

Discussion Questions

1. Cite reasons for and against rebuilding Greensburg as a "green town." Which reasons do you find most convincing and why?

2. Do you think Greensburg's decision-making process was effective, methodical, and capable of producing a good outcome? Explain.

3. What role did risk and uncertainty play in Greensburg's decision?

Case

3M's Conundrum of Efficiency and Creativity

Well-known innovative companies, like Minnesota Mining and Manufacturing (3M), that are successful share at least four fundamental characteristics: (1) putting people and ideas at the heart of the management philosophy; (2) giving people opportunities and latitude to develop, try new things, and learn from their mistakes; (3) building a strong sense of openness, trust, and community throughout the organization; and (4) facilitating the mobility of talent within the organization.[1] 3M believes in the power of ideas and individual initiative and "recognizes that entrepreneurial behavior will continue to flourish only if management is willing to accept and even applaud 'well-intentioned failure.'"[2] Innovation, the traditional hallmark of 3M's business operations and success, is "a process that thrives on multiple, diverse, independent and rapid experimentation, in a failure-tolerant environment that values and accommodates constructive conflict."[3]

Richard McKnight, 3M's president in the company's early days, "recognized that it was the individual inventor, enabled in pursuing his ideas, who could help the company develop new organizational knowledge with which to meet emerging customer needs. As a result, McKnight created the company's 15 Percent Rule, which still encourages technical employees to spend as much as 15 percent of their time pursuing their own ideas. ... Among the most successful of the products developed through the 15 Percent Rule are masking tape in the 1930s, Scotchgard fabric protector in the 1950s, and Post-it Notes in the 1970s."[4]

The creative and innovative orientation of 3M—and in particular a tolerance for failure or equivalently, defects or errors—came under serious attack in December 2000, when former General Electric executive James McNerney took over as CEO of 3M. McNerney immediately began implementing Six Sigma,[5] a type of management program that is designed to identify problems in work processes, and then use rigorous measurement to reduce variation, eliminate defects, and increase efficiency. Under McNerney's leadership, profits initially grew at about 22 percent annually but then sputtered. Some experts were critical of McNerney's unyielding commitment to Six Sigma, wondering if it was stifling 3M's creativity and innovation.[6]

When initiatives such as Six Sigma become embedded in a company's culture, as they did at 3M, creativity and innovation can easily get squelched.[7] In mid-2005, when McNerney departed 3M to take the CEO's job at Boeing, he left his successor, George Buckley, with the difficult question of "whether the relentless emphasis on efficiency had made 3M a less creative company."[8] According to management guru Tom Peters, McNerney's implementation of Six Sigma at 3M "more or less closed the lid on entrepreneurial behavior."[9] Vijay Govindarajan, a professor at Dartmouth's Tuck School of Business, observes that when more emphasis is placed on a program like Six Sigma, the more likely it is that breakthrough innovations will be harmed.[10] Art Fry, the inventor of 3M's Post-It notes, says, "[y]ou have to go through 5,000 to 6,000 raw ideas to find one successful business," but the Six Sigma program would ask "why not eliminate all that waste and just come up with the right idea the first time?"[11]

Some experts maintain that Six Sigma can absolutely co-exist with innovation in that Six Sigma can eliminate mundane, repetitive, and tedious tasks that impede creative thinking and innovation.[12] However, others assert that "[s]ome of the aspects that make Six Sigma powerful may in fact reduce its overall effectiveness. The methodology employs rigorous statistical analysis to identify defect areas, the correction of which produces better quality, lower costs, and increased efficiency. But while Six Sigma may be very effective at controlling processes, elements that are harder to control, such as employee behavior and innovation/ideation, can hinder long-term success."[13]

Six Sigma focuses on efficiency and quality in order to enhance profits, but the lifeblood of long-term profitability for most, if not all, businesses is innovation. Indeed, "to compete in the coming decades, creativity is one process that can't be left for later."[14] The proper balance between creativity and efficiency is essential. Effective innovation "requires a delicate balancing act between play and discipline, practice and process, creativity and efficiency, where firms need to 'learn how to walk the fine line between rigidity—which smothers creativity—and chaos—where creativity runs amok and nothing ever gets to market.'"[15]

Interestingly, over 60 percent of all corporate Six Sigma programs fail to produce the desired results.[16] When stacked up against the corporate need for creativity and innovation, this poses a significant challenge for executives and managers. Indeed, "[m]anaging the yin and yang of efficiency and creativity is one of the greatest challenges facing managers around the world. The 3M story illustrates that."[17]

Discussion Questions

1. What are the relative advantages and disadvantages of a company being committed to achieving efficiency through a program like Six Sigma versus encouraging and reinforcing creativity and innovation?

2. How would you describe 3M's efficiency and creativity conundrum in terms of programmed and nonprogrammed decisions?

3. How would you describe 3M's efficiency and creativity conundrum in terms of the rational, bounded rationality, and garbage can models of decision making?

4. What role(s) do intuition and creativity play in the decision making that is evident in 3M's efficiency and creativity conundrum?

5. Would you prefer to work in a company where decision making focuses on cost cutting and efficiency in order to achieve maximum profitability, or would you prefer a company where decision making leaves room for risk taking and possible failure in the pursuit innovative solutions and products which, hopefully, have significant commercial potential? Explain your answer.

SOURCE: This case was written by Michael K. McCuddy, The Louis S. and Mary L. Morgal Chair of Christian Business Ethics and Professor of Management, College of Business Administration, Valparaiso University.

Power and Political Behavior

LEARNING OBJECTIVES

After reading this chapter, you should be able to do the following:

1 Distinguish among power, influence, and authority.

2 Compare the interpersonal and intergroup sources of power.

3 Understand the ethical use of power.

4 Explain power analysis, an organizational-level theory of power.

5 Identify symbols of power and powerlessness in organizations.

6 Define organizational politics and understand the role of political skill and major influence tactics.

7 Develop a plan for managing employee–boss relationships.

8 Discuss how managers can empower others.

Deloitte has made great strides to empower its employees.

THINKING AHEAD: DELOITTE

Barbara Adachi: An Empowered Employee

Barbara Adachi was not always comfortable in corporate America, and she spent her early career jumping from job to job because she couldn't find a way to balance her career and her family responsibilities as a mother.[1] All of that changed

when she arrived at Deloitte in 1990. Deloitte has made great strides to empower its employees, focusing on programs to attract and retain women and minorities. Through Deloitte's empowerment initiatives, Adachi has been able to have a rewarding career while still being there for her family and her daughter.

Currently, Adachi is the national managing principal for Deloitte's award-winning Women's Initiative; she serves on the board of Deloitte Consulting and leads Deloitte Consulting's Human Capital practice in the west region. She also serves on several advisory boards and has been named one of the "100 Most Influential Women in Business" by *San Francisco Business Times* for five consecutive years and received a "working heroes" award by the Professional Business Women of California and ten San Francisco Bay Area corporations.[2] So what has Deloitte done to empower Adachi and other women like her? See the Looking Back feature to read about the company's initiatives and awards.

THE CONCEPT OF POWER

1 Distinguish among power, influence, and authority.

Power is the ability to influence someone else. As an exchange relationship, it occurs in transactions between an agent and a target. The agent is the person using the power, and the target is the recipient of the attempt to use power.[3]

Because power is an ability, individuals can learn to use it effectively. *Influence* is the process of affecting the thoughts, behavior, and feelings of another person. *Authority* is the right to influence another person.[4] It is important to understand the subtle differences among these terms. For instance, a manager may have authority but no power. She may have the right, by virtue of her position as boss, to tell someone what to do. But she may not have the skill or ability to influence other people.

In a relationship between the agent and the target, there are many influence attempts that the target considers legitimate. Working forty hours per week, greeting customers, solving problems, and collecting bills are actions that, when requested by the manager, are considered legitimate by a customer service representative. Requests such as these fall within the employee's *zone of indifference*—the range in which attempts to influence the employee are perceived as legitimate and are acted on without a great deal of thought.[5] The employee accepts that the manager has the authority to request such behaviors and complies with the requests. Some requests, however, fall outside the zone of indifference, so the manager must work to enlarge the employee's zone of indifference. Enlarging the zone is accomplished with power (an ability) rather than with authority (a right).

Suppose the manager asks the employee to purchase a birthday gift for the manager's wife or to overcharge a customer for a service call. The employee may think the manager has no right to ask these things. These requests fall outside the zone of indifference; they're viewed as extraordinary, and the manager has to operate from outside the authority base to induce the employee to fulfill them. In some cases, no power base is enough to induce the employee to comply, especially if the employee considers the behaviors requested by the manager unethical.

Failures to understand power and politics can be costly in terms of your career. In the wake of economic and ethical problems of the past several years, power has shifted in organizations. CEOs in many industries who in the past have had enormous power because board members had become disinterested and regulatory rules had been removed have recently come under great scrutiny. Public pressure has reduced their ability to make unquestioned decisions and even resulted in some high-profile CEOs' resignations.[6] The most publicized of these: Jack Wagoner, who, pressured by the U.S. government, stepped down from his position as CEO at General Motors. This example illustrates that managers must learn that power and politics come from many different sources in organizations; managers need to be able to use them effectively and manage the inevitable political behavior in organizations.[7]

power
The ability to influence another person.

influence
The process of affecting the thoughts, behavior, and feelings of another person.

authority
The right to influence another person.

zone of indifference
The range in which attempts to influence a person will be perceived as legitimate and will be acted on without a great deal of thought.

FORMS AND SOURCES OF POWER IN ORGANIZATIONS

Individuals have many forms of power to use in their work settings. Some of them are interpersonal—used in interactions with others. One of the earliest and most influential theories of power comes from French and Raven, who tried to determine the sources of power managers use to influence other people.

2 Compare the interpersonal and intergroup sources of power.

Interpersonal Forms of Power

French and Raven identified five forms of interpersonal power that managers use: reward, coercive, legitimate, referent, and expert power.[8]

Reward power is based on the agent's ability to control rewards that a target wants. For example, managers control the rewards of salary increases, bonuses, and promotions. Reward power can lead to better performance, but only as long as the employee sees a clear and strong link between performance and rewards. To use reward power effectively, then, the manager should be explicit about the behavior being rewarded and should make the connection clear between the behavior and the reward.

Coercive power is based on the agent's ability to cause the target to have an unpleasant experience. To coerce someone into doing something means to force the person to do it, often with threats of punishment. Managers using coercive power may verbally abuse employees or withhold support from them.

Legitimate power, which is similar to authority, is based on position and mutual agreement. The agent and target agree that the agent has the right to influence the target. It doesn't matter that a manager thinks he has the right to influence his employees; for legitimate power to be effective, the employees must also believe the manager has the right to tell them what to do. In some Native American societies, the chief has legitimate power; tribe members believe in his right to influence the decisions in their lives.

Referent power is based on interpersonal attraction. The agent has referent power over the target because the target identifies with or wants to be like the agent. Charismatic individuals are often thought to have referent power. Interestingly, the agent need not be superior to the target in any way. People who use referent power well are most often individualistic and respected by the target.

Expert power exists when the agent has specialized knowledge or skills that the target needs. For expert power to work, three conditions must be in place. First, the target must trust that the expertise given is accurate. Second, the knowledge involved must be relevant and useful to the target. Third, the target's perception of the agent as an expert is crucial. Using easy-to-understand language signals the target that the expert has an appreciation for real-world concerns and increases the target's trust in the expert.[9]

Which type of interpersonal power is most effective? Research has focused on this question since French and Raven introduced their five forms of power. Some of the results are surprising. Reward power and coercive power have similar effects.[10] Both lead to compliance. That is, employees will do what the manager asks them to, at least temporarily, if the manager offers a reward or threatens them with punishment. Reliance on these sources of power is dangerous, however, because it may require the manager to be physically present and watchful in order to apply rewards or punishment when the behavior occurs. Constant surveillance creates an uncomfortable situation for managers and employees and eventually results in a dependency relationship. Employees will not work unless the manager is present.

reward power
Power based on an agent's ability to control rewards that a target wants.

coercive power
Power that is based on an agent's ability to cause an unpleasant experience for a target.

legitimate power
Power that is based on position and mutual agreement; agent and target agree that the agent has the right to influence the target.

referent power
An elusive power that is based on interpersonal attraction.

expert power
The power that exists when an agent has specialized knowledge or skills that the target needs.

Legitimate power also leads to compliance. When told "Do this because I'm your boss," most employees will comply. However, the use of legitimate power has not been linked to organizational effectiveness or to employee satisfaction.[11] In organizations where managers rely heavily on legitimate power, organizational goals are not necessarily met.

Referent power is linked with organizational effectiveness. It is the most dangerous power, however, because it can be too extensive and intensive in altering the behavior of others. Charismatic leaders need an accompanying sense of responsibility for others. The late disabled actor Christopher Reeve's referent power made him a powerful spokesperson for research on spinal injuries and stem cell research.

Expert power has been called the power of the future.[12] Of the five forms of power, it has the strongest relationship with performance and satisfaction. It is through expert power that vital skills, abilities, and knowledge are passed on within the organization. Employees internalize what they observe and learn from managers they perceive to be experts.

The results on the effectiveness of these five forms of power pose a challenge in organizations. The least effective power bases—legitimate, reward, and coercive— are the ones most likely to be used by managers.[13]

Marissa Mayer, vice president of Google, has a lot of technical knowledge but is also comfortable in social environments.

Managers inherit these power bases as part of the position when they take a supervisory job. By contrast, the most effective power bases—referent and expert—are ones that must be developed and strengthened through interpersonal relationships with employees. Marissa Mayer, vice president of search products and user experience at Google, is well respected and liked by her colleagues. She is described as someone with a lot of technical knowledge, and she is comfortable in social environments. This represents her expert power and referent power—she has an advanced degree in computer science from Stanford University and is known for her ability to connect with people. At thirty-four years of age, she has had a very successful career at Google and is one of the most powerful female executives in the country.[14]

Using Power Ethically

3 Understand the ethical use of power

Managers can work at developing all five of these forms of power for future use. The key to using them well is using them ethically, as shown in Table 11.1. Coercive power, for example, requires careful administration if it is to be used in an ethical manner. Employees should be informed of the rules in advance, and any punishment should be used consistently, uniformly, and privately. The key to using all five types of interpersonal power ethically is to be sensitive to employees' concerns and to communicate well.

To French and Raven's five power sources, we can add a source that is very important in today's organizations. *Information power* is access to and control over important information. Consider, for example, the CEO's administrative assistant. He or she has information about the CEO's schedule that people need if they are going to get in to see the CEO. Central to the idea of information power is the person's position in the communication networks in the organization, both formal and informal. Also important is the idea of framing, which is the "spin" that managers put on information. Managers not only pass information on to subordinates but also interpret this information and influence the subordinates' perceptions of it. Information power not only occurs in the downward direction but may also flow

information power

Access to and control over important information.

TABLE

11.1   Guidelines for the Ethical Use of Power

Form of Power	Guidelines for Use
Reward power	Verify compliance. Make feasible, reasonable requests. Make only ethical requests. Offer rewards desired by subordinates. Offer only credible rewards.
Coercive power	Inform subordinates of rules and penalties. Warn before punishing. Administer punishment consistently and uniformly. Understand the situation before acting. Maintain credibility. Fit punishment to the infraction. Punish in private.
Legitimate power	Be cordial and polite. Be confident. Be clear and follow up to verify understanding. Make sure request is appropriate. Explain reasons for request. Follow proper channels. Exercise power consistently. Enforce compliance. Be sensitive to subordinates' concerns.
Referent power	Treat subordinates fairly. Defend subordinates' interests. Be sensitive to subordinates' needs and feelings. Select subordinates similar to oneself. Engage in role modeling.
Expert power	Maintain credibility. Act confident and decisive. Keep informed. Recognize employee concerns. Avoid threatening subordinates' self-esteem.

final

SOURCES: *Leadership in Organizations* by Gary A. Yukl. Copyright ©1981. Reprinted by permission of Prentice Hall, Upper Saddle River, N.J.

upward from subordinates to managers. In manufacturing plants, database operators often control information about plant metrics and shipping performance that is vital to managerial decision making. Information power can also flow laterally. Salespersons convey information from the outside environment (their customers) that is essential for marketing efforts.

Determining whether a power-related behavior is ethical is complex. Another way to look at the ethics surrounding the use of power is to ask three questions that show the criteria for examining power-related behaviors:[15]

1. *Does the behavior produce a good outcome for people both inside and outside the organization?* This question represents the criterion of *utilitarian outcomes.* The behavior should result in the greatest good for the greatest number

of people. If the power-related behavior serves only the individual's self-interest and fails to help the organization reach its goals, it is considered unethical. A salesperson might be tempted to discount a product deeply in order to make a sale that would win a contest. Doing so would be in her self-interest but would not benefit the organization.

2. *Does the behavior respect the rights of all parties?* This question emphasizes the criterion of *individual rights*. Free speech, privacy, and due process are individual rights that are to be respected, and power-related behaviors that violate these rights are considered unethical.

3. *Does the behavior treat all parties equitably and fairly?* This question represents the criterion of *distributive justice*. Power-related behavior that treats one party arbitrarily or benefits one party at the expense of another is unethical. Granting a day of vacation to one employee in a busy week in which coworkers must struggle to cover for him might be considered unethical.

To be considered ethical, power-related behavior must meet all three criteria. If the behavior fails to meet the criteria, then alternative actions should be considered. Unfortunately, most power-related behaviors are not easy to analyze. Conflicts may exist among the criteria; for example, a behavior may maximize the greatest good for the greatest number of people but may not treat all parties equitably. Individual rights may need to be sacrificed for the good of the organization. A CEO may need to be removed from power for the organization to be saved. Still, these criteria can be used on a case-by-case basis to sort through the complex ethical issues surrounding the use of power. The ethical use of power is one of the hottest topics in the current business arena, due to the abuse of power by top executives at several firms. Bernie Madoff alledgedly ran a $50 billion Ponzi scheme that ruined many people's lives financially. He was clearly the mastermind of the scheme but it is not clear how many employees at Bernard L. Madoff Investment Securities knew that clients were being scammed. And abuses of power are certainly not confined to U.S. organizations—unfortunately they are a global phenomenon. Volkswagen (VW) has been the subject of a long-running corruption scandal, which you can read about in Real World 11.1.

Personal power used for personal gain. Former Illinois Governor Rod Blagojevich allegedly tried to sell a Senate seat.

© Jonathan Krishner/epa/Corbis

Two Faces of Power: One Positive, One Negative

We turn now to a theory of power that takes a strong stand on the "right" versus "wrong" kind of power to use in organizations. David McClelland has spent a great deal of his career studying the need for power and the ways managers use power. As was discussed in Chapter 5, he believes there are two distinct faces of power, one negative and one positive.[16] The negative face of power is *personal power*—power used for personal gain. Managers who use personal power are commonly described as "power hungry." Former Illinois Governor Rod Blagojevich allegedly tried to sell President Barack Obama's Senate seat. Reports note that he attempted to trade the seat for money, ambassadorships, and even a $150,000 salary for his wife. People who approach relationships with an exchange orientation often use personal power to ensure that they get at least their fair share—and often more—in the relationship. They are most concerned with their own needs and interests. One way to encourage ethical behavior in organizations is to encourage principled dissent. This refers to valid

personal power
Power used for personal gain.

Volkswagen: Perks and Prostitutes Scandal

VW has been rocked by scandals that involve both executives and labor union leaders. VW company executives allegedly bribed labor union leaders with company-paid shopping sprees for spouses, holiday visits with prostitutes, and cash bonuses to obtain their cooperation. Germany has also seen scandals implicating executives at Siemens and Deutsche Bank, among others, and these scandals have tarnished the image of corporate Germany. The magnitude of the scandals is forcing Germany to embrace the trend of making companies more transparent and accountable—as opposed to the old way of doing business in which banks, corporations, labor unions, and government are closely intertwined.

At VW, as in other German organizations, a close relationship exists between management and labor, and organized labor has a voice in important company decisions. VW's former head of human resources, Peter Hartz, was found guilty of endorsing the perks and prostitutes deal. He confessed to attempting to buy support from Klaus Volkert, head of the company's employee works council, for plans to cut costs and restructure the automaker. Volkert demanded, and received, $2.5 million in bonuses, along with $786,000 for luxury vacations, clothes, jewelry, and fake consulting fees for his girlfriend.

During the trial, a VW secretary confirmed that she was ordered to rent an apartment to be used for company and union executives' liaisons with prostitutes. VW executive Hartz was found guilty, and given a two-year suspended sentence along with a $736,000 fine. Volkert, as the top labor leader at VW, was found guilty of inciting fraud and receiving nearly $4 million in improper bonuses. He was sentenced to three years in prison. Another VW executive, Klaus-Joachim Gebauer, was handed a one-year suspended sentence for arranging lavish company trips for labor leaders, with some of these including visits to prostitutes and gift certificates at upscale boutiques for wives. The VW executives insisted that labor leaders pressured them for the bonuses, and kept coming back for more.

Although VW has removed some of the offenders who were in power, a central issue has yet to be addressed—the atmosphere of close ties between labor and executives that gave rise to the scandal.

Sources: M. Landler, "Sentence in Volkswagen Scandal," *New York Times* (February 23, 2008), "Hit by an Earthquake: How Scandals Have Led to a Crisis in German Corporate Governance," *Knoweldge Wharton*, accessed at http://knowledge.wharton.upenn.edu/article.cfm?articleid=1695&specialid=64

---

criticism that can benefit the organization rather than mere complaints about working conditions. Much like whistle-blowers who can serve as checks on powerful people within the organization, dissenters can pinpoint wrongdoings, encourage employee voice in key issues, and create a climate conducive to the ethical use of power.[17]

Individuals who rely on personal power at its extreme might be considered Machiavellian—willing to do whatever it takes to get one's own way. Niccolo Machiavelli was an Italian statesman during the sixteenth century who wrote *The Prince*, a guide for acquiring and using power.[18] Among his methods was manipulating others, believing that it was better to be feared than loved. Machiavellians (or high Machs) are willing to manipulate others for personal gain, and are unconcerned with others' opinions or welfare.

The positive face of power is *social power*—power used to create motivation or to accomplish group goals. McClelland clearly favors the use of social power by managers. People who approach relationships with a communal orientation focus on the needs and interests of others. They rely on social power.[19] McClelland has found that managers who use power successfully have four power-oriented characteristics:

social power
Power used to create motivation or to accomplish group goals.

1. *Belief in the authority system.* They believe that the institution is important and that its authority system is valid. They are comfortable influencing and being influenced. The source of their power is the authority system of which they are a part.

2. *Preference for work and discipline.* They like their work and are very orderly. They have a basic value preference for the Protestant work ethic, believing that work is good for a person over and beyond its income-producing value.

3. *Altruism.* They publicly put the company and its needs before their own needs. They are able to do this because they see their own well-being as integrally tied to the corporate well-being.

4. *Belief in justice.* They believe justice is to be sought above all else. People should receive what they are entitled to and what they earn.

McClelland takes a definite stand on the proper use of power by managers. When power is used for the good of the group, rather than for individual gain, it is positive.

Intergroup Sources of Power

Groups or teams within an organization can also use power from several sources. One source of intergroup power is control of *critical resources*.[20] When one group controls an important resource that another group desires, the first group holds power. Controlling resources needed by another group allows the power-holding group to influence the actions of the less powerful group. This process can continue in an upward spiral. Groups seen as powerful tend to be given more resources from top management.[21]

Groups also have power to the extent that they control *strategic contingencies*—activities that other groups depend on in order to complete their tasks.[22] The dean's office, for example, may control the number of faculty positions to be filled in each department of a college. The departmental hiring plans are thus contingent on approval from the dean's office. In this case, the dean's office controls the strategic contingency of faculty hiring, and thus has power.

Three factors can give a group control over a strategic contingency.[23] One is the *ability to cope with uncertainty*. If a group can help another group deal with uncertainty, it has power. One organizational group that has gained power in recent years is the legal department. Faced with increasing government regulations and fears of litigation, many other departments seek guidance from the legal department.

Another factor that can give a group control power is a *high degree of centrality* within the organization. If a group's functioning is important to the organization's success, it has high centrality. The sales force in a computer firm, for example, has power because of its immediate effect on the firm's operations and because other groups (accounting and servicing groups, for example) depend on its activities.

The third factor that can give a group power is *nonsubstitutability*—the extent to which a group performs a function that is indispensable to an organization. A team of computer specialists may be powerful because of its expertise with a system. It may have specialized experience that another team cannot provide.

The strategic contingencies model thus shows that groups hold power over other groups when they can reduce uncertainty, when their functioning is central to the organization's success, and when the group's activities are difficult to replace.[24]

strategic contingencies
Activities that other groups depend on in order to complete their tasks.

The key to all three of these factors, as you can see, is dependency. When one group controls something that another group needs, it creates a dependent relationship—and gives one group power over the other.

POWER ANALYSIS: A BROADER VIEW

Amitai Etzioni takes a more sociological orientation to power. Etzioni has developed a theory of power analysis.[25] He says that there are three types of organizational power and three types of organizational involvement, or membership, that will lead to either congruent or incongruent uses of power. The three types of organizational power are the following:

4 Explain power analysis, an organizational-level theory of power.

1. *Coercive power*—influencing members by forcing them to do something under threat of punishment or through fear and intimidation.
2. *Utilitarian power*—influencing members by providing them with rewards and benefits.
3. *Normative power*—influencing members by using the knowledge that they want very much to belong to the organization and by letting them know that what they are expected to do is the "right" thing to do.

Along with these three types of organizational power, Etzioni proposes that we can classify organizations by the type of membership they have:

1. *Alienative membership*. The members have hostile, negative feelings about being in the organization. They don't want to be there. Prisons are a good example of alienative memberships.
2. *Calculative membership*. Members weigh the benefits and limitations of belonging to the organization. Businesses are good examples of organizations with calculative memberships.
3. *Moral membership*. Members have such positive feelings about organizational membership that they are willing to deny their own needs. Organizations with many volunteer workers, such as the American Heart Association, are examples of moral memberships. Religious groups are another.

Etzioni argues that the type of organizational power should be matched to the type of membership in the organization in order to achieve congruence. Figure 11.1 shows the matches in his power analysis theory.

In an alienative membership, members have hostile feelings. In prisons, for example, Etzioni would contend that coercive power is the appropriate type to use.

A calculative membership is characterized by an analysis of the good and bad aspects of being in the organization. In a business partnership, for example, each partner weighs the benefits from the partnership against the costs entailed in the contractual arrangement. Utilitarian or reward-based power is the most appropriate type to use.

In a moral membership, the members have strong positive feelings about the particular cause or goal of the organization. Normative power is the most appropriate to use because it capitalizes on the members' desires to belong.

Etzioni's power analysis is an organizational-level theory. It emphasizes that the characteristics of an organization play a role in determining the type of power appropriate for use in it. Etzioni's theory is controversial in its contention that a single type of power is appropriate in any organization.

11.1 Etzioni's Power Analysis

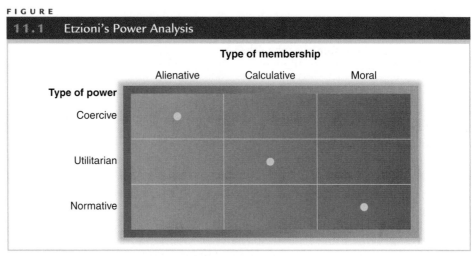

Type of membership

Type of power	Alienative	Calculative	Moral
Coercive	●		
Utilitarian		●	
Normative			●

SOURCE: Adapted from Amitai Etzioni, *Modern Organizations* (Upper Saddle River, NJ: Prentice Hall, 1964), 59–61. Reprinted by permission of Pearson Education, Inc., Upper Saddle River, NJ.

SYMBOLS OF POWER

5 Identify symbols of power and powerlessness in organizations.

Organization charts show who has authority but reveal little about who has power. We'll now look at two very different ideas about the symbols of power. The first comes from Rosabeth Moss Kanter. It is a scholarly approach to determining who has power and who feels powerless. The second is a semiserious look at the tangible symbols of power by Michael Korda.

Kanter's Symbols of Power

Kanter provides several characteristics of powerful people in organizations:[26]

1. *Ability to intercede for someone in trouble.* An individual who can pull someone out of a jam has power.

2. *Ability to get placements for favored employees.* Getting a key promotion for an employee is a sign of power.

3. *Exceeding budget limitations.* A manager who can go above budget limits without being reprimanded has power.

4. *Procuring above-average raises for employees.* One faculty member reported that her department head distributed 10 percent raises to the most productive faculty members although the budget allowed for only 4 percent increases. "I don't know how he did it; he must have pull," she said.

5. *Getting items on the agenda at meetings.* If a manager can raise issues for action at meetings, it's a sign of power.

6. *Access to early information.* Having information before anyone else does is a signal that a manager is plugged into key sources.

7. *Having top managers seek out their opinion.* When top managers have a problem, they may ask for advice from lower-level managers. The managers they turn to have power.

A theme that runs through Kanter's list is doing things for others: for people in trouble, for employees, for bosses. There is an active, other-directed element in her symbols of power.

You can use Kanter's symbols of power to identify powerful people in organizations. They can be particularly useful in finding a mentor who can effectively use power.

powerlessness
A lack of power.

organizational politics
The use of power and influence in organizations.

Kanter's Symbols of Powerlessness

Kanter also wrote about symptoms of *powerlessness*—a lack of power—in managers at different levels of the organization. First-line supervisors, for example, often display three symptoms of powerlessness: overly close supervision, inflexible adherence to the rules, and a tendency to do the job themselves rather than training their employees to do it. Staff professionals such as accountants and lawyers display different symptoms of powerlessness. When they feel powerless, they tend to resist change and try to protect their turf. Top executives can also feel powerless. They show symptoms such as focusing on budget cutting, punishing others, and using dictatorial, top-down communication. Acting in certain ways can lead employees to believe that a manager is powerless. By making external attributions (blaming others or circumstances) for negative events, a manager looks as if he or she has no power.[27]

What can you do when you recognize that employees are feeling powerless? The key to overcoming powerlessness is to share power and delegate decision-making authority to employees.

Korda's Symbols of Power

Michael Korda takes a different look at symbols of power in organizations.[28] He discusses three unusual symbols: office furnishings, time power, and standing by.

Furniture is not just physically useful; it also conveys a message about power. Locked file cabinets are signs that the manager has important and confidential information in the office. A rectangular (rather than round) conference table enables the most important person to sit at the head of the table. The size of one's desk may convey the amount of power. Most executives prefer large, expensive desks.

Time power means using clocks and watches as power symbols. Korda says that the biggest compliment a busy executive can pay a visitor is to remove his watch and place it face down on the desk, thereby communicating "my time is yours." He also notes that the less powerful the executive, the more intricate the watch. Moreover, managers who are really secure in their power wear no watch at all, since they believe nothing important can happen without them. A full calendar is also proof of power. Personal planners are left open on the desk to display busy schedules.

Standing by is a game in which people are obliged to keep their cell phones, pagers, etc. with them at all times so executives can reach them. The idea is that the more you can impose your schedule on other people, the more power you have. In fact, Korda defines *power* as follows: There are more people who inconvenience themselves on your behalf than there are people on whose behalf you would inconvenience yourself. Closely tied to this is the ability to make others perform simple tasks for you, such as getting your coffee or fetching the mail.

While Kanter's symbols focus on the ability to help others, Korda's symbols focus on status—a person's relative standing in a group based on prestige and having other people defer to him or her.[29] By identifying powerful people and learning from their modeled behavior, you can determine the keys to power use in the organization.

POLITICAL BEHAVIOR IN ORGANIZATIONS

Like power, the term *politics* in organizations may conjure up a few negative images. However, *organizational politics* is not necessarily negative; it is the use of power and influence in organizations. Organizations are arenas in which people have competing interests, which effective managers must reconcile. Organizational politics are

6 Define organizational politics and understand the role of political skill and major influence tactics.

central to managing. As people try to acquire power and expand their power base, they use various tactics and strategies. Some are sanctioned (acceptable to the organization); others are not. *Political behavior* refers to actions not officially sanctioned by an organization that are taken to influence others in order to meet one's personal goals.[30] Sometimes personal goals are aligned with team or organizational goals, and they can be achieved in support of others' interests. But other times personal goals and the interests of others collide, and individuals pursue politics at the expense of others' interests.[31]

Politics is a controversial topic among managers. Some managers take a favorable view of political behavior; others see it as detrimental to the organization. Some workers who perceive their workplace as highly political actually find the use of political tactics more satisfying and report greater job satisfaction when they engage in political behavior. Some people may therefore thrive in political environments, while others may find office politics distasteful and stressful.[32]

Most people are also amazingly good at recognizing political behavior at all levels of the firm. Employees are not only keenly aware of political behavior at their level but can also spot political behavior at both their supervisor's level and the topmost levels of the organization.[33]

Many organizational conditions encourage political activity. Among them are unclear goals, autocratic decision making, ambiguous lines of authority, scarce resources, and uncertainty.[34] Even supposedly objective activities may involve politics. One such activity is the performance appraisal process. A study of sixty executives who had extensive experience in employee evaluation indicated that political considerations were nearly always part of the performance appraisal process.[35]

Marissa Mayer of Google is charged with the key task of approving new ideas at Google to be presented to founders Sergey Brin and Larry Page. She takes several steps to ensure that politicking does not occur in choice of ideas that move forward. For this purpose, she has very clear criteria for objectively evaluating new ideas, holds meetings that allow ten minutes per idea with a timer ticking down, and has someone transcribe everything that is said in the meeting. She is also personally involved in the hiring process and conducts a summer trip abroad to stimulate creativity and build relationships with her design engineers.[36]

The effects of political behavior in organizations can be quite negative when such behavior is strategically undertaken to maximize self-interest. If people within the organization are competitively pursuing selfish ends, they're unlikely to be attentive to the concerns of others. The workplace can seem less helpful, more threatening, and more unpredictable. People focus on their own concerns rather than on organizational goals. This represents the negative face of power described earlier by David McClelland as personal power. If employees view the organization's political climate as extreme, they experience more anxiety, tension, fatigue, and burnout. They are also dissatisfied with their jobs and are more likely to leave.[37]

Not all political behavior is destructive. Positive political behavior still involves self-interest; however, when the self-interest is aligned with organizational goals, employees see this behavior as positive. Additionally, when political behavior is seen as the only means to accomplish something, it is often seen as positive. Positive and negative political behaviors influence satisfaction with one's job, supervisor, and coworkers.[38]

Influence Tactics

Influence is the process of affecting the thoughts, behavior, or feelings of another person. That other person could be the boss (upward influence), an employee (downward influence), or a coworker (lateral influence). There are eight basic types of influence tactics. They are listed and described in Table 11.2.[39]

political behavior
Actions not officially sanctioned by an organization that are taken to influence others in order to meet one's personal goals.

11.2 Influence Tactics Used in Organizations

Tactics	Description	Examples
Pressure	The person uses demands, threats, or intimidation to convince you to comply with a request or to support a proposal.	If you don't do this, you're fired. You have until 5:00 to change your mind, or I'm going without you.
Upward appeals	The person seeks to persuade you that the request is approved by higher management or appeals to higher management for assistance in gaining your compliance with the request.	I'm reporting you to my boss. My boss supports this idea.
Exchange	The person makes an explicit or implicit promise that you will receive rewards or tangible benefits if you comply with a request or support a proposal or reminds you of a prior favor to be reciprocated.	You owe me a favor. I'll take you to lunch if you'll support me on this.
Coalition	The person seeks the aid of others to persuade you to do something or uses the support of others as an argument for you to agree also.	All the other supervisors agree with me. I'll ask you in front of the whole committee.
Ingratiation	The person seeks to get you in a good mood or to think favorably of him or her before asking you to do something.	Only you can do this job right. I can always count on you, so I have another request.
Rational persuasion	The person uses logical arguments and factual evidence to persuade you that a proposal or request is viable and likely to result in the attainment of task objectives.	This new procedure will save us $150,000 in overhead. It makes sense to hire John; he has the most experience.
Inspirational appeals	The person makes an emotional request or proposal that arouses enthusiasm by appealing to your values and ideals or by increasing your confidence that you can do it.	Being environmentally conscious is the right thing. Getting that account will be tough, but I know you can do it.
Consultation	The person seeks your participation in making a decision or planning how to implement a proposed policy, strategy, or change.	This new attendance plan is controversial. How can we make it more acceptable? What do you think we can do to make our workers less fearful of the new robots on the production line?

SOURCE: First two columns from G. Yukl and C. M. Falbe, "Influence Tactics and Objectives in Upward, Downward, and Lateral Influence Attempts," *Journal of Applied Psychology* 75 (1990): 132–140. Copyright © 1990 by the American Psychological Association. Reprinted with permission.

Research has shown that the four tactics used most frequently are consultation, rational persuasion, inspirational appeals, and ingratiation. Upward appeals and coalition tactics are used moderately. Exchange tactics are used least often, while pressure is the least effective tactic.

Influence tactics are used for impression management, which was described in Chapter 3. In impression management, individuals use influence tactics to control others' impressions of them. One way in which people engage in impression management is through image building. Another way is to use impression management to get support for important initiatives or projects.

Ingratiation is an example of a tactic often used for impression management. Ingratiation can take many forms, including flattery, opinion conformity, and subservient behavior.[40] Exchange is another influence tactic that may be used for impression management. Offering to do favors for someone in an effort to create a favorable impression is an exchange tactic.

Which influence tactics are most effective? It depends on the target of the influence attempt and the objective. Individuals use different tactics for different purposes, and for different people. Influence attempts with subordinates, for example, usually involve assigning tasks or changing behavior. With peers, the objective is often to request help. With superiors, influence attempts are often made to request approval, resources, political support, or personal benefits. Rational persuasion and coalition tactics are used most often to get support from peers and superiors to change company policy. Consultation and inspirational appeals are particularly effective for gaining support and resources for a new project.[41] Overall, the most effective tactic in terms of achieving objectives is rational persuasion. Pressure is the least effective tactic.

Influence tactics are often used on bosses in order to get them to evaluate the employee more favorably or to give the employee a promotion. Two tactics, rational persuasion and ingratiation, appear to work effectively. Employees who use these tactics receive higher performance evaluations than employees who don't.[42] When supervisors believe an employee's motive for doing favors for the boss is simply to be a good citizen, they are likely to reward that employee. However, when the motive is seen as brownnosing (ingratiation), supervisors respond negatively.[43] And, as it becomes more obvious that the employee has something to gain by impressing the boss, the likelihood that ingratiation will succeed decreases. So, how does one use ingratiation effectively? A study conducted among supervisors and subordinates of a large state agency indicates that subordinates with higher scores on political skill used ingratiation regularly and received higher performance ratings, whereas individuals with lower scores on political skill who used ingratiation frequently received lower performance ratings.[44] Additionally, another research study demonstrated that supervisors rated subordinate ingratiation behavior as less manipulative if the subordinate was highly politically skilled.[45] These results indicate that political skill might be one factor that enables people to use ingratiation effectively. We'll describe political skill in more detail in the section of the chapter that follows.

Still, a well-disguised ingratiation is hard to resist. Attempts that are not obvious usually succeed in increasing the target's liking for the ingratiator.[46] Most people have trouble remaining neutral when someone flatters them or agrees with them. However, witnesses to the ingratiation are more likely to question the motive behind it. Observers are more skeptical than the recipients of the ingratiation.

There is evidence that men and women view politics and influence attempts differently. Men tend to view political behavior more favorably than do women. When both men and women witness political behavior, they view it more positively if the agent is of their gender and the target is of the opposite gender.[47] Women executives often view politics with distaste and expect to be recognized and promoted only on the merit of their work. A lack of awareness of organizational politics is a barrier that holds women back in terms of moving into senior executive ranks.[48] Women may have fewer opportunities to develop political skills because of a lack of mentors and role models and because they are often excluded from informal networks.[49]

Different cultures prefer different influence tactics at work. One study found that American managers dealing with a tardy employee tended to rely on pressure tactics such as "If you don't start reporting on time for work, I will have no choice but to start docking your pay." By contrast, Japanese managers relied on influence tactics that either appealed to the employee's sense of duty ("It is your duty as a responsible employee of this company to begin work on time.") or emphasized a consultative approach ("Is there anything I can do to help you overcome the problems that are preventing you from coming to work on time?").[50]

Influence can also stem from a person fitting with his or her work environment. A recent study found that extraverts have more influence in team-oriented work environments, whereas conscientious employees have more influence in environments where individuals work alone on technical tasks.[51]

It is important to note that influence tactics do have some positive effects. When investors form coalitions and put pressure on firms to increase their research and development efforts, it works.[52] However, some influence tactics, including pressure, coalition building, and exchange, can have strong ethical implications. There is a fine line between being an impression manager and being seen as a manipulator.

How can a manager use influence tactics well? First, she or he can develop and maintain open lines of communication in all directions: upward, downward, and lateral. Then the manager can treat the targets of influence attempts—whether managers, employees, or peers—with basic respect. Finally, the manager can understand that influence relationships are reciprocal—they are two-way relationships. As long as the influence attempts are directed toward organizational goals, the process of influence can be advantageous to all involved. When a manager is trying to influence employees, the choice of tactics is important, but so is the quality of the relationship between the manager and employee. In the Science feature, you can see how relationship quality and influence tactics interact to determine whether the manager can successfully influence the employee.

Political Skill

Researchers at Florida State University have generated an impressive body of research on political skill.[53] *Political skill* is the ability to get things done through positive interpersonal relationships outside the formal organization. Researchers suggest that it should be considered in hiring and promotion decisions. They found that leader political skill has a positive effect on team performance and on trust and support for the leader.[54,55] Furthermore, it buffers the negative effects of stressors such as role conflict in work settings. These findings point to the importance of developing political skill for managerial success.[56] Politically skilled individuals have the ability to accurately understand others and use this knowledge to influence them in order to meet personal or organizational goals. Political skill is made up of four key dimensions: social astuteness, interpersonal influence, networking ability, and sincerity.

1. *Social astuteness* refers to accurate perception and evaluation of social situations. Socially astute individuals manage social situations in ways that present them in the most favorable light.

political skill
The ability to get things done through favorable interpersonal relationships outside of formally prescribed organizational mechanisms.

Trying to Influence Your Employees? Consider the Relationship

As the preceding section indicates, managers have several options in regard to what types of influence tactics they can use; however, successful attempts at influence may depend on more than which particular tactic is chosen. Recent research indicates that the ways employees view their relationships with their leaders impact the effective of the influence tactic.

When leaders use ingratiation on their employees and those employees feel they have high-quality relationships with their leaders, they are less likely to resist change initiated by the leader. On the other hand, when the employees view the relationship as lesser in quality, they are more likely to resist change when ingratiation is used. Furthermore, when leaders use either legitimating

tactics (tactics that seek to establish credibility such as aligning with organization policies) or punishment, more resistance is seen when the relationship between the supervisor and employee is of low quality.

These findings indicate that before leaders determine how they should influence their followers, they need to consider the relationship. When the relationship is perceived as low quality by the employee, ingratiation, punishment, and legitimating tactics may cause increased resistance.

SOURCE: S. A. Furst and D. M. Cable "Employee Resistance to Change: Managerial Influence Tactics and Leader-Member Exchange," *Journal of Applied Psychology* 93 (2008): 453–462.

2. *Interpersonal influence* refers to a subtle and influential personal style that is effective in getting things done. Individuals with interpersonal influence are very flexible in adapting their behavior to differing targets of influence or differing contexts in order to achieve their goals.

3. *Networking ability* is an individual's capacity to develop and retain diverse and extensive social networks. People who have networking ability are effective in building successful alliances and coalitions, thus making them skilled at negotiation and conflict resolution.

4. *Sincerity* refers to an individual's ability to portray forthrightness and authenticity in all of their dealings. Individuals who can appear sincere inspire more confidence and trust, thus making them very successful in influencing other people.[57]

These four dimensions of political skill can each be learned. Several organizations now offer training to help develop this ability in their employees. And political skill is important at all levels of the organization. The biggest cause of failure among top executives is lack of social effectiveness.[58] High self-monitors and politically savvy individuals score higher on an index of political skill, as do individuals who are emotionally intelligent. You 11.1 helps you assess your political skill.

Military settings are particularly demanding in their need for leaders who can adapt to changing situations and maintain a good reputation. In such an environment, politically skilled leaders are seen as more sincere in their motives, can more readily perceive and adapt to work events, and can thus build a strong positive reputation among followers. In fact, political skill can be acquired through a social learning process and by having a strong mentor. Such a mentor then serves as a role model and helps the protégé navigate organizational politics and helps him/her learn the informal sources of power and politics in the organization.[59] Individuals who have political skill have been shown to be more likely to engage in OCBs, have more total promotions, have higher perceived career success, and have greater life satisfaction.[60,61]

You 11.1

Using the following 7-point scale, choose the number that best describes how much you agree with each statement about yourself.

> 1 = *strongly disagree*
> 2 = *disagree*
> 3 = *slightly disagree*
> 4 = *neutral*
> 5 = *slightly agree*
> 6 = *agree*
> 7 = *strongly agree*

1. _____ I spend a lot of time and effort at work networking with others.
2. _____ I am able to make most people feel comfortable and at ease around me.
3. _____ I am able to communicate easily and effectively with others.
4. _____ It is easy for me to develop good rapport with most people.
5. _____ I understand people very well.
6. _____ I am good at building relationships with influential people at work.
7. _____ I am particularly good at sensing the motivations and hidden agendas of others.
8. _____ When communicating with others, I try to be genuine in what I say and do.
9. _____ I have developed a large network of colleagues and associates at work who I can call on for support when I really need to get things done.
10. _____ At work, I know a lot of important people and am well connected.
11. _____ I spend a lot of time at work developing connections with others.
12. _____ I am good at getting people to like me.
13. _____ It is important that people believe I am sincere in what I say and do.
14. _____ I try to show a genuine interest in other people.
15. _____ I am good at using my connections and I network to make things happen at work.
16. _____ I have good intuition or savvy about how to present myself to others.
17. _____ I always seem to instinctively know the right things to say or do to influence others.
18. _____ I pay close attention to people's facial expressions.

A higher score indicates better political skill than a lower score.

SOURCE: G. Ferris, S. L. Davidson, & P. L. Perrewe, Political Skill at Work: Impact on Work Effectiveness, Davies-Black Publishing, 2005.

Managing Political Behavior in Organizations

Politics cannot and should not be eliminated from organizations. Managers can, however, take a proactive stance and manage the political behavior that inevitably occurs.[62] The first step in managing political behavior is recognizing it. Some of the tactics managers use often include networking, finding key players to support initiatives, making friends with powerful people, bending the rules, and self-promoting. Lesser used tactics include misinformation, spreading rumors, and keeping "dirt" files for blackmail.[63]

These tactics can be dealt with by open communication, which is one key to managing political behavior. Uncertainty tends to increase such behavior, and communication that reduces the uncertainty is important. One helpful form of communication is to clarify the sanctioned and nonsanctioned political behaviors in the organization. For example, you may want to encourage social power as opposed to personal power.[64]

Another key is to clarify expectations regarding performance. This can be accomplished through the use of clear, quantifiable goals and the establishment of a clear connection between goal accomplishment and rewards.[65]

Participative management is yet another key. Often, people engage in political behavior when they feel excluded from decision-making processes in the organization. By including such people, you will encourage positive input and eliminate behind-the-scenes maneuvering.

Encouraging cooperation among work groups is another strategy for managing political behavior. Managers can instill a unity of purpose among work teams by rewarding cooperative behavior and by implementing activities that emphasize the integration of team efforts toward common goals.[66]

Managing scarce resources well is also important. An obvious solution to the problem of scarce resources is to increase the resource pool, but few managers have this luxury. Clarifying the resource allocation process and making the connection between performance and resources explicit can help discourage dysfunctional political behavior.

Providing a supportive organizational climate is another way to manage political behavior effectively. A supportive climate allows employees to discuss controversial issues promptly and openly. This prevents the issue from festering and potentially causing friction among employees.[67]

Managing political behavior at work is important. The perception of dysfunctional political behavior can lead to dissatisfaction.[68] When employees perceive that there are dominant interest groups or cliques at work, they are less satisfied with pay and promotions. When they believe that the organization's reward practices are influenced by who you know rather than how well you perform, they are less satisfied.[69] In addition, when employees believe that their coworkers are exhibiting increased political behavior, they are less satisfied with their coworkers. Open communication, clear expectations about performance and rewards, participative decision-making practices, work group cooperation, effective management of scarce resources, and a supportive organizational climate can help managers prevent the negative consequences of political behavior.

MANAGING UP: MANAGING THE BOSS

7 Develop a plan for managing employee–boss relationships.

One of the least discussed aspects of power and politics is the relationship between you and your boss. This is a crucial relationship, because your boss is your most important link with the rest of the organization.[70] The employee–boss relationship is one of mutual dependence; you depend on your boss to give you performance feedback, provide resources, and supply critical information. He or she depends on you for performance, information, and support. Because it's a mutual relationship, you should take an active role in managing it. Too often the management of this relationship is left to the boss; but if the relationship doesn't meet your needs, chances are you haven't taken the responsibility to manage it proactively.

Table 11.3 shows the basic steps to take in managing your relationship with your boss. The first step is to try to understand as much as you can about him or her. What are his or her goals and objectives? What kind of pressures does he or she face in the job? Many individuals naively expect the boss to be perfect and are disappointed when they find that this is not the case. What are the boss's strengths, weaknesses, and blind spots? Because this is an emotionally charged relationship, it is difficult to be objective; but this is a critical step in forging an effective working

11.3   Managing Your Relationship with Your Boss

Make Sure You Understand Your Boss and Her Context, Including:

Her goals and objectives.

The pressures on her.

Her strengths, weaknesses, and blind spots.

Her preferred work style.

Assess Yourself and Your Needs, Including:

Your own strengths and weaknesses.

Your personal style.

Your predisposition toward dependence on authority figures.

Develop and Maintain a Relationship That:

Fits both your needs and styles.

Is characterized by mutual expectations.

Keeps your boss informed.

Is based on dependability and honesty.

Selectively uses your boss's time and resources.

SOURCE: Reprinted by permission of *Harvard Business Review*. From "Managing Your Boss," by J. J. Gabarro and J. P. Kotter (May–June 1993): p. 155. Copyright © 1993 by the Harvard Business School Publishing Corporation; all rights reserved.

relationship. What is the boss's preferred work style? Does he or she prefer everything in writing or hate detail? Does he or she prefer that you make appointments or is dropping in at his or her office acceptable? The point is to gather as much information about your boss as you can and to try to put yourself in his or her shoes.

The second step in managing this important relationship is to assess yourself and your own needs in the same way you analyzed your boss's. What are your strengths, weaknesses, and blind spots? What is your work style? How do you normally relate to authority figures? Some of us have tendencies toward counter-dependence; that is, we rebel against the boss as an authority and view him or her as a hindrance to our performance. Or, by contrast, we might take an overdependent stance, passively accepting the employee–boss relationship and treating him or her as an all-wise, protective parent. What is your tendency? Knowing how you react to authority figures can help you understand your interactions with your boss.

Once you have done a careful self-analysis and tried to understand your boss, the next step is to work to develop an effective relationship. Both parties' needs and styles must be accommodated. A fundraiser for a large volunteer organization related a story about a new boss, describing him as cold, aloof, unorganized, and inept. She made repeated attempts to meet with him and clarify expectations, and his usual reply was that he didn't have the time. Frustrated, she almost looked for a new job. "I just can't reach him!" was her refrain. Then she stepped back to consider her boss's style and her own. Being an intuitive-feeling type of person, she prefers constant feedback and reinforcement from others. Her boss, an intuitive thinker, works comfortably without feedback from others and has a tendency to fail to praise or reward others. She sat down with him and cautiously discussed the differences in their needs. This discussion became the basis for working out a comfortable relationship. "I still don't like him, but I understand him better," she said.

Another aspect of managing the relationship involves working out mutual expectations. One key activity is to develop a plan for work objectives and have the boss agree to it.[71] It is important to do things right, but it is also important to do the right things. Neither party to the relationship is a mind reader, and clarifying the goals is a crucial step.

Keeping the boss informed is also a priority. No one likes to be caught off guard, and there are several ways to keep the boss informed. Give the boss a weekly to-do list as a reminder of the progress toward goals. When you read something pertaining to your work, clip it out for the boss. Most busy executives appreciate being given materials they don't have time to find for themselves. Give the boss interim reports, and let the boss know if the work schedule is slipping. Don't wait until it's too late to take action.

The employee–boss relationship must be based on dependability and honesty. This means giving and receiving positive and negative feedback. Most of us are reluctant to give any feedback to the boss, but positive feedback is welcomed at the top. Negative feedback, while tougher to initiate, can clear the air. If given in a problem-solving format, it can even bring about a closer relationship.[72]

Finally, remember that the boss is on the same team you are. The golden rule is to make the boss look good, because you expect the boss to do the same for you.

SHARING POWER: EMPOWERMENT

8 Discuss how managers can empower others.

As modern organizations grow flatter, eliminating layers of management, empowerment becomes more and more important. Jay Conger defines *empowerment* as "creating conditions for heightened motivation through the development of a strong sense of personal self-efficacy."[73] Sharing power with others makes everyone in the organization more powerful. Kiva is an organization founded on the philosophy of empowering others. In The Real World 11.2, you can see how Kiva helps people empower other people worldwide.

Empowerment means sharing power in such a way that individuals learn to believe in their ability to do the job. The driving idea of empowerment is that the individuals closest to the work and to the customers should make the decisions and that this makes the best use of employees' skills and talents. You can empower yourself by developing your sense of self-efficacy. You 11.2 helps you assess your progress in terms of self-empowerment.

Four dimensions comprise the essence of empowerment: meaning, competence, self-determination, and impact.[74]

- *Meaning* is a fit between the work role and the employee's values and beliefs. It is the engine of empowerment that energizes employees about their jobs. If employees' hearts are not in their work, they cannot feel empowered.

- *Competence* is the belief that one has the ability to do the job well. Without competence, employees will feel inadequate and lack a sense of empowerment.

- *Self-determination* is having control over the way one does his or her work. Employees who feel they're just following orders from the boss cannot feel empowered.

- *Impact* is the belief that one's job makes a difference within the organization. Without a sense of contributing to a goal, employees cannot feel empowered.

empowerment
Sharing power within an organization.

The Real World 11.2

Kiva: Empowering Entrepreneurs

With a click of the mouse, you can make a loan to an entrepreneur in the Democratic Republic of the Congo, or Moldova, or Southern Sudan, or Peru, among other countries. Through Kiva, you can lend to an entrepreneur in the developing world; someone who needs the money for their business like raising and selling vegetables, making bricks, or raising goats. You are empowering them to lift themselves out of poverty!

Sophea Chum lives on an island in the Mekong River. She requested a loan through Kiva for $600 to purchase silk materials for her and her husband's weaving business.

Kiva was founded by Matt and Jessica Flannery, who witnessed microfinance firsthand on a trip to East Africa. They saw that small loans of $100 or so had the power to build small businesses, and they returned to the United States wondering how to lend money to African entrepreneurs. Their solution is a blend of microfinance and social networking.

On Kiva's Web site (http://www.kiva.org) are the loan opportunities, and each one has a picture of the entrepreneur along with a description of his or her business and how they plan to use their loan. You get updates of how the entrepreneur is doing, and when he or she pays the loan back, you get your money back. Lenders have the option to relend the money, donate it to Kiva's operations, or keep it. Kiva's loans are managed by microfinance institutions with plenty of experience. As of September 2009, the loan default rate was less than 2 percent, and approximately 98 percent of the loans are paid back in full.

Kiva expects to loan $1 billion within ten years, $25 at a time. Bill Clinton has featured Kiva in his book *Giving*, and Oprah Winfrey has featured Kiva in her television show. As of September 2009, there were approximately 550,000 Kiva lenders. The entrepreneurs who have been empowered through Kiva exceeds 105,000. Demand was so great in one particular month that lenders had to be turned away because all of the loans had been funded!

You could say that Kiva is people empowering people—a powerful idea.

Sources: *Kiva: Loans that Challenge Lives*, www.kiva.org; "When Small Loans Make a Big Difference," *Forbes.com*, June 3, 2008, accessed at http://www.forbes.com/2008/06/03/kiva-microfinance-uganda-ent-fin-cx_0603whartonkiva.html.

Employees need to experience all four of the empowerment dimensions in order to feel truly empowered. Only then will organizations reap the hoped-for rewards from empowerment efforts. Empowerment increases organizational commitment and job performance and reduces job stress.[75]

Empowerment is easy to advocate but difficult to put into practice. Conger offers some guidelines on how leaders can empower others.

First, managers should express confidence in employees and set high performance expectations. Positive expectations can go a long way toward enabling good performance, as the Pygmalion effect shows (Chapter 3).

Second, managers should create opportunities for employees to participate in decision making. This means participation in the forms of both voice and choice. Employees should not just be asked to contribute their opinions about any issue; they should also have a vote in the decision that is made. One method for increasing participation is using self-managed teams, as we discussed in Chapter 9. These are the ultimate in empowered teams, making all the decisions and conducting activities once reserved for managers.

Are You Self-Empowered?

Circle to indicate how you usually are in these situations:

1. If someone disagrees with me in a class or a meeting, I
   a. immediately back down.
   b. explain my position further.

2. When I have an idea for a project, I
   a. typically take a great deal of time to start it.
   b. get going on it fairly quickly.

3. If my boss or teacher tells me to do something that I think is wrong, I
   a. do it anyway, telling myself he or she is "the boss."
   b. ask for clarification and explain my position.

4. When a complicated problem arises, I usually tell myself I
   a. can take care of it.
   b. will not be able to solve it.

5. When I am around people of higher authority, I often
   a. feel intimidated and defer to them.
   b. enjoy meeting important people.

6. As I awake in the morning, I usually feel
   a. alert and ready to conquer almost anything.
   b. tired and have a hard time getting myself motivated.

7. During an argument I
   a. put a great deal of energy into "winning."
   b. try to listen to the other side and see if we have any points of agreement.

8. When I meet new people, I
   a. always wonder what they are "really" up to.
   b. try to learn what they are about and give them the benefit of the doubt until they prove otherwise.

9. During the day I often
   a. criticize myself on what I am doing or thinking.
   b. think positive thoughts about myself.

10. When someone else does a great job, I
    a. find myself picking apart that person and looking for faults.
    b. often give a sincere compliment.

11. When I am working in a group, I try to
    a. do a better job than the others.
    b. help the group function more effectively.

12. If someone pays me a compliment, I typically
    a. try not to appear boastful and I downplay the compliment.
    b. respond with a positive "thank you" or similar response.

13. I like to be around people who
    a. challenge me and make me question what I do.
    b. give me respect.

14. In love relationships, I prefer the other person to
    a. have his/her own selected interests.
    b. do pretty much what I do.

15. During a crisis, I try to
    a. resolve the problem.
    b. find someone to blame.

16. After seeing a movie with friends, I
    a. wait to see what they say before I decide whether I liked it.
    b. am ready to talk about my reactions right away.

17. When work deadlines are approaching, I typically
    a. get flustered and worry about completion.
    b. buckle down and work until the job is done.

18. If a job comes up I am interested in, I
    a. go for it and apply.
    b. tell myself I am not qualified enough.

19. When someone treats me unkindly or unfairly, I
    a. try to rectify the situation.
    b. tell other people about the injustice.

20. If a difficult conflict situation or problem arises, I
    a. try not to think about it, hoping it will resolve itself.
    b. look at various options and may ask others for advice before I figure out what to do.

Third, managers should remove bureaucratic constraints that stifle autonomy. Often, companies have antiquated rules and policies that prevent employees from managing themselves. An example is a collection agency where a manager's signature was once required to approve long-term payment arrangements for delinquent customers. Collectors, who spoke directly with customers, were the best judges of whether the payment arrangements were workable, and having to consult a manager made them feel closely supervised and powerless. The rule was dropped and collections increased.

Fourth, managers should set inspirational or meaningful goals. When individuals feel they "own" a goal, they are more willing to take personal responsibility for it.

Empowerment is a matter of degree. Jobs can be thought of in two dimensions: job content and job context. Job content consists of the tasks and procedures necessary for doing a particular job. Job context is broader. It is the reason the organization needs the job and includes the way the job fits into the organization's mission, goals, and objectives. These two dimensions are depicted in Figure 11.2, the employee empowerment grid.

Both axes of the grid contain the major steps in the decision-making process. As shown on the horizontal axis, decision-making authority over job content increases in terms of greater involvement in the decision-making process. Similarly, the vertical axis shows that authority over job context increases with greater involvement in that decision-making process. Combining job content and job context authority in this way produces five points that vary in terms of the degree of empowerment.[76]

No Discretion (point A) represents the traditional, assembly-line job: highly routine and repetitive, with no decision-making power. Recall from Chapter 7 that if these jobs have a demanding pace and if workers have no discretion, distress will result.

Task Setting (point B) is the essence of most empowerment programs in organizations today. In this case, the worker is empowered to make decisions about the best way to get the job done but has no decision responsibility for the job context.

Participatory Empowerment (point C) represents a situation that is typical of autonomous work groups that have some decision-making power over both job content and job context. Their involvement is in problem identification, developing

FIGURE

11.2   Employee Empowerment Grid

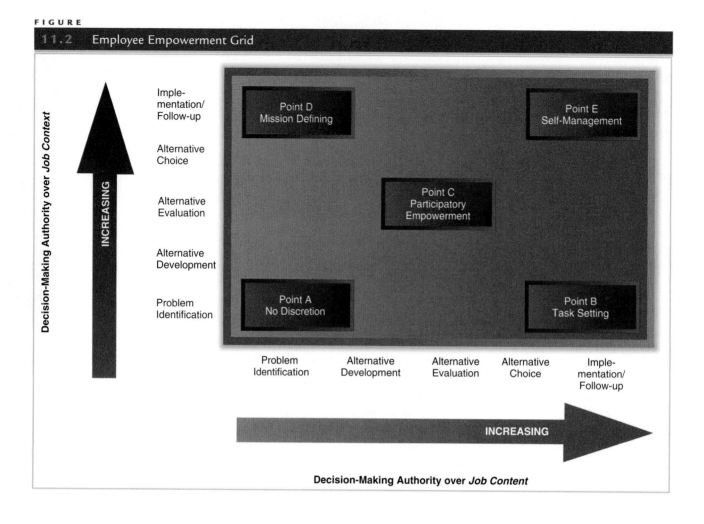

alternatives, and evaluating alternatives, but the actual choice of alternatives is often beyond their power. Participatory empowerment can lead to job satisfaction and productivity.

Mission Defining (point D) is an unusual case of empowerment and is seldom seen. Here, employees have power over job context but not job content. An example would be a unionized team that is asked to decide whether their jobs could be better done by an outside vendor. Deciding to outsource would dramatically affect the mission of the company but would not affect job content, which is specified in the union contract. Assuring these employees of continued employment regardless of their decision would be necessary for this case of empowerment.

Self-Management (point E) represents total decision-making control over both job content and job context. It is the ultimate expression of trust. One example is TXI Chaparral Steel (part of Texas Industries), where employees redesign their own jobs to add value to the organization.

Empowerment should begin with job content and proceed to job context. Because the workforce is so diverse, managers should recognize that some employees are more ready for empowerment than others. Managers must diagnose situations and determine the degree of empowerment to extend to employees. Recently, the management of change in organizations was identified as another area wherein empowerment can have a strong effect. Empowered employees are more likely to participate in and facilitate change processes in organizations as they feel more committed to the organizations' success.[77]

The empowerment process also carries with it a risk of failure. When you delegate responsibility and authority, you must be prepared to allow employees to fail; and failure is not something most managers tolerate well. At Merck, some say the CEO Ray Gilmartin empowered scientists too much and that their failures cost Merck its profitability and reputation as one of *Fortune*'s Most Admired Companies. One example of this empowerment involved a diabetes drug that early research showed caused tumors in mice. Scientists argued that despite early studies showing the drug wasn't viable, research should continue, and it did—until the drug was finally axed, costing the company considerably in terms of time and money.[78]

MANAGERIAL IMPLICATIONS: USING POWER EFFECTIVELY

Sydney Finkelstein, a professor at Dartmouth University, spends his time studying why executives fail. Interestingly, most of these failures involve the misuse of power and organizational politics. Here are several reasons why executives fail:

- *They see themselves and their companies as dominating their environments.* While confidence is helpful, the perception that a company is without peer is a recipe for failure. On a more personal level, CEOs who see themselves as uniquely gifted in comparison to their competitors and coworkers are generally ripe for a fall.

- *They think they have all the answers.* While decisive leadership and vision often lead to the executive suite, an unwillingness to admit ignorance or seek others' input may trigger disaster. A reluctance to empower others leads to failure.

- *They ruthlessly eliminate anyone who isn't 100 percent behind them.* Business history is replete with leaders who culled the ranks of those who were willing to voice different opinions, only to find themselves blundering down the road to catastrophe without anyone to yell "Stop!"

- *They stubbornly rely on what worked for them in the past.* Like most of us, business leaders tend to fall back on what has worked before. Unfortunately, yesterday's solution is rarely an ideal fit for today's challenge, and successes of the past may well inhibit success in the future.

- *They have no clear boundaries between their personal interests and corporate interests.* As a top leader invests more time and effort in a firm, it's easy for him or her to become convinced that the firm is simply a reflection of his or her own enormous ego. Ironically, leaders who fail to make this distinction tend to be far less careful about spending corporate resources, leading to often embarrassing revelations of executive excess at employee and stockholder expense.[79]

While Finkelstein is quick to point out that corporate executives are, almost without exception, amazingly bright and talented individuals, they also tend to succumb to the same temptations as lesser mortals. Given the extreme power they wield, their failures tend to be much more visible, painful, and far-reaching than most. Corporate executives need accountability to help them avoid these mistakes.

In addition to learning from failure, there is research on how to use power successfully. John Kotter argues that managers need to develop power strategies to operate effectively.[80] Kotter offers the following guidelines for managing dependence on others and for using power successfully:

- *Use power in ethical ways.* People make certain assumptions about the use of power. One way of using the various forms of power ethically is by applying the criteria of utilitarian outcomes, individual rights, and distributive justice.

- *Understand and use all of the various types of power and influence.* Successful managers diagnose the situation, understand the people involved, and choose a compatible influence method.
- *Seek jobs that allow you to develop your power skills.* Recognize that managerial positions are dependent ones, and look for positions that allow you to focus on a critical issue or problem.
- *Use power tempered by maturity and self-control.* Power for its own sake should not be a goal, nor should power be used for self-aggrandizement.
- *Accept that influencing people is an important part of the management job.*

Power means getting things accomplished; it is not a dirty word. Acquiring and using power well is a key to managerial success.

You can use these guidelines to enhance your own power skills. Mastering the power and politics within an organization takes respect and patience. When all people are empowered, the total amount of power within the organization will increase.

Diversity Dialogue

Barack Obama—A Different Kind of Power

When then-presidential candidate Barack Obama said that he would negotiate directly with Iranian leaders for peaceful relations as long as Iranian leaders agreed to set aside the nation's nuclear weapons program and support of terrorists, he received a great deal of criticism from members in both major political parties. Former President Bush (43) referred to Obama's proposal as a "foolish delusion," likening it to trying to appease Hitler during World War II through sensible conversation.

As president, Barack Obama has continued to display the same style of power that he displayed as a candidate regarding his stance toward peaceful diplomacy and negotiations. Obama's style is a significant departure from earlier policies, and it has changed the way that some in strong "anti-American" countries view the United States. A recent *Boston Globe* article suggests that Obama just might be making inroads toward that goal, citing posters and songs dedicated to the new American president popping up everywhere from Egypt to the Persian Gulf. Some believe that Obama's global popularity could foil attempts by some global leaders to use anti-American feelings to strengthen their own power.

By all accounts, Obama is not your "typical" American president in more than the obvious ways. The tactics that he uses to influence others, particularly those in countries considered U.S. adversaries, is unlike those used by past American presidents. Rather than a heavy-handed approach that includes fear of retribution and threat of punishment, Obama prefers a "softer," more conciliatory approach to achieve his desired objectives.

1. What role do you believe culture plays in Obama's decision to use a less coercive strategy to influence "anti-American" governments?
2. Do leaders who use softer influence tactics run the risk of being perceived as weak? Explain.

SOURCES: B. Bender, "Gentler Approach Challenges Anti-US Regimes, Analysts Say 'Great Satan' Images Suffers Under Obama," *Boston Globe* (February 11, 2009): A12; S. G. Stolberg, "Bush Speech Criticized as Attack on Obama," *New York Times* (May 16, 2008).

LOOKING BACK: DELOITTE

How Does Deloitte Empower Women?

After realizing the need to attract and retain female talent, Deloitte launched the women's initiative and made it a business imperative in 1994. Deloitte offers programs such as Mass Career Customization that allows employees to customize their careers as their priorities change in life. Deloitte also ensures gender-balanced representation by requiring it in assignment and proposal reviews. Deloitte offers networking programs to help women gain skills, connections and visibility. Career and succession planning programs map out paths to higher level positions for both men and women. Deloitte focuses on mentoring and guiding both male and female employees. Additionally, Deloitte offers a program called Personal Pursuits that allows Deloitte employees to go on leave for one to five years. During this leave, participants can utilize Deloitte-sponsored training, mentoring, networking, licensing accreditation, and ad hoc assignments to keep them connected.[81]

All of these programs are aimed at advancing and empowering women in the workplace, and Deloitte has been successful. Primarily, Deloitte's success can be seen in stories like Barbara Adachi's; however, the company has also experienced no difference between the number of men and women leaving the company, and they have been able to retain the company's top performers.[82] Deloitte has also received recognition for these efforts. To name a few, Deloitte is in *Working Mother* magazine's Hall of Fame for being listed on its 100 Best Companies list for 15 consecutive years and, in 2008, as one of *Fortune* magazine's "100 Best Companies to Work For." Deloitte has also been named one of *Working Mother*'s 2008 "Best Companies for Multicultural Women," *Working Mother*'s "Best Companies for Women of Color," and, in *Latina Style* magazine's "Latina Style 50," Deloitte has been listed as one of the best companies for Latinas for four consecutive years.[83]

Chapter Summary

1. Power is the ability to influence others. Influence is the process of affecting the thoughts, behavior, and feelings of others. Authority is the right to influence others.

2. French and Raven's five forms of interpersonal power are reward, coercive, legitimate, referent, and expert power. Information power is another form of interpersonal power.

3. The key to using all of these types of power well is to use them ethically.

4. McClelland believes personal power is negative and social power is positive.

5. Intergroup power sources include control of critical resources and strategic contingencies.

6. According to Etzioni's power analysis, the characteristics of the organization are an important factor in deciding the type of power to use.

7. Recognizing symbols of both power and powerlessness is a key diagnostic skill for managers.

8. Organizational politics is an inevitable feature of work life. Political behavior consists of actions not officially sanctioned that are taken to influence others in order to meet personal goals. Managers should take a proactive role in managing politics. Political skill is the ability to get things done through favorable interpersonal relationships outside of formally prescribed organizational mechanisms.

9. The employee–boss relationship is an important political relationship. Employees can use their skills to develop more effective working relationships with their bosses.

10. Empowerment is a positive strategy for sharing power throughout the organization.

Key Terms

authority (p. 364)
coercive power (p. 365)
empowerment (p. 382)
expert power (p. 365)
influence (p. 364)
information power (p. 366)

legitimate power (p. 365)
organizational politics (p. 373)
personal power (p. 368)
political behavior (p. 374)
political skill (p. 377)
power (p. 364)

powerlessness (p. 373)
referent power (p. 365)
reward power (p. 365)
social power (p. 369)
strategic contingencies (p. 370)
zone of indifference (p. 364)

Review Questions

1. What are the five types of power according to French and Raven? What are the effects of these types of power? What is information power?

2. What are the intergroup sources of power?

3. Distinguish between personal and social power. What are the four power-oriented characteristics of the best managers?

4. According to Rosabeth Moss Kanter, what are the symbols of power? The symptoms of powerlessness?

5. How do organizations encourage political activity?

6. Which influence tactics are most effective?

7. What are some of the characteristics of an effective relationship between you and your boss?

8. What are some ways to empower people at work?

Discussion and Communication Questions

1. Who is the most powerful person you know personally? What is it that makes the person so powerful?

2. Why is it hard to determine if power has been used ethically?

3. What kinds of membership (alienative, calculative, moral) do you currently have? Is the power used in these relationships congruent?

4. As a student, do you experience yourself as powerful, powerless, or both? On what symbols or symptoms are you basing your perception?

5. How does attribution theory explain the reactions supervisors can have to influence tactics? How can managers prevent the negative consequences of political behavior?

6. Are people in your work environment empowered? How could they become more empowered?

7. Chapter 2 discussed power distance as a dimension of cultural differences. How would empowerment efforts be different in a country with high-power distance?

8. *(communication question)* Think of a person you admire. Write a newspaper feature analyzing the person's use of power in terms of the ideas presented in the chapter.

Ethical Dilemma

Jesse Stockton is an employee at Norbury Manufacturing, and he approaches his boss, George Underhill, with a dilemma. Two of Norbury's main clients, Lowry Ltd. and Principal Contractors, have orders for motor components. Jesse explains to George that, due to an unexpected emergency order, there are only enough components to fulfill one of the two orders. Jesse informs George that Norbury will be able to fulfill the second order within two weeks, but that they will miss the deadline of one of the companies. Shipping incomplete orders to either client is not acceptable, so they must choose which company's order to fill. Jesse assures George that he will rush out the second order as quickly as possible. Jesse asks George what to do.

George knows that Lowry Ltd. has been a longtime client of Norbury, consistently ordering all of their parts from the company and never having been late in payments. Lowry, a company of about 150 people, completely depends on Norbury's strong track record of order fulfillment to maintain their day-to-day business. Lowry is also one of Norbury's largest clients with monthly invoice nearly double that of most of Norbury's other regular clients.

George has even greater insight into Principal Contractors' situation: George's sister-in-law is the head buyer. He knows that if Valerie's first attempt to order through Norbury falls through, it will be a disaster for her, since she is new and attempting to instigate change. He doesn't want his brother and his brother's wife to suffer if Valerie loses her new job because George's company couldn't meet its obligations.

George looks Jesse in the eye and tells him to fill Principal Contractors' order and to fill Lowry's order as soon as possible. Jesse leaves George's office very confused. He was certain that George would have told him to fill the Lowry order given the long and very successful relationship the two companies have always had. This is not the first time that George has made a decision that Jesse questions. But, it is the first time that the decision could have such negative outcomes. Jesse considers going over George's head to confirm the decision but if George's boss agreed, Jesse's job could be at stake.

Questions

1. Using consequential, rule-based and character theories, evaluate Jesse's options.

2. What should Jesse do? Why?

Experiential Exercises

11.1 Social Power Role Plays

1. Divide the class into five groups of equal size, each of which is assigned one of the French and Raven types of power.

2. Read the following paragraph and prepare an influence plan using the type of power that has been assigned to your group. When you have finished your planning, select one member to play the role of instructor. Then choose from your own or another group a "student" who is to be the recipient of the "instructor's" efforts.

You are an instructor in a college class and have become aware that a potentially good student has been repeatedly absent from class and sometimes is unprepared when he is there. He seems to be satisfied with the grade he is getting, but you would like to see him attend regularly, be better prepared, and thus do better in the class. You even feel that the student might get really turned on to pursuing a career in this field, which is an exciting one for you. You are respected and liked by your students, and it irritates you that this person treats your dedicated teaching with such a cavalier attitude. You want to influence the student to start attending regularly.

3. Role-playing.

   a. Each group role-plays its influence plan.

   b. During the role-playing, members in other groups should think of themselves as the student being influenced. Fill out the following "Reaction to Influence Questionnaire" for each role-playing episode, including your own.

4. Tabulate the results of the questionnaire within your group. For each role-playing effort, determine how many people thought the power used was reward, coercive, and so on; then add up each member's score for item 2, then for items 3, 4, and 5.

5. Group discussion.

a. As a class, discuss which influence strategy is the most effective in compliance, long-lasting effect, acceptable attitude, and enhanced relationships.

b. What are the likely side effects of each type of influence strategy?

Reaction to Influence Questionnaire

Role-Play #1

1. Type of power used (mark one):
Reward—Ability to influence because of potential reward.
Coercive—Ability to influence because of capacity to coerce or punish.
Legitimate—Stems from formal position in organization.
Referent—Comes from admiration and liking.
Expert—Comes from superior knowledge or ability to get things done.

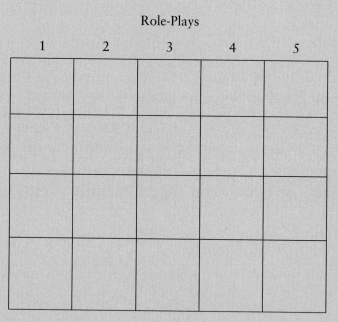

Think of yourself on the receiving end of the influence attempt just described and record your own reaction with an "X" in the appropriate box.

2. As a result of this influence attempt I will . . .
definitely not comply   definitely comply
1   2   3   4   5

3. Any change that does come about will be . . .
temporary   long-lasting
1   2   3   4   5

4. My own personal reaction is . . .
resistant   accepting
1   2   3   4   5

5. As a result of this influence attempt, my relationship with the instructor will probably be . . .
worse   better
1   2   3   4   5

SOURCE: Gib Akin, *Exchange* 3, No. 4 (1978): 38–39. Reprinted by permission of Gib Akin, McIntire School of Commerce, University of Virginia.

11.2 Empowerment in the Classroom

1. Divide the class into groups of six people.

2. Each group is to brainstorm ways in which students might be more empowered in the classroom. The ideas do not have to be either feasible or reasonable. They can be as imaginative as possible.

3. Each group should now analyze each of the empowerment ideas for feasibility, paying attention to administrative or other constraints that may hamper implementation. This feasibility discussion might include ideas about how the college or university could be altered.

4. Each group should present its empowerment ideas along with its feasibility analysis. Questions of clarification for each group should follow each presentation.

5. Discuss the following questions as a class:

a. Who is threatened by the power changes caused by empowerment?

b. Are there unintended or adverse consequences of empowerment? Explain.

BizFlix | Flash of Genius

Robert Kearns (Greg Kinnear), a college professor and part-time inventor, creates the intermittent windshield wiper. With the encouragement of his friend Gil Privick (Dermot Mulroney), Kearns presents his invention to Ford Motor Company executives. They accept his invention but do not give him either money or credit. Kearns enters into extended litigation with negative effects on himself, his marriage, and his family. The film is based on the true story about Kearns' triumph over Ford and the large settlement in the end.

Power and Political Behavior: Bob Kearns and Ford

This scene begins as a door opens and Mack a Ford executive (Mitch Pileggi) enters the room. It follows the family driving in the rain and testing the windshield wiper system for the first time. The scene ends with Bob and Mack shaking hands. Mack says, "Excellent. This is what it's all about, Bob. Corporate 'can do.' " Frank Sertin (Daniel Roebuck) says, "How about that."

What to Watch for and Ask Yourself

- This chapter defined power as "the ability to influence someone else." Who has power in this film scene?
- The chapter distinguished influence from authority. What is the example of the use of authority in the scene?
- Which interpersonal forms of power appear in this film scene? Draw examples of your choices from the scene.

Workplace Video | Numi Organic Tea: Managing the Value Chain, Information Technology, and E-Business

Numi is the tea maker of choice for high-end restaurants, hotel chains, colleges, and cruise lines. As pioneer of green marketing, the organic beverage company is dedicated to sustainability, fair trade, and a small carbon footprint. Unlike most businesses, Numi has a three-fold bottom line of "people, planet, and profit," which requires managers to evaluate performance on a range of criteria, including the overall "greenness" of supply chain operations.

But maintaining an eco-friendly business isn't easy. Many international businesses don't share Numi's perspectives on social responsibility, waste management, and workers' rights. Some don't even speak the same ethical language. While some disagreements are acceptable, others require shrewd political calculation and pressure to resolve.

Fortunately for Numi, the technical side of managing partnerships has become easier through information technology. Whether the task involves inventory, packaging, or transport, Numi's high-tech enterprise resource planning system (ERP) enables efficient coordination with strategic partners around the globe. An ERP is a computer system that processes vast organization data and provides real time information on specific companywide operations. Since members of Numi's supply chain—mostly growers, mills, and factories—are linked to the same computer system, the tea maker is able to monitor global operations from its headquarters in Oakland, California. "We're managing our inventories in multiple countries through the same software program," says Brian Durkee, director of operations. "All we do now is simply go into the system and push a button to say we want to make a particular product, and the system pulls all the lots and materials for us and allocates the inventory."

Despite the cultural and ethical differences between Numi and certain overseas partners, managers are committed to achieving a common vision through a variety of tactics, both political and technological. The tea maker's pursuit of an ethical and sustainable supply chain reduces waste in energy and natural resources. As a result, Numi's organic tea products not only taste great, but they are good for the planet as well.

Discussion Questions

1. Describe the power relationship between Numi and its supply chain partners.

2. In the video, what issues with China-based suppliers require Numi's managers to engage in organizational politics?

3. How does Numi get suppliers to comply with its policies?

Case

Power and Politics in the Fall and Rise of John Lasseter

John Lasseter grew up in a family heavily involved in artistic expression. Lasseter was drawn to cartoons as a youngster. Then as a freshman in high school he read a book entitled *The Art of Animation*. The book, about the making of the Disney animated film *Sleeping Beauty*, proved to be a revelation for Lasseter. He discovered that people could earn a living by developing cartoons. Lasseter started writing letters to The Walt Disney Company Studios regarding his interest in creating cartoons. Studio representatives, who corresponded with Lasseter many times, told him to get a great art education, after which they would teach him animation.[1]

When Disney started a Character Animation Program at the California Institute of Arts film school, the Disney Studio contacted Lasseter and he enrolled in the program. Classes were taught by extremely talented Disney animators who also shared stories about working with Walt Disney. During summer breaks from Cal Art classes, jobs at Disneyland further fueled Lasseter's passion for working as an animator for Disney Studios. Full of excitement, Lasseter joined the Disney animation staff in 1979 after graduation from the California Institute of Arts, but he met with disappointment.[2] According to Lasseter, "[t]he animation studio wasn't being run by these great Disney artists like our teachers at Cal Arts, but by lesser artists and businesspeople who rose through attrition as the grand old men retired."[3] Lasseter was told, "[y]ou put in your time for 20 years and do what you're told, and then you can be in charge."[4] Lasseter continues, "I didn't realize it then, but I was beginning to be perceived as a loose cannon. All I was trying to do was make things great, but I was beginning to make some enemies."[5]

In the early 1980s, Lasseter became enthralled with the potential of using computer graphics technology for animation but found little interest among Disney Studio executives for the concept. Nonetheless, a young Disney executive, Tom Willhite, eventually allowed Lasseter and a colleague to develop a thirty-second test film that combined "hand-drawn, two-dimensional Disney-style character animation with three-dimensional computer-generated backgrounds."[6] Lasseter found a story that would fit the test and could be developed into a full movie. When Lasseter presented the test clip and feature movie idea to the Disney Studio head, the only question the studio head asked concerned the cost of production. Lasseter told him the cost of production with computer animation would be about the same as a regular animated feature; and then the studio head informed Lasseter, "I'm only interested in computer animation if it saves money or time."[7]

Lasseter subsequently discovered that his idea was doomed before he ever presented it to the studio head. Says Lasseter, "[w]e found out later that others poked holes in my idea before I had even pitched it. In our enthusiasm, we had gone around some of my direct superiors, and I didn't realize how much of an enemy I had made of one of them. I mean, the studio head had made up his mind before we walked in. We could have shown him anything and he would have said the same thing."[8] Shortly after the studio head left the room, Lasseter received a call from the superior who didn't like him, informing Lasseter that his employment at Disney was being terminated immediately.[9]

Despite being fired, Lasseter did not speak negatively of the Disney organization, nor did he let others know anything other than the project on which he was working had ended. His personal admiration and respect for Walt Disney and animation were too great to allow him to do otherwise.[10]

Lasseter was recruited to Lucasfilm by Ed Catmull to work on a project that "turned out to be the very first character-animation cartoon done with a computer."[11] Not too long afterwards, Steve Jobs bought the animation business from George Lucas for $10 million and Pixar Animation Studios was born.[12] Lasseter became the chief creative genius behind Pixar's subsequent animated feature film successes like *Toy Story*, *Toy Story 2*, *A Bug's Life*, and *The Incredibles*, among others.[13]

In 2006, Disney CEO Robert Iger and Pixar CEO Steve Jobs consummated a deal for Pixar to become a wholly-owned subsidiary of Disney. Iger points out that, in making the Pixar acquisition, Disney wanted to protect Pixar's culture while giving it "a much broader canvas to paint on."[14] Instead of Disney absorbing Pixar into its culture, Iger gave Pixar executives "Ed Catmull and John Lasseter control of Disney's animation operations, with the mission to get the old studio's computer-generated efforts up to par."[15]

Iger wanted to reinvigorate animation at Disney, and as the top creative executive at Pixar, John Lasseter was viewed a key figure in achieving this objective.[16] Lasseter "is regarded by Hollywood executives as the modern Walt [Disney] himself [with capabilities] ... that have made Pixar a sure thing in the high stakes animated world."[17] Former Disney Studios head, Peter Schneider, says Lasseter "is a kid who has never grown up and continues to show the wonder and joy that you need in this business."[18] Current Disney Studio chief, Dick Cook, says that Lasseter is like the famous professional basketball player, Michael Jordan. "He makes all the players around him better."[19]

According to Iger, "[t]here's no question that animation is a great wavemaker for the company. We believe we have a very vibrant creative engine there, mostly driven by Pixar, and we hope that Disney Animation will once again experience glory days too. We believe we're on the right track."[20] Cook notes that Disney was the king of animation for a decade from the mid-1980s to the mid-1990s. Cook continues, "[b]ut I think the biggest challenge in any mature organization is how do you continue to evolve and press the edges of the envelope, and I think it's fair to say we stopped doing that." He also observes that getting Catmull and Lasseter "was like a giant shot of adrenaline to the system."[21]

Lasseter now oversees development of movies at both Pixar's and Disney's animation studios.[22] Says Lasseter, "I can't tell you how thrilled I am to have all these new roles. I do what I do in life because of Walt Disney—his films and his theme park and his characters and his joy in entertaining. The emotional feeling that his creations gave me is something that I want to turn around and give to others."[23]

Without a doubt, Lasseter is realizing his dream—and being very successful in doing so. *Bolt*, a recent production of Disney Animation Studios, received a Golden globe nomination in late 2008 for best animated feature film. And *Wall-E*, a Pixar Studios production, was nominated for the same award as well.[24] Jennie Yabroof, a reporter for *Newsweek*, writes that "Lasseter himself has played perhaps the biggest role in the elevation of the lowly cartoon" to the animated feature film.[25]

Lasseter's influence at Disney extends well beyond the animation studios. For example, Lasseter's impact can be seen in the reconstitution of the Disney theme parks' submarine ride. Refurbished as a take-off on the animated film *Finding Nemo*, "the ride resurfaced with whiz-bang video and audio effects that allow the animated sea creatures from *Finding Nemo* to seemingly swim and talk in the water."[26] "Disneyland's Finding Nemo Submarine Voyage is emblematic of Disney's efforts to keep its parks relevant in a digital age."[27] And Cars Land, a ride under development by Disney's Imagineers and which is based on *Bolt*, would not have been possible without Lasseter and his Pixar colleagues' hands-on input, says Bob Iger.[28]

What a professional journey. Being fired by Disney Animation Studios for trying to be too creative, then ultimately becoming the chief creative animation genius for both Disney and Pixar!

Discussion Questions

1. What forms of interpersonal power are evident in the case?

2. In what ways do the two faces of power appear in this case?

3. Does the firing of John Lasseter from Disney Studios and the events leading up to his firing demonstrate the ethical use of power? Explain your answer.

4. Did the firing of John Lasseter indicate the existence of political behavior in the Disney organization?

5. In his dual roles at the Pixar and Disney Studios, how does John Lasseter use power, influence, and organizational politics?

6. What useful lessons about power and politics in organizations are provided by John Lasseter's remarkable career?

SOURCE: This case was written by Michael K. McCuddy, The Louis S. and Mary L. Morgal Chair of Christian Business Ethics and Professor of Management, College of Business Administration, Valparaiso University.

12

Leadership and Followership

LEARNING OBJECTIVES

After reading this chapter, you should be able to do the following:

1 Define *leadership* and *followership*.

2 Discuss the differences between leadership and management and between leaders and managers.

3 Evaluate the effectiveness of autocratic, democratic, and laissez-faire leadership styles.

4 Explain initiating structure and consideration, leader behaviors, and the Leadership Grid.

5 Evaluate the usefulness of Fiedler's contingency theory of leadership.

6 Compare and contrast the path–goal theory, Vroom–Yetton–Jago theory, the Situational Leadership® model, leader–member exchange, and the Substitutes for Leadership model.

7 Distinguish among transformational, charismatic, and authentic leaders.

8 Discuss the characteristics of effective and dynamic followers.

RIM co-chief executives Jim Balsillie and Mike Lazaridis (right).

THINKING AHEAD: RESEARCH IN MOTION

Co-Leadership in Tough Economic Times

Mike Lazaridis and Jim Balsillie, co-CEOs of Research in Motion, will have their leadership skills put to the test over the coming years. Although the Blackberry has fared well in the economic downturn, with Apple's iPhone sales growth over 245 percent and new smartphones by Palm and Nokia hitting the market, the Blackberry has a lot of competition.[1]

Lazaridis and Balsillie both have formidable backgrounds to help handle the task. Lazaridis' path was unconventional, yet nonetheless impressive. As a teenager he developed a reputation as someone who could fix things. In high school, he got fed up with a buzzer used to practice for a game show competition so he made a new one that worked so well that other high schools started ordering from him. The money he earned went toward his first year in college. His big break came in college, where he won a half million dollar contract to build a network computer control display system. With the contract in hand, he left college and started Research in Motion at the age of twenty-four.[2] Lazaridis is credited with single-handedly developing the key concepts behind BlackBerry and its wireless e-mail service and is still known in the global wireless community as a visionary and innovator, earning Canada's most prestigious innovation prize—The Ernest C. Manning Principal Award. He has been quite influential in product strategy, research, and development ever since. He was also listed on the *Time* 100 List of Most Influential People.[3]

Balsillie, one of Canada's richest men, earned his MBA at Harvard University and is a fellow of the Ontario Institute of Chartered Accountants.[4] Balsillie joined Research in Motion in 1992, when it was still known primarily for making radio-based electronics. Balsillie provided the financial and marketing skills necessary to turn Research in Motion into a global company. It didn't come easy though. He has described the many rejections he received before finally selling the BlackBerry to one Canadian wireless company which is now notably Canadian's largest wireless carrier.[5]

How will Lazaridis and Balsillie use their experience and skill to lead their company in this highly competitive global market? See the Looking Back feature for the details.

Leadership in organizations is the process of guiding and directing the behavior of people in the work environment. The first section of this chapter distinguishes leadership from management. *Formal leadership* occurs when an organization officially bestows on a leader the authority to guide and direct others in the organization. *Informal leadership* occurs when a person is unofficially accorded power by others in the organization and uses influence to guide and direct their behavior. Leadership is among the most researched but least understood social processes in organizations.

Leadership has a long, rich history in organizational behavior. In this chapter, we explore many of the theories and ideas that have emerged along the way in that history. To begin, we examine the differences between leaders and managers. Next, we explore the earliest theories of leadership, the trait theories, which tried to identify a set of traits that leaders have in common. Following the trait theories came behavioral theories, which proposed that leader behaviors, not traits, are what counts. Contingency theories followed soon after. These theories argue that appropriate leader behavior depends on the situation and the followers. Next, we present some exciting contemporary theories of leadership, followed by the exciting new issues that are arising in leadership. We end by discussing *followership* and offering some guidelines for using this leadership knowledge.

LEADERSHIP AND MANAGEMENT

1 Define leadership and followership.

2 Discuss the differences between leadership and management and between leaders and managers.

John Kotter suggests that leadership and management are two distinct yet complementary systems of action in organizations.[6] Specifically, he believes that effective leadership produces useful change in organizations and that good management controls complexity in the organization and its environment. Fred Smith, who founded Federal Express (FedEx) in 1971, produced constant change from the company's beginning. FedEx began with primarily high-dollar medical and technology shipments. The company bought Kinko's to extend its reach from the back office to the front.[7] American Express CEO Ken Chenault believes that the key to leadership success is adaptability. Six attributes stand out in Chenault's mind while envisioning good leadership: integrity, courage, being a team player, emotional intelligence (as opposed to general intelligence), helping others succeed, and being proactive instead of reactive.[8] Healthy organizations need both effective leadership and good management.

For Kotter, the management process involves (1) planning and budgeting, (2) organizing and staffing, and (3) controlling and problem solving. The management process reduces uncertainty and stabilizes an organization. Alfred P. Sloan's integration and stabilization of General Motors after its early growth years are an example of good management.

American Express CEO Ken Chenault, left, believes that the key to leadership success is adaptability.

By contrast, the leadership process involves (1) setting a direction for the organization, (2) aligning people with that direction through communication, and (3) motivating people to action, partly through empowerment and partly through basic need gratification. The leadership process creates uncertainty and change in an organization. Effective leaders not only control the future of the organization but also act as enablers of change. They disturb existing patterns of behaviors, promote novel ideas, and help organizational members make sense of the change process.[9]

Abraham Zaleznik proposes that leaders have distinct personalities that stand in contrast to the personalities of a manager.[10] Zaleznik suggests that both leaders and managers make a valuable contribution to an organization and that each one's contribution is different. Whereas *leaders* agitate for change and new approaches, *managers* advocate stability and the status quo. There is a dynamic tension between leaders and managers that makes it difficult for each to understand the other. Leaders and managers differ along four separate dimensions of personality: attitudes toward goals, conceptions of work, relationships with other people, and sense of self. The differences between these two personality types are summarized in Table 12.1. Zaleznik's distinction between leaders and managers is similar to the distinction made between transactional and transformational leaders, or between leadership and supervision. Transactional leaders use formal rewards and punishment to engage in deal making and contractual obligations, which you will read about later in this chapter.

It has been proposed that some people are strategic leaders who embody both the stability of managers and the visionary abilities of leaders. Thus, strategic leaders combine the best of both worlds in a synergistic way. The unprecedented success of both Coca-Cola and Microsoft suggests that their leaders, the late Roberto Goizueta (of Coke) and Bill Gates, were strategic leaders.[11]

EARLY TRAIT THEORIES

The first studies of leadership attempted to identify what physical attributes, personality characteristics, and abilities distinguished leaders from other members of a group.[12] The physical attributes considered have been height, weight, physique, energy, health, appearance, and even age. This line of research yielded some interesting findings. However, very few valid generalizations emerged from this line of inquiry. Therefore, there is insufficient evidence to conclude that leaders can be distinguished from followers on the basis of physical attributes.

leadership
The process of guiding and directing the behavior of people in the work environment.

formal leadership
Officially sanctioned leadership based on the authority of a formal position.

informal leadership
Unofficial leadership accorded to a person by other members of the organization.

followership
The process of being guided and directed by a leader in the work environment.

leader
An advocate for change and new approaches to problems.

manager
An advocate for stability and the status quo.

TABLE 12.1 Leaders and Managers

Personality Dimension	Manager	Leader
Attitudes toward goals	Has an impersonal, passive, functional attitude; believes goals arise out of necessity and reality	Has a personal and active attitude; believes goals arise from desire and imagination
Conceptions of work	Views work as an enabling process that combines people, ideas, and things; seeks moderate risk through coordination and balance	Looks for fresh approaches to old problems; seeks high-risk positions, especially with high payoffs
Relationships with others	Avoids solitary work activity, preferring to work with others; avoids close, intense relationships; avoids conflict	Is comfortable in solitary work activity; encourages close, intense working relationships; is not conflict averse
Sense of self	Is once born; makes a straightforward life adjustment; accepts life as it is	Is twice born; engages in a struggle for a sense of order in life; questions life

SOURCE: Reprinted by permission of *Harvard Business Review*. From "Managers and Leaders: Are They Different?" by A. Zaleznik (January 2004). Copyright © 2004 by the Harvard Business School Publishing Corporation; all rights reserved.

Leader personality characteristics that have been examined include originality, adaptability, introversion–extraversion, dominance, self-confidence, integrity, conviction, mood optimism, and emotional control. There is some evidence that leaders may be more adaptable and self-confident than the average group member.

With regard to leader abilities, attention has been devoted to such constructs as social skills, intelligence, scholarship, speech fluency, cooperativeness, and insight. In this area, there is some evidence that leaders are more intelligent, verbal, and cooperative and have a higher level of scholarship than the average group member.

These conclusions suggest traits leaders possess, but the findings are neither strong nor uniform. For each attribute or trait claimed to distinguish leaders from followers, there were always at least one or two studies with contradictory findings. For some, the trait theories are invalid, though interesting and intuitively of some relevance. The trait theories have had very limited success in being able to identify the universal, distinguishing attributes of leaders. Recent research investigated the effects of heritability among 178 fraternal and 214 identical female twins. Results indicated that genetic factors contribute to the motivation to occupy leadership positions among women leaders. Similarly, prior work experience also has a significant impact on the motivation to lead. Thus, it seems that both personal factors and experience affect a person's desire to become a leader.[13]

BEHAVIORAL THEORIES

Behavioral theories emerged as a response to the deficiencies of the trait theories. Trait theories told us what leaders were like, but didn't address how they behaved. Three theories are the foundations of many modern leadership theories: the Lewin, Lippitt, and White studies; the Ohio State studies; and the Michigan studies.

autocratic style
A style of leadership in which the leader uses strong, directive, controlling actions to enforce the rules, regulations, activities, and relationships in the work environment.

3 Evaluate the effectiveness of autocratic, democratic, and laissez-faire leadership styles.

Lewin Studies

The earliest research on leadership style, conducted by Kurt Lewin and his students, identified three basic styles: autocratic, democratic, and laissez-faire.[14] Each leader uses one of these three basic styles when approaching a group of followers in a leadership situation. The specific situation is not an important consideration, because the leader's style does not vary with the situation. The *autocratic style* is directive, strong, and controlling in relationships. Leaders with an autocratic style use rules and regulations to run the work environment. Followers have little discretionary influence over the nature of the work, its accomplishment, or other aspects of the work environment. The leader with a *democratic style* is collaborative, responsive, and interactive in relationships and emphasizes rules and regulations less than the autocratic leader. Followers have a high degree of discretionary influence, although the leader has ultimate authority and responsibility. The leader with a *laissez-faire style* has a hands-off approach. A laissez-faire leader abdicates the authority and responsibility of the position, which often results in chaos. Laissez-faire leadership also causes role ambiguity for followers by the leader's failure to clearly define goals, responsibilities, and outcomes. It leads to higher interpersonal conflict at work.[15]

Ohio State Studies

The leadership research program at The Ohio State University also measured specific leader behaviors. The initial Ohio State research studied aircrews and pilots.[16] The aircrew members, as followers, were asked a wide range of questions about their lead pilots using the Leader Behavior Description Questionnaire (LBDQ). The results using the LBDQ suggested that there were two important underlying dimensions of leader behaviors.[17] These were labeled initiating structure and consideration.

Initiating structure is leader behavior aimed at defining and organizing work relationships and roles, as well as establishing clear patterns of organization, communication, and ways of getting things done. *Consideration* is leader behavior aimed at nurturing friendly, warm working relationships, as well as encouraging mutual trust and interpersonal respect within the work unit. These two leader behaviors are independent of each other. That is, a leader may be high on both, low on both, or high on one while low on the other. The Ohio State studies were intended to describe leader behavior, not to evaluate or judge it.[18]

Michigan Studies

Another approach to the study of leadership, developed at the University of Michigan, suggests that the leader's style has very important implications for the emotional atmosphere of the work environment and, therefore, for the followers who work under that leader. Two styles of leadership were identified: production oriented and employee oriented.[19]

A production-oriented style leads to a work environment characterized by constant influence attempts on the part of the leader, either through direct, close supervision or through the use of many written and unwritten rules and regulations for behavior. The focus is clearly on getting work done.

In comparison, an employee-oriented leadership style leads to a work environment that focuses on relationships. The leader exhibits less direct or less close supervision and establishes fewer written or unwritten rules and regulations for behavior. Employee-oriented leaders display concern for people and their needs.

4 Explain initiating structure and consideration, leader behaviors, and the Leadership Grid.

democratic style
A style of leadership in which the leader takes collaborative, responsive, interactive actions with followers concerning the work and work environment.

laissez-faire style
A style of leadership in which the leader fails to accept the responsibilities of the position.

initiating structure
Leader behavior aimed at defining and organizing work relationships and roles, as well as establishing clear patterns of organization, communication, and ways of getting things done.

consideration
Leader behavior aimed at nurturing friendly, warm working relationships, as well as encouraging mutual trust and interpersonal respect within the work unit.

How Does Your Supervisor Lead?

Answer the following sixteen questions concerning your supervisor's (or professor's) leadership behaviors using the seven-point Likert scale. Then complete the summary to examine your supervisor's behaviors.

	Not at All						Very Much
1. Is your superior strict about observing regulations?	1	2	3	4	5	6	7
2. To what extent does your superior give you instructions and orders?	1	2	3	4	5	6	7
3. Is your superior strict about the amount of work you do?	1	2	3	4	5	6	7
4. Does your superior urge you to complete your work by the time he or she has specified?	1	2	3	4	5	6	7
5. Does your superior try to make you work to your maximum capacity?	1	2	3	4	5	6	7
6. When you do an inadequate job, does your superior focus on the inadequate way the job was done instead of on your personality?	1	2	3	4	5	6	7
7. Does your superior ask you for reports about the progress of your work?	1	2	3	4	5	6	7
8. Does your superior work out precise plans for goal achievement each month?	1	2	3	4	5	6	7
9. Can you talk freely with your superior about your work?	1	2	3	4	5	6	7
10. Generally, does your superior support you?	1	2	3	4	5	6	7
11. Is your superior concerned about your personal problems?	1	2	3	4	5	6	7
12. Do you think your superior trusts you?	1	2	3	4	5	6	7
13. Does your superior give you recognition when you do your job well?	1	2	3	4	5	6	7
14. When a problem arises in your workplace, does your superior ask your opinion about how to solve it?	1	2	3	4	5	6	7
15. Is your superior concerned about your future benefits like promotions and pay raises?	1	2	3	4	5	6	7
16. Does your superior treat you fairly?	1	2	3	4	5	6	7

Add up your answers to Questions 1 through 8. This total indicates your supervisor's performance orientation:

Task orientation = _____

Add up your answers to Questions 9 through 16. This total indicates your supervisor's maintenance orientation:

People orientation = _____

A score above 40 is high, and a score below 20 is low.

SOURCE: Reprinted from "The Performance-Maintenance Theory of Leadership: Review of a Japanese Research Program" by J. Misumi and M. F. Peterson, published in *Administrative Science Quarterly* 30 (1985): 207. By permission of Administrative Science Quarterly © 1985.

These three groups of studies—Lewin, Lippitt, and White; Ohio State; and Michigan—taken together form the building blocks of many recent leadership theories. What the studies have in common is that two basic leadership styles were identified, with one focusing on tasks (autocratic, production oriented, initiating structure) and one focusing on people (democratic, employee oriented, consideration). Use You 12.1 to assess your supervisor's task- versus people-oriented styles.

The Leadership Grid: A Contemporary Extension

Robert Blake and Jane Mouton's *Leadership Grid*, originally called the Managerial Grid, was developed with a focus on attitudes.[20] The two underlying dimensions of the grid are labeled Concern for Results and Concern for People. These two attitudinal dimensions are independent of each other and in different combinations form various leadership styles. Blake and Mouton originally identified five distinct managerial styles, and further development of the grid has led to the seven distinct leadership styles shown in Figure 12.1.

Leadership Grid
An approach to understanding a leader's or manager's concern for results (production) and concern for people.

FIGURE

12.1   The Leadership Grid

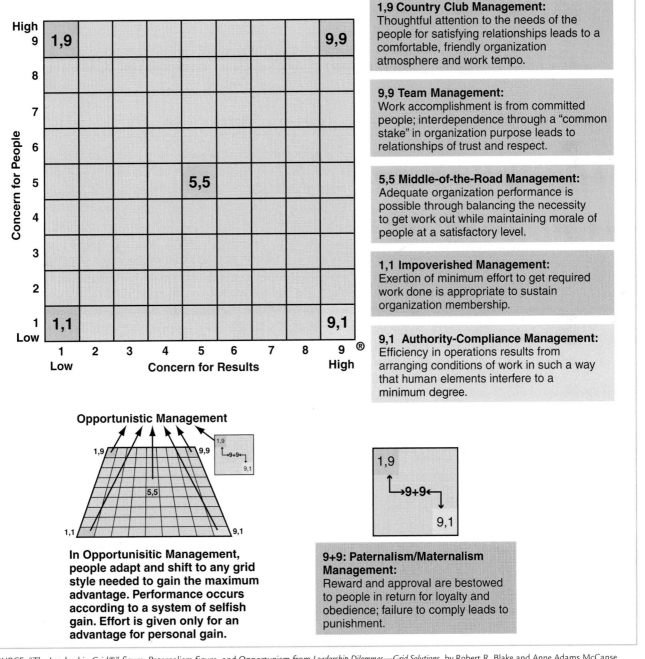

1,9 Country Club Management:
Thoughtful attention to the needs of the people for satisfying relationships leads to a comfortable, friendly organization atmosphere and work tempo.

9,9 Team Management:
Work accomplishment is from committed people; interdependence through a "common stake" in organization purpose leads to relationships of trust and respect.

5,5 Middle-of-the-Road Management:
Adequate organization performance is possible through balancing the necessity to get work out while maintaining morale of people at a satisfactory level.

1,1 Impoverished Management:
Exertion of minimum effort to get required work done is appropriate to sustain organization membership.

9,1 Authority-Compliance Management:
Efficiency in operations results from arranging conditions of work in such a way that human elements interfere to a minimum degree.

Opportunistic Management

In Opportunisitic Management, people adapt and shift to any grid style needed to gain the maximum advantage. Performance occurs according to a system of selfish gain. Effort is given only for an advantage for personal gain.

9+9: Paternalism/Maternalism Management:
Reward and approval are bestowed to people in return for loyalty and obedience; failure to comply leads to punishment.

SOURCE: "The Leadership Grid® figure, Paternalism figure, and Opportunism from *Leadership Dilemmas—Grid Solutions*, by Robert R. Blake and Anne Adams McCanse (formerly *The Managerial Grid* by Robert R. Blake and Jane S. Mouton). Houston: Gulf Publishing Company (Grid Figure: p. 29; Paternalism Figure: p. 30; Opportunism Figure: p. 31). Copyright 1991 by Blake and Mouton, and Scientific Methods, Inc. Reproduced by permission of the owners.

The *organization man manager (5,5)* is a middle-of-the-road leader who has a medium concern for people and production. This leader attempts to balance a concern for both people and production without a commitment to either.

The *authority-compliance manager (9,1)* has great concern for production and little concern for people. This leader desires tight control in order to get tasks done efficiently and considers creativity and human relations unnecessary. Authority-compliance managers may become so focused on running an efficient organization that they actually use tactics such as bullying. Some authority-compliance managers may intimidate, verbally and mentally attack, and otherwise mistreat subordinates. This form of abuse is quite common, with one in six U.S. workers reporting that they have been bullied by a manager.[21] The *country club manager (1,9)* has great concern for people and little concern for production, attempts to avoid conflict, and seeks to be well liked. This leader's goal is to keep people happy through good interpersonal relations, which are more important to him or her than the task. (This style is not a sound human relations approach but rather a soft Theory X approach.)

The *team manager (9,9)* is considered ideal and has great concern for both people and production. This leader works to motivate employees to reach their highest levels of accomplishment, is flexible, responsive to change, and understands the need for change. The *impoverished manager (1,1)* is often referred to as a laissez-faire leader. This leader has little concern for people or production, avoids taking sides, and stays out of conflicts; he or she does just enough to get by. Two new leadership styles have been added to these five original leadership styles within the grid. The *paternalistic "father knows best" manager (9+9)* promises reward for compliance and threatens punishment for noncompliance. The *opportunistic "what's in it for me" manager (Opp)* uses the style that he or she feels will return the greatest self-benefits.

The Leadership Grid is distinguished from the original Ohio State research in two important ways. First, it has attitudinal overtones that are not present in the original research. Whereas the LBDQ aims to describe behavior, the grid addresses both the behavior and the attitude of the leader. Second, the Ohio State approach is fundamentally descriptive and nonevaluative, whereas the grid is normative and prescriptive. Specifically, the grid evaluates the team manager (9,9) as the very best style of managerial behavior. This is the basis on which the grid has been used for team building and leadership training in an organization's development. As an organizational development method, the grid aims to transform the leader in the organization to lead in the "one best way," which according to the grid is the team approach. The team style is one that combines optimal concern for people with optimal concern for results.

CONTINGENCY THEORIES

5 Evaluate the usefulness of Fiedler's contingency theory of leadership.

Contingency theories involve the belief that leadership style must be appropriate for the particular situation. By their nature, contingency theories are "if–then" theories: If the situation is ____, then the appropriate leadership behavior is ____. We examine four such theories, including Fiedler's contingency theory, path–goal theory, normative decision theory, and situational leadership theory.

Fiedler's Contingency Theory

Fiedler's contingency theory of leadership proposes that the fit between the leader's need structure and the favorableness of the leader's situation determines the team's effectiveness in work accomplishment. This theory assumes that leaders are either task oriented or relationship oriented, depending on how the leaders obtain their primary need gratification.[22] Task-oriented leaders are primarily gratified

organization man manager (5,5)
A middle-of-the-road leader.

by accomplishing tasks and getting work done. Relationship-oriented leaders are primarily gratified by developing good, comfortable interpersonal relationships. Accordingly, the effectiveness of both types of leaders depends on the favorableness of their situation. The theory classifies the favorableness of the leader's situation according to the leader's position power, the structure of the team's task, and the quality of the leader–follower relationships.

The Least Preferred Coworker Fiedler classifies leaders using the Least Preferred Coworker (LPC) Scale.[23] The LPC Scale is a projective technique through which a leader is asked to think about the person with whom he or she can work least well (the *least preferred coworker*, or *LPC*).

The leader is asked to describe this coworker using sixteen eight-point bipolar adjective sets. Two of these sets follow (the leader marks the blank most descriptive of the LPC):

| Efficient | : | : | : | : | : | : | : | : | : | Inefficient |
| Cheerful | : | : | : | : | : | : | : | : | : | Gloomy |

Leaders who describe their LPC in positive terms (i.e., pleasant, efficient, cheerful, and so on) are classified as high LPC, or relationship-oriented, leaders. Those who describe their LPC in negative terms (i.e., unpleasant, inefficient, gloomy, and so on) are classified as low LPC, or task-oriented, leaders.

The LPC score is a controversial element in contingency theory.[24] It has been critiqued conceptually and methodologically because it is a projective technique with low measurement reliability.

Situational Favorableness The leader's situation has three dimensions: task structure, position power, and leader–member relations. Based on these three dimensions, the situation is either favorable or unfavorable for the leader. *Task structure* refers to the number and clarity of rules, regulations, and procedures for getting the work done. *Position power* refers to the leader's legitimate authority to evaluate and reward performance, punish errors, and demote group members.

The quality of *leader–member relations* is measured by the Group-Atmosphere Scale, composed of nine eight-point bipolar adjective sets. Two of these bipolar adjective sets follow:

| Friendly | : | : | : | : | : | : | : | : | : | Unfriendly |
| Accepting | : | : | : | : | : | : | : | : | : | Rejecting |

A favorable leadership situation is one with a structured task for the work group, strong position power for the leader, and good leader–member relations. By contrast, an unfavorable leadership situation is one with an unstructured task, weak position power for the leader, and moderately poor leader–member relations. Between these two extremes, the leadership situation has varying degrees of moderate favorableness for the leader.

Leadership Effectiveness The contingency theory suggests that low and high LPC leaders are each effective if placed in the right situation.[25] Specifically, low LPC (task-oriented) leaders are most effective in either very favorable or very unfavorable leadership situations. By contrast, high LPC (relationship-oriented) leaders are most effective in situations of intermediate favorableness. Figure 12.2 shows the nature of these relationships and suggests that leadership effectiveness is determined by the degree of fit between the leader and the situation. Recent research has shown that relationship-oriented leaders encourage team learning and innovativeness, which helps products get to market faster. This means that most relationship-oriented

authority-compliance manager (9,1)
A leader who emphasizes efficient production.

country club manager (1,9)
A leader who creates a happy, comfortable work environment.

team manager (9,9)
A leader who builds a highly productive team of committed people.

impoverished manager (1,1)
A leader who exerts just enough effort to get by.

paternalistic "father knows best" manager (9+9)
A leader who promises reward and threatens punishment.

least preferred coworker (LPC)
The person a leader has least preferred to work with over his or her career.

task structure
The degree of clarity, or ambiguity, in the work activities assigned to the group.

position power
The authority associated with the leader's formal position in the organization.

leader–member relations
The quality of interpersonal relationships among a leader and the group members.

opportunistic "what's in it for me" manager (Opp)
A leader whose style aims to maximize self-benefit.

FIGURE
12.2 Leadership Effectiveness in the Contingency Theory

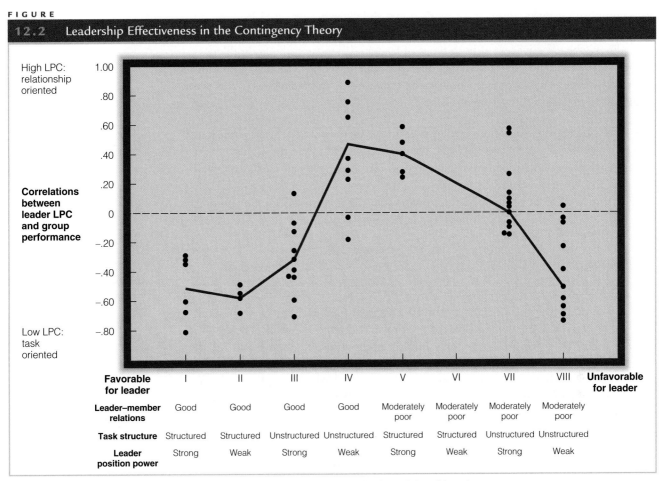

	I	II	III	IV	V	VI	VII	VIII	
Favorable for leader									**Unfavorable for leader**
Leader–member relations	Good	Good	Good	Good	Moderately poor	Moderately poor	Moderately poor	Moderately poor	
Task structure	Structured	Structured	Unstructured	Unstructured	Structured	Structured	Unstructured	Unstructured	
Leader position power	Strong	Weak	Strong	Weak	Strong	Weak	Strong	Weak	

SOURCE: F. E. Fiedler, *A Theory of Leader Effectiveness* (New York: McGraw-Hill, 1964). Reprinted with permission of the author.

leaders perform well in leading new product development teams. In short, the right team leader can help get creative new products out the door faster, while a mismatch between the leader and the situation can have the opposite effect.[26]

What, then, is to be done if there is a misfit? That is, what happens when a low LPC leader is in a moderately favorable situation or when a high LPC leader is in a highly favorable or highly unfavorable situation? It is unlikely that the leader can be changed, according to the theory, because the leader's need structure is an enduring trait that is hard to change. Fiedler recommends that the leader's situation be changed to fit the leader's style.[27] A moderately favorable situation would be reengineered to be more favorable and therefore more suitable for the low LPC leader. A highly favorable or highly unfavorable situation would be changed to one that is moderately favorable and more suitable for the high LPC leader. Fiedler's theory makes an important contribution in drawing our attention to the leader's situation.

Path–Goal Theory

6 Compare and contrast the path–goal theory, Vroom–Yetton–Jago theory, the Situational Leadership model, leader–member exchange, and the Substitutes for Leadership model.

Robert House developed a path–goal theory of leader effectiveness based on an expectancy theory of motivation.[28] From the perspective of path–goal theory, the basic role of the leader is to clear the follower's path to the goal. The leader uses the most appropriate of four leader behavior styles to help followers clarify the paths that lead them to work and personal goals. The key concepts in the theory are shown in Figure 12.3.

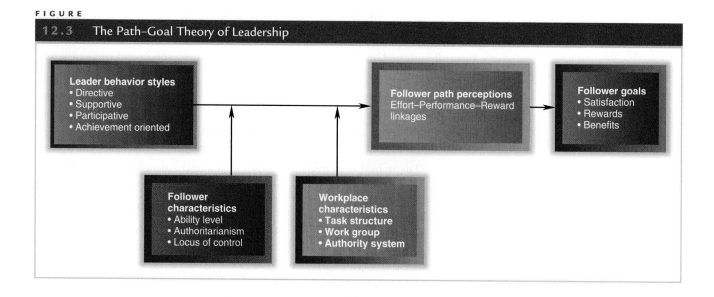

12.3 The Path–Goal Theory of Leadership

A leader selects from the four leader behavior styles, shown in Figure 12.3, the one that is most helpful to followers at a given time. The *directive style* is used when the leader must give specific guidance about work tasks, schedule work, and let followers know what is expected. The *supportive style* is used when the leader needs to express concern for followers' well-being and social status. The *participative style* is used when the leader must engage in joint decision-making activities with followers. The *achievement-oriented style* is used when the leader must set challenging goals for followers and show strong confidence in those followers.

In selecting the appropriate leader behavior style, the leader must consider both the followers and the work environment. A few characteristics are included in Figure 12.3. Let us look at two examples. In Example 1, the followers are inexperienced and working on an ambiguous, unstructured task. The leader in this situation might best use a directive style. In Example 2, the followers are highly trained professionals, and the task is a difficult yet achievable one. The leader in this situation might best use an achievement-oriented style. The leader always chooses the leader behavior style that helps followers achieve their goals.

The path–goal theory assumes that leaders adapt their behavior and style to fit the characteristics of the followers and the environment in which they work. Actual tests of the path–goal theory and its propositions provide conflicting evidence.[29] The path–goal theory does have intuitive appeal and reinforces the idea that the appropriate leadership style depends on both the work situation and the followers. Research is focusing on which style works best in specific situations. For example, in small organizations, leaders who used visionary, transactional, and empowering behaviors, while avoiding autocratic behaviors, were most successful.[30]

Vroom–Yetton–Jago Normative Decision Model

The Vroom–Yetton–Jago normative decision model helps leaders and managers know when to have employees participate in the decision-making process. Victor Vroom, Phillip Yetton, and Arthur Jago developed and refined the normative decision model, which helps managers determine the appropriate decision-making strategy to use. The model recognizes the benefits of authoritative, democratic, and consultative styles of leader behavior.[31] Five forms of decision making are described in the model:

- *Decide.* The manager makes the decision alone and either announces it or "sells" it to the group.

- *Consult individually.* The manager presents the problem to the group members individually, gets their input, and then makes the decision.

- *Consult group.* The manager presents the problem to the group members in a meeting, gets their inputs, and then makes the decision.

- *Facilitate.* The manager presents the problem to the group in a meeting and acts as a facilitator, defining the problem and the boundaries that surround the decision. The manager's ideas are not given more weight than any other group member's ideas. The objective is to get concurrence.

- *Delegate.* The manager permits the group to make the decision within the prescribed limits, providing needed resources and encouragement.[32]

The key to the normative decision model is that a manager should use the decision method most appropriate for a given decision situation. The manager arrives at the proper method by working through matrices like the one in Figure 12.4. The factors across the top of the model (decision significance, commitment, leader expertise, etc.) are the situational factors in the normative decision model. This matrix is for decisions that must be made under time pressure, but other matrices are also available. For example, there is a different matrix managers can use when their objective is to develop subordinates' decision-making skills. Vroom has also developed a Windows-based computer program called Expert System that can be used by managers to determine which style to use.

Although the model offers very explicit predictions as well as prescriptions for leaders, its utility is limited to the leader decision-making tasks.

One unique study applied the normative decision model of leadership to the battlefield behavior of ten commanding generals in six major battles of the American Civil War. When the commanders acted consistently with the prescriptions of the Vroom–Yetton–Jago model, they were more successful in accomplishing their military goals. The findings also suggested that a lack of information sharing and consensus building resulted in serious disadvantages.[33]

The Situational Leadership Model

The Situational Leadership model, developed by Paul Hersey and Kenneth Blanchard, suggests that the leader's behavior should be adjusted to the maturity level of the followers.[34] The model employs two dimensions of leader behavior as used in the Ohio State studies: one dimension is task oriented, and the other is relationship oriented. Follower maturity is categorized into four levels, as shown in Figure 12.5. Follower readiness is determined by the follower's ability and willingness to complete a specific task. Readiness can therefore be low or high depending on the particular task. In addition, readiness varies within a single person according to the task. One person may be willing and able to satisfy simple requests from customers (high readiness) but less able or willing to give highly technical advice to customers (low readiness). It is important that the leader be able to evaluate the readiness level of each follower for each task. The four styles of leader behavior associated with the four readiness levels are depicted in the figure as well.

According to the Situational Leadership model, a leader should use a telling style (S1) when a follower is unable and unwilling to do a certain task. This style involves providing instructions and closely monitoring performance. As such, the telling style involves considerable task behavior and low relationship behavior. When a follower is unable but willing and confident to do a task, the leader can use the selling style (S2) in which there is high task behavior and high relationship behavior. In this case, the leader explains decisions and provides opportunities for the employee to seek clarification or help. Sometimes a follower will be able to complete a task but may seem unwilling or

TIME-DRIVEN MODEL

Instructions: The matrix operates like a funnel. You start at the left with a specific decision problem in mind. The column headings denote situational factors which may or may not be present in that problem. You progress by selecting High or Low (H or L) for each relevant situational factor. Proceed down from the funnel, judging only those situational factors for which a judgment is called for, until you reach the recommended process.

Decision Significance	Importance of Commitment	Leader Expertise	Likelihood of Commitment	Group Support	Group Expertise	Team Competence	
H	H	H	H	–	–	–	Decide
			L	H	H	H	Delegate
						L	Consult (Group)
					L	–	Consult (Group)
				L	–	–	Consult (Group)
		L	H	H	H	–	Facilitate
					L	–	Consult (Individually)
				L	–	–	Consult (Individually)
			L	H	H	–	Facilitate
					L	–	Consult (Group)
				L	–	–	Consult (Group)
	L	H	–	–	–	–	Decide
		L	–	H	H	–	Facilitate
					L	–	Consult (Individually)
				L	–	–	Consult (Individually)
L	H	–	H	–	–	–	Decide
			L	–	–	H	Delegate
						L	Facilitate
	L	–	–	–	–	–	Decide

PROBLEM STATEMENT

SOURCE: Reprinted from *Organizational Dynamics,* 28 (Spring 2000), by V. H. Vroom, "Leadership and the Decision-Making Process," pp. 82–94 with permission from Elsevier.

insecure about doing so. In these cases, a participating style (S3) is warranted, which involves high relationship but low task behavior. The leader in this case encourages the follower to participate in decision making. Finally, for tasks in which a follower is able and willing, the leader is able to use a delegating style (S4), characterized by low task behavior and low relationship behavior. In this case, follower readiness is high, and low levels of leader involvement (task or relationship) are needed.

FIGURE

12.5   The Situational Leadership Model: The Hersey–Blanchard Model

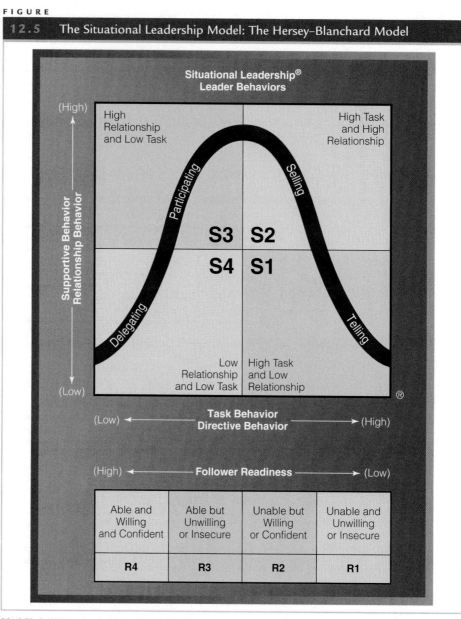

One key limitation of the Situational Leadership model is the absence of central hypotheses that could be tested, which would make it a more valid, reliable theory of leadership.[35] However, the theory has intuitive appeal and is widely used for training and development in corporations. In addition, the theory focuses attention on follower maturity as an important determinant of the leadership process.

Leader–Member Exchange

Leader–member exchange theory, or LMX, recognizes that leaders may form different relationships with followers. The basic idea behind LMX is that leaders form two groups of followers: in-groups and out-groups. In-group members tend to be similar to the leader and given greater responsibilities, more rewards, and more attention. They work within the leader's inner circle of communication. As a result, in-group members are more satisfied, have lower turnover, and have higher organizational commitment. By contrast, out-group members are outside the circle and receive less attention and fewer rewards. They are managed by formal rules and policies.[36]

Research on LMX is supportive. In-group members are more likely to engage in organizational citizenship behavior, while out-group members are more likely to retaliate against the organization.[37] And the type of stress varies by the group to which a subordinate belongs. In-group members' stress comes from the additional responsibilities placed on them by the leader, whereas out-group members' stress comes from being left out of the communication network.[38] One surprising finding is that more frequent communication with the boss may either help or hurt a worker's performance ratings, depending on whether the worker is in the in-group or the out-group. Among the in-group, more frequent communication generally leads to higher performance ratings, while members of the out-group who communicate more often with the superior tend to receive lower performance ratings. Perhaps the out-group members get to talk to the boss only when something has gone wrong![39]

Employees who enjoy more frequent contact with the boss also have a better understanding of what the boss's expectations are. Such agreement tends to lead to better performance by the employee and fewer misunderstandings between employer and employee.[40]

In-group members are also more likely to support the values of the organization and to become models of appropriate behavior. If the leader, for example, wants to promote safety at work, in-group members model safe work practices, which lead to a climate of workplace safety.[41]

LMX and empowerment can work together to produce positive outcomes in the workplace, as you can see in the Science feature.

Substitutes for Leadership

Sometimes situations can neutralize or even replace leader behavior. This is the central idea behind the substitutes for leadership theory.[42] When a task is very

Science

Relationship Focus or Empowerment Focus? What's a Leader to Do?

Research has supported the positive impact of both LMX and empowerment on work-related outcomes. But given limited time and resources, should a leader focus his or her efforts on empowering his or her employees and leaving those employees to do their job or should a leader focus on being present and cultivating the relationship between him or herself and the follower, as LMX would suggest?

A recent study investigating the effects of both empowerment and LMX found that when employees were empowered and perceived quality relationships with their supervisors, job satisfaction, job performance, and organizational citizenship behavior were high while turnover intentions were low. This finding supports LMX theory. In looking more closely at the findings, the researchers discovered that as long as subordinates felt empowered, the quality of the relationship did not significantly impact these outcomes; however, when employees did not feel empowered, the quality of the relationship had a significant and positive impact on these important outcomes. These findings suggest that leaders should focus on empowering their employees, but when empowerment is not possible, leaders should focus on improving the quality of the exchange relationship with employees.

SOURCE: K. J. Harris, A. R. Wheeler, and K. M. Kacmar, "Leader-Member Exchange and Empowerment: Direct and Interactive Effects on Job Satisfaction, Turnover Intentions and Performance." *The Leadership Quarterly* 20 (2009): 371–382.

satisfying and employees get feedback about performance, leader behavior is irrelevant, because the employee's satisfaction comes from the interesting work and the feedback. Other things that can substitute for leadership include high skill on the part of the employee, team cohesiveness, and formal controls on the part of the organization. Research on this idea is generally supportive, and other factors that act as substitutes are being identified.[43] Even a firm's customers can be a substitute for leadership. In service settings, employees with lots of customer contact actually receive significant leadership and direction from customer demands, allowing the firm to provide less formal supervision to these employees than to workers with little customer contact. This finding adds new weight to the old adage about the customer being boss.[44]

THE EMERGENCE OF INSPIRATIONAL LEADERSHIP THEORIES

7 Distinguish among transformational, charismatic, and authentic leaders.

Leadership is an exciting area of organizational behavior, one in which new research is constantly emerging. Three new developments are important to understand. These are transformational leadership, charismatic leadership, and authentic leadership. These three theories can be called inspirational leadership theories because in each one, followers are inspired by the leader to perform well.

Transformational Leadership

As we indicated earlier in the chapter, transactional leaders are those who use rewards and punishment to strike deals with followers and shape their behavior. By contrast, transformational leaders inspire and excite followers to high levels of performance.[45] They rely on their personal attributes instead of their official position to manage followers. There is some evidence that transformational leadership can be learned.[46] Transformational leadership consists of the following four sub dimensions: charisma, individualized consideration, inspirational motivation, and intellectual stimulation. We describe charisma in detail below. Individualized consideration refers to how much the leader displays concern for each follower's individual needs, and acts as a coach or a mentor. Inspirational motivation is the extent to which the leader is able to articulate a vision that is appealing to followers.[47] An extensive research study shows that transformational leadership predicts several criteria such as follower job satisfaction, leader effectiveness ratings, group or organizational performance, and follower motivation.[48] Transformational leadership research conducted in China, Kenya, and Thailand also showed that it had positive effects on employee commitment and negative effects on employee work withdrawal.[49]

Transformation leadership has been shown to increase firm performance.[50] U.S. corporations increasingly operate in a global economy, so there is a greater demand for leaders who can practice transformational leadership by converting their visions into reality[51] and by inspiring followers to perform "above and beyond the call of duty."[52] Howard Schultz, founder and chairman of Starbucks Coffee, is the transformational leader and visionary heart of Starbucks. He has grown his firm from a small specialty coffee bar into one of the best-known brands in the world. But with the flagging global economy, can he once again transform Starbucks? The Real World 12.1 captures the challenges Schultz faces.

The Real World 12.1

Can He Transform Starbucks Again?

Being a transformational leader is about bringing change to organizations, and Howard Schultz, Starbucks' CEO, is looking to transform the organization he founded. After an eight-year hiatus, he returned as CEO with a bold plan to reignite Starbucks' emotional attachment with the Starbucks brand and streamline the company's U.S. operations, including closing some underperforming stores and accelerating the company's international expansion. These actions, aimed at the chain of 16,000 stores, are in response to the toughest economic times in the company's thirty-eight-year history.

Starbucks' declining market share may be attributable to its image as catering to affluent professionals, which Schultz says is simply not true, pointing out several lower priced menu items. Starbucks has even lowered some prices and now offers value meals.

Schultz also wants to revive the ambiance of Starbucks locations. The new coffee machines are lower and in better view so customers can see the theater of baristas crafting their drinks. Smelly sandwiches are no longer on the menu so customers can smell the coffee bean aroma. Stores are being refurbished with recycled materials, local decorating themes, and funky lighting. They're even launching an instant coffee called Via to compete in the worldwide instant coffee market.

All of these changes, Schultz hopes, will revive Starbucks. To make sure this happens, he will need all of his skills as a transformational leader.

Sources: A. Clark, "Starbucks Boss: We're Not All Froth," *The Guardian* (March 20, 2009), accessed at http://www.guardian.co.uk/business/2009/mar/20/howard-schultz-starbucks-chairman-interview; L. J. Flynn, "Starbucks, Awaiting Recovery, Says Profits Fell 77%," *The New York Times* (April 29, 2009), accessed at http://www.nytimes.com/2009/04/30/business/30sbux.html?_r=1.

Leaders can be both transformational and transactional.[53] Transformational leadership adds to the effects of transactional leadership, but exceptional transactional leadership cannot substitute for transformational leadership.[54] One reason the latter is effective is that transformational leaders encourage followers to set goals congruent with the followers' own authentic interests and values. Because of this, followers see their work as important and their goals as aligned with who they are.[55]

There is some evidence that transformational leadership may work in military organizations. One study showed that military leaders who practiced transformational leadership produced both greater development and better performance among their subordinates than leaders who used other leadership styles.[56] Transformational leadership is very important in teams with diverse members. A recent study found that high diversity teams with transformation leaders outperformed teams with no transformational leadership.[57]

Charismatic Leadership

Steve Jobs, the pioneer behind the Macintosh computer and the growing music download market, has an uncanny ability to create a vision and convince others to become part of it. This was evidenced by Apple's continual overall success despite its major blunders in the desktop computer wars. Jobs's ability is so powerful that Apple employees coined a term in the 1980s for it, the *reality-distortion field*. This expression is used to describe the persuasive ability and peculiar charisma of managers like Steve Jobs. This reality-distortion field allows Jobs to convince even skeptics that his plans are worth supporting, no matter how unworkable they may appear. Those close to these managers become passionately committed to seemingly impossible projects, without regard to the practicality of their implementation or competitive forces in the marketplace.[58] Similarly, people who have worked with CEO Ken Chenault of American Express note that they admire him immensely and would do anything for him. He is known for chatting with executives and secretaries alike and is seen as someone who is free from the normal trappings of power.

Charismatic leadership results when a leader uses the force of personal abilities and talents to have profound and extraordinary effects on followers.[59] Some scholars see transformational leadership and charismatic leadership as very similar, but others believe they are different. *Charisma* is a Greek word meaning "gift"; the charismatic leader's unique and powerful gifts are the source of his or her great influence with followers.[60] In fact, followers often view the charismatic leader as one who possesses superhuman, or even mystical, qualities.[61] Charismatic leaders rely heavily on referent power, discussed in Chapter 11, and charismatic leadership is especially effective in times of uncertainty.[62] Charismatic leadership falls to those who are "chosen" (born with the "gift" of charisma) or who cultivate that gift. Some say charismatic leaders are born, and others say they are taught.

Some charismatic leaders rely on humor as a tool for communication. Charismatic leadership carries with it not only great potential for high levels of achievement and performance on the part of followers but also shadowy risks of destructive courses of action that might harm followers or other people. Several researchers have attempted to demystify charismatic leadership and distinguish its two faces.[63]

The ugly face of charisma is revealed in the personalized power motivations of Adolf Hitler in Nazi Germany and David Koresh of the Branch Davidian cult in Waco, Texas. Both men led their followers into struggle, conflict, and death. The brighter face of charisma is revealed in the socialized power motivations of U.S. President Franklin D. Roosevelt. Former presidents Bill Clinton and Ronald Reagan, while worlds apart in terms of their political beliefs, were actually quite similar in their use of personal charisma to inspire followers and motivate them to pursue the leader's vision. In each case, followers perceived the leader as imbued with a unique vision for America and unique abilities to lead the country there.

Photo by John Moore/Getty Images

Former South African President Nelson Mandela is considered an authentic leader.

charismatic leadership
A leader's use of personal abilities and talents in order to have profound and extraordinary effects on followers.

authentic leadership
A style of leadership that includes transformational, charismatic, or transactional approaches as the situation demands.

Authentic Leadership

Recently, a new form of leadership has started to garner attention thanks to the ethical scandals rocking the business world. In response to concerns about the potential negative side of inspirational forms of leadership, researchers have called for authentic leadership.[64] *Authentic leadership* includes transformational, charismatic, or transactional leadership as the situation demands. However, it differs from the other kinds in that authentic leaders have a conscious and well-developed sense of values. They act in ways that are consistent with their value systems, so authentic leaders have a highly evolved sense of moral right and wrong. Their life experiences (often labeled "moments that matter") lead to authentic leadership development, and allow authentic leaders to be their true selves.[65] Authentic leaders arouse and motivate followers to higher levels of performance by building a workforce characterized by high levels of hope, optimism, resiliency, and self-efficacy.[66] Followers also experience more positive emotions and trust leadership as a result of transparency and a collective caring climate engendered by the leader. Researchers contend that this is the kind of leadership embodied by Gandhi, Nelson Mandela, and others like them throughout history. Only time and solid management research will tell if this approach can yield results for organizational leadership. One recent development in the identification of authentic leaders stems from the area of emotions. Emotions act as checks and balances that not only keep the ugly side of charisma in check but also provide certain cues to followers. For example, a leader who espouses benevolence (as a value) and does not display compassion (an emotion) might not be very authentic in followers' eyes.[67] Similarly, a leader who displays compassion when announcing a layoff may be seen by followers as more morally worthy and held in higher regard.[68]

Despite the warm emotions charismatic leaders can evoke, some of them are narcissists who listen only to those who agree with them.[69] Whereas charismatic leaders with socialized power motivation are concerned about the collective well-being of their followers, charismatic leaders with a personalized power motivation are driven by the need for personal gain and glorification.[70]

Charismatic leadership styles are associated with several positive outcomes. One study reported that firms headed by more charismatic leaders outperformed other firms, particularly in difficult economic times. Perhaps even more important, charismatic leaders were able to raise more outside financial support for their firms than noncharismatic leaders, meaning that charisma at the top may translate to greater funding at the bottom.[71]

EMERGING ISSUES IN LEADERSHIP

Along with the recent developments in theory, some exciting issues have emerged of which leaders must be aware. These include emotional intelligence, trust, women leaders, and servant leadership.

Emotional Intelligence

It has been suggested that effective leaders possess emotional intelligence, which is the ability to recognize and manage emotion in oneself and in others. In fact, some researchers argue that emotional intelligence is more important for effective leadership than either IQ or technical skills.[72] Emotional intelligence is made up of several competencies, including self-awareness, empathy, adaptability, and self-confidence. While most people gain emotional intelligence as they age, not everyone starts with an equal amount. Fortunately, emotional intelligence can be learned. With honest feedback from coworkers and ongoing guidance, almost any leader can improve emotional intelligence, and with it, the ability to lead in times of adversity.[73]

Emotional intelligence affects the way leaders make decisions. Under high stress, leaders with higher emotional intelligence tend to keep their cool and make better decisions, while leaders with low emotional intelligence make poor decisions and lose their effectiveness.[74] Joe Torre, former manager of the New York Yankees, got the most out of his team, worked for a notoriously tough boss, and kept his cool. He was a model of emotional intelligence: compassionate, calm under stress, and a great motivator. He advocated "managing against the cycle," which means staying calm when situations are tough, but turning up the heat on players when things are going well.[75] Now the manager of the Los Angeles Dodgers, Torre has written that his "triple play" in managing others includes fairness, trust, and respect. [76]

Trust

Trust is an essential element in leadership. Trust is the willingness to be vulnerable to the actions of another.[77] This means that followers believe that their leader will act with the followers' welfare in mind. Trustworthiness is also one of the competencies in emotional intelligence. Trust among top management team members facilitates strategy implementation; this means that if team members trust each other, they have a better chance of getting "buy-in" from employees on the direction of the company.[78] And if employees trust their leaders, they will buy in more readily.

Trust in top business leaders may be at an all-time low given the highly publicized failures of many CEOs. Rick Wagoner, CEO of General Motors 2000–2009, lost more money than any CEO in history, yet he continued to express confidence in his company and his strategy. He was fired by the government just before GM went bankrupt.[79] Ed Zander, CEO of Motorola 2004–2008, reorganized the company's departments to compete with each other as warring tribes. He failed to capitalize on the success of Motorola's RAZR phone, and overlooked the transition to smartphones, sending Motorola into a downward spiral.[80]

Effective leaders also understand both *who* to trust and *how* to trust. At one extreme, leaders often trust a close circle of advisors, listening only to them and gradually cutting themselves off from dissenting opinions. At the opposite extreme, lone-wolf leaders may trust nobody, leading to preventable mistakes. Wise leaders carefully evaluate both the competence and the position of those they trust, seeking out a variety of opinions and input.[81]

Gender and Leadership

An important, emergent leadership question is this: Do women and men lead differently? Historical stereotypes persist, and people characterize successful managers as having more male-oriented attributes than female-oriented attributes.[82] Although legitimate gender differences may exist, the same leadership traits may be interpreted differently in a man and a woman because of stereotypes. The real issue should be leader behaviors that are not bound by gender stereotypes.

Early evidence shows that women tend to use a more people-oriented style that is inclusive and empowering. Women managers excel in positions that demand strong interpersonal skills.[83] More and more women are assuming positions of leadership in organizations. Andrea Jung of Avon is the longest-tenured female CEO in the Fortune 500. Read about how she reinvents herself and her company in the Real World 12.2. Interestingly, much of what we know about leadership is based on studies that were conducted on men. We need to know more about the ways women lead. Interestingly, recent research reports on the phenomenon of the *glass cliff* (as opposed to the *glass ceiling* effect discussed in Chapter 2). The *glass cliff* represents a trend in organizations of placing more women in difficult leadership situations. Women perceive these assignments as necessary due to difficulty in attaining leadership positions and lack of alternate opportunities combined with male in-group favoritism. On the other hand, men perceive that women are better suited to difficult leadership positions due to better decision making.[84]

The Real World 12.2

The CEO Who Fires Herself

Andrea Jung of Avon has been CEO for ten years, making her the longest-tenured CEO in the Fortune 500. Always a high achiever, she skipped first grade and started college at age sixteen. A magna cum laude grad of Princeton, she became Avon's CEO in 1999.

Along the way, she has learned several lessons. Jung says you have to reinvent yourself before you reinvent your company. Experience in the job is mostly a good thing, but it limits the CEO's ability to look at the business with fresh eyes, objectively. To overcome this, Jung fires herself every Friday. This means that she comes in every Monday as if she has just been hired as a new turnaround leader. She believes the skills that lead to her success each year become obsolete the following year, and she has to reinvent herself each year.

Andrea Jung, CEO of Avon.

stocklight/Shutterstock

Another lesson from Jung is communicate, communicate, communicate. In tough times, CEOs and all leaders must share the vision and the reasons behind difficult decisions. And, she says, do it frequently and face to face, not in e-mail. This will make the company healthier through trust and respect.

Jung also says people come first for the CEO, not just vision and strategy. Without the right people, vision and strategy go nowhere. Jung spends more than 25 percent of her time in talent development. To weather these tough economic times, Jung says you must have the best talent and grow them because, like her, they will need to reinvent themselves to stay ahead of the game.

Source: "Reinvent Yourself and Your Company," *USA Today* (June 15, 2009): 3B.

Servant Leadership

Robert Greenleaf was director of management research at AT&T for many years. He believed that leaders should serve employees, customers, and the community, and his essays are the basis for today's view called servant leadership. His personal and professional philosophy was that leaders lead by serving others. Other tenets of servant leadership are that work exists for the person as much as the person exists for work, and that servant leaders try to find out the will of the group and lead based on that. Servant leaders are also stewards who consider leadership a trust and desire to leave the organization in better shape for future generations.[85] Although Green-leaf's writings were completed thirty years ago, many have now been published and are becoming more popular.

Abusive Supervision

Recently research has begun to investigate not only what make leaders effective but also the dark side of leader behavior. The most common negative leader behaviors include sexual harassment, physical violence, angry outbursts, public ridicule, taking credit for employees' successes, and scapegoating employees.[86] Abusive supervision, as these behaviors are called, is estimated to effect about 13.6 percent of U.S. workers and leads to many negative consequences. Abused workers report diminished well-being, along with increased deviance behavior, problem drinking, psychological distress, and emotional exhaustion.[87,88,89,90] In addition, abusive supervision increases absenteeism and reduces productivity. In fact, the cost of abusive supervision to U.S. corporations has been estimated at $23.8 billion.[91] It is not clear why supervisors abuse others. Some research suggests that injustice experienced by supervisors increases the likelihood that they will abuse. Abusive supervisors are more likely to direct their aggression toward employees who are very negative, or toward those who appear weak or unwilling or unable to defend themselves.[92]

FOLLOWERSHIP

In contrast to leadership, the topic of followership has not been extensively researched. Much of the leadership literature suggests that leader and follower roles are highly differentiated. The traditional view casts followers as passive, whereas a more contemporary view casts the follower role as an active one with potential for leadership.[93] The follower role has alternatively been cast as one of self-leadership in which the follower assumes responsibility for influencing his or her own performance.[94] This approach emphasizes the follower's individual responsibility and self-control. Self-led followers perform naturally motivating tasks and do work that must be done but that is not naturally motivating. Self-leadership enables followers to be disciplined and effective, essential first steps if one is to become a leader.

Organizational programs such as empowerment and self-managed work teams may be used to further activate the follower role.[95]

Types of Followers

8 Discuss the characteristics of effective and dynamic followers.

Contemporary work environments are ones in which followers recognize their interdependence with leaders and learn to challenge them while at the same time respecting the leaders' authority.[96] Effective followers are active, responsible, and autonomous in their behavior and critical in their thinking without being insubordinate or disrespectful—in essence, they are highly engaged at work. Effective followers and four other types of followers are identified based on two dimensions: (1) activity versus passivity and (2) independent, critical thinking versus dependent, uncritical thinking.[97] Figure 12.6 shows these follower types.

Alienated followers think independently and critically, yet are very passive in their behavior. As a result, they become psychologically and emotionally distanced from their leaders. Alienated followers are potentially disruptive and a threat to the health of the organization. "Sheep" are followers who do not think independently or critically and are passive in their behavior. They simply do as they are told by their leaders. "Yes people" are followers who also do not think independently or critically, yet are very active in their behavior. They uncritically reinforce the thinking and ideas of their leaders with enthusiasm, never questioning or challenging the wisdom of the leaders' ideas and proposals. Yes people are the most dangerous to a leader because they are the most likely to give a false-positive reaction and give no warning of potential pitfalls. Survivors are the least disruptive and the lowest risk followers in an organization. They perpetually sample the wind, and their motto is "better safe than sorry."

Effective followers are the most valuable to a leader and an organization because of their active contributions. Effective followers share four essential qualities. First, they practice self-management and self-responsibility. A leader

12.6 Five Types of Followers

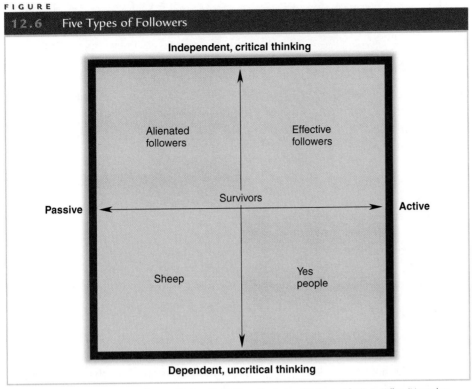

can delegate to an effective follower without anxiety about the outcome. Second, they are committed to both the organization and a purpose, principle, or person outside themselves. Effective followers are not self-centered or self-aggrandizing. Third, effective followers invest in their own competence and professionalism and focus their energy for maximum impact. Effective followers look for challenges and ways in which to add to their talents or abilities. Fourth, they are courageous, honest, and credible. You 12.2 gives you an opportunity to consider your effectiveness as a follower.

Effective followers might be thought of as self-leaders who do not require close supervision.[98] The notion of self-leadership, or superleadership, blurs the distinction between leaders and followers. Caring leaders are able to develop dynamic followers.

The Dynamic Follower

The traditional stereotype of the follower or employee is of someone in a powerless, dependent role rather than in a potent, active, significant role. The latter, in which the follower is dynamic, is a more contemporary, healthy role.[99] The *dynamic follower* is a responsible steward of his or her job, is effective in managing the relationship with the boss, and practices responsible self-management.

The dynamic follower becomes a trusted adviser to the boss by keeping the supervisor well informed and building trust and dependability into the relationship. He or she is open to constructive criticism and solicits performance feedback. The dynamic follower shares needs and is responsible.

It takes time and patience to nurture a good relationship between a follower and a supervisor. Once this relationship has been developed, it is a valuable resource for both.

dynamic follower
A follower who is a responsible steward of his or her job, is effective in managing the relationship with the boss, and practices self-management.

You 12.2

Are You an Effective Follower?

To determine whether you are an effective follower, read the text section on "Types of Followers," look back at your self-reliance results in You 7.2, and work through the following four steps. Answer each question in the four steps yes or no.

Step 1. Self-Management and Self-Responsibility

_____ Do you take the initiative at work?

_____ Do you challenge the system at work when appropriate?

_____ Do you ask questions when you need more information?

_____ Do you successfully bring your projects to completion?

Step 2. Commitment beyond Yourself

_____ Are you committed to your boss's and company's success?

_____ Is there a higher purpose in life that you value deeply?

_____ Is there a principle(s) that you will not compromise?

_____ Is there a person at work or elsewhere you admire greatly?

Step 3. Self-Development

_____ Do you attend a professional development class annually?

_____ Do you have a program of self-study or structured learning?

_____ Do you take at least one class each semester in the year?

_____ Have you identified new skills to learn for your job?

Step 4. Courage and Honesty

_____ Have you disagreed with your boss twice this year?

_____ Have you taken two unpopular positions at work this year?

_____ Have you given critical feedback to someone, kindly?

_____ Have you taken one risk at work to do a better job?

Scoring:

Count the number of "yes" answers in Steps 1 through 4: _____

If you have 10–16 "yes" answers, this would suggest that you are an effective follower. If you have 7 or fewer "yes" answers, this may suggest that you fall into one of the other four categories of followers.

People who are self-reliant may also be effective followers, and effective followers may also be self-reliant. If you are an effective follower, were you also self-reliant in You 7.2? If you were not self-reliant in You 7.2, did you fall into a category other than the effective follower category?

CULTURAL DIFFERENCES IN LEADERSHIP

The situational approaches to leadership would lead to the conclusion that a leader must factor in culture as an important situational variable when exercising influence and authority. Thus, global leaders should expect to be flexible enough to alter their approaches when crossing national boundaries and working with people from different cultures.[100]

We are beginning to learn more about how perspectives on effective leadership vary across cultures. You might assume that most Europeans view leadership in the same way. Research tells us instead that there are many differences among European countries. In Nordic countries like Finland, leaders who are direct and close to subordinates are viewed positively, while in Turkey, Poland, and Russia, this is not the case. And leaders who give subordinates autonomy are viewed more positively in Germany and Austria than in the Czech Republic and Portugal.[101] There are even differences between the American view of transformational leadership and that found in the United Kingdom. The UK approach to transformational leadership is much closer to what we in the United States refer to as servant leadership. It involves more connectedness between leaders and followers and more vulnerability on the part of the leader.[102]

To be effective, leaders must understand other cultures. U.S. executives often perceive specific global regions as being made up of relatively homogenous individuals. For example, some U.S. leaders think that most of Latin America is populated with people of similar values and beliefs. But a recent study of more than 1,000 small-business owners in the region demonstrated that despite similarities, these business leaders are quite diverse in terms of their individual goals. Mexican and Brazilian leaders had values that were very different from leaders in other countries in the region. This means that we cannot stereotype people from Latin America as being totally similar.[103]

Whereas most American workers follow traditional Protestant work values, workers from other countries base their work values on very different sets of beliefs, drawing in some cases from multiple philosophies. China, for instance, draws from not one but three perspectives, as Buddhism, Taoism, and Confucianism harmonize to create work values such as trust, hierarchy, loyalty, and networks.[104] Across cultures, leaders vary widely in their orientation toward the future. This translates into focus on either short-term benefits or longer term orientation toward employee development. For example, Singapore was the most future oriented of all cultures that were studied. This implies that leaders in Singapore are more focused on longer term benefits such as delayed gratification, long-term planning, and investing in employee development with longer-term pay-offs.[105]

GUIDELINES FOR LEADERSHIP

Leadership is a key to influencing organizational behavior and achieving organizational effectiveness. Studies of leadership succession show a moderately strong leader influence on organizational performance.[106] With this said, it is important to recognize that other factors also influence organizational performance. These include environmental factors (such as general economic conditions) and technological factors (such as efficiency).

Corporate leaders play a central role in setting the ethical tone and moral values for their organizations. While many corporate leaders talk about ethics, many never have to actually risk the firm's fortune on an ethical decision. In 1976, when James Burke, head of Johnson & Johnson, challenged his management team to reaffirm the company's historic commitment to ethical behavior, he had no idea he would be asked to demonstrate that commitment in action. But six years later, when poisoned packages of Tylenol appeared on store shelves, Burke did not hesitate to act on what he had pledged. The company pulled the product from the shelves at a cost of $100 million. It also offered a reward and revamped the product's packaging. In the end, Tylenol recovered and is once again the leading pain medication in the United States. Burke was recently recognized by *Fortune* as one of the ten greatest CEOs of all time, and Johnson & Johnson continues to be rated one of the best companies for which to work.[107]

Five useful guidelines have emerged from the extensive leadership research of the past sixty years:

- First, leaders and organizations should appreciate the unique attributes, predispositions, and talents of each leader. No two leaders are the same, and there is value in this diversity.

- Second, although there appears to be no single best style of leadership, there are organizational preferences in terms of style. Leaders should be chosen who challenge the organizational culture, when necessary, without destroying it.

- Third, participative, considerate leader behaviors that demonstrate a concern for people appear to enhance the health and well-being of followers in the work environment. This does not imply, however, that a leader must ignore the team's work tasks.

- Fourth, different leadership situations call for different leadership talents and behaviors. This may result in different individuals taking the leader role, depending on the specific situation in which the team finds itself.

- Fifth, good leaders are likely to be good followers. Although there are distinctions between their social roles, the attributes and behaviors of leaders and followers may not be as distinct as is sometimes thought.

Diversity Dialogue

White Males: Diversity Programs' Newest Leaders?

Keith Ruth was very surprised when he was approached by PricewaterhouseCoopers' (PwC) chief diversity officer, Chris Simmons, to help lead the firm's corporate diversity effort. Why was he so surprised? Because Ruth is a white male, and it is common knowledge that diversity programs aren't designed for white males, right? Not according to Simmons.

When he became PricewaterhouseCoopers' chief diversity officer in 2004, Simmons was given a directive by the U.S. chairman to move diversity "off the sidelines" and "into the mainstream." That meant fully integrating diversity into the firm's daily operations including client assignments and employee promotions. At the same time, diversity leaders were being named for PwC's four business units. Although Simmons is African American, he was concerned that none of the diversity leaders being named as a business unit diversity leader was a white male. He believed that having a Caucasian male champion diversity would be instrumental in helping to bring other white males on

board. After all, he reasoned, they are still the majority of workers in most large firms. Frank McCloskey, Georgia Power's first white male head of diversity, insists that it would be difficult to create a sustainable diversity initiative if the majority of the workforce felt there was nothing in it for them.

Since becoming a PwC diversity leader, Keith Ruth has had much success reaching many people Chris Simmons admits he had had a difficult time reaching.

1. Do you believe recruiting white males to lead diversity programs is a good strategy for garnering support for diversity? Why or why not?
2. What leadership skills must Keith Ruth and other Caucasians use in order to be effective diversity leaders? Contrast them with skills that minority leaders must use.

SOURCE: E. White, "Diversity Programs Look to Involve White Males as Leaders," *Wall Street Journal* (May 7, 2007): B4.

LOOKING BACK: RESEARCH IN MOTION

Breaking the Status Quo

So how do Lazaridis and Balsillie plan to weather the economic downturn and deal with popular competitors? They will continue to focus on innovation by encouraging

Courtesy of Research In Motion

teamwork and empowering, developing, and taking care of their employees. Lazaridis and Balsillie are big believers in hiring smart, innovative people and giving them the flexibility to work, focusing on both collaboration and collegiality. Fostering collegiality is so important to their leadership strategy that when they open offices in new places, often they will look for companies that are downsizing and hire whole staffs who are already integrated.[108] They also foster collegiality by supporting employee sports teams and company-subsidized social events. For example, in 2008, they organized a surprise holiday staff appreciation concert in which Tragically Hip and Van Halen played for over 14,000 employees, co-op students, and business partners.[109]

Lazaridis and Balsillie reduce the corporate bureaucracy and lead through empowering their employees, listening to them, and allowing them to participate in decisions. This creates an environment in which employees want to work and can be innovative. Lazaris and Balsillie are quite focused on communicating their innovation vision. Research in Motion has weekly vision meetings where the co-CEOs talk to various teams. They also have brainstorming leadership committees that focus on all parts of the organization from technology to research and development to the BlackBerry user interface. They don't limit membership on these committees to executives but base membership on capability, knowledge, and skill.

These co-CEOs also value quality of life for their employees. Research in Motion offers its employees on-site massages, flexible work hours, and subsidized tuition for continuing education. Their focus on employees has made them one of Canada's top 100 Employers in 2009.[110]

Chapter Summary

1. Leadership is the process of guiding and directing the behavior of followers in organizations. Followership is the process of being guided and directed by a leader. Leaders and followers are companions in these processes.

2. A leader creates meaningful change in organizations, whereas a manager controls complexity. Charismatic leaders have a profound impact on their followers.

3. Autocratic leaders create high pressure for followers, whereas democratic leaders create healthier environments for followers.

4. The five styles in the Leadership Grid are manager, authority-compliance manager, country club manager, team manager, and impoverished manager.

5. According to Fiedler's contingency theory, task-oriented leaders are most effective in highly favorable or highly unfavorable leadership situations, and relationship-oriented leaders are most effective in moderately favorable leadership situations.

6. The path–goal theory, Vroom–Yetton–Jago theory, and Situational Leadership model say that a leader should adjust his or her behavior to the situation and should appreciate diversity among followers.

7. There are many developments in leadership. Emerging issues include emotional intelligence, trust, women leaders, and servant leadership.

8. Effective, dynamic followers are competent and active in their work, assertive, independent thinkers, sensitive to their bosses' needs and demands, and responsible self-managers. Caring leadership and dynamic followership go together.

Key Terms

authentic leadership (p. 416)

authority-compliance
    manager (9,1) (p. 406)

autocratic style (p. 403)

charismatic leadership (p. 415)

consideration (p. 403)

country club manager (1,9) (p. 406)

democratic style (p. 403)

dynamic follower (p. 420)

followership (p. 400)

formal leadership (p. 400)

impoverished manager (1,1) (p. 406)

informal leadership (p. 400)

initiating structure (p. 403)

laissez-faire style (p. 403)

leader (p. 401)

leader–member relations (p. 407)

leadership (p. 400)

Leadership Grid (p. 403)

least preferred coworker (LPC) (p. 407)

manager (p. 401)

opportunistic "what's in it for me" manager (Opp)
    (p. 406)

organization man
    manager (5,5) (p. 406)

paternalistic "father knows best" manager (9, 9)
    (p. 406)

position power (p. 407)

task structure (p. 407)

team manager (9,9) (p. 406)

Review Questions

1. Define *leadership* and *followership*. Distinguish between formal leadership and informal leadership.

2. Discuss transformational, charismatic, and authentic leadership. Would you expect these styles of leadership to exist in all cultures? Differ across cultures?

3. Describe the differences between autocratic and democratic work environments. How do they differ from a laissez-faire workplace?

4. Define *initiating structure* and *consideration* as leader behaviors.

5. Describe the middle-of-the-road manager, authority-compliance manager, country club manager, team manager, and impoverished manager.

6. How does the LPC scale measure leadership style? What are the three dimensions of the leader's situation?

7. Describe the alternative decision strategies used by a leader in the Vroom–Yetton–Jago normative decision theory.

8. Compare House's path–goal theory of leadership with the Situational Leadership model.

9. Describe alienated followers, sheep, yes people, survivors, and effective followers.

Discussion and Communication Questions

1. Do you (or would you want to) work in an autocratic, democratic, or laissez-faire work environment? What might be the advantages and disadvantages of each?

2. Is your supervisor or professor someone who is high in concern for production and people? What is his or her Leadership Grid style?

3. What decision strategies does your supervisor use to make decisions? Are they consistent or inconsistent with the Vroom–Yetton–Jago model?

4. Discuss the similarities and differences between effective leadership and dynamic followership. Are you dynamic?

5. Describe the relationship you have with your supervisor or professor. What are the best and worst parts of the relationship? What could you do to make the relationship better?

6. *(communication question)* Who is the leader you admire the most? Write a description of this person's characteristics and attributes that you admire. Note any aspects of this leader's behavior that you find less than wholly admirable.

7. *(communication question)* Refresh yourself on the distinction between leaders (also called transformational leaders) and managers (also called transactional leaders) in the text. Then read about four contemporary business leaders. Prepare a brief summary of each and classify them as leaders or managers.

8. *(communication question)* Interview a supervisor or manager about the best follower the supervisor or manager has worked with. Ask questions about the characteristics and behaviors that made this person such a good follower. Note in particular how this follower responds to change. Be prepared to present your interview results in class.

Ethical Dilemma

Brent Jones is a manager at Anderson Advertising, leading a team of four people. Brent's team has just wrapped up their last project for one of the firm's main clients, and Brent is trying to decide what project to tackle next. Brent and his team have been doing well this year, and they are all hoping for a good year-end review, possibly including a raise for everyone.

Two projects have made their way to Brent's desk, each from major clients.

The first project requires the inclusion of a multi-media component, utilizing a significant amount of technologic savvy. It would be an opportunity for Brent's team to demonstrate their mastery of cutting-edge systems and formats for clients wishing to appeal to the Internet generation.

The second project is more straight-forward, but will require a clever, creative approach, at which Brent excels. Brent is a talented copyrighter, more so than any other member of his team. Brent knows that if he chooses the first project, his team as a whole will have a chance to impress the client and upper management. If he chooses the second assignment, he will have a chance to demonstrate his personal abilities on a high-profile project. Brent has been at Anderson for many years, and he feels that it is his time to move up the executive ladder. Both projects are on immediate deadlines, so Brent must make a choice and pass the other project on to another team.

Brent knows that if he chooses the creative project, he'll have a better shot at advancement, but at the expense of the good of his team. Brent doesn't want to be that kind of manager—he needs his team to trust him, and he wants them to believe that he has the team's interest at heart when making critical decisions. He knows that the team could do a great job on the first project, and everyone could share in the success.

Questions:

1. Using consequential, rule-based and character theories, evaluate Brent's options.

2. What should Brent do? Why?

Experiential Exercises

12.1 National Culture and Leadership

Effective leadership often varies by national culture, as Hofstede's research has shown. This exercise gives you the opportunity to examine your own and your group's leadership orientation compared to norms from ten countries, including the United States.

Exercise Schedule

1. **Preparation (before class)**
   Complete the 29-item questionnaire.

2. **Individual and Group Scoring**
   Your instructor will lead you through the scoring of the questionnaire, both individually and as a group.

3. **Comparison of Effective Leadership Patterns by Nation**
   Your instructor leads a discussion on Hofstede's value system and presents the culture dimension scores for the ten countries.

In the questionnaire below, indicate the extent to which you agree or disagree with each statement. For example, if you strongly agree with a particular statement, circle the 5 next to the statement.

1 = strongly disagree
2 = disagree
3 = neither agree nor disagree
4 = agree
5 = strongly agree

QUESTIONNAIRE

	STRONGLY DISAGREE				STRONGLY AGREE
1. It is important to have job instructions spelled out in detail so that employees always know what they are expected to do.	1	2	3	4	5
2. Managers expect employees to closely follow instructions and procedures.	1	2	3	4	5
3. Rules and regulations are important because they inform employees what the organization expects of them.	1	2	3	4	5
4. Standard operating procedures are helpful to employees on the job.	1	2	3	4	5
5. Instructions for operations are important for employees on the job.	1	2	3	4	5
6. Group welfare is more important than individual rewards.	1	2	3	4	5
7. Group success is more important than individual success.	1	2	3	4	5
8. Being accepted by the members of your work group is very important.	1	2	3	4	5
9. Employees should pursue their own goals only after considering the welfare of the group.	1	2	3	4	5
10. Managers should encourage group loyalty even if individual goals suffer.	1	2	3	4	5
11. Individuals may be expected to give up their goals in order to benefit group success.	1	2	3	4	5
12. Managers should make most decisions without consulting subordinates.	1	2	3	4	5
13. Managers should frequently use authority and power when dealing with subordinates.	1	2	3	4	5
14. Managers should seldom ask for the opinions of employees.	1	2	3	4	5
15. Managers should avoid off-the-job social contacts with employees.	1	2	3	4	5
16. Employees should not disagree with management decisions.	1	2	3	4	5
17. Managers should not delegate important tasks to employees.	1	2	3	4	5
18. Managers should help employees with their family problems.	1	2	3	4	5
19. Managers should see to it that employees are adequately clothed and fed.	1	2	3	4	5
20. A manager should help employees solve their personal problems.	1	2	3	4	5
21. Management should see that all employees receive health care.	1	2	3	4	5

(Continued)

	STRONGLY DISAGREE				STRONGLY AGREE
22. Management should see that children of employees have an adequate education.	1	2	3	4	5
23. Management should provide legal assistance for employees who get into trouble with the law.	1	2	3	4	5
24. Managers should take care of their employees as they would their children.	1	2	3	4	5
25. Meetings are usually run more effectively when they are chaired by a man.	1	2	3	4	5
26. It is more important for men to have a professional career than it is for women to have a professional career.	1	2	3	4	5
27. Men usually solve problems with logical analysis; women usually solve problems with intuition.	1	2	3	4	5
28. Solving organizational problems usually requires an active, forceful approach, which is typical of men.	1	2	3	4	5
29. It is preferable to have a man, rather than a woman, in a high-level position.	1	2	3	4	5

SOURCES: By Peter Dorfman, *Advances in International Comparative Management*, Vol. 3, pp. 127–150, 1988. Reprinted by permission of JAI Press Inc. D. Marcic and S. M. Puffer, "Dimensions of National Culture and Effective Leadership Patterns: Hofstede Revisited," *Management International* (Minneapolis/St. Paul: West Publishing, 1994), 10–15. All rights reserved. May not be reproduced without written permission of the publisher.

12.2 Leadership and Influence

To get a better idea of what your leadership style is and how productive it would be, fill out the following questionnaire. If you are currently a manager or have been a manager, answer the questions considering "members" to be your employees. If you have never been a manager, think of situations when you were a leader in an organization and consider "members" to be people working for you.

Response choices for each item:

A = always   B = often   C = occasionally
D = seldom   E = never

	A B C D E
1. I would act as the spokesperson of the group.	
2. I would allow the members complete freedom in their work.	
3. I would encourage overtime work.	
4. I would permit the members to use their own judgment in solving problems.	
5. I would encourage the use of uniform procedures.	
6. I would needle members for greater effort.	
7. I would stress being ahead of competing groups.	
8. I would let the members do their work the way they think best.	
9. I would speak as the representative of the group.	
10. I would be able to tolerate postponement and uncertainty.	

	A B C D E
11. I would try out my ideas in the group.	
12. I would turn the members loose on a job, and let them go on it.	
13. I would work hard for a promotion.	
14. I would get swamped by details.	
15. I would speak for the group when visitors are present.	
16. I would be reluctant to allow the members any freedom of action.	
17. I would keep the work moving at a rapid pace.	
18. I would let some members have authority that I should keep.	
19. I would settle conflicts when they occur in the group.	
20. I would allow the group a high degree of initiative.	

21. I would represent the group at outside meetings. A B C D E

22. I would be willing to make changes.

23. I would decide what will be done and how it will be done.

24. I would trust the members to exercise good judgment.

25. I would push for increased production.

26. I would refuse to explain my actions.

27. Things usually turn out as I predict.

28. I would permit the group to set its own pace.

29. I would assign group members to particular tasks. A B C D E

30. I would act without consulting the group.

31. I would ask the members of the group to work harder.

32. I would schedule the work to be done.

33. I would persuade others that my ideas are to their advantage.

34. I would urge the group to beat its previous record.

35. I would ask that group members follow standard rules and regulations.

Scoring

People oriented: Place a check mark by the number if you answered either A or B to any of these questions:

Question # 2 ____ 10 ____ 22 ____
            4 ____ 12 ____ 24 ____
            6 ____ 18 ____ 28 ____
            8 ____ 20 ____

Place a check mark by the number if you answered either D or E to any of these questions:

14 ____ 16 ____ 26 ____ 30 ____

Count your check marks to get your total people-oriented score. ____

Task oriented: Place a check mark by the number if you answered either A or B to any of these questions:

3 ____ 7 ____ 11 ____ 13 ____
17 ____ 25 ____ 29 ____ 31 ____
34 ____

Place a check mark by the number if you answered C or D to any of these questions:

1 ____ 5 ____ 9 ____ 15 ____
19 ____ 21 ____ 23 ____ 27 ____
32 ____ 33 ____ 35 ____

Count your check marks to get your total task-oriented score. ____

Range	Range		
People 0–7;	Task 0–10	You are not involved enough in either the task or the people.	Uninvolved
People 0–7;	Task 10–20	You tend to be autocratic, a whip-snapper. You get the job done, but at a high emotional cost.	Task-oriented
People 8–15;	Task 0–10	People are happy in their work, but sometimes at the expense of productivity.	People-oriented
People 8–15;	Task 10–20	People enjoy working for you and are productive. They naturally expend energy because they get positive reinforcement for doing a good job.	Balanced

As a leader, most people tend to be more task oriented or more people oriented. Task orientation is concerned with getting the job done, while people orientation focuses on group interactions and the needs of individual workers.

Effective leaders, however, are able to use both styles, depending on the situation. There may be times when a rush job demands great attention placed on task completion. During a time of low morale, though, sensitivity to workers' problems would be more appropriate.

The best managers are able to balance both task and people concerns. Therefore, a high score on both would show this balance. Ultimately, you will gain respect, admiration, and productivity from your workers.

Exercise Schedule

1. Preparation (before class)
Complete and score inventory.

2. Group discussion
The class should form four groups based on the scores on the Leadership Style Inventory. Each group will be given a separate task.

Uninvolved: Devise strategies for developing task-oriented and people-oriented styles.

Task-oriented: How can you develop a more people-oriented style? What problems might occur if you do not do so?

People-oriented: How can you develop a more task-oriented style? What problems might occur if you do not do so?

Balanced: Do you see any potential problems with your style? Are you a fully developed leader?

SOURCE: From Thomas Sergiovanni, Richard Metzcus, and Larry Burden, "Toward a Particularistic Approach to Leadership Style: Some Findings," *American Educational Research Journal*, 6(1) (January 1969). Copyright 1969. The American Educational Research Association. Reprinted with permission of AERA.

BizFlix | Doomsday

The Reaper Virus strikes Glasgow, Scotland, on April 3, 2008. It spreads and devastates the population throughout Scotland. Authorities seal off the borders, preventing anyone from entering or leaving the country. They also prohibit aircraft flyovers. Social decay spreads, and cannibalistic behavior develops among the few remaining survivors. Eventually, no one is left alive in the quarantined area. The Reaper Virus reemerges in 2032, this time in London, England. Classified satellite images show life in Glasgow and Edinburgh. Prime Minister John Hatcher (Alexander Siddig) and his assistant Michael Canaris (David O'Hara) assign the task of finding the cure to Security Chief Bill Nelson (Bob Hoskins).

Leadership: No Rules, No Backup

This sequence starts with a shot of the Department of Domestic Security emblem. The film cuts to Major Eden Sinclair (Rhona Mitra) standing in the rain smoking a cigarette while waiting for Chief Nelson. The sequence ends after Michael Canaris leaves the helicopter while saying to Sinclair, "Then you needn't bother coming back." He closes the helicopter's door. Major Sinclair blows her hair from her face while pondering his last statement.

What to Watch for and Ask Yourself

- Assess the behavior of both Major Sinclair and Michael Canaris. Which leadership traits described earlier in this chapter appear in their behavior?

- Apply the behavioral theories discussed earlier to this film sequence. Which parts apply to Sinclair and Canaris's behavior? Draw specific examples from the film sequence.

- Does this film sequence show any aspects of transformational and charismatic leadership? Draw some examples from the sequence.

Workplace Video | City of Greensburg, Kansas: Leadership

After working in Oklahoma City as a parks director, Steve Hewitt wanted to run an entire town. A smaller community seemed the perfect place to get hands-on leadership experience before tackling a bigger city, so Hewitt took the city administrator position in his hometown, Greensburg, Kansas (population: 1,500). But on May 4, 2007, while staring into a dark sky from the tattered remains of his kitchen, Hewitt realized that he got more than he'd bargained for—a tornado had struck the town.

The morning after the powerful EF-5 tornado whipped through the area, everyone knew Greensburg was gone—perhaps forever. But in a subsequent press conference, Mayor Lonnie McCollum announced that the town would rebuild as a model green community, and he convinced the city it needed a full-time administrator to make big changes. Hewitt was the man for the job.

Intense and fast-talking, Steve Hewitt provided the perfect complement to McCollum's humble, measured demeanor. Daniel Wallach, executive director of

Greensburg GreenTown, describes the young leader as "the kind of guy you want taking the last shot in a basketball game." Indeed, Hewitt had the ambition and confidence necessary to get the community back on its feet. While Mayor McCollum offered a vision for rebuilding Greensburg, it was Hewitt who stepped up to ensure that the vision became a reality.

Hewitt quickly went to work on a plan for rebuilding. He took a crash course on interpersonal influence tactics, increased his staff from 20 to 35 people, and established full-time fire, planning, and community development departments. To keep Greensburg on everyone's radar, Hewitt spent hours each week conducting interviews with news media. The press attention kept Greensburg on the map even though it lay in ruins.

City workers give Hewitt high marks for his handling of the crisis. "He has been very open as far as information," said recovery coordinator Kim Alderfer. "He's very good about delegating authority. He gives you the authority to do your job. He doesn't have time to micromanage."

Like most good leaders, Hewitt hasn't been afraid to ruffle feathers as needed. When certain residents opposed the strict environmental building codes, Hewitt found the courage and moral leadership to say, "No. You're going to build it right and you're going to do it to code." Asked about his management of conflict in the middle of a crisis, Hewitt answered, "I'm dumb enough not to care what people say, and young enough to have the energy to get through it."

Discussion Questions

1. Where does Hewitt's leadership fall on the Leadership Grid discussed in the chapter? Explain.

2. How does having two distinct leadership roles, mayor and city administrator, create a challenging environment for effective leadership and followership?

3. Is Hewitt's leadership style appropriate for Greensburg's situation? Explain using insights drawn from Fiedler's contingency theory.

Case

Ingvar Kamprad: Wealthy Man, Frugal Man, Entrepreneur Extraordinaire

Although octogenarian Ingvar Kamprad, the founder of Swedish-based IKEA, is one of the wealthiest individuals in the world, he nonetheless lives quite frugally. Kamprad avoids wearing suits, flies economy class, takes the subway to work, drives a ten-year-old Volvo, and frequents cheap restaurants.[1] "It has long been rumored in Sweden that when his self-discipline fails and he drinks an overpriced Coke out of a hotel minibar, he will go to a grocery store to buy a replacement."[2]

Kamprad, whose official home is Switzerland because of lower taxes, remains very active in running IKEA even though he relinquished his position as CEO in 1999 in order to comply with Dutch age retirement laws for chief executives.[3] "Kamprad has three sons, who all work for the company (he likes to say that IKEA is his fourth child)."[4]

Kamprad developed an entrepreneurial spirit in his youth. As a youngster, Kamprad rode his bicycle throughout the neighborhood, selling matches, pens, and Christmas cards to the local residents.[5] Then in 1943 when he was only seventeen years old, Kamprad used a cash gift from his father to form a company called IKEA. The name IKEA was derived from Ingvar Kamprad's initials plus the first letters of the farm and village where he grew up (Elmtaryd and Agunnaryd).[6]

Initially, IKEA was a catalog company that sold pens, picture frames, wallets, and other bargain goods. "Kamprad used his village's milk van to deliver his products when he first started the business. In 1951, IKEA began selling furniture made by local carpenters; six years later Kamprad opened the first IKEA store in Sweden. In 1985 the first U.S. IKEA—which measured three football fields long—opened in a Philadelphia suburb called Plymouth Meeting. Today IKEA is the largest furniture store in the world."[7] With its "hip furniture designs for the cost conscious … [IKEA] has stores in thirty-three countries, while continuing to expand markets in China and Russia."[8]

A signature characteristic of the company is that "all IKEA products—from furniture to the now famous mobile kitchens—could be packed in flat, stackable boxes that could be mailed or transported and reassembled at home."[9] Interestingly, the flatpack idea for furniture arose by accident when an employee took the legs off a table in order to load it into a customer's car.[10]

"[T]he IKEA way of doing business combines a very Scandinavian embrace of paternalistic employment policies and a social safety net with a hard-core drive for profits and market share that bows to no competitor, anywhere, anytime."[11] IKEA's unrelenting quest for profits reflects Kamprad's frugality. Indeed, Kamprad's thriftiness is infused into IKEA's culture; for example, employees become catalog models and managers share hotel rooms when they travel.[12] "Kamprad obviously appreciates what it takes to earn his money and realizes that there are no guarantees to economic success tomorrow apart from hard work."[13]

At different times throughout his career, Kamprad became reflective about what he had accomplished and proceeded to jot down bits of his management philosophy. One philosophical gem is: "By always asking why we are doing this or that, we can find new paths. By refusing to accept a pattern simply because it is well established, we make progress. We dare to do it a different way! Not just in large matters, but in solving small everyday problems, too."[14] Another of his lofty pronouncements is: "Wasting resources is 'a mortal sin'."[15] Kamprad also promises "a better life for many."[16]

Like many other wealthy people, Kamprad maintains a personal library, deeming personal intellectual development to be a more worthy pursuit than entertainment.[17]

Even with his long career and extraordinary success with IKEA, Kamprad had his share of challenges. "As IKEA grew, so did Kamprad's problems—alcoholism, allegations of a Nazi past, deaths at a store opening—but nothing deflected him."[18] Kamprad describes his association with the "new Swedish" wartime pro-Nazi party as "the greatest mistake of my life."[19]

On a more positive note, Paul Davis, writing for *EzineArticles.com*, observes, "Kamprad's age-old wisdom needs to be heard. His personal humility and modesty says a lot about his character."[20]

From the mistakes and the successes, what lessons should others—current leaders or those aspiring to become leaders—take away from Ingvar Kamprad's experiences?

Discussion Questions

1. In what ways is Ingvar Kamprad a manager? In what ways is he a leader?

2. Describe the nature of followership that Kamprad seems to have encouraged at IKEA.

3. Using the Leadership Grid and its underlying leader behaviors of "concern for results" and "concern for people," explain the leadership orientation of Ingvar Kamprad.

4. Use the concepts of transactional, transformational, charismatic, and authentic leaders to describe the leadership of Ingvar Kamprad.

5. What are the key leadership lessons provided by Kamprad's experiences?

6. What skills would you personally need to develop or refine to become a leader like Kamprad? What could you do to develop or refine these skills?

SOURCE: This case was written by Michael K. McCuddy, The Louis S. and Mary L. Morgal Chair of Christian Business Ethics and Professor of Management, College of Business Administration, Valparaiso University.

X transactional

X transformational

X charismatic

— authentic leader

X —>

Manager vrs

leader.

Key leadership lessons.

∠ Concern For results.

13

Conflict and Negotiation

LEARNING OBJECTIVES

After reading this chapter, you should be able to do the following:

1 Diagnose functional versus dysfunctional conflict.

2 Identify the causes of conflict in organizations.

3 Identify the different forms of conflict.

4 Understand the defense mechanisms that individuals exhibit when they engage in interpersonal conflict.

5 Describe effective and ineffective techniques for managing conflict.

6 Understand five styles of conflict management, and diagnose your own preferred style.

Carpet clipping and finishing in northern India.

THINKING AHEAD: IKEA

Conflict with Suppliers over Child Labor

IKEA has a strong focus on corporate social responsibility, and the company requires its suppliers to sign a Code of Conduct document forbidding the use of child labor. Despite

these precautions, IKEA ran into conflict with its suppliers concerning this issue. In 1994, a Swedish documentary showed children working on weaving looms in Pakistan and mentioned IKEA as an importer of these carpets. Later, Dutch media alleged that two of IKEA's rug suppliers exploited child labor.[1] The emergence of the allegations in news stories clearly indicated that simply using a Code of Conduct was not sufficient and IKEA leaders also realized that this conflict with suppliers was extremely complex.

The suppliers argued that children were better suited for this type of labor than adults because their fingers were smaller and more dexterous. Furthermore, they argued that if the children weren't working, abject poverty would make life unbearable. Although there is little credibility for the first argument, there was some truth to the second. Often, children are put to work in India and Pakistan because their parents are in debt. Loan sharks, who also own the looms, loan money to these parents at exorbitant interest rates. When they aren't paid back, the loan sharks suggest that the children go to work. To further complicate the issue, attempts at boycotting those using child labor have had negative consequences. When U.S. trade sanctions ordered Bangladeshi garment manufacturers to stop employing children, many of these children ended up with no alternatives. Hunger and desperation drove them to demonstrate to get their jobs back.[2] Furthermore, when foreign companies have tried to set up schools for these children, they find that most schools end up empty because the children go to work somewhere else.[3] IKEA found itself in a very difficult position and sought to do the right thing regarding child labor. Read about how IKEA handled this conflict in the Looking Back feature at the end of this chapter.

THE NATURE OF CONFLICTS IN ORGANIZATIONS

All of us have experienced conflict of various types, yet we probably fail to recognize the variety of conflicts that occur in organizations. *Conflict* is defined as any situation in which incompatible goals, attitudes, emotions, or behaviors lead to disagreement or opposition between two or more parties.[4]

Today's organizations may face greater potential for conflict than ever before in history. The marketplace, with its increasing competition and globalization, magnifies differences among people in terms of personality, values, attitudes, perceptions, languages, cultures, and national backgrounds.[5] With the increasing diversity of the workforce, furthermore, comes the potential for incompatibility and conflict.

Importance of Conflict Management Skills for the Manager

Estimates show that managers spend about 21 percent of their time dealing with conflict.[6] That is the equivalent of one day every week. And conflict management skills are a major predictor of managerial success.[7] Emotional intelligence (EI) relates to the ability to manage conflict. It is the power to control one's emotions and perceive emotions in others, adapt to change, and manage adversity. Conflict management skills may be more a reflection of EI than of IQ. People who lack EI, especially empathy or the ability to see life from another person's perspective, are more likely to be causes of conflict than managers of conflict.[8] EI seems to be valid across cultures. It is common among successful people not only in North America, but also in Nigeria, India, Argentina, and France.

1 Diagnose functional versus dysfunctional conflict.

conflict

Any situation in which incompatible goals, attitudes, emotions, or behaviors lead to disagreement or opposition for two or more parties.

Functional versus Dysfunctional Conflict

Not all conflict is bad. In fact, some types of conflict encourage new solutions to problems and enhance creativity in the organization. In these cases, managers will want to encourage the conflicts. Thus, the key to conflict management is to stimulate functional conflict and prevent or resolve dysfunctional conflict. The difficulty, however, is distinguishing between dysfunctional and functional conflicts. The consequences of conflict can be positive or negative, as shown in Table 13.1.

Conflict by its nature is an emotional interaction,[23] and the emotions of the parties involved in conflict play a pivotal role in how they perceive the negotiation and respond to one another. In fact, emotions are now considered critical elements of any negotiation that must be included in any examination of the process and how it unfolds.[24]

One important research finding has been that emotion can play a problematic role in negotiations. In particular, when negotiators begin to act based on emotions rather than on cognitions, they are much more likely to reach an impasse.[25]

Communication Barriers Communication barriers such as physical separation and language can create distortions in messages, and these can lead to conflict. Another communication barrier is value judgment, in which a listener assigns a worth to a message before it is received. For example, suppose a team member is a chronic complainer. When this individual enters the manager's office, the manager is likely to devalue the message before it is even delivered. Conflict can then emerge.

Cultural Differences Although cultural differences are assets in organizations, sometimes they can be seen as sources of conflict. Often, these conflicts stem from a lack of understanding of another culture. In one MBA class, for example, Indian students were horrified when American students challenged the professor. Meanwhile, the American students thought the students from India were too passive. Subsequent discussions revealed that professors in India expected to be treated deferentially and with great respect. While students might challenge an idea vigorously, they would rarely challenge the professor. Diversity training that emphasizes education on cultural differences can make great strides in preventing misunderstandings.

GLOBALIZATION AND CONFLICT

Large transnational corporations employ many different ethnic and cultural groups. In these multiethnic corporations, the widely differing cultures represent vast differences among individuals, so the potential for conflict increases.[26] As indicated in Chapter 2, Hofstede has identified five dimensions along which cultural differences may emerge: individualism/collectivism, power distance, uncertainty avoidance, masculinity/femininity, and long-term/short-term orientation.[27] These cultural differences have many implications for conflict management in organizations.

Individualism means that people believe that their individual interests take priority over society's interests. Collectivism, by contrast, means that people put the good of the group first. For example, the United States is a highly individualistic culture, whereas Japan is a very collectivist culture. The individualism/collectivism dimension of cultural differences strongly influences conflict management behavior. People from collectivist cultures tend to display a more cooperative approach to managing conflict.[28]

Hofstede's second dimension of cultural differences is power distance. In cultures with high-power distance, individuals accept that people in organizations have varying levels of power. By contrast, in cultures with low-power distance, individuals do not automatically respect those in positions of authority. For example, the United States is a country of low-power distance, whereas Brazil is a country with a high-power distance. Differences in power distance can lead to conflict. Imagine a U.S. employee managed by a Brazilian supervisor who expects deferential behavior. The supervisor would expect automatic respect based on legitimate power. When this respect is not given, conflict would arise.

Uncertainty avoidance also varies by culture. In the United States, employees can tolerate high levels of uncertainty, whereas employees in Israel tend to prefer certainty in their work settings. A U.S.-based multinational firm might run into

conflicts operating in Israel. Suppose such a firm is installing a new technology. Its expatriate workers from the United States would tolerate the uncertainty of the technological transition better than would their Israeli coworkers, and this might lead to conflicts among the employees.

Masculinity versus femininity illustrates the contrast between preferences for assertiveness and material goods versus preferences for human capital and quality of life. The United States is a masculine society, whereas Sweden is considered a feminine society. Adjustment to the assertive interpersonal style of U.S. workers may be difficult for Swedish coworkers.

Conflicts can also arise between cultures that vary in their time orientation of values. China, for example, has a long-term orientation; the Chinese prefer values that focus on the future, such as saving and persistence. The United States and Russia, by contrast, have short-term orientations. These cultures emphasize values in the past and present, such as respect for tradition and fulfillment of social obligations. Conflicts can arise when managers fail to understand the nature of differences in values.

The response to conflict may differ by country as well. A recent study found that U.S. employees were more likely to engage in indirect conflict at work or negative behavior behind someone's back, whereas Chinese employees were more likely to engage in direct conflict or face-to-face conflict. Direct conflict was reported as more stressful to U.S. employees while indirect conflict was more stressful for Chinese employees.[29]

An organization whose workforce consists of multiple ethnicities and cultures holds potential for many types of conflict because of the sheer volume of individual differences among workers. The key to managing conflict in a multicultural workforce is understanding cultural differences and appreciating their value.

FORMS OF CONFLICT IN ORGANIZATIONS

3 Identify the different forms of conflict.

Conflict can take on any of several different forms in an organization, including interorganizational, intergroup, intragroup, interpersonal, and intrapersonal conflicts. It is important to note that the prefix *inter* means "between," whereas the prefix *intra* means "within."

Interorganizational Conflict

Conflict that occurs between two or more organizations is called *interorganizational conflict*. Competition can heighten interorganizational conflict. Corporate takeovers, mergers, and acquisitions can also produce interorganizational conflict. What about the interorganizational conflict between major league baseball's players' union and management, which is sometimes characterized as a battle between millionaires and multimillionaires. The players regularly go on strike to extract more of the profits from management, while management cries that it is not making a dime.

Conflicts among organizations abound. Some of these conflicts can be functional, as when firms improve the quality of their products and services in the spirit of healthy competition. Other interorganizational conflicts can have dysfunctional results.

interorganizational conflict
Conflict that occurs between two or more organizations.

intergroup conflict
Conflict that occurs between groups or teams in an organization.

Intergroup Conflict

When conflict occurs between groups or teams, it is known as *intergroup conflict*. Conflict between groups can have positive effects within each group, such as increased group cohesiveness, increased focus on tasks, and increased loyalty to the

group. There are, however, negative consequences as well. Groups in conflict tend to develop an "us against them" mentality whereby each sees the other team as the enemy, becomes more hostile, and decreases its communication with the other group. Groups are even more competitive and less cooperative than individuals. The inevitable outcome is that one group gains and the other group loses.[30]

Competition between groups must be managed carefully so that it does not escalate into dysfunctional conflict. Research has shown that when groups compete for a goal that only one group can achieve, negative consequences like territoriality, aggression, and prejudice toward the other group can result.[31] Managers should encourage and reward cooperative behaviors across groups. Some effective ways of doing this include modifying performance appraisals to include assessing intergroup behavior and using an external supervisor's evaluation of intergroup behavior. Group members will be more likely to help other groups when they know that the other group's supervisor will be evaluating their behavior, and that they will be rewarded for cooperation.[32] In addition, managers should encourage social interactions across groups so that trust can be developed. Trust allows individuals to exchange ideas and resources with members of other groups and results in innovation when members of different groups cooperate.[33] Conflict often results when older employees fear that younger new-hires may take over their jobs. Social interaction can help reduce these perceived threats, creating trust and reducing the intergroup conflict in the process.[34] An emerging challenge identified by research in conflict management points at the intergenerational conflict brought about by the diversity in age in the U.S. workforce as discussed in Chapter 2. This type of intergenerational conflict can stem from the design of employee benefit packages that might appeal more to one age group than another. Organizations should design flexible employee benefit systems that have a broader appeal to a diverse age group to curtail this type of intergenerational conflict.[35]

Intragroup Conflict

Conflict that occurs within groups or teams is called *intragroup conflict*. Some conflict within a group is functional. It can help the group avoid groupthink, as we discussed in Chapter 10. Even the newest teams, virtual teams, are not immune to conflict. The nuances and subtleties of face-to-face communication are often lacking in these teams, and misunderstandings can result. To avoid dysfunctional conflicts, virtual teams should make sure their tasks fit their methods of interacting. Complex strategic decisions may require face-to-face meetings rather than e-mails or threaded discussions. Face-to-face and telephone interactions early on can eliminate later conflicts and allow virtual teams to move on to use electronic communication because trust has been developed.[36] For a greater understanding of how to manage conflict in teams for better performance, see the Science feature.

Teams can experience many types of conflict. Using You 13.1, you can assess the types of conflict in a team you belong to, as well as design ways to manage those conflicts.

Interpersonal Conflict

Conflict between two or more people is *interpersonal conflict*. Conflict between people can arise from many individual differences, including personalities, attitudes, values, perceptions, and the other differences we discussed in Chapters 3 and 4. Later in this chapter, we look at defense mechanisms that individuals exhibit in interpersonal conflict and at ways to cope with difficult people.

intragroup conflict
Conflict that occurs within groups or teams.

interpersonal conflict
Conflict that occurs between two or more individuals.

Intragroup Conflict: How Do Groups Deal with Conflict and Facilitate Performance and Satisfaction?

Recent research suggests that the type of conflict a group experiences (task, relationship, or process) may not directly impact the group's performance. Instead, what's important is conflict resolution strategies. Groups who improve or maintain top performance *and* member satisfaction maintain a focus on equity or finding viable ways for each team member to contribute given their constraints, and clearly articulate compromises and trade-offs made by individual members or the group in preventing destructive conflicts. These groups use a "dual concern" approach which focuses on concern for the task but also concern for integrating the interests of individual team members. By contrast, groups that maintained high performance but exhibited waning member satisfaction used a rules-focused strategy in which they dealt with conflict by establishing specific rules. This created a task-focused environment at the expense of integrating individual interests.

Low-performing groups with high member satisfaction took an equality focus where complete accommodation of individual concerns was observed. These groups avoided any interpersonal conflict, and thus, there was harmony in these group but poor performance. Groups that performed poorly and had low member satisfaction used an ad hoc approach to conflict resolution in which roles were not clear, the root cause of the problem was not identified or corrected, and there was no clear conflict management strategy. The bottom line? Good performance and satisfied team members result when teams emphasize both getting the work done and integrating the interests of team members, and acknowledge the members who help prevent dysfunctional conflicts.

SOURCE: K. J. Behfar, R. S. Peterson, E. A. Mannix, and W. M. K. Trochim, "The Critical Role of Conflict Resolution in Teams," *Journal of Applied Psychology* 93 (2008): 170–188.

Intrapersonal Conflict

When conflict occurs within an individual, it is called *intrapersonal conflict.* There are several types of intrapersonal conflict, including interrole, intrarole, and person–role conflicts. A role is a set of expectations placed on an individual by others.[37] The person occupying the focal role is the role incumbent, and the individuals who place expectations on the person are role senders. Figure 13.2 depicts a set of role relationships.

Interrole conflict occurs when a person experiences conflict among the multiple roles in his or her life. One interrole conflict that many employees experience is work/home conflict, in which their role as worker clashes with their role as spouse or parent.[38] Work/home conflict has many causes including time constraints, strain, and having responsibility for others in the workplace.[39] Work/home conflict has become even more common with the rise of work-at-home professionals and telecommuting because the home becomes the office, blurring the boundary between work and family life.[40] Recently, organizations are leveraging their use of information technology to gain a competitive edge. This has translated into ambitious and highly involved employees using office communications (e.g., voice mail, e-mail, etc.) even after-hours. Such after-hours communication usage is associated with increased work–life conflict as reported by the employee and a significant other.[41]

Intrarole conflict is conflict within a single role. It often arises when a person receives conflicting messages from role senders about how to perform a certain role. Suppose a manager receives counsel from her department head that she needs to socialize less with the nonmanagement employees. She also is told by her project manager that she needs to be a better team member, and that she can accomplish this by socializing more with the other nonmanagement team members. This situation is one of intrarole conflict.

intrapersonal conflict

Conflict that occurs within an individual.

interrole conflict

A person's experience of conflict among the multiple roles in his or her life.

intrarole conflict

Conflict that occurs within a single role, such as when a person receives conflicting messages from role senders about how to perform a certain role.

You 13.1

Assess Your Team's Conflict

Think of a team you're a member of or one you were part of in the past. Answer the following eight questions regarding that team.

1. How much emotional tension was there in your team?

No tension				Lots of tension
1	2	3	4	5

2. How much conflict of ideas was there in your team?

No idea conflict				Lots of idea conflict
1	2	3	4	5

3. How often did people get angry while working in your team?

Never				Often
1	2	3	4	5

4. How different were your views on the content of your project?

Very similar views				Very different views
1	2	3	4	5

5. How much were personality clashes evident in your team?

No clashes evident				Personality clashes very evident
1	2	3	4	5

6. How much did you talk through disagreements about your team projects?

Never talked through disagreements				Always talked through disagreements
1	2	3	4	5

7. How much interpersonal friction was there in your team?

No friction				Lots of friction
1	2	3	4	5

8. How much disagreement was there about task procedure in your team?

No disagreement about procedure				Lots of disagreement about procedure
1	2	3	4	5

Total for items 2, 4, 6, and 8 =_____ indicating task conflict.
Total for items 1, 3, 5, and 7 = _____ indicating relationship conflict.

- Did your team experience higher relationship or task conflict?
- What actions can you take to better manage task conflict? Relationship conflict?
- Was there an absence of both, or either, types of conflict in your team? What does this indicate?

SOURCE: Adapted from K. Jehn, "A Multimethod Examination of the Benefits and Detriments of Intragroup Conflict," *Administrative Science Quarterly* 40 (1995): 256–282.

Person–role conflict occurs when an individual in a particular role is expected to perform behaviors that clash with his or her values.[42] Salespeople, for example, may be required to offer the most expensive item in the sales line first to the customer, even when it is apparent that the customer does not want or cannot afford the item. A computer salesman may be required to offer a large, elaborate system to a student he knows is on a tight budget. This may conflict with the salesman's values, and he may experience person–role conflict.

Intrapersonal conflicts can have positive consequences. Often, professional responsibilities clash with deeply held values. A budget shortfall may force you to lay off a loyal, hardworking employee. Your daughter may have a piano recital on the same day your largest client is scheduled to be in town visiting the office. In such conflicts, we often have to choose between right and right; that is, there's no correct response. These may be thought of as *defining moments* that challenge us to choose between two or more things in which we believe.[43] Character is formed in defining moments because they cause us to shape our identities. They help us crystallize our values and serve as opportunities for personal growth.

person–role conflict
Conflict that occurs when an individual is expected to perform behaviors in a certain role that conflict with his or her personal values.

FIGURE

13.2   An Organization Member's Role Set

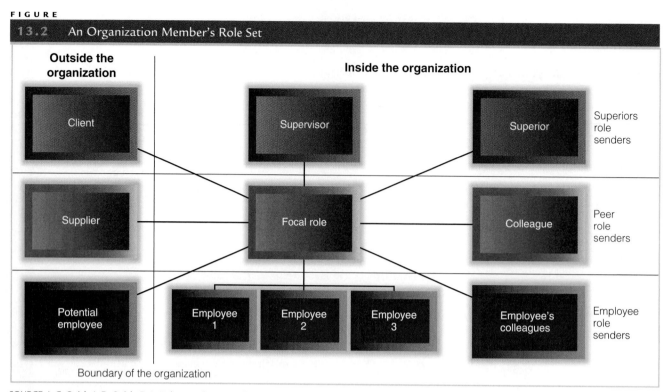

SOURCE: J. C. Quick, J. D. Quick, D. L. Nelson, and J. J. Hurrell, Jr., *Preventive Stress Management in Organizations*, 1997. Copyright © 1997 by the American Psychological Association. Reprinted with permission.

INTRAPERSONAL CONFLICT

Intrapersonal conflict can be managed with careful self-analysis and diagnosis of the situation. Three actions in particular can help prevent or resolve intrapersonal conflicts.

First, when seeking a new job, you should find out as much as possible about the values of the organization.[44] Many person–role conflicts center around differences between the organization's values and the individual's values. Research has shown that when there is a good fit between the values of the individual and the organization, the individual is more satisfied and committed and is less likely to leave the organization.[45]

Second, to manage intrarole or interrole conflicts, role analysis is a good tool.[46] In role analysis, the individual asks the various role senders what they expect of him or her. The outcomes are clearer work roles and the reduction of conflict and ambiguity.[47] Role analysis is a simple tool that clarifies the expectations of both parties in a relationship and reduces the potential for conflict within a role or between roles.

Third, political skills can help buffer the negative effects of stress that stem from role conflicts. Effective politicians, as we discussed in Chapter 11, can negotiate role expectations when conflicts occur. All these forms of conflict can be managed. An understanding of the many forms is a first step. The next section focuses more extensively on interpersonal conflict because of its pervasiveness in organizations.

INTERPERSONAL CONFLICT

When a conflict occurs between two or more people, it is known as interpersonal conflict. Such conflicts can be minor, or they can be extremely difficult. Workplace bullying, for example, can be difficult to handle. Most of us remember bullies from childhood playground days. They exist in the workplace as well. According to the

Workplace Bullying Institute (WBI), half of all workers have been bullied, and most bullies (72 percent) are bosses. Both sexes can be bullies, but most targets are women (57 percent). Just what constitutes bullying? It is repeated, health-harming mistreatment of one or more persons by one or more perpetrators. It can take the form of verbal abuse, offensive conduct, or work interference. It is driven by the bully's need to control the target. In 13.1 you can read about a real instance of bullying, along with the WBI guidelines on what to do if you're a target of bullying in the workplace.[48]

The Real World 13.1

Workplace Bullying on the Rise, According to the Workplace Bullying Institute

The senior nurse threw scissors and yelled at Nicole to pick them up. She framed Nicole for a disastrous medical error involving a patient. She verbally abused Nicole in front of patients, who were also scared to death of the senior nurse. In another case, a surgeon was sued by a hospital employee who accused him of intentionally inflicting emotional distress and assault. Although these two examples are from health care, workplace bullying is found across industries and organizations, and it is increasing. A survey of U.S workers indicated that half said they either had been bullied at work or had seen other employees bullied. The WBI estimates that 54 million people have been bullied at work. And, bullying is a global phenomenon. A recent study in Spain indicated that it is prevalent in that country, that women are most often the victims, and that the type of bullying varies by age. Those workers under thirty are more likely to be harassed, whereas those forty-five and older are more likely to be abused.

The WBI recommends the following three-step method that you can use should you find yourself the target of a workplace bully.

Workplace bullying can take the form of verbal abuse, offensive conduct, or work interference. Meryl Streep portrayed a bully in the movie *The Devil Wears Prada*.

20TH CENTURY FOX/THE KOBAL COLLECTION/WETCHER, BARRY

Research state and federal legal options. Gather data about the economic impact the bully has had on the company. If necessary, start your job search for a new position.

Step Three: Expose the Bully. Make the business case that the bully is too expensive to keep. Tell everyone about the bully for your health's sake. Give the employer ONE CHANCE to do the right thing.

WBI acknowledges that dealing with bullies is an uphill struggle. They also recommend that you not ask others (like HR) to make the bully stop for you. Instead, make the business case so that they will stop the bully for their own self-interests.

Step One: Name It! Legitimize Yourself. You did not invite this bullying and interference with your work, so don't let others tell you that because your problem is not illegal, you have no problem. Call it what it is: bullying, psychological harassment, psychological violence, emotional abuse.

Step Two: Seek Respite, Take Time Off to Bullyproof Yourself. Check your mental and physical health.

SOURCES: http://www.workplacebullying.org/targets/solution/three-step-method.html; S. Boesveld, "Beward the Office Bully—She's Baring Her Claws," *The Globe and Mail* (May 18, 2009), accessed at http://www.workplacebullying.org/2009/05/18/globemail/#more-514.

To manage interpersonal conflict, along with understanding workplace bullying, it is helpful to understand power networks in organizations and defense mechanisms exhibited by individuals when they are in conflict situations.

Power Networks

According to Mastenbroek, individuals in organizations are organized in three basic types of power networks.[49] Based on these power relationships, certain kinds of conflict tend to emerge. Figure 13.3 illustrates three basic kinds of power relationships in organizations.

The first relationship is equal versus equal, in which there is a horizontal balance of power among the parties. An example of this type of relationship would be a conflict between individuals from two different project teams. The behavioral tendency is toward suboptimization; that is, the focus is on a win–lose approach to problems, and each party tries to maximize its power at the expense of the other party. Conflict within this type of network can lead to depression, low self-esteem, and other distress symptoms. Interventions like improving coordination between the parties and working toward common interests can help manage these conflicts.

The second power network is high versus low, or a powerful versus a less powerful relationship. Conflicts that emerge here take the basic form of the powerful

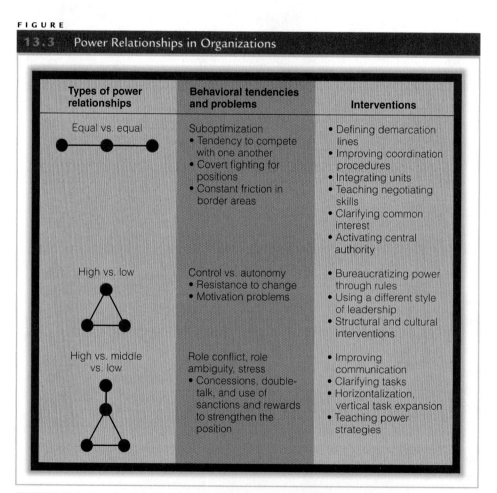

FIGURE
13.3 Power Relationships in Organizations

Types of power relationships	Behavioral tendencies and problems	Interventions
Equal vs. equal	Suboptimization • Tendency to compete with one another • Covert fighting for positions • Constant friction in border areas	• Defining demarcation lines • Improving coordination procedures • Integrating units • Teaching negotiating skills • Clarifying common interest • Activating central authority
High vs. low	Control vs. autonomy • Resistance to change • Motivation problems	• Bureaucratizing power through rules • Using a different style of leadership • Structural and cultural interventions
High vs. middle vs. low	Role conflict, role ambiguity, stress • Concessions, double-talk, and use of sanctions and rewards to strengthen the position	• Improving communication • Clarifying tasks • Horizontalization, vertical task expansion • Teaching power strategies

SOURCE: W. F. G. Mastenbroek, *Conflict Management and Organization Development*, 1987. Copyright John Wiley & Sons Limited. Reproduced with permission.

individuals trying to control others, with the less powerful people trying to become more autonomous. Conflict in this network can lead to job dissatisfaction, low organizational commitment, and turnover.[50] Organizations typically respond to these conflicts by tightening the rules. However, the more successful ways of managing these conflicts are to try a different style of leadership, such as a coaching and counseling style, or to change the structure to a more decentralized one.

The third power network is high versus middle versus low. This power network illustrates the classic conflicts felt by middle managers. Two particular conflicts are evident for middle managers: role conflict, in which conflicting expectations are placed on the manager from bosses and employees, and role ambiguity, in which the expectations of the boss are unclear. Improved communication among all parties can reduce role conflict and ambiguity. In addition, middle managers can benefit from training in positive ways to influence others.

Knowing the typical kinds of conflicts that arise in various kinds of relationships can help a manager diagnose conflicts and devise appropriate ways to manage them.

Defense Mechanisms

4 Understand the defense mechanisms that individuals exhibit when they engage in interpersonal conflict.

When individuals are involved in conflict with another human being, frustration often results.[51] Conflicts can often arise within the context of a performance appraisal session. Most people do not react well to negative feedback, as was illustrated in a classic study.[52] In this study, when employees were given criticism about their work, over 50 percent of their responses were defensive.

When individuals are frustrated, as they often are in interpersonal conflict, they respond by exhibiting defense mechanisms.[53] Defense mechanisms are common reactions to the frustration that accompanies conflict. Table 13.2 describes several defense mechanisms seen in organizations.

Aggressive mechanisms, such as fixation, displacement, and negativism, are aimed at attacking the source of the conflict. In *fixation*, an individual fixates on the conflict, or keeps up a dysfunctional behavior that obviously will not solve the conflict. An example of fixation occurred in a university, where a faculty member became embroiled in a battle with the dean because the faculty member felt he had not received a large enough salary increase. He persisted in writing angry letters to the dean, whose hands were tied because of a low budget allocation to the college. *Displacement* means directing anger toward someone who is not the source of the conflict. For example, a manager may respond harshly to an employee after a telephone confrontation with an angry customer. Another aggressive defense mechanism is *negativism*, which is active or passive resistance. Negativism is illustrated by a manager who, when appointed to a committee on which she did not want to serve, made negative comments throughout the meeting.

Compromise mechanisms, such as compensation, identification, and rationalization, are used by individuals to make the best of a conflict situation. *Compensation* occurs when an individual tries to make up for an inadequacy by putting increased energy into another activity. Compensation can be seen when a person makes up for a bad relationship at home by spending more time at the office. *Identification* occurs when one individual patterns his or her behavior after another's. One supervisor at a construction firm, not wanting to acknowledge consciously that she was not likely to be promoted, mimicked the behavior of her boss, even going so far as to buy a car just like the boss's. *Rationalization* is trying to justify one's behavior by constructing bogus reasons for it. Employees may rationalize unethical behavior like padding their expense accounts because "everyone else does it."

fixation
An aggressive mechanism in which an individual keeps up a dysfunctional behavior that obviously will not solve the conflict.

displacement
An aggressive mechanism in which an individual directs his or her anger toward someone who is not the source of the conflict.

negativism
An aggressive mechanism in which a person responds with pessimism to any attempt at solving a problem.

compensation
A compromise mechanism in which an individual attempts to make up for a negative situation by devoting himself or herself to another pursuit with increased vigor.

identification
A compromise mechanism whereby an individual patterns his or her behavior after another's.

rationalization
A compromise mechanism characterized by trying to justify one's behavior by constructing bogus reasons for it.

13.2 Common Defense Mechanisms

Defense Mechanism	Psychological Process
Aggressive Mechanisms	
• Fixation	Person maintains a persistent, nonadjustive reaction even though all the cues indicate the behavior will not cope with the problem.
• Displacement	Individual redirects pent-up emotions toward persons, ideas, or objects other than the primary source of the emotion.
• Negativism	Person uses active or passive resistance, operating unconsciously.
Compromise Mechanisms	
• Compensation	Individual devotes himself or herself to a pursuit with increased vigor to make up for some feeling of real or imagined inadequacy.
• Identification	Individual enhances own self-esteem by patterning behavior after another's, frequently also internalizing the values and beliefs of the other person; also vicariously shares the glories or suffering in the disappointments of other individuals or groups.
• Rationalization	Person justifies inconsistent or undesirable behavior, beliefs, statements, and motivations by providing acceptable explanations for them.
Withdrawal Mechanisms	
• Flight or withdrawal	Through either physical or psychological means, person leaves the field in which frustration, anxiety, or conflict is experienced.
• Conversion	Emotional conflicts are expressed in muscular, sensory, or bodily symptoms of disability, malfunctioning, or pain.
• Fantasy	Person daydreams or uses other forms of imaginative activity to obtain an escape from reality and obtain imagined satisfactions.

SOURCE: Timothy W. Costello and Sheldon S. Zalkind, adapted table from "Psychology in Administration: A Research Orientation" from *Journal of Conflict Resolution* III 1959, pp. 148–149. Reprinted by permission of Sage Publications, Inc.

flight/withdrawal

A withdrawal mechanism that entails physically escaping a conflict (flight) or psychologically escaping (withdrawal).

conversion

A withdrawal mechanism in which emotional conflicts are expressed in physical symptoms.

fantasy

A withdrawal mechanism that provides an escape from a conflict through daydreaming.

Withdrawal mechanisms are exhibited when frustrated individuals try to flee from a conflict using either physical or psychological means. Flight, withdrawal, conversion, and fantasy are examples of withdrawal mechanisms. Physically escaping a conflict is *flight*. When an employee takes a day off after a blowup with the boss is an example. *Withdrawal* may take the form of emotionally leaving a conflict, such as exhibiting an "I don't care anymore" attitude. *Conversion* is a process whereby emotional conflicts are expressed in physical symptoms. Most of us have experienced the conversion reaction of a headache following an emotional exchange with another person. *Fantasy* is an escape by daydreaming. In the Internet age, fantasy as an escape mechanism has found new meaning. A study conducted by International Data Corporation (IDC) showed that 30–40 percent of all Internet surfing at work is nonwork-related and that more than 70 percent of companies have had sex sites accessed from their networks, suggesting that employees' minds aren't always focused on their jobs.[54]

When employees exhibit withdrawal mechanisms, they often fake it by pretending to agree with their bosses or coworkers in order to avoid facing an immediate conflict. Many employees fake it because the firm informally rewards agreement and punishes dissent. The long-term consequence of withdrawal and faking it is emotional distress for the employee.[55]

Knowledge of these defense mechanisms can be extremely beneficial to a manager. By understanding the ways in which people typically react to interpersonal conflict, managers can be prepared for employees' reactions and help them uncover their feelings about a conflict.

CONFLICT MANAGEMENT STRATEGIES AND TECHNIQUES

The overall approach (or strategy) you use in a conflict is important in determining whether the conflict will have a positive or negative outcome.

These overall strategies are competitive versus cooperative strategies. Table 13.3 depicts the two strategies and four different conflict scenarios. The competitive strategy is founded on assumptions of win–lose and entails dishonest communication, mistrust, and a rigid position from both parties.[56] The cooperative strategy is founded on different assumptions: the potential for win–win outcomes, honest communication, trust, openness to risk and vulnerability, and the notion that the whole may be greater than the sum of the parts.

To illustrate the importance of the overall strategy, consider the case of two groups competing for scarce resources. Suppose budget cuts have to be made at an insurance company. The claims manager argues that the sales training staff should be cut, because agents are fully trained. The sales training manager argues that claims personnel should be cut, because the company is processing fewer claims. This could turn into a dysfunctional brawl, with both sides refusing to give ground. This would constitute a win–lose, lose–win, or lose–lose scenario. Personnel cuts could be made in only one department, or in both departments. In all three cases, with the competitive approach the organization winds up in a losing position.

Even in such intense conflicts as those over scarce resources, a win–win strategy can lead to an overall win for the organization. In fact, conflicts over scarce resources can be productive if the parties have cooperative goals—a strategy that seeks a winning solution for both parties. To achieve a win–win outcome, the conflict must be approached with open-minded discussion of opposing views. Through

TABLE

| 13.3 | Win–Lose versus Win–Win Strategies | | |

Strategy	Department A	Department B	Organization
Competitive	Lose	Lose	Lose
	Lose	Win	Lose
	Win	Lose	Lose
Cooperative	Win–	Win–	Win

open-minded discussion, both parties integrate views and create new solutions that facilitate productivity and strengthen their relationship; the result is feelings of unity rather than separation.[57]

In the example of the conflict between the claims manager and the sales training manager, open-minded discussion might reveal that there are ways to achieve budget cuts without cutting personnel. Sales support might surrender part of its travel budget, and claims might cut out overtime. This represents a win–win situation for the company. The budget has been reduced, and relationships between the two departments have been preserved. Both parties have given up something (note the "win–" in Table 13.3), but the conflict has been resolved with a positive outcome.

You can see the importance of the broad strategy used to approach a conflict. We now move from broad strategies to more specific techniques.

Ineffective Techniques

5 Describe effective and ineffective techniques for managing conflict.

There are many specific techniques for dealing with conflict. Before turning to techniques that work, it should be recognized that some actions commonly taken in organizations to deal with conflict are not effective.[58]

Nonaction is doing nothing in hopes that the conflict will disappear. Generally, this is not a good technique, because most conflicts do not go away, and the individuals involved in the conflict react with frustration.

Secrecy, or trying to keep a conflict out of view of most people, only creates suspicion. An example is an organizational policy of pay secrecy. In some organizations, discussion of salary is grounds for dismissal. When this is the case, employees suspect that the company has something to hide. Secrecy may result in surreptitious political activity by employees who hope to uncover the secret![59]

Administrative orbiting is delaying action on a conflict by buying time, usually by telling the individuals involved that the problem is being worked on or that the boss is still thinking about the issue. Like nonaction, this technique leads to frustration and resentment.

Due process nonaction is a procedure set up to address conflicts that is so costly, time-consuming, or personally risky that no one will use it. Some companies' sexual harassment policies are examples of this technique. To file a sexual harassment complaint, detailed paperwork is required, the accuser must go through appropriate channels, and the accuser risks being branded a troublemaker. Thus, the company has a procedure for handling complaints (due process), but no one uses it (nonaction).

Character assassination is an attempt to label or discredit an opponent. Character assassination can backfire and make the individual who uses it appear dishonest and cruel. It often leads to name-calling and accusations by both parties, both ending up losers in the eyes of those who witness the conflict.

Effective Techniques

Fortunately, there are effective conflict management techniques. These include appealing to superordinate goals, expanding resources, changing personnel, changing structure, and confronting and negotiating.

Superordinate Goals An organizational goal that is more important to both parties in a conflict than their individual or group goals is a *superordinate goal.*[60] Superordinate goals cannot be achieved by an individual or by one group alone. The achievement of these goals requires cooperation by both parties.

One effective technique for resolving conflict is to appeal to a superordinate goal—in effect, to focus the parties on a larger issue on which they both agree. This helps them realize their similarities rather than their differences.

nonaction
Doing nothing in hopes that a conflict will disappear.

secrecy
Attempting to hide a conflict or an issue that has the potential to create conflict.

administrative orbiting
Delaying action on a conflict by buying time.

due process nonaction
A procedure set up to address conflicts that is so costly, time-consuming, or personally risky that no one will use it.

character assassination
An attempt to label or discredit an opponent.

superordinate goal
An organizational goal that is more important to both parties in a conflict than their individual or group goals.

In the conflict between service representatives and cable television installers that was discussed earlier, appealing to a superordinate goal would be an effective technique for resolving the conflict. Both departments can agree that superior customer service is a goal worthy of pursuit and that this goal cannot be achieved unless cables are installed properly and in a timely manner, and customer complaints are handled effectively. Quality service requires that both departments cooperate to achieve the goal.

Expanding Resources One conflict resolution technique is so simple that it may be overlooked. If the conflict's source is scarce resources, providing more resources may be a solution. Of course, managers working with tight budgets may not have this luxury. Nevertheless, it is a technique to be considered. In the example earlier in this chapter, one solution to the conflict among managers over secretarial support would be to hire more secretaries.

Changing Personnel In some cases, long-running severe conflict may be traced to a specific individual. For example, managers with lower levels of EI have been demonstrated to have more negative work attitudes, to exhibit less altruistic behavior, and to produce more negative work outcomes. A chronically disgruntled manager who exhibits low EI may not only frustrate his employees but also impede his department's performance. In such cases, transferring or firing an individual may be the best solution, but only after due process.[61]

Changing Structure Another way to resolve a conflict is to change the structure of the organization. One way of accomplishing this is to create an integrator role. An integrator is a liaison between groups with very different interests. In severe conflicts, it may be best that the integrator be a neutral third party.[62] Creating the integrator role is a way of opening dialogue between groups that have difficulty communicating.

Using cross-functional teams is another way of changing the organization's structure to manage conflict. In the old methods of designing new products in organizations, many departments had to contribute, and delays resulted from difficulties in coordinating the activities of the various departments. Using a cross-functional team made up of members from different departments improves coordination and reduces delays by allowing many activities to be performed at the same time rather than sequentially.[63] The team approach allows members from different departments to work together and reduces the potential for conflict. However, recent research also suggests that such functional diversity can lead to slower informational processing in teams due to differences in members' perceptions of what might be required to achieve group goals. When putting together cross-functional teams, organizations should emphasize superordinate goals and train team members on resolving conflict. One such training technique could involve educating individual members in other functional areas so that everyone in the team can have a shared language.[64] In teamwork, it is helpful to break up a big task so that it becomes a collection of smaller, less complex tasks, and to have smaller teams work on the smaller tasks. This helps to reduce conflict, and organizations can potentially improve the performance of the overall team by improving the outcomes in each subteam.[65]

Confronting and Negotiating Some conflicts require confrontation and negotiation between the parties. Both these strategies require skill on the part of the negotiator and careful planning before engaging in negotiations. The process of negotiating involves an open discussion of problem solutions, and the outcome often is an exchange in which both parties work toward a mutually beneficial solution.

Negotiation is a joint process of finding a mutually acceptable solution to a complex conflict. Negotiating is a useful strategy under the following conditions:

- There are two or more parties. Negotiation is primarily an interpersonal or intergroup process.

- There is a conflict of interest between the parties such that what one party wants is not what the other party wants.

- The parties are willing to negotiate because each believes it can use its influence to obtain a better outcome than by simply taking the side of the other party.

- The parties prefer to work together rather than to fight openly, give in, break off contact, or take the dispute to a higher authority.

There are two major negotiating approaches: distributive bargaining and integrative negotiation.[66] *Distributive bargaining* is an approach in which the goals of one party are in direct conflict with the goals of the other party. Resources are limited, and each party wants to maximize its share of the resources (get its part of the pie). It is a competitive or win–lose approach to negotiations. Sometimes distributive bargaining causes negotiators to focus so much on their differences that they ignore their common ground. In these cases, distributive bargaining can become counterproductive. The reality is, however, that some situations are distributive in nature, particularly when the parties are interdependent. If a negotiator wants to maximize the value of a single deal and is not worried about maintaining a good relationship with the other party, distributive bargaining may be an option. Labor leaders in France took distributive bargaining to a new level when they engaged in "boss-napping" in order to get concessions from management. Read about this new, and disturbing, negotiation tactic in Real World 13.2.

By contrast, *integrative negotiation* is an approach in which the parties' goals are not seen as mutually exclusive and in which the focus is on making it possible for both sides to achieve their objectives. Integrative negotiation focuses on the merits of the issues and is a win–win approach. (How can we make the pie bigger?) For integrative negotiation to be successful, certain preconditions must be present. These include having a common goal, faith in one's own problem-solving abilities, a belief in the validity of the other party's position, motivation to work together, mutual trust, and clear communication.[67]

Cultural differences in negotiation must be acknowledged. Japanese negotiators, for example, when working with American negotiators, tend to see their power as coming from their role (buyer versus seller). Americans, by contrast, view their power as their ability to walk away from the negotiations.[68] Neither culture understands the other very well, and the negotiations can resemble a dance in which one person is waltzing and the other doing a samba. The collectivism–individualism dimension (discussed in Chapter 2) has a great bearing on negotiations. Americans, with their individualism, negotiate from a position of self-interest; Japanese focus on the good of the group. Cross-cultural negotiations can be more effective if you learn as much about other cultures as possible.

Gender may also play a role in negotiation. There appears to be no evidence that men are better negotiators than women or vice versa. The differences lie in how negotiators are treated. Women have historically been discriminated against in terms of the offers made to them in negotiations.[69] Gender stereotypes also affect the negotiating process. Women may be seen as accommodating, conciliatory, and emotional (negatives in negotiations), and men may be seen as assertive, powerful, and convincing (positive for negotiations) in accordance with traditional stereotypes. Sometimes, when women feel they're being stereotyped, they exhibit stereotype reactance, which is a tendency to display behavior inconsistent with

distributive bargaining
A negotiation approach in which the goals of the parties are in conflict, and each party seeks to maximize its resources.

integrative negotiation
A negotiation approach that focuses on the merits of the issues and seeks a win–win solution.

The Real World 13.2

3M, Sony, and Caterpillar in France: Executives, Pack Your Overnight Bags!

What do top executives at the 3M, Sony, and Caterpillar locations in France have in common? They have all been boss-napped—held hostage by workers who demanded concessions from management in the rash of downsizings due to the global economic crisis. The following are some examples:

Caterpillar bulldozer plant director Nicolas Polutnik was held hostage at the Caterpillar plant in Grenoble

JEAN-PIERRE CLATOT/AFP/Getty Images

- At the 3M factory at Orleans, employees demanding money for laid-off fellow workers and guarantees for the employees remaining held the company's industrial director for more than twenty-four hours until a deal was reached.

- At the Sony factory in southwest France, the CEO and human resources director were held until the unions bargained for better terms for dismissed workers. Angry employees barred the doors with branches and tree trunks until they were convinced to move to the police station to negotiate.

- At the Caterpillar plant in Grenoble, four executives were boss-napped by forty-eight employees who took over the executives' cell phones and made threatening phone calls to their families.

Why is boss-napping such a French phenomenon? It is mainly due to the unique structure of the labor unions, which have been given lucrative power by the government. France is the least unionized country in the developed world, with just 8 percent of dues-paying members (compared with 11.6 percent in the United States). Unions in France tend to be comprised of the most radical workers, and the unions compete with one another and compensate for low numbers of members with visible forms of protest.

Public sentiment seems to be in the boss-nappers' favor, because the majority believe that boss-napping may be the only way the employees' demands may be heard. And boss-napping seems to have worked. At the Sony factory, slated to close with a loss of 311 jobs, boss-nappers got 13 million euro added to the redundancy package, and at 3M, where 110 jobs were cut, the boss-nappers secured a deal for ten months' redundancy pay.

SOURCES: T. McNicoll, "Sure, Kidnap the Man," *Newsweek* (April 25, 2009), retrieved from http://www.newsweek.com/id/195092; A. Sage, "Angry French Workers Turn to Bossnapping to Solve their Problems," *TimesOnline* (April 4, 2009), retrieved from http://www. timesonline.co.uk/tol/news/world/europe/article6031822.ece.

(or opposite of) the stereotype. This means they become more assertive and convincing. Alternatively, men may hesitate when they're expected to fulfill the stereotype, fearing that they might not be able to live up to the stereotype.

One way to help men and women avoid stereotyping each other is to promote shared, positive identities between the negotiators. This means recognizing similarities between the two parties; for example, recognizing each other as highly successful professionals. This results in more cooperation because of shared and equal status, as opposed to more competition because of gender stereotypes.[70]

CONFLICT MANAGEMENT STYLES

Managers have at their disposal a variety of conflict management styles: avoiding, accommodating, competing, compromising, and collaborating. One way of classifying styles of conflict management is to examine the styles' assertiveness (the extent to which you want your goals met) and cooperativeness (the extent to which you

6 Understand five styles of conflict management, and diagnose your own preferred style.

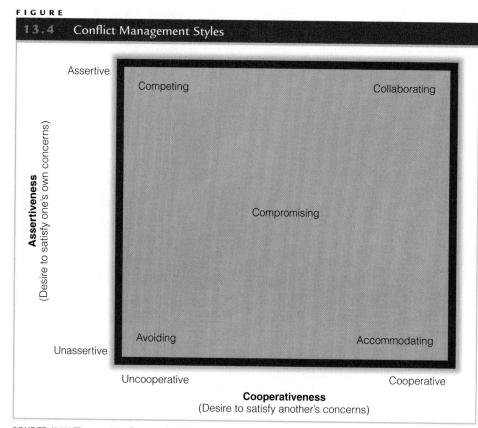

FIGURE

13.4 Conflict Management Styles

SOURCE: K. W. Thomas, "Conflict and Conflict Management," in M. D. Dunnette, ed. *Handbook of Industrial and Organizational Psychology* (Chicago: Rand McNally, 1976), 900. Used with permission of M. D. Dunnette.

want to see the other party's concerns met).[71] Figure 13.4 graphs the five conflict management styles using these two dimensions. Table 13.4 lists appropriate situations for using each conflict management style.

Avoiding

Avoiding is a style low on both assertiveness and cooperativeness. Avoiding is a deliberate decision to take no action on a conflict or to stay out of a conflict situation. In recent times, Airbus, a European manufacturer of aircraft, has faced massive intraorganizational conflict stemming from major expansions that included French, German, Spanish, and British subsidiaries within the same parent company. Power struggles among executives, combined with massive changes in organizational structure, are believed to have led to this type of conflict. Airbus seems to be adopting the avoidance strategy in an effort to let these conflicts subside on their own.[72] Some relationship conflicts, such as those involving political norms and personal tastes, may distract team members from their tasks and avoiding may be an appropriate strategy.[73] When the parties are angry and need time to cool down, it may be best to use avoidance. There is a potential danger in using an avoiding style too often, however. Research shows that overuse of this style results in negative evaluations from others in the workplace.[74]

Accommodating

Accommodating is a style in which you are concerned that the other party's goals be met but relatively unconcerned with getting your own way. It is cooperative but unassertive. Appropriate situations for accommodating include times when you find you are wrong, when you want to let the other party have his or her way so that that

13.4 Uses of Five Styles of Conflict Management

Conflict-Handling Style	Appropriate Situation
Competing	1. When quick, decisive action is vital (e.g., emergencies).
	2. On important issues where unpopular actions need implementing (e.g., cost cutting, enforcing unpopular rules, discipline).
	3. On issues vital to company welfare when you know you are right.
	4. Against people who take advantage of noncompetitive behavior.
Collaborating	1. To find an integrative solution when both sets of concerns are too important to be compromised.
	2. When your objective is to learn.
	3. To merge insights from people with different perspectives.
	4. To gain commitment by incorporating concerns into a consensus.
	5. To work through feelings that have interfered with a relationship.
Compromising	1. When goals are important but not worth the effort or potential disruption of more assertive modes.
	2. When opponents with equal power are committed to mutually exclusive goals.
	3. To achieve temporary settlements to complex issues.
	4. To arrive at expedient solutions under time pressure.
	5. As a backup when collaboration or competition is unsuccessful.
Avoiding	1. When an issue is trivial or more important issues are pressing.
	2. When you perceive no chance of satisfying your concerns.
	3. When potential disruption outweighs the benefits of resolution.
	4. To let people cool down and regain perspective.
	5. When gathering information supersedes immediate decision.
	6. When others can resolve the conflict more effectively.
	7. When issues seem tangential or symptomatic of other issues.
Accommodating	1. When you find you are wrong—to allow a better position to be heard, to learn, and to show your reasonableness.
	2. When issues are more important to others than to yourself—to satisfy others and maintain cooperation.
	3. To build social credits for later issues.
	4. To minimize loss when you are outmatched and losing.
	5. When harmony and stability are especially important.
	6. To allow employees to develop by learning from mistakes.

SOURCE: K. W. Thomas, "Toward Multidimensional Values in Teaching: The Example of Conflict Behaviors," *Academy of Management Review* 2 (1977): 309–325.

individual will owe you similar treatment later, or when the relationship is important. Overreliance on accommodating has its dangers. Managers who constantly defer to others may find that others lose respect for them. In addition, accommodating managers may become frustrated because their own needs are never met, and they may lose self-esteem.[75] Research has also shown that individuals will sometimes overestimate the importance of the relationship and focus too heavily on accommodating at the expense of the actual outcomes. The overuse of accommodating has been shown to be more prevalent when two females are involved in the conflict or negotiation than when the conflict or negotiation is between males.[76]

Competing

Competing is a style that is very assertive and uncooperative. You want to satisfy your own interests and are willing to do so at the other party's expense. In an emergency or in situations where you know you are right, it may be appropriate to put your foot down. For example, environmentalists forced Shell Oil Company (part of Royal Dutch/Shell Group) to scrap its plans to build a refinery in Delaware after a bitter "To Hell with Shell" campaign.[77] Relying solely on competing strategies is dangerous, though. Managers who do so may become reluctant to admit when they are wrong and may find themselves surrounded by people who are afraid to disagree with them. In team settings, it has been noted earlier that task conflict and relationship conflict could occur together although task conflict is seen as functional, whereas relationship conflict is seen as dysfunctional for the team. In a recent study, pairs of participants were exposed to task-based conflict. One of the two members of the pairs was trained on using either the competing conflict handling style or the collaborative style. Results indicated that the competing style led to the most relationship conflict, whereas the collaborative style led to the least relationship conflict after the task conflict was resolved.[78]

Compromising

Compromising style is an intermediate style in both assertiveness and cooperativeness, because each party must give up something to reach a solution to the conflict. Compromises are often made in the final hours of union–management negotiations, when time is of the essence. Compromise may be an effective backup style when efforts toward collaboration are not successful.[79]

It is important to recognize that compromises are not optimal solutions. Compromise means partially surrendering one's position for the sake of coming to terms. Often, when people compromise, they inflate their demands to begin with. The solutions reached may only be temporary, and often compromises do nothing to improve relationships between the parties in the conflict.

Collaborating

Collaborating is a win–win style that is high on both assertiveness and cooperativeness. Working toward collaborating involves an open and thorough discussion of the conflict and arriving at a solution that is satisfactory to both parties. Situations where collaboration may be effective include times when both parties need to be committed to a final solution or when a combination of different perspectives can be formed into a solution. Collaborating requires open, trusting behavior and sharing information for the benefit of both parties. Long term, it leads to improved relationships and effective performance.[80] Teams that use collaboration effectively view conflict as a mutual problem that needs common consideration to resolve. This understanding leads to a confidence that others will work for mutually beneficial solutions, which ultimately leads to a genuine exchange of diverse ideas that facilitates team performance.[81]

Research on the five styles of conflict management indicates that although most managers favor a certain style, they have the capacity to change styles as the

You 13.2

What Is Your Conflict-Handling Style?

Instructions:

For each of the fifteen items, indicate how often you rely on that tactic by circling the appropriate number.

		Rarely Always
1.	I argue my case with my coworkers to show the merits of my position.	①—2—3—4—5
2.	I negotiate with my coworkers so that a compromise can be reached.	1—2—③—4—5
3.	I try to satisfy the expectations of my coworkers.	1—2—3—④—5
4.	I try to investigate an issue with my coworkers to find a solution acceptable to us.	1—2—3—④—5
5.	I am firm in pursuing my side of the issue.	1—2—③—4—5
6.	I attempt to avoid being "put on the spot" and try to keep my conflict with my coworkers to myself.	1—2—③—4—5
7.	I hold on to my solution to a problem.	①—2—3—4—5
8.	I use "give and take" so that a compromise can be made.	1—2—3—4—⑤
9.	I exchange accurate information with my coworkers to solve a problem together.	1—2—3—4—5
10.	I avoid open discussion of my differences with my coworkers.	1—2—3—4—5
11.	I accommodate the wishes of my coworkers.	1—2—3—4—5
12.	I try to bring all our concerns out in the open so that the issues can be resolved in the best possible way.	1—2—3—4—5
13.	I propose a middle ground for breaking deadlocks.	1—2—3—4—5
14.	I go along with the suggestions of my coworkers.	1—2—3—4—5
15.	I try to keep my disagreements with my coworkers to myself in order to avoid hard feelings.	1—2—3—4—5

Scoring Key:

Collaborating		Accommodating		Competing		Avoiding		Compromising	
Item	Score	Item	Score	Item	Score	Item	Score	Item	Score
4.	_____	3.	_____	1.	_____	6.	_____	2.	_____
9.	_____	11.	_____	5.	_____	10.	_____	8.	_____
12.	_____	14.	_____	7.	_____	15.	_____	13.	_____
Total = _____		Total = _____		Total = _____		Total = _____		Total = _____	

Your primary conflict-handling style is: _____
(The category with the highest total.)

Your backup conflict-handling style is: _____
(The category with the second highest total.)

SOURCE: Reprinted with permission of Academy of Management, PO Box 3020, Briar Cliff Manor, NY 10510-8020. *A Measure of Styles of Handling Interpersonal Conflict* (adaptation), M. A. Rahim, *Academy of Management Journal*, June 1983. Reproduced by permission of the publisher via Copyright Clearance Center, Inc.

situation demands.[82] A study of project managers found that managers who used a combination of competing and avoiding styles were seen as ineffective by the engineers who worked on their project teams.[83] In another study of conflicts between R&D project managers and technical staff, competing and avoiding styles resulted in more frequent conflict and lower performance, whereas the collaborating style resulted in less frequent conflict and better performance.[84] Use You 13.2 to assess your dominant conflict management style.

Cultural differences also influence the use of different styles of conflict management. For example, one study compared Turkish and Jordanian managers with U.S. managers. All three groups preferred the collaborating style. Turkish managers also reported frequent use of the competing style, whereas Jordanian and U.S. managers reported that it was one of their least used styles.[85]

The human resources manager of one U.S. telecommunications company's office in Singapore engaged a consultant to investigate the conflict in the office.[86] Twenty-two expatriates from the United States and Canada and thirty-eight Singaporeans worked in the office. The consultant used the Thomas model (Figure 13.4) and distributed questionnaires to all managers to determine their conflict management styles. The results were not surprising: The expatriate managers preferred the competing, collaborating, and compromising styles, while the Asians preferred the avoiding and accommodating styles.

Workshops were conducted within the firm to develop an understanding of the differences and how they negatively affected the firm. The Asians interpreted the results as reflecting the tendency of Americans to "shout first and ask questions later." They felt that the Americans had an arrogant attitude and could not handle having their ideas rejected. The Asians attributed their own styles to their cultural background. The Americans attributed the results to the stereotypical view of Asians as unassertive and timid, and they viewed their own results as reflecting their desire to "get things out in the open."

The process opened a dialogue between the two groups, who began to work on the idea of harmony through conflict. They began to discard the traditional stereotypes in favor of shared meanings and mutual understanding.

China is one of the biggest marketplaces in the world, and negotiating with the Chinese is very frustrating for Americans due to a lack of understanding of Chinese conflict management styles. One study indicated that compromising and avoiding are the most preferred conflict handling styles among the Chinese. Interestingly, the Chinese reported the most satisfaction with a business negotiation when accommodating and competing approaches were used by both parties.[87] A recent study in China found some similarity between Chinese work teams and U.S. work teams in that when collaborative styles are used in these teams, team members feel the team has joint concerns which facilitates trust and ultimately team performance.[88]

It is important to remember that preventing and resolving dysfunctional conflict is only half the task of effective conflict management. Stimulating functional conflict is the other half.

MANAGERIAL IMPLICATIONS: CREATING A CONFLICT-POSITIVE ORGANIZATION

Dean Tjosvold argues that well-managed conflict adds to an organization's innovation and productivity.[89] He discusses procedures for making conflict positive. Too many organizations take a win–lose, competitive approach to conflict or avoid conflict altogether. These two approaches view conflict as negative. A positive view of conflict, by contrast, leads to win–win solutions. Figure 13.5 illustrates these three approaches to conflict management.

Four interrelated steps are involved in creating a conflict-positive organization:

1. *Value diversity and confront differences.* Differences should be seen as opportunities for innovation, and diversity should be celebrated. Open and honest confrontations bring out differences, and they are essential for positive conflict.

2. *Seek mutual benefits and unite behind cooperative goals.* Conflicts have to be managed together. Through conflict, individuals learn how much they depend

13.5 Three Organization Views of Conflict

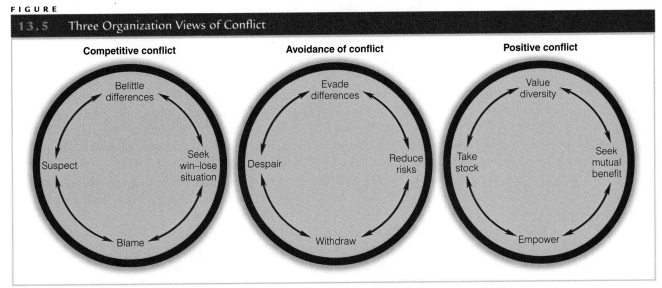

SOURCE: *The Conflict Positive Organization*, by Dean Tjosvold, © 1991. Reprinted by permission of Prentice-Hall, Inc., Upper Saddle River, NJ.

on one another. Even when employees share goals, they may differ on how to accomplish the goals. The important point is that they are moving toward the same objectives. Joint rewards should be given to the whole team for cooperative behavior.

3. *Empower employees to feel confident and skillful.* People must be made to feel that they control their conflicts and that they can deal with their differences productively. When they do so, they should be recognized.

4. *Take stock to reward success and learn from mistakes.* Employees should be encouraged to appreciate one another's strengths and weaknesses and to talk directly about them. They should celebrate their conflict management successes and work out plans for ways they can improve in the future.

Tjosvold believes that a conflict-positive organization has competitive advantages for the future.

A complementary perspective comes from Peter J. Frost, who proposed that over time, organizational practices like poor conflict management can "poison" the organization as well as those who work within it. He describes how compassionate leaders can help reduce the effects of organizational toxins on their coworkers and how these toxin handlers should be rewarded for this crucial role in maintaining organizational health. Frost's position echoes Tjosvold's, as he calls for firms to become emotionally healthy workplaces for the good of their employees as well as for the good of their stockholders.[90]

Managers should be aware, however, that positive conflict or conflict that has primarily positive consequences is rare and oftentimes, conflict that may have short-term positive outcomes may have longer term negative ones. Both task and relationship conflicts have been shown to have negative impacts on team member satisfaction and team effectiveness.[91] Managers should pay close attention to both types of conflict and carefully weigh the positive and negative consequences resulting from them.

Finally, don't overlook the importance of high EI in the work of a good conflict manager. The ability to influence your own and others' emotions is not just a practical tool, but it can also serve as an important tactical asset, making you a better negotiator in a variety of situations and helping reduce conflict and increase productivity in your organization.[92]

Diversity Dialogue

"Swimming" in Conflict

What do African-American and Hispanic summer camp children have in common with children from Huntingdon Valley, Pennsylvania, on a warm summer day? They all want to swim! Rather than swim, however, the sixty-five predominately black and Hispanic campers from Creative Steps day camp found themselves in the center of a huge controversy amid allegations of racism and discrimination.

Creative Steps, a Northeast Philadelphia day camp, paid The Valley Club, a predominately white suburban private club, a $1,950 membership fee in order for its campers to swim in the club pool each Monday afternoon. Surprisingly after the camp's first visit, the club refunded the camp's membership fee without explanation. Several of Creative Step's campers reported that they heard several club members making racial remarks and at least one person complain that the children did not belong there. According to the camp's attorney, "The kids were humiliated."

John Duesler, The Valley Club's president, insisted that it wasn't race that precipitated the refund of the camp's swim fee, rather it was safety. When The Valley Club initially contracted with the camp, it had not considered that the club might be short on lifeguards and wouldn't be able to handle additional swimmers—an important issue given that many of the campers could not swim. Duesler added that " ... the club's board had not properly thought through the demands of accommodating them [the campers]."

The controversy surrounding this conflict gathered steam as the NAACP filed a formal complaint with the Pennsylvania Human Relations Commission, the U.S. Justice Department began investigations into the club's conduct, and the public began to weigh in. Creative Steps declined The Valley Club's reinvitation to the club. Last reported, the camp was in negotiations with a local college for their children to swim there.

1. Would you describe the conflict between Creative Steps and The Valley Club as functional or dysfunctional? Explain.
2. Despite the obvious demographic differences, what additional diversity issues are relevant here?

SOURCES: I. Urbina, "Club in Philadelphia Suburb Faces Accusations of Racism," *New York Times* (July 11, 2009); S. Netter, "Specter Wants Probe Into Club's Rejection of Black Swimmers," *ABCNews.com* (July 9, 2009), http://abcnews.go.com.

LOOKING BACK: IKEA

Focusing on the Cause of the Conflict

When faced with a child exploitation allegation, IKEA was quick to respond by sending top executives to India to investigate. They considered an option to join a foundation made up of similar organizations that buy rugs and carpets from this region. This foundation stamps each carpet to guarantee no child labor was used and supervises the use of the label. IKEA executives, however, were very concerned about what would happen to the children if this approach was taken and decided to address what they determined to be the root cause of the problem: a lack of viable alternatives for the children and adults in this region.

They developed an ongoing initiative aimed at helping India's "carpet belt" where 85 percent of rugs exported from India are made. They worked with UNICEF and the World Health Organization to provide learning centers to ease children back into school. In fact, IKEA has made corporate commitments totaling more than $180 million from 2000 to 2015.[93] They helped develop women's groups that encourage women to put aside small sums of money so that they can get loans from banks at reasonable interest rates. IKEA acknowledges that this will not solve the problem entirely and they still do not guarantee that their rugs and carpets are made entirely without child labor, but many organizations like Save the Children and UNICEF agree that it's a big step in the right direction.

Chapter Summary

1. Conflict management skills are keys to management success. The manager's task is to stimulate functional conflict and prevent or resolve dysfunctional conflict.

2. Structural causes of conflict include specialization, interdependence, common resources, goal differences, authority relationships, status inconsistencies, and jurisdictional ambiguities.

3. Personal factors that lead to conflict include differences in skills and abilities, personalities, perceptions, or values and ethics; emotions; communication barriers; and cultural differences. The increasing diversity of the workforce and globalization of business have potential to increase conflict arising from these differences.

4. The levels of conflict include interorganizational, intergroup, interpersonal, and intrapersonal.

5. Individuals engaged in interpersonal conflict often display aggressive, compromise, or withdrawal defense mechanisms.

6. Ineffective techniques for managing conflict include nonaction, secrecy, administrative orbiting, due process nonaction, and character assassination.

7. Effective techniques for managing conflict include appealing to superordinate goals, expanding resources, changing personnel, changing structure, and confronting and negotiating.

8. In negotiating, managers can use a variety of conflict management styles, including avoiding, accommodating, competing, compromising, and collaborating.

9. Managers should strive to create a conflict-positive organization—one that values diversity, empowers employees, and seeks win–win solutions to conflicts.

Key Terms

administrative orbiting (p. 458)
character assassination (p. 458)
compensation (p. 455)
conflict (p. 442)
conversion (p. 456)
displacement (p. 455)
distributive bargaining (p. 460)
due process nonaction (p. 458)
dysfunctional conflict (p. 443)
fantasy (p. 456)

fixation (p. 455)
flight/withdrawal (p. 456)
functional conflict (p. 443)
identification (p. 455)
integrative negotiation (p. 460)
intergroup conflict (p. 448)
interorganizational conflict (p. 448)
interpersonal conflict (p. 449)
interrole conflict (p. 449)
intragroup conflict (p. 449)

intrapersonal conflict (p. 449)
intrarole conflict (p. 449)
jurisdictional ambiguity (p. 446)
negativism (p. 455)
nonaction (p. 458)
person–role conflict (p. 451)
rationalization (p. 456)
secrecy (p. 458)
superordinate goal (p. 458)

Review Questions

1. Discuss the differences between functional and dysfunctional conflict. Why should a manager understand conflict?

2. Identify the structural and personal factors that contribute to conflict.

3. Discuss the four major forms of conflict in organizations.

4. What defense mechanisms do people use in interpersonal conflict?

5. What are the most effective techniques for managing conflict at work? What are some ineffective techniques?

6. Identify and discuss five styles of conflict management.

Discussion and Communication Questions

1. What causes you the most conflict at work or school?

2. Identify the different intragroup, interrole, intrarole, and person–role conflicts that you experience.

3. Which defense mechanism do you see people exhibiting most frequently? Why do you think this is the case? How can you manage this type of reaction to a conflict?

4. Are you comfortable with your preferred conflict management style? Would you consider modifying it?

5. *(communication question)* Think of a person with whom you have had a recent conflict. Write a letter to this person, attempting to resolve the conflict. Use the concepts from the chapter to accomplish your objective. Be sure to address whether the conflict is functional or dysfunctional, what styles each party has used, effective strategies for resolving the conflict, and ineffective strategies that should be avoided.

Ethical Dilemma

Maria Vasquez has called a department meeting to address a critical issue affecting Universal Product Shipping as a whole. Maria's department seems unable to meet their deadline, and as a result, orders and fulfillment are constantly getting backlogged. Maria's supervisor has instructed her to divine the source of the problem through team brainstorming and exercises.

Maria asks everyone to share their role in the process so that the department can start determining where the bottlenecking problems are occurring. Jim, a long-time member of the team, explains that he thinks that when he passes his work onto Vincent, the files don't move forward in a timely manner. Vincent pushes back against this assessment, saying that he has to go through Jim's work a second time before he can add his component and pass it forward to Cassie.

Jim begins to get defensive, accusing Vincent of making a claim that Jim's age is negatively affecting his performance. Shelly, who works closely with Jim, mentions that she thinks there's a significant portion of information that is omitted when the files get to their step in the process, and thinks that the department needs to see why those data are absent.

Unfortunately, just as people start brainstorming about where that missing information is, Jim and Vincent begin to raise their voices. Maria tries to keep everyone on topic, but she realizes that Jim and Vincent seem to be at the heart of the problem. Jim's missing information is stymieing the process, and Vincent's tardiness with moving the files forward is further compounding the problem. Maria knows that they can't resolve the problem without keeping these two people staying engaged in the process.

However, Jim and Vincent's interaction is becoming louder and more personal. Maria has been trained to intervene when interpersonal conflict becomes problematic, and she thinks that Jim and Vincent have crossed the line. On the other hand, she has a mandate to solve this crisis immediately, and believes that she needs Jim and Vincent to stay in the brainstorming session in order to accomplish this.

Questions:

1. Using consequential, rule-based and character theories, evaluate Maria's options.

2. What should Maria do? Why?

Experiential Exercises

13.1 Conflicts over Unethical Behavior

Many conflicts in work organizations arise over differences in beliefs concerning what constitutes ethical versus unethical behavior. The following questionnaire

provides a list of behaviors that you or your coworkers might engage in when working for a company. Go over each item, and circle the number that best indicates the frequency with which you personally would (or do, if you work now) engage in that behavior. Then put an X over the number you think represents how often your coworkers would (or do) engage in that behavior.

Finally, put a check mark beside the item (in the "Needs Control" column) if you believe that management should control that behavior.

	At Every Opportunity	About Half Often	Needs the Time	Seldom	Never	Control
1. Passing blame for errors to an innocent coworker.	5	4	3	2	1	_____
2. Divulging confidential information.	5	4	3	2	1	_____
3. Falsifying time/quality/quantity reports.	5	4	3	2	1	_____
4. Claiming credit for someone else's work.	5	4	3	2	1	_____
5. Padding an expense account by over 10 percent.	5	4	3	2	1	_____
6. Pilfering company materials and supplies.	5	4	3	2	1	_____
7. Accepting gifts/favors in exchange for preferential treatment.	5	4	3	2	1	_____
8. Giving gifts/favors in exchange for preferential treatment.	5	4	3	2	1	_____
9. Padding an expense account by up to 10 percent.	5	4	3	2	1	_____
10. Authorizing a subordinate to violate company rules.	5	4	3	2	1	_____
11. Calling in sick to take a day off.	5	4	3	2	1	_____
12. Concealing one's errors.	5	4	3	2	1	_____
13. Taking longer than necessary to do a job.	5	4	3	2	1	_____
14. Using company services for personal use.	5	4	3	2	1	_____
15. Doing personal business on company time.	5	4	3	2	1	_____
16. Taking extra personal time (lunch hour, breaks, early departure, and so forth).	5	4	3	2	1	_____
17. Not reporting others' violations of company policies and rules.	5	4	3	2	1	_____
18. Overlooking a superior's violation of policy to prove loyalty to the boss.	5	4	3	2	1	_____

Discussion Questions

1. Would (do) your coworkers seem to engage in these behaviors more often than you would (do)? Why do you have this perception?

2. Which behaviors tend to be most frequent?

3. How are the most frequent behaviors different from the behaviors engaged in less frequently?

4. What are the most important items for managers to control? How should managers control these behaviors?

5. Select a particular behavior from the list. Have two people debate whether the behavior is ethical or not.

6. What types of conflicts could emerge if the behaviors in the list occurred frequently?

SOURCE: From *Managerial Experience*, 3rd ed. by L. Jauch © 1983. Reprinted with permission of South-Western, a part of Cengage Learning: academic. cengage.com.

13.2 The World Bank Game: An Intergroup Negotiation

The purposes of this exercise are to learn about conflict and trust between groups and to practice negotiation skills. In the course of the exercise, money will be won or lost. Your team's objective is to win as much money as it can. Your team will be paired with another team, and both teams will receive identical instructions. After reading these instructions, each team will have ten minutes to plan its strategy.

Each team is assumed to have contributed $50 million to the World Bank. Teams may have to pay more or may receive money from the World Bank, depending on the outcome.

Each team will receive twenty cards. These cards are the weapons. Each card has a marked side (*X*) and an unmarked side. The marked side signifies that the weapon is armed; the unmarked side signifies that the weapon is unarmed.

At the beginning, each team will place ten of its twenty weapons in their armed position (marked side up) and the remaining ten in their unarmed position (marked side down). The weapons will remain in the team's possession and out of sight of the other team at all times.

The game will consist of *rounds* and *moves*. Each round will be composed of seven moves by each team. There will be two or more rounds in the game, depending on the time available. Pay-offs will be determined and recorded after each round. The rules are as follows:

1. A move consists of turning two, one, or none of the team's weapons from armed to unarmed status, or vice versa.

2. Each team has one-and-a-half minutes for each move. There is a thirty-second period between each move. At the end of the one-and-a-half minutes, the team must have turned two, one, or none of its weapons from armed to unarmed status or from unarmed to armed status. If the team fails to move in the allotted time, no change can be made in weapon status until the next move.

3. The two-minute length of the period between the beginning of one move and the beginning of the next is unalterable.

Finances:

The funds each team has contributed to the World Bank are to be allocated in the following manner: $30 million will be returned to each team to be used as the team's treasury during the course of the game, and $20 million will be retained for the operation of the World Bank.

Pay-offs:

1. If there is an attack:

   a. Each team may announce an attack on the other team by notifying the banker during the thirty seconds following any minute-and-a-half period used to decide upon the move (including the seventh, or final, decision period in any round). The choice of each team during the decision period just ended counts as a move. An attack may not be made during negotiations.

   b. If there is an attack by one or both teams, two things happen: (1) the round ends, and (2) the World Bank assesses a penalty of $2.5 million on each team.

   c. The team with the greater number of armed weapons wins $1.5 million for each armed weapon it has over and above the number of armed weapons of the other team. These funds are paid directly from the treasury of the losing team to the treasury of the winning team. The banker will manage the transfer of funds.

2. If there is no attack: At the end of each round (seven moves), each team's treasury will receive from the World Bank $1 million for each of its weapons that is at that point unarmed; and each team's treasury will pay to the World Bank $1 million for each of its weapons remaining armed.

Negotiations:

Between moves, each team will have the opportunity to communicate with the other team through its negotiations. Either team may call for negotiations by notifying the banker during any of the thirty-second periods between decisions. A team is free to accept or reject any invitation to negotiate.

Negotiators from both teams are required to meet after the third and sixth moves (after the thirty-second period following the move, if there is no attack).

Negotiations can last no longer than three minutes. When the two negotiators return to their teams, the minute-and-a-half decision period for the next move will begin once again.

Negotiators are bound only by (1) the three-minute time limit for negotiations and (2) their required appearance after the third and sixth moves. They are always free to say whatever is necessary to benefit themselves or their teams. The teams are not bound by agreements made by their negotiators, even when those agreements are made in good faith.

Special Roles:

Each team has ten minutes to organize itself and plan team strategy. During this period, before the first round begins, each team must choose persons to fill the following roles:

- A *negotiator*—activities stated above.
- A *representative*—to communicate the team's decisions to the banker.
- A *recorder*—to record the moves of the team and to keep a running balance of the team's treasury.

- A *treasurer*—to execute all financial transactions with the banker.

The instructor will serve as the banker for the World Bank and will signal the beginning of each of the rounds.

At the end of the game, each participant should complete the following questionnaire, which assesses reactions to the World Bank Game.

World Bank Questionnaire:

1. To what extent are you satisfied with your team's strategy?

   Highly   1   2   3   4   5   6   7   Highly
   dissatisfied   satisfied

2. To what extent do you believe the other team is trustworthy?

   Highly   1   2   3   4   5   6   7   Highly
   untrustworthy   trustworthy

3. To what extent are you satisfied with the performance of your negotiator?

   Highly   1   2   3   4   5   6   7   Highly
   dissatisfied   satisfied

4. To what extent was there a consensus on your team regarding its moves?

   Very little   1   2   3   4   5   6   7   A great deal

5. To what extent do you trust the other members of your team?

   Very little   1   2   3   4   5   6   7   A great deal

6. Select one word that describes how you feel about your team: _____.

7. Select one word that describes how you feel about the other team: _____.

Negotiators only:

   How did you see the other team's negotiator?

   Phony and   1   2   3   4   5   6   7   Authentic
   insincere   and sincere

At the end of the game, the class will reconvene and discuss team members' responses to the World Bank Questionnaire. In addition, the following questions are to be addressed:

1. What was each team's strategy for winning? What strategy was most effective?

2. Contrast the outcomes in terms of win–win solutions to conflict versus win–lose solutions.

SOURCE: Adapted by permission from N. H. Berkowitz and H. A. Hornstein, "World Bank: An Intergroup Negotiation," in J. W. Pfeiffer and J. E. Jones, eds., *The 1975 Handbook for Group Facilitators* (San Diego: Pfeiffer), 58–62. Copyright © 1975 Pfeiffer/Jossey-Bass. This material is used by permission of John Wiley & Sons, Inc.

WORLD BANK RECORD SHEET

		Round One		Round Two		Round Three		Round Four	
		Armed	Unarmed	Armed	Unarmed	Armed	Unarmed	Armed	Unarmed
	Move	10	10	10	10	10	10	10	10
	1								
	2								
Required Negotiation	3								
	4								
	5								
	6								
Required Negotiation	7								

Funds in Team Treasury	$30 million				
Funds of Other Treasury	$30 million				
Funds in World Bank	$40 million				

BizFlix | Welcome Home Roscoe Jenkins

Hollywood talk-show host Roscoe Jenkins (Martin Lawrence) returns to his Georgia home for his parents' fiftieth wedding anniversary. Cultures clash between the big-city Roscoe and other family members. The culture clash becomes even more severe because of the presence of his upper-class fiancée, Bianca Kittles (Joy Bryant), who does not understand this family and feels superior to them.

Conflict: It Can Sneak Up on You

This sequence starts with Roscoe and his brother, Sheriff Otis Jenkins (Michael Clarke Duncan), carrying a tub of fish and ice from Monty's butcher shop to Sheriff Jenkins's pickup truck. It follows the baseball game during which Roscoe hit a ball that struck Mama Jenkins (Margaret Avery) in the head. This sequence ends after Sheriff Jenkins knocks out his brother.

What to Watch for and Ask Yourself

- This chapter defined conflict as "any situation in which incompatible goals, attitudes, emotions, or behaviors lead to disagreement or opposition between two or more parties." Does the interaction in this film sequence show this definition in action? Give examples from the sequence.

- Does this film sequence show functional or dysfunctional conflict? Give some examples from the sequence.

- Which conflict management style best fits the behavior shown in this film sequence? Give some examples from the sequence.

Workplace Video | Evo: Teams and Conflict

Evo has definitely evolved since CEO Bryce Phillip launched the company from his garage back in 2001. In the beginning, the organization functioned as a one-man operation. Today, however, the Seattle-based ski-and-boards retailer boasts more than 60 employees and is organized into well-managed departments including e-commerce, customer service, inventory, and information technology.

But Evo's rapid growth has not come without conflict. Until recently, the organization had been experiencing major problems with its advertising and promotion output. Though talented individually, Evo's copywriters, photographers, and graphic designers weren't on the same page. Even worse, they weren't in the same group.

To remedy this organizational breakdown, E-commerce Director Nathan Decker took on the role of integrator and brought Evo's creative folks together in a new team. The creative services team is composed of three full-time members: Tre Dauenhauer, staff photographer; Pubs One, graphic designer; and Sunny Fenton, copywriter. Together they produce magazine ads, all the content for Evo's Web site, and more.

Before forming a team, the members functioned individually and weren't sharing power or making group decisions. This was no surprise, as creative types are known for being independent and opinionated. In art school, students focus on expressing their creative voices, which can make for a very competitive atmosphere where team assignments are nonexistent. But with Decker's skillful negotiations, the creative members began learning how to communicate with each other in ways less likely to escalate into conflict. For example, the members figured out how to speak a common language. Instead of making vague and confusing comments such as, "The message needs to be bigger," the teammates learned to offer more specific feedback, such as "I think the text needs to pop off the page more," or "the message isn't reading well."

Under Decker's steady interim leadership, Evo's creative group is now combining images, copy, and designs into effective unified campaigns. While Dauenhauer thinks the group will eventually need a permanent leader with a creative background, Decker keeps the group working together on common goals for now. And while some intragroup conflict remains, Evo's advertising and promotion efforts are more integrated and on target than ever before.

Discussion Questions

1. What style did the team use to handle conflicts initially? What styles are they learning to use?

2. What type of conflict negotiation is Decker using: integrative or distributive?

3. What communication issues have sparked conflict between team members, and how are those issues being resolved?

Case

Customer Service at Nordstrom: Are There Potential Conflicts?

Nordstrom, an upscale retailer headquartered in Seattle, Washington, operates about 170 stores throughout the United States. [1] "While Nordstrom was growing nationally, it focused on catering to customers' needs, individually. Instead of categorizing departments by merchandise, Nordstrom created fashion departments that fit individuals' lifestyles. Today, Nordstrom has grown from one downtown Seattle shoe store into a nationwide fashion specialty chain with renowned services, generous size ranges and a selection of the finest apparel, shoes and accessories for the entire family. The company's philosophy has remained unchanged for more than 100 years since its establishment by John W. Nordstrom in 1901: offer the customer the best possible service, selection, quality and value." [2]

Nordstrom is famous for its exceptional customer service. Whether it's true or not, a classic story about Nordstrom's service tells the public a lot about the high-end retailer's approach to customer relationship management. According to the story, "[a] man walked into the Nordstrom department store in Fairbanks, Alaska, with two snow tires. He approached the counter, put the tires down and asked for his money back. The clerk, who'd been working there for two weeks, saw the price on the side of the tires, reached into the cash register and handed the man $145. It didn't matter that Nordstrom sells upscale clothing and not tires. The customer wanted to return the tires. The clerk accepted the return because that is what the customer wanted." [3] John Nordstrom, one of three brothers in senior executive positions at the retailer, "claims he was there and that the refund took place in a former tire store that had been converted [into] a Nordstrom outlet." [4]

Nordstrom handles customer returns on a case-by-case basis. [5] Sometimes Nordstrom will replace items years after their purchase—just to keep the customer happy. [6] "We really think a reason our customers shop with us is that we stand behind our merchandise," says a Nordstrom spokeswoman. [7] "Returns of Nordstrom products do not have to include a sales invoice or a Nordstrom price tag. ... Nordstrom knows it's not the price but the customer service that gains and retains loyal customers that generate strong profits." [8]

Without a doubt, Nordstrom provides extraordinary customer service and customer relationship management. But would Nordstrom's phenomenal efforts be enough to help the luxury retailer weather the economic realities of 2008 and 2009?

"The global economic downturn has hurt demand for luxury goods and Nordstrom, a key player in the lower-end of the luxury-goods market, hasn't been spared. Through 2008, Nordstrom's same-store sales declined every month but May. Like many stores, Nordstrom cut prices sharply to move merchandise during the [Christmas] holidays." [9]

Jennifer Saranow, reporting for the *Wall Street Journal*, writes, "[a]fter a decade of conspicuous consumption, many middle- and upper-income Americans are no longer comfortable showing off $300 Gucci sunglasses and $8,000 Hermes Birkin bags. They are developing a distaste for extravagance that promises to affect spending on everything from cars and travel to electronics, fashion and household goods—and to last at least as long as the recession." [10] Christina Binkley, also reporting for the *Wall Street Journal*, observes that "[a]fter years of gluttonous shopping, forgoing our wants feels virtuous, like using up leftovers. That's why many are boasting that they are 'shopping' in their closets." [11] Debbie Then, a New York psychologist who studies the luxury goods industry, says, "[p]eople are saddled with stuff they don't need ... I think the way people were shopping is over." [12] Pamela Danziger, president of the research firm Unity Marketing, points out that "some affluent Americans have simply 'given up the fight to keep up with the Joneses' ... while others have decided that 'spending money on luxury is a poor use of resources in a climate of high gas prices and rising carbon footprint.'" [13]

The change in consumers' buying habits regarding luxury goods isn't the only challenge confronting Nordstrom during the 2008/2009 recession. Customers' payments on their credit accounts also challenge the retailer. Nordstrom is but one of numerous blue-chip companies that experienced increased pressure on their accounts receivable during 2008 due to customers delaying payment. [14] Writing in *Business Week*, Matthew Boyle and Olga Kharif point out that "[d]ealing with deadbeats is tricky. Companies need to push enough to get customers to pay up, but not so much that they're driven away."[15]

Erik Nordstrom, one of the three Nordstrom brothers currently in senior management, says "[t]his is the toughest retail environment that I've been a part of." Despite this he remains "optimistic, noting that the retailer, founded in 1901 by his great-grandfather, has weathered other downturns, including the Great Depression. ... Some people will choose to take a little retail therapy [by going shopping], and we want to be there to serve them."[16]

So, how can Nordstrom serve customers beyond their already extraordinary customer service? Writing in *Brandweek*, Ann Beriault observes, "[f]inding ways for high-end goods to be viewed as experiential or as 'adding to my life experience' should be a priority on any luxury marketer's to-do list. If approached with a deft hand, the reward of spending time well will remain a potent promise, even when the economy swings north."[17]

Whatever Nordstrom does, can it avoid being trapped in circumstances that could significantly alter the relationship between the retailer and its customers? Can Nordstrom continue to defuse potential conflicts with customers?

Discussion Questions

1. Dealing with dissatisfied customers is, perhaps, the greatest source of conflict for retailers. Is Nordstrom's approach to customer service and customer relationship management an appropriate way to defuse potential conflict situations? Explain the reasoning behind your answer.

2. Using the assertiveness and cooperativeness dimensions that underlie the five conflict management styles, explain Nordstrom's approach to customer service and customer relationship management.

3. Drawing on your answer to the preceding question, discuss whether or not Nordstrom can continue with the same customer relationship management approach as the economy deteriorates.

4. What potential conflicts might arise for a luxury retailer like Nordstrom during a severe economic recession? What are some effective ways in which Nordstrom might deal with these potential conflicts?

SOURCE: This case was written by Michael K. McCuddy, The Louis S. and Mary L. Morgal Chair of Christian Business Ethics and Professor of Management, College of Business Administration, Valparaiso University.

Cohesion Case

Zappos.com: Behavioral Dynamics—Cause for Concern or for Celebration? (C)

Zappos gives its employees plenty of freedom to do their jobs. For example, employees in the Zappos call center are told to do whatever they think is necessary to solve a customer's problems—and they don't have to get a manager's approval to do it. With this level of freedom, one employee observes, "You have as much power to help a customer as Tony [Hsieh, Zappos CEO] does himself."[1]

This empowerment to do extraordinary things is due to the company's culture rather than specific policies or procedures.[2] Customer service representatives (CSRs) can take as much time with customers as they need in order to "wow" them, whether its resolving a shipping problem, helping a customer find a product on a competitor's Web site if Zappos doesn't have it in stock, sending flowers to a bereaved customer, or anything else.[3] "Although this laissez faire philosophy can cause chaos at times, the results are impressive: three-quarters of Zappos's sales come from repeat customers and its revenues are still growing this year [2009], albeit more slowly than before."[4]

To dissuade any doubters, Hsieh tells two stories, each about a distressed customer. According to one story, "when the payment deadline for shoes a customer ordered came and went, a Zappos rep e-mailed the woman to remind her the money was due. The woman told the rep the reason: She had meant to send back the shoes, which were for her ailing mother, but in the meantime, her mother had died. The company rep arranged to have UPS [United Parcel Service] pick up the shoes, then actually sent the woman a flower arrangement and condolence card."[5]

In the second story, also mentioned in Zappos.com (A), a woman's husband "died in a car accident after she had ordered boots for him from Zappos. The day after she called to ask for help with the return, she received a flower delivery. The call center rep had ordered the flowers without checking with a supervisor and billed them to the company. At the funeral, the widow told her friends and family about the experience. ... Not only was she a customer for life, but so were those 30 or 40 people at the funeral. ... [Hsieh says,] [s]tories like these are being created every single day, thousands and thousands of times. ... It's just an example that if you get the culture right, then most of the other stuff follows."[6]

As the CEO of Zappos, Hsieh is as unique as the organizational culture that he has fostered. Hsieh is not the typical CEO when it comes to doing most anything, whether it's developing and maintaining a quite unique company culture, encouraging unusual recruitment and hiring practices, communicating with people, or a host of other activities.

Hsieh, a computer whiz and adept at writing programming code, decided to attempt a similarly algorithmic approach to creating the Zappos culture with his list of ten core values—the Zappos version of the "Ten Commandments." Included on the Zappos list are values such as "be humble," "build open and honest relationships with communication," and "create fun and a little weirdness." These core values drive all the key decisions—from hiring to customer relations to the recent downsizing of the company.[7]

Max Chafkin, a reporter for *Inc.* magazine, notes that "Hsieh is hard to know and even harder to read. He's generous and smart, but so subdued in one-on-one conversation that it's easy to mistake his reticence for rudeness. When he does speak, it's in full paragraphs that sound as if they have been formulated in advance. He sometimes smiles—as he does when he's explaining the clever way Zappos manages its call center—but he doesn't laugh at other people's jokes and seldom tells his own."[8]

"And yet, this mild-mannered fellow leads a company that is entirely uninhibited. Interviews are held over vodka shots, bathrooms are plastered with 'urine color' charts (ostensibly to ensure that employees are hydrated but also just to be weird and funny), and managers are encouraged to goof off with the people they manage."[9]

"What most of Hsieh's admirers—and even some Zappos employees—don't know is that this openness doesn't come naturally. Hsieh has been exceptionally shy all his life and finds meeting strangers exhausting. (His trick to get over his shyness is to pretend he's interviewing you for a job.)"[10] Still he has become an accomplished public speaker, giving many talks without notes. Tony Hsieh "is held with a regard typically afforded rock stars and cult leaders."[11]

Frequent and transparent communication with employees and customers—and anyone else who cares to know—is a hallmark of the Zappos experience. "Hsieh has embraced an ethos of transparency, using social networking tools such as Facebook, Twitter and blogging to share information, both good and bad, with employees, customers and anyone else interested in Zappos."[12] For example, in just one week, Hsieh "had given away shoes on Twitter, sent out an open invitation to a company barbecue and solved a service problem a customer left in a blog comment," among numerous other customer and employee interactions.[13]

Approximately one-third of the company's 1,400 employees "actively use Twitter to promote the company. ... The goal is to respond to customer comments and form personal connections with their Twitter followers, as well as with friends on Facebook, where employees post blogs and videos. ... [Doing this gives] customers and other curious social network members a way to get a glimpse at the inside workings of the company."[14] For employees who are not Twitter users, Zappos offers classes to help them become familiar with the communications application.[15]

The frequent and transparent communication applies to bad news as well as good news. Like many companies, Zappos has been hit by the recession that started in December 2007. In late October of 2008, Sequoia Capital, the majority owner of privately held Zappos, insisted that all of the companies in its investment portfolio, including Zappos, cut costs. The Zappos management team decided to lay off 124 employees, approximately 8 percent of its workforce. But even in distressing economic times Zappos has shown that it can be great, this time with immediate communication of the bad news.[16] CEO Tony Hsieh wanted to inform employees quickly so as to help alleviate the inevitable stress the layoffs would cause. "He announced the move in an e-mail, on his blog, and with Twitter."[17] "The quick disclosure is part of a broader culture of electronic openness at Zappos.com. ... Our true belief here is that everything is transparent," says Rebecca Ratner, the company's HR director.[18]

Zappos managers are required to spend 10–20 percent of their time "goofing off" with the associates they manage. Hsieh says that 10–20 percent is "just kind of a random number we made up. ... But part of the way you build company culture is hanging out outside of the office."[19] After managers have spent time "goofing off" with their team members, they invariably tell Hsieh that "goofing off" has improved communication, generated greater trust, and fostered budding friendships within the team. Hsieh always asks the managers whether the activities helped make the team more efficient, and they report an efficiency increase in the range of 20–100 percent.[20]

Interviews of prospective employees are not ordinary either. They are sometimes conducted in a speed-dating format, in which applicants talk with five or six managers in fast-paced five-minute dialogues. However, if the applicant survives this initial round of conversations, then more traditional interviews are conducted to assess the candidate's technical abilities in the specific area in which they desire to work. Finally, the applicants are interviewed by human resources professionals to ascertain whether they will fit into the Zappos culture.[21]

For better or worse, alcohol is frequently a part of the company's hiring process. Rebecca Ratner, the current head of HR, describes her interview with CEO Hsieh: "I had three vodka shots with Tony during my interview. ... And I'm not atypical." She asked Hsieh whether this type of recruiting behavior didn't expose Zappos to unnecessary risks. Hsieh's reply: "It's a risk. ... But if we're building a culture where everyone is friends with everyone else, it's worth the risk."[22]

Calculated risks, unusually transparent communications, unique ways of promoting teamwork and group cohesion, extraordinary degrees of employee freedom and empowerment, and an unorthodox leader: Are these causes for concern or for celebration?

Discussion Questions

1. How would you describe Tony Hsieh's approach to leadership?

2. What type(s) of followers would work well with Tony Hsieh? What type(s) of followers would not work well with Hsieh?

3. Does the high level of employee empowerment and freedom put the company at risk more than it benefits the company? Explain the reasoning behind your answer.

4. Discuss the advantages and disadvantages associated with the way in which Zapponians utilize communications.

5. How does Tony Hsieh's leadership influence group dynamics at Zappos?

6. Do you think engaging in activities outside of work—like goofing off with followers—are useful ways to promote teamwork?

7. At the end of the case the question is posed regarding whether calculated risks, unusually transparent communications, unique ways of promoting teamwork and group cohesion, extraordinary degrees of employee freedom and empowerment, and an unorthodox leader are causes for concern or for celebration. What is your position—a cause for concern or a cause for celebration? Explain your answer.

SOURCE: This case was written by Michael K. McCuddy, The Louis S. and Mary L. Morgal Chair of Christian Business Ethics and Professor of Management, College of Business Administration, Valparaiso University.

PART 4

© Brand X Pictures

Organizational Processes and Structure

14

Jobs and the Design of Work

LEARNING OBJECTIVES

After reading this chapter, you should be able to do the following:

1 Define the term *job* and identify six patterns of defining *work*.

2 Discuss the four traditional approaches to job design.

3 Describe the Job Characteristics Model.

4 Compare the social information–processing (SIP) model with traditional job design approaches.

5 Explain ergonomics and the interdisciplinary framework for the design of work.

6 Compare Japanese, German, and Scandinavian approaches to work.

7 Explain how job control, uncertainty, and conflict can be managed for employee well-being.

8 Discuss five contemporary issues in the design of work.

CarMax sales consultants
stay with customers from
start to finish.

THINKING AHEAD: CARMAX

One Sales Consultant, from Start to Finish

CarMax had challenges in the 2008 and 2009 recession like
so many other companies. Their actual results were down as
much as 27 percent during one quarter of this period. While
CarMax is the nation's largest used-car retailer, the company

has less than 2 percent of the total used-car market, which gives a sense of the huge opportunity that
the company has in front of itself.[1] Therefore, in the midst of the dramatic changes in the American
automotive industry and car markets during possibly the worst economic conditions in seventy years,
CarMax is not in a bad place. One of the reasons for this opportunistic position is the company's
business model and how one of the key jobs is designed, executed, and incentivized.

The sales consultant job at CarMax is the key interface job with the customer. In the traditional
used-car business, the salesperson makes a hand off with the customer to a sales manager who
takes the sales process from there. The CarMax sales consultant job is designed to take the customer
through the entire transaction in a seamless way. Because CarMax operates at the high end of the

used-car range with an average retail around $16,000, almost all the cars they sell require a loan. The sales consultant is the one with whom the customer fills out a loan application, not a finance manager as in traditional used-car sales. The sales consultant is the one person who is with the customer from start to finish at CarMax.

The design of the sales consultant job at CarMax does not fit the stereotype of the used-car salesman. Neither does the incentive system for sales consultants. CarMax's incentives for salespeople are very different from the traditional used-car sales job. The company uses a flat, fixed commission. Therefore, the salesperson gets paid regardless of what car the customer chooses to buy and regardless of the profit the company makes. The sales consultant gets the same commission if they sell a customer a $5,000 car or a $50,000 car. Because most traditional used-car salespeople are paid a percentage of cross profit, their incentive is to push the customer to the car with the most profit for the salesperson. The "CarMax Way" is a transparent, customer-friendly sales process. Will this incentive strategy be enough to sustain them during the downturn? We will see in the Looking Back feature.

1 Define the term *job* and identify six patterns of defining *work*.

A *job* is defined as an employee's specific work and task activities in an organization. A job is not the same as an organizational position or a career. Organizational position identifies a job in relation to other parts of the organization; career refers to a sequence of job experiences over time.

This chapter focuses on jobs and the design of work as elements of the organization's structure. Jobs help people define their work and become integrated into the organization. The first section in the chapter examines the meaning of work in organizations. The second section addresses four traditional approaches to job design developed between the late 1800s and the 1970s. The third section examines four alternative approaches to job design developed over the past couple of decades. The final section addresses emerging issues in job design.

WORK IN ORGANIZATIONS

Work is effortful, productive activity resulting in a product or a service. It is one important reason why organizations exist. A job is composed of a set of specific tasks, each of which is an assigned piece of work to be done in a specific time period. Work is an especially important human endeavor because it has a powerful effect in binding a person to reality. Through work, people become securely attached to reality and securely connected in human relationships. *Work* has different meanings for different people. For all people, work is organized into jobs, and jobs fit into the larger structure of an organization. The structure of jobs is the concern of this chapter, and the structure of the organization is the concern of the next chapter. Both chapters emphasize organizations as sets of task and authority relationships through which people get work done.

The Meaning of Work

The *meaning of work* differs from person to person, from culture to culture, and from profession to profession.[2] In an increasingly global workplace, it is important

job
A set of specified work and task activities that engage an individual in an organization.

work
Mental or physical activity that has productive results.

meaning of work
The way a person interprets and understands the value of work as part of life.

to understand and appreciate differences among individuals and cultures with regard to the meaning of work. One study found six patterns people follow in defining *work*, and these help explain the cultural differences in people's motivation to work.[3]

Pattern A people define *work* as an activity in which value comes from performance and for which a person is accountable. It is generally self-directed and devoid of negative affect.

Pattern B people define *work* as an activity that provides a person with positive personal affect and identity. Work contributes to society and is not unpleasant.

Pattern C people define *work* as an activity from which profit accrues to others by its performance, and that may be done in various settings other than a working place. Work is usually physically strenuous and somewhat compulsive.

Pattern D people define *work* as primarily a physical activity a person must do that is directed by others and generally performed in a working place. Work is usually devoid of positive affect and is unpleasantly connected to performance.

Pattern E people define *work* as a physically and mentally strenuous activity. It is generally unpleasant and devoid of positive affect.

Pattern F people define *work* as an activity constrained to specific time periods that does not bring positive affect through its performance.

These six patterns were studied in six different countries: Belgium, Germany, Israel, Japan, the Netherlands, and the United States. Table 14.1 summarizes the percentage of workers in each country who defined work according to each of the six patterns. An examination of the table shows that a small percentage of workers in all six countries used either Pattern E or Pattern F to define *work*. Furthermore, there are significant differences among countries in how *work* is defined. In the Netherlands, it is defined most positively and with the most balanced personal and collective reasons for doing it. *Work* is defined least positively and with the most collective reason for doing it in Germany and Japan. Belgium, Israel, and the United States

TABLE

14.1   Work Definition Patterns by Nation

	Pattern*					
Sample	**A**	**B**	**C**	**D**	**E**	**F**
Total Sample (*N* × 4,950)	11%	28%	18%	22%	11%	12%
Nation						
Belgium	8%	40%	13%	19%	11%	9%
Germany	8%	26%	13%	28%	11%	14%
Israel	4%	22%	33%	23%	9%	9%
Japan	21%	11%	13%	29%	10%	17%
The Netherlands	15%	43%	12%	11%	9%	9%
United States	8%	30%	19%	19%	12%	11%

Note: X^2 = 680.98 (25 degrees of freedom). <.0001 Significance level.
*In Pattern A, work is valued for its performance. The person is accountable and generally self-directed. In Pattern B, work provides a person with positive affect and identity. It contributes to society. In Pattern C, work provides profit to others by its performance. It is physical and not confined to a working place. In Pattern D, work is a required physical activity directed by others and generally unpleasant. In Pattern E, work is physically and mentally strenuous. It is generally unpleasant. In Pattern F, work is constrained to specific time periods. It does not bring positive affect through performance.
SOURCE: From G. W. England and I. Harpaz, "How Working Is Defined: National Contexts and Demographic and Organizational Role Influences," from *Journal of Organizational Behavior*, 11, 1990. Copyright John Wiley & Sons, Limited. Reproduced with permission.

represent a middle position between these two. Future international studies should include Middle Eastern countries, India, Central and South American countries, and other Asian countries to better represent the world's cultures.

In another international study, 5,550 people across ten occupational groups in twenty different countries completed the Work Value Scales (WVS).[4] The WVS is composed of thirteen items measuring various aspects of the work environment, such as responsibility and job security. The study found two common basic work dimensions across cultures. Work content is one dimension, measured by items such as "the amount of responsibility on the job." Job context is the other dimension, measured by items such as "the policies of my company." This finding suggests that people in many cultures distinguish between the nature of the work itself and elements of the context in which work is done. This supports Herzberg's two-factor theory of motivation (see Chapter 5) and his job enrichment method discussed later in this chapter. Although the meaning of work differs among countries, new theorizing about crafting a job also suggests that individual employees can alter work meaning and work identity by changing task and relationship configurations in their work.[5]

Jobs in Organizations

Task and authority relationships define an organization's structure. Jobs are the basic building blocks of this task–authority structure and are considered the microstructural element to which employees most directly relate. Jobs are usually designed to complement and support other jobs in the organization. Isolated jobs are rare, although one was identified at Coastal Corporation during the early 1970s. Shortly after Oscar Wyatt moved the company from Corpus Christi, Texas, to Houston, Coastal developed organizational charts and job descriptions because the company had grown so large. In the process of charting the organization's structure, it was discovered that the beloved corporate economist reported to no one. Everyone assumed he worked for someone else. Such peculiarities are rare, however.

Jobs in organizations are interdependent and designed to make a contribution to the organization's overall mission and goals. For salespeople to be successful, the production people must be effective. For production people to be effective, the material department must be effective. These interdependencies require careful planning and design so that all of the "pieces of work" fit together into a whole. For example, an envelope salesperson who wants to take an order for 1 million envelopes from John Hancock Financial Services must coordinate with the production department to establish an achievable delivery date. The failure to incorporate this interdependence into his planning could create conflict and doom the company to failure in meeting John Hancock's expectations. The central concerns of this chapter are designing work and structuring jobs to prevent such problems and to ensure employee well-being. Inflexible jobs that are rigidly structured have an adverse effect and lead to stressed-out employees.

Chapter 15 addresses the larger issues in the design of organizations. In particular, it examines the competing processes of differentiation and integration in organizations. Differentiation is the process of subdividing and departmentalizing the work of an organization. Jobs result from differentiation, which is necessary because no one can do it all (contrary to the famous statement made by Harold Geneen, former chairman of ITT: "If I had enough arms and legs and time, I'd do it all myself"). Even small organizations must divide work so that each person is able to accomplish a manageable piece of the whole. At the same time the organization divides up the work, it must also integrate those pieces back into a whole. Integration is the process of connecting jobs and departments into a coordinated, cohesive whole. For example, if the envelope salesperson had coordinated with the production manager before finalizing the order with John Hancock, the company could have met the customer's expectations, and integration would have occurred.

TRADITIONAL APPROACHES TO JOB DESIGN

2 Discuss the four traditional approaches to job design.

Failure to differentiate, integrate, or both may result in badly designed jobs, which in turn cause a variety of performance problems in organizations. Good job design helps avoid these problems, improves productivity, and enhances employee well-being. Four approaches to job design that were developed during the twentieth century are scientific management, job enlargement/job rotation, job enrichment, and the job characteristics theory. Each approach offers unique benefits to the organization, the employee, or both, but each also has limitations and drawbacks. Furthermore, an unthinking reliance on a traditional approach can be a serious problem in any company. The later job design approaches were developed to overcome the limitations of traditional job design approaches. For example, job enlargement was intended to overcome the problem of boredom associated with scientific management's narrowly defined approach to jobs.

Scientific Management

Scientific management, an approach to work design first advocated by Frederick Taylor, emphasized work simplification. *Work simplification* is the standardization and the narrow, explicit specification of task activities for workers.[6] Jobs designed through scientific management have a limited number of tasks, and each task is scientifically specified so that the worker is not required to think or deliberate. According to Taylor, the role of management and the industrial engineer is to calibrate and define each task carefully. The role of the worker is to execute the task. The elements of scientific management, such as time and motion studies, differential piece-rate systems of pay, and the scientific selection of workers, all focus on the efficient use of labor to the economic benefit of the corporation. Employees who are satisfied with various aspects of repetitive work may like scientifically designed jobs.

Two arguments supported the efficient and standardized job design approach of scientific management in the early days of the American Industrial Revolution. The first argument was that work simplification allowed individuals of diverse ethnic and skill backgrounds to work together in a systematic way. This was important during the first great period of globalization in the late 1800s during which Germans, Scots, Hungarians, Poles, and other immigrants came to work in America.[7] Taylor's unique approach to work standardization allowed diverse individuals to be blended into a functional workforce.

The second argument for scientific management was that work simplification led to production efficiency in the organization and, therefore, to higher profits. This economic argument for work simplification tended to treat labor as a means of production and dehumanized it.

A fundamental limitation of scientific management is that it undervalues the human capacity for thought and ingenuity. Jobs designed through scientific management use only a portion of a person's capabilities. This underutilization makes work boring, monotonous, and understimulating. The failure to fully utilize the workers' capacity in a constructive fashion may cause a variety of work problems. Contemporary approaches to enhancing motivation through pay and compensation work to overcome these problems through modern job designs that retain talent and reduce turnover.[8]

work simplification
Standardization and the narrow, explicit specification of task activities for workers.

Job Enlargement/Job Rotation

Job enlargement is a traditional approach to overcome the limitations of highly specialized work, such as boredom[9] and the difficulty of coordinating work.[10] *Job enlargement* is a method of job design that increases the number of tasks in a job. *Job rotation,* a variation of job enlargement, exposes a worker to a variety of specialized job tasks over time. CarMax's sales consultant jobs are an example of job enlargement because they take the customer all the way through the used-car transaction. India-based Tata Consultancy Services (TCS), a software services and consulting company, considers job rotation a key workforce development strategy that delivers added value to customer as seen in The Real World 14.1. The reasoning behind these approaches to the problems of overspecialization is as follows.

First, the core problem with overspecialized work was believed to be lack of variety. That is, jobs designed by scientific management were too narrow and limited in the number of tasks and activities assigned to each worker. Second, a lack of variety led to understimulation and underutilization of the worker. Third, the worker would be more stimulated and better utilized by increasing the variety in the job. Variety

The Real World 14.1

Dual Value Proposition at TCS

TCS is a software services and consulting company based in India. TCS has operations in countries such China and Hungary, along with a presence in South America. Altogether, TCS has offices in forty-two countries globally and customers throughout the world. As a strategy for workforce development and delivery of added value to these worldwide cus-

TCS CEO Ramadorai (far right) and a TSC employee (far left) share a moment with two British leaders visiting TSC's Mumbai plant.

tomers, TCS implemented an overseas program of job rotation for employees native to India. Sending skilled Indian employees abroad is essential to employee development, and the overseas job rotation program allows TCS to provide better service by drawing on the strength of its entire workforce rather than only employee talent found in the office located closest to the customer. Vice president of human resources, Ajoy Mukherjee, sees this as a value added proposition for TCS customers from the point of view of quality and knowledge. TCS overseas assignments usually span eighteen to twenty-four months, with employees learning both from their work with the customer and from fellow TCS employees who are based permanently at that location. After returning to India, the employee often works on the same kinds of projects that were worked on abroad, thereby transferring the knowledge gained overseas to the home office. Job rotation is essential in building competency. On-site, face-to-face work with customers builds international people skills as well as enhances technical skills. Some TCS employees, but not all, in overseas assignments learn the language.

SOURCE: M Weinstein, "Foreign but Familiar," *Training* 46 (January 2009): 20–23.

could be increased by increasing the number of activities or by rotating the worker through different jobs. For example, job enlargement for a lathe operator in a steel plant might include selecting the steel pieces to be turned and performing all of the maintenance work on the lathe. As an example of job rotation, an employee at a small bank might take new accounts one day, serve as a cashier another day, and process loan applications on a third day.

One of the first studies of the problem of repetitive work was conducted at IBM after World War II. The company implemented a job enlargement program during the war and evaluated the effort after six years.[11] The two most important results were a significant increase in product quality and a reduction in idle time, both for people and for machines. Less obvious and measurable are the benefits of job enlargement to IBM through enhanced worker status and improved manager–worker communication. IBM concluded that job enlargement countered the problems of work specialization. A contemporary study in a Swedish electronics assembly plant used physiological measures of muscle tension.[12] Job enlargement had a positive effect on mechanical exposure variability.

A later study examined the effects of mass production jobs on assembly-line workers in the automotive industry.[13] Mass production jobs have six characteristics: mechanically controlled work pace, repetitiveness, minimum skill requirements, predetermined tools and techniques, minute division of the production process, and a requirement for surface mental attention, rather than thoughtful concentration. The researchers conducted 180 private interviews with assembly-line workers and found generally positive attitudes toward pay, security, and supervision. They concluded that job enlargement and job rotation would improve other job aspects, such as repetition and a mechanical work pace.

Job rotation and *cross-training* programs are variations of job enlargement. Pharmaceutical company Eli Lilly has found that job rotation can be a proactive means for enhancing work experiences for career development and can have tangible benefits for employees in the form of salary increases and promotions.[14] In cross-training, workers are trained in different specialized tasks or activities. While job rotation may be common practice for high-potential employees, they should remain in a position long enough to see the consequences of their decisions.[15] All three kinds of programs horizontally enlarge jobs; that is, the number and variety of an employee's tasks and activities are increased. Graphic Controls Corporation (now a subsidiary of Tyco International) used cross-training to develop a flexible workforce that enabled the company to maintain high levels of production.[16] Many of today's jobs require that employees manage several work activities as part of their normal business day. It is important that employees be able to disengage from one task before moving on to another to achieve high levels of performance.[17]

Job Enrichment

Whereas job enlargement increases the number of job activities through horizontal loading, job enrichment increases the amount of job responsibility through vertical loading. Both approaches to job design are intended, in part, to increase job satisfaction for employees. A study to test whether job satisfaction results from characteristics of the job or of the person found that an interactionist approach is most accurate and that job redesign can contribute to increased job satisfaction for some employees. Another two-year study found that intrinsic job satisfaction and job perceptions are reciprocally related to each other.[18]

Job enrichment is a job design or redesign method aimed at increasing the motivational factors in a job. Job enrichment builds on Herzberg's two-factor

cross-training
A variation of job enlargement in which workers are trained in different specialized tasks or activities.

job enrichment
Designing or redesigning jobs by incorporating motivational factors into them.

theory of motivation, which distinguishes between motivational and hygiene factors for people at work. Whereas job enlargement recommends increasing and varying the number of activities a person does, job enrichment recommends increasing the recognition, responsibility, and opportunity for achievement. For example, enlarging the lathe operator's job means adding maintenance activities, and enriching the job means having the operator meet with customers who buy the products.

Herzberg believes that only certain jobs should be enriched and that the first step is to select the jobs appropriate for job enrichment.[19] He recognizes that some people prefer simple jobs. Once jobs are selected for enrichment, management should brainstorm about possible changes, revise the list to include only specific changes related to motivational factors, and screen out generalities and suggestions that would simply increase activities or numbers of tasks. Those whose jobs are to be enriched should not participate in this process because of a conflict of interest. Two key problems can arise in the implementation of job enrichment. First, an initial drop in performance can be expected as workers accommodate to the change. Second, first-line supervisors may experience some anxiety or hostility as a result of employees' increased responsibility.

A seven-year implementation study of job enrichment at AT&T found the approach beneficial.[20] Job enrichment required a big change in management style, and AT&T found that it could not ignore hygiene factors in the work environment just because it was enriching existing jobs. Although the AT&T experience with job enrichment was positive, a critical review of job enrichment did not find that to be the case generally.[21] One problem with job enrichment as a strategy for work design is that it is based on an oversimplified motivational theory. Another problem is the lack of consideration for individual differences among employees. Job enrichment, like scientific management's work specialization and job enlargement/job rotation, is a universal approach to the design of work and thus does not differentiate among individuals.

Job Characteristics Theory

3 Describe the Job Characteristics Model.

The job characteristics theory, which was initiated during the mid-1960s, is a traditional approach to the design of work that makes a significant departure from the three earlier approaches. It emphasizes the interaction between the individual and specific attributes of the job; therefore, it is a person–job fit model rather than a universal job design model. It originated in a research study of 470 workers in forty-seven different jobs across eleven industries.[22] The study measured and classified relevant task characteristics for these forty-seven jobs and found four core job characteristics: job variety, autonomy, responsibility, and interpersonal interaction. The study also found that core job characteristics did not affect all workers in the same way. A worker's values, religious beliefs, and ethnic background influenced how the worker responded to the job. Specifically, workers with rural values and strong religious beliefs preferred jobs high in core characteristics, and workers with urban values and weaker religious beliefs preferred jobs low in core characteristics. One study tested the effect of job and work characteristics on employee turnover intentions and found that they consider both when deciding when to leave a company.[23]

Richard Hackman and his colleagues modified the original model by including three critical psychological states of the individual and refining the measurement of core job characteristics. The result is the *Job Characteristics Model* shown in Figure 14.1.[24] The *Job Diagnostic Survey (JDS)*, the most commonly used job design measure, was developed to diagnose jobs by measuring the five core job

Job Characteristics Model
A framework for understanding person–job fit through the interaction of core job dimensions with critical psychological states within a person.

Job Diagnostic Survey (JDS)
The survey instrument designed to measure the elements in the Job Characteristics Model.

14.1   The Job Characteristics Model

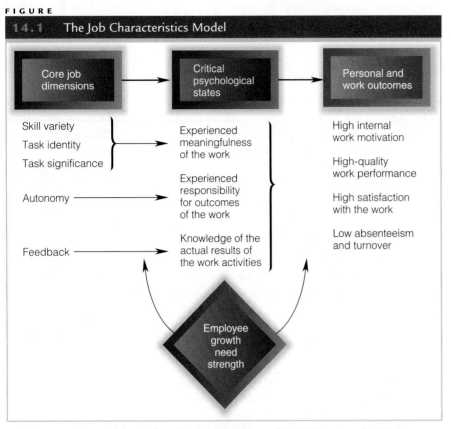

SOURCE: J. R. Hackman and G. R. Oldham, "The Relationship Among Core Job Dimensions, the Critical Psychological States, and On-the-Job Outcomes," *The Job Diagnostic Survey: An Instrument for the Diagnosis of Jobs and the Evaluation of Job Redesign Projects*, 1974. Reprinted by permission of Greg R. Oldham.

characteristics and three critical psychological states shown in the model. The core job characteristics stimulate the critical psychological states in the manner shown in Figure 14.1. This results in varying personal and work outcomes, as identified in the figure. A recent proposal to modify the job characteristics model suggests that psychological ownership is an important factor in job design.[25]

The five core job characteristics are defined as follows:

1. *Skill variety.* The degree to which a job includes different activities and involves the use of multiple skills and talents of the employee.

2. *Task identity.* The degree to which the job requires completion of a whole and identifiable piece of work—that is, doing a job from beginning to end with a tangible outcome.

3. *Task significance.* The degree to which the job has a substantial impact on the lives or work of other people, whether in the immediate organization or in the external environment.

4. *Autonomy.* The degree to which the job provides the employee with substantial freedom, independence, and discretion in scheduling the work and in determining the procedures to be used in carrying it out.

5. *Feedback from the job itself.* The degree to which carrying out the work activities results in the employee's obtaining direct and clear information about the effectiveness of his or her performance.

Hackman and his colleagues say that the five core job characteristics interact to determine an overall Motivating Potential Score (MPS) for a specific job. The MPS

Diagnosing Your Job

This questionnaire challenges you to examine the motivating potential in your job. If you are not currently working, complete the questionnaire for any job you have ever held for which you want to examine the motivating potential. For each of the following five questions, circle the number of the most accurate description of the job. Be as objective as you can in describing the job by answering these questions.

1. How much *autonomy* is there in the job? That is, to what extent does the job permit a person to decide *on his or her own* how to go about doing the work?

1	2	3	4	5	6	7

Very little; the job gives a person almost no personal say about how and when the work is done.

Moderate autonomy; many things are standardized and not under the control of the person, but he or she can make some decisions about the work.

Very much; the job gives the person almost complete responsibility for deciding how and when the work is done.

2. To what extent does the job involve doing a *whole* and *identifiable piece of work*? That is, is the job a complete piece of work that has an obvious beginning and end? Or is it a small part of the overall piece of work, which is finished by other people or by automatic machines?

1	2	3	4	5	6	7

The job is only a tiny part in the overall piece of work; the results of the person's activities cannot be seen in the final product or service.

The job is a moderate-sized "chunk" of the overall piece of work; the person's own contribution can be seen in the final outcome.

The job involves doing the whole piece of work, from start to finish; the results of the person's activities are easily seen in the final product or service.

3. How much *variety* is there in the job? That is, to what extent does the job require a person to do many different things at work, using a variety of his or her skills and talents?

1	2	3	4	5	6	7

Very little; the job requires the person to do the same routine things over and over again.

Moderate variety.

Very much; the job requires the person to do many different things, using a number of different skills and talents.

4. In general, how *significant* or *important* is the job? That is, are the results of the person's work likely to affect significantly the lives or well-being of other people?

1	2	3	4	5	6	7

Not at all significant; the outcome of the work is *not* likely to affect anyone in any important way.

Moderately significant.

Highly significant; the outcome of the work can affect other people in very important ways.

5. To what extent *does doing the job itself* provide the person with information about his or her work performance? That is, does the actual work itself provide clues about how well the person is doing—aside from any feedback coworkers or supervisors may provide?

1	2	3	4	5	6	7

Very little; the job itself is set up so a person could work forever without finding out how well he or she is doing.

Moderately; sometimes doing the job provides feedback to the person; sometimes it does not.

Very much; the job is set up so that a person gets almost constant feedback as he or she works about how well he or she is doing.

To score your questionnaire, place your responses to Questions 3, 2, 4, 1, and 5, respectively, in the blank spaces in the following equation:

Motivating
Potential   = $\dfrac{Q\#3 + Q\#2 + Q\#4}{3}$ × Q#1 × Q#5 = _____ .
Score (MPS)

If the MPS for the job you rated is between:

- 200 and 343, it is high in motivating potential.
- 120 and 199, it is moderate in motivating potential.
- 0 and 119, it is low in motivating potential.

SOURCE: J. R. Hackman and G. R. Oldham, "The Job Diagnostic Survey: An Instrument for the Diagnosis of Jobs and the Evaluation of Job Redesign Projects," *Technical Report No. 4*, 1974, 2–3 of the Short Form. Reprinted by permission of Greg R. Oldham.

indicates a job's potential for motivating incumbents. An individual's MPS is determined by the following equation:

$$\text{MPS} = \frac{[\text{Skill variety}] + [\text{Task identity}] + [\text{Task significance}]}{3} \times [\text{Autonomy}] \times [\text{Feedback}].$$

You 14.1 enables you to answer five questions from the JDS short form to get an idea about the motivating potential of your present job or any job you have held.

The Job Characteristics Model includes *growth-need strength* (the desire to grow and fully develop one's abilities) as a moderator. People with a high growth-need strength respond favorably to jobs with high MPSs, and individuals with low growth-need strength respond less favorably to such jobs. We see in the Science feature that one study found growth-need strength had a positive effect on individual creative performance. The job characteristics theory further suggests that core job dimensions stimulate three critical psychological states according to the relationships specified in the model. These critical psychological states are defined as follows:

1. *Experienced meaningfulness of the work*, or the degree to which the employee experiences the job as one that is generally meaningful, valuable, and worthwhile.

2. *Experienced responsibility for work outcomes*, or the degree to which the employee feels personally accountable and responsible for the results of the work he or she does.

3. *Knowledge of results*, or the degree to which the employee knows and understands, on a continuous basis, how effectively he or she is performing the job.

In one early study, Hackman and Oldham administered the JDS to 658 employees working on sixty-two different jobs in seven business organizations.[26] The JDS was useful for job redesign efforts through one or more of five implementing concepts: (1) combining tasks into larger jobs, (2) forming natural work teams to increase task identity and task significance, (3) establishing relationships with customers, (4) loading jobs vertically with more responsibility, and/or (5) opening feedback channels for the job incumbent. For example, if an automotive mechanic received little feedback on the quality of repair work performed, one redesign strategy would be to solicit customer feedback one month after each repair.

A more recent sequence of two studies conducted in Egypt aimed to disaggregate work autonomy, one important component in job design theory.[27] Study 1 included

Science

Growth-Need Strength, Work Context, and Creative Performance

This research used an interactionist perspective and focused on "growth-need strength" as an important individual factor for employees' creative performance. The study was based on a U.S. national survey that used probability sampling and random digital dialing to create the sample. Eligible participants were over eighteen years of age and worked at least thirty hours per week. Completed interview data were collected from 1,465 participants, which was a response rate of 61.4 percent of the qualified subjects. The sample included jobs across which there was a wide range of job complexity. Therefore, some jobs were low in complexity and other jobs very high in complexity. Self-reported creative performance was the outcome variable in this research. The researchers measured three additional variables: growth-need strength, job complexity, and supportiveness of the work context. The study controlled the effects of individual factors previously linked to creativity, which are creative personality, intrinsic motivation, and cognitive style. The results found that growth-need strength has both a positive main effect on creativity and an interactive effect with work context. In addition, job complexity moderated this relationship. The findings highlight that a supportive work context plays a critical role for creativity and organizational support contributes positively to the performance of both in-role and extra-role activities. The researchers conclude that understanding the nature of a job and individual differences are important in matching these with the work being performed and the work context.

SOURCE: C. E. Shalley, L. L. Gilson, and T. C. Blum, "Interactive Effects of Growth Need Strength, Work Context, and Job Complexity on Self-Reported Creative Performance," *Academy of Management Journal* 52 (2009): 489–505.

534 employees in two Egyptian organizations. Study 2 involved 120 managers in four organizations. The results indicated that separate work method, work schedule, and work criteria autonomy were three separate facets of work autonomy. An extension of job characteristics theory, the Work Design Questionnaire (WDQ), measures twenty-one distinct work characteristics in three categories. These are motivational work characteristics such as skill variety and task identity, social characteristics such as interdependence and social support, and work context characteristics such as physical demands and work conditions.[28]

In another international study, the Job Characteristics Model was tested in a sample of fifty-seven jobs from thirty-seven organizations in Hong Kong.[29] Job incumbents and their supervisors both completed questionnaires about the incumbents' jobs.[30] The supervisory version asked the supervisor to rate the employee's job. The study supported the model in general. However, task significance was not a reliable core job dimension in Hong Kong, which suggests either national differences in the measurement of important job dimensions or cultural biases about work. This result also suggests that value differences may exist between American and Asian people with regard to jobs.

An alternative to the Job Characteristics Model is the Job Characteristics Inventory (JCI) developed by Henry Sims and Andrew Szilagyi.[31] The JCI primarily measures core job characteristics. It is not as comprehensive as the JDS or the new WDQ because it does not incorporate critical psychological states, personal and work outcomes, or employee needs. The JCI does give some consideration to structural and individual variables that affect the relationship between core job characteristics and the individual.[32] One comparative analysis of the JCI and JDS found similarities in the measures and in the models' predictions.[33] The comparative analysis also found two differences. First, the variety scales in the two models appear to have different effects on performance. Second, the autonomy scales in the two models appear to have different effects on employee satisfaction. Overall, the

JCI, JDS, and new WDQ all support the usefulness of a person–job fit approach to the design of work over the earlier, universal theories.

Engagement

Psychological conditions related to job design features are a particular concern of the Job Characteristics Model.[34] One study of over 200 managers and employees in a Midwestern insurance company found that meaningfulness, safety, and availability were three important psychological conditions that affected employees' *engagement* in their jobs and work roles. Engagement at work is important for its positive individual and organizational outcomes. Although important to company success, only one-third of employees in a recent study reported that they were engaged.[35] Engagement is the harnessing of organizational members to their work roles. When engaged, people employ and express themselves physically, cognitively, and emotionally as they perform their jobs and their work roles. For example, Gallup's Q was used to improve engagement for a clinical nutrition group at St. Mary's/Duluth Clinic Health System.[36]

Full engagement requires the strategic management of one's energy in response to the environment.[37] Being fully engaged in one's work role and job can be highly appropriate and yet demand energy, time, and effort. To achieve balance and afford opportunity for recovery, there is a commensurate need to strategically and appropriately disengage from one's job and work role on a periodic basis. The effective management of energy in response to one's job and work role leads to both high performance and personal renewal. Thus, while the design of work is important, the human spirit's response to job characteristics and work design features is equally important.

ALTERNATIVE APPROACHES TO JOB DESIGN

Because each of the traditional job design approaches has limitations, several alternative approaches to job design have emerged over the past couple of decades. This section examines four of these alternatives that are in the process of being tried and tested. First, it examines the social information-processing model. Second, it reviews ergonomics and the interdisciplinary framework of Michael Campion and Paul Thayer. Their framework builds on the traditional job design approaches. Third, this section examines the international perspectives of the Japanese, Germans, and Scandinavians. Finally, it focuses on the health and well-being aspects of work design. Healthy work enables individuals to adapt, function well, and balance work with private life activities.[38] An emerging fifth approach to the design of work through teams and autonomous work groups was addressed in Chapter 9.

4 Compare the social information-processing (SIP) model with traditional job design approaches.

Social Information Processing

The traditional approaches to the design of work emphasize objective core job characteristics. By contrast, the *social information-processing (SIP) model* emphasizes the interpersonal aspects of work design. Specifically, the SIP model says that what others tell us about our jobs is important.[39] The SIP model has four basic premises about the work environment.[40] First, other people provide cues we use to understand the work environment. Second, other people help us judge what is important in our jobs. Third, other people tell us how they see our jobs. Fourth, other people's positive and negative feedback helps us understand our feelings about our jobs. This is very consistent with the dynamic model of the job design process that views it as a social one involving job-holders, supervisors, and peers.[41]

engagement

The expression of oneself as one performs in work or other roles.

social information-processing (SIP) model

A model that suggests that the important job factors depend in part on what others tell a person about the job.

People's perceptions and reactions to their jobs are shaped by information from other people in the work environment.[42] In other words, what others believe about a person's job may be important to understanding the person's perceptions of, and reactions to, the job. This does not mean that objective job characteristics are unimportant; rather, it means that others can modify the way these characteristics affect us. For example, one study of task complexity found that the objective complexity of a task must be distinguished from the subjective task complexity experienced by the employee.[43] While objective task complexity may be a motivator, the presence of others in the work environment, social interaction, or even daydreaming may be important additional sources of motivation. The SIP model makes an important contribution to the design of work by emphasizing the importance of other people and the social context of work. For example, relational job design may motivate employees to take prosocial action and make a positive difference in other people's lives.[44] In addition, the relational aspects of the work environment may be more important than objective core job characteristics. Therefore, the subjective feedback of other people about how difficult a particular task is may be more important to a person's motivation to perform than an objective estimate of the task's difficulty.

Ergonomics and Interdisciplinary Framework

5 Explain ergonomics and the interdisciplinary framework for the design of work.

Michael Campion and Paul Thayer use *ergonomics* based on engineering, biology, and psychology to develop an interdisciplinary framework for the design of work. Actually, they say that four approaches—the mechanistic, motivational, biological, and perceptual/motor approaches—are necessary because no one approach can solve all performance problems caused by poorly designed jobs. Each approach has its benefits as well as its limitations. One ergonomics study of eighty-seven administrative municipal employees found lower levels of upper body pain along with other positive outcomes of the workstation redesign.[45]

The interdisciplinary framework allows the job designer or manager to consider trade-offs and alternatives among the approaches based on desired outcomes. If a manager finds poor performance a problem, for example, she or he should analyze the job to ensure a design aimed at improving performance. The interdisciplinary framework is important because badly designed jobs cause far more performance problems than managers realize.[46]

Table 14.2 summarizes the positive and negative outcomes of each job design approach. The mechanistic and motivational approaches to job design are very similar to scientific management's work simplification and to the Job Characteristics Model, respectively. Because these were discussed earlier in the chapter, they are not further elaborated here.

The biological approach to job design emphasizes the person's interaction with physical aspects of the work environment and is concerned with the amount of physical exertion, such as lifting and muscular effort, required by the position. For example, an analysis of medical claims within TXI's steel operating company identified lower back problems as the most common physical problem experienced by steelworkers and managers alike. As a result, the company instituted an education and exercise program under expert guidance to improve care of the lower back. Program graduates received back cushions for their chairs with "Chaparral Steel Company" embossed on them. Herman Miller designed an office chair to support the lower back and other parts of the human body.[47] The chair was tested in several offices including that of the director of human resources for Valero Energy Corporation prior to large-scale production. Lower back problems associated with improper lifting may be costly, but they are not fatal. Campion describes the potentially catastrophic problem that occurred at Three Mile Island, when nuclear

ergonomics
The science of adapting work and working conditions to the employee or worker.

14.2   Summary of Outcomes from Various Job Design Approaches

Job Design Approach (Discipline)	Positive Outcomes	Negative Outcomes
Mechanistic Approach (mechanical engineering)	Decreased training time	Lower job satisfaction
	Higher personnel utilization levels	Lower motivation
	Lower likelihood of error	Higher absenteeism
	Less chance of mental overload	
	Lower stress levels	
Motivational Approach (industrial psychology)	Higher job satisfaction	Increased training time
	Higher motivation	Lower personnel utilization levels
	Greater job involvement	Greater chance of errors
	Higher job performance	Greater chance of mental overload and stress
	Lower absenteeism	
Biological Approach (biology)	Less physical effort	Higher financial costs because of changes in equipment or job environment
	Less physical fatigue	
	Fewer health complaints	
	Fewer medical incidents	
	Lower absenteeism	
	Higher job satisfaction	
Perceptual Motor Approach (experimental psychology)	Lower likelihood of error	Lower job satisfaction
	Lower likelihood of accidents	Lower motivation
	Less chance of mental stress	
	Decreased training time	
	Higher personnel utilization levels	

SOURCE: Reprinted from *Organizational Dynamics*, Winter/1987 Copyright © 1987, with permission from Elsevier Science.

materials contaminated the surrounding area and threatened disaster. Campion concluded that poor design of the control room operator's job caused the problem.

The perceptual/motor approach to job design also emphasizes the person's interaction with physical aspects of the work environment and is based on engineering that considers human factors such as strength or coordination, ergonomics, and experimental psychology. It places an important emphasis on human interaction with computers, information, and other operational systems. This approach addresses how people mentally process information acquired from the physical work environment through perceptual and motor skills. The approach emphasizes perception and fine motor skills as opposed to the gross motor skills and muscle strength emphasized in the mechanistic approach. The perceptual/motor approach is more likely to be relevant to operational and technical work, such as keyboard operations and data entry jobs, which may tax a person's concentration and attention, than to managerial, administrative, and custodial jobs, which are less likely to strain concentration and attention.

One study using the interdisciplinary framework to improve jobs evaluated 377 clerical, 80 managerial, and 90 analytical positions.[48] The jobs were improved by combining tasks and adding ancillary duties. The improved jobs provided greater motivation for the incumbents and were better from a perceptual/motor standpoint. The jobs were poorly designed from a mechanical engineering standpoint, however, and they were unaffected from a biological standpoint. Again, the interdisciplinary framework considers trade-offs and alternatives when evaluating job redesign efforts.

International Perspectives on the Design of Work

6 Compare Japanese, German, and Scandinavian approaches to work.

Each nation or ethnic group has a unique way of understanding and designing work.[49] As organizations become more global and international, an appreciation of the perspectives of other nations is increasingly important. A study of 2,359 call centers in sixteen countries found that an organization's management strategy and operational context influences variation in work design.[50] The Japanese, Germans, and Scandinavians in particular have distinctive perspectives on the design and organization of work.[51] Each country's perspective is forged within its unique cultural and economic system, and each is distinct from the approaches used in North America.

The Japanese Approach The Japanese began harnessing their productive energies during the 1950s by drawing on the product quality ideas of W. Edwards Deming.[52] In addition, the central government became actively involved in the economic resurgence of Japan, and it encouraged companies to conquer industries rather than merely to maximize profits.[53] Such an industrial policy, which built on the Japanese cultural ethic of collectivism, has implications for how work is done. Whereas Frederick Taylor and his successors in the United States emphasized the job of an individual worker, the Japanese work system emphasizes the strategic level and encourages collective and cooperative working arrangements.[54] As Table 14.1 shows, the Japanese emphasize performance, accountability, and other- or self-directedness in defining work, whereas Americans emphasize the positive affect, personal identity, and social benefits of work.

The Japanese success with lean production has drawn the attention of managers. *Lean production* methods are similar to the production concept of *sociotechnical systems (STS)*, although there are some differences.[55] In particular, STS gives greater emphasis to teamwork and self-managed and autonomous work groups, to the ongoing nature of the design process, and to human values in the work process. The approaches are similar, however, in that both differ from Taylor's scientific management and both emphasize job variety, feedback to work groups and teams, support of human resources, and control of production variance close to the point of origin. One three-year evaluation of lean teams, assembly lines, and workflow formalization as lean production practices was conducted in Australia.[56] Employees in all lean production groups were negatively affected, and the assembly-line employees the worst.

The German Approach The German approach to work has been shaped by Germany's unique educational system, cultural values, and economic system. The Germans are a highly educated and well-organized people. For example, their educational system has a multitrack design with technical and university alternatives. The German economic system puts a strong emphasis on free enterprise, private property rights, and management–labor cooperation. A comparison of voluntary and mandated management–labor cooperation in Germany found that productivity was superior under voluntary cooperation.[57] The Germans value hierarchy and authority relationships and, as a result, are generally disciplined.[58] Germany's workers are highly unionized, and their discipline and efficiency have enabled Germany to be highly productive while its workers labor substantially fewer hours than do Americans.

The traditional German approach to work design was *technocentric,* an approach that placed technology and engineering at the center of job design decisions. Recently,

lean production
Using committed employees with ever-expanding responsibilities to achieve zero waste, 100 percent good product, delivered on time, every time.

sociotechnical systems (STS)
Giving equal attention to technical and social considerations in job design.

technocentric
Placing technology and engineering at the center of job design decisions.

14.2   Hierarchical Model of Criteria for the Evaluation of Human Work

Scientific approaches of labor sciences	Levels of evaluation of human work	Problem areas and assignment to disciplines
View from natural science / Primarily oriented to individuals / Primarily oriented to groups / View from cultural studies	Practicability	Technical, anthropometric, and psychophysical problems (ergonomics)
	Endurability	Technical, physiological, and medical problems (ergonomics and occupational health)
	Acceptability	Economical and sociological problems (occupational psychology and sociology, personnel management)
	Satisfaction	Sociopsychological and economic problems (occupational psychology and sociology, personnel management)

SOURCE: H. Luczak, " 'Good Work' Design: An Ergonomic, Industrial Engineering Perspective," in J. C. Quick, L. R. Murphy, and J. J. Hurrell, eds., *Stress and Well-Being at Work* (Washington, DC). Copyright ©1997 by the American Psychological Association. Reprinted with permission.

German industrial engineers have moved to a more *anthropocentric* approach, which places human considerations at the center of job design decisions. The former approach uses a natural scientific process in the design of work, whereas the latter relies on a more humanistic process, as shown in Figure 14.2. In the anthropocentric approach, work is evaluated using the criteria of practicability and worker satisfaction at the individual level and the criteria of endurability and acceptability at the group level. Figure 14.2 also identifies problem areas and disciplines concerned with each aspect of the work design.

The Scandinavian Approach The Scandinavian cultural values and economic system stand in contrast to the German system. The social democratic tradition in Scandinavia has emphasized social concern rather than industrial efficiency. The Scandinavians place great emphasis on a work design model that encourages a high degree of worker control and good social support systems for workers.[59] Lennart Levi believes that circumstantial and inferential scientific evidence provides a sufficiently strong basis for legislative and policy actions for redesigns aimed at enhancing worker well-being. An example of such an action for promoting good working environments and occupational health was Swedish Government Bill 1976/77:149, which stated, "Work should be safe both physically and mentally *but also* provide opportunities for involvement, job satisfaction, and personal development." In 1991, the Swedish Parliament set up the Swedish Working Life Fund to finance research, intervention programs, and demonstration projects

A woman works at a Volvo plant in Sweden. The Scandinavians place great emphasis on a work design model that encourages a high degree of worker control.

Chad Ehlers/Photolibrary

anthropocentric
Placing human considerations at the center of job design decisions.

in work design. For example, a study of Stockholm police on shift schedules found that going from a daily, counterclockwise rotation to a clockwise rotation was more compatible with human biology and resulted in improved sleep, less fatigue, lower systolic blood pressure, and lower blood levels of triglycerides and glucose.[60] Hence, the work redesign improved the police officers' health.

Work Design and Well-Being

7 Explain how job control, uncertainty, and conflict can be managed for employee well-being.

An international group of scholars, including American social scientists, has been concerned about designing work and jobs that are both healthy and productive.[61] This issue was discussed briefly in Chapter 7. Economic and industry-specific upheavals in the United States during the 1990s led to job loss and unemployment, and the adverse health impact of these factors has received attention. [62] Attention has also been devoted to the effects of specific work design parameters on psychological health.[63] For example, by mixing cognitively challenging and "mindless" work throughout the day, one may reduce pressures for chronic overwork and enhance creativity. Frank Landy believes that organizations should redesign jobs to increase worker control and reduce worker uncertainty, while at the same time managing conflict and task/job demands. These objectives can be achieved in several ways.

Control in work organizations can be increased by (1) giving workers the opportunity to control several aspects of the work and the workplace; (2) designing machines and tasks with optimal response times and/or ranges; and (3) implementing performance-monitoring systems as a source of relevant feedback to workers. Uncertainty can be reduced by (1) providing employees with timely and complete information needed for their work; (2) making clear and unambiguous work assignments; (3) improving communication at shift change time; and (4) increasing employee access to information sources. Conflict at work can be managed through (1) participative decision making to reduce conflict; (2) using supportive supervisory styles to resolve conflict; and (3) having sufficient resources available to meet work demands, thus preventing conflict. Task/job design can be improved by enhancing core job characteristics and not patterning service work after assembly-line work.

Task uncertainty was shown to have an adverse effect on morale in a study of 629 employment security work units in California and Wisconsin.[64] More important, the study showed that morale was better predicted by considering both the overall design of the work unit and the task uncertainty. This study suggests that if one work design parameter, such as task uncertainty, is a problem in a job, its adverse effects on people may be mitigated by other work design parameters. For example, higher pay may offset an employee's frustration with a difficult coworker, or a friendly, supportive working environment may offset frustration with low pay. You 14.2 provides you with an opportunity to evaluate how psychologically healthy your work environment is. The American Psychological Association annually presents psychologically healthy workplace awards.[65]

CONTEMPORARY ISSUES IN THE DESIGN OF WORK

8 Discuss five contemporary issues in the design of work.

A number of contemporary issues related to specific aspects of the design of work have an effect on increasing numbers of employees. Rather than addressing job design or worker well-being in a comprehensive way, these issues address one or another aspect of a job. The issues include telecommuting, alternative work patterns, technostress, task revision, and skill development. One study found that employees stay motivated when their work is relationally designed to provide opportunities for respectful contact with those critical to their work.[66] Telecommuting and alternative work patterns such as job sharing can increase flexibility for employees. Companies

You 14.2

Is Your Work Environment a Healthy One?

To determine whether your work environment is a healthy one, read the text section on "Work Design and Well-Being," and then complete the following four steps. Answer each question in the five steps "yes" or "no."

Step 1. Control and Influence

_____ Do you have influence over the pace of your work?

_____ Are system response times neither too fast nor too slow?

_____ Do you have a say in your work assignments and goals?

_____ Is there an opportunity for you to comment on your performance appraisal?

Step 2. Information and Uncertainty

_____ Do you receive timely information to complete your work?

_____ Do you receive complete information for your work assignments?

_____ Is there adequate planning for changes that affect you at work?

_____ Do you have access to all the information you need at work?

Step 3. Conflict at Work

_____ Does the company apply policies clearly and consistently?

_____ Are job descriptions and task assignments clear and unambiguous?

_____ Are there adequate policies and procedures for the resolution of conflicts?

_____ Is your work environment an open, participative one?

Step 4. Job Scope and Task Design

_____ Is there adequate variety in your work activities and/or assignments?

_____ Do you receive timely, constructive feedback on your work?

_____ Is your work important to the overall mission of the company?

_____ Do you work on more than one small piece of a big project?

Scoring

Count the number of "yes" answers in Steps 1 through 4: _____

If you have 10 to 16 "yes" answers, this suggests that your work environment is a psychologically healthy one.

If you have 7 or fewer "yes" answers, this may suggest that your work environment is not as psychologically healthy as it could be.

use these and other approaches to the design of work as ways to manage a growing business while contributing to a better balance of work and family life for employees. In challenging economic times, companies like CarMax may engage in some job reshuffling, as we will see in the Looking Back feature.

Telecommuting

Telecommuting is when employees work at home or in other locations geographically separate from their company's main location. Estimates are that about 28 million Americans are telecommuting. Telecommuting may entail working in a combination of home, satellite office, and main office locations. This flexible arrangement is designed to achieve a better fit between the needs of the individual employee and the organization's task demands. Cisco Systems manager Christian Renaud moved from California and began telecommuting from Johnston, Iowa, when he and his wife began their family. Based on years of experience, CEO of leading company GE, Jack Welch, concludes that telecommuting can be an ideal situation for some but not for leaders.

Telecommuting has been around since the 1970s but was slower to catch on than some expected.[67] This was due to the inherent paradoxes associated with telecommuting.[68] Actually, with a greater emphasis on managing the work rather than the worker, managers can enhance control, effectively decentralize, and even encourage teamwork through telecommuting. A number of companies, such as AT&T in Phoenix and Bell Atlantic (now part of Verizon Communications), have programs in telecommuting for a wide range of employees. These flexible arrangements help some companies respond to changing demographics and a shrinking labor pool. The Travelers Group (now part of Citigroup) was one of the first companies to try telecommuting and was considered an industry leader in telecommuting. Because of its confidence in its employees, Travelers reaped rewards from telecommuting, including higher productivity, reduced absenteeism, expanded opportunities for workers with disabilities, and an increased ability to attract and retain talent.[69]

Pacific Bell (now part of AT&T) tried telecommuting on a large scale.[70] Pacific Bell had 1,500 managers who telecommuted. For example, an employee might work at home four days a week as an information systems designer and spend one day a week at the main office location in meetings, work exchanges, and coordination with others. Of 3,000 Pacific Bell managers responding to a mail survey, 87 percent said telecommuting would reduce employee stress, 70 percent said it would increase job satisfaction while reducing absenteeism, and 64 percent said it would increase productivity.

Telecommuting is neither a cure-all nor a universally feasible alternative. Many telecommuters feel a sense of social isolation. Some executives are concerned that while such workers are more productive, their lack of visibility may hold back their careers. Furthermore, not all forms of work are amenable to telecommuting. For example, firefighters and police officers must be at their duty stations to be successful in their work. Employees for whom telecommuting is not a viable option within a company may feel jealous of those able to telecommute. In addition, telecommuting may have the potential to create the sweatshops of the twenty-first century. Thus, it is a novel, emerging issue.

Alternative Work Patterns

Job sharing is an alternative work pattern in which more than one person occupies a single job. It may be an alternative to telecommuting for addressing demographic and labor pool concerns. Job sharing is found throughout a wide range of managerial and professional jobs, as well as in production and service jobs. It is not common among senior executives.

The *four-day workweek* is a second type of alternative work schedule. Information systems personnel at the United Services Automobile Association (USAA) in San Antonio, Texas, work four ten-hour days and enjoy a three-day weekend. This arrangement provides the benefit of more time for those who want to balance work and family life through weekend travel. However, the longer workdays may be a drawback for employees with many family or social activities on weekday evenings. Hence, the four-day workweek has both benefits and limitations.

Flextime, in which employees can set their own daily work schedules, is a third alternative work pattern. It has been applied in numerous ways in work organizations and can lead to reduced absenteeism. Companies in highly concentrated urban areas, like Houston, Los Angeles, and New York City, may allow employees to set their own daily work schedules as long as they start their eight hours at any thirty-minute interval from 6:00 A.M. to 9:00 A.M. This arrangement is designed to ease traffic and commuting pressures. It also is responsive to individual biorhythms, allowing early risers to go to work early and nighthawks to work late. Typically, 9:00 A.M. to 3:00 P.M. is the required core working time for everyone in the company. Even in companies without formal flextime programs, flextime may be an individual option arranged between supervisor and subordinate. For example, a first-line supervisor who wants to complete a college degree may negotiate a work

job sharing
An alternative work pattern in which more than one person occupies a single job.

flextime
An alternative work pattern that enables employees to set their own daily work schedules.

schedule accommodating both job requirements and course schedules at the university. Flextime options may be more likely for high performers who assure their bosses that work quality and productivity will not suffer.[71] In The Real World 14.2 feature, we see how Linda Skoglund implemented a "results only work environment" (ROWE) at J. A. Counter & Associates insurance and investment firm. On the cautionary side, one study found that a woman on a flexible work schedule was perceived to have less job–career dedication and less advancement motivation, though no less ability.[72]

Technology at Work

New technologies and electronic commerce are here to stay and are changing the face of work environments, dramatically in some cases. Many government jobs expect to change, and even disappear, with the advent of e-government using Internet technology. The concept involves work being where people are, rather than people moving to where the work is. New technologies make connectivity, collaboration, and communication easy. Critical voice mails and messages can be delivered to and from the central office, a client's office, the airport, the car, or home. Wireless

The Real World 14.2

Where Is Everybody? ROWEing

Sometimes Linda Skoglund wonders where everyone is because they are not in the office. J. A. Counter & Associates is a $2.5 million insurance and investment firm operating in Richmond, Wisconsin. After struggling with several efforts to improve the financial performance of the firm, Linda found that these efforts carried a cost in terms of

With the ROWE program, employees do not have to tell anyone where they are going or why.

taking the afternoon off to go to a baseball game, the rules say that no one is allowed to make muttering comments about the employee's work ethic. As one might anticipate, morale was boosted by ROWE. In addition, productivity increased as well. What is key to the success of a ROWEing program is that it applied to everyone, which includes assistants, secretaries,

morale. Therefore, she implemented the ultimate in flexible work schedules where everyone, even the receptionist, takes part. She calls the program ROWE for short. The flexible schedule's full name is "results only work environment." ROWEing is a new way of managing. Employees do not have to tell anyone where they are going or why. If an employee chooses to share the fact that he or she is

receptionists, and the managers and the boss. There is no two-tiered system here because it divides people and creates jealousy. The keys to successful ROWEing are to set measurable goals, to eradicate toxic language, and for the leaders to set positive examples.

SOURCE: S. Westcott, "Beyond Flextime: Trashing the Workweek," *Inc.* (August 2008): 30–31.

Internet access and online meeting software such as WebEx make it possible for employees to participate in meetings anywhere at any time.

As forces for change, new technologies are a double-edged sword that can be used to improve job performance or to create stress. On the positive side, modern technologies are helping to revolutionize the way jobs are designed and the way work gets done. The *virtual office* is a mobile platform of computer, telecommunication, and information technology and services that allows mobile workforce members to conduct business virtually anywhere, anytime, globally. While virtual offices have benefits, they may also lead to a lack of social connection or to technostress.

Technostress is stress caused by new and advancing technologies in the workplace, most often information technologies.[73] For example, the widespread use of electronic bulletin boards as a forum for rumors of layoffs may cause feelings of uncertainty and anxiety—technostress. However, the same electronic bulletin boards can be an important source of information and thus *reduce* uncertainty for workers.

New information technologies enable organizations to monitor employee work performance, even when the employee is not aware of the monitoring.[74] These new technologies also allow organizations to tie pay to performance because performance is electronically monitored.[75] Three guidelines can help make electronic workplace monitoring, especially of performance, less distressful. First, workers should participate in the introduction of the monitoring system. Second, performance standards should be seen as fair. Third, performance records should be used to improve performance, not to punish the performer. In the extreme, new technologies that allow for virtual work in remote locations take employees beyond such monitoring.[76]

Task Revision

A new concept in the design of work is *task revision*.[77] Task revision is an innovative way to modify an incorrectly specified role or job. Task revision assumes that organizational roles and job expectations may be correctly or incorrectly defined. Furthermore, a person's behavior in a work role has very different performance consequences depending on whether the role is correctly or incorrectly defined. Table 14.3 sets out the performance consequences of three categories of role behaviors based on the definition of the role or job. As indicated in the table, standard role behavior leads to good performance if the role is correctly defined, and it leads to poor performance if the role is incorrectly defined. These performances go to the extreme when incumbents exhibit extreme behavior in their jobs.[78] Going to extremes leads one to exceed expectations and display extraordinary behavior (extrarole behavior); this results in either excellent or poor performance, depending on the accuracy of the defined role.

virtual office

A mobile platform of computer, telecommunication, and information technology and services.

technostress

The stress caused by new and advancing technologies in the workplace.

task revision

The modification of incorrectly specified roles or jobs.

TABLE

14.3   Performance Consequences of Role Behaviors

Role Characteristics	Standard Role Behavior (Meets Expectations)	Extra Role Behavior (Goes Beyond Expectations)	Counter-Role Behavior (Differs From Expected)
Correctly specified role	Ordinary good performance	Excellent performance (organizational citizenship and prosocial behavior)	Poor performance (deviance, dissent, and grievance)
Incorrectly specified role	Poor performance (bureaucratic behavior)	Very poor performance (bureaucratic zeal)	Excellent performance (task revision and redirection, role innovation)

SOURCE: Republished with permission of Academy of Management, PO Box 3020, Briar Cliff Manor, NY 10510-8020. "Task Revision: A Neglected Form of Work Performance," (Table), R. M. Staw & R. D. Boettger, *Academy of Management Journal*, 1990, Vol. 33. Reproduced by permission of the publisher via Copyright Clearance Center, Inc.

Counter-role behavior is when the incumbent acts contrary to the expectations of the role or exhibits deviant behavior. This is a problem if the role is correctly defined. For example, poor performance occurred on a hospital ward when the nursing supervisor failed to check the administration of all medications for the nurses she was supervising, resulting in one near fatality because a patient was not given required medication by a charge nurse. The nursing supervisor exhibited counter-role behavior in believing she could simply trust the nurses and did not have to double-check their actions. The omission was caught on the next shift. When a role or task is correctly defined, such as the task of double-checking medication administration by nurses, the counter-role behavior leads to poor performance.

Task revision is counter-role behavior in an incorrectly specified role and is a useful way to correct the problem in the role specification (see Table 14.3). Task revision is a form of role innovation that modifies the job to achieve a better performance. Task revision is the basis for long-term adaptation when the current specifications of a job are no longer applicable.[79] For example, the traditional role for a surgeon is to complete surgical procedures in an accurate and efficient manner. Based on this definition, socio-emotional caregiving is counter-role behavior on the part of the surgeon. However, if the traditional role were to be labeled incorrect, the surgeon's task revision through socio-emotional caregiving would be viewed as leading to much better medical care for patients. In all, job analyses should include tasks that are relevant in today's business environment.[80]

Skill Development

Problems in work system design are often seen as the source of frustration for those dealing with technostress.[81] However, system and technical problems are not the only sources of technostress in new information technologies. Some experts see a growing gap between the skills demanded by new technologies and the skills possessed by employees in jobs using these technologies.[82] Although technical skills are important and are emphasized in many training programs, the largest sector of the economy is actually service oriented, and service jobs require interpersonal skills. Managers also need a wide range of nontechnical skills to be effective in their work.[83] Therefore, any discussion of jobs and the design of work must recognize the importance of incumbent skills and abilities to meet the demands of the work. Organizations must consider the talents and skills of their employees when they engage in job design efforts. The two issues of employee skill development and job design are interrelated.

MANAGERIAL IMPLICATIONS: THE CHANGING NATURE OF WORK

Work is an important aspect of a healthy life. The two central needs in human nature are to engage in productive work and to form healthy relationships with others. Work means different things to different ethnic and national groups. Therefore, job design efforts must be sensitive to cultural values and beliefs.

In crafting work tasks and assignments, managers should make an effort to fit the jobs to the people who are doing them. There are no universally accepted ways to design work, and early efforts to find them have been replaced by a number of alternatives. Early approaches to job design were valuable for manufacturing and administrative jobs of the mid-1900s. Now, however, the changing nature of work in the United States and the Americans with Disabilities Act (ADA) challenge managers to find new ways to define work and design jobs.

counter-role behavior
Deviant behavior in either a correctly or incorrectly defined job or role.

The distinguishing feature of job design in the foreseeable future is flexibility. Dramatic global, economic, and organizational changes dictate that managers be flexible in the design of work in their organizations. Jobs must be designed to fit the larger organizational structures discussed in Chapter 15. Organizations must ask, does the job support the organization's mission? Employees must ask, does the job meet my short- and long-term needs?

Technology is one of the distinguishing features of the modern workplace. Advances in information, mechanical, and computer technology are transforming work into a highly scientific endeavor demanding employees who are highly educated, knowledgeable workers. American workers can expect these technological advances to continue during their lifetimes and should expect to meet the challenge through continuous skill development and enhancement.

Diversity Dialogue

Making a Way for the Disabled Worker

When twenty-seven-year-old Natasha Frechette learned that she had multiple sclerosis, she wondered whether she would not only need someone to take care of her but whether she would be able to keep her data manager job at the small research firm where she worked. After all, the disease with which Frechette was diagnosed could lead to numbness, blindness, and eventual paralysis. Not to mention she would need to take time off for physical and occupational therapy.

In a related story, Joel Boswell could no longer work as a mechanic at United Airlines after he was treated for a brain tumor. The EEOC alleged in its class-action lawsuit against the airline that rather than hire Boswell for other jobs for which he was qualified, United placed him on involuntary leave until he retired. According to the EEOC attorney, "They [disabled workers] shouldn't have to be competing with everybody else. If they can do these jobs they should try to work out an accommodation with the disabled worker."

Frechette and Boswell are not alone. Millions of U.S. workers grapple with similar issues. In fact, over 7.4 million workers received Social Security Administration (SSA) disability benefits in 2008. Many of these workers suffer with serious or chronic illnesses that interfere with their ability to perform the work that bring

so much meaning to their lives. Yet, many disabled employees do not let their employers know for fear of being perceived as a cop-out or of being discriminated against. Failure to disclose one's illness, regardless of the reason, is risky. First, employers could mistake disability-related behaviors as dysfunctional behavior. For example, career coach Rosalind Joffe tells of client who, by not disclosing his illness to his employer, was accused of being a drug abuser. Most importantly, employers won't know if and in what ways to adjust the disabled employee's work if they don't know that an adjustment is required.

1. As a manager, how would you balance a disabled employee's needs for a work adjustment to your need to design jobs that meet organizational performance goals?
2. Do you believe United Airlines was justified in placing Boswell on involuntary leave? Explain.

SOURCES: L. Alderman, "Protecting Your Job While Coping With a Chronic Illness," *New York Times* (June 20, 2009); "Number of disabled workers and their dependents receiving benefits on December 31, 1970–2008," http://www.ssa.gov/OACT/STATS/DIbenies.html#foot, accessed July 25, 2005; "EEOC Sues United Over Handling of Disabled Workers," *Associated Press* (June 4, 2009), http://abcnews.go.com/Business/wireStory?id=7758295, accessed July 25, 2005.

LOOKING BACK: CARMAX

Well-Trained Employees for Reshuffled Jobs

Courtesy of CarMax

One of the keys to excellent job performance is exceptional training. CarMax offers exceptional training and is recognized for its programs. In 2008, *Training Magazine* named CarMax one of the top 1,245 training organizations in the country. Exceptional training can lead to benefits beyond excellent job performance. One such benefit is very engaged employees. In addition, the company experiences really low turnover for employee groups that are paid almost completely on commission, which applies to CarMax's sales consultant group of employees. Sales consultants can earn president's club recognition by selling more than fifteen cars each month. The result is a higher fixed commission per car, which is more than entry sales consultants are paid. Training and incentives lead to excellent employee retention.

Sales consultants who earn president's club level have less than a 20 percent annualized turnover rate, which is pretty strong in the commissioned area. This does create opportunities on a regular basis for new sales consultants to be hired and jobs to be filled. As a business strategy, CarMax did suspend store growth during the economic turmoil of the recession. Prior to that, the company had grown 15 percent annually for six consecutive years. Suspending store growth due to the huge drop-off in sales did not mean that all hiring was suspended with the company. Thus, the sales consultant turnover does create opportunities within the company for new hires and does keep up the demand for exceptional training to keep the company healthy.

CarMax found that the difficult economy changed some of its business needs and the jobs that support those business needs.[84] About 1 percent of the company's 13,000 jobs were affected by the changes. As the company shifted operations in response to the economy, some jobs were no longer necessary. As a result, 130 employees changed roles as the company reshuffled jobs at its headquarters and at some of its 100 stores. CarMax expected there to be jobs for every employee who chose to move into a new role because there were enough open jobs for that to happen. The open jobs into which employees could choose to move were full-time positions with benefits. Employees who decided not to take new jobs would be entitled to severance pay. Meeting business needs and employee needs at the same time can be a challenge for leaders in difficult economic times. CarMax aims to be an employer who is fair to all concerned.

Chapter Summary

1. Different countries have different preferences for one or more of six distinct patterns of defining work.

2. Scientific management, job enlargement/job rotation, job enrichment, and the job characteristics theory are traditional American approaches to the design of work and the management of workforce diversity.

3. The social information-processing (SIP) model suggests that information from others and the social context are important in a job.

4. Ergonomics and the interdisciplinary framework draw on engineering, psychology, and biology in considering the advantages and disadvantages of job and work design efforts.

5. The cultural values and social organizations in Japan, Germany, and Scandinavia lead to unique approaches to the design of work.

6. Control, uncertainty, conflict, and job/task demands are important job design parameters to consider when designing work for the well-being of the workers.

7. Telecommuting, alternative work patterns, technostress, task revision, and skill development are emerging issues in the design of work and the use of information technology.

Key Terms

anthropocentric (p. 499)
counter-role behavior (p. 505)
cross-training (p. 489)
engagement (p. 495)
ergonomics (p. 496)
flextime (p. 502)
job (p. 484)
Job Characteristics Model (p. 490)

Job Diagnostic Survey (JDS) (p. 490)
job enlargement (p. 488)
job enrichment (p. 489)
job rotation (p. 488)
job sharing (p. 502)
lean production (p. 498)
meaning of work (p. 484)
social information-processing (SIP) model (p. 495)

sociotechnical systems (STS) (p. 498)
task revision (p. 504)
technocentric (p. 498)
technostress (p. 504)
virtual office (p. 504)
work (p. 484)
work simplification (p. 487)

Review Questions

1. Define a job in its organizational context.

2. Describe six patterns of working that have been studied in different countries.

3. Describe four traditional approaches to the design of work in America.

4. Identify and define the five core job dimensions and the three critical psychological states in the Job Characteristics Model.

5. What are the salient features of the social information-processing (SIP) model of job design?

6. List the positive and negative outcomes of the four job design approaches considered by the interdisciplinary framework.

7. How do the Japanese, German, and Scandinavian approaches to work differ from one another and from the American approach?

8. Describe the key job design parameters considered when examining the effects of work design on health and well-being.

9. What are five emerging issues in jobs and the design of work?

Discussion and Communication Questions

1. Is there ever one best way to design a particular job?

2. What should managers learn from the traditional approaches to the design of work used in the United States?

3. It is possible for American companies to apply approaches to the design of work that were developed in other countries?

4. What is the most important emerging issue in the design of work?

5. *(communication question)* Read about new approaches to jobs, such as job sharing. Prepare a memo comparing what you have learned from your reading with one or more approaches to job design discussed in the chapter. What changes in approaches to jobs and job design do you notice from this comparison?

6. *(communication question)* Interview an employee in your organization or another organization and develop an oral presentation about how his or her job could be enriched. Make sure you ask questions about all aspects of the employee's work (e.g., what specific tasks are done and with whom the employee interacts on the job).

7. *(communication question)* Based on the materials in the chapter, prepare a memo detailing the advantages and disadvantages of flextime job arrangements. In a second part of the memo, identify the specific conditions and characteristics required for a successful flextime program. Would you like to work under a flextime arrangement?

Ethical Dilemma

Jen Gracie is a systems analyst for Lensher & Maximoff, a large IT consulting firm. Jen's job is to manage the knowledge dissemination of any system updates to everyone in her region. This is a difficult and demanding job. Jen must be responsive to all consultants in her area working on any project in which a change or adjustment in a system would have an impact. Jen is ultimately responsible that everyone in her region is fully knowable about all new systems information and she is great at accomplishing this.

Carson Xander, regional manager and Jen's direct supervisor, is aware that Jen's job is extremely demanding. Jen is the fourth person to hold this job in the ten years Carson has been with the company. The job just takes its toll on the person. It is a 24/7 kind of job. There is no such thing as a guaranteed day off. Jen must always be available by phone and, no matter what the day or time, ready to respond to a problem. The worst part is that there are always problems. The compensation is good but no matter how much money the position pays, money cannot prevent the burnout that every person in the position has experienced.

Carson has considered many times how he could best redesign the position. No question if the job was shared by several people, it would be much easier to handle. If the region was split into two and an additional person hired, the job would be better. However, the ability for everyone in his region to always be equally aware of new developments would be jeopardized. There would be another level of coordination between the section managers that would definitely slow down the process. That was going to be difficult to sell to upper management given that Lensher & Mazimoff's promise to their clients is the ultimate in timely service.

Carson likes Jen a lot. She is an incredible worker and done everything asked of her. Carson is already seeing Jen showing the negative effects of the stress of the job and is very concerned about her. He wants to do something to help but knows the negative impact changing the job will have on company.

Questions:

1. Using consequential, rule-based and character theories, evaluate Carson's options.

2. What should Carson do? Why?

Experiential Exercises

14.1 Chaos and the Manager's Job

Managers' jobs are increasingly chaotic as a result of high rates of change, uncertainty, and turbulence. Some managers thrive on change and chaos, but others have a difficult time responding to high rates of change and uncertainty in a positive manner. This questionnaire gives you an opportunity to evaluate how you would react to a manager's job that is rather chaotic.

Exercise Schedule

1. Preparation (preclass)
Complete the questionnaire.

2. Individual Scoring
Give yourself 4 points for each A, 3 points for each B, 2 points for each C, 1 point for each D, and 0 points for each E. Compute the total, divide by 24, and round to one decimal place.

3. Group Discussion
Your instructor may have you discuss your scores in groups of six students. The higher your score, the more you respond positively to change and chaos; the lower your score, the more difficulty you would have responding to this manager's job in a positive manner. In addition, answer the following questions.

a. If you could redesign this manager's job, what are the two or three aspects of the job that you would change first?

b. What are the two or three aspects of the job that you would feel no need to change?

SOURCE: "Chaos and the Manager's Job" in D. Marcic, "Option B. Quality and the New Management Paradigm," *Organizational Behavior: Experiences and Cases*, 4th ed. (Minneapolis/St. Paul: West Publishing, 1995), 296–297. Reprinted by permission.

A Manager's Job

Listed below are some statements a thirty-seven-year-old manager made about his job at a large and successful corporation. If your job had these characteristics, how would you react to them? After each statement are five letters, A–E. Circle the letter that best describes how you would react according to the following scale:

A. I would enjoy this very much; it's completely acceptable.

B. This would be enjoyable and acceptable most of the time.

C. I'd have no reaction one way or another, or it would be about equally enjoyable and unpleasant.

D. This feature would be somewhat unpleasant for me.

E. This feature would be very unpleasant for me.

1. I regularly spend 30–40 percent of my time in meetings.   A B C D E

2. A year and a half ago, my job did not exist, and I have been essentially inventing it as I go along.   A B C D E

3. The responsibilities I either assume or am assigned consistently exceed the authority I have for discharging them.   A B C D E

4. At any given moment in my job, I average about a dozen phone calls to be returned.   A B C D E

5. There seems to be very little relation in my job between the quality of my performance and my actual pay and fringe benefits.   A B C D E

6. I need about two weeks of management training a year to stay current in my job.   A B C D E

7. Because we have very effective equal employment opportunity in my company and because it is thoroughly multinational, my job consistently brings me into close contact at a professional level with people of many races, ethnic groups, and nationalities and of both sexes.   A B C D E

8. There is no objective way to measure my effectiveness.   A B C D E

9. I report to three different bosses for different aspects of my job, and each has an equal say in my performance appraisal.   A B C D E

10. On average, about a third of my time is spent dealing with unexpected emergencies that force all scheduled work to be postponed.   A B C D E

11. When I need to meet with the people who report to me, it takes my secretary most of a day to find a time when we are all available, and even then I have yet to have a meeting where everyone is present for the entire meeting.   A B C D E

12. The college degree I earned in preparation for this type of work is now obsolete, and I probably should return for another degree.   A B C D E

13. My job requires that I absorb about 100–200 pages a week of technical material.   A B C D E

14. I am out of town overnight at least one night a week.   A B C D E

15. My department is so interdependent with several other departments in the company that all distinctions about which department is responsible for which tasks are quite arbitrary.   A B C D E

16. I will probably get a promotion in about a year to a job in another division that has most of these same characteristics.   A B C D E

17. During the period of my employment here, either the entire company or the division I worked in has been reorganized every year or so.   A B C D E

18. While I face several possible promotions, I have no real career path.   A B C D E

19. While there are several possible promotions I can see ahead of me, I think I have no realistic chance of getting to the top levels of the company.   A B C D E

20. While I have many ideas about how to make things work better, I have no direct influence on either the business policies or the personnel policies that govern my division.   A B C D E

21. My company has recently put in an "assessment center" where I and other managers must go through an extensive battery of psychological tests to assess our potential.   A B C D E

22. My company is a defendant in an antitrust suit, and if the case comes to trial, I will probably have to testify about some decisions that were made a few years ago.   A B C D E

23. Advanced computer and other electronic office technology is continually being introduced into my division, necessitating constant learning on my part.   A B C D E

24. The computer terminal and screen I have in my office can be monitored in my boss's office without my knowledge.   A B C D E

SOURCE: "A Manager's Job" by Peter B. Vaill in *Managing as a Performing Art: New Ideas for a World of Chaotic Change*, 1989. Reprinted by permission of Jossey-Bass Inc., Publishers.

14.2 A Job Redesign Effort

This activity will help you consider ways in which work can be redesigned to improve its impact on people and its benefit to the organization. Consider the following case.

Eddie is a quality control inspector for an automotive manufacturer. His job is to inspect the body, interior, and engine of cars as they roll off the assembly line. Eddie's responsibility is to identify quality problems that either hinder the functioning of these parts of the car or noticeably mar the car's appearance. He is to report the problem so that it can be corrected. Sometimes late in the day, especially on Thursdays and Fridays, Eddie lets assembly problems slip past him. In addition, his back feels sore at the end of the day, and sometimes he is very stiff in the morning. There are times when he is not sure whether he is seeing a serious problem or just a glitch.

As part of a five-person team, your job is to evaluate two alternative approaches to redesigning Eddie's job using theories presented in the chapter. Answer the following questions as a team. Your team should be prepared to present its recommendations to the class as a whole.

Discussion Questions

Your instructor will lead a class discussion of each of the following questions:

1. For this particular job, which are the two best models to use in a redesign effort? Why?

2. Does your team need any additional information before it begins to redesign Eddie's job? If so, what information do you need?

3. Using the two models you chose in Question 1, what would your team specifically recommend to redesign Eddie's job?

BizFlix | Tyler Perry's Daddy's Little Girls

Monty (Idris Elba), a hardworking automobile mechanic, loses custody of his three daughters to his evil ex-wife, Jennifer (Tasha Smith). He begins working as a chauffeur for Julia (Gabriele Union), an upper-class attorney. Their relationship develops both romantically and professionally as she represents him in his court battle. The film twists and turns around Monty's past but closes in an unusual and happy way.

Job Design: Monty the Limousine Driver

This sequence begins with a panning shot of Julia's condominium building. The camera pans down to the Doorman (Steve Coulter) and Monty standing by the limousine. This sequence ends after Julia and Monty arrive at the courthouse. Julia says, "Next time follow my instructions, okay?" Monty responds, "Yes ma'am." as he gets out of the car.

What to Watch for and Ask Yourself

- This chapter opened with a discussion of "job" and "work." Apply that discussion to the film sequence. Include in your analysis the pattern of social interaction between Monty and Julia.

- Apply the job characteristics theory to the film sequence. What is the level of each core job characteristic for Monty's job? Calculate his Motivating Potential Score using the formula that appears earlier in this chapter.

- Estimate the levels of each critical psychological state for Monty. Use Figure 14.1, "The Job Characteristics Model," as a guide to your estimate. Use "low," "middle," or "high" for your estimate.

Workplace Video | Maine Media Workshops—Building a Contingent Workforce

Since 1973, Maine Media Workshops has seen some of the most talented filmmakers, photographers, and writers pass through its doors. The program began as a summer camp for amateur and professional artists wanting to hone their skills along the beautiful coast of Rockport, Maine. Over the years, the workshops have allowed students to work alongside some of Hollywood's heavy-hitters, including Vilmos Zsigmond (*The Black Dahlia*), Alan Myerson (*Boston Public*), and Gene Wilder (*Willy Wonka & the Chocolate Factory*).

Staff selection is difficult for Maine Media Workshops. From January through November, the organization hires instructors to teach weeklong classes for approximately 500 courses. With the exception of a few full-timers, the organization is staffed with temporary week-to-week instructors. In the time it takes new hires to get their employee handbook and complete W2 forms, most instructors at the Maine Media Workshops have finished their course and are moving on.

Job requirements for workshop instructors are unique. Instructors act as mentors and coaches who dine with students, participate in social events, teach, and discuss assignments and careers. "What makes a good teacher is someone who is generous enough and open enough to share her life, her experience, her career and her knowledge 24/7 with students," said Elizabeth Greenburg, director of education.

Keeping courses staffed requires constant recruitment, and there is no time for training. As a result, the HR department seeks people who, like Elizabeth Greenburg, were once students. That way a new hire already understands what it takes to perform according to the Maine Media Workshops standard.

Surprisingly, compensation is not an issue. Although the Maine Media Workshops pays a fair wage, the real compensation doesn't come in a check. "No one comes here for the money," said Mimi Edmunds, film program manager. "They come here because they love it."

Discussion Questions

1. What is the primary problem the directors have in recruiting instructors to teach at Maine Media Workshops? How might they solve this problem?

2. What is the social information-processing (SIP) model, and how does it relate to course instructor jobs at Maine Media Workshops?

3. Using the Internet, conduct a job analysis for one of the courses at the Maine Media Workshops and create a job posting for that position. Include a job description, qualifications, and a realistic preview of the job.

Case

Alternative Work Arrangements: Possible Solutions for a Plethora of Problems?

Alternative work arrangements—such as compressed work weeks, flexible work schedules, telecommuting, or job sharing, among others—can have positive and negative consequences for employers and/or employees. In general, alternative work arrangements can generate beneficial outcomes, particularly for employers, such as "increased employee retention, loyalty and morale; higher productivity; improved recruiting of highly qualified workers; decreased employee tardiness and unscheduled absences; and maximum use of facilities and equipment."[1] On the employees' side, for example, telecommuting—one type of alternative work arrangement—has favorable effects on perceived autonomy, the resolution of work–family conflicts, job performance, job satisfaction, and the experience of stress; and it does not harm perceived career prospects or the quality of workplace relationships.[2] On the downside, however, are the challenges associated with making these programs work for both employer and employees; handling issues regarding employee training, work monitoring, and performance evaluation; maintaining lines of communication with bosses and coworkers; and changing the attitudes of managers that are uncomfortable with anything other than traditional working arrangements.[3]

On balance the positives seem to outweigh the negatives.[4] "Organizations that offer flexible working arrangements are, and will continue to be, employers of choice. ... Employees consistently rank flexible schedules high on their list of desired benefits; employers who are reluctant to offer these popular perks will find themselves falling short in the bidding wars for talent."[5]

Although alternative work arrangements can be highly beneficial for both employers and employees, we need to ask the question: "What seems to be the underlying factors that are driving the movement toward the increased utilization of alternative work arrangements in many different workplaces?"

One factor reflects the needs and desires of workers. "Many people today are seeking flexibility at work. Parents...may want more time for family. Students hope to fit employment into a busy class schedule. And some people look for work after retirement. Whatever their situation, they're not alone in wanting a job that's a better match for their lives."[6]

Younger workers and those nearing retirement age are two particular segments of the workforce that can be meaningfully targeted by employers offering various alternative work arrangements.

Younger workers are entering the workforce with different expectations than previous generations of workers. Whereas their parents were work-centric, most members of Generations X and Y give priority to their personal lives; or at the very least they desire to balance their work lives and personal lives.[7] Sharif Khan, vice-president of human resources at Microsoft Canada, says, "Gen X and Gen Y are coming into the workplace with the expectation that they're going to be treated as individuals, [who] ... want to be able to fit their life and their work together comfortably, as opposed to focusing on work and dealing with life after the fact."[8]

Another important demographic group in the workforce consists of those individuals nearing retirement. "Baby Boomers are reaching retirement age. While many Boomers may choose to stretch their retirement date based on some combination of lifestyle choice and recent market developments, many are opting for less-demanding positions or reduced workloads."[9] "By 2020, 16 percent of the U.S. population will be age 65 and over, up from 12 percent in 1999. ... Yet leaders of many organizations ignore aging workforce issues despite the potential problems they see coming, and some damage seems likely to occur before the issues receive appropriate attention."[10] "[T]he size of the Baby Boomer demographic group exceeds current graduating classes, and replacing their experience will be a challenge for most firms."[11]

Increasingly, business and governmental organizations are adopting alternative work arrangements because of the condition of the economy. For example, a May 2008 poll conducted by the Society for Human Resource Management indicated that 18 percent of the responding organizations offered telecommuting in order to help employees with rising fuel costs. Four months later, with fuel prices continuing to soar, the percentage of organizations offering the telecommuting option had risen to 40 percent.[12] In October 2008, when gasoline prices were peaking, Ann Bednarz, writing in *Network World*, reported that "[g]as shortages in the Southeast United States are prompting companies to consider expanding their telework programs so employees can conserve fuel. Other options workers are weighing include greater use of carpools and public transit, along with alternative scheduling arrangements such as four-day work weeks."[13]

In addition to the dramatic increase in fuel costs in the summer and autumn of 2008, concerns about global warming and long commutes have fostered interest in alternative arrangements for working remotely.[14] Moreover, two recession-related factors could lead more employees to seek out long-distance telecommuting options for at least part of their time on the job. First, the slow housing market limits people's ability to move to new jobs. Consequently, rather than physically commuting a long distance for a new job, part-time, long-distance telecommuting could be an option. Second, the weak job market that has been caused by the recession appears to be increasing the number of commuter marriages wherein the spouses work in different cities due to economic necessity. Here too, part-time, long-distance telecommuting might be a viable option.[15]

Many nations have experimented successfully with various flexible work programs; and indeed, in some countries laws have been enacted to make alternative work arrangements more accessible to employees.

Although the United States has not enacted such legislation, the demographic and economic changes that are occurring may result in alternative work arrangements laws that "could play an important role in preparing the U.S. economy for the future."[16]

Will the U.S. government and American businesses be adequately prepared to meet future economic challenges, at least in part, by embracing the movement toward increasing use of alternative work arrangements?

Discussion Questions

1. How can employees benefit from alternative work arrangements? How can employers benefit from alternative work arrangements?

2. What are some of the possible negative outcomes for employers and/or employees regarding alternative work arrangements?

3. What types of factors are influencing organizations to consider using alternative work arrangements? Explain how alternative work arrangements can address the problems/issues that are raised by these factors.

4. Should the availability of alternative work arrangements to employees in the United States be mandated by law? Why or why not?

SOURCE: This case was written by Michael K. McCuddy, The Louis S. and Mary L. Morgal Chair of Christian Business Ethics and Professor of Management, College of Business Administration, Valparaiso University.

Organizational Design and Structure

LEARNING OBJECTIVES

After reading this chapter, you should be able to do the following:

1 Define *differentiation* and *integration* as organizational design processes.

2 Discuss six basic design dimensions of an organization.

3 Briefly describe five structural configurations for organizations.

4 Describe four contextual variables for an organization.

5 Explain the four forces reshaping organizations.

6 Discuss emerging organizational structures.

7 Identify two cautions about the effect of organizational structures on people.

Deloitte + Touche office in London.

THINKING AHEAD: DELOITTE

"One Firm" Design, Many Partnerships

Deloitte Touche Tohmatsu (Deloitte) has a single brand name that spans the world. People may think of Deloitte as a global company. The reality is more complex than a "one firm" design.[1] Deloitte is a global network of independent member

firms that provide audit, tax, consulting, and financial advisory services. About 165,000 professionals in 140 countries work for separate member partnerships coordinated under the Deloitte brand. This is true of all of the Big Four: Ernst & Young, PricewaterhouseCoopers, KPMG, and Deloitte. These Big Four are composed of hundreds of firms linked by knowledge, economics, and brand, each with one coordinating firm. While Ernst & Young and PricewaterhouseCoopers have their coordinating firms in the United Kingdom, Deloitte has its coordinating firms in Switzerland. The individual firms within the Deloitte structure are owned by partners who become co-owners or shareholders as they go on to become senior members of the organization.

The individual firms within the "one firm" design structure are largely unlimited liability partnerships doing auditing and/or accounting work. Even if some of the individual firms are limited liability companies, the senior members who become shareholders are still designated as partners. This design becomes a double-edged sword when a local affiliate is pulled up for accounting wrongdoing. For instance, PricewaterhouseCoopers will have to face the regulatory and possibly judicial review because an individual firm in India was involved in the Satyam fraud. In addition, because Satyam is listed on the New York Stock Exchange, PricewaterhouseCoopers is open to a Class Action Suit, which is very risky. The power and global reach of size are therefore offset by the risk of financial and material liability.

In Deloitte's case, the organization was the external auditor for General Motors in the United States. Deloitte was dragged into an accounting fraud allegedly perpetrated by the automobile giant and accused of falsely certifying General Motors' accounts, in which the automaker had apparently accelerated the booking of income between 2002 and 2006. This sort of allocation places the entire Deloitte "one firm" at risk unless it can differentiate and isolate the point where the real liability lies, if the accusations prove to be true. Even the hint of scandal can be problematic in a profession in which there is much ambiguity for some many people. What do accounting firms really do? What is the role of auditors? How are they regulated? How are they integrated? These are important questions to answer, especially when wrongdoing is alleged.

Organizational design is the process of constructing and adjusting an organization's structure to achieve its business strategy and goals. The design process begins with the organization's goals. These goals are broken into tasks as the basis for jobs, as discussed in Chapter 14. Jobs are grouped into departments, and departments are linked to form the *organizational structure*. Chapter 15 builds on Chapter 14 by examining the macro structure of the organization in a parallel fashion to the way Chapter 14 examines the micro structure of the organization.

The first section of the chapter examines the design processes of differentiation and integration. The second section addresses the six basic design dimensions of an organization's structure. The organization's structure gives it the form to fulfill its function in the environment. As Louis Sullivan, the father of the skyscraper, said, "Form ever follows function." The third section of the chapter presents five structural configurations for organizations. Based on its mission and purpose, an organization determines the best structural configuration for its unique situation. The fourth section examines size, technology, environment, and strategy and goals as *contextual variables* influencing organizational design. When these variables change, the organization must redesign itself to meet new demands and functions. The fifth section examines five forces shaping organizations today. The final section notes several areas in which managers should be cautious with regard to structural weaknesses and dysfunctional structural constellations.

organizational design
The process of constructing and adjusting an organization's structure to achieve its goals.

organizational structure
The linking of departments and jobs within an organization

contextual variables
A set of characteristics that influence the organization's design processes.

KEY ORGANIZATIONAL DESIGN PROCESSES

Differentiation is the design process of breaking the organizational goals into tasks. Integration is the design process of linking the tasks together to form a structure that supports goal accomplishment. These two processes are the keys to successful organizational design. The organizational structure is designed to prevent chaos through an orderly set of reporting relationships and communication channels. Understanding the key design processes and organizational structure helps a person understand the larger working environment and may prevent confusion in the organization.

The organization chart is the most visible representation of a company's structure and underlying components. Figure 15.1 is the organizational chart for the World Trade Organization (WTO). Most organizations have a series of such charts showing reporting relationships throughout the system. The underlying components are (1) formal lines of authority and responsibility (the organizational structure designates reporting relationships by the way jobs and departments are grouped) and (2) formal systems of communication, coordination, and integration (the organizational structure designates the expected patterns of formal interaction among employees).[2]

Differentiation

Differentiation is the process of deciding how to divide the work in an organization.[3] Differentiation ensures that all essential organizational tasks are assigned to one or more jobs and that the tasks receive the attention they need. Many dimensions of differentiation have been considered in organizations. Lawrence and Lorsch found four dimensions of differentiation in one study: (1) manager's goal orientation, (2) time orientation, (3) interpersonal orientation, and (4) formality of structure.[4] Table 15.1 shows some typical differences in orientation for various functional areas of an organization. Three different forms of differentiation are horizontal, vertical, and spatial.

Horizontal differentiation is the degree of differentiation between organizational subunits and is based on employees' specialized knowledge, education, or training. For example, two university professors who teach specialized subjects in different academic departments are subject to horizontal differentiation. Horizontal differentiation increases with specialization and departmentation.

Specialization refers to the particular grouping of activities performed by an individual.[5] The degree of specialization or the division of labor in the organization gives an indication of how much training is needed, what the scope of a job is, and what individual characteristics are needed for jobholders. Specialization can also lead to the development of a specialized vocabulary, as well as other behavioral norms. As the two college professors specialize in their subjects, abbreviations or acronyms take on unique meanings. For example, OB means "organizational behavior" to a professor of management but "obstetrics" to a professor of medicine.

Usually, the more specialized the jobs within an organization, the more departments are differentiated within that organization (the greater the departmentation). Departmentation can be by function, product, service, client, geography, process, or some combination of these. A large organization may departmentalize its structure using all or most of these methods at different levels of the organization. For example, the U.S. Army Reserve changed its departmentalization from divisional to an operational strategic reserve to an operational force structure.[6]

Vertical differentiation is the difference in authority and responsibility in the organizational hierarchy. Vertical differentiation occurs, for example, between a chief executive and a maintenance supervisor. Tall, narrow organizations have greater vertical differentiation, and flat, wide organizations have less vertical differentiation. The height of the organization is also influenced by level of horizontal

differentiation
The process of deciding how to divide the work in an organization.

15.1 Organization Chart for the World Trade Organization

WTO Structure

All WTO members may participate in all councils, committees, etc., except Appellate Body, Dispute Settlement panels, Textiles Monitoring Body, and plurilateral committees.

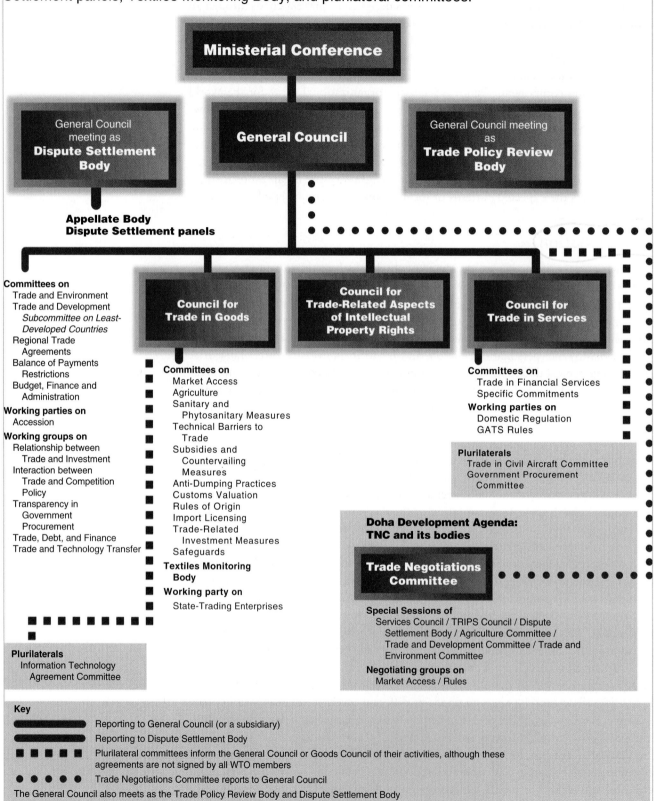

SOURCE: WTO Organization Chart, http://www.wto.org/english/thewto_e/whatis_e/tif_e/org2_e.htm.

15.1 Differentiation between Marketing and Engineering

Basis for Difference	Marketing	Engineering
Goal orientation	Sales volume	Design
Time orientation	Long run	Medium run
Interpersonal orientation	People oriented	Task oriented
Structure	Less formal	More formal

(handwritten note: Good! for final paper)

differentiation and span of control. The span of control refers to and defines the number of subordinates a manager can and should supervise.[7]

Tall structures—those with narrow spans of control—tend to be characterized by closer supervision and tighter controls. In addition, the communication becomes more burdensome, since directives and information must be passed through more layers. The banking industry has often had tall structures. Flat structures—those with wider spans of control—have simpler communication chains and reduced promotion opportunities due to fewer levels of management. Sears is an example of an organization that has gone to a flat structure. With the loss of more than a million middle-management positions, many organizations are now flatter. The degree of vertical differentiation affects organizational effectiveness, but there is no consistent finding that flatter or taller organizations are better.[8] Organizational size, type of jobs, skills and personal characteristics of employees, and degree of freedom must all be considered in determining organizational effectiveness.[9]

Spatial differentiation is the geographic dispersion of an organization's offices, plants, and personnel. A salesperson in New York and one in Portland experience spatial differentiation. An increase in the number of locations increases the complexity of organizational design but may be necessary for organizational goal achievement or organizational protection. For example, if an organization wants to expand into a different country, it may be best to form a separate subsidiary that is partially owned and managed by citizens of that country. Few U.S. citizens think of Shell Oil Company as being a subsidiary of Royal Dutch/Shell Group, a company whose international headquarters is in the Netherlands.

Spatial differentiation may give an organization political and legal advantages in a country because it is identified as a local company. Distance is as important as political and legal issues in making spatial differentiation decisions. For example, a salesperson in Lubbock, Texas, would have a hard time servicing accounts in Beaumont, Texas (over 500 miles away), whereas a salesperson in Delaware might be able to cover all of that state, as well as parts of one or two others.

Horizontal, vertical, and spatial differentiation indicate the amount of width, height, and breadth an organizational structure needs. Just because an organization is highly differentiated along one of these dimensions does not mean it must be highly differentiated along the others. The university environment, for example, is generally characterized by great horizontal differentiation but relatively little vertical and spatial differentiation. A company such as Coca-Cola is characterized by a great deal of all three types of differentiation. The more structurally differentiated an organization is, the more complex it is.[10]

Complexity refers to the number of activities, subunits, or subsystems within the organization. Lawrence and Lorsch suggest that an organization's complexity should mirror the complexity of its environment. As the complexity of an organization increases, its need for mechanisms to link and coordinate the differentiated parts also

The Real World 15.1

Speed, Skill, and Flexibility

Cisco Systems' organizational structure is so complex that it can take fifteen minutes and a whiteboard to fully explain. John Chambers describes the benefits simply: speed, skill, and flexibility. The core structural unit at the heart of Chambers' concept is the management team. Cisco managers, employees, and senior leaders are on more than one management team, actually many more. The existence of multiple teams, councils, boards, and working groups within Cisco creates a web of internal integrating structures that lead to fast decisions by the right people to ensure that the company is agile, with the potential to grow even in difficult times. Manny Rivelo is a senior vice president at Cisco and at one point was embedded in at least fourteen internal teams: three

John Chambers, CEO of Cisco Systems.

© Mark Harmel/Alamy

councils, six boards, and five working groups, all within the company. What led Chambers to this complex organizational structure was the realization that the company's hierarchical structure precluded it from moving quickly into new markets. By restructuring with an emphasis on horizontal integration and cross-functional teaming, Chambers flattened Cisco and increased the company's agility. A key benefit is speed of decision making. Fast decision making is good when the right skilled people are engaged in the process. The team approach through councils, boards, and working groups ensures that the right people are in the right place at the right time to make good decisions, quickly.

SOURCE: M. Kimes, "Cisco Systems Layers It On," *Fortune* 158 (December 8, 2008): 24.

---

increases. If these links do not exist, the departments or differentiated parts of the organization can lose sight of its larger mission, and the organization runs the risk of chaos. Cisco Systems' CEO John Chambers devised a complex organizational model that landed his company on the World's Most Admired Companies list partly for its management prowess, as we see in The Real World 15.1. The process of designing and building linkage and coordination mechanisms is known as *integration*. We saw Deloitte's need for the integration of its many "firms" in the Thinking Ahead feature.

Integration

Integration is the process of coordinating the different parts of an organization. Integration mechanisms are designed to achieve unity among individuals and groups in various jobs, departments, and divisions in the accomplishment of organizational goals and tasks.[11] Integration helps keep the organization in a state of dynamic equilibrium, a condition in which all the parts of the organization are interrelated and balanced.

Vertical linkages are used to integrate activities up and down the organizational chain of command. A variety of structural devices can be used to achieve vertical linkage. These include hierarchical referral, rules and procedures, plans and schedules, positions added to the structure of the organization, and management information systems.[12]

The vertical lines on an organization chart indicate the lines of hierarchical referral up and down the organization. When employees do not know how to solve a problem, they can refer it up the organization for consideration and resolution.

integration
The process of coordinating the different parts of an organization.

Work that needs to be assigned is usually delegated down the chain of command as indicated by the vertical lines.

Rules and procedures, as well as plans and schedules, provide standing information for employees without direct communication. These vertical integrators, such as an employee handbook, communicate through employees standard information or information that they can understand on their own. These integrators allow managers to have wider spans of control, because the managers do not have to inform each employee of what is expected and when it is expected. Vertical integrators encourage managers to use management by exception—to make decisions when employees bring problems up the hierarchy. Military organizations depend heavily on vertical linkages. The army, for example, has a well-defined chain of command. Certain duties are expected to be carried out, and proper paperwork is to be in place. In times of crisis, however, much more information is processed, and the proper paperwork becomes secondary to "getting the job done." Vertical linkages help individuals understand their roles in the organization, especially in times of crisis.

Adding positions to the hierarchy is used as a vertical integrator when a manager becomes overloaded by hierarchical referral or problems arise in the chain of command. Positions such as "assistant to" may be added, as may another level. Adding levels to the hierarchy often reflects growth and increasing complexity. This action tends to reduce the span of control, thus allowing more communication and closer supervision.

Management information systems that are designed to process information up and down the organization also serve as a vertical linkage mechanism. With the advent of computers and network technology, it has become easier for managers and employees to communicate through written reports that are entered into a network and then electronically compiled for managers in the hierarchy. Electronic mail systems allow managers and employees greater access to one another without having to be in the same place at the same time or even attached by telephone. These types of systems make information processing up and down the organization more efficient.

Generally, the taller the organization, the more vertical integration mechanisms are needed. This is because the chains of command and communication are longer. Additional length requires more linkages to minimize the potential for misunderstandings and miscommunications.

Horizontal integration mechanisms provide the communication and coordination that are necessary for links across jobs and departments in the organization. The need for horizontal integration mechanisms increases as the complexity of the organization increases. The horizontal linkages are built into the design of the organization by including liaison roles, task forces, integrator positions, and teams.

A liaison role is created when a person in one department or area of the organization has the responsibility for coordinating with another department (e.g., a liaison between the engineering and production departments). Task forces are temporary committees composed of representatives from multiple departments who assemble to address a specific problem affecting these departments.[13]

A stronger device for integration is to develop a person or department designed to be an integrator. In most organizations, the integrator has a good deal of responsibility but not much authority. Such an individual must have the ability to get people together to resolve differences within the perspective of organizational goals.[14]

The strongest method of horizontal integration is through teams. Horizontal teams cut across existing lines of organizational structure to create new entities that make organizational decisions. An example of this may occur in product development with the formation of a team that includes marketing, research, design, and production personnel. Ford used such a cross-functional team to develop the Taurus automobile, which was designed to regain market share in the United States. The information exchanged by such a product development team should lead to a product that is acceptable to a wider range of organizational groups, as well as to customers.[15]

The use of these linkage mechanisms varies from one organization to another, as well as within areas of the same organization. In general, the flatter the organization, the more necessary are horizontal integration mechanisms.

BASIC DESIGN DIMENSIONS

2 Discuss six basic design dimensions of an organization.

Differentiation, then, is the process of dividing work in the organization, and integration is the process of coordinating work in the organization. From a structural perspective, every manager and organization looks for the best combination of differentiation and integration for accomplishing the goals of the organization. There are many ways to approach this process. One way is to establish a desired level of each structural dimension on a high to low continuum and then develop a structure that meets the desired configuration. These structural dimensions include the following:[16]

1. *Formalization.* The degree to which an employee's role is defined by formal documentation (procedures, job descriptions, manuals, and regulations).

2. *Centralization.* The extent to which decision-making authority has been delegated to lower levels of an organization. An organization is centralized if the decisions are made at the top of the organization and decentralized if decision making is pushed down to lower levels.

3. *Specialization.* The degree to which organizational tasks are subdivided into separate jobs. The division of labor and the degree to which formal job descriptions spell out job requirements indicate the level of specialization in the organization.

4. *Standardization.* The extent to which work activities are described and performed routinely in the same way. Highly standardized organizations have little variation in the defining of jobs.

5. *Complexity.* The number of activities within the organization and the amount of differentiation needed within the organization.

6. *Hierarchy of authority.* The degree of vertical differentiation through reporting relationships and the span of control within the structure of the organization.

An organization that is high on formalization, centralization, specialization, standardization, and complexity and has a tall hierarchy of authority is said to be highly bureaucratic. Bureaucracies are not in themselves bad; however, they are often tainted by abuse and red tape. There are cases, however, where centralized structures can be beneficial. For example, one study found that a more centralized structure is effective for increased job satisfaction when perceptions of interactional and procedural justice are present.[17]

An organization that is on the opposite end of each of these continua is very flexible and loose. Control is very hard to implement and maintain in such an organization, but at certain times such an organization is appropriate. The research and development departments in many organizations are often more flexible than other departments in order to stimulate creativity. An important organizational variable, which is not included in the structural dimensions is trust.

Another approach to the process of accomplishing organizational goals is to describe what is and is not important to the success of the organization rather than worry about specific characteristics. Henry Mintzberg feels that the following questions can guide managers in designing formal structures that fit each organization's unique set of circumstances:[18]

1. How many tasks should a given position in the organization contain, and how specialized should each task be?

formalization
The degree to which the organization has official rules, regulations, and procedures.

centralization
The degree to which decisions are made at the top of the organization.

specialization
The degree to which jobs are narrowly defined and depend on unique expertise.

standardization
The degree to which work activities are accomplished in a routine fashion.

complexity
The degree to which many different types of activities occur in the organization.

hierarchy of authority
The degree of vertical differentiation across levels of management.

2. How standardized should the work content of each position be?

3. What skills, abilities, knowledge, and training should be required for each position?

4. What should be the basis for the grouping of positions within the organization into units, departments, divisions, and so on?

5. How large should each unit be, and what should the span of control be (i.e., how many individuals should report to each manager)?

6. How much standardization should be required in the output of each position?

7. What mechanisms should be established to help individuals in different positions and units adjust to the needs of other individuals?

8. How centralized or decentralized should decision-making power be in the chain of authority? Should most of the decisions be made at the top of the organization (centralized) or be made down in the chain of authority (decentralized)?

The manager who can answer these questions has a good understanding of how the organization should implement the basic structural dimensions. These basic design dimensions act in combination with one another and are not entirely independent characteristics of an organization. You 15.1 gives you (or a friend) an opportunity to consider how decentralized your company is.

FIVE STRUCTURAL CONFIGURATIONS

Differentiation, integration, and the basic design dimensions combine to yield various structural configurations. Very early organization structures were often based on either product or function. The matrix organization structure crossed these two ways of organizing.[19] Mintzberg moved beyond these early approaches and proposed five structural configurations: the simple structure, the machine bureaucracy, the professional bureaucracy, the divisionalized form, and the adhocracy.[20] Table 15.2 summarizes the prime coordinating mechanism, the key part of the organization, and the type of decentralization for each of these structural configurations. The five basic parts of the organization, for Mintzberg, are the upper echelon or strategic apex; the middle level; the operating core, where work is accomplished; the technical staff; and the support staff. Figure 15.2 depicts these five basic parts with a small strategic apex, connected by a flaring middle line to a large, flat operating core. Each configuration affects people in the organization somewhat differently and all organizational structures should support the firm's strategic goals.

3 Briefly describe five structural configurations for organizations.

Simple Structure

The *simple structure* is an organization with little technical and support staff, strong centralization of decision making in the upper echelon, and a minimal middle level. This structure has a minimum of vertical differentiation of authority and minimal formalization. It achieves coordination through direct supervision, often by the chief executive in the upper echelon. An example of a simple structure is a small, independent landscape practice in which one or two landscape architects supervise the vast majority of work with no middle-level managers. Even an organization with as few as thirty people can become dysfunctional as a simple structure after an extended period.

Machine Bureaucracy

The *machine bureaucracy* is an organization with a well-defined technical and support staff differentiated from the line operations of the organization, limited horizontal decentralization of decision making, and a well-defined hierarchy of

simple structure
A centralized form of organization that emphasizes the upper echelon and direct supervision.

machine bureaucracy
A moderately decentralized form of organization that emphasizes the technical staff and standardization of work processes.

You 15.1

How Decentralized Is Your Company?

Decentralization is one of the key design dimensions in an organization. It is closely related to several behavioral dimensions of an organization, such as leadership style, degree of participative decision making, and the nature of power and politics within the organization. In addition, decentralization has been linked to increased safety in organizations.[21]

The following questionnaire allows you to get an idea about how decentralized your organization is. (If you do not have a job, have a friend who does work complete the questionnaire to see how decentralized his or her organization is.) Which level in your organization has the authority to make each of the following eleven decisions? Answer the questionnaire by circling one of the following:

0 = The board of directors makes the decision.
1 = The CEO makes the decision.
2 = The division/functional manager makes the decision.
3 = A subdepartment head makes the decision.
4 = The first-level supervisor makes the decision.
5 = Operators on the shop floor make the decision.

Decision Concerning: | | | **Circle Appropriate Level** | | | |
|---|---|---|---|---|---|
| a. The number of workers required. | 0 | 1 | 2 | 3 | 4 | 5 |
| b. Whether to employ a worker. | 0 | 1 | 2 | 3 | 4 | 5 |
| c. Internal labor disputes. | 0 | 1 | 2 | 3 | 4 | 5 |
| d. Overtime worked at shop level. | 0 | 1 | 2 | 3 | 4 | 5 |
| e. Delivery dates and order priority. | 0 | 1 | 2 | 3 | 4 | 5 |
| f. Production planning. | 0 | 1 | 2 | 3 | 4 | 5 |
| g. Dismissal of a worker. | 0 | 1 | 2 | 3 | 4 | 5 |
| h. Methods of personnel selection. | 0 | 1 | 2 | 3 | 4 | 5 |
| i. Method of work to be used. | 0 | 1 | 2 | 3 | 4 | 5 |
| j. Machinery or equipment to be used. | 0 | 1 | 2 | 3 | 4 | 5 |
| k. Allocation of work among workers. | 0 | 1 | 2 | 3 | 4 | 5 |

Scoring

Add up all your circled numbers.
Total = _____.

The higher your number (e.g., 45 or more), the more decentralized your organization. The lower your number (e.g., 25 or less), the more centralized your organization.

SOURCE: From D. Miller and C. Droge, "Psychological and Traditional Determinants of Structure," *Administrative Science Quarterly* 31 (1986): 558. Reprinted by permission of the *Administrative Science Quarterly*.

authority. The technical staff is powerful in a machine bureaucracy. There is strong formalization through policies, procedures, rules, and regulations. Coordination is achieved through the standardization of work processes. An example of a machine bureaucracy is an automobile assembly plant with routinized operating tasks. The strength of the machine bureaucracy is efficiency of operation in stable, unchanging environments. The weakness of the machine bureaucracy is its slow responsiveness to external changes and to individual employee preferences and ideas.

Structural Configuration	Prime Coordinating Mechanism	Key Part of Organization	Type of Decentralization
Simple structure	Direct supervision	Upper echelon	Centralization
Machine bureaucracy	Standardization of work processes	Technical staff	Limited horizontal decentralization
Professional bureaucracy	Standardization of skills	Operating level	Vertical and horizontal decentralization
Divisionalized form	Standardization of outputs	Middle level	Limited vertical decentralization
Adhocracy	Mutual adjustment	Support staff	Selective decentralization

15.2 Five Structural Configurations of Organizations

SOURCE: From H. Mintzberg, *The Structuring of Organizations*, © 1979, 20. Reprinted by permission of Pearson Education, Inc., Upper Saddle River, NJ.

Professional Bureaucracy

The *professional bureaucracy* emphasizes the expertise of the professionals in the operating core of the organization. The technical and support staffs serve the professionals. There is both vertical and horizontal differentiation in the professional bureaucracy. Coordination is achieved through the standardization of the professionals' skills. Examples of professional bureaucracies are hospitals and universities. The doctors, nurses, and professors are given wide latitude to pursue their work based on professional training and indoctrination through professional training programs. Large accounting firms may fall into the category of professional bureaucracies.

professional bureaucracy
A decentralized form of organization that emphasizes the operating core and standardization of skills.

FIGURE

15.2 Mintzberg's Five Basic Parts of an Organization

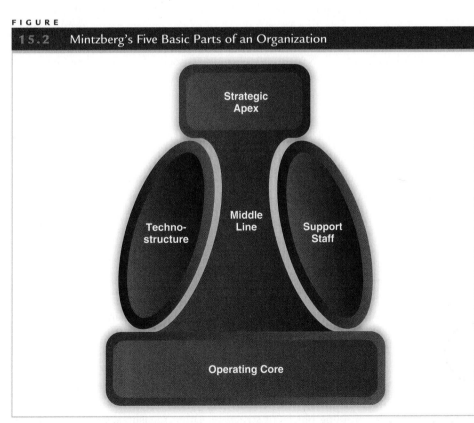

SOURCE: From H. Mintzberg, *The Structuring of Organizations*, © 1979, 20. Reprinted by permission of Pearson Education, Inc., Upper Saddle River, NJ.

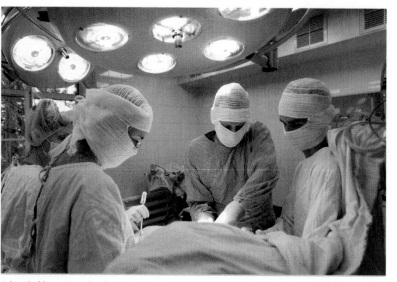

A hospital is an example of a professional bureaucracy. Doctors and nurses are given wide latitude to pursue their work based on professional training.

Divisionalized Form

The *divisionalized form* is a loosely coupled, composite structural configuration.[22] It is a configuration composed of divisions, each of which may have its own structural configuration. Each division is designed to respond to the market in which it operates. There is vertical decentralization from the upper echelon to the middle of the organization, and the middle level of management is the key part of the organization. This form of organization may have one division that is a machine bureaucracy, one that is an adhocracy, and one that is a simple structure. An example of this form of organization is Valero Energy Corporation, headquartered in San Antonio, Texas, with oil refining operations throughout the country. The divisionalized organization uses standardization of outputs as its coordinating mechanism.

Adhocracy

The *adhocracy* is a highly open and decentralized, rather than highly structured, configuration with minimal formalization and order. It is designed to fuse interdisciplinary experts into smoothly functioning ad hoc project teams. Liaison devices are the primary mechanism for integrating the project teams through a process of mutual adjustment. There is a high degree of horizontal specialization based on formal training and expertise. Selective decentralization of the project teams occurs within the adhocracy. An example of this form of organization is the National Aeronautics and Space Administration (NASA), which is composed of many talented experts who work in small teams on a wide range of projects related to America's space agenda. New high-technology businesses also often select an adhocracy design.

CONTEXTUAL VARIABLES

4 Describe four contextual variables for an organization.

The basic design dimensions and the resulting structural configurations play out in the context of the organization's internal and external environments. Four contextual variables influence the success of an organization's design: size, technology, environment, and strategy and goals. These variables provide a manager with key considerations for the right organizational design, although they do not determine the structure. The amount of change in the contextual variables throughout the life of the organization influences the amount of change needed in the basic dimensions of its structure.[23] For example, competitive pressures in many industries have led to outsourcing, one of the greatest shifts in organization structure in a century.[24]

divisionalized form

A moderately decentralized form of organization that emphasizes the middle level and standardization of outputs.

adhocracy

A selectively decentralized form of organization that emphasizes the support staff and mutual adjustment among people.

Size

The total number of employees is the appropriate definition of size when discussing the design of organizational structure. This is logical, because people and their interactions are the building blocks of structure. Other measures, such as net assets, production rates, and total sales, are usually highly correlated with the total number of employees but may not reflect the actual number of interpersonal relationships that are necessary to effectively structure an organization.

Electronic Data Systems (EDS) began as an entrepreneurial venture of H. Ross Perot, Sr. and had grown into an internationally prominent provider of information technology services when it was bought by General Motors Corporation (GM) in the early 1980s. Nearly half of EDS's revenues came from GM at the time of the buyout. The early culture of EDS placed a premium on technical competence, high achievement drive, an entrepreneurial attitude, and a maverick spirit. EDS grew well after the acquisition because GM exploited EDS's technological capability in a coordinated way while protecting EDS' autonomy as an information technology leader.[25] In 1996, it was spun off by GM and became an autonomous company once again.[26] However, following the spin-off, the company has struggled to find a clear focus and identity and has lost two chairmen (Les Alberthal and Dick Brown) in the process.

Although there is some argument over the degree of influence that size has on organizational structure, there is no question that it influences design options. In one study, Meyer found size to be the most important of all variables considered in influencing the organization's structure and design, whereas other researchers argue that the decision to expand the organization's business causes an increase in size as the structure is adjusted to accommodate the planned growth.[27] Downsizing is a planned strategy to reduce the size of an organization, and is often accompanied by related restructuring and revitalization activities.[28] Organizational size is one key predictor—along with industry type, firm diversification strategy, and network effects—of the likelihood of women on corporate boards.[29]

How much influence size exerts on the organization's structure is not as important as the relationship between size and the design dimensions of structure. In other words, when exploring structural alternatives, what should the manager know about designing structures for large and small organizations?

Table 15.3 illustrates the relationships among each of the design dimensions and organizational size. Formalization, specialization, and standardization all tend to be greater in larger organizations because they are necessary to control activities within the organization. For example, larger organizations are more likely to use documentation, rules, written policies and procedures, and detailed job descriptions than to rely on personal observation by the manager. The more relationships that have to be managed by the structure, the more formalized and standardized the processes need to be. McDonald's has several volumes that describe how to make all its products, how to greet customers, how to maintain the facilities, and so on. This level of standardization, formalization, and specialization helps McDonald's maintain the same quality of product no matter where a restaurant is located. By contrast, at a small, locally owned café, your hamburger and french fries may taste a little different every time you visit. This is evidence of a lack of standardization.

TABLE

15.3 Relationship between Organizational Size and Basic Design Dimensions

Basic Design Dimensions	Small Organizations	Large Organizations
Formalization	Less	More
Centralization	High	Low
Specialization	Low	High
Standardization	Low	High
Complexity	Low	High
Hierarchy of authority	Flat	Tall

Formalization and specialization also help a large organization decentralize decision making. Because of the complexity and number of decisions in a large organization, formalization and specialization are used to set parameters for decision making at lower levels. Can you imagine the chaos if the President of the United States, commander-in-chief of all U.S. military forces, had to make operational-level decisions in the war on terrorism? By decentralizing decision making, the larger organization adds horizontal and vertical complexity, but not necessarily spatial complexity. However, it is more common for a large organization to have more geographic dispersion. For example, the San Diego, California County government created a regionalized structure to decentralize decision making, share common resources and competencies, and meet its uniqueclient needs.[30]

Another dimension of design, hierarchy of authority, is related to complexity. As size increases, so does complexity; thus, more levels are added to the hierarchy of authority. This keeps the span of control from getting too large. However, there is a balancing force, because formalization and specialization are added. The more formalized, standardized, and specialized the roles within the organization, the wider the span of control can be.

Although some contend that the future belongs to small, agile organizations, others argue that size continues to be an advantage. To take advantage of size, organizations must become centerless corporations with a global core.[31] These concepts are pioneered by Booz Allen Hamilton based on its worldwide technology and management consulting. The global core provides strategic leadership, helps distribute and provide access to the company's capabilities and knowledge, creates the corporate identity, ensures access to low-cost capital, and exerts control over the enterprise as a whole.

Technology *final paper.*

An organization's technology is an important contextual variable in determining its structure, as noted in Chapter 2.[32] Technology is defined as the tools, techniques, and actions used by an organization to transform inputs into outputs.[33] Technology can be used as well to achieve coordination and integration, as we will see in examining video communication at Deloitte in the Looking Back feature.

The inputs of the organization include human resources, machines, materials, information, and money. The outputs are the products and services the organization offers to the external environment. Determining the relationship between technology and structure is complicated, because different departments may employ very different technologies. As organizations become larger, there is greater variation in technologies across its units. Joan Woodward, Charles Perrow, and James Thompson have developed ways to understand traditional organizational technologies. More work is needed to better understand the contemporary engineering, research and development, and knowledge-based technologies of the information age.

Woodward introduced one of the best-known classification schemes for technology, identifying three types: unit, mass, or process production. Unit technology is small-batch manufacturing technology and, sometimes, made-to-order production. Examples include Smith & Wesson's arms manufacture and the manufacture of fine furniture. Mass technology is large-batch manufacturing technology. Examples include American automotive assembly lines and latex glove production. Process production means continuous production. Examples include oil refining and beer making. Woodward classified unit technology as the least complex, mass technology as more complex, and process technology as the most complex. The more complex the organization's technology, the more complex the administrative component or structure of the organization needs to be.

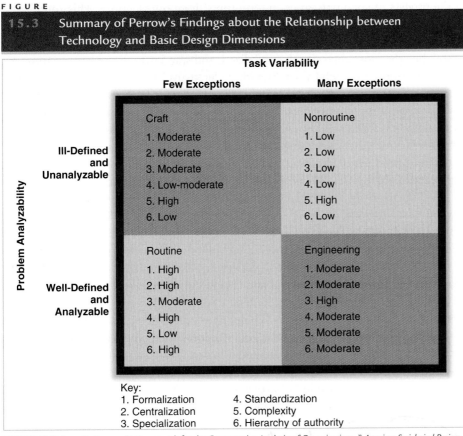

15.3 Summary of Perrow's Findings about the Relationship between Technology and Basic Design Dimensions

Task Variability

	Few Exceptions	Many Exceptions

Problem Analyzability

Ill-Defined and Unanalyzable

Craft
1. Moderate
2. Moderate
3. Moderate
4. Low-moderate
5. High
6. Low

Nonroutine
1. Low
2. Low
3. Low
4. Low
5. High
6. Low

Well-Defined and Analyzable

Routine
1. High
2. High
3. Moderate
4. High
5. Low
6. High

Engineering
1. Moderate
2. Moderate
3. High
4. Moderate
5. Moderate
6. Moderate

Key:
1. Formalization   4. Standardization
2. Centralization   5. Complexity
3. Specialization   6. Hierarchy of authority

SOURCE: Built from C. Perrow, "A Framework for the Comparative Analysis of Organizations," *American Sociological Review* (April 1967): 194–208.

Perrow proposed an alternative to Woodward's scheme based on two variables: task variability and problem analyzability. Task variability considers the number of exceptions encountered in doing the tasks within a job. Problem analyzability examines the types of search procedures followed to find ways to respond to task exceptions. For example, for some exceptions encountered while doing a task, the appropriate response is easy to find. If you are driving down a street and see a sign that says, "Detour—Bridge Out," it is very easy to respond to the task variability. When Thomas Edison was designing the first electric light bulb, however, the problem analyzability was very high for his task.

Perrow went on to identify the four key aspects of structure that could be modified to the technology. These structural elements are (1) the amount of discretion that an individual can exercise to complete a task, (2) the power of groups to control the unit's goals and strategies, (3) the level of interdependence among groups, and (4) the extent to which organizational units coordinate work using either feedback or planning. Figure 15.3 summarizes Perrow's findings about types of technology and basic design dimensions.[34]

Thompson offered yet another view of technology and its relationship to organizational design. This view is based on the concept of *technological interdependence* (i.e., the degree of interrelatedness of the organization's various technological elements) and the pattern of an organization's work flows. Thompson's research suggests that greater technological interdependence leads to greater organizational complexity and that the problems of this greater complexity may be offset by decentralized decision making.[35]

The research of these three early scholars on the influence of technology on organizational design can be combined into one integrating concept—routineness

technological interdependence
The degree of interrelatedness of the organization's various technological elements.

in the process of changing inputs into outputs in an organization. This routineness has a very strong relationship with organizational structure. The more routine and repetitive the tasks of the organization, the higher the degree of formalization that is possible; the more centralized, specialized, and standardized the organization can be; and the more hierarchical levels with wider spans of control that are possible.

Since the work of Woodward, Perrow, and Thompson, however, an important caveat to the discussion of technology has emerged: the advance of information technology has influenced how organizations transform inputs into outputs. The introduction of computer-integrated networks, CAD/CAM systems, and computer-integrated manufacturing has broadened the span of control, flattened the organizational hierarchy, decentralized decision making, and lowered the amount of specialization and standardization.[36] Advances in information technology have allowed for other advances in manufacturing, such as mass customization. Hewlett-Packard has found a key to mass customization in postponing the task of differentiating a product for a specific customer until the latest possible time.[37]

Further, the emergence of new digital technologies and the globalization of the economy are major forces for change. These two forces affect all organizations throughout the economy, ushering in a new economy that has four characteristics. Stanley M. Davis describes these as (1) *any time*—customers can get their goods and services 24/7; (2) *any place*—customers can order from anywhere if they have Internet access; (3) *no matter*—intangibles are adding value to products, such as through digital photography; and (4) *mass customization*—technology and information allow for rapid, responsive customization of products.[38] Thus, digital technology and economic change have resulted in downsizing and restructuring activities in the private sector.

Environment *final*

The third contextual variable for organizational design is *environment*. The environment of an organization is most easily defined as anything outside the boundaries of that organization. Different aspects of the environment have varying degrees of influence on the organization's structure. In one study of 318 CEOs between 1996 and 2000, strategic decision speed was found to moderate the relationship between the environment and the organization structure and performance.[39] For example, in response to the 9/11 terrorist attack on the World Trade Center, President George W. Bush acted swiftly to restructure the U.S. federal government and create the Department of Homeland Security. The general environment includes all conditions that may have an impact on the organization. These conditions could include economic factors, political considerations, ecological changes, sociocultural demands, and governmental regulation.

Task Environment When aspects of the general environment become more focused in areas of direct interest to the organization, those aspects become part of the *task environment*, or specific environment. The task environment is that part of the environment that is directly relevant to the organization. Typically, it includes stakeholders such as unions, customers, suppliers, competitors, government regulatory agencies, and trade associations.

The domain of the organization refers to the area the organization claims for itself with respect to how it fits into its relevant environments. The domain is particularly important because it is defined by the organization, and it influences how the organization perceives and acts within its environments.[40] For example, Wal-Mart and Neiman Marcus both sell clothing apparel, but their domains are very different.

The organization's perceptions of its environment and the actual environment may not be the same. The environment that the manager perceives is the one that the organization responds to and organizes for.[41] Therefore, two organizations may be in relatively

environment
Anything outside the boundaries of an organization.

task environment
The elements of an organization's environment that are related to its goal attainment.

the same environment from an objective standpoint, but if the managers perceive differences, the organizations may enact very different structures to deal with this same environment. For example, one company may decentralize and use monetary incentives for managers that lead it to be competitively aggressive, while another company may centralize and use incentives for managers that lead it to be less intense in its rivalry.[42]

Environmental Uncertainty The perception of *environmental uncertainty* or the perception of the lack of it is how the contextual variable of environment most influences organizational design. Some organizations have relatively static environments with little uncertainty, whereas others are so dynamic that no one is sure what tomorrow may bring. Binney & Smith, for example, has made relatively the same product for more than fifty years with very few changes in the design or packaging. The environment for its Crayola products is relatively static. In fact, customers rebelled when the company tried to get rid of some old colors and add new ones. By contrast, in the last two decades, competitors in the airline industry have encountered deregulation, mergers, bankruptcies, safety changes, changes in cost and price structures, changes in customer and employee demographics, and changes in global competition. In such uncertain conditions, fast-response organizations must use expertise coordination practices to ensure that distributed expertise is managed and applied in a timely manner.[43]

The amount of uncertainty in the environment influences the structural dimensions. Burns and Stalker labeled two structural extremes that are appropriate for the extremes of environmental uncertainty—*mechanistic structure* and *organic structure*.[44] Table 15.4 compares the structural dimensions of these two extremes. The mechanistic and organic structures are opposite ends of a continuum of organizational design possibilities. Although the general premise of environmental uncertainty and structural dimensions has been upheld by research, the organization must make adjustments for the realities of its perceived environment when designing its structure.[45] Some research suggests that the type of structure, either mechanistic or organic, depends on a manager's level of organizational design experience and formal training.[46]

The question for those trying to design organizational structures is how to determine environmental uncertainty. Dess and Beard defined three dimensions of environment that should be measured in assessing the degree of uncertainty: capacity, volatility, and complexity.[47] The *capacity* of the environment reflects the abundance or scarcity of resources. If resources abound, the environment supports expansion, mistakes, or both. By contrast, in times of scarcity, the environment demands survival of the fittest. *Volatility* is the degree of instability. The airline industry is in a volatile environment. This makes it difficult for managers to know what needs to be done. The *complexity* of the environment refers to the differences and variability among environmental elements.

TABLE 15.4 Mechanistic and Organic Organizational Forms

Basic Design Dimensions	Mechanistic	Organic
Formalization	High	Low
Centralization	High	Low
Specialization	High	Low
Standardization	High	Low
Complexity	Low	High
Hierarchy of authority	Strong, tall	Weak, flat

environmental uncertainty
The amount and rate of change in the organization's environment.

mechanistic structure
An organizational design that emphasizes structured activities, specialized tasks, and centralized decision making.

organic structure
An organizational design that emphasizes teamwork, open communication, and decentralized decision making.

If the organization's environment is uncertain, dynamic, and complex and resources are scarce, the manager needs an organic structure that is better able to adapt to its environment. Such a structure allows the manager to monitor the environment from a number of internal perspectives, thus helping the organization maintain flexibility in responding to environmental changes.[48]

Strategy and Goals

The fourth contextual variable that influences how the design dimensions of structure should be enacted is the strategies and goals of the organization. Strategies and goals provide legitimacy to the organization, as well as employee direction, decision guidelines, and criteria for performance.[49] In addition, they help the organization fit into its environment. The Science feature explores a study designed to examine whether strategy determines structure or structure determines strategy.

As more understanding of the contextual influence of strategies and goals has developed, several strategic dimensions that influence structure have been defined. One of these definitions was put forth by Danny Miller.[50] His framework for these strategic dimensions and their implications for organizational structure are shown in Table 15.5. Though strategic orientation influences organizational performance, most firms implement a mixed structural form to help themselves adapt to market changes.[51]

For example, when Apple Computer introduced personal computers to the market, its strategies were very innovative. The structure of the organization was relatively flat and very informal. Apple had Friday afternoon beer and popcorn discussion sessions, and eccentric behavior was easily accepted. As the personal computer market became more competitive, however, the structure of Apple changed to help it differentiate its products and to help control costs. The innovative strategies

Science

Strategy and Structure

The classic argument is that strategy precedes structure because an increase in diversification requires a new and more decentralized structure, often called the multidivisional form of structure. There is a long line of research supporting this "structure follows strategy" thesis. There are researchers with alternative perspectives and some argue that "strategy follows structure," just the reverse of the classic argument. A key argument against the strategy determines structure thesis is that the business environment is changed so much over several decades that a structure determines strategy thesis is at least equally viable. This research tested both theses over a ten-year period. Corporate strategy was measured using a scale that discriminated businesses as a single business, a dominant business, or a diversified

business. The organization structure was measured as a functional, a holding, a product divisional, or a geographic divisional company. The study was conducted in a new context (Spain) and during a new time (1993–2003). The results supported the classic thesis that strategy precedes structure yet found support too for the structure precedes strategy alternative perspective. This suggests that there is a dynamic, interactive effect between the strategy and the structure of an organization. While globalization and technological changes have led to new organizational forms, the classic strategy determines structure thesis is alive and well.

SOURCE: J. I. Galan and M. J. Sanchez-Bueno, "The Continuing Validity of the Strategy-Structure Nexus: New Findings, 1993–2003," *Strategic Management Journal* 30 (2009): 1234–1243.

15.5 Miller's Integrative Framework of Structural and Strategic Dimensions

Strategic Dimension	Predicted Structural Characteristics
Innovation—to understand and manage new processes and technologies	Low formalization
	Decentralization
	Flat hierarchy
Market differentiation—to specialize in customer preferences	Moderate to high complexity
	Moderate to high formalization
	Moderate centralization
Cost control—to produce standardized products efficiently	High formalization
	High centralization
	High standardization
	Low complexity

SOURCE: D. Miller, "The Structural and Environmental Correlates of Business Strategy," *Strategic Management Journal* 8 (1987): 55–76. Copyright © John Wiley & Sons Limited. Reproduced with permission.

and structures devised by Steve Jobs, one of Apple's founders, were no longer appropriate. The board of directors recruited John Scully, a marketing expert from PepsiCo, to help Apple better compete in the market it had created. In 1996 and 1997, Apple reinvented itself again and brought back Jobs to try to restore its innovative edge. Since his return, Apple has become a major player in the digital music market with its introduction of the iPod, selling over 200,000 units in one quarter.

Limitations exist, however, on how much strategy and goals influence structure. Because the structure of the organization includes the formal information-processing channels in the organization, it stands to reason that the need to change strategies may not be communicated throughout the organization. In such a case, the organization's structure influences its strategic choice. Changing that structure may not unlock value but rather drive up costs and difficulties. Therefore, strategic success may hinge on choosing an organization design that works reasonably well, and then fine-tuning the structure through a strategic system.[52]

The inefficiency of the structure in perceiving environmental changes may even lead to organizational failure. In the airline industry, several carriers failed to adjust quickly enough to deregulation and the highly competitive marketplace. Only those airlines that were generally viewed as lean structures with good information-processing systems have flourished in the turbulent years since deregulation. Examples of how different design dimensions can affect the strategic decision process are listed in Table 15.6.

The four contextual variables—size, technology, environment, and strategy and goals—combine to influence the design process. However, the existing structure of the organization influences how it interprets and reacts to information about each of the variables. Each of the contextual variables has management researchers who claim that it is the most important variable in determining the best structural design. Because of the difficulty in studying the interactions of the four contextual dimensions and the complexity of organizational structures, the argument about which variable is most important continues. What is apparent is that there must be some level of fit between the structure and the contextual dimensions of the organization. The better the fit, the more likely the organization will achieve its short-run goals. In addition, the better the fit, the more likely the organization will

15.6 Examples of How Structure Affects the Strategic Decision Process

Formalization

As the level of formalization increases, so does the probability of the following:

1. The strategic decision process will become reactive to crisis rather than proactive through opportunities.

2. Strategic moves will be incremental and precise.

3. Differentiation in the organization will not be balanced with integrative mechanisms.

4. Only environmental crises that are in areas monitored by the formal organizational systems will be acted upon.

Centralization

As the level of centralization increases, so does the probability of the following:

1. The strategic decision process will be initiated by only a few dominant individuals.

2. The decision process will be goal oriented and rational.

3. The strategic process will be constrained by the limitations of top managers.

Complexity

As the level of complexity increases, so does the probability of the following:

1. The strategic decision process will become more politicized.

2. The organization will find it more difficult to recognize environmental opportunities and threats.

3. The constraints on good decision processes will be multiplied by the limitations of each individual within the organization.

SOURCE: Republished with permission of Academy of Management, PO Box 3020, Briar Cliff Manor, NY 10510–8020. "The Strategic Decision Process and Organizational Structure" (table), J. Fredrickson, *Academy of Management Review* (1986): 284. Reproduced by permission of the publisher via Copyright Clearance Center, Inc.

process information and design appropriate organizational roles for long-term prosperity, as indicated in Figure 15.4.

FORCES RESHAPING ORGANIZATIONS

5 Explain the four forces reshaping organizations.

Managers and researchers traditionally examine organizational design and structure within the framework of basic design dimensions and contextual variables. Several forces reshaping organizations are causing managers to go beyond the traditional frameworks and to examine ways to make organizations more responsive to customer needs. Some of these forces include shorter life cycles within the organization, globalization, and rapid changes in information technology. These forces together increase the demands on process capabilities within the organization and emerging organizational structures. To successfully retain their health and vitality, organizations must function as open systems, as discussed in Chapter 1, that are responsive to their task environment.[53]

Life Cycles in Organizations

Organizations are dynamic entities. As such, they ebb and flow through different stages. Usually, researchers think of these stages as *organizational life cycles*. The total organization has a life cycle that begins at birth, moves through growth and maturity to decline, and possibly experiences revival.[54]

Organizational subunits may have very similar life cycles. Because of changes in technology and product design, many such subunits, especially those that are product based, are experiencing shorter life cycles. Hence, the subunits that compose the organization are changing more rapidly than in the past. These shorter life cycles enable the organization to respond quickly to external demands and changes. In

organizational life cycle
The differing stages of an organization's life from birth to death.

FIGURE

15.4   The Relationship among Key Organizational Design Elements

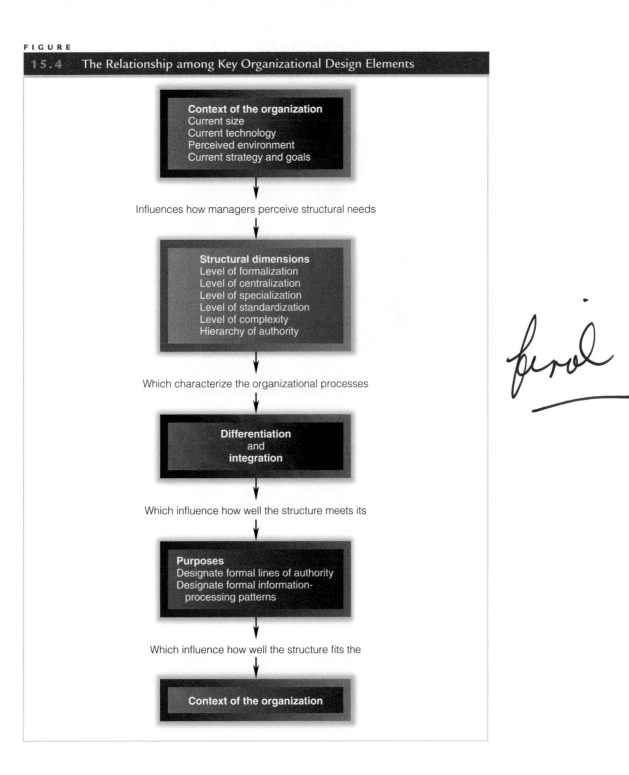

Context of the organization
Current size
Current technology
Perceived environment
Current strategy and goals

Influences how managers perceive structural needs

Structural dimensions
Level of formalization
Level of centralization
Level of specialization
Level of standardization
Level of complexity
Hierarchy of authority

Which characterize the organizational processes

Differentiation
and
integration

Which influence how well the structure meets its

Purposes
Designate formal lines of authority
Designate formal information-
   processing patterns

Which influence how well the structure fits the

Context of the organization

The Real World 15.2, we see that Yahoo! picked up speed with a new CEO through internal structural redesign.

When a new organization or subunit is born, the structure is organic and informal. If the organization or subunit is successful, it grows and matures. This usually leads to formalization, specialization, standardization, complexity, and a more mechanistic structure. If the environment changes, however, the organization must be able to respond. A mechanistic structure is not able to respond to a dynamic environment as well as an organic one. If the organization or subunit does respond, it becomes more organic and revives; if not, it declines and possibly dies. New research suggests temporarily cycling through mechanistic and organic designs in order to meet the often conflicting demands of organizations.[55]

The Real World 15.2

Faster on Its Feet

When Carol Barz assumed the position of CEO at Yahoo!, she inherited an organization with a complex matrix structure. The matrix structure handed multiple executives oversight over many products and new projects. This design had two key limitations, which were slow decision making and little accountability. To make Yahoo! faster on its feet, Barz acted quickly to centralize and flatten the organizational structure.

Yahoo! co-founders Jerry Yang (left) and David Filo.

REUTERS/Court Mast/Yahoo!/Landov

Two additional pluses are a sharper focus on the core business and a greater likeliness of identifying nonperforming groups for divestiture. Barz focuses on the external environment as well as the internal structure. She placed a special emphasis on customer feedback and viewed the flatter organization as a way to increase responsiveness to customers. Structurally, she created a Customer Advocacy Group as a formal mech-

The new structure has all major executives in the company reporting directly to Barz. Previously, too many decentralized product groups in the company led to duplication of engineering and other functional resources. On a cautionary note, too much centralization may stifle innovation. The new, streamlined structure aimed to quicken the pace of decision making while increasing accountability.

anism for ensuring a secure link between Yahoo and this important element of its task environment. The new organizational structure is no guarantee that things will improve for Yahoo and it demands successful execution by the full management team.

SOURCE: R. D. Hof, "Yahoo's Barz Shows Who's Boss" *BusinessWeek Online* 114 (March 2, 2009): 9.

Shorter life cycles put more pressure on the organization to be both flexible and efficient at the same time. Further, as flexible organizations use design to their competitive advantage, discrete organizational life cycles may give way to a kaleidoscope of continuously emerging, efficiency-seeking organizational designs.[56] The manager's challenge in this context becomes one of creating congruency among various organizational design dimensions to fit continuously changing markets and locations. Many fast-growing organizations face critical transition points thorough their life cycles that present growth and structural challenges. The organization should attempt to resolve these before moving on to the next phase of growth and development.[57]

Globalization

Another force that is reshaping organizations is globalization. In other words, organizations operate worldwide rather than in just one country or region. Global corporations can become pitted against sovereign nations when rules and laws conflict across national borders. Globalization makes spatial differentiation even more of a reality for organizations. Besides the obvious geographic differences, there may be deep cultural and value system differences. This adds another type of complexity to the structural design process and necessitates the creation of integrating mechanisms so that people are able to understand and interpret, as well as coordinate with, one another.

The choice of structure for managing an international business is generally based on the following three factors:

1. *The level of vertical differentiation.* A hierarchy of authority must be created that clarifies the responsibilities of both domestic and foreign managers.

2. *The level of horizontal differentiation.* Foreign and domestic operations should be grouped in such a way that the company effectively serves the needs of all customers.

3. *The degree of formalization, specialization, standardization, and centralization.* The global structure must allow decisions to be made in the most appropriate area of the organization. However, controls must be in place that reflects the strategies and goals of the parent firm.[58]

Changes in Information-Processing Technologies

Many of the changes in information-processing technologies have allowed organizations to move into new product and market areas more quickly. However, just as shorter life cycles and globalization have caused new concerns for designing organizational structures, so has the increased availability of advanced information-processing technologies. New business technologies are increasingly changing and shaping future business processes, initiatives, and organizational designs.[59]

Organizational structures are already feeling the impact of advanced information-processing technologies. More integration and coordination are evident, because managers worldwide can be connected through computerized networks. The basic design dimensions have also been affected as follows:

1. The hierarchy of authority has been flattened.

2. The basis of centralization has been changed. Now managers can use technology to acquire more information and make more decisions, or to push information and decision making lower in the hierarchy and thus decrease centralization.

3. Less specialization and standardization are needed, because people using advanced information-processing technologies have more sophisticated jobs that require a broader understanding of how the organization gets work done.[60]

Advances in information processing are leading to knowledge-based organizations, the outlines of which are now only seen dimly. Some of the hallmarks of these new organizational forms are virtual enterprising, dynamic teaming, and knowledge networking.[61] This fifth generation of management thought and practice leads to co-creation of products and services. Future organizations may well be defined by networks of overlapping teams.

Demands on Organizational Processes

Because of the forces reshaping organizations, managers find themselves trying to meet what seem to be conflicting goals: an efficiency orientation that results in on-time delivery *and* a quality orientation that results in customized, high-quality goods or services.[62] Traditionally, managers have seen efficiency and customization as conflicting demands.

To meet these conflicting demands, organizations need to become "dynamically stable."[63] To do so, an organization must have managers who see their roles as architects who clearly understand the "how" of the organizing process. Managers must combine long-term thinking with flexible and quick responses that help improve process and know-how. The organizational structure must help define, at least to some degree, roles for managers who hope to successfully address the conflicting demands of dynamic stability. The differences between the structural roles of managers today and managers of the future are illustrated in Table 15.7. You 15.2 allows you to examine the ways managers in your organization currently operate on the job.

Emerging Organizational Structures

6 Discuss emerging organizational structures.

The demands on managers and on process capabilities place demands on structures. The emphasis in organizations is shifting to organizing around processes. This process orientation emerges from the combination of three streams of applied organizational design: high-performance, self-managed teams; managing processes rather than functions; and the evolution of information technology. Information technology and advanced communication systems have led to internetworking. In a study of 469 firms, deeply internetworked firms were found to be more focused and specialized, less hierarchical, and more engaged in external partnering.[64] Three emerging organizational structures associated with these changes are network organizations, virtual organizations, and the circle organization. Virtuality in organizations is often broken down into four interlocking components: geographic dispersion, electronic interdependence, dynamic structure, and national diversity.[65]

Network organizations are weblike structures that contract some or all of their operating functions to other organizations and then coordinate their activities through managers and other employees at their headquarters. Information technology is the basis for building the weblike structure of the network organization and business unit managers that are essential to the success of these systems. This type of

T A B L E

15.7 Structural Roles of Managers Today versus Managers of the Future
Roles of Managers Today
1. Strictly adhering to boss–employee relationships.
2. Getting things done by giving orders.
3. Carrying messages up and down the hierarchy.
4. Performing a prescribed set of tasks according to a job description.
5. Having a narrow functional focus.
6. Going through channels, one by one by one.
7. Controlling subordinates.
Roles of Future Managers
1. Having hierarchical relationships subordinated to functional and peer relationships.
2. Getting things done by negotiating.
3. Solving problems and making decisions.
4. Creating the job by developing entrepreneurial projects.
5. Having broad cross-functional collaboration.
6. Emphasizing speed and flexibility.
7. Coaching their workers.

SOURCE: Reprinted by permission of the publisher, from *Management Review*, January 1991 © 1991. Thomas R. Horton. American Management Association, New York. All rights reserved.

Managers of Today and the Future

Are the roles for managers in your organization more oriented toward today or toward the future? (If you do not work, think of an organization where you have worked or talk with a friend about managerial roles in his or her organization.)

Step 1. Reread Table 15.7 and check which orientation (today or future) predominates in your organization for each of the following seven characteristics:

	Today	Future
1. Boss–employee relationships.	–––––	–––––
2. Getting work accomplished.	–––––	–––––
3. Messenger versus problem solver.	–––––	–––––
4. Basis for task accomplishment.	–––––	–––––
5. Narrow versus broad functional focus.	–––––	–––––
6. Adherence to channels of authority.	–––––	–––––
7. Controlling versus coaching subordinates.	–––––	–––––

Step 2. Examine the degree of consistency across all seven characteristics. Could the organization make one or two structural changes to achieve a better alignment of the manager's role with today or with the future?

Step 3. Identify one manager in your organization who fits very well into the organization's ideal manager's role. What does this manager do that creates a good person–role fit?

Step 4. Identify one manager in your organization who does not fit very well into the organization's ideal manager's role. What does this manager do that creates a poor person–role fit?

organization has arisen in the age of electronic commerce and brought into practice transaction cost economics, interorganizational collaborations, and strategic alliances. Network organizations can be global in scope.[66]

Virtual organizations are temporary network organizations consisting of independent enterprises. Many dot-coms were virtual organizations designed to come together swiftly to exploit an apparent market opportunity. They may function much like a theatrical troupe that comes together for a "performance."[67] Trust can be a challenge for virtual organizations because it is a complex phenomenon involving ethics, morals, emotions, values, and natural attitudes. However, trust and trustworthiness are important connective issues in virtual environments. Three key ingredients for the development of trust in virtual organizations are technology that can communicate emotion; a sharing of values, vision, and organizational identity; and a high standard of ethics.[68]

The circle organization is a third emerging structure crafted by Harley-Davidson in its drive to achieve teamwork without teams.[69] The company evolved the circle form of organization shown in Figure 15.5. The three organizational parts are those that (1) create demand, (2) produce product, and (3) provide support. As the figure indicates, these three parts are linked by the leadership and strategy council (LSC). The circle organization is a more open system and an organic structure for customer responsiveness. One innovation in this organizational scheme is the "circle coach," who possesses acute communication, listening, and influencing skills that make him or her highly respected by circle members and the company's president.

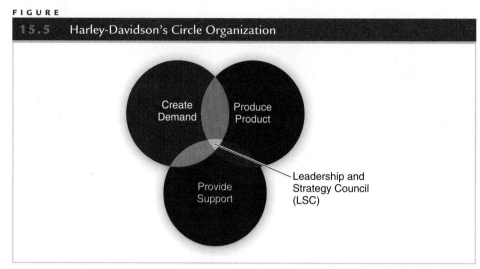

FIGURE

15.5 Harley-Davidson's Circle Organization

CAUTIONARY NOTES ABOUT STRUCTURE

7 Identify two cautions about the effect of organization structures on people.

This chapter has identified the purposes of structure, the processes of organizational design, and the dimensions and contexts that must be considered in structure. In addition, it has looked at forces and trends in organizational design. Two cautionary notes are important for the student of organizational behavior. First, an organizational structure may be weak or deficient. In general, if the structure is out of alignment with its contextual variables, one or more of the following four symptoms appears. First, decision making is delayed because the hierarchy is overloaded and too much information is being funneled through one or two channels. Second, decision making lacks quality because information linkages are not providing the correct information to the right person in the right format. Third, the organization does not respond innovatively to a changing environment, especially when coordinated effort is lacking across departments. Fourth, a great deal of conflict is evident when departments are working against one another rather than working for the strategies and goals of the organization as a whole; the structure is often at fault here.

The second caution is that the personality of the chief executive may adversely affect the structure of the organization.[70] Managers' personal, cognitive biases and political ideologies affect their good judgment and decision making.[71] Five dysfunctional combinations of personality and organization have been identified: the paranoid, the depressive, the dramatic, the compulsive, and the schizoid.[72] Each of these personality–organization constellations can create problems for the people who work in the organization. For example, in a paranoid constellation, people are suspicious of each other, and distrust in working relationships may interfere with effective communication and task accomplishment. For another example, in a depressive constellation, people feel depressed and inhibited in their work activities, which can lead to low levels of productivity and task accomplishment. The chief executive's personality is not always harmful.

MANAGERIAL IMPLICATIONS: FITTING PEOPLE AND STRUCTURES TOGETHER

Organizations are complex social systems composed of numerous interrelated components. They can be complicated to understand. Managers who design, develop, and improve organizations must have a mastery of the basic concepts related to the anatomy and processes of organizational functioning. It is essential for executives at the top to have a clear concept of how the organization can be differentiated and then integrated into a cohesive whole.

People can work better in organizations if they understand how their jobs and departments relate to other jobs and departments in the organization. An understanding of the whole organization enables people to better relate their contribution to its overall mission and to compensate for its structural deficiencies.

Different structural configurations place unique demands on the people who work within them. The diversity of people in work organizations suggests that some people are best suited to a simple structure, others work better in a professional bureaucracy, and still others are most productive in an adhocracy. Organizational structures are not independent of the people who work within them. This is especially true for organizations operating in a global work environment.

Managers must pay attention to the technology of the organization's work, the amount of change occurring in its environment, and the regulatory pressures created by governmental agencies as the managers design effective organizations and subunits to meet emerging international demands and a diverse, multicultural workforce.

Diversity Dialogue

Restructuring for the New Reality—Male Beauty

Once upon a time ... women made up the market for skin and hair care products, cosmetics, and fragrances. Many women now regard these items as a part of their normal routines. Packaged goods manufacturers counted on personal care items becoming a necessity, and female consumers did not disappoint. Women continue to splurge on beauty products despite overall decreases in discretionary income. According to *Male Grooming Trends: Profiting in 2009 and Beyond*, women dominate spending in the personal care industry. But personal care is not just for women anymore. The male grooming market, though not as lucrative as the women's market, is expanding and has great potential for companies that position their products to meet the needs of beauty-conscious men. Proctor & Gamble (P&G) is "making a play" for these men and announced plans in early April 2009 to restructure its beauty and grooming division to "better serve 'Him and Her.'"

Ed Shirley, P&G's global division chief, acknowledges that the company's redesign will be a challenge. After all, P&G does not have a reputation for being the most operationally agile organizations. To the contrary, it has one of the most bureaucratic structures in the

industry. According to Shirley, the new structure "will require a cultural shift" in order to repair its fledgling beauty business unit and reach out to a relatively "ignored" market.

Male beauty is one aspect of the new reality. Men's needs extend beyond a simple haircut, shower, and shave. Men may no longer be satisfied with personal care products and brands that are targeted for women and may relish at the chance to buy male-only products. After all, men have distinct needs and concerns. Companies will have to change the way they do business in order to capitalize on the concerns of today's male. That may mean following in P&G's footsteps and redesigning their operations to fit this new reality.

1. How will P&G's redesign affect their employment recruitment and selection practices?
2. Discuss the contextual variables that led to P&G's restructuring.

SOURCES: E. Byron, "P&G Makes a Bigger Play for Men," *Wall Street Journal* (April 29, 2009): B8; "Male Grooming Continues to Grow," *GCIMagazine.com* (March 11, 2009), http://www.gcimagazine.com/marketstrends/consumers/men/41099052.html, accessed July 26, 2009.

LOOKING BACK: DELOITTE

Connecting Employees, Business Strategy, and Senior Leaders

© Clive Sawyer/Alamy

The Deloitte worldwide network of partnership firms in 140 countries creates a major organizational design and structural challenge for coordination and integration. The differentiation process within Deloitte is accomplished in a relatively straightforward manner based upon independent firms and partnership structure under a single umbrella. The more difficult task in a naturally differentiated structure is one of integration. Deloitte has accomplished these critical tasks of coordination and integration through video.[73] Yes, video! The company has been able to reach more employees and keep its costs down through this new media. Video as a media may be an especially great way to reach the Gen Y generation in the workforce along with the other generations of employees.

Deloitte made a strategic decision to launch a video department in 2005. The company did this for at least three reasons. First, the demand for Web video is increasing. The number of videos viewed by Americans increased 34 percent between 2007 and 2008, from 9.5 billion to 12.7 billion. Second, video can be a critical communication tool that actually saves money. For the fifty videos that Deloitte's video department produced during 2008, they estimated a 300 percent return on investment (ROI), excluding savings on travel. Third, online communication skills have evolved dramatically in the past decade, both in consuming online communication and in producing online communication. Companies may already have professional staff with necessary skills for video communication without fully realizing that they do.

Deloitte's years of successful experience with video as a coordination and integration mechanism has found that employees can be better connected to the business strategy and senior leaders. Employees can be well connected to each other as well. Deloitte has come away with six concrete lessons learned on how to produce engaging videos. First, have one big idea per video so that people come away with one main point. Second, think about what people want and/or need to hear rather than what someone wants to say. Third, tell a story with a beginning, middle, and end because video is linear. Fourth, make the video authentic with sound bites that provide information and stir emotion. Fifth, keep videos short because most people tune out after about one minute. Finally, get metrics from viewers to ensure that the videos are connecting and making the intended positive impact. Ultimately, organization design and structure is about getting lots of people well connected and working together.

Chapter Summary

1. Three basic types of differentiation occur in organizations: horizontal, vertical, and spatial.

2. The greater the complexity of an organization because of its degree of differentiation, the greater the need for integration.

3. Formalization, centralization, specialization, standardization, complexity, and hierarchy of authority are the six basic design dimensions in an organization.

4. Simple structure, machine bureaucracy, professional bureaucracy, divisionalized form, and adhocracy are five structural configurations of an organization.

5. The contextual variables important to organizational design are size, technology, environment, and strategy and goals.

6. Life cycles, globalization, changes in information-processing technologies, and demands on process capabilities are forces reshaping organizations today.

7. Network organizations, virtual organizations, and the circle organization are emerging organizational structures.

8. Organizational structures may be inherently weak, or chief executives may create personality–organization constellations that adversely affect employees.

Key Terms

adhocracy (p. 528)
centralization (p. 524)
complexity (p. 524)
contextual variables (p. 518)
differentiation (p. 519)
divisionalized form (p. 528)
environment (p. 532)
environmental uncertainty (p. 533)

formalization (p. 524)
hierarchy of authority (p. 524)
integration (p. 522)
machine bureaucracy (p. 526)
mechanistic structure (p. 533)
organic structure (p. 533)
organizational design (p. 518)
organizational life cycle (p. 536)

organizational structure (p. 518)
professional bureaucracy (p. 527)
simple structure (p. 526)
specialization (p. 524)
standardization (p. 524)
task environment (p. 532)
technological interdependence (p. 531)

Review Questions

1. Define the processes of differentiation and integration.

2. Describe the six basic dimensions of organizational design.

3. Discuss five structural configurations from the chapter.

4. Discuss the effects of the four contextual variables on the basic design dimensions.

5. Identify four forces that are reshaping organizations today.

6. Discuss the nature of emerging organizational structures.

7. List four symptoms of structural weakness and five unhealthy personality–organization combinations.

Discussion and Communication Questions

1. How would you describe the organization you work for (or your college) on each of the basic design dimensions? For example, is it a very formal organization or an informal organization?

2. Do the size, technology, and mission of your organization directly affect you? How?

3. Who are your organization's competitors? What changes do you see in information technology where you work?

4. Does your company show any one or more of the four symptoms of structural deficiency discussed at the end of the chapter?

5. *(communication question)* Write a memo classifying and describing the structural configuration of your university based on the five choices in Table 15.2. Do you need more information than you have to be comfortable with your classification and description? Where could you get the information?

6. *(communication question)* Interview an administrator in your college or university about possible changes in size (Will the college or university get bigger? Smaller?) and technology (Is the college or university making a significant investment in information technology?). What effects does the administrator anticipate from these changes? Be prepared to present your results orally to the class.

Ethical Dilemma

Even as Cecily Blake reads the latest news in an industry trade publication, she's well aware that Blake-Lyon Tech is falling behind its competitors. Years ago, when Cecily founded Blake-Lyon, she centered it in a pure hierarchal structure, where all of the engineers and technicians reported upward to her. At the time, she was able to steer the organization toward new and more innovative products and procedures; now, as competition grows, Cecily is aware that Blake-Lyon cannot keep up.

One significant problem facing the company is the slow pace of communication. Blake-Lyon is committed to hiring the finest technicians and personnel, but lags behind its competitors because it is slow to respond to market changes. Because every new concept must go through each channel, including departments that have little to no impact on decision making, Blake-Lyon is no longer at the forefront of the industry—even though Cecily knows that her workers are more than capable of creating better technology quicker.

Part of Cecily's great reservation in changing the structure of her company is the impact on her top executives. They are effective managers who have been with the company a long time and have been loyal, effective employees. Most of them have been with her from the beginning and are largely responsible for the growth of Blake-Lyon, especially in such a competitive, high-turnover environment. Cecily doesn't want to turn her back on the very people who help her create such a successful organization. However, so many layers of managers through which all decisions need to pass are making Blake-Lyon a dinosaur in the fast-paced technology industry. She won't allow her company to go under; everyone would be hurt by that. But the change would force the elimination of these well respected, loyal executives who are at an age that would make it difficult for them to find new jobs.

Questions:

1. Using consequential, rule-based and character theories, evaluate Cecily's options.

2. What should Cecily do? Why?

Experiential Exercises

15.1 Words-in-Sentences Company

Purpose: To design an organization for a particular task and carry through to production; to compare design elements with effectiveness.

Group Size: Any number of groups of six to fourteen persons.

Time Required: Fifty to ninety minutes.

Related Topics: Dynamics within groups and work motivation.

Background

You are a small company that manufactures words and then packages them in meaningful English-language sentences. Market research has established that sentences of at least three words but not more than six words are in demand. Therefore, packaging, distribution, and sales should be set up for three- to six-word sentences.

The "words-in-sentences" (WIS) industry is highly competitive; several new firms have recently entered what appears to be an expanding market. Since raw materials, technology, and pricing are all standard for the industry, your ability to compete depends on two factors: (1) volume and (2) quality.

Your Task

Your group must design and participate in running a WIS Company. You should design your organization to be as efficient as possible during each ten-minute production run. After the first production run, you will have an opportunity to reorganize your company if you want.

Raw Materials

For each production you will be given a "raw material word or phrase." The letters found in the word or phrase serve as raw materials available to produce new words in sentences. For example, if the raw material word is "organization," you could produce the words and sentence: "Nat ran to a zoo."

Production Standards

Several rules must be followed in producing "words-in-sentences." If these rules are not followed, your output will not meet production specifications and will not pass quality-control inspection.

1. The same letter may appear only as often in a manufactured word as it appears in the raw material word or phrase; for example, "organization" has two o's.

Thus, "zoo" is legitimate, but not "zoonosis." It has too many o's and s's.

2. Raw material letters can be used again in different manufactured words.

3. A manufactured word may be used only once in a sentence and in only one sentence during a production run; if a word—for example, "a"—is used once in a sentence, it is out of stock.

4. A new word may not be made by adding "s" to form the plural of an already manufactured word.

5. A word is defined by its spelling, not its meaning.

6. Nonsense words or nonsense sentences are unacceptable.

7. All words must be in the English language.

8. Names and places are acceptable.

9. Slang is not acceptable.

Measuring Performance

The output of your WIS Company is measured by the total number of acceptable words that are packaged in sentences. The sentences must be legible, listed on no more than two sheets of paper, and handed to the Quality Control Review Board at the completion of each production run.

Delivery

Delivery must be made to the Quality Control Review Board thirty seconds after the end of each production run, or else all points are lost.

Quality Control

If any word in a sentence does not meet the standards set forth above, all the words in the sentence will be rejected. The Quality Control Review Board (composed of one member from each company) is the final arbiter of acceptability. In the event of a tie on the Review Board, a coin toss will determine the outcome.

Exercise Schedule

	Unit Time	Total Time
1. **Form groups, organizations, and assign workplaces** Groups should have between six and fourteen members (if there are more than eleven or twelve persons in a group, assign one or two observers). Each group is a company.	2–5 min	2–5 min
2. **Read "Background"** Ask the instructor about any points that need clarification.	5 min	10 min
3. **Design organizations** Design your organizations using as many members as you see fit to produce your "words-in-sentences." You may want to consider the following. a. What is your objective? b. What technology would work here? c. What type of division of labor is effective? Assign one member of your group to serve on the Quality Review Board. This person may also take part in production runs.	7–15 min	14–25 min
4. **Production Run 1** The instructor will hand each WIS Company a sheet with a raw material word or phrase. When the instructor announces "Begin production," you are to manufacture as many words as possible and package them in sentences for delivery to the Quality Control Review Board. You will have ten minutes. When the instructor announces "Stop production," you will have thirty seconds to deliver your output to the Quality Control Review Board. Output received after thirty seconds does not meet the delivery schedule and will not be counted.	7–10 min	21–35 min
5. **Quality Review Board meets, evaluates output** While that is going on, groups discuss what happened during the previous production run.	5–10 min	26–45 min

6. **Companies evaluate performance and type of organization**   5–10 min   31–55 min
Groups may choose to restructure and reorganize for the next production run.

7. **Production Run 2 (same as Production Run 1)**   7–10 min   38–65 min

8. **Quality Review Board meets**   5–10 min   43–75 min
Quality Review Board evaluates output while groups draw their organization charts (for Runs 1 and 2) on the board.

9. **Class discussion**   7–15 min   50–90 min
Instructor leads discussion of exercise as a whole. Discuss the following questions:

    a. What were the companies' scores for Runs 1 and 2?

    b. What type of structure did the "winning" company have? Did it reorganize for Run 2?

    c. What type of task was there? Technology? Environment?

    d. What would Joan Woodward, Henry Mintzberg, Frederick Taylor, Lawrence and Lorsch, or Burns and Stalker say about WIS Company organization?

SOURCE: "Words-in-Sentences Company" in Dorothy Marcic, *Organizational Behavior: Experiences and Cases*, 4th ed. (St. Paul: West, 1995), 303–305. Reprinted by permission.

15.2 Design and Build a Castle

This exercise is intended to give your group an opportunity to design an organization and produce a product.

Your group is one of three product-development teams working within the research and development division of the GTM (General Turret and Moat) Corporation. GTM has decided to enter new markets by expanding the product line to include fully designed and produced castles, rather than selling components to other companies, as it has in the past.

Each of the three teams has been asked to design a castle for the company to produce and sell. Given its limited resources, GTM cannot put more than one design on the market. Therefore, it will have to decide which of the three designs it will use and will discard the other two designs.

Your task is to develop and design a castle. You will have forty-five minutes to produce a finished product. At the end of this period, several typical consumers, picked by scientific sampling techniques, will judge which is the best design. Before the consumers make their choice, each group will have one to two minutes to make a sales presentation.

Step 1. Each group is designated 1, 2, or 3. The instructor will provide group members a memorandum appropriate for their group. One observer (or two for larger groups) is selected for each group. Observers read their materials.

Step 2. Groups design their organization in order to complete their goal.

Step 3. Each group designs its own castle and draws it on newsprint.

Step 4. "Typical consumers" (may be observers) tour building locations and hear sales pitches. Judges caucus to determine winner.

Step 5. Groups meet again and write up their central goal statement. They also write the organization chart on newsprint with the goal written beneath. These are posted around the room.

Step 6. Instructor leads a class discussion on how the different memos affected organization design. Which design seemed most effective for this task?

NOTE: Your instructor may allow more time and actually have you *build* the castles.

SOURCE: "Design and Build a Castle" from Dorothy Marcic and Richard C. Housley, *Organizational Behavior: Experiences and Cases* (St. Paul: West, 1989), 221–225. Reprinted by permission.

BizFlix | Rendition

U.S. government operatives suddenly take Anwar El-Ibrahimi (Omar Metwally) from his flight from Cape Town, South Africa, after it arrives in Washington, D.C. He is a suspected terrorist whom the government sends to North Africa for torture and interrogation (extraordinary rendition). Douglas Freeman (Jake Gyllenhaal), a CIA analyst, becomes involved. He reacts negatively to the torture techniques and urges El-Ibrahimi's release. The story has other complications in the form of his pregnant wife at home who desperately works for her husband's safe return.

Organizational Structure: A Simple Look

This scene opens with a night shot of the Washington Monument. It follows Kahlid's (Moa Khouas) discussion with Hamadi (Hassam Ghancy), the leader of the terrorist bomb group. Congressional aide Alan Smith's (Peter Sarsgaard) voice-over says, "She called you?" The scene ends after Senator Hawkins (Alan Arkin) tells Alan to back off. The film cuts to a panning shot of a market area and Douglas Freeman drinking.

Alan Smith's question, "She called you?" refers to Corrine Whitman (Meryl Streep), head of U.S. intelligence. She authorized the extraordinary rendition of El-Ibrahimi. Alan Smith, earlier in the film, pressed her for El-Ibrahimi's release and his return to the United States. Whitman lied about El-Ibrahimi's existence. This scene does not explicitly discuss organizational structure, but you can infer several aspects of structure from the scene.

What to Watch for and Ask Yourself

- Review the earlier section, "Basic Design Dimensions." Which dimensions does this scene show or imply?

- Can you sense the division of labor represented by Senator Hawkins and Alan Smith? Corrine Whitman does not appear in this scene but is also part of a division of labor.

- Review the five structural configurations described earlier in this chapter. Which of those configurations best describes the likely structure of Senator Hawkins' office? Which configurations do not apply? Why?

Workplace Video | Evo: Designing Adaptive Organizations

When ski-enthusiast Bryce Phillips started selling ski and snowboard equipment on eBay, he managed everything—customer care, supply chain, technology, buying, and finance— all from his apartment. Nine years later, Phillips's company, Evo, runs a hugely successful e-commerce site, employs more than 60 people, manages its Seattle flagship store, and operates a 40,000 square foot distribution center. Evo has grown at least 70 percent every year and recently hit $10 million in sales. To effectively lead this expanding venture, Phillips continually looks for ways to delegate responsibilities to capable managers around him.

As a straightforward business, Evo is well served by its flat, functional structure. A recent companywide meeting showcased this organizational structure. Department heads introduced themselves and their staffs and explained the function of their departments so new employees and the whole company would have a better understanding of how all the pieces of the company fit together.

Beyond its formal structure, Evo works within a set of core values called "The Great 8," which provides another important operating framework. The Great 8 includes authenticity, balanced ambition, credibility, style, leadership, respect, communication, and evolución. On Evo's Web site, Phillips explained, "Even with all of the changes, many things have remained constant, and we are where we are because we have stayed true to the Great 8. We established the Great 8 to guide us through the decisions, big and small, that we make every day."

In 2004, when Evo employed only six people, flexibility was a way of life. Everyone wore multiple hats and did everything necessary to get the job done. As the number of employees on payroll approached 60, it was time to make sure the people who dealt directly with customers possessed the authority and flexibility to deliver excellent service. This organizational soul-searching yielded a new customer care policy titled "Just Say YES!" As a result, customer service representatives now make their own decisions about how to make customers happy.

Today, Phillips is looking for ways to adapt again—this time to the troubled U.S. economy. Luckily, tackling monster moguls on the ski slopes has prepared him for almost anything.

Discussion Questions

1. Is Evo a centralized or decentralized company? Explain.

2. Are Evo's top managers likely to seek a more mechanistic type of organization to accommodate growth and change? Why or why not?

3. Given Evo's current structure and pace of growth, what organizational challenges might arise in the future?

Case

NASA: Organizational Design Frontiers for Exploring Space Frontiers

In its current strategic plan, published in 2006, the United States' National Aeronautics and Space Administration (NASA) articulated the following strategic goals:

- "Fly the Shuttle as safely as possible until its retirement, not later than 2010."

- "Complete the International Space Station in a manner consistent with NASA's International partner commitments and the needs of human exploration."

- "Develop a balanced overall program of science, exploration, and aeronautics consistent with the redirection of the human spaceflight program to focus on exploration."

- "Bring a new Crew Exploration Vehicle into service as soon as possible after Shuttle retirement."

- "Encourage the pursuit of appropriate partnerships with the emerging commercial space sector."

- "Establish a lunar return program having the maximum possible utility for later missions to Mars and other destinations."[1]

A variety of external factors—over which NASA says it has little, if any, control—influence its strategic goals and how it goes about achieving those goals. These external factors include the following:

- Legislative and Policy Framework—NASA's Strategic Plan assumes continued Congressional support through appropriate legislative acts and annual appropriations.

- Economy and Public Support—NASA's Strategic Plan assumes that the economy and public support will remain strong.

- Changing Relationships with Other Nations—NASA recognizes the contributions that can be derived from partnerships with other nations as well as the risks associated with those partnerships.

- National Security/Homeland Security—NASA will continue providing support to the United States Department of Defense and other federal and local agencies where there is a mutual interest in achieving goals that can meet both civil and national security needs.

- Markets—NASA recognizes that space exploration presents enormous future business opportunities.

- Discovery—New discoveries could change NASA's strategic goals, even though at the present time the agency believes it has developed a balanced and feasible program for the future.

- Technology—NASA recognizes that many of its current strategic goals rely on future technological breakthroughs, which can either delay or accelerate its achievement.[2]

Like many other organizations, NASA, in its efforts to achieve its strategic goals, faces an increasingly complex and unstable external environment. A prominent concern for executives and managers in all of these organizations is how to best design them to achieve their strategic goals. Effective organization design in turbulent environments requires these executives and managers to make numerous decisions about complex, inter-related variables such as how specialization should be used to maximize output, how specialists' work should be integrated, who makes various types of decisions, and how communication should occur within work teams and with management.[3] For an increasingly large number of organizations, these decisions result in some sort of *network* organization design—a design that has recently been called a *lattice* design. Some of the key features of a lattice design are crucial elements of organizations that are designed to achieve success in the twenty-first century. Among these key features are process differentiation rather than functional differentiation, process champions in place of multilevel management pyramids, activity teams instead of specialized departments, curtailing hierarchy to enable empowerment, and multidirectional flow of information among process teams.[4]

In pursuing its strategic goals within the context of what NASA considers to be essentially uncontrollable external factors, the Space Agency has transformed its organizational structure. In mid-2004, Sean O'Keefe, then NASA's head administrator, announced a transformation of the agency's organization structure. This massive transformation effort was in response to the President's Commission on Implementation of U.S. Space Exploration Policy, which found that "NASA needs to transform itself into a leaner, more focused agency by developing an organizational structure that recognizes the need for a more integrated approach to science requirements, management, and implementation of systems development and exploration missions."[5] O'Keefe said, "[o]ur task is to … promote synergy across the agency, and support the long-term exploration vision in a way that is sustainable and affordable. … We need to take these critical steps to streamline the organization and create a structure that affixes clear authority and accountability."[6] The new structure revolved around four Mission Directorates—Aeronautics Research, Science, Exploration Systems, and Space Operations—and some headquarters support functions.[7] The new organization structure would be "a large matrix between projects (managed by Exploration Systems) and functional areas (overseen by Space Operations, Science, and Aeronautics Research.)"[8]

"The Aeronautics Research Mission Directorate conducts research in aeronautical disciplines and develops capabilities, tools, and technologies to enable safe, reliable, capable, and efficient flight vehicles and aviation systems. The Science Mission Directorate carries out the scientific exploration of the Earth, Sun, solar system, and universe. … The Exploration Systems Mission Directorate develops capabilities and supporting research and technology that enable sustained and affordable human and robotic exploration and that ensure the health and performance of crews during long-duration space exploration. … The Space Operations Mission Directorate directs spaceflight operations, space launches, and space communications and manages the operation of integrated systems in low Earth orbit and beyond, including the International Space Station."[9]

The supporting functional areas that are overseen by Space Operations, Science, and Aeronautics Research include a variety of NASA Centers and Mission Support Offices. The NASA Centers are Ames Research Center, Dryden Flight Research Center, Glenn Research Center, Goddard Space Flight Center, Jet Propulsion Laboratory, Johnson Space Center, Kennedy Space Center, Langley Research Center, Marshall Space Flight Center, and Stennis Space Center.[10] The Mission Support Offices include the following: Chief Financial Officer, Chief Information Officer, General Counsel, Integrated Enterprise Management Program, Innovative Partnership Program, Security and Program Protection, Chief Health and Medical Officer, Institutions and Management, and Strategic Communications.[11]

An important element—but certainly not the only element—that NASA has considered in building and maintaining a strong organization design is ensuring that the NASA Centers share certain critical attributes. In December of 2005, NASA's Strategic Management Council described the following set of attributes for strong, healthy Centers: "[c]lear, stable, and enduring roles and responsibilities; [c]lear program/project management leadership roles; [m]ajor in-house, durable spaceflight responsibility; [s]killed and flexible blended workforce with sufficient depth and breadth to meet the Agency's challenges; [t]echnically competent and value-centered leadership; [c]apable and effectively utilized infrastructure; and [s]trong stakeholder support."[12]

Given all that NASA has already accomplished and the challenges that it faces, will its organizational design transformations effectively position the Space Agency to achieve its strategic goals?

Discussion Questions

1. Explain the context that NASA's *strategic goals* provide for the design of its organization structure.

2. Explain the context that NASA's *external environment* provides for both its strategic goals and the design of its organization structure.

3. What is a network (or lattice) organization, and how does it differ from more traditional organization structures?

4. Why have network (or lattice) organizations come into existence?

5. How does the network (or lattice) organization relate to NASA's organization design of four Mission Directorates supported by various NASA Centers and Mission Support Offices?

6. What advantages and disadvantages do you think arise from utilizing a network (or lattice) organization?

SOURCE: This case was written by Michael K. McCuddy, The Louis S. and Mary L. Morgal Chair of Christian Business Ethics and Professor of Management, College of Business Administration, Valparaiso University.

16

Organizational Culture

LEARNING OBJECTIVES

After reading this chapter, you should be able to do the following:

1 Describe organizational culture.

2 Critically evaluate the roles of the three levels of culture.

3 Evaluate the four functions of culture within an organization.

4 Explain the relationship between organizational culture and performance.

5 Contrast the characteristics of adaptive and nonadaptive cultures.

6 Describe five ways leaders reinforce organizational culture.

7 Describe the three stages of organizational socialization and the ways culture is communicated in each step.

8 Identify ways of assessing organizational culture.

9 Explain actions managers can take to change organizational culture.

Nordstrom representatives adorn 17-year-old Brittany Claunch with jewelry, dress, and shoes for her prom. Claunch recently had a tumor removed from her brain.

THINKING AHEAD: NORDSTROM

A Customer Service Culture

Since Wallin and Nordstrom opened their first store in 1901, one of their primary foundations of business has been "Do whatever it takes to take care of the customer, and do whatever it takes to make sure the customer doesn't leave the store without buying something." Nordstrom asks their employees to write down stories that exemplify the organization's culture. Many stories exist of Nordstrom employees going the extra mile to help a customer as well as Nordstrom's employees' focus on teamwork.

When a couple from out of town stopped at a Nordstrom store, the wife tried on an outfit she wanted to wear that night but was hesitant to buy it because she didn't have the right jewelry to wear. To make the sale and please the customer, the salesperson loaned the customer the jewelry she was wearing. From the Nordstrom store in Oakbrook, Illinois comes a story of a cosmetic salesperson who regularly interacts with a customer from out of town who has never been to the store. Sadly, the customer has cancer and says the service and make-up she receives is one of the only things that

still make her feel pretty. In New Jersey, a customer who was about to leave for Milan the next day came to Nordstrom for a pair of pants and mentioned that he needed other things but didn't have time for alterations so he was going to buy these items once he arrived in Milan. The salesperson contacted Alterations and the Tailor Shop and the team worked together to get the customer all the clothes he needed altered by the next morning.

So how has Nordstrom been able to maintain this customer-focused culture for over 100 years? See the Looking Back section at the end of this chapter for the answers.

THE KEY ROLE OF ORGANIZATIONAL CULTURE

The concept of organizational culture has its roots in cultural anthropology. As in larger human society, there are cultures within organizations. These cultures are similar to societal cultures. They are shared, communicated through symbols, and passed down from generation to generation of employees.

The concept of cultures in organizations was alluded to as early as the Hawthorne studies, which described work group culture. The topic came into its own during the early 1970s, when managers and researchers alike began to search for keys to survival for organizations in a competitive and turbulent environment. Then, in the early 1980s, several books on corporate culture were published, including Deal and Kennedy's *Corporate Cultures*,[1] Ouchi's *Theory Z*,[2] and Peters and Waterman's *In Search of Excellence*.[3] These books found wide audiences, and research began in earnest on the elusive topic of organizational cultures. Executives indicated that these cultures were real and could be managed.[4]

Culture and Its Levels

1 Describe organizational culture.

Many definitions of *organizational culture* have been proposed. Most of them agree that there are several levels of culture and that these levels differ in terms of their visibility and their ability to be changed. The definition adopted in this chapter is that *organizational (corporate) culture* is a pattern of basic assumptions that are considered valid and that are taught to new members as the way to perceive, think, and feel in the organization.[5]

2 Critically evaluate the roles of the three levels of culture.

Edgar Schein, in his comprehensive book on organizational culture and leadership, suggests that organizational culture has three levels. His view of culture is presented in Figure 16.1. The levels range from visible artifacts and creations to testable values to invisible and even preconscious basic assumptions. To achieve a complete understanding of an organization's culture, all three levels must be studied.

organizational (corporate) culture
A pattern of basic assumptions that are considered valid and that are taught to new members as the way to perceive, think, and feel in the organization.

artifacts
Symbols of culture in the physical and social work environment.

Artifacts

Symbols of culture in the physical and social work environment are called *artifacts*. They are the most visible and accessible level of culture. The key to understanding culture through artifacts lies in figuring out what they mean. Artifacts are also the most frequently studied manifestation of organizational culture, perhaps because of their accessibility. Among the artifacts of culture are personal enactment, ceremonies and rites, stories, rituals, and symbols.[6]

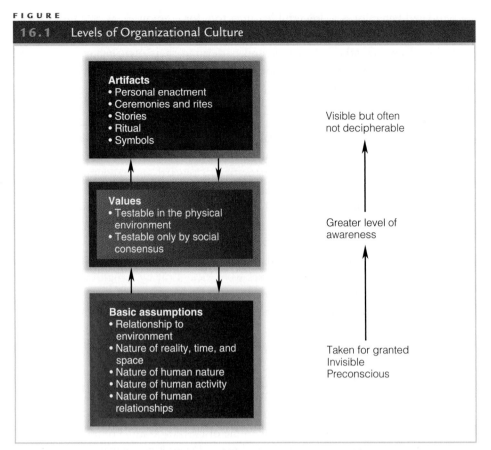

16.1 Levels of Organizational Culture

Artifacts
- Personal enactment
- Ceremonies and rites
- Stories
- Ritual
- Symbols

Visible but often not decipherable

Values
- Testable in the physical environment
- Testable only by social consensus

Greater level of awareness

Basic assumptions
- Relationship to environment
- Nature of reality, time, and space
- Nature of human nature
- Nature of human activity
- Nature of human relationships

Taken for granted
Invisible
Preconscious

SOURCE: From Edgar H. Schein, *Organizational Culture and Leadership: A Dynamic View.* Copyright © 1985 Jossey-Bass Inc. Reprinted by permission of Jossey-Bass, Inc., a subsidiary of John Wiley & Sons, Inc.

The big "Blue Bag" that IKEA sells to customers for less than $1 rather than using plastic bags serves as an artifact for IKEA's cultural stance of protecting the planet.[7] Similarly, the corporate culture of Google is apparent in the offices of its headquarters in Mountain View, California. The lobby is replete with lava lamps, pianos, and live searches on the Google search engine from around the world. The hallways house bikes and exercise machines, while office spaces are laid-back, featuring couches and occupied by dogs that go with their owners to work.[8]

Personal Enactment Culture can be understood, in part, through an examination of the behavior of organization members. Personal enactment is behavior that reflects the organization's values. In particular, personal enactment by the top managers provides insight into these values. Steve Irby is the founder and CEO of Stillwater Designs, the company that created Kicker audio speakers. He values good relationships and believes that people are the most important part of his company. Irby builds trust with his employees by sharing the financial results of the business each month. The employees know that if monthly sales are higher than the sales in the same month of the previous year, Irby will hold a cookout for the employees on the following Friday. Irby and the general manager always do the cooking. Eskimo Joe's, a Stillwater, Oklahoma, restaurant chain and one of the largest T-shirt sellers in the United States, could probably have become a national franchise years ago. But founder Stan Clark, who began as co-owner of the once-tiny bar, says his intent is to become better, not bigger. Clark still meets personally with new hires for the restaurant's serving staff, ensuring that they receive a firm grounding in his philosophy of food and fun.[9]

Modeled behavior is a powerful learning tool for employees, as Bandura's social learning theory demonstrated.[10] As we saw in Chapter 5, individuals learn vicariously by observing others' behavior and patterning their own behavior similarly. Culture can be an important leadership tool. Managerial behavior can clarify what is important and coordinate the work of employees, in effect negating the need for close supervision.[11]

Ceremonies and Rites Relatively elaborate sets of activities that are enacted time and again on important occasions are known as organizational ceremonies and rites.[12] These occasions provide opportunities to reward and recognize employees whose behavior is congruent with the values of the company. Ceremonies and rites send a message that individuals who both espouse and exhibit corporate values are heroes to be admired.

The ceremonies also bond organization members together. Southwestern Bell (now part of SBC Communications) emphasized the importance of management training to the company. Training classes were kicked off by a high-ranking executive (a rite of renewal), and completion of the classes was signaled by a graduation ceremony (a rite of passage). Six kinds of rites in organizations have been identified:[13]

1. *Rites of passage* show that an individual's status has changed. Retirement dinners are an example.

2. *Rites of enhancement* reinforce the achievement of individuals. An example is the awarding of certificates to sales contest winners.

3. *Rites of renewal* emphasize change in the organization and commitment to learning and growth. An example is the opening of a new corporate training center.

4. *Rites of integration* unite diverse groups or teams within the organization and renew commitment to the larger organization. Company functions such as annual picnics fall into this category.

5. *Rites of conflict reduction* focus on dealing with conflicts or disagreements that arise naturally in organizations. Examples are grievance hearings and the negotiation of union contracts.

6. *Rites of degradation* are used by some organizations to visibly punish persons who fail to adhere to values and norms of behavior. Some CEOs, for example, are replaced quite publicly for unethical conduct or for failure to achieve organizational goals. In some Japanese organizations, employees who perform poorly are given ribbons of shame as punishment.

Berkshire Hathaway Inc. is an Omaha-based company that owns and operates a number of insurance firms and several other subsidiaries. Its chairman and CEO is Warren Buffett, known for his business acumen and for ensuring good returns on shareholder investments. Berkshire's annual shareholder meeting is a ceremony of celebration and appears more like a rock music festival than a corporate meeting. Each annual meeting starts with a short film poking fun at Berkshire's CEO and his cantankerous sidekick, Charlie Munger. Susan Lucci starred last year, and then showed up to try to take Buffett's job. Others who have made cameos include Arnold Schwarzenegger, Donald Trump, and the women of Desperate Housewives. Jimmy Buffett sang "Margaritaville" at the meeting with some of the lyrics changed to "wasting away in Berkshire-Hathaway-a-ville"! Bill Gates, who is on the board of directors at Berkshire Hathaway, made it to the meeting as well and was seen playing ping-pong with Warren Buffett. Over 20,000 shareholders, employees, and Warren Buffett attend the star-studded event annually.[14]

Stories Some researchers have argued that the most effective way to reinforce organizational values is through stories.[15] As they are told and retold, stories give meaning and identity to organizations and are especially helpful in orienting new employees. Part of the strength of organizational stories is that the listeners are left to draw their own conclusions—a powerful communication tool.[16]

Some corporate stories even transcend cultural and political boundaries. Visit the Web site of Wal-Mart China, and you will read the true story of Jeff, a pharmacist in Harrison, Arkansas, a small town deep in the Ozarks. When Jeff received an early morning weekend call

Bill Gates, who is on the board of directors at Berkshire Hathaway, plays a game of bridge with Warren Buffett during the Berkshire Hathaway shareholders annual meeting.

telling him that a diabetic patient needed insulin, he quickly opened his pharmacy and filled the prescription.[17] While Arkansas and Beijing are worlds apart, stories such as this one help transfer Wal-Mart's corporate "personality" to its new Asian associates. Research by Joanne Martin and her colleagues has indicated that certain themes recur in stories across different types of organizations:[18]

1. *Stories about the boss.* These stories may reflect whether the boss is "human" or how the boss reacts to mistakes.

2. *Stories about getting fired.* Events leading to employee firings are recounted.

3. *Stories about how the company deals with employees who have to relocate.*

These stories relate to the company's actions toward employees who have to move—whether the company is helpful and takes family and other personal concerns into account.

4. *Stories about whether lower-level employees can rise to the top.* Often, these stories describe a person who started out at the bottom and eventually became the CEO. QuikTrip is well known for promoting from within and is one reason they have been voted to *Fortune*'s "100 Best Companies to Work For" seven years running. In fact, two-thirds of QuikTrip's top 100 managers started at an entry-level position in the organization.[19]

5. *Stories about how the company deals with crisis situations.* AIG's payout of $73 million in bonuses to seventy-three employees in the unit that lost the so much money that it forced a taxpayer bailout made AIG the poster child for Wall Street greed, excess, and bad management.[20]

6. *Stories about how status considerations work when rules are broken.* When Tom Watson, Sr., was CEO of IBM, he was once confronted by a security guard because he was not wearing an ID badge.

These are the themes that can emerge when stories are passed down. The information from these stories serves to guide the behavior of organization members.

To be effective cultural tools, stories must be credible. You can't tell a story about your flat corporate hierarchy and then have reserved parking spaces for managers. Stories that aren't backed by reality can lead to cynicism and mistrust. For example, Steve Jobs, the founder and CEO of Apple, made a commencement address at Stanford University and told stories relating his successful battle with cancer, his struggles with keeping Apple afloat, and his being fired and getting back on top. These stories were meant to reinforce his lesson that one should work toward whatever his or her passion might be.[21]

Effective stories can also reinforce culture and create renewed energy. Lucasfilm is the home of director and producer George Lucas and the birthplace of such blockbusters as *Star Wars* and *Forrest Gump*. Stories of the company's legendary accomplishments are used to reinforce the creative culture and to rally the troops. When Gail Currey, former head of the company's digital division, found her 300 designers were grumbling, she reminded them of how they did *Gump* when everyone else said it was impossible and what a hit the film was. The designers would then head back to their computers to contribute to the company's success.[22]

Rituals Everyday organizational practices that are repeated over and over are rituals. They are usually unwritten, but they send a clear message about "the way we do things around here." While some companies insist that people address each other by their titles (Mr., Mrs., Ms., Miss) and surnames to reinforce a professional image, others prefer that employees operate on a first-name basis—from the top manager on down. Hewlett-Packard values open communication, so its employees address one another by first names only.

In the fast-paced world of automotive manufacturing, the endless grind of the assembly line makes it tough for workers to imagine the person who will actually drive the car they are building. But at Saturn's Tennessee assembly plant, each car travels down the assembly line with the customer's name attached to it. And upon delivery, the customer is handed the keys and photographed by the dealer in a small ceremony commemorating the event. Not surprisingly, Saturn owners are among the most loyal in the industry.[23]

As everyday practices, rituals reinforce the organizational culture by establishing role identities, and fixing values, beliefs, and norms.[24] Insiders who commonly practice the rituals may be unaware of their subtle influence, but outsiders recognize it easily.

Symbols Symbols communicate organizational culture by unspoken messages. Symbols are representative of organizational identity and membership to employees. Nike's trademark "swoosh" is proudly tattooed above the ankles of some Nike employees. Apple Computer employees readily identify themselves as "Apple People." Symbols are used to build solidarity in the organizational culture.[25]

Personal enactment, rites and ceremonies, stories, rituals, and symbols serve to reinforce the values that are the next level of culture.

Values

espoused values
What members of an organization say they value.

enacted values
Values reflected in the way individuals actually behave.

Values are the second, and deeper, level of culture. They reflect a person's underlying beliefs of what should be or should not be. Values are often consciously articulated, both in conversation and in a company's mission statement or annual report. However, there may be a difference between a company's *espoused values* (what the members say they value) and its *enacted values* (values reflected in the way the members actually behave).[26] Values also may be reflected in the behavior of individuals, which is an artifact of culture. One study investigating the gender gap in a Canadian sports organization found that coaches and athletes believed that inequities resulting from this gap were normal or natural or completely denied such inequities existed even though they were widespread. This was because even though the organization espoused gender equity as a value, its practices did not demonstrate and support gender equity.[27]

A firm's values and how it promotes and publicizes them can also affect how workers feel about their jobs and themselves. A study of 180 managers looked at their employers' effectiveness in communicating concern for employees' welfare. Managers in organizations that consistently communicated concern for workers' well-being and that focused on treating employees fairly reported feeling better about themselves and their role in the organization.[28] The lesson? *Treat* employees like valuable team members, and they are more likely to *feel* like valuable team members.

Values underlie the customer, environment, and high quality–focused culture at Whole Foods Market. As guides for behavior, they are reinforced in the aspirations statement and in the reward system of the organization. Whole Foods Market states that these values do not change from time to time, from person to person, or as the company grows but are the "soul" of the company's culture.[29]

Some organizational cultures are characterized by values that support healthy lifestyle behaviors. When the workplace culture values worker health and psychological needs, there is enhanced potential for high performance and improved well-being.[30] Clif Bar, the energy bar maker, even has a twenty-two-foot rock-climbing wall in its corporate office.

When Harley-Davidson hires new customer service employees, they had better be ready to do more than just answer telephones. Working at Harley-Davidson is not only a job, it's about an entire subculture that revolves around Harleys. New employees are immersed in this culture, typically through working at a Harley owners' rally and taking demonstration rides. Over time, most employees become Harley riders or owners, which helps them provide better service to other Harley lovers.[31]

Charles Schwab Corporation, a financial services firm, is a model of a values-driven business. Its core organizational values are as follows:

- Be fair, empathetic, and responsive in serving our clients.
- Respect and reinforce our fellow employees and the power of teamwork.
- Strive relentlessly to innovate what we do and how we do it.
- Always earn and be worthy of our clients' trust.[32]

Assumptions

Assumptions are the deeply held beliefs that guide behavior and tell members of an organization how to perceive and think about things. As the deepest and most fundamental level of an organization's culture, according to Edgar Schein, they are the essence of culture. They are so strongly held that a member behaving in any fashion that would violate them would be unthinkable. Another characteristic of assumptions is that they are often unconscious. Organization members may not be aware of their assumptions and may be reluctant or unable to discuss them or change them.

While unconscious assumptions often guide a firm's actions and decisions, some companies are quite explicit in their assumptions about employees. NetApp, a data storage solution provider, operates under the cultural assumption that treating their employees fairly reduces the need for too many rules or regulations. For example, their travel policy simply states, "We are a frugal company but don't show up dog-tired to save a few bucks."[33] NetApp was named the "Best Company to Work For"

assumptions
Deeply held beliefs that guide behavior and tell members of an organization how to perceive and think about things.

in part due to its focus on trust and openness. Read more about the NetApp culture in The Real World 16.1.

Now that you understand Schein's three levels of culture, you can use You 16.1 to assess a culture you'd like to learn more about.

FUNCTIONS AND EFFECTS OF ORGANIZATIONAL CULTURE

3 Evaluate the four functions of culture within an organization.

In an organization, culture serves four basic functions. First, culture provides a sense of identity to members and increases their commitment to the organization.[34] When employees internalize the values of the company, they find their work intrinsically rewarding and identify with their fellow workers. Motivation is enhanced, and employees are more committed.[35]

Second, culture is a sense-making device for organization members. It provides a way for employees to interpret the meaning of organizational events.[36] Leaders can use organizational symbols like corporate logos as sense-making devices to help

The Real World 16.1

NetApp's Culture of Openness Makes it *Fortune*'s "Best Company to Work For"

The data storage and management company NetApp has survived the dot.com crash and has enjoyed tremendous success under long-time CEO Dan Warmenhoven. Top executives at NetApp are quick to credit the open, trusting culture for the company's success—and employees agree, catapulting NetApp to the top of *Fortune*'s "Best Companies to Work For" list.

A culture of trust and openness gives NetApp a distinct competitive advantage. The office design supports these values. Everyone, including the CEO, works in an open air cubicle. Information is shared fully and openly. A Vice President's Forum is held every two weeks in which information about the company and the economy is shared, but its main purpose is for the VP to hear what's on the mind of NetApp employees. Key to the culture is the commitment to simplicity and common sense. Bureaucracy is at a minimum, and products are designed in order to do the job as simply as possible for customers. A twelve-page travel policy was canned in favor of a simple statement asking employees to use their common sense.

Recruiting is done to attract brilliant people to the organization, and care is taken to let employees know how brilliant and appreciated they are. NetApp provides exciting work, provides flexible scheduling for work–life balance, and encourages volunteer efforts in the community. Five paid days off are given to each employee for volunteer work. Unique benefits are provided, too, like adoption aid and autism coverage.

NetApp's culture of trust, openness, simplicity, and common sense has garnered not only recognition, but highly performing employees and loyal customers, both keys to competitive advantage.

SOURCES: R. Levering and M. Moskowitz, "And the Winners Are ...." *Fortune* (February 2, 2009): 67–78; http://greatplacetowork.com/best/100best-2009/100best2009-netapp.php.

employees understand the changing nature of their organizational identity. This is specifically so in an environment that is constantly changing.[37] Sometimes symbols can remain the same to ensure that some things stay constant despite changing conditions; other times symbols may have to change to reflect the new culture in the organization. For example, McDonald's is known worldwide for its golden arches that have remained the same since its inception in 1955.[38] By contrast, Southwest Airlines changed its logo in 2002 to mark its leadership in the airline industry as the "fun" airline and to capitalize on one of its most important trademarks, being "the love airline."

Third, culture reinforces the values in the organization. The culture at SSM Health Care emphasizes patient care and continuous improvement. The St. Louis-based company, which owns and manages twenty-one acute-care hospitals in four states, values compassionate, holistic, high-quality care. SSM was the first health care organization to win the Malcolm Baldrige National Quality Award.

Finally, culture serves as a control mechanism for shaping behavior. Norms that guide behavior are part of culture. If the norm the company wants to promote is teamwork, its culture must reinforce that norm. The company's culture must be characterized by open communication, cooperation between teams, and integration of teams.[39] Culture can also be used as a powerful tool to discourage dysfunctional and deviant behaviors in organizations. Norms can send clear messages that certain behaviors are unacceptable.[40] For example, the workgroup that an employee is involved with can have an impact on her or his absenteeism behavior. That is, if the work group does not have explicit norms in place discouraging absenteeism, members are more likely to be engaged in excessive absenteeism.[41]

The effects of organizational culture are hotly debated by organizational behaviorists and researchers. Managers attest strongly to the positive effects of culture in organizations, but it is difficult to quantify these effects. John Kotter and James Heskett have reviewed three theories about the relationship between organizational culture and performance and the evidence that either supports or refutes these theories.[42] The three are the strong culture perspective, the fit perspective, and the adaptation perspective.

The Strong Culture Perspective

4 Explain the relationship between organizational culture and performance.

The strong culture perspective states that organizations with "strong" cultures perform better than other organizations.[43] A *strong culture* is an organizational culture with a consensus on the values that drive the company and with an intensity that is recognizable even to outsiders. Thus, a strong culture is deeply held and widely shared. It also is highly resistant to change. One example of a strong culture is IBM's. Its culture is one we are all familiar with: conservative, with a loyal workforce and an emphasis on customer service.

Strong cultures are thought to facilitate performance for three reasons. First, they are characterized by goal alignment; that is, all employees share common goals. Second, they create a high level of motivation because of the values shared by the members. Third, they provide control without the oppressive effects of a bureaucracy.

To test the strong culture hypothesis, Kotter and Heskett selected 207 firms from a wide variety of industries. They used a questionnaire to calculate a culture strength index for each firm, and they correlated that index with the firm's economic performance over a twelve-year period. They concluded that strong cultures were associated with positive long-term economic performance, but only modestly.

There are also two perplexing questions about the strong culture perspective. First, what can be said about evidence showing that strong economic performance can create strong cultures, rather than the reverse? Second, what if the strong culture leads the firm down the wrong path? Sears, for example, is an organization with a strong culture, but in the 1980s, it focused inward, ignoring competition and consumer preferences and damaging its performance. Changing Sears' strong but stodgy culture has been a tough task, with financial performance only recently showing an upward trend.[44]

The Fit Perspective

The fit perspective argues that a culture is good only if it "fits" the industry or the firm's strategy. For example, a culture that values a traditional hierarchical structure and stability would not work well in the computer manufacturing industry, which demands fast response and a lean, flat organization. Three particular characteristics of an industry may affect culture: the competitive environment, customer requirements, and societal expectations.[45] In the computer industry, firms face a highly competitive environment, customers who require highly reliable products, and a society that expects state-of-the-art technology and high-quality service.

A study of twelve large U.S. firms indicated that cultures consistent with industry conditions help managers make better decisions. It also indicated that cultures need not change as long as the industry doesn't change. If the industry does change, however, many cultures change too slowly to avoid negative effects on firms' performance.[46]

The fit perspective is useful in explaining short-term performance but not long-term performance. It also indicates that it is difficult to change culture quickly, especially if the culture is widely shared and deeply held. But it doesn't explain how firms can adapt to environmental change.

The Adaptation Perspective

The third theory about culture and performance is the adaptation perspective. Its theme is that only cultures that help organizations adapt to environmental change are associated with excellent performance. An *adaptive culture* is one that

strong culture
An organizational culture with a consensus on the values that drive the company and with an intensity that is recognizable even to outsiders.

adaptive culture
An organizational culture that encourages confidence and risk taking among employees, has leadership that produces change, and focuses on the changing needs of customers.

encourages confidence and risk taking among employees,[47] has leadership that produces change,[48] and focuses on the changing needs of customers.[49] 3M is a company with an adaptive culture in that it encourages new product ideas from all levels within the company.

To test the adaptation perspective, Kotter and Heskett interviewed industry analysts about the cultures of twenty-two firms. The contrast between adaptive cultures and nonadaptive cultures was striking. The results of the study are summarized in Table 16.1.

Adaptive cultures facilitate change to meet the needs of three groups of constituents: stockholders, customers, and employees. Nonadaptive cultures are characterized by cautious management that tries to protect its own interests. Adaptive firms showed significantly better long-term economic performance in Kotter and Heskett's study. One contrast that can be made is between Hewlett-Packard (HP), a high performer, and Xerox, a lower performer. The analysts viewed HP as valuing excellent leadership more than Xerox did and as valuing all three key constituencies more than Xerox did. Economic performance from 1977 through 1988 supported this difference: HP's index of annual net income growth was 40.2, as compared with Xerox's 13.1. Kotter and Heskett concluded that the cultures that promote long-term performance are those that are most adaptive.

5 Contrast the characteristics of adaptive and nonadaptive cultures.

Given that high-performing cultures are adaptive ones, it is important to know how managers can develop adaptive cultures. Would you think that the military is an adaptive culture or nonadaptive? In the Science feature, discover how West Point Military Academy is struggling with implementing change due to a gap between its cultural artifacts and espoused values.

In the next section, we will examine the leader's role in managing organizational culture.

TABLE

16.1 Adaptive versus Nonadaptive Organizational Cultures

	Adaptive Organizational Cultures	Nonadaptive Organizational Cultures
Core values	Most managers care deeply about customers, stockholders, and employees. They also strongly value people and processes that can create useful change (e.g., leadership up and down the management hierarchy).	Most managers care mainly about themselves, their immediate work group, or some product (or technology) associated with that work group. They value the orderly and risk-reducing management process much more highly than leadership initiatives.
Common behavior	Managers pay close attention to all their constituencies, especially customers, and initiate change when needed to serve their legitimate interests, even if that entails taking some risks.	Managers tend to behave somewhat insularly, politically, and bureaucratically. As a result, they do not change their strategies quickly to adjust to or take advantage of changes in their business environments.

SOURCE: Reprinted with the permission of The Free Press, a Division of Simon & Schuster, Inc. from *Corporate Culture and Performance* by John P. Kotter and James L. Heskett. Copyright © 1992 by Kotter Associates, Inc. and James L. Heskett.

New Job? You'll Need Supervisor Support to Succeed

Organizational socialization is quite important for both new employees and the organization. The ways in which new employees learn how things are done in an organization have long-lasting effects on their job attitudes and behaviors. Also, support from organizational insiders is thought to play a role in how successful this socialization is. A recent study investigated supervisor support during the period from six to twenty-one months after a newcomer entered an organization. Results showed that supervisor support diminished over the time period. And, the more this support declined during this time period, the less job clarity and job satisfaction the newcomer had and the slower the newcomer's salary increased over time. These findings have several implications. First, if supervisors want to reap the most benefits from organizational socialization, they should continue to support their new employees steadily for at least the first two years. Additionally, supervisors should encourage employees to seek support from coworkers when they enter the organization because the supervisor may need help in providing support to the new employee for the full two years.

SOURCES: M. Jokisaari and J. Nurmi, "Change in Newcomers' Supervisor Support and Socialization Outcomes after Organizational Entry," *Academy of Management Journal* 52 (2009): 527–544.

THE LEADER'S ROLE IN SHAPING AND REINFORCING CULTURE

6 Describe five ways leaders reinforce organizational culture.

According to Edgar Schein, leaders play crucial roles in shaping and reinforcing culture.[50] The five most important elements in managing culture are (1) what leaders pay attention to; (2) how leaders react to crises; (3) how leaders behave; (4) how leaders allocate rewards; and (5) how leaders hire and fire individuals.

The Enron Corporation fiasco illustrates each of these roles. *Enron ethics* is the term applied to the gap between words and deeds, and it illustrates that leader behavior deeply affects organizational culture.[51] Enron created deceptive partnerships and used questionable accounting practices to maintain its investment-grade rating. Employees recorded earnings before they were realized; they thought this was merely recording them early, not wrongly. Enron's culture was shaping the ethical boundaries of its employees, and Enron executives bent the rules for personal gain.

What Leaders Pay Attention To

Leaders in an organization communicate their priorities, values, and beliefs through the themes that consistently emerge from what they focus on. These themes are reflected in what they notice, comment on, measure, and control. If leaders are consistent in what they pay attention to, measure, and control, employees receive clear signals about what is important in the organization. If, however, leaders are inconsistent, employees spend a lot of time trying to decipher and find meaning in the inconsistent signals.

Enron leader Jeffrey Skilling paid attention to money and profit at all costs. Employees could take as much vacation as they wanted as long as they were delivering results; they could deliberately break company rules as long as they were making money. By contrast, leaders at Badger Mining Company pay attention to the environment. Their environmental stewardship, along with their cultural emphasis on trust, earned them the top spot as the "Best Small Company to Work for in America." You can learn about what they do to focus on the environment in The Real World 16.2.

The Real World 16.2

Badger Mining's Cultural Commitment to the Environment

Headquartered in Berlin, Wisconsin, family-owned Badger Mining Company (BMC) has a deep sense of responsibility to the community and to the environment. Combined with their trust-based culture, this landed them at the number one spot as "Best Small Company to Work for in America" from the Society for Human Resource Management. Many companies' approaches to environmental stewardship require strict compliance with regulations and guidelines. Badger Mining's commitment goes beyond this standard. They want to serve as stewards of the land they utilize.

What began as a non-metallic mining operation for the company is now known as White Sand Lake. BMC developed a reclamation program such that once the sandstone had been mined, the company created a gradual slope to form the shoreline of what would become the lake—a great recreation and fishing area. The idea in all of the reclamation efforts is to put the land back better than it was if possible, and many former mining sites are turned into fish ponds or wetlands such that

Badger Mining Corporation releases pheasants on an annual basis to help restore wild pheasant populations.

they blend with the natural environment. And what company would build its new Corporate Center on top of an abandoned landfill site? Badger Mining did, and the center is now a beautiful entrance to the small town of Berlin. It is also a home to wildlife like ducks, geese, and turtles. When wild birds nest in the grasslands around the buildings, particular care is taken to protect the nests and to avoid any grass mowing in the vicinity.

BMC's commitment to recreation extends to employees as well. The company pays the dues for recreational teams when 50 percent or more of the members are employees or family members. BMC compiles a photo history of the recreational teams and their season records.

The payoff of this cultural commitment to employees and the environment is an average length of service in the company of 16 years, and a turnover rate of 2 percent.

SOURCES: http://greatplacetowork.com/best/sme2009/best-small-and-medium-2009-badger-mining.php; http://www2.shrm.org/bptw/index.html

How Leaders React to Crises

The way leaders deal with crises communicates a powerful message about culture. Emotions are heightened during a crisis, and learning is intense. With mergers and acquisitions, the way in which the leader reacts to change, transparency of the procedures used, and communication quality affect how followers perceive change and ultimately acceptance of any associated changes in the organizational culture.[52]

Difficult economic times present crises for many companies and illustrate their different values. Some organizations do everything possible to prevent laying off workers. Others may claim that employees are important but quickly institute major layoffs at the first signal of an economic downturn. Employees may perceive that the company shows its true colors in a crisis and thus may pay careful attention to the reactions of their leaders.

When the Enron crisis became public, managers quickly shifted blame and pointed fingers. Before bankruptcy was declared, managers began systematically firing any employee they could lay blame on, while denying that there was a problem with accounting irregularities. During the crisis, managers responded with anonymous whistle-blowing, hiding behind the Fifth Amendment and shredding documents.

How Leaders Behave

Through role modeling, teaching, and coaching, leaders reinforce the values that support the organizational culture. Employees often emulate leaders' behavior and look to the leaders for cues to appropriate behavior. Many companies are encouraging employees to be more entrepreneurial—to take more initiative and be more innovative in their jobs. A study showed that if managers want employees to be more entrepreneurial, they must demonstrate such behaviors themselves.[53] This is the case with any cultural value. Employees observe the behavior of leaders to find out what the organization values.

The behavior of Enron's managers spoke volumes; they broke the law as they created fake partnerships. They ignored and then denied that problems existed. While employees were unable to dump their Enron stocks, managers were hastily getting rid of their shares, all the while telling employees that the company would be fine.

How Leaders Allocate Rewards

To ensure that values are accepted, leaders should reward behavior that is consistent with the values. Some companies, for example, may claim that they use a pay-for-performance system that distributes rewards on the basis of performance. When the time comes for raises, however, the increases are awarded according to length of service with the company. Imagine the feelings of a high-performing newcomer who has heard leaders espouse the value of rewarding individual performance and then receives only a tiny raise.

Some companies may value teamwork. They form cross-functional teams and empower them to make important decisions. However, when performance is appraised, the criteria for rating employees focus on individual performance. This sends a confusing signal to employees about the company's culture: Is individual performance valued, or is teamwork the key?

At Enron, employees were rewarded only if they produced consistent results, with little regard for ethics. Managers were given extremely large bonuses to keep the stock price up at any cost. Performance reviews were done in public, and poor performers were ridiculed.

How Leaders Hire and Fire Individuals

A powerful way that leaders reinforce culture is through the selection of newcomers to the organization. With the advent of electronic recruitment practices, applicant perceptions of organizational culture are shaped by what the organization advertises on their recruitment Web site. Typical perception-shaping mechanisms are organizational values, policies, awards, and goals.[54] Leaders often unconsciously look for individuals who are similar to current organizational members in terms of values and assumptions. Some companies hire individuals on the recommendation of a current employee; this tends to perpetuate the culture because the new employees typically hold similar values. Jeffrey Swartz, CEO of Timberland, has a unique way of hiring people. He has his recruiter call the applicant in advance and have them wear anything they feel passionately about other than Timberland shoes. Senior applicants go through a day of community service with Timberland executives because Swartz claims that anyone can be smarter than him in an interview, but service brings out the real person and this is who they try to hire.[55]

The way a company fires an employee and the rationale behind the firing also communicate the culture. Some companies deal with poor performers by trying to find a place within the organization where they can perform better and make a contribution. Other companies seem to operate under the philosophy that those who cannot perform are out quickly.

The reasons for terminations may not be directly communicated to other employees, but curiosity leads to speculation. An employee who displays unethical behavior and is caught may simply be reprimanded even though such behavior is clearly against the organization's values. Other employees may view this as a failure to reinforce the values within the organization.

Enron hired employees who had aggressiveness, greed, a desire to win at all costs, and a willingness to break rules. It fired nonproductive employees, using a "rank and yank" system whereby the bottom 15–20 percent of employees were let go each year. Peers were required to rank each other, which led to cutthroat competition and extreme distrust among employees.

In summary, leaders play a critical role in shaping and reinforcing organizational culture. The Enron case illustrates how powerful, and potentially damaging, that influence can be. The lesson for future managers is to create a positive culture through what they pay attention to, how they react to crises, how they behave, the way they allocate rewards, and how they hire and fire employees. Research results from a study of finance professionals in Greece support this view. Transformational leaders create a more adaptive culture, which in turn increases business unit performance.[56]

ORGANIZATIONAL SOCIALIZATION

We have seen that leaders play key roles in shaping an organization's culture. Another process that perpetuates culture is the way it is handed down from generation to generation of employees. Newcomers learn the culture through *organizational socialization*—the process by which newcomers are transformed from outsiders to participating, effective members of the organization.[57] The process is also a vehicle for bringing newcomers into the organizational culture. As we saw earlier, cultural socialization begins with the careful selection of newcomers who are likely to reinforce the organizational culture.[58] Once selected, newcomers pass through the socialization process.

The Stages of the Socialization Process

The organizational socialization process is generally described as having three stages: anticipatory socialization, encounter, and change and acquisition. Figure 16.2 presents a model of the process and the key concerns at each stage of it.[59]

It also describes the outcomes of the process, which will be discussed in the next section of the chapter.

7 Describe the three stages of organizational socialization and the ways culture is communicated in each step.

Anticipatory Socialization *Anticipatory socialization,* the first stage, encompasses all of the learning that takes place prior to the newcomer's first day on the job. It includes the newcomer's expectations. The two key concerns at this stage are realism and congruence.

Realism is the degree to which a newcomer holds realistic expectations about the job and about the organization. One thing newcomers should receive information about during entry into the organization is the culture. Information about values at this stage can help newcomers begin to construct a scheme for interpreting their organizational experiences. A deeper understanding of the organization's culture will be possible through time and experience in the organization. Furthermore, a recent study found that when organizations not only give realistic job previews that highlight major stressors *but also* teach various coping strategies to deal with these stressors, newcomers feel less stressed and report higher levels of adjustment six and nine months post entry.[60]

There are two types of *congruence* between an individual and an organization: congruence between the individual's abilities and the demands of the job, and the

organizational socialization
The process by which newcomers are transformed from outsiders to participating, effective members of the organization.

anticipatory socialization
The first socialization stage, which encompasses all of the learning that takes place prior to the newcomer's first day on the job.

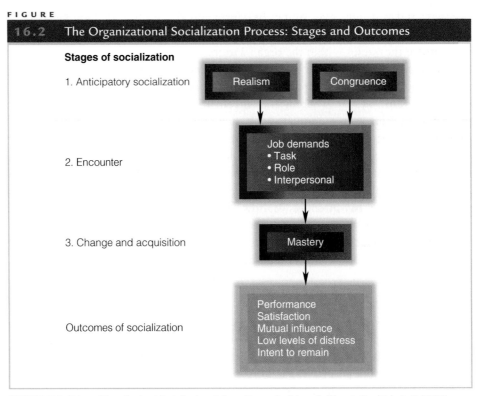

16.2   The Organizational Socialization Process: Stages and Outcomes

Stages of socialization

1. Anticipatory socialization — Realism   Congruence

2. Encounter — Job demands
- Task
- Role
- Interpersonal

3. Change and acquisition — Mastery

Outcomes of socialization — Performance
Satisfaction
Mutual influence
Low levels of distress
Intent to remain

SOURCE: D. L. Nelson, "Organizational Socialization: A Stress Perspective," *Journal of Organizational Behavior* 8 (1987): 311–324.

fit between the organization's values and the individual's values. Organizations disseminate information about their values through their Web pages, annual reports, and recruitment brochures.[61] Value congruence is particularly important for organizational culture. It is also important in terms of newcomer adjustment. Newcomers whose values match the company's values are more satisfied with their new jobs, adjust more quickly, and say they intend to remain with the firm longer.[62]

Encounter The second stage of socialization, *encounter,* is when newcomers learn the tasks associated with the job, clarify their roles, and establish new relationships at work. This stage commences on the first day at work and is thought to encompass the first six to nine months on the new job. Newcomers face task demands, role demands, and interpersonal demands during this period.

Task demands involve the actual work performed. Learning to perform tasks is related to the organization's culture. In some organizations, newcomers are given considerable latitude to experiment with new ways to do the job, and creativity is valued. In others, newcomers are expected to learn the established procedures for their tasks. Early experiences with trying to master task demands can affect employees' entire careers. Auditors, for example, are often forced to choose between being thorough, on the one hand, and being fast in completing their work, on the other. By pressuring auditors in this way, firms often set themselves up for problems later, when these pressures may lead auditors to make less-than-ethical decisions.

Role demands involve the expectations placed on newcomers. Newcomers may not know exactly what is expected of them (role ambiguity) or may receive conflicting expectations from other individuals (role conflict). The way newcomers approach these demands depends in part on the culture of the organization. Are newcomers expected to operate with considerable uncertainty, or is the manager expected to clarify the newcomers' roles? Some cultures even put newcomers through considerable stress in the socialization process, including humility-inducing

encounter
The second socialization stage in which the newcomer learns the tasks associated with the job, clarifies roles, and establishes new relationships at work.

experiences, so newcomers will be more open to accepting the firm's values and norms. Long hours, tiring travel schedules, and an overload of work are part of some socialization practices.

Interpersonal demands arise from relationships at work. Politics, leadership style, and group pressure are interpersonal demands. All of them reflect the values and assumptions that operate within the organization. Most organizations have basic assumptions about the nature of human relationships. The Korean *chaebol* (business conglomerate) LG Group strongly values harmony in relationships and in society, and its decision-making policy emphasizes unanimity.

In the encounter stage, the expectations formed in anticipatory socialization may clash with the realities of the job. It is a time of facing the task, role, and interpersonal demands of the new job.

Change and Acquisition In the third and final stage of socialization, *change and acquisition,* newcomers begin to master the demands of the job. They become proficient at managing their tasks, clarifying and negotiating their roles, and engaging in relationships at work. The time when the socialization process is completed varies widely, depending on the individual, the job, and the organization. The end of the process is signaled by newcomers being considered by themselves and others as organizational insiders.

Outcomes of Socialization

Newcomers who are successfully socialized should exhibit good performance, high job satisfaction, and the intention to stay with the organization. In addition, they should exhibit low levels of distress symptoms.[63] High levels of organizational commitment are also marks of successful socialization.[64] This commitment is facilitated throughout the socialization process by the communication of values that newcomers can buy into. Successful socialization is also signaled by mutual influence; that is, the newcomers have made adjustments in the job and organization to accommodate their knowledge and personalities. Newcomers are expected to leave their mark on the organization and not to be completely conforming.

When socialization is effective, newcomers understand and adopt the organization's values and norms. This ensures that the company's culture, including its central values, survives. It also provides employees a context for interpreting and responding to things that happen at work, and it ensures a shared framework of understanding among employees.[65]

Newcomers adopt the company's norms and values more quickly when they receive positive support from organizational insiders. Sometimes this is accomplished through informal social gatherings.[66] Although socialization occurs when an employee enters the organization, a recent study shows how this support from organizational leaders can impact socialization outcomes for close to two years after entry. See the Science feature for more information.

Socialization as Cultural Communication

Socialization is a powerful cultural communication tool. While the transmission of information about cultural artifacts is relatively easy, the transmission of values is more difficult. The communication of organizational assumptions is almost impossible, since organization members themselves may not be consciously aware of them.

The primary purpose of socialization is the transmission of core values to new organization members.[67] Newcomers are exposed to these values through the role models they interact with, the training they receive, and the behavior they observe

change and acquisition
The third socialization stage, in which the newcomer begins to master the demands of the job.

Steve Vidler/Photolibrary

Disney transmits its culture to employees through careful selection, socialization, and training.

being rewarded and punished. Newcomers are vigilant observers, seeking clues to the organization's culture and consistency in the cultural messages they receive. If they are expected to adopt these values, it is essential that the message reflect the underlying values of the organization.

One company known for its culture is The Walt Disney Company. Disney transmits its culture to employees though careful selection, socialization, and training. The Disney culture is built around customer service, and its image serves as a filtering process for applicants. Peer interviews are used to learn how applicants interact with each other. Disney tries to secure a good fit between employee values and the organization's culture. To remind employees of the image they are trying to project, employees are referred to as "cast members" and they occupy a "role." They work either "on stage" or "backstage" and wear "costumes" rather than uniforms. Disney operates its own "universities," which are attended by all new employees. Once trained at a Disney university, cast members are paired with role models to continue their learning on-site.

Companies such as Disney use the socialization process to communicate messages about organizational culture. Both individuals and organizations can take certain actions to ensure the success of the socialization process.

ASSESSING ORGANIZATIONAL CULTURE

8 Identify ways of assessing organizational culture.

Although some organizational scientists argue for assessing organizational culture with quantitative methods, others say qualitative methods yield better results.[68] Quantitative methods, such as questionnaires, are valuable because of their precision, comparability, and objectivity. Qualitative methods, such as interviews and observations, are valuable because of their detail, descriptiveness, and uniqueness.

Two widely used quantitative assessment instruments are the Organizational Culture Inventory (OCI) and the Kilmann–Saxton Culture-Gap Survey. Both assess the behavioral norms of organizational cultures, as opposed to the artifacts, values, or assumptions of the organization.

Organizational Culture Inventory

The OCI focuses on behaviors that help employees fit into the organization and meet the expectations of coworkers. Using Maslow's motivational need hierarchy as its basis, it measures twelve cultural styles. The two underlying dimensions of the OCI are task/people and security/satisfaction. There are four satisfaction cultural styles and eight security cultural styles.

A self-report instrument, the OCI contains 120 questions. It provides an individual assessment of culture and may be aggregated to the work group and to the organizational level.[69] It has been used in firms throughout North America, Western Europe, New Zealand, and Thailand, as well as in U.S. military units, the Federal Aviation Administration, and nonprofit organizations.

Kilmann–Saxton Culture-Gap Survey

The Kilmann–Saxton Culture-Gap Survey focuses on what actually happens and on the expectations of others in the organization.[70] Its two underlying dimensions are technical/human and time (the short term versus the long term). With these two dimensions, the actual operating norms and the ideal norms in four areas are assessed. The areas are task support (short-term technical norms), task innovation (long-term technical norms), social relationships (short-term human orientation norms), and personal freedom (long-term human orientation norms). Significant gaps in any of the four areas are used as a point of departure for cultural change to improve performance, job satisfaction, and morale.

A self-report instrument, the Gap Survey provides an individual assessment of culture and may be aggregated to the work group. It has been used in firms throughout the United States and in nonprofit organizations.

Triangulation

A study of a rehabilitation center in a 400-bed hospital incorporated *triangulation* (the use of multiple methods to measure organizational culture) to improve inclusiveness and accuracy in measuring the organizational culture.[71] Triangulation has been used by anthropologists, sociologists, and other behavioral scientists to study organizational culture. Its name comes from the navigational technique of using multiple reference points to locate an object. In the rehabilitation center study, the three methods used to triangulate on the culture were (1) obtrusive observations by eight trained observers, which provided an outsider perspective; (2) self-administered questionnaires, which provided quantitative insider information; and (3) personal interviews with the center's staff, which provided qualitative contextual information.

The study showed that each of the three methods made unique contributions toward the discovery of the rehabilitation center's culture. The complete picture could not have been drawn with just a single technique. Triangulation can lead to a better understanding of the phenomenon of culture and is the best approach to assessing organizational culture.

CHANGING ORGANIZATIONAL CULTURE

Changing situations may require changes in the existing culture of an organization. With rapid environmental changes such as globalization, workforce diversity, and technological innovation, the fundamental assumptions and basic values that drive the organization may need to be altered. One particular situation that may require cultural change is a merger or acquisition. The blending of two distinct organizational cultures may prove difficult.

Despite good-faith efforts, combining cultures is difficult. When established media giant Time Warner merged with Internet upstart America Online in 2001, few could imagine the fireworks that would result when these two "oil and water" firms tried to mix. Typical of the conflicts that followed was a client dinner in which AOL executive Neil Davis horrified Time Warner executives by describing how AOL preferred to handle weakened competitors. Taking a steak knife from the table, Davis raised his arm and drove the knife into the table top, explaining that "What we like

triangulation

The use of multiple methods to measure organizational culture.

to do to a competitor that is damaged is drive the knife in their heart." The shocked client ultimately declined to buy ads on AOL, and the entire merger was eventually deemed a multibillion-dollar failure due, at least in part, to the culture clash between the two partners.[72]

Prior to the Daimler–Chrysler merger, both automotive giants enjoyed good performance. After the merger, however, it was a different story. The Chrysler division started losing money and instituted major, unanticipated layoffs. Differences in culture were cited as responsible for this failure. Daimler–Benz had a culture that was formal, with a very structured management style. Chrysler, by contrast, had a relaxed management style that accounted for its premerger success. The two divisions had vastly different views on pay scales and travel expenses. Chrysler executives and engineers began leaving in great numbers, and Chrysler employees believed that Daimler was trying to control the company and impose its culture on Chrysler. The stock price after the merger fell to half of its previous value following the initial postmerger high.[73,74]

Alterations in culture may also be required when an organization employs people from different countries. Research indicates that some organizational cultures actually enhance differences in national cultures.[75] One study compared foreign employees working in a multinational organization with employees working in different organizations within their own countries. The assumption was that the employees from various countries working for the same multinational organization would be more similar than employees working in diverse organizations in their native countries. The results were surprising, in that there were significantly greater differences among the employees of the multinational than among managers working for different companies within their native countries. In the multinational, Swedes became more Swedish, Americans became more American, and so forth. It appears that employees enhance their national culture traditions even when working within a single organizational culture.[76] This is more likely to occur when diversity is moderate. When diversity is very high, employees are more likely to develop a shared identity in the organization's culture instead of relying on their own national culture.[77]

9 Explain actions managers can take to change organizational culture.

Changing an organization's culture is feasible but difficult.[78] One reason for the difficulty is that assumptions—the deepest level of culture—are often unconscious. As such, they are often nonconfrontable and nondebatable. Another reason for the difficulty is that culture is deeply ingrained and behavioral norms and rewards are well learned.[79] In a sense, employees must unlearn the old norms before they can learn new ones. Managers who want to change the culture should look first to the ways culture is maintained. Research among hospitals found that change was welcomed in private hospitals with a collaborative culture, whereas change was met with opposition in public hospitals with an autocratic culture.[80]

A model for cultural change that summarizes the interventions managers can use is presented in Figure 16.3. In this model, the numbers represent the actions managers can take. There are two basic approaches to changing the existing culture: (1) helping current members buy into a new set of values (actions 1, 2, and 3); or (2) adding newcomers and socializing them into the organization and removing current members as appropriate (actions 4 and 5).[81]

The first action is to change behavior in the organization. Even if behavior does change, however, this is not sufficient for cultural change to occur. Behavior is an artifact (level 1) of culture. Individuals may change their behavior but not the values that drive it. They may rationalize, "I'm only doing this because my manager wants me to."

Therefore, managers must use action 2, which is to examine the justifications for the changed behavior. Are employees buying into the new set of values, or are they just complying?

16.3 Interventions for Changing Organizational Culture

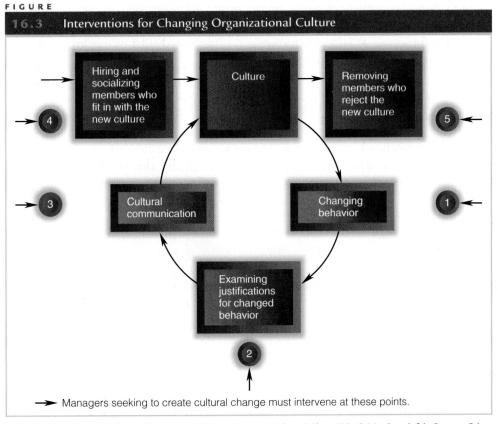

➤ Managers seeking to create cultural change must intervene at these points.

SOURCE: From Vijay Sathe, "How to Decipher and Change Corporate Culture," Chap. 13 in *Gaining Control of the Corporate Culture* (R. H. Kilmann et al., eds.), Fig. 1, p. 245. Copyright © 1985 Jossey-Bass, Inc. Reprinted by permission of Jossey-Bass, Inc., a subsidiary of John Wiley & Sons, Inc.

The third action, cultural communication, is extremely important. All of the artifacts (personal enactment, stories, rites and ceremonies, rituals, and symbols) must send a consistent message about the new values and beliefs. It is crucial that the communication be credible; that is, managers must live the new values and not just talk about them. Leaders should pay attention to the informal social networks rather than just structural positions in leading organizational change. These informal network communication channels, combined with employee's values and the belief that managers are highly committed to the change effort, can go a long way in making the change a success.[82]

The two remaining actions (4 and 5) involve shaping the workforce to fit the intended culture. First, the organization can revise its selection strategies to more accurately reflect the new culture. Second, the organization can identify individuals who resist the cultural change or who are no longer comfortable with the values in the organization. Reshaping the workforce should not involve a ruthless pursuit of nonconforming employees; it should be a gradual and subtle change that takes considerable time. Changing personnel in the organization is a lengthy process; it cannot be done effectively in a short period of time without considerable problems.

Evaluating the success of cultural change may be best done by looking at behavior. Cultural change can be assumed to be successful if the behavior is intrinsically motivated—on "automatic pilot." If the new behavior would persist even if rewards were not present, and if the employees have internalized the new value system, then the behavior is probably intrinsically motivated. If employees automatically respond to a crisis in ways consistent with the corporate culture, then the cultural change effort can be deemed successful.

Given the current business environment, managers may want to focus on three particular cultural modifications: (1) support for a global view of business, (2) reinforcement of ethical behavior, and (3) empowerment of employees to excel in product and service quality.

Developing a Global Organizational Culture

The values that drive the organizational culture should support a global view of the company and its efforts. To do so, the values should be clear to everyone involved so that everyone understands them. The values should also be strongly supported at the top. Management should embody the shared values and reward employees who support the global view. Finally, the values should be consistent over time. Consistent values give an organization a unifying theme that competitors may be unable to emulate.[83]

Global corporations suffer from the conflicting pressures of centralization and decentralization. An overarching corporate culture that integrates the decentralized subsidiaries in locations around the world can be an asset in the increasingly competitive global marketplace.

Following are six specific guidelines for managers who want to create a global culture:[84]

1. Create a clear and simple mission statement. A shared mission can unite individuals from diverse cultural backgrounds.

2. Create systems that ensure an effective flow of information. Coordination councils and global task forces can be used to ensure that information flows throughout the geographically dispersed organization are consistent.

3. Create "matrix minds" among managers; that is, broaden managers' minds to allow them to think globally. IBM does this through temporary overseas assignments. Managers with international experience share that experience when they return to the home organization.

4. Develop global career paths. This means ensuring not only that home country executives go overseas but also that executives from other countries rotate into service in the home office.

5. Use cultural differences as a major asset. The former Digital Equipment Corporation (now part of Hewlett-Packard), for example, transferred its research and development functions to Italy to take advantage of the free-flowing Italian management style that encouraged creativity. Its manufacturing operations went to Germany, which offered a more systematic management style.

6. Implement worldwide management education and team development programs. Unified training efforts that emphasize corporate values can help establish a shared identity among employees.

These guidelines are specifically aimed at multinational organizations that want to create a global corporate culture, but other organizations can also benefit from them. Companies that want to broaden employees' views or to use the diversity of their workforce as a resource will find several of these recommendations advantageous.

Developing an Ethical Organizational Culture

While a majority of U.S. firms have rushed to create and publicize codes of ethics in an effort to help their employees discern right from wrong, the impact of these codes is not always as positive as might be expected. While the implementation of formal ethics guidelines might be expected to improve ethical behavior, some studies have shown the exact opposite, with institution of formal ethics codes actually leading to less ethical behavior among employees. While the reasons for this are not clear, it appears that in some cases employees see the code of ethics as simply a management showpiece, leading to cynicism and resentment. In other cases, a heavy reliance on a strict set of rules may reduce the perceived need for employees to think about and be involved in ethical decision making, leading to inferior choices in the long run.[85]

The organizational culture, however, can have profound effects on the ethical behavior of organization members.[86] When a company's culture promotes ethical norms, individuals behave accordingly. Managers can encourage ethical behavior by being good role models for employees. They can institute the philosophy that ethical behavior makes good business sense and puts the company in congruence with the larger values of society.[87] Managers can also communicate that rationalizations for unethical behavior are not tolerated. For example, some salespersons justify padding their expense accounts because everyone else does it. Declaring these justifications illegitimate sends a clear message about the lack of tolerance for such behavior. Leaders can also use storytelling as a tool to build an ethical culture and create a sense of identity for organizational members with a higher purpose or goal within the organization.[88] For example, Cisco's CEO John Chambers is known for his ability to give inspiring speeches. Yet Cisco is in the business of selling routers and switches—items that are crucial for Internet connectivity but that most users don't even see. Chambers tells stories of how such connectivity can change lives and make the world a better place and thus creates a sense of identity and higher purpose for his investors as well as employees.[89]

Trust is another key to effectively managing ethical behavior, especially in cultures that encourage whistle-blowing (as we saw in Chapter 2). Employees must trust that whistle-blowers will be protected, that procedures used to investigate ethical problems will be fair, and that management will take action to solve problems that are uncovered.

The reasons most often cited for unethical corporate conduct are interesting.[90] They include the belief that a behavior is not really unethical, that it is in the organization's best interest, that it will not be discovered, and that the organization will support it because it offers a good outcome for the organization. An ethical corporate culture can eliminate the viability of these excuses by clearly communicating the boundaries of ethical conduct, selecting employees who support the ethical culture, rewarding organization members who exhibit ethical behavior, and conspicuously punishing members who engage in unethical behavior.

Organizations that seek to encourage ethical behavior can do so by using their organizational culture. By completing You 16.2, you can assess the ethical culture of an organization you're familiar with.

Developing a Culture of Empowerment and Quality

Throughout this book, we have seen that successful organizations promote a culture that empowers employees and excels in product and service quality. Empowerment serves to unleash employees' creativity and productivity. It requires eliminating traditional hierarchical notions of power. Cultures that emphasize empowerment and quality are preferred by employees. Companies that value empowerment and continuous improvement have cultures that promote high product and service quality.[91] Furthermore, an integral part of empowerment and improvement involves the manager trusting his or her employees. Organizations with employees who feel as though management trusts them perform better. When an organization focuses on

You 16.2

Organizational Culture and Ethics

Think about the organization you currently work for or one you know something about and complete the following Ethical Climate Questionnaire.

Use the scale below and write the number that best represents your answer in the space next to each item.

To what extent are the following statements true about your company?

Completely false	Mostly false	Somewhat false	Somewhat true	Mostly true	Completely true
0	1	2	3	4	5

_____ 1. In this company, people are expected to follow their own personal and moral beliefs.

_____ 2. People are expected to do anything to further the company's interests.

_____ 3. In this company, people look out for each other's good.

_____ 4. It is very important here to follow the company's rules and procedures strictly.

_____ 5. In this company, people protect their own interests above other considerations.

_____ 6. The first consideration is whether a decision violates any law.

_____ 7. Everyone is expected to stick by company rules and procedures.

_____ 8. The most efficient way is always the right way in this company.

_____ 9. Our major consideration is what is best for everyone in the company.

_____ 10. In this company, the law or ethical code of the profession is the major consideration.

_____ 11. It is expected at this company that employees will always do what is right for the customer and the public.

To score the questionnaire, first add up your responses to questions 1, 3, 6, 9, 10, and 11. This is subtotal number 1. Next, reverse the scores on questions 2, 4, 5, 7, and 8 (5 = 0, 4 = 1, 3 = 2, 2 = 3, 1 = 4, 0 = 5). Add the reverse scores to form subtotal number 2. Add subtotal number 1 to subtotal number 2 for an overall score.

Subtotal 1 _____ + Subtotal 2 _____ = Overall Score _____.

Overall scores can range from 0 to 55. The higher the score, the more the organization's culture encourages ethical behavior.

SOURCE: Reprinted from *Organizational Dynamics*, Autumn 1989, "An Ethical Weather Report: Assessing the Organization's Ethical Climate" by John B. Cullen et al. Copyright © 1989, with permission from Elsevier Science.

instilling a culture of trust, employees feel accountable for their performance, and sales performance improves as well as customer service performance.[92]

Corporate culture can also support values that help firms compete. New Balance Athletic Shoe competes with low-wage suppliers in Asia (where the average wage is less than $2 per hour), even though one-fourth of its products are produced in the United States. Part of the firm's success comes from its willingness to empower its employees by sharing information with them. For instance, the firm often shares cost data with employees, pointing out that a competitor's shoe can be made overseas for $15 and challenging them to meet that cost point. Today, New Balance workers in the United States receive twenty-two hours of training when they are hired and continual training on the factory floor. The result is that New Balance's U.S. workers can produce a pair of shoes in twenty-four minutes, compared with almost three hours in Asia.[93,94]

Harley-Davidson might well be the ultimate old-line manufacturing firm trying to develop a culture of quality. From 1985, with the firm literally minutes from bankruptcy, to today, with demand for its high-quality cycles at an all-time high, Harley-Davidson has gone from the valley to the mountaintop. Like many other old manufacturing firms, Harley tried to compete in the 1970s with techniques developed in the 1950s. Huge forklifts wandered the shop floor, shuffling millions of dollars worth of components among workstations; quality was poor—in short, Harley was fat and inefficient. Over the last two decades, Harley has reinvented itself. Manufacturing has been streamlined to reflect more modern thinking on efficiency. Product quality has improved immensely, and the firm's workforce continues to improve, with close to half the company's employees taking training courses in any given year.

Harley's high level of quality is not merely an artifact of better shop practices. The company's management has worked to foster a unique congenial relationship with its unions, ensuring that continuous improvement is an organizational priority rather than simply the latest management fad. Today's Harley "hog" costs less to make and is more reliable than any before it, due in large part to the firm's incessant drive to make a better product.[95]

Medrad, Inc., won the 2003 Malcolm Baldrige Award for quality in manufacturing. Medrad makes devices that allow doctors to see through you; using diagnostic imaging technology, doctors get an inside view of the human body. It sells these products to hospitals and imaging centers around the world. CEO John Friel is committed to continuous improvement and quality, as well as employee empowerment. He spends at least one day a month in company shop floor operations—including customer service, tech support, and even sweeping the floor in maintenance. Friel's employees are committed to him, to Medrad, and to quality.[96]

Managers can learn from the experiences of New Balance, Harley-Davidson, and Medrad that employee empowerment is a key to achieving quality. Involving employees in decision making, removing obstacles to their performance, and communicating the value of product and service quality reinforce the values of empowerment and quality in the organizational culture.

MANAGERIAL IMPLICATIONS: THE ORGANIZATIONAL CULTURE CHALLENGE

Managing organizational culture is a key challenge for leaders in today's organizations. With the trend toward downsizing and restructuring, maintaining an organizational culture in the face of change is difficult. In addition, such challenges as globalization, workforce diversity, technology, and managing ethical behavior often require that an organization change its culture. Adaptive cultures that can respond to changes in the environment can lead the way in terms of organizational performance.

Managers have at their disposal many techniques for managing organizational culture. These techniques range from manipulating the artifacts of culture, such as ceremonies and symbols, to communicating the values that guide the organization. The socialization process is a powerful cultural communication process. Managers are models who communicate the organizational culture to employees through personal enactment. Their modeled behavior sets the norms for the other employees to follow. Their leadership is essential for developing a culture that values diversity, supports empowerment, fosters innovations in product and service quality, and promotes ethical behavior.

Diversity Dialogue

Culture Change Ordered for Cola Giant

Coca-Cola was given five years to change its corporate culture and treatment of people of color as part of a $192.5 million discrimination lawsuit settlement, the largest in U.S. history. For years, the cola giant highlighted its commitment to African Americans outside the company: consumers, suppliers, and members of the community. However many believed the organization did not show the same level of commitment to its employees *inside* the firm.

The case began when African-American Linda Ingram's manager made derogatory remarks to her, calling her the N-word to her face. Says Ingram, "She did it around some other peers ... I was so appalled and shocked that something of that nature would happen at that company in that day and time." Ingram's manager was subsequently fired for her remarks, but the investigation increased tension between Ingram and her coworkers (all of whom were white) so much that she requested a transfer to another department. After her requests were continually ignored by the company's

human resource manager, Ingram felt she had no other recourse but to seek relief outside of the firm.

Ingram did not sue Coca-Cola because her former manager called her the N-word. She brought legal action against Coca-Cola as a result of the company's culture of indifference after the fact. Cyrus Mehri, the attorney who won a landmark $176 million judgment in the 1997 Texaco discrimination case, took on Ingram's case, charging Coca-Cola with engaging in systematic race discrimination that extended throughout its employment policies and practices.

1. Why do you believe Coca-Cola was ordered to change its culture and not only its treatment of employees of color?
2. What are the first steps you would you take to initiate such a culture change?

SOURCE: S. Spruell, "Coca-Cola: From Discrimination Suit to Diversity Leader," *DiversityInc* (January/February 2007): 21–30.

LOOKING BACK: NORDSTROM

NORDSTROM

Maintaining Customer Service Excellence for Over 100 Years

The Nordstrom family understands how to maintain a customer service culture. First, leading by example has always been a focus. The executive members of the Nordstrom family have all worked in the stores since they were young. They understand the daily life in these stores and they set a good example. A former employee tells a story about Bruce Nordstrom, who cleaned off counters in one of the Nordstrom's stores because he saw it needed doing. He didn't ask an employee to do it; he just did it. Furthermore, Nordstrom does everything it can to keep employees who excel in their customer service-focused culture; whenever possible, they promote from within.

Nordstrom also uses stories to spread the culture. The company encourages its employees to write up "heroics" or stories of customer service and teamwork above and beyond the call of duty. In fact, the examples in the Looking Ahead section are all heroics written by employees about other employees. The company also relies on experienced "Nordies" to socialize new employees to the culture. When Nordstrom expands into a new market, veteran Nordies speak to new employees and give their own personal stories of the company. All these tactics have allowed Nordstrom to become

known for its exceptional customer service and maintain that reputation for more than 100 years.

Chapter Summary

1. Organizational (corporate) culture is a pattern of basic assumptions that are considered valid and that are taught to new members as the way to perceive, think, and feel in the organization.

2. The most visible and accessible level of culture is artifacts, which include personal enactment, ceremonies and rites, stories, rituals, and symbols.

3. Organizational culture has four functions: giving members a sense of identity and increasing their commitment, serving as a sense-making device for members, reinforcing organizational values, and serving as a control mechanism for shaping behavior.

4. Three theories about the relationship between culture and performance are the strong culture perspective, the fit perspective, and the adaptation perspective.

5. Leaders shape and reinforce culture by what they pay attention to, how they react to crises, how they

behave, how they allocate rewards, and how they hire and fire individuals.

6. Organizational socialization is the process by which newcomers become participating, effective members of the organization. Its three stages are anticipatory socialization, encounter, and change and acquisition. Each stage plays a unique role in communicating organizational culture.

7. The Organizational Culture Inventory and Kilmann–Saxton Culture-Gap Survey are two quantitative instruments for assessing organizational culture. Triangulation, using multiple methods for assessing culture, is an effective measurement strategy.

8. It is difficult but not impossible to change organizational culture. Managers can do so by helping current members buy into a new set of values, by adding newcomers and socializing them into the organization, and by removing current members as appropriate.

Key Terms

adaptive culture (p. 564)
anticipatory socialization (p. 569)
artifacts (p. 556)
assumptions (p. 561)
change and acquisition (p. 571)

enacted values (p. 560)
encounter (p. 570)
espoused values (p. 560)
organizational (corporate) culture
  (p. 556)

organizational socialization (p. 569)
strong culture (p. 564)
triangulation (p. 573)

Review Questions

1. Explain the three levels of organizational culture. How can each level be measured?

2. Describe five artifacts of culture and give an example of each.

3. Explain three theories about the relationship between organizational culture and performance. What does the research evidence say about each one?

4. Contrast adaptive and nonadaptive cultures.

5. How can leaders shape organizational culture?

6. Describe the three stages of organizational socialization. How is culture communicated in each stage?

7. How can managers assess the organizational culture? What actions can they take to change the organizational culture?

8. How does a manager know that cultural change has been successful?

9. What can managers do to develop a global organizational culture?

Discussion and Communication Questions

1. Name a company with a visible organizational culture. What do you think are the company's values? Has the culture contributed to the organization's performance? Explain.

2. Name a leader you think manages organizational culture well. How does the leader do this? Use Schein's description of how leaders reinforce culture to analyze the leader's behavior.

3. Suppose you want to change your organization's culture. What sort of resistance would you expect from employees? How would you deal with this resistance?

4. Given Schein's three levels, can we ever truly understand an organization's culture? Explain.

5. To what extent is culture manageable? Changeable?

6. *(communication question)* Select an organization that you might like to work for. Learn as much as you can about that company's culture, using library resources, online sources, contacts within the company, and as many creative means as you can. Prepare a brief presentation to the class summarizing the culture.

Ethical Dilemma

Lisbeth Kakutani is committed to making sure that her teams run as efficiently and as harmoniously as possible. When an opening comes up, she is relentless in working to find the right person, someone who has the skills and abilities to do the job but also someone who will fit the culture. Part of Lisbeth's commitment stems from what had been fostered in the culture of Larson-Knoff, Inc. well before she arrived. The community atmosphere at Larson-Knoff is one that is supportive of family and oriented in group-work. Larson-Knoff's mission speaks of working for the good of the many rather than the advancement of the individual, and for those who have been with the organization for years, it has become a true family atmosphere.

As Lisbeth sorts through applications for an opening in her department, she finds herself struck by one in particular—Graham Williams. Graham has every academic and professional qualification Lisbeth could want for to fill the position, and she immediately calls him in for an interview. Graham impresses Lisbeth during the interview. His education and experience should allow him to become effective as soon as he joins the team. He is the best candidate she has seen. Lisbeth's only reservation is that Graham seems to be something of a loner although he assures her that he can work very effectively with others.

As soon as Graham joins the team, Lisbeth is aware that her concerns are well founded. Graham prefers to work on projects alone. He willingly shares his information but rarely does the work in conjunction with the other members of the department. Lisbeth is worried that Graham is completely disinterested in being a good team member. However, Graham's work is superb, and she is well aware that clients approve whole-heartedly regarding his designs and his approaches. In fact, Graham's work on existing clients' accounts has enticed new ones to come aboard.

Lisbeth is willing to give Graham time to develop his team skills but already the complaints are coming in from the other members of the group. Everyone has noticed Graham's unwillingness to be a team player and they are not happy. Graham is creating a divide in Lisbeth's department and serious problems are developing. Lisbeth really likes Graham and wants to keep him but is he worth disrupting the culture that is at the heart of Larson-Knoff?

Questions:

1. Using consequential, rule-based and character theories, evaluate Lisbeth's options.

2. What should Lisbeth do? Why?

Experiential Exercises

16.1 Identifying Behavioral Norms

This exercise asks you to identify campus norms at your university. Every organization or group has a set of norms that help determine individuals' behavior. A norm is an unwritten rule for behavior in a group. When a norm is not followed, negative feedback is given. It may include negative comments, stares, harassment, and exclusion.

1. As a group, brainstorm all the norms you can think of in the following areas:
   Dress
   Classroom behavior

Studying
Weekend activities
Living arrangements
Campus activities
Dating (who asks whom)
Relationships with faculty
Eating on campus versus off campus
Transportation

2. How did you initially get this information?
3. What happens to students who don't follow these norms?
4. What values can be inferred from these norms?

SOURCE: Dorothy Marcic, "Identifying Behavioral Norms," *Organizational Behavior: Experiences and Cases* (St. Paul, MN: West Publishing, 1989). Reprinted by permission.

16.2 Contrasting Organizational Cultures

To complete this exercise, groups of four or five students should be formed. Each group should select one of the following pairs of organizations:

American Airlines and Northwest Airlines
Anheuser-Busch and Coors
Hewlett-Packard and Xerox
Albertsons and Winn-Dixie
Dayton-Hudson (Target) and J. C. Penney Company

Use your university library's resources to gather information about the companies' cultures. Contrast the cultures of the two organizations using the following dimensions:

- Strength of the culture.
- Fit of the culture with the industry's environment.
- Adaptiveness of the culture.

Which of the two is the better performer? On what did you base your conclusion? How does the performance of each relate to its organizational culture?

SOURCE: Adapted with the permission of The Free Press, a Division of Simon & Schuster, Inc., from *Corporate Culture and Performance* by John P. Kotter and James L. Heskett. Copyright © 1992 by Kotter Associates, Inc., and James L. Heskett.

BizFlix | Charlie Wilson's War

Democratic Congressman Charlie Wilson (Tom Hanks) from East Texas lives a reckless life that includes heavy drinking and chasing attractive women. The film focuses on the Afghanistan rebellion against the Soviet troop invasion in the 1980s. Wilson becomes the unlikely champion of the Afghan cause through his role in two major congressional committees that deal with foreign policy and covert operations. Houston socialite Joanne Herring (Julia Roberts) strongly urges the intervention. CIA agent Gust Avrakotos (Philip Seymour Hoffman) helps with some details.

Organizational Culture: Some Observations

This sequence appears early in the film after the scene showing Charlie Wilson, Paul Brown (Brian Markinson), Crystal Lee (Jud Tyler), and two strippers drinking and partying in a hot tub. It opens with a shot of the Capitol Building. Congressman Charlie Wilson talks to his assistant Bonnie Bach (Amy Adams) while walking to chambers for a vote. The sequence ends after Wilson enters the chambers.

What to Watch for and Ask Yourself

- This chapter described organizational culture as having three levels of visibility. Artifacts are at the first level and are the easiest to see. Which artifacts did you observe in this sequence?

- Values appear at the next level of organizational culture. You can infer a culture's values from the behavior of organizational members. Which values appear in this sequence?

- Organizational members will unconsciously behave according to an organization culture's assumptions. You also can infer these from observed behavior. Which assumptions appear in this sequence?

Workplace Video | The Environment and Corporate Culture at Recycline

Ever since green became the new black, U.S. companies have been scrambling to change their products, packaging, and energy consumption to stay in the game. Thanks to Eric Hudson's perceptive scanning of the external environment in the mid-1990s, recycled products firm Recycline discovered an opportunity others missed.

Hudson broke into the natural product arena with an innovative toothbrush made from recycled materials—a bold decision in 1996. Hudson named his first product the Preserve Toothbrush, and Recycline was born. The toothbrush, with its nylon bristles and ergonomically curved handle made of 100 percent recycled material, was a hit with eco-conscious consumers. New converts flocked to it, and Hudson gradually added personal care and kitchenware items to his line of recycled products. Today, Preserve products can be found at top retail chains including Target, Whole Foods Market, and Wal-Mart.

For environmentally sensitive consumers, integrity is everything. Recycline believes that customers are getting wise to the "green-washing effect" in which businesses cultivate a superficial green image without the substance to back it up. A close look at Recycline's internal culture confirms that Hudson's company is authentically green. First, as Preserve's cultural leader, Hudson practices what he preaches; When he isn't pedaling 22 miles to and from work on his bicycle, he's cruising in a Volkswagen that has been converted to run on french-fry grease—an emerging symbol of the modern-day eco-hero. Additionally, everyone at Preserve tries to do right by the natural environment, whether it's composting, conserving energy, or using eco-friendly cleaning products.

But Recycline's organizational culture isn't just green—it's effective. Because of Recycline's small size, anyone interested in taking on a new initiative is encouraged to do so, regardless of position. The vice president of sales, John Turcott, believes that Preserve's size is critical for rapid response: "Our decision-making process is quicker. We pull together the resources we need to solve a problem, we get it done and move on to the next thing." Since everything at Preserve happens at high-speed, everyone has to be driven, creative, and adaptable.

Discussion Questions

1. What are some visible aspects of Recycline's culture that reflect the company's values and commitment to green issues?
2. What role do leaders play in shaping Recycline's organizational culture? Explain.
3. Could Recycline easily change its organizational culture if the green products market encounters a backlash? How would management know if a permanent change in culture has occurred?

Case

Developing Chinks in the Vaunted *Toyota Way*

In 2005, *The Economist* noted the increasing dominance of Toyota in automotive manufacturing, commenting that "[t]here is the world car industry, and then there is Toyota."[1] For fiscal year 2009, Toyota produced slightly over 7 million vehicles, with approximately 40 percent of those being produced outside of Japan. In the same fiscal year, Toyota sold almost 7.6 million vehicles, and 74.3 percent of the sales were overseas. As of June 2009, Toyota employed over 320,000 people throughout its globally dispersed parts manufacturing, vehicle assembly, and marketing operations.[2]

Toyota's strong corporate culture is the "glue" that holds these far-flung operations together and makes them part of a single entity.[3] "Spend some time with Toyota people and ... you realize there is something different about them. The rest of the car industry raves about engines, gearboxes, acceleration, fuel economy, handling, ride quality and sexy design. Toyota's people talk about *The Toyota Way* [italics added] and about customers."[4] Toyota's customer focus is legendary. Says one Toyota executive, "[t]he Toyota culture is inside all of us. Toyota is a customer's company. ... Everything is done to make ... [the customer's] life better."[5]

Toyota's culture, known as *The Toyota Way*, is embodied in fourteen principles, which are as follows:

- "Base your management decisions on a long-term philosophy, even at the expense of short-term financial goals."

- "Create a continuous process flow to bring problems to the surface."

- "Use 'pull' systems to avoid overproduction."

- "Level out the workload (*heijunka*). (Work like the tortoise, not the hare.)"

- "Build a culture of stopping to fix problems, to get quality right the first time."

- "Standardized tasks and processes are the foundation for continuous improvement and employee empowerment."

- "Use visual control so no problems are hidden."

- "Use only reliable, thoroughly tested technology that serves your people and processes."

- "Grow leaders who thoroughly understand the work, live the philosophy, and teach it to others."

- "Develop exceptional people and teams who follow your company's philosophy."

- "Respect your extended network of partners and suppliers by challenging them and helping them improve."

- "Go and see for yourself to thoroughly understand the situation (*genchi genbutsu*)."

- "Make decisions slowly by consensus, thoroughly considering all options; implement decisions rapidly (*nemawashi*)."

- "Become a learning organization through relentless reflection (*hansei*) and continuous improvement (*kaizen*)."[6]

The Toyota Production System (TPS), which puts *The Toyota Way* into practice, focuses on "making cars, making cars better, and teaching everyone how to make cars better. At its Olympian best, Toyota adds one more level: [i]t is always looking to improve the process by which it improves all the other processes."[7]

Toyota's culture has served the company very well for many years. Indeed, competitors marvel at Toyota's culture and its ongoing success.[8] As one General Motors' planner observed privately, "the only way to stop Toyota would be the business equivalent of germ warfare, finding a 'poison pill' or 'social virus' that could be infiltrated into the company to destroy its culture."[9]

Over the years, "Toyota has adapted well to changes facing the automotive industry by establishing sound processes and procedures. It has made continuous change and improvement the essence of its business philosophy: each year thousands of improvements are suggested by employees and many are implemented. ... It has built its success with products that are made according to the all-embracing *Toyota Way* [italics added]. In fact, so confident is Toyota of its quality and reliability record, that it allows rival companies to visit its factories all over the world."[10]

In recent years, however, some chinks seem to be developing in the armor of Toyota's vaunted culture. An internal Toyota study compared the company's products against its competitors' products—component by component, car by car—and found Toyota's products to be superior in just over half of hundreds of components and vehicle systems. Toyota judged such quality performance to be unacceptably mediocre.[11] In reference to the U.S. market, some business analysts say that Toyota's rapid growth is one cause of the company's growing quality-control problems.[12] Charles Fishman, writing in *Fast Company*, says, "Toyota is far from infallible ... recalls for quality and safety problems have spiked dramatically [and are] evidence of the strain that rapid growth puts on even the best systems. But those quality issues have seized the attention of Toyota's senior management. In the larger arena, when the strategy isn't to build cars but to build cars better, you create perpetual competitive advantage."[13]

Toyota has long desired to become the Number One Car Company in the world. However, the pursuit of this ambitious goal has strained Toyota's fable production system as "a series of unToyota-like quality problems have begun to nibble away at the firm's reputation as the world's most admired manufacturer and as a byword for reliable vehicles."[14]

Given that Toyota makes nearly as many vehicles outside Japan as it does at home, the company has been challenged in effectively inculcating *The Toyota Way* into its foreign manufacturing operations. And this has contributed to the quality problems that Toyota has experienced in its foreign operations.[15] Katsuaki Watanabe, Toyota's CEO, "thinks Toyota is losing its competitive edge as it expands around the world." He frets that quality, the foundation of its U.S. success, is slipping. He grouses that Toyota's factories and engineering practices aren't efficient enough.[16]

Will *The Toyota Way* enable this company to solve it quality problems—or will Toyota need to part from its *Way*?

Discussion Questions

1. Describe Toyota's culture from the perspective of *espoused values* and *enacted values*.

2. Using the perspective of the *functions* of organizational culture, explain the impact of *The Toyota Way*.

3. Using the perspective of the *effects* of organizational culture, explain the impact of *The Toyota Way*.

4. What challenges does Toyota face as it attempts to maintain *The Toyota Way* while pursuing vigorous global expansion?

SOURCE: This case was written by Michael K. McCuddy, The Louis S. and Mary L. Morgal Chair of Christian Business Ethics and Professor of Management, College of Business Administration, Valparaiso University.

Career Management

LEARNING OBJECTIVES

After reading this chapter, you should be able to do the following:

1 Define *career* and *career management*.

2 Explain occupational and organizational choice decisions.

3 Describe the four stages of the career model.

4 Explain the psychological contract.

5 Describe how mentors help organizational newcomers.

6 Describe ways to manage conflicts between work and home.

7 Explain how career anchors help form a career identity.

Employers might use
Facebook to screen job
candidates.

THINKING AHEAD: FACEBOOK

Using Facebook as a Hiring Tool

A 2009 study conducted by CareerBuilder.com indicated that
45 percent of employers admit to using Facebook or another
social networking site to screen candidates. And, 35 percent
of employers who used a social networking site state that due

to the content discovered on the site, the applicant was struck from the list of potential hires.[1] Not all

potential employees, particularly graduating students, are surprised by this usage. A study conducted

by the National Association of Colleges and Employees found 51.1 percent of graduating students

expected employers to look at their social networking profile.[2]

Clearly, applicants are advised to keep these sites respectable and not include any information

that might hurt their chances of getting a job or at the very least add a security feature to their

personal pages so potential employers do not have access to what the employee or the employee's

friends may post. But what about the legality of using these pages for recruiting purposes? Facebook

pages allow recruiters to make assessments as to the race of the candidates. And some organizations have taken it further; Yahoo sports reported that one NFL team made fake Facebook profiles to send "friend requests" to recruits. These fake profiles appeared to be an attractive female fan. When a recruit accepted the "fan's" friend request, recruiters had access to the recruit's personal Facebook pages and all the potentially damaging personal information within.[3] What are the legal implications of these issues in terms of equal opportunity employment? See the Looking Back feature for the rest of the story.

CAREERS AS JOINT RESPONSIBILITIES

1 Define *career* and *career management*.

Career management is an integral activity in our lives. There are three reasons why it is important to understand careers. First, if we know what to look forward to over the course of our careers, we can take a proactive approach to planning and managing them. Second, as managers, we need to understand the experiences of our employees and colleagues as they pass through the various stages of careers over their life spans. Third, career management is good business. It makes good financial sense to have highly trained employees keep up with their fields so that organizations can protect valuable investments in human resources.

A *career* is a pattern of work-related experiences that span the course of a person's life.[4] The two elements in a career are the objective element and the subjective element.[5] The objective element of the career is the observable, concrete environment. For example, you can manage a career by getting training to improve your skills. By contrast, the subjective element involves your perception of the situation. Rather than getting training (an objective element), you might change your aspirations (a subjective element). Thus, both objective events and the individual's perception of those events are important in defining a career.

Career management is a lifelong process of learning about self, jobs, and organizations; setting personal career goals; developing strategies for achieving the goals; and revising the goals based on work and life experiences.[6] Whose responsibility is career management? It is tempting to place the responsibility on individuals, and it is appropriate. However, it is also the organization's duty to form partnerships with individuals in managing their careers. Careers are made up of exchanges between individuals and organizations. Inherent in these exchanges is the idea of reciprocity, or give and take.

The balance between individuals and organizations in terms of managing careers has shifted in recent times. With restructuring and reengineering has come a new perspective of careers and career management.

career
The pattern of work-related experiences that span the course of a person's life.

career management
A lifelong process of learning about self, jobs, and organizations; setting personal career goals; developing strategies for achieving the goals, and revising the goals based on work and life experiences.

THE NEW CAREER

The time of the fast track to the top of the hierarchical organization is past. Also gone is the idea of lifetime employment in a single organization. Today's environment demands leaner organizations. The paternalistic attitude that organizations take care of employees no longer exists. Individuals now take on more responsibility for managing their own careers. The concept of the career is undergoing a paradigm shift, as shown in Table 17.1. The old career is giving way to a new career characterized by discrete exchange, occupational excellence, organizational empowerment,

TABLE

17.1   The New versus Old Career Paradigms

New Career Paradigm	Old Career Paradigm
Discrete exchange means:	**The mutual loyalty contract meant:**
• explicit exchange of specified rewards in return for task performance	• implicit trading of employee compliance in return for job security
• basing job rewards on the current market value of the work being performed	• allowing job rewards to be routinely deferred into the future
• engaging in disclosure and renegotiation on both sides as the employment relationship unfolds	• leaving the mutual loyalty assumptions as a political barrier to renegotiation
• exercising flexibility as each party's interests and market circumstances change	• assuming employment and career opportunities are standardized and prescribed by the firm
Occupational excellence means:	**The one-employer focus meant:**
• performance of current jobs in return for developing new occupational expertise	• relying on the firm to specify jobs and their associated occupational skill base
• employees identifying with and focusing on what is happening in their adopted occupation	• employees identifying with and focusing on what is happening in their particular firm
• emphasizing occupational skill development over the local demands of any particular firm	• forgoing technical or functional development in favor of firm-specific learning
• getting training in anticipation of future job opportunities; having training lead jobs	• doing the job first to be entitled to new training: making training follow jobs
Organizational empowerment means:	**The top-down firm meant:**
• strategic positioning is dispersed to separate business units	• strategic direction is subordinated to "corporate headquarters"
• everyone is responsible for adding value and improving competitiveness	• competitiveness and added value are the responsibility of corporate experts
• business units are free to cultivate their own markets	• business unit marketing depends on the corporate agenda
• new enterprise, spinoffs, and alliance building are broadly encouraged	• independent enterprise is discouraged, and likely to be viewed as disloyalty
Project allegiance means:	**Corporate allegiance meant:**
• shared employer and employee commitment to the overarching goal of the project	• project goals are subordinated to corporate policy and organizational constraints
• a successful outcome of the project is more important than holding the project team together	• being loyal to the work group can be more important than the project itself
• financial and reputational rewards stem directly from project outcomes	• financial and reputational rewards stem from being a "good soldier" regardless of results
• upon project completion, organization and reporting arrangements are broken up	• social relationships within corporate boundaries are actively encouraged

and project allegiance.[7] Moreover, one recent study found that both individuals and organizations are actively involved in the management of the new career of employees. As such, the new career involves a type of participatory management technique on the part of the individual, but the organization responds to each individual's needs and thus is more flexible in its career development programs.[8] One company that understands the new career very well is Cisco Systems. In Real World 17.1, you can see how Cisco uses innovative work arrangements that help them attract and retain good employees, and benefit the environment as well.

Cisco Systems: Supporting the New Career

Cisco Systems is a pioneer in telecommuting technologies. Its Cisco Virtual Office, Cisco OfficeExtend, and Cisco WebEx are remote connectivity and virtual collaboration solutions that facilitate work from home, or from anywhere. High-quality voice and video allow employees to attend meetings while at home, and these solutions permit a seamless transition between working in the office and working remotely.

The company practices what it preaches, and it is also a leader in telecommuting among employees. A Cisco survey of 2,000 telecommuters from five regions (United States/Canada, Asia Pacific, European markets, Japan, and emerging markets) revealed that employees who telecommute experienced higher productivity, work/life flexibility, and job satisfaction. In addition, 75 percent reported more timely work from telecommuting, and 67 percent said the overall quality of their work improved. Employees reported fuel cost savings of $10.3 million per year from telecommuting.

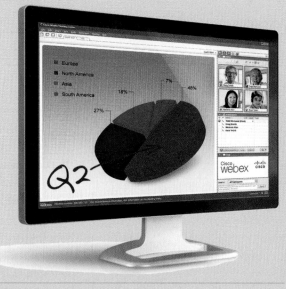

Cisco WebEx is a remote connectivity and virtual collaboration solution that facilitates work from home.

The benefits to the company are numerous, including a savings of $277 million per year in time and productivity costs. At Cisco, telecommuting is a green practice as well—in a single year, Cisco telecommuters stopped 47,320 metric tons of greenhouse gases from being released.

Cisco's commitment to telecommuting, both in terms of offering it to employees and designing new technologies, reflects the way modern careers evolve and globalize. By enabling people to work together no matter where they are located, barriers of time and distance are broken down, and business becomes borderless.

SOURCES: A. Schwartz, "Cisco Says Telecommuting Saves Money, and the World," *Fast Company* (June 26, 2009), accessed at http://www.fastcompany.com/blog/ariel-schwartz/sustainability/cisco-telecommuting-increases-productivity-saves-money-and-cuts-c; http://newsroom.cisco.com/dlls/2009/prod_062609.html.

Discrete exchange occurs when an organization gains productivity while a person gains work experience. It is a short-term arrangement that recognizes that job skills change in value and that renegotiation of the relationship must occur as conditions change. This contrasts sharply with the mutual loyalty contract of the old career paradigm in which employee loyalty was exchanged for job security.

Occupational excellence means continually honing skills that can be marketed across organizations. The individual identifies more with the occupation ("I am an engineer") than the organization ("I am an IBMer"). By contrast, the old one-employer focus meant that training was company specific rather than preparing the person for future job opportunities. A recent research study that focused on ethnographic data (interviews and stories) was conducted among software engineers in three European firms and two U.S. firms. Software engineers did not have much respect for their immediate supervisors, the organization, or formal dress codes. The only thing they did believe in was occupational excellence so that they could be better at what they do. In this regard, the authors of the study note that software engineers represent a unique group in terms of career development, and that they fit well within the model of the "new career."[9]

Organizational empowerment means that power flows down to business units and in turn to employees. Employees are expected to add value and help the organization remain competitive by being innovative and creative. The old top-down approach meant that control and strategizing were only done by the top managers, and individual initiative might be viewed as disloyalty or disrespect.

Project allegiance means that both individuals and organizations are committed to the successful completion of a project. The firm's gain is the project outcome; the individual's gain is experience and shared success. On project completion, the project team breaks up as individuals move on to new projects. Under the old paradigm, corporate allegiance was paramount. The needs of projects were overshadowed by corporate policies and procedures. Work groups were long term, and keeping the group together was often a more important goal than project completion.

While spending an entire career in one company was the old career model, times have changed, and job hopping and company hopping are becoming more the norm. You can expect to change jobs many times in your career. College graduates typically change jobs four times in their first ten years of work, a number that is projected to increase. At that rate, you could easily hold twenty different jobs in a typical career. In fact, the stigma associated with frequent job changes has largely disappeared. Some recruiters now view a résumé littered with different companies and locations as a sign of a smart self-promoter. The key is to know *why* you are making each job move, including both what it will cost and gain for you. By presenting your job-hopping career path as a growth process rather than a series of impulsive changes, you may set yourself apart in the minds of recruiters.[10] Individuals must prepare for the new career and manage their careers with change in mind.

Becoming Your Own Career Coach

The best way to stay employed is to see yourself as being in business for yourself, even if you work for someone else. Know what skills you can package for other employers and what you can do to ensure that your skills are state of the art. Organizations need employees who have acquired multiple skills and are adept at more than one job. Employers want employees who have demonstrated competence in dealing with change.[11] To be successful, think of organizational change not as a disruption to your work but as its central focus. You will also need to develop self-reliance, as we discussed in Chapter 7, to deal effectively with the stress of change. Self-reliant individuals take an interdependent approach to relationships and are comfortable both giving and receiving support from others.

The people who will be most successful in the new career paradigm are those who are flexible, team oriented (rather than hierarchical), energized by change, and tolerant of ambiguity. The people who will become frustrated in the new career are those who are rigid in their thinking and learning styles and who have high needs for control. A commitment to continuous, lifelong learning will prevent you from becoming a professional dinosaur.[12] An intentional and purposeful commitment to taking charge of your professional life will be necessary in managing the new career.

In the current business environment of ethical scandals, behaving in an ethical manner, standing by your values, and building a professional image of integrity are very important qualities. Major corporations such as Google conduct extensive reference checks on their applicants—not just with the references supplied by the applicants but also with friends of friends of such references. Recall that we mentioned earlier in this book that managing ethical behavior is one of the most significant challenges facing managers today. Ever wonder why highly respected and well-paid top management executives engage in fraud and endanger their careers? One study suggests that this happens as top executives feel the pressure to keep up with inflated expectations and changes in cultural norms, short-term versus long-term orientations, board of directors' composition, and senior leadership in the organization.[13]

Emotional Intelligence and Career Success

Almost 40 percent of new managers fail within the first eighteen months on the job. What are the reasons for the failure? Newly hired managers flame out because they fail to build good relationships with peers and subordinates (82 percent of failures), are confused or uncertain about what their bosses expect (58 percent of failures), lack internal political skills (50 percent of failures), and are unable to achieve the two or three most important objectives of the new job (47 percent of failures).[14] You'll note that these failures are all due to a lack of human skills.

In Chapter 13, we introduced the concept of emotional intelligence (EI) as an important determinant of conflict management skills. Daniel Goleman argues that EI is a constellation of the qualities that mark a star performer at work. These attributes include self-awareness, self-control, trustworthiness, confidence, and empathy, among others. Goleman's belief is that emotional competencies are twice as important to people's success today as raw intelligence or technical know-how. He also argues that the further up the corporate ranks you go, the more important EI becomes.[15,16] Employers, either consciously or unconsciously, look for EI during the hiring process. In addition to traditionally recognized competencies such as communication and social skills, interns with higher levels of EI are rated as more hireable by their host firms than those with lower levels of EI.[17] Neither gender seems to have cornered the market on EI. Both men and women who can demonstrate high levels of EI are seen as particularly gifted and may be promoted more rapidly.[18]

EI is important to career success in many cultures. A recent study in Australia found that high levels of EI are associated with job success. EI improves one's ability to work with other team members and to provide high-quality customer service, and workers with high EI are more likely to take steps to develop their skills. This confirms U.S. studies that portray high EI as an important attribute for the upwardly mobile worker.[19] You can assess your own EI using You 17.1.

L'Oreal has found EI to be a profitable selection tool. Salespeople selected on the basis of emotional competence outsold those selected using the old method by an average of $91,370 per year. As an added bonus for the firm, these salespeople also had 63 percent less turnover during the first year than those selected in the traditional way.[20]

The good news is that EI can be developed and does tend to improve throughout life. Some companies are providing training in EI competencies. American Express began sending managers through an emotional competence training program. It found that trained managers outperformed those who lacked this training. In the year after completing the course, managers trained in emotional competence grew their businesses by an average of 18.1 percent compared with 16.2 percent for those businesses whose managers were untrained.[21]

Before turning to the stages of an individual's career, we will examine the process of preparation for the world of work. Prior to beginning a career, individuals must make several important decisions.

Preparing for the World of Work

2 Explain occupational and organizational choice decisions.

When viewed from one perspective, you might say that we spend our youth preparing for the world of work. Educational experiences and personal life experiences help an individual develop the skills and maturity needed to enter a career.

You 17.1

What's Your EI at Work?

Answering the following 25 questions will allow you to rate your social skills and self-awareness.

EI, the social equivalent of IQ, is complex in no small part because it depends on some pretty slippery variables—including your innate compatibility, or lack thereof, with the people who happen to be your coworkers. But if you want to get a rough idea of how your EI stacks up, this quiz will help.

As honestly as you can, estimate how you rate in the eyes of peers, bosses, and subordinates on each of the following traits, on a scale of 1 to 4, with 4 representing strong agreement, and 1, strong disagreement.

_____ 1. I usually stay composed, positive, and unflappable even in trying moments.

_____ 2. I can think clearly and stay focused on the task at hand under pressure.

_____ 3. I am able to admit my own mistakes.

_____ 4. I usually or always meet commitments and keep promises.

_____ 5. I hold myself accountable for meeting my goals.

_____ 6. I'm organized and careful in my work.

_____ 7. I regularly seek out fresh ideas from a wide variety of sources.

_____ 8. I'm good at generating new ideas.

_____ 9. I can smoothly handle multiple demands and changing priorities.

_____ 10. I'm results-oriented, with a strong drive to meet my objectives.

_____ 11. I like to set challenging goals and take calculated risks to reach them.

_____ 12. I'm always trying to learn how to improve my performance, including asking advice from people younger than I am.

_____ 13. I readily make sacrifices to meet an important organizational goal.

_____ 14. The company's mission is something I understand and can identify with.

_____ 15. The values of my team—or of our division or department, or the company—influence my decisions and clarify the choices I make.

_____ 16. I actively seek out opportunities to further the overall goals of the organization and enlist others to help me.

_____ 17. I pursue goals beyond what's required or expected of me in my current job.

_____ 18. Obstacles and setbacks may delay me a little, but they don't stop me.

_____ 19. Cutting through red tape and bending outdated rules are sometimes necessary.

_____ 20. I seek fresh perspectives, even if that means trying something totally new.

_____ 21. My impulses or distressing emotions don't often get the best of me at work.

_____ 22. I can change tactics quickly when circumstances change.

_____ 23. Pursuing new information is my best bet for cutting down on uncertainty and findings ways to do things better.

_____ 24. I usually don't attribute setbacks to a personal flaw (mine or someone else's).

_____ 25. I operate from an expectation of success rather than a fear of failure.

A score below 70 indicates a problem. If your total is somewhere in the basement, don't despair: EI is not unimprovable. "Emotional intelligence can be learned, and in fact we are each building it, in varying degrees, throughout life. It's sometimes called maturity," says Daniel Goleman. "EI is nothing more or less than a collection of tools that we can sharpen to help ensure our own survival."

SOURCE: A. Fisher, "Success Secret: A High Emotional IQ." Reprinted from the October 26, 1998, issue of *Fortune* by special permission; copyright 1998, Time Inc. All rights reserved.

Preparation for work is a developmental process that gradually unfolds over time.[22] As the time approaches for beginning a career, individuals face two difficult decisions: the choice of occupation and the choice of organization.

Occupational Choice

In choosing an occupation, individuals assess their needs, values, abilities, and preferences and attempt to match them with an occupation that provides a fit. Personality plays a role in the selection of occupation. John Holland's theory of occupational choice contends that there are six types of personalities and that each is characterized by a set of interests and values.[23] Holland's six types are as follows:

1. *Realistic:* stable, persistent, and materialistic.
2. *Artistic:* imaginative, emotional, and impulsive.
3. *Investigative:* curious, analytical, and independent.
4. *Enterprising:* ambitious, energetic, and adventurous.
5. *Social:* generous, cooperative, and sociable.
6. *Conventional:* efficient, practical, and obedient.

Holland also states that occupations can be classified using this typology. For example, realistic occupations include mechanic, restaurant server, and mechanical engineer. Artistic occupations include architect, voice coach, and interior designer. Investigative occupations include physicist, surgeon, and economist. Real estate agent, human resource manager, and lawyer are enterprising occupations. The social occupations include counselor, social worker, and member of the clergy. Conventional occupations include word processor, accountant, and data entry operator.

Holland's typology has been used to predict career choices with a variety of international participants, including Mexicans, Australians, Indians, New Zealanders, Taiwanese, Pakistanis, South Africans, and Germans.[24]

An assumption that drives Holland's theory is that people choose occupations that match their own personalities. People who fit Holland's social types are those who prefer jobs that are highly interpersonal in nature. They may see careers in physical and math sciences, for example, as not affording the opportunity for interpersonal relationships.[25] To fulfill the desire for interpersonal work, they may instead gravitate toward jobs in customer service or counseling in order to better match their personalities.

Although personality is a major influence on occupational choice, it is not the only influence. There is a host of other ones, including social class, parents' occupations, economic conditions, and geography.[26] Once a choice of occupation has been made, another major decision individuals face is the choice of organizations.

Organizational Choice and Entry

Several theories of how individuals choose organizations exist, ranging from those that postulate very logical and rational choice processes to those that offer seemingly irrational processes. Expectancy theory, which we discussed in Chapter 5, can be applied to organizational choice.[27] According to the expectancy theory view, individuals choose organizations that maximize positive outcomes and avoid negative outcomes. Job candidates calculate the probability that an organization will provide a certain outcome and then compare the probabilities across organizations.

Other theories propose that people select organizations in a much less rational fashion. Job candidates may satisfice—that is, select the first organization that meets one or two important criteria—and then justify their choice by distorting their perceptions.[28]

The method of selecting an organization varies greatly among individuals and may reflect a combination of the expectancy theory and theories that postulate less rational approaches. Entry into an organization is further complicated by the conflicts that occur between individuals and organizations during the process. Figure 17.1 illustrates these potential conflicts. The arrows in the figure illustrate four types of conflicts that can occur as individuals choose organizations and organizations choose individuals. The first two conflicts (1 and 2) occur between individuals and organizations. The first is a conflict between the organization's effort to attract candidates and the individual's choice of an organization. The individual needs complete and accurate information to make a good choice, but the organization may not provide it. The organization is trying to attract a large number of qualified candidates, so it presents itself in an overly attractive way.

The second conflict is between the individual's attempt to attract several organizations and the organization's need to select the best candidate. Individuals want good offers, so they do not disclose their faults. They describe their preferred job in terms of the organization's opening instead of describing a job they would really prefer.

Conflicts 3 and 4 are internal to the two parties. The third is a conflict between the organization's desire to recruit a large pool of qualified applicants and the organization's need to select and retain the best candidate. In recruiting, organizations tend to give only positive information, which results in mismatches between the individual and the organization. The fourth conflict is internal to the individual; it is between the individual's desire for several job offers and the need to make a good choice. When individuals present themselves as overly attractive, they risk being offered positions that are poor fits in terms of their skills and career goals.[29]

The organizational choice and entry process is very complex due to the nature of these conflicts. Partial responsibility for preventing these conflicts rests with the individual. Individuals should conduct thorough research of the organization through published reports and industry analyses. They also should conduct a careful self-analysis and be as honest as possible with organizations to ensure a good match. The job interview process can be stressful, but also fun.

Partial responsibility for good matches also rests with the organization. One way of avoiding the conflicts and mismatches is to utilize a realistic job preview.

FIGURE

17.1   Conflicts during Organizational Entry

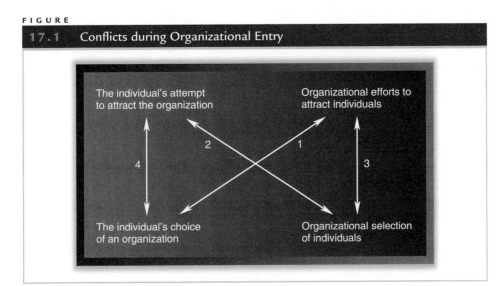

SOURCE: Figure in L. W. Porter, E. E. Lawler III, and J. R. Hackman, *Behavior in Organizations*, New York: McGraw-Hill, Inc., 1975, p. 134. Reproduced with permission of The McGraw-Hill Companies.

Realistic Job Previews

The conflicts just discussed may result in unrealistic expectations on the part of the candidate. People entering the world of work may expect, for example, that they will receive explicit directions from their boss, only to find that they are left with ambiguity about how to do the job. They may expect that promotions will be based on performance and find that in fact they are based mainly on political considerations. Some new hires expect to be given managerial responsibilities right away; however, this is not often the case.

Giving potential employees a realistic picture of the job they are applying for is known as a *realistic job preview (RJP)*. When candidates are given both positive and negative information, they can make more effective job choices. Traditional recruiting practices produce unrealistically high expectations, which produce low job satisfaction when these unrealistic expectations hit the reality of the job situation. RJPs tend to create expectations that are much closer to reality, and they increase the numbers of candidates who withdraw from further consideration.[30] This occurs because candidates with unrealistic expectations tend to look for employment elsewhere. The Idaho State Police Department's online employment site provides an RJP, which begins with these words: "[Y]ou should put aside the images you have seen on television or in the movies and read carefully about the tasks an Idaho State Police Trooper performs."[31] It then goes on to provide an exhaustive list of tasks ranging from the exciting (manhunts and serving warrants) to the mundane (inspecting heavy trucks), as well as noting that troopers currently work rotating ten-hour shifts. While the site concludes with a summary of the rewards that accompany the job, it clearly notes that the work is at times tedious and far less glamorous than might be expected.

Idaho State Police cadets at this academy graduation ceremony are about to become Troopers. The Idaho State Police Department's online employment site provides a specific RJP.

RJPs can also be thought of as inoculation against disappointment. If new recruits know what to expect in the new job, they can prepare for the experience. Newcomers who are not given RJPs may find that their jobs don't measure up to their expectations. They may then believe that their employer was deceitful in the hiring process, become unhappy and mishandle job demands, and ultimately leave the organization.[32]

Job candidates who receive RJPs view the organization as honest and also have a greater ability to cope with the demands of the job.[33] RJPs perform another important function: uncertainty reduction.[34] Knowing what to expect, both good and bad, gives a newcomer a sense of control that is important to job satisfaction and performance.

With today's emphasis on ethics, organizations need to do all they can to be seen as operating consistently and honestly. RJPs are one way companies can provide ethically required information to newcomers. Ultimately, RJPs result in more effective matches, lower turnover, and higher organizational commitment and job satisfaction.[35] There is much to gain, and little to risk, in providing realistic job information.[36]

In summary, the needs and goals of individuals and organizations can clash during entry into the organization. To avoid potential mismatches, individuals should conduct a careful self-analysis and provide accurate information about themselves to potential employers. Organizations should present RJPs to show candidates both the positive and negative aspects of the job, along with the potential career paths available to the employee.

realistic job preview (RJP)
Both positive and negative information given to potential employees about the job they are applying for, thereby giving them a realistic picture of the job.

After entry into the organization, individuals embark on their careers. A person's work life can be traced through successive stages, as we see in the career stage model.

THE CAREER STAGE MODEL

A common way of understanding careers is viewing them as a series of stages through which individuals pass during their working lives.[37] Figure 17.2 presents the career stage model, which will form the basis for our discussion in the remainder of this chapter.[38] The career stage model shows that individuals pass through four stages in their careers: establishment, advancement, maintenance, and withdrawal. It is important to note that the age ranges shown are approximations; that is, the timing of the career transitions varies greatly among individuals.

Establishment is the first stage of a person's career. The activities that occur in this stage center around learning the job and fitting into the organization and occupation. *Advancement* is a high-achievement-oriented stage in which people focus on increasing their competence. The *maintenance* stage finds the individual trying to maintain productivity while evaluating progress toward career goals. The *withdrawal* stage involves contemplation of retirement or possible career change.

Along the horizontal axis in Figure 17.2 are the corresponding life stages for each career stage. These life stages are based on the pioneering research on adult development conducted by Levinson and his colleagues. Levinson conducted extensive biographical interviews to trace the life stages of men and women. He interpreted his research in two books, *The Seasons of a Man's Life* and *The Seasons of a Woman's Life*.[39] Levinson's life stages are characterized by an alternating pattern of stability and transition.[40] Throughout the discussion of career stages that follows, we weave in the transitions of Levinson's life stages. Work and personal life are inseparable, and to understand a person's career experiences, we must also examine the unfolding of her or his personal experiences.

You can see that adult development provides unique challenges for the individual and that there may be considerable overlap between the stages. Now let us examine each career stage in detail.

3 Describe the four stages of the career model.

establishment
The first career stage in which the person learns the job and begins to fit into the organization and occupation.

advancement
The second, high-achievement-oriented career stage in which the individual focuses on increasing competence.

maintenance
The third career stage in which the individual tries to maintain productivity while evaluating progress toward career goals.

withdrawal
The final career stage in which the individual contemplates retirement or possible career changes.

FIGURE

17.2   The Career Stage Model

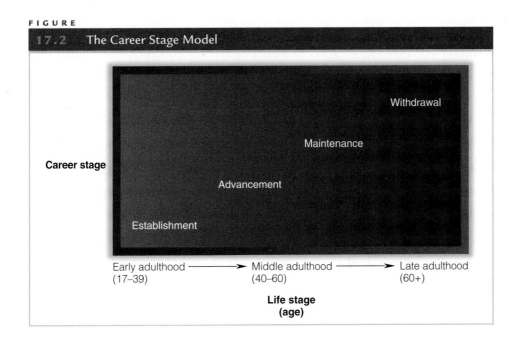

Career stage

Withdrawal

Maintenance

Advancement

Establishment

Early adulthood ⟶ Middle adulthood ⟶ Late adulthood
(17–39)   (40–60)   (60+)

**Life stage
(age)**

THE ESTABLISHMENT STAGE

During the establishment stage, the individual begins a career as a newcomer to the organization. This is a period of great dependence on others, as the individual is learning about the job and the organization. The establishment stage usually occurs during the beginning of the early adulthood years (ages eighteen to twenty-five). During this time, Levinson notes, an important personal life transition into adulthood occurs: the individual begins to separate from his or her parents and becomes less emotionally and financially dependent. Following this period is a fairly stable time of exploring the adult role and settling down.

The transition from school to work is a part of the establishment stage. Many graduates find the transition a memorable experience. The following description was provided by a newly graduated individual who went to work at a large public utility:

> We all tried to one-up each other about jobs we had just accepted . . . bragging that we had the highest salary, the best management training program, the most desirable coworkers, the most upward mobility . . . and believed we were destined to become future corporate leaders. . . . Every Friday after work we met for happy hour to visit and relate the events of the week. It is interesting to look at how the mood of those happy hours changed over the first few months . . . at first, we jockeyed for position in terms of telling stories about how great these new jobs were, or how weird our bosses were. . . . Gradually, things quieted down at happy hour. The mood went from "Wow, isn't this great?" to "What in the world have we gotten ourselves into?" There began to be general agreement that business wasn't all it was cracked up to be.[41]

Establishment is thus a time of big transitions in both personal and work life. At work, three major tasks face the newcomer: negotiating effective psychological contracts, managing the stress of socialization, and making a transition from organizational outsider to organizational insider.

Psychological Contracts

A *psychological contract* is an implicit agreement between the individual and the organization that specifies what each is expected to give and receive in the relationship.[42] Individuals expect to receive salary, status, advancement opportunities, and challenging work to meet their needs. Organizations expect to receive time, energy, talents, and loyalty in order to meet their goals. Working out the psychological contract with the organization begins with entry, but the contract is modified as the individual proceeds through the career.

Psychological contracts form and exist between individuals.[43] During the establishment stage, newcomers form attachment relationships with many people in the organization. Working out effective psychological contracts within each relationship is important. Newcomers need social support in many forms and from many sources. Table 17.2 shows the type of psychological contracts, in the form of social support, that newcomers may work out with key insiders in the organization.

One common newcomer concern, for example, is whose behavior to watch for cues to appropriate behavior. Senior colleagues can provide modeling support by displaying behavior that the newcomer can emulate. This is only one of many types of support that newcomers need. Newcomers should contract with others to receive each of the needed types of support so that they can adjust to the new job. Organizations should help newcomers form relationships early and

psychological contract
An implicit agreement between an individual and an organization that specifies what each is expected to give and receive in the relationship.

17.2 Newcomer–Insider Psychological Contracts for Social Support

Type of Support	Function of Supportive Attachments	Newcomer Concern	Examples of Insider Response/ Action
Protection from stressors	Direct assistance in terms of resources, time, labor, or environmental modification	What are the major risks/ threats in this environment?	*Supervisor* cues newcomer to risks/ threats.
Informational	Provision of information necessary for managing demands	What do I need to know to get things done?	*Mentor* provides advice on informal political climate in organization.
Evaluative	Feedback on both personal and professional role performances	How am I doing?	*Supervisor* provides day-to-day performance feedback during first week on new job.
Modeling	Evidence of bahavioral standards provided through modeled behavior	Whom do I follow?	Newcomer is apprenticed to *senior colleague.*
Emotional	Empathy, esteem, caring, or love	Do I matter? Who cares if I'm here or not?	*Other newcomers* empathize with and encourage individual when reality shock sets in.

SOURCE: Table from D. L. Nelson, J. C. Quick, and J. R. Joplin, "Psychological Contracting and Newcomer Socialization: An Attachment Theory Foundation," from *Journal of Social Behavior and Personality* 6 (1991): 65. Reprinted with permission.

should encourage the psychological contracting process between newcomers and insiders.

Broken or breached psychological contracts can have very negative outcomes. When a breach occurs, employees can have very negative emotional reactions which can lead to loss of trust, reduced job satisfaction, and lower commitment to the organization and higher turnover intentions.[44] However, not all employees

Science

Broken Psychological Contracts: People React Differently

When an employee's psychological contract is broken with the organization, the employee often attempts to deal with the breach. He or she might do so by trying to get back at the organization, and as a result, turnover, absenteeism, or even more deviant behavior like employee theft may occur. A recent study, however, found that conscientious individuals will respond differently to psychological breach than individuals with low conscientiousness. Specifically, conscientious employees respond to breach by reducing their levels of task performance but nonconscientious employees are more likely to decrease their organizational loyalty and job satisfaction and increase their

desire to withdraw from the organization or quit. These distinctions may be important for organizations to recognize. Because of the sometimes serious negative toll that psychological contract breaches take, organizations should, of course, avoid them; however, when they are unavoidable, organizations need to understand how to intervene to reduce some of the negative impacts. Understanding how people may react differently to psychological breaches may help in that aim.

SOURCE: K. A. Orvis, N. M. Dudley, and J. M. Cortina, "Conscientiousness and Reactions to Psychological Contract Breach," *Journal of Applied Psychology*, 93 (2008): 1183–1193.

react to psychological contract breach in the same way. See the Science feature for details.

The influence of a broken psychological contract is often felt even after an employee leaves a job. Laid-off employees who feel that a psychological contract breach has occurred are not only unhappy with their former firms but may also be both more cynical and less trusting of their new employers.[45]

The Stress of Socialization

In Chapter 16, we discussed three phases that newcomers go through in adjusting to a new organization: anticipatory socialization, encounter, and change and acquisition. (You may want to review Figure 16.2.) Another way to look at these three phases is to examine the kinds of stress newcomers experience during each stage.[46]

In anticipatory socialization, the newcomer is gathering information from various sources about the job and organization. The likely stressor in this stage is ambiguity, so the provision of accurate information is important. During this stage, the psychological contract is formed. It is essential that both parties go into it with good intentions of keeping up their end of the agreement.

In the encounter phase, the demands of the job in terms of the role, task, interpersonal relationships, and physical setting become apparent to the newcomer. The expectations formed in anticipatory socialization may clash with the realities of organizational life, and reality shock can occur.[47] This very predictable "surprise" reaction may find the new employee thinking, "What have I gotten myself into?"[48] The degree of reality shock depends on the expectations formed in the anticipatory socialization stage. If these expectations are unrealistic or unmet, reality shock may be a problem.

While most organizations allow some time for newcomers to adapt, as little as two to three months may be allotted for new hires to reach some level of independence. This unwritten rule will mean that new hires who cannot quickly get up to speed on the organization's and their work group's norms and procedures will quickly find themselves experiencing negative feedback from coworkers.[49]

In the change and acquisition phase, the newcomer begins to master the demands of the job. Newcomers need to feel that they have some means of control over job demands.

Easing the Transition from Outsider to Insider

Being a newcomer in an organization is stressful. The process of becoming a functioning member of the organization takes time, and the newcomer needs support in making the transition. A successful transition from outsider to insider can be ensured if both the newcomer and the organization work together to smooth the way.

Individual Actions Newcomers should ask about the negative side of the job if they were not given an RJP. In particular, newcomers should ask about the stressful aspects of the job. Other employees are good sources of this information. Research has shown that newcomers who underestimate the stressfulness of job demands do not adjust well.[50] In addition, newcomers should present honest and accurate information about their own weaknesses. Both actions can promote good matches.

During the encounter phase, newcomers must prepare for reality shock. Realizing that slight depression is natural when adjusting to a new job can help alleviate the distress. Newcomers can also plan ways to cope with job stress ahead of time. If, for example, long assignments away from home are typical, newcomers can plan for these trips in advance. Part of the plan for dealing with reality shock should include ways to seek support from others. Networking with other newcomers who empathize can help individuals cope with the stress of the new job.

In the change and acquisition stage of adjusting to a new organization, newcomers should set realistic goals and take credit for the successes that occur as they master the job. Newcomers must seek feedback on job performance from their supervisors and coworkers. Newcomers should be proactive, because proactive personality in newcomers has been shown to relate to creativity on the job and increased career satisfaction.[51] Organizations also can assist newcomers in their transition from outsiders to insiders.

Organizational Actions RJPs start the relationship between the newcomer and the organization with integrity and honesty. Careful recruitment and selection of new employees can help ensure good matches.

During the encounter phase, organizations should provide early job assignments that present opportunities for the new recruit to succeed. Newcomers who experience success in training gain increased self-efficacy and adjust to the new job more effectively.[52] Newcomers who face early job challenges successfully tend to be higher performers later in their careers.[53] Providing encouragement and feedback to the newcomer during this stage is crucial. The immediate supervisor, peers, other newcomers, and support staff are important sources of support during encounter.[54] Otis Elevator has experimented with a program in which new hires, regardless of their specific job function (sales, manufacturing, finance, etc.), all complete a six-week training course covering all aspects of the elevator industry. During this program, they not only visit Otis's manufacturing and headquarters sites, they also visit construction sites to experience the gritty world of elevator installation.[55]

By contrast, some firms do little to help newcomers adjust. A recent survey of information technology firms found that only 38 percent have formal company policies regarding training for new employees. The remaining 62 percent answered that when it comes to new-hire training, they simply "wing it."[56]

During the change and acquisition phase, rewards are important. Organizations should tie the newcomers' rewards as explicitly as possible to performance.[57]

Feedback is also crucial. Newcomers should receive daily, consistent feedback. This communicates that the organization is concerned about their progress and wants to help them learn the ropes along the way. Supervisory support is important during and even beyond the first few months. A recent study found that on average, newcomers perceived less supervisory support during the six to twenty-one months after starting the job, and this resulted in role confusion and lower job satisfaction, and even delayed the receipt of salary increases over time.[58]

The establishment stage marks the beginning of an individual's career. Its noteworthy transitions include the transition from school to work, from dependence on parents to dependence on self, from organizational outsider to organizational insider. Individuals who successfully complete the establishment stage go through many positive changes, including increased self-confidence, interpersonal skills, and self-knowledge.[59] Once they have met their need to fit in, individuals move on to the advancement stage of their careers.

THE ADVANCEMENT STAGE

The advancement stage is a period when individuals strive for achievement. They seek greater responsibility and authority and strive for upward mobility. Usually around age thirty, an important life transition occurs.[60] Individuals reassess their goals and feel the need to make changes in their career dreams. The transition at age thirty is followed by a period of stability during which the individual tries to find a role in adult society and wants to succeed in the career. During this stage, several issues are important: exploring career paths, finding a mentor, working out dual-career partnerships, and managing conflicts between work and personal life.

Career Paths and Career Ladders

Career paths are sequences of job experiences along which employees move during their careers.[61] At the advancement stage, individuals examine their career dreams and the paths they must follow to achieve them. For example, suppose a person dreams of becoming a top executive in the pharmaceutical industry. She majors in chemistry in undergraduate school and takes a job with a nationally recognized firm. After she has adjusted to her job as a quality control chemist, she reevaluates her plan and decides that further education is necessary. She plans to pursue an MBA degree part-time, hoping to gain expertise in management. From there, she hopes to be promoted to a supervisory position within her current firm. If this does not occur within five years, she will consider moving to a different pharmaceutical company. An alternate route would be to try to transfer to a sales position, from which she might advance into management.

The career paths of many women have moved from working in large organizations to starting their own businesses. Currently, there are 10.6 million women-owned firms in the United States, comprising almost half of all privately held firms in the country. What is the motivation for this exodus to entrepreneurship? The main reasons are to seek additional challenge and self-fulfillment and to have more self-determination and freedom.[62]

A *career ladder* is a structured series of job positions through which an individual progresses in an organization. For example, at Southwestern Bell, it is customary to move through a series of alternating line and staff supervisory assignments to advance toward upper management. Supervisors in customer service might be assigned next to the training staff and then rotate back as line supervisors in network services to gain experience in different departments.

Some companies use the traditional concept of career ladders to help employees advance in their careers. Other organizations take a more contemporary approach to career advancement. Sony encourages creativity in its engineers by using nontraditional career paths. At Sony, individuals have the freedom to move on to interesting and challenging job assignments without notifying their supervisors. If they join a new project team, their current boss is expected to let them move on. This self-promotion philosophy at Sony is seen as a key to high levels of innovation and creative new product designs. There has been heightened interest in international assignments by multinational corporations in response to globalization and global staffing issues. One challenge in this regard has been that most expatriate assignments are not successful, and organizations have been facing the challenge of properly training and preparing individuals for such assignments. Alternative international work assignments (e.g., commuter work assignments, virtual assignments, short-term assignments) can be used to help individuals gain international work experience in preparation for higher levels in the organization.[63]

Another approach used by some companies to develop skills is the idea of a "career lattice"—an approach to building competencies by moving laterally through different departments in the organization or by moving through different projects. Top management support for the career lattice is essential because in traditional terms an employee who has made several lateral moves might not be viewed with favor. However, the career lattice approach is an effective way to develop an array of skills to ensure one's employability.[64]

career path

A sequence of job experiences that an employee moves along during his or her career.

career ladder

A structured series of job positions through which an individual progresses in an organization.

Exploring career paths is one important activity in advancement. Another crucial activity during advancement is finding a mentor.

Finding a Mentor

A *mentor* is an individual who provides guidance, coaching, counseling, and friendship to a protégé. Mentors are important to career success because they perform both career and psychosocial functions.[65]

5 Describe how mentors help organizational newcomers.

The career functions provided by a mentor include sponsorship, facilitating exposure and visibility, coaching, and protection. Sponsorship means actively helping the individual get job experiences and promotions. Facilitating exposure and visibility means providing opportunities for the protégé to develop relationships with key figures in the organization in order to advance. Coaching involves providing advice in both career and job performance. Protection is provided by shielding the protégé from potentially damaging experiences. Career functions are particularly important to the protégé's future success. One study found that the amount of career coaching received by protégés was related to more promotions and higher salaries four years later.[66]

A mentor is an individual who provides guidance, coaching, counseling, and friendship to a protégé.

The mentor also performs psychosocial functions. Role modeling occurs when the mentor displays behavior for the protégé to emulate. This facilitates social learning. Acceptance and confirmation is important to both the mentor and protégé. When the protégé feels accepted by the mentor, it fosters a sense of pride. Likewise, positive regard and appreciation from the junior colleague provide a sense of satisfaction for the mentor. Counseling by a mentor helps the protégé explore personal issues that arise and require assistance. Friendship is another psychosocial function that benefits both mentor and protégé alike.

There are characteristics that define good mentoring relationships. In effective mentoring relationships, there is regular contact between mentor and protégé that has clearly specified purposes. Mentoring should be consistent with the corporate culture and the organization's goals. Both mentors and protégés alike should be trained in ways to manage the relationship. Mentors should be held accountable and rewarded for their role. Mentors should be perceived (accurately) by protégés as having considerable influence within the organization.[67] While it may be tempting to go after the "top dog" as your mentor, personality compatibility is also an important factor in the success or failure of a mentoring relationship. Mentors who are similar to their protégés in terms of personality traits like extraversion, and whose expectations are largely met by the relationship, are more likely to show interest in continuing the arrangement.[68] Cigna Financial Advisors takes a proactive approach to integrating new employees. As part of the company's Partnership Program, all new hires work for up to twenty-seven months under the oversight of an experienced, successful mentor. This relationship provides the new hires with hands-on instruction in how to sell more effectively, as well as increasing sales levels for the mentors themselves. Cigna demonstrates its commitment to this approach by hiring no more new producers than it can assign to individual mentors.[69]

Mentoring programs are also effective ways of addressing the challenge of workforce diversity. The mentoring process, however, presents unique problems, including the availability of mentors, issues of language and acculturation, and cultural sensitivity, for minority groups such as Hispanic Americans. Negative stereotypes can limit

mentor
An individual who provides guidance, coaching, counseling, and friendship to a protégé.

minority members' access to mentoring relationships and the benefits associated with mentoring.[70] To address this problem, companies can facilitate access to mentors in organizations. Informal mentoring programs identify pools of mentors and protégés, give training in the development of effective mentoring and diversity issues, and then provide informal opportunities for the development of mentoring relationships. Network groups are another avenue for mentoring. Network groups help members identify with those few others who are like them within an organization, build relationships with them, and build social support. Network groups enhance the chance that minorities will find mentors.[71] Dell, for example, has several Employee Resource Groups that serve networking functions. Some of these groups are aDellante, for Hispanic Americans; Asians in Motion, for Asian Americans; Building Relationships in Diverse Group Environments, for African Americans; and PRIDE, for gay, lesbian, and bisexual individuals. These groups serve as links to their respective communities within Dell. Networks also increase the likelihood that individuals have more than one mentor. Employees with multiple mentors, such as those gained from mentoring networks, have even greater career success than those with only one mentor.[72]

Some companies have formal mentoring programs. PricewaterhouseCoopers (PWC) also uses the mentoring model to help its interns. Each intern is assigned both a peer mentor to help with day-to-day questions and an experienced mentor to help with larger issues such as career path development. As an international firm, PWC also employs similar methods overseas. In PWC's Czech Republic operations, a team of two mentors—one of whom is called a "counselor"—fills the same guidance role as the two mentors generally fill for U.S. employees.[73]

Mentoring has had a strong impact in shaping the identities of the Big Four accounting firms. In one study, every partner who was interviewed reported having at least one mentor who played a critical role in his or her attainment of the partnership and beyond. Protégés' identities are shaped through mentoring, and their work goals, language, and even lifestyles reflect the imperatives of the Big Four firm.[74] Protégés are schooled on partners' "hot buttons" (what not to talk about), what to wear, to "tuck in the tie," and not to cut the grass without wearing a shirt.

Although some companies have formal mentoring programs, junior employees more often are left to negotiate their own mentoring relationships. The barriers to finding a mentor include lack of access to mentors, fear of initiating a mentoring relationship, and fear that supervisors or coworkers might not approve of the mentoring relationship. Individuals may also be afraid to initiate a mentoring relationship because it might be misconstrued as a sexual advance by the potential mentor or others. This is a fear of potential mentors as well. Some are unwilling to develop a relationship because of their own or the protégé's gender. Women report more of these barriers than men, and individuals who lack previous experience report more barriers to finding a mentor.[75] There are other gender differences found in mentoring relationships. Male protégés report receiving less psychological support than female protégés. Additionally, male mentors report giving more career development support, whereas female mentors report giving more psychological support.[76]

Organizations can encourage junior workers to approach mentors by providing opportunities for them to interact with senior colleagues. The immediate supervisor is not always the best mentor for an individual, so exposure to other senior workers is important. Seminars, multilevel teams, and social events can serve as vehicles for bringing together potential mentors and protégés.

Mentoring relationships go through a series of phases: initiation, cultivation, separation, and redefinition. There is no fixed time length for each phase, because each relationship is unique. In the *initiation* phase, the mentoring relationship begins to take on significance for both the mentor and the protégé. In the *cultivation* phase, the relationship becomes more meaningful, and the protégé shows rapid progress because of the career and psychosocial support provided by the mentor. Protégés influence mentors as well.

In the *separation* phase, the protégé feels the need to assert independence and work more autonomously. Separation can be voluntary, or it can result from an involuntary change (the protégé or mentor may be promoted or transferred). The separation phase can be difficult if it is resisted, either by the mentor (who is reluctant to let go of the relationship) or by the protégé (who resents the mentor's withdrawal of support). Separation can proceed smoothly and naturally or can result from a conflict that disrupts the mentoring relationship.

The *redefinition* phase occurs if separation has been successful. In this phase, the relationship takes on a new identity as both parties consider themselves colleagues or friends. The mentor feels pride in the protégé, and the protégé develops a deeper appreciation for the support from the mentor.

Why are mentors so important? Aside from the support they provide, the research shows that mentors are vital to the protégé's future success. For example, studies have demonstrated that individuals with mentors have higher promotion rates and higher incomes than individuals without them.[77] In fact, mentorship has been shown to add increase career success above and beyond an individual's education, training, work experience, proactivity in their careers, and networking.[78] Professionals who have mentors earn between $5,600 and $22,000 more per year than those who do not.[79] Individuals with mentors also are better decision makers.[80] And it is not just the presence of the mentor that yields these benefits. The quality of the relationship is most important.[81]

During the advancement stage, many individuals face another transition: They settle into a relationship with a life partner. This lifestyle transition requires adjustment in many respects: learning to live with another person, being concerned with someone besides yourself, dealing with an extended family, and many other demands. The partnership can be particularly stressful if both members are career oriented.

Dual-Career Partnerships

The two-career lifestyle has increased in recent years due in part to the need for two incomes to maintain a preferred standard of living. *Dual-career partnerships* are relationships in which both people have important career roles. This type of partnership can be mutually beneficial, but it can also be stressful. Often these stresses center around stereotypes that providing income is a man's responsibility and taking care of the home is the woman's domain. Among married couples, working women's satisfaction with the marriage is affected by how much the husband helps with childcare. Men who adhere to traditional gender beliefs may be threatened when the wife's income exceeds their own. Beliefs about who should do what in the partnership complicate the dual-career issue.[82]

One stressor in a dual-career partnership is time pressure. When both partners work outside the home, there may be a time crunch in fitting in work, family, and leisure time. Another potential problem is jealousy. When one partner's career blooms before the other's, the less successful partner may feel threatened.[83]

Another issue to work out is whose career takes precedence. For example, what happens if one partner is transferred to another city? Must the other partner make a move that might threaten his or her own career in order to be with the individual who was transferred? Who, if anyone, will stay home and take care of a new baby?

Working out a dual-career partnership takes careful planning and consistent communication between the partners. Each partner must serve as a source of social support for the other. Couples can also turn to other family members, friends, and professionals for support if the need arises.

dual-career partnership
A relationship in which both people have important career roles.

Work–Home Conflicts

6 Describe ways to manage conflicts between work and home.

An issue related to dual-career partnerships that is faced throughout the career cycle, but often first encountered in the advancement phase, is the conflicts that occur between work and personal life. Experiencing a great deal of work–home conflict negatively affects an individual's overall quality of life. Such conflicts can lead to emotional exhaustion. Dealing with customer complaints all day, failed sales calls, and missed deadlines can magnify negative events at home, and vice versa.[84] Responsibilities at home can clash with responsibilities at work, and these conflicts must be planned for. For example, suppose a child gets sick at school. Who will pick up the child and stay home with him or her? Couples must work together to resolve these conflicts. Even at Eli Lilly and Company, only 36 percent of workers said it is possible to get ahead in their careers and still devote sufficient time to family. This is surprising, because Lilly has a reputation as one of the world's most family-friendly workplaces.[85] When one partner has a lot of work–home conflict, it negatively affects the other partner. A recent study found that one partner's work–home conflict impacts how couples interact with one another and increases behaviors aimed at expressing negative feelings, criticizing or actually negatively impacting the other's goal attainment which eventually leads to exhaustion in that other partner.[86]

Work–home conflicts are particular problems for working women.[87] Women have been quicker to share the provider role than men have been to share responsibilities at home.[88] When working women experience work–home conflict, their performance declines, and they suffer more strain. Work–home conflict is a broad topic. It can be narrowed further into work–family conflict, in which work interferes with family, versus family–work conflict, in which family or home life interferes with work.[89] Additionally, egalitarian individuals who believe men and women should identify equally with their contributions at home and work experience more guilt associated with work–home conflict than individuals who are more traditional. In fact, traditional individuals tend to feel more guilt associated with home interfering with work.[90]

Cultural differences arise in these types of conflicts. One study showed that while Americans experience more family–work conflict, Chinese experience more work–family conflict.[91] For example, women in management positions in China were very positive about future advancements and carried a strong belief in their ability to succeed. This, in turn, caused them to reevaluate their personal and professional identities. Such an identity transformation is marked by happiness associated with career advancement, even though many women foresaw emotional costs with such career advancement. This study indicated that female Chinese managers experience work–family conflict in part because the Chinese culture emphasizes close social ties and guanxi, or personalized networks of influence.[92]

To help individuals deal with work–home conflict, companies can offer *flexible work schedules*.[93] These programs, such as flextime, which we discussed in Chapter 14, give employees freedom to take care of personal concerns while still getting their work done. Company-sponsored childcare is another way to help. Companies with on-site day-care centers include Johnson & Johnson, Perdue Farms, and Campbell Soup. Mitchell Gold, an award-winning furniture maker, believes that treating people right must come first. Its 2,700-square-foot on-site day-care center is education based rather than activity based and operates at break-even rates to make it more accessible. The day-care facility was named the county's "Provider of the Year" in 2003.[94] Whereas large companies may offer corporate day care, small companies can also assist their workers by providing referral services for locating the type of childcare the workers need. For smaller organizations, this is a cost-effective

flexible work schedule
A work schedule that allows employees discretion in order to accommodate personal concerns.

alternative.[95] At the very least, companies can be sensitive to work–home conflicts and handle them on a case-by-case basis with flexibility and concern.

A program of increasing interest that organizations can provide is *eldercare*. Often workers find themselves part of the sandwich generation: They are expected to care for both their children and their elderly parents. This extremely stressful role is reported more often by women than men.[96] The impact of caring for an aging loved one is often underestimated. But 17 percent of those who provide care eventually quit their jobs due to time constraints, and another 15 percent cut back their work hours for the same reason.[97] Caring for an elderly dependent at home can create severe work–home conflicts for employees and also takes a toll on the employee's own well-being and performance at work. This is especially true if the organization does not provide a supportive climate for discussion of eldercare issues.[98] Harvard University has taken steps to help its faculty and staff deal with eldercare issues by contracting with Parents in a Pinch, a firm that specializes in nanny services and now also offers eldercare.[99]

John Beatrice is one of a handful of men making work fit their family, rather than trying to fit family around career. John remembers his father working most of the night so he could be at John's athletic events during the day, and John wants the same for his family. So while job sharing, flexible scheduling, and telecommuting have traditionally been viewed as meeting the needs of working mothers, John and other men are increasingly taking advantage of such opportunities. In John's case, flexible work hours at Ernst & Young allow him to spend part of his mornings and afternoons coaching a high school hockey team. In John's assessment, flexible work hours actually lead him to work more hours than he would otherwise, and he's happier about doing it. Not surprisingly, John's employer also benefits from the arrangement; after nineteen years, John is more loyal than ever and still loves what he does.[100]

Alternative work arrangements such as flextime, compressed workweeks, work-at-home arrangements, part-time hours, job sharing, and leave options can help employees manage work–home conflicts. A leader in offering innovative programs to help the sandwich generation is the accounting firm KPMG, and you can read about the variety of programs they offer in the Real World. Managers must not let their biases get in the way of these benefits. Top managers may be less willing to grant alternative work arrangements to men than to women, to supervisors than to subordinates, and to employees caring for elderly parents rather than children. It is important that family-friendly policies be applied fairly.[101]

The advancement stage is filled with the challenges of finding a mentor, balancing dual-career partnerships, and dealing with work–home conflicts. Developmental changes that occur in either the late advancement stage or the early maintenance stage can prove stressful, too. The midlife transition, which takes place approximately between ages forty and forty-five, is often a time of crisis. Levinson points out three major changes that contribute to the midlife transition. First, people realize that their lives are half over and that they are mortal. Second, age forty is considered by people in their twenties and thirties to be "over the hill" and not part of the youth culture. Finally, people reassess their dreams and evaluate how close they have come to achieving those dreams. All of these factors make up the midlife transition.

THE MAINTENANCE STAGE

Maintenance may be a misnomer for this career stage because some people continue to grow in their careers, although the growth is usually not at the rate it was earlier. A career crisis at midlife may accompany the midlife transition. A senior product manager at Borden found himself in such a crisis and described it this way: "When

eldercare
Assistance in caring for elderly parents and/or other elderly relatives.

The Real World 17.2

KPMG Provides Help for the Sandwich Generation

Many workers find themselves caught between taking care of their children and their elderly parents. KPMG, the audit, tax, and advisory accounting firm, recognized these needs and took steps to address them. At KPMG, a fluid and supportive program focuses on work–life balance, including alternative work arrangements like compressed workweeks, flextime, and telecommuting. If babysitting arrangements fall through for employees, KPMG offers a backup childcare service. In addition, they have a shared leave program, in which employees can donate personal time to colleagues experiencing a family emergency like sudden illness or death of a loved one.

Most unique of their work–life balance initiatives is the three-part eldercare benefit. It started with an online information and referral service that connected employees with aging and health-related resources and facilities. Next, the firm began to offer backup care for elderly relatives, which provides up to twenty days care per year. The backup care can be facility-based, or it can consist of in-home care by aides who help the parent or family member with situations like coming

home from a hospital stay, or with daily activities like bathing or getting dressed. As with the shared leave program, employees can donate unused backup care to colleagues who have exhausted their own allotment for the year. Finally, if an employee needs to take time off work to plan for eldercare or to deliver that care in person, KPMG's paid time off policy can be used, or employees can obtain a leave of absence. If the elderly relative is local, the employee's work schedule can be adjusted through flextime.

The pay-offs for providing these benefits are many. Sandwich generation workers can be relieved of worries about caring for kids or elderly parents, and can show up for work and be productive. For KPMG, the programs led to reduced turnover and improved employee morale, along with an award from Catalyst (the leading nonprofit promoting inclusive workplaces for women) for the firm's transformation into an employer of choice.

SOURCES: http://www.catalyst.org/file/280/difinalpracticekpmg_pdf.pdf; https://www.web1.lifebenefits.com/MMG/resources/aware_newsletter/aware0408/ef_print.html

---

I was in college, I had thought in terms of being president of a company. . . . But at Borden I felt used and cornered. Most of the guys in the next two rungs above me had either an MBA or fifteen to twenty years of experience in the food business. My long-term plans stalled."[102]

Some individuals who reach a career crisis are burned out, and a month's vacation will help, according to Carolyn Smith Paschal, who owns an executive search firm. She recommends that companies give employees in this stage sabbaticals instead of bonuses. This would help rejuvenate them.

Some individuals reach the maintenance stage with a sense of achievement and contentment, feeling no need to strive for further upward mobility. Whether the maintenance stage is a time of crisis or contentment, however, there are two issues to grapple with: sustaining performance and becoming a mentor.

Sustaining Performance

Remaining productive is a key concern for individuals in the maintenance stage. This becomes challenging when one reaches a *career plateau*, a point where the probability of moving further up the hierarchy is low. Some people handle career plateauing fairly well, but others may become frustrated, bored, and dissatisfied with their jobs.

To keep employees productive, organizations can provide challenges and opportunities for learning. Lateral moves are one option. Another option is to involve the

career plateau
A point in an individual's career in which the probability of moving further up the hierarchy is low.

employee in project teams that provide new tasks and skill development. The key is keeping the work stimulating and involving. Individuals at this stage also need continued affirmation of their value to the organization. They need to know that their contributions are significant and appreciated.[103]

Becoming a Mentor

During maintenance, individuals can make a contribution by sharing their wealth of knowledge and experience with others. Opportunities to be mentors to new employees can keep senior workers motivated and involved in the organization and lead to positive job attitudes.[104] It is important for organizations to reward mentors for the time and energy they expend. Some employees adapt naturally to the mentor role, but others may need training on how to coach and counsel junior workers.

Kathy Kram notes that there are four keys to the success of a formal mentoring program. First, participation should be voluntary. No one should be forced to enter a mentoring relationship, and careful matching of mentors and protégés is important. Second, support from top executives is needed to convey the intent of the program and its role in career development. Third, training should be provided to mentors so they understand the functions of the relationship. Finally, a graceful exit should be provided for mismatches or for people in mentoring relationships that have fulfilled their purpose.[105]

Maintenance is a time of transition, like all career stages. It can be managed by individuals who know what to expect and plan to remain productive, as well as by organizations that focus on maximizing employee involvement in work. According to Levinson, during the latter part of the maintenance stage, another life transition occurs. The age-fifty transition is another time of reevaluating the dream and working further on the issues raised in the midlife transition. Following the age-fifty transition is a fairly stable period. During this time, individuals begin to plan seriously for withdrawing from their careers.

THE WITHDRAWAL STAGE

The withdrawal stage usually occurs later in life and signals that a long period of continuous employment will soon come to a close. Older workers may face discrimination and stereotyping. They may be viewed by others as less productive, more resistant to change, and less motivated. However, older workers are one of the most undervalued groups in the workforce. They can provide continuity in the midst of change and can serve as mentors and role models to younger generations of employees.

Discrimination against older workers is prohibited under the Age Discrimination in Employment Act.[106] Organizations must create a culture that values older workers' contributions. With their level of experience, strong work ethic, and loyalty, these workers have much to contribute. In fact, older workers have lower rates of tardiness and absenteeism, are more safety conscious, and are more satisfied with their jobs than are younger workers.[107]

Planning for Change

The decision to retire is an individual one, but the need for planning is universal. A retired sales executive from Boise Cascade said that the best advice is to "plan no unplanned retirement."[108] This means carefully planning not only the transition but also the activities you will be involved in once the transition is made. All options should be open for consideration. One recent trend is the need for temporary top-level executives. Some companies are hiring senior managers from the outside on a temporary basis. The qualities of a good temporary executive include substantial high-level management experience, financial security that allows the executive to choose only assignments that really interest him or her, and a willingness to relocate.[109] Some individuals at the withdrawal stage find this an attractive option.

Planning for retirement should include not only financial planning but also a plan for psychologically withdrawing from work. The pursuit of hobbies and travel, volunteer work, or more time with extended family can all be part of the plan. The key is to plan early and carefully, as well as to anticipate the transition with a positive attitude and a full slate of desirable activities.

Retirement

There are several retirement trends right now, ranging from early retirement to phased retirement to never retiring. Some adults are choosing a combination of these options, leaving their first career for some time off before reentering the workforce either part-time or full-time doing something they enjoy. For more and more Americans, the idea of a retirement spent sitting beside the swimming pool lacks appeal. Factors that influence the decision of when to retire include company policy, financial considerations, family support or pressure, health, and opportunities for other productive activities.[110]

During the withdrawal stage, the individual faces a major life transition that Levinson refers to as the late adulthood transition (ages sixty to sixty-five). One's own mortality becomes a major concern, and the loss of one's family members and friends becomes more frequent. The person works to achieve a sense of integrity—that is, the encompassing meaning and value—in life.

Some retirement-agers may go through a second midlife crisis. People are living longer and staying more active. Vickie Ianucelli, for example, bought a condo on a Mexican beach, celebrated a birthday in Paris, bought herself a 9.5-karat ring, and got plastic surgery. And it's her second midlife crisis. She's a psychologist who is also a sixty-plus grandmother of two.[111]

Retirement need not be a complete cessation of work. Many alternative work arrangements can be considered, and many companies offer flexibility in these options. *Phased retirement* is a popular option for retirement-age workers who want to gradually reduce their hours and/or responsibilities. There are many forms of phased retirement, including reduced workdays or workweeks, job sharing, and consulting and mentoring arrangements. Many organizations cannot afford the loss of large numbers of experienced employees at once. In fact, although 50 percent of all U.S. workers are officially retired by age sixty, only 11 percent fully withdraw from work. This means there is an increase in *bridge employment*, which takes place after a retirement from a full-time position but before permanent withdrawal from the workforce. Bridge employment is related to retirement satisfaction and overall life satisfaction.[112]

Some companies are helping employees transition to retirement in innovative ways. Retired individuals can continue their affiliation with the organization by serving as mentors to employees who are embarking on retirement planning or other career transitions. This helps diminish the fear of loss some people have about retirement, because the retiree has an option to serve as a mentor or consultant to the organization.

Lawrence Livermore National Labs (LLNL) employs some of the best research minds in the world. And when these great minds retire from full-time work, they have numerous opportunities to continue contributing. LLNL's retiree program

phased retirement

An arrangement that allows employees to reduce their hours and/or responsibilities in order to ease into retirement.

bridge employment

Employment that takes place after retiring from a full-time position but before permanent withdrawal from the workforce.

Web site lists a wide variety of requests, ranging from leading tours and making phone calls to providing guidance on current research and helping researchers make contact with other researchers.[113] Programs like these help LLNL avoid the typical knowledge drain that takes place when seasoned veteran employees retire.

Now that you understand the career stage model, you can begin to conduct your own career planning. It is never too early to start.

Career Anchors

Much of an individual's self-concept rests on a career. Over the course of a person's work life, career anchors are developed. *Career anchors* are self-perceived talents, motives, and values that guide an individual's career decisions.[114] Edgar Schein developed the concept of career anchors based on a twelve-year study of MBA graduates from the Massachusetts Institute of Technology (MIT). Schein found great diversity in the graduates' career histories but great similarities in the way they explained the career decisions they had made.[115] From extensive interviews with the graduates, Schein developed five career anchors:

7 Explain how career anchors help form a career identity.

1. *Technical/functional competence.* Individuals who hold this career anchor want to specialize in a given functional area (e.g., finance or marketing) and become competent. The idea of general management does not interest them.

2. *Managerial competence.* Adapting this career anchor means individuals want general management responsibility. They want to see their efforts have an impact on organizational effectiveness.

3. *Autonomy and independence.* Freedom is the key to this career anchor, and often these individuals are uncomfortable working in large organizations. Autonomous careers such as writer, professor, or consultant attract these individuals.

4. *Creativity.* Individuals holding this career anchor feel a strong need to create something. They are often entrepreneurs.

5. *Security/stability.* Long-term career stability, whether in a single organization or in a single geographic area, fits people with this career anchor. Some government jobs provide this type of security.

Career anchors emerge over time and may be modified by work or life experiences.[116] The importance of knowing your career anchor is that it can help you find a match between yourself and an organization. For example, individuals with creativity as an anchor may find themselves stifled in bureaucratic organizations. Textbook sales may not be the place for an individual with a security anchor because of the frequent travel and seasonal nature of the business.

MANAGERIAL IMPLICATIONS: MANAGING YOUR CAREER

The challenges of globalization, diversity, technology, and ethics have provided unique opportunities and threats for career management. The ongoing restructuring of American organizations with its accompanying downsizing has resulted in a reduction of 25 percent of the jobs held in the Fortune 500 companies.[117] The flattening of the organizational hierarchy has resulted in fewer opportunities for promotion. Forty-year careers with one organization, a phenomenon baby boomers saw their parents experience, are becoming less and less the norm. Negotiating the turbulent waters of the U.S. employment market will be a challenge in the foreseeable future.

career anchors
A network of self-perceived talents, motives, and values that guide an individual's career decisions.

Many industries are experiencing sinking employment, but there are some bright spots. According to Labor Department projections, the U.S. economy will add approximately 21.3 million jobs by the year 2012, most of them in service industries. Figure 17.3 shows where the new jobs will be found. Of all the occupations

Over the 2002–2012 decade, career choices abound for those seeking high earnings and lots of opportunities. High-paying occupations that are projected to have many openings are varied. This diverse group includes teachers, managers, and construction trades workers.

The job openings shown in the chart represent the total that are expected each year for workers who are entering these occupations for the first time. The job openings result from each occupation's growth and from the need to replace workers who retire or leave the occupation permanently for some other reason. Not included among these openings are ones that are created when workers move from job to job within an occupation.

Median earnings, such as those listed below, indicate that half of the workers in an occupation made more than that amount, and half made less. The occupations in the chart ranked in the highest or second-highest earnings quartiles for 2002 median earnings. This means that median earnings for workers in these occupations were higher than the earnings for at least 50 percent of all occupations in 2002.

Most of these occupations had another thing going for them in 2002: low or very low unemployment. Workers in occupations that had higher levels of unemployment—truck drivers, carpenters, and electricians—were more dependent on a strong economy or seasonal employment.

	Annual average job openings due to growth and net replacement needs, projected 2002–2012	Median annual earnings, 2002
Registered nurses	110,119	$48,090
Postsecondary teachers	95,980	49,090
General and operations managers	76,245	68,210
Sales representatives, wholesale and manufacturing, except technical and scientific products	66,239	42,730
Truck drivers, heavy and tractor-trailer	62,517	33,210
Elementary school teachers, except special education	54,701	41,780
First-line supervisors or managers of retail sales workers	48,645	29,700
Secondary school teachers, except special and vocational education	45,761	43,950
General maintenance and repair workers	44,978	29,370
Executive secretaries and administrative assistants	42,444	33,410
First-line supervisors or managers of office and administrative support workers	40,909	38,820
Accountants and auditors	40,465	47,000
Carpenters	31,917	34,190
Automotive service technicians and mechanics	31,887	30,590
Police and sheriff's patrol officers	31,290	42,270
Licensed practical and licensed vocational nurses	29,480	31,440
Electricians	28,485	41,390
Management analysts	25,470	60,340
Computer systems analysts	23,735	62,890
Special education teachers	23,297	43,450

SOURCE: Bureau of Labor Statistics, "High-Paying Occupations with Many Openings, Projected 2002–2012," *Occupational Outlook Quarterly* 48 (Spring 2004), http://www.bls.gov/opub/ooq/2004/spring/oochart.pdf.

expected to have faster-than-average employment growth, above-average earnings, and below-average unemployment, the ones shown in this chart have the largest number of projected openings. These occupations will account for 5 million new jobs, or 27 percent of all job growth. Most of these jobs require at least a bachelor's degree.

Andy Grove, chairman of Intel Corporation, suggests that as a general rule, you must accept that no matter where you work, you are not an employee. Instead, you are in a business with one employee: yourself. You face tremendous competition with millions of other businesses. You own your career as a sole proprietor. Grove poses three key questions that are central to managing your career. Continually ask the following questions:

1. *Am I adding real value?* You add real value by continually looking for ways to make things truly better in your organization. In principle, every hour of your workday should be spent increasing the value of the output of the people for whom you're responsible.

2. *Am I plugged into what's happening around me?* Inside the company? The industry? Are you a node in a network of plugged-in people, or are you floating around by yourself?

3. *Am I trying new ideas, new techniques, and new technologies?* Try them personally—don't just read about them.[118]

The key to survival is to add more value every day and to be flexible. You can use You 17.2 to assess the current state of your flexibility skills.

You 17.2

Assess Your Flexibility Skills

Use the following scale to rate the frequency with which you perform the behaviors described in each question. Place the corresponding number (1–7) in the blank preceding the statement.

Rarely	Irregularly	Occasionally	Usually	Frequently	Almost Always	Consistently
1	2	3	4	5	6	7

_____ 1. I manage a variety of assignments with varying demands and complexities.

_____ 2. I adjust work plans to account for new circumstances.

_____ 3. I modify rules and procedures in order to meet operational needs and goals.

_____ 4. I work with ambiguous assignments when necessary and use these when possible to further my goals and objectives.

_____ 5. I rearrange work or personal schedules to meet deadlines.

_____ 6. In emergencies, I respond to the most pressing needs first.

_____ 7. I change my priorities to accommodate unexpected events.

_____ 8. I manage my personal work overload by seeking assistance or by delegating responsibility to others.

_____ 9. I vary the way I deal with others according to their needs and personalities.

_____ 10. I help others improve their job performance, or I assign tasks that will further their development.

_____ 11. I accept the authority of my manager but continue to demonstrate my initiative and assertiveness.

_____ 12. I work well with all types of personalities.

(Continued)

_____ 13. I measure my performance on the job against the feedback I receive.

_____ 14. I correct performance deficits that have been brought to my attention.

_____ 15. When I disagree with my manager's appraisal of my work, I discuss our differences.

_____ 16. I seek training and assignments that can help me improve my job-related skills.

_____ 17. In disagreements concerning work-related issues, I look at matters impersonally and concentrate on the facts.

_____ 18. I make compromises to get problems moving toward resolution.

_____ 19. I look for new and better ways to accomplish my duties and responsibilities.

_____ 20. I offer to negotiate all areas of disagreement.

FIGURE A

Flexible Behaviors Questionnaire (FBQ) Scoring

Skill Area	Items	Score
Working with new, changing, and ambiguous situations	1, 2, 3, 4	
Working under pressure	5, 6, 7, 8	
Dealing with different personal styles	9, 10, 11, 12	
Handling feedback	13, 14, 15, 16	
Resolving conflicts	17, 18, 19, 20	
TOTAL SCORE		

FIGURE B

Flexible Behaviors Questionnaire (FBQ) Evaluation

Total Score

Lowest score   Highest score

20   50   80   110   40

Category Scores

Working with new, changing, and ambiguous situations

| 4 | 10 | 16 | 22 | 28 |

Working under pressure

| 4 | 10 | 16 | 22 | 28 |

Dealing with different personality styles

| 4 | 10 | 16 | 22 | 28 |

Handling feedback

| 4 | 10 | 16 | 22 | 28 |

Resolving conflicts

| 4 | 10 | 16 | 22 | 28 |

FBQ Scoring

The scoring sheet in Figure A summarizes your responses for the FBQ. It will help you identify your existing strengths and pinpoint areas that need improvement.

FBQ Evaluation

Figure B shows score lines for your total score and for each category measured on the FBQ. Each line shows a continuum from the lowest score to the highest.

The score lines in Figure B show graphically where you stand with regard to the five flexible behaviors. If you have been honest with yourself, you now have a better idea of your relative strengths and weaknesses in the categories that make up the skills of flexibility.

SOURCE: From Fandt, _Management Skills: Learning Through Practice and Experience_, 1st ed. pp. 431–433. Copyright © 1994 Cengage Learning. Reprinted with permission of Cengage Learning, www.cengage.com/permissions.

Diversity Dialogue

Retirees Find New Careers Working for Their Children

Robert Shipman is a sixty-four-year-old retired CEO of a clothing manufacturing company who carries pink business cards with a picture of a pug on them. Why does he do that? Because his daughter told him he had to. After Shipman retired, he began working for his then-twenty-eight-year-old daughter at her cosmetics firm. The pug is the company mascot and as for the color of the business card, well . . . his daughter likes pink. Shipman retired from a company that boasted $130 million in annual sales, and though he is fond of neither pugs nor pink, he carries the business cards anyway as a condition of his employment.

Shipman is not alone. Working for their children is a growing trend among retirees, with many notable parents having worked for their children at some point in their careers. For example, after helping him find an attorney to defend Microsoft in a government lawsuit, Bill Gates hired William H. Gates, Sr. as the chairman of the Gates Foundation. After G. Harry Huizenga retired, he was hired to oversee the real estate for his son H. Wayne Huizenga's company, Blockbuster Entertainment.

Shipman, Gates, and Huizenga are reminders about the changing nature of retirement. Many retirees are no longer satisfied to withdraw to the golf course or trade in their business suits and ties for shorts and sandals. Instead, more and more retirement-age executives are using their knowledge and expertise to fill important roles in new companies—in many cases where their children are their bosses.

1. Imagine you are hiring your retired parent in an executive position in your firm. What issues should you address to ensure the partnership is a healthy one?
2. Older workers are the most undervalued groups in the workforce, often the target of age discrimination. Can working for their children help change this perception? How?

SOURCES: T. Demos, "Hiring Parents," *Fortune* 155(12) (June 25, 2007): 134; A. Fisher, "Working for Your Kids," *Fortune* 155(12) (June 25, 2007): 130–138.

LOOKING BACK: FACEBOOK

What Is Legal?

Under Title VII of the Civil Rights Act of 1964, the Americans with Disabilities Act (ADA), and the Age Discrimination in Employment Act (ADEA), it is illegal to discriminate in any aspect of employment, including hiring and firing. Discriminatory practices under these laws also include "employment decisions based on stereotypes or assumptions about the abilities, traits, or performance of individuals of a certain sex, race, age, religion, or ethnic group, or individuals with disabilities" and "denying employment opportunities to a person because of marriage to, or association with, an individual of a particular race, religion, national origin, or an individual with a disability." Title VII also prohibits discrimination because of "participation in schools or places of worship associated with a particular racial, ethnic, or religious group".[119]

If an employer is using Facebook to screen candidates and avoids interviewing an individual because of race, gender, or any of the above conditions, this would be illegal. Research has investigated the impact of black-sounding names on a resume and the likelihood of getting a job interview. In these studies, two fictitious but very similar resumes are sent to potential employers with the only difference being the name; one is an African American–sounding name whereas one is a white-sounding name. Those resumes with the white-sounding name are more likely to get a job interview. In fact, one such study found that the white-sounding name would receive an interview 50 percent more often than the African American–sounding name.[120] Thus, the questions that remain for Facebook users, employers, and the EEOC are if this sort of discrimination can exist when the only indication of race is a name, what kind of discrimination will exist with the use of Facebook and, perhaps, more importantly, how will the EEOC prevent it?

Chapter Summary

1. Career management is a joint responsibility of individuals and organizations.

2. Good matches between individuals and organizations can be promoted with a realistic job preview (RJP).

3. The four stages in an individual's career are establishment, advancement, maintenance, and withdrawal. Each stage has unique challenges.

4. Psychological contracts are implicit agreements between individuals and organizations.

5. Mentoring is crucial to both the career success of young workers and the needs of older workers.

6. Childcare, eldercare, and flexible work schedules can help employees manage work–home conflicts.

7. Career anchors help an individual form a career identity and formulate an effective career plan.

Key Terms

advancement (p. 597)
bridge employment (p. 610)
career (p. 588)
career anchors (p. 611)
career ladder (p. 602)
career management (p. 588)

career path (p. 602)
career plateau (p. 608)
dual-career partnership (p. 604)
eldercare (p. 607)
establishment (p. 597)
flexible work schedule (p. 606)

maintenance (p. 597)
mentor (p. 603)
phased retirement (p. 610)
psychological contract (p. 598)
realistic job preview (RJP) (p. 596)
withdrawal (p. 597)

Review Questions

1. What is career management?

2. What is the new career, and how does it differ from older notions about careers?

3. What are the sources of potential conflict during organizational entry? How can they be avoided?

4. What is a realistic job preview, and why is it important?

5. What are psychological contracts?

6. What stressors are associated with socialization?

7. What are the career functions provided by a mentor?

8. What are some of the most likely causes of home–work conflicts?

9. What are the two key issues to deal with during the maintenance career stage?

10. What is the key to career survival?

Discussion and Communication Questions

1. What are the realities of the new career? How can developing your emotional intelligence help you turn these realities into opportunities to improve your career?

2. What do you think will be the most stressful career stage? What type of stressors led you to make this choice?

3. Does the career stage model have exceptions? In other words, can it be applied to all careers? If not, what are the exceptions?

4. Do men and women have different expectations of a dual-career partnership? How do these expectations differ?

5. Given the downsizing and restructuring in many organizations, how can organizations help employees with career management if there are fewer opportunities for promotion?

6. How has each of the four challenges (globalization, diversity, technology, and ethics) affected career management in recent years?

7. *(communication question)* Contact the human resources manager of a local business. Ask if he or she would take a few minutes to discuss some issues about résumés with you. Structure your discussion around the following questions:

a. How often do you encounter "padded" résumés? What is the most common padding, and how do you react to it?

b. Do you verify the information on résumés? How do you do this? How long does it take for you to be sure that an applicant has been honest about his or her qualifications?

c. What would you do if you found that a productive, loyal employee had lied on a résumé when applying for a job? Is "résumé fraud" an offense that warrants firing?

Summarize the findings from your interview in a memo to your instructor.

8. *(communication question)* Select an individual in the field you want to work in or in a company you might want to work for. Contact the individual and ask if you might take a minute of her or his time for some career advice. Ask the following two questions, along with others you design yourself. First, how has the idea of a "career" changed over the past few years? Second, what advice would the person give to college students just beginning a new career? Be prepared to present your interview results in class.

Ethical Dilemma

Lynn Kingston graduated at the top of her class at law school, and she has long dreamed of becoming partner at a top corporate law firm. When she is offered an associate position with Smith & Johnson, she is elated—this is a full-service firm that serves high-profile clients, and Lynn thinks she will be able to distinguish herself here. She has always wanted to work in diverse areas of corporate law and Smith & Johnson is also known for their work upholding the kind of ethical and moral goals she admires.

Lynn also knows that the work load at Smith & Johnson is quite rigorous. Clients of the firm anticipate that their lawyers will be available at all hours. That's what makes Smith & Johnson so successful, and during the interview process, these expectations are made overtly clear to Lynn. The hiring manager explains that associates are always on call; however, the compensation is superior. Lynn knows that she and her new husband, Brian, will be able to afford a new house and build up their nest egg on this kind of salary.

However, Lynn and Brian were also hoping to start a family soon. After reviewing the maternity leave policy in the benefits handbook, she learns that the company has a very generous approach to new mothers.

However, it is clear that after the eight-week leave, the employee is expected to return to the same full-time schedule as prior to the birth. Lynn is ready to commit herself to the workload, but she's not sure if she will be so willing to commit herself to that lifestyle after the birth of a child.

Lynn also considers how much she respects Smith & Johnson; as an associate, she would feel compelled to give the firm and her clients the highest level of commitment possible. She is aware that if she is promoted to a senior associate, the intensity of the time demands level off. Lynn believes that she has the talent and energy to be an essential contributor.

As she contemplates saying yes to what she believes to be her dream job, she also realizes that she doesn't want to compromise Smith & Johnson by accepting their offer if she knows, from the onset, that she might not be willing or able to be the highest-performing employee she can.

Questions:

1. Using consequential, rule-based, and character theories, evaluate Lynn's options.

2. What should Lynn do? Why?

Experiential Exercises

17.1 The Individual–Organizational Dialogue

The purpose of this exercise is to help you gain experience in working out a psychological contract from both perspectives—the individual's and the organization's.

Students should form groups of six to eight members. Within each group, half of the students will be job candidates, and half will represent organization members (insiders).

Step 1. Each half should make two lists as follows:

List 1, candidate version. What information should you, as a job candidate, provide the organization to start an effective psychological contract?

List 2, candidate version. What information should you, as a job candidate, seek from the organization?

List 1, insider version. What information should you, as an organization insider, seek from potential employees?

List 2, insider version. What information should you, as an organization insider, provide to potential employees to start an effective psychological contract?

Step 2. Within each group, compare lists by matching the two versions of List 1. What were the similarities and differences in your lists? Then compare List 2 from each half of the group. What were the similarities and differences in these lists?

Step 3. Review the lists, and select the most difficult information to obtain from the candidate and the organization. Select one person to play the candidate and one to play the insider. First, have the candidate role-play an interaction with the insider in which the candidate tries to get the difficult information from the organization. Then have the insider try to obtain the difficult information from the candidate.

Step 4. Reconvene as a class, and discuss the following questions:

1. What did you find to be the most difficult questions asked by candidates?

2. What did you find to be the most difficult questions asked by insiders?

3. What information is necessary for an effective psychological contract?

4. What keeps each party from fully disclosing the information needed for a good psychological contract?

5. What can organizations do to facilitate the process of forming good psychological contracts?

6. What can individuals do to facilitate the process?

17.2 The Ethics of Résumés and Recommendations

The purpose of this exercise is to explore ethical issues concerning résumés and recommendations. First, read the following brief introductory scenario.

Jason Eckerle returned to his desk from lunch with a single mission in mind: to select the half-dozen best candidates for a regional customer service manager's position. As he hung up his suit jacket, Eckerle sized up the stack of résumés and recommendations he'd been dealing with all morning—more than 100 of them.

The work had been slow but steady, gradually forming into three distinct piles: one contained absolute rejects (not enough work experience, wrong academic credentials, or poor recommendations from former employers), the second contained a few definite candidates for personal interviews, and the third held the applications of those about whom he still had questions or reservations.

His task for the afternoon—selecting three more applicants to bring to the company headquarters for interviews—was complicated by the résumés and recommendation letters themselves. Some questions were obvious: "This guy lists five years' full-time sales and marketing experience, yet he's only twenty-two years old. How can he go to school full-time and have that kind of experience?" Here's another: "This young lady says she went to school at the Sorbonne in Paris for two years; yet on the application form, under the heading 'Foreign Languages' she's checked 'none.' " Here's one more: "This fella says he has a degree from the University of Texas, yet nowhere on his résumé does he say he lived or spent time there. Did he get that diploma by correspondence?"

Other issues are even more mysterious: "This young lady's résumé lists education and work experience, but there's a three-year gap from 1989 to 1992. What's that all about? Is she trying to conceal something, or just absentminded?" As Eckerle thumbed through another résumé, he noticed the application form declaring "fluency in Japanese, French, and Spanish." "How do you get to be *fluent* in a language unless you've lived where it's spoken?" he wondered. The résumé didn't list any of those languages as native, nor did the application mention living abroad.

"Some of this stuff is outright fraud," he observed. As he sifted through the "reject" pile, Eckerle pulled out one application with an education block that lists a degree the applicant didn't have. "When we checked," he said, "they told us he was close to finishing a master's degree, but he hadn't yet finished his thesis. The applicant said he had the degree in hand." Another listed work experience no one could verify. "This guy's résumé says he was a client service representative for Litiplex, Inc., of Boston, but the phone book doesn't list any firm by that name, no one in our business has ever heard of it, and we can't check out his claims. I asked the applicant about the company, and he says, 'Maybe they went out of business.'"

Résumés weren't Eckerle's only problem. Recommendations were almost as bad. "Letters of recommendation aren't particularly useful," he said. "In the first place, almost no one is dumb enough to ask for a recommendation from someone who'll give them a bad one. Second, most recommenders write in broad, general, vague terms that don't tell me much about an applicant's work history, aptitude, or potential. They use glowing, nonspecific words that tell me the applicant's a marvelous human being but don't say whether the guy's had any comparable work experience that I could use to help make a decision."

Eckerle mentioned one other recommendation problem. "Most of the people who write letters in support of a job applicant are fairly close friends of the applicant. They'll often say things that are laudatory, but just aren't true. By the time you're done reading the letter, you'd think the young man in question could walk on water. When he comes for an interview, he can't get his own name straight." Excessive praise in letters of recommendation, Eckerle noted, can be expensive for a firm when the recommendation just doesn't reflect the applicant's true potential. "It costs us nearly $1,000 to bring in an entry-level management candidate for interviews," he said, "and it's my job to make sure we don't bring in someone who's just not competitive." Inflated recommendations, he thought, can make that job much more difficult.

Next, the class should be divided into ten groups. Each group will be assigned one ethical issue. The group should formulate an answer to the dilemma and be ready to present the group's solution to the class.

1. Is a job applicant obligated to list *all employment* or *every work experience* on a résumé? What about jobs in which an applicant has had a bad relationship with a supervisor? Is it fair to "load up" a résumé only with positive work experience?

2. What if an applicant has been fired? Is a résumé *required* to reveal the exact circumstances under which he or she left the job?

3. Is it ethical to list educational institutions or degree programs that an applicant has attended but not completed? How much detail is necessary? Should an applicant explain *why* he or she left a degree program or school without finishing?

4. Is a job applicant *obliged* to list offenses against the law on a résumé? What about convictions or incarceration—say, ninety days' jail time for DWI?

5. Under such résumé categories as "Foreign Languages," how does an applicant determine whether he or she is "fluent," "conversant," or merely "familiar with" a language? Do the same general rules apply to listing technical skills, such as computer languages and software applications?

6. In a letter of recommendation, is it ethical to lavish praise on a young man or woman just because you know the person is in need of a job? Conversely, does faint praise mean that a job applicant will likely be refused?

7. Is it better to turn away a student for asking for a letter of recommendation, or should you do what's *honest* and tell a graduate school (or potential employer) exactly what you think of the person?

8. Is a résumé something like a *certificate of authenticity*, listing specifics and details with absolute adherence to honesty and accuracy? Or is it more like a *sales brochure*, offering the best possible picture of a person in search of employment?

9. How well do you have to know someone before you can write an authentic, honest letter of recommendation? Is there a minimum time requirement before you can do so in good conscience?

10. Is the author of a letter of recommendation required to reveal *everything relevant* that he or she knows about an applicant? What about character or integrity flaws that may stand in the way of a job applicant's success? To whom is the author of such letters obligated—the potential employer or the applicant?

SOURCE: J. S. O'Rourke, "The Ethics of Résumés and Recommendations: When Do Filler and Fluff Become Deceptions and Lies?" *Business Communication Quarterly* 58 (1995): 54–56. Reprinted with permission by the author.

Biz Flix | Baby Mama

Meet Kate Holbrook (Tina Fey), single, late thirties, successful in her career, but childless. She loves children and wants a child but does not want to take chances with a pregnancy at her age. Kate enlists the help of Angie Ostrowiski (Amy Poehler) from South Philadelphia to act as her surrogate mother. Former attorney, now Super Fruity Fruit Smoothies owner, Rob Ackerman (Greg Kinnear) enters the scene and begins dating Kate. Angie becomes pregnant but it is not clear whether the child is Kate's or Angie's. The complex, intertwined relationships and social interactions create an enjoyable comedy experience.

Emotional Intelligence: Some Observations

These sequences appear at two different places in the film. A title screen appears between the two scenes.

The first scene appears at the end of DVD Chapter 12, "Deal Breaker." It follows the scene of Kate talking to Rob in his shop. Angie walks along the sidewalk and says "Hi, Carl." Carl Loomis (Dax Shepherd) leans against his car while pretending to read a newspaper (it is inverted and in an Asian language). This scene ends as Carl speeds away. Angie shrugs her shoulders and sighs.

The second scene appears within DVD Chapter 16, "Party's Over." It begins with a night shot of Kate's car parked in front of a Marriott Hotel. The scene follows Kate's discussion with Chaffee Bicknell (Sigourney Weaver) about Angie possibly not carrying Kate's baby. Kate says to Angie, "I booked you a room here, until we sort this out." This scene ends after Angie leaves the car. Kate sighs and lays her head on the steering wheel.

What to Watch for and Ask Yourself

- Assess the emotional intelligence of each of the three characters shown in these scenes. What level of emotional intelligence does Carl exhibit? Assess him on self-awareness, empathy, and self-control.

- What level of emotional intelligence does Angie show? Assess her on self-awareness, empathy, and self-control.

- What level of emotional intelligence does Kate exhibit? Assess her on self-awareness, empathy, and self-control.

Workplace Video | Numi Organic Tea: Danielle Oviedo

When Danielle Oviedo showed up for her first day as the manager of the Distribution Center at Numi Organic Tea in Oakland, California, her new direct reports were not happy about the change. They loved Oviedo's predecessor, who was more like a friend than a boss to them. But Numi's director of operations, Brian Durkee, was looking for someone with specific skills and experience when he hired Danielle, and popularity wasn't on the list. Durkee hired Danielle because of her effectiveness and success as a manager in previous positions. She also had experience leading much big teams in similar departments.

Prior to Danielle's arrival, lead times for Numi's customer orders were not competitive. Although Numi's loyal food service customers were happy with Numi products, some customers were considering taking their business elsewhere because deliveries were unpredictable. Upon her arrival at Numi, Danielle identified the problem: employees were performing tasks in isolation with little attention to anything else.

To solve the issue, Danielle trained the Distribution Center employees in every critical task and process, explaining how all the pieces fit together. Going forward, her staff would perform multiple tasks depending on what pressing deadlines loomed. Importantly, Danielle helped her team understand their jobs on a conceptual level so they could see how their work linked directly to Numi's larger goals. With newfound effectiveness aided by Danielle's planning and organizing, the team cut lead times for international orders by about 75 percent.

Numi's customer service manager, Cindy Graffort, is thrilled about Danielle's achievements and said none of these changes were possible before Danielle arrived. According to Cindy, the dramatic changes were a direct result of Danielle's ability to come up with innovative solutions to problems plaguing the Distribution Center.

When asked for specific insight into Danielle's managerial success, Cindy highlighted her impressive human skills. Unlike old-school managers who hide in their offices and manage employees from afar, Danielle is out on the floor working with teammates, ensuring they understand the process, and being supportive.

Discussion Questions

1. At what stage of the Career Stage Model is manager Danielle Oviedo? Explain.

2. Has working numerous jobs with different companies made Oviedo more or less valuable in the eyes of Numi's senior management?

3. Do you think Danielle Oviedo will attain senior leadership at Numi or elsewhere? Why or why not?

Case

Maxine Clark: Building Mentoring Capability from Build-A-Bear Workshop

"Build-A-Bear Workshop, Inc. is the only global company that offers an interactive 'make your own stuffed animal' retail-entertainment experience."[1] As of early 2009, Build-A-Bear operates more than 400 stores worldwide. Company-owned stores are located in the United States, Puerto Rico, Canada, Ireland, the United Kingdom, and France. Franchise stores are found in Africa, Asia, Australia, and Europe.[2]

Although Build-A-Bear Workshop was "the brainchild" of Maxine Clark, she credits the company's successful business plan to her godchild Katie. Caught up in the Beanie Baby craze of the mid-1990s, Clark and her godchild talked about "how it would be 'cool' to build your own Beanie Babies"—and a business plan for what would become Build-A-Bear Workshops began emerging.[3]

"Since the retailer opened its first store in a St. Louis mall in 1997, skeptics have warned that the concept wouldn't last."[4] However, the company "keeps defying critics with strong gains as it broadens its geography, customer types and menagerie."[5] Build-A-Bear's core customer demographic is the group known as "female tweens"—but the Build-A-Bear product line appeals to a wide range of customers.[6] Locating stores at zoos and ballparks, which is part of the company's ongoing expansion plan, is intended to enhance the product line's appeal for boys, who, in mid-2006, represented only about a quarter of the company's customers.[7] Building on the Build-A-Bear success, the company also has launched two additional make-your-own business lines: friends2Bmade for customers to make dolls, and Build-A-Dino, located in T-Rex cafe restaurants, where customers create their own dinosaurs.[8]

So, who is Maxine Clark, the woman behind the Build-A-Bear Workshop success story? Dubbed "the Oprah Winfrey of the retail industry—compassionate, creative and charismatic," Maxine Clark "is a feisty, seasoned ex-May Department Stores veteran who doesn't let one detail get by her."[9] As the founder and CEO of Build-A-Bear Workshop, Maxine Clark "charmed consumers and wowed Wall Street with a concept that set a new template for interactive experiential retailing. She also defied the odds, growing her business, which celebrated its 10th anniversary in October [2007] . . . while other, bigger-brand toy stores languished or faded from the scene."[10] Clark's

success has captured the intense interest of others. "In fact, it's been the inspiration for numerous imitators; Clark herself is a majority investor and key driver behind the launch of Ridemakerz, a toy-car customizing experience."[11]

Clark's remarkable success has put her in a position to mentor others, particularly other women. She has taken on this role with gusto!

According to a report in *Chain Store Age*, many retail executives give little thought to mentoring before they assume management positions. Maxine Clark, however, "has always been very aware that how she conducts herself can positively or negatively affect the development of those around her."[12] Clark says, "I'm an older sister, so my parents were always telling me to set an example . . . I was even a volunteer in the Big Sister program in high school."[13]

Clark believes that women tend to seek her out as a mentor because there aren't a lot of women in management positions. One issue on which women commonly seek advice from her concerns whether they can be as successful as Clark is and still have children of their own. Clark says, "[t]hat's a tough question to answer for someone else. I couldn't do both, and that's why I don't have children."[14]

"Clark's real test as a retail mentor came in 1997 when she began mentoring students enrolled in a program on entrepreneurship at the Olin School of Business at St. Louis' Washington University. The program, called The Hatchery, provides seed capital to students with good business plans and a lot of energy. Andrew Rubin, a student assigned to Clark, had both. . . . He had a lot of energy and a vision. And I could see more potential in him than he could because I had been there," says Clark. Under Clark's guidance, Rubin developed the winning business plan in The Hatchery competition.[15]

"I can't ever have imagined starting a business at 22, but here this guy did it," says Clark. Reflecting on her mentoring relationship with Andrew Rubin, Clark reveals, "I tell him all the time that I don't care if he ever pays me back. I enjoyed this. I'd just like to see him do the same for someone else sometime."[16]

In considering her own experience with being mentored, Clark mentions Dave Farrell, a person for whom she worked at May Department Stores. She asserts that Farrell "had the greatest influence on her career." Clark says the mentoring relationship between her and Farrell was informal rather than formal. She continues, "while I think of him as a mentor, there never was any sort of formalized mentoring relationship between us. We never talked about it that way. He was my boss. I think mentoring is sort of an unwritten part of the job description when you move up the management ranks. And I think that's probably the way Dave saw it."[17]

What lessons can Maxine Clark's experiences and successes provide for others who seek to be effective mentors?

Discussion Questions

1. How can Maxine Clark's business experiences help her to be an effective mentor?

2. In which career stage would you place Maxine Clark? Why?

3. How does Maxine Clark's career stage relate to her mentoring activities?

4. Do you think a formal mentoring program is superior to an informal mentoring program, or vice versa? Explain the reasoning behind your answer.

5. Suppose that you are seeking out a mentor? What attributes would you look for in a mentoring relationship? Why would you seek these attributes?

SOURCE: This case was written by Michael K. McCuddy, The Louis S. and Mary L. Morgal Chair of Christian Business Ethics and Professor of Management, College of Business Administration, Valparaiso University.

18

Managing Change

LEARNING OBJECTIVES

After reading this chapter, you should be able to do the following:

1 Examine the major external and internal forces for change in organizations.

2 Understand *incremental change, strategic change, transformational change*, and *change agent*.

3 Evaluate the reasons for resistance to change, and discuss methods organizations can use to manage resistance.

4 Apply force field analysis to a problem.

5 Explain Lewin's organizational change model.

6 Describe the use of organizational diagnosis and needs analysis as a first step in organizational development.

7 Discuss the major organization development interventions.

8 Identify the ethical issues that must be considered in organization development efforts.

parker/Alamy

An IKEA warehouse collection area in the United Kingdom.

THINKING AHEAD: IKEA

Catalyst for Change

Norbert Michalke/ Photolibrary

IKEA was founded in 1943 by Ingvar Kamprad with a cost leadership focus. IKEA designs and sells furniture in "flat packs" that require customer assembly. The idea for flat packs was cost related in that it takes one truck to deliver flat what six trucks could deliver fully furnished.[1] However, a couple of wake-up calls changed IKEA's focus from low costs to "Low prices but not at any price."

In the early 1980s, formaldehyde emissions were found to cause health issues such as watery eyes, headaches, and a burning sensation in the throat, so regulatory bodies in Denmark and Germany began to regulate these emissions. Formaldehyde is used as binding glue in plywood and particle-board. Higher than acceptable concentrations were found in many IKEAs products. When this information was publicized, IKEA sales dropped 20 percent in Denmark. The company reacted by setting strict guidelines, but this was not enough. In the early 1990s, a best-selling IKEA book case was again found to have higher than acceptable levels of formaldehyde. Once again, sales dropped.[2]

Because of the large financial impact and IKEA's desire to be socially responsible, IKEA CEO Anders Dalhvig knew changes had to be made. He began by asking a series of questions: "Is environmental and social work good for business? What right do we have to put demands on our suppliers? How fast should a company like IKEA move on sustainability?" Struggling with these questions led to IKEA becoming a company that is well known for its commitment to the environment.[3] What changes did IKEA make? See the Looking Back feature for the journey.

FORCES FOR CHANGE IN ORGANIZATIONS

Change has become the norm in most organizations. Plant closings, business failures, mergers and acquisitions, and downsizing are experiences common to American companies. *Adaptiveness, flexibility,* and *responsiveness* are characteristics of the organizations that will succeed in meeting the competitive challenges that businesses face.[4] In the past, organizations could succeed by claiming excellence in one area—quality, reliability, or cost, for example—but this is not the case today. The current environment demands excellence in all areas and vigilant leaders. A recent survey of CEOs who were facing crises found that 50 percent said they believed the problems arrived "suddenly" and that they had not prepared adequately for them. More than 10 percent said they were, in fact, the last to know about the problems.[5]

As we saw in Chapter 1, change is what's on managers' minds. The pursuit of organizational effectiveness through downsizing, restructuring, reengineering, productivity management, cycle-time reduction, and other efforts is paramount. Organizations are in a state of tremendous turmoil and transition, and all members are affected. Continued downsizings may have left firms leaner but not necessarily richer. Although downsizing can increase shareholder value by better aligning costs with revenues, firms may suffer from public criticism for their actions. Laying off employees may be accompanied by increases in CEO pay and stock options, linking the misery of employees with the financial success of owners and management.[6]

Organizations must also deal with ethical, environmental, and other social issues. Competition is fierce, and companies can no longer afford to rest on their laurels. American Airlines has developed a series of programs to constantly reevaluate and change its operating methods to prevent the company from stagnating. General Electric (GE) holds off-site WorkOut sessions with groups of managers and employees whose goal is to make GE a faster, less complex organization that can respond effectively to change. In the WorkOut sessions, employees recommend specific changes, explain why they are needed, and propose ways the changes can be implemented. Top management must make an immediate response: an approval, a disapproval (with an explanation), or a request for more information. The GE WorkOut sessions eliminate the barriers that keep employees from contributing to change.

There are two basic forms of change in organizations. *Planned change* is change resulting from a deliberate decision to alter the organization. Companies that wish to move from a traditional hierarchical structure to one that facilitates self-managed teams must use a proactive, carefully orchestrated approach. Not all change is planned, however. *Unplanned change* is imposed on the organization and is often unforeseen. Changes in government regulations and in the economy, for example, are often unplanned. Responsiveness to unplanned change requires tremendous flexibility and adaptability on the part of organizations. Managers must be prepared to handle both planned and unplanned forms of change in organizations.

planned change
Change resulting from a deliberate decision to alter the organization.

unplanned change
Change that is imposed on the organization and is often unforeseen.

Forces for change can come from many sources. Some of these are external, arising from outside the company, whereas others are internal, arising from sources within the organization.

External Forces

The four major managerial challenges we have described throughout the book—globalization, workforce diversity, technological change, and managing ethical behavior—are significant external forces that precipitate change in organizations.

1 Examine the major external and internal forces for change in organizations.

Globalization The power players in the global market are the multinational and transnational organizations. NAFTA's impact has been felt across numerous industries. American agriculture has been a tremendous beneficiary, with annual U.S. exports of fruits and vegetables to Mexico climbing by more than $1 billion since 1993. This expanded market has been a tremendous windfall for U.S. producers, but trouble may be looming. Mexican farm leaders have accused the United States of unfairly dumping fruits and vegetables into the Mexican market.[7] They also claim that small Mexican farms cannot compete with large industrialized U.S. operations, and they have asked the Mexican government to renegotiate NAFTA to give them greater protection.[8] Because global business implicitly involves multiple governments and legal systems, it carries unique risks not found by firms competing within a single nation.

The United States is but one nation in the drive to open new markets. Japan and Germany are responding to global competition in powerful ways, and the emergence of the European Union as a powerful trading group will have a profound impact on world markets. By joining with their European neighbors, companies in smaller countries will begin to make major progress in world markets, thus increasing the fierce competition that already exists.

Coca-Cola faced a crisis when it introduced its Dasani bottled water in Great Britain. Coke had chosen a particularly compelling theme for its advertising, touting Dasani as more pure than other bottled waters. After Coke had invested more than £7 million in this project, government regulators found that the water contained illegally high levels of bromate, a potentially cancer-causing chemical. To make matters worse, Coke was forced to admit that the contamination was introduced by its own production process. Coke's response was swift: it quickly pulled half a million bottles of Dasani from London shelves and postponed plans for product launches in France and Germany. Some British writers rank Coke's introduction of Dasani among the worst marketing disasters in Britain's history.[9]

All of these changes, along with others, have led companies to rethink the borders of their markets and to encourage their employees to think globally. Jack Welch, former CEO of GE, was among the first to call for a boundaryless company, in which there are no mental distinctions between domestic and foreign operations or between managers and employees.[10] GE has locations in 160 countries across the globe and has become a truly multinational corporation. The thought that drives the boundaryless company is that barriers that get in the way of people's working together should be removed. Globalizing an organization means rethinking the most efficient ways to use resources, disseminate and gather information, and develop people. It requires not only structural changes but also changes in the minds of employees. India's Tata conglomerate, for example, has gone through an impressive list of mergers and acquisitions over the last several years. The healthy economy in India in the early- to mid-2000s resulted in the acquisition of over forty companies, including Tetley Tea, Jaguar, and Land Rover.[11]

Workforce Diversity Related to globalization is the challenge of workforce diversity. As we have seen throughout this book, workforce diversity is a powerful force for change in organizations. Let us recap the demographic trends contributing to workforce diversity that we discussed at length in Chapter 2. First, the workforce will see increased participation from women, because the majority of new workers will be women.[12] In fact, in the most recent recession in 2008 and 2009, men were the hardest hit in terms of lay-offs increasing the percentage of female workers in the labor force.[13]

Second, the workforce will be more culturally diverse than ever. Part of this is attributable to globalization, but in addition, U.S. demographics are changing. The participation of African Americans and Hispanic Americans is increasing in record numbers. Third, the workforce is aging. There will be fewer young workers and more middle-aged Americans working.[14]

Following a high-profile bribery scandal during which top executives resigned, Siemans, a 160-year-old technology and equipment firm, decided it was time to expand beyond a group of German male executives and better represent the diversity of their over 2 million customers. As a result, they hired a Chief Diversity Officer who has launched several programs focusing on mentoring and increasing diversity in their management ranks.[15]

Technological Change Rapid technological innovation is another force for change in organizations, and those who fail to keep pace can quickly fall behind. *Smart tags*, for example, are replacing bar codes for tracking and scanning products. Bar codes are passive identification markers whose stripes are unchangeable, and items must be lined up individually for scanning (like in a grocery store checkout line). Manufacturers are starting to use radio-frequency identification (RFID) tags that are as small as two matches laid side by side, and hold digital memory chips the size of a pinhead. RFIDs are also used in show dogs and cats. The tags are injected under a pet's skin with a syringe.

RFIDs contain a lot more information than bar codes, and users can alter that information. As many as fifty tags per second can be read—forty times faster than bar-code scanners. Ford uses RFIDs to track parts. Data such as a unique ID, part type, plant location, and time/date stamps are included on the tag. Because RFIDs are reusable, the long-term costs are about the same as bar codes.[16] American Express Business Travel Program has gained widespread popularity in the corporate world, but American Express has not lost sight of the fact that competing through technology also should be coupled with excellent customer service. It invests in employee engagement, skill training, and leadership development programs. Furthermore, it emphasizes quality of customer care through what it calls the Great Call Experience. Employees are trained on a standard set of protocols to enhance customer satisfaction.[17]

Technological innovations bring about profound change because they are not just changes in the way work is performed. Instead, the innovation process promotes associated changes in work relationships and organizational structures.[18] The team approach adopted by many organizations leads to flatter structures, decentralized decision making, and more open communication between leaders and team members.

One organization that has evolved through several changes is Amazon. In Real World 18.1, you can read about how Kindle (the e-reader) has changed Amazon, and also may change an entire industry.

Managing Ethical Behavior Recent ethical scandals have brought ethical behavior in organizations to the forefront of public consciousness. Ethical issues, however, are not always public and monumental. Employees face ethical dilemmas in their daily work lives. The need to manage ethical behavior has brought about several changes

The Real World 18.1

Will Amazon's Kindle Revolutionize the Publishing Industry?

The plain-looking, pricey gadget has been referred to as the iPod of reading, and has been showing up especially among business travelers. Will the Amazon Kindle DX do the same thing to publishing that the iPod and iTunes did to the music business? Jeff Bezos, CEO of Amazon, the world's largest bookstore, thinks so, and he thinks that Kindle creates a new platform for news and advertising. Newspapers are in trouble, and rather than offering them free online, consumers can subscribe and read them via the Kindle.

Amazon founder and CEO Jeff Bezos holds the new Kindle DX electronic reader.

ERIC THAYER/Reuters/Landov

And, if he is right, Amazon could phase out book publishers entirely, because they would become unnecessary with Kindle technology. Amazon could bypass the publishers by making deals with best-selling authors to write e-books. Much the same way Apple did with music using iTunes, Amazon hopes to create a price that sticks in consumers' minds ($9.99 per book). In fact, Amazon users have boycotted Kindle books that retail for more than that price.

Amazon's challenges for publishing domination are many. Will a stand-alone product like the Kindle work, when consumers are attracted to devices like smart phones that do everything? The Kindle is simply an e-reader and a fairly primitive piece of technology. Is Apple planning a move into e-books? If so, a touch-screen color media tablet with multiple functions could make Kindle's grayscale display much less appealing.

Prognosticators argue that as readers adopt the e-book format, the very notion of what constitutes a book may change. It could evolve from simply words on a page to a multimedia blend of text, video, and audio. Magazines and newspapers could take the same form. If so, the current version of the Kindle could not take advantage of the new dynamic book format. In terms of change, the Kindle has not only changed Amazon, but is poised to change publishing, and the way we all read.

SOURCES: A. L. Penenberg, "The Evolution of Amazon," *Fast Company* (July/August 2009): 66–72; J. M. O'Brien, "Amazon's Next Revolution," *Fortune* (June 8, 2009): 68–76.

---

in organizations. Most center around the idea that an organization must create a culture that encourages ethical behavior.

All public companies issue annual financial reports. Gap Inc. has gone a step further by issuing an annual ethical report. The clothing industry is almost synonymous with the use of sweatshops—low-paying overseas factories in which third-world workers (including children) labor for fifty to sixty hours each week for a few dollars in pay. Gap is hardly alone in facing these issues. What sets the company apart is its candor, beginning with its open admission that none of its 3,000 suppliers fully complies with the firm's ethical code of conduct. But rather than run from these problems, Gap has chosen to work with its suppliers to improve conditions overseas. The firm has more than ninety full-time employees charged with monitoring supplier operations around the world.[19]

The annual report includes extensive descriptions of these workers' activities, including which factories were monitored, what violations were found, and which factories are no longer used by Gap because of violations. It also addresses media reports critical of Gap and its operations.

Gap tries to improve worker conditions by providing training and encouraging suppliers to develop their own conduct codes. For example, in China it has encouraged lunchtime sessions in which workers are advised of their rights. While most facilities respond positively to these efforts, some don't, and Gap pulled its business from 136 factories it concluded were not going to improve. It also terminated contracts with two factories that had verifiable use of child labor. Gap's approach to overseas labor offers a model for other garment firms.[20]

Society expects organizations to maintain ethical behavior both internally and in relationships with other organizations. Ethical behavior is expected in relationships with customers, the environment, and society. These expectations may be informal, or they may come in the form of increased legal requirements. These four challenges are forces that place pressures to change on organizations. There are other forces as well. Legal developments, changing stakeholder expectations, and shifting consumer demands can also lead to change.[21] And some companies change simply because others are changing.[22] Other powerful forces for change originate from within the organization.

Internal Forces

Pressures for change that originate inside the organization are generally recognizable in the form of signals indicating that something needs to be altered. A declining effectiveness is a pressure to change. A company that experiences its third quarterly loss within a fiscal year is undoubtedly motivated to do something about it. Some companies react by instituting layoffs and massive cost-cutting programs, whereas others look at the bigger picture, view the loss as symptomatic of an underlying problem, and seek the cause of the problem.

A crisis may also stimulate change in an organization. Strikes or walkouts may lead management to change the wage structure. The resignation of a key decision maker may cause the company to rethink the composition of its management team and its role in the organization. An economic crisis such as a recession may also bring about change in many organizations. Vineet Nayer, CEO of HCL Technologies, a leading IT and software development company, argues that the relentless, powerful CEO primarily in search of shareholder value must change to become a more responsible CEO pursuing sustainability while embedding corporate responsibility into the core business strategy.[23]

Changes in employee expectations can also trigger change in organizations. A company that hires a group of young newcomers may find that their expectations are very different from those expressed by older workers. The workforce is more educated than ever before. Although this has its advantages, workers with more education demand more of employers. Today's workers are also concerned with career and family balance issues, such as dependent care. The many sources of workforce diversity hold potential for a host of differing expectations among employees.

Changes in the work climate at an organization can also stimulate change. A workforce that seems lethargic, unmotivated, and dissatisfied must be addressed. These symptoms are common in organizations that have experienced layoffs. Workers who have escaped a layoff may grieve for those who have lost their jobs and may find it hard to continue to be productive. They may fear they will be laid off as well.

CHANGE IS INEVITABLE

We have seen that organizations face substantial pressures to change from both external and internal sources. Change in organizations is inevitable, but change is a process that can be managed. The scope of change can vary from small to quantum.

The Scope of Change

Change can be of a relatively small scope, such as a modification in a work procedure (an *incremental change*). Such changes, in essence, are a fine-tuning of the organization, or the making of small improvements. Intel and other chip producers must continually upgrade their manufacturing equipment just to stay competitive. Intel's new Arizona chip-making plant opened in 2007 and cost $3 billion; it is so large that more than 17 football fields can fit inside it.[24] While radical change is more exciting and interesting to discuss, most research on change has focused on evolutionary (incremental) rather than revolutionary change.[25] Change can also be of a larger scale, such as the restructuring of an organization (a *strategic change*).[26] In strategic change, the organization moves from an old state to a known new state during a controlled period of time. Strategic change usually involves a series of transition steps. AT&T, the granddaddy of long-distance companies, made a strategic decision in 2004 to get out of the residential long-distance market entirely. When eBay purchased Skype, whose software allows people to make phone calls via the Internet, it departed from its core business, but it opened up huge potential in e-commerce. Only time will tell whether the strategic change paid off.[27]

The most massive scope of change is *transformational change*, in which the organization moves to a radically different, and sometimes unknown, future state.[28] In transformational change, the organization's mission, culture, goals, structure, and leadership may all change dramatically.[29] Just over a century ago, two successful bicycle makers decided to leave the safety of the bike business to devote their time to building and selling an amazing new invention—the airplane. This invention would transform travel, warfare, communications, and indeed the entire world. Of all the tasks a leader undertakes, many say that changing the form and nature of the organization itself may be the most difficult, an observation supported by research.[30]

One of the toughest decisions faced by leaders is the proper "pace" of change. Some scholars argue that rapid change is more likely to succeed, since it creates momentum,[31] while others argue that these short, sharp changes are actually rare and not experienced by most firms.[32] Still others observe that change in a large organization may occur incrementally in parts of the firm and quickly in others.[33] In summary, researchers agree that the pace of change is important, but they can't quite agree on which pace of change is most beneficial.

Very little long-term research has looked at change over a significant time period. One twelve-year study examined change in the structure of Canadian National Sports Organizations (NSOs). It found that within NSOs, radical transition did not always require a fast pace of change. It also found that successful transitions often involve changing the high-impact elements of an organization (in this case, their decision-making structures) early in the process.[34]

The Change Agent's Role

The individual or group that undertakes the task of introducing and managing a change in an organization is known as a *change agent*. Change agents can be internal, such as managers or employees who are appointed to oversee the change process. In her book *The Change Masters*, Rosabeth Moss Kanter notes that at companies like Hewlett-Packard and Polaroid, managers and employees alike are developing the needed skills to produce change and innovation in the organization.[35] Change agents can also be external, such as outside consultants.

Internal change agents have certain advantages in managing the change process. They know the organization's past history, its political system, and its culture. Because they must live with the results of their change efforts, internal change agents are likely

2 Understand *incremental change, strategic change, transformational change,* and *change agent.*

incremental change
Change of a relatively small scope, such as making small improvements.

strategic change
Change of a larger scale, such as organizational restructuring.

transformational change
Change in which the organization moves to a radically different, and sometimes unknown, future state.

change agent
The individual or group that undertakes the task of introducing and managing a change in an organization.

to be very careful about managing change. There are disadvantages, however, to using internal change agents. They may be associated with certain factions within the organization and may easily be accused of favoritism. Furthermore, internal change agents may be too close to the situation to have an objective view of what needs to be done.

Change leaders within organizations tend to be young, in the twenty-five to forty age range. They are more flexible than ordinary general managers and much more people oriented. A high number of change leaders are women. The change leaders have a balance of technical and interpersonal skills. They are tough decision makers who focus on performance results. They also know how to energize people and get them aligned in the same direction. They get more out of people than ordinary managers can. In addition, they have the ability to operate in more than one leadership style and can shift from a team mode to command and control, depending on the situation. They are also comfortable with uncertainty.[36]

If change is large scale or strategic in nature, it may take a team of leaders to make change happen. A team assembling leaders with a variety of skills, expertise, and influence who can work together harmoniously may be needed to accomplish change of large scope.[37]

External change agents bring an outsider's objective view to the organization. They may be preferred by employees because of their impartiality. External change agents face certain problems, however; not only is their knowledge of the organization's history limited, but they may also be viewed with suspicion by organization members. External change agents have more power in directing changes if employees perceive the change agents as being trustworthy, possessing important expertise, having a track record that establishes credibility, and being similar to them.[38]

Different change agent competencies are required at different stages of the change process. Leadership, communication, training, and participation have varying levels of impact as the change proceeds, meaning change agents must be flexible in how they work through the different phases of the process.[39] Effective change leaders build strong relationships within their leadership team, between the team and organizational members, and between the team and key environmental players. Strong relationships between leaders and followers lead to less resistance to change.[40] Maintaining all three relationships simultaneously is quite difficult, so successful leaders are continually "coupling" and "uncoupling" with the different groups as the change process proceeds. Adaptability is a key skill for both internal and external change leaders.[41]

THE PROCESS OF CHANGE IN ORGANIZATIONS

Organizations tend to respond to change by continuing to do what they are good at. After all, these strategies have been successful in the past. After periods of success, organizations can lose the ability to recognize when it is necessary to give up past strategies and try something new. This is not the case at Under Armour, best known for their moisture-wicking compression T-shirts. Read about how Under Armour is trying something new in Real World 18.2.

Once an organization has made the decision to change, careful planning and analysis must take place. Change processes such as business process reengineering cannot ensure the success of the change. The people aspects of change are the most critically important for successful transformations.[42] Even Michael Hammer, who launched the reengineering movement, admits that he forgot about the "human aspects" of change. "I was reflecting on my engineering background and was insufficiently appreciative of the human dimension. I've learned that it's critical."[43] If people are not taken into account, a change process will be negatively affected or may even fail. Like organizations, people tend to cling to what has worked in the past, especially if they have been successful and they see no need for change.[44] One

The Real World 18.2

Under Armour Steps into the Shoe Market

Under Armour's head-quarters in Baltimore has walls covered with photos of professional athletes and a treadmill in the hall. Most of its employees are jocks; in fact, CEO Kevin Plank is a former University of Maryland football player. Competitive athletes have always been customers for Under Armour, but they have moved into the casual athlete market with apparel—and now they want to become a mainstream brand. One step in their strategy to appeal to women and older consumers is by entering the highly competitive athletic shoe market.

The treadmill in the hall is hooked to a digital camera that uses software to record biometric data about how feet and legs move in motion. 3-D technology is used to create images that are used to design shoes without

Product display at a launch event for Under Armour's running shoes.

AP Photo/Rick Maiman

spending the time and money involved in creating a physical sample of the shoe. At Under Armour, young designers are sought after because they're more likely to excel at thinking and designing in 3-D. The technologies are not exclusive to Under Armour; competitors like Nike, Asics, and Saucony take advantage of these technologies and the competition has never been tougher.

The good news is that the athletic footwear market is so large ($5 billion annually in the United States on running shoes alone) that even a small portion of the market would add significantly to Under Armour's financial status. And, of course, the company is hoping that the change pays off.

SOURCE: S. N. Mehta, "Under Armour Reboots," *Fortune* (February 2, 2009): 29–33.

---

major aspect that change agents need to consider is the altered psychological contracts that employees perceive with their employers after a merger or acquisition. Change agents can typically help people adjust to these corporate culture changes by working with them to enhance their coping abilities.[45]

The challenge of managing the change process involves harnessing the energy of diverse individuals who hold a variety of views of change. It is important to recognize that most changes will be met with varying degrees of resistance and to understand the basis of resistance to change.

Resistance to Change

People often resist change in a rational response based on self-interest. However, there are countless other reasons people resist change. Many of these center around the notion of reactance—that is, a negative reaction that occurs when individuals feel that their personal freedom is threatened.[46] Some of the major reasons for resisting change follow.

3 Evaluate the reasons for resistance to change, and discuss methods organizations can use to manage resistance.

Fear of the Unknown Change often brings with it substantial uncertainty. Employees facing a technological change, such as the introduction of a new computer system, may resist the change simply because it introduces ambiguity into what was once a comfortable situation for them. This is especially a problem when there has been little communication about the change.

Fear of Loss When a change is impending, some employees may fear losing their jobs; this fear is particularly acute when an advanced technology like robotics is introduced.

Employees may also fear losing their status because of a change.[47] Computer systems experts, for example, may feel threatened when they believe their expertise is eroded by the installation of a more user-friendly networked information system. Another common fear is that changes may diminish the positive qualities the individual enjoys in the job. Computerizing the customer service positions at Southwestern Bell (now part of AT&T), for example, threatened the autonomy that representatives previously enjoyed.

Fear of Failure Some employees fear changes because they fear their own failure. Employees may fear that changes will result in increased workloads or increased task difficulty, and they may question their own competencies for handling these. They may also fear that performance expectations will be elevated following the change, and that they may not measure up.[48] Resistance can also stem from a fear that the change itself will not really take place. In one large library that was undergoing a major automation effort, employees were doubtful that the vendor could really deliver the state-of-the-art system that was promised. In this case, the implementation never became a reality—the employees' fears were well founded.[49]

Disruption of Interpersonal Relationships Employees may resist change that threatens to limit meaningful interpersonal relationships on the job. Librarians facing the automation effort described previously feared that once the computerized system was implemented, they would not be able to interact as they did when they had to go to another floor of the library to get help finding a resource. In the new system, with the touch of a few buttons on the computer, they would get their information without consulting another librarian.

Personality Individuals with an internal locus of control, high growth needs, and strong motivation are more likely to embrace changes at work.[50] Positively oriented people (those with hope, optimism, self-efficacy, and resiliency) are also more positive about organizational change.[51] Personality conflicts can impact acceptance of change. When the change agent's personality engenders negative reactions, employees may resist the change. A change agent who appears insensitive to employee concerns and feelings may meet considerable resistance, because employees perceive that their needs are not being taken into account.

Politics Organizational change may also shift the existing balance of power in the organization. Individuals or groups who hold power under the current arrangement may be threatened with losing these political advantages in the advent of change.

Cultural Assumptions and Values Sometimes cultural assumptions and values can be impediments to change, particularly if the assumptions underlying the change are alien to employees. Other times, employees might interpret strategic change initiatives from the standpoint of the organization's value system and ideologies of the management team. In fact, research indicates that employees pay attention to the informal sense-making process prevalent in organizations, and hence top-down change initiatives often fail.[52] This form of resistance can be very difficult to overcome, because some cultural assumptions are unconscious. As we discussed in Chapter 2, some cultures tend to avoid uncertainty. In Mexican and Greek cultures, for example, change that creates a great deal of uncertainty may be met with great resistance.

Some individuals are more tolerant of ambiguity than others. You can assess your own attitude toward ambiguity in You 18.1.

We have described several sources of resistance to change. The reasons for resistance are as diverse as the workforce itself and vary with different individuals and organizations. The challenge for managers is introducing change in a positive manner and managing employee resistance.

Managing Resistance to Change

The traditional view of resistance to change treated it as something to be overcome, and many organizational attempts to reduce the resistance have only intensified it. The contemporary view holds that resistance is simply a form of feedback and that this feedback can be used very productively to manage the change process.[53] One key to managing resistance is to plan for it and to be ready with a variety of strategies for using the resistance as feedback and helping employees negotiate the transition. Three key strategies for managing resistance to change are communication, participation, and empathy and support.[54]

Communication about impending change is essential if employees are to adjust effectively.[55] The details of the change should be provided, but equally important is the rationale behind the change. Keeping employees informed about anticipated events and the possible consequences of change can reduce uncertainty and decrease resistance to change.[56] Employees want to know why change is needed. If there is no good reason for it, why should they favor the change? Providing accurate and timely information about the change can help prevent unfounded fears and potentially damaging rumors from developing. Delaying the announcement of a change and handling information in a secretive fashion can fuel the rumor mill. Open communication in a culture of trust is a key ingredient for successful change.[57] It is also beneficial to inform people about the potential consequences of the change. Managers should pay attention to the informal communication networks in an organization because they can serve as power channels of disseminating change-related information.[58] Educating employees on new work procedures is often helpful. In addition, mentors and mentees both derive benefits from going through the process of organizational change together. Mentees are assisted by mentors who help them make sense of the change, and mentors experience satisfaction in having helped the mentee through the change process.[59] Studies on the introduction of computers in the workplace indicate that providing employees with opportunities for hands-on practice helps alleviate fears about the new technology. Employees who have experience with computers display more positive attitudes and greater efficacy—a sense that they can master their new tasks.[60] Another key ingredient that can help employees adjust to change is a supervisor they can trust. When employees trust their supervisors, it serves as a social support mechanism, making them more committed to the organization even if they feel they can't control the change process.[61]

There is substantial research support underscoring the importance of participation in the change process. Employees must be engaged and involved in order for change to work—as evidenced by the notion "That which we create, we support." Participation helps employees become involved in the change and establish a feeling of ownership in the process. Designer retailer Prada, famous for its extravagant clothing, decided to create an equally remarkable retail location. The company opened perhaps the world's most sophisticated boutique in New York City, spending one-fourth of its IT budget on the experiment. Wireless networks linked each item in inventory to a single database, allowing staff to walk the floor armed with wireless PDAs to check inventory. Automated dressing rooms with touch screens offered additional information to customers. But within three years, most of the technology sat abandoned, some of it malfunctioning, some of it simply too difficult to use. Like many firms before it, Prada appears to have fallen in love with the idea of going high tech without bothering to get the actual users (its employees) onboard.[62] Prada fell

Designer retailer Prada, famous for its extravagant clothing, decided to create an equally remarkable retail location. Prada clothes and accessories are displayed in this shop window on Madison Avenue in New York City.

You 18.1

Tolerance for Ambiguity

Tolerance for Ambiguity Survey Form

Read each of the following statements carefully. Then rate each of them in terms of the extent to which you either agree or disagree with the statement using the following scale:

Completely Disagree			Neither Agree nor Disagree			Completely Agree
1	2	3	4	5	6	7

Place the number that best describes your degree of agreement or disagreement in the blank to the left of each statement.

_____ 1. An expert who doesn't come up with a definite answer probably doesn't know much.

_____ 2. I would like to live in a foreign country for a while.

_____ 3. The sooner we all acquire similar values and ideals, the better.

_____ 4. A good teacher is one who makes you wonder about your way of looking at things.

_____ 5. I like parties where I know most of the people more than ones where all or most of the people are complete strangers.

_____ 6. Teachers or supervisors who hand out vague assignments give a chance for one to show initiative and originality.

_____ 7. A person who leads an even, regular life in which few surprises or unexpected happenings arise really has a lot to be grateful for.

_____ 8. Many of our most important decisions are based upon insufficient information.

_____ 9. There is really no such thing as a problem that can't be solved.

_____ 10. People who fit their lives to a schedule probably miss most of the joy of living.

_____ 11. A good job is one where what is to be done and how it is to be done are always clear.

_____ 12. It is more fun to tackle a complicated problem than to solve a simple one.

_____ 13. In the long run, it is possible to get more done by tackling small, simple problems rather than large and complicated ones.

_____ 14. Often the most interesting and stimulating people are those who don't mind being different and original.

_____ 15. What we are used to is always preferable to what is unfamiliar.

Scoring: For even-numbered questions, add the total points.
For odd-numbered questions, use reverse scoring and add the total points.
Your score is the total of the even- and odd-numbered questions.

Norms Using the Tolerance for Ambiguity Scale

Basis: The survey asks fifteen questions about personal and work-oriented situations with ambiguity. You were asked to rate each situation on a scale from 1 (tolerant) to 7 (intolerant). (Alternating questions have the response scale reversed.) The index scores the items. A perfectly tolerant person would score 15 and a perfectly intolerant person 105. Scores between 20 and 80 are reported, with means of 45. The responses to the even-numbered questions with 7 minus the score are added to the response for the odd-numbered questions.

(Continued)

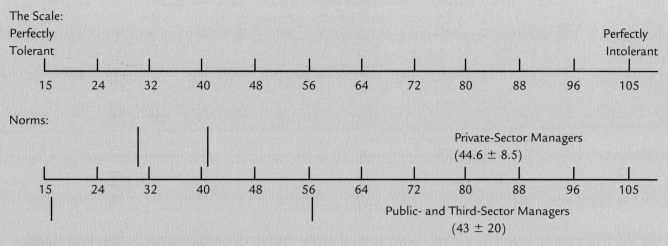

The Scale:

Perfectly Tolerant — Perfectly Intolerant

15　24　32　40　48　56　64　72　80　88　96　105

Norms:

15　24　32　40　48　56　64　72　80　88　96　105

Private-Sector Managers
(44.6 ± 8.5)

Public- and Third-Sector Managers
(43 ± 20)

SOURCE: "Tolerance for Ambiguity" from D. Marcic, *Organizational Behavior: Experiences and Cases* (St. Paul, MN: West Publishing, 1992), 339–340. Adapted from Paul Nutt. Used with permission.

victim to the utopian idea of going high tech without doing a due diligence reality check—convincing employees to buy into the idea.

Another strategy for managing resistance is providing empathy and support to employees who have trouble dealing with the change. Active listening is an excellent tool for identifying the reasons behind resistance and for uncovering fears. An expression of concerns about the change can provide important feedback that managers can use to improve the change process. Emotional support and encouragement can help an employee deal with the anxiety that is a natural response to change. Employees who experience severe reactions to change can benefit from talking with a counselor. Some companies provide counseling through their employee assistance plans. Managers should not make the mistake of assuming that when employees resist change, they are acting irrationally. In some cases, could the resistance actually

Science

Resistance to Change Can Sometimes Be a Good Thing

Most research on resistance to change assumes that the people who resist change are irrational or are unreasonable and that change agents are the undeserving victims of the irrational and dysfunctional responses of those resistant to change. Researchers looked at the resistance process from another angle and argued that resistance can be a valuable resource on three levels: existence, engagement, and strengthening. Oftentimes, it is difficult to get new ideas heard, let alone repeated in enough places by enough people to get a change implemented. Resistance actually provides this opportunity and can keep the change topic or idea in existence long enough to garner support. With resistance can also come commitment or engagement. Individuals who resist are typically more invested in what

is impacted by the change than those who are ambivalent. Change agents should take note of these engaged individuals, listen to them, and consider changing the pace, scope, or sequencing of the change based on their arguments. Resistance can be functional and strengthen an organization much like functional conflict, and the actions managers use to counter resistance can actually be beneficial to the change process. Sometimes resistance can lead to increased communication, and greater participation, along with better working relationships. The lesson for managers is that resistance is not necessarily a bad thing.

SOURCE: J. D. Ford, L. W. Ford, and A. D'Amelio "Resistance to Change: The Rest of the Story," *Academy of Management Review* 33 (2008): 362–377.

be a result of well-thought out strategies and objectives and if so, could that be a good thing? See the Science feature for more details.

Open communication, participation, and emotional support can go a long way toward managing resistance to change. Managers must realize that some resistance is inevitable, however, and should plan ways to deal with it early in the change process.

The Hartford Financial Services Group encountered resistance to change in going global. When the company attempted to enter the lucrative British and Dutch insurance markets by acquiring British and Dutch companies, the overseas staff resisted changes suggested by Hartford, such as using laptops and introducing new financial products. The introduction of such U.S. business practices is often referred to as "economic imperialism" by employees who feel they are being forced to substitute corporate values for personal or national values.

Hartford needed its European staff to understand that they were part of a transnational company. Its solution was to offer a stock ownership plan that tied the personal fortunes of the staff to the company. This gave employees a considerable interest in Hartford's success and helped them identify with the company.[63]

Behavioral Reactions to Change

In spite of attempts to minimize the resistance to change in an organization, some reactions to change are inevitable. Negative reactions may be manifested in overt behavior or through more passive resistance to change. People show four basic, identifiable reactions to change: disengagement, disidentification, disenchantment, and disorientation.[64] Managers can use interventions to deal with these reactions, as shown in Table 18.1.

Disengagement is psychological withdrawal from change. The employee may appear to lose initiative and interest in the job. Employees who disengage may fear the change but approach it by doing nothing and simply hoping for the best. Disengaged employees are physically present but mentally absent. They lack drive and commitment, and they simply comply without real psychological investment in their work. Disengagement can be recognized by behaviors such as being hard to find or doing only the basics to get the job done. Typical disengagement statements include "No problem" or "This won't affect me."

One oil and gas company that started ventures in Russia found that the very idea of change was alien to Russian managers. These managers felt that their task was to establish procedures and ensure continuity. When Western managers tried to institute change, the Russian managers disengaged, believing that their job was to secure stability rather than change.[65]

The basic managerial strategy for dealing with disengaged individuals is to confront them with their reaction and draw them out so that they can identify the concerns that need to be addressed. Disengaged employees may not be aware of the change in their behavior, and they need to be assured of your intentions. Drawing

disengagement
Psychological withdrawal from change.

disidentification
Feeling that one's identity is being threatened by a change.

TABLE

18.1	Reactions to Change and Managerial Interventions	
Reaction	**Expression**	**Managerial Intervention**
Disengagement	Withdrawal	Confront, identify
Disidentification	Sadness, worry	Explore, transfer
Disenchantment	Anger	Neutralize, acknowledge
Disorientation	Confusion	Explain, plan

SOURCE: Table adapted from H. Woodward and S. Buchholz, *Aftershock: Helping People Through Corporate Change,* p. 15. Copyright © 1987 John Wiley & Sons, Inc. Reprinted by permission of John Wiley & Sons.

them out and helping them air their feelings can lead to productive discussions. Disengaged people seldom become cheerleaders for the change, but they can be brought closer to accepting and working with a change by open communication with an empathetic manager who is willing to listen.

Another reaction to change is *disidentification*. Individuals reacting in this way feel that their identity has been threatened by the change, and they feel very vulnerable. Many times they cling to a past procedure because they had a sense of mastery over it, and it gave them a sense of security. "My job is completely changed" and "I used to . . ." are verbal indications of disidentification. Disidentified employees often display sadness and worry. They may appear to be sulking and dwelling on the past by reminiscing about the old ways of doing things.

Because disidentified employees are so vulnerable, they often feel like victims in the change process. Managers can help them through the transition by encouraging them to explore their feelings and helping them transfer their positive feelings into the new situation. One way to do this is to help them identify what they liked in the old situation and then show them how it is possible to have the same positive experience in the new situation. Disidentified employees need to see that work itself and emotion are separable—that is, that they can let go of old ways and experience positive reactions to new ways of performing their jobs.

Disenchantment is also a common reaction to change. It is usually expressed as negativity or anger. Disenchanted employees realize that the past is gone, and they are mad about it. They may try to enlist the support of other employees by forming coalitions. Destructive behaviors like sabotage and backstabbing may result. Typical verbal signs of disenchantment are "This will never work" and "I'm getting out of this company as soon as I can." The anger of a disenchanted person may be directly expressed in organizational cultures where it is permissible to do so. This behavior tends to get the issues out in the open. More often, however, cultures view the expression of emotion at work as improper and unbusinesslike. In these cultures, the anger is suppressed and emerges in more passive-aggressive ways, such as badmouthing and starting rumors. One of the particular dangers of disenchantment is that it is quite contagious in the workplace. Managers should try to bring the employee to a more neutral emotion state and acknowledge that her or his anger is valid.

It is often difficult to reason with disenchanted employees. Thus, the first step in managing this reaction is to bring these employees from their highly negative, emotionally charged state to a more neutral state. To neutralize the reaction does not mean to dismiss it; rather, it means to allow the individuals to let off the necessary steam so that they can come to terms with their anger. The second part of the strategy for dealing with disenchanted employees is to acknowledge that their anger is normal and that you do not hold it against them. Sometimes disenchantment is a mask for one of the other three reactions, and it must be worked through to get to the core of the employee's reaction. Employees may also become cynical about change and lose faith in the leaders of change.

A final reaction to change is *disorientation*. Disoriented employees are lost and confused, and often unsure of their feelings. They waste energy trying to figure out what to do instead of how to do things. Disoriented individuals ask a lot of questions and become very detail oriented. They may appear to need a good deal of guidance and may leave their work undone until all of their questions have been answered. "Analysis paralysis" is characteristic of disoriented employees. They feel that they have lost touch with the priorities of the company, and they may want to analyze the change to death before acting on it. Disoriented employees may ask questions like "Now what do I do?" or "What do I do first?"

Disorientation is a common reaction among people who are used to clear goals and unambiguous directions. When change is introduced, it creates uncertainty and a

disenchantment
Feeling negativity or anger toward a change.

disorientation
Feelings of loss and confusion due to a change.

lack of clarity. The managerial strategy for dealing with this reaction is to explain the change in a way that minimizes the ambiguity that is present. The information about the change needs to be put into a framework or an overall vision so that the disoriented individual can see where he or she fits into the grand scheme of things.[66] Once the disoriented employee sees the broader context of the change, you can plan a series of steps to help him or her adjust. The employee needs a sense of priorities to work on.

Managers need to be able to diagnose these four reactions to change. Because each reaction brings with it significant and different concerns, no single universal strategy can help all employees adjust. By recognizing each reaction and applying the appropriate strategy, it is possible to help even strong resisters work through a transition successfully.

Lewin's Change Model

4 Apply force field analysis to a problem.

Kurt Lewin developed a model of the change process that has stood the test of time and continues to influence the way organizations manage planned change. Lewin's model is based on the idea of force field analysis.[67] Figure 18.1 shows a force field analysis of a decision to engage in exercise behavior.

This model contends that a person's behavior is the product of two opposing forces; one force pushes toward preserving the status quo, and the other force pushes for change. When the two opposing forces are approximately equal, current behavior is maintained. For behavioral change to occur, the forces maintaining the status quo must be overcome. This can be accomplished by increasing the forces for change, by weakening the forces for the status quo, or by a combination of these actions. You 18.2 asks you to apply force field analysis to a problem in your life.

5 Explain Lewin's organizational change model.

Lewin's change model is a three-step process, as shown in Figure 18.2. The process begins with *unfreezing*, which is a crucial first hurdle in the change process. Unfreezing involves encouraging individuals to discard old behaviors by shaking up the equilibrium state that maintains the status quo. Change management literature has long advocated that certain individuals have personalities that make them more resistant to change. However, recent research indicates that only a small portion of a study's respondents (23 percent) displayed consistency in their reactions to three different kinds of change: structural, technological, and office relocation. The majority of respondents (77 percent) reacted differently to these various kinds of change, suggesting that

unfreezing
The first step in Lewin's change model, in which individuals are encouraged to discard old behaviors by shaking up the equilibrium state that maintains the status quo.

FIGURE

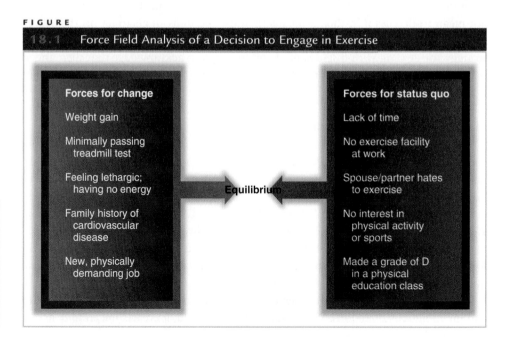

18.1   Force Field Analysis of a Decision to Engage in Exercise

Forces for change	Forces for status quo
Weight gain	Lack of time
Minimally passing treadmill test	No exercise facility at work
Feeling lethargic; having no energy	Spouse/partner hates to exercise
Family history of cardiovascular disease	No interest in physical activity or sports
New, physically demanding job	Made a grade of D in a physical education class

Equilibrium

18.2 Lewin's Change Model

Unfreezing	Moving	Refreezing
Reducing forces for status quo	Developing new attitudes, values, and behaviors	Reinforcing new attitudes, values, and behaviors

reactions to change might be more situationally driven than was previously thought.[68] Organizations often accomplish unfreezing by eliminating the rewards for current behavior and showing that current behavior is not valued. By unfreezing, individuals accept that change needs to occur. In essence, individuals surrender by allowing the boundaries of their status quo to be opened in preparation for change.[69]

The second step in the change process is *moving*. In the moving stage, new attitudes, values, and behaviors are substituted for old ones. Organizations accomplish moving by initiating new options and explaining the rationale for the change, as well as by providing training to help employees develop the new skills they need. Employees should be given the overarching vision for the change so that they can establish their roles within the new organizational structure and processes.[70]

Refreezing is the final step in the change process. In this step, new attitudes, values, and behaviors are established as the new status quo. The new ways of operating are cemented in and reinforced. Managers should ensure that the organizational culture and formal reward systems encourage the new behaviors and avoid rewarding the old ways of operating. Changes in the reward structure may be needed to ensure

moving
The second step in Lewin's change model, in which new attitudes, values, and behaviors are substituted for old ones.

refreezing
The final step in Lewin's change model, in which new attitudes, values, and behaviors are established as the new status quo.

You 18.2

Applying Force Field Analysis

Think of a problem you are currently facing. An example would be trying to increase the amount of study time you devote to a particular class.

1. Describe the problem, as specifically as possible.
2. List the forces driving change on the arrows at the left side of the diagram.
3. List the forces restraining change on the arrows at the right side of the diagram.
4. What can you do, specifically, to remove the obstacles to change?
5. What can you do to increase the forces driving change?
6. What benefits can be derived from breaking a problem down into forces driving change and forces restraining change?

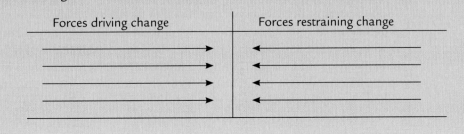

Forces driving change	Forces restraining change

that the organization is not rewarding the old behaviors and merely hoping for the new behaviors. A study by Exxon Research and Engineering showed that framing and displaying a mission statement in managers' offices may eventually change the behavior of 2 percent of the managers. By contrast, changing managers' evaluation and reward systems will change the behavior of 55 percent of the managers almost overnight.[71]

The approach used by Monsanto to increase opportunities for women within the company is an illustration of how to use Lewin's model effectively. First, Monsanto emphasized unfreezing by helping employees debunk negative stereotypes about women in business. This also helped overcome resistance to change. Second, Monsanto moved employees' attitudes and behaviors by diversity training in which differences were emphasized as positive, and supervisors learned ways of training and developing female employees. Third, Monsanto changed its reward system so that managers were evaluated and paid according to how they coached and promoted women, which helped refreeze the new attitudes and behaviors.

One frequently overlooked issue is whether or not the change is consistent with the company's deeply held core values. Value consistency is critical to making a change "stick." Organizations whose members perceive the changes to be consistent with the firm's values adopt the changes much more easily and fully. Conversely, organizations whose members' values conflict with the changes may display "superficial conformity," in which members pay lip service to the changes but ultimately revert to their old behaviors.[72]

Organizations that wish to change can select from a variety of methods to make a change become reality. Organization development is a method that consists of various programs for making organizations more effective.

ORGANIZATION DEVELOPMENT INTERVENTIONS

Organization development (OD) is a systematic approach to organizational improvement that applies behavioral science theory and research in order to increase individual and organizational well-being and effectiveness.[73] This definition implies certain characteristics. First, OD is a systematic approach to planned change. It is a structured cycle of diagnosing organizational problems and opportunities and then applying expertise to them. Second, OD is grounded in solid research and theory. It involves the application of our knowledge of behavioral science to the challenges that organizations face. Third, OD recognizes the reciprocal relationship between individuals and organizations. It acknowledges that for organizations to change, individuals must change. Finally, OD is goal oriented. It is a process that seeks to improve both individual and organizational well-being and effectiveness.

OD has a rich history. Some of the early work in OD was conducted by Kurt Lewin and his associates during the 1940s. This work was continued by Rensis Likert, who pioneered the use of attitude surveys in OD. During the 1950s, Eric Trist and his colleagues at the Tavistock Institute in London focused on the technical and social aspects of organizations and how they affect the quality of work life. These programs on the quality of work life migrated to the United States during the 1960s. During this time, a 200-member OD network was established, and it has grown to more than 4,100 members worldwide. As the number of practitioners has increased, so has the number of different OD methods. One compendium of organizational change methods estimates that more than 300 different methods have been used.[74]

OD is also being used internationally. OD has been applied in Canada, Sweden, Norway, Germany, Japan, Australia, Israel, and Mexico, among others. Some OD

organization development (OD)

A systematic approach to organizational improvement that applies behavioral science theory and research in order to increase individual and organizational well-being and effectiveness.

methods are difficult to implement in other cultures. As OD becomes more internationally widespread, we will increase our knowledge of how culture affects the success of different OD approaches.

Prior to deciding on a method of intervention, managers must carefully diagnose the problem they are attempting to address. Diagnosis and needs analysis are a critical first step in any OD intervention. Following this, an intervention method is chosen and applied. Finally, a thorough follow-up of the OD process is conducted. Figure 18.3 presents the OD cycle, a continuous process of moving the organization and its employees toward effective functioning.

Diagnosis and Needs Analysis

Before any intervention is planned, a thorough organizational diagnosis should be conducted. Diagnosis is an essential first step for any OD intervention.[75] The term *diagnosis* comes from *dia* (through) and *gnosis* (knowledge of). Thus, the diagnosis should pinpoint specific problems and areas in need of improvement. Problems can arise in any part of the organization. Six areas to examine carefully are the organization's purpose, structure, reward system, support systems, relationships, and leadership.[76]

6 Describe the use of organizational diagnosis and needs analysis as a first step in organizational development.

Harry Levinson's diagnostic approach asserts that the process should begin by identifying where the pain (the problem) in the organization is, what it is like, how long it has been happening, and what has already been done about it.[77] Then a four-part, comprehensive diagnosis can begin. The first part of the diagnosis involves achieving an understanding of the organization's history. In the second part, the organization as a whole is analyzed to obtain data about its structure and processes. In the third part, interpretive data about attitudes, relationships, and current organizational functioning are gathered. In the fourth part of the diagnosis, the data are analyzed and conclusions are reached. In each stage of the diagnosis, the data can be gathered using a variety of methods, including observation, interviews, questionnaires, and archival records.

The diagnostic process may yield the conclusion that change is necessary. As part of the diagnosis, it is important to address the following issues:

- What are the forces for change?
- What are the forces preserving the status quo?
- What are the most likely sources of resistance to change?
- What are the goals to be accomplished by the change?

FIGURE

18.3 The Organization Development Cycle

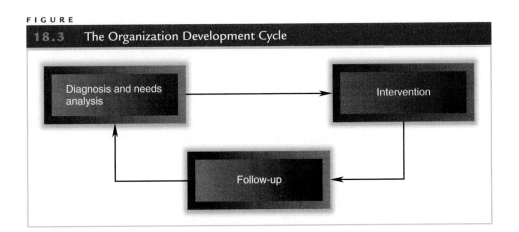

This information constitutes a force field analysis, as discussed earlier in the chapter.

A needs analysis is another crucial step in managing change. This is an analysis of the skills and competencies that employees must have to achieve the goals of the change. A needs analysis is essential because interventions such as training programs must target these skills and competencies.

Hundreds of alternative OD intervention methods exist. One way of classifying these methods is by the target of change. The target of change may be the organization, groups within the organization, or individuals.

Organization- and Group-Focused Techniques

7 Discuss the major organization development interventions.

Some OD intervention methods emphasize changing the organization itself or changing the work groups within the organization. Intervention methods in this category include survey feedback, management by objectives, product and service quality programs, team building, and process consultation.

Survey Feedback *Survey feedback* is a widely used intervention method whereby employee attitudes are solicited using a questionnaire. Once the data are collected, they are analyzed and fed back to the employees to diagnose problems and plan other interventions. Survey feedback is often used as an exploratory tool and then is combined with some other intervention. The effectiveness of survey feedback in actually improving outcomes (absenteeism or productivity, for example) increases substantially when this method is combined with other interventions.[78] The effectiveness of this technique is contingent on trust between management and subordinates, and this can be reinforced through the anonymity and confidentiality of survey responses.

For survey feedback to be an effective method, certain guidelines should be used. Unless the assurance of confidentiality and anonymity is given, employee responses may not be honest. Feedback should be reported in a group format; that is, no individual responses should be identified. Employees must be able to trust that there will be no negative repercussions from their responses. They should be informed of the purpose of the survey. Failing to do this can set up unrealistic expectations about the changes that might come from the surveys. One recent study found that the personality characteristic *change-specific self-efficacy*, which reflects an individual's belief that he or she can successfully cope with change, had a positive impact on employees' attitudes toward and commitment to change. Thus, managers could help build employee change efficacy by presenting them with smaller changes and helping them succeed. Providing positive feedback and rewarding efforts directed at coping with change can further build change self-efficacy. In addition, role-playing related to managing change, mentoring, and coaching can also help build change self-efficacy. Leaders might focus on developing this trait among employees while implementing major changes.[79]

In addition, management must be prepared to follow up on the survey results. If some things cannot be changed, the rationale (e.g., prohibitive cost) must be explained to employees. Without appropriate follow-through, employees will not take the survey process seriously the next time.

Management by Objectives As an organization-wide technique, management by objectives (MBO) involves joint goal setting between employees and managers. The MBO process includes the setting of initial objectives, periodic progress reviews, and problem solving to remove any obstacles to goal achievement.[80] All these steps are joint efforts between managers and employees.

MBO is a valuable intervention because it meets three needs. First, it clarifies what is expected of employees. This reduces role conflict and ambiguity. Second, MBO provides knowledge of results, an essential ingredient in effective job

survey feedback
A widely used method of intervention whereby employee attitudes are solicited using a questionnaire.

performance. Finally, MBO provides an opportunity for coaching and counseling by the manager. The problem-solving approach encourages open communication and discussion of obstacles to goal achievement.[81]

Companies that have used MBO successfully include the former Tenneco, Mobil (now part of ExxonMobil), and GE. The success of MBO in effecting organizational results hinges on the linking of individual goals to the goals of the organization.[82] MBO programs should be used with caution, however. An excessive emphasis on goal achievement can result in cutthroat competition among employees, falsification of results, and striving for results at any cost.

Product and Service Quality Programs *Quality programs*—programs that embed product and service quality excellence in the organizational culture—are assuming key roles in the OD efforts of many companies. For example, the success or failure of a service company may depend on the quality of customer service it provides.[83]

The Ritz-Carlton Hotel Company (now part of Marriott International) integrated its comprehensive service quality program into marketing and business objectives. The Atlanta-based company, which managed twenty-eight luxury hotels, won the Malcolm Baldrige Award for service quality. Key elements of Ritz-Carlton's quality program included participatory executive leadership, thorough information gathering, coordinated execution, and employees who were empowered to "move heaven and earth" to satisfy customers.[84]

At Ritz-Carlton, the company president and thirteen senior executives made up the senior quality management team, which met weekly to focus on service quality. Quality goals were established at all levels of the company. The crucial product and service requirements of travel consumers were translated into Ritz-Carlton Gold Standards, which included a credo, a motto, three steps of service, and twenty Ritz-Carlton Basics. These standards guided service quality throughout the organization.

Employees were required to act on a customer complaint at once and were empowered to provide "instant pacification," no matter what it took. Quality teams set action plans at all levels of the company. Each hotel had a quality leader, who served as a resource to the quality teams. Daily quality production reports provided an early warning system for identifying areas that needed quality improvement.

After celebrating an award as the best hotel in the world, Ritz-Carlton did not stop its quality improvement process. At one hotel, the chief complaint was that room service was always late. A quality team was put together, including a cook, a waiter, and a room service order taker. They studied how the process flowed. When they discovered that the service elevator was slow, they added an engineer and a representative from the elevator company to the team. They found that the elevators worked fine. Next, they posted a team member in the elevator twenty-four hours a day for a week. Every time the door opened, the team member had to find out why. Finally, a team member noticed that housemen who helped the maids got on the elevator a lot. It turned out that the housemen were taking towels from other floors because their maids needed more. The problem with room service was that the hotel didn't own enough towels. Ritz-Carlton bought more towels, and room service complaints fell 50 percent.[85] Toyota Motor Corporation, like Ritz-Carlton, constantly finds ways to integrate cutting-edge technological innovations with the growing pains of global expansion. The famed "Toyota Way" of doing business is based on two key principles: continuous improvement focused on innovation and respect for people.[86]

Team Building *Team building* programs can improve the effectiveness of work groups. Team building usually begins with a diagnostic process through which team members identify problems, and it continues with the team's planning actions to

quality program
A program that embeds product and service quality excellence in the organizational culture.

team building
An intervention designed to improve the effectiveness of a work group.

take in order to resolve those problems. The OD practitioner in team building serves as a facilitator, and the work itself is completed by team members.[87]

Team building is a very popular OD method. A survey of Fortune 500 companies indicated that human resource managers considered team building the most successful OD technique.[88] Managers are particularly interested in building teams that can learn. To build learning teams, members must be encouraged to seek feedback, discuss errors, reflect on successes and failures, and experiment with new ways of performing. Mistakes should be analyzed for ways to improve, and a climate of mutual support should be developed. Leaders of learning teams are good coaches who promote a climate of psychological safety so that team members feel comfortable discussing problems.[89]

One popular technique for team building is the use of outdoor challenges. Participants go through a series of outdoor activities, such as climbing a fourteen-foot wall. Similar physical challenges require the participants to work as a team and focus on trust, communication, decision making, and leadership. GE and Weyerhaeuser use outdoor challenges at the beginning of their team-building courses, and later in the training, team members apply what they have learned to actual business situations.[90] Now that adventure courses, paintball, and even high-powered gokarting have become common corporate training exercises, what's the next big thing? One innovative firm called Teambuilding Inc. uses rowing as team-building exercise. It enlisted the services of an Olympic gold medalist, Dan Lyons, to design a seminar focused on team building using rowing as the central organizing theme. This activity encourages participants to practice leadership, communication, goal setting, conflict management, and motivation. GE Healthcare, ING Direct, and Wyeth Corporate Communications have all used this technique for their team-building programs.[91,92] Preliminary studies indicate that team building can improve group processes.[93]

Process Consultation Pioneered by Edgar Schein, *process consultation* is an OD method that helps managers and employees improve the processes that are used in organizations.[94] The processes most often targeted are communication, conflict resolution, decision making, group interaction, and leadership.

One of the distinguishing features of the process consultation approach is that an outside consultant is used. The role of the consultant is to help employees help themselves. In this way, the ownership of a successful outcome rests with the employees.[95] The consultant guides the organization members in examining the processes in the organization and in refining them. The steps in process consultation are entering the organization, defining the relationship, choosing an approach, gathering data and diagnosing problems, intervening, and gradually leaving the organization.

Process consultation is an interactive technique between employees and an outside consultant, so it is seldom used as a sole OD method. Most often, it is used in combination with other OD interventions.

All the preceding OD methods focus on changing the organization or the work group. Other OD methods are aimed at facilitating change within individuals.

Individual-Focused Techniques

OD efforts that are targeted toward individuals include skills training, leadership training and development, executive coaching, role negotiation, job redesign, health promotion programs, and career planning.

Skills Training The key question addressed by *skills training* is "What knowledge, skills, and abilities are necessary to do this job effectively?" Skills training is

process consultation
An OD method that helps managers and employees improve the processes that are used in organizations.

skills training
Increasing the job knowledge, skills, and abilities that are necessary to do a job effectively.

accomplished either in formal classroom settings or on the job. The challenge of integrating skills training into OD is the rapid change that most organizations face. The job knowledge in most positions requires continual updates to keep pace with rapid change.

FedEx depends on more than 218,000 full- and part-time employees in 215 countries to deliver 100 percent customer satisfaction. The company is constantly changing its products and services, sometimes at the rate of 1,700 changes per year. FedEx decided to accomplish its mission using Web-based training and job skills testing. Employees find the training easy to use, convenient, and individualized. FedEx has found it to be economical as well because it eliminates travel expenses and the need for instructors. In job skills testing, every customer service employee takes a test every six months via computer. The test generates a unique prescription that informs employees what they do well and how they need to improve. It also directs employees to the interactive video lesson they need to practice to improve their skills.[96]

Leadership Training and Development Companies invest millions of dollars in *leadership training and development,* a term that encompasses a variety of techniques designed to enhance individuals' leadership skills. One popular technique is sending future leaders to off-site training classes. Research shows that this type of education experience can have some impact, but participants' enthusiastic return to work may be short-lived due to the challenges and realities of work life. Classroom learning alone thus has a limited effect on leadership skills.

The best leadership training and development programs combine classroom learning with on-the-job experiences. One way of accomplishing development is through the use of action learning, a technique that was pioneered in Europe.[97] In action learning, leaders take on unfamiliar problems or familiar problems in unfamiliar settings. The leaders work on the problems and meet weekly in small groups made up of individuals from different organizations. The outcome of action learning is that leaders learn about themselves through the challenges of their comrades. Other techniques that provide active learning for participants are simulation, business games, role-playing, and case studies.[98]

Eli Lilly has an action learning program that pulls together eighteen future company leaders and gives them a strategic business issue to resolve. For six weeks, the trainees meet with experts, best-practices organizations, and customers and then present their recommendations to top brass. One action learning team was charged with coming up with an e-business strategy; their plan was so good that executives immediately implemented it. At Eli Lilly and other firms, action learning programs provide developmental experiences for leaders and result in useful initiatives for the company.[99]

Leadership training and development is an ongoing process that takes considerable time and effort. There are no quick fixes. At IBM, managers are strongly held accountable for leadership development. In fact, IBM's managers will not be considered for promotion into senior executive positions unless they have a record of developing leaders. Top management must be committed to the process of leadership training and development if they want to create a pipeline of high-potential employees to fill leadership positions.[100]

Executive Coaching *Executive coaching* is a technique in which managers or executives are paired with a coach in a partnership to help the executive perform more effectively at work and, sometimes, even in personal life. Although coaching is usually done in a one-on-one manner, it is sometimes done in groups. The popularity of executive coaching has increased dramatically in recent years. In just two years of existence, the International Coach Federation, a group that trains and accredits executive coaches, doubled its membership, which is now at 7,000 members in thirty-five countries.

leadership training and development
A variety of techniques that are designed to enhance individuals' leadership skills.

executive coaching
A technique in which managers or executives are paired with a coach in a partnership to help the executive perform more efficiently.

Coaching is typically a special investment in top-level managers. Coaches provide another set of eyes and ears and help executives see beyond their own blinders. They elicit solutions and ideas from the client rather than making suggestions; thus, they enhance the talents and capabilities within the client, in addition to developing new ones. Many coaching arrangements focus on developing the emotional intelligence of the client executive and may use a 360-degree assessment in which the executive, his or her boss, peers, subordinates, and even family members rate the executive's emotional competencies.[101,102] This information is then fed back to the executive, and along with the coach, a development plan is put in place.

Good coaches form strong connections with clients, exhibit professionalism, and deliver forthright, candid feedback. The top reasons executives seek out coaches are to make personal behavior changes, enhance their effectiveness, and foster stronger relationships. Does executive coaching pay off? Evidence suggests that successful coaching can result in sustained changes in executives' behavior, increased self-awareness and understanding, and more effective leadership competencies.[103] In one study, for example, executives who worked with executive coaches were more likely to set specific goals, ask for feedback from their supervisors, and were rated as better performers by their supervisors and subordinates when compared to executives who simply received feedback from surveys.[104] Effective coaching relationships depend on a professional, experienced coach, an executive who is motivated to learn and change, and a good fit between the two.

Role Negotiation Individuals who work together sometimes have differing expectations of one another within the working relationship. *Role negotiation* is a simple technique whereby individuals meet and clarify their psychological contract. In doing this, the expectations of each party are clarified and negotiated. The outcome of role negotiation is a better understanding between the two parties of what each can be expected to give and receive in the reciprocal relationship. When both parties have a mutual agreement on expectations, there is less ambiguity in the process of working together.

Job Redesign As an OD intervention method, *job redesign* emphasizes the fit between individual skills and the demands of the job. Chapter 14 outlined several approaches to job design. Many of these methods are used as OD techniques for realigning task demands and individual capabilities or for redesigning jobs to fit new techniques or organizational structures better.

Ford Motor Company has redesigned virtually all of its manufacturing jobs, shifting workers from individual to team-based roles in which they have greater control of their work and can take the initiative to improve products and production techniques. Ford began trying this technique more than a decade ago and found that it improved not only employee job satisfaction but also productivity and product quality.

Another form of job redesign is telecommuting, in which employees perform some or all of their work from home. Companies including American Express, AT&T, and Merrill Lynch have significant numbers of employees who work this way. When AT&T surveyed its managers to assess the impact of telecommuting, 76 percent were happier with their jobs, and 79 percent were happier with their careers in general since they began telecommuting.[105]

Health Promotion Programs As organizations have become increasingly concerned with the costs of distress in the workplace, health promotion programs have become a part of larger OD efforts. In Chapter 7, we examined stress and strain

role negotiation
A technique whereby individuals meet and clarify their psychological contract.

job redesign
An OD intervention method that alters jobs to improve the fit between individual skills and the demands of the job.

at work. Companies that have successfully integrated health promotion programs into their organizations include AT&T, Caterpillar, Kimberly-Clark, and Johnson & Johnson.

The American Psychological Association recognizes companies for innovative programs that support psychologically healthy work environments. Green Mountain Coffee Roasters has in place yoga, meditation, and physical therapy programs to reduce work-related stress and injury. It pays for 90 percent of health care costs of its full-time employees. Furthermore, the company reimburses each employee up to $400 per year for participation in wellness programs, health club memberships, or smoking cessation programs.[106]

Although companies have long recognized the importance of maintenance on their machinery, many are only recently learning that their human assets need maintenance as well, in the form of employee wellness and health promotion activities. The components of these programs can include education about stress and coping, relaxation training, company-sponsored exercise, and employee assistance programs. All are focused on helping employees manage their stress and health in a preventive manner.

Career Planning Matching an individual's career aspirations with the opportunities in the organization is *career planning*. This proactive approach to career management is often part of an organization's development efforts. Career planning is a joint responsibility of organizations and individuals. Companies like IBM, Travelers Life & Annuity (part of Citigroup), and 3M have implemented career-planning programs.

Career-planning activities benefit the organization as well as its workers. Through counseling sessions, employees identify their skills and skill deficiencies. The organization then can plan its training and development efforts based on this information. In addition, the process can be used to identify and nurture talented employees for potential promotion.

Managers can choose from a host of OD techniques to facilitate organizational change. Some of these techniques are aimed toward organizations or groups, and others focus on individuals. Large-scale changes in organizations require the use of multiple techniques. For example, implementing a new technology like robotics may require simultaneous changes in the structure of the organization, the configuration of work groups, and individual attitudes.

We should recognize at this point that the OD methods just described are means to an end. Programs do not drive change; business needs do. The OD methods are merely vehicles for moving the organization and its employees in a more effective direction.

ETHICAL CONSIDERATIONS IN ORGANIZATION DEVELOPMENT

OD is a process of helping organizations improve. It may involve resistance to change, shifts in power, losses of control, and redefinition of tasks.[107] These are all sensitive issues. Further, the change agent, whether a manager from within the organization or a consultant from outside, is in a position of directing the change. Such a position carries the potential for misuse of power. The ethical concerns surrounding the use of OD center around four issues.[108]

8 Identify the ethical issues that must be considered in organization development efforts.

The first issue is the *selection* of the OD method to be used. Every change agent has inherent biases about particular methods, but these biases must not enter into the decision process. The OD method used must be carefully chosen in accordance with the problem as diagnosed, the organization's culture, and the employees concerned. All alternatives should be given fair consideration in the choice of a method. In addition, the OD practitioner should never use a method he or she is not skilled in delivering. Using a method you are not an expert in is unethical, because the client assumes you are.

The second ethical issue is *voluntary participation*. No employee should be forced to participate in any OD intervention.[109] To make an informed decision about participation, employees should be given information about the nature of the intervention and what will be expected of them. They should also be afforded the option to discontinue their participation at any time they choose.

The third issue of ethical concern is *confidentiality*. Change agents gather a wealth of information during organizational diagnoses and interventions. Successful change agents develop a trusting relationship with employees. They may receive privileged information, sometimes unknowingly. It is unethical for a change agent to reveal information in order to give some group or individual political advantage or to enhance the change agent's own standing. Consultants should not reveal information about an organization to its competitors. The use of information gathered from OD efforts is a sensitive issue and presents ethical dilemmas.

A final ethical concern in OD is the potential for *manipulation* by the change agent. Because any change process involves influence, some individuals may feel manipulated. The key to alleviating the potential for manipulation is open communication. Participants should be given complete knowledge of the rationale for change, what they can expect of the change process, and what the intervention will entail. No actions should be taken that limit the participants' freedom of choice.[110]

ARE ORGANIZATION DEVELOPMENT EFFORTS EFFECTIVE?

Because OD is designed to help organizations manage change, it is important to evaluate the effectiveness of these efforts. The success of any OD intervention depends on a host of factors, including the technique used, the competence of the change agent, the organization's readiness for change, and top management commitment. No single method of OD is effective in every instance. Instead, multiple-method OD approaches are recommended because they allow organizations to capitalize on the benefits of several approaches.[111]

Evaluations of OD efforts have focused on outcomes such as productivity. One review of more than 200 interventions indicated that worker productivity improved in 87 percent of the cases.[112] A separate analysis of ninety-eight of these interventions revealed impressive productivity gains.[113] We can conclude that when properly applied and managed, OD programs have positive effects on performance.[114]

MANAGERIAL IMPLICATIONS: MANAGING CHANGE

Several guidelines can be used to facilitate the success of management change efforts.[115] First, managers should recognize the forces for change. These forces can come from a combination of sources both internal and external to the organization.

A shared vision of the change should be developed that includes participation by all employees in the planning process. Top management must be committed to the change and should visibly demonstrate support, because employees look to these leaders to model appropriate behavior. A comprehensive diagnosis and needs analysis should be conducted. The company then must ensure that there are adequate resources for carrying out the change.

Resistance to change should be planned for and managed. Communication, participation, and empathetic support are ways of helping employees adjust. The reward system within the organization must be carefully evaluated to ensure that new behaviors, rather than old ones, are being reinforced. Participation in the change process should also be recognized and rewarded.

The OD technique used should be carefully selected to meet the goals of the change. Finally, OD efforts should be managed in an ethical manner and should preserve employees' privacy and freedom of choice. Employees must be treated fairly, and management's explanations for change must be congruent with their actions. The congruence between talk and actions, or "walking the talk," is critical in managing organizational change.[116] By using these guidelines, managers can meet the challenges of managing change while enhancing productivity in their organizations.

Diversity Dialogue

Changing Racial Attitudes One Dorm Room at a Time

Many U.S. colleges and universities are taking the saying, "familiarity breeds content" to a new level by assigning students of different races as roommates. Many times these assignments are out of necessity due to a decreased number of minority students on some college campuses. Other times, the roommate assignments are due to the limited number of available on-campus housing. And when students have roommate problems, they are usually told to work it out whether the roommate is of the same or a different race. Whatever the reason, this "natural experiment" has yielded some surprising results. The most interesting finding from a study of Ohio State students was that students who remained with different-race roommates for at least ten weeks saw an improvement in their racial attitudes. How? Just ask Sam Boakye.

Ghana-born Boakye enrolled in Ohio State as a freshman and was the only black student on his dorm-room floor. He was determined to get good grades, in part, so that his white roommate would not have a basis for negative racial views. "If you're surrounded by whites," Boakye explains, "you have something to prove. You're pushed to do better, to challenge the stereotype that black people are not that smart." Racial attitudes are typically formed early in life. Many college students

have had very little exposure to diversity when they arrive on campus, and as a result, have few different-race friends. And while most college classrooms have sufficient levels of diversity, one Ohio State professor suggests that classroom diversity does not have the same effect on increasing different-race friendships that living together in residence halls do.

Are there conflicts between interracial roommates? Sure there are. But most of those are no different than the things that drive conflict in same-race relationships—personal property, loud music, cleanliness, or coming in late at night. Could the key to challenging racial stereotypes and negative perceptions be as simple as making a good impression? Boakye believes it could be. According to him, ". . . when their [white students'] first experience with a black guy isn't so bad, they go and make more black friends."

1. What deep-level diversity issues may be relevant here?

2. Would you support college residence policies that required different-race roommate pairings to increase campus diversity? Why or why not?

SOURCE: T. Lewin, "Interracial Roommates Can Reduce Prejudice," *New York Times* (July 8, 2009).

LOOKING BACK: IKEA

IKEA Goes Green

To become more green, IKEA rallied company support around five primary areas where environmental criteria needed to be applied to their business: forestry, adapting the product range, working with suppliers, transport and distribution, and ensuring environmentally conscious stores. In regard to forestry, IKEA gets its timber from responsibly managed forests. The company employs forest managers whose job it is to monitor this on-site. IKEA is also working with the World Wildlife Fund to help the countries where they get their timber to improve their practices. The company substitutes wood using wood veneer products to reduce the amount of wood used.[117]

IKEA's code of conduct (called IWAY) inspectors visit suppliers at least three days a week to ensure they are meeting the IKEA code of conduct and adhering to the environmental principals.[118] Their aim is to make products that have a minimum impact on the environment and do so in a socially responsible way. Although much of their impact on the environment comes from transportation, the "flat packs" allow IKEA to ship more in one truck. IKEA's direct emissions are about 3.2 million tons (compared to the biggest emitter among coal-fired power plants in the United States which resides in Juliette, Georgia, and emits about 25 million tons).

Like IKEA's other social responsibility initiatives, focus on the environment is an ongoing process and IKEA hopes to continue to reduce their environmental footprint. The employees that CEO Dahlvig once set out to convince to change are now driving the environmental effort, demanding that the company do more.

Chapter Summary

1. Organizations face many pressures to change. Some forces are external, including globalization, workforce diversity, technological innovation, and ethics. Other forces are internal, such as declining effectiveness, crises, changing employee expectations, and a changing work climate.

2. Organizations face both planned and unplanned change. Change can be of an incremental, strategic, or transformational nature. The individual who directs the change, known as a change agent, can be internal or external to the organization.

3. Individuals resist change for many reasons, and many of these reasons are rooted in fear.

Organizations can help manage resistance by educating workers and openly communicating the change, encouraging worker participation in the change efforts, and providing empathy and support to those who have difficulty dealing with change.

4. Reactions to change may be manifested in behaviors reflecting disengagement, disidentification, disenchantment, and disorientation. Managers can use separate interventions targeted toward each reaction.

5. Force field analysis states that when the forces for change are balanced by the forces restraining change, an equilibrium state exists. For change to

occur, the forces for change must increase or the restraining forces must decrease.

6. Lewin's change model proposes three stages of change: unfreezing, moving, and refreezing.

7. A thorough diagnosis and needs analysis is a critical first step in any organization development (OD) intervention.

8. OD interventions targeted toward organizations and groups include survey feedback, management by objectives, product and service quality programs, team building, and process consultation.

9. OD interventions that focus on individuals include skills training, leadership training and development, executive coaching, role negotiation, job redesign, health promotion programs, and career planning.

10. OD efforts should be managed ethically and should preserve individual freedom of choice and privacy.

11. When properly conducted, OD can have positive effects on performance.

Key Terms

change agent (p. 633)
disenchantment (p. 641)
disengagement (p. 640)
disidentification (p. 641)
disorientation (p. 641)
executive coaching (p. 649)
incremental change (p. 633)
job redesign (p. 650)
leadership training and
   development (p. 649)

moving (p. 643)
organization development (OD)
   (p. 644)
planned change (p. 628)
process consultation (p. 648)
quality program (p. 647)
refreezing (p. 643)
role negotiation (p. 650)

skills training (p. 648)
strategic change (p. 633)
survey feedback (p. 646)
team building (p. 647)
transformational change
   (p. 633)
unfreezing (p. 642)
unplanned change (p. 628)

Review Questions

1. What are the major external and internal forces for change in organizations?

2. Contrast incremental, strategic, and transformational change.

3. What is a change agent? Who plays this role?

4. What are the major reasons individuals resist change? How can organizations deal with resistance?

5. Name the four behavioral reactions to change. Describe the behavioral signs of each reaction, and identify an organizational strategy for dealing with each reaction.

6. Describe force field analysis and its relationship to Lewin's change model.

7. What is organization development? Why is it undertaken by organizations?

8. Name six areas to be critically examined in any comprehensive organizational diagnosis.

9. What are the major organization-focused, group-focused, and individual-focused OD intervention methods?

10. Which OD intervention is most effective?

Discussion and Communication Questions

1. What are the major external forces for change in today's organizations?

2. What are the advantages of using an external change agent? An internal change agent?

3. Review You 18.1. What can you learn from this challenge about how individuals' tolerance for ambiguity can lead to resistance?

4. Can organizations prevent resistance to change? If so, how?

5. What organization development techniques are the easiest to implement? What techniques are the most difficult to implement? Why?

6. Suppose your organization experiences a dramatic increase in turnover. How would you diagnose the underlying problem?

7. Downsizing has played a major role in changing U.S. organizations. Analyze the internal and external forces for change regarding downsizing an organization.

8. If you were in charge of designing the ideal management development program, what topics would you include? Why?

9. *(communication question)* Find an article that describes an organization that has gone through change and managed it well. Develop a Real World feature of your own about the example you find using the format in this book. Prepare a brief oral presentation of your Real World feature for your class.

10. *(communication question)* Think of a change you would like to make in your life. Using Figure 18.1 as a guide, prepare your own force field analysis for that change. How will you overcome the forces for the status quo? How will you make sure to "refreeze" following the change? Summarize your analysis in an action plan.

Ethical Dilemma

Robert Tamarin stares at a questionnaire and considers his options.

He's just completed a meeting with Wendy Preston, the consultant who has been hired to evaluate company productivity and procedure in order to streamline processes and aim for efficiency at Wiffendorf Corp. Wendy is looking at duplicated efforts that exist in the present hierarchy, and she's meeting with managers such as Robert to evaluate where changes can be made.

Robert's meeting with Wendy was pretty straightforward: She took some notes about who reported to him directly and to whom he reported.

Now he has been instructed to complete a form regarding some procedural issues at the company.

Robert knows that there is a lot of wasted time due to repetitive procedures at Wiffendorf—and he thinks that, in general, hiring a consultant was the right thing to do. Money and time are being wasted, and an outsider could have a clear perspective of what changes need to be made to improve the processes. Wiffendorf Corp. has an opportunity right now to take a significant position in the market, but it's got to be able to grow efficiently. In order to do that, Robert's certain that significant changes will need to be made, and almost certainly, positions will be cut.

As he starts to write down his thoughts, he thinks about how he wants to word his recommendations and impressions. Robert knows that if he omitted some details and rephrased certain procedures, he might be able to structure the change to ensure that he and his team feel the least impact. Robert wants to make sure that neither he nor anyone else in his department loses their jobs. He can see how his job and another manager's job could be combined—however, he can also show how restructuring some of the teams could make his department more important than it is now. While these changes that favored him and his department would definitely improve Wifferdorf's productivity, it would probably not improve it as much as a restructure done on complete disclosure could.

Questions:

1. Using consequential, rule-based and character theories, evaluate Robert's options.

2. What should Robert do? Why?

Experiential Exercises

18.1 Organizational Diagnosis of the University

The purpose of this exercise is to give you experience in organizational diagnosis. Assume that your team has been hired to conduct a diagnosis of problem areas in your university and to make preliminary recommendations for organization development (OD) interventions.

Each team member should complete the following University Profile. Then, as a team, evaluate the strengths and weaknesses within each area (academics, teaching, social, cultural, and administrative) using the accompanying University Diagnosis form. Finally, make recommendations concerning OD interventions for each area. Be as specific as possible in both your diagnosis and your recommendations. Each team should then present its diagnosis to the class.

University Profile

Not True   1   2   3   4   5   Very True

I. Academics

1 2 3 4 5   1. There is a wide range of courses to choose from.

1 2 3 4 5   2. Classroom standards are too easy.

1 2 3 4 5   3. The library is adequate.

1 2 3 4 5   4. Textbooks are helpful.

II. Teachers

1 2 3 4 5   1. Teachers here are committed to quality instruction.

1 2 3 4 5   2. We have a high-quality faculty.

III. Social

1 2 3 4 5   1. Students are friendly to one another.

1 2 3 4 5   2. It is difficult to make friends.

1 2 3 4 5   3. Faculty get involved in student activities.

1 2 3 4 5   4. Too much energy goes into drinking and goofing off.

IV. Cultural Events

1 2 3 4 5   1. There are ample activities on campus.

1 2 3 4 5   2. Student activities are boring.

1 2 3 4 5   3. The administration places a high value on student activities.

1 2 3 4 5   4. Too much emphasis is placed on sports.

1 2 3 4 5   5. We need more "cultural" activities.

V. Organizational/Management

1 2 3 4 5   1. Decision making is shared at all levels of the organization.

1 2 3 4 5   2. There is unity and cohesiveness among departments and units.

1 2 3 4 5   3. Too many departmental clashes hamper the organization's effectiveness.

1 2 3 4 5   4. Students have a say in many decisions.

1 2 3 4 5   5. The budgeting process seems fair.

1 2 3 4 5   6. Recruiting and staffing are handled thoughtfully with student needs in mind.

University Diagnosis

	STRENGTH	WEAKNESS	INTERVENTION
1. Academic			
2. Teaching			
3. Social			
4. Cultural			
5. Administrative			

SOURCE: "Organizational Diagnosis of the University" by D. Marcic, *Organizational Behavior: Experiences and Cases* (St. Paul, MN: West Publishing Company, 1989), 326–329. Reprinted by permission.

18.2 Team Building for Team Effectiveness

This exercise will allow you and your team to engage in an organization development activity for team building. The two parts of the exercise are diagnosis and intervention.

Part 1. Diagnosis

Working as a team, complete the following four steps:

1. Describe how you have worked together this semester as a team.

2. What has your team done especially well? What has enabled this?

3. What problems or conflicts have you had as a team? (Be specific.) What was the cause of the problems your team experienced? Have the conflicts been over ideas, methods, or people?

4. Would you assess the overall effectiveness of your team as excellent, good, fair, poor, or a disaster? Explain your effectiveness rating.

Part 2. Intervention

A diagnosis provides the basis for intervention and action in organization development. Team building is a way to improve the relationships and effectiveness of teams at work. It is concerned with the results of work activities and the relationships among the members of the team. Complete the following three steps as a team.

Step 1. Answer the following questions with regard to the relationships within the team:

a. How could conflicts have been handled better?

b. How could specific relationships have been improved?

c. How could the interpersonal atmosphere of the team have been improved?

Step 2. Answer the following questions with regard to the results of the team's work:

a. How could the team have been more effective?

b. Are there any team process changes that would have improved the team's effectiveness?

c. Are there any team structure changes that would have improved the team's effectiveness?

Step 3. Answer the following questions with regard to the work environment in your place of employment:

a. What have you learned about team building that you can apply there?

b. What have you learned about team building that would not be applicable there?

Biz Flix | Field of Dreams

Ray Kinsella (Kevin Costner) hears a voice while working in his Iowa cornfield that says, "If you build it, he will come." Ray concludes that "he" is legendary "Shoeless Joe" Jackson (Ray Liotta), a Chicago White Sox player suspended for rigging the 1919 World Series. With the support of his wife Annie (Amy Madigan), Ray jeopardizes his farm by replacing some cornfields with a modern baseball diamond. "Shoeless Joe" soon arrives, followed by the rest of the suspended players. This charming fantasy film, based on W. P. Kinsellas's novel *Shoeless Joe*, shows the rewards of pursuing a dream.

Forces for Change: Some Internal and External Forces

This scene is part of the "People Will Come" sequence toward the end of the film. By this time in the story, Ray has met Terrence Mann (James Earl Jones). They have traveled together from Boston to Minnesota to find A. W. "Moonlight" Graham (Burt Lancaster). At this point, the three are at Ray's Iowa farm.

This scene follows Mark's (Timothy Busfield) arrival to discuss the foreclosure of Ray and Annie's mortgage. Mark, who is Annie's brother, cannot see the players on the field. Ray and Annie's daughter Karin (Gaby Hoffman) has proposed that people will come to Iowa City and buy tickets to watch a baseball game.

What to Watch for and Ask Yourself

- Who is the target of change in this scene?

- Apply a force field analysis to this scene. What are the forces for change? What are the forces for the status quo?

- Is there any evidence of resistance to change in this scene? Give specific examples of resistance behavior from the scene.

Workplace Video | Scholfield Honda: Change and Innovation

Not long ago, the phrase "hybrid SUV" would have been considered an oxymoron, but almost overnight, hybrid cars of all shapes and sizes became mainstream. As gas prices soared and concerns about the environment deepened, many people were looking for innovative solutions to energy problems and wondering about the cars of the future.

Enter Lee Lindquist, alternative fuels specialist at Scholfield Honda in Wichita, Kansas. Lindquist loves technology, is a passionate environmentalist, and has found the perfect way to make a difference at work. While researching alternative fuel vehicles for his upcoming presentation at the local Sierra Club, he learned Honda had been selling a natural gas vehicle in New York and California since 1998, where it was marketed as a way for municipalities and fleet customers to address air quality issues. He also discovered that the Honda Civic GX was the greenest model currently available for sale in the United States.

Lindquist couldn't believe Honda's most innovative car had been on the market for ten years and still hadn't been embraced by Honda dealerships or consumers. One challenge of offering the Civic GX to the public was the lack of natural gas fueling stations and the high cost of purchasing and installing individual fueling stations for home use. With any new technology, a critical mass of early adopters helped lay groundwork for others. In the case of the Civic GX, Honda dealerships weren't adopting or promoting the new technology, and Lindquist viewed this lack of entrepreneurship as unacceptable.

Rising fuel prices provided the perfect opportunity to introduce cost-conscious and green-minded customers to the Civic GX. When Lindquist brought the Civic GX idea to his boss, owner Roger Scholfield was skeptical. He had long been promoting the Honda brand as fuel-efficient and didn't want to confuse customers with the "new" vehicle. Nevertheless, he eventually warmed to the idea and with Lindquist's help began marketing the car to corporate and government customers.

Since that time, Scholfield Honda has seen many green-oriented changes. The dealership has stocked up on recycling bins and compostable cups, launched tree giveaway promotions, donated a Civic GX to a nearby tornado-stricken town, and formed a "Green Team," which meets regularly to identify what's next for Scholfield's ever-changing workplace.

Discussion Questions

1. What might explain dealers' failure to promote the Civic GX, beyond fueling issues?

2. How might Scholfield Honda expand on the changes put into motion by Lindquest?

3. How could the Honda Corporation capitalize on innovation at the dealer level?

Case

CarMax, the Used-Car Superstore: Smooth Ride or a Rocky Road?

CarMax, the nation's largest retailer of used cars, is headquartered in Richmond, Virginia, and as of mid-2009, it operated 100 used-car superstores in 46 markets. In its most recent fiscal year, which ended February 28, 2009, the company sold 345,465 used vehicles at retail and 194,081 vehicles at its wholesale in-store auctions.[1]

"The concept for CarMax was developed by Circuit City in the early 1990s, when Circuit City began searching for future growth opportunities beyond the consumer electronics sector. The automotive retail sector was identified as having the greatest potential based on its huge size, fragmented competition, and reputation for unmet consumer needs."[2] The first CarMax superstore was opened in Richmond, Virginia, in September 1993,[3] operating with a mission "to offer consumers a larger selection of cars than independent dealers, a no-haggle environment, low pricing, a quality guarantee, and exceptional customer service."[4] David MacMillan, then a spokesperson for Circuit City Stores, observed, "CarMax represents an opportunity to expand the company's [i.e., Circuit City's] growth beyond the 1990s."[5] However, on October 1, 2002, Circuit City completed a spin-off of the CarMax business, in which the auto superstores became an independent company.[6] CarMax survives to this day, whereas Circuit City Stores filed for bankruptcy protection in late 2008 and subsequently commenced liquidating its business a few months later.

True to its founding principles, CarMax provides "customers the opportunity to shop for vehicles the way they shop for items at other national retailers, and it is structured around four customer benefits: low, no-haggle prices; a broad selection; high quality vehicles; and a customer-friendly sales process."[7] "Industry observers say CarMax has carved out a solid niche with its used-car superstores that feature no-haggle pricing and financing, a five-day money-back guarantee, and a national database of cars that can be delivered anywhere. It also will buy used cars, whether a customer is buying a car from them or not."[8]

Money manager Doug Schaller believes that CarMax has a proven business model, and "that few competitors are expected to challenge CarMax nationally." He continues, "CarMax spent years honing its business model and sales-data trends, which creates entry barriers."[9]

Although the prospects for Carmax looked bright, this position was not achieved without some suffering. "It hasn't always been a smooth ride—CarMax bled money for its first seven years—but today [September 2006] the company stands as an unlikely American success story. . . . Through a blend of technology and an inspired reimagination of how to treat customers, CarMax has managed to outsmart any credible competitors. Now it has Hummer-size ambitions, with plans to build at least 300 more stores in the next 12 years."[10]

In September 2006, Tom Folliard, CarMax's current president and CEO, opined that the company can become a $20 billion operation within a decade. But naysayers warned that he must remember the mantra of founding CEO Austin Ligon: "If you don't offer the customer something special, then you're just another used-car dealer."[11]

As of May 2007 CarMax had "plans to grow its store base 15% to 20% a year for at least the next several years" and analysts believed that rate could continue for about a decade.[12] Building on this growth environment, business for CarMax auto superstores was essentially smooth ride throughout 2007. "CarMax concedes that a lot went right in fiscal 2007. Same-store sales were strong, as were results from its wholesale and financing arm."[13] Katharine Kenny, executive vice president of investor relations for Carmax, characterizes 2007 as the year of the perfect storm—"[t]he external environment, the internal environment, everything went right." But she added, "[w]e don't think that's a realistic situation every time."[14]

Some analysts and commentators said that natural disasters and gas prices could stall the company's growth, but others doubt that will happen. "Sept. 11 should have been the end of CarMax," says George Hoffer, an economics professor at Virginia Commonwealth University who has studied CarMax since its founding.[15] But 9/11 wasn't the end of CarMax!

Then in mid-2008 the road for Carmax's auto superstores became a lot rockier.

In June and July 2008, CarMax's sales fell dramatically after the price of gasoline spiked to about $4 a gallon. Citing same-store sales that were down an average 17 percent in July and August 2008, CarMax announced that it would "slash used-vehicle inventory levels and slow store expansion.... [It also had been] aggressively cutting store staffing levels, mainly through scheduling and attrition, and ... [would continue] to focus on controlling overhead expenses."[16] In navigating through a very difficult economic environment, CarMax continually looked for ways to align overhead costs with sales levels.[17]

President and CEO Tom Folliard blamed the sales decline on the environment. He observed, "[h]istorically, our earnings have funded a significant portion of our store growth, and the current slowdown in customer traffic and sales is pressuring this source of funding. While this is clearly a difficult environment for us, we remain confident in our superior consumer offer and our long-term growth opportunity."[18]

Outside of high gasoline prices, another reason that CarMax experienced significant sales declines was the massive inventory clearance undertaken by the major automobile companies, wherein they increased incentives and lowered prices. The inventory clearance initiatives of the major auto manufacturers hurt CarMax because CarMax had to reduce its own prices. Moreover, the price pressure was intensified because CarMax primarily sells late-model used cars, which is a more volatile market than used cars in general. However, "with car companies curtailing their use of leases, late-model used cars could become 'a more attractive option for some consumers'," which in turn could eventually benefit CarMax.[19]

The tough auto market continued well into 2009. Indeed, in June 2009, CarMax reported that customer traffic remained weak, and that its cutback on auto loans also had dampened sales.[20]

As CarMax continues to deal with the numerous changes affecting the used-car market, will it continue to have a rocky road or will it return to a smoother ride?

Discussion Questions

1. Describe the *external* forces for change that seem to be affecting CarMax.

2. Describe the *internal* forces for change that seem to be affecting CarMax.

3. Using force field analysis, explain CarMax's development as a business enterprise.

4. Explain the development of CarMax from the perspectives of incremental, strategic, and transformational changes.

SOURCE: This case was written by Michael K. McCuddy, The Louis S. and Mary L. Morgal Chair of Christian Business Ethics and Professor of Management, College of Business Administration, Valparaiso University.

Cohesion Case

PART IV

Zappos.com: Are Culture and Technology the Super Highway to the Future? (D)

Zappos.com isn't the first business venture pursued by entrepreneur Tony Hsieh. He cofounded LinkExchange shortly after graduating from Harvard with a computer science degree. LinkExchange "allowed amateur Web publishers to barter for advertising by agreeing to publish one another's ads."[1] LinkExchange proved to be a successful business venture, but Hsieh became depressed because the work was no longer fun.[2] "When it was just five or ten people, it was a lot of fun. We were working around the clock, no idea what day of the week it was, sleeping under our desks," says Hsieh. . . . [Continuing, he explains,] "[w]e hired all the right people in terms of skill sets, but by the time it was 100 or so, I dreaded going to the office."[3]

Hsieh increasingly felt "that the people he had hired were not committed to the venture's long-term growth. . . . Work, which once had felt liberating, had become a chore. He resolved that his next company would not be about a short-term payday. It would be about long-term growth, about creating a place to which he and his employees would want to come every day."[4]

Then at age twenty-four, Hsieh sold LinkExchange to Microsoft for $265 million.[5] He used the money to help fund his second company, which was cofounded in 1999 with Alfred Lin, a Harvard classmate. Called Venture Frogs, the business was a venture capital firm investing in start-up businesses. "A few of Venture Frogs' investments succeeded—notably the search engine Ask.com and the restaurant reservation system OpenTable—but as the dot-com bubble burst, most struggled to survive, and some were shuttered. Hsieh had been attracted to investing because it seemed to bring all the fun of start-ups on a larger scale; instead, it became a treadmill of meetings full of bad news. . . . What Hsieh wanted, he realized, was the unstructured fun of a new company. As he puts it, 'I wanted to be involved in building something.' "[6]

One of the start-ups funded by Venture Frogs was the online shoe store Shoesite.com, founded in San Francisco by Nicholas Swinmurn.[7] In reflecting on Shoesite.com, Hsieh says, "It was the most interesting opportunity, and the people were the most fun."[8] Hsieh invested $500,000 in Shoesite.com, joined the company, and subsequently renamed it Zappos. By the summer of 2000, Hsieh and Swinmurn were co-chief executives, and Zappos was operating out of Hsieh's living room.[9] Zappos grew rapidly and soon was moved from San Francisco to Henderson, Nevada, just outside of Las Vegas. When Swinmurn left the company in 2006, Hsieh became the sole chief executive.[10]

The Zappos Culture

Tony Hsieh, as chief cultural architect, and his team have focused their efforts on creating a distinctive culture at Zappos.[11] This distinctive culture is built upon a foundation of ten core values that all Zapponians—the name that Zappos personnel give themselves—follow in their work lives. These values are as follows:

- deliver WOW through service;
- embrace and drive change;
- create fun and a little weirdness;
- be adventurous, creative, and open-minded;
- pursue growth and learning;
- build open and honest relationships with communication;
- build a positive team and family spirit;
- do more with less;
- be passionate and determined; and be humble.[12]

"Defining core values as a company is one thing. Performing them on a daily basis is another."[13] So, how does Zappos put its core values into practice? First and foremost, Zappos builds its culture, brand, and business strategies on these core values.[14]

Developing and maintaining the Zappos culture starts with the hiring process. Tony Hsieh says, "[t]here are plenty of candidates who would be great individual contributors, but if they are not a cultural fit we would not hire them. . . .We want people who are eager to live the Zappos lifestyle and promote the Zappos culture—not a typical nine-to-five office employee."[15]

Culture building continues after the hiring process is over. In fact, it is an important ingredient of everyone's job. "[A] passion for having fun is the unwritten requirement in everyone's job description."[16] And annually, the company publishes a "Culture Book" in which many of the associates explain what the Zappos culture means to them. Moreover,

Zappos "bases half of an employee's performance review on how well he/she has lived up to the company's values."[17]

Another important way in which the Zappos staff lives the company's core values is always striving to maintain the firm's reputation for developing lifelong customer relationships. According to Hsieh, "[i]f you get the culture right, you don't need to come up with a policy and procedure for everything."[18]

Technology at Zappos

While organizational culture drives Zappos.com, technology supports that culture and the work of all Zappos employees in delivering great customer service. A prime example of the role that technology plays is provided by the Zappos distribution center (DC).

Zappos has one central warehousing/distribution location rather than numerous regional sites. Physically situated in Shepherdsville, Kentucky, the DC is close to the United Parcel Service (UPS) World Port, the main air hub of UPS in Louisville. This enables Zappos to fill orders less than two hours after they are placed and to take advantage of the UPS late-night pickup schedule.[19]

Craig Adkins, vice president of fulfillment operations for Zappos.com, explains the company's reasoning for one central DC as opposed to a distributed network with several regional locations. "Zappos would have to carry more inventory to spread it across multiple facilities.... If we were spread out throughout the country, we would be regionally closer, but we would actually be no closer to the customer than we are now.... If, for example, I had a building in Reno, and I wanted to serve my customers in California from there, I can actually get goods into Los Angeles faster from Louisville than I could from Nevada."[20]

How does technology enable the DC to contribute to fulfilling of the core value: Deliver WOW Through Service? It starts with the company's information technology, nearly all of which is developed in-house, linking its storage and shipping systems to the e-commerce site through a central database.[21]

Inside the DC, all incoming shipments from suppliers are unpackaged immediately and placed on pickable shelves. This helps to make inventory management, product distribution, and customer ordering processes integrated and seamless. Craig Adkins explains, "There are a million individual SKUs and 4 million items in inventory, so there's no need for a deep level of reserve storage. If you see it on our web site, it's on our shelf. If the last item sells out, it comes off the web site automatically. We don't do back orders. It's a live inventory system, which almost nobody does."[22]

A recent technological leap forward at the DC was the installation in the summer of 2008 of 72 Kiva robots at a cost of $5 million. The Kiva "bots" pack 12 percent of the shipped items at the DC, and the results have been tremendous. "The Kiva system is killing our old conveyor-based fulfillment process," says Adkins. "The labor costs are 50%, and electrically it's only using half as much power as our old system."[23] The Kiva "bot" system allows the Zappos DC to ship a pair of shoes in as little as eight minutes.[24]

The Kiva system is extraordinarily flexible and can be adapted to other product lines as Zappos expands. The system can be reconfigured very easily, and it can be moved to any geographic location.[25]

Craig Adkins describes the company's experience with the Kiva "bots" with enthusiasm and a definite view to the future: "We were amazed that Kiva transformed our new warehouse from bare concrete to fully operational readiness—with trained supervisors and associates—just four months after we signed the purchase order. We're already working on designs to cube out the building with Kiva's mobile fulfillment system (MFS) on the multi-level mezzanines."[26]

A Concluding Question

So, will the Zappos culture and its creative use of technology propel the company to even greater heights in the future?

Discussion Questions

1. What insights can be gained from Tony Hsieh's career progression that might be helpful to aspiring entrepreneurs?
2. How would you describe the culture at Zappos?
3. Explain what each of the company's core values contributes to the Zappos culture.
4. How does Zappos maintain the organizational culture that it has developed?
5. How does the Zappos culture influence organizational design and work design?
6. How does technology support the efforts of Zappos employees to provide extraordinary customer service?
7. What opportunities might the innovative use of technology provide for Zappos in the future?
8. Do you think Zappos is well positioned to deal with the changing world of modern business? Explain your answer.

SOURCE: This case was written by Michael K. McCuddy, The Louis S. and Mary L. Morgal Chair of Christian Business Ethics and Professor of Management, College of Business Administration, Valparaiso University.

*In a lengthy e-mail sent to Zappos employees on July 22, 2009, Tony Hsieh announced that Zappos had entered into a definitive agreement for Amazon to acquire Zappos. Hsieh emphasized to the employees that Zappos would continue to operate as it had in the past.

Appendix A

A Brief Historical Perspective

Organizational behavior may be traced back thousands of years, as noted in Sterba's analysis of the ancient Mesopotamian temple corporations. However, we focus on the modern history of organizational behavior, which dates to the late 1800s. One of the more important series of studies conducted during this period was the Hawthorne studies. As these and other studies have unfolded, the six disciplines discussed in Chapter 1 of the text have contributed to the advancement of organizational behavior. An overview of the progress during the past century is presented in Table A.1 and the accompanying text. This is followed by a discussion of the Hawthorne studies.

ONE HUNDRED PLUS YEARS OF PROGRESS

Progress in any discipline, practice, or field of study is measured by significant events, discoveries, and contributions over time. The history of organizational behavior begins, as noted in Table A.1, with the work of Frederick Taylor in scientific management at Midvale Steel Company, Bethlehem Steel Company, and elsewhere.[1] Taylor applied engineering principles to the study of people and their behavior at work. He pioneered the use of performance standards for workers, set up differential piece-rate systems of pay, and argued for the scientific selection of employees. He hoped to ultimately improve labor–management relationships in American industry. Taylor's lasting contributions include organizational goal-setting programs, incentive pay systems, and modern employee selection techniques.

The late 1800s saw the United States make the transition from an agricultural society to an industrial one, and Taylor was part of this transformation process. About the same time Taylor was developing a uniquely American approach to the design of work, Max Weber was undertaking a classic work on religion and capitalism in Germany.[2] Weber's lasting legacies to management and organizational behavior are found in his notions of bureaucracies and the Protestant ethic, the latter an important feature of Chapter 5 in the text. Another major event of this era, as noted in Table A.1, was Walter Cannon's discovery of the stress response in about 1915. This discovery laid a foundation for psychosomatic medicine, industrial hygiene, and an understanding of the emotional components of health at work and play.[3] Finally, the first quarter of the twentieth century saw the initiation of the Hawthorne studies, a major research advancement in understanding people at work.[4] The Hawthorne studies are discussed in some depth in the second half of this brief history.

A.1	One Hundred Years Plus of Progress in Organizational Behavior
1890s	· Frederick Taylor's development of scientific management
1900s	· Max Weber's concept of bureaucracy and the Protestant ethic
1910s	· Walter Cannon's discovery of the "emergency (stress) response"
1920s	· Elton Mayo's illumination studies in the textile industry
	· The Hawthorne studies at Western Electric Company
1930s	· Kurt Lewin, Ronald Lippitt, and Ralph White's early leadership studies
1940s	· Abraham Maslow's need hierarchy motivation theory
	· B. F. Skinner's formulation of the behavioral approach
	· Charles Walker and Robert Guest's studies of routine work
1950s	· Ralph Stogdill's Ohio State leadership studies
	· Douglas McGregor's examination of the human side of enterprise
	· Frederick Herzberg's two-factor theory of motivation and job enrichment
1960s	· Arthur Turner and Paul Lawrence's studies of diverse industrial jobs
	· Robert Blake and Jane Mouton's Leadership Grid
	· Patricia Cain Smith's studies of satisfaction in work and retirement
	· Fred Fiedler's contingency theory of leadership
1970s	· J. Richard Hackman and Greg Oldham's job characteristics theory
	· Edward Lawler's approach to pay and organizational effectiveness
	· Robert House's path–goal and charismatic theories of leadership
1980s	· Peter Block's political skills for empowered managers
	· Charles Manz's approach to self-managed work teams
	· Edgar Schein's approach to leadership and organizational culture
1990s	· Robert Solomon's personal integrity, character, and virtue ethics
	· Martin Seligman's positive psychology of hope and strength
2000s	· Fred Luthan's new framework of positive organizational behavior (POB)
	· Bruce Avolio's approach to authentic leadership

From the end of the 1930s through the 1950s, major contributions were made to the understanding of leadership, motivation, and behavior in organizations, as noted in Table A.1.[5] Lewin, Lippitt, and White's early examination of autocratic, democratic, and laissez-faire leadership styles was followed over a decade later by Ralph Stogdill's extensive studies at The Ohio State University focusing on leader behaviors. This marked a point of departure from earlier leadership studies, which had focused on the traits of the leader. Abraham Maslow proposed a need hierarchy of human motivation during the early 1940s, which served as a foundation for Douglas McGregor's theorizing in the 1950s about assumptions concerning the human side of a business enterprise. The 1950s was the decade in which Frederick Herzberg developed a new theory of motivation, which he later translated into an approach to job design, called *job enrichment*. This is quite different from the approach to designing work that Charles Walker and Robert Guest formulated a decade earlier in response to the problems they found with routine work. Attention was also given to group dynamics during this era in an effort to explain small group behavior.[6]

The 1960s and 1970s saw continued attention to theories of motivation, leadership, the design of work, and job satisfaction.[7] For example, Arthur Turner and Paul Lawrence's studies of diverse industrial jobs in various industries were forerunners for the research program of Richard Hackman and Greg Oldham, which led to their job characteristics theory a decade later. Robert Blake and Jane Mouton's Leadership Grid was a variation on the Ohio State leadership studies of a decade earlier, whereas Fred Fiedler's contingency theory of leadership was an entirely new approach to leadership that emerged during the 1960s. Robert House proposed path–goal and charismatic theories of leadership during this era, and Edward Lawler drew attention to the importance of pay in performance and organizational effectiveness.

The 1980s saw attention shift to organizational culture, teamwork, and political skills in organizations. Peter Block drew our attention to the political skills required to empower managers in increasingly challenging work environments, whereas Charles Manz directed attention to teamwork and self-managed teams. Leadership continued to be an important topic, and Edgar Schein formulated a framework for understanding how leaders created, embedded, and maintained an organizational culture. Throughout the changing and unfolding story of the study of organizational behavior during the twentieth century, there has been a common theme: How do we understand people, their psychology, and their behavior in the workplace?[8]

The 1990s saw an emerging concern for personal integrity, character, and virtue ethics as well as the new domain of positive psychology. The political scandals and impeachment hearings during the Clinton administration led to discussions in corporate boardrooms and college campuses about personal integrity and character. Robert Solomon framed an approach to personal virtues using an Aristotelian approach to business ethics.[9] Solomon extends his philosophy of personal integrity and character by articulating how they can lead to corporate success.[10] A second important development during the 1990s was the emergence of positive psychology, which Martin Seligman suggested was an underdeveloped aspect of the science of human behavior. The focus of positive psychology is building upon human strength and encouraging hope and optimism.[11] Joy, exhilaration, mirth, and happiness are positive emotions within this domain.[12] Since the year 2000, Fred Luthans has extended positive psychology with his emphasis on positive organizational behavior (POB), which emphasizes confidence, hope, optimism, and other positive attributes at work.[13] Bruce Avolio draws upon POB research in his approach to authentic leadership.[14]

The intention of this brief historical review and time line in Table A.1 is to give you a sense of perspective on the drama of unfolding research programs, topics, and investigators who have brought us to the present state of knowledge and practice in organizational behavior. Although the text addresses the field in a topical manner by chapter, we think it is important that students of organizational behavior have a sense of historical perspective of the whole field. We now turn to the Hawthorne studies, one of the seminal research programs from the early part of the twentieth century.

THE HAWTHORNE STUDIES

Initiated in 1925 with a grant from Western Electric, the Hawthorne studies were among the most significant advances in the understanding of organizational behavior during the past century. They were preceded by a series of studies of illumination conducted by Elton Mayo in the textile industry of Philadelphia. The research at the Hawthorne Works (an industrial manufacturing facility in Cicero, Illinois) was directed by Fritz Roethlisberger and consisted of four separate studies throughout a seven-year period.[15] These studies included (1) experiments in illumination, (2) the relay assembly test room study, (3) experiments in interviewing workers, and (4) the bank wiring room study. We will briefly examine this research program.

Experiments in Illumination

The experiments in illumination were a direct follow-up to Mayo's earlier work in the textile industry. At Hawthorne, the experiments in illumination consisted of a series of studies of test groups, in which the researchers varied illumination levels, and control groups, in which conditions were held constant. The purpose was to examine the relation of the quality and quantity of illumination to the efficiency of industrial workers. The experiments began in 1925 and extended over several years.

The researchers were surprised to discover that productivity increased to roughly the same rate in both test and control groups. It was only in the final experiment, in which they decreased illumination levels to 0.06 footcandle (roughly moonlight intensity), that an appreciable decline in output occurred. The anticipated finding of a positive, linear relationship between illumination and industrial efficiency was simply not found. The researchers concluded that the results were "screwy" in the absence of this simple, direct cause-and-effect relationship.

It is from these first experiments that the term *Hawthorne Effect* was coined, referring originally to the fact that people's knowledge that they are being studied leads them to modify their behavior. A closer consideration of the Hawthorne Effect reveals that it is poorly understood and has taken on different meanings with the passage of time.[16] Hence, it has become somewhat an imprecise concept.

Relay Assembly Test Room Study

The researchers next set out to study workers segregated according to a range of working condition variables, such as workroom temperature and humidity, work schedule, rest breaks, and food consumption. The researchers chose five women in the relay assembly test room and kept careful records of the predictor variables, as well as output (measuring the time it took each woman to assemble a telephone relay of approximately forty parts).

Again, there was little the researchers were able to conclude from the actual data in this study in terms of a relationship between the predictor variables and industrial efficiency. However, they began to suspect that employee attitudes and sentiments were critically important variables not previously taken into account. Therefore, the researchers underwent a radical change of thought.

Experiments in Interviewing Workers

In 1928, a number of the researchers began a program of going into the workforce, without their normal tools and equipment, for the purpose of getting the workers to talk about what was important to them. Nearly 20,000 workers were interviewed over a period of two years, and in this interviewing process a major breakthrough occurred. The interview study was a form of research in which the investigators did not have a set of preconceptions concerning what they would find, as was the case in the two earlier phases of research. Rather, they set out to sympathetically and skillfully listen to what each worker was saying. As the interviewing progressed, the researchers discovered that the workers would open up and talk freely about what were the most important, and at times problematic, issues on their minds. The researchers discovered a rich and intriguing world previously unexamined within the Hawthorne Works.

Ultimately, Roethlisberger and his colleagues formulated guidelines for the conduct of interviews, and these guidelines became the basis for contemporary interviewing and active listening skills.[17] The discovery of the informal organization and its relationship to the formal organization began during the interview study. This led to a richer understanding of the social, interpersonal dynamics of people at work.

The Bank Wiring Room Study

The concluding study at Hawthorne was significant because it confirmed the importance of one aspect of the informal organization on worker productivity. Specifically, the researchers studied workers in the bank wiring room and found that the behavioral norms set by the work group had a powerful influence over the productivity of the group. The higher the norms, the greater the productivity. The lower the norms, the lower the productivity. The power of the peer group and the importance of group influence on individual behavior and productivity were confirmed in the bank wiring room.

The Hawthorne studies laid a foundation for understanding people's social and psychological behavior in the workplace. Some of the methods used at Hawthorne, such as the experimental design methods and the interviewing technique, are used today for research in organizations. However, the discipline of organizational behavior is more important than the psychology of people at work and the sociology of their behavior in organizations. Organizational behavior emerges from a wide range of interdisciplinary influences.

How Do We Know What We Know about Organizational Behavior?

By Uma Sekaran

This book has examined the skills and knowledge that managers need to be successful in their jobs. But how do you know how much faith to put in all the information you acquire from textbooks and management journals? Are some theories and statements more applicable than others? Even when applicable, will they apply at all times and under all circumstances? You can find answers to these important questions once you know the foundation on which theories and assertions rest. This appendix provides that foundation. It first examines why managers need to know about research and then discusses the basis for knowledge in this field. It then looks at the research process and research design and ends with a discussion of how research knowledge affects you.

WHY MANAGERS SHOULD KNOW ABOUT RESEARCH

Why is it necessary for you to know about research? First, this knowledge helps you determine how much of what is offered in textbooks is of practical use to you as a manager. Second, a basic understanding of how good empirical research is done can make you an effective manager by helping you to make intelligent decisions about research proposals and reports that reach your desk. Third, it enables you to become an informed and discriminating consumer of research articles published in the management journals that you need to read to keep up with new ideas and technology. For your convenience, a list of the current academic and practitioner-oriented journals that frequently publish articles on organizational behavior is provided in Table B.1

B.1   Journals with Organizational Behavior Articles

Academic Journals	Practitioner-Oriented Journals
Academy of Management Journal	Academy of Management Learning & Education
Academy of Management Review	Business Horizons
Administrative Science Quarterly	California Management Review
Advances in International Comparative Management	Columbia Journal of World Business
Group and Organization Studies	Harvard Business Review
Human Relations	Human Resource Development Quarterly
Human Resource Management	Industrial Relations
Human Resource Management Review	Industry Week
Human Resource Planning	Organizational Dynamics
Industrial and Labor Relations Review	Personnel Journal
International Journal of Human Resource Management	SAM Advanced Management Journal
International Journal of Management	Sloan Management Review
Journal of Applied Behavioral Science	Supervision
Journal of Applied Business Research	Training
Journal of Applied Psychology	Training and Development Journal
Journal of Business	
Journal of Business Ethics	
Journal of Business Research	
Journal of International Business Studies	
Journal of Management	
Journal of Management Studies	
Journal of Occupational Psychology	
Journal of Organizational Behavior	
Journal of Organizational Behavior Management	
Journal of Vocational Behavior	
Organizational Behavior and Human Decision Processes	
Personnel Administrator	
Sex Roles	
Women in Business	

Understanding scientific research methods enables you to differentiate between good and appropriate research, which you can apply in your setting, and flawed or inappropriate research, which you cannot use. Moreover, knowledge of techniques such as sampling design enables you to decide whether the results of a study using a particular type of sample in certain types of organizations are applicable to your setting.

Managers need to understand, predict, and control the research-oriented problems in their environment. Some of these problems may be relatively simple and can be solved through simple data gathering and analysis. Others may be relatively complex, needing the assistance of researchers or consultants. In either case, without some basic knowledge of scientific research, managers will be unable to solve the problems themselves or to work effectively with consultants.

Managers need to discuss their problems with consultants in a useful way. This includes informing the problem solvers right at the start of the consulting process of any constraints (such as company records that are off limits to outsiders) or of types of recommendations that will not be considered (such as laying off or hiring more people). Such discussions not only save time but also help the managers and researchers start off on the right foot. Managers who don't understand the important aspects of research will not be equipped to anticipate and forestall the inevitable hurdles in manager–researcher interactions. Also, paying a consultant handsomely for a research report will not help the company unless the manager is capable of determining how much scientific value can be placed on the findings. For these and other reasons, a working knowledge of the scientific research process and research design is necessary.

OUR BASIS FOR KNOWLEDGE

Observation and scientific data gathering have led to some of our knowledge about management. For instance, very early on, Frederick Winslow Taylor observed, studied, experimented, and demonstrated how coal-mining operations could be managed more efficiently by changing the way men shoveled coal—changing how the shovel was handled, how the body movements were made, and so on. The era of scientific management that Taylor's work ushered in provided much knowledge about how management could improve efficiency. This type of knowledge is not easy to come by, however, when we are examining employees' feelings, attitudes, and behaviors. Our knowledge of organizational behavior stems instead from armchair theories, case studies, and scientific research.

Armchair Theories

In trying to understand organizational behavior, management experts and scholars initially resorted to *armchair theorizing*—theorizing based on the observation of various phenomena and behaviors in the workplace. For instance, Douglas McGregor, through observation and experience, theorized that managers have two different world views of employees. Some managers (Theory X) assume that employees are, by nature, lazy and not very bright, that they dislike responsibility and prefer to be led rather than to lead, and that they resist change. Other managers (Theory Y) assume that employees have the opposite characteristics. McGregor's concept of Theory X and Theory Y managers has become a classic armchair theory.

Few people either totally accept or totally dispute this theory because of the lack of hard data to either substantiate or negate this interesting notion. Armchair theories are based on natural observation with no systematic experimentation and hence are not very useful for application in organizations.

Case Studies

Case studies—studies that examine the environment and background in which events occur in specific organizations in a particular period of time—help us to understand behavior in those organizations at that time. For example, we could study a particular organization in depth to determine the contributing factors that led to its fast recovery after a prolonged recession. We might find several factors, including price reductions, the offering of good incentives to a highly motivated workforce, and the taking of big risks. However, the findings from this one-time study of an organization offer only limited knowledge about fast recovery from recessions, because the findings may not hold true for other organizations or for even the same organization at another time. The replication of case studies is almost impossible, since environmental and background factors are rarely the same from organization to organization. Most of the companies whose problems you have been asked to solve are from real cases written by management scholars who studied the companies. The solutions they found may not work for other organizations experiencing similar problems, since differences in size, technology, environment, labor force, clientele, and other internal and external factors may exist. However, through case studies, we do gather information and gain insights and knowledge that might help us to develop theories and test them later.

Scientific Research

Empirical or data-based *scientific research* identifies a problem and solves it after a systematic gathering and analysis of the relevant data. This type of research offers in-depth understanding, confidence in the findings, and the capability of applying the knowledge gained to similar organizations. Scientific research is the main focus of this appendix.

SCIENTIFIC INQUIRY

Scientific inquiry involves a well-planned and well-organized systematic effort to identify and solve a problem. It encompasses a series of well-thought-out and carefully executed activities that help to solve the problem—as opposed to the symptoms—that is identified.

Purposes of Scientific Research: Applied and Basic Research

Scientific inquiry can be undertaken for two different purposes: (1) to solve an existing problem that a particular organization faces or (2) to examine problems that organizations generally encounter and to generate solutions, thereby expanding the knowledge base. Research undertaken to solve an existing problem in a specific setting is *applied research*. In this type of research, the findings are immediately applied to solve the problem. Many professors acting as consultants to organizations do applied research.

Research undertaken to add information to our existing base of knowledge is *basic research*. A large number of issues are of common interest to many organizations—for example, how to increase the productivity of a diverse workforce or how to eradicate sexual harassment in the workplace. The knowledge gained from research on such general issues can become useful later for application in organizational settings, but that is not the primary goal of basic research. The goal is to generate knowledge with which to build better theories that can be tested later. Basic research is often published in academic journals.

The Two Faces of Science: Theory and Empirical Research

Theory and empirical research are the two faces of science. Organizations benefit when good theories are developed and then substantiated through scientific research, because the results can then be confidently used for problem solving.

Theory A *theory* is a postulated network of associations among various factors that a researcher is interested in investigating. For example, given what has been published thus far, you might theorize that self-confident employees perceive their work environment positively, which fosters their productivity, which in turn generates more profits for the company. In constructing this theory, you have postulated a positive relationship among (1) the self-confidence of employees and their positive attitude toward their work environment, (2) their attitude toward the work environment and their productivity, and (3) their productivity and the company's profits.

No doubt, this theory appeals to common sense. But in order to establish whether or not it holds true, we need to actually test it in organizations. Thus, theories offer the basis for doing scientific, data-based research; the theories and research together add to our knowledge. Conducting empirical research without the basis of sound theories does not steer us in the right direction, and building theories without empirically testing them limits their value.

The usefulness of good theories cannot be overstated. A good theory is formulated only after a careful examination of all the previous research and writings on the topic of interest, so that no factor already established as important is inadvertently omitted. Theory building offers unique opportunities to look at phenomena from different perspectives or to add new dimensions to existing ways of examining a phenomenon. New insights and creative ideas for theory building can come through personal observation, intuition, or even informal discussions with employees.

Testable theories are theories whose hypothesized relationships among measurable variables can be empirically tested and verified. When tested and substantiated repeatedly, such theories become the foundation on which subsequent theory building progresses. The next issue of interest is how theories are affirmed through empirical research.

Empirical Research As we have just seen, theories are of no practical use unless we have confidence that they work and can be applied to problem solving in organizational settings. Empirical research allows us to test the value of theories.

Empirical research is research that involves identifying the factors to be studied, gathering the relevant data, analyzing them, and drawing conclusions from the results of data analysis. It could involve simple qualitative analysis of the data, or it could be more complex, using a hypothetico-deductive approach. In *qualitative analysis*, responses to open-ended questions are obtained and meaningfully classified, and certain conclusions are drawn. In the *hypothetico-deductive approach*, a problem is identified, defined, and studied in depth. Then, a theory is formulated. From that theory, testable hypotheses are generated. Next, a research design is developed, relevant data are gathered and analyzed, results are interpreted, and conclusions (or deductions) are drawn from the results. Figure B.1 illustrates this approach.

To be called "scientific," research should conform to certain basic principles. It should be conducted objectively (without subjective biases). It should have a good

B.1   Steps in the Hypothetico-Deductive Approach to Research

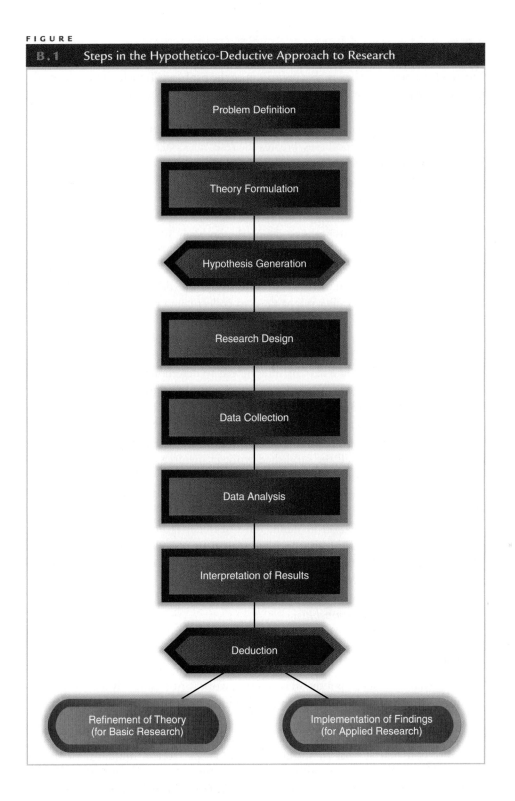

and rigorous design (which we will examine shortly). It should be testable; that is, the conjectured relationships among factors in a setting should be capable of being tested. It should be replicable; that is, the results must be similar each time similar research is conducted. Finally, the findings should be generalizable (applicable to similar settings). It goes without saying, then, that scientific research offers precision (a good degree of exactitude) and a high degree of confidence in the results of the research (e.g., the researcher can say that 95 percent of the time, the results generated by the research will hold true, with only a 5 percent chance of its not being so).

THE RESEARCH PROCESS

The research process starts with a definition of the problem. To help define the problem, the researcher may interview people and study published materials in the area of interest in order to better understand what is happening in the environment. After defining the problem in clear and precise terms, the researcher develops a theoretical framework, generates hypotheses, creates the research design, collects data, analyzes data, interprets results, and draws conclusions.

Problem Definition

The first job for the researcher is to define the problem. It is often difficult to state precisely the specific research question to be investigated. The researcher might simply know the broad area of interest—for instance, discrimination—without being clear about which aspect of discrimination to study. In order to focus on the issue to be investigated, the researcher might need to collect some preliminary information that will help to narrow down the issue.

Such information can be obtained by interviewing people in organizations and by doing a literature survey. For example, employees of different gender, race, age, physical ability, and the like may be interviewed to determine the specific aspect of discrimination on which to focus. These interviews also provide insight into what the employees (rather than the researchers) consider important. The literature survey ensures that no pertinent variable is inadvertently omitted and that there is a credible and defensible basis for the research to be done. The researcher conducts an exhaustive search of all the published work in the area of interest to determine what research has been done thus far in the particular area and with what results. The search consumes a lot of time, as one must wade through several psychological, sociological, anthropological, and other relevant journals.

With all this information in hand, the researcher is now ready to define the problem. A well-defined, precise problem statement is a must for any study. The problem definition for the broad topic of discrimination could be this: *What are the important factors that contribute to employees' beliefs that they are being discriminated against by their immediate supervisor in cross-gender or cross-racial supervisor–employee relationships?*

Theoretical Framework

The next step is to develop a theoretical framework for the study. It involves focusing on the pertinent variables for the study and discussing the anticipated or theorized network of connections among the variables. For the discrimination problem, the framework might identify three factors related to employees' beliefs that they were discriminated against by the supervisor: (1) the level of mutual trust that is perceived by the employee to exist between the supervisor and employee (high to low), (2) the manner in which the supervisor offers performance feedback to the employee (in a forthright and helpful manner rather than in a derogatory and hurtful way), and (3) the extent to which the supervisor plays the role of mentor to the employee (training the subordinate and promoting the person's interests in career advancement to being indifferent toward the employee's career progress).

A network of logical connections among these four variables of interest to the study—discrimination (the dependent variable) and trust, performance feedback, and mentoring (the three independent variables)—can then be formulated. These connections with the anticipated nature and direction of the relationships among the variables are postulated in the theoretical framework.

Hypotheses

On the basis of the theoretical framework, the researcher next generates hypotheses. A *hypothesis* is a testable statement of the conjectured relationship between two or more variables. It is derived from the connections postulated in the theoretical framework. An example of a hypothesis is this: The more the employee perceives the supervisor as performing the mentoring role, the less the employee will feel discriminated against by the supervisor. The statement can be tested through data gathering and correlational analysis to see if it is supported.

Research Design

The next step in the research process is research design. Because this step is complex, it is covered in a separate section of the appendix, after the research process.

Data Collection

After creating the research design, the researcher must gather the relevant data. In our example of the discrimination problem, we would collect data on the four variables of interest from employees in one or more organizations, obtain information about their race and gender and that of their supervisors, and seek such demographic data as age, educational level, and position in the organization. This information helps us describe the sample and enables us to see later if demographic characteristics make a difference in the results. For example, we might discover during data analysis that older employees sense less discrimination than their younger counterparts. Such information could even provide a basis for further theory development.

Data Analysis

Having collected the data, the researcher must next analyze it, using statistical procedures to test whether the hypotheses have been substantiated. In the case of the discrimination hypothesis, if a correlational analysis between the variables of mentoring and discrimination indicates a significant negative correlation, the hypothesis will have been supported. In other words, we have been correct in conjecturing that the more the supervisor is perceived as a mentor, the less the employee feels discriminated against. Each of the hypotheses formulated from the theoretical framework is tested, and the results are examined.

Interpreting Results and Drawing Conclusions

The final step is to interpret the results of the data analysis and draw conclusions about them. In our example, if a significant negative relationship is indeed found between mentoring and discrimination, then one of our conclusions might be that mentoring helps fight feelings of discrimination. We might therefore recommend that if the organization wants to create a climate where employees do not feel discriminated against, supervisors should actively engage in mentoring. If the organization accepts this recommendation, it might conduct training programs to make supervisors better mentors. By testing and substantiating each of the hypotheses, we might find a multitude of solutions to overcome the perception of discrimination by employees.

Summary

We can see that every step in the research process is important. Unless the problem is well defined, the research endeavor will be fruitless. If a thorough literature survey is not done, a defensible theoretical framework cannot be developed and useful hypotheses cannot be generated—which compromises effective problem solving. Using the correct methods in data gathering and analysis and drawing relevant conclusions are all indispensable methodological steps for conducting empirical research. We next examine some of the research design issues that are integral to conducting good research.

RESEARCH DESIGN

Issues regarding research design relate particularly to how the variables are measured, how the data are collected, what sampling design is used, and how the data are analyzed. Before decisions in these areas are made, some details about the nature and purpose of the study have to be determined so there is a good match between the purpose of the study and the design choices. If the research design does not mesh with the research goals, the right solutions will not be found.

Important Concepts in Research Design

Five important concepts in research design must be understood before an adequate design can be created: nature of study, study setting, types of study, researcher interference, and time horizon. The *nature of study* is the purpose of the study—whether it is to establish correlations among variables or causation. The *study setting* could either be the environment in which the phenomena studied normally and naturally occur—the *field*—or be in a contrived, artificial setting, such as a laboratory. The *type of study* is either experimental (to establish causal connections) or correlational (to establish correlations). An experiment could be conducted in an artificial setting—a *lab experiment*, or it could be conducted in the organization itself where events naturally occur—*field experiment*. *Researcher interference* is the extent to which the researcher manipulates the independent variable and controls other contaminating factors in the study setting that are likely to affect the cause–effect relationship. The *time horizon* is the number of data collection points in the study; the study could be either one-shot (various types of data are collected only once during the investigation) or longitudinal (same or similar data are collected more than once from the same system during the course of the study).

Purpose of Study and Design Choices

One of the primary issues to consider before making any research design decision is the purpose of the study. Is the research to establish a causal relationship (that variable *X* causes variable *Y*), or is it to detect any correlations that might exist between two or more variables? A study to establish a cause–effect relationship differs in many areas (e.g., the setting, type of study, extent of researcher interference with the ongoing processes, and time frame of the study) from a study to examine correlations among factors. Figure B.2 depicts the fit between the goal of the study and the characteristics of the study.

Causal Studies

Studies conducted to detect causal relationships call for an experimental design, considerable researcher interference, and a longitudinal time span. The design could consist of laboratory experiments, field experiments, or simulations.

B.2   Fit between Goal of Study and Study Characteristics

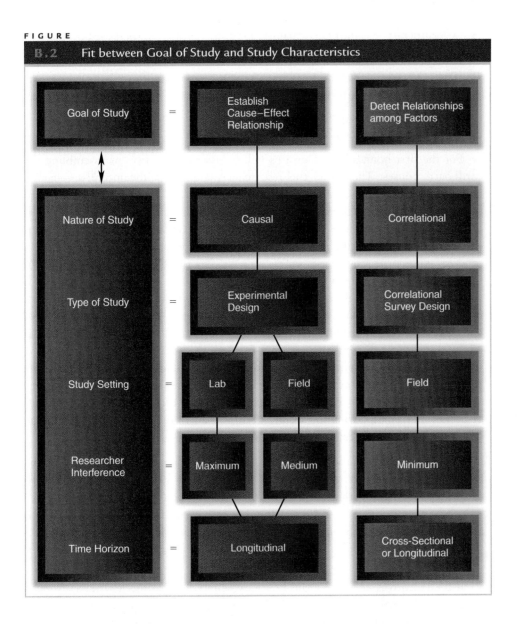

Laboratory Experiments   A rigorous causal study may call for a *laboratory experiment*, in which participants are exposed to an artificial environment and an artificial stimulus in order to establish a cause–effect relationship. The experiment is set up with maximum researcher interference; both manipulation and controls (described later) are used, and data are collected from the subjects more than once during the experiment (longitudinally). Following is an example of how a lab experiment is conducted.

Suppose a manager wants to know which of two incentives—offering stock options or giving a bonus—would better improve employee productivity. To determine this, the manager has to experiment with each of the two types of incentives to see which offers better results. Not knowing how to proceed, the manager might hire a researcher who is likely to recommend conducting a lab experiment first and then a field experiment. The lab experiment firmly establishes the causal relationship, and the field experiment confirms whether or not the causal relationship established during the lab experiment holds good in the organizational setting.

To set up a lab experiment in which thirty subjects participate, perform the following:

1. An artificial setting is created. It will consist of three conference rooms in which the experiment is conducted after regular work hours.

2. A simple task—assembling cardboard houses—is given to the subjects, who take part in the experiment for two hours.

3. The subjects are given an imaginary bonus in the form of cardboard chips and stock options in the form of fake certificates.

4. Each subject is randomly assigned to one of three conference rooms, thus forming three ten-member groups.

For the first hour, all three groups will be assigned the task of assembling the cardboard houses. Thereafter, the researcher manipulates the incentives—giving one group stock options, another a bonus, and a third, called the control group, no incentives at all. The researcher has already exercised tight control to ensure that all three groups have more or less the same types of members in terms of ability, experience, and the like by randomly assigning members to each of the groups. In random assignment, every member has an equal chance of being assigned to any of the groups. This control helps avoid contamination of the cause–effect relationship, since all factors that might affect the causal relationship (age, ability, and so on) are randomly distributed among the groups.

The data are collected at two different times in the following manner. At the end of the first hour, when all three groups have worked without any incentives, the number of cardboard houses built by each group will be recorded by the researcher. The numbers are again counted and recorded at the end of the second hour, after the introduction of the incentives. Determining the difference between the number of houses assembled during the second hour and the number assembled during the first hour for the three groups clarifies the following two issues:

• Do the incentives make any difference at all to performance? Obviously, if the performance has increased during the second hour for either or both of the two groups provided with incentives, while there is no difference for the control group, then it is safe to surmise that either or both of the incentives have caused performance to rise. If there is no difference in the production between the second and first hour for all three groups, then, of course, the incentives have not caused an increase in performance.

• If the incentives do make a difference, which of the two incentives has worked better? By examining which group—the group that received the stock options or the group that received the bonus—performed better during the second hour, we know which of the two incentives worked better. The incentive that increases performance more will obviously be preferred by the company.

Because all possible contaminating factors have been controlled by the random assignment of members to the three groups, the cause–effect relationships found can be accepted with a high degree of confidence.

Field Experiments What occurred in the tightly controlled artificial lab setting may or may not happen in an organizational setting, where many of the factors (such as employees' ages and experience) cannot be controlled and the jobs to be done might be quite complex. But having established a strong causal relationship in the lab setting, the researcher is eager to see if that relationship is generalizable to the organization, or field setting.

For the field experiment, three experimental cells (three branches or departments of the company, or whatever other units are appropriate for the organization) can be chosen. Real bonus and stock options can be offered to two groups, whereas the third group is treated as a control group and given no incentives. Work performance data can be collected for the three cells before the incentives are introduced and again six months after the incentives are introduced.

While it is possible to manipulate the incentive in a field experiment, it is not possible to control the contaminating factors (ability, experience, and so on). Because employees are already placed, members cannot be randomly assigned to the three units. Under these circumstances, researcher interference can be only partial, since the independent variable can be manipulated but other factors cannot be controlled. Even manipulating the independent variable is not easy, because people in organizations get suspicious and anxious as the word spreads that some strange changes are being made at some sites. Not only does this cause apprehension among employees, but it may also produce invalid results. Because of these difficulties, very few field experiments are conducted in organizational behavior research. However, if the manipulation is successful and the results of the field experiment are similar to those of the lab experiment, the manager can confidently introduce the changes needed to obtain the desired results.

If you read journal articles describing experimental designs, you will want to see how well the manipulations were done and how tightly the contaminating variables were controlled. Were the independent variables successfully manipulated, or did the subjects see through the manipulations? If the subjects in the various groups differed in some characteristics that are relevant to the cause–effect relationship, then it cannot be said with confidence that only the manipulated independent variable caused the dependent variable. Other factors in the setting might also have influenced the dependent variable, and they might be impossible to trace.[1]

Simulations Somewhere between lab and field experiments are *simulations*—experiments that are conducted in settings that closely resemble field settings. The specially created settings look much like actual environments in which events normally occur—for example, offices with desks, computers, and phones. Members of the experimental group are randomly selected and exposed to real-world experiences over a period of time, during which their behavior is studied. A free simulation for studying leadership styles, called "Looking Glass," has been used in management classes. This simulation enables students to study different kinds of behavior as the researcher manipulates some of the stimuli while allowing the flow of events to be governed by the reactions of the participants.[2]

Correlational Studies

Researchers and managers may not be interested in establishing causal connections. Instead, they may want to understand, describe, or predict occurrences in the workplace. In general, they want to know which factors are related to desirable outcomes (such as employee loyalty to the organization) and which to undesirable outcomes (such as high turnover rates). *Correlational studies* are studies that are not specifically geared toward establishing cause–effect relationships. Such studies may be *exploratory*—trying to understand certain relationships; *descriptive*—trying to describe certain phenomena at the workplace; or *analytical*—focusing on testing hypotheses. Correlational studies are always conducted in the field setting with minimum researcher interference, and they can be either one-shot or longitudinal. The vast majority of the research articles published in organizational behavior journals are field studies examining correlations among factors.

To conduct a scientific study, whether causal or correlational, certain research design decisions must be made. As Figure B.3 shows, these decisions involve measurement issues, data collection methods, sampling design, and data analysis procedures.

Measurement Issues

We saw earlier that it is difficult to measure attitudes, feelings, and other abstract concepts. Since the measurement of variables in the organizational sciences is not

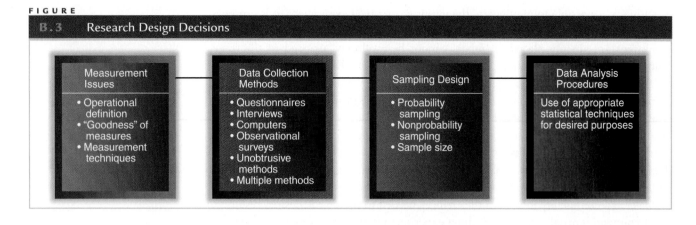

Measurement Issues	Data Collection Methods	Sampling Design	Data Analysis Procedures
• Operational definition • "Goodness" of measures • Measurement techniques	• Questionnaires • Interviews • Computers • Observational surveys • Unobtrusive methods • Multiple methods	• Probability sampling • Nonprobability sampling • Sample size	Use of appropriate statistical techniques for desired purposes

as exact as in the physical sciences, management research cannot be completely scientific. It is possible, however, to minimize biases in measurement by carefully developing valid and reliable measures for even abstract concepts. The primary aspects in measurement are operational definition, the "goodness" of measures, and the measurement techniques to be used.

Operational Definition Attitudes such as job satisfaction and organizational commitment do not easily lend themselves to measurement. To measure them, we first need to translate them into observable behaviors. *Operational definition* is the reduction of the level of abstraction of concepts so as to identify the observable behaviors and measure them.

For example, how can we measure the motivational level of individuals? We know that highly motivated people engage in the following types of behaviors, among others. They are driven by work, and they keep persevering even if they initially fail to accomplish what they want. We can measure the abstract concept of motivation by developing an instrument that asks subjects to respond to several suitably worded questions tapping these behaviors.[3] Most of the abstract concepts that are important to the study of organizational behavior have been operationally defined by scholars, who have developed "good" instruments for measuring them.[4]

"Goodness" of Measures "Good" measurement instruments offer researchers the confidence that they do indeed measure what is desired to be measured and do so in a thorough and accurate manner. The goodness of instruments is established through their validity and reliability.

Validity is our confidence that the instrument used does indeed measure the concept it is supposed to measure. For instance, if a twenty-item instrument is developed to measure job satisfaction, we need to know that it does indeed measure job satisfaction, not employees' general happiness.

Researchers usually establish various types of validity for the measures they use. Among them are content validity, criterion-related validity, predictive validity, construct validity, and convergent and discriminant validity. Journal articles often explain the types of validity established for the instrument used, especially if it is newly developed. In general, only such measures as are both valid and reliable are frequently used by researchers.[5]

Reliability is the ability of an instrument to accurately and stably measure a concept over time and across situations. For example, it is not enough for an instrument to measure job satisfaction; it must do so consistently and accurately time and again in all settings. Most researchers discuss the reliability of their instruments in terms of stability and consistency. Test–retest reliability is one indicator of the stability of a measure over time. Cronbach's alpha and split-half reliability are two indicators of the internal consistency of instruments. These are the terms you are likely to come across in published empirical research.

Authors of studies usually provide details of the measures they use and, at a minimum, cite their source. Journal editors and reviewers try to ensure that studies to be published have used valid and reliable measures. Discriminant readers of journals reporting empirical studies pay attention to the "goodness" of the measures. If variables are not validly and reliably measured, how can we place any confidence in the results of the study?

Measurement Techniques Concepts are not measured solely through questionnaires or interviews. Sometimes, in order to tap certain ideas, feelings, and thoughts that are not easily verbalized, researchers use *projective tests*—word association, sentence completion, thematic apperception tests, and ink-blot tests are some familiar projective tests. In word association (e.g., work could be associated with excitement or drudgery) and sentence completion ("I like") tests, it is expected that the respondent will draw on deeply embedded feelings, attitudes, and orientations when answering. Marketing researchers use these techniques to assess consumer preferences. Thematic apperception tests and ink-blot tests ask the subject to offer a story or interpret an ink blot. They can be interpreted only by trained psychologists.

Data Collection Methods

Data can be collected through questionnaires, interviews, computers, observation, unobtrusive methods, or a combination of these. The most frequently used method in organizational behavior research is data collection through questionnaires.

Questionnaires A *questionnaire* is a written set of questions to which respondents record their answers, usually within a close range of alternatives given to them. Questionnaires can be mailed to respondents or administered personally.

Mail questionnaires are commonly used because of the large number of people who can be reached economically even when they are geographically dispersed. As a rule, however, they do not elicit a good response rate, even when stamped, self-addressed envelopes are enclosed for their return. (Researchers sometimes even include, as a small token of their appreciation, a one-dollar bill.) A 30 percent response rate for mail questionnaires is considered good. Mail responses generally fall far short of even this low percentage. Because of the low response rate, certain types of nonresponse biases can creep into research. For example, we cannot know if those who responded to the survey differ from those who did not. Thus, we cannot be sure that the data are representative of the population we are trying to study.

Personally administered questionnaires are questionnaires given to groups of subjects by the researcher, who collects the responses immediately after completion. This method ensures practically a 100 percent response rate. However, many organizations are reluctant to spare company time for the research effort unless the study is of vital importance to them.

Interviews *Interviews* have the potential to elicit a good deal of information. In *structured interviews*, specific questions are asked of all respondents, and the responses are noted by the interviewer. In *unstructured interviews*, there is no predetermined format; questions are framed according to responses given to the previous question. Structured interviews are conducted when the interviewer knows precisely what sort of information is needed. They are efficient in terms of the amount of time involved in both obtaining the required information and categorizing the data obtained. Unstructured interviews are conducted when the researcher wants to explore a problem or become more knowledgeable about particular situations.

Face-to-face interviews offer the researcher the advantage of being able to observe the interviewees as they respond to questions. Nonverbal messages transmitted by the interviewees can be observed and explored further. *Telephone interviews*, on the other hand, help the researcher reach a vast number of geographically dispersed individuals. In both face-to-face and telephone interviews, certain types of biases can enter. The way a question is worded and asked, the inflection of a voice, the frame of mind of the interviewee at the time the interview is conducted, and other factors can all contribute to biases in the data.

Computers *Computer-assisted interviewing* and *computer-aided surveys* will become more popular in the future as more and more people become comfortable using their computers at home and responding to questions contained on diskettes or displayed on Web sites. Interview and questionnaire methods of data collection are greatly facilitated through computers. However, computer literacy of respondents is a prerequisite for using computer-assisted data collection techniques effectively.

Observational Surveys *Observational surveys* are another data collection method whereby information is obtained without asking questions of subjects. In this method, the researcher observes firsthand what is going on and how people are behaving in the work setting. The data are collected by either nonparticipant observers (researchers who observe behavior as outsiders) or participant observers (integral members of the work team). An example of a nonparticipant study is one done by Henry Mintzberg, who observed the nature of managerial work over a period of time.

Like interviews, observational surveys can be either structured or unstructured. In a structured observational survey, the observer identifies the factors that are to be observed. For example, the observer might want to note the number of times a manager gives instructions to staff members and how much time this takes. In an unstructured observational survey, the observer might simply want to know how the manager spends the day at the workplace and might jot down all the activities the manager engages in and the time periods and frequencies involved.

Observational studies help prevent respondent bias, since information is not given by the subjects directly. Any bias that might creep in through the self-consciousness of subjects usually lasts only a few days. Then, subjects begin to function and behave normally, oblivious to the presence of the observer.

However, observer fatigue and observer bias cannot be totally avoided in observational studies. Moreover, when several observers are involved in a large research project, interobserver reliability could become an issue for concern; different observers might interpret and categorize the same behavior differently. This problem can be minimized by training the observers before the start of the project.

Unobtrusive Methods Data collection by *unobtrusive methods* offers valid and reliable information; bias is minimized because the source of the data is tangible elements rather than people. For example, the usage of library books can be determined by the wear and tear on them, a source of information more reliable than surveys of users of the library. The number of empty cans or bottles of pop in the recycling bins outside houses on garbage collection days would offer a good idea of the beverage consumption patterns in households. The personnel records of a company would indicate the absenteeism patterns of employees. Unobtrusive methods thus have the potential to offer the most reliable and unbiased data. They are, however, time consuming and labor intensive; also, the researcher must obtain the company's permission to gain access to such data.

Multiple Methods Each data collection method has advantages and disadvantages. The best approach is using multiple methods of collecting data, since it offers researchers a chance to cross-check the information obtained through the various methods. This approach, however, is expensive and thus is used infrequently in organizational behavior research.

When you read journal articles, you should assess the data collection methods used by the researchers to determine if they are adequate. Authors of published studies often discuss the limitations of their research and the biases they have attempted to minimize. The biases could relate to the types of measures used, the data collection methods adopted, the sampling design, and other research process and design issues. Sophisticated managers pay attention to all research design details in order to evaluate the quality of the research.

Sampling Design

Sampling is the process of drawing a limited number of subjects from a larger population or universe. Since researchers cannot possibly survey the entire universe of people they are interested in studying, they usually draw a sample of subjects from the population for investigation. The sampling design used makes a difference in the generalizability of the findings and determines the usefulness and scientific nature of the study. Sample size is another important issue. There are two broad categories of sampling—probability sampling and nonprobability sampling.

Probability Sampling *Probability sampling* is sampling that ensures that the elements in the population have some known chance, or probability, of being selected for the sample. Because of this, probability sampling designs offer more generalizability than nonprobability designs. There are many probability designs. The *simple random sampling* design, wherein every element in the population has a known and equal chance of being chosen, lends itself to the greatest generalizability. However, other probability designs can be more efficient and offer good generalizability as well. Among them are systematic sampling, stratified random sampling, cluster sampling, and area sampling.

In *systematic sampling*, every *n*th element in the population is chosen as a subject. In *stratified random sampling*, the population is first divided into meaningful strata (e.g., blue-collar and white-collar employees); a sample is then drawn from each stratum using either simple random sampling or systematic sampling. *Cluster sampling* is the random selection of chunks (clusters or groups) of elements from the population; every chunk has an equal chance of being selected, and all the members in each chosen chunk participate in the research. For example, in an attitude survey, three departments in an organization can be randomly chosen; all the members of the three departments are the subjects. *Area sampling* is cluster sampling confined to particular geographical areas, such as counties or city blocks. Marketing researchers use cluster and area sampling extensively for surveys.

Nonprobability Sampling For some research projects, probability sampling may be impossible or inappropriate. In such cases, *nonprobability sampling* may be used, even if generalizability is impaired or lost. In nonprobability sampling, the subjects do not have a known probability of being chosen for the study. For instance, the sample of subjects in a study of sexual harassment must come from those who have experienced such harassment; there is nothing to be gained by researching all the employees of the organization. When the choice of subjects for a study involves a limited number of people who are in a position to provide the required information, a probability sampling design is infeasible. The results of such a study are not generalizable; nevertheless, this type of sampling is the best way to learn about certain problems, such as sexual harassment.

Nonprobability sampling includes convenience sampling, judgment sampling, and quota sampling. In *convenience sampling*, information is collected from whoever is conveniently available. In *judgment sampling*, subjects who are in the best position to provide the required information are chosen. In *quota sampling*, people from different groups—some of which are underrepresented—are sampled for comparison purposes. One example might be a study of middle-class African Americans and whites.

As noted earlier, nonprobability sampling does not lend itself to generalizability. In reading research articles, you should determine the type of sampling design being used and how much generalizability the author claims for the research.

Sample Size Another critical issue in sampling is *sample size*. Too small or too large a sample could distort the results of the research. Tables providing ideal sample sizes for desired levels of precision and confidence are available to researchers. In examining any business report or journal article, you should note the sampling design and the sample size used by the researcher to assess the generalizability of the findings.

Data Analysis Procedures

Beyond good measures, appropriate data collection methods, and an acceptable sampling design, a good research project should also have suitable *data analysis procedures*. Some data cannot be subjected to sophisticated statistical tests. One example is data collected on a *nominal scale*, which divides subjects into mutually exclusive groups, such as men and women or the poor and the rich. Another example is data collected on an *ordinal scale*, which rank-orders the subjects and indicates a preference (X is better than Y). Various simple ways are available to analyze such data that are qualitative or nonparametric in nature. For instance, if we have categorized under distinct headings the verbal responses of organizational members to an open-ended question on how they perceive their work environment, a frequency count of the responses in each category would be adequate to describe how the work environment is perceived. Likewise, to detect if the gender of the worker (male versus female) is independent of members' commitment to the organization (less committed versus more committed), a simple x^2 (chi-square) test would suffice.

Sophisticated statistical tests are possible when data have been gathered on interval or ratio scales. Data collected on interval scales—through individuals' responses to questions on equal-appearing multipoint scales—allow for the computation of the arithmetic mean and standard deviation. Data collected on ratio scales also allow us to compute proportions and ratios. For example, an individual who weighs 250 pounds is twice as heavy as one who weighs 125 pounds. Pearson correlations can be calculated, and multiple regression and many multivariate analyses can be made with data obtained on interval and ratio scales. These sorts of analyses cannot be made with data obtained on nominal and ratio scales. Illustrations of the four scales appear in Figure B.4.

One decision that needs to be made before collecting the data is what kinds of analyses are needed to find answers to the research question. This decision will determine which scales should be used in data collection. Sometimes researchers are tempted to apply more sophisticated statistical analyses to data that do not lend themselves to such analyses (this includes sample sizes below thirty). Using inappropriate methods can negatively affect the interpretation of the results and can compromise the problem solution.

B.4 Illustrations of Four Data Analysis Scales

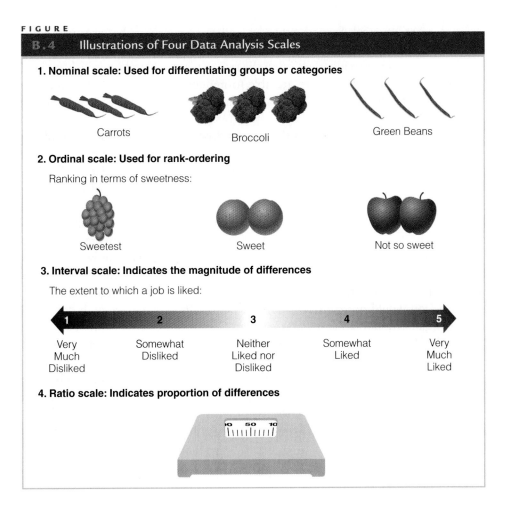

1. Nominal scale: Used for differentiating groups or categories

Carrots

Broccoli

Green Beans

2. Ordinal scale: Used for rank-ordering

Ranking in terms of sweetness:

Sweetest

Sweet

Not so sweet

3. Interval scale: Indicates the magnitude of differences

The extent to which a job is liked:

| 1 | 2 | 3 | 4 | 5 |

Very Much Disliked

Somewhat Disliked

Neither Liked nor Disliked

Somewhat Liked

Very Much Liked

4. Ratio scale: Indicates proportion of differences

Biases in Interpretation of Results

Thus far, we have examined the biases that would result from poor research process and design decisions. Another source of bias is in the interpretation of results. Objectivity plays a large part in the validity of interpretations from the results of data analysis. Objectivity may be difficult, however, if the results of the study do not substantiate the theories painstakingly developed by the researcher.

When data analysis does not substantiate one or more of the hypotheses generated, the researcher may be tempted to downplay the results or try to explain them away. For example, a researcher may say that the results were actually in the expected direction even though they were not statistically significant. If a hypothesis has not passed the appropriate statistical test, the hypothesis is just not substantiated, regardless of whether the results were in the theorized direction. When authors try to explain their results, you have to decide for yourself whether the explanations offered are valid.

ORGANIZATIONAL BEHAVIOR RESEARCH AND YOU

It is seldom possible to do completely scientific research in the field of organizational behavior. First, adherence to good research design principles may not always be possible, since certain choices (such as obtaining the most representative sample for better generalizability or utilizing the best data collection methods) may be beyond the researcher's control. Second, attitudes and feelings cannot be measured accurately. Hence, there are likely to be several types of biases in research in this field. However, by paying careful attention to the research process and rigorously making good research design choices, we are able to minimize the biases and enhance the objectivity, testability, replicability, precision and confidence, and generalizability of our research.

Bias can enter at every stage of the process, from problem definition to problem solution. Errors can creep into experimental designs by way of poor or inadequate manipulations and controls. They can enter into measurement, data collection, sampling, data analysis, interpretation of results, and the drawing of conclusions therefrom.

Unless managers are knowledgeable about some of the methodological flaws that can adversely affect research results, they may inappropriately apply the conclusions drawn in published research to their own settings. Having been exposed to the rudiments of scientific research, *you* can critically examine and evaluate all published works before you assess their usefulness for your organization. For instance, you would not consider applying the results of good research done in a service organization to a manufacturing firm. Good research results in the hands of knowledgeable managers are highly useful tools. That is where research knowledge becomes invaluable. By grasping the essentials of good research, you will become a discriminating consumer of business reports and published articles and can become an effective manager. Research knowledge can often make the difference between managerial excellence and mediocrity.

References

Chapter 1

1. L. Llovio, "The CarMax Way: Changing the Used-Car Business," *McClatchy—Tribune Business News* (June 23, 2008): D12.

2. H. Schwartz, "The Clockwork or the Snakepit: An Essay on the Meaning of Teaching Organizational Behavior," *Organizational Behavior Teaching Review* 11(2) (1987): 19–26.

3. M. Matcho, "Idea Fest," *Fast Company* 66 (January 2003): 95–105, http://www.fastcompany.com/online/66/ideafest.html.

4. H. G. Barkem, J. A. C. Baum, and E. A. Mannix, "Management Challenges in a New Time," *Academy of Management Journal* 45 (2002): 916–930.

5. K. Lewin, "Field Theory in Social Science," selected theoretical papers (edited by Dorin Cartwright) (New York: Harper, 1951).

6. N. Schmitt, ed., Industrial/Organizational Section in *Encyclopedia of Psychology* (Washington, DC: American Psychological Association, and New York: Oxford University Press, 2000).

7. R. M. Yerkes, "The Relation of Psychology to Military Activities," *Mental Hygiene* 1 (1917): 371–376.

8. N. Gross, W. Mason, and A. McEachen, *Explorations in Role Analysis: Studies of the School Superintendency Role* (New York: Wiley, 1958).

9. J. S. Adams, A. Tashchian, and T. H. Stone, "Codes of Ethics as Signals for Ethical Behavior," *Journal of Business Ethics* 29 (2001): 199–211.

10. F. W. Taylor, *The Principles of Scientific Management* (New York: Norton, 1911).

11. E. A. Locke and G. P. Latham, *A Theory of Goal Setting and Task Performance* (Englewood Cliffs, NJ: Prentice Hall, 1990).

12. A. L. Wilkins and W. G. Ouchi, "Efficient Cultures: Exploring the Relationship between Culture and Organizational Performance," *Administrative Science Quarterly* 28 (1983): 468–481.

13. M. F. R. Kets de Vries and D. Miller, "Personality, Culture, and Organization," *Academy of Management Review* 11 (1986): 266–279.

14. H. Schwartz, *Narcissistic Process and Corporate Decay: The Theory of the Organizational Ideal* (New York: New York University Press, 1990).

15. J. G. March and H. A. Simon, *Organizations* (New York: John Wiley & Sons, 1958).

16. H. B. Elkind, *Preventive Management: Mental Hygiene in Industry* (New York: B. C. Forbes, 1931).

17. J. C. Quick, "Occupational Health Psychology: Historical Roots and Future Directions," *Health Psychology* 18 (1999).

18. K. R. Pelletier, *Mind as Healer, Mind as Slayer: A Holistic Approach to Preventing Stress Disorders* (New York: Delacorte, 1977).

19. D. R. Ilgen, "Health Issues at Work," *American Psychologist* 45 (1990): 273–283.

20. B. M. Staw, L. E. Sandelands, and J. E. Dutton, "Threat-Rigidity Effects in Organizational Behavior: A Multilevel Analysis," *Administrative Science Quarterly* 26 (1981): 501–524.

21. J. D. Ford and L. W. Ford, "Decoding Resistance to Change," *Harvard Business Review* 87 (April 2009): 99–103.

22. D. Kirkpatrick, "The Net Makes It All Easier—Including Exporting U.S. Jobs," *Fortune* (May 26, 2003): 146.

23. E. V. Brown, President of Proline International, Inc., "Commencement Address—College of Business Administration, the University of Texas at Arlington" (December 2003).

24. T. Reay, K. Golden-Biddle, and K. Germann, "Legitimizing a New Role: Small Wins and Microprocesses of Change," *Academy of Management Journal* 49 (2006): 977–998.

25. R. L. A. Sterba, "The Organization and Management of the Temple Corporations in Ancient Mesopotamia," *Academy of Management Review* 1 (1976): 16–26; S. P. Dorsey, *Early English Churches in America* (New York: Oxford University Press, 1952).

26. Sir I. Moncreiffe of That Ilk, *The Highland Clans: The Dynastic Origins, Chiefs, and Background of the Clans and of Some Other Families Connected to Highland History*, rev. ed. (New York: C. N. Potter, 1982).

27. D. Shambaugh, "The Soldier and the State in China: The Political Work System in the People's Liberation Army," *Chinese Quarterly* 127 (1991): 527–568.

28. L. L'Abate, ed., *Handbook of Developmental Family Psychology and Psychopathology* (New York: John Wiley & Sons, 1993).

29. J. A. Hostetler, *Communitarian Societies* (New York: Holt, Rinehart & Winston, 1974).

30. J. M. Lewis, "The Family System and Physical Illness," in *No Single Thread: Psychological Health in Family Systems* (New York: Brunner/ Mazel, 1976).

31. D. Katz and R. L. Kahn, *The Social Psychology of Organizations*, 2nd ed. (New York: John Wiley & Sons, 1978; H. J. Leavitt, "Applied Organizational Change in Industry: Structural, Technological, and Humanistic Approaches," in J. G. March, ed., *Handbook of Organizations* (Chicago: Rand McNally, 1965), 1144–1170.

32. J. D. Thompson, *Organizations in Action* (New York: McGraw-Hill, 1967).

33. M. Malone, "The Twitter Revolution," *Wall Street Journal* (April 18, 2009): A11.

34. F. J. Roethlisberger and W. J. Dickson, *Management and the Worker* (Cambridge, MA: Harvard University Press, 1939).

35. W. L. French and C. H. Bell, *Organization Development*, 4th ed. (Englewood Cliffs, NJ: Prentice Hall, 1990).

36. S. G. Barsade and D. E. Gibson, "Why Does Affect Matter in Organizations?," *Academy of Management Perspectives* 21 (2007): 36–59.

37. J. P. Kotter, "Managing External Dependence," *Academy of Management Review* 4 (1979): 87–92.

38. H. K. Steensma and D. G. Corley, "Organizational Context as a Moderator of Theories on Firm Boundaries for Technology Sourcing," *Academy of Management Journal* 44 (2001): 271–291.

39. "The CarMax Timeline," http://www.carmax.com/enUS/company-info/about-us-timeline.html (accessed May 7, 2009); L. Llovio (June 23, 2008), "The CarMax way: Changing the Used-Car Business," *McClatchy-Tribune Business News*; CarMax Annual Report, Fiscal Year 2009.

40. http://www.facebook.com/facebook?v=app_7146470109&viewas=0

41. http://shop.nordstrom.com/c/6022693/0~2377475~6022693; R. Spector and P. McCarthy, *The Nordstrom Way to Customer Service Excellence* (Hoboken, New Jersey: John Wiley & Sons, Inc, 2005)

42. http://www.ikea.com/ms/en_US/about_ikea/index.html

43. http://press.rim.com/financial/release; A. Abkowitz. "The BlackBerry boss," *Fortune* 159(8) (April 27, 2009): 20; "How the BlackBerry Duo Plans to Stay in Motion," *BusinessWeek* (Issue 4127) (April 20, 2009): 47.

44. http://www.deloitte.com; http://nyjobsource.com/deloitte.html; S. Layak "When Small is Big," *Business Today* 18(4) (February 22, 2009): 65.

45. T. B. Lawrence and V. Corwin, "Being There: The Acceptance and Marginalization of Part-Time Professional Employees," *Journal of Organizational Behavior* 24 (2003): 923–943.

46. M. K. Gowing, J. D. Kraft, and J. C. Quick, *The New Organizational Reality: Downsizing, Restructuring and Revitalization* (Washington, DC: American Psychological Association, 1998); T. Tang and R. M. Fuller, "Corporate Downsizing: What Managers Can Do to Lessen the Negative Effects of Layoffs," *SAM Advanced Management Journal* 60 (1995): 12–15, 31.

47. L. R. Offermann and M. K. Gowing, "Organizations of the Future," *American Psychologist* 45 (1990): 95–108.

48. J. Chatman, J. Polzer, S. Barsade, and M. Neale, "Being Different Yet Feeling Similar: The Influence of Demographic Composition and Organizational Culture on Work Processes and Outcomes," *Administrative Science Quarterly* 43 (1998): 749–780.

49. L. E. Thurow, *Head to Head: The Coming Economic Battle among Japan, Europe, and America* (New York: William Morrow, 1992).

50. J. E. Patterson, *Acquiring the Future: America's Survival and Success in the Global Economy* (Homewood, IL: Dow Jones-Irwin, 1990); H. B. Stewart, *Recollecting the Future: A View of Business, Technology, and Innovation in the Next 30 Years* (Homewood, IL: Dow Jones-Irwin, 1989).

51. M. W. Peng and H. Shin, "How Do Future Business Leaders View Globalization?," *Thunderbird International Business Review* 50 (May/June 2008): 175–182.

52. D. Ciampa, *Total Quality* (Reading, MA: Addison-Wesley, 1992).

53. R. J. David and D. Strang, "When Fashion Is Fleeting: Transitory Collective Beliefs and the Dynamics of TQM Consulting," *Academy of Management Journal* 49 (2006): 215–233.

54. T. J. Douglas and W. Q. Judge, Jr., "Total Quality Management Implementation and Competitive Advantage: The Role of Structural Control and Exploration," *Academy of Management Journal* 44 (2001): 158–169.

55. American Management Association, *Blueprints for Service Quality: The Federal Express Approach* (New York: American Management Association, 1991); P. R. Thomas, L. J. Gallace, and K. R. Martin, *Quality Alone Is Not Enough* (New York: American Management Association, 1992).

56. J. de Mast, "A Methodological Comparison of Three Strategies for Quality Improvement," *International Journal of Quality & Reliability Management* 21 (2004): 198–213.

57. M. Barney, "Motorola's Second Generation," *Six Sigma Forum Magazine* 1(3) (May 2002): 13.

58. J. A. Edosomwan, "Six Commandments to Empower Employees for Quality Improvement," *Industrial Engineering* 24 (1992): 14–15.

59. J. T. Prince and D. H. Simon, "Multimarket Contact and Service Quality: Evidence from On-Time Performance in the U.S. Airline Industry," *Academy of Management Journal* 52 (2009): 336–354.

60. D. Pitts, "Diversity Management, Job Satisfaction, and Performance: Evidence from U.S. Federal Agencies," *Public Administration Review* 69 (March/April 2009): 328–338.

61. P. Norberg, " 'I Don't Care that People Don't Like What I Do'—Business Codes Viewed as Invisible or Visible Restrictions," *Journal of Business Ethics* 86 (2009): 211–225.

62. Staff, "To count or not to count," *Economist* 390 (Issue 8624) (2009).

63. See also the five articles in the Special Research Forum on Teaching Effectiveness in the Organizational Sciences, *The Academy of Management Journal* 40 (1997): 1265–1398.

64. L. Proserpio and D. A. Gioia. "Teaching the Virtual Generation," *Academy of Management Learning and Education* 6 (2007): 69–80.

65. R. M. Steers, L. W. Porter, and G. A. Bigley, *Motivation and Leadership at Work* (New York: McGraw-Hill, 1996).

66. H. Levinson, *Executive Stress* (New York: New American Library, 1975).

67. D. L. Whetzel, "The Department of Labor Identifies Workplace Skills," *Industrial/Organizational Psychologist* 29 (1991): 89–90.

68. D. A. Whetton and K. S. Cameron, *Developing Management Skills*, 3rd ed. (New York: HarperCollins, 1995).

69. C. Argyris and D. A. Schon, *Organizational Learning: A Theory of Action Perspective* (Reading, MA: Addison-Wesley, 1978).

70. A. Y. Kolb and D. A. Kolb. "Learning Styles and Learning Spaces: Enhancing Experiential Learning in Higher Education," *Academy of Management Learning and Education* 4 (2005): 193–212.

71. R. Ramanjuam and D. M. Rousseau. "The Challenges Are Organizational not Just Clinical," *Journal of Organizational Behavior* 27 (2006): 811–827.

72. "CarMax Named one of the '100 Best Companies to Work For' by Fortune Magazine for the Fifth Straight Year," *Business Wire* (January 22, 2009).

73. "CarMax Named to Training Magazine's Top 125," *Business Wire* (February 12, 2009).

Chapter 1 Case

1. R. Richmond, "Enterprise: Some Facebook Applications Thrive, Others Flop; Popular Programs Are Useful, Entertain and Let Friends Mingle," *Wall Street Journal* (Eastern edition) (June 10, 2008): B7.

2. Ibid.

3. C. S. Tang, "Business Insight (A Special Report): Marketing; United We May Stand: In Their First Incarnation, Group Buying Services Failed; A Similar Concept in China May Provide a Road Map for How to Do It Right," *Wall Street Journal* (Eastern edition) (May 12, 2008): R10.

4. Ibid.

5. Ibid.

6. Ibid.

7. R. Rothenberg, "Facebook's Flop," *Wall Street Journal* (Eastern edition) (December 14, 2007): A21.

8. C. S. Tang, "Business Insight (A Special Report)," R10.

9. J. Tsai, "Facebook's About-face: The Social Networking Company Introduced a Marketing Plan Many of Its Members Hated—and Changed Course Accordingly," *Customer Relationship Management* 12(1) (January 1, 2008): 17.

10. V. Vara, "Facebook Rethinks Tracking; Site Apologizes, Makes It Easier to Retain Privacy," *Wall Street Journal* (Eastern edition) (December 7, 2007): B4.

11. L. Musthaler, "Facebook Fiasco Highlights Privacy Concerns," *Network World* 25(1) (January 7, 2008): 30.

12. "Business: Everywhere and Nowhere; Online Social Networks," *The Economist* 386(8572) (March 22, 2008): 81.

13. Rothenberg, "Facebook's Flop," A21.

14. Vara, "Facebook Rethinks Tracking," B4.

Chapter 2

1. J. Hempel, "BlackBerry Battles Back," *Fortune* (November 24, 2008): 45.

2. M. A. Hitt, R. E. Hoskisson, and J. S. Harrison, "Strategic Competitiveness in the 1990s: Challenges and Opportunities

for U.S. Executives," *Academy of Management Executive* 5 (1991): 7–22.

3. H. G. Barkem, J. A. C. Baum, and E. A. Mannix, "Management Challenges in a New Time," *Academy of Management Journal* 45 (2002): 916–930.

4. S. C. Harper, "The Challenges Facing CEOs: Past, Present, and Future," *Academy of Management Executive* 6 (1992): 7–25.

5. T. R. Mitchell and W. G. Scott, "America's Problems and Needed Reforms: Confronting the Ethic of Personal Advantage," *Academy of Management Executive* 4 (1990): 23–25.

6. B. Spindle, "Sinking in Sync—The Global Slowdown Surprises Economists and Many Companies," *Wall Street Journal* (December 21, 2000): A1–A10.

7. D. A. Harrison, J. H. Gavin, and A. T. Florey, "Time, Teams, and Task Performance: Changing Effects of Surface- and Deep-Level Diversity on Group Functioning," *Academy of Management Journal* 45 (2003): 1029–1045.

8. J. H. Gavin, J. C. Quick, C. L. Cooper, and J. D. Quick, "A Spirit of Personal Integrity: The Role of Character in Executive Health," *Organizational Dynamics* 32 (2003): 165–179.

9. K. Sera, "Corporate Globalization: A New Trend," *Academy of Management Executive* 6 (1992): 89–96.

10. K. Ohmae, *Borderless World: Power and Strategies in the Interlinked Economy* (New York: Harper & Row, 1990).

11. C. Whitlock, "VW's Home Town Finds Ways to Cope with Globalization," *Washington Post* (June 5, 2007): A10.

12. C. A. Bartlett and S. Ghoshal, *Managing across Borders: The Transnational Solution* (Boston: Harvard Business School Press, 1989).

13. F. Warner, "Learning How to Speak to Gen Y," *Fast Company* 72 (July 2003): 36–37.

14. K. R. Xin and J. L. Pearce, "Guanxi: Connections as Substitutes for Formal Institutional Support," *Academy of Management Journal* 39 (1996): 1641–1658.

15. P. S. Chan, "Franchise Management in East Asia," *Academy of Management Executive* 4 (1990): 75–85.

16. H. Weihrich, "Europe 1992: What the Future May Hold," *Academy of Management Executive* 4 (1990): 7–18.

17. E. H. Schein, "Coming to a New Awareness of Organizational Culture," *MIT Sloan Management Review* 25 (1984): 3–16.

18. S. S. Sarwano and R. M. Armstrong, "Microcultural Differences and Perceived Ethical Problems: An International Business Perspective," *Journal of Business Ethics* 30 (2001): 41–56.

19. R. Sharpe, "Hi-Tech Taboos," *Wall Street Journal* (October 31, 1995): A1.

20. G. Hofstede, *Culture's Consequences: International Differences in Work-Related Values* (Beverly Hills, CA: Sage Publications, 1980).

21. G. Hofstede, "Motivation, Leadership, and Organization: Do American Theories Apply Abroad?" *Organizational Dynamics* (Summer 1980): 42–63.

22. R. Buda and S. M. Elsayed-Elkhouly, "Cultural Differences between Arabs and Americans," *Journal of Cross-Cultural Psychology* 29 (1998): 487–492.

23. G. Hofstede, "Gender Stereotypes and Partner Preferences of Asian Women in Masculine and Feminine Countries," *Journal of Cross Cultural Psychology* 27 (1996): 533–546.

24. G. Hofstede, "Cultural Constraints in Management Theories," *Academy of Management Executive* 7 (1993): 81–94.

25. G. M. Spreitzer, M. W. McCall, Jr., and J. D. Mahoney, "Early Identification of International Executive Potential," *Journal of Applied Psychology* 82 (1997): 6–29.

26. M. A. Hitt, L. Bierman, K. Uhlenbruck, and K. Shimizu, "The Importance of Resources in the Internationalization of Professional Service Firms: The Good, the Bad, and the Ugly," *Academy of Management Journal* 49 (2006): 1137–1157.

27. L. Nardon and R. M. Steers. "The New Global Manager: Learning Cultures on the Fly," *Organizational Dynamics*, 37(1): 47–59.

28. A. J. Michel, "Goodbyes Can Cost Plenty in Europe," *Fortune* (April 6, 1992): 16.

29. M. Adams, "Building a Rainbow One Stripe at a Time," *HR Magazine* 9 (August 1999): 72–79; Intel, "Diversity at Intel: Our Commitment," 2003, http://www.intel.com/jobs/Diversity/commitment.htm.

30. E. Brandt, "Global HR," *Personnel Journal* 70 (1991): 38–44.

31. M. Bell, *Diversity in Organizations* (Mason, OH: Cengage/South-Western, 2007).

32. P. Chattopadhyay, "Can Dissimilarity Lead to Positive Outcomes: The Influence of Open versus Closed Minds," *Journal of Organizational Behavior* 24 (2003): 295–312.

33. J. C. Quick, J. H. Gavin, C. L. Cooper, and J. D. Quick, "Working Together: Balancing Head and Heart," in R. H. Rozensky, N. G. Johnson, C. D. Goodheart, and W. R. Hammond, eds., *Psychology Builds a Healthy World: Opportunities for Research and Practice*: (Washington, DC: American Psychological Association, 2004), 219–232.

34. J. A. Gilbert and J. M. Ivancevich, "Valuing Diversity: A Tale of Two Organizations," *Academy of Management Executive* 4 (2000): 93–105.

35. R. W. Judy and C. D'Amico, *Workforce 2020* (Indianapolis, IN: Hudson Institute, 1997); U.S. Department of Labor, "Usual Weekly Earnings Summary," *Labor Force Statistics from the Current Population Survey* (Washington, DC: U.S. Government, 2002).

36. S. Caudron, "Task Force Report Reveals Coke's Progress on Diversity," *Workforce* 82 (2003): 40; http://www.workforceonline.com/section/03/feature/23/42/44/234246.html.

37. L. S. Gottfredson, "Dilemmas in Developing Diversity Programs," in S. E. Jackson, ed., *Diversity in the Workplace: Human Resources Initiatives* (New York: Guilford Press, 1992), 279–305.

38. U.S. Department of Labor, "Employment Status of the Civilian Population by Sex and Age," http://stats.bls.gov/news.release/empsit.t01.htm (accessed July 2004).

39. "Catalyst Releases 2005 Censuses of Women Board Directors and Corporate Officers," Perspective. Catalyst.org, http://www.catalyst.org/ bookstore/perspective/06August.pdf (accessed February 7, 2007.

40. Ibid.

41. Ibid.

42. "Xerox Names Burns Chief as Mulcahy Retires Early," *Wall Street Journal* (May 22, 2009): 1.

43. U.S. Department of Labor, "Highlights of Women's Earnings in 2005," Report 995 (September 2006).

44. D. C. Wyld and R. Maurin, "How Do Women Fare When the Promotion Rules Change?" *Academy of Management Perspectives*, 22(4): 83–85.

45. A. M. Morrison, R. P. White, E. Van Velsor, and the Center for Creative Leadership, *Breaking the Glass Ceiling: Can Women Reach the Top of America's Largest Corporations?* (Reading, MA: Addison-Wesley, 1987).

46. D. E. Arfken, S. L. Bellar, and M. M. Helms, "The Ultimate Glass Ceiling Revisited: The Presence of Women on Corporate Boards," *Journal of Business Ethics* 50 (March 2004): 177–186.

47. A. M. Konrad, V. Kramer, and S. Erkut, "Critical Mass: The Impact of Three or More Women on Corporate Boards," *Organizational Dynamics*, 37(2): 145–164.

48. "Top Facts about Women-Owned Businesses," Center for Women's Business Research, http://www.womensbusinessresearch.org/facts/index.php (accessed February 2, 2007).

49. L. L. Martins and C. K. Parsons. "Effects of Gender Diversity Management on Perceptions of Organizational Attractiveness: The Role of Individual Differences in Attitudes and Beliefs," *Journal of Applied Psychology* 92 (2007): 865–875.

50. A. Eyring and B. A. Stead, "Shattering the Glass Ceiling: Some Successful Corporate Practices," *Journal of Business Ethics* 17 (1998): 245–251.

51. Catalyst, *Advancing Women in Business: The Catalyst Guide* (San Francisco: Jossey-Bass, 1998).

52. D. L. Nelson and M. A. Hitt, "Employed Women and Stress: Implications for Enhancing Women's Mental Health in the Workplace," in J. C. Quick, L. R. Murphy, and J. J. Hurrell, Jr., eds., *Stress and*

Well-Being at Work (Washington, DC: American Psychological Association, 1992), 164–177.

53. L. E. Atwater and D. D. Van Fleet, "Another Ceiling: Can Males Compete for Traditionally Female Jobs?" *Journal of Management* 23 (1997): 603–626.

54. U.S. Department of Health and Human Services, *Profile of Older Americans* (Washington, DC: U.S. Government, 1997).

55. W. B. Johnston, "Global Workforce 2000: The New World Labor Market," *Harvard Business Review* 69 (1991): 115–127.

56. S. E. Jackson and E. B. Alvarez, "Working Through Diversity as a Strategic Imperative," in S. E. Jackson, ed., *Diversity in the Workplace: Human Resources Initiatives* (New York: Guilford Press, 1992), 13–36.

57. "Managing Generational Diversity," *HR Magazine* 36 (1991): 91–92.

58. K. Tyler, "The Tethered Generation," *HR* magazine (May 2007): 41–46.

59. C. M. Solomon, "Managing the Baby Busters," *Personnel Journal* (March 1992): 52–59.

60. S. R. Rhodes, "Age-Related Differences in Work Attitudes and Behavior: A Review and Conceptual Analysis," *Psychological Bulletin* 93 (1983): 338–367.

61. B. L. Hassell and P. L. Perrewe, "An Examination of Beliefs about Older Workers: Do Stereotypes Still Exist?" *Journal of Organizational Behavior* 16 (1995): 457–468.

62. U.S. Bureau of the Census, *Population Profile of the United States, 1997* (Washington, DC: U.S. Government Printing Office, 1997).

63. W. J. Rothwell, "HRD and the Americans with Disabilities Act," *Training and Development Journal* (August 1991): 45–47.

64. J. Waldrop, "The Cost of Hiring the Disabled," *American Demographics* (March 1991): 12.

65. J. J. Laabs, "The Golden Arches Provide Golden Opportunities," *Personnel Journal* (July 1991): 52–57.

66. C. T. Kulik, M. B. Pepper, L. Robertson, and S. K. Parker, "The Rich Get Richer: Predicting Participation in Voluntary Diversity Training," *Journal of Organizational Behavior*, 28 (2007): 753–769.

67. L. Winfield and S. Spielman, "Making Sexual Orientation Part of Diversity," *Training and Development* (April 1995): 50–51.

68. N. E. Day and P. Schoenrade, "Staying in the Closet versus Coming Out: Relationships between Communication about Sexual Orientation and Work Attitudes," *Personnel Psychology* 50 (1997): 147–163.

69. J. Landau, "The Relationship of Race and Gender to Managers' Ratings of Promotion Potential," *Journal of Organizational Behavior* 16 (1995): 391–400.

70. P. Barnum, "Double Jeopardy for Women and Minorities: Pay Differences with Age," *Academy of Management Journal* 38 (1995): 863–880.

71. J. E. Rigdon, "PepsiCo's KFC Scouts for Blacks and Women for Its Top Echelons," *Wall Street Journal* (November 13, 1991): A1.

72. P. A. Galagan, "Tapping the Power of a Diverse Workforce," *Training and Development Journal* 26 (1991): 38–44.

73. C. L. Holladay, J. L. Knight, D. L. Paige, and M. A. Quinones, "The Influence of Framing on Attitudes Toward Diversity Training," *Human Resource Development Quarterly* 14 (2003): 245–263.

74. R. Thomas, "From Affirmative Action to Affirming Diversity," *Harvard Business Review* 68 (1990): 107–117.

75. T. H. Cox, Jr., *Cultural Diversity in Organizations: Theory, Research and Practice* (San Francisco: Berrett-Koehler, 1994).

76. J. Gordon, "Different from What?" *Training* (May 1995): 25–33.

77. N. Andreoli and J. Lefkowitz, "Individual and Organizational Antecedents of Misconduct in Organizations," *Journal of Business Ethics*, 85: 309–332.

78. M. R. Fusilier, C. D. Aby, Jr., J. K. Worley, and S. Elliott, "Perceived Seriousness of Business Ethics Issues," *Business and Professional Ethics Journal* 15 (1996): 67–78.

79. J. S. Mill, *Utilitarianism, Liberty, and Representative Government* (London: Dent, 1910).

80. K. H. Blanchard and N. V. Peale, *The Power of Ethical Management* (New York: Morrow, 1988).

81. C. Fried, *Right and Wrong* (Cambridge, MA: Harvard University Press, 1978).

82. I. Kant, *Groundwork of the Metaphysics of Morals*, trans. H. J. Paton (New York: Harper & Row, 1964).

83. A. Smith, *An Inquiry into the Nature and Causes of the Wealth of Nations*, vol. 10 of The Harvard Classics, ed. C. J. Bullock (New York: P. F. Collier & Son, 1909).

84. S. Finkelstein, J. Whitehead, and A. Campbell, "How Inappropriate Attachments can Drive Good Leaders to Make Bad Decision," *Organizational Dynamics*, 38(2): 83–92.

85. R. C. Solomon, "Corporate Roles, Personal Virtues: Aristotelean Approach to Business Ethics," *Business Ethics Quarterly* 2 (1992): 317–339; R. C. Solomon, *A Better Way to Think about Business: How Personal Integrity Leads to Corporate Success* (New York: Oxford University Press, 1999).

86. S. Bowles, "When Economic Incentives Backfire," *Harvard Business Review*, 87(3): 22–23.

87. D. Kemp, "Employers and AIDS: Dealing with the Psychological and Emotional Issues of AIDS in the Workplace," *American Review of Public Administration* 25 (1995): 263–278.

88. J. J. Koch, "Wells Fargo's and IBM's HIV Policies Help Protect Employees' Rights," *Personnel Journal* (April 1990): 40–48.

89. A. Arkin, "Positive HIV and AIDS Policies at Work," *Personnel Management* (December 1994): 34–37.

90. U.S. EEOC. 1980. Discrimination because of Sex under Title VII of the 1964 Civil Rights Act as amended: Adoption of interim guidelines—sexual harassment. *Federal Register* 45: 25024–25025; S. J. Adler, "Lawyers Advise Concerns to Provide Precise Written Policy to Employees," *Wall Street Journal* (October 9, 1991): B1.

91. L. F. Fitzgerald, F. Drasgow, C. L. Hulin, M. J. Gelfand, and V. J. Magley, "Antecedents and Consequences of Sexual Harassment in Organizations: A Test of an Integrated Model," *Journal of Applied Psychology* 82 (1997): 578–589.

92. E. Felsenthal, "Rulings Open Way for Sex-Harass Cases," *Wall Street Journal* (June 29, 1998): A10.

93. K. T. Schneider, S. Swan, and L. F. Fitzgerald, "Job-Related and Psychological Effects of Sexual Harassment in the Workplace: Empirical Evidence from Two Organizations," *Journal of Applied Psychology* 82 (1997): 401–415.

94. A. M. O'Leary-Kelly, L. Bowes-Sperry, C. A. Bates, and E. R. Lean, "Sexual Harassment at Work: A Decade (Plus) of Progress," *Journal of Management*, 35(3): 503–536.

95. L. M. Goldenhar, N. G. Swanson, J. J. Hurrell, Jr., A. Ruder, and J. Deddens, "Stressors and Adverse Outcomes for Female Construction Workers," *Journal of Occupational Health Psychology* 3 (1998): 19–32; C. S. Piotrkowski, "Gender Harassment, Job Satisfaction and Distress Among Employed White and Minority Women," *Journal of Occupational Health Psychology* 3 (1998): 33–42.

96. G. N. Powell and S. Foley, "Something to Talk About: Romantic Relationships in Organizational Settings," *Journal of Management* 24 (1998): 421–448.

97. R. A. Posthuma, C. P. Maertz, Jr., and J. B. Dworkin. "Procedural Justice's Relationship with Turnover: Explaining Past Inconsistent Findings," *Journal of Organizational Behavior* 28 (2007): 381–398.

98. D. Fields, M. Pang, and C. Chio, "Distributive and Procedural Justice as Predictors of Employee Outcomes in Hong Kong," *Journal of Organizational Behavior* 21 (2000): 547–562.

99. H. L. Laframboise, "Vile Wretches and Public Heroes: The Ethics of Whistleblowing in Government," *Canadian Public Administration* (Spring 1991): 73–78.

100. A. Nyberg, "Whistle-Blower Woes," *CFO Magazine* 19 (October 2003): 50, http://www.cfo.com/article/1,5309,10790,00.html.

101. D. B. Turban and D. W. Greening, "Corporate Social Performance and Organizational Attractiveness to Prospective Employees," *Academy of Management Journal* 40 (1996): 658–672.

102. S. Amnbec and P. Lanoie. "Does It Pay to be Green? A Systematic Overview," *Academy of Management Perspectives* 22(4): 45–62.

103. J. Goolsby, D. A. Mack, and J. C. Quick. "Winning by Staying In Bounds: Good Outcomes for Positive Ethics," *Organizational Dynamics* 39(2): in press.

104. T. Simons, R. Friedman, L. A. Liu, and J. M. Parks. "Racial Differences in Sensitivity to Behavioral Integrity: Attitudinal Consequences, In-Group Effects and 'Trickle Down' among Black and Non-Black Employees," *Journal of Applied Psychology* 92 (2007): 650–665.

105. A. Abkowitz, "The BlackBerry Boss," *Fortune* 159(8) (April 27, 2009): 20; G. Marchial, "Betting on the Blackberry," *Business Week* (Issue 4128) (April 27, 2009): 68.

Chapter 2 Case

1. "About Timberland," Timberland Web site, http://www.timberland.com/corp/index.jsp?clickid+topnow_corp.txt (accessed July 2, 2009).

2. BellwetherReport.com, "Current Research on Timberland Co.," *M2PressWire* (February 13, 2007), from Newspaper Source database (accessed August 21, 2007).

3. "Timberland Co. (TBL)," Yahoo!® Finance, http://finance.yahoo.com/q/is?s=TBL&annual (accessed July 2, 2009).

4. "About Timberland."

5. "CSR Strategy," Timberland Web site, http://www.timberland.com/corp/index.jsp?page=csr_strategy (accessed July 2, 2009).

6. J. Reingold, "Walking the Walk," *Fast Company* (100) (November 2005): 80.

7. Ibid., pp. 80–85.

8. D. Rigby and S. Tager, "Learning the Advantages of Sustainable Growth," *Strategy and Leadership*, 36(4) (2008): 25.

9. "CSR: Global Human Rights," Timberland Web site, http://www.timberland.com/corp/index.jsp?page=ghr (accessed August 20, 2009).

10. Reingold, "Walking the Walk," 80–85.

11. J. Swartz, "19. Take Off from Work," *Time* 172(12) (September 22, 2008): 62.

12. Ibid.

13. S. O'Laughlin, "Heart and Sole," *Brandweek* 44(13) (March 31, 2003): 17.

14. Ibid., p. 16.

15. Ibid.

16. Ibid.

17. S. Migliore, "For-Profits and Nonprofits Achieve Missions Together," *Nonprofit World*, 25(4) (July/August 2007): 22.

18. Rigby and Tager, "Learning the Advantages of Sustainable Growth," 24.

19. J. Swartz, "19. Take Off from Work," *Time* 172(12) (September 22, 2008): 62.

20. Rigby and Tager, "Learning the Advantages of Sustainable Growth," 26.

Chapter 2 Cohesion Case: Part 1

1. N. Zmuda, "Zappos," **Advertising Age** (Midwest Region Edition) 79(39) (October 20, 2008): 36.

2. "Business: Keeper of the Flame; Face Value," **The Economist** 391(8627) (April 18, 2009): 75.

3. M. Zager, "Zappos Delivers Service...With Shoes on the Side," *Apparel Magazine* (January 2009), http://www.apparelmag.com?ME2/dirmod.asp?sid=23B25809...(accessed June 9, 2009).

4. Ibid.

5. H. Coster, "A Step Ahead," *Forbes* (June 2, 2008), http://www.forbes.com/global/2008/0602/064.html (accessed June 20, 2009); Zager, "Zappos Delivers Service."

6. Coster, "A Step Ahead."

7. Ibid.

8. K. Magill, "New Dogs Learn Old Tricks," Multichannel Merchant 24(9) (September 2007): 21.

9. Ibid.

10. Coster, "A Step Ahead."

11. J. M. O'Brien, "Zappos Knows How to Kick It," *Fortune* 159(2) (February 2, 2009): 56.

12. M. Chafkin, "Get Happy: How Tony Hsieh Uses Relentless Innovation, Stellar Service, and a Staff of Believers to Make Zappos.com and E-commerce Juggernaut—and One of the Most Blissed-out Businesses in America," *Inc.* 31(4) (May 2009): 71.

13. B. Morrisey, "Communal Branding: How These Web 2.0 Companies Build Good Relationships to Build Their Brands," *Adweek* 49(16) (May 12, 2008): 9.

14. O'Brien, "Zappos Knows How to Kick It."

15. Zager, "Zappos Delivers Service."

16. Chafkin, "Get Happy", p. 72.

17. "Business: Keeper of the Flame."

18. Coster, "A Step Ahead."

19. Ibid.

20. B. Morrisey, "Communal Branding: How These Web 2.0 Companies Build Good Relationships to Build Their Brands," *Adweek* 49(16) (May 12, 2008): 9.

21. S. Murphy, "Culture Conscious," *Chain Store Age* 83(9) (September 2007): 55.

22. "Retail's Power 25: The 25 Most Influential People in Retailing," *Chain Store Age* 84(1) (January 2008): 3A.

23. Coster, "A Step Ahead."

24. C. R. Bell and J. R. Patterson, "Imaginative Service," *Leadership Excellence* 26(5) (May 2009): 10.

25. "Business."

26. Bell and Patterson, "Imaginative Service."

27. "Business."

28. Zmuda, "Zappos."

Chapter 3

1. K. Lewin, "Formalization and Progress in Psychology," in D. Cartwright, ed., *Field Theory in Social Science* (New York: Harper, 1951).

2. N. S. Endler and D. Magnusson, "Toward an Interactional Psychology of Personality," *Psychological Bulletin* 83 (1976): 956–974.

3. J. R. Terborg, "Interactional Psychology and Research on Human Behavior in Organizations," *Academy of Management Review* 6 (1981): 561–576.

4. C. Spearman, "General Intelligence: Objectively Determined and Measured," *American Journal of Psychology* 15 (1904): 201–293.

5. F. L. Schmidt and J. Hunter, "General Mental Ability in the World of Work: Occupational Attainment and Job Performance," *Journal of Personality and Social Psychology* 86(1) (2004): 162–173.

6. C. Bertua, N. Anderson, and J. F. Salgado, "The Predictive Validity of Cognitive Ability Tests: A UK Meta-Analysis," *Journal of Occupational and Organizational Psychology* 78 (2004): 387–409.

7. M. J. Ree and J. A. Earles, "Intelligence Is the Best Predictor of Job Performance," *Current Directions in Psychological Science* 1 (2008): 86–89.

8. T. J. Bouchard, Jr., "Twins Reared Together and Apart: What They Tell Us about Human Diversity," in S. W. Fox, ed., Individuality and Determinism (New York: Plenum Press, 1984).

9. R. D. Arvey, T. J. Bouchard, Jr., N. L. Segal, and L. M. Abraham, "Job Satisfaction: Environmental and Genetic Components," *Journal of Applied Psychology* 74 (1989): 235–248.

10. G. Allport, *Pattern and Growth in Personality* (New York: Holt, 1961).

11. R. B. Cattell, *Personality and Mood by Questionnaire* (San Francisco: Jossey-Bass, 1973).

12. J. M. Digman, "Personality Structure: Emergence of a Five-Factor Model," *Annual Review of Psychology* 41 (1990): 417–440.

13. M. Komarraju, S. J. Karau, R. R. Schmeck, "Role of the Big Five Personality Traits in Predicting College Students Academic Motivation and Achievement," *Learning and Individual Differences* 19 (2009): 47–52.

14. T. A. Judge, J. J. Martocchio, and C. J. Thoresen, "Five-Factor Model of Personality and Employee Absence," *Journal of Applied Psychology* 82 (1997): 745–755.

15. H. J. Bernardin, D. K. Cooke, and P. Villanova, "Conscientiousness and Agreeableness as Predictors of Rating Leniency," *Journal of Applied Psychology* 85 (2000): 232–234.

16. S. E. Seibert and M. L. Kraimer, "The Five-Factor Model of Personality and Career Success," *Journal of Vocational Behavior* 58 (2001): 1–21.

17. T. A. Judge and R. Ilies, "Relationships of Personality to Performance Motivation: A Meta-Analytic Review," *Journal of Applied Psychology* 87 (2002): 797–807.

18. G. M. Hurtz and J. J. Donovan, "Personality and Job Performance: The Big Five Revisited," *Journal of Applied Psychology* 85 (2000): 869–879.

19. S. T. Bell. "Deep-Level Composition Variables as Predictors of Team Performance: A Meta-Analysis," *Journal of Applied Psychology* 92(3) (2007): 595–615.

20. J. F. Salgado, S. Moscoso, and M. Lado, "Evidence of Cross-Cultural Invariance of the Big Five Personality Dimensions in Work Settings," *European Journal of Personality* 17 (2003): S67–S76; C. Rodriguez and T. H. Church, "The Structure and Personality Correlates of Affect in Mexico: Evidence of Cross-Cultural Comparability Using the Spanish Language," *Journal of Cross-Cultural Psychology* 34 (2003): 211–230.

21. M. Schaller and D. R. Murray, "Pathogens, Personality, and Culture: Disease Prevalence Predicts Worldwide Variability in Sociosexuality, Extraversion, and Openness to Experience," *Journal of Personality and Social Psychology* 95 (July 2008): 212–221.

22. M. R. Barrick and M. K. Mount, "The Big Five Personality Dimensions and Job Performance: A Meta-Analysis," *Personnel Psychology* 44 (1991): 1–26.

23. D. D. Clark and R. Hoyle, "A Theoretical Solution to the Problem of Personality-Situational Interaction," *Personality and Individual Differences* 9 (1988): 133–138.

24. D. Byrne and L. J. Schulte, "Personality Dimensions as Predictors of Sexual Behavior," in J. Bancroft, ed., *Annual Review of Sexual Research*, vol. 1 (Philadelphia: Society for the Scientific Study of Sex, 1990).

25. T. A. Judge, E. A. Locke, and C. C. Durham, "The Dispositional Causes of Job Satisfaction: A Core Self-Evaluation Approach," *Research in Organizational Behavior* 19 (1997): 151–188.

26. M. Erez and T. A. Judge, "Relationship of Core Self-Evaluations to Goal Setting, Motivation and Performance," *Journal of Applied Psychology* 86 (2001):1270–1279.

27. R. F. Piccolo, T. A. Judge, K. Takahashi, N. Watanabe, and E. A Locke, "Core Self-Evaluations in Japan: Relative Effects on Job Satisfaction, Life Satisfaction, and Happiness," *Journal of Organizational Behavior* 26(8) (2005): 965–984.

28. J. B. Rotter, "Generalized Expectancies for Internal vs. External Control of Reinforcement," *Psychological Monographs* 80, whole No. 609 (1966).

29. T. A. Judge and J. E. Bono, "Relationship of Core Self-Evaluations Traits—Self-Esteem, Generalized Self-Efficacy, Locus of Control, and Emotional Stability—with Job Satisfaction and Job Performance: A Meta-Analysis," *Journal of Applied Psychology* 86 (2001): 80–92.

30. S. S. K. Lam and J. Shaubroeck, "The Role of Locus of Control in Reactions to Being Promoted and to Being Passed Over: A Quasi Experiment," *Academy of Management Journal* 43 (2000): 66–78.

31. G. Chen, S. M. Gully, J. Whiteman, and R. N. Kilcullen, "Examination of Relationships Among Trait-Like Individual Differences, State-Like Individual Differences, and Learning Performance," *Journal of Applied Psychology* 85 (2000): 835–847; G. Chen, S. M. Gully, and D. Eden, "Validation of a New General Self-Efficacy Scale," *Organizational Research Methods* 4 (2001): 62–83.

32. A. Bandura, *Self-Efficacy: The Exercise of Control* (San Francisco: Freeman, 1997).

33. D. R. Avery, "Personality as a Predictor of the Value of Voice," *The Journal of Psychology* 137 (2003): 435–447.

34. B. W. Pelham and W. B. Swann, Jr., "From Self-Conceptions to Self-Worth: On the Sources and Structure of Global Self-Esteem," *Journal of Personality and Social Psychology* 57 (1989): 672–680.

35. A. H. Baumgardner, C. M. Kaufman, and P. E. Levy, "Regulating Affect Interpersonally: When Low Esteem Leads to Greater Enhancement," *Journal of Personality and Social Psychology* 56 (1989): 907–921.

36. J. Schimel, T. Pyszczynski, J. Arndt, and J. Greenberg, "Being Accepted for Who We Are: Evidence That Social Validation of the Intrinsic Self Reduces General Defensiveness," *Journal of Personality and Social Psychology* 80 (2001): 35–52.

37. P. Tharenou and P. Harker, "Moderating Influences of Self-Esteem on Relationships between Job Complexity, Performance, and Satisfaction," *Journal of Applied Psychology* 69 (1984): 623–632.

38. R. T. Keller. "Predicting Job Performance from Individual Characteristics among R&D Engineers," *The Business Review*, Cambridge 8(1) (2007): 12–18.

39. R. A. Ellis and M. S. Taylor, "Role of Self-Esteem within the Job Search Process," *Journal of Applied Psychology* 68 (1983): 632–640.

40. J. Brockner and T. Hess, "Self-Esteem and Task Performance in Quality Circles," *Academy of Management Journal* 29 (1986): 617–623.

41. B. R. Schlenker, M. F. Weingold, and J. R. Hallam, "Self-Serving Attributions in Social Context: Effects of Self-Esteem and Social Pressure," *Journal of Personality and Social Psychology* 57 (1990): 855–863.

42. M. K. Duffy, J. D. Shaw, and E. M. Stark, "Performance and Satisfaction in Conflicted Interdependent Groups: When and How Does Self-Esteem Make a Difference?" *Academy of Management Journal* 43 (2000): 772–782.

43. T. Mussweiler, S. Gabriel, and G. V. Bodenhausen, "Shifting Social Identities as a Strategy for Deflecting Threatening Social Comparisons," *Journal of Personality and Social Psychology* 79 (2000): 398–409.

44. Erez and Judge, "Relationship of Core Self-Evaluations to Goal Setting."

45. Ibid.

46. M. Snyder and S. Gangestad, "On the Nature of Self-Monitoring: Matters of Assessment, Matters of Validity," *Journal of Personality and Social Psychology* 51 (1986): 123–139.

47. G. Toegel, N. Anand, and M. Kilduff, " Emotion Helpers: The Role of High Positive Affectivity and High Self Monitoring Managers," *Personnel Psychology* 60(2) (2007): 337–365.

48. A. Mehra, M. Kilduff, and D. J. Brass, "The Social Networks of High and Low Self-Monitors: Implications for Workplace Performance," *Administrative Science Quarterly* 46 (2001): 121–146.

49. W. H. Turnley and M. C. Bolino, "Achieving Desired Images While Avoiding Undesired Images: Exploring the Role of Self-Monitoring in Impression Management," *Journal of Applied Psychology* 86 (2001): 351–360.

50. M. Kilduff and D. V. Day, "Do Chameleons Get Ahead? The Effects of Self-Monitoring on Managerial Careers," *Academy of Management Journal* 37 (1994): 1047–1060.

51. A. H. Church, "Managerial Self-Awareness in High-Performing Individuals in Organizations," *Journal of Applied Psychology* 82 (1997): 281–292.

52. A. Mehra and M. T. Schenkel, "The Price Chameleons Pay: Self-monitoring, Boundary Spanning and Role Conflict in the Workplace," *British Journal of Management* 19 (2008): 138–144.

53. C. Douglas and W. L. Gardner, "Transition to Self-Directed Work Teams: Implications of Transition Time and Self-Monitoring for Managers' Use of Influence Tactics," *Journal of Organizational Behavior* 25 (2004): 45–67.

54. A. M. Isen and R. A. Baron, "Positive Affect and Organizational Behavior," in B. M. Staw and L. L. Cummings, eds., *Research in Organizational Behavior*, vol. 12 (Greenwich, CT: JAI Press, 1990).

55. D. Watson and L. A. Clark, "Negative Affectivity: The Disposition to Experience Aversive Emotional States," *Psychological Bulletin* 96 (1984): 465–490.

56. R. Ilies and T. Judge, "On the Heritability of Job Satisfaction: The Mediating Role of Personality," *Journal of Applied Psychology* 88 (2003): 750–759.

57. J. M. George, "State or Trait," *Journal of Applied Psychology* 76 (1991): 299–307.

58. J. M. George, "Mood and Absence," *Journal of Applied Psychology* 74 (1989): 287–324.

59. S. Lyubormirsky, L. King, and E. Diener, "The Benefits of Frequent Positive Affect: Does Happiness Lead to Success?" *Psychological Bulletin* 131(6) (2005): 803–855.

60. M. J. Burke, A. P. Brief, and J. M. George, "The Role of Negative Affectivity in Understanding Relations between Self-Reports of Stressors and Strains: A Comment on the Applied Psychology Literature," *Journal of Applied Psychology* 78 (1993): 402–412.

61. S. Barsade, A. Ward, J. Turner, and J. Sonnenfeld, "To Your Heart's Content: A Model of Affective Diversity in Top Management Teams," *Administrative Science Quarterly* 45 (2000): 802–836.

62. J. Schaubroeck, F. O. Walumbwa, D. C. Ganster, and S. Kepes, "Destructive Leader Traits and the Neutralizing Influence of an 'Enriched' Job," *Leadership Quarterly* 18(3) (2007): 236–251.

63. S. Kaplan, J. C. Bradley, J. N. Luchman, and D. Haynes, "On the Role of Positive and Negative Affectivity in Job Performance: A Meta-Analytic Investigation," *Journal of Applied Psychology* 94 (January 2009): 162–176.

64. W. Mischel, "The Interaction of Person and Situation," in D. Magnusson and N. S. Endler, eds., *Personality at the Crossroads: Current Issues in Interactional Psychology* (Hillsdale, NJ: Erlbaum, 1977).

65. H. Rorschach, *Psychodiagnostics* (Bern: Hans Huber, 1921).

66. C. G. Jung, *Psychological Types* (New York: Harcourt & Brace, 1923).

67. Consulting Psychologists Press, http://www.cpp.com.

68. R. Benfari and J. Knox, *Understanding Your Management Style* (Lexington, MA: Lexington Books, 1991).

69. I. B. Myers, M. H. McCaulley, N. L. Quenk, and A. L. Hammer, *MBTI® Manual: A Guide to the Development and Use of the Myers-Briggs Type Indicator®*, 3rd ed. (Palo Alto, CA: Consulting Psychologists Press, 1998).

70. S. Hirsch and J. Kummerow, *Life Types* (New York: Warner Books, 1989).

71. Myers et al., *MBTI® Manual*; ibid.

72. G. P. Macdaid, M. H. McCaulley, and R. I. Kainz, *Myers-Briggs Type Indicator®: Atlas of Type Tables* (Gainesville, FL: Center for Application of Psychological Type, 1987).

73. J. B. Murray, "Review of Research on the Myers-Briggs Type Indicator®," *Perceptual and Motor Skills* 70 (1990): 1187–1202.

74. J. G. Carlson, "Recent Assessment of the Myers-Briggs Type Indicator®," *Journal of Personality Assessment* 49 (1985): 356–365.

75. A. Thomas, M. Benne, M. Marr, E. Thomas, and R. Hume, "The Evidence Remains Stable: The MBTI® Predicts Attraction and Attrition in an Engineering Program," *Journal of Psychological Type* 55 (2000): 35–42.

76. C. Walck, "Training for Participative Management: Implications for Psychological Type," *Journal of Psychological Type* 21 (1991): 3–12.

77. J. Michael, "Using the Myers-Briggs Indicator as a Tool for Leadership Development: Apply with Caution," *Journal of Leadership & Organizational Studies* 10 (2003): 68–78.

78. E. C. Webster, *The Employment Interview: A Social Judgment Process* (Schomberg, Canada: SIP, 1982).

79. A. J. Ward, M. J. Lankau, A. C. Amason, J. A. Sonnenfeld, and B. R. Agle, "Improving the Performance of Top Management Teams," *MIT Sloan Management Review* 48(3) (2007): 85–90.

80. N. Adler, *International Dimensions of Organizational Behavior*, 2nd ed. (Boston: PWS-Kent, 1991).

81. L. R. Offerman and M. K. Gowing, "Personnel Selection in the Future: The Impact of Changing Demographics and the Nature of Work," in N. Schmitt, W. C. Borman and Associates, eds., *Personnel Selection in Organizations* (San Francisco: Jossey-Bass, 1993).

82. J. Park and M. R. Banaji, "Mood and Heuristics: The Influence of Happy and Sad States on Sensitivity and Bias in Stereotyping," *Journal of Personality and Social Psychology* 78 (2000): 1005–1023.

83. M. W. Levine and J. M. Shefner, *Fundamentals of Sensation and Perception* (Reading, MA: Addison-Wesley, 1981).

84. R. L. Dipboye, H. L. Fromkin, and K. Willback, "Relative Importance of Applicant Sex, Attractiveness, and Scholastic Standing in Evaluations of Job Applicant Resumes," *Journal of Applied Psychology* 60 (1975): 39–43.

85. I. H. Frieze, J. E. Olson, and J. Russell, "Attractiveness and Income for Men and Women in Management," *Journal of Applied Social Psychology* 21 (1991): 1039–1057.

86. P. Ekman and W. Friesen, *Unmasking the Face* (Englewood Cliffs, NJ: Prentice Hall, 1975).

87. J. E. Rehfeld, "What Working for a Japanese Company Taught Me," *Harvard Business Review* (November–December 1990): 167–176.

88. M. W. Morris and R. P. Larrick, "When One Cause Casts Doubt on Another: A Normative Analysis of Discounting in Causal Attribution," *Psychological Review* 102 (1995): 331–355.

89. G. B. Sechrist and C. Stangor, "Perceived Consensus Influences Intergroup Behavior and Stereotype Accessibility," *Journal of Personality and Psychology* 80 (2001): 645–654; A. Lyons and Y. Kashima, "How Are Stereotypes Maintained Through Communication? The Influence of Stereotype Sharedness," *Journal of Personality and Social Psychology* 85 (2003): 989–1005.

90. L. Copeland, "Learning to Manage a Multicultural Workforce," *Training* (May 1988): 48–56.

91. S. Ferrari, "Human Behavior in International Groups," *Management International Review* 7 (1972): 31–35.

92. M. Johns, M. Inzlicht and T. Schamder. "Stereotype Threat and Executive Resource Depletion: Examining the Influence of Emotion Regulation" *Journal of Experimental Psychology* 137 (2008): 691–705.

93. A. Feingold, "Gender Differences in Effects of Physical Attractiveness on Romantic Attraction: A Comparison across Five Research Paradigms," *Journal of Personality and Social Psychology* 59 (1990): 981–993.

94. M. Snyder, "When Belief Creates Reality," *Advances in Experimental Social Psychology* 18 (1984): 247–305.

95. M. Biernat, "Toward a Broader View of Social Stereotyping," *American Psychologist* 58 (2003): 1019–1027.

96. E. Burnstein and Y. Schul, "The Informational Basis of Social Judgments: Operations in Forming an Impression of Another Person," *Journal of Experimental Social Psychology* 18 (1982): 217–234.

97. T. DeGroot and S. Motowidlo, "Why Visual and Vocal Cues Can Affect Interviewers' Judgments and Predict Job Performance," *Journal of Applied Psychology* 84. (1999): 986–993; M. C. L. Greene and L. Mathieson, *The Voice and Its Disorders* (London: Whurr, 1989).

98. R. L. Gross and S. E. Brodt, "How Assumptions of Consensus Undermine Decision Making," *MIT Sloan Management Review* 42 (Winter 2001): 86–94.

99. R. Rosenthal and L. Jacobson, *Pygmalion in the Classroom: Teacher Expectations and Pupils' Intellectual Development* (New York: Holt, Rinehart & Winston, 1968).

100. D. Eden and Y. Zuk, "Seasickness as a Self-Fulfilling Prophecy: Raising Self-Efficacy to Boost Performance at Sea," *Journal of Applied Psychology* 80 (1995): 628–635.

101. N. M. Kierein and M. A. Gold, "Pygmalion in Work Organizations: A Meta-Analysis," *Journal of Organizational Behavior* 21 (2000): 913–928.

102. D. Eden, "Pygmalion without Interpersonal Contrast Effects: Whole Groups Gain from Raising Manager Expectations," *Journal of Applied Psychology* 75 (1990): 394–398.

103. R. A. Giacolone and P. Rosenfeld, eds., *Impression Management in Organizations* (Hillsdale, NJ: Erlbaum, 1990); J. Tedeschi and V. Melburg, "Impression Management and Influence in the Organization," in S. Bacharach and E. Lawler, eds., *Research in the Sociology of Organizations* (Greenwich, CT: JAI Press, 1984), 31–58.

104. A. Colella and A. Varma, "The Impact of Subordinate Disability on Leader–Member Exchange Relationships," *Academy of Management Journal* 44 (2001): 304–315.

105. L. M. Roberts, "Changing Faces: Professional Image Construction in Diverse Organizational Settings," *Academy of Management Review* 30 (2005): 85–711.

106. D. C. Gilmore and G. R. Ferris, "The Effects of Applicant Impression Management Tactics on Interviewer Judgments," *Journal of Management* (December 1989): 557–564.

107. C. K. Stevens and A. L. Kristof, "Making the Right Impression: A Field Study of Applicant Impressions Management during Job Interviews," *Journal of Applied Psychology* 80 (1995): 587–606.

108. S. J. Wayne and R. C. Liden, "Effects of Impression Management on Performance Ratings: A Longitudinal Study," *Academy of Management Journal* 38 (1995): 232–260.

109. R. A. Baron, "Impression Management by Applicants during Employment Interviews: The 'Too Much of a Good Thing' Effect," in R. W. Eder and G. R. Ferris, eds., *The Employment Interview: Theory, Research, and Practice* (Newbury Park, CA: Sage Publications, 1989).

110. F. Heider, *The Psychology of Interpersonal Relations* (New York: John Wiley & Sons, 1958).

111. B. Weiner, "An Attributional Theory of Achievement Motivation and Emotion," *Psychological Review* (October 1985): 548–573.

112. P. D. Sweeney, K. Anderson, and S. Bailey, "Attributional Style in Depression: A Meta-Analytic Review," *Journal of Personality and Social Psychology* 51 (1986): 974–991.

113. P. Rosenthal, D. Guest, and R. Peccei, "Gender Differences in Managers' Causal Explanations for Their Work Performance," *Journal of Occupational and Organizational Psychology* 69 (1996): 145–151.

114. J. Silvester, "Spoken Attributions and Candidate Success in Graduate Recruitment Interviews," *Journal of Occupational and Organizational Psychology* 70 (1997): 61–71.

115. L. Ross, "The Intuitive Psychologist and His Shortcomings: Distortions in the Attribution Process," in L. Berkowitz, ed., *Advances in Experimental Social Psychology* (New York: Academic Press, 1977); M. O'Sullivan, "The Fundamental Attribution Error in Detecting Deception: The Boy-Who-Cried Wolf Effect," *Personality & Social Psychology Bulletin* 29 (2003): 1316–1327.

116. D. T. Miller and M. Ross, "Self-Serving Biases in the Attribution of Causality: Fact or Fiction?" *Psychological Bulletin* 82 (1975): 313–325.

117. J. R. Schermerhorn, Jr., "Team Development for High-Performance Management," *Training and Development Journal* 40 (1986): 38–41.

118. J. G. Miller, "Culture and the Development of Everyday Causal Explanation," *Journal of Personality and Social Psychology* 46 (1984): 961–978.

119. G. Si, S. Rethorst, and K. Willimczik, "Causal Attribution Perception in Sports Achievement: A Cross-Cultural Study on Attributional Concepts in Germany and China," *Journal of Cross-Cultural Psychology* 26 (1995): 537–553.

120. R. Spector and P. McCarthy, *The Nordstrom Way to Customer Service Excellence.* (Hobokan, NJ: John Wiley & Sons, 2005).

Chapter 3 Case

1. "About Deloitte," http://www.deloitte.com (accessed June 18, 2009).

2. J. Felix, "Teach Your Way to the Top," *Director* 60(2) (September 2006): 70.

3. Ibid.

4. Ibid.

5. Ibid., p. 71.

6. E. Keelan, "Personal File: Psychometric Tests—Psychokiller?," *Accountancy* (May 1, 2003): 1.

7. Ibid.

8. "How Coaching Helps a 'Big Four' Accounting Firm Retain Staff," *HR Focus* 83(1) (January 2006): 5.

9. Ibid.

10. Ibid., p. 6.

Chapter 4

1. http://www.facebook.com/press/info.php?statistics

2. http://www.facebook.com/terms/english.php

3. J. Wortham, "Facebook Won't Budge on Breastfeeding Photos," *New York Times* (January 2, 2009), http://bits.blogs.nytimes.com/2009/01/02/breastfeeding-facebook-photos/

4. L. Phillips, "Brussels Blasts Facebook Over Hate Groups," *Business Week Europe* (November 12, 2008), http://www.businessweek.com/globalbiz/content/nov2008/gb20081112_457292.htm

5. D. MacMillan, "Facebooks Holocaust Controversy," *Business Week Internet* (May 12, 2009), http://www.businessweek.com/technology/content/may2009/tc20090512_104433.htm

6. C. Parsons, "Hate Goes Viral on Social Network Sites: Group," *Rueters.com* (May 13, 2009), http://www.reuters.com/article/technologyNews/idUSTRE54C4KW20090513

7. MacMillan, "Facebooks Holocaust Controversy."

8. A. H. Eagly and S. Chaiken, *The Psychology of Attitudes* (Orlando, FL: Harcourt Brace Jovanovich, 1993).

9. M. J. Rosenberg, C. I. Hovland, W. J. McGuire, R. P. Abelson, and J. H. Brehm, *Attitude Organization and Change* (New Haven, CT: Yale University Press, 1960).

10. R. H. Fazio and M. P. Zanna, "On the Predictive Validity of Attitudes: The Roles of Direct Experience and Confidence," *Journal of Personality* 46 (1978): 228–243.

11. A. Tversky and D. Kahneman, "Judgment Under Uncertainty: Heuristics and Biases," in D. Kahneman, P. Slovic, and A. Tversky, eds., *Judgment Under Uncertainty* (New York: Cambridge University Press, 1982): 3–20.

12. D. Rajecki, *Attitudes*, 2nd ed. (Sunderland, MA: Sinauer Associates, 1989).

13. I. Ajzen and M. Fishbein, "Attitude–Behavior Relations: A Theoretical Analysis and Review of Empirical Research," *Psychological Bulletin* 84 (1977): 888–918.

14. B. T. Johnson and A. H. Eagly, "Effects of Involvement on Persuasion: A Meta-Analysis," *Psychological Bulletin* 106 (1989): 290–314.

15. K. G. DeBono and M. Snyder, "Acting on One's Attitudes: The Role of History of Choosing Situations," *Personality and Social Psychology Bulletin* 21 (1995): 629–636.

16. I. Ajzen and M. Fishbein, *Understanding Attitudes and Predicting Social Behavior* (Englewood Cliffs, NJ: Prentice Hall, 1980).

17. I. Ajzen, "From Intentions to Action: A Theory of Planned Behavior," in J. Kuhl and J. Beckmann, eds., *Action-Control: From Cognition to Behavior* (Heidelberg: Springer, 1985).

18. I. Ajzen, "The Theory of Planned Behavior," *Organizational Behavior and Human Decision Processes* 50 (1991): 1–33.

19. L. Festinger, *A Theory of Cognitive Dissonance* (Evanston, IL: Row, Peterson, 1957).

20. A. Sagie and M. Krausz, "What Aspects of the Job Have Most Effect on Nurses?" *Human Resource Management Journal* 13 (2003): 46–62.

21. C. P. Parker, B. B. Baltes, S. A. Young, J. W. Huff, R. A. Altman, H. A. LaCost, and J. E. Roberts, "Relationships Between Psychological Climate Perceptions and Work Outcomes: A Meta-Analytic Review," *Journal of Organizational Behavior* 24 (2003): 389–416.

22. J. Lemmick and J. Mattsson, "Employee Behavior, Feelings of Warmth and Customer Perception in Service Encounters," *International Journal of Retail & Distribution Management* 30 (2002): 18–44.

23. E. A. Locke, "The Nature and Causes of Job Satisfaction," in M. Dunnette, ed., *Handbook of Industrial and Organizational Psychology* (Chicago: Rand McNally, 1976).

24. P. C. Smith, L. M. Kendall, and C. L. Hulin, *The Measurement of Satisfaction in Work and Retirement* (Skokie, IL: Rand McNally, 1969).

25. R. Ilies and T. A. Judge, "On the Heritability of Job Satisfaction: The Mediating Role of Personality," *Journal of Applied Psychology* 88 (2003): 750–759.

26. D. J. Weiss, R. V. Davis, G. W. England, and L. H. Lofquist, *Manual for the Minnesota Satisfaction Questionnaire* (Minneapolis: Industrial Relations Center, University of Minnesota, 1967).

27. C. D. Fisher, "Why Do Lay People Believe That Satisfaction and Performance Are Correlated? Possible Sources of a Commonsense Theory," *Journal of Organizational Behavior* 24 (2003): 753–777.

28. M. T. Iaffaldano and P. M. Muchinsky, "Job Satisfaction and Job Performance: A Meta-Analysis," *Psychological Bulletin* 97 (1985): 251–273.

29. L. A. Bettencourt, K. P. Gwinner, and M. L. Meuter, "A Comparison of Attitude, Personality, and Knowledge Predictors of Service-Oriented Organizational Citizenship Behaviors," *Journal of Applied Psychology* 86 (2001): 29–41.

30. Aplus.Net, "Aplus.Net Is Put to the Test with Firestorm 2003 and Passes with Flying Colors," http://www.aplus.net/comp_info_20031105.html (accessed November 6, 2003).

31. D. W. Organ, *Organizational Citizenship Behavior: The Good Soldier Syndrome* (Lexington, MA: Lexington Books, 1988).

32. P. M. Podsakoff, S. B. Mackenzie, and C. Hui, "Organizational Citizenship Behaviors and Managerial Evaluations of Employee Performance: A Review and Suggestions for Future Research," G. Ferris, ed., in *Research in Personnel and Human Resources Management* (Greenwich, CT: JAI Press, 1993): 1–40.

33. K. Lee. and N. J. Allen, "Organizational Citizenship Behavior and Workplace Deviance: The Role of Affect and Cognitions," *Journal of Applied Psychology* 87(1) (2002): 131–142.

34. O. Christ, R. Van Dick, and U. Wagner, "When Teachers Go the Extra Mile: Foci of Organizational Identification as Determinants of Different Forms of Organizational Citizenship Behavior Among Schoolteachers," *British Journal of Educational Psychology* 73 (2003): 329–341.

35. G. L. Blakely, M. C. Andrews, and J. Fuller, "Are Chameleons Good Citizens: A Longitudinal Study of the Relationship between Self-Monitoring and Organizational Citizenship Behavior," *Journal of Business & Psychology* 18 (2003): 131–144.

36. W. H. Bommer, E. W. Miles, and S. L. Grover, "Does One Good Turn Deserve Another? Coworker Influences on Employee Citizenship," *Journal of Organizational Behavior* 24 (2003): 181–196.

37. C. Ostroff, "The Relationship Between Satisfaction, Attitudes and Performance: An Organizational Level Analysis," *Journal of Applied Psychology* 77 (1992): 963–974.

38. R. Griffin and T. Bateman, "Job Satisfaction and Organizational Commitment," in C. Cooper and I. Robertson, eds., *International Review of Industrial and Organizational Psychology* (New York: John Wiley & Sons, 1986).

39. A. R. Wheeler, V. C. Gallagher, R. L. Brouer, and C. J. Sablynski, "When Person-Organization (Mis)fit and (Dis)satisfaction Lead to Turnover: The Moderating Role of Perceived Job Mobility," *Journal of Managerial Psychology* 22(2): 203–219.

40. X. Huang and E. Van De Vliert, "Where Intrinsic Job Satisfaction Fails to Work: National Moderators of Intrinsic Motivation," *Journal of Organizational Behavior* 24 (2003): 133–250.

41. L. Sun, S. Aryee, and K. S. Law, "High-Performance Human Resource Practices, Citizenship Behavior, and Organizational Performance: A Relational Perspective," *Academy of Management Journal* 50(3): 558–577.

42. S. L. Robinson and R. J. Bennett, "A Typology of Deviant Workplace Behaviors: A Multidimensional Scaling Study," *Academy of Management Journal* 38(2) (1995): 555–572.

43. M. E. Heilman and V. B. Alcott, "What I Think You Think of Me: Women's Reactions to Being Viewed as Beneficiaries of Preferential Selection," *Journal of Applied Psychology* 86 (2001): 574–582.

44. M. E. Heilman, C. J. Block, and P. Stathatos, "The Affirmative Action Stigma of Incompetence: Effects of Performance Information Ambiguity," *Academy of Management Journal* 40 (1997): 603–625.

45. B. J. Tepper, J. C. Carr, D. M. Breaux, S. Geider, C. Hu, and W. Hua, "Abusive Supervision, Intentions to Quit, and Employees' Workplace Deviance: A Power/Dependence Analysis," *Organizational Behavior and Human Decision Processes* (in press).

46. R. T. Mowday, L. W. Porter, and R. M. Steers, *Employee–Organization Linkages: The Psychology of Commitment* (New York: Academic Press, 1982).

47. H. S. Becker, "Notes on the Concept of Commitment," *American Journal of Sociology* 66 (1960): 32–40.

48. J. P. Meyer, N. J. Allen, and C. A. Smith, "Commitment to Organizations and Occupations: Extension and Test of a Three-Component Model," *Journal of Applied Psychology* 78 (1993): 538–551.

49. J. P. Curry, D. S. Wakefield, J. L. Price, and C. W. Mueller, "On the Causal Ordering of Job Satisfaction and Organizational Commitment," *Academy of Management Journal* 29 (1986): 847–858.

50. T. N. Bauer, T. Bodner, B. Erdogan, D. M. Truxillo, and J. S. Tucker, "Newcomer Adjustment during Organizational Socialization: A Meta-Analytic Review of Antecedents, Outcomes, and Methods," *Journal of Applied Psychology* 92(3) (2007): 707–721.

51. B. Benkhoff, "Ignoring Commitment Is Costly: New Approaches Establish the Missing Link between Commitment and Performance," *Human Relations* 50 (1997): 701–726; N. J. Allen and J. P. Meyer, "Affective, Continuance, and Normative Commitment to the Organization: An Examination of Construct Validity," *Journal of Vocational Behavior* 49 (1996): 252–276.

52. M. J. Somers, "Organizational Commitment, Turnover, and Absenteeism: An Examination of Direct and Interaction Effects," *Journal of Organizational Behavior* 16 (1995): 49–58; L. Lum, J. Kervin, K. Clark, F. Reid, and W. Sirola, "Explaining Nursing Turnover Intent: Job Satisfaction, Pay Satisfaction, or Organizational Commitment?" *Journal of Organizational Behavior* 19 (1998): 305–320.

53. F. Stinglhamber and C. Vandenberghe, "Organizations and Supervisors as Sources of Support and Targets of Commitment," *Journal of Organizational Behavior* 24 (2003): 251–270.

54. R. Eisenberger *et al.*, "Reciprocation of Perceived Organizational Support," *Journal of Applied Psychology* 86 (2001): 42–51; J. E. Finegan, "The Impact of Person and Organizational Values on Organizational Commitment," *Journal of Occupational and Organizational Psychology* 73 (2000): 149–169.

55. E. Snape and T. Redman, "Too Old or Too Young? The Impact of Perceived Age Discrimination," *Human Resource Management Journal* 13 (2003): 78–89.

56. Y. Gong, K. S. Law, S. Chang, and K. R. Xin, "Human Resources Management and Firm Performance: The Differential Role of Managerial Affective and Continuance Commitment," *Journal of Applied Psychology* 94 (January 2009): 263–275.

57. F. Luthans, H. S. McCaul, and N. C. Dodd, "Organizational Commitment: A Comparison of American, Japanese, and Korean Employees," *Academy of Management Journal* 28 (1985): 213–219.

58. C. Wong and I. Wong, "The Role of Perceived Quality of Social Relationships within Organizations in Chinese Societies," *International Journal of Management* 20 (2003): 216–223.

59. D. J. Koys, "The Effects of Employee Satisfaction, Organizational Citizenship Behavior, and Turnover on Organizational Effectiveness: A Unit-Level, Longitudinal Study," *Personnel Psychology* 54 (2001): 101–114.

60. J. A. Conger, "The Necessary Art of Persuasion," *Harvard Business Review* 76 (1998): 84–96.

61. J. Cooper and R. T. Croyle, "Attitudes and Attitude Change," *Annual Review of Psychology* 35 (1984): 395–426.

62. P. Sellers, "The Trials of John Mack," *Fortune* (August 11, 2003): 98–102.

63. D. M. Mackie and L. T. Worth, "Processing Deficits and the Mediation of Positive Affect in Persuasion," *Journal of Personality and Social Psychology* 57 (1989): 27–40.

64. J. W. Brehm, *Responses to Loss of Freedom: A Theory of Psychological Reactance* (New York: General Learning Press, 1972).

65. D. DeSteno, R. E. Petty, and D. D. Rucker, "Discrete Emotions and Persuasion: The Role of Emotion-Induced Expectancies," *Journal of Personality & Social Psychology* 86 (2004): 43–56.

66. J. Cesario and E.T. Higgins, "Making Message Recipients 'Feel Right': How Nonverbal Cues Can Increase Persuasion," *Psychological Science* 19 (May 2008): 415–420.

67. R. Petty, D. T. Wegener, and L. R. Fabrigar, "Attitudes and Attitude Change," *Annual Review of Psychology* 48 (1997): 609–647.

68. P. Brinol and R. E. Petty, "Overt Head Movements and Persuasion: A Self-Validation Analysis," *Journal of Personality & Social Psychology* 84 (2003): 1123–1139.

69. L. C. Levitan and P. S. Visser, "The Impact of the Social Context on Resistance to Persuasion: Effortful versus Effortless Responses to Counter-Attitudinal Information," *Journal of Experimental Social Psychology* 44 (2008): 640–649.

70. W. Wood, "Attitude Change: Persuasion and Social Influence," *Annual Review of Psychology* 51 (2000): 539–570.

71. D. Watson and L. A. Clark, "Affects Separable and Inseparable: On the Hierarchical Arrangement of Negative Affects," *Journal of Personality and Social Psychology* 62 (1992): 489–505.

72. A. Ortony, G. L. Clore, and A. Collins, *The Cognitive Structure of Emotions* (Cambridge, England: Cambridge University Press, 1988).

73. R. S. Lazarus, *Emotion and Adaptation* (New York: Oxford University Press, 1991).

74. H. M. Weiss, K. Suckow, and R. Cropanzano, "Effects of Justice Conditions on Discrete Emotions," *Journal of Applied Psychology* 84 (1999): 786–794.

75. B. M. Staw and S. G. Barsade, "Affect and Managerial Performance: A Test of the Sadder but Wiser vs Happier and Smarter Hypothesis," *Administrative Science Quarterly* 38, (1993): 304–331.

76. P. T. Van Katwyk, S. Fox, P. E. Spector, and E. K. Kelloway, "Using the Job-Related Affective Well-Being Scale to Investigate Affective Responses to Work Stressors," *Journal of Occupational Health Psychology* 52 (2000): 219–230.

77. S. Kaplan, J. C. Bradley, J. N. Luchman, and D. Haynes, "On the Role of Positive and Negative Affectivity in Job Performance: A Meta-Analytic Investigation," *Journal of Applied Psychology* 94 (2009): 16278. T. B. Lawrence and S. L. Robinson, "Ain't Misbehavin: Workplace Deviance as Organizational Resistance," *Journal of Management* 33(3) (2007): 378–394.

79. B. L. Fredrickson and C. Brannigan, "Positive Emotions," in G. Bonnano and T. Mayne, eds., *Emotions: Current Issues and Future Directions* (New York: Guilford Press, 2001): 123–152.

80. A. M. Isen and R. A. Baron, "Positive Affect as a Factor in Organizational Behavior," *Research in Organizational Behavior* 13 (1991): 1–53.

81. S. G. Barsade, "The Ripple Effect: Emotional Contagion and Its Influence on Group Behavior," *Administrative Science Quarterly* 47 (2002): 644–675.

82. J. E. Dutton, P. J. Frost, M. C. Worline, J. M. Lilius, and J. M., Kanov, "Leading in Times of Trauma," *Harvard Business Review* 80(1) (2002): 54–61.

83. F. Navran, "Your Role in Shaping Ethics," *Executive Excellence* 9 (1992): 11–12.

84. K. Labich, "The New Crisis in Business Ethics," *Fortune* (April 20, 1992): 167–176.

85. L. S. Paine, *Value Shift: Why Companies Must Merge Social and Financial Imperatives to Achieve Superior Performance* (New York: McGraw-Hill, 2003).

86. D. B. Turban and D. M. Cable, "Firm Reputation and Applicant Pool Characteristics," *Journal of Organizational Behavior* 24 (2003): 733–751.

87. E. A. Lind, J. Greenberg, K. S. Scott, and T. D. Welchans, "The Winding Road from Employee to Complainant: Situational and Psychological Determinants of Wrongful-Termination Claims," *Administrative Science Quarterly* 45 (2000): 557–590.

88. Miriam Schulman, "LittleBrother Is Watching You," http://www.scu.edu/ethics/publications/iie/v9n2/brother.html.

89. G. Flynn, "Make Employee Ethics Your Business," *Personnel Journal* (June 1995): 30–40.

90. M. Oneal, P. Callahan, and E. Osnos, "Mattel Recalls 18 Million Toys," *Chicago Tribune* (August 15, 2007), http://www.chicagotribune.com/business/chi-toysaug15,0,7223810.story

91. P. Bansal, "Experts Say Mattel Image Hit and Recall Suits a Risk," *Reuters.com* (August 14, 2007), http://uk.reuters.com/article/topNews/idUKN1429386120070814?pageNumber=1&virtualBrandChannel=0

92. M. S. Baucus and D. A. Baucus, "Paying the Piper: An Empirical Examination of Longer-Term Financial Consequences of Illegal Corporate Behavior," *Academy of Management Journal* 40 (1997): 129–151.

93. J. O. Cherrington and D. J. Cherrington, "A Menu of Moral Issues: One Week in the Life of *Wall Street Journal*," *Journal of Business Ethics* 11 (1992): 255–265.

94. B. L. Flannery and D. R. May, "Environmental Ethical Decision Making in the U.S. Metal-Finishing Industry," *Academy of Management Journal* 43 (2000): 642–662.

95. K. R. Andrews, "Ethics in Practice," *Harvard Business Review* 89 (1989): 99–104.

96. M. Rokeach, *The Nature of Human Values* (New York: Free Press, 1973).

97. M. Rokeach and S. J. Ball-Rokeach, "Stability and Change in American Value Priorities, 1968–1981," *American Psychologist* 44 (1989): 775–784.

98. S. P. Eisner, "Managing Generation Y," *S.A.M. Advanced Management Journal* 70(4) (2005): 4–15.

99. G. W. England, "Organizational Goals and Expected Behavior of American Managers," *Academy of Management Journal* 10 (1967): 107–117.

100. E. C. Ravlin and B. M. Meglino, "Effects of Values on Perception and Decision Making: A Study of Alternative Work Values Measures," *Journal of Applied Psychology* 72 (1987): 666–673.

101. E. C. Ravlin and B. M. Meglino, "The Transitivity of Work Values: Hierarchical Preference Ordering of Socially Desirable Stimuli," *Organizational Behavior and Human Decision Processes* 44 (1989): 494–508.

102. B. M. Meglino, E. C. Ravlin, and C. L. Adkins, "A Work Values Approach to Corporate Culture: A Field Test of the Value Congruence Process and Its Relationship to Individual Outcomes," *Journal of Applied Psychology* 74 (1989): 424–432.

103. T. A. Judge and R. D. Bretz, Jr., "Effects of Work Values on Job Choice Decisions," *Journal of Applied Psychology* 77 (1992): 261–271.

104. Tony Jones, "Survey Finds Big Business Lacking in Social Responsibility," *Australian Broadcasting Corporation* (October 13, 2003), http://www.abc.net.au/lateline/content/2003/s966137.htm; RepuTex, http://www.reputex.com.au.

105. R. H. Doktor, "Asian and American CEOs: A Comparative Study," *Organizational Dynamics* 18 (1990): 46–56.

106. R. L. Tung, "Handshakes across the Sea: Cross-Cultural Negotiating for Business Success," *Organizational Dynamics* (Winter 1991): 30–40.

107. C. Gomez, B. L. Kirkman, and D. L. Shapiro, "The Impact of Collectivism and In-Group/Out-Group Membership on the Evaluation Generosity of Team Members," *Academy of Management Journal* 43 (2000): 1097–1106; J. Zhou and J. J. Martocchio, "Chinese and American Managers' Compensation Award Decisions: A Comparative Policy-Capturing Study," *Personnel Psychology* 54 (2001): 115–145.

108. A. J. Ali and M. Amirshahi, "The Iranian Manager: Work Values and Orientations," *Journal of Business Ethics* 40 (2002): 133–143.

109. R. Neale and R. Mindel, "Rigging Up Multicultural Teamworking," *Personnel Management* (January 1992): 27–30.

110. K. Hodgson, "Adapting Ethical Decisions to a Global Marketplace," *Management Review* 81 (1992): 53–57.

111. J. B. Rotter, "Generalized Expectancies for Internal versus External Control of Reinforcement," *Psychological Monographs* 80 (1966): 1–28.

112. L. K. Trevino and S. A. Youngblood, "Bad Apples in Bad Barrels: A Causal Analysis of Ethical Decision-Making Behavior," *Journal of Applied Psychology* 75 (1990): 378–385.

113. H. M. Lefcourt, *Locus of Control: Current Trends in Theory and Research*, 2nd ed. (Hillsdale, NJ: Erlbaum, 1982).

114. N. Machiavelli, *The Prince*, trans. George Bull (Middlesex, England: Penguin Books, 1961).

115. R. Christie and F. L. Geis, *Studies in Machiavellianism* (New York: Academic Press, 1970).

116. R. A. Giacalone and S. B. Knouse, "Justifying Wrongful Employee Behavior: The Role of Personality in Organizational Sabotage," *Journal of Business Ethics* 9 (1990): 55–61.

117. S. B. Knouse and R. A. Giacalone, "Ethical Decision Making in Business: Behavioral Issues and Concerns," *Journal of Business Ethics* 11 (1992): 369–377.

118. L. Kohlberg, "Stage and Sequence: The Cognitive Developmental Approach to Socialization," in D. A. Goslin, ed., *Handbook of Socialization Theory and Research* (Chicago: Rand McNally, 1969): 347–480.

119. C. I. Malinowski and C. P. Smith, "Moral Reasoning and Moral Conduct: An Investigation Prompted by Kohlberg's Theory," *Journal of Personality and Social Psychology* 49 (1985): 1016–1027.

120. M. Brabeck, "Ethical Characteristics of Whistleblowers," *Journal of Research in Personality* 18 (1984): 41–53.

121. W. Y. Penn and B. D. Collier, "Current Research in Moral Development as a Decision Support System," *Journal of Business Ethics* 4 (1985): 131–136.

122. Trevino and Youngblood, "Bad Apples in Bad Barrels."

123. C. Gilligan, *In a Different Voice: Psychological Theory and Women's Development* (Cambridge, MA: Harvard University Press, 1982).

124. S. Jaffee and J. S. Hyde, "Gender Differences in Moral Orientation: A Meta-Analysis," *Psychological Bulletin* 126 (2000): 703–726.

125. G. R. Franke, D. F. Crown, and D. F. Spake, "Gender Differences in Ethical Perceptions of Business Practices: A Social Role Theory Perspective," *Journal of Applied Psychology* 82 (1997): 920–934.

126. S. A. Goldman and J. Arbuthnot, "Teaching Medical Ethics: The Cognitive-Developmental Approach," *Journal of Medical Ethics* 5 (1979): 171–181.

127. MacMillan, "Facebooks Holocaust Controversy."

Chapter 4 Case

1. "About Whole Foods Market," Whole Foods Market Web site, http://www.wholefoodsmarket.com/company/index.php (accessed July 2, 2009).

2. "Our History," Whole Foods Market, http://www.wholefoodsmarket.com/company/history.html (accessed October 10, 2007).

3. D. Kesmodel and J. Eig, "Unraveling Rahodeb: A Grocer's Brash Style-2-," *Wall Street Journal* (Eastern edition) (July 20, 2007): A1.

4. D. Kesmodel, "Court Clears Whole Foods Deal; FTC Loses Appeal to Delay Acquisition of Wild Oats, But Other Options Remain," *Wall Street Journal* (Eastern edition) (August 24, 2007): A2.

5. D. Kesmodel, "Whole Foods Wins Ruling on Wild Oats," *Wall Street Journal* (Eastern edition) (August 17, 2007): A3.

6. Kesmodel and Eig, "Unraveling Rahodeb,"A1.

7. Ibid.

8. D. Kesmodel, "SEC Opens Informal Inquiry of Whole Foods CEO Postings," *Wall Street Journal* (Eastern edition) (July 14, 2007): A2.

9. D. Kesmodel and J. R. Wilke, "Whole Foods Is Hot, Wild Oats a Dud—So Said 'Rahodeb'; Then Again, Yahoo Poster was a Whole Foods Staffer, the CEO to Be Precise," *Wall Street Journal* (Eastern edition) (July 12, 2007): A1.

10. Ibid.

11. Kesmodel and Eig, "Unraveling Rahodeb,"A1.

12. Ibid.

13. Ibid.

14. Ibid.

15. H. W. Jenkins, Jr., "Business World: Lessons of a Food Fight," *Wall Street Journal* (Eastern edition) (August 29, 2007): A14.

16. J. R. Wilke, "Corporate News: Whole Foods Returns FTC's Fire—Grocer Files Rare Suit Against U.S. Agency in Fight Over Wild Oats Merger," *Wall Street Journal* (Eastern edition) (December 9, 2008): B3.

17. "Blogger's Shameless Spin," *Workforce Management* 87(10) (June 9, 2008): 41.

18. Ibid.

19. H. Havenstein, "SEC Ruling Lets Whole Foods CEO Blog Again," *Computerworld* 42(23) (June 2, 2008): 8.

20. H. Mummert, "Is That You, John Mackey?," *Target Marketing* 32(6) (June 2009): 9.

21. "Blogger's Shameless Spin,"41.

22. J. R. Wilke, "Corporate News: Whole Foods Returns FTC's Fire—Grocer Files Rare Suit Against U.S. Agency in Fight Over Wild Oats Merger," *Wall Street Journal* (Eastern edition) (December 9, 2008): B3.

23. "Retail's Power 25: The 25 Most Influential People in Retailing," *Chain Store Age* 84(1) (January 2008): 6A.

Chapter 5

1. "Aiming for the Same Target." *The Sunday Times* (March 8, 2009): 18-18

2. L. W. Porter, G. Bigley, and R. M. Steers, *Motivation and Leadership at Work*, 7th ed. (New York: McGraw-Hill, 2002).

3. J. P. Campbell and R. D. Pritchard, "Motivation Theory in Industrial and Organizational Psychology," in M. D. Dunnette, ed., *Handbook of Industrial and Organizational Psychology* (Chicago: Rand McNally, 1976), 63–130.

4. M. Weber, *The Protestant Ethic and the Spirit of Capitalism* (London: Talcott Parson, tr., 1930).

5. S. Freud, *Civilization and Its Discontents*, trans. and ed. J. Strachey (New York: Norton, 1961).

6. P. D. Dunlop and K. Lee, "Workplace Deviance, Organizational Citizenship Behavior, and Business Unit Performance: The Bad Apples Do Spoil the Whole Barrel," *Journal of Organizational Behavior* 25 (2004): 67–80.

7. K. J. Sweetman, "Employee Loyalty Around the Globe," *Sloan Management Review* 42 (2001): 16.

8. B. S. Frey, *Not Just for the Money: An Economic Theory of Personal Motivation* (Brookfield, VT: Edgar Elger, 1997).

9. N. Nohria, B. Groysberg, and L. Lee, "Employee Motivation: A Powerful New Model," *Harvard Business Review* (July–August 2008): 78–84.

10. J. L. Matjasko and A. F. Feldman, "Bringing Work Home: The Emotional Experiences of Mothers and Fathers," *Journal of Family Psychology* 20 (2006): 47–55.

11. F. J. Roethlisberger, *Management and Morale* (Cambridge, MA: Harvard University Press, 1941).

12. C. Boardman and E. Sundquist, "Toward Understanding Work Motivation," *The American Review of Public Administration* (2008), doi: 10.1177/0275074008324567.

13. A. Smith, *An Inquiry into the Nature and Causes of the Wealth of Nations*, Vol. 10 of *The Harvard Classics*, C. J. Bullock, ed. (New York: Collier, 1909).

14. J. Jennings, *Less Is More: How Great Companies Use Productivity as a Competitive Tool in Business* (New York: Portfolio, 2002).

15. F. W. Taylor, *The Principles of Scientific Management* (New York: Norton, 1911).

16. Hearings before Special Committee of the House of Representatives to Investigate the Taylor and Other Systems of Shop Management under Authority of House Resolution 90, Vol. 3, 1377–1508 contains Taylor's testimony before the committee from Thursday, January 25, through Tuesday, January 30, 1912.

17. J. Breal, "Secret sauce," *Fast Company* 115 (May 2007): 61–63.

18. L. Van Dyne and J. L. Pierce, "Psychological Ownership and Feelings of Possession: Three Field Studies Predicting Employee Attitudes and Organizational Citizenship Behavior," *Journal of Organizational Behavior* 25 (2004): 439–459.

19. A. H. Maslow, "A Theory of Human Motivation," *Psychological Review* 50 (1943): 370–396.

20. W. James, *The Principles of Psychology* (New York: H. Holt & Co., 1890; Cambridge, MA: Harvard University Press, 1983).

21. J. Dewey, *Human Nature and Conduct: An Introduction to Social Psychology* (New York: Holt, 1922).

22. S. Freud, *A General Introduction to Psycho-Analysis: A Course of Twenty-Eight Lectures Delivered at the University of Vienna* (New York: Liveright, 1963); A. Adler, *Understanding Human Nature* (Greenwich, CT: Fawcett, 1927).

23. L. W. Porter, "A Study of Perceived Need Satisfactions in Bottom and Middle Management Jobs," *Journal of Applied Psychology* 45 (1961): 1–10.

24. E. E. Lawler, III and J. L. Suttle, "A Causal Correlational Test of the Need Hierarchy Concept," *Organizational Behavior and Human Performance* 7 (1973): 265–287.

25. D. M. McGregor, *The Human Side of Enterprise* (New York: McGraw-Hill, 1960).

26. D. M. McGregor, "The Human Side of Enterprise," *Management Review* (November 1957): 22–28, 88–92.

27. E. E. Lawler, G. E. Lawford, S. A. Mohrman, and G. E. Ledford, Jr., *Strategies for High Performance Organizations—The CEO Report: Employee Involvement, TQM, and Reengineering Programs in Fortune 1000 Corporations* (San Francisco: Jossey-Bass, Inc., 1998).

28. J. Boorstin, "No Preservatives. No Unions. Lots of Dough," *Fortune* 148 (September 15, 2003): 127–129.

29. G. E. Forward, D. E. Beach, D. A. Gray, and J. C. Quick, "Mentofacturing: A Vision for American Industrial Excellence," *Academy of Management Executive* 5 (1991): 32–44.

30. C. P. Alderfer, *Human Needs in Organizational Settings* (New York: Free Press, 1972).

31. B. Schneider and C. P. Alderfer, "Three Studies of Need Satisfactions in Organizations," *Administrative Science Quarterly* 18 (1973): 489–505.

32. H. A. Murray, *Explorations in Personality: A Clinical and Experimental Study of Fifty Men of College Age* (New York: Oxford University Press, 1938).

33. D. C. McClelland, *Motivational Trends in Society* (Morristown, NJ: General Learning Press, 1971).

34. J. P. Chaplin and T. S. Krawiec, *Systems and Theories of Psychology* (New York: Holt, Rinehart & Winston, 1960).

35. D. C. McClelland, "Achievement Motivation Can Be Learned," *Harvard Business Review* 43 (1965): 6–24.

36. S. Chen, H. Wang, C. Wei, B. Fwu, and K. Hwang, "Taiwanese Students' Self-Attributions for Two Types of Achievement Goals," *The Journal of Social Psychology*, 149(2): 179–193.

37. L. Houser-Marko and K. M. Sheldon, "Eyes on the Prize or Nose to the Grindstone? The Effects of Level of Goal Evaluation on Mood and Motivation," *Personality and Social Psychology Bulletin*, 34(11) (2008): 1556–1569.

38. E. A. Ward, "Multidimensionality of Achievement Motivation Among Employed Adults," *Journal of Social Psychology* 134 (1997): 542–544.

39. A. Sagie, D. Elizur, and H. Yamauchi, "The Structure and Strength of Achievement Motivation: A Cross-Cultural Comparison," *Journal of Organizational Behavior* 17 (1996): 431–444.

40. D. C. McClelland and D. Burnham, "Power Is the Great Motivator," *Harvard Business Review* 54 (1976): 100–111; J. Hall and J. Hawker, *Power Management Inventory* (The Woodlands, TX: Teleometrics International, 1988).

41. F. Luthans, "Successful versus Effective Real Managers," *Academy of Management Executive* 2 (1988): 127–131.

42. S. Schachter, *The Psychology of Affiliation* (Stanford, CA: Stanford University Press, 1959).

43. N. W. van Yperen and M. Hagedoorn, "Do High Job Demands Increase Intrinsic Motivation or Fatigue or Both? The Role of Job Control and Job Social Support," *Academy of Management Journal* 46 (2003): 339–348.

44. F. Herzberg, B. Mausner, and B. Snyderman, *The Motivation to Work* (New York: John Wiley & Sons, 1959).

45. F. Herzberg, *Work and the Nature of Man* (Cleveland: World, 1966).

46. D. S. Hamermesh, "The Changing Distribution of Job Satisfaction," *Journal of Human Resources* 36 (2001): 1–30.

47. J. H. Karriker and M. L. Williams, "Organizational Justice and Organizational Citizenship Behavior: A Mediated Multifoci Model," *Journal of Management*, 35(1) (2009): 112–135.

48. J. Marquez, "Winning Women Back," *Workforce Management* 86(7) (April 9, 2007): 20–21.

49. B. B. Baltes, L. S. Zhdanova, and S. P. Parker, "Psychological Climate: A Comparison of Organizational and Individual Level Referents," *Human Relations*, 62 (5) (2009): 669–700.

50. F. J. Leach and J. D. Westbrook, "Motivation and Job Satisfaction in One Government Research and Development Environment," *Engineering Management Journal* 12 (2000): 3–8.

51. A. D. Stajkovic, "Development of a Core Confidence—Higher Order Construct," *Journal of Applied Psychology* 91 (2006): 1208–1224.

52. D. L. Nelson and B. L. Simmons, "Health Psychology and Work Stress: A More Positive Approach," in J. C. Quick and L. E. Tetrick, eds., *Handbook of Occupational Health Psychology* (Washington, DC: American Psychological Association, 2003), 97–119.

53. K. S. Cameron, J. E. Dutton, and R. E. Quinn, eds., *Positive Organizational Scholarship: Foundations of a New Discipline* (San Francisco: Berrett-Koehler, 2003).

54. J. Loehr and T. Schwartz, "The Making of a Corporate Athlete," *Harvard Business Review* 79 (2001): 120–129.

55. J. Loehr and T. Schwartz, *The Power of Full Engagement: Managing Energy, Not Time, Is the Key to High Performance and Personal Renewal* (New York: Free Press, 2003).

56. P. M. Blau, *Exchange and Power in Social Life* (New York: John Wiley & Sons, 1964).

57. A. Etzioni, "A Basis for Comparative Analysis of Complex Organizations," in A. Etzioni, ed., *A Sociological Reader on Complex Organizations*, 2nd ed. (New York: Holt, Rinehart & Winston, 1969), 59–76.

58. O. Janssen, "Job Demands, Perceptions of Effort–Reward Fairness and Innovative Work Behavior," *Journal of Occupational & Organizational Psychology* 73 (2000): 287–302.

59. R. Cropanzano, B. Goldman, and R. Folger, "Deontic Justice: The Role of Moral Principles in Workplace Fairness," *Journal of Organizational Behavior* 24 (2003): 1019–1024.

60. J. P. Campbell, M. D. Dunnette, E. E. Lawler, III, and K. E. Weick, Jr., *Managerial Behavior, Performance and Effectiveness* (New York: McGraw-Hill, 1970).

61. S. S. Masterson and C. L. Stamper, "Perceived Organizational Membership: An Aggregate Framework Representing the Employee—Organization Relationship," *Journal of Organizational Behavior* 24 (2003): 473–490.

62. J. S. Adams, "Inequity in Social Exchange," in L. Berkowitz, ed., *Advances in Experimental Social Psychology*, Vol. 2 (New York: Academic Press, 1965), 267–299; J. S. Adams, "Toward an Understanding of Inequity," *Journal of Abnormal and Social Psychology* 67 (1963): 422–436.

63. J. Nelson-Horchler, "The Best Man for the Job Is a Man," *Industry Week* (January 7, 1991): 50–52.

64. P. D. Sweeney, D. B. McFarlin, and E. J. Inderrieden, "Using Relative Deprivation Theory to Explain Satisfaction with Income and Pay Level: A Multistudy Examination," *Academy of Management Journal* 33 (1990): 423–436.

65. R. C. Huseman, J. D. Hatfield, and E. A. Miles, "A New Perspective on Equity Theory: The Equity Sensitivity Construct," *Academy of Management Review* 12 (1987): 222–234.

66. D. McLoughlin and S. C. Carr, "Equity and Sensitivity and Double Demotivation," *Journal of Social Psychology* 137 (1997): 668–670.

67. K. E. Weick, M. G. Bougon, and G. Maruyama, "The Equity Context," *Organizational Behavior and Human Performance* 15 (1976): 32–65.

68. R. Coles, *Privileged Ones* (Boston: Little, Brown, 1977).

69. J. A. Colquitt and J. Greenberg, "Organizational Justice: A Fair Assessment of the State of the Literature," in J. Greenberg, ed., *Organizational Behavior: The State of the Science*, 2nd ed. (Mahwah, NJ: Erlbaum Associates, 2003).

70. J. Greenberg, "Equity and Workplace Status: A Field Experiment," *Journal of Applied Psychology* 73 (1988): 606–613.

71. C. P. Zapata-Phelan, J. A. Colquitt, B. A. Scott, and B. Livingston," Procedural Justice, Interactional Justice, and Task Performance: The Mediating Role of Intrinsic Motivation," *Organizational Behavior and Human Decision Processes*, 108 (2009): 93–105.

72. J. Greenberg, "Losing Sleep over Organizational Justice: Attenuating Insomniac Reactions to Underpayment Inequity with Supervisory Training in Interactional Justice," *Journal of Applied Psychology* 91 (2006): 58–69.

73. J. Greenberg and B. Alge, "Aggressive Reactions to Workplace Injustice," in R. W. Griffin, A. O'Leary-Kelly, and J. Collins, eds., *Dysfunctional Behavior in Organizations, Vol. 1: Violent Behaviors in Organizations* (Greenwich, CT: JAI Press, 1998), 119–145.

74. R. A. Cosier and D. R. Dalton, "Equity Theory and Time: A Reformulation," *Academy of Management Review* 8 (1983): 311–319.

75. J. E. Martin and M. W. Peterson, "Two-Tier Wage Structures: Implications for Equity Theory," *Academy of Management Journal* 30 (1987): 297–315.

76. V. H. Vroom, *Work and Motivation* (New York: Wiley, 1964/1970).

77. E. Mickel and L. A. Barron, "Getting 'More Bang for the Buck': Symbolic Value of Monetary Rewards in Organizations," *Journal of Management Inquiry*, 17(4) (2008): 329–338.

78. U. R. Larson, "Supervisor's Performance Feedback to Subordinates: The Effect of Performance Valence and Outcome Dependence," *Organizational Behavior and Human Decision Processes* 37 (1986): 391–409.

79. M. C. Kernan and R. G. Lord, "Effects of Valence, Expectancies, and Goal-Performance Discrepancies in Single and Multiple Goal Environments," *Journal of Applied Psychology* 75 (1990): 194–203.

80. R. J. Sanchez, D. M. Truxillo, and T. N. Bauer, "Development and Examination of an Expectancy-Based Measure of Test-Taking Motivation," *Journal of Applied Psychology* 85 (2000): 739–750.

81. L. Lim, "A Two-Factor Model of Defensive Pessimism and Its Relations with Achievement Motives," The *Journal of Psychology*, 143 (2009): 318–336.

82. W. VanEerde and H. Thierry, "Vroom's Expectancy Models and Work-Related Criteria: A Meta-Analysis," *Journal of Applied Psychology* 81 (1996): 575–586.

83. E. D. Pulakos and N. Schmitt, "A Longitudinal Study of a Valence Model Approach for the Prediction of Job Satisfaction of New Employees," *Journal of Applied Psychology* 68 (1983): 307–312.

84. F. J. Landy and W. S. Becker, "Motivation Theory Reconsidered," in L. L. Cummings and B. M. Staw, eds., *Research in Organizational Behavior*, Vol. 9 (Greenwich, CT: JAI Press, 1987), 1–38.

85. L. Kohlberg, "The Cognitive-Developmental Approach to Socialization," in D. A. Goslin, ed., *Handbook of Socialization Theory and Research* (Chicago: Rand McNally, 1969).

86. N. J. Adler, *International Dimensions of Organizational Behavior*, 4th ed. (Mason, OH: South-Western, 2001).

87. G. Hofstede, "Motivation, Leadership, and Organization: Do American Theories Apply Abroad?" *Organizational Dynamics* 9 (1980): 42–63.

88. G. H. Hines, "Cross-Cultural Differences in Two-Factor Theory," *Journal of Applied Psychology* 58 (1981): 313–317.

89. M. C. Bolino and W. H. Turnley, "Old Faces, New Places: Equity Theory in Cross-Cultural Contexts," *Journal of Organizational Behavior* 29 (2008): 29–50.

90. L. Fitzpatrick, "We're Getting Off the Ladder," *Time* 173.20 (25 May 2009): 45–45.

Chapter 5 Case

1. S. Ng and L. Pleven, "An AIG Unit's Quest to Juice Profit—Securities-Lending Business Made Risky Bets; They Backfired on Insurer," *Wall Street Journal* (Eastern edition) (February 5, 2009): C1.

2. H. W. Jenkins, Jr., "The Real AIG Disgrace," *Wall Street Journal* (Eastern edition) (March 25, 2009): A11.

3. Ibid.

4. Ibid.

5. R. Smith and L. Pleven, "Some Will Pay Back AIG Bonuses," *Wall Street Journal* (Eastern edition) (March 19, 2009): A1.

6. R. Smith, J. Weisman, and L. Pleven, "Some at AIG Buck Efforts to Give Back Bonus Pay," *Wall Street Journal* (Eastern edition) (March 26, 2009): C1.

7. Smith and Pleven, "Some Will Pay Back AIG Bonuses," A1.

8. Ibid.

9. Ibid.

10. Ibid.

11. "The AIG Mess Gets Worse," *BusinessWeek* (4125) (April 6, 2009): 6.

12. Smith et al., "Some at AIG Buck Efforts to Give Back Bonus Pay," C1.

13. Ibid.

14. Ibid.

15. Ibid.

16. J. DeSantis, "Op-Ed Contributor: Dear A.I.G., I Quit!," *New York Times*, March 25, 2009, http://www.nytimes.com/2009/03/25/opinion/25desantis.html.

17. Ibid.

Chapter 6

1. R. Spector and P.D. McCarthy, *The Nordstrom Way: The Inside Story of America's #1 Customer Service Company*, 2nd ed. (New York: John Wiley & Sons, Inc., 1995), 116–119.

2. I. P. Pavlov, *Conditioned Reflexes* (New York: Oxford University Press, 1927).

3. B. Cannon, "Walter B. Cannon: Reflections on the Man and His Contributions," *Centennial Session*, American Psychological Association Centennial Convention, Washington, DC, 1992.

4. B. F. Skinner, *The Behavior of Organisms: An Experimental Analysis* (New York: Appleton-Century-Crofts, 1938).

5. B. F. Skinner, *Science and Human Behavior* (New York: Free Press, 1953).

6. F. Luthans and R. Kreitner, *Organizational Behavior Modification and Beyond* (Glenview, IL: Scott, Foresman, 1985).

7. A. D. Stajkovic and F. Luthans, "A Meta-Analysis of the Effects of Organizational Behavior Modification on Task Performance, 1975–95," *Academy of Management Journal* 40 (1997): 1122–1149.

8. C. B. Cadsby, F. Song, and F. Tapon. "Sorting and Incentive Effects of Pay for Performance: An Experimental Investigation," *Academy of Management Journal* 50 (2007): 387–405.

9. J. Hale, "Strategic Rewards: Keeping Your Best Talent from Walking Out the Door," *Compensation & Benefits Management* 14 (1998): 39–50.

10. B. F. Skinner, *Contingencies of Reinforcement: A Theoretical Analysis* (New York: Appleton-Century-Crofts, 1969).

11. J. P. Chaplin and T. S. Krawiec, *Systems and Theories of Psychology* (New York: Holt, Rinehart & Winston, 1960).

12. M. Maccoby, J. Hoffer Gittell, and M. Ledeen, "Leadership and the Fear Factor," *Sloan Management Review* 148 (Winter 2004): 14–18.

13. Y. Liberman, "The Perfect Punishment," *The Conference Board* 46 (2009): 32–39.

14. A. Bandura, *Social Learning Theory* (Englewood Cliffs, NJ: Prentice Hall, 1977); A. Bandura, "Self-Efficacy: Toward a Unifying Theory of Behavioral Change," *Psychological Review* 84 (1977): 191–215.

15. T. M. Egan, "The Relevance of Organizational Subculture for Motivation to Transfer Learning," *Human Resource Development Quarterly* 19 (2009): 299–322.

16. J. J. Martocchio and E. J. Hertenstein, "Learning Orientation and Goal Orientation Context: Relationships with Cognitive and Affective Learning Outcomes," *Human Resource Development Quarterly* 14 (2003): 413–434.

17. A. Bandura, "Regulation of Cognitive Processes through Perceived Self-Efficacy," *Developmental Psychology* (September 1989): 729–735.

18. J. M. Phillips and S. M. Gully, "Role of Goal Orientation, Ability, Need for Achievement, and Locus of Control in the Self-Efficacy and Goal-Setting Process," *Journal of Applied Psychology* 82 (1997): 792–802.

19. J. C. Weitlauf, R. E. Smith, and D. Cervone, "Generalization Effects of Coping-Skills Training: Influence of Self-Defense Training on Women's Efficacy Beliefs, Assertiveness, and Aggression," *Journal of Applied Psychology* 85 (2000): 625–633.

20. A. D. Stajkovic and F. Luthans, "Social Cognitive Theory and Self-Efficacy: Going Beyond Traditional Motivational and Behavioral Approaches," *Organizational Dynamics* (Spring 1998): 62–74.

21. A. D. Stajkovic and F. Luthans, "Self-Efficacy and Work-Related Performance: A Meta-Analysis," *Psychological Bulletin* 124 (1998): 240–261.

22. V. Gecas, "The Social Psychology of Self-Efficacy," *Annual Review of Sociology* 15 (1989): 291–316.

23. J. B. Vancouver and L. N. Kendall. "When Self-Efficacy Negatively Relates to Motivation and Performance in a Learning Context," *Journal of Applied Psychology* 91 (2006): 1146–1153.

24. O. Isachsen and L. V. Berens, *Working Together: A Personality Centered Approach to Management* (Coronado, CA: Neworld Management Press, 1988); O. Krueger and J. M. Thuesen, *Type Talk* (New York: Tilden Press, 1988).

25. E. A. Locke and G. P. Latham, *A Theory of Goal Setting and Task Performance* (Englewood Cliffs, NJ: Prentice Hall, 1990).

26. G. Yeo, S. Loft, T. Xiao, and C. Kiewitz, "Goal Orientations and Performance: Differential Relationships Across Levels of Analysis and as Function of Task Demands," *Journal of Applied Psychology* 94 (2009): 710–726.

27. A. D. Stajkovic, E. A. Locke, and E. S. Blair, "A First Examination of the Relationships between Primed Subconscious Goals, Assigned Conscious Goals, and Task Performance," *Journal of Applied Psychology* 91 (2006): 1172–1180.

28. T. O. Murray, *Management by Objectives: A Systems Approach to Management* (Fort Worth, TX: Western Company, n.d.).

29. W. T. Brooks and T. W. Mullins, *High Impact Time Management* (Englewood Cliffs, NJ: Prentice Hall, 1989).

30. G. H. Seijts, G. P. Latham, K. Tasa, and B. W. Latham, "Goal Setting and Goal Orientation: An Integration of Two Different Yet Related Literatures," *Academy of Management Journal* 47 (2004): 227–239.

31. E. A. Locke, "Toward a Theory of Task Motivation and Incentives," *Organizational Behavior and Human Performance* 3 (1968): 157–189.

32. J. C. Quick, "Dyadic Goal Setting within Organizations: Role Making and Motivational Considerations," *Academy of Management Review* 4 (1979): 369–380.

33. D. McGregor, "An Uneasy Look at Performance Appraisal," *Harvard Business Review* 35 (1957): 89–94.

34. J. R. Hollenbeck, C. R. Williams, and H. J. Klein, "An Empirical Examination of the Antecedents of Commitment to Difficult Goals," *Journal of Applied Psychology* 74 (1989): 18–23.

35. R. C. Rodgers and J. E. Hunter, "The Impact of Management by Objectives on Organizational Productivity," unpublished paper (Lexington: University of Kentucky, 1989).

36. E. A. Locke, K. N. Shaw, L. M. Saari, and G. P. Latham, "Goal Setting and Task Performance: 1969–1980," *Psychological Bulletin* 90 (1981): 125–152.

37. D. B. Fedora, W. D. Davis, J. M. Maslync, and K. Mathiesond, "Performance Improvement Efforts in Response to Negative Feedback: The Roles of Source Power and Recipient Self-Esteem," *Journal of Management* 27 (2001): 79–98.

38. A. M. Schmidt, C. M. Dolis, and A. P. Tolli, "A Matter of Time: Individual Differences, Contextual Dynamics, and Gal Progress Effects on Multiple-Goal-Self-Regulation," *Journal of Applied Psychology* 94 (2009): 692–709.

39. J. C. Quick, "Dyadic Goal Setting and Role Stress," *Academy of Management Journal* 22 (1979): 241–252.

40. G. S. Odiorne, *Management by Objectives: A System of Managerial Leadership* (New York: Pitman, 1965).

41. American Management Association, *Blueprints for Service Quality: The Federal Express Approach* (New York: American Management Association, 1991).

42. G. P. Latham and G. A. Yukl, "A Review of Research on the Application of Goal Setting in Organizations," *Academy of Management Journal* 18 (1975): 824–845.

43. P. F. Drucker, *The Practice of Management* (New York: Harper & Bros., 1954).

44. R. D. Prichard, P. L. Roth, S. D. Jones, P. J. Galgay, and M. D. Watson, "Designing a Goal-Setting System to Enhance Performance: A Practical Guide," *Organizational Dynamics* 17 (1988): 69–78.

45. C. L. Hughes, *Goal Setting: Key to Individual and Organizational Effectiveness* (New York: American Management Association, 1965).

46. M. E. Tubbs and S. E. Ekeberg, "The Role of Intentions in Work Motivation: Implications for Goal-Setting Theory and Research," *Academy of Management Review* 16 (1991): 180–199.

47. S. Vatave, "Managing Risk," *Supervision* 65 (2004): 6–9.

48. L. D. Ordonez, M. E. Schweitzer, A. D. Galinskly, and M. H. Bazerman, "Goals Gone Wild: The Systematic Side Effects of Overprescribing Goal Setting," *Academy of Management Perspectives*, 23 (2009): 6–16; E. A. Locke and G. P. Latham, "Has Goal Setting One Wild, or Have Its Attackers Abandoned Good Scholarship?" *Academy of Management Perspectives* 23 (2009): 17–23.

49. J. R. Hollenbeck and A. P. Brief, "The Effects of Individual Differences and Goal Origin on Goal Setting and Performance," *Organizational Behavior and Human Decision Processes* 40 (1987): 392–414.

50. R. A. Katzell and D. E. Thompson, "Work Motivation: Theory and Practice," *American Psychologist* 45 (1990): 144–153; M. W. McPherson, "Is Psychology the Science of Behavior?" *American Psychologist* 47 (1992): 329–335.

51. E. A. Locke, "The Ideas of Frederick W. Taylor: An Evaluation," *Academy of Management Review* 7 (1982): 15–16; R. M. Yerkes and J. D. Dodson, "The Relation of Strength of Stimulus to Rapidity of Habit-Formation," *Journal of Comparative Neurology and Psychology* 18 (1908): 459–482.

52. F. L. Schmidt and J. Hunter, "General Mental Ability in the World of Work: Occupational Attainment and Job Performance," *Journal of Personality and Social Psychology* 86 (2004): 162–173.

53. R. L. Cardy, *Performance Management: Concepts, Skills, and Exercises* (Armonk, New York and London, England: M.E. Sharpe, 2004).

54. P. Cappelli and N. Rogovsky, "Employee Involvement and Organizational Citizenship: Implications for Labor Law Reform and 'Lean Production,'" *Industrial & Labor Relations Review* 51 (1998): 633–653.

55. R. D. Goffin, R. B. Jelley, D. M. Powell, and N. G. Johnston. "Taking Advantage of Social Comparisons in Performance Appraisal: The Relative Percentile Method," *Human Resource Management*, 48 (2009): 251–268.

56. B. Erdogan, M. L. Kraimer, and R. C. Liden, "Procedural Justice as a Two-Dimensional Construct: An Examination in the Performance Appraisal Account," *Journal of Applied Behavioral Science* 37 (2001): 205–222.

57. P. A. Heslin and D. Vandewalle. Performance Appraisal Procedural Justice: The Role of a Manager's Implict Person Theory," *Journal of Management* 36 (2010): in press.

58. S. E. DeVoe and S. S. Iyengar, "Managers' Theories of Subordinates: A Cross-Cultural Examination of Manager Perceptions of Motivation and Appraisal of Performance," *Organizational Behavior and Human Decision Processes* 93 (2004): 47–61.

59. I. M. Jawahar and C. R. Williams, "Where All the Children Are Above Average: The Performance Appraisal Purpose Effect," *Personnel Psychology* 50 (1997): 905–925.

60. M. E. Tubbs and M. L. Trusty, "Direct Reports of Motivation for Task Performance Levels: Some Construct-Related Evidence," *Journal of Psychology* 135 (2001): 185–205.

61. R. R. Kilburg, *Executive Coaching: Developing Managerial Wisdom in a World of Chaos* (Washington, DC: American Psychological Association, 2000).

62. H. H. Meyer, E. Kay, and J. R. P. French, "Split Roles in Performance Appraisal," *Harvard Business Review* 43 (1965): 123–129.

63. W. Lam, X. Huang, and E. Snape, "Feedback-Seeking Behavior and Leader-Member Exchange: Do Supervisor-Attributed Motives Matter?" *Academy of Management Journal* 50 (2007): 348–363.

64. W. A. Fisher, J. C. Quick, L. L. Schkade, and G. W. Ayers, "Developing Administrative Personnel through the Assessment Center Technique," *Personnel Administrator* 25 (1980): 44–46, 62.

65. J. S. Goodman, R. E. Wood, and M. Hendrickx, "Feedback Specificity, Exploration, and Learning," *Journal of Applied Psychology* 89 (2004): 248–262.

66. M. B. DeGregorio and C. D. Fisher, "Providing Performance Feedback: Reactions to Alternative Methods," *Journal of Management* 14 (1988): 605–616.

67. G. C. Thornton, "The Relationship between Supervisory and Self-Appraisals of Executive Performance," *Personnel Psychology* 21 (1968): 441–455.

68. A. S. DeNisi and A. N. Kluger, "Feedback Effectiveness: Can 360-Degree Appraisals Be Improved?" *Academy of Management Executive* 14 (2000): 129–140.

69. F. Luthans and S. J. Peterson, "360-Degree Feedback with Systematic Coaching: Empirical Analysis Suggests a Winning Combination," *Human Resource Management* 42 (2003): 243–256.

70. G. Toegel and J. A. Conger, "360-Degree Assessment: Time for Reinvention," *Academy of Management Learning and Education* 2 (2003): 297–311.

71. F. Shipper, R. C. Hoffman, and D. M. Rotondo, "Does the 360 Feedback Process Create Actionable Knowledge Equally Across Cultures?" *Academy of Management Learning & Education* 6 (2007): 33–50.

72. L. Hirschhorn, "Leaders and Followers in a Postindustrial Age: A Psychodynamic View," *Journal of Applied Behavioral Science* 26 (1990): 529–542.

73. F. M Jablin, "Superior-Subordinate Communication: The State of the Art," *Psychological Bulletin* 86 (1979): 1201–1222.

74. A. Salimaki, A. Hakonen, and R. L. Heneman. "Managers Generating Meaning for Pay: A Test for Reflection Theory," *Journal of Managerial Psychology* 24 (2009): 161–177.

75. J. Pfeffer, "Six Dangerous Myths about Pay," *Harvard Business Review* 76 (1998): 108–119.

76. "Six Employee Types Prefer Different Rewards," *HRFocus* 84(4) (April 2007): 12.

77. M. Erez, "Work Motivation from a Cross-Cultural Perspective," in A. M. Bouvy, F. J. R. Van de Vijver, P. Boski, and P. G. Schmitz, eds., *Journeys into Cross-Cultural Psychology* (Amsterdam, Netherlands: Swets & Zeitlinger, 1994), 386–403.

78. George T. Milkovich and Jerry M. Newman, *Compensation*, 4th ed. (Homewood, IL: Irwin, 1993).

79. S. Kerr, "On the Folly of Rewarding A, While Hoping for B," *Academy of Management Journal* 18 (1975): 769–783.

80. D. F. Giannetto, "Get Your Money's Worth from Incentives," *Business Performance Management* 7 (2009): 12.

81. J. M. Bardwick, *Danger in the Comfort Zone* (New York: American Management Association, 1991).

82. M. J. Martinko and W. L. Gardner, "The Leader/Member Attributional Process," *Academy of Management Review* 12 (1987): 235–249.

83. K. N. Wexley, R. A. Alexander, J. P. Greenawalt, and M. A. Couch, "Attitudinal Congruence and Similarity as Related to Interpersonal Evaluations in Manager-Subordinate Dyads," *Academy of Management Journal* 23 (1980): 320–330.

84. H. H. Kelley, *Attribution in Social Interaction* (New York: General Learning Press, 1971).

85. H. H. Kelley, "The Processes of Causal Attribution," *American Psychologist* 28 (1973): 107–128.

86. B. Raabe and T. A. Beehr, "Formal Mentoring versus Supervisor and Coworker Relationships: Differences in Perceptions and Impact," *Journal of Organizational Behavior* 24 (2003): 271–293.

87. A. M. Young and P. L. Perrewe, "What Did You Expect? An Examination of Career-Related Support and Social Support among Mentors and Protégés," *Journal of Management* 26 (2000): 611–633.

88. K. Doherty, "The Good News about Depression," *Business and Health* 3 (1989): 1–4.

89. K. E. Kram, "Phases of the Mentor Relationship," *Academy of Management Journal* 26 (1983): 608–625.

90. T. D. Allen, L. T. Eby, M. L. Poteet, E. Lentz, and L. Lima, "Career Benefits Associated with Mentoring for Protégés: A Meta-Analysis," *Journal of Applied Psychology* 89 (2004): 127–136.

91. S. J. Wells, "Choices Flourish at IBM," *HR Magazine* (May 2009): 52–57.

92. T. N. Bauer and S. G. Green, "Development of Leader–Member Exchange: A Longitudinal Test," *Academy of Management Journal* 39 (1996): 1538–1567.

93. K. E. Kram and L. A. Isabella, "Mentoring Alternatives: The Role of Peer Relationships in Career Development," *Academy of Management Journal* 28 (1985): 110–132.

94. J. Greco, "Hey, Coach!" *Journal of Business Strategy* 22 (2001): 28–32.

95. Spector and McCarthy, *The Nordstrom Way*, 119–123.

Chapter 6 Case

1. American Express Company, "Our History: Becoming American Express," *AmericanExpress.com*, http://home3.americanexpress.com/corp/os/history.asp (accessed July 10, 2009).

2. R. Hill, "Analysis for the American Express Learning Network (AELN)" (November 3, 2008): 2, http://www.robertphill.com/portfolio/media/artifacts/AELN_analysis.pdf (accessed July 9, 2009).

3. B. Summerfield, "CLO Profile: American Express' Jeanette Harrison: Learning as a Service," *Chief Learning Officer* (March 2008): 28.

4. Ibid., p. 26.

5. Ibid., p. 28.

6. Ibid.

7. Hill, "Analysis for the American Express Learning Network," 2.

8. Summerfield, "American Express' Jeanette Harrison," 26.

9. Hill, "Analysis for the American Express Learning Network," 6; B. Howells, "Blended Learning? That'll do nicely . . . ," *Human Capital Management* (May–June 2008), http://www.humancapitalmanagement.org/pdf/Resource%20Management%20-%20Leadership%20Development%20-%20Case%20Study.pdf (accessed July 10, 2009); Simba Information, "AMEX Finds Manager Support Trumps Delivery in Sustaining Performance Improvement," *Corporate Training & Development Advisor* 11(19) (September 29, 2006): 3.

10. Howells, "Blended Learning?"; Simba Information, "AMEX Finds," 3.

11. Ibid.

12. Summerfield, "American Express' Jeanette Harrison," 28.

Chapter 7

1. M. Leroux, "Thinking Outside the Box Finally Flusters Ikea's Growth," *Times of London* (June 24, 2009); A. E. Kramere, "Ikea Curtails Russia Plans, Citing Corruption; Retailer's Investments Are Put on Hold Because of 'Unpredictability,'" *New York Times/International Herald Tribune* (June 26, 2009).

2. J. Barling, E. K. Kelloway, and M. R. Frone, eds., *Handbook of Work Stress* (Thousand Oaks, CA: Sage Publications, 2005).

3. J. C. Quick, J. D. Quick, D. L. Nelson, and J. J. Hurrell, Jr., *Preventive Stress Management in Organizations* (Washington, DC: American Psychological Association, 1997).

4. S. Benison, A. C. Barger, and E. L. Wolfe, *Walter B. Cannon: The Life and Times of a Young Scientist* (Cambridge, MA: Harvard University Press, 1987).

5. W. B. Cannon, "Stresses and Strains of Homeostasis," *American Journal of the Medical Sciences* 189 (1935): 1–14.

6. W. B. Cannon, *The Wisdom of the Body* (New York: Norton, 1932).

7. R. S. Lazarus, *Psychological Stress and the Coping Process* (New York: McGraw-Hill, 1966).

8. C. Liu, P. E. Spector, and L. Shi, "Cross-National Job Stress: A Quantitative and Qualitative Study," *Journal of Organizational Behavior* 28 (2007): 209–239.

9. J. D. Kammeyer-Mueller, T. A. Judge, and B. A. Scott, "The Role of Core Self-Evaluations in the Coping Process," *Journal of Applied Psychology* 94 (2009): 177–195.

10. D. Katz and R. L. Kahn, *The Social Psychology of Organizations*, 2nd ed. (New York: John Wiley & Sons, 1978), 185–221.

11. H. Levinson, "A Psychoanalytic View of Occupational Stress," *Occupational Mental Health* 3 (1978): 2–13.

12. P. L. Perrewé, K. L. Zellars, G. R. Ferris, A. M. Rossi, C. J. Kacmar, and D. A. Ralston, "Neutralizing Job Stressors: Political Skill as an Antidote

to the Dysfunctional Consequences of Role Conflict," *Academy of Management Journal* 47 (2004): 141–152.

13. T. L. Friedman, *The Lexus and the Olive Tree* (New York: Vintage Anchor, 2000).

14. T. Theorell and R. A. Karasek, "Current Issues Relating to Psychosocial Job Strain and Cardiovascular Disease," *Journal of Occupational Health Psychology* 1 (1996): 9–26.

15. D. T. Hall and J. Richter, "Career Gridlock: Baby Boomers Hit the Wall," *Academy of Management Executive* 4 (1990): 7–22.

16. N. P. Podsakoff, J. A. LePine, and M. A. LePine, "Differential Challenge Stressor-Hindrance Stressor Relationships with Job Attitudes, Turnover Intentions, Turnover, and Withdrawal Behavior: A Meta-Analysis," *Journal of Applied Psychology* 92 (2007): 438–454.

17. S. Zuboff, *In the Age of the Smart Machine: The Future of Work and Power* (New York: Basic Books, 1988).

18. R. L. Kahn, D. M. Wolfe, R. P. Quinn, J. D. Snoek, and R. A. Rosenthal, *Organizational Stress: Studies in Role Conflict and Ambiguity* (New York: John Wiley & Sons, 1964).

19. L. B. Hammer, T. N. Bauer, and A. A. Grandey, "Work-Family Conflict and Work-Related Withdrawal Behaviors," *Journal of Business and Psychology* 17 (2003): 419–436.

20. M. F. Peterson, et al., "Role Conflict, Ambiguity, and Overload: A 21-Nation Study," *Academy of Management Journal* 38 (1995): 429–452.

21. S. Pal, and P. O. Saksvik, "Work-Family Conflict and Psychosocial Work Environment Stressors as Predictors of Job Stress in a Cross-Cultural Study," *International Journal of Stress Management* 15 (2008): 22–42.

22. P. D. Bliese and C. A. Castro, "Role Clarity, Work Overload and Organizational Support: Multilevel Evidence of the Importance of Support," *Work & Stress* 14 (2000): 65–74.

23. A. Skogstad, S. Einarsen, T. Torsheim, M. S. Aasland, and H. Hetland, "The Destructiveness of Laissez-Faire Leadership Behavior," *Journal of Occupational Health Psychology* 12 (2007): 80–92.

24. P. J. Frost, *Toxic Emotions at Work: How Compassionate Managers Handle Pain and Conflict* (Boston, MA: Harvard Business School Press, 2003).

25. S. Grebner, N. K. Semmer, L. L. Faso, S. Gut, W. Kalin, and A. Elfering, "Working Conditions, Well-Being, and Job-Related Attitudes Among Call Centre Agents," *European Journal of Work and Organizational Psychology* 12 (2003): 341–365.

26. M. P. Bell, J. C. Quick, and C. Cycota, "Assessment and Prevention of Sexual Harassment: An Applied Guide to Creating Healthy Organizations," *International Journal of Selection and Assessment* 10 (2002): 160–167.

27. L. T. Hosmer, "Trust: The Connecting Link between Organizational Theory and Philosophical Ethics," *Academy of Management Review* 20 (1995): 379–403; V. J. Doby and R. D. Caplan, "Organizational Stress as Threat to Reputation: Effects on Anxiety at Work and at Home," *Academy of Management Journal* 38 (1995): 1105–1123.

28. R. T. Keller, "Cross-Functional Project Groups in Research and New Product Development: Diversity, Communications, Job Stress, and Outcomes," *Academy of Management Journal* 33 (2001): 547–555.

29. M. F. Peterson and P. B. Smith, "Does National Culture or Ambient Temperature Explain Cross-National Differences in Role Stress? No Sweat!" *Academy of Management Journal* 40 (1997): 930–946.

30. K. K. Gillingham, "High-G Stress and Orientational Stress: Physiologic Effects of Aerial Maneuvering," *Aviation, Space, and Environmental Medicine* 59 (1988): A10–A20.

31. R. S. DeFrank, "Executive Travel Stress: Perils of the Road Warrior," *Academy of Management Executive* 14 (2000): 58–72.

32. M. Westman, "Strategies for Coping with Business Trips: A Qualitative Exploratory Study," *International Journal of Stress Management* 11 (2004): 167–176.

33. R. Weiss, "Health," *Washington Post* (June 5, 2007): F-1.

34. R. S. Bhagat, S. J. McQuaid, S. Lindholm, and J. Segovis, "Total Life Stress: A Multimethod Validation of the Construct and Its Effect on Organizationally Valued Outcomes and Withdrawal Behaviors," *Journal of Applied Psychology* 70 (1985): 202–214.

35. J. C. Quick, J. R. Joplin, D. A. Gray, and E. C. Cooley, "The Occupational Life Cycle and the Family," in L. L'Abate, ed., *Handbook of Developmental Family Psychology and Psychopathology* (New York: John Wiley & Sons, 1993).

36. S. Shellenbarger, "Work & Family," *Wall Street Journal* (January 31, 1996): B1.

37. S. A. Lobel, "Allocation of Investment in Work and Family Roles: Alternative Theories and Implications for Research," *Academy of Management Review* 16 (1991): 507–521.

38. G. Porter, "Organizational Impact of Workaholism: Suggestions for Researching the Negative Outcomes of Excessive Work," *Journal of Occupational Health Psychology* 1 (1996): 70–84.

39. J. W. Pennebaker, C. F. Hughes, and R. C. O'Heeron, "The Psychophysiology of Confession: Linking Inhibitory and Psychosomatic Processes," *Journal of Personality and Social Psychology* 52 (1987): 781–793.

40. J. Loehr and T. Schwartz, "The Making of a Corporate Athlete," *Harvard Business Review* 79 (2001): 120–129.

41. J. R. B. Halbesleben and W. M. Bowler, "Emotional Exhaustion and Job Performance: The Mediating Role of Motivation," *Journal of Applied Psychology* 92 (2007): 93–106.

42. J. D. Quick, R. S. Horn, and J. C. Quick, "Health Consequences of Stress," *Journal of Organizational Behavior Management* 8 (1986): 19–36.

43. R. M. Yerkes and J. D. Dodson, "The Relation of Strength of Stimulus to Rapidity of Habit-Formation," *Journal of Comparative Neurology and Psychology* 18 (1908): 459–482.

44. J. E. McGrath, "Stress and Behavior in Organizations," in M. D. Dunnette, ed., *Handbook of Industrial and Organizational Psychology* (Chicago: Rand McNally, 1976), 1351–1395.

45. T. A. Wright, R. Cropanzano, and D. G. Meyer, "State and Trait Correlates of Job Performance: A Tale of Two Perspectives," *Journal of Business and Psychology* 18 (2004): 365–383.

46. W. B. Cannon, *Bodily Changes in Pain, Hunger, Fear, and Rage* (New York: Appleton, 1915).

47. P. A. Herbig and F. A. Palumbo, "Karoshi: Salaryman Sudden Death Syndrome," *Journal of Managerial Psychology* 9 (1994): 11–16.

48. S. Sauter, L. R. Murphy, and J. J. Hurrell, Jr., "Prevention of Work-Related Psychological Distress: A National Strategy Proposed by the National Institute for Occupational Safety and Health," *American Psychologist* 45 (1990): 1146–1158.

49. R. Cropanzano, D. E. Rupp, and Z. S. Byrne, "The Relationship of Emotional Exhaustion to Work Attitudes, Job Performance, and Organizational Citizenship Behaviors," *Journal of Applied Psychology* 88 (2003): 160–169.

50. A. A. Grandey, "When 'The Show Must Go On': Surface Acting and Deep Acting as Determinants of Emotional Exhaustion and Peer-Rated Service Delivery," *Academy of Management Journal* 46 (2003): 86–96.

51. I. Wylie, "Routing Rust-Out," © 2004 Gruner & Jahr USA Publishing. First published in *Fast Company* Magazine (January 2004): 40. Reprinted with permission, http://www.fastcompany.com/magazine/78/5things.html.

52. H. Selye, *Stress in Health and Disease* (Boston: Butterworth, 1976).

53. B. G. Ware and D. L. Block, "Cardiovascular Risk Intervention at a Work Site: The Ford Motor Company Program," *International Journal of Mental Health* 11 (1982): 68–75.

54. B. S. Siegel, *Love, Medicine, and Miracles* (New York: Harper & Row, 1986).

55. D. B. Kennedy, R. J. Homant, and M. R. Homant, "Perceptions of Injustice as a Predictor of Support for Workplace Aggression," *Journal of Business and Psychology* 18 (2004): 323–336.

56. N. Bolger, A. DeLongis, R. C. Kessler, and E. A. Schilling, "Effects of Daily Stress on Negative Mood," *Journal of Personality and Social Psychology* 57 (1989): 808–818.

57. B. Moreno-Jimenez, A. Rodrguez-Munoz, J. C. Pastor, A. I. Sanz-Vergel, and E. Garrosa, "The Moderating Effecting of Psychological Detachment and Thoughts of Revenge in Workplace Bullying," *Personality and Individual Differences* 46 (2009): 359–364.

58. B. A. Macy and P. H. Mirvis, "A Methodology for Assessment of Quality of Work Life and Organizational Effectiveness in Behavioral-Economic Terms," *Administrative Science Quarterly* 21 (1976): 212–226.

59. F. K. Cocchiara and J. C. Quick, "The Negative Effects of Positive Stereotypes: Ethnicity-Related Stressors and Implications on Organizational Health," *Journal of Organizational Behavior* 25 (2004): 781–785.

60. J. M. Ivancevich, M. T. Matteson, and E. Richards, "Who's Liable for Stress on the Job?" *Harvard Business Review* 64 (1985): 60–72.

61. *Frank S. Deus v. Allstate Insurance Company*, civil action no. 88-2099, U.S. District Court, Western District of Louisiana.

62. R. S. DeFrank and J. M. Ivancevich, "Stress on the Job: An Executive Update," *Academy of Management Executive* 12 (1998): 55–66.

63. P. Wilson and M. Bronstein, "Employers: Don't Panic about Work-Place Stress," *Personnel Today* (November 4, 2003): 10.

64. J. E. Bono and M. A. Vey, "Personality and Emotional Performance: Extraversion, Neuroticism, and Self-Monitoring," *Journal of Occupational Health Psychology* 12 (2007): 177–192.

65. C. S. Troutman, K. G. Burke, and J. D. Beeler, "The Effects of Self-Efficacy, Assertiveness, Stress, and Gender on Intention," *Journal of Applied Business Research* 16 (2000): 63–75.

66. S. E. Taylor, L. C. Klein, G. P. Lewis, T. L. Gruenewald, R. A. R. Burung, and J. A. Updegraff, "Biobehavioral Responses to Stress in Females: Tend-and-Befriend, Not Fight-or-Flight," *Psychological Review* 107 (2000): 411–429.

67. D. L. Nelson and J. C. Quick, "Professional Women: Are Distress and Disease Inevitable?" *Academy of Management Review* 10 (1985): 206–218; T. D. Jick and L. F. Mitz, "Sex Differences in Work Stress," *Academy of Management Review* 10 (1985): 408–420.

68. K. M. Rospenda, K. Fujishiro, C. A. Shannon, and J. A. Richman, "Workplace Harassment, Stress, and Drinking Behavior over Time: Gender Differences in a National Sample," *Addictive Behaviors* 33 (2008): 964–967.

69. L. Verbrugge, "Recent, Present, and Future Health of American Adults," *Annual Review of Public Health* 10 (1989): 333–361.

70. M. D. Friedman and R. H. Rosenman, *Type A Behavior and Your Heart* (New York: Knopf, 1974).

71. L. Wright, "The Type A Behavior Pattern and Coronary Artery Disease," *American Psychologist* 43 (1988): 2–14.

72. J. M. Ivancevich and M. T. Matteson, "A Type A–B Person–Work Environment Interaction Model for Examining Occupational Stress and Consequences," *Human Relations* 37 (1984): 491–513.

73. S. O. C. Kobasa, "Conceptualization and Measurement of Personality in Job Stress Research," in J. J. Hurrell, Jr., L. R. Murphy, S. L. Sauter, and C. L. Cooper, eds., *Occupational Stress: Issues and Developments in Research* (New York: Taylor & Francis, 1988), 100–109.

74. J. K. Ito and C. M. Brotheridge, "Predictors and Consequences of Promotion Stress: A Bad Situation Made Worse by Employment Dependence," *International Journal of Stress Management* 16 (2009): 65–85.

75. J. Borysenko, "Personality Hardiness," *Lectures in Behavioral Medicine* (Boston: Harvard Medical School, 1985).

76. O. Siu, C. H. Hui, D. R. Phillips, L. Lin, T. Wong, and K. Shi, "A Study of Resiliency Among Chinese Health Care Workers: Capacity to Cope with Workplace Stress," *Journal of Research in Personality*, In press.

77. J. S. House, K. R. Landis, and D. Umberson, "Social Relationships and Health," *Science* 241 (1988): 540–545.

78. J. Bowlby, *A Secure Base* (New York: Basic Books, 1988).

79. C. Hazan and P. Shaver, "Love and Work: An Attachment-Theoretical Perspective," *Journal of Personality and Social Psychology* 59 (1990): 270–280.

80. J. C. Quick, D. L. Nelson, and J. D. Quick, *Stress and Challenge at the Top: The Paradox of the Successful Executive* (Chichester, England: John Wiley & Sons, 1990).

81. Staff, "Partner Relationship Could Be a Buffer Against Work-Related Stress," *Asian News International* (June 24, 2009).

82. J. C. Quick, J. R. Joplin, D. L. Nelson, and J. D. Quick, "Self-Reliance for Stress and Combat" (*Proceedings of the 8th Combat Stress Conference*, U.S. Army Health Services Command, Fort Sam Houston, Texas, September 23–27, 1991): 1–5.

83. J. C. Dvorak, "Baffling," *PC Magazine* 3 (November 4, 2003): 61, http://www.pcmag.com/article2/0,4149,1369270,00.asp.

84. O. Janssen, "How Fairness Perceptions Make Innovative Behavior More or Less Stressful," *Journal of Organizational Behavior* 25 (2004): 201–215; T. A. Judge and J. A. Colquitt, "Organizational Justice and Stress: The Mediating Role of Work–Family Conflict," *Journal of Applied Psychology* 89 (2004): 395–404.

85. K. Hickox, "Content and Competitive," *Airman* (January 1994): 31–33.

86. A. Drach-Zahavy and A. Freund, "Team Effectiveness under Stress: A Structural Contingency Approach," *Journal of Organizational Behavior* 28 (2007): 423–450.

87. R. W. Griffin, A. O'Leary-Kelly, and J. M. Collins, eds., *Dysfunctional Behavior in Organizations: Violent and Deviant Behavior* (Stamford, CT: JAI Press, 1998).

88. N. Williams, "Employers Set Out to Reduce Workplace Stress," *Personnel Today* (February 10, 2009): 39.

89. J. L. Xie, J. Schaubroeck, and S. S. K. Lam, "Theories of Job Stress and Role of Traditional Values: A Longitudinal Study in China," *Journal of Applied Psychology* 93(4) (2008): 831–848.

90. W. L. French and C. H. Bell, Jr., *Organizational Development: Behavioral Science Interventions for Organization Improvement*, 4th ed. (Englewood Cliffs, NJ: Prentice Hall, 1990).

91. M. Macik-Frey, J. C. Quick, and J. D. Quick, "Interpersonal Communication: The Key to Unlocking Social Support for Preventive Stress Management," in C. L. Cooper, ed., *Handbook of Stress, Medicine, and Health, Second Edition* (Boca Raton, FL: CRC Press, 2005), 265–292.

92. J. C. Quick and C. L. Cooper, *FAST FACTS: Stress and Strain*, 2nd ed. (Oxford, England: Health Press, 2003).

93. M. E. P. Seligman, *Learned Optimism* (New York: Knopf, 1990).

94. F. Luthans, "Positive Organizational Behavior: Developing and Managing Psychological Strengths for Performance Improvement," *Academy of Management Executive* 16 (2002): 57–75.

95. W. T. Brooks and T. W. Mullins, *High-Impact Time Management* (Englewood Cliffs, NJ: Prentice Hall, 1989).

96. M. Westman and D. Eden, "Effects of a Respite from Work on Burnout: Vacation Relief and Fade-Out," *Journal of Applied Psychology* 82 (1997): 516–527.

97. C. P. Neck and K. H. Cooper, "The Fit Executive: Exercise and Diet Guidelines for Enhancing Performance," *Academy of Management Executive* 14 (2000): 72–84.

98. M. Davis, E. R. Eshelman, and M. McKay, *The Relaxation and Stress Reduction Workbook*, 3rd ed. (Oakland, CA: New Harbinger, 1988).

99. H. Benson, "Your Innate Asset for Combating Stress," *Harvard Business Review* 52 (1974): 49–60.

100. D. Ornish, *Dr. Dean Ornish's Program for Reversing Cardiovascular Disease* (New York: Random House, 1995).

101. J. W. Pennebaker, *Opening Up: The Healing Power of Expressing Emotions* (New York: Guilford, 1997).

102. M. E. Francis and J. W. Pennebaker, "Putting Stress into Words: The Impact of Writing on Physiological, Absentee, and Self-Reported Emotional Well-Being Measures," *American Journal of Health Promotion* 6 (1992): 280–287.

103. Z. Solomon, B. Oppenheimer, and S. Noy, "Subsequent Military Adjustment of Combat Stress Reaction Casualties: A Nine-Year Follow-Up Study," in N. A. Milgram, ed., *Stress and Coping in Time of War: Generalizations from the Israeli Experience* (New York: Brunner/Mazel, 1986), 84–90.

104. D. Wegman and L. Fine, "Occupational Health in the 1990s," *Annual Review of Public Health* 11 (1990): 89–103; J. C. Quick, "Occupational Health Psychology: Historical Roots and Future Directions," *Health Psychology* 17 (1999): 82–88.

105. D. Gebhardt and C. Crump, "Employee Fitness and Wellness Programs in the Workplace," *American Psychologist* 45 (1990): 262–272.

106. T. Wolf, H. Randall, and J. Faucett, "A Survey of Health Promotion Programs in U.S. and Canadian Medical Schools," *American Journal of Health Promotion* 3 (1988): 33–36.

107. S. Weiss, J. Fielding, and A. Baum, *Health at Work* (Hillsdale, NJ: Erlbaum, 1990).

108. J. B. Bennett, R. F. Cook, and K. R. Pelletier, "Toward an Integrated Framework for Comprehensive Organizational Wellness: Concepts, Practices, and Research in Workplace Health Promotion," in J. C. Quick and L. E. Tetrick, eds., *Handbook of Occupational Health Psychology*: (Washington, DC: American Psychological Association, 2003), 69–95.

109. D. Wighton, "Is Ikea's Business Model Coming Apart?" *Times of London* (June 24, 2009).

110. M. Sasso, "IKEA Theory: 'Do-It-Yourself' Creates Loyalty, Business," *Tampa Tribune* (May 1, 2009).

Chapter 7 Case

1. "Corporate Overview," Genentech: About US: Corporate Overview, http://www.gene.com/gene/about/corporate/ (accessed July 8, 2009).

2. M. Chase, "Boss Talk: How Genentech Wins at Blockbuster Drugs; CEO to Critics of Prices: 'Give Me a Break'," *Wall Street Journal* (Eastern edition) (June 5, 2007): B1.

3. "Product Information," Genentech: About Us: Product Information, http://www.gene.com/gene/products/information/ (accessed July 8, 2009).

4. Chase, "Boss Talk," B1.

5. "Awards and Recognition," Genentech: About Us: Awards and Recognition, http://www.gene.com/gene/about/corporate/awards/ (accessed July 8, 2009).

6. "Our Culture," Genentech: Careers: Culture, http://www.gene.com/gene/careers/culture/ (accessed July 8, 2009).

7. Ibid.

8. Ibid.

9. J. McGregor, A. McConnon, A. Weintraub, and S. Holmes, "The 25 Most Innovative Companies; The leaders in Nurturing Cultures of Creativity," *Business Week* (May 14, 2007): 52.

10. M. Stallard and J. Pankau, "Connection Cultures: Great Leaders Create Strong Bonds," *Leadership Excellence* 24(11) (November 2007): 4.

11. Ibid.

12. E. White, "Theory & Practice: Corporate Tuition Aid Appears to Keep Workers Loyal; Studies Reinforce View of Improved Retention; UTC's Plan Stands Out," *Wall Street Journal* (Eastern edition) (May 21, 2007): B4.

13. D. A. Reiss and M. R. Costello, "Location Alone Can't Retain Today's Workforce," *Financial Executive* 23(7) (September 2007): 50.

14. Ibid.

15. Ibid.

Chapter 7 Cohesion Case: Part 2

1. J. M. O'Brien, "Zappos Knows How to Kick It," *Fortune* 159(2) (February 2, 2009): 56.

2. Ibid.

3. M. Chafkin, "Get Happy: How Tony Hsieh Uses Relentless Innovation, Stellar Service, and a Staff of Believers to Make Zappos.com and E-commerce Juggernaut—and One of the Most Blissed-Out Businesses in America," *Inc.* 31(4) (May 2009): 68.

4. Ibid., p. 72.

5. O'Brien, "Zappos Knows How to Kick It," 58.

6. S. Murphy, "Culture Conscious," *Chain Store Age* 83(9) (September 2007): 55.

7. O'Brien, "Zappos Knows How to Kick It," 58.

8. Ibid., p. 60.

9. Ibid., p. 58.

10. Chafkin, "Get Happy," 68.

11. Ibid., p. 72.

12. J. McGregor, "Zappos' Secret: It's an Open Book," *Business Week* (March 23, 2009): 62.

13. Chafkin, "Get Happy," 68.

14. Ibid.

15. C. Gentry, "Cultural Revolution," *Chain Store Age* 83(12) (December 2007): 34.

16. Ibid.

17. Ibid.

18. Ibid.

19. O'Brien, "Zappos Knows How to Kick It," 58.

20. Gentry, "Cultural Revolution," 34.

21. N. Zmuda, "Zappos," *Advertising Age* (Midwest Region Edition) 79(39) (October 20, 2008): 36.

22. Chafkin, "Get Happy," 72.

23. Ibid.

24. Ibid., p. 68.

25. Gentry, "Cultural Revolution," 34.

26. Ibid.

Chapter 8

1. B. Schmidt, "So Much for that Window of Opportunity...," *The Oregonian* (June 15, 2009).

2. Staff, "CarMax CEO Optimistic," *The Richmond Times-Dispatch* (June 24, 2009).

3. D. L. Whetzel, "The Department of Labor Identifies Workplace Skills," *The Industrial/Organizational Psychologist* (July 1991): 89–90.

4. M. Macik-Frey, J. C. Quick, and J. D. Quick, "Interpersonal Communication: The Key to Unlocking Social Support for Preventive Stress Management," in C. L. Cooper, ed., *Handbook of Stress, Medicine, and Health, Revised Edition* (Boca Raton, FL: CRC Press, 2005), 265–292.

5. J. M. Brett, M. Olekalns, R. Friedman, N. Goats, C. Anderson, and C. C. Lisco, "Sticks and Stones: Language, Face, and Online Dispute Resolution," *Academy of Management Journal* 50 (2007): 85–99.

6. *Richness* is a term originally coined by W. D. Bodensteiner, "Information Channel Utilization under Varying Research and Development Project Conditions" (Ph.D. diss., University of Texas at Austin, 1970).

7. B. Barry and I. S. Fulmer, "The Medium and the Message: The Adaptive Use of Communication Media in Dyadic Influence," *Academy of Management Review* 29 (2004): 272–292.

8. R. Reik, *Listen with the Third Ear* (New York: Pyramid, 1972).

9. E. Rautalinko and H. O. Lisper, "Effects of Training Reflective Listening in a Corporate Setting," *Journal of Business and Psychology* 18 (2004): 281–299.

10. A. G. Athos and J. J. Gabarro, *Interpersonal Behavior: Communication and Understanding in Relationships* (Englewood Cliffs, NJ: Prentice Hall, 1978).

11. A. D. Mangelsdorff, "Lessons Learned from the Military: Implications for Management" (Distinguished Visiting Lecture, University of Texas at Arlington, January 29, 1993).

12. D. A. Morand, "Language and Power: An Empirical Analysis of Linguistic Strategies Used in Superior–Subordinate Communication," *Journal of Organizational Behavior* 21 (2000): 235–249.

13. S. Bates, "How Leaders Communicate Big Ideas to Drive Business Results," *Employment Relations Today* 33 (Fall 2006): 13–19.

14. F. Luthans, "Successful versus Effective Real Managers," *Academy of Management Executive* 2 (1988): 127–132.

15. L. E. Penley, E. R. Alexander, I. E. Jernigan, and C. I. Henwood, "Communication Abilities of Managers: The Relationship of Performance," *Journal of Management* 17 (1991): 57–76.

16. J. A. LePine and L. Van Dyne, "Voice and Cooperative Behavior as Contrasting Forms of Contextual Performance: Evidence of Differential Relationships with Big Five Personality Characteristics and Cognitive Ability," *Journal of Applied Psychology* 86 (2001): 326–336.

17. F. M. Jablin, "Superior-Subordinate Communication: The State of the Art," *Psychological Bulletin* 86 (1979): 1201–1222; W. C. Reddin, *Communication within the Organization: An Interpretive Review of Theory and Research* (New York: Industrial Communication Council, 1972).

18. B. Barry and J. M. Crant, "Dyadic Communication Relationships in Organizations: An Attribution Expectancy Approach," *Organization Science* 11 (2000): 648–665.

19. A. Rosenberg and J. Hirschberg, "Charisma perception from text and speech," *Speech Communication* 51 (2009): 640–655.

20. J. C. Quick, D. L. Nelson, and J. D. Quick, *Stress and Challenge at the Top: The Paradox of the Successful Executive* (Chichester, England: John Wiley & Sons, 1990).

21. J. Silvester, F. Patterson, A. Koczwara, and E. Ferguson, " 'Trust Me…': Psychological and Behavioral Predictors of Perceived Physician Empathy," *Journal of Applied Psychology* 92 (2007): 519–527.

22. S. E. Moss and J. I. Sanchez, "Are Your Employees Avoiding You? Managerial Strategies for Closing the Feedback Gap," *Academy of Management Executive* 18 (2004): 32–44.

23. G. T. Kumkale and D. Albarracin, "The Sleeper Effect in Persuasion: A Meta-Analytic Review," *Psychological Bulletin* 130 (2004): 143–172.

24. M.J. Hornsey, E. Robson, J. Smith, S. Esposo, and R. M. Sutton, "Sugaring the Pill: Assessing Rhetorical Strategies Designed to Minimize Defensive Reactions to Group Criticism," *Human Communication Research* 34 (2008): 70–98

25. A. Furhham and P. Stringfield, "Congruence in Job-Performance Ratings: A Study of 360 Degree Feedback Examining Self, Manager, Peers, and Consultant Ratings," *Human Relations* 51 (1998): 517–530.

26. J. W. Gilsdorf, "Organizational Rules on Communicating: How Employees Are—and Are Not—Learning the Ropes," *Journal of Business Communication* 35 (1998): 173–201.

27. E. A. Gerloff and J. C. Quick, "Task Role Ambiguity and Conflict in Supervision–Subordinate Relationships," *Journal of Applied Communication Research* 12 (1984): 90–102.

28. E. H. Schein, "Reassessing the 'Divine Rights' of Managers," *Sloan Management Review* 30 (1989): 63–68.

29. D. Tannen, *That's Not What I Mean! How Conversational Style Makes or Breaks Your Relations with Others* (New York: Morrow, 1986); D. Tannen, *You Just Don't Understand* (New York: Ballentine, 1990).

30. R. I. Swaab and D. F. Swaab, "Sex Differences in the Effects of Visual Contact and Eye Contact in Negotiations," *Journal of Experimental Social Psychology* 45 (2009): 129–136.

31. D. G. Allen and R. W. Griffeth, "A Vertical and Lateral Information Processing: The Effects of Gender, Employee Classification Level, and Media Richness on Communication and Work Outcomes," *Human Relations* 50 (1997): 1239–1260.

32. K.L. Ashcraft, "Empowering 'Professional' Relationships," *Management Communication Quarterly* 13 (2000): 347–393.

33. G. Hofstede, *Culture's Consequences: International Differences in Work-Related Values* (Beverly Hills, CA: Sage Publications, 1980).

34. G. Hofstede, "Motivation, Leadership, and Organization: Do American Theories Apply Abroad?" *Organizational Dynamics* 9 (1980): 42–63.

35. H. Levinson, *Executive* (Cambridge, MA: Harvard University Press, 1981).

36. P. Benimadhu, "Adding Value through Diversity: An Interview with Bernard F. Isautier," *Canadian Business Review* 22 (1995): 6–11.

37. M. J. Gannon and Associates, *Understanding Global Cultures: Metaphorical Journeys through 17 Countries* (Thousand Oaks, CA: Sage Publications, 1994).

38. T. M. Karelitz and D. V. Budescu, "You Say 'Probable' and I Say 'Likely': Improving Interpersonal Communication with Verbal Probability Phrases," *Journal of Experimental Psychology: Applied* 10 (2004): 25–41.

39. T. Wells, *Keeping Your Cool under Fire: Communicating Nondefensively* (New York: McGraw-Hill, 1980).

40. R. D. Laing, *The Politics of the Family and Other Essays* (New York: Pantheon, 1971).

41. H. S. Schwartz, *Narcissistic Process and Corporate Decay: The Theory of the Organizational Ideal* (New York: New York University Press, 1990).

42. W. R. Forrester and M. F. Maute, "The Impact of Relationship Satisfaction on Attribution, Emotions, and Behaviors Following Service Failure," *Journal of Applied Business Research* 17 (2000): 1–14.

43. M. L. Knapp, *Nonverbal Communication in Human Interaction* (New York: Holt, Rinehart & Winston, 1978); J. McCroskey and L. Wheeless, *Introduction to Human Communication* (New York: Allyn & Bacon, 1976).

44. A. M. Katz and V. T. Katz, eds., *Foundations of Nonverbal Communication* (Carbondale, IL: Southern Illinois University Press, 1983).

45. M. D. Lieberman, "Intuition: A Social Cognitive Neuroscience Approach," *Psychological Bulletin* 126 (2000): 109–138.

46. R. Friedman and A. J. Elliott, "The Effect of Arm Crossing on Persistence and Performance," *European Journal of Social Psychology* 33 (2008): 449–461.

47. M. Weisbuch and N. Ambady, "Unspoken Cultural Influence: Exposure to and Influence of Nonverbal Bias," *Journal of Personality and Social Psychology* 96 (2009): 1104–1119.

48. E. T. Hall, *The Hidden Dimension* (Garden City, NY: Doubleday Anchor, 1966).

49. E. T. Hall, "Proxemics," in A. M. Katz and V. T. Katz, eds., *Foundations of Nonverbal Communication* (Carbondale, IL: Southern Illinois University Press, 1983).

50. R. T. Barker and C. G. Pearce, "The Importance of Proxemics at Work," *Supervisory Management* 35 (1990): 10–11.

51. R. L. Birdwhistell, *Kinesics and Context* (Philadelphia: University of Pennsylvania Press, 1970).

52. K. I. Ruys and D. A. Stapel, "Emotion Elicitor or Emotion Messenger?" *Psychological Science* 19 (2008): 593–600.

53. M. G. Frank and P. Ekman, "Appearing Truthful Generalizes Across Different Deception Situations," *Journal of Personality and Social Psychology* 86 (2004): 486–495.

54. S. L. Sporer and B. Schwandt, "Moderators of Nonverbal Indicators of Deception," *Psychology, Public Policy, and Law* 13 (2007): 1–34.

55. P. Ekman and W. V. Friesen, "Research on Facial Expressions of Emotion," in A. M. Katz and V. T. Katz, eds., *Foundations of Nonverbal Communication* (Carbondale, IL: Southern Illinois University Press, 1983).

56. H. H. Tan, M. D. Foo, C. L. Chong, and R. Ng, "Situational and Dispositional Predictors of Displays of Positive Emotions," *Journal of Organizational Behavior* 24 (2003): 961–978.

57. C. Barnum and N. Wolniansky, "Taking Cues from Body Language," *Management Review* 78 (1989): 59.

58. Katz and Katz, *Foundations of Nonverbal Communication*, p. 181.

59. R. Gifford, C. F. Ng, and M. Wilkinson, "Nonverbal Cues in the Employment Interview: Links between Applicant Qualities and Interviewer Judgments," *Journal of Applied Psychology* 70 (1985): 729–736.

60. A. Drahota, A. Costall and V. Reddy. "The Vocal Communication of Different Kinds of Smile," *Speech Communication* 50 (2008): 278–287.

61. P. J. DePaulo and B. M. DePaulo, "Can Deception by Salespersons and Customers Be Detected through Nonverbal Behavioral Cues?" *Journal of Applied Social Psychology* 19 (1989): 1552–1577.

62. P. Ekman, *Telling Lies* (New York: Norton, 1985); D. Goleman, "Nonverbal Cues Are Easy to Misinterpret," *New York Times* (September 17, 1991): B5.

63. J. P. Forgas and R. East, "On Being Happy and Gullible: Mood Effects on Skepticism and the Deception of Deception," *Journal of Experimental Social Psychology* 44 (2008): 1362–1367.

64. J. J. Lynch, *A Cry Unheard: New Insights into the Medical Consequences of Loneliness* (Baltimore, MD: Bancroft Press, 2000).

65. J. C. Quick, J. H. Gavin, C. L. Cooper, and J. D. Quick, "Working Together: Balancing Head and Heart," in N. G. Johnson, R. H. Rozensky, C. D. Goodheart, and R. Hammond, eds., *Psychology Builds a Healthy World*: (Washington, DC: American Psychological Association, 2004), 219–232.

66. J. C. Quick, C. L. Cooper, J. D. Quick, and J. H. Gavin, *The Financial Times Guide to Executive Health* (London, UK: Financial Times–Prentice Hall, 2003).

67. K. M. Wasylyshyn, "Coaching the Superkeepers," in L. A. Berger and D. R. Berger, eds., *The Talent Management Handbook: Creating*

Organizational Excellence by Identifying, Developing, and Positioning Your Best People: (New York, NY: McGraw-Hill, 2003), 320–336.

68. J. C. Quick and M. Macik-Frey, "Behind the Mask: Coaching through Deep Interpersonal Communication," *Consulting Psychology Journal: Practice and Research* 56 (2004): 67–74.

69. B. Drake and K. Yuthas, "It's Only Words—Impacts of Information Technology on Moral Dialogue," *Journal of Business Ethics* 23 (2000): 41–60.

70. N. Frohlich and J. Oppenheimer, "Some Consequences of E-Mail vs. Face-to-Face Communication in Experiment," *Journal of Economic Behavior & Organization* 35 (1998): 389–403.

71. C. E. Naquin, T. R. Kurtzberg, and L. Y. Belkin, "E-Mail Communication and Group Cooperation in Mixed Motive Contexts," *Social Justice Research* 21 (2008): 470–489.

72. J. Kruger, N. Epley, J. Parker, and Z. Ng, "Egocentrism over E-mail: Can We Communicate as Well as We Think?"`, *Journal of Personality and Social Psychology* 89 (2005): 925–936.

73. R. Donkin, "Irrational Resistance to Innovation," *Human Resources* (August 2008): 20.

74. C. Brod, *Technostress: The Human Cost of the Computer Revolution* (Reading, MA: Addison-Wesley, 1984).

75. S. Kiesler, "Technology and the Development of Creative Environments," in Y. Ijiri and R. L. Kuhn, eds., *New Directions in Creative and Innovative Management* (Cambridge, MA: Ballinger Press, 1988).

76. S. Kiesler, J. Siegel, and T. W. McGuire, "Social Psychological Aspects of Computer-Mediated Communication," *American Psychologist* 39 (1984): 1123–1134.

77. P. Shachaf, "Cultural Diversity and Information and Communication Technology Impacts on Global Virtual Teams: An Exploratory Study," *Information & Management* 45 (2008): 131–142.

78. Staff, "CarMax Receives Award for Business Practices," *The Richmond Times-Dispatch* (January 14, 2009).

79. Staff, "CarMax Launches New Advance Search Tool," *Business Wire* (January 20, 2009).

Chapter 8 Case

1. J. E. Vascellaro, "BlackBerry Outage Leaves Sour Taste; RIM's Partners Not as Forgiving as Its Customers," *Wall Street Journal* (Eastern edition) (February 13, 2008): A28.

2. J. E. Vascellaro, "RIM BlackBerries Hit by Large-Scale Outage," *Wall Street Journal* (Eastern edition) (February 12, 2008): B4; Vascellaro, "BlackBerry Outage Leaves Sour Taste," A28.

3. Vascellaro, "RIM BlackBerries Hit by Large-Scale Outage," B4.

4. Ibid.

5. Vascellaro, "BlackBerry Outage Leaves Sour Taste," A28.

6. Vascellaro, "RIM BlackBerries Hit by Large-Scale Outage," B4.

7. Vascellaro, "BlackBerry Outage Leaves Sour Taste," A28.

8. N. Wingfield, "Technology (A Special Report); Why It May Be Time to Leave the Laptop Behind; For More Mobile Workers, Phone Increasingly Give Them Much of What They Need—With a Lot Less Hassle," *Wall Street Journal* (Eastern edition) (October 27, 2008): R4.

9. Ibid.

10. Ibid.

11. Ibid.

Chapter 9

1. A. Wahl, "Jim Balsille Mike Lazaridis," *Canadian Business* 82 (2008): 53–54.

2. T. Tedesco, "Balsille's Eye on the Puck," *Financial Post* (June 13, 2009): FP1.

3. G. Garcia, "Measuring Performance at Northrop Grumman," *Knowledge Management Review* 3 (2001): 22–25.

4. A. M. Towsend, S. M. DeMarie, and A. R. Hendrickson, "Virtual Teams: Technology and the Workplace of the Future," *Academy of Management Executive* 12 (1998): 17–29.

5. D. M. McGregor, *The Human Side of Enterprise* (New York: McGraw-Hill, 1960).

6. J. R. Katzenbach and D. K. Smith, "The Discipline of Teams," *Harvard Business Review* 71 (1993): 111–120.

7. N. Ellemers, S. Pagliaro, M. Barreto, and C. W. Leach, "Is It Better to Be Moral than Smart? The Effects of Morality and Competence Norms on the Decision to Work at Group Status Improvement," *Journal of Personality and Social Psychology* 95 (2008), 1397–1410.

8. K. L. Bettenhausen and J. K. Murnighan, "The Development and Stability of Norms in Groups Facing Interpersonal and Structural Challenge," *Administrative Science Quarterly* 36 (1991): 20–35.

9. I. Adarves-Yorno, T. Postmes, and S. A. Haslam, "Creative Innovation or Crazy Irrelevance? The Contribution of Group Norms and Social Identity to Creative Behavior," *Journal of Experimental Social Psychology* 43 (2007): 410–416.

10. D. Tjosvold and Z. Yu, "Goal Interdependence and Applying Abilities for Team In-Role and Extra-Role Performance in China," *Group Dynamics: Theory, Research, and Practice* 8 (2004): 98–111.

11. M. S. Cole, F. Walter, and H. Bruch, "Affective Mechanisms Linking Dysfunctional Behavior to Performance in Work Teams: A Moderated Mediation Study," *Journal of Applied Psychology* 93 (2008), 945–958.

12. V. U. Druskat and S. B. Wolff, "Building the Emotional Intelligence of Groups," *Harvard Business Review* 79 (2001): 80–90.

13. I. Summers, T. Coffelt, and R. E. Horton, "Work-Group Cohesion," *Psychological Reports* 63 (1988): 627–636.

14. D. C. Man and S. S. K. Lam, "The Effects of Job Complexity and Autonomy on Cohesiveness in Collectivistic and Individualistic Work Groups: A Cross-Cultural Analysis," *Journal of Organizational Behavior* 24 (2003): 979–1001.

15. K. H. Price, "Working Hard to Get People to Loaf," *Basic and Applied Social Psychology* 14 (1993): 329–344.

16. R. Albanese and D. D. Van Fleet, "Rational Behavior in Groups: The Free-Riding Tendency," *Academy of Management Review* 10 (1985): 244–255.

17. E. Diener, "Deindividuation, Self-Awareness, and Disinhibition," *Journal of Personality and Social Psychology* 37 (1979): 1160–1171.

18. S. Prentice-Dunn and R. W. Rogers, "Deindividuation and the Self-Regulation of Behavior," in P. Paulus, ed., *Psychology of Group Influence* (Hillsdale, NJ: Erlbaum, 1989), 87–109.

19. B. M. Bass and E. C. Ryterband, *Organizational Psychology*, 2nd ed. (Boston: Allyn & Bacon, 1979).

20. W. G. Bennis and H. A. Shepard, "A Theory of Group Development," *Human Relations* 9 (1956): 415–438.

21. S. Caudron, "Monsanto Responds to Diversity," *Personnel Journal* (November 1990): 72–80.

22. D. L. Fields and T. C. Bloom, "Employee Satisfaction in Work Groups with Different Gender Composition," *Journal of Organizational Behavior* 18 (1997): 181–196.

23. D. C. Lau and J. K. Murnighan, "Demographic Diversity and Fault-lines: The Compositional Dynamics of Organizational Groups," *Academy of Management Review* 23 (1998): 325–340.

24. B. Tuckman, "Developmental Sequence in Small Groups," *Psychological Bulletin* 63 (1965): 384–399; B. Tuckman and M. Jensen, "Stages of Small-Group Development," *Group and Organizational Studies* 2 (1977): 419–427.

25. D. Nichols, "Quality Program Sparked Company Turnaround," *Personnel* (October 1991): 24. For a commentary on Wallace's hard times and subsequent emergence from Chapter 11 bankruptcy, see R. C. Hill, "When the Going Gets Tough: A Baldrige Award Winner on the Line," *Academy of Management Executive* 7 (1993): 75–79.

26. S. Weisband and L. Atwater, "Evaluating Self and Others in Electronic and Face-to-Face Groups," *Journal of Applied Psychology* 84 (1999): 632–639.

27. C. J. G. Gersick, "Time and Transition in Work Teams: Toward a New Model of Group Development," *The Academy of Management Journal* 31 (1988): 9–41.

28. M. Hardaker and B. K. Ward, "How to Make a Team Work," *Harvard Business Review* 65 (1987): 112–120.

29. C. R. Gowen, "Managing Work Group Performance by Individual Goals and Group Goals for an Interdependent Group Task," *Journal of Organizational Behavior Management* 7 (1986): 5–27.

30. K. L. Bettenhausen and J. K. Murnighan, "The Emergence of Norms in Competitive Decision-Making Groups," *Administrative Science Quarterly* 30 (1985): 350–372; K. L. Bettenhausen, "Five Years of Groups Research: What We Have Learned and What Needs to Be Addressed," *Journal of Management* 17 (1991): 345–381.

31. J. E. McGrath, *Groups: Interaction and Performance* (Englewood Cliffs, NJ: Prentice Hall, 1984).

32. K. L. Gammage, A. V. Carron, and P. A. Estabrooks, "Team Cohesion and Individual Productivity," *Small Group Research* 32 (2001): 3–18.

33. F. Walter and H. Bruch, "The Positive Group Affect Spiral: A Dynamic Model of the Emergence of Positive Affective Similarity in Work Groups," *Journal of Organizational Behavior* 29 (2008), 239–261.

34. S. E. Seashore, *Group Cohesiveness in the Industrial Work Group* (Ann Arbor, MI: University of Michigan, 1954).

35. S. M. Klein, "A Longitudinal Study of the Impact of Work Pressure on Group Cohesive Behaviors," *International Journal of Management* 12 (1996): 68–75.

36. N. Steckler and N. Fondas, "Building Team Leader Effectiveness: A Diagnostic Tool," *Organizational Dynamics* 23 (1995): 20–35.

37. A. Carter and S. Holmes, "Curiously Strong Teamwork," *BusinessWeek* 4023 (February 26, 2007): 90–92.

38. G. Parker, *Team Players and Teamwork* (San Francisco: Jossey-Bass, 1990).

39. N. R. F. Maier, "Assets and Liabilities in Group Problem Solving: The Need for an Integrative Function," *Psychological Review* 74 (1967): 239–249.

40. T. A. Stewart, "The Search for the Organization of Tomorrow," *Fortune* (May 18, 1992): 92–98.

41. J. R. Goktepe and C. E. Schneier, "Role of Sex, Gender Roles, and Attraction in Predicting Emergent Leaders," *Journal of Applied Psychology* 74 (1989): 165–167.

42. W. R. Lassey, "Dimensions of Leadership," in W. R. Lassey and R. R. Fernandez, eds., *Leadership and Social Change* (La Jolla, CA: University Associates, 1976), 10–15.

43. B. Broysberg and L. Lee, "The Effect of Colleague Quality on Top Performance: The Case of Security Analysts," *Journal of Organizational Behavior* 29 (2008): 1123–1144.

44. J. D. Quick, G. Moorhead, J. C. Quick, E. A. Gerloff, K. L. Mattox, and C. Mullins, "Decision Making among Emergency Room Residents: Preliminary Observations and a Decision Model," *Journal of Medical Education* 58 (1983): 117–125.

45. W. J. Duncan and J. P. Feisal, "No Laughing Matter: Patterns of Humor in the Workplace," *Organizational Dynamics* 17 (1989): 18–30.

46. A. Hunter, "Best Practice Club," *Personnel Today* (April 15, 2003): 8.

47. S. S. Webber and R. J. Klimoski, "Crews: A Distinct Type of Work Team," *Journal of Business and Psychology* 18 (2004): 261–279.

48. P. F. Drucker, "There's More than One Kind of Team," *Wall Street Journal* (February 11, 1992): A16.

49. B. L. Kirkman, C. B. Gibson, and D. L. Shapiro, " 'Exporting' Teams: Enhancing the Implementation and Effectiveness of Work Teams in Global Affiliates," *Organizational Dynamics* 30 (2001): 12–29.

50. A. Taylor and H. R. Greve, "Superman or the Fantastic Four? Knowledge Combination and Experience in Innovative Teams," *Academy of Management Journal* 49 (2006): 723–740.

51. P. M. Podsakoff, M. Ahearne, and S. B. MacKenzie, "Organizational Citizenship Behavior and the Quantity and Quality of Work Group Performance," *Journal of Applied Psychology* 82 (1997): 262–270.

52. L. Hirschhorn, *Managing in the New Team Environment* (Upper Saddle River, NJ: Prentice Hall, 2002), 521A.

53. S. E. Humphrey, F. P. Morgeson, and M. J. Mannor, "Developing a Theory of the Strategic Core of Teams: A Role Composition Model of Team Performance," *Journal of Applied Psychology* 94 (2009): 48–61.

54. G. Chen and R. J. Klimoski, "The Impact of Expectations on Newcomer Performance in Teams as Mediated by Work Characteristics, Social Exchanges, and Empowerment," *Academy of Management Journal* 46 (2003): 591–607.

55. B. Beersma, J. R. Hollenbeck, S. E. Humphrey, H. Moon, D. E. Conlon, and D. R. Ilgen, "Cooperation, Competition, and Team Performance: Toward a Contingency Approach," *Academy of Management Journal* 46 (2003): 572–590.

56. S. Faraj and A. Yan, "Boundary Work in Knowledge Teams," *Journal of Applied Psychology* 94 (2009): 604–617.

57. W. L. Mohr and H. Mohr, *Quality Circles: Changing Images of People at Work* (Reading, MA: Addison-Wesley, 1983).

58. R. W. Griffin, "A Longitudinal Assessment of the Consequences of Quality Circles in an Industrial Setting," *Academy of Management Journal* 31 (1988): 338–358.

59. P. Shaver and D. Buhrmester, "Loneliness, Sex-Role Orientation, and Group Life: A Social Needs Perspective," in P. Paulus, ed., *Basic Group Processes* (New York: Springer-Verlag, 1985), 259–288.

60. P. Chattopadhyay, M. Tluchowska, and E. George, "Identifying the Ingroup: A Closer Look at the Influence of Demographic Dissimilarity on Employee Social Identity," *Academy of Management Review* 29 (2004): 180–202.

61. M. M. Stewart and P. Garcia-Prieto, "A Relational Demography Model of Workgroup Identification: Testing the Effects of Race, Race Dissimilarity, Racial Identification, and Communication Behavior," *Journal of Organizational Behavior,* 29 (2008): 657–680.

62. F. Balkundi, M. Kilduff, Z. I. Barsness, and J. H. Michael, "Demographic Antecedents and Performance Consequences of Structural Holes in Work Teams," *Journal of Organizational Behavior* 28 (2007): 241–260.

63. E. V. Hobman, P. Bordia, and C. Gallois, "Consequences of Feeling Dissimilar from Others in a Work Team," *Journal of Business and Psychology* 17 (2003): 301–325.

64. A. E. Randel and K. S. Jaussi, "Functional Background Identity, Diversity, and Individual Performance in Cross-Functional Teams," *Academy of Management Journal* 46 (2003): 763–774.

65. J. S. Bunderson, "Team Member Functional Background and Involvement in Management Teams: Direct Effects and the Moderating Role of Power Centralization," *Academy of Management Journal* 46 (2003): 458–474.

66. G. S. Van Der Vegt, E. Van De Vliert, and A. Oosterhof, "Informational Dissimilarity and Organizational Citizenship Behavior: The Role of Intrateam Interdependence and Team Identification," *Academy of Management Journal* 46 (2003): 715–727.

67. A. Pirola-Merlo and L. Mann, "The Relationship between Individual Creativity and Team Creativity: Aggregating Across People and Time," *Journal of Organizational Behavior* 25 (2004): 235–257.

68. L. Thompson, "Improving the Creativity of Organizational Work Groups," *Academy of Management Executive* 17 (2003): 96–111.

69. C. Ford and D. M. Sullivan, "A Time for Everything: How the Timing of Novel Contributions Influences Project Team Outcomes," *Journal of Organizational Behavior* 25 (2004): 279–292.

70. B. L. Kirman and D. L. Shapiro, "The Impact of Cultural Values on Job Satisfaction and Organizational Commitment in Self-Managing Work Teams: The Mediating Role of Employee Resistance," *Academy of Management Journal* 44 (2001): 557–569.

71. J. W. Dean, Jr. and J. Evans. *Total Quality: Management, Organization, and Strategy* (St. Paul, MN: West, 1994).

72. R. R. Blake, J. S. Mouton, and R. L. Allen, *Spectacular Teamwork: How to Develop the Leadership Skills for Team Success* (New York: John Wiley & Sons, 1987).

73. American Management Association, *Blueprints for Service Quality: The Federal Express Approach*, AMA Management Briefing (New York: AMA, 1991).

74. J. C. Quick, J. H. Gavin, C. L. Cooper, and J. D. Quick, "Working Together: Balancing Head and Heart," in R. H. Rozensky, N. G. Johnson, C. D. Goodheart, and W. R. Hammond, eds., *Psychology*

Builds a Healthy World (Washington, DC: American Psychological Association, 2004), 219–232.

75. A. G. Athos and J. J. Gabarro, *Interpersonal Behavior: Communication and Understanding in Relationships* (Englewood Cliffs, NJ: Prentice Hall, 1978).

76. C. C. Moskos and J. S. Butler, *All That We Can Be: Black Leadership and Racial Integration The Army Way* (New York: Basic Books, 1996).

77. E. Aronson, N. Blaney, C. Stephan, J. Sikes, and M. Snapp, *The Jigsaw Classroom* (Beverly Hills and London: Sage, 1978).

78. D. A. Harrison, K. H. Price, and M. P. Bell, "Beyond Relational Demography: Time and the Effect of Surface—Versus Deep-Level Diversity on Group Cohesiveness," *Academy of Management Journal*, 41 (1998): 96–107.

79. C. Douglas and W. L. Gardner, "Transition to Self-Directed Work Teams: Implications of Transition Time and Self-Monitoring for Managers' Use of Influence Tactics," *Journal of Organizational Behavior* 25 (2004): 47–65.

80. C. Douglas, J. S. Martin, and R. H. Krapels, "Communication in the Transition to Self-Directed Work Teams," *Journal of Business Communication* 43 (2006): 295–321.

81. J. L. Cordery, W. S. Mueller, and L. M. Smith, "Attitudinal and Behavioral Effects of Autonomous Group Working: A Longitudinal Field Study," *Academy of Management Journal* 34 (1991): 464–476.

82. M. Workman and W. Bommer, "Redesigning Computer Call Center Work: A Longitudinal Field Experiment," *Journal of Organizational Behavior* 25 (2004): 317–337.

83. G. Moorhead, C. P. Neck, and M. S. West, "The Tendency Toward Defective Decision Making within Self-Managing Teams: The Relevance of Groupthink for the 21st Century," *Organizational Behavior & Human Decision Processes* 73 (1998): 327–351.

84. B. M. Staw and L. D. Epstein, "What Bandwagons Bring: Effects of Popular Management Techniques on Corporate Performance, Reputation, and CEO Pay," *Administrative Science Quarterly* 45 (2000): 523–556.

85. R. M. Robinson, S. L. Oswald, K. S. Swinehart, and J. Thomas, "Southwest Industries: Creating High-Performance Teams for High-Technology Production," *Planning Review* 19, published by the Planning Forum (November–December 1991): 10–47.

86. A. Lienert, "Forging a New Partnership," *Management Review* 83 (1994): 39–43.

87. S. Thiagaraian, "A Game for Cooperative Learning," *Training and Development* (May 1992): 35–41.

88. D. C. Hambrick and P. Mason, "Upper Echelons: The Organization as a Reflection of Its Top Managers," *Academy of Management Review* 9 (1984): 193–206.

89. D. C. Hambrick, "The Top Management Team: Key to Strategic Success," *California Management Review* 30 (1987): 88–108.

90. G. A. Van Kleef, A. C. Homan, B. Beersma, D. Van Knippenberg, B. Van Knippenberg, and F. Damen, "Searing Sentiment or Cold Calculation? The Effects of Leader Emotional Displays on Team Performance Depend on Follower Epistemic Motivation," *Academy of Management Journal* 52 (2009): 562–580.

91. A. D. Henderson and J. W. Fredrickson, "Top Management Team Coordination Needs and the CEO Pay Gap: A Competitive Test of Economic and Behavioral Views," *Academy of Management Journal* 44 (2001): 96–117.

92. D. C. Hambrick and G. D. S. Fukutomi, "The Seasons of a CEO's Tenure," *Academy of Management Review* 16 (1991): 719–742.

93. J. C. Quick, D. L. Nelson, and J. D. Quick, "Successful Executives: How Independent?" *Academy of Management Executive* 1 (1987): 139–145.

94. I. Adizes, "Communication Strategies for Leading Teams," *Leader to Leader* (Winter 2004): 10–15.

95. A. A. Cannella Jr, J. Park, and H. Lee, "Top Management Team Functional Background Diversity and Firm Performance: Examining the Roles of Team Member Colocation and Environmental Uncertainty," *Academy of Management Journal* 51 (2008): 768–784.

96. L. G. Love, "The Evolving Pinnacle of the Corporation: An Explanatory Study of the Antecedents, Processes, and Consequences of CoCEOs" (The University of Texas at Arlington, 2003).

97. N. J. Adler, *International Dimensions of Organizational Behavior* (Mason, OH: South-Western, 2001).

98. I. D. Steiner, *Group Process and Productivity* (New York: Academic Press, 1972).

99. U. Glunk, M. G. Heijltjes, and R. Olie, "Design Characteristics and Functioning of Top Management Teams in Europe," *European Management Journal* 19 (2001): 291–300.

100. E. Kearney, D. Gebert, and S. C. Voelpel, "When and How Diversity Benefits Teams: The Importance of Team Members' Need for Cognition," *Academy of Management Journal* 52 (2009): 581–598.

101. J. W. Pfeiffer and C. Nolde, eds., *The Encyclopedia of Team-Development Activities* (San Diego: University Associates, 1991).

102. M. Walcoff, "Change Has Come: 10 Years of BlackBerry," *Waterloo Region Record* (January 24, 2009).

Chapter 9 Case

1. "Stryker History," Stryker Corporation Web site, http://www.stryker.com/en-us/corporate/AboutUs/History/index.htm (accessed July 13, 2009).

2. K. Yung, "Kalamazoo Firm Finds Success in Innovation," *Detroit Free Press* (August 12, 2007), from Newspaper Source database (accessed September 26, 2007).

3. K. Norris, "Kalamazoo, Mich., Firm Makes Instruments and Body Parts for an Aging Nation," *Detroit Free Press* (January 3, 2007), from Newspaper Source database (accessed September 26, 2007).

4. "Stryker History"; "Stryker: Company Profile," *Datamonitor.com* (August 2006), reference code 3629: 4–5; A. Weintraub, "Stryker," *BusinessWeek* (March 26, 2007): 66–67; K. Yung, "Kalamazoo Firm Finds Success in Innovation," *Detroit Free Press* (August 12, 2007), from Newspaper Source database (accessed September 26, 2007).

5. R. Wagner and J. K. Harter, "Assembling the Right Talents at Stryker," *Gallup Management Journal* (September 14, 2006), http://gmj.gallup.com (accessed September 26, 2007): 1–2.

6. Ibid., p. 2.

7. Ibid., p. 3.

8. Ibid., p. 4.

9. Ibid.

10. Ibid., p. 5.

11. D. Bogoslaw, "Stryker: A Strong Quarter," *BusinessWeek Online* (January 25, 2008), http://www.businessweek.com/investor/contents/jan2008/pi20080124_300920.htm (accessed July 13, 2009).

12. J. Kamp, "Stryker's Growth Streak Runs into Doubts," *Wall Street Journal* (Eastern edition): (September 17, 2008): B5A.

13. Bogoslaw, "Stryker."

14. K. J. Winstein, "Senate Panel to Question Payments to Surgeons," *Wall Street Journal* (Eastern edition) (February 27, 2008): B6.

15. Ibid.

16. Kamp, "Stryker's Growth," B5A.

17. J. Kamp, "Stryker Dispute with U.S. Could Continue for Months," *Wall Street Journal* (Eastern edition) (October 1, 2008): D8.

Chapter 10

1. http://www.facebook.com/photo.php?pid=1705632&id=829502718&saved#/group.php?sid=117ac309f77ebca5d59c832559a2374d&gid=21225988060&ref=search.

2. J. Hempel, "How Facebook Is Taking Over Our Lifes," *Fortune* Magazine Online (February 17, 2009), http://money.cnn.com/2009/02/16/technology/hempel_facebook.fortune/.

3. B. Stone and B. Stetler, "Facebook Withdraws Changes in Data Use", *New York Times* online (February 18, 2009), http://www.nytimes.com/2009/02/19/technology/internet/19facebook.html.

4. H. A. Simon, *The New Science of Management Decision* (New York: Harper & Row, 1960).

5. G. Huber, *Managerial Decision Making* (Glenview, IL: Scott, Foresman, 1980).

6. H. A. Simon, *Administrative Behavior* (New York: Macmillan, 1957).

7. E. F. Harrison, *The Managerial Decision-Making Process* (Boston: Houghton Mifflin, 1981).

8. R. L. Ackoff, "The Art and Science of Mess Management," *Interfaces* (February 1981): 20–26.

9. L. Rubel, "The Availability Heuristic: A Redux," *Journal of Statistics Education* 15 (2007): 1–9.

10. M. E. Bazerman and D. A. Moore, *Judgment in Managerial Decision Making*, 7th ed. (New York: John Wiley & Sons, 2008).

11. A. Tversky and D. Kahneman, "Judgment Under Uncertainty, Heuristics and Biases," *Science* 185 (1974): 1124–1131.

12. Bazerman and Moore, *Judgment in Managerial Decision Making*.

13. S. Hayibor and D. M. Wasieleski, "Effects of the Use of the Availability Heuristic on Ethical Decision Making in Organizations," *Journal of Business Ethics* 84 (2008): 151–165.

14. R. M. Cyert and J. G. March, eds., *A Behavioral Theory of the Firm* (Englewood Cliffs, NJ: Prentice Hall, 1963).

15. M. D. Cohen, J. G. March, and J. P. Olsen, "A Garbage Can Model of Organizational Choice," *Administrative Science Quarterly* 17 (1972): 1–25.

16. J. G. March and J. P. Olsen, "Garbage Can Models of Decision Making in Organizations," in J. G. March and R. Weissinger-Baylon, eds., *Ambiguity and Command* (Marshfield, MA: Pitman, 1986), 11–53.

17. D. van Knippenberg, B. van Knippenberg, and E. van Dijk, "Who Takes the Lead in Risky Decision Making? Effects of Group Members' Risk Preferences and Prototypicality," *Organizational Behavior and Human Decision Processes* 83 (2000): 213–234.

18. K. R. MacCrimmon and D. Wehrung, *Taking Risks* (New York: Free Press, 1986).

19. T. S. Perry, "How Small Firms Innovate: Designing a Culture for Creativity," *Research Technology Management* 28 (1995): 14–17.

20. B. M. Staw, "Knee-Deep in the Big Muddy: A Study of Escalating Commitment to a Chosen Course of Action," *Organizational Behavior and Human Performance* 16 (1976): 27–44; B. M. Staw, "The Escalation of Commitment to a Course of Action," *Academy of Management Review* 6 (1981): 577–587.

21. B. M. Staw and J. Ross, "Understanding Behavior in Escalation Situations," *Science* 246 (1989): 216–220.

22. T. Freemantle and M. Tolson, "Space Station Had Political Ties in Tow," *Houston Chronicle* (August 4, 2003), http://www.chron.com/cs/CDA/ssistory.mpl/space/2004947.

23. L. Festinger, *A Theory of Cognitive Dissonance* (Evanston, IL: Row, Peterson, 1957).

24. B. M. Staw, "The Escalation of Commitment: An Update and Appraisal," in Z. Shapira, ed., *Organizational Decision Making* (Cambridge, England: Cambridge University Press, 1997).

25. D. M. Boehne and P. W. Paese, "Deciding Whether to Complete or Terminate an Unfinished Project: A Strong Test of the Project Completion Hypothesis," *Organizational Behavior and Human Decision Processes* 81 (2000): 178–194; H. Moon, "Looking Forward and Looking Back: Integrating Completion and Sunk Cost Effects within an Escalation-of-Commitment Progress Decision," *Journal of Applied Psychology* 86 (2000): 104–113.

26. J. A. Sonnenfeld, "How Rick Wagoner Lost GM," *BusinessWeek* (June 1, 2009). http://www.businessweek.com/managing/content/jun2009/ca2009061_966638.htm?chan=rss_topDiscussed_ssi_5.

27. N. Sivanathan, D. C. Molden, A. D. Galinsky, and G. Ku, "The Promise and Peril of Self-affirmation in the De-escalation of Commitment," *Organizational Behavior and Human Decision Processes* 107 (2008): 1–14.

28. G. McNamara, H. Moon, and P. Bromiley, "Banking on Commitment: Intended and Unintended Consequences of an Organization's Attempt to Attenuate Escalation of Commitment," *Academy of Management Journal* 45 (2002): 443–452.

29. G. Whyte, "Diffusion of Responsibility: Effects on the Escalation Tendency," *Journal of Applied Psychology* 76 (1991): 408–415.

30. C. G. Jung, *Psychological Types* (London: Routledge & Kegan Paul, 1923).

31. W. Taggart and D. Robey, "Minds and Managers: On the Dual Nature of Human Information Processing and Management," *Academy of Management Review* 6 (1981): 187–195; D. Hellriegel and J. W. Slocum, Jr., "Managerial Problem-Solving Styles," *Business Horizons* 18 (1975): 29–37.

32. G. A. Stevens and J. Burley, "Piloting the Rocket of Radical Innovation," *Research Technology Management* 46 (2003): 16–26.

33. J. C. White, P. R. Varadarajan, and P. A. Dacin, "Market Situation Interpretation and Response: The Role of Cognitive Style, Organizational Culture, and Information Use," *Journal of Marketing* 67 (2003): 63–73.

34. I. I. Mitroff and R. H. Kilmann, "On Organization Stories: An Approach to the Design and Analysis of Organization through Myths and Stories," in R. H. Killman, L. R. Pondy, and D. P. Slevin, eds., *The Management of Organization Design* (New York: Elsevier–North Holland, 1976).

35. I. B. Myers, *Gifts Differing* (Palo Alto, CA: Consulting Psychologists Press, 1980).

36. A. Saleh, "Brain Hemisphericity and Academic Majors: A Correlation Study," *College Student Journal* 35 (2001): 193–200.

37. N. Khatri, "The Role of Intuition in Strategic Decision Making," *Human Relations* 53 (2000): 57–86.

38. H. Mintzberg, "Planning on the Left Side and Managing on the Right," *Harvard Business Review* 54 (1976): 51–63.

39. D. J. Isenberg, "How Senior Managers Think," *Harvard Business Review* 62 (1984): 81–90.

40. R. N. Beck, "Visions, Values, and Strategies: Changing Attitudes and Culture," *Academy of Managment Executive* 1 (1987): 33–41.

41. K. G. Ross, G. A. Klein, P. Thunholm, J. F. Schmitt, and H. C Baxter, "The Recognition-Primed Decision Model," *Military Review, Fort Leavenworth* 84 (2004): 6–10.

42. C. I. Barnard, *The Functions of the Executive* (Cambridge, MA: Harvard University Press, 1938).

43. R. Rowan, *The Intuitive Manager* (New York: Little, Brown, 1986).

44. W. H. Agor, *Intuition in Organizations* (Newbury Park, CA: Sage, 1989).

45. Isenberg, "How Senior Managers Think."

46. H. A. Simon, "Making Management Decisions: The Role of Intuition and Emotion," *Academy of Management Executive* 1 (1987): 57–64.

47. J. L. Redford, R. H. McPhierson, R. G. Frankiewicz, and J. Gaa, "Intuition and Moral Development," *Journal of Psychology* 129 (1994): 91–101.

48. R. Wild, "Naked Hunch; Gut Instinct Is Vital to Your Business," *Success* (June 1998), L. Iacocca and W. Novak, *Iacocca: An Autobiography*, New York, Bantam Books, 1984.

49. W. H. Agor, "How Top Executives Use Their Intuition to Make Important Decisions," *Business Horizons* 29 (1986): 49–53.

50. O. Behling and N. L. Eckel, "Making Sense Out of Intuition," *Academy of Management Executive* 5 (1991): 46–54.

51. L. R. Beach, *Image Theory: Decision Making in Personal and Organizational Contexts* (Chichester, England: John Wiley & Sons, 1990).

52. E. Bonabeau, "Don't Trust Your Gut," *Harvard Business Review* 81 (2003): 116–126.

53. L. Livingstone, "Person-Environment Fit on the Dimension of Creativity: Relationships with Strain, Job Satisfaction, and Performance" (Ph.D. diss., Oklahoma State University, 1992).

54. M. A. West and J. L. Farr, "Innovation at Work," in M. A. West and J. L. Farr, eds., *Innovation and Creativity at Work: Psychological and Organizational Strategies* (New York: John Wiley & Sons, 1990), 3–13.

55. G. Wallas, *The Art of Thought* (New York: Harcourt Brace, 1926).

56. H. Benson and W. Proctor, *The Break-Out Principle* (Scribner: New York, 2003).

57. G. L. Fricchione, B. T. Slingsby, and H. Benson, "The Placebo Effect and the Relaxation Response: Neural Processes and Their Coupling to Constitutive Nitric Oxide," *Brain Research Reviews* 35 (2001): 1–19.

58. M. D. Mumford and S. B. Gustafson, "Creativity Syndrome: Integration, Application, and Innovation," *Psychological Bulletin* 103 (1988): 27–43.

59. T. Poze, "Analogical Connections—The Essence of Creativity," *Journal of Creative Behavior* 17 (1983): 240–241.

60. I. Sladeczek and G. Domino, "Creativity, Sleep, and Primary Process Thinking in Dreams," *Journal of Creative Behavior* 19 (1985): 38–46.

61. F. Barron and D. M. Harrington, "Creativity, Intelligence, and Personality," *Annual Review of Psychology* 32 (1981): 439–476.

62. R. J. Sternberg, "A Three-Faced Model of Creativity," in R. J. Sternberg, ed., *The Nature of Creativity* (Cambridge, England: Cambridge University Press, 1988), 125–147.

63. A. M. Isen, "Positive Affect and Decision Making," in W. M. Goldstein and R. M. Hogarth, eds., *Research on Judgment and Decision Making* (Cambridge, England: Cambridge University Press, 1997).

64. G. L. Clore, N. Schwartz, and M. Conway, "Cognitive Causes and Consequences of Emotion," in R. S. Wyer and T. K. Srull (eds.), *Handbook of Social Cognition* (Hillsdale, NJ: Erlbaum, 1994): 323–417.

65. B. L. Frederickson, "What Good Are Positive Emotions?" *Review of General Psychology* 2 (1998): 300–319.

66. B. L. Frederickson, "The Role of Positive Emotions in Positive Psychology," *American Psychologist* 56 (2001): 218–226.

67. T. M. Amabile, S. G. Barsade, J. S. Mueller, and B. M. Staw, "Affect and Creativity at Work," *Administrative Science Quarterly* 50(3) (2005): 367–403.

68. E. R. Hirt, G. M. Levine, H. E. McDonald, R. J. Melton, and L. L. Martin, "The Role of Mood in Quantitative and Qualitative Aspects of Performance: Single or Multiple Mechanisms?" *Journal of Experimental Social Psychology* 33 (1997): 602–629.

69. J. M. George and Z. Zhou, "Understanding When Bad Moods Foster Creativity and Good Ones Don't: The Role of Context and Clarity of Feelings," *Journal of Applied Psychology* 87 (2002): 687–697.

70. J. Zhou, "When the Presence of Creative Coworkers Is Related to Creativity: Role of Supervisor Close Monitoring, Developmental Feedback, and Creative Personality," *Journal of Applied Psychology* 88 (2003): 413–422.

71. C. Axtell, D. Holman, K. Unsworth, T. Wall, and P. Waterson, "Shop-floor Innovation: Facilitating the Suggestion and Implementation of Ideas," *Journal of Occupational Psychology* 73 (2000): 265–285.

72. B. Kijkuit and J. van den Ende, "The Organizational Life of an Idea: Integrating Social Network, Creativity, and Decision-Making Perspectives," *Journal of Management Studies* 44(6) (2007): 863–882.

73. T. M. Amabile, R. Conti, H. Coon, J. Lazenby, and M. Herron, "Assessing the Work Environment for Creativity," *Academy of Management Journal* 39 (1996): 1154–1184.

74. T. Tetenbaum and H. Tetenbaum, "Office 2000: Tear Down the Wall," *Training* (February 2000): 58–64.

75. D. M. Harrington, "Creativity, Analogical Thinking, and Muscular Metaphors," *Journal of Mental Imagery* 6 (1981): 121–126; R. M. Kanter, *The Change Masters* (New York: Simon & Schuster, 1983).

76. T. M. Amabile, B. A. Hennessey, and B. S. Grossman, "Social Influences on Creativity: The Effects of Contracted-for Reward," *Journal of Personality and Social Psychology* 50 (1986): 14–23.

77. Livingstone, "Person-Environment Fit."

78. R. L. Firestein, "Effects of Creative Problem-Solving Training on Communication Behaviors in Small Groups," *Small Group Research* (November 1989): 507–521.

79. R. Von Oech, *A Whack on the Side of the Head* (New York: Warner, 1983).

80. A. G. Robinson and S. Stern, *How Innovation and Improvement Actually Happen* (San Francisco: Berrett-Koehler, 1997).

81. K. Unsworth, "Unpacking Creativity," *Academy of Management Review* 26 (2001): 289–297.

82. M. F. R. Kets de Vries, R. Branson, and P. Barnevik, "Charisma in Action: The Transformational Abilities of Virgin's Richard Branson and ABBS's Percy Barnevik," *Organizational Dynamics* 26 (1998): 7–21.

83. M. Kostera, M. Proppe, and M. Szatkowski, "Staging the New Romantic Hero in the Old Cynical Theatre: On Managers, Roles, and Change in Poland," *Journal of Organizational Behavior* 16 (1995): 631–646.

84. J. Pfeffer, "Seven Practices of Successful Organizations," *California Management Review* 40 (1998): 96–124.

85. L. A. Witt, M. C. Andrews, and K. M. Kacmar, "The Role of Participation in Decision Making in the Organizational Politics—Job Satisfaction Relationship," *Human Relations* 53 (2000): 341–358.

86. J. He and W. R. King, "The Role of User Participation in Information Systems Development: Implications from a Meta-Analysis," *Journal of Management Information Systems* 25 (2008): 301–331.

87. C. R. Leana, E. A. Locke, and D. M. Schweiger, "Fact and Fiction in Analyzing Research on Participative Decision Making: A Critique of Cotton, Vollrath, Froggatt, Lengnick-Hall, and Jennings," *Academy of Management Review* 15 (1990): 137–146; J. L. Cotton, D. A. Vollrath, M. L. Lengnick-Hall, and K. L. Froggatt, "Fact: The Form of Participation Does Matter—A Rebuttal to Leana, Locke, and Schweiger," *Academy of Management Review* 15 (1990): 147–153.

88. G. Hamel, "Reinvent Your Company," *Fortune* 141 (June 12, 2000): 98–118.

89. T. W. Malone, "Is Empowerment Just a Fad? Control, Decision Making, and Information Technology," *Sloan Management Review* 38 (1997): 23–35.

90. IBM Customer Success Stories, "City and County of San Francisco Lower Total Cost of Ownership and Build on Demand Foundation" (February 3, 2004), http://www-306.ibm.com/software/success/cssdb.nsf/cs/LWRT-5VTLM2?OpenDocument&Site=lotusmandc.

91. T. L. Brown, "Fearful of 'Empowerment': Should Managers Be Terrified?" *Industry Week* (June 18, 1990): 12.

92. P. G. Gyllenhammar, *People at Work* (Reading, MA: Addison-Wesley, 1977).

93. R. Tannenbaum and F. Massarik, "Participation by Subordinates in the Managerial Decision-Making Process," *Canadian Journal of Economics and Political Science* 16 (1950): 408–418.

94. H. Levinson, *Executive* (Cambridge, MA: Harvard University Press, 1981).

95. J. S. Black and H. B. Gregersen, "Participative Decision Making: An Integration of Multiple Dimensions," *Human Relations* 50 (1997): 859–878.

96. G. Stasser, L. A. Taylor, and C. Hanna, "Information Sampling in Structured and Unstructured Discussion of Three- and Six-Person Groups," *Journal of Personality and Social Psychology* 57 (1989): 67–78.

97. E. Kirchler and J. H. Davis, "The Influence of Member Status Differences and Task Type on Group Consensus and Member Position Change," *Journal of Personality and Social Psychology* 51 (1986): 83–91.

98. R. F. Maier, "Assets and Liabilities in Group Problem Solving," *Psychological Review* 74 (1967): 239–249.

99. M. E. Shaw, *Group Dynamics: The Psychology of Small Group Behavior*, 3rd ed. (New York: McGraw-Hill, 1981).

100. P. W. Yetton and P. C. Bottger, "Individual versus Group Problem Solving: An Empirical Test of a Best Member Strategy," *Organizational Behavior and Human Performance* 29 (1982): 307–321.

101. W. Watson, L. Michaelson, and W. Sharp, "Member Competence, Group Interaction, and Group Decision Making: A Longitudinal Study," *Journal of Applied Psychology* 76 (1991): 803–809.

102. M. A. Serva, M. A. Fuller, and R. C. Mayer, "The Reciprocal Nature of Trust: A Longitudinal Study of Interacting Teams," *Journal of Organizational Behavior* 26 (2005): 625–649.

103. I. Janis, *Victims of Groupthink* (Boston: Houghton Mifflin, 1972).

104. M. A. Hogg and S. C. Hains, "Friendship and Group Identification: A New Look at the Role of Cohesiveness in Groupthink," *European Journal of Social Psychology* 28 (1998): 323–341.

105. P. E. Jones and H. M. P. Roelofsma, "The Potential for Social Contextual and Group Biases in Team Decision Making: Biases, Conditions, and Psychological Mechanisms," *Ergonomics* 43 (2000): 1129–1152; J. M. Levine, E. T. Higgins, and H. Choi, "Development of Strategic Norms in Groups," *Organizational Behavior and Human Decision Processes* 82 (2000): 88–101.

106. A. L. Brownstein, "Biased Predecision Processing," *Psychological Bulletin* 129 (2003): 545–568.

107. C. P. Neck and G. Moorhead, "Groupthink Remodeled: The Importance of Leadership, Time Pressure, and Methodical Decision-Making Procedures," *Human Relations* 48 (1995): 537–557.

108. J. Schwartz and M. L. Ward, "Final Shuttle Report Cites 'Broken Safety Culture' at NASA," *New York Times* (August 26, 2003), http://www.nytimes.com/2003/08/26/national/26CND-SHUT.html?ex=1077253200&en=882575f2c17ed8ff&ei=5070.

109. C. Ferraris and R. Carveth, "NASA and the Columbia Disaster: Decision Making by Groupthink?" in Proceedings of the 2003 Convention of the Association for Business Communication Annual Convention, http://www.businesscommunication.org/conventions/Proceedings/2003/PDF/03ABC03.pdf.

110. V. Anand, B. E. Ashforth, and M. Joshi, "Business as Usual: The Acceptance and Perpetuation of Corruption in Organizations," *Academy of Management Executive* 19, (2005): 9–23.

111. A. C. Homan, D. van Knippenberg, G. A. Van Kleef, and K. W. C. De Dreu, "Bridging Faultlines by Valuing Diversity: Diversity Beliefs, Information Elaboration, and Performance in Diverse Work Groups," *Journal of Applied Psychology* 92(5) (2007): 1189–1199.

112. G. Moorhead, R. Ference, and C. P. Neck, "Group Decision Fiascoes Continue: Space Shuttle Challenger and a Revised Groupthink Framework," *Human Relations* 44 (1991): 539–550.

113. J. R. Montanari and G. Moorhead, "Development of the Groupthink Assessment Inventory," *Educational and Psychological Measurement* 49 (1989): 209–219.

114. P. t'Hart, "Irving L. Janis' Victims of Groupthink," *Political Psychology* 12 (1991): 247–278.

115. A. C. Mooney, P. J. Holahan, and A. C. Amason, "Don't Take it Personally: Exploring Cognitive Conflict as a Mediator of Affective Conflict," *Journal of Management Studies* 44(5) (2007): 733–758.

116. J. A. F. Stoner, "Risky and Cautious Shifts in Group Decisions: The Influence of Widely Held Values," *Journal of Experimental Social Psychology* 4 (1968): 442–459.

117. S. Moscovici and M. Zavalloni, "The Group as a Polarizer of Attitudes," *Journal of Personality and Social Psychology* 12 (1969): 125–135.

118. G. R. Goethals and M. P. Zanna, "The Role of Social Comparison in Choice of Shifts," *Journal of Personality and Social Psychology* 37 (1979): 1469–1476.

119. A. Vinokur and E. Burnstein, "Effects of Partially Shared Persuasive Arguments on Group-Induced Shifts: A Problem-Solving Approach," *Journal of Personality and Social Psychology* 29 (1974): 305–315.

120. J. K. Palmer and J. M. Loveland, "The Influence of Group Discussion on Performance Judgments: Rating Accuracy, Contrast Effects and Halo," *The Journal of Psychology: Interdisciplinary and Applied* 142 (2008): 117–130.

121. B. A. Nijstad, W. Stroebe, and H. F. M. Lodewijkx, "Production Blocking and Idea Generation: Does Blocking Interfere with Cognitive Processes?" *Journal of Experimental Social Psychology* 39 (2003): 531–549.

122. W. H. Cooper, R. B. Gallupe, S. Pollard, and J. Cadsby, "Some Liberating Effects of Anonymous Electronic Brainstorming," *Small Group Research* 29 (1998): 147–178.

123. A. Van de Ven and A. Delbecq, "The Effectiveness of Nominal, Delphi and Interacting Group Decision-Making Processes," *Academy of Management Journal* 17 (1974): 605–621.

124. A. L. Delbecq, A. H. Van de Ven, and D. H. Gustafson, *Group Techniques for Program Planning: A Guide to Nominal, Group, and Delphi Processes* (Glenview, IL: Scott, Foresman, 1975).

125. R. A. Cosier and C. R. Schwenk, "Agreement and Thinking Alike: Ingredients for Poor Decisions," *Academy of Management Executive* 4 (1990): 69–74.

126. D. M. Schweiger, W. R. Sandburg, and J. W. Ragan, "Group Approaches for Improving Strategic Decision Making: A Comparative Analysis of Dialectical Inquiry, Devil's Advocacy, and Consensus," *Academy of Management Journal* 29 (1986): 149–159.

127. G. Whyte, "Decision Failures: Why They Occur and How to Prevent Them," *Academy of Management Executive* 5 (1991): 23–31.

128. E. E. Lawler III and S. A. Mohrman, "Quality Circles: After the Honeymoon," *Organizational Dynamics* (Spring 1987): 42–54.

129. T. L. Tang and E. A. Butler, "Attributions of Quality Circles' Problem-Solving Failure: Differences among Management, Supporting Staff, and Quality Circle Members," *Public Personnel Management* 26 (1997): 203–225.

130. S. R. Olberding, "Toyota on Competition and Quality Circles," *The Journal for Quality and Participation* 21 (1998): 52–54.

131. J. Schilder, "Work Teams Boost Productivity," *Personnel Journal* 71 (1992): 67–72.

132. L. I. Glassop, "The Organizational Benefits of Teams," *Human Relations* 55 (2002): 225–249.

133. C. J. Nemeth, "Managing Innovation: When Less Is More," *California Management Review* 40 (1997): 59–68.

134. L. Scholten, D. van Knippenberg, B. A. Nijstad, and K. W. C. De Dreu, "Motivated Information Processing and Group Decision-Making: Effects of Process Accountability on Information Processing and Decision Quality," *Journal of Experimental Social Psychology* 43(4) (2007): 539–552.

135. N. Adler, *International Dimensions of Organizational Behavior*, 3rd ed. (Cincinnati, OH: South-Western, 1997).

136. S. C. Peppas, "Attitudes of Hispanics and Non-Hispanics in the US: A Comparative Study of Business Ethics," *Management Research News* 29(3) (2006): 92–105.

137. G. K. Stephens and C. R. Greer, "Doing Business in Mexico: Understanding Cultural Differences," *Organization Dynamics* 24 (1995): 39–55.

138. C. R. Greer and G. K. Stephens, "Escalation of Commitment: A Comparison of Differences between Mexican and U. S. Decision Makers," *Journal of Management* 27 (2001): 51–78.

139. K. W. Phillips and D. L. Lloyd, "When Surface and Deep-Level Diversity Collide: The Effects on Dissenting Group Members," *Organizational Behavior and Human Decision Processes* 99(2) (2006): 143–160.

140. T. Simons, L. H. Pelled, and K. A. Smith, "Making Use of Difference: Diversity, Debate, and Decision Comprehensiveness in Top Management Teams," *Academy of Management Journal* 42(6) (1999): 662–673.

141. S. Elbanna and J. Child, "The Influence of Decision, Environmental and Firm Characteristics on the Rationality of Strategic Decision-Making," *Journal of Management Studies* 44(4) (2007): 561–591.

142. A. M. Townsend, S. M. DeMarie, and A. R. Hendrickson, "Virtual Teams: Technology and the Workplace of the Future," *Academy of Management Executive* 12 (1998): 17–29.

143. M. S. Poole, M. Holmes, and G. DeSanctis, "Conflict Management in a Computer-Supported Meeting Environment," *Management Science* 37 (1991): 926–953.

144. S. S. K. Lam and J. Schaubroeck, "Improving Group Decisions by Better Pooling Information: A Comparative Advantage of Groups Decision Support Systems," *Journal of Applied Psychology* 85 (2000): 565–573.

145. L. M. Jessup and J. F. George, "Theoretical and Methodological Issues in Group Support Systems," *Small Group Research* 28 (1997): 394–413.

146. E. Bonabeau, "Predicting the Unpredictable," *Harvard Business Review* 80 (2002): 109–117.

147. K. Blanchard and N. V. Peale, *The Power of Ethical Management* (New York: Fawcett Crest, 1988).

148. C. Schneider, "War Dance: Will SEC Go Light on DOD Contractors?" *CFO Magazine* April 7, 2003, http://www.informationweek.com/news/internet/social_network/showArticle.jhtml?articleID=217702151.

149. M. McGraw, "Another Whistleblower Down the Tubes," *Bulletin of the Atomic Scientists* 46 (June 1990), http://www.thebulletin.org/issues/1990/j90/j90mcgraw.html.

150. "Facebook Opens Governance of Service and Policy Process to Users" (February, 26, 2009), http://www.facebook.com/press/releases.php?p=85587.

151. B. Stone and B. Stelter, "Facebook Withdraws Changes in Data Use," *New York Times* online (February 18, 2009), http://www.nytimes.com/2009/02/19/technology/internet/19facebook.html.

Chapter 10 Case

1. B. Leavy, "Leader's Guide to Creating an Innovation Culture," *Strategy & Leadership* 33(4) (2005): 39.

2. Ibid.

3. Ibid., p. 42.

4. K. Baskin, "Storied Spaces: The Human Equivalent of Complex Adaptive Systems," *Emergence: Complexity and Organization* 10(2) (2008): 9.

5. B. Hindo, "At 3M, A Struggle between Efficiency and Creativity; How CEO George Buckley Is managing the Yin and Yang of Discipline and Imagination," *BusinessWeek* (4038) (June 11, 2007): 8.

6. C. Del Angel and J. Froelich, "Six Sigma: What Went Wrong?" *Customer Relationship Management* 12(11) (November 2008): 14; C. Del Angel and C. Pritchard, "Behavior Tests Six Sigma," *Industrial Engineer* 40(8) (August 2008): 41.

7. Hindo, "At 3M, A Struggle between Efficiency and Creativity," 10.

8. Ibid., p. 8.

9. "Scrutinizing Six Sigma; The Story on 3M's Evaluation of the Program Triggered a Vigorous Debate among Readers," *BusinessWeek* (4041) (July 2, 2007): 90.

10. Hindo, "At 3M, A Struggle between Efficiency and Creativity," 10.

11. Ibid., p. 14.

12. "Scrutinizing Six Sigma," 90; S. Sanders, "The Quality/Creativity Paradox," *Quality Progress* 40(8) (August 2007): 1.

13. C. Del Angel and J. Froelich, "Six Sigma: What Went Wrong?" *Customer Relationship Management* 12(11) (November 2008): 14.

14. P. Georgescu, "Creativity to the Rescue," *Fortune* 156(8) (October 15, 2007): 74.

15. B. Leavy, "Leader's Guide to Creating an Innovation Culture," *Strategy & Leadership* 33(4) (2005): 42.

16. Del Angel and Froelich, "Six Sigma," 14.

17. B. Nussbaum, "The Fragility of Innovation," *BusinessWeek* (4038) (June 11, 2007): 3.

Chapter 11

1. H. Cassell, "CEO Moms: Barbara Adachi, Deloitte LLP" theglasshammer.com (January 13, 2009), http://www.theglasshammer.com/news/2009/01/13/ceo-moms-barbara-adachi-deloitte-llp/

2. "Meet Barbara Adachi" http://www.deloitte.com/dtt/employee_profile/0,1007,cid%253D3120,00.html

3. G. C. Homans, "Social Behavior as Exchange," *American Journal of Sociology* 63 (1958): 597–606.

4. R. D. Middlemist and M. A. Hitt, *Organizational Behavior: Managerial Strategies for Performance* (St. Paul, MN: West Publishing, 1988).

5. C. Barnard, *The Functions of the Executive* (Cambridge, MA: Harvard University Press, 1938).

6. F. Aguila, "CEO Diminished Power Could Prove Costly," *BusinessWeek* (May 4, 2009), http://www.businessweek.com/investor/content/may2009/pi2009054_028764.htm.

7. Reuters Limited, "Canadian Carty Had Rough Ride at American Airlines," *USA Today* (April 25, 2003), http://www.usatoday.com/travel/news/2003/2003-04-25-aa-carty-profile.htm.

8. J. R. P. French and B. Raven, "The Bases of Social Power," in D. Cartwright, ed., *Group Dynamics: Research and Theory* (Evanston, IL: Row, Peterson, 1962); T. R. Hinkin and C. A. Schriesheim, "Development and Application of New Scales to Measure the French and Raven (1959) Bases of Social Power," *Journal of Applied Psychology* 74 (1989): 561–567.

9. K. D. Elsbach and G. Elofson, "How the Packaging of Decision Explanations Affects Perceptions of Trustworthiness," *Academy of Management Journal* 43 (1) (2000): 80–89.

10. P. M. Podsakoff and C. A. Schriesheim, "Field Studies of French and Raven's Bases of Power: Critique, Reanalysis, and Sugges tions for Future Research," *Psychological Bulletin* 97 (1985): 387–411.

11. M. A. Rahim, "Relationships of Leader Power to Compliance and Satisfaction with Supervision: Evidence from a National Sample of Managers," *Journal of Management* 15 (1989): 545–556.

12. C. Argyris, "Management Information Systems: The Challenge to Rationality and Emotionality," *Management Science* 17 (1971): 275–292; J. Naisbitt and P. Aburdene, *Megatrends 2000* (New York: Morrow, 1990).

13. P. P. Carson, K. D. Carson, E. L. Knight, and C. W. Roe, "Power in Organizations: A Look through the TQM Lens," *Quality Progress* (November 1995): 73–78.

14. J. Guthrie, "The Adventures of Marissa," *San Francisco Magazine* (February 27, 2008), http://www.sanfranmag.com/story/adventures-marissa

15. M. Velasquez, D. J. Moberg, and G. F. Cavanaugh, "Organizational Statesmanship and Dirty Politics: Ethical Guidelines for the Organizational Politician," *Organizational Dynamics* 11 (1982): 65–79.

16. D. E. McClelland, *Power: The Inner Experience* (New York: Irvington, 1975).

17. N. Shahinpoor and B. F Matt, "The Power of One: Dissent and Organizational Life," *Journal of Business Ethics* 74(1) (2007): 37–49.

18. N. Machiavelli, *The Prince*, trans. by G. Bull (Middlesex, England: Penguin Books, 1961).

19. S. Chen, A. Y. Lee-Chai, and J. A. Bargh, "Relationship Orientation as a Moderator of the Effects of Social Power," *Journal of Personality and Social Psychology* 80(2) (2001): 173–187.

20. J. Pfeffer and G. Salancik, *The External Control of Organizations* (New York: Harper & Row, 1978).

21. T. M. Welbourne and C. O. Trevor, "The Roles of Departmental and Position Power in Job Evaluation," *Academy of Management Journal* 43(4) (2000): 761–771.

22. R. H. Miles, *Macro Organizational Behavior* (Glenview, IL: Scott, Foresman, 1980).

23. D. Hickson, C. Hinings, C. Lee, R. E. Schneck, and J. M. Pennings, "A Strategic Contingencies Theory of Intraorganizational Power," *Administrative Science Quarterly* 14 (1971): 219–220.

24. C. R. Hinings, D. J. Hickson, J. M. Pennings, and R. E. Schneck, "Structural Conditions of Intraorganizational Power," *Administrative Science Quarterly* 19 (1974): 22–44.

25. A. Etzioni, *Modern Organizations* (Upper Saddle River, NJ: Prentice Hall, 1964).

26. R. Kanter, "Power Failure in Management Circuits," *Harvard Business Review* (July–August 1979): 31–54.

27. F. Lee and L. Z. Tiedens, "Who's Being Served? 'Self-Serving' Attributions in Social Hierarchies," *Organizational Behavior and Human Decision Processes* 84(2) (March 2001): 254–287.

28. M. Korda, *Power: How to Get It, How to Use It* (New York: Random House, 1975).

29. S. R. Thye, "A Status Value Theory of Power in Exchange Relations," *American Sociological Review* (2000): 407–432.

30. B. T. Mayes and R. T. Allen, "Toward a Definition of Organizational Politics," *Academy of Management Review* 2 (1977): 672–678.

31. M. Valle and P. L. Perrewe, "Do Politics Perceptions Relate to Political Behaviors? Tests of an Implicit Assumption and Expanded Model," *Human Relations* 53 (2000): 359–386.

32. W. A. Hochwarter, "The Interactive Effects of Pro-Political Behavior and Politics Perceptions on Job Satisfaction and Affective Commitment," *Journal of Applied Social Psychology* 33 (2003): 1360–1378.

33. W. A. Hochwarter, K. M. Kacmar, D. C. Treadway, and T. S. Watson, "It's All Relative: The Distinction and Prediction of Political Perceptions Across Levels," *Journal of Applied Social Psychology* 33 (2003): 1955–2016.

34. D. A. Ralston, "Employee Ingratiation: The Role of Management," *Academy of Management Review* 10 (1985): 477–487; D. R. Beeman and T. W. Sharkey, "The Use and Abuse of Corporate Politics," *Business Horizons* (March–April 1987): 25–35.

35. C. O. Longnecker, H. P. Sims, and D. A. Gioia, "Behind the Mask: The Politics of Employee Appraisal," *Academy of Management Executive* 1 (1987): 183–193.

36. Inside Innovation, "Marissa Mayer: The Talent Scout."

37. M. Valle and P. L. Perrewe, "Do Politics Perceptions Relate to Political Behaviors? Tests of an Implicit Assumption and Expanded Model," *Human Relations* 53(3) (2000): 359–386.

38. D. Fedor, J. Maslyn, S. Farmer, K. Bettenhausen, "The Contribution of Positive Politics to the Prediction of Employee Reactions," *Journal of Applied Social Psychology* 38(1) (2008): 76–96.

39. D. Kipnis, S. M. Schmidt, and I. Wilkinson, "Intraorganizational Influence Tactics: Explorations in Getting One's Way," *Journal of Applied Psychology* 65 (1980): 440–452; D. Kipnis, S. Schmidt, C. Swaffin-Smith, and I. Wilkinson, "Patterns of Managerial Influence: Shotgun Managers, Tacticians, and Bystanders," *Organizational Dynamics* (Winter 1984): 60–67; G. Yukl and C. M. Falbe, "Influence Tactics and Objectives in Upward, Downward, and Lateral Influence Attempts," *Journal of Applied Psychology* 75 (1990): 132–140.

40. G. R. Ferris and T. A. Judge, "Personnel/Human Resources Management: A Political Influence Perspective," *Journal of Management* 17 (1991): 447–488.

41. G. Yukl, P. J. Guinan, and D. Sottolano, "Influence Tactics Used for Different Objectives with Subordinates, Peers, and Superiors," *Groups & Organization Management* 20 (1995): 272–296.

42. C. A. Higgins, T. A. Judge, and G. R. Ferris, "Influence Tactics and Work Outcomes: A Meta-Analysis," *Journal of Organizational Behavior* 24 (2003): 89–106.

43. K. K. Eastman, "In the Eyes of the Beholder: An Attributional Approach to Ingratiation and Organizational Citizenship Behavior," *Academy of Management Journal* 37 (1994): 1379–1391.

44. K. J. Harris, K. M. Kacmar, S. Zivnuska, and J. D. Shaw, "The Impact of Political Skill on Impression Management Effectiveness," *Journal of Applied Psychology* 92(1) (2007): 278–285.

45. D. C. Treadway, G. R. Ferris, A. B. Duke, G. L. Adams, and J. B. Thatcher, "The Moderating Role of Subordinate Political Skill on Supervisors' Impressions of Subordinate Ingratiation and Ratings of Subordinate Interpersonal Facilitation," *Journal of Applied Psychology* 92(3) (2007): 848–855.

46. R. A. Gordon, "Impact of Ingratiation on Judgments and Evaluations: A Meta-Analytic Investigation," *Journal of Personality and Social Psychology* 71 (1996): 54–70.

47. A. Drory and D. Beaty, "Gender Differences in the Perception of Organizational Influence Tactics," *Journal of Organizational Behavior* 12 (1991): 249–258.

48. S. Wellington, M. B. Kropf, and P. R. Gerkovich, "What's Holding Women Back?" *Harvard Business Review* (June 2003): 2–4.

49. P. Perrewe and D. Nelson, "Gender and Career Success: The Facilitative Role of Political Skill," *Organizational Dynamics* 33 (2004): 366–378.

50. R. Y. Hirokawa and A. Miyahara, "A Comparison of Influence Strategies Utilized by Managers in American and Japanese Organizations," *Communication Quarterly* 34 (1986): 250–265.

51. C. Anderson, S. E. Spataro, and F. J. Flynn, "Personality and Organizational Culture as Determinants of Influence," *Journal of Applied Psychology* 93 (May 2008): 702–710.

52. P. David, M. A. Hitt, and J. Gimeno, "The Influence of Activism by Institutional Investors on R&D," *Academy of Management Journal* 44(1) (2001): 144–157.

53. G. R. Ferris, P. L. Perrewe, W. P. Anthony, and D. C. Gilmore, "Political Skill at Work," *Organizational Dynamics* 28 (2000): 25–37.

54. D. C. Treadway, W. A. Hochwarter, G. R. Ferris, C. J. Kacmar, C. Douglas, A. P. Ammeter, and M. R. Buckley, "Leader Political Skill and Employee Reactions," *Leadership Quarterly* 15 (2004): 493–513.

55. K. K. Ahearn, G. R. Ferris, W. A. Hochwarter, C. Douglas, A. P. Ammeter, "Leader Political Skill and Team Performance," *Journal of Management* 30(3) (2004): 309–327.

56. P. L. Perrewé, K. L. Zellars, G. R. Ferris, A. M. Rossi, C. J. Kacmar, and D. A. Ralston, "Neutralizing Job Stressors: Political Skill as an Antidote to the Dysfunctional Consequences of Role Conflict Stressors," *Academy of Management Journal* 47 (2004): 141–152.

57. G. R. Ferris, D. C. Treadway, R. W. Kolodinsky, W. A. Hochwarter, C. J. Kacmar, C. Douglas, and D. D. Frink, "Development and Validation of the Political Skill Inventory," *Journal of Management* 31 (2005): 126–152.

58. G. Ferris, S. Davidson, and P. Perrewé, "Developing Political Skill at Work," *Training* 42 (2005): 40–45.

59. F. R. Blass and G. R. Ferris, "Leader Reputation: The Role of Mentoring, Political Skill, Contextual Learning, and Adaptation," *Human Resource Management* 46(1) (2007): 5–19.

60. S. Y. Todd, K. J. Harris, R. B. Harris, and A. R. Wheeler, "Career Success Implications of Political Skill," The *Journal of Social Psychology* 149(3) (June 2009): 179–204.

61. I. M. Jawahar, J. A. Meurs, G. R. Ferris, and W. A. Hochwarter, "Self-Efficacy and Political Skill as Comparative Predictors of Task and Contextual Performance: A Two-Study Constructive Replication," *Human Performance* 21 (2008): 138–157.

62. K. Kumar and M. S. Thibodeaux, "Organizational Politics and Planned Organizational Change," *Group and Organization Studies* 15 (1990): 354–365.

63. D. Buchanan, "You Stab My back, I'll Stab Yours: Management Experience and Perceptions of Organization Political Behaviour," *British Journal of Management* 19 (March 2008): 49–64.

64. McClelland, *Power*.

65. Beeman and Sharkey, "Use and Abuse of Corporate Politics," p. 37.

66. C. P. Parker, R. L. Dipboye, and S. L. Jackson, "Perceptions of Organizational Politics: An Investigation of Antecedents and Consequences," *Journal of Management* 21 (1995): 891–912.

67. S. J. Ashford, N. P. Rothbard, S. K. Piderit, and J. E. Dutton, "Out on a Limb: The Role of Context and Impression Management in Selling Gender-Equity Issues," *Administrative Science Quarterly* 43 (1998): 23–57.

68. J. Zhou and G. R. Ferris, "The Dimensions and Consequences of Organizational Politics Perceptions: A Confirmatory Analysis," *Journal of Applied Social Psychology* 25 (1995): 1747–1764.

69. M. L. Seidal, J. T. Polzer, and K. J. Stewart, "Friends in High Places: The Effects of Social Networks on Discrimination in Salary Negotiations," *Administrative Science Quarterly* 45 (2000): 1–24.

70. J. J. Gabarro and J. P. Kotter, "Managing Your Boss," *Harvard Business Review* (January–February 1980): 92–100.

71. P. Newman, "How to Manage Your Boss," Peat, Marwick, Mitchell & Company's *Management Focus* (May–June 1980): 36–37.

72. F. Bertolome, "When You Think the Boss Is Wrong," *Personnel Journal* 69 (1990): 66–73.

73. J. Conger and R. Kanungo, *Charismatic Leadership: The Elusive Factor in Organizational Effectiveness* (New York: Jossey-Bass, 1988).

74. G. M. Spreitzer, M. A. Kizilos, and S. W. Nason, "A Dimensional Analysis of the Relationship between Psychological Empowerment and Effectiveness, Satisfaction, and Strain," *Journal of Management* 23 (1997): 679–704.

75. M. Butts, R.J. Vandenberg, D.M. DeJoy, B.S. Schaffer, and M.G. Wilson "Individual Reactions to High Involvement Work Processes: Investigating the Role of Empowerment and Perceived Organizational Support." *Journal of Occupational Health Psychology* 14 (April 2009): 122–136.

76. R. C. Ford and M. D. Fottler, "Empowerment: A Matter of Degree," *Academy of Management Executive* 9 (1995): 21–31.

77. M. Holbrook, "Employee Commitment Is Crucial," *Human Resources* (May 2007): 66.

78. J. Simons, "Merck's Man in the Hot Seat," *Fortune* (February 23, 2004): 111–114.

79. S. Finkelstein, *Why Smart Executives Fail: And What You Can Learn from Their Mistakes* (New York: Portfolio, 2003).

80. J. P. Kotter, "Power, Dependence, and Effective Management," *Harvard Business Review* 55 (1977): 125–136; J. P. Kotter, *Power and Influence* (New York: Free Press, 1985).

81. http://www.deloitte.com/dtt/section_node/0,1042,sid%253D2262,00.html

82. H. Cassell, "CEO Moms: Barbara Adachi, Deloitte LLP" theglasshammer.com (January 13, 2009), http://www.theglasshammer.com/news/2009/01/13/ceo-moms-barbara-adachi-deloitte-llp/

83. http://www.deloitte.com/dtt/section_node/0,1042,sid%253D2263,00.html

Chapter 11 Case

1. B. Schlender and C. Tkaczyk, "Pixar's Magic Man," *Fortune* 153(10) (May 29, 2006): 142.

2. Ibid., pp. 142–143.

3. Ibid., p. 143.

4. Ibid.

5. Ibid., pp. 143–144.

6. Ibid., p. 145.

7. Ibid.

8. Ibid.

9. Ibid.

10. Ibid.

11. Ibid., p. 145–146.

11. P. Burrows, R. Grover, and H. Green, "Steve Jobs' Magic Kingdom," *BusinessWeek* (3970) (February 6, 2006): 62.

12. Pixar, "Pixar Corporate Overview," *Pixar.com*, http://www.pixar.com/companyinfo/about_us/overview.htm, accessed July 30, 2009.

13. R. Siklos, "Q&A: The Iger Difference," *Fortune* 157(8) (April 28, 2008): 94.

14. P. Sanders, "Disney Learns Lessons from Pixar; Storied Animation Studio's New 3-D Computer-Generated Film Showcases Melding of Pixar Talent," *Wall Street Journal* (Eastern edition) (October 27, 2008): B1.

15. R. Grover, "How Bob Iger Unchained Disney," *BusinessWeek* (4020) (February 5, 2007): 74.

16. R. Grover, "A Pixar Exec's Fairy-Tale Story," *BusinessWeek Online* (January 26, 2006), http://www.businessweek.com?technology/content/jan2006/tc20060126_466477.htm, accessed July 30, 2009.

17. Ibid.

18. Ibid.

19. Siklos, "Q&A: The Iger Difference," p. 92.

20. Sanders, "Disney Learns Lessons from Pixar," p. B1.

21. Burrows, Grover, and Green, "Steve Jobs' Magic Kingdom," pp. 62+.

22. Schlender and Tkaczyk, "Pixar's Magic Man," p. 149.

23. J. Yabroff, "John Lasseter; Pixar's Animation Guru Dominates the Global Box Office, Even in Tough Times," *Newsweek* 153(1) (January 5, 2009): 35.

24. Ibid.

25. D. J. Jefferson, "Disney's New Magic," *Newsweek* 149(25) (June 25, 2007): 14.

26. Ibid.

27. R. Siklos, "Bob Iger Rocks Disney," *Fortune* 159(1) (January 19, 2009): 94.

28. Ibid.

Chapter 12

1. P. Elmer-DeWitt, "Apple 2.0: Mac News from Outside the Reality Distortion Field," *Fortune* (March 12, 2009). http://apple20.blogs.fortune.cnn.com/2009/03/12/iphone-sales-grew-245-in-2008-gartner/

2. A. Abkowitz, "The Blackberry Boss," *Fortune* 159 (April 27, 2009): 8.

3. http://www.rim.net/newsroom/media/executive/index.shtml.

4. Ibid.

5. I. Austen, "Blackberry Billionaire has the N.H.L. Buzzing," *New York Times* (May 9, 2009), http://www.nytimes.com/pages/sports/basketball/index.html.

6. J. P. Kotter, "What Leaders Really Do," *Harvard Business Review* 68 (1990): 103–111.

7. E. Florian, "2004 America's Most Admired Companies: Fred Smith of FedEx," *Fortune* (March 8, 2004): 88a, http://www.fortune.com/fortune/subs/article/0,15114,592448,00.html.

8. "AmEx's Ken Chenault Talks about Leadership, Integrity, and the Credit Card Business," Published in Knowledge@Wharton (April, 10, 2005), http://knowledge.wharton.upenn.edu/articlepdf/1179.pdf?CFID=19898527&CFTOKEN=39534433&jsessionid=a830dfb2436748503819.

9. D. A. Plowman, S. Solansky, T. E. Beck, L. Baker, M. Kulkarni, and D. V. Travis, "The Role of Leadership in Emergent, Self-Organization," *Leadership Quarterly* 18(4) (2007): 341–356.

10. A. Zaleznik, "HBR Classic—Managers and Leaders: Are They Different?" *Harvard Business Review* 70 (1992): 126–135.

11. W. G. Rowe, "Creating Wealth in Organizations: The Role of Strategic Leadership," *Academy of Management Executive* 15 (2001): 81–94.

12. R. M. Stogdill, "Personal Factors Associated with Leadership: A Survey of the Literature," *Journal of Psychology* 25 (1948): 35–71.

13. R. D. Arvey, Z. Zhang, B. J. Avolio, and R. F. Krueger, "Developmental and Genetic Determinants of Leadership Role Occupancy among Women," *Journal of Applied Psychology* 92(3) (2007): 693–706.

14. K. Lewin, R. Lippitt, and R. K. White, "Patterns of Aggressive Behavior in Experimentally Created 'Social Climates,' " *Journal of Social Psychology* 10 (1939): 271–299.

15. S. D. Sidle, "The Danger of Do Nothing Leaders," *The Academy of Management Perspectives* 21(2) (2007): 75–77.

16. R. M. Stogdill and A. E. Coons, eds., *Leader Behavior: Its Description and Measurement*, research monograph no. 88 (Columbus, OH: Bureau of Business Research, The Ohio State University, 1957).

17. A. W. Halpin and J. Winer, "A Factorial Study of the Leader Behavior Description Questionnaire," in R. M. Stogdill and A. E. Coons, eds., *Leader Behavior: Its Description and Measurement*, research monograph no. 88 (Columbus, OH: Bureau of Business Research, The Ohio State University, 1957), 39–51.

18. E. A. Fleishman, "Leadership Climate, Human Relations Training, and Supervisory Behavior," *Personnel Psychology* 6 (1953): 205–222.

19. R. Kahn and D. Katz, "Leadership Practices in Relation to Productivity and Morale," in D. Cartwright and A. Zander, eds., *Group Dynamics, Research and Theory* (Elmsford, NY: Row, Paterson, 1960).

20. R. R. Blake and J. S. Mouton, *The Managerial Grid III: The Key to Leadership Excellence* (Houston: Gulf, 1985).

21. W. Vandekerckhove and R. Commers, "Downward Workplace Mobbing: A Sign of the Times?" *Journal of Business Ethics* 45 (2003): 41–50.

22. F. E. Fiedler, *A Theory of Leader Effectiveness* (New York: McGraw-Hill, 1964).

23. F. E. Fiedler, *Personality, Motivational Systems, and Behavior of High and Low LPC Persons*, tech. rep. no. 70-12 (Seattle: University of Washington, 1970).

24. J. T. McMahon, "The Contingency Theory: Logic and Method Revisited," *Personnel Psychology* 25 (1972): 697–710; L. H. Peters, D. D. Hartke, and J. T. Pohlman, "Fiedler's Contingency Theory of Leadership: An Application of the Meta-Analysis Procedures of Schmidt and Hunter," *Psychological Bulletin* 97 (1985): 224–285.

25. F. E. Fiedler, "The Contingency Model and the Dynamics of the Leadership Process," in L. Berkowitz, ed., *Advances in Experimental and Social Psychology*, Vol. 11 (New York: Academic Press, 1978).

26. S. Arin and C. McDermott, "The Effect of Team Leader Characteristics on Learning, Knowledge Application, and Performance of Cross-Functional New Product Development Teams," *Decision Sciences* 34 (2003): 707–739.

27. F. E. Fiedler, "Engineering the Job to Fit the Manager," *Harvard Business Review* 43 (1965): 115–122.

28. R. J. House, "A Path–Goal Theory of Leader Effectiveness," *Administrative Science Quarterly* 16 (1971): 321–338; R. J. House and T. R. Mitchell, "Path–Goal Theory of Leadership," *Journal of Contemporary Business* 3 (1974): 81–97.

29. C. A. Schriescheim and V. M. Von Glinow, "The Path–Goal Theory of Leadership: A Theoretical and Empirical Analysis," *Academy of Management Journal* 20 (1977): 398–405; E. Valenzi and G. Dessler, "Relationships of Leader Behavior, Subordinate Role Ambiguity, and Subordinate Job Satisfaction," *Academy of Management Journal* 21 (1978): 671–678; N. R. F. Maier, *Leadership Methods and Skills* (New York: McGraw-Hill, 1963).

30. J. P. Grinnell, "An Empirical Investigation of CEO Leadership in Two Types of Small Firms," *S.A.M. Advanced Management Journal* 68 (2003): 36–41.

31. V. H. Vroom and P. W. Yetton, *Leadership and Decision Making* (Pittsburgh: University of Pittsburgh, 1973).

32. V. H. Vroom, "Leadership and the Decision-Making Process," *Organizational Dynamics* 28 (2000): 82–94.

33. W. J. Duncan, K. G. LaFrance, and P. M. Ginter, "Leadership and Decision Making: A Retrospective Application and Assessment," *Journal of Leadership & Organizational Studies* 9 (2003): 1–20.

34. P. Hersey and K. H. Blanchard, "Life Cycle Theory of Leadership," *Training and Development* 23 (1969): 26–34; P. Hersey, K. H. Blanchard, and D. E. Johnson, *Management of Organizational Behavior: Leading Human Resources*, 8th ed. (Upper Saddle River, NJ: Prentice Hall, 2001).

35. B. M. Bass, *Bass and Stogdill's Handbook of Leadership: Theory, Research, and Managerial Applications*, 3rd ed. (New York: Free Press, 1990).

36. G. B. Graen and M. Uhl-Bien, "Relationship-Based Approach to Leadership: Development of Leader–Member Exchange (LMX) Theory of Leadership over 25 Years," *Leadership Quarterly* 6 (1995): 219–247; C. R. Gerstner and D. V. Day, "Meta-Analytic Review of Leader–Member Exchange Theory: Correlates and Construct Issues," *Journal of Applied Psychology* 82 (1997): 827–844; R. C. Liden, S. J. Wayne, and R. T. Sparrowe, "An Examination of the Mediating Role of Psychological Empowerment on the Relations between the Job, Interpersonal Relationships, and Work Outcomes," *Journal of Applied Psychology* 85 (2001): 407–416.

37. J. Townsend, J. S. Phillips, and T. J. Elkins, "Employee Retaliation: The Neglected Consequence of Poor Leader–Member Exchange Relations," *Journal of Occupational Health Psychology* 5 (2000): 457–463.

38. D. Nelson, R. Basu, and R. Purdie, "An Examination of Exchange Quality and Work Stressors in Leader–Follower Dyads," *International Journal of Stress Management* 5 (1998): 103–112.

39. K. M. Kacmar, L. A. Witt, S. Zivnuska, and S. M. Gully, "The Interactive Effect of Leader–Member Exchange and Communication Frequency on Performance Ratings," *Journal of Applied Psychology* 88 (2003): 764–772.

40. A. G. Tekleab and M. S. Taylor, "Aren't There Two Parties in an Employment Relationship? Antecedents and Consequences of Organization–Employee Agreement on Contract Obligations and Violations," *Journal of Organizational Behavior* 24 (2003): 585–608.

41. D. A. Hoffman, S. J. Gerras, and F. P. Morgeson, "Climate as a Moderator of the Relationship Between Leader–Member Exchange and Content Specific Citizenship: Safety Climate as an Exemplar," *Journal of Applied Psychology* 88 (2003): 170–178.

42. S. Kerr and J. M. Jermier, "Substitutes for Leadership: Their Meaning and Measurement," *Organizational Behavior and Human Performance* 22 (1978): 375–403.

43. P. M. Podsakoff, S. B. MacKenzie, and W. H. Bommer, "Meta-Analysis of the Relationships between Kerr and Jermier's Substitutes for Leadership and Employee Job Attitudes, Role Perceptions, and Performance," *Journal of Applied Psychology* 81 (1996): 380–399.

44. B. C. Skaggs and M. Youndt, "Strategic Positioning, Human Capital, and Performance in Service Organizations: A Customer Interaction Approach," *Strategic Management Journal* 25 (2004): 85–99.

45. J. M. Burns, *Leadership* (New York: Harper & Row, 1978); T. O. Jacobs, *Leadership and Exchange in Formal Organizations* (Alexandria, VA: Human Resources Research Organization, 1971).

46. B. M. Bass, "From Transactional to Transformational Leadership: Learning to Share the Vision," *Organizational Dynamics* 19 (1990): 19–31; B. M. Bass, *Leadership and Performance beyond Expectations* (New York: Free Press, 1985).

47. P. M. Podsakoff, S. B. MacKenzie, and W.H. Bommer, "Transformational Leader Behaviors and Substitutes for Leadership as Determinants of Employee Satisfaction, Commitment, Trust, and Organizational Citizenship Behaviors," *Journal of Management* 22 (1996): 259–298.

48. T. A. Judge and R. F. Piccolo, "Transformational and Transactional Leadership: A Meta-Analytic Test of their Relative Validity," *Journal of Applied Psychology* 89 (2004): 755–768.

49. P. Wang and F. O. Walumbwa, "Family-Friendly Programs, Organizational Commitment, and Work Withdrawal: The Moderating Role of Transformational Leadership," *Personnel Psychology* 60(2) (2007): 397–427.

50. S. J. Peterson, F. O. Walumbwa, K. Bryon, and J. Mtrowitz, "CEO Positive Psychological Traits, Transformational Leadership, and Firm Performance in High-Technology Start-up and Established Firms," *Journal of Management* 35 (2009): 348–368.

51. W. Bennis, "Managing the Dream: Leadership in the 21st Century," *Training* 27 (1990): 43–48.

52. P. M. Podsakoff, S. B. MacKenzie, R. H. Moorman, and R. Fetter, "Transformational Leader Behaviors and Their Effects on Followers' Trust in Leader, Satisfaction, and Organizational Citizenship Behaviors," *Leadership Quarterly* 1 (1990): 107–142.

53. C. P. Egri and S. Herman, "Leadership in the North American Environmental Sector: Values, Leadership Styles, and Contexts of Environmental Leaders and Their Organizations," *Academy of Management Journal* 43 (2000): 571–604.

54. T. A. Judge and J. E. Bono, "Five-Factor Model of Personality and Transformational Leadership," *Journal of Applied Psychology* 85 (2001): 751–765.

55. J. E. Bono and T. A. Judge, "Self-Concordance at Work: Toward Understanding the Motivational Effects of Transformational Leaders," *Academy of Management Journal* 46 (2003): 554–571.

56. T. Dvir, D. Eden, B. J. Avolio, and B. Shamir, "Impact of Transformational Leadership on Follower Development and Performance: A Field Experiment," *Academy of Management Journal* 45 (2002): 735–744.

57. E. Kearney and D. Gebert, "Managing diversity and enhancing team outcomes: The promise of transformational leadership," *Journal of Applied Psychology* 94 (2009): 77–89.

58. The Urban Dictionary, accessed at http://www.urbandictionary.com/define.php?term=reality+distortion+field

59. R. J. House and M. L. Baetz, "Leadership: Some Empirical Generalizations and New Research Directions," in B. M. Staw, ed., *Research in Organizational Behavior*, Vol. 1 (Greenwood, CT: JAI Press, 1979), 399–401.

60. J. A. Conger and R. N. Kanungo, "Toward a Behavioral Theory of Charismatic Leadership in Organizational Settings," *Academy of Management Review* 12 (1987): 637–647.

61. A. R. Willner, *The Spellbinders: Charismatic Political Leadership* (New Haven, CT: Yale University Press, 1984).

62. D. Waldman, G. G. Ramirez, R. J. House, and P. Puranam, "Does Leadership Matter? CEO Leadership Attributes and Profitability under Conditions of Perceived Environmental Uncertainty," *Academy of Management Journal* 44 (2001): 134–143.

63. J. M. Howell, "Two Faces of Charisma: Socialized and Personalized Leadership in Organizations," in J. A. Conger, ed., *Charismatic Leadership: Behind the Mystique of Exceptional Leadership* (San Francisco: Jossey-Bass, 1988).

64. F. Luthans and B. J. Avolio, "Authentic Leadership: A Positive Development Approach," in K. S. Cameron, J. E. Dutton, and R. E. Quinn, eds., *Positive Organizational Scholarship: Foundations of a New Discipline* (San Francisco, Calif.: Berrett-Koehler, 2004), 241–261.

65. W. L. Gardner, B. J. Avolio, F. Luthans, D. R. May, and F. O. Walumbwa, "Can You See the Real Me? A Self-based Model of Authentic Leader and Follower Development," *The Leadership Quarterly* 16 (2005): 343–372.

66. B. J. Avolio, W. L. Gardner, F. O. Walumbwa, F. Luthans, and D. R. May, "Unlocking the Mask: A Look at the Process by Which Authentic

Leaders Impact Follower Attitudes and Behaviors," *The Leadership Quarterly* 15 (2004): 801–823.

67. S. Michie and J. Gooty, "Values, Emotions, and Authentic Leadership Behaviors: Will the Real Leader Please Stand Up?" *The Leadership Quarterly* 16 (2005): 441–457.

68. S. Michie and D. L. Nelson, "The Effects of Leader Compassion Display on Follower Attributions: Building a Socialized Leadership Image," Paper presented at the *Academy of Management Conference* in Honolulu, Hawaii (2005).

69. M. Maccoby, "Narcissistic Leaders: The Incredible Pros, the Inevitable Cons," *Harvard Business Review* 78 (2000): 68–77.

70. D. Sankowsky, "The Charismatic Leader as Narcissist: Understanding the Abuse of Power," *Organizational Dynamics* 23 (1995): 57–71.

71. F. J. Flynn and B. M. Staw, "Lend Me Your Wallets: The Effect of Charismatic Leadership on External Support for an Organization," *Strategic Management Journal* 25 (2004): 309–330.

72. D. Goleman, "What Makes a Leader?" *Harvard Business Review* 82 (2004): 82–91.

73. D. Goleman, "Never Stop Learning," *Harvard Business Review* 82 (2004): 28–30.

74. C. L. Gohm, "Mood Regulation and Emotional Intelligence: Individual Differences," *Journal of Personality and Social Psychology* 84 (2003): 594–607.

75. J. Useem, "A Manager for All Seasons," *Fortune* (April 30, 2001): 66–72.

76. J. Torre and H Dreher, *Joe Torre's Ground Rules for Winners: 12 Keys to Managing Team Players, Tough Bosses, Setbacks and Success.* (New York: Hyperion Books, 2000).

77. R. C. Mayer, J. H. Davis, and F. D. Schoorman, "An Integrative Model of Organizational Trust," *Academy of Management Review* 20 (1995): 709–734.

78. R. S. Dooley and G. E. Fryxell, "Attaining Decision Quality and Commitment from Dissent: The Moderating Effects of Loyalty and Competence in Strategic Decision-Making Teams," *Academy of Management Journal* 42 (1999): 389–402.

79. J. Flint, "Why Rick Wagoner Had to Go," *Forbes* (March 30, 2009), http://www.forbes.com/2009/03/30/rick-wagoner-gm-jerry-flint-business-autos-backseat-driver.html.

80. http://news.cnet.com/Motorolas-Zander-out-after-Razr-deemed-one-hit-wonder/2100-1036_3-6220913.html.

81. Saj-nicole A. Joni, "The Geography of Trust," *Harvard Business Review* 82 (2003): 82–88.

82. M. E. Heilman, C. J. Block, R. F. Martell, and M. C. Simon, "Has Anything Changed? Current Characteristics of Men, Women, and Managers," *Journal of Applied Psychology* 74 (1989): 935–942.

83. A. H. Eagly, S. J. Darau, and M. Makhijani, "Gender and the Effectiveness of Leaders: A Meta-Analysis," *Psychological Bulletin* 117 (1995): 125–145.

84. M. K. Ryan, S. A. Haslam, and T. Postmes, "Reactions to the Glass Cliff: Gender Differences in the Explanations for the Precariousness of Women's Leadership Positions," *Journal of Organizational Change Management* 20(2) (2007): 182–197.

85. R. K. Greenleaf, L. C. Spears, and D. T. Frick, eds., *On Becoming a Servant-Leader* (San Francisco: Jossey-Bass, 1996).

86. A. C. H. Schat, M. R. Frone, and E. K. Kelloway, "Prevelence of Workplace Aggression in the U.S. Workforce: Findings from a National Study," in E. K. Kelloway, J. Barling, and J. J. Hurrell (Eds.) *Handbook of Workplace Violence* (Thousand Oaks, CA: Sage, 2006), 47–89.

87. B. J. Tepper, C. A. Henle, L. S. Lambert, R. A. Giacalone, and M. K. Duffy, "Abusive Supervision and Subordinates' Organization Deviance," *Journal of Applied Psychology* 93 (2008): 721–732.

88. P. A. Bamberger and S. B. Bacharach, "Abusive Supervision and Subordinate Problem Drinking: Taking Resistance, Stress and Subordinate Personality into Account," *Human Relations* 59 (2006): 1–30.

89. B. J. Tepper, "Consequences of Abusive Supervision," *Academy of Management Journal* 43 (2000): 178–190.

90. A. A. Grandey, J. Kern, and M. Frone, "Verbal Abuse from Outsiders versus Insiders: Comparing Frequency, Impact on Emotional Exhaustion, and the Role of Emotional Labor," *Journal of Occupation Health Psychology* 12 (2007): 63–79.

91. B. J. Tepper, M. K. Duffy, C. A. Henle, and L. S. Lambert, "Procedural Injustice, Victim Precipitation and Abusive Supervision," *Personnel Psychology* 59 (2006): 101–123.

92. B. J. Tepper, "Abusive Supervision in Work Organizations: Review, Synthesis and Research Agenda," *Journal of Management* 33 (2007) 261–289.

93. E. P. Hollander and L. R. Offerman, "Power and Leadership in Organizations: Relationships in Transition," *American Psychologist* 45 (1990): 179–189.

94. H. P. Sims, Jr., and C. C. Manz, *Company of Heros: Unleashing the Power of Self-Leadership* (New York: John Wiley & Sons, 1996).

95. C. C. Manz and H. P. Sims, "Leading Workers to Lead Themselves: The External Leadership of Self-Managing Work Teams," *Administrative Science Quarterly* 32 (1987): 106–128.

96. L. Hirschhorn, "Leaders and Followers in a Postindustrial Age: A Psychodynamic View," *Journal of Applied Behavioral Science* 26 (1990): 529–542.

97. R. E. Kelley, "In Praise of Followers," *Harvard Business Review* 66 (1988): 142–148.

98. C. C. Manz and H. P. Sims, "SuperLeadership: Beyond the Myth of Heroic Leadership," *Organizational Dynamics* 20 (1991): 18–35.

99. W. J. Crockett, "Dynamic Subordinancy," *Training and Development Journal* (May 1981): 155–164.

100. N. J. Adler, *International Dimensions in Organizational Behavior* (Boston: PWS-Kent, 1991).

101. F. C. Brodback, et al., "Cultural Variation of Leadership Prototypes across 22 European Countries," *Journal of Occupational and Organizational Psychology* 73 (2000): 1–29.

102. B. Alimo-Metcalfe and R. J. Alban-Metcalfe, "The Development of a New Transformational Leadership Questionnaire," *Journal of Occupational and Organizational Psychology* 74 (2001): 1–27.

103. T. Lenartowicz and J. P. Johnson, "A Cross-National Assessment of the Values of Latin American Managers: Contrasting Hues or Shades of Gray?" *Journal of International Business Studies* 34 (2003): 266–281.

104. Y. Hui-Chun and P. Miller, "The Generation Gap and Cultural Influence: A Taiwan Empirical Investigation," *Cross Cultural Management* 10 (2003): 23–42.

105. M. Javidan, "Forward-Thinking Cultures," *Harvard Business Review* 85(7, 8) (2007): 20.

106. G. A. Yukl, *Leadership in Organizations*, 2nd ed. (Upper Saddle River, NJ: Prentice Hall, 1989).

107. Harvard Business School, "James E. Burke," *Working Knowledge* (October 27, 2003), http://hbswk.hbs.edu/pubitem.jhtml?id=3755&t=leadership.

108. P.W. Beamish, R.E. White, and D. Mazutis, "Research in Motion: Managing Explosive Growth," *Harvard Business Case* (May 15, 2008).

109. http://www.CanadasTop100.com/national.

110. http://www.eluta.ca/top-employer-rim.

Chapter 12 Case

1. C. Daniels, "Create Ikea, Make Billions, Take Bus," *Fortune* 149(9) (May 3, 2004): 44; P. Davis, "Billionaire Attributes—Modesty: Ingvar Kamprad, Ikea's Founder & Owner," http://EzineArticles.com/?expert=Paul_Davis, accessed June 28, 2009.

2. C. Daniels, "Create Ikea, Make Billions, Take Bus," *Fortune* 149(9) (May 3, 2004): 44.

3. Ibid.

4. Ibid.

5. "How He Made His Pile: Ingvar Kamprad," *Management Today* (September 2008): 20.

6. Daniels, "Create Ikea, Make Billions, Take Bus," Ibid., p. 44; J. Scully, "Ikea," *Time* (Summer 2004): 16.

7. Daniels, "Create Ikea, Make Billions, Take Bus," p. 44.

8. Davis, "Billionaire Attributes."

9. Scully, "Ikea," p. 16.

10. "How He Made His Pile," p. 20.

11. A. Meisler, "Success, Scandinavian Style," *Workforce Management* 83(8) (August 2004): 27.

12. "How He Made His Pile," p. 20.

13. Davis, "Billionaire Attributes."

14. A. Meisler, "Family Values, Warm and Fuzzy Math," *Workforce Management* 83(8) (August 2004): 30.

15. "History Lessons: Be Persistent, Ingvar Kamprad," *Management Today* (April 2006): 13.

16. Ibid.

17. Davis, "Billionaire Attributes."

18. "History Lessons," p. 13.

19. "How He Made His Pile," p. 20.

20. Davis, "Billionaire Attributes."

Chapter 13

1. C. A. Bartlett, V. Dessain, and A. Sjoman, "IKEA's Global Sourcing Challenge: Indian Rugs and Child Labor," *Harvard Business School Case* (November 14, 2006).

2. "IKEA Investigates Child Labor Allegations," *Los Angeles Times* (October 24, 1997), http://articles.latimes.com/1997/oct/24/business/fi-46077.

3. E. Luce, "IKEA Strives to Confront Child Labor Issue," *Los Angeles Times* (September 20, 2004), http://articles.latimes.com/2004/sep/20/business/ft-ikea20.

4. Definition adapted from D. Hellriegel, J. W. Slocum, Jr., and R. W. Woodman, *Organizational Behavior* (St. Paul: West, 1992) and from R. D. Middlemist and M. A. Hitt, *Organizational Behavior* (St. Paul: West, 1988).

5. D. Tjosvold, *The Conflict-Positive Organization* (Reading, MA: Addison-Wesley, 1991).

6. K. Thomas and W. Schmidt, "A Survey of Managerial Interests with Respect to Conflict," *Academy of Management Journal* 19 (1976): 315–318; G. L. Lippitt, "Managing Conflict in Today's Organizations," *Training and Development Journal* 36 (1982): 66–74.

7. M. Rajim, "A Measure of Styles of Handling Interpersonal Conflict," *Academy of Management Journal* 26 (1983): 368–376.

8. D. Goleman, *Emotional Intelligence* (New York: Bantam Books, 1995); J. Stuller, "Unconventional Smarts," *Across the Board* 35 (1998): 22–23.

9. Tjosvold, *The Conflict-Positive Organization*, 4.

10. R. A. Cosier and D. R. Dalton, "Positive Effects of Conflict: A Field Experiment," *International Journal of Conflict Management* 1 (1990): 81–92.

11. D. Tjosvold, "Making Conflict Productive," *Personnel Administrator* 29 (1984): 121–130.

12. A. C. Amason, W. A. Hochwarter, K. R. Thompson, and A. W. Harrison, "Conflict: An Important Dimension in Successful Management Teams," *Organizational Dynamics* 24 (1995): 25–35.

13. M. Inness, M. M. LeBlanc, and J. Barling, "Psychological Predictors of Supervisor-, Peer-, Subordinate-, and Service-Provider-Targeted Aggression," *Journal of Applied Psychology* 93 (2008): 1401–1411.

14. T. L. Simons and R. S. Peterson, "Task Conflict and Relationship Conflict in Top Management Teams: The Pivotal Role of Intergroup Trust," *Journal of Applied Psychology* 85 (2000): 102–111.

15. R. Nibler and K. L. Harris, "The Effects of Culture and Cohesiveness on Intragroup Conflict and Effectiveness," *The Journal of Social Psychology* 143 (2003): 613–631.

16. I. Janis, *Groupthink*, 2nd ed. (Boston: Houghton Mifflin, 1982).

17. J. D. Thompson, *Organizations in Action* (New York: McGraw-Hill, 1967).

18. G. Walker and L. Poppo, "Profit Centers, Single-Source Suppliers, and Transaction Costs," *Administrative Science Quarterly* 36 (1991): 66–87.

19. R. Miles, *Macro Organizational Behavior* (Glenview, IL: Scott, Foresman, 1980).

20. H. Levinson, "The Abrasive Personality," *Harvard Business Review* 56 (1978): 86–94.

21. J. C. Quick and J. D. Quick, *Organizational Stress and Preventive Management* (New York: McGraw-Hill, 1984).

22. F. N. Brady, "Aesthetic Components of Management Ethics," *Academy of Management Review* 11 (1986): 337–344.

23. J. R. Ogilvie and M. L. Carsky, "Building Emotional Intelligence in Negotiations," *The International Journal of Conflict Management* 13 (2002): 381–400.

24. A. M. Bodtker and R. L. Oliver, "Emotion in Conflict Formation and Its Transformation: Application to Organizational Conflict Management," *International Journal of Conflict Management* 12 (2001): 259–275.

25. D. E. Conlon and S. H. Hunt, "Dealing with Feeling: The Influence of Outcome Representations on Negotiation," *International Journal of Conflict Management* 13 (2002): 35–58.

26. V. K. Raizada, "Multi-Ethnic Corporations and Inter-Ethnic Conflict," *Human Resource Management* 20 (1981): 24–27; T. Cox, Jr., "The Multicultural Organization," *Academy of Management Executive* 5 (1991): 34–47.

27. G. Hofstede, *Culture's Consequences: International Differences in Work-related Values* (Beverly Hills, CA: Sage, 1980); G. Hofstede and M. H. Bond, "The Confucius Connection: From Cultural Roots to Economic Growth," *Organizational Dynamics* (Spring 1988): 4–21; G. Hofstede, "Cultural Constraints in Management Theories," *Academy of Management Executive* 7 (1993): 81–94.

28. T. H. Cox, S. A. Lobel, and P. L. McLead, "Effects of Ethnic Group Cultural Differences on Cooperative and Competitive Behavior in a Group Task," *Academy of Management Journal* 34 (1991): 827–847.

29. C. Lui, M. M. Nauta, P. E. Spector, and C. Li "Direct and indirect conflicts at work in China and the US: A Cross-Cultural Comparison," *Work and Stress* 22 (2008): 295–313.

30. J. Schopler, C. A. Insko, J. Wieselquist, et al., "When Groups Are More Competitive than Individuals: The Domain of the Discontinuity Effect," *Journal of Personality and Social Psychology* 80 (2001): 632–644.

31. M. Sherif and C. W. Sherif, *Social Psychology* (New York: Harper & Row, 1969).

32. C. Song, S. M. Sommer, and A. E. Hartman, "The Impact of Adding an External Rater on Interdepartmental Cooperative Behaviors of Workers," *International Journal of Conflict Management* 9 (1998): 117–138.

33. W. Tsai and S. Ghoshal, "Social Capital and Value Creation: The Role of Intrafirm Networks," *Academy of Management Journal* 41 (1998): 464–476.

34. M. A. Zarate, B. Garcia, A. A. Garza, and R. T. Hitlan, "Cultural Threat and Perceived Realistic Group Conflict as Dual Predictors of Prejudice," *Journal of Experimental Social Psychology* 40 (2004): 99–105.

35. J. C. Dencker, A. Joshi, and J. J. Martocchio, "Employee Benefits as Context for Intergenerational Conflict," *Human Resource Management Review* 17(2) (2007): 208–220.

36. M. L. Maznevski and K. M. Chudoba, "Bridging Space over Time: Global Virtual-Team Dynamics and Effectiveness," *Organization Science* 11 (2000): 473–492.

37. D. Katz and R. Kahn, *The Social Psychology of Organizations*, 2nd ed. (New York: John Wiley & Sons, 1978).

38. D. L. Nelson and J. C. Quick, "Professional Women: Are Distress and Disease Inevitable?" *Academy of Management Review* 10 (1985): 206–218; D. L. Nelson and M. A. Hitt, "Employed Women and Stress: Implications for Enhancing Women's Mental Health in the Workplace," in J. C. Quick, J. Hurrell, and L. A. Murphy, eds., *Stress and Well-Being at Work: Assessments and Interventions for Occupational Mental Health* (Washington, DC: American Psychological Association, 1992).

39. E. C. Dierdorff and J. K. Ellington, "It's the Nature of Work: Examining Behavior-Based Sources of Work-Family Conflict Across Occupations" *Journal of Applied Psychology* 93 (2008): 883–892.

40. M. G. Pratt and J. A. Rosa, "Transforming Work-Family Conflict into Commitment in Network Marketing Organizations," *Academy of Management Journal* 46 (2003): 395–418.

41. W. R. Boswell and J. B. Olson-Buchanan, "The Use of Communication Technologies After Hours: The Role of Work Attitudes and Work-Life Conflict," *Journal of Management* 33(4) (2007): 592–610.

42. R. L. Kahn, et al., *Organizational Stress: Studies in Role Conflict and Ambiguity* (New York: John Wiley & Sons, 1964).

43. J. L. Badaracco, Jr., "The Discipline of Building Character," *Harvard Business Review* (March–April 1998): 115–124.

44. B. Schneider, "The People Make the Place," *Personnel Psychology* 40 (1987): 437–453.

45. C. A. O'Reilly, J. Chatman, and D. F. Caldwell, "People and Organizational Culture: A Profile Comparison Approach to Assessing Person-Organization Fit," *Academy of Management Journal* 34 (1991): 487–516.

46. I. Dayal and J. M. Thomas, "Operation KPE: Developing a New Organization," *Journal of Applied Behavioral Science* 4 (1968): 473–506.

47. R. H. Miles, "Role Requirements as Sources of Organizational Stress," *Journal of Applied Psychology* 61 (1976): 172–179.

48. http://www.workplacebullying.org/research.html.

49. W. F. G. Mastenbroek, *Conflict Management and Organization Development* (Chichester, England: John Wiley & Sons, 1987).

50. M. R. Frone, "Interpersonal Conflict at Work and Psychological Outcomes: Testing a Model among Young Workers," *Journal of Occupational Health Psychology* 5 (2000): 246–255.

51. K. Thomas, "Conflict and Conflict Management," in M. D. Dunnette, ed., *Handbook of Industrial and Organizational Psychology* (New York: John Wiley & Sons, 1976).

52. H. H. Meyer, E. Kay, and J. R. P. French, "Split Roles in Performance Appraisal," *Harvard Business Review* 43 (1965): 123–129.

53. T. W. Costello and S. S. Zalkind, *Psychology in Administration: A Research Orientation* (Englewood Cliffs, NJ: Prentice Hall, 1963).

54. Snapshot Spy, "Employee Computer & Internet Abuse Statistics," http://www.snapshotspy.com/employee-computer-abuse-statistics.htm; Data sources include U.S. Department of Commerce—Economics and Statistics Administration and the National Telecommunications and Information Administration—Greenfield and Rivet, "Employee Computer Abuse Statistics."

55. P. F. Hewlin, "And the Award for Best Actor Goes to…: Facades of Conformity in Organizational Settings," *Academy of Management Review* 28 (2003): 633–642.

56. C. A. Insko, J. Scholper, L. Gaertner, et al., "Interindividual–Intergroup Discontinuity Reduction through the Anticipation of Future Interaction," *Journal of Personality and Social Psychology* 80 (2001): 95–111.

57. D. Tjosvold and M. Poon, "Dealing with Scarce Resources: Open-Minded Interaction for Resolving Budget Conflicts," *Group and Organization Management* 23 (1998): 237–255.

58. R. Miles, *Macro Organizational Behavior*; R. Steers, *Introduction to Organizational Behavior*, 4th ed. (Glenview, IL: Harper-Collins, 1991).

59. C. Morrill, M. N. Zold, and H. Rao, "Covert Political Conflict in Organizations: Challenges from Below," *Annual Review of Sociology* 29 (2003): 391–415.

60. A. Tyerman and C. Spencer, "A Critical Text of the Sherrif's Robber's Cave Experiments: Intergroup Competition and Cooperation between Groups of Well-Acquainted Individuals," *Small Group Behavior* 14 (1983): 515–531; R. M. Kramer, "Intergroup Relations and Organizational Dilemmas: The Role of Categorization Processes," in B. Staw and L. Cummings, eds., *Research in Organizational Behavior*, Vol. 13 (Greenwich, CT: JAI Press, 1991), 191–228.

61. A. Carmeli, "The Relationship between Emotional Intelligence and Work Attitudes, Behavior and Outcomes: An Examination among Senior Managers," *Journal of Managerial Psychology* 18 (2003): 788–813.

62. R. Blake and J. Mouton, "Overcoming Group Warfare," *Harvard Business Review* 64 (1984): 98–108.

63. D. G. Ancona and D. Caldwell, "Improving the Performance of New Product Teams," *Research Technology Management* 33 (1990): 25–29.

64. M. A. Cronin and L. R. Weingart, "Representational Gaps, Information Processing, and Conflict in Functionally Diverse Teams," *Academy of Management Review* 32(3) (2007): 761–773.

65. C. K. W. DeDreu and L. R. Weingart, "Task versus Relationship Conflict, Team Performance, and Team Member Satisfaction: A Meta-Analysis," *Journal of Applied Psychology* 88 (2003): 741–749.

66. R. J. Lewicki, J. A. Litterer, J. W. Minton, and D. M. Saunders, *Negotiation*, 2nd ed. (Burr Ridge, IL: Irwin, 1994).

67. C. K. W. De Dreu, S. L. Koole, and W. Steinel, "Unfixing the Fixed Pie: A Motivated Information-Processing Approach to Integrative Negotiation," *Journal of Personality and Social Psychology* 79 (2000): 975–987.

68. M. H. Bazerman, J. R. Curhan, D. A. Moore, and K. L. Valley, "Negotiation," *Annual Review of Psychology* 51 (2000): 279–314.

69. I. Ayers and P. Siegelman, "Race and Gender Discrimination in Bargaining for a New Car," *American Economic Review* 85 (1995): 304–321.

70. L. J. Kray, L. Thompson, and A. Galinsky, "Battle of the Sexes: Gender Stereotype Confirmation and Reactance in Organizations," *Journal of Personality and Social Psychology* 80 (2001): 942–958.

71. K. W. Thomas, "Conflict and Conflict Management," in M. D. Dunnette, ed., *Handbook of Industrial and Organizational Psychology* (Chicago: Rand McNally, 1976), 900.

72. S. Steinberg, "Airbus Workers in France, Germany Strike against Massive Job Cuts" (March 1, 2007), http://www.wsws.org/articles/2007/mar2007/airb-m01.shtml.

73. C. K. W. De Dreu and A. E. M. Van Vianen, "Managing Relationship Conflict and the Effectiveness of Organizational Teams," *Journal of Organizational Behavior* 22 (2001): 309–328.

74. R. A. Baron, S. P. Fortin, R. L. Frei, L. A. Hauver, and M. L. Shack, "Reducing Organizational Conflict: The Role of Socially Induced Positive Affect," *International Journal of Conflict Management* 1 (1990): 133–152.

75. S. L. Phillips and R. L. Elledge, *The Team Building Source Book* (San Diego: University Associates, 1989).

76. J. R. Curhan, M.A. Neale, L. Ross, J. Rosencranz-Engelmann, "Relational Accommodation in Negotiation: Effects of Egalitarianism and Gender on Economic Efficiency and Relational Capital," *Organizational Behavior and Human Decision Processes* 107 (2008): 192–205.

77. T.N. Gladwin and I. Walter, "How Multinationals Can Manage Social and Political Forces," *Journal of Business Strategy* 1 (1980): 54–68.

78. L. A. Dechurch, K. L. Hamilton, and C. Haas, "Effects of Conflict Management Strategies on Perceptions of Intragroup Conflict," *Group Dynamics: Theory, Research, and Practice* 11(1) (2007): 66–78.

79. K. W. Thomas, "Toward Multidimensional Values in Teaching: The Example of Conflict Behaviors," *Academy of Management Review* 2 (1977): 484–490.

80. S. Alper, D. Tjosvold, and K. S. Law, "Conflict Management, Efficacy, and Performance in Organizational Teams," *Personnel Psychology* 53 (2000): 625–642.

81. A. Somech, H. S. Desvililya, and H. Lidogoster, "Team Conflict Management and Team Effectiveness: The Effects of Task Interdependence and Team Identification," *Journal of Organizational Behavior* 30 (2009): 359–378.

82. W. King and E. Miles, "What We Know and Don't Know about Measuring Conflict," *Management Communication Quarterly* 4 (1990): 222–243.

83. J. Barker, D. Tjosvold, and I. R. Andrews, "Conflict Approaches of Effective and Ineffective Project Managers: A Field Study in a Matrix Organization," *Journal of Management Studies* 25 (1988): 167–178.

84. M. Chan, "Intergroup Conflict and Conflict Management in the R&D Divisions of Four Aerospace Companies," *IEEE Transactions on Engineering Management* 36 (1989): 95–104.

85. M. K. Kozan, "Cultural Influences on Styles of Handling Interpersonal Conflicts: Comparisons among Jordanian, Turkish, and U.S. Managers," *Human Relations* 42 (1989): 787–799.

86. S. McKenna, "The Business Impact of Management Attitudes towards Dealing with Conflict: A Cross-Cultural Assessment," *Journal of Managerial Psychology* 10 (1995): 22–27.

87. Z. Ma, "Chinese Conflict Management Styles and Negotiation Behaviours: An Empirical Test," *International Journal of Cross Cultural Management* 7(1) (2007): 101–119.

88. P. S. Hempel, Z. Zhang, and D. Tjosvold, "Conflict Management Between and Within Teams for Trusting Relationships and Performance in China," *Journal of Organizational Behavior* 30 (2009): 41–65.

89. Tjosvold, *The Conflict-Positive Organization.*

90. P. J. Frost, *Toxic Emotions at Work: How Compassionate Managers Handle Pain and Conflict* (Harvard Business School Press, 2003).

91. C. K. W. DeDrue, "The Virtue and Vice of Workplace Conflict: Food for (Pessimistic) Thought," *Journal of Organizational Behavior* 29 (2008): 5–18.

92. J. R. Ogilvie and M. L. Carsky, "Building Emotional Intelligence in Negotiations," *The International Journal of Conflict Management* 13 (2002): 381–400.

93. http://www.unicef.org/corporate_partners/index_25092.html.

Chapter 13 Case

1. "Corporate News: Nordstrom, Kohl's Net Goes on Markdown—Rack Retailers Offer Dim Holiday Forecasts, Cut Full-Year Profit Estimates as Quarterly Earnings Fall," *Wall Street Journal* (Eastern edition) (November 14, 2008): B3.

2. "Nordstrom Today," Nordstrom Web Site, http://aboutnordstrom.com/aboutus/ companyhist/companyhist.asp (accessed August 5, 2009).

3. B. Janet, "Customers Never Tire of Great Service," *Dealerscope* 50(7) (July 2008): 40.

4. Ibid.

5. N. Templin, "Cheapskate: How It Felt to Be Kicked by a Running Shoe," *Wall Street Journal* (Eastern edition) (November 13, 2008): D3.

6. Ibid.

7. Ibid.

8. B. Janet, "Customers Never Tire of Great Service."

9. V. O'Connell, "Nordstrom Net Falls," *Wall Street Journal* (Eastern edition) (February 24, 2009): B6.

10. J. Saranow, "Currents: Luxury Consumers Scrimp for Sake of Planet, and Because It's Cheaper," *Wall Street Journal* (Eastern edition) (November 4, 2008): A14.

11. C. Binkley, "Style—On Style: The Latest Style: Self-Denial; In a Troubled Economy, Splurges Seem Shameful, and Cheap Is Cool; Needs vs. Wants," *Wall Street Journal* (Eastern edition) (November 6, 2008): D12.

12. Ibid.

13. Saranow, "Currents."

14. M. Boyle and O. Kharif, "Getting Tough with Customers," *Business Week* (4122) (March 9, 2009): 30.

15. Ibid.

16. K. Maher, "U.S. News: For Nordstrom Launch, Business as Usual — Sort of; Christening of a Store in a Lousy Economy Is Unsettling, but for Those Seeking Retail Therapy, Company Says, 'We Want to Be There'," *Wall Street Journal* (Eastern edition) (October 25, 2008): A2.

17. A. Beriault, "What's a Poor Little Yatch Brand to Do?," *Brandweek* 49(39) (November 3, 2008): 16.

Chapter 13 Cohesion Case: Part 3

1. "Business: Keeper of the Flame; Face Value," *The Economist* 391(8627) (April 18, 2009): 75.

2. M. Chafkin, "Get Happy: How Tony Hsieh Uses Relentless Innovation, Stellar Service, and a Staff of Believers to Make Zappos.com and E-commerce Juggernaut—and One of the Most Blissed-out Businesses in America," *Inc.* 31(4) (May 2009): 73.

3. M. Zager, "Zappos Delivers Service … With Shoes on the Side," *Apparel Magazine* (January 2009), http://www.apparelmag.com?ME2/dirmod.asp?sid=23B25809… (accessed June 9, 2009).

4. "Business: Keeper of the Flame; Face Value."

5. B. Morrisey, "Communal Branding: How These Web 2.0 Companies Build Good Relationships to Build Their Brands," *Adweek* 49(16) (May 12, 2008): 9.

6. Chafkin, "Get Happy," 73.

7. J. M. O'Brien, "Zappos Knows How to Kick It," *Fortune* 159(2) (February 2, 2009): 56.

8. Chafkin, "Get Happy," 68.

9. Ibid., pp. 68–69.

10. Ibid., p. 69.

11. Ibid.

12. Zager, "Zappos Delivers Service."

13. Morrisey, "Communal Branding," 8.

14. S. Gaudin, "Web 2.0 Tools Can Foster Growth in Hard Times," *Computerworld* 43(11) (March 16, 2009): 12.

15. D. M. Amato-McCoy, "Blending Technology and Tradition," *Chain Store Age* 84(10) (October 2008): 50.

16. E. Frauenheim, "Technology Forcing Firms to Shed More Light on Layoffs," *Workforce Management* 88(1) (January 19, 2009): 8; O'Brien, "Zappos Knows," 56.

17. O'Brien, "Zappos Knows," 60.

18. E. Frauenheim, "Technology Forcing Firms to Shed More Light on Layoffs," *Workforce Management* 88(1) (January 19, 2009): 8.

19. Chafkin, "Get Happy," 73.

20. O'Brien, "Zappos Knows," 58.

21. C. Gentry, "Cultural Revolution," *Chain Store Age* 83(12) (December 2007): 32.

22. Chafkin, "Get Happy," 73.

Chapter 14

1. C. Kennison, "CarMax, Inc at Robert W. Baird & Co., Inc. Growth Stock Conference," *CQ FD*, May 13, 2009.

2. J. S. Bunderson and J. A. Thompson, "The Call of the Wild: Zookeepers, Callings, and the Double-Edged Sword of Deeply Meaningful Work," *Administrative Science Quarterly* 54 (2009): 32–57.

3. G. W. England and I. Harpaz, "How Working Is Defined: National Contexts and Demographic and Organizational Role Influences," *Journal of Organizational Behavior* 11 (1990): 253–266.

4. L. R. Gomez-Mejia, "The Cross-Cultural Structure of Task-Related and Contextual Constructs," *Journal of Psychology* 120 (1986): 5–19.

5. A. Wrzesniewski and J. E. Dutton, "Crafting a Job: Revisioning Employees as Active Crafters of Their Work," *Academy of Management Review* 26 (2001): 179–201.

6. F. W. Taylor, *The Principles of Scientific Management* (New York: Norton, 1911).

7. T. Bell, *Out of This Furnace* (Pittsburgh: University of Pittsburgh Press, 1941).

8. P. Cappelli, "A Market-Driven Approach to Retaining Talent," *Harvard Business Review* 78 (2000): 103–111.

9. N. D. Warren, "Job Simplification versus Job Enlargement," *Journal of Industrial Engineering* 9 (1958): 435–439.

10. J. H. Gittell, D. B Weinberg, A. L. Bennett, and J. A. Miller, "Is the Doctor in? A Relational Approach to Job Design and the Coordination of Work," *Human Resource Management* 47 (Winter 2008): 729–755.

11. C. R. Walker, "The Problem of the Repetitive Job," *Harvard Business Review* 28 (1950): 54–58.

12. T. Moller, S. E. Mathiassen, H. Franzon, and S. Kihlberg, "Job Enlargement and Mechanical Exposure Variability in Cyclic Assembly Work," *Ergonomics* 47 (2004): 19–40.

13. C. R. Walker and R. H. Guest, *The Man on the Assembly Line* (Cambridge, MA: Harvard University Press, 1952).

14. M. A. Campion, L. Cheraskin, and M. J. Stevens, "Career-Related Antecedents and Outcomes of Job Rotation," *Academy of Management Journal* 37 (1994): 1518–1542.

15. H. R. Nalbantian and R. A. Guzzo, "Making Mobility Matter," *Harvard Business Review* (March 2009): 76–84.

16. E. Santora, "Keep Up Production Through Cross-Training," *Personnel Journal* (June 1992): 162–166.

17. S. Leroy, "Why Is It So Hard to Do My Work? The Challenge of Attention Residue When Switching between Work Tasks," *Organizational Behavior and Human Decision Processes* 109 (2009): 168–181.

18. R. P. Steel and J. R. Rentsch, "The Dispositional Model of Job Attitudes Revisited: Findings of a 10-Year Study," *Journal of Applied Psychology* 82 (1997): 873–879; C.-S. Wong, C. Hui, and K. S. Law, "A Longitudinal Study of the Job Perception–Job Satisfaction Relationship: A Text of the Three Alternative Specifications," *Journal of Occupational & Organizational Psychology* 71 (Part 2, 1998): 127–146.

19. F. Herzberg, "One More Time: How Do You Motivate Employees?" *Harvard Business Review* 46 (1968): 53–62.

20. R. N. Ford, "Job Enrichment Lessons from AT&T," *Harvard Business Review* 51 (1973): 96–106.

21. R. J. House and L. A. Wigdor, "Herzberg's Dual-Factor Theory of Job Satisfaction and Motivation: A Review of the Evidence and a Criticism," *Personnel Psychology* 20 (1967): 369–389.

22. A. N. Turner and P. R. Lawrence, *Industrial Jobs and the Worker* (Cambridge, MA: Harvard University Press, 1965).

23. D. H. McKnight, B. Phillips, and B.C. Hardgrave, "Which Reduces IT Turnover Intention the Worst: Workplace Characteristics or Job Characteristics?" *Information & Management* 46 (2009): 167–174.

24. J. R. Hackman and G. R. Oldham, "The Job Diagnostic Survey: An Instrument for the Diagnosis of Jobs and the Evaluation of Job Redesign Projects," *Technical Report No. 4* (New Haven, CT: Department of Administrative Sciences, Yale University, 1974).

25. J. L Pierce, I. Jussila, and A. Cummings, "Psychological Ownership within the Job Design Context: Revision of the Job Characteristics Model," *Journal of Organizational Behavior* 30 (2009): 477–496.

26. J. R. Hackman and G. R. Oldham, "Development of the Job Diagnostic Survey," *Journal of Applied Psychology* 60 (1975): 159–170.

27. E. Sadler-Smith, G. El-Kot, and M. Leat, "Differentiating Work Autonomy Facets in a Non-Western Context," *Journal of Organizational Behavior* 24 (2003): 709–731.

28. F. P. Morgeson and S. E. Humphrey, "The Work Design Questionnaire (WDQ): Developing and Validating a Comprehensive Measure for Assessing Job Design and the Nature of Work," *Journal of Applied Psychology* 91 (2006): 1321–1329.

29. P. H. Birnbaum, J. L. Farh, and G. Y. Y. Wong, "The Job Characteristics Model in Hong Kong," *Journal of Applied Psychology* 71 (1986): 598–605.

30. J. R. Hackman and G. R. Oldham, *Work Design* (Reading, MA: Addison-Wesley, 1980).

31. H. P. Sims, A. D. Szilagyi, and R. T. Keller, "The Measurement of Job Characteristics," *Academy of Management Journal* 19 (1976): 195–212.

32. H. P. Sims and A. D. Szilagyi, "Job Characteristic Relationships: Individual and Structural Moderators," *Organizational Behavior and Human Performance* 17 (1976): 211–230.

33. Y. Fried, "Meta-Analytic Comparison of the Job Diagnostic Survey and Job Characteristic Inventory as Correlates of Work Satisfaction and Performance," *Journal of Applied Psychology* 76 (1991): 690–698.

34. D. R. May, R. L. Gilson, and L. M. Harter, "The Psychological Conditions of Meaningfulness, Safety, and Availability and the Engagement of the Human Spirit at Work," *Journal of Occupational and Organizational Psychology* 77 (2004): 11–37.

35. M. Soyars and J. Brusino, "Essentials of Engagement," *T&D* (March 2009): 62–65.

36. R. Wagner, "Nourishing Employee Engagement," *Gallup Management Journal* (February 12, 2004): 1–7, http://gmj.gallup.com/content/default.asp?ci=10504.

37. J. Loehr and T. Schwartz, *The Power of Full Engagement: Managing Energy, Not Time, Is the Key to High Performance and Personal Renewal* (New York: Free Press, 2003).

38. M. F. R. Kets de Vries, "Creating Authentizotic Organizations: Well-Functioning Individuals in Vibrant Companies," *Human Relations* 54 (2001): 101–111.

39. G. R. Salancik and J. Pfeffer, "A Social Information Processing Approach to Job Attitudes and Task Design," *Administrative Science Quarterly* 23 (1978): 224–253.

40. J. Pfeffer, "Management as Symbolic Action: The Creation and Maintenance of Organizational Paradigms," in L. L. Cummings and B. M. Staw, eds., *Research in Organizational Behavior*, vol. 3 (Greenwich, CT: JAI Press, 1981), 1–52.

41. C. Clegg and C. Spencer, "A Circular and Dynamic Model of the Process of Job Design," *Journal of Occupational & Organizational Psychology* 80 (2007): S321–S339.

42. J. Thomas and R. Griffin, "The Social Information Processing Model of Task Design: A Review of the Literature," *Academy of Management Review* 8 (1983): 672–682.

43. D. J. Campbell, "Task Complexity: A Review and Analysis," *Academy of Management Review* 13 (1988): 40–52.

44. A. M. Grant, "Relational Job Design and the Motivation to Make a Prosocial Difference," *Academy of Management Review* 32 (2007): 393–417.

45. D. R. May, K. Reed, C. E. Schwoerer, and P. Potter, "Ergonomic Office Design and Aging: A Quasi-Experimental Field Study of Employee Reactions to an Ergonomics Intervention Program," *Journal of Occupational Health Psychology* 9 (2004): 123–135.

46. M. A. Campion and P. W. Thayer, "Job Design: Approaches, Outcomes, and Trade-Offs," *Organizational Dynamics* 16 (1987): 66–79.

47. J. Teresko, "Emerging Technologies," *Industry Week* (February 27, 1995): 1–2.

48. M. A. Campion and C. L. McClelland, "Interdisciplinary Examination of the Costs and Benefits of Enlarged Jobs: A Job Design Quasi-Experiment," *Journal of Applied Psychology* 76 (1991): 186–199.

49. B. Kohut, *Country Competitiveness: Organizing of Work* (New York: Oxford University Press, 1993).

50. D. Holman, S. Frenkel, O. Sorensen, and S. Wood, "Work Design Variation and Outcomes in Call Centers: Strategic Choice and Institutional Explanations," *Industrial and Labor Relations Review* 62 (July 2009): 510–532.

51. J. C. Quick and L. E. Tetrick, eds., *Handbook of Occupational Health Psychology, Revised Edition* (Washington, DC: American Psychological Association, 2011).

52. W. E. Deming, *Out of the Crisis* (Cambridge, MA: MIT Press, 1986).

53. L. Thurow, *Head to Head: The Coming Economic Battle among Japan, Europe, and America* (New York: Morrow, 1992).

54. M. A. Fruin, *The Japanese Enterprise System—Competitive Strategies and Cooperative Structures* (New York: Oxford University Press, 1992).

55. W. Niepce and E. Molleman, "Work Design Issue in Lean Production from a Sociotechnical System Perspective: Neo-Taylorism or the Next Step in Sociotechnical Design?" *Human Relations* 51 (1998): 259–287.

56. S. K. Parker, "Longitudinal Effects of Lean Production on Employee Outcomes and the Mediating Role of Work Characteristics," *Journal of Applied Psychology* 88 (2003): 620–634.

57. E. Furubotn, "Codetermination and the Modern Theory of the Firm: A Property-Rights Analysis," *Journal of Business* 61 (1988): 165–181.

58. H. Levinson, *Executive: The Guide to Responsive Management* (Cambridge, MA: Harvard University Press, 1981).

59. B. Gardell, "Scandinavian Research on Stress in Working Life" (Paper presented at the IRRA Symposium on Stress in Working Life, Denver, September 1980).

60. L. Levi, "Psychosocial, Occupational, Environmental, and Health Concepts; Research Results and Applications," in G. P. Keita and S. L. Sauter, eds., *Work and Well-Being: An Agenda for the 1990s* (Washington, DC: American Psychological Association, 1992), 199–211.

61. L. R. Murphy and C. L. Cooper, eds., *Healthy and Productive Work: An International Perspective* (London and New York: Taylor & Francis, 2000).

62. R. L. Kahn, *Work and Health* (New York: John Wiley & Sons, 1981); M. Gowing, J. Kraft, and J. C. Quick, *The New Organizational Reality: Downsizing, Restructuring, and Revitalization* (Washington, DC: American Psychological Association, 1998).

63. F. J. Landy, "Work Design and Stress," in G. P. Keita and S. L. Sauter, eds., *Work and Well-Being: An Agenda for the 1990s* (Washington, DC: American Psychological Association, 1992), 119–158.

64. C. Gresov, R. Drazin, and A. H. Van de Ven, "Work-Unit Task Uncertainty, Design, and Morale," *Organizational Studies* 10 (1989): 45–62.

65. M. Macik-Frey, J. D. Quick, J. C. Quick, and D. L. Nelson. "Chapter 1: Occupational Health Psychology: From Preventive Medicine to Psychologically Healthy Workplaces," in A.-S. G. Antoniou, C. L. Cooper, G. P. Chrousos, C. D. Spielberger, and M. W. Eysenck, eds., *Handbook of Managerial Behavior and Occupational Health* (Cheltenham, UK: Edward Elgar, 2009), 3–19.

66. A. M. Grant, E. M. Campbell, G. Chen, K. Cottone, D. Lapedis, and K. Lee, "Impact and the Art of Motivation Maintenance: The Effects of Contact with Beneficiaries on Persistence Behavior," *Organizational Behavior and Human Decision Processes* 103 (2007): 53–67.

67. Y. Baruch, "The Status of Research on Teleworking and an Agenda for Future Research," *International Journal of Management Review* 3 (2000): 113–129.

68. K. E. Pearlson and C. S. Saunders, "There's No Place Like Home: Managing Telecommuting Paradoxes," *Academy of Management Executive* 15 (2001): 117–128.

69. S. Caudron, "Working at Home Pays Off," *Personnel Journal* (November 1992): 40–47.

70. D. S. Bailey and J. Foley, "Pacific Bell Works Long Distance," *HRMagazine* (August 1990): 50–52.

71. S. M. Pollan and M. Levine, "Asking for Flextime," *Working Women* (February 1994): 48.

72. S. A. Rogier and M. Y. Padgett, "The Impact of Utilizing a Flexible Work Schedule on the Perceived Career Advancement Potential of Women," *Human Resource Development Quarterly* 15 (2004): 89–106.

73. S. Zuboff, *In the Age of the Smart Machine: The Future of Work and Power* (New York: Basic Books, 1988).

74. B. A. Gutek and S. J. Winter, "Computer Use, Control over Computers, and Job Satisfaction," in S. Oskamp and S. Spacapan, eds., *People's Reactions to Technology in Factories, Offices, and Aerospace: The Claremont Symposium on Applied Social Psychology* (Newbury Park, CA: Sage, 1990), 121–144.

75. L. M. Schleifer and B. C. Amick III, "System Response Time and Method of Pay: Stress Effects in Computer-Based Tasks," *International Journal of Human-Computer Interaction* 1 (1989): 23–39.

76. K. Voight, "Virtual Work: Some Telecommuters Take Remote Work to the Extreme," *Wall Street Journal Europe* (February 1, 2001): 1.

77. B. M. Staw and R. D. Boettger, "Task Revision: A Neglected Form of Work Performance," *Academy of Management Journal* 33 (1990): 534–559.

78. H. S. Schwartz, "Job Involvement as Obsession Compulsion," *Academy of Management Review* 7 (1982): 429–432.

79. C. J. Nemeth and B. M. Staw, "The Tradeoffs of Social Control and Innovation in Groups and Organizations," in L. Berkowitz, ed., *Advances in Experimental Social Psychology*, vol. 22 (New York: Academic Press, 1989), 175–210.

80. P. Singh, "Job Analysis for a Changing Workplace," *Human Resource Management Review* 18 (2008): 87–99.

81. G. Salvendy, *Handbook of Industrial Engineering: Technology and Operations Management* (New York: John Wiley & Sons, 2001).

82. D. M. Herold, "Using Technology to Improve Our Management of Labor Market Trends," in M. Greller, ed., "Managing Careers with a Changing Workforce," *Journal of Organizational Change Management* 3 (1990): 44–57.

83. D. A. Whetten and K. S. Cameron, *Developing Management Skills*, 6th ed. (Upper Saddle River, N.J.: Prentice Hall, 2004).

84. "CarMax Reshuffling 130 Workers," *The Richmond Times-Dispatch*, May 7, 2009.

Chapter 14 Case

1. S. Meisinger, "Flexible Schedules Make Powerful 'Perks,'" *HRMagazine* 52(4) (April 2007): 12.

2. Newswise, "Telecommuting Has Mostly Positive Consequences for Employees and Employers," *CPA Practice Management Forum* (December 2007): 19.

3. Meisinger, "Flexible Schedules Make Powerful 'Perks.'"

4. Newswise, "Telecommuting Has Mostly Positive."

5. Meisinger, "Flexible Schedules Make Powerful 'Perks.'"

6. E. M. Torpey, "Flexible Work: Adjusting the When and Where of Your Job," *Occupational Outlook Quarterly* (Summer 2007): 14.

7. S. Klie, "Flexibility a Growing Global Issue," *Canadian HR Reporter* 20(19) (November 5, 2007): 11.

8. Ibid.

9. L. Murphy, "Shining the Brass Ring—Making Partnership Attractive to the New Generation," *CPA Practice Management Forum* (January 2007): 5.

10. J. M. Phillips, M. Pomerantz, and S. M. Gully, "Plugging the Boomer Drain," *HRMagazine* 52(12) (December 2007): 54.

11. Murphy, "Shining the Brass Ring."

12. J. Schramm, "Work Turns Flexible," *HRMagazine* 54(3) (March 2009): 88.

13. A. Bednarz, "Gas Shortage Spurs Teleworking," *Network World* 25(39) (October 6, 2008): 16.

14. A. Holmes, "Telework," *Government Executive* 40(7) (June 15, 2008): 44.

15. Schramm, "Work Turns Flexible."

16. "What U.S. Employers Can Learn About Flexible Work in Other Nations," *HR Focus* 85(8) (August 2008): 8.

Chapter 15

1. S. Layak and P. Mehra, "Inside the Secret World of Auditing," *Business Today* (February 22, 2009).

2. J. Child, *Organization* (New York: Harper & Row, 1984).

3. P. Lawrence and J. Lorsch, "Differentiation and Integration in Complex Organizations," *Administrative Science Quarterly* 12 (1967): 1–47.

4. P. Lawrence and J. Lorsch, *Organization and Environment: Managing Differentiation and Integration*, rev. ed. (Cambridge, MA: Harvard University Press, 1986).

5. J. Hage, "An Axiomatic Theory of Organizations," *Administrative Science Quarterly* 10 (1965): 289–320.

6. "The Army Reserve at 100: An Emerging Operational Force," *Army Logistician* (November–December, 2008): 15–16.

7. W. Ouchi and J. Dowling, "Defining the Span of Control," *Administrative Science Quarterly* 19 (1974): 357–365.

8. L. Porter and E. Lawler, III, "Properties of Organization Structure in Relation to Job Attitudes and Job Behavior," *Psychological Bulletin* 65 (1965): 23–51.

9. J. Ivancevich and J. Donnelly, Jr., "Relation of Organization and Structure to Job Satisfaction, Anxiety-Stress, and Performance," *Administrative Science Quarterly* 20 (1975): 272–280.

10. R. Dewar and J. Hage, "Size, Technology, Complexity, and Structural Differentiation: Toward a Theoretical Synthesis," *Administrative Science Quarterly* 23 (1978): 111–136.

11. Lawrence and Lorsch, "Differentiation and Integration," 1–47.

12. J. R. R. Galbraith, *Designing Complex Organizations* (Reading, MA: Addison-Wesley-Longman, 1973).

13. W. Altier, "Task Forces: An Effective Management Tool," *Management Review* 76 (1987): 26–32.

14. P. Lawrence and J. Lorsch, "New Managerial Job: The Integrator," *Harvard Business Review* 45 (1967): 142–151.

15. J. Lorsch and P. Lawrence, "Organizing for Product Innovation," *Harvard Business Review* 43 (1965): 110–111.

16. D. Pugh, D. Hickson, C. Hinnings, and C. Turner, "Dimensions of Organization Structure," *Administrative Science Quarterly* 13 (1968): 65–91; B. Reimann, "Dimensions of Structure in Effective Organizations: Some Empirical Evidence," *Academy of Management Journal* 17 (1974): 693–708; S. Robbins, *Organization Theory: The Structure and Design of Organizations*, 3rd ed. (Englewood Cliffs, NJ: Prentice Hall, 1990).

17. M. C. Andrews, T. L. Baker, and T. G. Hunt, "The Interactive Effects of Centralization on the Relationship between Justice and Satisfaction," *Journal of Leadership & Organizational Studies* 15 (2008): 135–144.

18. H. Mintzberg, *The Structuring of Organizations* (Englewood Cliffs, NJ: Prentice Hall, 1979).

19. J. A. Kuprenas, "Implementation and Performance of a Matrix Organization Structure," *International Journal of Project Management* 21 (2003): 51–62.

20. Mintzberg, *Structuring of Organizations*.

21. K. J. Lauver and C. Q. Trank, "Safety and Organizational Design Factors: Decentralization, Alignment, and Influence," *Academy of Management Proceedings* (2008): 106–111.

22. K. Weick, "Educational Institutions as Loosely Coupled Systems," *Administrative Science Quarterly* (1976): 1–19.

23. D. Miller and C. Droge, "Psychological and Traditional Determinants of Structure," *Administrative Science Quarterly* 31 (1986): 540; H. Tosi, Jr., and J. Slocum, Jr., "Contingency Theory: Some Suggested Directions," *Journal of Management* 10 (1984): 9–26.

24. C. B. Clott, "Perspectives on Global Outsourcing and the Changing Nature of Work," *Business and Society Review* 109 (2004): 153–170.

25. P. Puranam, H. Singh, and M. Zollo, "Organizing for Innovation: Managing the Coordination-Automony Dilemma in Technology Acquisitions," *Academy of Management Journal* 49 (2006): 263–280.

26. D. Mack and J. C. Quick, "EDS: An Inside View of a Corporate Life Cycle Transition," *Organizational Dynamics* 30 (2002): 282–293.

27. M. Meyer, "Size and the Structure of Organizations: A Causal Analysis," *American Sociological Review* 37 (1972): 434–441; J. Beyer and H. Trice, "A Reexamination of the Relations between Size and Various Components of Organizational Complexity," *Administrative Science Quarterly* 24 (1979): 48–64; B. Mayhew, R. Levinger, J. McPherson, and T. James, "Systems Size and Structural Differentiation in Formal Organizations: A Baseline Generator for Two Major Theoretical Propositions," *American Sociological Review* 37 (1972): 26–43.

28. M. Gowing, J. Kraft, and J. C. Quick, *The New Organizational Reality: Downsizing, Restructuring, and Revitalization* (Washington, DC: American Psychological Association, 1998).

29. Amy J. Hillman and Albert A. Cannella Jr., "Organizational Predictors of Women on Corporate Boards," *Academy of Management Journal* 50 (2007): 941–952.

30. J. Werth and D. Fleming, "Creating a 'Super' Agency in San Diego County," *The Public Manager* (Fall 2008): 21–26.

31. B. A. Pasternack and A. J. Viscio, *The Centerless Corporation: A New Model for Transforming Your Organization for Growth and Prosperity* (New York: Simon & Schuster, 1999).

32. J. Woodward, *Industrial Organization: Theory and Practices* (London: Oxford University Press, 1965).

33. C. Perrow, "A Framework for the Comparative Analysis of Organizations," *American Sociological Review* 32 (1967): 194–208; D. Rosseau, "Assessment of Technology in Organizations: Closed versus Open Systems Approaches," *Academy of Management Review* 4 (1979): 531–542.

34. Perrow, "A Framework for the Comparative Analysis of Organizations," 194–208.

35. J. D. Thompson, *Organizations in Action* (New York: McGraw-Hill, 1967).

36. P. Nemetz and L. Fry, "Flexible Manufacturing Organizations: Implication for Strategy Formulation and Organization Design," *Academy of Management Review* 13 (1988): 627–638; G. Huber, "The Nature and Design of Post-Industrial Organizations," *Management Science* 30 (1984): 934.

37. E. Feitzinger and H. L. Lee, "Mass Customization at Hewlett-Packard: The Power of Postponement," *Harvard Business Review* 75 (1997): 116–121.

38. S. M. Davis, *Future Perfect* (Reading, MA: Addison-Wesley, 1987).

39. J. R. Baum and S. Wally, "Strategic Decision Speed and Firm Performance," *Strategic Management Journal* 24 (2003): 1107–1129.

40. Thompson, *Organizations in Action*.

41. H. Downey, D. Hellriegel, and J. Slocum, Jr., "Environmental Uncertainty: The Construct and Its Application," *Administrative Science Quarterly* 20 (1975): 613–629.

42. G. Vroom, "Organizational Design and the Intensity of Rivalry," *Management Science* 52 (2006): 1689–1702.

43. S. Faraj and Y. Xiao, "Coordination in Fast-Response Organizations," *Management Science* 52 (2006): 1155–1169.

44. T. Burns and G. Stalker, *The Management of Innovation* (London: Tavistock, 1961); Mintzberg, *Structuring of Organizations*.

45. M. Chandler and L. Sayles, *Managing Large Systems* (New York: Harper & Row, 1971).

46. M. Sanchez-Manzanares, R. Rico, and F. Gil, "Designing Organizations: Does Expertise Matter?," *Journal of Business Psychology* 23 (2008): 87–101.

47. G. Dess and D. Beard, "Dimensions of Organizational Task Environments," *Administrative Science Quarterly* 29 (1984): 52–73.

48. J. Courtright, G. Fairhurst, and L. Rogers, "Interaction Patterns in Organic and Mechanistic Systems," *Academy of Management Journal* 32 (1989): 773–802.

49. R. Daft, *Organization Theory and Design*, 7th ed. (Mason, OH: South-Western/Thomson Learning, 2000).

50. D. Miller, "The Structural and Environmental Correlates of Business Strategy," *Strategic Management Journal* 8 (1987): 55–76.

51. L. Pleshko, and I. Nickerson, "Strategic Orientation, Organizational Structure, and the Associated Effects on Performance in Industrial Firms," *Academy of Strategic Management Journal* 7 (2008): 95–110.

52. R. S. Kaplan and D. P. Norton, "How to Implement a New Strategy without Disrupting Your Organization," *Harvard Business Review* (March 2006): 100–109.

53. W. R. Scott, *Organizations: Rational, Natural, and Open Systems*, 4th ed. (Upper Saddle River, NJ: Prentice Hall, 1997).

54. D. Miller and P. Friesen, "A Longitudinal Study of the Corporate Life Cycle," *Management Science* 30 (1984): 1161–1183.

55. S. Raisch, "Balanced structures: Designing Organizations for Profitable Growth," *Long Range Planning* 41 (2008): 483–508.

56. M. H. Overholt, "Flexible Organizations: Using Organizational Design as a Competitive Advantage," *Human Resource Planning* 20 (1997): 22–32; P. W. Roberts and R. Greenwood, "Integrating Transaction Cost and Institutional Theories: Toward a Constrained-Efficiency Framework for Understanding Organizational Design Adoption," *Academy of Management Review* 22 (1997): 346–373.

57. G. Davidson, "Organisation Structure: The Life Cycle of an Organization," *New Zealand Management* 56 (2008): 58–60.

58. C. W. L. Hill and G. R. Jones, *Strategic Management Theory*, 5th ed. (Boston: Houghton Mifflin, 2000).

59. F. Hoque, "Designing the Right Kind of Organization," *Baseline* (January/February 2009): 46.

60. Daft, *Organization Theory and Design*.

61. C. M. Savage, *5th Generation Management, Revised Edition: Co-creating through Virtual Enterprising, Dynamic Teaming, and Knowledge Networking* (Boston: Butterworth-Heinemann, 1996).

62. S. M. Davis, *Future Perfect* (Perseus Publishing, 1997).

63. A. Boynton and B. Victor, "Beyond Flexibility: Building and Managing a Dynamically Stable Organization," *California Management Review* 8 (Fall 1991): 53–66.

64. P. J. Brews and C. L. Tucci, "Exploring the Structural Effects of Internetworking," *Strategic Management Journal* 25 (2004): 429–451.

65. J. Fulk, "Global Network Organizations: Emergence and Future Prospects," *Human Relations* 54 (2001): 91–100.

66. C. B. Gibson and J. L. Gibbs, "Unpacking the Concept of Virtuality: Geographic Dispersion, Electronic Dependence, Dynamic Structure, and National Diversity on Team Innovation," *Administrative Science Quarterly* 51 (2006): 451–495.

67. The use of the theatrical troupe as an analogy for virtual organizations was first used by David Mack, circa 1995.

68. E. C. Kasper-Fuehrer and N. M. Ashkanasy, "Communicating Trustworthiness and Building Trust in Interorganizational Virtual Organizations," *Journal of Management* 27 (2001): 235–254.

69. R. Teerlink and L. Ozley, *More than a Motorcycle: The Leadership Journey at Harley-Davidson* (Boston: Harvard Business School Press, 2000).

70. W. A. Cohen and N. Cohen, *The Paranoid Organization and 8 Other Ways Your Company Can Be Crazy: Advice from an Organizational Shrink* (New York: American Management Association, 1993).

71. P. E. Tetlock, "Cognitive Biases and Organizational Correctives: Do Both Disease and Cure Depend on the Politics of the Beholder?" *Administrative Science Quarterly* 45 (2000): 293–326.

72. M. F. R. Kets de Vries and D. Miller, "Personality, Culture, and Organization," *Academy of Management Review* 11 (1986): 266–279.

73. K. Frankola, "How Deloitte Build Video into the Corporate Strategy," *Strategic Communication Management* 13 (2009): 28–31.

Chapter 15 Case

1. National Aeronautics and Space Administration, *2006 NASA Strategic Plan*, http://www.nasa.gov/pdf/142302main_NASA_Strategic_Plan.pdf (accessed August 1, 2009): 4.

2. Ibid., pp. 35–36.

3. G. B. Friesen, "Organization Design for the 21st Century," *Consulting to Management* 16(3) (September, 2005): 32.

4. Ibid., p. 50.

5. Goddard Space Flight Center, "Administrator Unveils Next Steps of NASA Transformation," *Goddard News* 1(7) (July, 2004): 1.

6. Ibid.

7. Ibid.; National Aeronautics and Space Administration, *2006 NASA Strategic Plan*, 22.

8. T. N. Carroll, T. J. Gormley, V. J. Bilardo, R. M. Burton, and K. L. Woodman, "Designing a New Organization at NASA: An Organization Design Process Using Simulation," *Organization Science* 17(2): 203.

9. National Aeronautics and Space Administration, *2006 NASA Strategic Plan*, 23.

10. Ibid., p. 22.

11. Ibid.

12. Ibid., p. 23.

Chapter 16

1. T. E. Deal and A. A. Kennedy, *Corporate Cultures* (Reading, MA: Addison-Wesley, 1982).

2. W. Ouchi, *Theory Z* (Reading, MA: Addison-Wesley, 1981).

3. T. J. Peters and R. H. Waterman, *In Search of Excellence* (New York: Harper & Row, 1982).

4. M. Gardner, "Creating a Corporate Culture for the Eighties," *Business Horizons* (January–February 1985): 59–63.

5. Definition adapted from E. H. Schein, *Organizational Culture and Leadership* (San Francisco: Jossey-Bass, 1985), 9.

6. C. D. Sutton and D. L. Nelson, "Elements of the Cultural Network: The Communicators of Corporate Values," *Leadership and Organization Development* 11 (1990): 3–10.

7. M. Gunther, "At IKEA, green is gold" *Fortune Magazine* (November, 26, 2008) http://money.cnn.com/2008/11/25/news/companies/gunther_ikea.fortune/

8. http://www.google.com/corporate/culture.html.

9. J. Pagel, "Eskimo Joe's Getting Older, But Still Fun at 21," Amarillo *Business Journal* (November 20, 1996), http://www.businessjournal.net/entrepreneur1196.html.

10. A. Bandura, *Social Learning Theory* (Englewood Cliffs, NJ: Prentice Hall, 1977).

11. J. A. Chatman, "Leading by Leveraging Culture," *California Management Review* 45 (2003): 20–34.

12. J. M. Beyer and H. M. Trice, "How an Organization's Rites Reveal Its Culture," *Organizational Dynamics* 16 (1987): 5–24.

13. H. M. Trice and J. M. Beyer, "Studying Organizational Cultures through Rites and Ceremonials," *Academy of Management Review* 9 (1984): 653–669.

14. 16. H. Levinson and S. Rosenthal, *CEO: Corporate Leadership in Action* (New York: Basic Books, 1984).

15. K. Rockwood, "Meet the Famous Faces at Berkshire Hathaway's Annual Meeting," *Fast Company*, (May 2009), http://www.fastcompany.com/magazine/135/gather-berkshire-hathaway-annual-meeting.html.

16. V. Sathe, "Implications of Corporate Culture: A Manager's Guide to Action," *Organizational Dynamics* 12 (1987): 5–23.

17. "Wal-Mart Culture Stories—The Sundown Rule," http://www.wal-martchina.com/english/walmart/rule/sun.htm.

18. J. Martin, M. S. Feldman, M. J. Hatch, and S. B. Sitkin, "The Uniqueness Paradox in Organizational Stories," *Administrative Science Quarterly* 28 (1983): 438–453.

19. J. Lofstock, "Aplauding the QuikTrip Culture" http://www.quiktrip.com/aboutqt/news.asp

20. L. Story, "Cuomo Details Million-Dollar Bonuses at A.I.G." *New York Times* (March 17, 2009), http://www.nytimes.com/2009/03/18/business/18cuomo.html.

21. http://news-service.stanford.edu/news/2005/june15/jobs-061505.html.

22. B. Durrance, "Stories at Work," *Training and Development* (February 1997): 25–29.

23. B. Siuru, "2003 Saturn L Series," http://www.autowire.net/2002-40.html.

24. R. Goffee and G. Jones, "What Holds the Modern Company Together?" *Harvard Business Review* (November–December 1996): 133–143.

24. G. Islam and M. J. Zyphur, "Rituals in Organizations: A Review and Expansion of Current Theory," *Group and Organization Management* 34 (2009): 114–139.

25. C. Argyris and D. A. Schon, *Organizational Learning* (Reading, MA: Addison-Wesley, 1978).

26. L. Hoeber, "Exploring the Gaps between Meanings and Practices of Gender Equity in a Sport Organization," *Gender Work and Organization* 14(3) (2007): 259–280.

27. D. J. McAllister and G. A. Bigley, "Work Context and the Definition of Self: How Organizational Care Influences Organization-Based Self-Esteem," *Academy of Management Journal* 45 (2002): 894–905.

28. http://www.wholefoodsmarket.com/company/corevalues.php

28. "Sounds Like a New Woman," *New Woman* (February 1993): 144.

29. M. Peterson, "Work, Corporate Culture, and Stress: Implications for Worksite Health Promotion," *American Journal of Health Behavior* 21 (1997): 243–252.

30. R. Targos, "Big Bad Hog—Harley-Davidson Customer Service," *Child Care Business*, http://www.childcarebusiness.com/articles/161cover.html.

31. J. Rosenthal and M. A. Masarech, "High-Performance Cultures: How Values Can Drive Business Results," *Journal of Organizational Excellence* (Spring 2003): 3–18.

32. http://money.cnn.com/magazines/fortune/bestcompanies/2009/snapshots/1.html

33. L. Smircich, "Concepts of Culture and Organizational Analysis," *Administrative Science Quarterly* (1983): 339–358.

34. Y. Weiner and Y. Vardi, "Relationships between Organizational Culture and Individual Motivation: A Conceptual Integration," *Psychological Reports* 67 (1990): 295–306.

35. M. R. Louis, "Surprise and Sense Making: What Newcomers Experience in Entering Unfamiliar Organizational Settings," *Administrative Science Quarterly* 25 (1980): 209–264.

36. D. Ravasi and M. Schultz, "Responding to Organizational Identity Threats: Exploring the Role of Organizational Culture," *Academy of Management Journal*, 49(3) (2006): 433–458.

37. http://www.mcdonalds.com/corp/about/mcd_history_pg1.html.

38. T. L. Doolen, M. E. Hacker, and E. M. van Aken, "The Impact of Organizational Context on Work Team Effectiveness: A Study of Production Teams," *IEEE Transactions on Engineering Management* 50 (2003): 285–296.

39. D. D. Van Fleet and R. W. Griffin, "Dysfunctional Organization Culture: The Role of Leadership in Motivating Dysfunctional Work Behaviors," *Journal of Managerial Psychology* 21(8) (2006): 698–708.

40. P. Bamberger and M. Biron, "Group Norms and Excessive Absenteeism: The Role of Peer Referent Others," *Organizational Behavior and Human Decision Processes* 103(2) (2007): 179–196.

41. J. P. Kotter and J. L. Heskett, *Corporate Culture and Performance* (New York: Free Press, 1992).

42. Deal and Kennedy, *Corporate Cultures*.

43. D. R. Katz, *The Big Store* (New York: Viking, 1987).

44. G. G. Gordon, "Industry Determinants of Organizational Culture," *Academy of Management Review* 16 (1991): 396–415.

45. G. Donaldson and J. Lorsch, *Decision Making at the Top* (New York: Basic Books, 1983).

46. R. H. Kilman, M. J. Saxton, and R. Serpa, eds., *Gaining Control of the Corporate Culture* (San Francisco: Jossey-Bass, 1986).

47. J. P. Kotter, *A Force for Change: How Leadership Differs from Management* (New York: Free Press, 1990); R. M. Kanter, *The Change Masters* (New York: Simon & Schuster, 1983).

48. T. Peters and N. Austin, *A Passion for Excellence: The Leadership Difference* (New York: Random House, 1985).

49. Schein, *Organizational Culture and Leadership*.

50. R. R. Sims and J. Brinkmann, "Enron Ethics (or Culture Matters More than Codes)," *Journal of Business Ethics* 45 (2003): 243–256.

51. M. H. Kavanagh and N. M. Ashkanasy, "The Impact of Leadership and Change Management Strategy on Organizational Culture and Individual Acceptance of Change during a Merger," *British Journal of Management Supplement* 17(1) (2006): S81–S103.

52. J. A. Pearce II, T. R. Kramer, and D. K. Robbins, "Effects of Managers' Entrepreneurial Behavior on Subordinates," *Journal of Business Venturing* 12 (1997): 147–160.

53. P. W. Braddy, A. W. Meade, and C. M. Kroustalis, "Organizational Recruitment Website Effects on Viewers' Perceptions of Organizational Culture," *Journal of Business and Psychology* 20(4) (2006): 525–543.

54. http://money.cnn.com/magazines/fortune/fortune_archive/2006/01/23/8366992/index.htm.

55. A. Xenikou and M. Simosi, "Organizational Culture and Transformational Leadership as Predictors of Business Unit Performance," *Journal of Managerial Psychology* 21(6) (2006): 566–579.

56. D. C. Feldman, "The Multiple Socialization of Organization Members," *Academy of Management Review* 6 (1981): 309–318.

57. R. Pascale, "The Paradox of Corporate Culture: Reconciling Ourselves to Socialization," *California Management Review* 27 (1985): 26–41.

58. D. L. Nelson, "Organizational Socialization: A Stress Perspective," *Journal of Occupational Behavior* 8 (1987): 311–324.

59. J. Fan and J. P. Wanous, "Organizational and Cultural Entry: A New Type of Orientation Program for Multiple Boundary Crossings," *Journal of Applied Psychology* 93 (2008): 1390–1400.

60. D. M. Cable, L. Aiman-Smith, P. W. Mulvey, and J. R. Edwards, "The Sources and Accuracy of Job Applicants' Beliefs about Organizational Culture," *Academy of Management Journal* 43 (2000): 1076–1085.

61. J. Chatman, "Matching People and Organizations: Selection and Socialization in Public Accounting Firms," *Administrative Science Quarterly* 36 (1991): 459–484.

62. D. L. Nelson, J. C. Quick, and M. E. Eakin, "A Longitudinal Study of Newcomer Role Adjustment in U.S. Organizations," *Work and Stress* 2 (1988): 239–253.

63. N. J. Allen and J. P. Meyer, "Organizational Socialization Tactics: A Longitudinal Analysis of Links to Newcomers' Commitment and Role Orientation," *Academy of Management Journal* 33 (1990): 847–858.

64. T. N. Bauer, E. W. Morrison, and R. R. Callister, "Organizational Socialization: A Review and Directions for Future Research," *Research in Personnel and Human Resources Management* 16 (1998): 149–214.

65. D. M. Cable and C. K. Parsons, "Socialization Tactics and Person–Organization Fit," *Personnel Psychology* 54 (2001): 1–23.

66. M. R. Louis, "Acculturation in the Workplace: Newcomers as Lay Ethnographers," in B. Schneider, ed., *Organizational Climate and Culture* (San Francisco: Jossey-Bass, 1990), 85–129.

67. D. M. Rousseau, "Assessing Organizational Culture: The Case for Multiple Methods," in B. Schneider, ed., *Organizational Climate and Culture* (San Francisco: Jossey-Bass, 1990).

68. R. A. Cooke and D. M. Rousseau, "Behavioral Norms and Expectations: A Quantitative Approach to the Assessment of Organizational Culture," *Group and Organizational Studies* 12 (1988): 245–273.

69. R. H. Kilmann and M. J. Saxton, *Kilmann-Saxton Culture-Gap Survey* (Pittsburgh: Organizational Design Consultants, 1983).

70. W. J. Duncan, "Organizational Culture: 'Getting a Fix' on an Elusive Concept," *Academy of Management Executive* 3 (1989): 229–236.

71. C. Yang, "Merger of Titans, Clash of Cultures," *Business Week Online* (July 14, 2003), http://www.businessweek.com/magazine/content/03_8/b3841042_mz005.htm.

72. R. A. Weber and C. F. Camerer, "Cultural Conflict and Merger Failure: An Experimental Approach," *Management Science* 49 (2003): 400–415.

73. S. Buchheit, W. R. Pasewark, and J. R. Strawser, "No Need to Compromise: Evidence of Public Accounting's Changing Culture Regarding Budgetary Performance," *Journal of Business Ethics* 42 (2003): 151–163.

74. N. J. Adler, *International Dimensions of Organizational Behavior*, 2nd ed. (Boston: PWS Kent, 1991).

75. A. Laurent, "The Cultural Diversity of Western Conceptions of Management," *International Studies of Management and Organization* 13 (1983): 75–96.

76. P. C. Earley and E. Mosakowski, "Creating Hybrid Team Cultures: An Empirical Test of Transnational Team Functioning," *Academy of Management Journal* 43 (2000): 26–49.

77. P. Bate, "Using the Culture Concept in an Organization Development Setting," *Journal of Applied Behavior Science* 26 (1990): 83–106.

78. K. R. Thompson and F. Luthans, "Organizational Culture: A Behavioral Perspective," in B. Schneider, ed., *Organizational Climate and Culture* (San Francisco: Jossey-Bass, 1990).

79. S. Seren and U. Baykal, "Relationships between Change and Organizational Culture in Hospitals," *Journal of Nursing Scholarship* 39(2) (2007): 191–197.

80. V. Sathe, "How to Decipher and Change Corporate Culture," in R. H. Kilman et al., ed., *Managing Corporate Cultures* (San Francisco: Jossey-Bass, 1985).

81. M. E. Johnson-Cramer, S. Parise, and R. L. Cross, "Managing Change through Networks and Values," *California Management Review* 49(3) (2007): 85–109.

82. D. Lei, J. W. Slocum, Jr., and R. W. Slater, "Global Strategy and Reward Systems: The Key Roles of Management Development and Corporate Culture," *Organizational Dynamics* 19 (1990): 27–41.

83. S. H. Rhinesmith, "Going Global from the Inside Out," *Training and Development Journal* 45 (1991): 42–47.

84. A. Pater and A. van Gils, "Stimulating Ethical Decision Making in a Business Context: Ethics of Ethical and Professional Codes," *European Management Journal* 21 (December 2003): 762–772.

85. L. K. Trevino and K. A. Nelson, *Managing Business Ethics: Straight Talk about How to Do It Right* (New York: John Wiley & Sons, 1995).

86. A. Bhide and H. H. Stevenson, "Why Be Honest if Honesty Doesn't Pay?" *Harvard Business Review* (September–October 1990): 121–129.

87. C. Driscoll and M. McKee, "Restoring a Culture of Ethical and Spiritual Values: A Role for Leader Storytelling," *Journal of Business Ethics* 73(2) (2007): 205–217.

88. C. Gallo, "How Cisco's CEO Works the Crowd," *Business Week* (October, 11, 2006), http://www.businessweek.com/smallbiz/content/oct2006/sb20061011_917113.htm?campaign_id=nws_insdr_oct13&link_position=link15.

89. S. W. Gellerman, "Why Good Managers Make Bad Ethical Choices," *Harvard Business Review* 64 (1986): 85–90.

90. J. R. Detert, R. G. Schroeder, and J. J. Mauriel, "A Framework for Linking Culture and Improvement Initiatives in Organizations," *Academy of Management Review* 25 (2000): 850–863.

91. S. D. Salamon and S. L. Robinson, "Trust that Binds: The Impact of Collective Felt Trust on Organizational Performance," *Journal of Applied Psychology* 93 (2008): 593–601.

92. P. Panchak, "Executive Word—Manufacturing in the U.S. Pays Off," *Industry Week* (December 1, 2002), http://www.industryweek.com /CurrentArticles/Asp/articles.asp?ArticleId=1365.

93. A. Bernstein, "Low-Skilled Jobs: Do They Have to Move?" *Business Week* (February 26, 2001): 92.

94. R. Bruce, "A Case Study of Harley-Davidson's Business Practices," http://stroked.virtualave.net/casestudy.shtml.

95. T. A. Williams, "Do You Believe in Baldrige?" *Quality Magazine* 43 (2004): 6.

96. R. Spector and P. McCarthy, *The Nordstrom Way to Customer Service Excellence* (Hobokan, New Jersey: John Wiley & Sons, Inc, 2005).

Chapter 16 Case

1. "Special Report: The Car Company in Front—Toyota," *The Economist* 374(8411) (January 29, 2005): 73.

2. Toyota Motor Corporation, "Company Profile: Overview," *Toyota*, http://www2.toyota.co.jp/en/about_toyota/overview/index.html (accessed July 31, 2009).

3. "Survey: Inculcating Culture," *The Economist* 378(8461) (January 21, 2006): 13.

4. "Special Report: The Car Company in Front—Toyota."

5. Ibid.

6. J. K. Liker, *The Toyota Way* (New York: McGraw-Hill, 2003), pp. 37–41.

7. C. Fishman, "No satisfaction," *Fast Company* (111) (December 2006/January 2007): 86. C.

8. A. Smalley and T. Harada, "Lean Lives on the Floor," *Manufacturing Engineering* 142(5) (May 2009): 83.

9. "Special Report: The Car Company in Front—Toyota."

10. S. Cook, S. Macaulay, and H. Coldicott, "Facing the Devil in the Detail," *Training Journal* (October 2005): 33.

11. N. Shirouzu, "Paranoid Tendency: As Rivals Catch Up, Toyota CEO Spurs Big Efficiency Drive; Culture of Institutional Worry Drives Mr. Watanabe; How Paint Is Like 'Fondue'; Finding Limits to Improvement," *Wall Street Journal* (Eastern edition) (December 9, 2006): A1.

12. N. Shirouzu, "Paranoid Tendency."

13. C. Fishman, "No satisfaction," p. 87.

14. "A Wobble on the Road to the Top—Toyota," *The Economist* 385(8554) (November 10, 2007): 105.

15. I. Rowley, "Even Toyota Isn't Perfect; A Raft of Recalls Lately Has It Scrambling to Safeguard Its Reputation for Quality," *Business Week* (4018) (January 22, 2007): 54.

16. N. Shirouzu, "Paranoid Tendency."

Chapter 17

1. http://www.careerbuilder.com/Article/CB-1337-Getting-Hired-More-Employers-Screening-Candidates-via-Social-Networking-Sites/

2. http://www.naceweb.org/press/display.asp?year=&prid=2873.

3. http://scitech.blogs.cnn.com/2009/04/22/have-you-seen-a-facebook-ghost/

4. J. H. Greenhaus, *Career Management* (Hinsdale, IL: CBS College Press, 1987).

5. D. T. Hall, *Careers in Organizations* (Pacific Palisades, CA: Goodyear, 1976).

6. J. H. Greenhaus, *Career Management*; T. G. Gutteridge and F. L. Otte, "Organizational Career Development: What's Going On Out There?" *Training and Development Journal* 37 (1983): 22–26.

7. M. B. Arthur, P. H. Claman, and R. J. DeFillippi, "Intelligent Enterprise, Intelligent Careers," *Academy of Management Executive* (November 1995): 7–22.

8. M. Lips-Wiersma and D. T. Hall, "Organizational Career Development Is Not Dead: A Case Study on Managing the New Career During Organizational Change," *Journal of Organizational Behavior* 28(6) (2007): 771–792.

9. D. Jemielniak, "Managers as Lazy, Stupid Careerists?" *Journal of Organizational Change Management* 20(4) (2007): 491–508.

10. T. Lee, "Should You Stay Energized by Changing Jobs Frequently?" *CareerJournal* (January 11, 1998), http://www.careerjournal.com/jobhunting/strategies/19980111-reisberg.html.

11. P. Buhler, "Managing in the '90s," *Supervision* (July 1995): 24–26.

12. D. T. Hall and J. E. Moss, "The New Protean Career Contract: Helping Organizations and Employees Adapt," *Organizational Dynamics* (Winter 1998): 22–37.

13. S. A. Zahra, R. L. Priem, and A. A. Rasheed, "Understanding the Causes and Effects of Top Management Fraud," *Organizational Dynamics* 36(2) (2007): 122–139.

14. A. Fisher, "Don't Blow Your New Job," *Fortune* (June 22, 1998): 159–162.

15. D. Goleman, *Working with Emotional Intelligence* (New York: Bantam, 1998).

16. A. Fisher, "Success Secret: A High Emotional IQ," *Fortune* (October 26, 1998): 293–298.

17. M. L. Maynard, "Emotional Intelligence and Perceived Employability for Internship Curriculum," *Psychological Reports* 93 (December 2003): 791–792.

18. K. V. Petrides, A. Furnham, and G. N. Martin, "Estimates of Emotional and Psychometric Intelligence," *Journal of Social Psychology* 144 (April 2004): 149–162.

19. C. Stough and D. de Guara, "Examining the Relationship between Emotional Intelligence and Job Performance," *Australian Journal of Psychology* 55 (2003): 145.

20. C. Chermiss, "The Business Case for Emotional Intelligence," *The Consortium for Research on Emotional Intelligence in Organizations* (2003), http://www.eiconsortium.org/research/business_case_for_ei.htm; L. M. Spencer, Jr. and S. Spencer, *Competence at Work: Models*

for *Superior Performance* (New York: John Wiley & Sons, 1993); L. M. Spencer, Jr., D. C. McClelland, and S. Kelner, *Competency Assessment Methods: History and State of the Art* (Boston: Hay/McBer, 1997).

21. Chermiss, "The Business Case for Emotional Intelligence."

22. D. E. Super, *The Psychology of Careers* (New York: Harper & Row, 1957); D. E. Super and M. J. Bohn, Jr., *Occupational Psychology* (Belmont, CA: Wadsworth, 1970).

23. J. L. Holland, *The Psychology of Vocational Choice* (Waltham, MA: Blaisdell, 1966); J. L. Holland, *Making Vocational Choices: A Theory of Careers* (Englewood Cliffs, NJ: Prentice Hall, 1973).

24. F. T. L. Leong and J. T. Austin, "An Evaluation of the Cross-Cultural Validity of Holland's Theory: Career Choices by Workers in India," *Journal of Vocational Behavior* 52 (1998): 441–455.

25. C. Morgan, J. D. Isaac, and C. Sansone, "The Role of Interest in Understanding the Career Choices of Female and Male College Students," *Sex Roles* 44 (2001): 295–320.

26. S. H. Osipow, *Theories of Career Development* (Englewood Cliffs, NJ: Prentice Hall, 1973).

27. J. P. Wanous, T. L. Keon, and J. C. Latack, "Expectancy Theory and Occupational/Organizational Choices: A Review and Test," *Organizational Behavior and Human Performance* 32 (1983): 66–86.

28. P. O. Soelberg, "Unprogrammed Decision Making," *Industrial Management Review* 8 (1967): 19–29.

29. J. P. Wanous, *Organizational Entry: Recruitment, Selection, and Socialization of Newcomers* (Reading, MA: Addison-Wesley, 1980).

30. S. L. Premack and J. P. Wanous, "A Meta-Analysis of Realistic Job Preview Experiments," *Journal of Applied Psychology* 70 (1985): 706–719.

31. Idaho State Police, "Realistic Job Preview," http://www.isp.state.id.us/hr/trooper_info/realistic_job.html.

32. P. W. Hom, R. W. Griffeth, L. E. Palich, and J. S. Bracker, "An Exploratory Investigation into Theoretical Mechanisms Underlying Realistic Job Previews," *Personnel Psychology* 41 (1998): 421–451.

33. J. A. Breaugh, "Realistic Job Previews: A Critical Appraisal and Future Research Directions," *Academy of Management Review* 8 (1983): 612–619.

34. G. R. Jones, "Socialization Tactics, Self-Efficacy, and Newcomers' Adjustment to Organizations," *Academy of Management Journal* 29 (1986): 262–279.

35. M. R. Buckley, D. B. Fedor, J. G. Veres, D. S. Wiese, and S. M. Carraher, "Investigating Newcomer Expectations and Job-Related Outcomes," *Journal of Applied Psychology* 83 (1998): 452–461.

36. M. R. Buckley, D. B. Fedor, S. M. Carraher, D. D. Frink, and D. Marvin, "The Ethical Imperative to Provide Recruits Realistic Job Previews," *Journal of Managerial Issues* 9 (1997): 468–484.

37. J. O. Crites, "A Comprehensive Model of Career Adjustment in Early Adulthood," *Journal of Vocational Behavior* 9 (1976): 105–118; S. Cytrynbaum and J. O. Crites, "The Utility of Adult Development in Understanding Career Adjustment Process," in M. B. Arthur, D. T. Hall, and B. S. Lawrence, eds., *Handbook of Career Theory* (Cambridge: Cambridge University Press, 1989), 66–88.

38. D. E. Super, "A Life-Span, Life-Space Approach to Career Development," *Journal of Vocational Behavior* 16 (1980): 282–298; L. Baird and K. Kram, "Career Dynamics: Managing the Superior/Subordinate Relationship," *Organizational Dynamics* 11 (1983): 46–64.

39. D. J. Levinson, *The Seasons of a Man's Life* (New York: Knopf, 1978); D. J. Levinson, *The Seasons of a Woman's Life* (New York, NY: Alfred A. Knopf, 1997).

40. D. J. Levinson, "A Conception of Adult Development," *American Psychologist* 41 (1986): 3–13.

41. D. L. Nelson, "Adjusting to a New Organization: Easing the Transition from Outsider to Insider," in J. C. Quick, R. E. Hess, J. Hermalin, and J. D. Quick, eds., *Career Stress in Changing Times* (New York: Haworth Press, 1990), 61–86.

42. J. P. Kotter, "The Psychological Contract: Managing the Joining Up Process," *California Management Review* 15 (1973): 91–99.

43. D. M. Rousseau, "New Hire Perceptions of Their Own and Their Employers' Obligations: A Study of Psychological Contracts," *Journal of Organizational Behavior* 11 (1990): 389–400; D. L. Nelson, J. C.

Quick, and J. R. Joplin, "Psychological Contracting and Newcomer Socialization: An Attachment Theory Foundation," *Journal of Social Behavior and Personality* 6 (1991): 55–72.

44. H. Zhao, S. Wayne, B. Glibkowski, and J. Bravo "The Impact of Psychological Breach on Work-Related Outcomes" *Personnel Psychology* 60 (2007): 647–680.

45. S. D. Pugh, D. P. Skarlicki, and B. S. Passell, "After the Fall: Layoff Victims' Trust and Cynicism in Reemployment," *Journal of Occupational and Organizational Psychology* 76 (June 2003): 201–212.

46. D. L. Nelson, "Organizational Socialization: A Stress Perspective," *Journal of Occupational Behavior* 8 (1987): 311–324.

47. R. A. Dean, K. R. Ferris, and C. Konstans, "Reality Shock: Reducing the Organizational Commitment of Professionals," *Personnel Administrator* 30 (1985): 139–148.

48. Nelson, "Adjusting to a New Organization," 61–86.

49. G. Chen and R. J. Kilmoski, "The Impact of Expectations on Newcomer Performance in Teams as Mediated by Work Characteristics, Social Exchanges, and Empowerment," *Academy of Management Journal* 46 (October 2003): 591–607.

50. D. L. Nelson and C. D. Sutton, "The Relationship between Newcomer Expectations of Job Stressors and Adjustment to the New Job," *Work and Stress* 5 (1991): 241–254.

51. T. Kim, A. Hon, and J. M. Crant, "Proactive Personality, Employee Creativity, and Newcomer Outcomes: A Longitudinal Study," *Journal of Business and Psychology* 24 (2009): 93–103

52. A. M. Saks, "Longitudinal Field Investigation of the Moderating and Mediating Effects of Self-Efficacy on the Relationship between Training and Newcomer Adjustment," *Journal of Applied Psychology* 80 (1995): 211–225.

53. G. F. Dreher and R. D. Bretz, Jr., "Cognitive Ability and Career Attainment: Moderating Effects of Early Career Success," *Journal of Applied Psychology* 76 (1991): 392–397.

54. D. L. Nelson and J. C. Quick, "Social Support and Newcomer Adjustment in Organizations: Attachment Theory at Work?" *Journal of Organizational Behavior* 12 (1991): 543–554.

55. Author conversation with Mark Phillips, Assistant Professor of Management, Abilene Christian University (July 2004).

56. TechRepublic Staff, "Most Organizations Wing It with New Employees," *TechRepublic* (April 5, 2002), http://techrepublic.com.com/5100-6317_111051414.html.

57. R. Pascale, "The Paradox of Corporate Culture: Reconciling Ourselves to Socialization," *California Management Review* 27 (1985): 27–41.

58. M. Jokisaari and J. Nurmi, "Change in Newcomers' Supervisor Support and Socialization Outcomes after Organizational Entry," *Academy of Management Journal* 52 (2009): 527–544.

59. K. M. Davey and J. Arnold, "A Multi-Method Study of Accounts of Personal Change by Graduates Starting Work: Self-Ratings, Categories, and Women's Discourses," *Journal of Occupational and Organizational Psychology* 73 (2000): 461–486.

60. Levinson, "A Conception of Adult Development," 3–13.

61. J. W. Walker, "Let's Get Realistic about Career Paths," *Human Resource Management* 15 (1976): 2–7.

62. E. H. Buttner and D. P. Moore, "Women's Organizational Exodus to Entrepreneurship: Self-Reported Motivations and Correlates," *Journal of Small Business Management* 35 (1997): 34–46; Center for Women's Business Research Press Release, "Privately Held, 50% or More Women-Owned Businesses in the United States" (2004), http://www.nfwbo.org/pressreleases/nationalstatetrends/total.htm.

63. D. G. Collings, H. Scullion, and M. J. Morley, "Changing Patterns of Global Staffing in the Multinational Enterprise: Challenges to the Conventional Expatriate Assignment and Emerging Alternatives," *Journal of World Business* 42(2) (2007): 198–213.

64. B. Filipczak, "You're on Your Own," *Training* (January 1995): 29–36.

65. K. E. Kram, *Mentoring at Work: Developmental Relationships in Organizational Life* (Glenview, IL: Scott, Foresman, 1985).

66. C. Orpen, "The Effects of Monitoring on Employees' Career Success," *Journal of Social Psychology* 135 (1995): 667–668.

67. J. Arnold and K. Johnson, "Mentoring in Early Career," *Human Resource Management Journal* 7 (1997): 61–70.

68. B. P. Madia and C. J. Lutz, "Perceived Similarity, Expectation–Reality Discrepancies, and Mentors' Expressed Intention to Remain in the Big Brothers/Big Sisters Programs," *Journal of Applied Social Psychology* 34 (March 2004): 598–622.

69. "A Guide to the Mentor Program Listings," *Mentors Peer Resources*, http://www.mentors.ca/mentorprograms.html.

70. B. R. Ragins, "Diversified Mentoring Relationships in Organizations: A Power Perspective," *Academy of Management Review* 22 (1997): 482–521.

71. R. Friedman, M. Kan, and D. B. Cornfield, "Social Support and Career Optimism: Examining the Effectiveness of Network Groups among Black Managers," *Human Relations* 51 (1998): 1155–1177.

72. http://content.dell.com/us/en/corp/cr-diversity-employee-resource-groups.aspx

73. S. E. Seibert, M. L. Kraimer, and R. C. Liden, "A Social Capital Theory of Career Success," *Academy of Management Journal* 44 (2001): 219–237.

74. PricewaterhouseCoopers Czech Republic, "Graduate Recruitment— FAQs," http://www.pwcglobal.com/cz/eng/car-inexp/main/faq.html.

75. M. A. Covaleski, M. W. Dirsmuth, J. B. Heian, and S. Samuel, "The Calculated and the Avowed: Techniques of Discipline and Struggles over Identity in Big Six Public Accounting Firms," *Administrative Science Quarterly* 43 (1998): 293–327.

76. B. R. Ragins and J. L. Cotton, "Easier Said Than Done: Gender Differences in Perceived Barriers to Gaining a Mentor," *Academy of Management Journal* 34 (1991): 939–951; S. D. Phillips and A. R. Imhoff, "Women and Career Development: A Decade of Research," *Annual Review of Psychology* 48 (1997): 31–4.

77. W. Whiteley, T. W. Dougherty, and G. F. Dreher, "Relationship of Career Mentoring and Socioeconomic Origin to Managers' and Professionals' Early Career Progress," *Academy of Management Journal* 34 (1991): 331–351; G. F. Dreher and R. A. Ash, "A Comparative Study of Mentoring among Men and Women in Managerial, Professional, and Technical Positions," *Journal of Applied Psychology* 75 (1990): 539–546; T. A. Scandura, "Mentorship and Career Mobility: An Empirical Investigation," *Journal of Organizational Behavior* 13 (1992): 169–174.

78. R. Singh, B. R. Regins, and P. Tharenou "What Matters Most? The Relative Role of Mentoring and Career Capital in Career Success," *Journal of Vocational Behavior* (2009): 56–67.

79. G. F. Dreher and T. H. Cox, Jr., "Race, Gender, and Opportunity: A Study of Compensation Attainment and Establishment of Mentoring Relationships," *Journal of Applied Psychology* 81 (1996): 297–309.

80. D. D. Horgan and R. J. Simeon, "Mentoring and Participation: An Application of the Vroom–Yetton Model," *Journal of Business and Psychology* 5 (1990): 63–84.

81. B. R. Ragins, J. L. Cotton, and J. S. Miller, "Marginal Mentoring: The Effects of Type of Mentor, Quality of Relationship, and Program Design on Work and Career Attitudes," *Academy of Management Journal* 43 (2000): 1177–1194.

82. R. T. Brennan, R. C. Barnett, and K. C. Gareis, "When She Earns More Than He Does: A Longitudinal Study of Dual-Earner Couples," *Journal of Marriage and Family* 63 (2001): 168–182.

83. F. S. Hall and D. T. Hall, *The Two-Career Couple* (Reading, MA: Addison-Wesley, 1979).

84. J. S. Boles, M. W. Johnston, and J. F. Hair, Jr., "Role Stress, Work–Family Conflict, and Emotional Exhaustion: Inter-Relationships and Effects on Some Work-Related Consequences," *Journal of Personal Selling and Sales Management* 17 (1998): 17–28.

85. B. Morris, "Is Your Family Wrecking Your Career? (and Vice Versa)," *Fortune* (March 17, 1997): 70–80.

86. A. B. Bakker, E. Demeroutie, and M. F. Dollard, "How Job Demands Affect Partners' Experience of Exhaustion: Integrating Work-Family Conflict and Crossover Theory," *Journal of Applied Psychology* (2008): 901–911.

87. D. L. Nelson, J. C. Quick, M. A. Hitt, and D. Moesel, "Politics, Lack of Career Progress, and Work/Home Conflict: Stress and Strain for Working Women," *Sex Roles* 23 (1990): 169–185.

88. L. E. Duxbury and C. A. Higgins, "Gender Differences in Work–Family Conflict," *Journal of Applied Psychology* 76 (1991): 60–74.

89. R. G. Netemeyer, J. S. Boles, and R. McMurrian, "Development and Validation of Work–Family Conflict and Family–Work Conflict Scales," *Journal of Applied Psychology* 81 (1996): 400–410.

90. B. Livingston and T. A. Judge "Emotional Responses to Work-Family Conflict: An Examination of Gender Role Orientation Among Working Men and Women," *Journal of Applied Psychology* (2008): 207–216.

91. N. Yang, C. C. Chen, J. Choi, and Y. Zou, "Sources of Work–Family Conflict: A Sino–U.S. Comparison of the Effects of Work and Family Demands," *Academy of Management Journal* 43 (2000): 113–123.

92. A. Iiris Aaltio and H. Jiehua Huang, "Women Managers' Careers in Information Technology in China: High Flyers with Emotional Costs?" *Journal of Organizational Change Management* 20(2) (2007): 227–244.

93. D. L. Nelson and M. A. Hitt, "Employed Women and Stress: Implications for Enhancing Women's Mental Health in the Workplace," in J. C. Quick, L. R. Murphy, and J. J. Hurrell, eds., *Stress and Well-Being at Work: Assessments and Interventions for Occupational Mental Health* (Washington, DC: American Psychological Association, 1992), 164–177.

94. Mitchell Gold Co., "Day Care," http://www.mitchellgold.com/daycare .asp.

95. D. Machan, "The Mommy and Daddy Track," *Forbes* (April 6, 1990): 162.

96. E. M. Brody, M. H. Kleban, P. T. Johnsen, C. Hoffman, and C. B. Schoonover, "Work Status and Parental Care: A Comparison of Four Groups of Women," *Gerontological Society of America* 27 (1987): 201–208; J. W. Anastas, J. L. Gibson, and P. J. Larson, "Working Families and Eldercare: A National Perspective in an Aging America," *Social Work* 35 (1990): 405–411.

97. Cincinnati Area Senior Services, "Corporate Elder Care Program," http://www.senserv.org/elder.htm.

98. E. E. Kossek, J. A. Colquitt, and R. A. Noe, "Caregiving, Well-Being, and Performance: The Effects of Place and Provider as a Function of Dependent Type and Work–Family Climates," *Academy of Management Journal* 44 (2001): 29–44.

99. Harvard University Office of Human Resources, "Work/Life Support Services—Elder Care Resources," http://atwork.harvard.edu/worklife / eldercare/.

100. M. Richards, "'Daddy Track' Is Road Taken More Often," *The Morning Call* (July 28, 2004), http://www.mcall.com/business/local/ alldaddyjul28,0,1869593.story?coll=all-businesslocal-hed.

101. L. J. Barham, "Variables Affecting Managers' Willingness to Grant Alternative Work Arrangements," *Journal of Social Psychology* 138 (1998): 291–302.

102. J. Kaplan, "Hitting the Wall at Forty," *Business Month* 136 (1990): 52–58.

103. E. Lentz and T. D. Allen, "The Role of Mentoring Others in the Career Plateauing Phenomenon," *Group and Organization Management* (2009): 358–384.

104. M. B. Arthur and K. E. Kram, "Reciprocity at Work: The Separate Yet Inseparable Possibilities for Individual and Organizational Development," in M. B. Arthur, D. T. Hall, and B. S. Lawrence, eds., *Handbook of Career Theory* (Cambridge: Cambridge University Press, 1989).

105. K. E. Kram, "Phases of the Mentoring Relationship," *Academy of Management Review* 26 (1983): 608–625.

106. B. Rosen and T. Jerdee, *Older Employees: New Roles for Valued Resources* (Homewood, IL: Irwin, 1985).

107. J. W. Gilsdorf, "The New Generation: Older Workers," *Training and Development Journal* (March 1992): 77–79.

108. J. F. Quick, "Time to Move On?" in J. C. Quick, R. E. Hess, J. Hermalin, and J. D. Quick, eds., *Career Stress in Changing Times* (New York: Haworth Press, 1990), 239–250.

109. D. Machan, "Rent-an-Exec," *Forbes* (January 22, 1990): 132–133.

110. E. McGoldrick and C. L. Cooper, "Why Retire Early?" in J. C. Quick, R. E. Hess, J. Hermalin, and J. D. Quick, eds., *Career Stress in Changing Times* (New York: Haworth Press, 1990), 219–238.

111. E. Daspin, "The Second Midlife Crisis," *The Baltimore Sun* (originally published in *Wall Street Journal*) (May 10, 2004), http:// www.baltimoresun.com/business/bal-crisis051004,0,614944.story? coll=bal-business-headlines.

112. S. Kim and D. C. Feldman, "Working in Retirement: The Antecedents of Bridge Employment and Its Consequences for Quality of Life in Retirement," *Academy of Management Journal* 43 (2000): 1195–1210.

113. Lawrence Livermore Retiree Program, "Tasks Requested by Lab Programs," http://www.llnl.gov/aadp/retiree/tasks.html.

114. E. Schein, *Career Anchors* (San Diego: University Associates, 1985).

115. G. W. Dalton, "Developmental Views of Careers in Organizations," in M. B. Arthur, D. T. Hall, and B. S. Lawrence, eds., *Handbook of Career Theory* (Cambridge: Cambridge University Press, 1989), 89–109.

116. D. C. Feldman, "Careers in Organizations: Recent Trends and Future Directions," *Journal of Management* 15 (1989): 135–156.

117. B. O'Reilly, "The Job Drought," *Fortune* (August 24, 1992): 62–74.

118. A. S. Grove, "A High-Tech CEO Updates His Views on Managing and Careers," *Fortune* (September 18, 1995): 229–230.

119. http://www.eeoc.gov/abouteeo/overview_practices.html

120. M. Bertrand and S. Mullainathan, "Are Emily and Greg More Employable than Lakisha and Jamal: A Field Experiment on Labor Market Discrimination," *American Economic Review* 94 (2004): 991–1013.

Chapter 17 Case

1. Build-A-Bear Workshop, Inc., "Fact Sheet," *Build-A-Bear.com*, http://media.corporate-ir.net/ media_files/irol/18/182478/factSheet_010709.pdf (accessed August 7, 2009).

2. Ibid.

3. D. M. Amato-McCoy, "Where 'Everybear' Knows Your Name," *Chain Store Age* 84(8) (August 2008): 48.

4. G. Edwards, "Build-A-Bear Is Stretching at Seams," *Wall Street Journal* (Eastern edition) (April 5, 2006): B3C.

5. Ibid.

6. Amato-McCoy, "Where 'Everybear' Knows Your Name."

7. Edwards, "Build-A-Bear Is Stretching at Seams."

8. "Retails Power 25: The 25 Most Influential People in Retailing," *Chain Store Age*, 84(1) (January 2008): 8A; Edwards, "Build-A-Bear Is Stretching at Seams."

9. "Retails Power 25."

10. Ibid.

11. Ibid.

12. M. Nannery, J. Orton, J. Dennis, L. H Roberts, et al., "Helping Hands," *Chain Store Age* 77(1) (January 2001): 52.

13. Ibid.

14. Ibid., p. 58.

15. Ibid., p. 52.

16. Ibid., p. 54.

17. Ibid.

Chapter 18

1. M. Gunther, "At IKEA, Green Is Gold," *Fortune* (November 26, 2008), http://money.cnn.com/2008/11/25/news/companies/gunther_ikea.fortune/

2. C. A. Bartlett, V. Dessain, and A. Sjoman, "IKEA's Global Sourcing Challenge: Indian Rugs and Child Labor," *Harvard Business School Case* (November 14, 2006).

3. Gunther, "At IKEA, Green is Gold."

4. M. A. Verespej, "When Change Becomes the Norm," *Industry Week* (March 16, 1992): 35–38.

5 P. Mornell, "Nothing Endures but Change," *Inc.* 22 (July 2000): 131–132, http://www.inc.com/magazine/20000701/19555.html.

6. H. J. Van Buren III, "The Bindingness of Social and Psychological Contracts: Toward a Theory of Social Responsibility in Downsizing," *Journal of Business Ethics* 25 (2000): 205–219.

7. United States Embassy in Mexico press release, "Response to Criticism of U.S. Agricultural Policy and NAFTA" (December 5, 2002), http://www.usembassy-mexico.gov/releases/ep021205realitiesNAFTA.htm.

8. M. Stevenson, "Mexican Farmers Renew NAFTA Protests," *Yahoo! News* (January 20, 2003).

9. M. McCarthy, "PR Disaster as Coke Withdraws 'Purest' Bottled Water in Britain," *The New Zealand Herald* (March 20, 2004), http://www.nzherald.co.nz/business/businessstorydisplay.cfm?storyID=3555911&thesection= business&thesubsection=world&thesecondsubsection=europe.

10. L. Hirschhorn and T. Gilmore, "The New Boundaries of the 'Boundaryless' Company," *Harvard Business Review* (May–June 1992): 104–115.

11. http://www.tata.com/htm/Group_MnA_YearWise.htm

12. L. R. Offerman and M. Gowing, "Organizations of the Future: Changes and Challenges," *American Psychologist* (February 1990): 95–108.

13. J. Goudreau, "Overworked, Overextended and Overstressed," *Time* (August 26, 2009) http://www.forbes.com/2009/08/26/household-responsibility-husband-wife-forbes-woman-time-equality.html

14. W. B. Johnston, "Global Work Force 2000: The New World Labor Market," *Harvard Business Review* (March–April 1991): 115–127.

15. H. Brown, "Diversity Does Matter," *ForbesWoman Q&A* (July 21, 2009), http://www.forbes.com/2009/07/21/diversity-jill-lee-business-forbes-woman-q-and-a-competitive.html

16. G. Bylinsky, "Hot New Technologies for American Factories," *Fortune* (June 26, 2000): 288A–288K.

17. http://home3.americanexpress.com/corp/pc/2007/axiom.asp.

18. R. M. Kanter, "Improving the Development, Acceptance, and Use of New Technology: Organizational and Interorganizational Challenges," in *People and Technology in the Workplace* (Washington, DC: National Academy Press, 1991), 15–56.

19. Gap Inc. press release, "Gap Inc. Joins the Ethical Trading Initiative," *CSRwire* (April 28, 2004), http://www.csrwire.com/article.cgi/2683.html.

20. "Gap Inc. 2003 Social Responsibility Report," *Gap Inc.* (September 17, 2004), http://ccbn.mobular.net/ccbn/7/645/696/index.html.

21. S. A. Mohrman and A. M. Mohrman, Jr., "The Environment as an Agent of Change," in A. M. Mohrman, Jr., et al., eds., *Large-Scale Organizational Change* (San Francisco: Jossey-Bass, 1989), 35–47.

22. T. D'Aunno, M. Succi, and J. A. Alexander, "The Role of Institutional and Market Forces in Divergent Organizational Change," *Administrative Science Quarterly* 45 (2000): 679–703.

23. V. Nayer, "There Is Life after the Recession. But It Calls for a More Evolved, Employee-Centric CEO," *Fortune Brainstorm Tech* (September 8, 2009), http://brainstormtech.blogs.fortune.cnn.com/2009/09/09/the-reincarnate-ceo/

24. Intel press release, Santa Clara, CA (April 21, 2004), http://www.manufacturing.net/Intel-Opening-Arizona-Chip-Plant.aspx?menuid=278.

25. Q. N. Huy, "Emotional Balancing of Organizational Continuity and Radical Change: The Contribution of Middle Managers," *Administrative Science Quarterly* 47 (March 1, 2002): 31–69.

26. D. Nadler, "Organizational Frame-Bending: Types of Change in the Complex Organization," in R. Kilmann and T. Covin, eds., *Corporate Transformation* (San Francisco: Jossey-Bass, 1988), 66–83.

27. K. Belson, "AT&T Plans to Raise Its Rates for Residential Calling Plans," *New York Times* (August 4, 2004), http://www.businessweek.com/technology/content/nov2007/tc20071128_603655.htm.

28. L. Ackerman, "Development, Transition, or Transformation: The Question of Change in Organizations," *OD Practitioner* (December 1986): 1–8.

29. T. D. Jick, *Managing Change* (Homewood, IL: Irwin, 1993), 3.

30. J. M. Bloodgood and J. L. Morrow, "Strategic Organizational Change: Exploring the Roles of Environmental Structure, Internal Conscious Awareness, and Knowledge," *Journal of Management Studies* 40 (2003): 1761–1782.

31. D. Miller and M. J. Chen, "Sources and Consequences of Competitive Inertia. A Study of the U.S. Airline Industry," *Administrative Science Quarterly* 39 (1994): 1–23.

32. S. L. Brown and K. M. Eisenhardt, "The Art of Continuous Change: Linking Complexity Theory and Time-Paced Evolution in Relentlessly Shifting Organizations," *Administrative Science Quarterly* 42 (1997): 1–34.

33. J. Child and C. Smith, "The Context and Process of Organizational Transformation: Cadbury Ltd. in Its Sector," *Journal of Management Studies* 12 (1987): 12–27.

34. J. Amis, T. Slack, and C. R. Hinings, "The Pace, Sequence, and Linearity of Radical Change," *Academy of Management Journal* 47 (2004): 15–39.

35. R. M. Kanter, *The Change Masters* (New York: Simon & Schuster, 1983).

36. J. R. Katzenbach, *Real Change Leaders* (New York: Times Business, 1995).

37. J. L. Denis, L. Lamothe, and A. Langley, "The Dynamics of Collective Leadership and Strategic Change in Pluralistic Organizations," *Academy of Management Journal* 44 (2001): 809–837.

38. M. Beer, *Organization Change and Development: A Systems View* (Santa Monica, CA: Goodyear, 1980): 78.

39. K. Whalen-Berry and C. R. Hinings, "The Relative Effect of Change Drivers in Large-Scale Organizational Change: An Empirical Study," in W. Passmore and R. Goodman, eds., *Research in Organizational Change and Development*, Vol. 14 (New York: JAI Press, 2003): 99–146.

40. S.A. Furst and D. M. Cable, "Employee Resistance to Organizational Change: Managerial Influence Tactics and Leader-Member Exchange," *Journal of Applied Psychology* 92 (2008): 453–462.

41. J. L. Denis, L. Lamothe, and A. Langley, "The Dynamics of Collective Leadership and Strategic Change in Pluralistic Organizations," *Academy of Management Journal* 44 (2001): 809–837.

42. F. Cheyunski and J. Millard, "Accelerated Business Transformation and the Role of the Organizational Architect," *Journal of Applied Behavioral Science* 34 (1998): 268–285.

43. N. A. M. Worren, K. Ruddle, and K. Moore, "From Organizational Development to Change Management: The Emergence of a New Profession," *Journal of Applied Behavioral Science* 35 (1999): 273–286.

44. P. G. Audia, E. A. Locke, and K. G. Smith, "The Paradox of Success: An Archival and a Laboratory Study of Strategic Persistence Following Radical Environmental Change," *Academy of Management Journal* 43 (2000): 837–853.

45. V. Bellou, "Psychological Contract Assessment after a Major Organizational Change: The Case of Mergers and Acquisitions," *Employee Relations* 29(1) (2007): 68–88.

46. J. W. Brehm, *A Theory of Psychological Reactance* (New York: Academic Press, 1966).

47. J. A. Klein, "Why Supervisors Resist Employee Involvement," *Harvard Business Review* 62 (1984): 87–95.

48. B. L. Kirkman, R. G. Jones, and D. L. Shapiro, "Why Do Employees Resist Teams? Examining the 'Resistance Barrier' to Work Team Effectiveness," *International Journal of Conflict Management* 11 (2000): 74–92.

49. D. L. Nelson and M. A. White, "Management of Technological Innovation: Individual Attitudes, Stress, and Work Group Attributes," *Journal of High Technology Management Research* 1 (1990): 137–148.

50. S. Elias, "Employee Commitment in Times of Change: Assessing the Importance of Attitudes Toward Organizational Change," *Journal of Management* 35 (2009): 37–55.

51. J. B. Avey, T. S. Wernsing, and F. Luthans "Can Positive Employees Help Positive Organizational Change? Impact of Psychological Capital and Emotions on Relevant Attitudes and Behaviors," *Journal of Applied Behavioral Science* 44 (2008): 48–70.

52. D. Klein, "Some Notes on the Dynamics of Resistance to Change: The Defender Role," in W. G. Bennis, K. D. Benne, R. Chin, and K. E. Corey, eds., *The Planning of Change*, 3rd ed. (New York: Holt, Rinehart & Winston, 1969), 117–124.

53. T. Diefenbach, "The Managerialistic Ideology of Organisational Change Management," *Journal of Organizational Change Management* 20(1) (2007): 126–144.

54. T. G. Cummings and E. F. Huse, *Organizational Development and Change* (St. Paul, MN: West, 1989).

55. N. L. Jimmieson, D. J. Terry, and V. J. Callan, "A Longitudinal Study of Employee Adaptation to Organizational Change: The Role of Change-Related Information and Change-Related Self Efficacy," *Journal of Occupational Health Psychology* 9 (2004): 11–27.

56. K. van Dam, S. Oreg, and B. Schyns, "Daily Work Contexts and Resistance to Organisational Change: The Role of Leader-Member Exchange, Development Climate, and Change Process Characteristics," *Applied Psychology: An International Review* 57 (2008): 313–334.

57. N. DiFonzo and P. Bordia, "A Tale of Two Corporations: Managing Uncertainty during Organizational Change," *Human Resource Management* 37 (1998): 295–303.

58. J. de Vries, C. Webb, and J. Eveline, "Mentoring for Gender Equality and Organisational Change," *Employee Relations* 28(6) (2006): 573–587.

59. M. Johnson-Cramer, S. Parise, and R. Cross, "Managing Change through Networks and Values," *California Management Review* 49(3) (2007): 85–109.

60. L. P. Livingstone, M. A. White, D. L. Nelson, and F. Tabak, "Delays in Technological Innovation Implementations: Some Preliminary Results on a Common but Understudied Occurrence," working paper, Oklahoma State University.

61. P. Neves and A. Caetano, "Social Exchange Processes in Organizational Change: The Roles of Trust and Control," *Journal of Change Management* 6(4) (2006): 351–364.

62. G. Lindsay, "Prada's High-Tech Misstep," *Business 2.0* (February 25, 2004): 72–75, http://www.business2.com/b2/web/articles/0,17863, 594365,00.html.

63. M. Hickins, "Reconcilable Differences," *Management Review* 87 (1998): 54–58.

64. J. P. Kotter and L. A. Schlesinger, "Choosing Strategies for Change," *Harvard Business Review* 57 (1979): 109–112; W. Bridges, *Transitions: Making Sense of Life's Changes* (Reading, MA: Addison-Wesley, 1980); H. Woodward and S. Buchholz, *Aftershock: Helping People through Corporate Change* (New York: John Wiley & Sons, 1987).

65. S. Michailova, "Contrasts in Culture: Russian and Western Perspectives on Organizational Change," *Academy of Management Executive* 14 (2000): 99–112.

66. S. E. Herzig and N. L. Jimmieson, "Middle Managers' Uncertainty Management during Organizational Change," *Leadership & Organization Development Journal* 27(8) (2006): 628–645.

67. K. Lewin, "Frontiers in Group Dynamics," *Human Relations* 1 (1947): 5–41.

68. C. Bareil, A. Savoie, and S. Meunier, "Patterns of Discomfort with Organizational Change," *Journal of Change Management* 7(1) (2007): 13–24.

69. W. McWhinney, "Meta-Praxis: A Framework for Making Complex Changes," in A. M. Mohrman, Jr., et al., eds., *Large-Scale Organizational Change* (San Francisco: Jossey-Bass, 1989), 154–199.

70. M. Beer and E. Walton, "Developing the Competitive Organization: Interventions and Strategies," *American Psychologist* 45 (1990): 154–161.

71. B. Bertsch and R. Williams, "How Multinational CEOs Make Change Programs Stick," *Long Range Planning* 27 (1994): 12–24.

72. J. Amis, T. Slack, and C. R. Hinings, "Values and Organizational Change," *Journal of Applied Behavioral Science* 38 (2002): 356–385.

73. W. L. French and C. H. Bell, *Organization Development: Behavioral Science Interventions for Organization Improvement*, 4th ed. (Englewood Cliffs, NJ: Prentice Hall, 1990); W. W. Burke, *Organization Development: A Normative View* (Reading, MA: Addison-Wesley, 1987).

74. A. Huczynski, *Encyclopedia of Organizational Change Methods* (Brookfield, VT: Gower, 1987).

75. A. O. Manzini, *Organizational Diagnosis* (New York: AMACOM, 1988).

76. M. R. Weisbord, "Organizational Diagnosis: Six Places to Look for Trouble with or without a Theory," *Group and Organization Studies* (December 1976): 430–444.

77. H. Levinson, *Organizational Diagnosis* (Cambridge, MA: Harvard University Press, 1972).

78. J. Nicholas, "The Comparative Impact of Organization Development Interventions," *Academy of Management Review* 7 (1982): 531–542.

79. D. M. Herold, D. B. Fedor, and S. D. Caldwell, "Beyond Change Management: A Multilevel Investigation of Contextual and Personal Influences on Employees' Commitment to Change," *Journal of Applied Psychology* 92(4) (2007): 942–951.

80. G. Odiorne, *Management by Objectives* (Marshfield, MA: Pitman, 1965).

81. E. Huse, "Putting in a Management Development Program That Works," *California Management Review* 9 (1966): 73–80.

82. J. P. Muczyk and B. C. Reimann, "MBO as a Complement to Effective Leadership," *Academy of Management Executive* (May 1989): 131–138.

83. L. L. Berry and A. Parasuraman, "Prescriptions for a Service Quality Revolution in America," *Organizational Dynamics* 20 (1992): 5–15.

84. "Five Companies Win 1992 Baldrige Quality Awards," *Business America* (November 2, 1992): 7–16.

85. D. M. Anderson, "Hidden Forces," *Success* (April 1995): 12.

86. T. A. Stewart and A. P. Raman, "Lessons from Toyota's Long Drive," *Harvard Business Review* 85(7/8) (2007): 74–83.

87. W. G. Dyer, *Team Building: Issues and Alternatives*, 2nd ed. (Reading, MA: Addison-Wesley, 1987).

88. E. Stephan, G. Mills, R. W. Pace, and L. Ralphs, "HRD in the Fortune 500: A Survey," *Training and Development Journal* (January 1988): 26–32.

89. A. Edmondson, "Psychological Safety and Learning Behavior in Work Teams," *Administrative Science Quarterly* 44 (1999): 350–383.

90. M. Whitmire and P. R. Nienstedt, "Lead Leaders into the '90s," *Personnel Journal* (May 1991): 80–85.

91. http://www.teambuildinginc.com/services4_teamconcepts.htm.

92. http://www.teambuildinginc.com/services5.htm.

93. E. Salas, T. L. Dickinson, S. I. Tannenbaum, and S. A. Converse, *A Meta-Analysis of Team Performance and Training, Naval Training System Center Technical Reports* (Orlando, FL: U.S. Government, 1991).

94. E. Schein, *Its Role in Organization Development*, vol. 1 of *Process Consultation* (Reading, MA: Addison-Wesley, 1988).

95. H. Hornstein, "Organizational Development and Change Management: Don't Throw the Baby Out with the Bath Water," *Journal of Applied Behavioral Science* 37 (2001): 223–226.

96. D. Filipowski, "How Federal Express Makes Your Package Its Most Important," *Personnel Journal* (February 1992): 40–46; P. Galagan, "Training Delivers Results to Federal Express," *Training and Development* (December 1991): 27–33.

97. R. W. Revans, *Action Learning* (London: Blonde & Briggs, 1980).

98. I. L. Goldstein, *Training in Organizations*, 3rd ed. (Pacific Grove, CA: Brooks/Cole, 1993).

99. J. A. Conger and R. M. Fulmer, "Developing Your Leadership Pipeline," *Harvard Business Review* 81 (2003): 76–84.

100. D. A. Ready and J. A. Conger, "Why Leadership Development Efforts Fail," *MIT Sloan Management Review* 44 (2003): 83–89.

101. M. Jay, "Understanding How to Leverage Executive Coaching," *Organization Development Journal* 21 (2003): 6–13.

102. D. Goleman, R. Boyasis, and A. McKee, *Primal Leadership: Learning to Lead with Emotional Intelligence* (Boston: Harvard Business School Press, 2004).

103. K. M. Wasylyshyn, "Executive Coaching: An Outcome Study," *Consulting Psychology Journal* 55 (2003): 94–106.

104. J. W. Smither, M. London, R. Flautt, Y. Vargas, and I. Kucine, "Can Working with an Executive Coach Improve Multisource Feedback Ratings over Time? A Quasi-Experimental Field Study," *Personnel Psychology* 56 (2003): 23–44.

105. "Occupational Stress and Employee Stress," *American Psychological Association* (June 6, 2004), http://www.psychologymatters.org/karasek.html.

106. American Psychological Association, "Psychologically Healthy Workplace Awards," http://apahelpcenter.mediaroom.com/file.php/mr_apahelpcenter/spinsite_docfiles/134/phwa_magazine_2007.pdf.

107. D. A. Nadler, "Concepts for the Management of Organizational Change," in J. R. Hackman, E. E. Lawler III, and L. W. Porter, eds., *Perspectives on Organizational Behavior* (New York: McGraw-Hill, 1983).

108. Cummings and Huse, *Organizational Development*; P. E. Connor and L. K. Lake, *Managing Organizational Change* (New York: Praeger, 1988).

109. R. L. Lowman, "Ethical Human Resource Practice in Organizational Settings," in D. W. Bray, ed., *Working with Organizations* (New York: Guilford Press, 1991).

110. H. Kelman, "Manipulation of Human Behavior: An Ethical Dilemma for the Social Scientist," in W. Bennis, K. Benne, and R. Chin, eds., *The Planning of Change* (New York: Holt, Rinehart, & Winston, 1969).

111. A. M. Pettigrew, R. W. Woodman, and K. S. Cameron, "Studying Organizational Change and Development: Challenges for Future Research," *Academy of Management Journal* 44 (2001): 697–713.

112. R. A. Katzell and R. A. Guzzo, "Psychological Approaches to Worker Productivity," *American Psychologist* 38 (1983): 468–472.

113. R. A. Guzzo, R. D. Jette, and R. A. Katzell, "The Effects of Psychologically Based Intervention Programs on Worker Productivity," *Personnel Psychology* 38 (1985): 275–291.

114. Goldstein, *Training in Organizations*.

115. T. Covin and R. H. Kilmann, "Participant Perceptions of Positive and Negative Influences on Large-Scale Change," *Group and Organization Studies* 15 (1990): 233–248.

116. C. M. Brotheridge, "The Role of Fairness in Mediating the Effects of Voice and Justification on Stress and Other Outcomes in a Climate of Organizational Change," *International Journal of Stress Management* 10 (2003): 253–268.

117. http://www.ikea.com/ms/en_US/about_ikea/our_responsibility/index.html

118. M. Gunther "At IKEA, Green is Gold," *Fortune* (November 26, 2008), http://money.cnn.com/2008/11/25/news/companies/gunther_ikea.fortune/

Chapter 18 Case

1. CarMax Business Services, LLC, "Corporate Profile," *CarMax.com*, http://phx.corporate-ir.net/phoenix.zhtml?c=125417&p=irol-IRHome (accessed August 4, 2009).

2. CarMax Business Services, LLC, "FAQ," *CarMax.com*, http://phx.corporate-ir.net/phoenix.zhtml?c=125417&p=irol-faq (accessed August 4, 2009).

3. Ibid.

4. L. Allison, "Driving Car Dealers Crazy," *Sales and Marketing Management*, 148(10) (October 1996): 22.

5. Ibid.

6. CarMax Business Services, LLC, "FAQ."

7. CarMax Business Services, LLC, "Corporate Profile."

8. T. Kosdrosky, "CarMax Looks Fueled to Grow," *Wall Street Journal* (Eastern edition) (May 2, 2007): B2E.

9. Ibid.

10. M. Myser, "The Wal-Mart of Used Cars," *Business 2.0* 7(8) (September 2006): 58.

11. Ibid.

12. Kosdrosky, "CarMax Looks Fueled to Grow."

13. Ibid.

14. Ibid.

15. Myser, "The Wal-Mart of Used Cars."

16. M. Barris, "Corporate News: CarMax to Pare Inventory, Slow Store Growth," *Wall Street Journal* (Eastern edition) (August 7, 2008): B3.

17. "Corporate News: CarMax Earnings Take a Tumble; Quarterly Profit Drops 78% as Weak Economy, High Gas Prices Put a Dent in Sales," *Wall Street Journal* (Eastern edition) (September 23, 2008): B6.

18. Barris, "Corporate News."

19. D. Gaffen, "MarketBeat/Market Insight from WSJ.com," *Wall Street Journal* (Eastern edition) (August 7, 2008): C6.

20. Barris, "Corporate News," B5.

Chapter 18 Cohesion Case: Part 4

1. M. Chafkin, "Get Happy: How Tony Hsieh Uses Relentless Innovation, Stellar Service, and a Staff of Believers to Make Zappos.com and E-commerce Juggernaut—and One of the Most Blissed-out Businesses in America," *Inc.* 31(4) (May 2009): 69.

2. Ibid.

3. J. M. O'Brien, "Zappos Knows How to Kick It," *Fortune* 159(2) (February 2, 2009): 56.

4. Chafkin, "Get Happy," 69.

5. O'Brien, "Zappos Knows," 56.

6. Chafkin, "Get Happy," 70.

7. H. Coster, "A Step Ahead," *Forbes* (June 2, 2008), http://www.forbes.com/global/2008/0602/064.html (accessed June 20, 2009).

8. Chafkin, "Get Happy," 70.

9. Chafkin, "Get Happy," 70; Coster, "A Step Ahead."

10. Coster, "A Step Ahead."

11. "Business: Keeper of the Flame; Face Value," *The Economist* 391(8627) (April 18, 2009): 75.

12. "Zappos Core Values," http://about.zappos.com/our-unique-culture/zappos-core-values (accessed June 20, 2009).

13. C. S. Cross, "Dot-com Distribution," *Industrial Engineer* 40(11) (November 2008): 52.

14. "Zappos Core Values," http://about.zappos.com/our-unique-culture/zappos-core-values (accessed June 20, 2009).

15. C. Gentry, "Cultural Revolution," *Chain Store Age* 83(12) (December 2007): 32 and 34.

16. Gentry, "Cultural Revolution," 32.

17. "Business: Keeper of the Flame; Face Value."

18. S. Murphy, "Culture Conscious," *Chain Store Age* 83(9) (September 2007): 55.

19. W. Hoffman, "From Bricks to Clicks," *Journal of Commerce* (December 22, 2008), http://www.joc.com/node/408765 (accessed June 9, 2009).

20. P. Barnard, "The New Big Thing: Super-size DCs," *Multichannel Merchant* 25(11) (November 2008): 51.

21. M. Zager, "Zappos Delivers Service … With Shoes on the Side," *Apparel* (January 2009), http://www.apparelmag.com?ME2/dirmod.asp?sid=23B25809… (accessed June 9, 2009).

22. Ibid.

23. C. Steiner, "A Bot in Time Saves Nine," *Forbes* (March 16, 2009), http://www.forbes.com/forbes/2009/0316/040_bot_times_saves_nine.html (accessed June 20, 2009).

24. Chafkin, "Get Happy," 68.

25. W. Atkinson, "Robotics in Action" sidebar to "The Future Is Flexible," *Modern Materials Management* (Warehousing Management Edition) 63(9) (September 2008): 31.

26. J. Teresko, "Getting Lean with Armless Robots," *Industry Week* 257(9) (September 2008): 26.

Appendix A

1. F. W. Taylor, *The Principles of Scientific Management* (New York: Norton, 1911).

2. M. Weber, *The Protestant Ethic and the Spirit of Capitalism* (London: Talcott Parson, tr., 1930).

3. W. B. Cannon, *Bodily Changes in Pain, Hunger, Fear, and Rage* (New York: Appleton, 1915/1929).

4. F. J. Roethlisberger and W. J. Dickson, *Management and the Worker* (Cambridge, MA: Harvard University Press, 1939).

5. K. Lewin, R. Lippitt, and R. K. White, "Patterns of Aggressive Behavior in Experimentally Created 'Social Climates,' " *Journal of Social Psychology* 10 (1939): 271–299; A. H. Maslow, *Motivation and Personality* (New York: Harper & Row, 1954); F. Herzberg, B. Mausner, and B. Snyderman, *The Motivation to Work*, 2nd ed. (New York: John Wiley & Sons, 1959); E. A. Locke, "Toward a Theory of Task Motivation and Incentives," *Organizational Behavior and Human Performance* 3 (1968): 157–189; R. M. Stogdill, *Handbook of Leadership: A Survey of Theory and Research* (New York: Free Press, 1974); G. A. Yukl, *Leadership in Organizations*, 3rd ed. (Englewood Cliffs, NJ: Prentice Hall, 1995).

6. G. C. Homans, *The Human Group* (New York: Harcourt Brace Jovanovich, 1950).

7. J. R. Hackman and G. Oldham, *Work Redesign* (Reading, MA: Addison-Wesley, 1980); P. C. Smith, L. M. Kendall, and C. L. Hulin, *The Measurement of Satisfaction in Work and Retirement* (Chicago: Rand McNally, 1969).

8. N. R. F. Maier, *Psychology in Industry: A Psychological Approach to Industrial Problems*, 2nd ed. (Boston: Houghton Mifflin, 1955).

9. R. C. Solomon, "Corporate Roles, Personal Virtues: An Aristotelian Approach to Business Ethics," *Business Ethics Quarterly*, 2 (1992): 317–339.

10. R. C. Solomon, *A Better Way to Think about Business: How Personal Integrity Leads to Corporate Success* (New York: Oxford University Press, 1999).

11. M. E. P. Seligman, *Learned Optimism* (New York: Knopf, 1990) and M. E. P. Seligman and M. Csikszentmihalyi, "Positive Psychology," *American Psychologist*, 55 (2000): 5–14.

12. M. Lewis, J. M. Haviland-Jones, and L.F. Barrett (Eds.), *Handbook of Emotions*, 3rd ed. (New York: Guilford Press, 2008).

13. F. Luthans, "Positive Organizational Behavior: Developing and Managing Psychological Strengths," *Academy of Management Executive*, 16 (2002): 57–72; "The Need for and Meaning of Positive Organizational Behaviors," *Journal of Organizational Behavior*, 23 (2002): 695–706.

14. B. J. Avolio, *Full Leadership Development: Building the Vital Forces in Organizations* (Thousand Oaks, CA: Sage Publications, 1999).

15. F. J. Roethlisberger, *Management and Morale* (Cambridge, MA: Harvard University Press, 1941).

16. J. G. Adair, "The Hawthorne Effect: A Reconsideration of Methodological Artifact," *Journal of Applied Psychology* 69 (1984): 334–345.

17. F. J. Roethlisberger, W. J. Dickson, and H. A. Wright, *Management and the Worker: An Account of a Research Program Conducted by the Western Electric Company, Hawthorne Works, Chicago* (Cambridge, MA: Harvard University Press, 1950); A. G. Athos and J. J. Gabarro, *Interpersonal Behavior: Communication and Understanding in Relationships* (Englewood Cliffs, NJ: Prentice Hall, 1978).

Appendix B

1. Two sources for further reference on experimental design are D. T. Campbell and J. C. Stanley, *Experimental and Quasi-Experimental Designs for Research* (Chicago: Rand McNally, 1966); and T. D. Cook and D. T. Campbell, *Quasi-Experimentation: Design and Analysis Issues for Field Settings* (Boston: Houghton Mifflin, 1979).

2. M. L. Lombardo, M. McCall, and D. L. DeVries, *Looking Glass* (Glenview, IL: Scott, Foresman, 1983).

3. Elaboration of how such measures are developed is beyond the scope of this appendix but can be found in U. Sekaran, *Research Methods for Business: A Skill Building Approach*, 2nd ed. (New York: Wiley, 1992).

4. Several measures are available in *Psychological Measurement Year-books*; J. L. Price, *Handbook of Organizational Measurement* (Lexington, MA: D. C. Heath, 1972); and *Michigan Organizational Assessment Packages* (Ann Arbor, MI: Institute of Survey Research).

5. One such instrument is the Job Descriptive Index, which is used to measure job satisfaction. It was developed by P. C. Smith, L. Kendall, and C. Hulin. See their book *The Measurement of Satisfaction in Work and Retirement* (Chicago: Rand McNally, 1969), pp. 79–84.

Glossary

A

adaptive culture An organizational culture that encourages confidence and risk taking among employees, has leadership that produces change, and focuses on the changing needs of customers.

adhocracy A selectively decentralized form of organization that emphasizes the support staff and mutual adjustment among people.

administrative orbiting Delaying action on a conflict by buying time.

advancement The second, high-achievement-oriented career stage in which the individual focuses on increasing competence.

affect The emotional component of an attitude.

affective commitment A type of organizational commitment based on an individual's desire to remain in an organization.

anthropocentric Placing human considerations at the center of job design decisions.

anthropology The science of the learned behavior of human beings.

anticipatory socialization The first socialization stage, which encompasses all of the learning that takes place prior to the newcomer's first day on the job.

artifacts Symbols of culture in the physical and social work environment.

assumptions Deeply held beliefs that guide behavior and tell members of an organization how to perceive and think about things.

attitude A psychological tendency expressed by evaluating an entity with some degree of favor or disfavor.

attribution theory A theory that explains how individuals pinpoint the causes of their own behavior and that of others. •

authentic leadership A style of leadership that includes transformational, charismatic, or transactional approaches as the situation demands.

authority The right to influence another person.

authority-compliance manager (9,1) A leader who emphasizes efficient production.

autocratic style A style of leadership in which the leader uses strong, directive, controlling actions to enforce the rules, regulations, activities, and relationships in the work environment.

B

barriers to communication Aspects of the communication content and context that can impair effective communication in a workplace.

behavioral measures Personality assessments that involve observing an individual's behavior in a controlled situation.

benevolent An individual who is comfortable with an equity ratio less than that of his or her comparison other.

bounded rationality A theory that suggests there are limits to how rational a decision maker can actually be.

brainstorming A technique for generating as many ideas as possible on a given subject, while suspending evaluation until all the ideas have been suggested.

bridge employment Employment that takes place after retiring from a full-time position but before permanent withdrawal from the workforce.

C

career The pattern of work-related experiences that span the course of a person's life.

career anchors A network of self-perceived talents, motives, and values that guide an individual's career decisions.

career ladder A structured series of job positions through which an individual progresses in an organization.

career management A lifelong process of learning about self, jobs, and organizations; setting personal career goals; developing strategies for achieving the goals; and revising the goals based on work and life experiences.

career path A sequence of job experiences that an employee moves along during his or her career.

career plateau A point in an individual's career in which the probability of moving further up the hierarchy is low.

centralization The degree to which decisions are made at the top of the organization.

challenge The call to competition, contest, or battle.

change The transformation or modification of an organization and/or its stakeholders.

change agent The individual or group that undertakes the task of introducing and managing a change in an organization.

change and acquisition The third socialization stage, in which the newcomer begins to master the demands of the job.

character assassination An attempt to label or discredit an opponent.

character theory An ethical theory that emphasizes the character, personal virtues, and integrity of the individual.

charismatic leadership A leader's use of personal abilities and talents in order to have profound and extraordinary effects on followers.

classical conditioning Modifying behavior so that a conditioned stimulus is paired with an unconditioned stimulus and elicits an unconditioned response.

coercive power Power that is based on an agent's ability to cause an unpleasant experience for a target.

cognitive dissonance A state of tension that is produced when an individual experiences conflict between attitudes and behavior.

cognitive moral development The process of moving through stages of maturity in terms of making ethical decisions.

cognitive style An individual's preference for gathering information and evaluating alternatives.

collectivism A cultural orientation in which individuals belong to tightly knit social frameworks, and they depend strongly on large extended families or clans.

communication The evoking of a shared or common meaning in another person.

communicative disease The absence of heartfelt communication in human relationships leading to loneliness and social isolation.

communicator The person originating a message.

compensation A compromise mechanism in which an individual attempts to make up for a negative situation by devoting himself or herself to another pursuit with increased vigor.

compensation award An organizational cost resulting from court awards for job distress.

complexity The degree to which many different types of activities occur in the organization.

conflict Any situation in which incompatible goals, attitudes, emotions, or behaviors lead to disagreement or opposition for two or more parties.

consensus An informational cue indicating the extent to which peers in the same situation behave in a similar fashion.

consequential theory An ethical theory that emphasizes the consequences or results of behavior.

consideration Leader behavior aimed at nurturing friendly, warm working relationships, as well as encouraging mutual trust and interpersonal respect within the work unit.

consistency An informational cue indicating the frequency of behavior over time.

contextual variables A set of characteristics that influence the organization's design processes.

continuance commitment A type of organizational commitment based on the fact that an individual cannot afford to leave.

conversion A withdrawal mechanism in which emotional conflicts are expressed in physical symptoms.

counterdependence An unhealthy, insecure pattern of behavior that leads to separation in relationships with other people.

counter-role behavior Deviant behavior in either a correctly or incorrectly defined job or role.

country club manager (1,9) A leader who creates a happy, comfortable work environment.

creativity A process influenced by individual and organizational factors that results in the production of novel and useful ideas, products, or both.

cross-training A variation of job enlargement in which workers are trained in different specialized tasks or activities.

D

data Uninterpreted and unanalyzed facts.

defensive communication Communication that can be aggressive, attacking, and angry, or passive and withdrawing.

Delphi technique Gathering the judgments of experts for use in decision making.

democratic style A style of leadership in which the leader takes collaborative, responsive, interactive actions with followers concerning the work and work environment.

devil's advocacy A technique for preventing groupthink in which a group or individual is given the role of critic during decision making.

dialectical inquiry A debate between two opposing sets of recommendations.

differentiation The process of deciding how to divide the work in an organization.

discounting principle The assumption that an individual's behavior is accounted for by the situation.

disenchantment Feeling negativity or anger toward a change.

disengagement Psychological withdrawal from change.

disidentification Feeling that one's identity is being threatened by a change.

disorientation Feelings of loss and confusion due to a change.

displacement An aggressive mechanism in which an individual directs his or her anger toward someone who is not the source of the conflict.

distinctiveness An informational cue indicating the degree to which an individual behaves the same way in other situations.

distress The adverse psychological, physical, behavioral, and organizational consequences that may arise as a result of stressful events.

distributive bargaining A negotiation approach in which the goals of the parties are in conflict, and each party seeks to maximize its resources.

distributive justice The fairness of the outcomes that individuals receive in an organization.

diversity All forms of individual differences, including culture, gender, age, ability, religion, personality, social status, and sexual orientation.

divisionalized form A moderately decentralized form of organization that emphasizes the middle level and standardization of outputs.

dual-career partnership A relationship in which both people have important career roles.

due process nonaction A procedure set up to address conflicts that is so costly, time-consuming, or personally risky that no one will use it.

dynamic follower A follower who is a responsible steward of his or her job, is effective in managing the relationship with the boss, and practices self-management.

dysfunctional conflict An unhealthy, destructive disagreement between two or more people.

E

effective decision A timely decision that meets a desired objective and is acceptable to those individuals affected by it.

ego-ideal The embodiment of a person's perfect self.

eldercare Assistance in caring for elderly parents and/or other elderly relatives.

emotional contagion A dynamic process through which the emotions of one person are transferred to another either consciously or unconsciously through nonverbal channels.

emotions Mental states that typically include feelings, physiological changes, and the inclination to act.

empowerment Sharing power within an organization.

enacted values Values reflected in the way individuals actually behave.

encounter The second socialization stage in which the newcomer learns the tasks associated with the job, clarifies roles, and establishes new relationships at work.

engagement The expression of oneself as one performs in work or other roles.

engineering The applied science of energy and matter.

entitled An individual who is comfortable with an equity ratio greater than that of his or her comparison other.

environment Anything outside the boundaries of an organization.

environmental uncertainty The amount and rate of change in the organization's environment.

equity sensitive An individual who prefers an equity ratio equal to that of his or her comparison other.

ergonomics The science of adapting work and working conditions to the employee or worker.

escalation of commitment The tendency to continue to support a failing course of action.

espoused values What members of an organization say they value.

establishment The first career stage in which the person learns the job and begins to fit into the organization and occupation.

ethical behavior Acting in ways consistent with one's personal values and the commonly held values of the organization and society.

eustress Healthy, normal stress.

executive coaching A technique in which managers or executives are paired with a coach in a partnership to help the executive perform more efficiently.

expatriate manager A manager who works in a country other than his or her home country.

expectancy The belief that effort leads to performance.

expert power The power that exists when an agent has specialized knowledge or skills that the target needs.

extinction The attempt to weaken a behavior by attaching no consequences to it.

extraversion A preference indicating that an individual is energized by interaction with other people.

F

fantasy A withdrawal mechanism that provides an escape from a conflict through daydreaming.

feedback Information fed back that completes two-way communication.

feeling Making decisions in a personal, value-oriented way.

femininity The cultural orientation in which relationships and concern for others are valued.

first-impression error The tendency to form lasting opinions about an individual based on initial perceptions.

fixation An aggressive mechanism in which an individual keeps up a dysfunctional behavior that obviously will not solve the conflict.

flexible work schedule A work schedule that allows employees discretion in order to accommodate personal concerns.

flextime An alternative work pattern that enables employees to set their own daily work schedules.

flight/withdrawal A withdrawal mechanism that entails physically escaping a conflict (flight) or psychologically escaping (withdrawal).

followership The process of being guided and directed by a leader in the work environment.

formal leadership Officially sanctioned leadership based on the authority of a formal position.

formal organization The official, legitimate, and most visible part of the system.

formalization The degree to which the organization has official rules, regulations, and procedures.

functional conflict A healthy, constructive disagreement between two or more people.

fundamental attribution error The tendency to make attributions to internal causes when focusing on someone else's behavior.

G

garbage can model A theory that contends that decisions in organizations are random and unsystematic.

gateways to communication Pathways through barriers to communication and antidotes to communication problems.

general self-efficacy An individual's general belief that he or she is capable of meeting job demands in a wide variety of situations.

glass ceiling An intangible barrier that keeps women and minorities from rising above a certain level in organizations.

goal setting The process of establishing desired results that guide and direct behavior.

group Two or more people with common interests, objectives, and continuing interaction.

group cohesion The "interpersonal glue" that makes members of a group stick together.

group polarization The tendency for group discussion to produce shifts toward more extreme attitudes among members.

groupthink A deterioration of mental efficiency, reality testing, and moral judgment resulting from pressures within the group.

guanxi The Chinese practice of building networks for social exchange.

H

Hawthorne studies Studies conducted during the 1920s and 1930s that discovered the existence of the informal organization.

heuristics Shortcuts in decision making that save mental activity.

hierarchy of authority The degree of vertical differentiation across levels of management.

homeostasis A steady state of bodily functioning and equilibrium.

hygiene factor A work condition related to dissatisfaction caused by discomfort or pain.

I

identification A compromise mechanism whereby an individual patterns his or her behavior after another's.

impoverished manager (1,1) A leader who exerts just enough effort to get by.

impression management The process by which individuals try to control the impressions others have of them.

incremental change Change of a relatively small scope, such as making small improvements.

individual differences The way in which factors such as skills, abilities, personalities, perceptions, attitudes, values, and ethics differ from one individual to another.

individualism A cultural orientation in which people belong to loose social frameworks, and their primary concern is for themselves and their families.

inequity The situation in which a person perceives he or she is receiving less than he or she is giving, or is giving less than he or she is receiving.

influence The process of affecting the thoughts, behavior, and feelings of another person.

informal leadership Unofficial leadership accorded to a person by other members of the organization.

informal organization The unofficial and less visible part of the system.

information Data that have been interpreted and analyzed and have meaning to some user.

Information Communication Technology (ICT) The various new technologies, such as e-mail, voice mail, teleconferencing, and wireless access, which are used for interpersonal communication.

information power Access to and control over important information.

initiating structure Leader behavior aimed at defining and organizing work relationships and roles, as well as establishing clear patterns of organization, communication, and ways of getting things done.

instrumental values Values that represent the acceptable behaviors to be used in achieving some end state.

instrumentality The belief that performance is related to rewards.

integrated involvement Closeness achieved through tasks and activities.

integration The process of coordinating the different parts of an organization.

integrative approach The broad theory that describes personality as a composite of an individual's psychological processes.

integrative negotiation A negotiation approach that focuses on the merits of the issues and seeks a win–win solution.

interactional psychology The psychological approach that says in order to understand human behavior, we must know something about the person and about the situation.

intergroup conflict Conflict that occurs between groups or teams in an organization.

interorganizational conflict Conflict that occurs between two or more organizations.

interpersonal communication Communication between two or more people in an organization.

interpersonal conflict Conflict that occurs between two or more individuals.

interrole conflict A person's experience of conflict among the multiple roles in his or her life.

intragroup conflict Conflict that occurs within groups or teams.

intrapersonal conflict Conflict that occurs within an individual.

intrarole conflict Conflict that occurs within a single role, such as when a person receives conflicting messages from role senders about how to perform a certain role.

introversion A preference indicating that an individual is energized by time alone.

intuiting Gathering information through "sixth sense" and focusing on what could be rather than what actually exists. (Chapter 3)

intuition A fast, positive force in decision making that is utilized at a level below consciousness and involves learned patterns of information. (Chapter 10)

J

job A set of specified work and task activities that engage an individual in an organization.

Job Characteristics Model A framework for understanding person–job fit through the interaction of core job dimensions with critical psychological states within a person.

Job Diagnostic Survey (JDS) The survey instrument designed to measure the elements in the Job Characteristics Model.

job enlargement A method of job design that increases the number of activities in a job to overcome the boredom of overspecialized work.

job enrichment Designing or redesigning jobs by incorporating motivational factors into them.

job redesign An OD intervention method that alters jobs to improve the fit between individual skills and the demands of the job.

job rotation A variation of job enlargement in which workers are exposed to a variety of specialized jobs over time.

job satisfaction A pleasurable or positive emotional state resulting from the appraisal of one's job or job experiences.

job sharing An alternative work pattern in which more than one person occupies a single job.

Judging Preference Preferring closure and completion in making decisions.

jurisdictional ambiguity The presence of unclear lines of responsibility within an organization.

L

laissez-faire style A style of leadership in which the leader fails to accept the responsibilities of the position.

language The words, their pronunciation, and the methods of combining them used and understood by a group of people.

leader An advocate for change and new approaches to problems.

leader–member relations The quality of interpersonal relationships among a leader and the group members.

leadership The process of guiding and directing the behavior of people in the work environment.

Leadership Grid An approach to understanding a leader's or manager's concern for results (production) and concern for people.

leadership training and development A variety of techniques that are designed to enhance individuals' leadership skills.

lean production Using committed employees with ever-expanding responsibilities to achieve zero waste, 100 percent good product, delivered on time, every time.

learning A change in behavior acquired through experience.

least preferred coworker (LPC) The person a leader has least preferred to work with over his or her career.

legitimate power Power that is based on position and mutual agreement; agent and target agree that the agent has the right to influence the target.

locus of control An individual's generalized belief about internal control (self-control) versus external control (control by the situation or by others).

loss of individuality A social process in which individual group members lose self-awareness and its accompanying sense of accountability, inhibition, and responsibility for individual behavior.

M

Machiavellianism A personality characteristic indicating one's willingness to do whatever it takes to get one's own way.

machine bureaucracy A moderately decentralized form of organization that emphasizes the technical staff and standardization of work processes.

maintenance The third career stage in which the individual tries to maintain productivity while evaluating progress toward career goals.

maintenance function An activity essential to effective, satisfying interpersonal relationships within a team or group.

management The study of overseeing activities and supervising people in organizations.

management by objectives (MBO) A goal-setting program based on interaction and negotiation between employees and managers. (Chapter 6)

manager An advocate for stability and the status quo.

masculinity The cultural orientation in which assertiveness and materialism are valued.

meaning of work The way a person interprets and understands the value of work as part of life.

mechanistic structure An organizational design that emphasizes structured activities, specialized tasks, and centralized decision making.

medicine The applied science of healing or treatment of diseases to enhance an individual's health and well-being.

mentor An individual who provides guidance, coaching, counseling, and friendship to a protégé.

mentoring A work relationship that encourages development and career enhancement for people moving through the career cycle.

message The thoughts and feelings that the communicator is attempting to elicit in the receiver.

moral maturity The measure of a person's cognitive moral development.

motivation The process of arousing and sustaining goal-directed behavior.

motivation factor A work condition related to satisfaction of the need for psychological growth.

moving The second step in Lewin's change model, in which new attitudes, values, and behaviors are substituted for old ones.

Myers–Briggs Type Indicator (MBTI®) instrument An instrument developed to measure Carl Jung's theory of individual differences.

N

need for achievement A manifest (easily perceived) need that concerns individuals' issues of excellence, competition, challenging goals, persistence, and overcoming difficulties.

need for affiliation A manifest (easily perceived) need that concerns an individual's need to establish and maintain warm, close, intimate relationships with other people.

need for power A manifest (easily perceived) need that concerns an individual's need to make an impact on others, influence others, change people or events, and make a difference in life.

need hierarchy The theory that behavior is determined by a progression of physical, social, and psychological needs, including lower-order needs and higher-order needs.

negative affect An individual's tendency to accentuate the negative aspects of himself or herself, other people, and the world in general.

negative consequences Results of a behavior that a person finds unattractive or aversive.

negativism An aggressive mechanism in which a person responds with pessimism to any attempt at solving a problem.

nominal group technique (NGT) A structured approach to group decision making that focuses on generating alternatives and choosing one.

nonaction Doing nothing in hopes that a conflict will disappear.

nondefensive communication Communication that is assertive, direct, and powerful.

nonprogrammed decision A new, complex decision that requires a creative solution.

nonverbal communication All elements of communication that do not involve words.

normative commitment A type of organizational commitment based on an individual's perceived obligation to remain with an organization.

norms of behavior The standards that a work group uses to evaluate the behavior of its members.

O

objective knowledge Knowledge that results from research and scientific activities.

one-way communication Communication in which a person sends a message to another person and no feedback, questions, or interaction follow.

operant conditioning Modifying behavior through the use of positive or negative consequences following specific behaviors.

opportunistic "what's in it for me" manager (Opp) A leader whose style aims to maximize self-benefit.

opportunities Favorable times or chances for progress and advancement.

organic structure An organizational design that emphasizes teamwork, open communication, and decentralized decision making.

organization development (OD) A systematic approach to organizational improvement that applies behavioral science theory and research in order to increase individual and organizational well-being and effectiveness.

organization man manager (5,5) A middle-of-the-road leader.

organizational behavior The study of individual behavior and group dynamics in organizations.

organizational citizenship behavior Behavior that is above and beyond the call of duty.

organizational commitment The strength of an individual's identification with an organization.

organizational (corporate) culture A pattern of basic assumptions that are considered valid and that are taught to new members as the way to perceive, think, and feel in the organization.

organizational design The process of constructing and adjusting an organization's structure to achieve its goals.

organizational life cycle The differing stages of an organization's life from birth to death.

organizational politics The use of power and influence in organizations.

organizational socialization The process by which newcomers are transformed from outsiders to participating, effective members of the organization.

organizational structure The linking of departments and jobs within an organization.

overdependence An unhealthy, insecure pattern of behavior that leads to preoccupied attempts to achieve security through relationships.

P

participation problem A cost associated with absenteeism, tardiness, strikes and work stoppages, and turnover.

participative decision making Decision making in which individuals who are affected by decisions influence the making of those decisions.

paternalistic "father knows best" manager (9+9) A leader who promises reward and threatens punishment.

people The human resources of the organization.

Perceiving Preference Preferring to explore many alternatives and flexibility.

perceptual screen A window through which we interact with people that influences the quality, accuracy, and clarity of the communication.

performance appraisal The evaluation of a person's performance.

performance decrement A cost resulting from poor quality or low quantity of production, grievances, and unscheduled machine downtime and repair.

performance management A process of defining, measuring, appraising, providing feedback on, and improving performance.

personal power Power used for personal gain.

personality A relatively stable set of characteristics that influence an individual's behavior.

personality hardiness A personality resistant to distress and characterized by commitment, control, and challenge.

person–role conflict Conflict that occurs when an individual is expected to perform behaviors in a certain role that conflict with his or her personal values.

phased retirement An arrangement that allows employees to reduce their hours and/or responsibilities in order to ease into retirement.

planned change Change resulting from a deliberate decision to alter the organization.

political behavior Actions not officially sanctioned by an organization that are taken to influence others in order to meet one's personal goals.

political skill The ability to get things done through favorable interpersonal relationships outside of formally prescribed organizational mechanisms.

position power The authority associated with the leader's formal position in the organization.

positive affect An individual's tendency to accentuate the positive aspects of himself or herself, other people, and the world in general.

positive consequences Results of a behavior that a person finds attractive or pleasurable.

power The ability to influence another person.

power distance The degree to which a culture accepts unequal distribution of power.

powerlessness A lack of power.

preventive stress management An organizational philosophy that holds that people and organizations should take joint responsibility for promoting health and preventing distress and strain.

primary prevention The stage in preventive stress management designed to reduce, modify, or eliminate the demand or stressor causing stress.

procedural justice The fairness of the process by which outcomes are allocated in an organization.

process consultation An OD method that helps managers and employees improve the processes that are used in organizations.

professional bureaucracy A decentralized form of organization that emphasizes the operating core and standardization of skills.

programmed decision A simple, routine matter for which a manager has an established decision rule.

projection Overestimating the number of people who share our own beliefs, values, and behaviors.

projective test A personality test that elicits an individual's response to abstract stimuli.

proxemics The study of an individual's perception and use of space, including territorial space.

psychoanalysis Sigmund Freud's method for delving into the unconscious mind to better understand a person's motives and needs.

psychological contract An implicit agreement between an individual and an organization that specifies what each is expected to give and receive in the relationship.

psychological intimacy Emotional and psychological closeness to other team or group members.

psychology The science of human behavior.

punishment The attempt to eliminate or weaken undesirable behavior by either bestowing negative consequences or withholding positive consequences.

Q

quality circle (QC) A small group of employees who work voluntarily on company time, typically one hour per week, to address work-related problems such as quality control, cost reduction, production planning and techniques, and even product design.

quality program A program that embeds product and service quality excellence in the organizational culture.

quality team A team that is part of an organization's structure and is empowered to act on its decisions regarding product and service quality.

R

rationality A logical, step-by-step approach to decision making, with a thorough analysis of alternatives and their consequences.

rationalization A compromise mechanism characterized by trying to justify one's behavior by constructing bogus reasons for it.

realistic job preview (RJP) Both positive and negative information given to potential employees about the job they are applying for, thereby giving them a realistic picture of the job.

receiver The person receiving a message.

referent power An elusive power that is based on interpersonal attraction.

reflective listening A skill intended to help the receiver and communicator clearly and fully understand the message sent.

refreezing The final step in Lewin's change model, in which new attitudes, values, and behaviors are established as the new status quo.

reinforcement The attempt to develop or strengthen desirable behavior by either bestowing positive consequences or withholding negative consequences.

reward power Power based on an agent's ability to control rewards that a target wants.

richness The ability of a medium or channel to elicit or evoke meaning in the receiver.

risk aversion The tendency to choose options that entail fewer risks and less uncertainty.

role negotiation A technique whereby individuals meet and clarify their psychological contract.

rule-based theory An ethical theory that emphasizes the character of the act itself rather than its effects.

S

satisfice To select the first alternative that is "good enough" because the costs in time and effort are too great to optimize.

secondary prevention The stage in preventive stress management designed to alter or modify the individual's or the organization's response to a demand or stressor.

secrecy Attempting to hide a conflict or an issue that has the potential to create conflict.

selective perception The process of selecting information that supports our individual viewpoints while discounting information that threatens our viewpoints.

self-esteem An individual's general feeling of self-worth.

self-fulfilling prophecy The situation in which our expectations about people affect our interaction with them in such a way that our expectations are confirmed.

self-image How a person sees himself or herself, both positively and negatively.

self-interest What is in the best interest and benefit to an individual.

self-managed team A team that makes decisions that were once reserved for managers.

self-monitoring The extent to which people base their behavior on cues from other people and situations.

self-reliance A healthy, secure, *interdependent* pattern of behavior related to how people form and maintain supportive attachments with others.

self-report questionnaire A common personality assessment that involves an individual's responses to a series of questions.

self-serving bias The tendency to attribute one's own successes to internal causes and one's failures to external causes.

sensing Gathering information through the five senses.

simple structure A centralized form of organization that emphasizes the upper echelon and direct supervision.

Six Sigma A high-performance system to execute business strategy that is customer driven, emphasizes quantitative decision making, and places a priority on saving money.

skill development The mastery of abilities essential to successful functioning in organizations.

skills training Increasing the job knowledge, skills, and abilities that are necessary to do a job effectively.

social decision schemes Simple rules used to determine final group decisions.

social information-processing (SIP) model A model that suggests that the important job factors depend in part on what others tell a person about the job.

social learning The process of deriving attitudes from family, peer groups, religious organizations, and culture.

social loafing The failure of a group member to contribute personal time, effort, thoughts, or other resources to the group.

social perception The process of interpreting information about another person.

social power Power used to create motivation or to accomplish group goals.

social responsibility The obligation of an organization to behave in ethical ways.

sociology The science of society.

sociotechnical systems (STS) Giving equal attention to technical and social considerations in job design.

specialization The degree to which jobs are narrowly defined and depend on unique expertise.

standardization The degree to which work activities are accomplished in a routine fashion.

status structure The set of authority and task relations among a group's members.

stereotype A generalization about a group of people.

strain Distress.

strategic change Change of a larger scale, such as organizational restructuring.

strategic contingencies Activities that other groups depend on in order to complete their tasks.

stress The unconscious preparation to fight or flee that a person experiences when faced with any demand.

stressor The person or event that triggers the stress response.

strong culture An organizational culture with a consensus on the values that drive the company and with an intensity that is recognizable even to outsiders.

strong situation A situation that overwhelms the effects of individual personalities by providing strong cues for appropriate behavior.

structure The systems of communication, authority and roles, and workflow.

superordinate goal An organizational goal that is more important to both parties in a conflict than their individual or group goals.

survey feedback A widely used method of intervention whereby employee attitudes are solicited using a questionnaire.

synergy A positive force that occurs in groups when group members stimulate new solutions to problems through the process of mutual influence and encouragement within the group.

T

task An organization's mission, purpose, or goal for existing.

task environment The elements of an organization's environment that are related to its goal attainment.

task function An activity directly related to the effective completion of a team's work.

task revision The modification of incorrectly specified roles or jobs.

task structure The degree of clarity, or ambiguity, in the work activities assigned to the group.

task-specific self-efficacy An individual's beliefs and expectancies about his or her ability to perform a specific task effectively.

team building An intervention designed to improve the effectiveness of a work group.

team diversity It is the differences in ability, skills, experience, personality, and demographic characteristics within a team.

team manager (9,9) A leader who builds a highly productive team of committed people.

teamwork Joint action by a team of people in which individual interests are subordinated to team unity.

technocentric Placing technology and engineering at the center of job design decisions.

technological interdependence The degree of interrelatedness of the organization's various technological elements.

technology The intellectual and mechanical processes used by an organization to transform inputs into products or services that meet organizational goals.

technology The tools, knowledge, and/or techniques used to transform inputs into outputs.

technostress The stress caused by new and advancing technologies in the workplace.

terminal values Values that represent the goals to be achieved or the end states of existence.

territorial space Bands of space extending outward from the body, which constitute comfort zones.

tertiary prevention The stage in preventive stress management designed to heal individual or organizational symptoms of distress and strain.

Theory X A set of assumptions of how to manage individuals who are motivated by lower-order needs.

Theory Y A set of assumptions of how to manage individuals who are motivated by higher-order needs.

thinking Making decisions in a logical, objective fashion.

360-degree feedback A process of self-evaluation and evaluations by a manager, peers, direct reports, and possibly customers.

time orientation Whether a culture's values are oriented toward the future (long-term orientation) or toward the past and present (short-term orientation).

trait theory The personality theory that states that in order to understand individuals, we must break down behavior patterns into a series of observable traits.

transformational change Change in which the organization moves to a radically different, and sometimes unknown, future state.

transformational coping A way of managing stressful events by changing them into less subjectively stressful events.

transnational organization An organization in which the global viewpoint supersedes national issues.

triangulation The use of multiple methods to measure organizational culture.

two-way communication A form of communication in which the communicator and receiver interact.

Type A behavior pattern A complex of personality and behavioral characteristics, including competitiveness, time urgency, social status insecurity, aggression, hostility, and a quest for achievements.

U

uncertainty avoidance The degree to which a culture tolerates ambiguity and uncertainty.

unfreezing The first step in Lewin's change model, in which individuals are encouraged to discard old behaviors by shaking up the equilibrium state that maintains the status quo.

unplanned change Change that is imposed on the organization and is often unforeseen.

upper echelon A top-level executive team in an organization.

V

valence The value or importance one places on a particular reward.

values Enduring beliefs that a specific mode of conduct or end state of existence is personally or socially preferable to an opposite or converse mode of conduct or end state of existence.

virtual office A mobile platform of computer, telecommunication, and information technology and services.

W

whistle-blower An employee who informs authorities of the wrongdoings of his or her company or coworkers.

withdrawal The final career stage in which the individual contemplates retirement or possible career changes.

work Mental or physical activity that has productive results.

work simplification Standardization and the narrow, explicit specification of task activities for workers.

work team A group of people with complementary skills who are committed to a common mission, performance goals, and approach for which they hold themselves mutually accountable.

workaholism An imbalanced preoccupation with work at the expense of home and personal life satisfaction.

workplace deviance behavior Any voluntary counterproductive behavior that violates organizational norms and causes some degree of harm to organizational functioning.

Z

zone of indifference The range in which attempts to influence a person will be perceived as legitimate and will be acted on without a great deal of thought.

Company Index

Name Index

Subject Index